Arabic for

Nerds two

A GRAMMAR COMPENDIUM

Understanding إِعْرَاب

450 Questions and Answers

Expanded and Revised
First Edition

by
Gerald Drißner

Gerald Drißner (Drissner),

born 1977 in a mountain village in Austria, is an economist and award-winning journalist. He has lived in the Middle East and North Africa for more than ten years, where he has intensively studied Arabic.

He is the author of *Arabic for Nerds 1* (Fill the Gaps: 270 Questions about Arabic Grammar; 2015) and *Islam for Nerds* (500 Questions and Answers; 2016).

IMPRINT/IMPRESSUM – Arabic for Nerds 2

1st edition, fully revised, December 2019 (070621)

Copyright © by Gerald Drißner (Drissner)

Cover design, layout: © by Gerald Drißner

Publisher:	pochemuchka (Gerald Drißner)
Internet:	https://pochemuchka-books.com
E-Mail:	comment@pochemuchka-books.com
Address:	Postfach 35 03 30, D-10212 Berlin, Germany
ISBN-13:	978-3-9819848-0-4 (Paperback)
ISBN-13:	978-3-9819848-1-1 (Hardcover)

Dedication

In memory of

Yasmine Ryan,

a journalist from New Zealand,

who died too young.

She was the first English-language journalist

to start in-depth reporting on the events in Tunisia

that preceded what later became known as the Arab Spring.

Her articles on the English website of Al-Jazeera

gave the desperately fighting people in Tunisia a voice

and made the Western world start listening.

Acknowledgments

I would like to express my gratitude

to *Paul Ammann*, from Switzerland, for his generous support and

Kenan Kalajdzic, from Sarajevo,

for his thorough reading and insightful suggestions.

Above all, I want to thank my wife *Mey*.

Although she regards grammar as an instrument of torture,

Mey has always supported and encouraged me.

ARABIC FOR NERDS *TWO*

Misleading signs – the need for virtual case markers

In any case the same – indeclinable words

The relationship of words – cases

Shaping the verb

Sentences / clauses which do the job of a single word

Neutral clauses - outside the scope of إِعْرابٌ

PART TWO: LETTERS, FORMS, AND WORDS

CHAPTER 3: SECRETS OF LETTERS AND FORMS

Linking two nouns (الإِضافةُ) - possession & belonging

The مَصْدَرٌ

CHAPTER 4: PRONOUNS AND PREPOSITIONS

Pronouns (الضَّمِيرُ) and what we call in English pronouns

Prepositions (حَرْفُ الْجَرِّ)

Extra letters & prepositions to emphasize the meaning

The quasi-sentence (شِبْهُ الْجُمْلةِ)

CHAPTER 5: TINY TRICKY WORDS

The inquiry / question words (كَلِماتُ الْإِسْتِفْهامِ)

CHAPTER 6: THE FOLLOWER (التّابِعُ)
WORDS THAT BLUEPRINT GRAMMATICAL FEATURES

The adjective (الصّفةُ or النّعْتُ)

The emphasis (التَّوْكِيدُ)

The apposition (الْبَدَلُ)

Conjunctions – coordinators, connectors & couplers (الْعَظْفُ)

CHAPTER 7: THE NUMBERS

PART THREE: THE SENTENCE

CHAPTER 8: THE NOMINAL SENTENCE

The predicate (الْخَبَرُ)

The verb كَانَ (to be, to exist)

The sisters of كَانَ

Still, to remain

Verbs of approaching

Optical twins: إِنَّ and أَنَّ

The reported or indirect speech

The negation of a nominal sentence

The absolute negation (the categorical denial)

CHAPTER 10: THE VERBAL SENTENCE

The subject of a verbal sentence

The subject of the passive verb (نائِبُ الْفاعِلِ)

CHAPTER 11: THE OBJECTS (الْمَفاعِيلُ)

Verbs with two (or three) objects

The absolute or inner object (الْمَفْعُولُ الْمُطْلَقُ)

The purpose of the action (الْمَفْعُولُ لِأَجْلِهِ)

Adverbial expression of time and place (الْمَفْعُولُ فِيهِ)

The tricky وَ - the object of accompaniment (الْمَفْعُولُ مَعَهُ)

The state or circumstance (الْحالُ)

The specification (التَّمْييزُ)

CHAPTER 12: FINE WAYS OF WORDING (الْجُمَلُ الْأُسْلُوبِيّةُ)

The conditional sentence (جُمْلةُ الشَّرْطِ)

The exclusion (جُمْلةُ الْاسْتِثْناءِ)

The particularization (أُسْلُوبُ الْإِخْتِصاصِ)

The occupied regent (الْإِشْتِغالُ) or: emphasis by word order

Two regents want to rule over one patient (التَّنازُعُ)

The vocative (النِّداءُ)

Warnings (التَّحْذِيرُ) and instigations (الْإِغْراءُ)

Sorrow and pain (النُّدْبةُ)

The call for help (الْإِسْتِغاثةُ)

Prohibition (النَّهْيُ) and proposal (الْعَرْضُ)

Exclamations: Admiration & Astonishment (جُمْلةُ التَّعَجُّبِ)

Praise and blame (جُمْلةُ الْمَدْحِ وَالذَّمِّ)

The oath – taking a vow (جُمْلةُ الْقَسَمِ)

Epilogue

0. Introduction

"Denial ain't just a river in Egypt."
Mark Twain

This book was born out of my struggles and failures. Learning Arabic could be frustrating – especially when I knew the meaning of every word in an Arabic sentence, but I didn't have a clue what it meant. Even worse: I didn't understand the reason why I failed. The books on Arabic I relied on at that time provided no answers.

The simple truth is that if you don't understand a sentence but know all the words, then you don't understand the grammar. Grammar is the system that puts words together into meaningful units. Grammar tells you who does what to whom, why, when, and how. Unfortunately, I have met many students who learned to hate grammar in school.

This book aims to transform the most dreaded subject into an understandable and enjoyable tool. Because – believe it or not – grammar can be fascinating and fun.

Books on Arabic grammar are usually written by people who either try to make it as complicated as possible because they are academics – or by those who purposely avoid grammar assuming that the reader doesn't even understand his native English grammar. My best teachers forced me to approach grammar in the same manner as the Arabs do. As a result, I am not a big fan of the Western approach of teaching Arabic by using Latin terms that need a translation themselves.

I aim to provide something new to Arabic language students. I wanted to write a book that I wished I had myself – a book that explains the approach of native Arabic grammarians to people who were educated in the West. My first book *Arabic for Nerds 1* (Fill the Gaps: 270 Questions about Arabic Grammar) covered basic grammar constructions and topics dealing with morphology (صَرْفٌ). It didn't follow a specific structure and mainly served the purpose of filling gaps.

Part two digs deeper and is thoughtfully structured. It explores the core of the language from letter to word to sentence and will teach you how to dissect a sentence. Imagine pushing entire sentences into an

MRI machine. After we will have examined the structure, we will put single words under a microscope. We will know how and why sentences work. We will analyze sentences consisting of few words but enough to give you a headache as well as verses of the Qur'an.

We will examine the peculiarities of Modern Standard Arabic as well as the beauty of Classical Arabic. We will learn how to form sophisticated sentences and how to avoid mistakes. I understand that many readers have limited time for studying and do not wish to read an entire book. For this reason, *questions* are largely self-contained, while similar *questions* will be found close to one another. You should have a good foundation of Arabic under your belt. This book should be both a learning tool and a reference book for advanced learners of Arabic.

I consider this book a work in progress. Since I am not very fond of academic writing, I am sure that experts and linguists may find inaccuracies. I wanted to keep it understandable on purpose. I don't insist on writing helping vowels which are needed for pronunciation but at the same time might confuse readers. Many Arabic grammar terms can't be translated exactly. For this reason, I try to use various translations now and then. I usually give the indefinite, singular form of Arabic grammar terms, though I may use different forms in the English text.

Before the feminine ending ة ـة, I do not write the short vowel *"a"* because by definition it must be either the vowel *"a"* (فَتْحةٌ) or Aleph (ا), a so-called أَلِفٌ ساكِنةٌ, like in فَتاةٌ (*young girl*), مُجاراةٌ (*conformity*), or قُضاةٌ (*judges*). Regarding the Aleph Maqsūra (أَلِفٌ مَقْصُورةٌ), I write ى and not ئ due to limitations of the Arabic fonts; for the same reason, you may find a فَتْحةٌ instead of the dagger Aleph. If the root of a verb is special, I use the letter R plus a number. *R1* is the ف, *R2* the ع, and *R3* the ل in a triliteral root. E.g., a I-verb like قال will be marked as R2=و.

I welcome and highly appreciate comments and suggestions. I can be reached by e-mail: *comment@pochemuchka-books.com*

I can't promise that you will love Arabic grammar because you went through this book. However, I am pretty sure that you will understand Arabic sentences much better.

Berlin, July 2018

PART ONE: THE BASICS

Chapter 1:
The Dawn of Arabic Grammar

1. How old is Arabic grammar?

Most of the Arabic grammar rules we apply today were defined around 1,200 years ago.

The rules are based on a certain kind of Arabic that is used in the Qur'an. Muslims believe that Allah's words were transferred to the Islamic Prophet Muhammad by an archangel in that particular language. Later on, Muslim scholars derived hundreds of grammar rules by analyzing verses of the Qur'an which serves as a perfect model of Classical Arabic. They did not stop until every sentence in the Qur'an could be reasonably explained.

Linguists have stated that the system of Classical Arabic (اللُّغَةُ الْعَرَبِيَّةُ الْفُصْحَى) was fully developed around the year 800 (184 AH) thanks to the works of three men: Sībawayhi (سيبويه), al-Farrā' (الْفَرَّاء), and al-Khalīl (الْخَلِيل) who wrote the first Arabic dictionary (*see question #3*).

2. What is Classical Arabic?

Classical Arabic (اللُّغَةُ الْعَرَبِيَّةُ الْفُصْحَى) is the literary form of the northern dialects of Arabia of the 7th century AD.

Classical Arabic was laid down mainly by the composition of the Qur'an as well as poetry. At that time there were two main varieties of Arabic in northern Arabia:

FAMILY 1: the dialect of the **Hijāz** (الْحِجازُ), the western part of Arabia along the Red Sea coast. This region was the cradle of Islam.

Muslims believe that the Qur'an was transmitted in the Hijāzi dialect. Hijāzi Arabic, however, was not pure even in the days of Prophet Muhammad. Some Arabs of the Hijāz were living in towns and maintained trade relations with foreigners (Syrians and Abyssinians).

FAMILY 2: the dialect of the **Najd** (النَّجْدُ) which is the speech of the desert tribes of the *hinterland*; for example, the Banū Tamīm (بَنُو تَميم). It is also called Eastern Arabic. The language of the Najd people was not influenced by foreigners and was considered purer than the Arabic spoken in the Hijāz.

The dialect of the Najd was set as the standard for good Arabic by the grammarians who made big efforts to make the Qur'an conform to it. When the text of the Qur'an was vowelled for the first time by Abū al-'Aswad al-Du'alī (أَبُو الأَسْوَد الدُّؤَلِيّ), it is said that he did not refer to the speech of the Hijāz – but to the dialect of the tribes living in the highlands of the Najd. So, the text of the Qur'an was carefully adapted to a dialect purer than that in which it had been composed originally.

A rule of thumb: Whenever there are differences between Eastern Arabic (Banū Tamīm) and Western Arabic (Hijāz; the language of Mecca and Medina), the Qur'an usually reflects the Eastern dialect.

The formal Arabic we use today is called *Modern Standard Arabic* (الْعَرَبِيَّةُ الْحَدِيثَةُ الْمِعْيارِيّةُ or اللُّغَةُ الْعَرَبِيَّةُ الْفُصْحَى الْحَدِيثَةُ). It basically follows the rules of Classical Arabic but has been influenced by foreign languages over the centuries.

3. Who wrote the first Arabic dictionary?

Al-Khalīl ibn 'Ahmad al-Farāhīdī (الْخَلِيل بن أَحْمَد الْفَراهِيدِيّ), *a grammarian who was born in 718 (100 AH) in present-day Oman.*

Al-Khalīl's work *Kitāb al-'Ayn* (كِتاب الْعَيْن), *the Book of the Letter Ayn,* is regarded as the first dictionary of the Arabic language and one of the earliest known dictionaries of any language.

In the early days of Islam, scholars and commentators had already started to paraphrase words of the Qur'an. 'Abd Allah ibn 'Abbās (عَبْد الله بن عَبّاس), a cousin and companion of Prophet Muhammad, compiled a list of words of foreign origin. These compilations were mainly based on topics, e.g., words that dealt with a camel or a horse. al-Khalīl, often just called al-Farāhīdī, lived in Basra in present-day Iraq and was a grammarian of the Basra school (الْبَصْرِيُّونَ) of grammar.

He was the first scholar to classify the consonants of Arabic and explained why they are important: **the root**. He discovered that every quadriliteral root (= 4 root letters) contains at least one of the following consonants: ‫ب - ف - م - ر - ن - ل‬.

Al-Farāhīdī's arrangement of the letters does not follow the alphabetical order we use today. He used a **phonetic order** according to the place of articulation in the mouth and throat, from the pharyngeal consonants (‫ع, ح‬) to the labials (‫ف, ب‬). You produce pharyngeals by making the muscles in your throat tighter so that air can't flow freely. Labials are made with the lips. According to this system, the order begins with the letter ‫ع‬ which is also the reason for the dictionary's name. Al-Farāhīdī saw in the ‫ع‬ the first and **most essential sound** of Arabic because no letter comes deeper from the throat. His dictionary ends with the letter ‫م‬ which is the last letter pronounced with the lips.

Later on, roots were sorted alphabetically, starting with the **last** of the three radicals, then the first, and then the second. This is called *rhyming order*. For poets, the last letter is often the most important one.

Remark: The most **famous Arabic dictionary** is *Lisān al-ʿArab* (‫لِسان‬ ‫الْعَرَب‬) by Ibn Manẓūr (‫ابن مَنْظُور‬), completed in 1290/689 AH. It is the first dictionary that was fully based on the system of ordering by roots and contains around 80,000 entries.

4. What does the Arabic word for *dictionary* (‫قامُوسٌ‬) mean?

‫قامُوسٌ‬ *means ocean* (‫مُحِيطٌ‬) *or sea* (‫بَحْرٌ‬).

The reason why ‫قامُوسٌ‬ (plural: ‫قَوامِيسُ‬) is used for *lexicon* has to do with the name of a famous dictionary.

In the 14th century, al-Fīrūzābādī (‫الْفِيرُوزآبادِى‬), a Persian lexicographer, wrote a large dictionary and called it *al-Qāmūs* (‫الْقامُوسُ‬). The word is of Persian origin (‫اقيانوس‬) and denotes *ocean*. ‫قامُوسٌ‬ has since become an Arabic term for *dictionary, lexicon*. The idea of using *ocean* as a metaphor for the abundance of words is common in Arabic.

There is another prominent word for *dictionary*: ‫مُعْجَمٌ‬ (plural: ‫مَعاجِمُ‬). Nowadays, people tend to use ‫قامُوسٌ‬ for dictionaries which translate Arabic words into other languages. Purist linguists, however, reject that. They suggest to use الْقامُوسُ only for al-Fīrūzābādī's dictionary. All other dictionaries should be called مُعْجَمٌ. Today, dictionaries often have titles like al-Munjid (الْمُنْجِدُ; *the rescuer; helper*), al-Marjiʿ (الْمَرْجِعُ; *the source; reference*), or al-Faysal (الْفَيْصَلُ; *the decisive word; the standard*).

Excursus: What is the form and origin of مُعْجَمٌ? It is a special type of the infinitive (مَصْدَرٌ مِيمِيٌّ) of IV-verb أَعْجَمَ - يُعْجِمُ which denotes *getting rid of the lack of clarity in Arabic speech* but also *to provide (a letter) with diacritical points*. But what is the corresponding I-verb of أَعْجَمَ? Is it عَجَمَ or عَجُمَ? Let's see the nuances:

- IV-verb أَعْجَمَ can be related to I-verb عَجَمَ which denotes that a person does **not** speak pure Arabic. For example: *The words were not well-spoken* (عَجَمَ الْكَلَامُ) in the sense of لَمْ يَكُنْ فَصِيحًا. The *"u"* in the middle will be decisive later.

- IV-verb أَعْجَمَ could also be linked to I-verb عَجَمَ. This verb denotes *to bite, to chew something for the purpose of eating or trial*; e.g.: he bit a piece of wood to know whether it was hard or fragile; or *to shake the sword to test it* (عَجَمَ السَّيْفَ).

The respective I-verbs have different مَصْدَرٌ-forms:

meaning	مَصْدَرٌ	I-verb
to bite; chew; to examine the hardness of a thing; also: to test; to try.	عُجُومٌ or عَجْمٌ	عَجَمَ - يَعْجُمُ
Having an inability, difficulty, or lack of clarity in his speech, especially when speaking Arabic.	عُجْمَةٌ	عَجُمَ - يَعْجُمُ

He tried/tested a person. Person here is the **direct object!**	عَجَمَ فُلانًا
He (a person) had difficulties in proper Arabic. Person = **subject!**	عَجُمَ فُلانٌ

عَجُمَ is an intransitive verb and cannot have a direct object. By adding the letter أ (which produces stem IV) we make such verbs transitive. In our example, we get the action of *clearing the vagueness or incorrectness related to Arabic of **something*** (= direct object).

Very well, but then why does the vowel in the middle matter at all since form IV is the same anyway? Let's open the *Hans Wehr* dictionary. Under ع-ج-م, we find أَعْجَمُ which is translated as *speaking incorrect Arabic; dumb; speechless*. What on earth is that all of a sudden? Is it a *noun of preference* (اِسْمُ التَّفْضِيلِ)? A verb in the first person? Nope.

It is a quasi (active) participle (صِفةٌ مُشَبَّهةٌ) which usually functions as an adjective. Such words are built from verbs which cannot form active participles and denote a state (you know corrupted Arabic) and not a process or action. An indicator is often the vowel "*u*" on the middle root letter (*see question #87*). A special pattern points to colors or human deficiencies which is exactly what we need here:

other plural	sound plural	singular	pattern (both are diptotes!)	
عُجْمٌ	أَعْجَمُونَ	أَعْجَمُ	أَفْعَلُ	masculine
	عَجْماواتٌ	عَجْماءُ	فَعْلاءُ	feminine

Note: مُعْجَمٌ is also the passive participle (اِسْمُ الْمَفْعُولِ) of IV-verb أَعْجَمَ since both share the same pattern (*see Arabic for Nerds 1, #172*).

5. What prompted the first grammarian to write down rules?

A mistake in Arabic, uttered by his daughter.

Many linguists regard Abū al-'Aswad al-Du'alī (أَبُو الْأَسْوَد الدُّؤَلِيّ), born ca. 603 (16 BH) in Yemen, as the first grammarian of the Arabic language. He invented the dots (points) that are placed under or above consonants as well as the vowel signs.

Legend has it that it was his daughter who made him do it. At least it clearly shows how critical grammar mistakes can be. When the Caliph, 'Alī ibn Abū Tālib (عَلِيّ بن أَبِي طالِب), asked him to write down the rules of grammar, Abū al-'Aswad al-Du'alī first refused to do so. Then one night he was sitting under the stars along with his daughter when she asked him: *"What's most beautiful in the sky?"* (ما أَحْسَنُ السَّماءِ؟)

"The stars," he replied. His daughter was confused by his answer and said that she wasn't looking for an answer – but rather wanted to make

a **statement of wonder and admiration**. Such constructions are called أُسْلُوبُ التَّعَجُّبِ and follow special rules (→ #434). The misunderstanding was based on incorrect case endings. By using the wrong vowels, she turned the statement into a question. His daughter tried to say: *"How beautiful the sky is!"* In Arabic, this would be: مَا أَحْسَنَ السَّماءَ!

Abū al-'Aswad al-Du'alī suddenly realized that the corruption of speech had started to affect native speakers. Thus, he decided to write the first grammatical treatise on Arabic.

Remark: There are several versions of this anecdote. For example, his daughter wanted to exclaim the following: *How strong is the heat!* But by mispronouncing the vowels, she actually asked a question: *What is the hottest (kind of) heat?* To which her father replied: الْقَيْظُ, which is the Arabic word for the most vehement heat of summer.

6. Why do we use the word نَحْوٌ for *grammar*?

It has to do with a command.

When the caliphate moved to Iraq (less than thirty years after Muhammad's death in 632), many Muslim converts made mistakes when reciting the Qur'an which prompted an urgent need to codify the language.

The fourth Caliph, 'Alī ibn Abū Tālib (عَلِيّ بن أَبِي طالِب), who himself had started to set up rules for Arabic, commanded one of his students with this task: Abū al-'Aswad al-Du'alī (أَبُو الْأَسْوَد الدُّؤَلِيّ).

Legend has it that 'Alī used the following words: "Follow this **method**, O Abū al-'Aswad!" (اُنْحُ هٰذا النَّحْوَ يا أَبا الْأَسْوَدِ); see *Arabic for Nerds 1, #6*.

نَحْوٌ means *direction; way* and gave this new field a name. 'Alī was murdered soon after. Finally, Abū al-'Aswad al-Du'alī invented the dots and made sure that the words of the Qur'an were pronounced correctly.

7. How did the inventor of the dots guide his calligrapher?

He used a description of his mouth.

In the oldest manuscripts of the Qur'an, vowels are expressed by dots (often marked in red) and not by the symbols we use today.

A single dot above the letter was used for فَتْحَةٌ, a dot underneath for كَسْرَةٌ, and one in the middle or on the line for ضَمَّةٌ. Nunation (تَنْوِينٌ) was expressed by two dots.

˝ equals ◌ً	.. equals ◌ِ	: equals ◌ُ
"-an" (فَتْحةٌ)	"-in" (كَسْرةٌ)	"-un" (ضَمَّةٌ)

There is a famous legend about this. Around the year 664 (42 AH), the inventor of the dot-system, Abū al-'Aswad al-Du'alī (أَبُو الْأَسْوَد الدُّؤَلِيّ), gave the following directives to his calligrapher:

"If you see me open my mouth (my two lips) to pronounce the letter, put a dot on the upper edge (فَتْحةٌ), if I bring together my lips, place a dot between the two sides of the letter (ضَمَّةٌ). And if I reduce my lips, put the dot under the letter (كَسْرةٌ). But if I follow up each of those movements with a modulation (humming, nasal sound), then replace each dot with two others (تَنْوِينٌ)."[1]

The notation of the Hamza (هَمْزةٌ) is attributed to Abū al-'Aswad as well. He used a small version of the ع above the Aleph and the semi-consonants و and ي to indicate a guttural sound (glottal stop).

Remark: Similar vowel signs were also used in Aramaic. Some scholars suggested that Abū al-'Aswad al-Du'alī, perhaps familiar with Aramaic, merely added them to Arabic, thereby enriching the Qur'an and the Arabic idiom.

8. Who invented the vowels and markers which we use today?

al-Khalīl ibn 'Ahmad al-Farāhīdī (الْخَلِيل بن أَحْمَد الْفَرَاهِيدِي)*, the author of the first Arabic dictionary.*

He replaced the system of dots with the following signs: a small و (◌ُ) for the vowel "u", a small ا (Aleph) for the vowel "a" (◌َ), and part of a small ي for the vowel "i" (◌ِ)

---

1   إِذَا رَأَيْتَنِي قَدْ فَتَحْتُ شَفَتَيَّ بِالْحَرْفِ فَانْقُطْ نُقْطَةً فَوْقَهُ، عَلَى أَعْلَاهُ، وَإِنْ ضَمَمْتُ شَفَتَيَّ فَانْقُطْ نُقْطَةً بَيْنَ يَدَيِ الْحَرْفِ، وَإِنْ كَسَرْتُ شَفَتَيَّ فَاجْعَلِ النُّقْطَةَ مِنْ تَحْتِ الْحَرْفِ، وَإِنْ أَتْبَعْتُ شَيْئًا مِنْ ذَلِكَ غُنَّةً (تَنْوِينًا) فَاجْعَلْ مَكَانَ النُّقْطَةِ نُقْطَتَيْنِ.

Al-Khalīl also changed the sign for the شَدّةٌ and opted for a small س which is short for شَدِيدٌ (*intense*). The new system was much more accurate compared to the dots which had various functions and could be confused. The system of Arabic orthography was almost complete at this point and is used as such until now.

9. Are there consonants which do not go well with each other?

Yes, Arabic doesn't like the co-occurrence of similar consonants.

Al-Khalīl ibn ʾAhmad al-Farāhīdī (الْخَلِيل بن أَحْمَد الْفَراهِيديّ), a genius of the 8th century AD, had investigated which letters get along well and which can't stand each other. His four main rules are still valid and fascinating. They help to better understand the nature of Arabic roots.

1	The **first two radicals** of a triliteral root are usually **not** identical.
2	The **first two radicals** should **not** belong to the **same class of letters** in terms of articulation, i.e., emphatic, non-emphatic, etc. They should not be *homorganic*, as linguists would say. Therefore, there are no roots in Arabic that begin with **b-m** (ب-م), i.e., two labials. Also the root **j-k** (ج-ك), i.e., two velars, would be strange because the ج originally resembles a "*g*" (pronounced like the English word *good*) rather than a "*j*" (like the English word *genuine*).
3	The **last two radicals** may be **identical**. It is not a problem to have a root like **m-d-d** (م-د-د).
4	The **last two radicals** should **not** be of the **same class of articulation**. A root like **m-d-t** (م-د-ت) doesn't exist, i.e., with two colliding dentals.
5	A root like **kh-h-q** (خ-ح-ق) is almost **impossible** in Arabic because the three consonants belong to the same class of articulation.

10. Who wrote the first book about Arabic grammar?

Sībawayhi (سيبويه).

Sībawayhi was born in the middle of the 8th century in Shiraz, Persia.

Later he moved to Basra (الْبَصْرَةُ) in present-day Iraq where he studied the early history of Islam, jurisprudence (الْفِقْهُ), and the traditions and sayings of the Prophet Muhammad (الْحَدِيثُ). He took lessons from Hammād ibn Salama (حمّاد ابْن سَلَمة), a highly respected Islamic scholar – an encounter which, as it turned out later, was of great importance for Arabic. It appears to me that Sībawayhi's linguistic inability almost forced him to study grammar in the presence of his mentor.

Like a man possessed, he began to analyze every aspect of Arabic. His findings about syntax, morphology, and phonology later became the founding text of Arabic grammatical science. Sībawayhi died at a relatively young age (between 32 and 40 years) before he could finish his work. As for the reason for his death there are two accounts: illness or that he died of grief after his humiliation in Baghdad (see *question #17*). His tomb is in Shiraz in present-day Iran.

Al-'Akhfash al-'Awsat (الْأَخْفَش الْأَوْسَط), a student of him, eventually published his work and gave it a rather simple title for such a monumental work: *al-Kitāb* (الْكِتاب) - t*he Book*. In more than 900 pages, *al-Kitāb* set the rules and defined what is correct and incorrect in Arabic. Al-'Akhfash al-'Awsat was born in Balkh (Afghanistan) and became a student of Sībawayhi in Basra. He was a famous grammarian himself.

Sībawayhi is not only the greatest Arabic linguist. He is certainly one of the greatest linguists of all time. He was of Persian descent and learned Arabic later in life which may explain his systematic approach.

Sībawayhi always tried to find a logical explanation. He was interested in the behavior of words rather than their meaning. His approach was different to that of the classical Greek grammarians who saw in the meanings of words and their logical relationships the most important aspects of language.

Remark 1: Before the Arabs were introduced to Islam, despite having a strong language, there wasn't any formalized grammar. Scholars have suggested that Sībawayhi was perhaps familiar with Aramaic and took some rules of Aramaic as his guide for recording the Arabic grammar.

Remark 2: Al-'Akhfash (الْأَخْفَشُ) is a strange Arabic word. It means *nyctalope* (someone who can see more/better by night than by day) or *devoid of eyelashes*, or *having small eyes and naturally weak sight*. It is the nickname of eleven exceptional people listed by the Islamic scholar al-Suyūtī (السُّيَوطيّ). The following three men are the most famous. The first two belong to the school of Basra:

- **al-'Akhfash al-'Akbar** (الْأَخْفَش الْأَكْبَر; died 793/177 AH): he was the first to provide ancient poems with (interlinear) commentary. Note: الْأَكْبَر here means *oldest* and not *greatest*.

- **al-'Akhfash al-'Awsat** (الْأَخْفَش الْأَوْسَط; died sometime between 210 and 221/825-835 AH): the most famous of all al-'Akhfash. He was a student of Sībawayhi whom he survived, although he was superior in age. It was he who made Sībawayhi's book known.

- **al-'Akhfash al-'Asghar** (الْأَخْفَش الْأَصْغَر; died 927/315 AH)): student of al-Mubarrad (الْمُبَرَّد). He made a name for himself by introducing the grammatical studies of Baghdad to Egypt.

11. What does the name Sībawayhi mean?

It denotes "little apple".

The name Sībawayhi (سيبويه) is a Persian diminutive for سيب, the Persian word for *apple*. Some authors claim that he was called Sībawayhi because his cheeks looked like apples.

However, the Arabs at that time did not know about this and treated the last element of his name as the Persian word for *scent* (بوي). That is why his name was frequently translated as *apple fragrance*. Others mistakenly interpreted the name as *30 scents* because سى means *thirty* in Persian. His name was further corrupted by assimilating its last element with the Persian suffix *-wayhi*, which is found in several proper names of Persian origin. This probably happened because *ūye* and *wayhi* are both spelled the same in the non-vocalized script (ويه).

How should you **pronounce** his name? It depends on the language. The Persian suffix ويه is pronounced *ūye* in contemporary Farsi. Therefore, سيبويه would be pronounced like *Sībūye*. In Middle Persian, it would sound like *Sēbōē*. In contemporary Arabic, people usually say *Sībawèih*, in English pronounced like "*Seebawe*".

Watch out: In Arabic, foreign proper nouns (names) that end in وَيْهِ such as سِيبَوَيْهِ are treated as **indeclinable** (مَبْنِيٌّ) which means that they always stay the same – regardless of their function in the sentence.

12. What is the first sentence of Sībawayhi's grammar book?

Nouns are man, horse, and wall.

Traditionally, works on Arabic grammar begin with a series of definitions that introduce the main categories of the language. *Nouns are man, horse, and wall* is only the most famous part of Sībawayhi's first sentence. The entire first sentence of *al-Kitāb* (الْكِتاب) reads as follows:

Chapter of the knowledge of words in the Arabic language:	بَابُ عِلْم الْكَلِم مِنَ الْعَرَبِيَّةِ:
Words are noun, verb, or particle intended for a meaning which is neither noun nor verb. Nouns are *man*, *horse*, and *wall*.	فَالْكَلِمُ: اسْمٌ وَفِعْلٌ وَحَرْفٌ جَاءَ لِمَعْنًى لَيْسَ بِاسْم وَلَا فِعْلٍ. فَالِاسْمُ: رَجُلٌ وَفَرَسٌ وَحَائِطٌ

13. What was the aim of the first Arabic grammarians?

The explanation of case endings in a sentence.

This process is called إِعْرابٌ, a term that originally referred to the correct use of Arabic according to the language of the Bedouins. Later it simply meant *declension*.

Case endings are produced by a *regent* or *governor* (عامِلٌ), i.e., a word in the sentence that influences (= governs) another word. In simple words, the عامِل is the **reason why words get cases**. The first grammarians developed an analytical framework that should give answers to every possible grammatical situation in a sentence. When analyzing a sentence, the grammarians tried to find the عامِل of nouns and verbs. If no such word could be identified, they had to reconstruct (تَقْدِيرٌ) the underlying level on which the عامِل could be seen to operate.

For example, when a person shouts *"help!"* (النَّجْدةَ!), we use the word in the accusative case (مَنْصُوبٌ). But if there is only one word, what could be the regent? We can explain it by assuming that the corresponding **verb** has been **deleted**. So النَّجْدَة could be understood as follows: *I request help* (!أَطْلُبُ النَّجْدَةَ). In this sentence, *help* is the direct object (مَفْعُولٌ بِهِ) of the verb and is therefore in the accusative case.

What is the difference to *morphology* (صَرْفٌ or تَصْرِيفٌ) which is another big part of teaching Arabic? In the area of صَرْفٌ we examine the **structure of words** and focus on explaining changes they go through that are **not caused by a regent** (عَامِلٌ). Linguists call that non-syntactic changes. Students should have a good foundation of صَرْفٌ to understand grammar (نَحْوٌ). The first Arabic grammarians did not distinguish between نَحْوٌ and صَرْفٌ for good reason.

Karīm is writing a book.	كَرِيمٌ كَاتِبٌ كِتَابًا.

You cannot know the place, the position in which an element is used (مَوْضِعٌ, lit.: *where something is placed*) of كِتَابًا unless you know that كَاتِبٌ is an active participle (اِسْمُ الْفَاعِلِ) that has the force of a verb. Only then you can know the job/function (الْوَظِيفَةُ النَّحْوِيّةُ) of كِتَابًا; in our example: the direct object. Each place (مَوْضِعٌ) represents a specific linguistic act. For example, the place for calling is realized by the word يا expressing the meaning of calling.

➤ صَرْفٌ is the tool to understand a word in its **independent form**.

➤ نَحْوٌ is the tool to understand the **meaning** of that word **in a sentence**.

14. What are the two most famous Arabic grammar schools?

The schools of Basra (الْبَصْرِيُّونَ) *and Kūfa* (الْكُوفِيُّونَ).

The 8th century was the heyday of Arabic grammar. Two opposing schools of grammar had dominated the scene and were named after the cities in which they operated: Basra and Kūfa (both located in present-day Iraq). Both were the two leading cultural centers before the foundation of Baghdad, which was established in 762 (145 AH) by the Abbasid Caliph al-Mansūr (الْمَنْصُور). Many of the superstars of Arabic grammar were not native Arabic speakers, but mostly of Persian origin. Both schools had their figureheads:

- **Basrans**: Sībawayhi (سيبويه), one of the greatest grammarians in history. Al-Khalīl (الْخَلِيل), who wrote the first Arabic dictionary.

- **Kūfans:** Al-Kisā'i (الْكِسائي), a controversial figure in the history of Arabic grammar. Some say he who knew everything about Arabic grammar; others that he knew nothing about it. His dispute with Sībawayhi is legendary and is discussed in *question #17*.

    Another important figure of this school was al-Farrā' (الْفَرّاء) who provided many explanations for difficult grammar points in the Qur'an. In general, the Kūfans focused more on poetry.

Both schools had different views on syntax, semantics, and the philosophy of language. The **Basrans** preferred analogy for solving problems and are known to be normative. The **Kūfans** stressed on the existence of exceptions to general rules and are known to be descriptive. **So, who won the competition?** We could say it was Basra.

Sībawayhi's grammar book became the model for a standardized Arabic grammar. The main problem that separated the Basrans from the Kūfans, however, had nothing to do with grammar.

- The Basrans insisted on closing the linguistic corpus. In other words, even if new texts were discovered, they would not be used to justify a change of rules. They wanted to adopt Sībawayhi's book as the source of all their data.

- The Kūfans, on the other hand, said that further data (i.e., texts) could always be discovered. In modern terms, we could say that the Kūfans saw grammar as a rolling software distribution.

The Kūfan position didn't fit into the ideological demands of the Islamic State, as M.G. Carter (2004) suggests in his book *Sibawayhi*. Thus, the Kūfan approach was forced into irrelevance. Islamic scholars couldn't tolerate a situation in which the rules were likely to be broken at any minute by newly discovered usages. Islamic jurisprudence faced the same dilemma. At some point, the scholars had to decide to seal the data. They feared that newly discovered sources would invalidate old judgments. Carter suggests that it is no coincidence that both the *principles of law* (أُصُولُ الْفِقْه) and the *principles of grammar* (أُصُولُ النَّحْوِ) came into being at the same time and with the same purpose.

Remark: It is estimated that more than 4,000 Arabic grammarians developed the core of the language over 750 years (from ~750 to ~1500).

15. How do we know that a scholar belongs to the Kūfa school?

We should check which term the author uses for the genitive case.

Both schools of Grammar (Basra and Kūfa) shared many grammar terms, but they used different terms for the genitive case:

- The **Kūfa** school of Arabic grammar uses خَفْضٌ which means *lowering, reduction*.
- The **Basra** school favors جَرٌّ which means *pulling, dragging*.

➤ What's most important to us: Both terms denote the same thing – the pronunciation of the final consonant with "*i*".

16. What role did the Bedouins play in the creation of grammar?

They played a big part.

The Bedouins were considered the true speakers of Arabic. Early works on grammar and the first dictionaries were heavily based on the spoken Arabic of the Bedouins. Caliphs who wanted their sons to speak Arabic correctly sent them to the Bedouins in the desert. There are many anecdotes about scholars who went into the desert to find Bedouins who could answer their questions about Arabic grammar.

A famous legend tells the story of Abū Mansūr al-ʾAzharī (أَبُو مَنْصُور الْأَزْهَرِيّ), a grammarian and lexicographer (895/282 AH – 980/370 AH). In the year 924 (312 AH) he was with the pilgrim caravan on the way back from Mecca to Kūfa when they were attacked by the Qarāmita tribe (الْقَرامِطة), a Shia (Ismāʿīlī) offshoot in eastern Arabia near modern-day Bahrain. Many travelers were massacred; al-ʾAzharī was taken captive. As a prisoner, al-ʾAzharī spent about two years with the Bedouins of the Hawāzin tribe (قَبِيلة هَوازِن) who grazed their cattle in the east of the Arabian Peninsula.

After his release he began to compose his famous work: *Tahdhīb al-Lugha* (تَهْذِيب اللُّغة), *The Reparation of Speech*, and wrote in the introduction: "They [the Bedouins] speak according to their desert nature and their ingrained instincts. In their speech, you hardly ever hear a linguistic error or a terrible mistake."[2]

Around the year 980 (370 AH), al-'Azharī died where he was born, in Herat, Khorasan (present-day Afghanistan). His lexicon was one of the most important sources for Ibn Manzūr's monumental dictionary *Lisān al-'Arab* (لِسان الْعَرَب).

Remark: The attackers were led by Abū Tāhir al-Jannābī. He outraged the Muslim world five years later (317 AH) when he raided Mecca and stole the Black Stone (الْحَجَرُ الْأَسْوَدُ) from the Kaaba (الْكَعْبَةُ). He forced the Abbasids to pay a huge sum for its return which happened around 941 (330 AH).

17. What does a *wasp* have to do with Arabic grammar?

The wasp stars in one of the most famous linguistic disputes in history.

Legend has it that the *question concerning the wasp – al-Mas'ala al-Zunbūrīya* (الْمَسْأَلَةُ الزُّنْبُورِيَّةُ) – caused Sībawayhi, the most famous grammarian of Arabic, to withdraw and die of anger and sadness.

According to several accounts, Sībawayhi (سيبويه) was challenged by his rival from Kūfa, al-Kisā'i (الْكِسائي), to pronounce himself on an abstruse question.

In the following sentence in Arabic, should you use both pronouns in the nominative case (i.e., هُوَ هِيَ) or do you use the second pronoun in the accusative case (i.e., هُوَ إِيَّاها)?

I used to think that the sting of a scorpion was more intense than that of a wasp (or hornet), **but** [I discovered that] **it was the same.**	كُنْتُ أَظُنُّ أَنَّ الْعَقْرَبَ أَشَدُّ لَسْعَةً مِنَ الزُّنْبُورِ فَإِذا هُوَ هِيَ (or هُوَ إِيَّاها).

The following translation clarifies what the pronouns refer to: *I used to think that the scorpion was more vehement in stinging than the wasp/hornet, and lo, he is (as vehement as) she.* The gender is important: زُنْبُورٌ is masculine (مُذَكَّرٌ) whereas عَقْرَبٌ is usually treated as feminine (مُؤَنَّثٌ).

---

2   يَتَكَلَّمُونَ بِطِباعِهِمِ الْبَدَوِيّةِ، وَقَرائِحِهِمِ الَّتِي اِعْتادُوها وَلا يَكادُ (يَقَعُ) فِي مَنْطِقِهِم لَحْنٌ أَوْ خَطَأٌ فاحِشٌ.

Sībawayhi said that هُوَ هِيَ was correct. Al-Kisā'i said the opposite.

Sībawayhi	هِيَ must be in the **nominative** (مَرْفُوعٌ).	فَإذا هُوَ هِيَ
Al-Kisā'i	إيّاها must be in the **accusative** (مَنْصُوبٌ).	فَإذا هُوَ إيّاها
To illustrate the problem: A similar question in English would be whether *it is she* or it *is her* is correct. In other words, whether the word in question should be in the nominative (*she*) or in the accusative case (*her*).		

Let's analyze what Sībawayhi proposed:

Conjunction (حَرْفُ عَطْفٍ). It does not have a place in إِعْرابٌ.	ف
Particle of surprise (حَرْفُ مُفَاجَأةٍ). It does not have a place in إِعْرابٌ.	إذا
Personal pronoun (ضَمِيرٌ مُنْفَصِلٌ) which relates to *scorpion*. It is the **subject** (مُبْتَدَأ) of the **nominal sentence** (جُمْلَةٌ اِسْمِيّةٌ). Although not visible due to the cemented, indeclinable shape, هُوَ is located in the position of a nominative (فِي مَحَلّ رَفْعٍ) since it is the subject.	هُوَ
Personal pronoun (ضَمِيرٌ مُنْفَصِلٌ); serves as the **predicate** (خَبَرٌ). It has a fixed, indeclinable shape (مَبْنِيٌّ عَلَى الْفَتْحِ), so we can't visibly mark the case. Nevertheless, the word occupies the position of a nominative case (فِي مَحَلّ رَفْعٍ) since it is the predicate.	هِيَ

And al-Kisā'i? He agreed with everything we've said so far, except for the last word. He insisted on إيّاها. There are two ways to treat إيّاها.

Option 1 إيّاها is an indeclinable, separated personal pronoun (ضَمِيرٌ مُنْفَصِلٌ) which serves as the **direct object** (مَفْعُولٌ بِهِ), so it is located in the position of an accusative case (فِي مَحَلّ نَصْبٍ). But how can it be the direct object since there is apparently <u>no</u> verb in the sentence? He assumed that there is a deleted verb (فِعْلٌ مَحْذُوفٌ) which is still understood. It could have been the verb *to be equivalent to* (يُساوِيها). Thus, we apply the rules of a **verbal sentence** (جُمْلَةٌ فِعْلِيّةٌ). The result is a primary nominal sentence starting with هُوَ, followed by a verbal sentence.

Now it all gets a little more complicated. Although many people say that إيّاها is the accusative case of هِيَ, this is not entirely correct. إيّاها has a fixed shape and theoretically would always look like this in any case. So we have to be precise and say that إيّاها is placed in the position of an accusative case (فِي مَحَلّ نَصْبٍ). It is, roughly speaking, the word you use when you need the accusative case of هِيَ.

We still need to fix one problem. Where is the **predicate (خَبَرٌ)** of the subject (مُبْتَدَأٌ), i.e., هُوَ, of the **primary (nominal) sentence?** Sībawayhi said that it is هِيَ. However, if we use option 1, then it is the entire verbal sentence (with the estimated, deleted verb). It is quite common for an entire sentence to serve as a خَبَرٌ. In such a situation, we assign a place value and say that the sentence occupies the position or place of a nominative case (فِي مَحَلّ رَفْعٍ) because the rule says that the predicate has to be in the nominative case. This is all rather confusing, but it is a way to justify why you see the personal pronoun in the accusative case.

Option 2 The personal pronoun إِيَّاها is the **predicate of the deleted verb** كَانَ (خَبَرُ كَانَ الْمَحْذُوفةِ مَعَ اسْمِها). The rules say that the predicate of كَانَ must be in the accusative case (مَنْصُوبٌ), so we arrive at إِيَّاها.

We already said that هُوَ is the subject (مُبْتَدَأٌ) of the primary nominal sentence. This subject needs a predicate. Now, where is the خَبَرٌ? The predicate is represented by كَانَ including its two governed factors (كَانَ وَمَعْمُولَاها): the "subject" of كَانَ (اسْمُ كَانَ) and the predicate of كَانَ (خَبَرُ كَانَ). They together supply the position of the predicate of the nominal sentence and are placed in the location of a nominative (فِي مَحَلّ رَفْعٍ).

Back then public debates about grammar were a form of entertainment in which the goal was not so much to establish a truth as to defeat an opponent in front of an audience. Sībawayhi was convinced that an accusative (مَنْصُوبٌ), which would be إِيَّاها, can't be the predicate of a nominal sentence. According to some traditions, his rival, al-Kisā'i, presented thereupon four Bedouins who were pretending to have just happened to be waiting at the door. They announced that a true Bedouin would only say إِيَّاها.

Followers of the Basra school claimed that al-Kisā'i had bribed them beforehand to support his answer. Followers of the Kūfa school rejected this and stated that it would be an insult to throw such allegations on al-Kisā'i's name. In the end, the four Bedouins testified that هُوَ إِيَّاها was correct. Sībawayhi, it seemed, was wrong. He left Baghdad and went to Shiraz in Persia where he soon died of anger and grief at the result of the debate, consoled by a payment of 10,000 dirhams solicited for him by al-Kisāʾī, as legend has it. Others say that he died of illness.

The argument most likely took place and is well recorded, e.g., by Ibn al-ʾAnbārī (اِبْن الْأَنْبَارِيّ; died 1181/577 AH). The story of the bribe, however, is not well founded. The dispute was typical for the discussions at that time because it dealt with **"what can be said"** and **"what can't be said"** in Arabic. Sībawayhi was being judged on this ability to speak correctly and not on the logic of his analysis. If one made a mistake, it only meant that he didn't say it in the way the Bedouins speak.

Watch out! The translation of the last part of the *wasp question* is tricky. It is not entirely clear to which words the feminine pronouns relate. Such problems occur in English too. For example: *The father hit his son because **he** was drunk.* What do you think – which of them was drunk? The father or the son? → See #113 for a deep analysis of such constructions. Let us now look at possible translations of the last part:

Slane (1842-1871)	and behold! It was so.
Blau (1963)	and behold, the one is (like) the other.
Carter (2004)	and sure enough it is.(Cart. relates لَسْعة to إِيّاهَا/هِيَ)
Ramzi Baalbaki (2014)	but [I discovered that] it was the same.
Versteegh (2014)	but it was the other way round.
Lutz Edzard (2016)	(however,) the former is (like) the latter.
In my mother tongue (German), I would say: *Ich glaubte, der Skorpion stäche heftiger als die Hornisse/Wespe, und siehe, sie ist (in dieser Beziehung wie) er.*	

18. What came first: noun or verb?

Nouns (اِسْمٌ) are probably older.

Unfortunately, we cannot step into a time machine and witness the beginnings of the Arabic language. There are, however, some indications that nouns are older than verbs.

- As for Semitic languages, we know from archaeological finds that forms of nouns are almost certainly older than those of verbs.

- In Arabic, there are verbs which are based on nouns (لِاتِّخاذِ الْفِعْلِ مِن الْإِسْم). They are called denominal verbs (derived from nouns) and are usually II-verbs, IV-verbs, or X-verbs. E.g.: *to greet* (سَلَّمَ).

- The number of noun patterns is significantly higher compared to the stereotyped verb forms. This could support the idea that nouns are an earlier type than verbs.

- The grammarian Ibn Jinnī (ابن جِنّي; died 1002/392 AH) was an expert on phonology and morphology. He suggested that nouns have a better ability to change because they were the first, and therefore must be considered the origin (الْأَصْلُ).

- Some Arabic nouns have biliteral roots: words with only two radicals. → There is often a reference to Ancient Egyptian and Hebrew.

Some examples of biliteral roots and their relation to other languages:

meaning	Ancient Egyptian	Hebrew	Arabic
son	bn	ben (בֶּן)	ابْنٌ
name	sm	shem (שֵׁם)	اسْمٌ
hand	yd	yad (יָד)	يَدٌّ

19. How can you tell that a word in Arabic is of foreign origin?

Check if the meaning deviates from the core meaning of the root.

The first Arabic scholars who started to compile dictionaries assumed that words which share the same root are related in meaning. Why is that important? Well, if a word deviates from the core meaning, it is usually a reliable sign that it is of foreign origin.

For example, words with the root letters ح-ب-ب are usually related to *love* or *loving*. There is a word that not only consists of the same root letters, but also has the same form as the Arabic word for *love:* the word for *water container* (حُبٌّ). Scholars suggested that this word was probably taken from Persian.

20. What does أَكَلُونِي الْبَراغِيثُ mean?

It means: the fleas devoured (ate) me.

In Classical and Modern Standard Arabic, the verb precedes the subject. It must be in the **third person singular** because it only agrees with the subject in **gender** (and not in number!). In some variants (ancient dialects) of Arabic, this rule was violated.

Grammarians use the expression أَكَلُونِي الْبَراغِيثُ (*the fleas consumed* [masculine plural!] *me*) to signify that a verb at the beginning **agrees in number with the subject** → natural agreement between subject and verb. Although the verb starts a sentence, it can get the dual or plural form, i.e., the verb has the و of the plural, the Aleph of the dual, or the ن of the feminine person attached. It is even possible that a plural verb refers to a singular collective noun (since it is understood as a plural).

		فُصْحَى	certain dialects
dual (هُما, f.)	*His eyes were red.*	إحْمَرَّتْ عَيْناهُ.	احْمَرَّتا عَيْناهُ.
Sing. collective	*My people aided you.*	نَصَرَكَ قَوْمِي.	نَصَرُوكَ قَوْمِي.

Such constructions are rare in Classical Arabic. Let's see the difference:

Classical Arabic (فُصْحَى)		أَكَلَتْنِي الْبَراغِيثُ.
certain ancient dialects	*The fleas ate me.*	أَكَلُونِي الْبَراغِيثُ.

Note: The expression أَكَلُونِي الْبَراغِيثُ goes back to the dialect of an ancient Arab tribe called Tayy' (طيّء). Their original homeland was Yemen. In the 2nd century CE, they migrated to the northern Arabian mountain ranges.

21. How did the scribes of the Qur'an set the rules for the Hamza?

They came up with a mix.

English speakers often insert a glottal stop before initial vowels, like in the words *it* or *ate* (which is, by the way, very much the same in Arabic). In English, we usually don't notice glottal stops because they do not change the meaning – which is different in Arabic! The Hamza (glottal stop) is a letter of the alphabet which can be a root letter.

The text of the Qur'an is the basis of Arabic orthography. The text was mainly written down in accordance with the local pronunciation of the people living in the Hijāz (الْحِجَازُ), a region in the west of present-day Saudi Arabia.

In the Hijāz, the هَمْزَةٌ was probably not known or discarded. The Quraysh (قُرَيْشٌ), a merchant tribe, were the rulers of Mecca during the time of the Islamic Prophet Muhammad. The locals traded with people from Syria and Egypt which affected their dialect. Scholars suggest that the Quraysh more or less did not pronounce the هَمْزَةٌ.

This was different in the *hinterland* of Arabia, the Najd, where the Banū Tamīm (بَنُو تَمِيمٍ) and the Qays tribe (قَيْسٌ) lived. They both sounded it true at the time of the establishment of Islam. Also in pre-Islamic poems, the هَمْزَةٌ was pronounced.

Because of the prestige of poetry and of the *hinterland* people, the Qur'an scribes of the Hijāz had to find a way to record the glottal stop. In their own speech, the هَمْزَةٌ was often replaced by a long vowel. They used this approach and spelled words containing a هَمْزَةٌ with a long vowel represented by a semi-consonant (و or ي) or a glide (l).

If you see one of them in a word, it may indicate that there once was a Hamza (هَمْزَةٌ) with a corresponding preceding short vowel. Nevertheless, Classical Arabic knows many words with the old guttural هَمْزَةٌ (glottal stop), i.e., ء - ئ - ؤ. Some examples:

meaning	Najd (also used in the Qur'an)	Hijāz
head	رَأْسٌ	راس
I came	جِئْتُ	جيت

22. Did Prophet Muhammad pronounce the هَمْزَةٌ (glottal stop)?

At least the Islamic prophet did not like the هَمْزَةٌ very much.

Native speakers today tend to avoid or neglect the Hamza in dialects, and so did some Arab tribes at the time of the establishment of Islam.

The **Quraysh** (قُرَيْشٌ) most probably did **not** pronounce the هَمْزة in the Arabic word for *prophet* (i.e., نَبِيٌّ), but other tribes did (i.e., نَبِيءٌ). This was of great importance for the Islamic Prophet Muhammad who belonged to the Quraysh.

There is an anecdote about that. A man had addressed him and pronounced the هَمْزة in the Arabic word for *prophet*.

Muhammad noticed it and referred to it in his answer.

A man said to the prophet: *"O Prophet of Allah!"*	يا نَبِيْءَ اللهِ !
And the prophet replied: *"Don't pronounce my name with Hamza!"*	لا تَنْبِرْ بِاسْمِي !
Note: The I-verb نَبَرَ - يَنْبِرُ has many meanings, among them are *to lay the stress on; to pronounce or mark a letter with Hamza* (هَمْزَةٌ).	

Why was that important to Muhammad?

Only then could he claim to be a leader. Muhammad disapproved pronouncing the Arabic word for *prophet* with هَمْزة because it would have suggested that he had not been from Mecca since the Quraysh pronounced this word most probably without هَمْزة.

His clearly recognizable Meccan origin, however, was important to be accepted as a leader. Hence, the Arabic word for *prophet*, especially when it relates to Muhammad, is written without Hamza: نَبِيٌّ.

Instead of the Hamza, the ي was doubled (شَدَّةٌ) as compensation.

→ See *Arabic for Nerds 1, quest. #64*, for the spelling rules of Hamza.

Chapter 2:
Decoding Arabic Grammar

WHAT YOU NEED TO KNOW ABOUT إِعْرابٌ

23. What is the formula (steps) to analyze a word in Arabic?

There are three main formulas.

Reading grammar books in Arabic is difficult if you cannot decipher the language of the grammarians. Unfortunately, many authors rarely use commas or dashes which makes it even more complicated. Let's start with the standard situation.

Situation 1: <u>noun</u> (اِسْمٌ مُعْرَبٌ) without anomalies or special features.

The dog is at home.	الْكَلْبُ فِي الْبَيْتِ

Let's put الْكَلْبُ under the microscope. We need three steps (formula):

STEP 1: State the **function of the word** in the sentence. In our example: *subject of a nominal sentence* (مُبْتَدَأٌ). Other examples *circumstantial qualifier* (حالٌ), direct object (مَفْعُولٌ بِهِ), specification (تَمْيِيزٌ), etc.

STEP 2: State the **case**. In our example: nominative (مَرْفُوعٌ).

STEP 3: State **how the case is expressed**. In our example: by a visible marker for the nominative case (بِالضَّمَّةِ الظَّاهِرةِ) or if you prefer the extended version: وَعَلامةُ رَفْعِهِ الضَّمّةُ الظّاهِرةُ

step 3	step 2	step 1	noun
وَعَلامةُ رَفْعِهِ الضَّمّةُ الظّاهِرةُ	مَرْفُوعٌ	مُبْتَدَأٌ	الْكَلْبُ:
the sign for the nominative is a visible ُ	nominative	subject	*the dog*

Some nouns, though they are inflected (= get cases) don't show their end vowels for certain reasons. Then we need to **assume** the case marker. We will use the term مُقَدَّرٌ (*assumed, estimated*). → See #38.

Situation 2: words that <u>cannot receive case markers</u> (مَبْنِيٌّ).

Now, what happens, if the word in question is not a declinable noun? We get this situation, e.g., when we analyze a particle (حَرْفٌ) or a word with a fixed (indeclinable) shape (مَبْنِيٌّ). We can use the following formula made of four steps:

STEP 1: You should first state the **type and nature** of the word. You do this only when the word is indeclinable and cannot get case markers. This happens, for example, with pronouns (ضَمِيرٌ), *demonstratives* (اسْمُ إِشارةٍ), *relative pronouns* (اسْمٌ مَوْصُولٌ), *adverbs of place* (ظَرْفُ زَمانٍ). You may also examine entire sentences, which are mingled into the larger sentence and are placed where you would usually expect a single word. A possible wording would be: *the sentence consisting of the subject and the predicate* (الْجُمْلةُ مِن الْمُبْتَدَإِ وَالْخَبَرِ).

STEP 2: When you deal with an indeclinable word (مَبْنِيٌّ), you should state the **sound on which the word is structured/built.** For example: *fixed/structured on "a"* (مَبْنِيٌّ عَلَى الْفَتْحِ).

STEP 3: This is the most important part: Since you can't put case markers on indeclinable words, you need to **assign a place value.** In grammar, we use the term مَحَلٌّ which means *place*. The *place* in syntax concerns the grammatical function fulfilled by the **noun**, the **verb**, or the **sentence** after the application of the referential relation to them or between them. The مَحَلٌّ is the spot that is assigned to a certain grammatical function in a sentence. Normally this function is evident by the case marker. However, indeclinable words do not show signs that indicate their function. That is why you need to mention the *place*. For example: *located in the position (place) of a nominative case* (فِي مَحَلِّ رَفْعٍ).

STEP 4: State the **grammatical function** of the word. For example: *subject of a verbal sentence* (فاعِلٌ), *predicate of a nominal sentence* (خَبَرٌ).

In the following example, we will analyze two words: the letter ه at the end of the verb and the last word (غَدًا).

| I will visit him tomorrow. | سَأَزُورُهُ غَدًا. |

step 4	step 3	step 2	step 1	letter
مَفْعُولٌ بِهِ	فِي مَحَلّ نَصْبٍ	مَبْنِيٌّ عَلَى الضَّمِّ	ضَمِيرٌ مُتَّصِلٌ	ه (الْهاءُ):
direct object of the verb visit (أَزُورُ)	in the location of an accusative case	indeclinable; structured (fixed) on the vowel "u"	pronoun suf- fix	him

مَفْعُولٌ فِيهِ	فِي مَحَلّ نَصْبٍ	مَبْنِيٌّ عَلَى الْفَتْحِ	ظَرْفُ زَمانٍ	غَدًا
adverbial ob- ject of time or place	in the location of an accusative case	indeclinable (fixed/structured) on the vowel "a"	adverb of time	tomorrow

Situation 3: a verb (فِعْلٌ).

Only the present tense verb (فِعْلٌ مُضارِعٌ) gets إِعْرابٌ (mood markers). When you analyze a present tense verb, you have to choose one of the following three: "u"/indicative (مَرْفُوعٌ), "a"/subjunctive (مَنْصُوبٌ), or clipping the ending/jussive (مَجْزُومٌ); see *question #62* for the reason.

We should go through six steps (formula), although we may not need all of them.

STEP 1: State the tense. For example: present tense (فِعْلٌ مُضارِعٌ)

STEP 2: If the verb is used in a conditional sentence, state whether it is used in the "if"-part (فِعْلُ الشَّرْطِ) or main part (جَوَابُ الشَّرْطِ).

STEP 3: State the mood: indicative (مَرْفُوعٌ), jussive (مَجْزُومٌ), or sub-junctive (مَنْصُوبٌ).

STEP 4: Give the reason for the إِعْرابٌ, i.e., which word is responsible for the mood?

STEP 5: Give the marker of the إِعْرابٌ. For ex., سُكُونٌ for the jussive.

STEP 6: If the subject of the verb is hidden – which means that it is not a noun nor a pronoun) -, state the implied pronoun.

| If you study, you will succeed. | | | | | إِنْ تَدْرُسْ تَنْجَحْ. |

step 6	step 5	step 3 + 4	step 2	step 1	verb
الْفَاعِلُ: ضَمِيرٌ مُسْتَتِرٌ تَقْدِيرُهُ (أَنْتَ)	وَعَلامةُ جَزْمِهِ السُّكُنُ	مَجْزُومٌ بِإِنْ	فِعْلُ الشَّرْطِ	فِعْلٌ مُضَارِعٌ	تَدْرُسْ: فِعْلٌ
subject: hidden, implied pronoun with the assumed meaning of *you*	mood is marked by سُكُونْ	jussive induced by إ نْ	conditional	present tense	you study

What about the past tense verb (الْماضِي)?

The past tense verb and the imperative (فِعْلُ أَمْرٍ) are both uninflected. The past tense verb has a fixed, cemented shape and doesn't get any grammatical inflection (مَبْنِيٌّ عَلَى الْفَتْحِ) → see *question #43*. In other words, you don't have to worry about mood markers because the past tense verb doesn't occur in the jussive or subjunctive mood. Only in very rare situations this may happen. Then you have to use a place value – *see #391*.

It's kind of logical. In Arabic, the الْماضِي says less about time itself and more about whether an action is completed or not. The past tense expresses a completed action, which is why special markings that make something seem possible or important would not really make sense.

| Muhammad went to school. | | | ذَهَبَ مُحَمَّدٌ إِلَى الْمَدْرَسِةِ. |

step 4 + 5	step 3	step 1	verb
لا مَحَلَّ لَهُ مِن الْإِعْرابِ	مَبْنِيٌّ عَلَى الْفَتْحِ	فِعْلٌ ماضِي	ذَهَبَ:
The verb doesn't have a place in the grammatical analysis. In other words, it does not express a certain mood and is not influenced by any other device.	indeclinable; fixed shape	past tense verb	*(he) went*

Most authors use similar formulas. Commas and colons would make life much easier. Don't forget that the explanations are only chunks of information. Whenever you read the إِعْرابٌ, don't treat the information as a meaningful sentence.

غَدًا: ظَرْفُ زَمانٍ, مَبْنِيٌّ عَلَى الْفَتْحِ, في مَحَلِّ نَصْبٍ, مَفْعُولٌ فِيهِ

In the following example, you want to express that a verbal sentence serves as the predicate:

وَالْجُمْلَةُ مِن الْفِعْلِ وَالْفاعِلِ: في مَحَلِّ رَفْعٍ, خَبَرٌ

Remark: If you want to learn how to express a grammatical analysis in Arabic, there aren't many books. You could try Mughnī al-Labīb (مُغْنِي اللَّبِيبِ) by ʿAbd Allāh ibn Yūsuf Ibn Hishām (عَبْد اللَّه بن يُوسُف ابن هشام; died 1360/761 AH) who was a scholar from Cairo. His book *Mughnī al-Labīb* is one of the finest works on Arabic syntax.

The word مُغْنِي is the active participle (اسْمُ الْفاعِلِ) of the IV-verb أَغْنَى which has many meanings: *to be of use/help, to enrich, to be enough*. The word لَبِيب denotes *reasonable, sensible*. We could translate the title of his work as: *Sufficient knowledge of the sensible one*. A loose translation would be: *the sensible approach*.

24. How much do English and Arabic grammar differ?

Not as much as you might think.

If you read grammar books, you may feel that both languages could not be more different. In my opinion, this is true for the vocabulary, but not for the grammar. Let's look at the main points.

1. Case endings and word order. *Big differences.*

Let's assume you don't know English grammar and hear the following sentence: *The man bites the dog.*

Intuitively, you'd probably say that it most probably means: *The dog bites the man* – because it is more logical. Since we don't use case endings in English, word-order is crucial. English grammar puts the doer of an action (subject) before the verb and the receiver of the action (object) after the verb. Knowing only the words without knowing the grammar could terribly mislead you. See also *Arabic for Nerds 1, #28.*

Arabic is more flexible. Although we usually put the verb at the beginning and let subject and object follow, words can be moved around, thanks to the invention of case markers. We use them to clearly mark the function and position of a word in a sentence.

Let's take the I-verb ضَرَبَ (*hit*) and assume that it is followed by two nouns: وَلَد (*boy*) and زَيْد (*Zayd*). Without case markers, the sentence can have 5 possible meanings.	ضَرَبَ وَلَد زَيْد.

1	A boy hit Zayd.	ضَرَبَ وَلَدٌ زَيْدًا.
2	Zayd hit a boy.	ضَرَبَ وَلَدًا زَيْدٌ.
3	Zayd's boy hit… (someone else); this is a إضافةٌ.	ضَرَبَ وَلَدُ زَيْدٍ...
4	He hit Zayd's boy.	ضَرَبَ وَلَدَ زَيْدٍ.
5	He hit a boy, Zayd. (Zayd is an apposition for *boy*.)	ضَرَبَ وَلَدًا زَيْدًا.

2. Tenses. *Little differences.*

It might be surprising, but Arabic and English work pretty similar regarding tenses and time. In Arabic as well as in English, there is only one form for the past and one for the present tense. Wait – but what about the future, the conditional, … in English? Germanic languages exhibit only two tense forms. English is a Germanic language. In French or Spanish, this is different.

The key word is <u>form</u>. Tense in English is a form as well as an idea. The future is formed by making the main verb conditional and by adding an adverb of time to the sentence. We need to introduce two linguistic terms in order to understand the concept of tenses in Arabic:

- **Tense**: a **form** of the verb which usually indicates the time when an action happened – in relation to the speaker.
- **Aspect**: deals with the degree of completeness of an action or state. Is the action completed, ongoing, or yet to happen?

When I use *tense* in this book, I mean the basic form of the verb and not the actual time of the event. Arabic doesn't have accurate time-points. In French the *imparfait* clearly describes a continuing state or action in the past. If you translate an Arabic sentence, you have to understand the situation of an event. Otherwise you can't find an appropriate tense for the translation.

The **past tense** usually relates to actions that happened in the past. However, in English and Arabic, the past tense can also refer to the future or convey a conditional meaning. Linguists say that the past tense is just a form – it doesn't necessarily tell you about the time.

The **present tense** can describe actions that are ongoing or that are habitual. For example: *Peter watches TV.* This can mean that Peter is watching <u>now</u> or that he does it regularly.

Arabic dialects, probably due to the influence of foreign languages, make the difference clearer. In dialects, you use the active particle (اِسْمُ الْفاعِلِ) when you want to stress that the action of the verb is taking place at the present time (right now).

In English, a verb has one of **two tenses** (past or present), a **mood** (indicative/normal, future, conditional), and an **aspect** (is the action or event completed or ongoing – present and progressive). Mood (modality) relates to the purpose of a sentence – whether it gives an order or indicates possibility or probability.

In Arabic, we have the same. We have **two tenses**: past (الْماضِي) and present (الْمُضارِعُ) tense. We have **moods**: indicative (مَرْفُوعٌ), subjunctive (مَنْصُوبٌ) and jussive (مَجْزُومٌ). And we can express a future or conditional meaning by auxiliary words (particles) such as سَوْفَ, س or لَوْ.

3. Types of words. *Big differences.*

This may be the most confusing part. English knows **nouns, verbs, adjectives, and adverbs**. They are the so-called basic constituents of sentences, those words that work together as single units.

Arabic knows three kinds of words: **nouns** (اِسْمٌ), **verbs** (فِعْلٌ), and **particles** (حَرْفٌ). The English translations are fuzzy and only give an approximate meaning. Only nouns and verbs (in the present tense) get markers for cases and moods. The adjective in Arabic is not a special type of word – it is a noun (اِسْمٌ). Thus, a word like *beautiful* (جَمِيلٌ) is, generally said, nothing but a derived noun (اِسْمٌ مُشْتاقٌّ). It belongs to the subcategory quasi-participle (صِفَةٌ مُشَبَّهَةٌ).

The **adverb** in Arabic may be a اِسْمٌ or a حَرْفٌ. It is important to classify such words correctly because a اِسْمٌ receives case endings. In Arabic, adverbs are more or less treated as certain objects (مَفْعُولٌ) of verbs.

4. Sentence structure. *Big differences.*

English doesn't know a sentence without a verb. In Arabic, this is no problem. A *nominal sentence* (جُمْلَةٌ اِسْمِيّةٌ) doesn't have a verb.

25. What gender should you use for Arabic grammar terms?

You can use both: masculine and feminine.

When you read grammar books, you get the impression that there are no rules for the correct gender of grammar terms. Let's take the Arabic term for *indeclinable. Some* authors choose the masculine form (مَبْنِيٌّ), others the feminine (مَبْنِيّةٌ). So, what is correct?

Both are correct. Both forms are actually adjectives – but for two different words which are not there, but understood anyway. What are these hidden words? Both are Arabic terms for *word*. Arabic has several words for *word*: لُغَةٌ or لَفْظٌ, كَلِمةٌ.

Now we get closer to the answer. Grammar terms like *indeclinable (word)* are regarded as...

- **masculine** – when they implicitly refer to the word لَفْظٌ;
- **feminine** – when they relate to the gender of كَلِمْةٌ or لُغةٌ.

Since مَبْنِيٌّ is an adjective and needs to be in grammatical agreement with the word to which it relates, it is a matter of taste whether the author had لَفْظٌ مَبْنِيٌّ or كَلِمةٌ مَبْنِيّةٌ in mind. So, you can use either form.

What about other grammar terms?

- Grammar terms which relate to اِسْمٌ: **adjectives** are **masculine**, taking the gender of اِسْمٌ. For ex.: *indeclinable noun* (اِسْمٌ مَبْنِيٌّ).
- Grammar terms relating to a particle (حَرْفٌ) are usually masculine.

However, they may also be **feminine** – because the author relates to أَداةٌ (*tool; instrument*) and not to the masculine حَرْفٌ. See #27.

- The verb كانَ (*to be*) seems by common consent to be taken as **feminine**, e.g., كانَ النّاقِصةُ (*defective "to be"*) or كانَ التّامّةُ (*complete verb "to be"*). Mere words like كانَ are treated as proper names and do not take the article.

- What about the letters of the alphabet? They can have both genders, but are usually treated as **feminine** – *see question #88.*

26. How many parts of speech does Arabic know?

Three types.

Noun (اِسْمٌ), verb (فِعْلٌ), and particle (حَرْفٌ). Three different categories doesn't sound much for such a rich language.

The main idea behind this classification relies on the fact that nouns and verbs have a well-defined morphology and range of meanings. There are very few overlaps. Particles, on the other hand, have no specific form – the only thing that particles have in common is that both their forms and meanings are different from those of nouns and verbs.

A **noun** (اِسْمٌ) is defined as a word that denotes a complete meaning by itself, having no reference to past or present tense. *Complete* here means that the word can be understood independently and without reference to anything else. The اِسْمٌ is equivalent to the noun in English, but it is much wider in scope. The term اِسْمٌ includes all pronouns, the infinitive (مَصْدَرٌ), adjectives, participles, and some adverbs.

A **verb** (فِعْلٌ) is a self-significant word having reference to past or present tense. It can only get mood markers.

A **particle** (حَرْفٌ) doesn't convey any complete meaning until another word is added to it. It depends on another word for its signification. Prepositions are the most important example of particles.

What's the benefit of identifying a word's nature correctly?

➢ NOUN: When you see a **noun** (اِسْمٌ), you have to think about the correct ending (case marker) because a اِسْمٌ gets a case marker. Linguists say that Arabic nouns are *declinable* (مُعْرَبٌ). The case marker can be visible (ظاهِرٌ) or invisible (مُقَدَّرَةٌ).

➤ **VERB:** Sentences are put together around **verbs**. Verbs determine the other components in sentences and define the relationships among those components.

Verbs tell you that certain nouns or phrases function as subjects and that other work as objects. They can **govern** other nouns and induce case endings therein, for example, the direct object (مَفْعُولٌ بِه) gets the accusative case (مَنْصُوبٌ) due to the influence of a verb. Verbs may have a position in إِعْرابٌ themselves which explains why they get mood markers. In other words, verbs can be **governed** which is expressed by *moods: indicative* (مَرْفُوعٌ), *subjunctive* (مَنْصُوبٌ), *jussive* (مَجْزُومٌ).

➤ **PARTICLE:** When you see a **particle** (حَرْفٌ) – for example, a **preposition** (حَرْفُ الْجَرِّ) –, you can be sure that it will stay the same and never change its form/shape, no matter what the position in the sentence is.

Such words are called مَبْنِيّ which means *set up, fixed, structured*; in linguistics: *indeclinable*. Basically, they have a cemented shape. You never have to think about which vowel you should put at the end.

A حَرْفٌ is never influenced by other words. We say that a حَرْفٌ does not have a place in the analysis (لا مَحَلَّ لَهُ مِن الْإِعْرابِ). A حَرْفٌ doesn't take different jobs or functions in a sentence. It can't serve as a *direct object* (مَفْعُولٌ بِه), *circumstantial description* (حالٌ), etc. A حَرْفٌ is often what we call a preposition. The Arabs call a *preposition* حَرْفُ الْجَرِّ which means *particle of dragging,* in the meaning of *subordination*.

You might also read الْجارُّ وَالْمَجْرُورُ which is used for *prepositional phrase*. جارٌّ - جَرَّ - يَجُرُّ is the active participle (اِسْمُ الْفاعِلِ) of the I-verb (R2=R3) which literally means *to drag; to pull*. In grammar, it denotes *governing the genitive*. مَجْرُورٌ is its passive participle (اِسْمُ الْمَفْعُولِ) and means *governed by a preposition; word in the genitive case.*

27. Are there *particles* in Arabic?

Purist Arabic grammarians would probably say no.

In English grammar, a particle is a word that often has little or no meaning. It is a nebulous term for a variety of short words that do not conveniently fit into other classes of words. For example, the word *up* in *look up* or the word *so* in the adverb *so far*.

Although I use the English term *particle* in this book too, we should bear in mind that this is not entirely correct in the Arabic framework. Unfortunately, there is some confusion here between English and Arabic grammatical logic. Grammarians mainly use two words to translate the term "particle". Some use أَداةٌ - لَأَدَواتٌ (tool, device), others use حَرْفٌ - حُرُوفٌ (single letter; consonant; particle). Both translations have problems. Not every English particle is a حَرْفٌ as we will see below. So, is it better to use the generic أَداةٌ for particle? On an abstract level, this is possible, but grammatically it makes little sense. We'll see why.

Every Arabic word must be a noun (اِسْمٌ), a verb (فِعْلٌ), or other than that (حَرْفٌ). Strictly speaking, we can't say *question particle* (أَداةُ اِسْتِفْهامٍ) or *negation particle* (أَداةُ نَفْيٍ) or *conditional particle* (أَداةُ شَرْطٍ) because Arabic doesn't know the category *particle*. *Question words* (كَلِماتُ الْإِسْتِفْهامِ) also do not form a special category in Arabic. They are either a حَرْفٌ or a اِسْمٌ with seriously different grammatical implications (although you might not see it). English grammar expressions cannot reflect this. In practice, only one thing is really important. You should be able to identify whether a "particle" is a حَرْفٌ or a اِسْمٌ.

Did Karīm come?	هَلْ جاءَ كَرِيمٌ؟
حَرْفُ اِسْتِفْهامٍ	هَلْ

The word هَلْ is a question (interrogative) particle. Since it is a حَرْفٌ, it can't get case inflections. It does **not** have a position in إِعْرابٌ.

When did Karīm come?	مَتَى جاءَ كَرِيمٌ؟
اِسْمُ اِسْتِفْهامٍ	مَتَى

مَتَى is a اِسْمٌ, so it may take different jobs in a sentence depending on its position. However, مَتَى is مَبْنِيٌّ and ends by definition in سُكُونٌ. Putting case markers is impossible. What do we do? We don't use visual markers. Instead, for the analysis, we use a "place value" according to the position

in the sentence. We say that مَتَى serves as an *adverb of time* (ظَرْفُ زَمانٍ);
therefore it is found in the position of an accusative case (فِي مَحَلِّ نَصْبٍ).

Who did come today?	مَنْ جاءَ الْيَوْمَ؟
اِسْمُ اِسْتِفْهامٍ	مَنْ

مَنْ is the subject (مُبْتَدَأ) of the nominal sentence (جُمْلَةٌ اِسْمِيّةٌ). A اِسْمٌ in
such a position, it should receive the marker of a nominative case. But this is
impossible because مَنْ is indeclinable (مَبْنِيٌّ). So we can only say that مَنْ -
as a subject - occupies the position of a nominative case (فِي مَحَلِّ رَفْعٍ مُبْتَدَأً).

IN SHORT: How should we deal with English particles in Arabic?

اِسْمٌ	What we call particle in English may be a noun in Arabic. As soon as we have identified that a "particle" is a اِسْمٌ, we have to check its function and thus its position in the sentence (e.g., subject, object, adverb, etc.). Eventually, we mark the function by the appropriate case ending which can be visible or not.	إِعْرابٌ
حَرْفٌ	When the "particle" is a حَرْفٌ in Arabic, we don't have to worry about its position in the sentence. Watch out: A حَرْفٌ does influence <u>other</u> words – but never gets affected by others.	NO إِعْرابٌ

28. What does إِعْرابٌ mean?

A practical translation of إِعْرابٌ *is declension.*

إِعْرابٌ is the grammatical analysis of a sentence. What is the function
of each word? Linguists call this process *parsing* or *syntax analysis*.
Only when you identify the function of a word do you know what the
word means in a sentence. Many languages use diacritical marks (case
endings) to indicate the function and to avoid any misunderstandings.

إِعْرابٌ is the مَصْدَرٌ of the IV-verb أَعْرَبَ - يُعْرِبُ which means *to use
good Arabic; to pronounce the final short vowels of a word.*

The grammar genius Mālik ibn 'Anas (مالِك بن أَنَس) had put it like
this: "إِعْرابٌ is the jewelry of your tongue, so do not deprive your

tongue of its jewelry."[3] Unfortunately, the Arabs did not really follow his advice. Scholars assume that in spoken Arabic the use of declensional endings (the pronunciation of case markers) had already died out around the year 600 CE (23 BH).

Applying إِعْرَابٌ involves the explicit (ظَاهِرٌ) or implicit (مُقَدَّرٌ) change at the end of nouns (اِسْمٌ) and verbs (فِعْلٌ). We achieve this by vowel markers (حَرَكَاتٌ) or letters (حُرُوفٌ) according to the place a word occupies, i.e., the places of جَرٍّ, نَصْبٍ, رَفْعٍ, or جَزْمٍ. Those places are governed by a particular regent (عَامِلٌ).

إِعْرَابٌ is as much fun as solving logic puzzles and will eventually give you a better feeling and understanding of Arabic. Whenever you see a word, always ask yourself: Is it **master** (عَامِلٌ) or **slave** (مَعْمُولٌ)? Does it occupy a **neutral place** (لا مَحَلَّ لَهُ مِن الْإِعْرَابِ)?

The master/slave-model (or less loaded: doctor/patient; boss/employee; operator/operated on model) explains quite well the concept of إِعْرَابٌ. The master is called **regent** or **governor** (عَامِلٌ). It is the device which causes case endings in another word: in the passive element or **slave** (مَعْمُولٌ). We say that the عَامِلٌ *governs* other words.

What should we do if we can't put case markers on a word? This happens in two situations:

1. A word has a fixed (structured), cemented shape (مَبْنِيٌّ). Grammarians call such words **indeclinable**; for example, the word هذا (*this*).

2. A word **can't carry any vowel** on the last letter. This is the situation when a word ends in Aleph (ى or ا); e.g., مَبْنًى (*building*). You can't put case markers on the last letter ى.

The grammarians found a solution for such situations: *the place of a word* (الْمَحَلُّ مِن الْإِعْرَابِ). Let's assume you have a verbal sentence, and the subject is the word *building* (مَبْنًى). We know that the subject takes the nominative case (مَرْفُوعٌ). How do we mark مَبْنًى as the subject? We can't use case endings. We say that it occupies *the place* of the subject, marked by a virtual, estimated marker of the nominative case (فِي مَحَلِّ رَفْعِ فَاعِلٍ) which is neither written nor pronounced!

---

3   الْإِعْرَابُ حَلْيُ اللِّسَانِ فَلَا تَمْنَعُوا أَلْسِنَتَكُمْ حَلْيَهَا.

Verbs and nouns usually have a role in a sentence. But what about **particles** (حَرْفٌ) like prepositions, conjunctions, or even single letters?

Particles and letters don't get case inflections and are immune to changes – but they may work as regents and cause case endings in other words. We call that *syntactical action* (عَمَلٌ نَحْوِيٌّ). They trigger something, but they can never be governed by anyone else – which means, they don't occupy the position of a certain case in the sentence. This is true for negation particles (لا, ما), prepositions, particles of a conditional clause, etc.

29. Which sounds are used for إِعْرابٌ?

It mainly comes down to three sounds and the marker of quiescence.

Grammarians in the West refer to the three Arabic cases as *nominative* (مَرْفُوعٌ), *genitive* (مَجْرُورٌ), and *accusative* (مَنْصُوبٌ). The nominative indicates **independence**, the accusative that a word **depends** on another one, and the genitive expresses **subordination** or **possession**.

Let's take, for example, the expression بَيْتُ الْمُدَرِّسِ. It means *the house of the teacher = the teacher's house*. We have a إضافة-construction which can be interpreted as *A of B*. → The second part (B = the teacher) gets the genitive case.

Usually the last letter matters for the إِعْرابٌ. There are four situations:

mood (verbs)	marker	case (nouns)	marker	marker	place
indicative	ُ	nominative	ُ or ٌ	الضَّمّةُ	الرَّفْعُ
subjunctive	َ	accusative	َ or ً	الْفَتْحةُ	النَّصْبُ
---	---	genitive	ِ or ٍ	الْكَسْرةُ	الْجَرُّ
jussive	ْ	---	---	السُّكُونُ	الْجَزْمُ

Karīm reads a book at home.	يَقْرَأُ كَرِيمٌ فِي الْبَيْتِ كِتابًا.

Verb in the present tense, **indicative mood**, first person singular. The mood is marked by a vowel	فِعْلٌ مُضارِعٌ مَرْفُوعٌ بِالضَّمّةِ الظّاهِرةِ	يَقْرَأُ

which is also pronounced: *"u"*.		
Subject of the verbal sentence; **nominative case** marked by the visible + pronounced ending *"-un"*.	فاعِلٌ مَرْفُوعٌ بِالضّمّةِ الظّاهِرةِ	كَرِيمٌ
Preposition. فِي never changes its **shape** (مَبْنِيٌّ); it also **never** gets a case. Why? Because a حَرْفٌ does not have a place in إِعْرابٌ.	حَرْفُ جَرٍّ مَبْنِيٌّ عَلَى السُّكُونِ لا مَحَلَّ لَهُ مِن الْإِعْرابِ	فِي
Noun which was dragged into the **genitive case** by the preposition فِي. The case is marked by the visible and pronounced ending *"-i"*.	اِسْمٌ مَجْرُورٌ بِفِي وَعَلامةُ جَرِّهِ الْكَسْرةُ الظّاهِرةُ	الْبَيْتِ
Direct object, in the **accusative case**, marked by the visible and pronounced ending *"-an"*.	مَفْعُولٌ بِهِ مَنْصُوبٌ بِالْفَتْحةِ الظّاهِرةِ	كِتابًا

30. Is each اِسْمٌ capable of showing the full range of case markers?

No. Some nouns express two endings only; others use different operations.

Let's start with the easy part. Words that express the full spectrum of case (nouns) or mood (verbs) endings. There are two situations:

1	**Nouns** which don't have a fixed, structured, cemented ending. They are **declinable** (الْإِسْمُ الْمُعْرَبُ).

- If you can't mistake a noun for a particle, and if a noun doesn't look like a verb by pattern, we call it a *declinable noun* (الْإِسْمُ الْمُتَمَكِّنُ) or *perfectly declinable* (مُتَمَكِّنٌ أَمْكَنُ) = triptote, with nunation. E.g.: *a book* (كِتابٌ), *a man* (رَجُلٌ).
- Otherwise, we call a noun *diptote* (مَمْنُوعٌ مِن الصَّرْفِ) or *noun with short inflection/declinable in two cases* (مُتَمَكِّنٌ غَيْرُ أَمْكَنَ).
  Note: مُتَمَكِّنٌ means *proficient*, *lasting*, or *strengthened*; in grammar, it denotes *declinable*. Thus, غَيْرُ مُتَمَكِّنٍ = مَبْنِيٌّ and means *indeclinable*.

2	A **verb** in the **present tense (imperfect)** – except if the verb ends in نَ.	الْفِعْلُ الْمُضارِعُ غَيْرُ الْمُتَّصِلِ بِنُونِ التَّوْكِيدِ أَوْ نُونِ النِّسْوةِ

When does a verb end in نَ?

a) The feminine form of *you* (in singular and plural) and *they* (feminine) always end in نَ.

b) Feminine or masculine forms of the emphasized imperative also end in نَ or نَّ.

Some examples of verbs ending in ن:

Singular, second person, feminine	You sit.	تَجْلِسِينَ
Plural, third person, feminine	They sit.	يَجْلِسْنَ
Energetic form; emphasis by a *light* Nūn (نُونٌ ساكِنةٌ خَفِيفةٌ)	He sits.	يَجْلِسَنْ
Energetic form with a *heavy* or *doubled* Nūn (نونُ التَّوْكِيدِ الثَّقِيلةُ), i.e. نَّ	Sit!	إِجْلِسَنَّ!
Energetic form with a *doubled* Nūn	He will surely be imprisoned! (Sura Yusuf; 12:32)	لَيُسْجَنَنَّ!

Now let's look at a few tricky situations.

> 1 What happens if a **sound feminine plural** (جَمْعُ الْمُؤَنَّثِ السّالِمُ) should get the مَنْصُوبٌ-case?

There is a **famous rule**: A sound feminine plural uses the ending اتٍ (if indefinite) or اتِ (if definite) to mark the accusative or genitive case.

If you see اتٍ or اتِ where you would expect "*-a*" or "*-an*" for the accusative, the plural is correctly marked as مَنْصُوبٌ. E.g: *I know the (fem.) teachers* (أَعْرِفُ الْمُدَرِّساتِ). The nominative is marked as usual.

> 2 What happens if we need the accusative for an indefinite noun that doesn't take nunation (تَنْوِينٌ), i.e., a **diptote** (مَمْنُوعٌ مِن الصَّرْفِ)?

Then the noun takes only <u>one</u> فَتْحةٌ in the accusative case. Note: If you are not sure how to mark the case in diptotes, check out *Arabic for Nerds 1*, #239 and #240.

Let's look at an example where both of the above situations occur.

| I saw beautiful cars in many places. | رَأَيْتُ سَيّاراتٍ جَمِيلَةً فِي أَماكِنَ كَثِيرَةٍ. |

Direct object (مَفْعُولٌ بِهِ), indefinite, so it should be in the accusative case and get nunation. But since we have a **sound feminine plural**, it is مَنْصُوبٌ by كَسْرَةٌ (-"in"). In Arabic, we say: جَمْعُ الْمُؤَنَّثِ السّالِمِ مَنْصُوبٌ، وَعَلامَةُ نَصْبِهِ الكَسْرَةُ الظّاهِرَةُ عَلَى آخِرِهِ	سَيّاراتٍ
Adjective (صِفَةٌ) for the direct object *cars*. It has to agree with the noun to which it refers (in gender, definiteness or indefiniteness, _and_ case). Since we said that *cars* is grammatically مَنْصُوبٌ, the adjective takes the regular مَنْصُوبٌ-ending: "-an".	جَمِيلَةً
Noun in the genitive case (مَجْرُورٌ) as it follows the preposition فِي. Since it is indefinite it should get nunation (كَسْرَةٌ) resulting in the ending "-in". However, this is the **broken plural** (جَمْعُ التَّكْسِيرِ) of the singular form مَكانٌ. Unfortunately, the plural pattern is a diptote and does not get nunation (مَمْنُوعٌ مِن الصَّرْفِ). Instead, it takes a single فَتْحَةٌ to mark the genitive case.	أَماكِنَ
Adjective (صِفَةٌ); thus, it has to agree with the noun to which it refers: *places* (أَماكِنَ). The noun أَماكِنَ is grammatically (though you don't see it) in the genitive ➡ كَثِيرَةٍ gets nunation (كَسْرَةٌ).	كَثِيرَةٍ

➤ If you have to mark an adjective with case endings, check the grammatical function and case of the noun to which the adjective refers. Don't copy the endings since the visible and pronounced case markers of the main noun may not reflect the actual case and may mislead you.

31. How do you put case or mood markers on indeclinable words?

That is impossible. You can't use visible markers.

Past tense verbs, e.g., *he went* (ذَهَبَ) and prepositions, e.g., *to* (إِلَى) are indeclinable words (مَبْنِيٌّ) and always stay the same, no matter what their function in a sentence may be. It is like a house with a pointed roof which can't get another floor. Let's look at two examples to illustrate the difference:

هذا is indeclinable (مَبْنِيٌّ)			كَرِيم is declinable (مُعْرَبٌ)		
This came.	هذا	جاءَ	Karīm came.	كَرِيمٌ	جاءَ
I saw this.	هذا	رَأَيْتُ	I saw Karīm.	كَرِيمًا	رَأَيْتُ
I passed (by) this.	بِهذا	مَرَرْتُ	I passed (by) Karīm.	بِكَرِيمٍ	مَرَرْتُ

كَريم (Karīm) is a noun (اِسْمٌ) and gets different case endings depending on the function in the sentence. هذا (this) is also a اِسْمٌ. In all the above examples, هذا has exactly the same functions as *Karīm* – but does not change its shape at all. How come? That's because هذا has a structured, cemented shape (مَبْنِيٌّ). → The word هذا is indeclinable.

32. Can you use letters to mark cases?

Yes, you can. We call it الإِعْرابُ بِالْحُرُوفِ.

Four Arabic letters can mark cases: ا – و – ي – ن. They are used for the dual (الْمُثَنَّى), the sound masculine plural (جَمْعُ الْمُذَكَّرِ السّالِمُ), and the so-called *six nouns* (الْأَسْماءُ السِّتّةُ). Let's see the details.

- In the **dual**, the Aleph (ا) marks the nominative case (مَرْفُوعٌ); the ي marks the accusative (مَنْصُوبٌ) and genitive (مَجْرُورٌ) case.

- In a **sound masculine plural,** the و marks the nominative and the ي the other two cases.

- The so-called six nouns: You use و to mark the nominative case. For the accusative (مَنْصُوبٌ), you use the ا (Aleph); for the genitive case (مَجْرُورٌ), you use ي. For example: *your brother* (أَخُوكَ).

What are the *six nouns*?

أَبٌ	father		أَخٌ	brother
حَمٌ	father-in-law		فَمٌ	mouth
ذُو	owner of		هَنٌ	thing (in a bad sense; something paltry)

In some grammar books, they are called *five nouns* (الْأَسْماءُ الْخَمْسةُ). Both terms mean the same. It is just a matter of counting. The word هَنٌ (plural: هَنُونَ) is not used anymore. You might encounter it in ancient texts. The special thing about these five (six) nouns is the إِعْرابٌ, i.e., when they receive case. Two conditions must be met to use a letter to mark the case in one of the *six nouns* (see *Arabic for Nerds 1, #220):*

1. The word has to be singular (نَكِرةٌ).

2. The word must be the first part of a إِضافة, i.e., the مُضافٌ. Watch out if the second part of the إِضافةٌ is the pronoun *my* (ي)!

My brother came.	جاءَ أَخِي.

The word *brother* is the subject (فَاعِلٌ) of the verbal sentence (جُمْلَةٌ فِعْلِيَّةٌ) and therefore must be in the nominative case (مَرْفُوعٌ). But how do we mark the case أَخٌ?

We use an *estimated, assumed, virtual* vowel (ضَمَّةٌ مُقَدَّرَةٌ) because we are not allowed to show the vowel. There must be a كَسرةٌ before the ي in any case as the كَسْرةٌ ("i") is the *suitable vowel* (حَرَكَةٌ مُناسِبةٌ) for the ي (long vowel ī). This means that the preceding letter (which would normally get the case marker) can't carry the actual marker. We have to make room for the كَسْرةٌ by deleting the vowel of the إِعْرابٌ as we can't put it there.

Your (*addressing a man*) two brothers came.	جاءَ أَخَواكَ.

أَخَوانِ means *two brothers*. The **dual** form is the subject (فَاعِلٌ) of the verbal sentence. Since we add a pronominal suffix (*your*=كَ), the ن must drop in the dual. → The Aleph expresses the nominative case (مَرْفُوعٌ).

What about the so-called **five verbs** (الْأَفْعال الْخَمسة)؟

The endings of some present tense verb forms resemble that of the noun which is the main reason why the present tense verb is declinable. The ending of the *five verbs* consists of a visible pronoun in form of a letter (و or ي or ا) expressing the subject (فَاعِلٌ). For example: *they write* (يَكْتُبُونَ).

This is true for the dual (هُما and أَنْتُما), *you* masculine plural (أَنْتُمْ) and feminine singular (أَنْتِ) as well as *they* masculine (هُمْ). If you count them, you will get *five* – see *Arabic for Nerds 1, question #83*.

These verb forms do not use ضَمَّةٌ to mark the present tense, **indicative mood** (الْمُضارِعُ), like in *he writes* (يَكْتُبُ). They use a **final ن** like in *they write* (يَكْتُبُونَ). In fact, the fixation of the *Nūn* (ثُبُوتُ النُّونِ) is the marker of the indicative. If such a verb needs the مَنْصُوبٌ (*subjunctive*) or مَجْزُومٌ (*jussive*) mood, the final ن gets elided (= the marker of the indicative). This happens after لَمْ or لَنْ. For example: *they didn't write* (لَمْ يَكْتُبُوا). We say that the marker of the jussive and subjunctive is the **deletion** of the *Nūn* (حَذْفُ النُّونِ).

All this gets interesting as soon as there is a weak letter involved (و or ي or ا). If such a verb is مَجْزُومٌ, the weak letter has to be elided.

Sura 17:37	And do not walk upon the earth ex- ultantly.	وَلَا تَمْشِ فِي الْأَرْضِ مَرَحًا.
Here we deal with a *prohibition* (لَا النَّاهِيَةُ). In such construc- tions, the verb in the present tense after لا must be in the jussive (مَجْزُومٌ), induced by the particle لا. The marker for the مَجْزُوم- mood is the deletion of the weak letter (حَرْفُ الْعِلّةِ).		لَا تَمْشِ

33. What is a *governor* or *operator* (عامِلٌ) in Arabic grammar?

A word that causes grammatical states.

When you analyze a word in a sentence, you need to look for its *gov- ernor* or *regent* (عامِلٌ). The عامِلٌ is the operator that assigns a job to a word. A عامِلٌ has the power over a certain position in a sentence. Ev- ery position in a sentence is associated with a certain case ending.

The case marker is an indication for the function of a word and somewhat more generally, a sign that a word is located in a certain po- sition in a sentence. We could say that the effect of the government is a case ending. Words that don't have governing power are called غَيْرُ عامِلٍ. All constituents of a sentence are either *governors* (عامِلٌ) or *gov- erned* (مَعْمُولٌ).

- All parts of speech – nouns (اِسْمٌ), verbs (فِعْلٌ), particles (حَرْفٌ) – can work as **governors** (عامِلٌ).
- But only nouns (اِسْمٌ) and present tense verbs (الْمُضارِعُ) can be **governed** and are **declinable** (i.e., they get case or mood markers).
- Particles (حَرْفٌ) and past tense verbs (الْماضِي) are indeclinable – we can't put a case/mood marker on them. That is why we say that they don't have a place in the case analysis (لا مَحَلَّ لَها مِن الْإِعْرابِ).

The following terms are essential for the analysis of any sentence.

The **operator** or **regent**; governor. Also called: active element. عامِلٌ literally means *factor; worker; operating*. In grammar, this term is used for the word that **imposes a case** on another word and brings along its marker (الْعَلامةُ). The عامِلٌ is a word governing an- other word, and the relationship is regulated by a case or mood.	عامِلٌ (plural: عَوامِلُ)

Although I use the term *regent*, there's no connection between عَمِلَ فِي – *to operate (grammatically) on;* the original idea of the Arabic grammarians – and the Latin expression *gubernare* or *regere* which would be عَمِلَ عَلَى (*to rule over*). Even so, in later works about Arabic grammar, the expression تَسَلَّطَ عَلَى does occur which, in fact, literally mean *to rule over.*	
This term is used for the word that **carries the sign** (الْعَلامةُ), i.e., the case or mood marker. The expression مَعْمُولٌ فِيهِ means *(the thing) operated on.* Grammarians call it *patient or passive element.*	مَعْمُولٌ
This word means *mark; sign.* In grammar, it denotes the **sign that marks the position** and function of a word (case marker).	عَلامةٌ

You may also encounter the following three terms:

This word literally means *where something occurs;* in grammar, it denotes the place **of a word in the sentence** without (necessarily) giving reference to its meaning or function. It is purely distributional and gives a general interpretation. In the language of computer science, we could say that this would be the place where an item occurs in the data.	مَوْقِعٌ
This is the *place* (in speech) of a word that determines its function. It is the micro-level. In linguistic terms, we could translate it as **function.** If we use the above analogy, we could say that this would be the place where an item occurs in the system.	مَوْضِعٌ
This is the **status** of a word. This term was taken over from ethics and law where rights and status depend on status. For example, a particle like إِنَّ which emphasizes the subject has the status of a verb because its meaning could be interpreted by a verb. This explains why إِنَّ has the grammatical power of a verb and is followed by dependent nouns → dependent is a sign of the accusative case (مَنْصُوبٌ). Another example: In Classical Arabic, ما may have the same power as the negation لَيْسَ.	مَنْزِلةٌ

34. Can there be more than one operator (عامِلٌ) in a sentence?

Yes, of course.

Although the verb is a powerful operator (عامِلٌ) and can guard many words at the same time (direct object, حالٌ, adverbs, etc.), there may be other regents in a sentence as well. Let's check an example.

Karīm went to the city in the morning.	ذَهَبَ كَرِيمٌ إِلَى الْمَدِينةِ صَباحًا.

عامِلٌ	*went*	ذَهَبَ

Verb (فِعْلٌ) in the past tense (الْماضِي). The ending of a past tense verb is always the same; it is fixed, structured – or as linguists say: they lack inflection. ذَهَبَ determines the <u>case</u> of two words. It operates (الْعامِـلُ) on *Karīm* (which makes it the subject and induces the nominative case) and of *in the morning* (adverb; it gives us information about when the action happened).

مَعْمُولٌ	Karīm	كَرِيمٌ

This **noun** (اسْمٌ) is the **subject** (فاعِلٌ) of the verbal sentence. It is the **agent** that carries out the action of the verb (the doer). Thus, it has to be in the nominative case (مَرْفُوعٌ). Since it is <u>in</u>definite, it gets nunation (تَنْوِينٌ): *"-un"*.

عامِلٌ	*to*	إِلَى

Preposition (حَرْفُ الْجَرِّ). It is the regent (عامِلٌ) of the expression *the city* and determines its <u>case</u> (the genitive). إِلَى is a حَرْفٌ; it doesn't have a place in إِعْرابٌ and doesn't take any case marker. It is not governed by any word.

مَعْمُولٌ	*the city*	الْمَدِينةِ

This noun gets the **genitive case** (اسْمٌ مَجْرُورٌ) due to the preposition إِلَى.

مَعْمُولٌ	*in the morning*	صَباحًا

صَباحًا is a noun (اسْمٌ) and serves here as an **adverb of time** (ظَرْفُ زَمانٍ). In this function, it has to be in the accusative case (مَنْصُوبٌ), marked by the ending *"-an"*. The governor or operator of this adverb is the verb ذَهَبَ.

It might not be of any practical use but try to use the correct terms for the إِعْرابٌ and for structured words (بِناءٌ) when you talk about vowels.

Let's first analyze the terms for **indeclinable words** (حالةُ الْبِناءِ):

meaning	incorrect	CORRECT
Fixed ending on the vowel "a"; thus indeclinable.	مَبْنِيٌّ بِالْفَتْحةِ مَبْنِيٌّ عَلَى الْفَتْحةِ	مَبْنِيٌّ عَلَى الْفَتْحِ
We want to describe that the word's final letter is fixed and always has the vowel "*a*" (إِنْهاءُ الْكَلِمةِ الْمَبْنِيّةِ بِفَتْحةٍ). The فَتْحةٌ is the **original sign of the accusative** (نَصْبٌ); in Arabic we'd say الْعَلامةُ الْأَصْلِيّةُ لِلنَّصْبِ في الْإِعْرابِ. But this is not our business here as we only want to describe the indeclinable shape of a word (فَتْحٌ = *openness*). This has nothing to do with case endings! →We should not use the term فَتْحةٌ.		

Now let's switch to the realms of إِعْرابٌ:

meaning	incorrect	CORRECT
In the nominative case by the vowel "u" on the final radical.	مَرْفُوعٌ بِالضَّمِّ مَرْفُوعٌ عَلَى الضَّمِّ	مَرْفُوعٌ بِالضَّمّةِ
Here we talk about a **case ending**. The ضَمّةٌ ("*u*") is the sign of the nominative case (رَفْعٌ) of declinable nouns (عَلامةٌ لِلرَّفْعِ في الْمُعْرَبِ).		

We can derive a rule from it:

➤ If we want to point to the fixed, structured <u>condition</u> of a word (حالةُ الْبِناءِ), i.e., the <u>cemented</u> vowel (or سُكُونٌ) on its final letter, we use the term without ة.

grammatical term – for الْبِناءُ			example	
Word that has a **fixed shape, cemented/built on the final vowel.**	("u") ـُ	مَبْنِيٌّ عَلَى الضَّمِّ	*where; since*	حَيْثُ
	("i") ـِ	مَبْنِيٌّ عَلَى الْكَسْرِ	*yesterday*	أَمْسِ
	("a") ـَ	مَبْنِيٌّ عَلَى الْفَتْحِ	*who; whom*	الَّذينَ
	(NO vowel) ـْ	مَبْنِيٌّ عَلَى السُّكُونِ	*no*	لَا

For the **case** (حالةُ الْإِعْرابِ), we use the passive participle of the same root: مَرْفُوعٌ for *nominative*, مَنْصُوبٌ for *accusative*, and مَجْرُورٌ for *geni-*

tive. In إعْرابٌ, we don't talk about the nature and condition of a word's shape. Cases are flexible vowel signs that change according to the function and position of a word in a sentence.

grammatical function	literal meaning	Arabic term
Nominative case when talking about nouns; regarding verbs, it denotes indicative mood (present tense).	*lifted; raised*	مَرْفُوعٌ بِالضَّمّة
Generally speaking, this case expresses an **independent** meaning.		
Accusative case (in nouns) or subjunctive mood (in verbs)	*set up; installed*	مَنْصُوبٌ بِالْفَتْحةِ
This case is used for words that are **dependent**. You set things, make things clearer, etc. Direct objects receive this case. Regarding verbs, the مَنْصُوبٌ mood denotes intention, hope, possibility, etc.		
Genitive case of a noun	*dragged; pulled*	مَجْرُورٌ بِالْكَسْرةِ
This case expresses subordination (process of embedding clauses in which one clause is dependent on the main clause) or possession (إضافةٌ). The preposition literally *drags* a following word into the genitive case.		
Jussive mood of a verb	*cut short, clipped*	مَجْزُومٌ بِالسُّكُونِ
By keeping the ending short (clipped), you either demand something (imperative) or you indicate vagueness. Remark: The original last vowel of this mood was perhaps كَسْرةٌ. I have seen that in ancient Arabic poetry.		

35. What does تَقْدِيرٌ mean?

Linguists call it supposition; restoration. Practically speaking, it means to guess what is missing in a sentence in order to make a sentence work.

The idea of تَقْدِيرٌ has many applications. It may denote the supposition of case markers or the supposition of an underlying governing element. The latter is tricky and probably the most abstract idea for learners of Arabic. It is this concept that makes Arabic an almost mathematical language that only has few exceptions.

The term تَقْدِيرٌ is the مَصْدَرٌ of the II-verb يُقَدِّرُ - قَدَّرَ which means *to appoint, to estimate, to anticipate*. The meaning of تَقْدِيرٌ can be *predestination, decreeing*, semantically connected with قَدْرٌ in the sense of Allah's decree: *fate*. The root also produces words that are related to measure, quantity, in the sense of *estimation of value*. Let's stick to this idea as it will bring us closer to the meaning of the grammar term.

تَقْدِيرٌ tells us something about something that does not exist in the state of the existent (sentence). Its aim in grammar is the **recovery of deleted items**. Grammarians say that تَقْدِيرٌ denotes *the implication of a missing syntactical part*. They use this term to explain suppressed elements. These missing words were intended by the speaker but not expressed in the actual utterance. So we assume that a word or expression is implicitly understood. تَقْدِيرٌ can denote a virtual reality. It is a hypothetical insertion of a word, used to show the underlying harmony.

Whenever the **surface structure** doesn't agree with our grammar framework, we need to identify the missing element by which we get to the **deeper structure** of a sentence.

With the concept of تَقْدِيرٌ, we can explain, for example,

- why there is no verb in a nominal sentence (*question #140*);
- why شُكْرًا ("*thanks*") is in the accusative case (مَنْصُوبٌ) – see *#320*;
- what we actually express when we say صَباحُ الْخَيْرِ ("*good morning*"). There are many ways to justify this expression. A common explanation is the following: صَباحُ الْخَيْرِ is a إِضافةٌ that is placed as the predicate (خَبَرٌ) of a deleted subject (مُبْتَدَأً مَحْذُوفٌ). What you say is the remaining fraction of صَباحُكُمْ صَباحُ الْخَيْرِ which means: *Your morning is a morning of good things.*

For the same reason, you say in German "*Guten Morgen*" with the adjective in the accusative because it is only the remaining part of "*Ich wünsche dir einen guten Morgen*". (*I wish you a good morning.*)

Sībawayhi used this concept to show phonological harmony (field of صَرْفٌ) but also to explain, how certain grammatical situations can be explained without just saying it is an exception. Usually, it is the assumption of the virtual occurrence of the operator (عامِلٌ) which was believed by Sībawayhi to have been elided.

تَقْدِيرُ الْمَحْذُوفِ (*defining the deleted*) has been the quest of scholars attempting to explain the exact meaning. Critics say that this leads to interpretation what the speaker or writer intended to say – which may be problematic when we analyze the Qur'an. But there is no alternative.

36. Which verb forms hide the subject?

The third person masculine and feminine form (he/she) in the past tense. And many forms in the present tense.

Every conjugated Arabic verb goes along with a subject (فاعِلٌ). This subject is found in the verb itself – which is different to English. In English, you need a personal pronoun to express the subject. For example: *I went; you went; she went.*

In Arabic, we use **fragments** of the personal pronoun. They are either *visible* (بارِزٌ) and attached as suffixes to the verb (ضَمِيرٌ مُتَّصِلٌ): *connected pronouns.* Or they are *hidden, concealed* (ضَمِيرٌ مُسْتَتِرٌ) in speech and writing. ➡ *See Arabic for Nerds 1, #72.*

We now examine the verb and how it expresses the subject.

1. The **past** tense (فِعْلٌ ماضٍ)

In the past tense, the subject (فاعِلٌ) is represented by the <u>suffix</u>. Only in the 3rd person singular (*he/she*), the pronoun <u>**may**</u> be **hidden** (ضَمِيرٌ مُسْتَتِرٌ جَوازًا). Why?

Because we could also use an apparent noun (اِسْمٌ ظاهِرٌ) as the subject which is only possible with هُوَ and هِيَ. For example: *The student wrote* (الطّالِبُ كَتَبَ). You can't do this with *I, you, we, they.*

What is the subject?	Reason for the preceding vowel/letter	...the vowel	fixed on...	verb	
فاعِلُهُ ضَمِيرٌ مُسْتَتِرٌ تَقْدِيرُهُ هُوَ Subject is a **hidden** pronoun: *he*.	---	أَلْفَتْح... a –	past tense verb, active voice, fixed on... فعْلٌ ماضٍ مَبْنِيٌّ يَبْنى على...	كَتَبَ *he wrote*	1
فاعِلُهُ ضَمِيرٌ مُسْتَتِرٌ تَقْدِيرُهُ هِيَ Subject is a **hidden** pronoun: *she*.	التّاءُ حَرْفُ تَأْنِيثٍ The ت is a sign of feminization, **not** a pronoun! Unlike a pronoun suffix it doesn't represent the subject. Thus, the subject can be mentioned after it.			كَتَبَتْ *she wrote*	2
الْأَلِفُ ضَمِيرٌ في مَحَلّ رَفْعِ فاعِلٌ The Aleph is a pronoun, serves as the subject, and is in the position of a nominative case.				كَتَبَتا *they (both, f.) wrote*	3
	---			كَتَبَا *they (b.) wrote*	4
الْواوُ ضَمِيرٌ في مَحَلّ رَفْعِ فاعِلٌ The *Wāw* is a pronoun, serving as the subject, in the place of a nominative.	لِاتِّصالِهِ بِواوِ الْجَمْعِ The fixation on the "u" is needed to connect the *Wāw* of the plural.	أَلضَّمّ... u –		كَتَبُوا *they wrote*	5
النّونُ ضَمِيرٌ في مَحَلّ رَفْعِ فاعِلٌ The *Nūn* is a pronoun, serving as the subject, in the spot of a nominative.	لِاتِّصالِهِ بِنُونِ الْإِناثِ The fixation on the non-vowel is needed to connect the *Nūn* of the female.			كَتَبْنَ *they (f.) wrote*	6
نا ضَمِيرٌ في مَحَلّ رَفْعِ فاعِلٌ The *na* is a pronoun, serving as the subject, in the place of a nominative case.	لِاتِّصالِهِ بِنا The fixation on the non-vowel is needed to connect the so-called نا الفاعِلِين.	quiescent – السُّكُون...		كَتَبْنا *we wrote*	7
التّاءُ ضَمِيرٌ في مَحَلّ رَفْعِ فاعِلٌ The *Tā'* serves as the subject and is in the position of a nominative case.	لِاتِّصالِهِ بِالضَّمِيرِ: ت The fixation on the non-vowel is needed to connect the pronoun ت.			كَتَبْتُ *I wrote*	8

Number 8 is also true for *you* (masculine/feminine: كَتَبْتَ/كَتَبْتِ), *you both* (كَتَبْتُما), *you* plural (كَتَبْتُمْ), *you* (feminine, plural: كَتَبْتُنَّ).

2. The **present tense** (فِعْلٌ مُضارِعٌ)

In the <u>present</u>, the subject **must** be **concealed** (ضَمِيرٌ مُسْتَتِرٌ وُجُوبًا) in many situations (*he, she, I, we*). You can't replace it by a noun. In the other situations, we express it by a letter. Don't forget: In the present tense, we don't use suffixes; instead, we add letters to the beginning.

These prefixes are called حُرُوفُ الْمُضارَعَةِ, i.e., the four letters أ, ت, ي, and ن. They can be summarized in the word نَأتِي. You can remember it easily since نَأتِي means *we come*. They are additional letters (حُرُوفٌ زائِدَةٌ). They are not part of the root and don't have a position in إعْرابٌ. The letters do not serve as the subject – the subject is expressed by something else as we will see. The only purpose of the extra letters is to give you an indication of the number.

What is the subject?	Marker of the indicative	1st letter	Which type?	verb	
فاعِلُهُ ضَمِيرٌ مُسْتَتِرٌ تَقْدِيرُهُ هُوَ Subject is a <u>hidden</u> pronoun: he.	مَرْفُوعٌ بِالضَّمّةِ indicative mood, marked by "*u*".	ياءٌ		يَكْتُبُ *he writes*	1
فاعِلُهُ ضَمِيرٌ مُسْتَتِرٌ تَقْدِيرُهُ هِيَ Subject is a <u>hidden</u> pronoun: she.				تَكْتُبُ *she writes*	2
الْأَلِفُ ضَمِيرٌ فِي مَحَلِّ رَفْعٍ فاعِلٌ The Aleph is a pronoun, serving as the subject; in the position of a nominative case.	مَرْفُوعٌ بِثُبُوتِ النُّونِ لِأَنَّهُ مِن الْأَفْعالِ الْخَمْسةِ The indicative mood is expressed by the cemented *Nūn* because it is one of the forms which we call *five verbs* (see #32).	تاءٌ	فِعْلٌ مُضارِعٌ مَعْلُومٌ present tense verb, active voice	تَكْتُبانِ *they (both, f.) write*	3
		ياءٌ		يَكْتُبانِ *they (both) write*	4
الْواوُ ضَمِيرٌ فِي مَحَلِّ رَفْعٍ فاعِلٌ The *Wāw* is a pronoun, serving as the subject; in the position of a nominative case.				يَكْتُبُونَ *they write*	5
فاعِلُهُ ضَمِيرٌ مُسْتَتِرٌ تَقْدِيرُهُ نَحْنُ Subject is a <u>hidden</u> pronoun: we.	مَرْفُوعٌ بِالضَّمّةِ indicative mood, marked by the vowel "*u*".	نُونٌ		نَكْتُبُ *we write*	6
فاعِلُهُ ضَمِيرٌ مُسْتَتِرٌ تَقْدِيرُهُ أَنا Subject is a <u>hidden</u> pronoun: I.		هَمْزةٌ		أَكْتُبُ *I write*	7

Some remarks:

- In the **imperative**, we also have a hidden pronoun that is inter-preted (implicitly understood) as *you* (الضَّمِيرُ الْمُسْتَتِرُ فِي فِعْلِ الْأَمْرِ تَقْدِيرُهُ أَنْتَ).
- The *hidden, concealed pronoun* (ضَمِيرٌ مُسْتَتِرٌ) can only occur in the position of a nominative case (فِي مَحَلِ رَفْعٍ).

37. The cryptic grammar term سَدَّ مَسَدَّ. Can a word be the subject (فَاعِلٌ) and serve as the predicate (خَبَرٌ)?

Yes, this is possible.

Sounds complicated. So, let's start with an example.

| Your two brothers are not traveling to an emigration country. | ما مُسافِرٌ أَخَواكَ إِلَى الْإِغْتِرابِ. |

Note: The VIII-verb اغْتَرَبَ - يَغْتَرِبُ means *to go to a foreign country, to emi-grate; to be (far) away from one's homeland; to live as a foreigner in a country*. We use the مَصْدَر here which denotes: *separation from one's native country, emigration; exile*. In a different context, it may denote: *Westernism*.

The weird thing here is the word مُسافِرٌ. What is its **function**? Why is it in the singular form, but the word which follows is in the dual (*two brothers*)? Is this a grammatical mistake? No, it isn't! We will see why.

ما	Negation device (حَرْفُ نَفْيٍ).
مُسافِرٌ	**Subject** (مُبْتَدَأٌ) of the <u>nominal</u> sentence; therefore, it has to take the nominative case (مَرْفُوعٌ بِالضَّمّةِ).
أَخَواكَ	**Subject** (فَاعِلٌ) of the <u>verbal</u> sentence. Wait, where is the verb? The active participle does that job and has a verbal force (فَاعِلٌ لِاسْمِ الْفاعِلِ: مُسافِر). أَخَواكَ is in the nominative case, and since we have a **dual**, the case is marked by the Aleph (مَرْفُوعٌ بِالْأَلِفِ لِأَنَّهُ مُثَنَّى). It is also the first part of the إِضافة; the second part (مُضافٌ إِلَيْهِ) is the pronoun suffix *Kāf* (الْكافُ ضَمِيرٌ). But there's more. أَخَواكَ has a **double function:** It also **replaces/"fills the place"** of the <u>predi-cate</u> of the nominal sentence (سَدَّ مَسَدَّ الْخَبَرِ).

Preposition that is connected to the active participle (حَرْفُ جَرٍّ). (مُتَعَلِّقٌ بِمُسافِر).	إِلَى
This word is dragged into the genitive by the previous preposition (مَجْرُورٌ بِالْكَسْرَةِ). It is part of a prepositional clause.	الْإِغْتِرابِ

So much for the theory. But what does it practically mean? سَدَّ مَسَدَّ is a grammar term which basically denotes the following: *in replacement, to be able to dispense, to do without, to dismiss the mentioning of one of the fundamentals/foundations or supplements* (الْإِسْتِغْناءُ عَنْ ذِكْرِ أَحَدِ أَرْكانِ الْعُمْدةِ أَوِ الْفَضْلَةِ).

The concept, which was already applied by the grammarians of Basra (الْبَصْرِيُّونَ), is a nice trick. It helps us understand sentences that look grammatically wrong – sentences which lack important parts; syntactical parts, as linguists put it. When can we apply this concept? There are **five situations**. We will list them at the end of this *question*. Let's first focus on the DNA of such sentences and use our example:

ما مُسافِرٌ أَخَواكَ إِلَى الْإِغْتِرابِ.

Two things are important here:

- We have a **subject** (مُبْتَدَأٌ) that does not have a predicate (خَبَرٌ). The subject is the word مُسافِرٌ.

- We also have a **word** in the **nominative case** (مَرْفُوعٌ) which is associated with the مُبْتَدَأ: the word أَخَواكَ. This word replaces the predicate (لَهُ مَرْفُوعٌ سَدَّ مَسَدَّ الْخَبَرِ).

Why is that possible? In Arabic, the subject (مُبْتَدَأٌ) of a nominal sentence can be stated in two ways:

OPTION 1 – the normal situation: The subject has a **predicate** (مُبْتَدَأٌ لَهُ خَبَرٌ). For ex.: *Is the man standing?* (أَالرَّجُلُ قائِمٌ؟). The خَبَرٌ is قائِمٌ.

OPTION 2 – the tricky situation: The subject (مُبْتَدَأٌ) of a nominal sentence goes along with an **agent** (= subject of a verbal sentence; the one who is acting) which **replaces the predicate** (مُبْتَدَأٌ لَهُ فاعِلٌ سَدَّ مَسَدَّ الْخَبَرِ). The مُبْتَدَأٌ works as a description/qualification (وَصْفٌ). For example: *Are the two men standing?* (أَقائِمٌ الرَّجُلَانِ؟)

How can we understand the last example? We'll start from the rear.

- الرَّجُلَانِ is the **subject** (فَاعِلٌ) of the active participle (اِسْمُ الْفَاعِلِ), i.e. قائِمٌ. The power of an active participle is similar to that of a verb which explains why we use the term فَاعِلٌ for "subject".

Now comes the hard part.

- Here, the فَاعِلٌ **replaces the predicate** of the **primary nominal sentence** (فَاعِلٌ سَدَّ مَسَدَّ الْخَبَرِ). But where is the subject (مُبْتَدَأٌ) of the nominal sentence actually? It is the active participle: قائِمٌ.

➡ **To sum it up:** The مُبْتَدَأ does not have a predicate (خَبَرٌ). The فَاعِلٌ replaces the predicate. Looking at the function, we have two "subjects".

RULE OF THUMB: When you have a sentence with *two nouns* in the nominative case in which the **first** noun is **singular** (the qualification) and the **second noun** is in the **dual** or **plural**, you can only make the sentence work grammatically by applying option 2.

However, if the 2nd word in the nominative is singular, you can either use option 1 or 2 for your analysis – both make sense and are correct.

فاعِلٌ	مُبْتَدَأ		خَبَرٌ مُقَدَّمٌ			
	الْغائِبُ؟		قادِمٌ	هَلْ		option 1
الْغائِبُ؟	قادِمٌ	هَلْ				option 2

- The sentence means: *Is the absentee coming?*
- In option 1 - the standard situation – the **word-order** is **reversed:** We have a fronted predicate and a delayed, postponed subject.

Constructions using the logic of option 2 are rare; mainly, because they often look wrong at first glance. Furthermore, **four conditions** must be fulfilled – otherwise option 2 won't work. We will check them now.

CONDITION 1. The subject (الْمُبْتَدَأ) is a description – a وَصْفٌ (أَنْ يَكُونَ الْمُبْتَدَأ وَصْفًا). The term وَصْفٌ denotes *description, qualification*.
➡ See *question #210* for a detailed explanation.

Practically speaking this implies that the الْمُبْتَدَأُ is a **derived word** from the **root** (مُشْتَقٌّ) such as an active participle (إِسْمُ الْفَاعِلِ), a passive participle (إِسْمُ الْمَفْعُولِ), a comparative (إِسْمُ التَّفْضِيلِ), etc.

CONDITION 2. The subject (الْوَصْفُ) **has to be linked** to a <u>question</u> or <u>negation</u> (أَنْ يَعْتَمِدَ الْوَصْفُ عَلَى اسْتِفْهَامٍ أَوْ نَفْيٍ). Note The grammarians of Kūfa (الْكُوفِيُّونَ) stated that this is <u>not</u> a necessary condition.

Fine, but if a sentence lacks a question or negation device, how should you treat the sentence? The Basra grammarians (الْبَصْرِيُّونَ), except for the grammarian الْأَخْفَش, said that you have to apply **option 1**:

The two men come.	قَائِمٌ الرَّجُلَانِ.
Here قَائِمٌ is the **fronted predicate** (خَبَرٌ مُقَدَّمٌ) and <u>not</u> the subject (مُبْتَدَأٌ).	

The Kūfan scholars, however, stated that it is possible to treat the sentence with the above mentioned trick. Let's see what they proposed:

The word قَائِمٌ is the **subject** (مُبْتَدَأٌ) of the **nominal** sentence.	قَائِمٌ
What follows قَائِمٌ has two faces: It is the **subject** of a nested **verbal sentence** (فَاعِلٌ): the فَاعِلٌ of the active particle قَائِمٌ. If we look at the broader picture, we also see that it replaces the *missing* **predicate** (سَدَّ مَسَدَّ الْخَبَرِ) of the nominal sentence.	الرَّجُلَانِ

The Kufa analysis sounds more intuitive to me. By the way, it doesn't matter whether the question word is a particle (e.g., أ) or a noun (e.g., كَيْفَ). The same is true for the negation. You can use a particle (ما), verb (لَيْسَ), or a noun (e.g., غَيْر). For ex.: غَيْرُ قَائِمٍ الرَّجُلَانِ.

غَيْرُ is the subject (مُبْتَدَأٌ). The word قَائِمٍ is the second part of the إِضَافَة-construction. The word الرَّجُلَانِ is the subject (فَاعِلٌ) of the active participle (i.e., قَائِمٍ) which replaces the predicate (سَدَّ مَسَدَّ الْخَبَرِ) because the sentence actually just means: ما قَائِمٌ الرَّجُلَانِ

CONDITION 3. The word in the nominative case after the مُبْتَدَأٌ has to be a **visible, apparent noun** or a (detached, separated, free) **personal pronoun** (ضَمِيرٌ مُنْفَصِلٌ). It cannot be a hidden pronoun nor a pronoun suffix (أَنْ يَكُونَ مَرْفُوعُهُ اسْمًا ظَاهِرًا أَوْ ضَمِيرًا مُنْفَصِلًا).

Are you two (both of you) standing?	أَقَائِمٌ أَنْتُما؟
The first word is singular and the pronoun is a dual. The pronoun is a separated personal pronoun. ➡ We can use option 2 for the analysis.	

CONDITION 4. The **second** word in the nominative case **completes** the meaning (أَنْ يَتِمُّ الْكَلامُ بِمَرْفُوعِهِ).

Let's see what this is about and analyze a pretty sophisticated sentence.

Are Zayd's parents laughing?	أَضاحِكٌ أَبَواهُ زَيْدٌ؟

- *Zayd* is the **delayed subject** (مُبْتَدَأٌ مُؤَخَّرٌ) of the <u>nominal</u> sentence.
- *His parents* is the **subject** (the one who is doing the action) of the active participle (فاعِلٌ بِضاحِكٍ) which *laughing*.
- The active participle ضاحِكٌ is the **fronted predicate** (خَبَرٌ مُقَدَّمٌ) and **not** the subject (لَيْسَ مُبْتَدَأً).

➡ We have to use **option 1** for the analysis.

Why can't we use option 2 (i.e., we'd replace the predicate)**?** Because the sentence does not get its final meaning by the word in the nominative case (i.e., الْفاعِلُ). That being said, the intended statement (meaning) would be incomplete if you said: أَضاحِكٌ أَبَواهُ؟

The reason is the pronoun (هـ) which is a <u>returner</u> (ضَمِيرٌ عائِدٌ) and not a possessive pronoun. A referential pronoun has to relate to another word in the sentence (الضَّمِيرُ لا بُدَّ لَهُ مِن عائِدٍ), but there is no such word here.

Let's conclude with the **five situations** we mentioned at the beginning:

When can a sentence lack an important part because another word steps in and substitutes for it (سَدَّ مَسَدَّ)?

Situation 1	The subject of a <u>nominal sentence</u> is deleted when the **complement/answer of an oath replaces** (fills the place of) the **subject** (يُحْذَفُ الْمُبْتَدَأُ مَتَى كانَ جَوابُ الْقَسَمِ سادًّا مَسَدَّهُ).

Upon my word/conscience (truly), I do it!	فِي ذِمَّتِي لَأَفْعَلَنَّ!
The virtual meaning (التَّقْدِيرُ) of this sentence is:	فِي ذِمَّتِي يَمِينٌ لَأَفْعَلَنَّ!

Preposition (حَرْفُ جَرٍّ)	فِي
Word in the genitive case by the preposition (مَجْرُورٌ بِالْكَسْرةِ), the ي is a possessive pronoun serving as the second part of the إِضافة (الْياءُ ضَمِيرٌ مُضافٌ إِلَيْهِ). The entire prepositional phrase appears in the place of a fronted predicate and is connected to a deleted word to fit into the sentence (حَرْفُ جَرٍّ مُتَعَلِّقٌ بِمَحْذُوفٍ خَبَرٌ مُقَدَّمٌ).	ذِمَّتِي
The ل is necessary for the oath (حَرْفُ جَوابٍ); *see question #449.* The verb has the energetic form (*heavy Nūn*). The subject of the verb is hidden (فَاعِلُهُ ضَمِيرٌ مُسْتَتِرٌ) and expresses *I* (أنا). The complement of the oath replaces the **deleted subject** of the nominal sentence (جَوابُ الْقَسَمِ سَدَّ مَسَدَّ الْمُبْتَدَإِ الْمَحْذُوفِ), i.e., the word يَمِينٌ (see above – virtual meaning).	لَأْفَعَلَنَّ

Situation 2	The **qualification** (وَصْفٌ) is a word in the **singular** (الصِّفةُ مُفْرَدةٌ) and **what follows** is a dual or plural. Then, you <u>must</u> <u>start</u> the sentence with that <u>singular</u> word (الابْتِداءُ بِها).

In situation 2, you have a nominal sentence (جُمْلةٌ اسْمِيّةٌ) with the description/qualification serving as the subject (مُبْتَدَأٌ). What is placed after the description (i.e., the dual or plural) **replaces** (takes over the role of) the **predicate** (إِذا كانَتِ الصِّفةُ مُفْرَدةً وَما بَعْدَها مُثَنَّى أَوْ جَمْعًا تَحَتَّمَ الابْتِداءُ بِها وَكانَ ما بَعْدَها مَرْفُوعًا سَدَّ مَسَدَّ الْخَبَرِ). This is what we had analyzed at the beginning of this *question*. See also *questions #211, #405.*

Now, what would happen if the description is **singular** and the word after it is **also a singular form**? Then you have two options. You **may** apply the concept of سَدَّ مَسَدَّ (option B below) – or you apply the logic of a fronted predicate and delayed subject (option A). We have already mentioned this previously after the *rule of thumb.*

Is the child sleeping?	أَنائِمٌ الطِّفْلُ؟

We have two options for the analysis:

option A	option B	
fronted **predicate** (خَبَرٌ مُقَدَّمٌ)	Subject (مُبْتَدَأٌ)	نائِمٌ

| delayed subject (مُبْتَدَأٌ مُؤَخَّرٌ) | **Subject** (فاعِلٌ) of the (verbal) sentence. There is no verb but the active participle has some kind of verbal power. It replaces the predicate of نائِمٌ. We say: فاعِلٌ سَدَّ مَسَدَّ الْخَبَرِ | الطِّفْلُ |

| Situation 3 | A word may fill the place (replace) one of the **two objects** if a *verb of meaning/verb of the heart* (أَفْعالُ الْقُلُوبِ) is involved. → See *questions #308, #318, and #557.* |

| Situation 4 | You <u>must delete</u> the regent (عامِلٌ) of a **circumstantial quali-fier** (حالٌ) if a حالٌ replaces the predicate of a nominal sentence (يَجِبُ حَذْفُ عامِلِ الْحالِ قِياسًا فِي الْحالِ السّادَّةِ مَسَدَّ الْخَبَرِ). |

| I beat up the slave when he is insulting. | ضَرْبِي الْعَبْدَ مُسِيئًا. |

This sentence may be disturbing for some readers. Well, it is a famous ex-ample of the book *Sharh 'ala Alfīya(t) Ibn Mālik* (شَرْح ابْن عَقِيل عَلَى أَلْفِيَّةِ ابْن مالِك; *Explanation of the book Alfīya*) by Ibn 'Aqīl (ابْن عَقِيل) which is the reason why I give it here as an example.

This word is a مَصْدَرٌ. It serves as the subject (مُبْتَدَأٌ) of the nomi-nal sentence. The case marker is virtual/assumed (مَرْفُوعٌ بِالضَّمَّةِ الْمُقَدَّرَةِ) because we need a كَسْرَةٌ in any case to add the posses-sive pronoun *my* (ي).	ضَرْبِي
This is the direct object (مَفْعُولٌ بِهِ); it is governed by the infini-tive noun (عامِلُهُ الْمَصْدَرُ).	الْعَبْدَ
This is a *circumstantial qualifier* (حالٌ). However, that is not the end of the story. The word مُسِيئًا replaces the predicate of the nominal sentence because the predicate was deleted (حالٌ سَدَّتْ مَسَدَّ الْخَبَرِ، وَالْخَبَرُ مَحْذُوفٌ).	مُسِيئًا

How can we you understand the above sentence? It is tricky. It depends on what you intend to say – it is mainly about the intended time.

| If you want to point to the **future** (إذا أَرَدْتَ الاسْتِقْبالَ). | ضَرْبِي الْعَبْدَ إذا كانَ مُسِيئًا. | I will beat him when/if…. |

If you want to point to the **past** tense (إِنْ أَرَدْتَ الْمَاضِي).	ضَرَبْتُ الْعَبْدَ إِذْ كَانَ مُسِيئًا.	I have beaten him, because...
Notice: The expressions إِذَا كَانَ and إِذْ كَانَ are **adverbs** that step in for the predicate (ظَرْفٌ نَائِبٌ عَنِ الْخَبَرِ).		

Let's focus again on the word مُسِيئًا (*insulting*; it is the active participle of the IV-verb أَساءَ - يُسِيءُ; R2=و, R3=ء). It works as a حَالٌ for the hidden/concealed pronoun (الضَّمِيرُ الْمُسْتَتِرُ) of the verb كَانَ. This non-visible pronoun refers to the word الْعَبْد (الْعَائِدُ إِلَى الْعَبْد).

Could the word مُسِيئًا be the predicate? No, that is impossible – because you don't say: *My beating is insulting* (ضَرْبِي مُسِيءٌ). In other words, the *beating* (الضَّرْب) is not described as being *insulting*. But if we fix the structure and say that مُسِيئًا serves as a حَالٌ that takes over the role of the predicate as well, then we are fine and get a sound meaning because we move away from a permanent description.

However, in several other situations, it would be possible that the word serving as the حَالٌ may work as the predicate itself.

Zayd kept standing.	زَيْدٌ قَائِمًا.
Here, *Zayd* is the subject (مُبْتَدَأٌ) of the nominal sentence. The **predicate** is **deleted** (الْخَبَرُ مَحْذُوفٌ). The assumed meaning of the sentence could be: زَيْدٌ ثَبَتَ قَائِمًا (*Zayd remained/kept standing.*)	

Here, it would be fine to use the حَالٌ as the predicate. We could say:

Zayd stands.	زَيْدٌ قَائِمٌ.

In such examples, it is correct to either delete **or** show the predicate.

Situation 5	We have the situation that we would **expect to find a derived word** from the root (الْمُشْتَقُّ) at a certain position in the sentence – but instead, we see the **standard** مَصْدَرٌ. In this situation, we say that the مَصْدَرٌ replaces the الْمُشْتَقُّ.

This only works if the مَصْدَرٌ is the original, standard مَصْدَرٌ - and not a الْمَصْدَرُ الْمِيمِيُّ ➔ see #173 and *Arabic for Nerds 1 #77*. Note that we must use the singular, masculine form of the مَصْدَرٌ. For example: *spilled* or *running water* (مَاءٌ سَكْبٌ) conveying the meaning of مُنْسَكِبٌ or جَارٍ.

MISLEADING SIGNS – THE NEED FOR VIRTUAL CASE MARKERS

38. What do you do when you can't put case markers on words?

You use virtual (assumed, estimated) markers.

Some Arabic words, though they are inflected, do not show their final vowel for certain reasons. You may even see different, visible markers than the ones you would expect. We say that their sign of إِعْرابٌ is assumed (مُقَدَّرٌ), we imagine it in our mind to be there in order to mark the position and function of such words in a sentence. In Arabic, we use the term الْإِعْرابُ الْمُقَدَّرُ for this process.

This "hidden" marker is neither pronounced nor written, but it is important to get the correct meaning. We will thoroughly and gradually analyze the concept of الْإِعْرابُ الْمُقَدَّرُ. We start by looking at when we get into such a situation. We mainly have to look at three situations.

1	The last letter isn't strong enough to carry the case or mood marker.

In other words, the last letter is **weak** (حَرْفُ الْعِلَّةِ). See *question #39*.

2	The last letter requires a certain vowel no matter what the case is. This means that the place for the marker is occupied by the كَسْرةٌ.

This happens when you add the pronominal suffix *my* (ي) to a noun. Such a ي is called ياءُ الْمُتَكَلِّم and serves as the مُضافٌ إِلَيْهِ, i.e., the second part of the إِضافة. Since we are talking about a specific thing – indicated by *my* – the expression must be definite which is achieved by the ي. And since it is the second part of the إِضافة, it must be genitive (مَجْرورٌ).

What happens then? The ي is added to the last letter of the noun. This last latter, in theory, also carries the case marker (= sign of إِعْرابٌ) which could be theoretically any case: nominative (ضَمّةٌ), genitive (كَسْرةٌ), or accusative (فَتْحةٌ). However, the ي requires a كَسْرةٌ by definition because otherwise, it is impossible to pronounce it as a long *"ee/ii"* (long vowel).

Let's take the expression *my book* (كِتابِي), pronounced *"kitaaabee"*. If *book* is the subject and would need the nominative case marker (ضَمّةٌ), you'd get a word which cannot be pronounced: كِتابُِي – because it is impossible that one letter carries two vowels at the same time.

We say that the spot for the case marker is **occupied by a (necessary)** suitable vowel (اِشْتِغالُ الْمَحَلّ بِالْحَرَكةِ الْمُناسِبةِ). All vowels are under-stood to be prevented from appearing due to this كَسْرةٌ, even if the origi-nal case marker happens to be كَسْرةٌ (in such a case, you still need to ap-ply virtual case markers as the visible كَسْرة is there for another reason).

3 | There is an extra/additional preposition involved (حَرْفُ جَرٍّ زائِدٌ). We will deal with this in several questions, for example, *question #127.*

39. Why is the Aleph the weakest letter in Arabic?

The Aleph (ى or l) can't show (carry) any of the three vowels which are used to mark cases or moods (i.e, كَسْرةٌ or ضَمّةٌ, فَتْحةٌ).

Weak letters (حَرْفُ الْعِلّةِ) are a bit of a spoiler in the otherwise logical Arabic grammar. All three weak letters – l and و and ي – may occur as the final letter of a word – the position, which usually causes the most problems. So, which case or mood markers can you put on them?

- On the **Aleph – none!**
- The other two weak letters, و and ي, can carry exactly one of the three vowels: فَتْحةٌ.
- This refers only to weak letters which work as long vowels at the end of a word.

Otherwise, both و and ي can take a ضَمّةٌ when used in the passive voice as in وُلِدَ (*he was born*) or يُكْتَبُ (*he/it is written*). If they don't work as long vowels (which means that the previous vowel is not the short version of the weak letter), then they can take other case markers as well, e.g., أَيُّ or أَيَّ or أَيِّ or وِزْرٌ (*burden, sin*).

To understand why, we need to introduce the following two terms:

→ Impossibility (تَعَذُّرٌ). This grammar term means that the visibility of the vowel marker is <u>impossible</u>. This is the situation in words like *Moses* (مُوسى) or *stick* (عَصا). **All three vowels** (ضَمّةٌ - فَتْحةٌ - كَسْرةٌ) are prevented from appearing because the Aleph simply can't carry it. **This is the situation for the Aleph.**

→ Heaviness (ثِقَلٌ). This term describes that it is theoretically <u>possible</u>

to show the vowel marker on the last radical. However, it would be difficult to pronounce the result (صُعُوبَةُ النُّطْقِ بِهِ) because of its disharmonious sounds, also called *mutual aversion* (تَنافُر). This applies to **words ending in** و or ي, e.g., *judge* (الْقاضِي) or *he calls* (يَدْعُو). Therefore, the vowels are prevented from appearing due to the heaviness of pronunciation **except** for فَتْحَةٌ. The فَتْحَةٌ appears as usual.

All of this has to do with the nature of weak letters. They are actually a portion or fraction of a حَرْفُ مَدٍّ (letter of prolongation) which is more or less what we would call a long vowel. The ضَمَّةٌ is a part of the و, the فَتْحَةٌ is a part of the Aleph (ا), and the كَسْرةٌ is a part of the ي.

That brings us to the crucial question: **Why is the Aleph different?** The Aleph can't carry any vowel because the **Aleph can't be a consonant**. The Aleph is a **pure vowel**; no vowel can have another vowel. Pure vowel here means that it must end in سُكُونْ, i.e., ئ ـْ or أ ـْ.

Let's take the Arabic word for *young boy; juvenile* in the definite form: الْفَتَى. In all three grammatical cases, الْفَتَى looks the same. In the following examples, the case markers can't be put on the last vowel. All of them have a virtual, estimated vowel marker.

ضَمّةٌ مُقَدَّرةٌ	The boy came.	جاءَ الْفَتَى.
فَتْحةٌ مُقَدَّرةٌ	I met the boy.	قابَلْتُ الْفَتَى.
كَسْرةٌ مُقَدَّرةٌ	I greeted the boy.	سَلَّمْتُ عَلَى الْفَتَى.

It is simply impossible (تَعَذُّرٌ) to put vowel markers for cases on the Aleph because you can't pronounce it! Would it help if we wrote the Aleph differently? No. We'd better keep our hands off it.

| **wrong** (incorrect) | This would change the nature of the word and therefore the meaning! | جاءَ الْفَتَأُ |
| | | جاءَ الْفَتَوُ |

Regarding ي and و, we could **theoretically** mark them with the appropriate vowels, pronounce the result with a lot of effort and end up with a very heavy sound. But this is not done.

The ضَمّةٌ could be pronounced with the ي.	جاءَ الْقاضِيُ.
The كَسْرةٌ could be pronounced with the ي.	سَلَّمْتُ عَلَى الْقاضِيِ.

40. Can you put case or mood markers on weak letters?

It depends on the case.

You probably came across the term weak letter (حَرْفُ الْعِلّةِ) relatively early in your Arabic studies. Often, however, the term is introduced so early that the subtleties are not addressed or simply overlooked.

That's why we want to start again here with a tour d'horizon. We will only focus on the last part of a word and analyze three situations in which a word **ends** in a weak letter.

1	Noun ending in a *permanent Aleph* (أَلِفٌ لازِمةٌ). This Aleph is not a sign of declension; it is in the DNA of the word.	إِسْمٌ مَقْصُورٌ

The final Aleph can have two shapes depending on the root:

- It can occur in the **standard shape of an Aleph** – ا – like in the Arabic word for *stick* (عَصًا). This usually happens when the root letter is, in fact, و. In the example of عَصًا, the root is ع-ص-و.

- It can occur as a ي **without dots:** ى. We call such ى an Aleph Maqsūra (أَلِفٌ مَقْصورةٌ). The term can be translated as an *Aleph that can be shortened*. If a word consists of the three root letters only, ى is a sign that the root letter is, in fact, ي. For example, *guidance* (هُدًى). The root is: ه-د-ي. Although it is often transliterated as *ā*, this letter is usually pronounced very close to a short "*a*" (unless you stop or pause after the word; then you pronounce it as long "*aa*"; see the excursus below).

The (long) Aleph is always written as ى + ٰ (i.e., an Aleph maqsūra) in words of **more than three letters** – unless the letter before the long a is ي. For example:

he lives; he will live	Notice the ي!	يَحْيَا		*Moses (Mūsā)*	مُوسَى
world; (lit.: nearer/lower)		دُنْيَا		hospital	مُسْتَشْفَى

Let's see how such words behave in grammar.

nominative (مَرْفُوعٌ)	A boy came.	جاءَ فتًى.
We say that the subject (فاعِلٌ) is مَرْفُوع by a virtual case marker (ضَمّةٌ مُقَدَّرةٌ) since the last letter can't carry any case marker (التَّعَذُّرُ).		

accusative (مَنْصُوبٌ)	You saw a boy.	رَأَيْتَ فَتًى.
Here, *boy* is the direct object (مَفْعُولٌ بِهِ) and therefore مَنْصُوبٌ. Since the last letter can't show any marker, we say that it is marked by an estimated, imaginary فَتْحَةٌ, a so-called فَتْحَةٌ مُقَدَّرَةٌ.		
genitive (مَجْرُورٌ)	We greeted a boy.	سَلَّمْنا عَلَى فَتًى.
The word *boy* comes after a preposition and must be genitive (مَجْرُورٌ). We can't put a marker on the last letter, we mark it by a كَسْرَةٌ مُقَدَّرَةٌ.		

The indefinite noun *boy* in the above examples never changes its shape due to the impossibility of the Aleph to carry anything (عَلامَاتُ الْإِعْرَابِ تَكُونُ مُقَدَّرَةً فِي آخِرِهِ لِلتَّعَذُّرِ); see #39. From the examples above, we also see how to mark an **indefinite noun** ending in ى. The **Aleph is eliminated by pronunciation** but not by spelling! (إذا نُوِّنَ الْمَقْصُورُ حُذِفَتْ أَلِفُهُ لَفْظًا لا خَطًّا). As for the case, you use estimated markers.

Let's turn to a special situation. A اِسْمٌ مَقْصُورٌ with more than 3 letters (الْمَقْصُورَةُ الزَّائِدَةُ) is **not allowed** to take nunation (تَنْوِينٌ) because it counts as a **diptote** (مَمْنُوعٌ مِن الصَّرْفِ). This is the situation when the Aleph (ى) is not part of the root, e.g., words like *Moses* (مُوسَى), *Layla* (لَيْلَى), or *Salwa* (سَلْوَى).

nominative (مَرْفُوعٌ)	Moses came.	جَاءَ مُوسَى.
accusative (مَنْصُوبٌ)	You saw Moses.	رَأَيْتَ مُوسَى.
genitive (مَجْرُورٌ)	We greeted Moses.	سَلَّمْنا عَلَى مُوسَى.
Remark: All names of prophets in the Qur'an (أَسْماء الْأَنْبِياء) are diptotes – except for *Muhammad* (مُحَمَّدٌ), *Lūt/Lot* (لُوطٌ), *Sālih* (صالِحٌ), *Hūd/Eber* (هُودٌ), *Shu'ayb/Jethro* (شُعَيْبٌ), and *Nūh/Noah* (نُوحٌ). Why are most of the names diptotes? Because they are foreign, non-Arabic names (الْعَلَمُ الْأَعْجَمِيُّ). Only names derived from Arabic roots (صالِحٌ) and names consisting of three letters with a سُكُونٌ on the second letter (e.g., لُوطٌ) do get nunation.		

The above examples demand some thoughts. *Moses*, since it is a proper name, is treated as a <u>definite</u> word. In the previous examples, we dealt with an indefinite word (*a boy*). Nouns that can't take nunation are special because the get special case markers. The **genitive case** is tricky:

The word مُوسَى must get the genitive case (مَجْرُورٌ), but the marker can't be shown. So far, so good.	عَلَى مُوسَى

However, the case marker for the genitive is a فَتْحةٌ because it is a diptote. Therefore, we say that it is genitive by an estimated فَتْحةٌ, in Arabic: مَجْرُورٌ بِفَتْحةٍ مُقَدَّرةٍ. This is because definite "diptote" nouns only have two case markers: a single ضَمّةٌ for the nominative and single فَتْحةٌ for the other 2 cases. Although the word hides this, we should be aware of it.

We can now summarize all of this input about the Aleph maqsūra: in four rules:

1. In verbs, you use ى in the past tense (الْماضِي) except for verbs which have و as a **last** root letter → then you use I. For ex.: *to throw* د-ع-و. (R3=و) ➡ (R3=ي); يَرْمِي - رَمَى). *To call* (دَعا - يَدْعُو) (R3=و). ر-م-ي.

2. You pronounce it short when it is followed by another **word**.

3. You write it as I when it is followed by a **pronoun**. For example, *commemoration*: ذِكْرَى - ذِكْراها.

4. Special situation: ي before the final ā ("aa") ➡ you write يَا. E.g.: *world; nearer* (دُنْيَا). Note: If you add my (ي) to words ending in long vowel, the ‑ + يْ changes to يَ. So we get: دُنْيايَ (*my world*).

Excursus: Why is the ى called *Aleph that can be shortened*? Two ideas.

1. The pronunciation. The Aleph maqsūra may got its name because when it comes in contact with a *connecting Hamza* (هَمْزةُ وَصْلٍ), also called *Hamza of liaison*, it is shortened in pronunciation before the following consonant (الْأَلِفُ الَّتِي اخْتَصَرَتْ لَفْظًا).

A *connecting Hamza* is found in the definite article الـ because the first letter I is only pronounced as a Hamza (= glottal stop) at the beginning of the speech.

A rule says that a **long vowel is shortened in pronunciation before the definite article**. For ex.: among men (فِي النَّاسِ) or the father of the teacher (أَبُو الْمُدَرِّسِ). Don't say: *"Abuuuu-l-Mudarris"* – it is *"Abu-l-mudarris"*. This is exactly what happens with the Aleph maqsūra.

There is even a more theoretical reason. If you did pronounce a Hamza in the definite article after the Aleph maqsūra, you would end up with an Aleph Mamdūda: (اء). The Aleph Mamdūda (أَلِفٌ مَمْدُودَةٌ), also called the *lengthened Aleph*, is a term used for the ending اء. If you encounter this combination at the end of a word, you know for sure that the Aleph is **additional** (أَلِفٌ زَائِدَةٌ) and does not belong to the root! Furthermore, the Hamza protects the Aleph, so the Aleph will always remain in any case. See *Arabic for Nerds 1 – question #14*.

2. Impossibility of showing case endings. The root ق-ص-ر means *to be or become short*; however, it may also convey the meaning of *to lock up; to confine* – like in the word for *castle* (قَصْرٌ) which may also be interpreted in the meaning of الْحَبْسُ – *confinement*.

A اسْمٌ مَقْصُورٌ gets virtual (estimated, assumed) case markers in all three cases. We call that الْإِعْرَابُ الْمُقَدَّرُ. That's perhaps a reason for the term مَقْصُورَةٌ as some scholars – e.g., Ibn Mālik (ابْن مالِك) – suggested.
➡ Because of their *inner confinement*, words with أَلِفٌ مَقْصُورَةٌ cannot get case endings (لِأَنَّهُ مَحْبُوسٌ عَنِ الْمَدِّ أَوْ عَنْ ظُهُورِ الْإِعْرَابِ).

2 Noun ending in a **permanent Yā'** (يَاءٌ لازِمَةٌ) which has no شَدَّةٌ. There must be a كَسْرةٌ before ي, so we end up having a long vowel: *"ii/ee"*. The اسْمٌ مَنْقُوصٌ is often translated as *noun with curtailed ending*. For ex.: قاضٍ / الْقاضِي (*judge*)	اسْمٌ مَنْقُوصٌ

A إسْمٌ مَنْقُوصٌ can take **one visible**, true marker (فَتْحةٌ) and **two virtual**, estimated markers (ضَمّةٌ and كَسْرةٌ). The *long vowel* ي (so-called يَاءٌ مَمْدُودَةٌ) needs a preceding كَسْرةٌ (*"i"*). But why can we only have one standard, true marker?

- The ضَمّةٌ is a heavy vowel which would compete with the *"i"* and would suppress the formation of ي. Thus, we can't put the ـُ.

- The كَسْرةٌ is actually a fraction of the ي, so it is troublesome to vocalize the ي with a part of its own (it's pretty hard to imagine).

- Only فَتْحةٌ, the **lightest** of the vowels, __can be shown__ on the ي.

Let's start the analysis when such nouns are **definite**.

nominative (مَرْفُوعٌ)	The judge came.	جاءَ الْقاضِي.

Judge is the subject (فاعِلٌ) and must be in the nominative case (مَرْفُوع). However, the last letter has great difficulties to carry a ضَمّةٌ, so we say that it is marked by an imaginary, estimated ضَمّةٌ, a ضَمّةٌ مُقَدَّرةٌ.

| accusative (مَنْصُوبٌ) | You saw the judge. | رَأَيْتَ الْقَاضِيَ. |

Judge is the direct object (مَفْعُولٌ بِهِ) and in the accusative (مَنْصُوبٌ) by فَتْحةٌ. This فَتْحةٌ isn't hidden but **shown** and **pronounced**! We call it a فَتْحةٌ ظَاهِرةٌ.

| genitive (مَجْرُورٌ) | We greeted the judge. | سَلَّمْنا عَلَى الْقَاضِي. |

Judge follows a preposition and must be genitive (مَجْرُورٌ). However, the last letter can't carry a كَسْرةٌ; the marker is hidden. We use a كَسْرةٌ مُقَدَّرةٌ.

What happens if the noun is <u>indefinite</u>?

In the nominative (مَرْفُوعٌ) and genitive case (مَجْرُورٌ), the ي is eliminated. It is **replaced/compensated** with nunation (تُقَدَّرُ الضَّمةُ وَالْكَسْرةُ في آخِرِهِ لِلثِّقَلِ). The nunation, however, is phonological and **not** grammatical and occurs since we omit the ي.

Grammarians call this process تَنْوِين العِوَض. The word عِوَض means *substitute* or *compensation*. Such nouns are treated as *defective* because they are derived from a root with the following characteristics: a final weak radical (ي or و) **plus** a كَسْرةٌ on the preceding letter. If the weak radical were to remain, the resulting ending would harm some phonological rules of Arabic. Two examples:

	What we use instead of the usual nominative and genitive case markers:	If we applied the standard nominative and genitive case markers, the final word would be difficult to pronounce:
judge	قاضٍ	قاضِيٍ or قاضِيٌ
host	داعٍ	داعِوٍ or داعِوٌ

Only in the accusative case, we can apply the standard case marker.

| nominative (مَرْفُوعٌ) | A judge came. | جاءَ قاضٍ. |

Judge is the subject (فاعِل) and has to get the nominative case (مَرْفُوعٌ). Since we cannot visibly put a ضَمّةٌ on قاضٍ, we say that it gets an estimated, virtual ضَمّةٌ. Okay, but on which letter should we place it? It is (picture that in your

| mind) on the <u>deleted</u> ي! In Arabic, we say: ضَمَّةٌ مُقَدَّرَةٌ عَلَى الْيَاءِ الْمَحْذُوفةِ. |||

| ACCUSATIVE (مَنْصُوبٌ) | You saw a judge. | رَأَيْتَ قَاضِيًا. |

Judge is the direct object (مَفْعُولٌ بِهِ). Nothing special; we apply the **standard rules**. *Judge* is مَنْصُوبٌ, takes فَتْحةٌ, and since it is indefinite, we use *nunation*.

| genitive (مَجْرُورٌ) | We greeted a judge. | سَلَّمْنا عَلَى قَاضٍ. |

Judge follows a preposition, so it must get the genitive case (مَجْرُورٌ). We see the كَسْرةٌ (-"*in*"), so it seems that everything is normal. But it is not! We still need an estimated, virtual case marker here! How come?

The "-*in*" (كَسْرةٌ) should be on the last letter, but the last letter (ي) was deleted. We therefore say that it is مَجْرُورٌ by an estimated كَسْرةٌ on the deleted ي (مَجْرُورٌ بِكَسْرةٍ مُقَدَّرةٍ عَلَى الْيَاءِ الْمَحْذُوفةِ). Strange, but true.

Now, what happens if the noun is a **diptote** (مَمْنُوعٌ مِن الصَّرْفِ) and is therefore not allowed to take nunation?

- If the إِسْمٌ مَنْقُوصٌ is in the nominative (مَرْفُوعٌ) or genitive (مَجْرُورٌ):
  → delete ي and **compensate** it with *nunation* (تَنْوِينُ الْعِوَضِ), i.e., ٍ
- If the إِسْمٌ مَنْقُوصٌ is in the **accusative** (مَنْصُوبٌ), show the actual sign of the case. You use the **standard rules**; nothing special.

Let's take the word جَارِيَةٌ which has two plural forms: جَارِياتٌ or the broken form جَوارٍ. The word is derived from the root ج-ر-ي which denotes *to flow, to take place*. It has many meanings depending on the context: *girl; maid, servant* (because of her activity); *ship* (because of its "running" upon the sea). The plural جَوارٍ is a إِسْمٌ مَنْقُوصٌ:

| nominative (مَرْفُوعٌ) | These are maids. | هٰذِهِ جَوارٍ. |

Maids is the predicate (خَبَرٌ) of the nominal sentence (جُمْلةٌ إِسْمِيّةٌ) and has to be مَرْفُوعٌ. However, it is an **indefinite** noun which can't take nunation (**diptote**). In such a situation, we would only put **one** ضَمّةٌ on the last letter. But the last letter here, the ي, was deleted and wouldn't be able to carry it anyway. Thus, we use a virtual case marker (ضَمّةٌ مُقَدَّرةٌ) which we put in our mind on the <u>deleted</u> ي. The nunation (تَنْوِينُ الْعِوَضِ) is a substitute for it.

| genitive (مَجْرُورٌ) | We greeted maids. | سَلَّمْنا عَلَى جَوارٍ. |

The word *maids* follows a preposition and has to be genitive (مَجْرُورٌ). The usual case marker for this is nunation (كَسْرةٌ): "-in". We got that here...

But wait! That would be <u>incorrect</u> as we deal with an **indefinite** noun that does not take **nunation** (مَمْنُوعٌ مِن الصَّرْفِ). In this situation, we would only need **one** فَتْحةٌ. For this reason, we must use an imaginary case marker – on a letter that is not there anymore: the ي. This was the letter, where we should put the case marker, but it was deleted. In Arabic, we would say: مَجْرُورٌ بِفَتْحةٍ مُقَدَّرةٍ عَلَى الْيَاءِ الْمَحْذُوفةِ.

ACCUSATIVE (مَنْصوبٌ)	You saw maids.	رَأَيْتَ جَوارِيَ.

The word *maids* is the direct object (مَفْعُولٌ بِهِ). Since it is a diptote, it doesn't get nunation. That's why we only use **one** فَتْحةٌ to mark the مَنْصوبٌ-case. The standard rule for a diptote is applied, nothing special.

Remark: Don't confuse جَوارٍ with جِوارٌ. It means *neighborhood*, *proximity* and relates to the root ج-و-ر. In the III-form (يُجاوِرُ - جاوَرَ; R2=و), it denotes *to neighbor; to border*. This root has a normal, sound letter at the end and does not cause any problems with case endings.

Now, let's turn to the last special situation:

3	A **VERB** in the present tense (الْمُضـارِعُ) with a final weak letter.	فِعْلٌ مُضارِعٌ مُعْتَلُّ الآخِرِ

In the indicative (رَفْعٌ) and subjunctive mood (نَصْبٌ), we use a virtual, estimated marker. However, in the **jussive** (جَزْمٌ) mood, the sign of the إِعْرابٌ is **apparent** because the weak letter is deleted.

Let's first check the **Aleph** (in the shape of ى).

She seeks (strives for) goodness.	تَسْعَى إِلَى الْخَيْرِ.

We have a present tense verb in the 3rd person singular (*she*). The **indicative mood** (standard form) of a verb is marked by ضَمّةٌ on the last letter, e.g., *she writes* (تَكْتُبُ). What can we do here since the Aleph can't carry a (ُ)-vowel? We use a virtual mood marker (ضَمّةٌ مُقَدَّرةٌ)! In the analysis, we'd say: فِعْلٌ مُضارِعٌ وَعَلامةُ رَفْعِهِ الضَّمّةُ الْمُقَدَّرةُ، مَنَعَ مِنْ ظُهُورِها التَّعَذُّرُ

He won't be satisfied with the food.	لَنْ يَرْضَى بِالأَكْلِ.

We have a **negated future tense,** formed by لَنْ plus a verb in the present tense, subjunctive mood (مَنْصوبٌ). However, we can't put a فَتْحةٌ on the last letter since it is an Aleph. We have to use a virtual فَتْحةٌ to mark it:

فِعْلٌ مُضارِعٌ مَنْصوبٌ بِلَنْ وَعَلامةُ نَصْبِهِ فَتْحةٌ مُقَدَّرةٌ, مَنَعَ مِنْ ظُهورِها التَّعَذُّرُ.

| Don't be afraid of anything except for Allah! | لا تَخْشَ غَيْرَ اللّٰهِ! |

We deal with a verb in the present tense which is placed after a **prohibitive لا** (لا النّاهِيةُ). Therefore, the verb must be in the jussive (مَجْزُومٌ) mood. A verb ending in Aleph is put into the jussive by deleting the last (the weak) letter and by putting the vowel "a" (ـَ) on the now final letter:

فِعْلٌ مُضارِعٌ مَجْزُومٌ بِلا النّاهِيةِ, وَعَلامةُ جَزْمِهِ حَذْفُ حَرْفِ الْعِلّةِ.

When the last **letter is و** or **ي**, the situation is different.

→ We can show the فَتْحةٌ. It is written on top of the letter.

→ Regarding the مَجْزُومٌ, we do the same as above in the Aleph case: The jussive mood is marked by the deletion of the weak letter. Then, we add a vowel that is related to the deleted letter.

→ Only the indicative marker "u" (ـُ) is a virtual sign and has to be estimated (مُقَدَّرة).

| و | Karīm invites a (f.) friend to the party. | يَدْعو كَريمٌ صَديقةً إِلَى الْحَفْلةِ. |

The verb is in the **present tense indicative (مَرْفوعٌ)**, so we would need a ضَمّةٌ on top of the last letter. However, since the last letter is و which is preceded by the vowel "u" (عُوْ), the و must have سُكونٌ and can't carry a ضَمّةٌ. We say that it is مَرْفوعٌ by a virtual, estimated ضَمّةٌ:

فِعْلٌ مُضارِعٌ مَرْفوعٌ, وَعَلامةُ رَفْعِهِ الضَّمّةُ الْمُقَدَّرةُ, مَنَعَ مِنْ ظُهورِها الثِّقَلُ.

| لا و + | Don't invite her to the party! | لا تَدْعُها إِلَى الْحَفْلةِ! |

Here we need to put the verb into the jussive (مَجْزُومٌ) mood because it comes after a **prohibitive لا**, a so-called لا النّاهِيةُ. The marker for the جَزْم is the deletion of the weak letter. In such situations, the deleted letter "hands over" the vowel to the preceding letter. Since we delete و, the former middle and now last letter gets a ضَمّةٌ ("u").

However, the ضَمّةٌ doesn't mark the mood! The mood is marked by the deletion of the letter و (عَلامةُ الْجَزْمِ حَذْفُ حَرْفِ الْعِلّةِ)!

| أَنْ و + | She wants to forgive. | تُريدُ أَنْ تَعْفُوَ. |

Here we use an **interpreted infinitive**, a so-called مَصْدَرٌ مُؤَوَّلٌ, created by the device أَنْ plus a verb in the subjunctive (مَنْصُوبٌ) mood. Since و (as well as ي) can carry a فَتْحةٌ, we can put it on top of the last letter of the verb (i.e., the و). So everything is **normal** here:

فِعْلٌ مُضارِعٌ مَنْصُوبٌ بِأَنْ, وَعَلامةُ نَصْبِهِ الْفَتْحةُ الظّاهِرةُ.

ي	I will come over tomorrow.	سَآتِيكُمْ غَدًا.

Present tense verb in the **indicative** (مَرْفُوعٌ) mood. We would need to put a ضَمّةٌ on top of ي, but this is impossible as this letter can't carry any vowel. We need a virtual, estimated (imaginary) marker:

فِعْلٌ مُضارِعٌ مَرْفُوعٌ, وَعَلامةُ رَفْعِهِ الضّمّةُ الْمُقَدَّرةُ, مَنَعَ مِنْ ظُهُورِها الثِّقَلُ.

لَنْ + ي	He won't come tomorrow.	لَنْ يَأْتِيَ غَدًا.

We want to express the **negation in the future** with the help of the device لَنْ. We need a verb in the subjunctive (مَنْصُوبٌ) mood after لَنْ. We show the فَتْحةٌ because the ي can carry a فَتْحةٌ! So everything is **normal:**

فِعْلٌ مُضارِعٌ مَنْصُوبٌ بِأَنْ, وَعَلامةُ نَصْبِهِ الْفَتْحةُ الظّاهِرةُ.

لَمْ + ي	He didn't come yesterday.	لَمْ يَأْتِ أَمْسِ.

We need a present tense verb in the مَجْزُومٌ-mood (jussive) because we use لَمْ to express the **negation in the past**. How do we mark it correctly? We delete the weak letter. Since we delete ي, the former middle and now last letter gets كَسْرةٌ , but this is not the marker of the mood. The marker is the deletion of the ي; in Arabic, we say:

فِعْلٌ مُضارِعٌ مَجْزُومٌ بِلَمْ, وَعَلامةُ جَزْمِهِ حَذْفُ حَرْفِ الْعِلّةِ.

41. Why can an extra (additional) preposition be annoying?

You might misunderstand the meaning of a sentence because you get misled by the marker of the genitive case induced by the preposition.

Preposition, as the name indicates, are devices that precede a noun or pronoun. They add a new meaning to the sentence and show a relationship in space or time or a logical relationship between two or more people, places, or things.

Now, what is an *extra preposition* (حَرْفُ جَرٍّ زائِدٌ)? An additional preposition does not add any new meaning to the sentence. It only **gives emphasis to a following word** by "freeing" it from the other parts. An extra preposition doesn't have the same job as a "true" preposition – but it does come with the same grammatical effects! ➤ It operates on a following noun (اِسْمٌ) and drags it into the genitive (مَجْرُورٌ).

How can you know that a preposition is extra? If you could delete the preposition and the sentence would still make sense and convey the basic meaning, then it is an extra, redundant preposition. This is not possible with a "normal", true preposition. Thus, some linguists call the additional preposition *expletive*. From this, we get an idea how we could treat the these extra devices and the words after it grammatically. We have to use virtual case markers that mark the word after the extra preposition according to its actual function and role in a sentence (i.e., as if the preposition was not there).

Technically speaking, we say that the place for the original case marker according to the function in the sentence is occupied by the extra preposition as a word can't carry two markers at the same time.

No man came. (Not a single man came.)	ما جاءَ مِنْ رَجُلٍ.

This is an extra preposition (حَرْفُ جَرٍّ زائِدٌ).	مِنْ
Subject (فاعِلٌ), so it needs the **nominative** (مَرْفُوعٌ) case. How can we mark it as such? What we see is the marker of the genitive…	رَجُلٍ

First of all, the place of the case marker is occupied by the extra preposition which has priority regarding the case markers. This is the reason why you see the كَسْرة (nunation: "-*in*"). At the same time, the markers of the genitive disguise that the word is the subject! We need to fix that with a trick. We use an **estimated, virtual** case marker (ضَمّة مُقَدَّرة) for the nominative case because the place for the case marker is taken:

فاعِلٌ مَرْفُوعٌ بِضَمّةٍ مُقَدَّرةٍ مَنَعَ مِنْ ظُهُورِها اشْتِغالُ الْمَحَلّ بِحَرَكةِ حَرْفِ الْجَرِّ الزّائِدِ.

Additional prepositions often occur together with لَيْسَ. The extra preposition is mainly there for emphasis (تَوْكِيد). The Qur'an uses this construction occasionally. Here is a famous example:

| Sura 88:22 | You are not there to control them. | لَسْتَ عَلَيْهِم بِمُصَيْطِرٍ. |

Note: Is there a spelling mistake? Shouldn't it be بِمُسَيْطِرٍ? Yes and no. The original word for control is مُسَيْطِر. But in the Qur'an, the س turns into a ص in rare occasions, mainly if there is a ط after the س.

In the above sentence, مُسَيْطِر is the predicate of لَيْسَ, the so-called خَبَرُ لَيْسَ. According to the rules, this predicate needs to be in the accusative (مَنْصُوبٌ) case and should take nunation (فَتْحَةٌ - "-an"). But the extra preposition بـ overshadows the standard rules and induces the كَسْرَةٌ ("-in") instead. Nevertheless, the predicate is مَنْصُوبٌ by a virtual or implied فَتْحَةٌ because the original marker cannot be shown.

Now, what about the following sentence?

| Are there any faithful people who would do that? | هَلْ مِنْ مُخْلِصِينَ يَفْعَلُونَ ذلِكَ؟ |

Also here مِنْ is an extra preposition which conveys emphasis. مُخْلِصِينَ is a sound masculine plural which functions as the subject (مُبْتَدَأ) of the nominal sentence (جُمْلَةٌ اِسْمِيّةٌ). Thus, it has to be in the nominative (مَرْفُوعٌ) case. The marker for the nominative case of a sound masculine plural is the و in the ending ـُونَ. The extra preposition triggers the genitive case which is marked in a sound masculine plural by the ي in the plural ending. For this reason, we can only say that مُخْلِصِينَ is nominative by a virtual و, a so-called واوٌ مُقَدَّرةٌ. In the analysis, we say:

مُبْتَدَأٌ مَرْفُوعٌ بِواوٌ مُقَدَّرةٍ مَنَعَ مِن ظُهُورِها اشْتِغالُ الْمَحَلِّ بِحَرَكةِ حَرْفِ الْجَرِّ الزَّائِدِ

It is of secondary importance what is shown in the word. The function is what matters! The following example looks perfectly fine, but some might misinterpret what they see. Let's see why.

| We are not believers. | لَسْنا بِمُؤْمِنِينَ. |

Believers (مُؤْمِنِينَ) is a sound masculine plural (جَمْعُ الْمُذَكَّرِ السّالِمُ). The بـ is a redundant, extra preposition (حَرْفُ جَرٍّ زائِدٌ) and drags the word into the genitive case (مَجْرُورٌ). Sound masculine plurals form the genitive (and the accusative) by changing the و (مُؤْمِنُونَ) into ي (مُؤْمِنِينَ). The function of the word in the above sentence is the predicate of لَيْسَ

which has to be in the accusative (مَنْصُوبٌ) case according to the rules.

Although we would visually get the same result without the preposition بـ, the analysis is different because of the بـ. We have to say that مُؤْمِنِينَ is مَنْصُوبٌ by a virtual, estimated ي (يَاءٌ مُقَدَّرَةٌ) because the preposition has occupied the position. The analysis is as follows:

$$\text{خَبَرُ لَيْسَ مَنْصُوبٌ بِفَتْحةٍ مُقَدَّرةٍ مَنَعَ مِنْ ظُهُورِها اشْتِغالُ بِعَلامةِ حَرْفِ}$$
$$\text{الْجَرِّ الزَّائِدِ}$$

Sounds complicated? It is. But once you have understood the underlying logic, it will become easy.

In summary, we can say that an **extra, redundant preposition** (حَرْفُ جَرٍّ زائِدٌ) should be analyzed from two different angles:

1. The visual, pronounced case marker. You use the term لَفْظًا. It tells you **what you see and hear**.

All *followers* (تَوابِعُ) – e.g., the attribute/adjective (نَعْتٌ), the apposition (بَدَلٌ), and the word following a conjunction (مَعْطُوفٌ) – usually follow the visible إِعْرابٌ especially when there is an extra preposition involved. If you want to **pronounce** a word correctly, you need to look at the visible markers.

2. The virtual case marker **according to the place** in the sentence. For this viewpoint, we use the term *as its place-value dictates* (مَحَلًّا).

The place that a word occupies in a sentence has a value regarding the grammatical analysis (الْإِعْرابُ الْمَحَلِّيُّ). If you want to **translate** a sentence correctly, you need to identify the place and function of a word.

IN ANY CASE THE SAME – INDECLINABLE WORDS

42. Which kinds of words are entirely indeclinable?

All particles and prepositions (كُلُّ الْحُرُوفِ).

Indeclinable (مَبْنِيٌّ or بِناءٌ) means that a word has only one shape – regardless of its position in the sentence. It never changes its shape and always looks the same. If you want to "mark" the case in **indeclinable** nouns, there is no other option but to use invisible **place values** in the analysis. We say, for example, فِي مَحَلِّ رَفْعٍ (*in the position of a nominative case*). This is the opposite of *declinable* (مُعْرَبٌ). Declinable words get visible case endings.

Now it gets tricky. This does not apply to particles (حَرْفٌ) and prepositions (حَرْفُ الْجَرِّ) because such words **do not have a place** in إِعْرابٌ. We say in Arabic: لا مَحَلَّ لَهُ مِن الْإِعْرابِ. They do not occupy a certain position in the sentence and therefore do not take on one of the various functions. For example, they cannot serve as the subject (فاعِلٌ), an object (مَفْعُولٌ), a specification (تَمْيِيزٌ) or as an absolute object, etc. Thus, they do not get visible or invisible case markers nor a place value.

The following words marked in gray never change their shape and don't get case endings nor place values. They all don't have a position in إِعْرابٌ (لا مَحَلَّ لَها مِن الْإِعْرابِ), but they may operate on other words.

هَلْ	**1** Question particle	حَرْفُ إِسْتِفْهامٍ مَبْنِيٌّ عَلَى السُّكُونِ
	Did Karīm come?	هَلْ جاءَ كَرِيمٌ؟
ما	**2** Negation particle	حَرْفُ نَفْيٍ مَبْنِيٌّ عَلَى السُّكُونِ
	Karīm didn't come.	ما جاءَ كَرِيمٌ.
بِ	**3** Preposition	حَرْفُ جَرٍّ مَبْنِيٌّ عَلَى الْكَسْرِ
	I was (felt) bored.	شَعَرْتُ بِالْمَلَلِ.
يا	**4** Particle of attention	حَرْفُ نِداءٍ مَبْنِيٌّ عَلَى السُّكُونِ
	Oh my son!	يَا بُنَيَّ!
Sura 12:5	**My son**, tell your brothers nothing of this dream, or they may plot to harm you.	يَا بُنَيَّ لَا تَقْصُصْ رُؤْيَاكَ عَلَى إِخْوَتِكَ فَيَكِيدُوا لَكَ كَيْدًا۔

Excursus: A deep analysis of يَا بُنَيَّ

We start with the noun بُنَيٌّ. Without vowels بني may denote *brown* (بُنّيٌّ) but this is far from our intended meaning. بُنَيٌّ is a diminutive (تَصْغِيرٌ) of اِبْنٌ (*son*) using the pattern فُعَيْلٌ. So, how did we get from اِبْنٌ to بُنَيٌّ? We need to look at the origin of اِبْنٌ which is the root ب-ن-و. If we now apply the pattern فُعَيْلٌ, we get بُنَيْوٌ. Since ي and و collide and the first of the two weak letters has سُكُونٌ, the و turns into ي → so we get بُنَيْيٌ. Arabic doesn't like the occurrence of a quiescent letter and a vocalized letter that resembles it. Thus, we incorporate the vowelless ي and get: بُنَيٌّ. Note: The feminine form is بُنَيَّةٌ, *a little daughter*; it is the diminutive of بِنْتٌ (*daughter*).

يا بُنَيَّ equals يا ابْنِيَ الصَّغِيرَ and is an affectionate way of calling a child. It literally means: *O my little son!*

What about the analysis? If you add the pronominal suffix *my* (ي), the vocative becomes a challenge. In the vocative, the suffix ي (*my*) is often shortened to a simple كسرةٌ, e.g., يا رَبِّ (*O my Lord!*). Thus, we can use the form يا بُنَيِّ (A) which is one possibility. Another form is يا بُنَيَّ (B) which is used in the Qur'an. Both versions were mentioned by the grammarian al-Farrāʾ (الْفَرَّاءُ) giving the analogy of يا أَبَتِ and يا أَبَتَ meaning *O my father!* → *see #417*. Let's try to understand the grammatical background. First of all, in both options (A+B), the pronoun ي was deleted! Let's see the details.

Option A: The expression was originally يا بُنَيْيِي with 3 Yāʾs: The first ي is for the diminutive, the second ي is the third root letter and the last ي is the pronoun my. بُنَيِّ is the *called person* (مُنادًى) in the **accusative** case by a virtual, estimated marker (عَلامةُ نَصْبِهِ الْفَتْحةُ الْمُقَدَّرةُ) placed on the ي. The case marker cannot be shown because the spot of the marker is occupied by the كَسرةٌ which signifies the deleted pronoun ي.

Option B: This time we work with يا بُنَيَّا. (If you don't know why there is an Aleph, see #417). Also here, بُنَيَّ is the *called person* (مُنادًى) in the **accusative** case by a virtual marker (عَلامةُ نَصْبِهِ الْفَتْحةُ الْمُقَدَّرةُ). Wait! But why do we call it a virtual, estimated marker since we have a فَتْحة at the end? The ي – the pronoun (ضَمِيرُ الْمُتَكَلِّم) - is the second part of the إضافةٌ but this ي was deleted to make the phrase a little lighter (مَحْذُوفٌ لِلتَّخْفِيفِ). The فَتْحة occupies the spot of the case marker to indicate the **deleted last letter Aleph** (الدَّالَّةُ عَلَى الْأَلِفِ الْمَحْذُوفةِ الْمُبْدَلَةِ مِنْ ضَمِيرِ الْمُتَكَلِّمِ) which originally came about through a conversion from the pronoun *my* (ي).

5	Particle of emphasis	إنَّ حَرْفُ تَوْكِيدٍ وَنَصْبٍ مَبْنِيٌّ عَلَى الْفَتْحِ

Indeed, the weather is nice.	إِنَّ الْجَوَّ جَمِيلٌ.

43. Are there indeclinable (مَبْنِيٌّ) verbs in Arabic?

Yes, there are. Actually most of the verb forms are مَبْنِيٌّ.

The term مَبْنِيٌّ describes one of the most important concepts in Arabic. It can be translated as *indeclinable,* some people prefer to say *structured* or *fixed,* or *cemented.* Regarding verbs, it means that the ending of a verb doesn't change if we put the verb into a different **mood**.

In my opinion, it is critical to understand how tenses, forms, and moods of Arabic verbs are constructed. For example, in many grammar books, it is stated that only **present tense verbs** can be used in the jussive mood (مَجْزُومٌ). This is only half of the truth. When we talk about the **visual** marker of the jussive (مَجْزُومٌ), i.e., the سُكُونْ, then yes, this is correct – because present tense verbs are not مَبْنِيٌّ and therefore can have different endings.

Although it is very, very rare, **past tense verbs** may serve in the **position** of a jussive verb in conditional sentences (*see #391*). You just can't see the jussive mood because past tense verbs are مَبْنِيٌّ and never change their shape. This happens, for example, in Sura 17:8.

Your Lord may yet have mercy on you, but if you do the same again, so shall We: We have made Hell a prison for those who defy [Our warning].	عَسَى رَبُّكُمْ أَن يَرْحَمَكُمْ وَإِنْ عُدتُّمْ عُدْنَا وَجَعَلْنَا جَهَنَّمَ لِلْكَـٰفِرِينَ حَصِيرًا.

إِنْ is a device for the conditional that induces the jussive mood in a following verb. However, the verb here (عُدتُّمْ) is in the past tense and immune to any changes. So, how can we fix that? We apply a place value. We say that the past tense verb is located in the position of a jussive (فِي مَحَلِّ جَزْمٍ فِعْلُ الشَّرْطِ).

As a rule of thumb, we can even say:

- **Nouns** should be <u>declined</u> (الْأَصْلُ فِي الْأَسْماءِ الْإِعْرابُ).
- **Verbs** should be structured (<u>indeclinable</u>). Those which are declined go outside the rule (الْأَصْلُ فِي الْأَفْعالِ الْبِناءُ). *See also qu. #45.*

Let's focus now on the verbs that have a fixed, indeclinable shape.

1. Past tense verbs (فِعْلٌ ماضٍ) - the most common type of indeclinable verbs. The last vowel is fixed on a vowel or quiescence (= zero-vowel) in accordance to the vowel that follows. We get three shapes:

A) The last root letter of the past tense verb is fixed/built on the vowel "*a*" (مَبْنِيٌّ عَلَى الْفَتْحِ). This is the situation for the standard form, e.g., *he wrote* (كَتَبَ). Furthermore, we use this shape for the third person singular *she* (كَتَبَتْ) and the dual (3ʳᵈ person) *they both* (هُما); e.g., *they both/masculine wrote* (كَتَبَا); *they both/feminine write* (كَتَبَتا).

B) The last root letter has سُكُونٌ. This enables us to connect the verb stem to a vowelled pronominal suffix. This is true for most suffixes.

			بْ	
I wrote	كَتَبْتُ	تُ	That is why we call the verb **indeclinable**. We cement the third root letter on the سُكُون.	
You (m.) wrote	كَتَبْتَ	تَ		
You (f.) wrote	كَتَبْتِ	تِ		
You (both) wrote	كَتَبْتُما	تُما	This makes it possible to add a (vowelled) pronominal **suffix** which serves as the subject (فِي مَحَلِّ رَفْعٍ	كَتَ +
We wrote	كَتَبْنا	نا		
You (m. pl.) wrote	كَتَبْتُمْ	تُمْ	فاعِلٌ) in the **nominative case** in accordance to the rules of Arabic phonology (فِعْلٌ ماضٍ مَبْنِيٌّ عَلَى	
You (f. pl.) wrote	كَتَبْتُنَّ	تُنَّ	السُّكُونِ لِاتِّصالِهِ بِضَمِيرِ رَفْعٍ مُتَحَرِّك).	
They (f. pl.) wrote	كَتَبْنَ	نَ		

Remark: The suffix ت is called تاءُ الْفاعِلِ. The نا is called نا الْمُتَكَلِّمِينَ, the نَ is called نا الْفاعِلِينَ. Notice that we use the term فاعِل as these letters are serving as the subject/doer.

Now, don't get confused. Why did we leave out the 3ʳᵈ person, feminine form *she wrote* (كَتَبَتْ)? Answer: The ت here is silent and just a تاءُ التَّأْنِيثِ to mark the feminine form – it **doesn't** have a place in إِعْرابٌ. ➡ It doesn't work as the subject! But where is the subject? It is a hidden pronoun (ضَمِيرٌ مُسْتَتِرٌ) and has the implicit meaning of *she* (هِيَ).

C) In the masculine plural (*they*), we need a different fixed form, built and cemented on "*u*" (مَبْنِيٌّ عَلَى الضَّمِّ). Only then, we can add the suffix وا which is called واوُ الْجَماعَةِ. For example: *they understood* (فَهِمُوا) because the و, in fact, looks like this: وْ. In Arabic, we can't have two سُكُون in a row which explains why we need the ضَمّة here <u>before</u> the و.

2. The imperative (فِعْلُ الْأَمْرِ). The imperative verb has a fixed, cemented shape and (usually) ends in سُكُونٌ (مَبْنِيٌّ عَلَى السُّكُونِ).

How do you form the imperative? You take the present tense form of the verb and delete the pronominal **prefix**. However, if we do that, we get an unvowelled first letter (سُكُونٌ) - an issue, we need to solve.

For example: *Write!* The present tense (3rd person singular) is يَكْتُبُ. We delete the prefix and get كْتُبُ. This would be impossible because you cannot start an Arabic utterance with two consonants: *ktubu* (see *Arabic for Nerds 1*, #8). So we need to add a connecting Hamza (هَمْزَةُ الْوَصْلِ) and finally get أُكْتُبْ. If it marks the beginning of speech, we pronounce the first letter as a glottal stop (أ). Furthermore, we use the vowel "*u*" because the second root vowel is "*u*" as well (يَكْتُبُ).

Remark: The Kūfa school of grammar (الْكُوفِيُّونَ) suggests that the verb in the imperative is, in fact, in the jussive (مَجْزُومٌ) mood and not indeclinable (مَبْنِيٌّ). They justify that by saying that the origin of the imperative is the present tense (فِعْلٌ مُضارِعٌ) in the jussive (مَجْزُومٌ). The jussive was evoked by the so-called لامُ الْأَمْرِ, written with a كَسْرَةٌ underneath (لِ). Thus, the origin of أُكْتُبْ would be لِتَكْتُبْ. Most grammarians, nevertheless, treat Arabic imperative forms as مَبْنِيٌّ.

3. Present tense verbs which end in Nūn (ن). This could be a feminine marker (نُونُ النِّسْوةِ) or a *Nūn of emphasis* (نُونُ التَّوْكِيدِ).

The students (fem., plural) *write.*	الطّالِبا يَكْتُبْنَ.
The verb has a fixed shape and is built/fixed on the سُكُون. This enables us to connect it to the appropriate suffix – the نَ.	

Now let's analyze a tricky one. **What happens if the last letter of a verb is an Aleph?** First of all, an Aleph can never be part of the root. When you see an Aleph, it is originally و or ي in the root. The final Aleph (ى or ا) changes its form according to the vowel right before it (see *Arabic for Nerds 1*, question #11). For this reason, we call it an *Aleph that can be shortened* (أَلِفٌ مَقْصُورةٌ) because such Aleph is not protected and can be deleted.

Let's assume that we have a verb ending in a أَلِفٌ مَقْصُورةٌ. For example, the Arabic verb for *to go*: مَشَى - يَمْشِي; R3=ي. In the root, there is a ي and not an Aleph but for pronunciation reasons, you cannot write مَشِيَ. Now we want to form the plural form *they*. For past tense verbs, this is done by adding وا, the so-called وَاوُ الْجَمَاعَةِ.

The student (singular) walked.	الطَّالِبُ مَشَى. 1
The students (plural, m.) walked.	الطُّلَابُ مَشَوْا. 2

What happened with the last letter (ى) in the second example? First of all, we have an indeclinable past tense verb (فِعْلٌ مَاضٍ). Fine, but which letter fixes the verb and, by doing that, makes it indeclinable? In our example, the verb's fixed shape is based on the <u>deleted</u> (!) letter ي.

How can we picture that? Let's use the standard formula and add the suffix وا to the root. Theoretically, we would get مَشَيُوا. For Arabs, this is difficult to pronounce. For this reason, the letter ئ (which is the pillar of the fixed shape) was deleted. The final result is مَشَوْا. This has to be done if we want to add وا. In Arabic, we say: فِعْلٌ مَاضٍ مَبْنِيٌّ عَلَى الضَّمِّ عَلَى الْيَاءِ الْمَحْذُوفَةِ.

Let's check another example with و in the root, e.g., *to invite; to call* which is دَعَا in the past tense and يَدْعُو in the present tense.

	original building of the verb	what we finally get
They call for...	هُمْ دَعَوُوا إِلَى...	هُمْ دَعَوْا إِلَى...
The past tense verb has a cemented, structured, indeclinable shape. By looking at the verb form, you can't see that. So, which part is unchangeable? It is the deleted letter وُ. We wanted to get rid of it mainly to facilitate the pronunciation (فِعْلٌ مَاضٍ مَبْنِيٌّ عَلَى الضَّمِّ عَلَى الْوَاوِ الْمَحْذُوفَةِ).		

THE RELATIONSHIP OF WORDS – CASES

44. What do case markers express?

They are more than just mere sounds. They have an almost philosophical basis and give you a rough idea of what a word might express.

A case shows a word's relationship with the other words in a sentence. Cases tell you more about the function of words in a sentence. In

English, nouns do not change their forms in any of the cases other than the genitive case (e.g., *Peter* becomes *Peter's* in a possessive construction). Pronouns, however, change their forms depending on the case (e.g., *he* becomes *his* or *him*). In Arabic, we have three cases for nouns and three moods for verbs.

	ending	What does it express?	Arabic	Latin, English
1	ـُ or ـٌ	regularity; independence	رَفْعٌ	subject; nominative case or indicative mood

Reserved for normal situations of the word, **for essential things.** Any word that is not under some syntactic influence should end in the vowel "*u*". In other words, if the influence is lifted (which is the literal translation of مَرْفُوعٌ), then it will end in regularity. We thus also call it the **independent case** or **regular ending.** The nominative case indicates that a noun serves as the subject (مُبْتَدَأٌ or فاعِلٌ) or predicate (خَبَرٌ).

	ending	What does it express?	Arabic	Latin, English
2	ـَ or ـً	openness; dependency; subordination	نَصْبٌ	direct object; accusative case, subjunctive mood

The root ن-ص-ب means *to set up, to elevate; to assign.* نَصْبٌ denotes that the voice is raised or elevated in singing or chanting [by which camels are urged or excited]. The analogy can be used for the grammar term نَصْبٌ, so called because the sound of a word of which the final letter is so pronounced rises to the highest cavity of the mouth. Thus, you pronounce the final letter with نَصْبٌ, i.e., with ـَ or ـً .

The فَتْحَةٌ, the vowel "*a*", which is used to mark this case is not a sharp vowel; it is an open vowel, used for situations of openness, thereby **enriching a sentence with additional information.** This information is related to the action of the verb when it is unfolding. It can be information about the time or place, how the action is performed, or why, etc.

	ending	What does it express?	Arabic	Latin, English
3	ـِ or ـٍ	reduction; subordination	جَرٌّ or خَفْضٌ	indirect/oblique; genitive case

The meaning of the root ج-ر-ر is *to break; to fold.* The pronunciation of this case marker requires a reduction (خَفْضٌ) of the lips. It may **narrow** (جَرَّ) the **circumstances** or the meaning of the action (حَدَثٌ) or demand precision in the use of words and coordination in the expression of ideas.

Such parts of the sentence are usually a **supplement** (فَضْلةٌ) which may create or add a new meaning to the sentence. Linguists say that they are non-predicative elements. Such nouns are kept in a state of **submission** (خَفْضٌ) regarding their regent. This submission is equivalent to reduction (جَرٌّ), i.e., **dragging** the noun (جَرُّ الْإِسْمِ) towards more **exactness**. This can be achieved by a preposition (حَرْفُ الْجَرِّ) or possessive construction (إِضافةٌ).

What about the سُكُونٌ? This is not a case marker. It marks a mood.

4	ْ	marker of non-occur-ring events	جَزْمٌ	apocopate, jussive mood

The root ج-ز-م means *to cut off; to clip*; in grammar: *to be without a vowel*. This mood marker is **only used with verbs**. The sign of this mood is the cutting of the verb's ending (جَزْمٌ), achieved by سُكُونٌ. If you see this sign at the end of a verb, you know that you don't deal with a standard situation (which would be marked by ُ, the indicative mood). Instead, it expresses a command/imperative, an interdiction, or a conditional meaning. Therefore, we can summarize them as non-occurring events.

45. Do verbs take cases in Arabic?

No, they don't (if we you use the grammatical understanding of English).

In Arabic, declension covers both noun (إِسْمٌ) and verb (فِعْلٌ). The term nominative (رَفْعٌ) is applied for the ُ ending of nouns and verbs in the present tense. In English grammar, we would call the noun *a noun in the nominative case* and the verb *a verb in the indicative mood*.

Let's dig a bit in the grammatical soil. Arabic nouns (إِسْمٌ) possess case endings by basic attested usage (أَصْلٌ) whereas verbs acquire it only by their resemblance/similarity (مُضارِعٌ) to nouns (see #62). This resemblance is found only in the present tense verb (imperfect). That is why in Arabic we treat the past tense verb as indeclinable (مَبْنِيٌّ).

46. What is the underlying concept of *nunation* (تَنْوِينٌ)?

It will tell you something about the "personality" of a word.

Nunation or *Tanwīn* (تَنْوِينٌ) stands for an extra نْ at the end of a noun (اِسْمٌ), which you pronounce (لَفْظًا) but do not write (لا خَطًّا). It practically means that you add a pronounced "*n*"-ending to an **indefinite noun** if you mark it with case endings.

The term تَنْوِينٌ is the مَصْدَرٌ of the II-verb نَوَّنَ - يُنَوِّنُ (R2=و) denoting *adding Nun(-ation) to a noun*. At the early stages of Arabic, it indicated the nasalization of the final vowel of the word in the case ending of the noun. Therefore, تَنْوِينٌ is nothing but an extra ن without a vowel (نُونٌ زائِدَةٌ ساكِنَةٌ) at the end of a word. In the early stages of Arabic, *Tanwīn* was not primarily a marker of indefiniteness (*a; an*) which explains why it is found on proper names like مُحَمَّدٌ (*Muhammad-un*). Instead, it simply marked the absence of the definite article. The sign of the *Nunation* is the doubling of the relevant vowel sign.

Let's see an example: *a book* (كِتابٌ), pronounced "*kitābun*". Scholars disagree whether the word, in early stages of Arabic, used to be written like this: كِتابُنْ. In other ancient Semitic languages, the letter Mīm had been used for a similar purpose. Nevertheless, the form with the written ن helps us to understand what *nunation* means: adding a نُونٌ. In Classical Arabic, such نُونٌ can't be expressed by the letter ن of the alphabet. Instead, we use diacritical signs such as ـٌ.

What is the difference between nunation (تَنْوِينٌ) and the letter نُونٌ?

- تَنْوِينٌ: It may occur at the final position of a noun depending on the function of the word. If you stop at the word, you don't pronounce it. E.g.: كِتابٌ - كِتابْ. You pronounce it "*kitābun*" or "*kitāb*".

- نُونٌ: If you see the letter ن in the basic form of a noun (singular), it is a root letter. You can't get rid of it. If you stop at the end of the word, you have to say the ن. For example: مُؤْمِنٌ - مُؤْمِنْ. You pronounce it "*mu'minun*" or "*mu'min*".

The concept and value of the *Nūn* in the application of the *Tanwīn* is deeply rooted in the fields of syntax and morphology. To determine whether a noun gets nunation or not, we have to look at the characteristics of a word, its shape, gender, and pattern. The grammarian Sībawayhi examined many words and organized them hierarchically. He used the terms *light* and *heavy*.

Lighter words (أَخَفُّ) are **better established** (أَشَدُّ تَمَكُّنٍ) and usually were first. By *first*, we mean that it is the origin and from that source other forms were derived. Let's see what Sībawayhi found out.

---

1. The lighter form is usually the **shorter** one.

This means that...

- ...the indefinite is lighter than the definite;
- ...the masculine is lighter than the feminine. In other words, the feminine form is heavier than the masculine, because it is derived from the masculine form. We could also say that the masculine form comes first.

---

2. The **noun is lighter** than the verb because a verb must have a noun with it, while a noun does not necessarily need a verb.

In the words of Sībawayhi: *"Can't you see that the verb needs the noun, without which there wouldn't be an utterance, whereas the noun can do without the verb?"*[4] Practically speaking, this means that a transitive verb needs an object. This makes the verb heavier than the noun, even if that heaviness is just the result of an insertion. Furthermore, verbs are heavier, mainly because they are derived from nouns.

We can derive the following hierarchy.

lighter and better established; what came first	heavier; less declinable
noun	verb
indefinite	definite
singular	plural
masculine	feminine

---

4 أَلَا تَرَى أَنَّ الْفِعْلَ لَا بُدَّ لَهُ مِنَ الِاسْمِ وَإِلَّا لَمْ يَكُنْ كَلَامًا وَالِاسْمُ قَدْ يَسْتَغْنِي عَنْ الْفِعْلِ.

In other words, when you drop the تَنْوِين, this was a sign for Bedouins in ancient times that a word becomes *heavier*.

But Sībawayhi did not only analyze forms and gender to determine whether a word is light or heavy. He also had a look at the **sounds** (phonological sense).

- The letter ي is lighter and more frequent than the و.
- The marker of the genitive case (كَسْرة) is **lighter** for the Arabs than the sound of the nominative (ضَمّة) case.

Okay, but what should we make out of that? What does *light* and *heavy* tell us? Sībawayhi concluded that...

- ...the **indefinite** form is **more declinable** (أَشَدُّ تَمَكُّنٍ) than the definite. Most words are declinable when indefinite.
- ...the **singular** is **more declinable** than the plural. This explains why some plural patterns are <u>diptotes</u> (مَمْنُوعٌ مِن الصَّرْفِ) and cannot get تَنْوِين when indefinite. Such plural forms follow patterns that are exclusively used for plurals and could not be used for singular patterns! E.g., *keys* (مَفاتِيحُ).
- ...the **masculine** is **more declinable** than the feminine because تَنْوِين is the sign of the more declinable. Why is this important? When you deal with diptotes (مَمْنُوعٌ مِن الصَّرْفِ), you will find out that feminine nouns are more often diptotes than masculine.

Now, what about *heavy* words?

- **Verbs** have heavy endings and do not carry nunation because they are heavier than nouns.
- Heavy words **don't get a** كَسْرة in the **genitive** case. Words such as *red* (أَحْمَرُ) are considered *heavy* by the Arabs, which is why they have a فَتْحة ("-*a*") in the genitive case.
- Adjectives like أَحْمَر, although they are nouns (اِسْمٌ) in Arabic, are heavy because they **resemble a verb in the present tense** – and verbs, in the logic of Sībawayhi, are *heavier* than nouns.

47. What does *nunation* (تَنْوِينٌ) actually express?

*Grammarians treat it is as an **indefinite article** (English: "a" or "an") or as a marker of indetermination. But the idea is much deeper.*

Some scholars have suggested that the function of the *nunation* is to mark the absence of the article الـ. In English, we use words to mark indefiniteness (*a* or *an*). In Arabic, we don't use words; we use **diacritical marks**: nunation. The value of the *Nūn*, however, is not entirely clear. For Sībawayhi nunation (تَنْوِينٌ) is the sign that the noun has "the quality of being firmly established" which he calls تَمَكُّنٌ or أَمْكَنِيّةٌ.

Practically speaking, this means that the Arabic noun may receive the entire range of case inflections which Sībawayhi calls تَصَرُّفٌ (*unrestricted circulation, free movement*). As a rule we can say that the more the noun is kept away from resembling a particle (حَرْفٌ) or verb (فِعْلٌ) regarding form and structure, the more it is **compatible with the signs of the noun** (مُتَمَكِّنٌ فِي الْإِسْمِيّةِ).

For Sībawayhi, marking indefiniteness was only a secondary function of nunation. Why? In Arabic, we do have definite nouns that take *nunation*. Proper nouns are a good example of that (زَيْدٌ, "*Zaydun*"). But we also have indefinite nouns without *nunation* (diptotes): أَسْوَدُ (*black*) or مَساجِدُ which is the plural of *mosque*. Since the primary function of nunation is perhaps not marking indefiniteness, you can also have nunation in proper names like *Muhammad* (مُحَمَّدٌ) or *Zayd*.

The noun Zayd is very well *established* (مُتَمَكِّنٌ أَمْكَنُ) as a noun; its case ending changes according to its position in the sentence. It accepts nunation, and it accepts all the signs of declension (cases). Therefore, the noun زَيْدٌ is very **pure** (أَصالةُ الْكَلِمةِ فِي مُناسَبةِ عَلاماتِ الْإِسْمِيّةِ). For example, it doesn't resemble a verb nor a particle.

What about the noun أَسْوَدُ? If we look at the form of أَسْوَدُ, it resembles a verb, and verbs are *heavier* than nouns (see #46). We say that it is not fully compatible with the full range of the signs of nouns (مُتَمَكِّنٌ غَيْرُ أَمْكَنَ) and thus can only receive and carry some of them. We therefore call it a diptote (مَمْنُوعٌ مِن الصَّرْفِ).

48. Does an indefinite word in the accusative case (مَنْصُوبٌ) always need a final Aleph?

No, it doesn't.

In Arabic, indefiniteness is expressed by nunation (تَنْوِينٌ). We use small signs, so-called diacritical marks. However, in the accusative case (تَنْوِينُ الْفَتْح), nunation also induces a typographic change: an **extra Aleph**. For example: إِشْتَرَيْتُ كِتَابًا (*I bought a book*).

Important question: Should we pronounce the Aleph in كِتَابًا ("*kitāban*") as a long vowel? Never! Such Aleph in no way affects the quantity of the vowel. It is **always short!**

Let's dig deeper. We don't write an extra و for the nominative or ي for the genitive case. So, why do we have to write an extra Aleph if a word is indefinite and has to be in the accusative case (مَنْصُوبٌ)? Simple answer: because we pronounce an "*a*"!

The key for understanding Arabic morphology is the سُكُونٌ. It is the essential sign of a pause (وَقْفٌ). Before a pause, it is normal to decrease the sound of the final word. From this natural reflex we can derive some rules. In the so-called **pausa form**...

* long vowels are pronounced short;
* letters like the ة are lowered down to a ه (whispered "*h*");
* nunation is totally dropped. For example, "*kitabun*" just becomes "*kitab*" if you stop after كِتَابٌ - with one exception as we will see.

There are two golden rules that you should always bear in mind:

Rule 1	An Arabic speaker **never starts** his utterance with a سُكُونٌ. You need a consonant followed by a vowel. ➡ C+V and never C+C.
Rule 2	An Arabic speaker **never stops** or pauses his speech with a vowel. The indicator of a stop is usually the "full stop" (.)

You stop after Muhammad. ➡ You don't pronounce the ending. ➡ "*Muhammad*"	Muhammad went.	ذَهَبَ مُحَمَّدْ.
You continue after Muhammad. ➡ You pronounce the ending. ➡ "*Muhammadun*"	Muhammad went to...	ذَهَبَ مُحَمَّدٌ إلى...

Now it gets interesting. If you add an extra Aleph, by definition, the preceding vowel has to be *"a"* (فَتْحَةٌ). This means that if you stop after a word with nunation in the accusative case, you have to pronounce an *"a"* since the final letter is the Aleph which always carries سُكُونٌ. Pausa forms in which the accusative ending *-an* is completely dropped and not pronounced as *"a"* are extremely rare but worth looking at.

You stop after Muhammad. ➡ You pronounce the vowel on the original last letter د. ➡ *"Muhammada"*	You saw Muhammad.	رَأَيْتَ مُحَمَّدًا.
You continue after Muhammad. ➡ You pronounce it *"Muhammadan"*	You saw Muhammad in...	رَأَيْتَ مُحَمَّدًا فِي...

So now we have the theoretical tools together. Let's return to our question: **When can we skip writing the Aleph in the accusative case?**

There are **five situations** in which you don't need a *supporting Aleph* and only put the diacritical marks (ً) on the regular last letter (عَلَى الْحَرْفِ الْمُنَوَّنِ).

	situation (reason for **not writing** the Aleph)	examples
1	The word ends in a Hamza that is spelled as an Aleph (هَمْزَةٌ مَرْسُومَةٌ عَلَى أَلِفٍ)	مُبْتَدَأٌ (subject), خَطَأٌ (mistake)
2	The word ends in a Hamza and is preceded by the long vowel *"ā"* in the shape of an Aleph (هَمْزَةٌ مَسْبُوقَةٌ بِأَلِفٍ مَدٍّ). In short: -ā'	بِنَاءٌ (building), سَماءٌ (sky)
3	The last letter is the feminine ending ة. The word ends in a تاءٌ مَرْبُوطَةٌ.	مَدْرَسةٌ (school), حَياةٌ (life)
4	The word ends in a weak letter (أَلِفٌ مَقْصُورَةٌ) in the shape of an Aleph (ى).	مُسْتَشْفًى (hospital), هُدًى (right guidance)
5	The word ends in a long vowel ā (أَلِفُ مَدٍّ).	عَصًا (stick)

Two examples of the Qur'an:

...and either [confer] favor afterwards or ransom [them] until... (*Sura 47:4*)	فَإِمَّا مَنًّا بَعْدُ وَإِمَّا فِدَاءً حَتَّى...	1

Let's assume, you would stop after فِدَاءً. How would you pronounce it? ➡ with "a": (أْ)فِدَاءً

| Did they think that they could take My servants as masters instead of Me? We have prepared Hell as the disbelievers' resting place. (Sura *The Cave*; 18:102) | أَفَحَسِبَ الَّذِينَ كَفَرُوا أَن يَتَّخِذُوا عِبَادِي مِن دُونِي أَوْلِيَاءَ إِنَّا أَعْتَدْنَا جَهَنَّمَ لِلْكَافِرِينَ نُزُلًا. | 2 |

Let's assume, you'd stop after أَوْلِيَاءَ. How would you pronounce it? ➡ **Without "a":** أَوْلِيَاءَ. Why? أَوْلِيَاءَ is a **diptote** and cannot receive nunation. It is the plural form of وَلِيٌّ which means *successor; protector*.

There remains an important question to consider in this context.

Where should you place the diacritical mark in the مَنْصُوبٌ-case in all other situations? Before the Aleph or on top of it?

In other words, should it be كِتَابًا or كِتَابًا? This has been a long debate. In my opinion, the form كِتَابًا, i.e., before the Aleph, is more logical.

First of all, all other diacritical marks for the nunation are written on the last letter. Moreover, by definition, the Aleph cannot carry any other vowel. It must carry سُكُونٌ, resulting in ا. This is primary not a spelling problem, but a problem of pronunciation. If we write it like كِتَابًا, then we will pronounce it like كِتَابَنْ.

However, if we write it like كِتَابًا, then we will suddenly get two سُكُونٌ in a row which is impossible in Arabic (عَدَمُ الْتِقَاءِ سَاكِنَتَيْنِ). We would have such a construction: كِتَابًاْ + نْ.

Now, imagine that we would stop after كِتَابًا. You can't add the نْ then (لَنْ يَجْتَمِعُ سُكُونُ التَّنْوِينِ مَعَ سُكُونِ أَلِفِ الْإِطْلَاقِ الْمَمْدُودَةِ).

How can you justify the spelling on top of the Aleph (e.g., كِتَابًا)? You may say that the other signs of declension are also put on the last letter which is true (e.g., كِتَابٌ or كِتَابٍ); furthermore, you may say that you are aware that there can't be two subsequent سُكُونٌ which is the reason why they come together in one place.

Today the spelling is more a matter of taste and depends on the region.

• **Before the Aleph** (كِتَابًا): mainly in Egypt and in the Hijāz.

- **On top of the Aleph (كِتاباً):** You will primarily encounter this spelling in Syria and Lebanon (أَهْلُ الشّامِ).

49. How do you mark cases in words with final هَمْزة, e.g., in شَيْءٍ؟

You have to check the preceding vowel.

The Hamza (هَمْزةٌ) is a tricky letter and a source of spelling mistakes in Arabic – especially if the Hamza is the last letter of a word. It is actually not that difficult once you know that the only thing that matters is the preceding vowel or non-vowel. Let's see why.

example		resulting letter		preceding vowel	
mocker	مُسْتَهْزِئٌ	ئ		ِ	1
to be thirsty	ظَمِئَ				
pearl	لُؤْلُؤٌ	ؤ	plus ء	ُ	2
to risk	جَرُؤَ				
to read	قَرَأَ	أ		َ	3
news item	نَبَأٌ				
thing	نَشْءٌ	ء		ْ	4
friends	أَصْدِقاءُ				

How do we mark cases in such words? The most challenging situation is the **accusative** case if the word with final Hamza is **<u>indefinite</u>** (الْهَمْزةُ الْمُنَوَّنةُ بِفَتْحَتَيْنِ). In other words, we have to deal with the ending *'-an*.

meaning	example	correct spelling	plus ء	preceding vowel	
thing*	شَيْئًا	ئًا		يْ	1
innocent	بَرِيْئًا				
sky	سَماءً	ءً		◌َ or Aleph (ا)	2
news item	نَبَأً				

pearl	لُؤْلُؤًا	ءً	non-vowel (ـْ) or	3
part	جُزْءًا		"u" (ـُ) or "i" (ـِ)	

* The older spelling of شَيْئًا is شَيْءٌ. Note: Many people write شِئ instead of شَيْءٌ. That's a mistake! شِئ (with "i") is the imperative of شَاءَ (to want/wish).

Let's go back to number 3 in the first table. The هَمْزَة is usually written **between** the ا and the **vowel** that accompanies it. This will become important if we have to mark a word in the genitive case (مَجْرُورٌ) by placing a كَسْرَة. Why? Because the vowel "i" (ـِ) is underneath the letter which means that the Hamza must drop to the bottom.

- **Nominative:** You write ـُ or ـٌ on top of the ا resulting in أُ or أٌ.
- **Accusative:** You write ـَ or ـً on top of it resulting in أَ or أً.
- **Genitive:** The كَسْرَة transforms the shape of the أ. So we get إ or إٍ.

Two examples:

subject (in grammar)	مُبْتَدَأٌ		mistake	خَطَأٌ	nominative (مَرْفُوعٌ)
	مُبْتَدَإٍ			خَطَإٍ	genitive (مَجْرُورٌ)
	مُبْتَدَأً			خَطَأً	accusative (مَنْصُوبٌ)

50. What is the function of the subject?

*It marks the **doer** in a sentence.*

Without a subject, there is no sentence. English grammar knows only one type of subject. Arabic knows two because Arabic distinguishes between two types of sentences: the verbal (جُمْلَةٌ فِعْلِيَّةٌ) and nominal sentence (جُمْلَةٌ اِسْمِيَّةٌ). Sometimes it is difficult to apply Indo-European language terms to Arabic. It would make more sense to analyze sentences by looking at the semantic relationship. However, many Western people aren't used to such terms because they didn't learn them in school. Let's see what such an analysis might look like.

		Peter	*gave*	*Michael*	*a book.*
1	grammatical	subject	verb	indirect ob-	direct object

	relationship			ject	
2	**semantic relationship**	agent	action	recipient of the action	patient
3	Arabic term	فاعِلٌ	فِعْلٌ	مَفْعُولٌ أَوَّلٌ first patient	مَفْعُولٌ ثانٍ second patient

What are the differences between English and Arabic regarding word order and grammar?

- In English, the subject always comes before a verb – no matter if the sentence starts with an adverb of time or place. For example: *Yesterday in the shopping mall **I met** Peter.* The subject (*I*) can never be put after the verb. **In Arabic**, on the other hand, the **verb comes first** and the subject follows.

- If there is no verb involved, it is different. In a nominal Arabic sentence (جُمْلةٌ اِسْمِيّةٌ), the subject is called مُبْتَدَأٌ and comes first. مُبْتَدَأٌ literally means *that which comes first*.

- In a verbal sentence (جُمْلةٌ فِعْلِيّةٌ), the subject is called فاعِلٌ which means *doer*. The verb is a fact that comes true by the subject. The verb commands the فاعِلٌ (= the one who executes the action).

- In the passive voice, we don't have information about the doer. Strictly speaking, the term *passive* is not a good one for Arabic. In Arabic, the verb we use is called فِعْلٌ مَجْهُولٌ. It means that the agent/doer of the verb is *ignored* or *unknown* (مَجْهُولٌ فاعِلُهُ).

Note: The Arabic passive verb brings along some issues. How would you translate the following English sentence into Arabic?

*A letter has been written **by xy**.*

The translation is, in fact, not trivial. The English passive designates the agent (the one who wrote the letter). Can we formulate the sentence in English in this way in Arabic? In Arabic, it would be awkward and strictly speaking, we can't do it because the **Arabic (passive) verb form completely ignores the agent/doer.**

*A letter has been written **by xy**.*	كُتِبَتْ رِسالةٌ مِنْ قِبَلِ فُلانٍ.

Translators use indirect ways to indicate the agent. They add a prepositional phrase: عَلَى يَد or مِنْ جانِب or مِنْ قِبَل or مِنْ طَرَف. They all mean
the same: *on the part of xy, from xy, by xy*. Note that they all form a إِضافةٌ.

51. When does a noun have to be in the nominative case (مَرْفُوعٌ)?

*There are mainly **eight** situations.*

Whenever you see a ـُ or ـٌ, i.e., a word in the state of رَفْع (nominative), you know that the noun has one of the following roles:

1. Subject of a verbal sentence (فاعِلٌ).

2. The noun that functions as a subject in a passive construction –
   passive-subject or deputy subject (نائِبُ الْفاعِلِ).

3. Subject of a nominal sentence (مُبْتَدَأٌ).

4. Predicate of a nominal sentence (خَبَرٌ).

5. The اِسْمُ كانَ, i.e., the "subject" in a construction with كانَ.

6. The "subject" of words resembling the negation with لَيْسَ (الْأَحْرُفُ
   الْمُشَبَّهةُ بِلَيْسَ). Such devices are: إِنْ - لاتَ - لا - ما. Regarding ما
   and لا, this is only true if you apply the rules of the ancient Hijāz
   variation (فِي لُغةِ أَهْلِ الْحِجازِ) because only then the device has
   governing power. → See question #272.

7. The predicate of إِنَّ and its sisters.

8. The predicate of the absolute negation (خَبَرُ لا النّافِيةُ لِلْجِنْسِ).

Note: Always look for *followers* (التّابِعُ لِلْمَرْفُوعِ) which mirror features
(also the case) of a previous word. They are four: adjective (اَلنَّعْتُ),
words after a "coupler" (الْعَطْفُ), apposition (الْبَدَلُ), emphasis (التَّوْكِيدُ).

52. What causes the مُبْتَدَأٌ of a nominal sentence to be مَرْفُوعٌ?

Simply said, it is the initial position in a nominal sentence.

In English, there is no sentence without a verb. In an Arabic nominal
sentence (جُمْلةٌ اِسْمِيّةٌ), as the name indicates, there is no verb, so there

is also no verb *to be*. Furthermore, nothing precedes the subject in an Arabic nominal sentence. So it is not that trivial to explain why the subject (مُبْتَدَأٌ) gets the nominative case (مَرْفُوعٌ).

The first grammarians struggled to find an answer why the first constituent (the first word of a nominal sentence) has to be مَرْفُوعٌ. They were looking for an underlying rule that fitted into the system of Arabic grammar and then found what they were looking for. They had found a brilliant reason for the nominative case: The governor (عامِلٌ) of the مُبْتَدَأ in a جُمْلةٌ اِسْمِيّةٌ is its **position**.

In other words, an *implicit, abstract regent*, also called *covert governor* (عامِلٌ مَعْنَوِيٌّ), operates on the subject. Grammarians call this concept اِبْتِداءٌ which literally means *beginning, start*. In grammar, it denotes the initial position in a sentence. The grammarians concluded that the مُبْتَدَأ gets the nominative case **due to the effect** of الاِبْتِداءُ.

Since it is an abstract concept, the underlying idea is deep. It does not mean that the مُبْتَدَأ gets the nominative case because it is placed at the beginning of a sentence. What the grammarians actually meant is that the مُبْتَدَأ gets the nominative case because of the effect of some grammatical qualities which the word acquires as a result of showing up at the beginning of a sentence. The regent of the مُبْتَدَأ is not the fact that it is placed at the beginning of the sentence, but rather the grammatical consequences deriving from its occurrence in this position.

Let's go a little further and put our eyes on the second part of a nominal sentence: the predicate (خَبَرٌ). So, what is the **regent of the predicate (الْعامِلُ فِي الْخَبَرِ)**? What causes the خَبَرٌ to be in the nominative case? It is the subject (مُبْتَدَأٌ); so we could say that it is indirectly also the *beginning* (الاِبْتِداءُ).

The idea that the position triggers the basic case is fundamentally present in Arabic and can also be found in the verb So, what causes a **verb** getting the **indicative mood (مَرْفُوعٌ)**? It is a similar concept! The reason for the مَرْفُوعٌ-ending of a present tense verb (indicative mood) has to do with its position, i.e., the occurrence of the verb in a position where a noun could appropriately be placed. In Arabic, a verbal sentence usually starts with a verb. This first position is also the place where a مُبْتَدَأ could occur.

53. What is the purpose of an object in Arabic?

An object in Arabic gives us further information.

The concept of "objects" (مَنْصُوباتٌ) is different from English. In English, a direct object is mainly the target of the action (verb) which the doer (subject) executes. In Arabic, the concept of objects is much broader. An object is something that enriches the action and gives us further information; it may also fix an issue or make a point clearer.

The concept of الْمَنْصُوباتُ is translated as *accusative* or **dependent case**. The مَنْصُوبٌ-ending *"a"* (ـَ or ـً) indicates that a word depends on another and is a *patient*. If we focus on the idea of providing more information, we can identify **five *patients*** (مَعْمُولٌ), or let's say, *objects*:

absolute object	مَفْعُولٌ مُطْلَقٌ	direct object	مَفْعُولٌ بِه
local or temporal object/adverb	مَفْعُولٌ فِيه	object of reason; causal object	مَفْعُولٌ لِأَجْلِه
		object of accompaniment	مَفْعُولٌ مَعَهُ

There are **three more** left for providing further information. Hence, they also take the مَنْصُوبٌ-ending.

circumstantial qualifier; status	حالٌ	distinction; the specifying element	تَمْيِيزٌ
exclusion	اسْتِثْناءٌ		

Remark: There are more situations when we have to use the مَنْصُوبٌ-case, but they have nothing to do with the idea of providing further information (they are related to "dependency") – see *question #54*.

54. When does a noun have to be in the مَنْصُوبٌ-case?

*There are **thirteen** situations.*

When you see the ending ـَ or ـً, i.e., a noun in the state of نَصْب, the word must have one of the following jobs/functions in the sentence.

1. The direct object (مَفْعُولٌ بِهِ); the thing or person that undergoes the action of a verb.

2. The absolute object (مَفْعُولٌ مُطْلَقٌ); used for giving intensity to the core meaning of the verb.

3. The purposive object (مَفْعُولٌ لَهُ); it expresses the cause or motive of the action.

4. The local or temporal object (مَفْعُولٌ فِيهِ); it gives us information about the time or place when or where the action takes place.

5. The associative object (مَفْعُولٌ مَعَهُ), prefixed by وَ; it denotes association of the former (subject) with the latter (object).

6. The specification (تَمْيِيزٌ); it determines and limits the object or specifies the relation of the predicate to its subject.

7. The circumstantial clause/qualifier (حَالٌ); it expresses the state or condition of the subject (or object) while the action takes place.

8. The thing that is excluded (الْمُسْتَثْنَى); it expresses *except/only*,

9. The vocative (الْمُنَادَى), i.e., the person that is being called.

10. The predicate of كَانَ *and its sisters* (خَبَرُ كَانَ وَأَخَوَاتِها).

11. The predicate of devices that resemble لَيْسَ, so-called خَبَرُ الْأَحْرُفِ الْمُشَبَّهِةِ بِلَيْسَ. Such devices are إِنْ – لَاتَ – لَا – مَا. Regarding مَا and لَا, this is true if you apply the rules of the ancient Hijāz variation of Arabic because only then the device has governing power. → see #272.

12. The "subject" of إِنَّ *and its sisters* (اِسْمُ إِنَّ وَأَخَوَاتِها).

13. The "subject" of an absolute negation (اِسْمُ لَا النَّافِيةِ لِلْجِنْسِ).

55. When does a noun have to be in the مَجْرُورٌ-case?

*There are only **two** situations.*

A اِسْمٌ is in the state of جَرٍّ (i.e, مَجْرُورٌ) only...

1. ...if it follows a preposition (الْاِسْمُ الْمَجْرُورُ بِحَرْفِ جَرٍّ);

2. ...if it is the second part of a possessive construction (إِضافةٌ), also called الْجَرُّ بِالْإِضافةِ, e.g., *the teacher's house* (بَيْتُ الْمُدَرِّسِ).

56. Does it matter whether we use a verbal or nominal sentence?

Yes, it does – but it is a finesse.

The English translation of the following two sentences is the same.

جُمْلةٌ إِسْميّةٌ	nominal sentence		زَيْدٌ أَكَلَ.	1
جُمْلةٌ فِعْليّةٌ	verbal sentence	*Zayd ate.*	أَكَلَ زَيْدٌ.	2

Some linguists claim that there is no difference since زَيْدٌ is the subject in both sentences: the مُبْتَدَأٌ in #1 and the فاعِلٌ in #2. However, if we use the logic of Classical Arabic, we can dispute that for two reasons:

> 1. Purist grammarians say that there is a **difference in meaning**.

The **nominal** sentence, which starts with *Zayd*, informs us <u>about the person</u> who ate, and this is Zayd. This means that the action of eating has actually happened, and it **originated from Zayd**, and not from Ahmed or Peter or whomsoever.

    The **verbal** sentence, on the other hand, gives us information about the <u>action</u> (حَدَثٌ) of *to eat* (أَكَلَ) and not about any other action. In other words: *Zayd <u>ate</u>.* He did not *read* (قَرَأَ) or *write* (كَتَبَ).

> 2. There is a **grammatical difference**.

If the subject consists of a word in the singular form, then the nominal and verbal sentence will use the same form of the verb (= singular).

    However, if the subject is other than that (غَيْرُ مُفْرَدٍ), the verb will go along with the form of the subject **only in the nominal sentence**.

dual (m.): هُما	The two teachers wrote.	الْمُدَرِّسانِ كَتَبا.
plural (masculine): هُمْ	The teachers (many) wrote.	الْمُدَرِّسُونَ كَتَبُوا.
plural (feminine): هُنَّ	The girls wrote.	الْبَناتُ كَتَبْنَ.

Since the verb is placed after the subject, the verb relates to the subject of the main (nominal) sentence which could be: the pronoun (ضَمِيرٌ), the Aleph in the dual, or the و in the plural like in the above examples. The entire (subsidiary) verbal sentence functions as the predicate (خَبَرٌ) of the primary nominal sentence.

57. Can you have two subjects in only one sentence?

Yes, this is possible. It is actually pretty common.

A (nominal or verbal) sentence can serve as the predicate (خَبَرٌ) of a **larger nominal sentence**. In such a situation, both sentences are analyzed separately. For example:

Karīm's father appeared.	كَرِيمٌ حَضَرَ أَبُوهُ.

Karīm is the **subject** (مُبْتَدَأٌ) of the **nominal** sentence. Thus, it takes the nominative case (مَرْفُوعٌ), marked by nunation; ضَمَّةٌ.

The I-verb حَضَرَ doesn't get any marker because it is a past tense form which has a fixed, indeclinable shape (مَبْنِيٌّ). It does not have a position in إِعْرابٌ.

The expression *his father* is the **subject** (فاعِلٌ) of the **verbal** sentence. Therefore, it needs the nominative (مَرْفُوعٌ) case, marked by the و in أَبُو (*father*) which serves as the first part of the إِضافةٌ.

The هـ is a pronoun suffix (ضَمِيرٌ مُتَّصِلٌ) which functions as a connector: it interlinks both parts of the sentence. Regarding its grammatical function, it is the second part of the إِضافةٌ. The pronoun suffix is indeclinable (مَبْنِيٌّ); it doesn't get any visible marker. Grammatically, however, it is located in the position of a **genitive** (فِي مَحَلِّ جَرٍّ) case.

The entire verbal sentence (marked in gray) functions as the **predicate** (خَبَرٌ) of the **first subject** (مُبْتَدَأٌ), i.e., the subject of the primary sentence. Thus, the entire sentence occupies the position of a nominative case (فِي مَحَلِّ رَفْعٍ). The sentence itself, nevertheless, gets its own analysis (إِعْرابٌ).

SHAPING THE VERB

58. What is a فِعْلٌ ناقِصٌ؟

It is an incomplete verb, also called defective, deficient verb.

There are two possibilities to apply this term:

> 1. Regarding the **grammar** (النَّحْوُ): كانَ and its sisters.

Why do we call such a verb *defective* or *incomplete*? A verb usually conveys two things: action (حَدَثٌ) and time (زَمَنٌ). A defective verb only conveys the meaning of time, but no action. In order to repair this "deficiency", it needs a predicate (خَبَرٌ).

The nominative case of the subject alone is not enough for a defective verb to convey a meaning. It needs more information in the accusative (مَنْصُوبٌ) to complete the meaning: a predicate (خَبَرُ كانَ). Note: There's also a "full" version of كانَ which is called كانَ التّامّةُ (see #232).

> 2. Regarding **morphology** (الصَّرْفُ): verbs ending in a weak letter.

The final radical could be any of the two weak letters (حَرْفُ الْعِلّةِ), i.e., و or ي. Remember that an Aleph is never part of the root; it is a transformed و or ي. In the I-verb دَعَا - يَدْعُو (R3=و; *to call*), the final ا is the root letter و. This I-verb follows the pattern فَعَلَ and يَفْعُلُ (present tense) which explains why we eventually get دَعَا and يَدْعُو.

Let's analyze another verb: رَضِيَ - يَرْضَى (R3=ي; *to be pleased, to approve*). This I-verb follows the pattern فَعِلَ and يَفْعَلُ (present tense). Originally, the past tense verb رَضِيَ was رَضِوَ (present tense: يَرْضَوُ). So, what happened?

In the past tense, the و was changed into ي due to the كَسْرةٌ in the verb pattern. With "i" under the second root letter, it is impossible to write the و as an Aleph like in the above example دَعَا.

The كَسْرةٌ ("i") is stronger than the other sounds. If the vowel before a weak letter is كَسْرةٌ ("i"), we need to write the و as ي. In the present tense, the و became ى (without the two dots underneath, so-called أَلِفٌ مَقْصُورةٌ) due to the vowel "a" on the second root letter in the present tense. In many dictionaries, you will find this verb under ر-ض-ى implying that the last root letter is ي. Nevertheless, it was originally و. The مَصْدَر-forms usually indicate the original root letter. In our example, it is رِضْوانٌ which means *approval; satisfaction*.

The conjugation of such verbs can be tricky. There is the principle of shortening the weak letter. Sometimes the suffix and the final radical will blend. Let's analyze the I-verb نَجَا - يَنْجُو (R3=و; *to be rescued*). If we build the past tense form for the third person feminine singular (*she*), we theoretically get نَجَاْتْ. However, the Aleph carries a (usually) un-written سُكُونٌ which would produce two سُكُونٌ in a row, and this is impossible in Arabic. Therefore, the first سُكُونٌ is dropped along with the long vowel. Only the فَتحةٌ, the short counterpart of the Aleph, re-mains. The final result is نَجَتْ.

59. Why do we sometimes find an extra ن at the end of verbs?

To prevent losing an important vowel.

First of all, what do we mean by extra ن? It is a ن which is mingled into a verb and is not part of the root nor the conjugation. An example would be يُسْعِدُني which means *he/it makes me happy*.

→ The vowel before ي **must** be كَسْرةٌ by definition. The ن helps us to keep the core body of the verb untouched.	يُسْعِدُني

What would happen without the extra ن? The ـُ, which marks the indicative mood of the verb (فِعْلٌ مُضارِعٌ مَرْفُوعٌ), would become ـِ resulting in يُسْعِدِي. This would be a grammatical error. However, if we insisted on the correct case marker ـُ, we would produce a word – يُسْعِدُي – which is impossible to pronounce. Therefore, the extra ن is inserted. It has no other function than safeguarding the main part; the ن doesn't have a position in إعْرابٌ.

The ن with كَسْرةٌ is called *guarding* or *preventive Nūn* (النُّونُ لِلْوِقاية) because it prevents the final vowel of the verb from being absorbed by the long vowel "ee/ii". Therefore, we fix this Nūn with a كَسْرةٌ حَرْفٌ (مَبْنِيٌّ عَلَى الْكَسْرِ). Some linguists call it *supporting Nūn* (نُونُ الْعِمادِ) be-cause it provides a كَسْرةٌ. The "i"-vowel is needed by the following letter ي and forms an essential part of the suffix *me* (ي). Otherwise, it could not be pronounced as "ee/ii".

60. Why do we say كَتَبْتُ for *I wrote* – and not كَتَبَتُ?

We want to avoid four consecutive letters with a vowel.

Let's try to pronounce كَتَبَتُ (*ka-ta-ba-tu*) or even كَتَبَتَ (*ka-ta-ba-ta*). This would be difficult, at least for Arabs. They find **four consecutive vowelled letters** distasteful.

For this reason, the place for the فَتْحَة on the last root letter (ب in our example) is occupied by the سُكُون. As a result, we get بْ which prevents the occurrence of a cluster of four vowels (اشْتِغَالُ الْمَحَلِّ). (بِالسُّكُونِ الْعَارِضِ لِدَفْعِ كَرَاهةِ تَوَالِى أَرْبَعِ مُتَحَرِّكَاتٍ).

61. Does an Arabic verb indicate time?

This is (still) a debate.

The discussion is focused on the following question: Does a verb mark *tense* (past versus non-past) or does it denote *aspect* (an action that was done versus an action that is still ongoing)? Or is it probably a combination of both?

The crucial point in this debate is whether there is such a thing as the present tense. The terms الماضِي and الْمُضارِعُ are among the oldest Arabic grammar terms, occurring already in the first pages of Sībawayhi's *al-Kitāb*. Sībawayhi classified verbs as ماضٍ which literally means *having passed, elapsed* and as مُضارِعٌ which means *resembling*. The grammar term مُضارِعٌ is the short form of *verb resembling the active participle* (فِي الْمُضَارِعِ لِاسْمِ الْفَاعِلِ). *See question #62 for details.*

The الماضِي refers to the completed state of the action. It is commonly (but misleadingly) translated as *past tense*. A better translation would be *perfect* tense. In this book, I also use the term *past tense* because I don't want to confuse readers who are familiar with English grammar terms. The الْمُضارِعُ is called *imperfect* as it indicates an action that has not been completed. In English, we call it *present tense*.

Sībawayhi gives the example of يَضْرِبُ which could mean *he strikes* or *he will strike*. For Sībawayhi, **time** is referenced in the مَفْعُولٌ فِيهِ, the adverbial component, which provides more information about time or place of the action.

His rivals, the Kūfa grammarians (الْكُوفِيُّونَ), had a different approach. They said that the **active participle** (اسْمُ الْفَاعِلِ) fulfills the role of the **present tense** and is used for an ongoing, lasting action. The past tense is the الْماضِي. And what about the **future**? The future is expressed by the الْمُضارِعُ! Such concept of time and tense is found in other languages as well, e.g., Modern Hebrew.

This shows that the present (German: *Gegenwart*) can't be a point of time, but only an interval of time. Grammatically speaking, however, this approach has a weak point. The اسْمُ الْفَاعِلِ is not a verb. It is a noun as its Arabic name says. It is important to remind ourselves once again that the active participle itself doesn't point to time. For example:

I am/will be standing tomorrow.	أَنا قائِمٌ غَدًا.
I was standing yesterday.	أَنا قائِمٌ أَمْسِ.

The grammarians of Basra followed Sībawayhi and accepted only two verb tenses, i.e., الْماضِي and الْمُضارِع, the latter being ambiguous as it could indicate both present and future tense. The active participle has a special connection to the verb in the present tense (الْمُضارِعُ) which is deeply rooted in grammar. For example, both, present tense verb and active participle can be preceded by the *Lām for emphasis*:

Verily, he is indeed writing!	إِنَّهُ لَكاتِبٌ!
	إِنَّهُ لَيَكْتُبُ!

Today, we often use a flexible approach. Arabic verbs are interpreted in the sense of time as well and not only, whether an action is completed or not (no matter in which time frame). Many grammarians say that verbs by necessity indicate time/tense because a verb indicates an action, and actions take place in the past, present, or future time. Interestingly, in the Hebrew Bible, the notion of time in verb tenses was developed over time as well.

The highly respected medieval scholar al-Zamakhsharī (الزّمخشري) suggests in *al-Mufaṣṣal* (الْمُفَصَّل) that the verb indicates a combination of event (حَدَثٌ) and time (زَمَنٌ). The title of his famous manual on Arabic grammar, الْمُفَصَّل, means *elaborately* or *in great detail*. He used a new approach therein. Instead of the classic arrangement in syntax, morphology, and phonology, al-Zamakhsharī divided his analysis according to the three parts of speech: noun (اِسْمٌ), verbs (فِعْلٌ), and particles (حَرْفٌ) plus a section with topics that affect all of them (مُشْتَرَكٌ) like weak letters. The الْمُفَصَّل had a huge influence on Western Arabic grammar books. It formed the basis for the Arabic grammar (1848) of Carl Paul Caspari, a Norwegian-German theologian and Orientalist. And Caspari's grammar, in turn, was the main basis for the world-renowned grammar of the English Orientalist William Wright.

Al-Zamakhsharī was of Persian descent, born around 1075 (467 AH) in Chorasmia (Khwārizm), a historic oasis region in western Central Asia which would today belong partly to Uzbekistan, Kazakhstan, and Turkmenistan. After extensive travels to the Arab world, he died in Gurgandj (al-Jurjāniyya) in Khwārizm in 1144 (538 AH) where the famous Arab explorer Ibn Battūta (اِبْن بَطُّوطة) was still able to see his tomb. His nickname (لَقَبٌ) was جارُ اللهِ which has a deep meaning. It denotes that *someone is a guest of God* (and thus was received under His protection), i.e., one who has resided in the sacred city. Al-Zamakhsharī most probably got this name after his travels to Mecca.

62. What does الْمُضارِعُ mean?

It means resembling.

ضارِعٌ means *resembling* and is the active participle (اِسْمُ الْفاعِلِ) of III-verb يُضارِعُ - ضارَعَ which means *to look like; to resemble*.

Therefore, the term الْفِعْلُ الْمُضارِعُ means *the resembling verb*. But resembling what? Answer: the **active participle** (اِسْمُ الْفاعِلِ). Now it gets interesting. الْمُضارِعُ is just an abbreviation for *verb resembling the active participle* (فِي الْمُضارِعِ لِاسْمِ الْفاعِلِ). What a stunning description! The entire meaning of the term will help us many times because it can explain why some things we know from present tense verbs also take place in a similar form in nouns.

What's the idea here? It all goes back to the debate whether a "real" present tense exists at all. (see *question #61*). The similarity to the active participle is mainly the reason why the verb in the مُضارِعٌ-tense shares

two of the three case markers (marked in gray in the table) that are used with nouns (اِسْمٌ) because the active participle in Arabic is a اِسْمٌ and gets cases. In the table below, the jussive (مَجْزُومٌ) mood is only found in the مُضَارِعٌ-tense of verbs (but not with nouns!).

1	indicative	مَرْفُوعٌ	He strikes.	يَضرِبُ.
2	subjunctive	مَنْصُوبٌ	to strike	أَنْ يَضرِبَ
3	jussive	مَجْزُومٌ	did not strike	لَمْ يَضرِبْ

Note: We don't use the term *case* when we talk about verbs; we use the term *mood*. However, Arabic does not really make a distinction between *mood* and *case* of verbs in the nominative/indicative as both states are called مَرْفُوعٌ. I nevertheless use the term mood.

63. What is the connection between verbs and diptotes?

The shape.

Arabic nouns are called مُنْصَرِفٌ when they are capable of receiving all three case endings, including nunation (تَنْوِينٌ). Those nouns which lose part of their repertoire of case endings are called غَيْرُ مُنْصَرِفٍ or, more generally, مَمْنُوعٌ مِن الصَّـرْفِ – *diptotes*. Such nouns **resemble verbs and particles** because they follow a similar (morphological) pattern and shape. For example, a proper name like *Yazīd* (يَزِيدُ) looks like a present tense verb. For that reason, يَزِيدُ loses part of its case inflections (إِعْرابٌ) and is a diptote. The same is true for *Ahmad* (أَحْمَدُ).

64. Why is there no *to be* in the Arabic present tense?

It is understood that the event or action is happening right now or is of permanent nature.

Grammarians know the term *copula* which is used to link subject and predicate. Copula verbs are verbs that have no inherent meaning and serve only to link the subject of the sentence to its predicate. The copula, however, is missing in Arabic. Let's take the sentence: أَنا طالِبٌ which means *I am a student*. The English linking word *am* is missing in Arabic. Why is that? Tenses work differently in Arabic. The idea of tense is more related to whether the action is ongoing or completed. In general, we could say that the *copula* (= the verb *to be*) is absent when the described event or action is <u>not</u> located <u>prior</u> to the moment of speech. When the event happened prior to the moment of speech or when we talk about the future, then it must be there.

He is a student.	هُوَ طالِبٌ.
He was a student.	هُوَ كانَ طالِبًا.

If you express events that are **habitual** or have a **conditional meaning**, you will need an **additional word** or expression – to indicate that what you talk about is <u>**not** happening now</u>. Moreover, you have to link that information to the predicate – by using the verb *to be* (= the copula).

The man is in the house.	الرَّجُلُ فِي الْبَيْتِ.
The man is **usually** in the house.	عادَةً ما يَكُونُ الرَّجُلُ فِي الْبَيْتِ.
When the man is in the house...	عِنْدَما يَكُونُ الرَّجُلُ فِي الْبَيْتِ...
The man **will** be in the house.	سَوْفَ يَكُونُ الرَّجُلُ فِي الْبَيْتِ.
The man **may** be in the house.	قَدْ يَكُونُ الرَّجُلُ فِي الْبَيْتِ.
Don't be silly!	لا تَكُنْ غَبِيًّا!

What about the prepositional phrase *in the house* (فِي الْبَيْتِ) in the first sentence? Some call it the predicate.

But in fact, it is a prepositional phrase (الْجارُّ وَالْمَجْرُورُ). In English, a prepositional phrase which behaves adverbially is called an adverbial phrase (of place or time). Now comes the tricky part. An adverb, as the name says, has to be linked to a verb or a word that does the verb's job or resembles it, e.g., an active participle – but in the sentence الرَّجُلُ فِي الْبَيْتِ there is nothing like that.

Well, sometimes a word or phrase may be linked to something that is not mentioned, not visible in the sentence. This happens when the prepositional phrase **appears** in the position of the predicate (خَبَر) of a nominal sentence. In this situation, the "real", deleted خَبَر has to be assumed which can be done by hypothetically inserting كَائِنٌ (being) or مُسْتَقِرٌّ (permanent) which both had to be deleted (مَحْذُوفٌ وُجُوبًا).

Wait a moment. Why was the "real" predicate deleted? This was done for grammatical reasons because we do not state the verb *to be* when it denotes something permanent or something that is happening now.

65. Which imperative form of a regular verb doesn't end in سُكُونٌ?

The feminine plural (see example 5 below).

The imperative, by looking at its core, is a verbal sentence (جُمْلَةٌ فِعْلِيَّةٌ) that uses a special form of the verb: the فِعْلُ أَمْرٍ. It has a fixed, indeclinable ending and is counted as one of the الْأَفْعَالُ الْمَبْنِيَّةُ.

We build it by cutting the prefix of the present tense verb and by applying the marker of the مَجْزُومٌ-mood which is a سُكُونٌ. An imperative (فِعْلُ أَمْرٍ) is only used for a *person spoken to* (الْمُخَاطَبُ).

1	أَنْتَ	masculine singular	Write!	بْ	اُكْتُبْ
2	أَنْتِ	feminine singular	Write!	ي	اُكْتُبِي
3	أَنْتُما	dual	You (both) write!	ا	اُكْتُبَا
4	أَنْتُمْ	masculine plural	You (men) write!	و	اُكْتُبُوا
5	أَنْتُنَّ	feminine plural	You (women) write!	نَ	اُكْتُبْنَ

In the first four examples, the verb ends in سُكُونٌ. For this reason, we call the verb in the imperative also مَبْنِيٌّ عَلَى السُّكُونِ. How did we achieve to get a سُكُونٌ? Let's see.

1	We add a سُكُونٌ to the final letter – under the condition that it is neither a weak letter nor a long vowel.
2, 3, 4	We get the سُكُونٌ by deleting the final ن which produces a long vowel. Every long vowel has, in fact, a سُكُونٌ. Therefore, we can say that this form is مَبْنِيٌّ عَلَى السُّكُونِ.
5	This is the only form <u>without</u> a سُكُونٌ. Why? The نَ has to be retained to mark the **gender**. Note that this form is **fixed** on the ending ـَ. Therefore, we call it مَبْنِيٌّ عَلَى الْفَتْحِ.

What happens if the last root letter is a weak letter (حَرْفُ الْعِلّةِ)? We delete and substitute the weak letter with the corresponding vowel.

Sura 16:125	[Prophet], call [people] to the way of your Lord with wisdom and good teaching!	ادْعُ إِلَى سَبِيلِ رَبِّكَ بِالْحِكْمَةِ وَالْمَوْعِظَةِ الْحَسَنَةِ!

The verb *to call* has the form دَعَا in the past tense and يَدْعُو in the present tense. We delete the final و and cement the imperative's ending on the ضَمّ, resulting in ادْعُ.

SENTENCES / CLAUSES WHICH DO THE JOB OF A SINGLE WORD

The following *questions* will deal with pretty hard stuff. It's the idea that you can find a whole sentence where you would normally expect just one word. These concepts require some abstraction. We'll learn that in grammar, it isn't so much about words, but more about **positions** in a sentence that are guarded and influenced by an operator/regent.

66. Having (or not having) a position in إِعْرابٌ - What does it mean?

It means that a word or sentence takes on a certain job (مَوْقِعٌ) in the sentence and occupies the respective location (مَحَلٌّ); therefore, it is affected (governed) by an operator (عامِلٌ) and gets a certain state (case ending).

Cases define the function of words in a sentence, for example, subject, predicate, direct object, etc. When you read Arabic grammar books, you will come across the expression مَحَلٌّ لَهُ مِن الْإِعْرابِ. The term مَحَلٌّ denotes the *syntactical function of a word*; in other words, a grammar role such as the subject. Instead of لَهُ you also see لَها depending on the word's gender to which the pronoun refers to (see #25). Now, what does it mean if a word *does **not** have a place in* إِعْرابٌ?

Let's start with the opposite. If a word **does have** a position in إِعْرابٌ, it means that this location could be filled by a single noun (اسْمٌ) or perhaps a verb. If you cannot fill a certain spot by a single noun, we usually cannot assign a grammatical role to that spot. Why? We can only charge nouns with jobs like the subject or direct object – but not prepositions or any other helping device like negation particles (حَرْفٌ).

So you have to know what kind of jobs there are to be distributed, because some functions that may be available in English are not available in Arabic. This is the situation for several sentence fragments in Arabic. The relative clause (صِلةُ الْمَوْصُولِ) and all sentences that work as a complement or consequent (جَوابٌ) do **not** have a place in إِعْرابٌ. This includes the second part of a conditional sentence (جَوابُ الشَّرْطِ) and what comes after an oath (جَوابُ الْقَسَمِ) – see #84 and #85.

67. How is it possible that a sentence does the job of a single word?

Because all that matters are the function and position. They are like variables in mathematics and can be filled with many things.

In Arabic, entire sentences can have a specific function or task that is normally performed by a single word (الْجُمْلةُ الَّتِي لَها مَحَلٌّ مِن الْإِعْرابِ). For example:

The students write.	الطُّلابُ يَكْتُبُونَ.
The verb يَكْتُبُونَ is, in fact, an entire (verbal) sentence that consists of a verb and a subject (*he*). This sentence serves in the position of the **predicate** (خَبَرٌ) of the primary (larger) nominal sentence (subject: الطُّلابُ). Therefore, we say that يَكْتُبُونَ has the grammatical role of the predicate and is in the position of a nominative case (فِي مَحَلِّ رَفْعٍ خَبَرٌ).	

> What is the key here?
> Since we can't put case endings, such sentences get a **"place value"**.

Every sentence conveys an **independent meaning** (مَعْنًى مُسْتَقِلٌّ). The sentence itself, however, may have a grammatical job inside a larger, primary sentence. For this reason, an entire sentence can be placed in the grammatical position (فِي مَحَلّ) of the state of...

3	genitive	جَرّ		1	nominative	رَفْع
4	jussive	جَزْم		2	accusative	نَصْب

فِي مَحَلّ

What does that practically mean? A sentence **occupies the position** which a single word (مَحَلٌّ مُفْرَدٌ) would normally take. Why do we say that the sentence occupies *the position of a grammatical state* and not that it takes a certain case? Because only a single word can <u>visibly</u> be marked with a grammatical case or mood.

But there are limits. According to most grammarians, a sentence **cannot** stand in place of the <u>subject</u> of a nominal sentence (مُبْتَدَأٌ), verbal sentence (فَاعِلٌ) or serve as the *passive subject* (نائِبٌ عَنِ الْفاعِلِ). Some scholars object that and allow that a sentence stands in place for the فَاعِلٌ or نائِبُ الْفاعِلِ – but never for the مُبْتَدَأٌ. See *question #299*. So, what are the sentences that can stand in place of a single word? We will check that in the following *questions*.

68. Can a sentence supply the place of the predicate?

Yes, this is pretty standard. If it is a verbal sentence, then it is nothing special. If it is a nominal sentence, it will be a more complex issue.

Such constructions (الْجُمْلَةُ الْواقِعةُ خَبَرًا) can be tricky to translate.

A) If we place a **nominal sentence** (جُمْلةٌ اِسْمِيّةٌ) as the predicate instead of just a word, we must not forget an important rule: This sentence must contain a (referential) **pronoun** (ضَمِيرٌ عائِدٌ) which relates to the subject (مُبْتَدَأٌ).

Zayd has a generous character.	زَيْدٌ خُلُقُهُ كَرِيمٌ.

Subject of the nominal sentence (مُبْتَدَأٌ). Therefore, it must get the nominative case (مَرْفُوعٌ بِالضَّمّةِ الظّاهِرةِ) which is clearly marked.	زَيْدٌ
Second subject (مُبْتَدَأٌ ثانٍ); in the nominative case as well. This word is also the first part of the إِضافةٌ.	خُلُقُ
Pronominal suffix (ضَمِيرٌ مُتَّصِلٌ); the *returning, referential pronoun* (ضَمِيرٌ عائِدٌ) serves as the second part of the إِضافةٌ (i.e., the مُضافٌ إِلَيْهِ). A word in such a position gets the genitive (مَجْرُورٌ) case. This pronoun, however, can't carry case inflections because it is indeclinable (مَبِنِيٌّ). Thus, we can't put the necessary genitive marker and can only assign a place value. We say that this pronoun holds the position of a genitive case (فِي مَحَلّ جَرّ).	هُ

Predicate of the <u>second</u> subject (خَبَرُ الْمُبْتَدَإِ الثَّانِي); it has to get the nominative case (مَرْفُوعٌ), marked by ضَمَّةٌ (nunation).	كَرِيمٌ

What about the **predicate of the <u>first</u> subject** (الْمُبْتَدَأُ الْأَوَّلُ)? The sentence consisting of the <u>second</u> subject plus its predicate takes on that task. We therefore say that it is placed in the location of a nominative case (فِي مَحَلِّ رَفْعٍ خَبَرُ الْمُبْتَدَإِ الْأَوَّلِ).

B) A **verbal sentence** placed as the خَبَر is easier to grasp.

Zayd studies medicine.	زَيْدٌ يَدْرُسُ الطِّبَّ.
Subject of the nominal sentence (مُبْتَدَأٌ), nominative (مَرْفُوعٌ).	زَيْدٌ
Verb in the present tense; indicative (فِعْلٌ مُضَارِعٌ مَرْفُوعٌ). The subject of the verb (فَاعِلٌ) is a hidden pronoun (ضَمِيرٌ مُسْتَتِرٌ) with the implied meaning of *he* (هُوَ).	يَدْرُسُ

What about the predicate of the nominal sentence (which is the primary sentence)? The verbal sentence *he studies medicine* (يَدْرُسُ) takes on the task of the predicate. Therefore, it occupies the position of a nominative state (الْجُمْلَةُ مِنَ الْفِعْلِ وَالْفَاعِلِ فِي مَحَلِّ رَفْعٍ خَبَرٌ).

C) What about a **sentence with** كَانَ?

Zayd had a generous character.	كَانَ زَيْدٌ خُلُقُهُ كَرِيمٌ.
Defective past tense verb (فِعْلٌ مَاضٍ نَاقِصٌ) which turns some grammatical case endings upside down.	كَانَ
This is the "subject", more correctly, the اِسْمُ كَانَ. It is in the nominative case (مَرْفُوعٌ بِالضَّمَّةِ الظَّاهِرَةِ).	زَيْدٌ
Subject of the <u>second</u> nominal sentence (مُبْتَدَأٌ); so, it has to be in the nominative (مَرْفُوعٌ) case. It serves as the first part of a إِضَافَةٌ.	خُلُقُ
Pronominal suffix; second part of the إِضَافَةٌ. Indeclinable (مَبْنِيٌّ); grammatically in the position of a genitive case (فِي مَحَلِّ جَرٍّ).	هُ
Predicate of the second subject (of the nominal sentence). It therefore has to be in the nominative case (مَرْفُوعٌ بِالضَّمَّةِ الظَّاهِرَةِ).	كَرِيمٌ

Where is the **predicate of** كانَ? The entire nominal sentence (جُمْلةٌ
اسْمِيّةٌ) – subject (مُبْتَدَأ) plus predicate (خَبَرٌ) – takes on that task.
Therefore, it occupies the position of an **accusative** case (مِن الْجُمْلةُ
الْمُبْتَدَإِ والْخَبَرِ فِي مَحَلِّ نَصْبٍ خَبَرُ كانَ).

D) What about the **emphatic particle** إِنَّ? That is pretty similar to what
we have seen so far.

Verily, Zayd's character is generous.	إِنَّ زَيْدًا خُلُقُهُ كَرِيمٌ.
Particle of emphasis (حَرْفُ تَوْكِيدٍ وَنَصْبٍ).	إِنَّ
اسْمُ إِنَّ ("subject"), in the accusative case (مَنْصُوبٌ بِالْفَتْحةِ الظّاهِرةِ) because the particle إِنَّ turns the usual case upside down.	زَيْدًا
Subject of the nominal sentence (مُبْتَدَأٌ); nominative case (مَرْفُوعٌ).	خُلُقُ
Pronominal suffix; second part of the إِضافة, see example above.	هُ
Predicate of the nominal sentence (خَبَرُ الْمُبْتَدَإِ) in the nominative case (مَرْفُوعٌ بِالضّمّةِ الظّاهِرةِ).	كَرِيمٌ

The nominal sentence marked in gray, consisting of مُبْتَدَأٌ and خَبَرٌ, is
the **predicate** of إِنَّ. It is therefore placed in the position of a nominative case (الْجُمْلةُ مِن الْمُبْتَدَإِ وخَبَرِهِ فِي مَحَلِّ رَفْعٍ خَبَرُ إِنَّ).

69. What is a جُمْلةٌ إِنْشائِيّة?

A non-informative sentence.

Usually a sentence carries a statement of fact or a claim – the predicate. Such sentences are called *informative sentences* (جُمْلةٌ خَبَرِيّةٌ). For
example: *The boy is nice. Nice* is the predicate = the information. The
Arabic term for predicate is خَبَرٌ which literally means *news; message*.

However, there is also another type of sentence which is called جُمْلةٌ
إِنْشائِيّةٌ. Such sentences carry a command, an order, a prohibition, a
question, or a wish. We call these sentences **non**-informative.

A teacher once told me a rule of thumb which may be helpful. If
someone says a sentence and you can accuse him or her of lying, then

it is an informative sentence. For example, if I say: *"I read a book to-day"*. Then you could reply: *"You are lying!"* If I say: *"Can I read this book?"*, then you can't accuse me of that.

Let's see two examples of a جُمْلَةٌ إِنْشائِيَّةٌ.

Do you have a pen?	هَلْ عِنْدَكَ قَلَمٌ؟
Drink the water!	اشْرَبْ الْماءَ!

Most grammarians say that a wish or command may be placed as the خَبَر, but this only works when the predicate is a **question** (اِسْتِفْهامِيَّةٌ) or it carries an **order** or **request** (طَلَبِيَّةٌ).

Zayd, reward him!	زَيْدٌ كافِئْهُ!

Subject (مُبْتَدَأٌ) of the nominal sentence; nominative (مَرْفُوعٌ).	زَيْدٌ
Imperative (فِعْلُ أَمْرٍ). Its source is the III-verb كافَأَ - يُكافِئُ (R3=ء; *to reward*). Subject is a hidden pronoun (ضَميرٌ مُسْتَتِرٌ) with the implied meaning of *you* (أَنْتَ).	كافِئْ
Pronominal suffix which serves as the direct object (مَفْعُولٌ بِهِ). It is indeclinable; however, grammatically speaking, it takes the position of an accusative case (فِي مَحَلِّ نَصْبٍ).	هُ
Where is the **predicate** (خَبَرٌ)? It is the <u>verbal sentence</u>, i.e., the imperative plus its hidden subject (الْجُمْلَةُ مِنَ الْفِعْلِ وَالْفاعِلِ فِي مَحَلِّ رَفْعٍ خَبَرٌ).	

An example of a question:

Has Zayd come?	زَيْدٌ هَلْ حَضَرَ؟

Subject (مُبْتَدَأٌ) of the nominal sentence in the nominative case.	زَيْدٌ
Question word (حَرْفُ اِسْتِفْهامٍ); this device does not have a position in إِعْرابٌ and does not operate on any word in the sentence.	هَلْ
Past tense verb, subject is a hidden pronoun, expressing *he* (هُوَ).	حَضَرَ
What about the predicate? It is the verbal sentence (i.e., حَضَرَ). In Arabic, we would say: الْجُمْلَةُ مِنَ الْفِعْلِ وَالْفاعِلِ فِي مَحَلِّ رَفْعٍ خَبَرٌ.	

70. Can a whole sentence take on the job of an object?

Yes, an entire sentence can be placed as an object.

When you have two sentences in English, you need to link them with a subordinate clause. For example: I *think* that he *had committed the crime*. In Arabic, this is different. You can place an **entire sentence as an object** (الْجُمْلَةُ الْوَاقِعَةُ مَفْعُولًا بِهِ). This, however, is only possible in certain situations. We will examine them now.

1. The sentence is a spoken utterance (quote) – **reported speech**.

Zayd said that ʿAlī is successful.	قالَ زَيْدٌ إِنَّ عَلِيًّا ناجِحٌ.
Subject (فاعِل) of the verb *to say*, مَرْفُوعٌ (nominative).	زَيْدٌ
Particle of emphasis/strengthening (حَرْفُ تَوْكِيدٍ وَنَصْبٍ).	إِنَّ
"Subject" (اِسْمُ إِنَّ) which has to be in the accusative (مَنْصُوبٌ).	عَلِيًّا
Predicate (خَبَرُ إِنَّ); therefore, it is in the nominative case (مَرْفُوعٌ).	ناجِحٌ

Didn't we miss something in our analysis? What about the *direct object* of قالَ, the *spoken object* (مَقُولُ الْقَوْلِ)? Well, it's there! It is the part marked in gray – the sentence that consists of إِنَّ and its governed factors (الْجُمْلَةُ مِنْ إِنَّ وَمَعْمُولَيْها فِي مَحَلِّ نَصْبٍ مَقُولُ الْقَوْلِ). Most grammarians agree that if the spoken part relates to a **passive verb** (الْمَبْنِيُّ لِلْمَجْهُولِ), it works as the **passive subject** (نائِبٌ عَنِ الْفاعِلِ). This means that it is placed in the position of a nominative case (فِي مَحَلِّ رَفْعٍ).

It was said that Zayd is successful.	قِيلَ إِنَّ زَيْدًا ناجِحٌ.

2. A tricky situation: The sentence is placed after the utterance (الْقَوْلُ), but the verb *to say* actually expresses *to think/assume*.

Do you think Muhammad plays?	أَتَقُولُ مُحَمَّدٌ يَلْعَبُ؟
Question particle (حَرْفُ اِسْتِفْهامٍ). It does not have a place in إِعْرابٌ.	أ
Subject (مُبْتَدَأ) of the nominal sentence in the nominative (مَرْفُوعٌ).	مُحَمَّدٌ

Present tense verb (فِعْلٌ مُضارِعٌ). The subject (فاعِلٌ) is a hidden pronoun (ضَمِيرٌ مُسْتَتِرٌ) with the implied meaning of *he*.	يَلْعَبُ

Two things are missing in the analysis: the **predicate** (خَبَر) of the subject *Muhammad* and the object of the speech (مَقُولُ الْقَوْلِ).

- The **verbal sentence** (يَلْعَبُ) is the **predicate**; therefore, it occupies the place of a nominative case (فِي مَحَلِّ رَفْعٍ خَبَرُ الْمُبْتَدَإِ).
- The **nominal sentence** consisting of subject and predicate is the **object of the speech** of *to think*; it is placed in the position of an accusative case (الْجُمْلَةُ مِن الْمُبْتَدَإِ وَخَبَرِهِ فِي مَحَلِّ نَصْبٍ مَقُولُ الْقَوْلِ).

There is another way to treat this sentence which brings along different cases. We assume that *to say* has the meaning of a <u>hypothetical verb</u> that **literally** means *to think*. Such verbs can take **two direct objects!**

Do you think Muhammad plays?	أَتَقُولُ مُحَمَّدًا يَلْعَبُ؟
➡ Virtual, estimated meaning of the above sentence: *Do you think that Muhammad is playing?*	أَتَظُنُّ مُحَمَّدًا لاعِبًا؟

In this version, Muhammad (مُحَمَّدًا) is in the **accusative** case!

First direct object (مَفْعُولٌ أَوَّلٌ); therefore مَنْصُوبٌ (accusative).	مُحَمَّدًا
Where is the **second** <u>direct object</u> (مَفْعُولٌ ثانٍ)? It is the verbal sentence يَلْعَبُ. It is placed in the position of an accusative case (الْجُمْلَةُ مِن الْفِعْلِ وَالْفاعِلِ فِي مَحَلِّ نَصْبٍ مَفْعُولٌ ثانٍ لِتَقُولُ). However, some conditions have to be fulfilled for this option – see #315!	

71. Can a sentence function as an object of ظَنَّ?

Yes, but it can only serve as the second direct object.

ظَنَّ *and its sisters* are crafty verbs because they can carry more than one direct object. We need some tricks to translate such sentences into good English – often by the help of the word *that*. It is even possible that the first direct object is just a plain word and the **second object is a sentence** – but not the other way round as we will later see.

I thought that Zayd is reading.	ظَنَنْتُ زَيْدًا يَقْرَأُ.

First direct object (مَفْعُولٌ أَوَّلٌ); in the accusative case (مَنْصُوبٌ).	زَيْدًا
Verb in the present tense (فِعْلٌ مُضَارِعٌ); its subject is an implied pronoun (ضَمِيرٌ مُسْتَتِرٌ) expressing the meaning of *he* (هُوَ): *he reads/is reading.* So, this is not just a verb – it is a full verbal sentence which serves as the **second object** (مَفْعُولٌ ثَانٍ). In Arabic, we say: (الْجُمْلَةُ مِنَ الْفِعْلِ وَالْفَاعِلِ فِي مَحَلِّ نَصْبٍ مَفْعُولٌ ثَانٍ).	يَقْرَأُ

Question: Why is it not possible to place a sentence as the **first** object?

The first direct object (الْمَفْعُولُ الْأَوَّلُ) of such verbs, as far as its actual true nature and origin is concerned, is the subject (مُبْتَدَأٌ) of a nominal sentence. A sentence, however, can never serve as the مُبْتَدَأٌ. See *question #203* for more details. For details about ظَنَّ, see *#306*.

72. Can a sentence function as the third object of certain verbs?

Yes, it can – as the third of the three.

Arabic knows pretty weird verbs that may carry three objects. To be honest, you don't encounter them often. Since they are very special, it is fun to analyze them. They are usually verbs of the IV-form (أَفْعَلَ); for a deep analysis and how they work, see *#316*.

Let's focus now on the nature of the objects. A sentence can serve as one of the three objects of such verbs – but the sentence can only be placed <u>after</u> the <u>second</u> object (بَعْدَ الْمَفْعُولِ الثَّانِي). In other words, it can only be the **third object**. We frequently encounter that when we deal with verbs denoting *to notify, to inform* (أَعْلَمَ) and *to show, to demonstrate* (أَرَى).

I told Zayd that Amr's brother is successful.	أَعْلَمْتُ زَيْدًا عَمْرًا أَخُوهُ نَاجِحٌ.

First direct object (مَفْعُولٌ أَوَّلٌ); in the accusative case (مَنْصُوبٌ).	زَيْدًا
Second direct object (مَفْعُولٌ ثَانٍ); in the accusative (مَنْصُوبٌ).	عَمْرًا
Subject (مُبْتَدَأٌ) of the nominal sentence. The و marks the nominative case (مَرْفُوعٌ) since أَخٌ is one of the *six nouns* (الْأَسْماءُ السِّتَّةُ). أَخُو also serves as the first part of the إِضافةٌ.	أَخُو

The مُضافٌ إِلَيْهِ, i.e., the second part of the إِضافةٌ. The pronoun has an indeclinable (مَبْنِيٌّ عَلَى الضَّمِّ) shape; we can't put the marker of the genitive. We can only say that it occupies the position of a genitive case (فِي مَحَلِّ جَرٍّ).	هُ
Predicate (خَبَرٌ) of the nominal sentence; nominative (مَرْفُوعٌ) case.	ناجِحٌ
What about the **third object** (مَفْعُولٌ ثالِثٌ)? The <u>nominal sentence</u> consisting of مُبْتَدَأ and خَبَرٌ is doing this job. It is placed in the position of an accusative (الْجُمْلةُ مِنَ الْمُبْتَدَإِ وَخَبَرِهِ فِي مَحَلِّ نَصْبٍ مَفْعُولٌ ثالِثٌ).	

Could the sentence be placed as the second object as well? No, because the true nature of the second object is the subject (مُبْتَدَأٌ) of a nominal sentence, and a sentence can't serve as the مُبْتَدَأٌ.

73. Can you use a sentence where you would expect a حالٌ?

Yes, you can. A sentence can serve in the position of a circumstantial description (حالٌ) without any problem.

In fact, to be honest, this happens very often. If the حالٌ is a **verbal sentence** (جُمْلةٌ فِعْلِيّةٌ), we don't have to worry much about the grammar. The sentence can be placed there without further assistance.

I saw Zayd reading.	رَأَيْتُ زَيْدًا يَقْرَأُ.
The **verbal sentence** (جُمْلةٌ فِعْلِيّةٌ), consisting of verb and subject (يَقْرَأُ), is the circumstantial qualifier (حالٌ) for Zayd. A حالٌ has to be in the accusative case (مَنْصُوبٌ) → we assign the place value of an accusative case to the verbal sentence (الْجُمْلةُ مِنَ الْفِعْلِ وَالْفاعِلِ فِي مَحَلِّ نَصْبٍ حالٌ مِنْ زَيْدٍ).	

Let's turn to the exciting part. If the حالٌ is a **nominal sentence** (جُمْلةٌ إِسْمِيّةٌ), we'll have to add a device: a **connector** (رابِطٌ) which is either وَ or a referential pronoun (ضَمِيرٌ عائِدٌ) referring to the صاحِبُ الْحالِ.

a) The construction with the pronoun.

I saw Zayd having his book in his hand.	رَأَيْتُ زَيْدًا كِتابُهُ فِي يَدِهِ.
Direct object (مَفْعُولٌ بِهِ) of the verb *to see* (رَأَى); therefore, it is	زَيْدًا

in the accusative case (مَنْصُوبٌ).	
Subject (مُبْتَدَأٌ) of the nominal sentence; nominative (مَرْفُوعٌ) case. It is also the first part of the إِضَافَةٌ.	كِتَابُ
Second part of the إِضَافَةٌ (مُضَافٌ إِلَيْهِ). Therefore, it should be in the genitive case (مَجْرُورٌ). But we can't put the marker as we are not allowed to change the shape of the pronoun's final letter (مَبْنِيٌّ عَلَى الضَّمِّ). Nevertheless, it holds the place of a genitive case (فِي مَحَلِّ جَرٍّ).	هُ
Prepositional phrase (الْجَارُّ وَالْمَجْرُورُ). The pronoun is the second part of the إِضَافَةٌ.	فِي يَدِهِ
Watch out: It is not enough to say that the شِبْهُ الْجُمْلَةِ is the predicate (خَبَرٌ) of the nominal sentence though it appears at the place of a predicate. We assume that the شِبْهُ الْجُمْلَةِ is connected to a deleted predicate in the sentence which is implicitly understood (مُتَعَلِّقٌ بِخَبَرٍ مَحْذُوفٍ). So, we need to find a virtual verb to which the prepositional phrase can relate (الْمُتَعَلَّقُ). In #140, we discuss the nature of a شِبْهُ الْجُمْلَةِ in a جُمْلَةٌ اِسْمِيَّةٌ. See also #369.	

Now, where is the حَالٌ? It is the **nominal sentence** consisting of subject (مُبْتَدَأٌ) and predicate (خَبَرٌ). This sentence is placed in the position of an accusative case (الْجُمْلَةُ مِنَ الْمُبْتَدَإِ وَخَبَرِهِ فِي مَحَلِّ نَصْبِ حَالٍ مِنْ زَيْدٍ) because it serves as a status, circumstantial qualifier (حَالٌ) for *Zayd* (زَيْدٍ).

b) Let's rewrite the sentence – and use وَ.

I saw Zayd having the book in his hand.	رَأَيْتُ زَيْدًا وَالْكِتَابُ فِي يَدِهِ.

This device (حَرْفٌ) is called *Wāw of the Hāl* (وَاوُ الْحَالِ). Watch out: It is not the conjunction *and* (وَ) although it may get translated as *and*. وَ has a different grammatical job in this sentence.	وَ
Subject (مُبْتَدَأٌ) of the nominal sentence which exists within the primary verbal sentence. Since it is the subject, it must be in the nominative case (مَرْفُوعٌ), clearly marked by the ضَمَّةٌ.	الْكِتَابُ
Prepositional phrase (جَارٌّ وَمَجْرُورٌ) which supplies the position of the predicate (خَبَرٌ). The pronoun serves as the مُضَافٌ إِلَيْهِ, the second part of the إِضَافَةٌ.	فِي يَدِهِ
Grammarians say that the شِبْهُ الْجُمْلَةِ is linked to a deleted predicate (مُتَعَلِّقٌ	

(بِخَبَرٍ مَحْذُوفٍ), e.g., the word مَوْجُودٌ (which was the real predicate); otherwise this sentence fragment would be disconnected, and a prepositional phrase must be associated with a verb or something with verbal power. Others, however, say that the prepositional phrase is the predicate itself. It is a debate that we will deal with from time to time.

What is the circumstantial qualifier (حالٌ) for *Zayd*? It is the **nominal sentence** (جُمْلَةٌ اسميّةٌ) with subject (مُبْتَدَأٌ) and predicate (خَبَرٌ). We say that this sentence is placed in the position of an accusative (مَنْصُوبٌ) case since it serves as a حالٌ for **Zayd** (زَيْدٌ), and a حالٌ must be مَنْصُوبٌ.

Let's put some spices on the sentence.

I only saw Zayd with his book in his hand.	ما رَأَيْتُ زَيْدًا إلّا كِتابُهُ في يَدِه.

A more literal translation would be: *I did not see Zayd in a position other than one in which he had his book in his hand.*

Negation particle (حَرْفُ نَفْيٍ).	ما
Direct object (مَفْعُولٌ بِه), in the accusative case (مَنْصُوبٌ).	زَيْدًا
Particle of exception (حَرْفُ اسْتِثْناءٍ مُلْغًى) that does not exercise its governing power. (We will examine that in *question #403*.) The particle does not have a position in إعْرابٌ.	إلّا
Here too, the entire **nominal sentence** (جُمْلَةٌ اسميّةٌ) consisting of the subject (مُبْتَدَأٌ) and the predicate (خَبَرٌ) is the حالٌ for *Zayd*; so we can say that the sentence is placed in the position of an accusative case.	

I only saw Zayd with his book in his hand walking.	ما رَأَيْتُ زَيْدًا إلّا كِتابُهُ في يَدِه يَمْشي.

What about the حالٌ? There are **two!**

The **nominal sentence** with subject (مُبْتَدَأٌ) and predicate (خَبَرٌ), like in the previous example (الجُمْلَةُ مِنَ الْمُبْتَدَإِ وَخَبَرِهِ في مَحَلِّ نَصْبٍ حالٍ مِن زَيْدٍ).

The **verbal sentence** (يَمْشي), consisting of verb plus subject. This is also a حالٌ for *Zayd*. Also this sentence is grammatically placed in the place of an accusative (الجُمْلَةُ مِنَ الْفِعْلِ وَالْفاعِلِ في مَحَلِّ نَصْبٍ حالٍ مِن زَيْدٍ).

74. Can a sentence function as an adjective (صِفةٌ)?

Yes, it can. Such sentences are called جُمْلةُ الصِّفة *(or* جُمْلةُ النَّعْتِ).

The idea of adjective in Arabic is not limited to single words. In many situations, we use entire sentences to describe a person, a place, or a thing. Now comes the sophisticated part. Such sentences are often translated into English as **relative clauses**.

This is a trick, because in Arabic we could not use a relative clause in such a situation. In Arabic, a relative clause must relate to a <u>definite</u> noun which is not the situation in English. The Arabs do not have a relative pronoun that refers to an indefinite word. Let's see some action.

1	A book (that) I like is in the library.	فِي الْمَكْتَبةِ كِتابٌ أُحِبُّهُ.
	We are not allowed to use a relative clause here as we would in English. In Arabic, we use a sentence and place it as an adjective, a so-called *descriptive* or *qualificative sentence* (جُمْلةُ النَّعْتِ or جُمْلةُ الصِّفة). Notice the word order! We can't start a nominal sentence with an **indefinite** word! The trick is that you move the prepositional phrase to the front – and the sentence will be grammatically fine. See *question #213*.	
2	**The** book (that) I like is in the library.	الْكِتابُ الَّذي أُحِبُّهُ فِي الْمَكْتَبةِ.
	We refer to a definite word. ➡ We need a relative pronoun (الَّذي).	

1	I saw **a** man who speaks Arabic.	رَأَيْتُ رَجُلًا يَتَكَلَّمُ الْعَرَبِيّةَ.
	The verbal sentence (يَتَكَلَّمُ الْعَرَبِيّةَ) serves as an adjective for *man*. In English, this would be a relative clause.	
2	I saw **the** man who speaks Arabic.	رَأَيْتُ الرَّجُلَ الَّذي يَتَكَلَّمُ الْعَرَبِيّةَ.

The adjective in the shape of a sentence needs a *referring, referential pronoun* (الْعائِدُ or الرّاجِعُ), referring to the qualified noun. In English grammar terms, we would call that a *relative pronoun*. The *referential pronoun* is either...

- ...**already contained** in the verb. This is the situation when the noun, which the adjective describes, is in the <u>nominative case</u>.

A man who came....	رَجُلٌ جاءَ...

- ...or **expressed** by a **separate pronoun** which is the situation when the adjective is a nominal sentence. This suffix may be suppressed when the connection between the noun and the *qualificative, adjectival clause* (جُمْلَةُ النَّعْتِ) is implicitly understood. In the genitive and accusative case, we will find the pronoun as a suffix.

A man who is my teacher...	رَجُلٌ هُوَ أُسْتاذِي...
I saw a child whose father was asleep.	رَأَيْتُ طِفْلًا أَبُوهُ نائِمٌ.

In the following examples, the adjective is a full sentence.

An eloquent man spoke at the conference.	تَحَدَّثَ فِي الْمُؤْتَمَرِ رَجُلٌ لِسانُهُ فَصِيحٌ.
Alternatively, we could say in English: *A man, who expresses himself elegantly, spoke at the conference.*	

Subject (فاعِل) of the verb تَحَدَّثَ; nominative case (مَرْفُوعٌ).	رَجُلٌ
What happens here is the following: We have a primary verbal sentence (جُمْلَةٌ فِعْلِيَّةٌ). *Tongue* starts a (subordinate) nominal sentence (جُمْلَةٌ اِسْمِيّةٌ) and is the subject (مُبْتَدَأ) in the nominative case (مَرْفُوعٌ). The attached pronoun is a *returning, referential pronoun* (الْعائِدُ) and functions as the 2nd part of the إِضافَةٌ.	لِسانُهُ
Predicate (خَبَرٌ) of the nominal sentence; nominative (مَرْفُوعٌ).	فَصِيحٌ

What is the **adjective** (صِفَةٌ or نَعْتٌ) for *man* (رَجُلٌ)؟

It is the **entire nominal sentence** (جُمْلَةٌ اِسْمِيّةٌ) consisting of subject (مُبْتَدَأ) and predicate (خَبَرٌ). The sentence supplies the place of the adjective. The جُمْلَةُ النَّعْتِ here describes a word in the nominative case. Since an adjective has to agree with the word it describes, we say that this sentence is located in the position of a nominative case (الْجُمْلَةُ مِن الْمُبْتَدَإِ وَخَبَرِهِ فِي مَحَلِّ رَفْعِ صِفَةٌ). Another example:

I heard a singer with a beautiful voice.	سَمِعْتُ مُغَنِّيًا صَوْتُهُ جَمِيلٌ.

Direct object (مَفْعُولٌ بِهِ) of the verb; accusative case (مَنْصُوبٌ).	مُغَنِّيًا
Subject (مُبْتَدَأ) of the nominal sentence, مَرْفُوعٌ. The attached pro-	صَوْتُهُ

noun is a "returner" (relative) pronoun and serves as the second part of the إضافةٌ. It is indeclinable which is the reason why we can only assign a "place value", i.e., the genitive case (فِي مَحَلِّ جَرٍّ).	
Predicate (خَبَرٌ) of the nominal sentence; nominative (مَرْفُوعٌ) case.	جَمِيلٌ
What about the **adjective** for *singer* (مُغَنِّيًا)? *Singer* is مَنْصُوبٌ which implies that the adjective has to take that case as well. The adjective, however, is not a word – it is a sentence with subject (مُبْتَدَأٌ) and predicate (خَبَرٌ). We can only assign a "place value" and say about the entire nominal sentence that it was placed in the location of an accusative case (اَلْجُمْلَةُ مِن الْمُبْتَدَإِ وَخَبَرِهِ فِي مَحَلِّ نَصْبِ صِفةٍ).	

75. Why does it matter in Arabic whether a noun is truly indefinite?

Because only then, two very famous grammar rules work.

First of all, what are the famous rules we will talk about? Many students learn them at the beginning of their studies:

- A sentence after an **indefinite** noun (نَكِرةٌ) is an **adjective** (صِفةٌ).
- A sentence after a **definite** noun (مَعْرِفةٌ) is a حالٌ.

The early Arabic grammarians have not stated this rule. Moreover, they have restricted it. Let's first look at the things which are not debated.

A **sentence** (اَلْجُمْلةُ الْخَبَرِيّةُ) following a noun...

- ...works as an adjective (صِفةٌ) if it is linked to a **purely, genuinely indefinite** (نَكِرةٌ مَحْضةٌ) noun;
- works as a circumstantial description (حالٌ) if it refers to a **purely, genuinely definite** (مَعْرِفةٌ مَحْضةٌ) noun.

Sounds complicated. If we look again at the two points, we see that there is only one difference from the famous rules mentioned above: the term **genuine**. What does *of pure, genuine descent* mean in that context? It means that it is indefinite or definite without any doubt, i.e., **definite** or **indefinite by its very nature**, no matter how you pronounce or mark it. For example, proper nouns (names) are understood as definite although we don't use a definite marker (ال), e.g., Muhammad (مُحَمَّدٌ).

Now, what happens if they are not genuine (غَيْرُ مَحْضةٍ)? Then you can choose. You treat the word according to the visible shape of the word (لَفْظًا) or according to the actual meaning (مَعْنًى). Practically speaking, you can treat it as a حالٌ or a صِفةٌ. This only works under the prerequisite that there is no hindrance that would prevent the sentence from becoming a صِفةٌ or حالٌ. Sounds abstract, let's make it practical.

a) The **purely, genuinely indefinite** (النَّكِرة الْمَحْضة).

I saw **a student** who was reading.	رَأَيْتُ طالِبًا يَقْرَأُ.
Without any doubt we are talking about an unspecific, indefinite person. There is no way to understand the word *student* as definite; it can't be a specific, concrete person. So, the verbal sentence يَقْرَأُ serves an **adjective** (صِفةٌ).	

b) The **purely, genuinely definite** (الْمَعْرِفةُ الْمَحْضةُ).

I saw **Zayd** reading.	رَأَيْتُ زَيْدًا يَقْرَأُ.
Zayd is without doubt definite. The sentence يَقْرَأُ is a حالٌ.	

c) The indefinite that is **not purely indefinite** (النَّكِرةُ غَيْرُ الْمَحْضةِ).

1	I saw **a diligent student** reading.	رَأَيْتُ طالِبًا مُجِدًّا يَقْرَأُ.
2	I saw **a student (of knowledge)** reading.	رَأَيْتُ طالِبَ عِلْمٍ يَقْرَأُ.

In both sentences, يَقْرَأُ could be treated as a صِفةٌ or a حالٌ. The indefinite word *student* is not genuinely indefinite because *student* is specified and distinguished by an adjective (نَعْتٌ) in the first example (*diligent*) and by a إِضافةٌ in the second example. Grammarians, however, suggest that it is better to treat such expressions as **adjectives** (صِفةٌ).

d) The definite that is **not purely definite** (الْمَعْرِفةُ غَيْرُ الْمَحْضةِ).

Zayd is like the lion **whose courage is authentic**.	زَيْدٌ مِثْلُ الْأَسَدِ جُرْأَتُهُ أَصِيلةٌ.

The sentence جُرْأَتُهُ أَصِيلةٌ is placed after *the lion* (الْأَسَد) which is definite by the article ال. However, it is further described which ironically weakens the definiteness because it indicates that there are more types than just *the lion.*

In other words, the definite article here classifies the lion as a certain kind of animal (generic name) and not a specific lion. This kind of definiteness is called التَّعْرِيفُ الْجِنْسِيُّ. From a grammatical perspective, this type of definiteness is close to leaving it undefined (تَنْكِيرٌ). For this reason, we could treat the expression in the above sentence as a حالٌ or a صِفةٌ. It is recommended, however, to treat it as a حالٌ.

Now what could prevent us from considering a sentence as a حالٌ or a صِفةٌ? What could be a hindrance (الْمَانِعُ)?

a) Giving an order ➤ a non-informative sentence (جُمْلةٌ إِنْشائِيّةٌ)

1	This is a careless (person), don't accompany him!	هذا مُهْمِلٌ لا تُصاحِبْهُ!
2	This is Zayd, don't insult him!	هذا زَيْدٌ لا تُهِنْهُ!
	Note: تُهِنْ is the jussive mood (مَجْزُومٌ), second person أَنْتَ, of the IV-verb أَهانَ - يُهِينُ (R2=و) which means *to insult; to humiliate.*	

- The sentence لا تُصاحِبْهُ conveys a command (جُمْلةٌ إِنْشائِيّةٌ) which is placed after the **indefinite** noun (نَكِرةٌ).

- In the second example, it is the other way round. The sentence لا تُهِنْهُ is placed after the **definite** noun (مَعْرِفةٌ).

Notice: A جُمْلةٌ إِنْشائِيّةٌ can <u>never</u> serve as a صِفةٌ or حالٌ. For this reason, we exclude it from the إِعْرابٌ. We say that the non-informative sentence doesn't have a position in the analysis (لا مَحَلَّ لَها مِن الْإِعْرابِ) which means that no other word or device operates on it.

b) A future particle

When a definite noun is followed by a verb with a prefix such as لَنْ or سَوْفَ or سَ, then it can <u>never</u> be a حالٌ! This is deeply rooted in the character of the حالٌ. The حالٌ **does not** support or provide the **meaning of the future** tense! Therefore, we should treat such sentences as an exception which also do not have a position in إِعْرابٌ – in other words, they don't fill a grammatical position that is governed by other words.

| Zayd visited me, I will reward him. | زَارَنِي زَيْدٌ سَأُكَافِئُهُ. |
| Zayd apologized, I will not punish him. | اِعْتَذَرَ زَيْدٌ لَنْ أُعَاقِبَهُ. |

c) The particle of exception

| Only a man talking good things came to me. | مَا جَاءَنِي رَجُلٌ إِلَّا قَالَ خَيْرًا. |

The sentence قَالَ خَيْرًا is placed after *a man* (رَجُلٌ) which is a purely indefinite word (نَكِرَةٌ مَحْضَةٌ). Applying the standard rules, the analysis should tell us that the sentence is placed as a صِفَةٌ.

However, the sentence after إِلَّا in the above example gets the إِعْرَابٌ of a حَالٌ – and <u>not</u> that of a صِفَةٌ. Why is that? It is a special case: In Arabic, the device إِلَّا does <u>not</u> separate the adjective/attribute (صِفَةٌ) from the noun to which it refers (مَوْصُوفٌ).

76. Can a sentence fill the location of *the excluded* (الْمُسْتَثْنَى)?

Yes, but this is quite tricky.

We get this situation when we deal with an *interrupted* or *detached exclusion* (اِسْتِثْنَاءٌ مُنْقَطِعٌ). This means that *the thing excepted* (مُسْتَثْنَى) is not of the same kind (جِنْس) as the thing from which the exception is made (الْمُسْتَثْنَى مِنْهُ).

| I will not punish the **diligent**, but will punish the **careless**, for his (the latter's) punishment is severe. | لَنْ أُعَاقِبَ مُجِدًّا إِلَّا الْمُهْمِلُ فَعِقَابُهُ شَدِيدٌ. |

Let's focus on the second part: إِلَّا الْمُهْمِلُ فَعِقَابُهُ شَدِيدٌ

Particle of exception (حَرْفُ اِسْتِثْنَاءٍ). No position in إِعْرَابٌ.	إِلَّا
First subject (مُبْتَدَأٌ) in the nominative case (مَرْفُوعٌ).	الْمُهْمِلُ
This letter is placed before the predicate (الْفَاءُ وَاقِعَةٌ فِي الْخَبَرِ).	ف
Second subject (مُبْتَدَأٌ ثَانٍ) in the nominative case (مَرْفُوعٌ). It is the first part of the إِضَافَة. The pronominal suffix (ه) is the second part of it. We can't mark it as such due to its indeclinable	عِقَابُهُ

| shape. So we can only assign the "place value" of a genitive case. | |
| Predicate of the **second** subject (خَبَرُ الْمُبْتَدَإِ الثَّانِي); nominative. | شَدِيدٌ |

So what is so special about this sentence?

- The sentence consisting of the <u>**second**</u> subject (الْمُبْتَدَأُ الثَّانِي) together with its predicate serves as the **predicate** of the first subject (خَبَرُ الْمُبْتَدَإِ الْأَوَّلِ). Therefore, the sentence supplies the position of a nominative case (فِي مَحَلِّ رَفْعٍ) – we assign a place value.

- The sentence consisting of the <u>**first**</u> subject (الْمُبْتَدَأُ الْأَوَّلُ) plus its predicate is *the thing excepted* (مُسْتَثْنًى) – marked in gray. So it takes the position of an accusative case (فِي مَحَلِّ نَصْبٍ).

77. Can you place a sentence as the second part of a إِضَافَةٌ?

Yes, this happens quite often.

Sentences that are placed as the مُضَافٌ إِلَيْهِ, i.e., the second part of a إِضَافَةٌ, can be difficult to translate. To make such constructions work, you need to keep an eye on the first part (مُضَافٌ).

What kind of word do we need as a مُضَافٌ so that we can add a sentence as the second part مُضَافٌ إِلَيْهِ?

1. Words that convey and point to the meaning of **time**, no matter whether they are an adverb (ظَرْفٌ) or not.

| I met Zayd on the day he came. | قَابَلْتُ زَيْدًا يَوْمَ حَضَرَ. |

Adverb of time (ظَرْفُ زَمَانٍ); it is in the accusative case (مَنْصُوبٌ). It is also the first part of the إِضَافَةٌ.	يَوْمَ
Past tense verb (فِعْلٌ مَاضٍ). Its subject (فَاعِلٌ) is a hidden pronoun (ضَمِيرٌ مُسْتَتِرٌ) with the implied meaning of *he* (هُوَ).	حَضَرَ
Where is the second part of the إِضَافَةٌ? The verbal sentence (حَضَرَ) takes on that job and serves as the مُضَافٌ إِلَيْهِ; this means that it grammatically takes the position of a genitive case (فِي مَحَلِّ جَرٍّ).	

Sura 5:119	This is a Day when the truthful will benefit from their truthfulness.	هَذَا يَوْمُ يَنْفَعُ الصَّادِقِينَ صِدْقُهُمْ.

This demonstrative word (اِسْمُ إِشارةٍ) is the subject (مُبْتَدَأٌ) of the nominal sentence (جُمْلَةٌ اِسْمِيّةٌ).	هذا
Watch out: The word يَوْمُ here is <u>not</u> placed as an adverb of time (ظَرْفٌ)! It is the **predicate** (خَبَرٌ) of the nominal sentence and therefore gets the nominative case (مَرْفُوعٌ). An adverb would get the accusative case (مَنْصُوبٌ).	يَوْمُ
Verb in the present tense; indicative (فِعْلٌ مُضارِعٌ مَرْفُوعٌ).	يَنْفَعُ
Direct object (مَفْعُولٌ بِهِ) of the verb (يَنْفَعُ); the letter ي marks the accusative case (مَنْصُوبٌ) here.	الصَّادِقِينَ
Subject (فاعِلٌ); in the nominative case.	صِدْقُهُمْ

In the above example, the verbal sentence takes on the task of the مُضافٌ إِلَيْهِ. Therefore, grammatically speaking, it gets the place value of a genitive case (الْجُمْلَةُ فِي مَحَلِّ جَرٍّ بِالإِضافةِ).

2. Some adverbs of time (ظَرْفُ زَمانٍ) can work as the مُضافٌ.

لَمّا	إذا	إذْ
when; after	*when (denoting future time and implying a condition)*	*when, since; then; at that time*

- The particle إذْ can work as the first part of a إِضافةٌ and can be followed by a nominal <u>**or**</u> verbal sentence.
- The particle إذا, however, can only work as the first part of a إِضافةٌ if the second part is a <u>verbal</u> sentence!

I was born when the war started. Note: The word *war* (حَرْبٌ) is feminine in Arabic.	وُلِدْتُ إذْ بَدَأَتْ الْحَرْبُ.
How happy we were as (when we were) children!	كَمْ سَعَدَنا إذْ كُنّا أَطْفالًا!

Adverb of time (ظَرْفُ زَمانٍ); we can't put case markers as it has a	إذْ

fixed, indeclinable shape. Nevertheless, it is placed in the position of an accusative case (فِي مَحَلِّ نَصْبٍ). It is also the first part of a إِضَافَةٌ.

What comes after إِذْ is the second part of the إِضَافَةٌ. In the second example, it is the sentence consisting of كَانَ and its governed factors (الْجُمْلَةُ مِن كَانَ وَمَعْمُولَيْها): the implicit pronoun (we) and أَطْفالًا. The sentence is located in the position of a genitive case (فِي مَحَلِّ جَرٍّ مُضافٌ إلَيْهِ).

| Do you remember when we were children? | هَلْ تَذْكُرُ إِذْ نَحْنُ أَطْفالٌ؟ |

Direct object (مَفْعُولٌ بِهِ). We can't use the markers of the accusative (مَنْصُوبٌ) case because إِذْ is indeclinable (مَبْنِيٌّ). Therefore, we can only apply a "place value" (فِي مَحَلِّ نَصْبٍ).	إِذْ
Subject (مُبْتَدَأٌ) of the nominal sentence. It has a fixed shape; we say that it is located in the spot of a nominative (فِي مَحَلِّ رَفْعٍ).	نَحْنُ
Predicate (خَبَرٌ) in the nominative case (مَرْفُوعٌ).	أَطْفالٌ

The **nominal sentence** consisting of subject (مُبْتَدَأٌ) and predicate (خَبَرٌ) is in the **position of the second part** of the إِضَافَةٌ.

Now, let's analyze إِذا and لَمّا. The word إِذا is one of the more complicated Arabic words because it produces quite complex grammatical structures - *see question #393.*

| I will treat Zayd with respect if he comes. | إِذا حَضَرَ زَيْدٌ أَكْرَمْتُهُ. |
| Treat him politely if he comes! | أَكْرِمْهُ إِذا جاءَ! |

| Adverb denoting the future (ظَرْفٌ لِما يُسْتَقْبَلُ مِن الزَّمانِ). | إِذا |
| Subject (فاعِلٌ) of the verbal sentence; nominative case (مَرْفُوعٌ). | زَيْدٌ |

The verbal sentence (حَضَرَ زَيْدٌ) is charged with the role of the second part of the إِضَافَةٌ; thus, it is grammatically treated as having the position of a genitive case (فِي مَحَلِّ جَرٍّ مُضافٌ إلَيْهِ).

| I met Zayd when he came. | قابَلْتُ زَيْدًا لَمّا حَضَرَ. |
| I treated him with respect whenever he came! | لَمّا جاءَ أَكْرَمْتُهُ! |

Adverb of time (ظَرْفُ زَمانٍ); as such it should get the marker of the accusative case – but the word is indeclinable. We cannot mark it as such and can only say that it is placed in the position of an accusative (فِي مَحَلِّ نَصْبٍ).	لَمّا
The verbal sentence حَضَرَ (and جاءَ respectively) is the second part of the إضافةٌ. Therefore, it is grammatically in the position of a genitive case.	

78. Why do adverbs of place may produce complex sentences?

Because some adverbs of place (ظَرْفُ مَكانٍ) serve as the first part of a إضافةٌ and are followed by an entire sentence functioning as the 2nd part.

Usually you can translate such Arabic sentences word by word into English, and you'll be fine. The grammar, however, is complex. Let's take the word حَيْثُ which means *where*. It can serve as the first part of a إضافةٌ and can be followed by a verbal or nominal sentence serving as the second part (مُضافٌ إلَيْهِ). This means that where you would normally find a word, there is now a whole sentence.

I sat where Zayd was sitting.	جَلَسْتُ حَيْثُ زَيْدٌ جالِسٌ.

Adverb of place (ظَرْفُ مَكانٍ); it has an indeclinable shape, so we can't mark it as مَنْصوبٌ (accusative) – but we treat it grammatically as such (فِي مَحَلِّ نَصْبٍ) and assign a place value.	حَيْثُ
Subject (مُبْتَدَأٌ) of a nominal sentence; nominative case (مَرْفوعٌ).	زَيْدٌ
Predicate (خَبَرٌ) of a nominal sentence; nominative case (مَرْفوعٌ).	جالِسٌ

In the above example, the word *Zayd* (زَيْدٌ) is not in the genitive case although we said that it starts the مُضافٌ إلَيْهِ, i.e., the second part of the إضافةٌ, which has to be مَجْرورٌ. Instead, the whole nominal sentence plays this role and occupies the place of a genitive case (فِي مَحَلِّ جَرٍّ).

The same is true for a verbal sentence.

I sat where Zayd sat.	جَلَسْتُ حَيْثُ جَلَسَ زَيْدٌ.

The verbal sentence جَلَسَ زَيْدٌ is considered to be the مُضافٌ إلَيْهِ; thus, it is in the position of a genitive case (فِي مَحَلِّ جَرٍّ).	

Watch out: حَيْثُ is a noun (اِسْم) in Arabic which means that it can fill several places and functions in a sentence. In most situations, it serves as an adverb of place or time (ظَرْفٌ). But that is not the end of the story since it's <u>not</u> necessary that حَيْثُ is placed as an adverb.

I started where Zayd had ended.	بَدَأْتُ مِنْ حَيْثُ اِنْتَهَى زَيْدٌ.
Preposition (حَرْفُ الْجَرِّ).	مِنْ
This is **not** an adverb. This noun serves in the position of a genitive case (فِي مَحَلِّ جَرٍّ), induced by the preceding preposition. Since it has an indeclinable shape (مَبْنِيٌّ عَلَى الضَّمِّ), it is impossible to put case markers. Therefore, we can't mark it visibly as such. Nevertheless, also here حَيْثُ is the first part of the إِضافَةٌ, i.e., the مُضافٌ.	حَيْثُ
The verbal sentence (اِنْتَهَى زَيْدٌ) is charged with the role of the مُضافٌ إِلَيْهِ. So, it is grammatically in the position of a genitive (فِي مَحَلِّ جَرٍّ).	

Note: The expression مِنْ حَيْثُ does not only mean *from where*. It can denote many meanings and is part of several expressions.

1	*as far as; with respect to; because of*	مِنْ حَيْثُ
	With regard to culture; as far as ... is concerned.	مِنْ حَيْثُ الثَّقافَةُ
2	*As such; in itself.* Same meaning as بِحَدِّ ذاتِهِ.	مِنْ حَيْثُ هُوَ
	The human being as such...	الْإِنْسانُ مِنْ حَيْثُ هُوَ
3	*Whether he knows it or not...*	مِنْ حَيْثُ يَدْرِي وَلا يَدْرِي

79. Can a nominal sentence take on the task of a مَجْزُومٌ-verb?

Yes, this is possible.

We should clarify some things before we start our analysis. First of all, what we say in this *question* is true for **conditional sentences**. The second part of a conditional sentence (*apodosis*), which we will analyze now, is called the *answer* or *result clause of the condition* (جَوابُ الشَّرْطِ). We will show that a **nominal sentence** (جُمْلَةٌ اِسْمِيَّةٌ) can hold the position where you would expect a verb in the jussive (مَجْزُومٌ) mood.

Such a situation (الْجُمْلَةُ الْواقِعةُ جَوابًا لِشَّرْطٍ) is possible if the sentence is placed after...

- فَ;
- the إذا الْفُجائِيّةُ – the إذا *of the unexpected* (particle of surprise);
- or if the conditional particle (كَلِمةُ الشَّرْطِ) has the power to govern words in the مَجْزُومٌ-mood.

1	The diligent will be successful. (Whoever strives, the success will be his ally.)	مَنْ جَدَّ فَالنَّجاحُ حَليفُهُ.
2	If you are sincere with Ali, he'll be loyal.	إنْ تُصادِقْ عَلِيًّا فَهُوَ مُخْلِصٌ.

2	This letter is needed to link the result clause (جَوابُ الشَّرْطِ) with the conditional (الشَّرْطِ).	فَ
	Subject (مُبْتَدَأٌ) of the nominal sentence (جُمْلَةٌ اسْمِيّةٌ).	هُوَ
	Predicate (خَبَرٌ) of the nominal sentence; nominative case.	مُخْلِصٌ
	The nominal sentence (subject and predicate) is the جَوابُ الشَّرْطِ. It is located in the position of a verb in the jussive mood (فِي مَحَلِّ جَزْمٍ).	

Now, let's look at an example with a *particle of surprise* (إذا).

If we get forceful on the enemy, then (suddenly) he will flee.	إنْ نُشَدِّدْ عَلَى الْعَدُوِّ إذا هُو هارِبٌ.

Particle of surprise (حَرْفُ مُفاجَأَةٍ); no position in إعْرابٌ.	إذا
Subject (مُبْتَدَأٌ) of the nominal sentence.	هُوَ
Predicate (خَبَرٌ) of the nominal sentence; nominative (مَرْفُوعٌ).	هارِبٌ
The nominal sentence (الْجُمْلَةُ مِنَ الْمُبْتَدَإ وَخَبَرِهِ) is the complement/answer (جَوابُ الشَّرْطِ) of the conditional. We say that it supplies the spot where a word in the jussive (مَجْزُومٌ) would be located (فِي مَحَلِّ جَزْمٍ).	

So far, so good – but why are we allowed to do this? The grammarians showed that we could add a verbal sentence after the nominal sentence which then would be a مَعْطُوفٌ (the term denotes *coupled, joined together*) and would take the same case or mood as the preceding word –

in our example: the مَجْزُومٌ-mood. This shows that our analysis is fine!

Let's enhance example number 2:

If you are sincere with Ali, he will be loyal and fulfill his duty.	إِنْ تُصَادِقْ عَلِيًّا فَهُوَ مُخْلِصٌ وَيَقُمْ بِوَاجِبِهِ.
Note that the I-verb (قَامَ - يَقُومُ) marked in gray is in the **jussive** (مَجْزُومٌ).	

80. What is the tricky thing if a sentence follows another sentence?

They might be grammatically linked.

It is about the following question: When does a sentence, which follows after another sentence, need to be analyzed in relation to the first? This happens in two situations:

1. If the sentence is **joined** with the first (عَطْفٌ) by the word *and* (وَ).

2. If the sentence works as an **apposition** (بَدَلٌ).

Zayd succeeded and won the prize.	زَيْدٌ نَجَحَ وَفَازَ بِالْجَائِزَةِ.
Conjunction (حَرْفُ عَطْفٍ). It does not have a place in إِعْرَابٌ.	وَ
Past tense verb (فِعْلٌ مَاضٍ). The subject (فَاعِلٌ) is a hidden pronoun (ضَمِيرٌ مُسْتَتِرٌ), expressing *he* (هُوَ).	فَازَ
The verbal sentence (فَازَ) is in the location of a nominative case (فِي مَحَلِّ رَفْع) because it is coupled with the preceding sentence (i.e., نَجَحَ). In Arabic, we would say: مَعْطُوفَةٌ عَلَى جُمْلةِ نَجَحَ. The verb نَجَحَ itself is the predicate (خَبَرٌ) of the primary nominal sentence.	

2. What about the **apposition**? Let's check an example:

I said to him, "go and don't stay here"!	قُلْتُ لَهُ إِذْهَبْ لا تَبْقَ هُنَا!
The verb قَالَ has a direct object (مَفْعُولٌ بِهِ), a so-called *spoken object* (مَقُولُ الْقَوْلِ) which is the imperative إِذْهَبْ. Thus, إِذْهَبْ is located the position of an accusative (فِي مَحَلِّ نَصْبٍ).	إِذْهَبْ
Particle of interdiction (حَرْفُ نَهْي); used to request leaving a matter; to refuse it; to forbid it. It does not have a position in إِعْرَابٌ.	لا

Present tense verb (فِعْلٌ مُضارِعٌ) in the مَجْزُومٌ-mood because we have a negative imperative (interdiction). We mark it as مَجْزُومٌ by deleting the weak letter (حَذْفُ حَرْفِ الْعِلَّةِ) of the I-verb بَقِيَ - بَقِيَ (R3=ي). The hidden, implied subject is *you* (أَنْتَ).	تَبْقَ
What about the verbal sentence (تَبْقَ)? It is an apposition (بَدَلٌ) for the verbal sentence (اِذْهَبْ). So, تَبْقَ takes the same case and also fills the place of a direct object (مَقُولُ الْقَوْلِ) in the accusative (فِي مَحَلِّ نَصْبٍ).	

NEUTRAL CLAUSES – OUTSIDE THE SCOPE OF إِعْرابٌ

إِعْرابٌ involves the explicit or implicit change at the endings (= cases) of words (اِسْمٌ and فِعْلٌ) due to particular places they occupy, i.e., the places of رَفْعٌ, نَصْبٌ, جَرٌّ or جَزْمٌ. These positions (مَحَلٌّ) are governed by a particular regent or operator (عامِلٌ) which induces and triggers certain cases, moods, and states.

If a sentence doesn't have a place in إِعْرابٌ, it means that it is not influenced by an operator. Such a sentence doesn't take on the role of a single word (كَلِمَةٌ مُفْرَدَةٌ) and doesn't get its "place value". We could say that we deal with "neutral" clauses or sentences. We do not have to think about their relationship to other words in the sentence.

Nevertheless, they are still sentences or clauses on their own – but within the larger sentence/framework. We will analyze many of these constructions in detail in *chapter 12*.

81. Does the independent clause have a position in إِعْرابٌ?

No, it hasn't.

The *independent clause* (الْجُمْلَةُ الْمُسْتَأْنَفةُ) is a sentence that is broken off – which makes it a sentence with an elementary, introductory meaning (جُمْلَةٌ اِبْتِدائِيَّةٌ). A جُمْلَةٌ اِبْتِدائِيَّةٌ is elementary in the sense that it is impossible to replace it with a single word (لَفْظٌ مُفْرَدٌ) because the meaning would get lost.

Zayd died, may Allah have mercy on him.	ماتَ زَيْدٌ - رَحِمَهُ اللَّهُ.

The sentence رَحِمَهُ اللّٰهُ is placed after the definite word *Zayd* – but it is <u>not</u> a حَالٌ. It is cut off from the other part (مُنْقَطِعَةٌ عَنِ الْجُمْلَةِ السَّابِقَةِ) and is an independent clause (جُمْلَةٌ مُسْتَأْنَفَةٌ); in our example, an *invocation* (call for mercy). This entire verbal sentence **does not have a place** in إِعْرَابٌ. Another example:

Sura 2:19	أَوْ كَصَيِّبٍ مِّنَ السَّمَاءِ فِيهِ ظُلُمَاتٌ وَرَعْدٌ وَبَرْقٌ، يَجْعَلُونَ، أَصَابِعَهُمْ فِي آذَانِهِم مِّنَ الصَّوَاعِقِ حَذَرَ الْمَوْتِ وَاللّٰهُ مُحِيطٌ بِالْكَافِرِينَ.
	Or [like people who, under] a cloudburst from the sky, with its darkness, thunder, and lightning, put their fingers into their ears to keep out the thunderclaps for fear of death – Allah surrounds the disbelievers.

Among the independent clauses are also those sentences which have the verb at the end and convey the meaning of *"I think"*.

Zayd is generous, I think.	زَيْدٌ كَرِيمٌ أَظُنُّ.

Subject (مُبْتَدَأٌ) and predicate (خَبَرٌ) of the **nominal** sentence.	زَيْدٌ كَرِيمٌ
Verb in the present tense (فِعْلٌ مُضَارِعٌ).	أَظُنُّ

The verbal sentence does not have a place in إِعْرَابٌ because it is an independent clause (جُمْلَةٌ مُسْتَأْنَفَةٌ). This is important because otherwise, we would have <u>different</u> case endings and would treat the first nominal sentence as the object of the verb!

Why is that important? If we don't treat such sentences as *independent*, the meaning might be different. Let's see why.

1	Sura 36:76	So let not their speech grieve you – indeed, We know what they conceal and what they declare.	فَلَا يَحْزُنْكَ قَوْلُهُمْ إِنَّا نَعْلَمُ مَا يُسِرُّونَ وَمَا يُعْلِنُونَ.
2	Sura 10:65	And let not their speech grieve you – indeed, honor [due to power] belongs to Allah entirely.	وَلَا يَحْزُنْكَ قَوْلُهُمْ إِنَّ الْعِزَّةَ لِلّٰهِ جَمِيعًا.

Both sentences marked in gray are independent clauses (جُمْلةٌ مُسْتَأْنَفةٌ) and have no place in إِعْرابٌ. What would happen if we treated them differently? In other words, if they were governed by a regent (عامِلٌ)?

Then, they would be the <u>direct object</u> (spoken object) of the verb *to say*; so, they would fill the location of an accusative case (فِي مَحَلِّ نَصْبٍ مَقُولٌ لِلْقَوْلِ). But where is the verb *to say* (قالَ)? In the above examples, the مَصْدَرٌ is used instead because a مَصْدَرٌ can do the job of a verb – see #305. If we did this operation, we would arrive at a corrupted meaning.

What is meant in the original verse in 36:76 is that Allah addresses his prophet, Muhammad, to not be saddened by the sayings of the polytheists. Then Allah tells Muhammad that Allah knows what these polytheists conceal and declare. The verse doesn't indicate that the polytheists say anything.

In Sura 10:65, if we treated the part marked in gray as a direct object of the verb *to say*, it would mean that the polytheists said the following: *"indeed, honor belongs to Allah entirely"* (إِنَّ الْعِزَّةَ لِلَّهِ جَمِيعًا) – which is very unlikely. Even if they had said it, how could this saying had made the prophet sad?

82. How should we deal with a parenthesis in Arabic grammar?

We don't have to think about cases; a parenthesis has no place in إِعْرابٌ.

The *parenthesis* or *inserted clause* (جُمْلةٌ مُعْتَرِضةٌ) is frequently used in spoken Arabic. A good example is the expression *by God!* (وَاللهِ), placed in various positions in the sentence.

What is the purpose of a parenthesis? It confirms the information in the sentence and strengthens it. In English, you usually use dashes before and after a parenthesis. In Arabic, dashes are rarely used which makes it more difficult. **The parenthesis is found in many positions:**

1. Between the verb and what is governed by the verb in the nominative (بَيْنَ الْفِعْلِ وَمَرْفُوعِهِ). In other words: verb – parenthesis – subject.

Zayd, I was told, has traveled.	سافَرَ - أُخْبِرْتُ - زَيْدٌ.

This passive verbal sentence was squeezed into the primary verbal sentence. The sentence does **not** have a place in إِعْرَابٌ because it forms a parenthesis.	أُخْبِرْتُ

2. You can squeeze a parenthesis into a passive construction.

In the following example, the parenthesis is found between the verb and the subject of the passive (نَائِبُ الْفَاعِلِ).

Zayd, I think, was rewarded.	كُوفِئَ - أَظُنُّ - زَيْدٌ.

3. The parenthesis can be found in a nominal sentence (جُمْلَةٌ اِسْمِيَّةٌ) between the subject (مُبْتَدَأٌ) and the predicate (خَبَرٌ).

Zayd, I am convinced, is generous.	زَيْدٌ - أَنا مُوقِنٌ - كَرِيمٌ.
Indeed, Zayd is – I know (found out) – generous.	إِنَّ زَيْدًا - أَعْلَمُ - كَرِيمٌ.

4. A parenthesis can be placed between the verb (فِعْلٌ) and its direct object (مَفْعُولٌ بِهِ). This can be tricky!

I treated Zayd with respect, I swear!	أَكْرَمْتُ - أُقْسِمُ - زَيْدًا!

5. In an oath, the parenthesis can be put between the first part and the complement (جَوَابٌ). Note: The English translation often uses a different word order.

Sura 56:76	A mighty oath, if you only knew.	وَإِنَّهُ لَقَسَمٌ لَوْ تَعْلَمُونَ عَظِيمٌ.

I swear to God – this is a mighty oath – the patient people will be successful.	وَاللهِ - إِنَّهُ لَقَسَمٌ عَظِيمٌ - لَيُفْلِحَنَّ الصَّابِرُونَ.

Particle of strengthening that induces the accusative (حَرْفُ تَوْكِيدٍ وَنَصْبٍ). The pronominal suffix serves as the "subject" (اِسْمُ إِنَّ) in the position of an accusative case (فِي مَحَلِّ نَصْبٍ).	إِنَّهُ
Lām that is pushed away (from its proper place), in Arabic: اللَّامُ الْمُزَحْلَقَةُ; see *question #260*.	ل

Predicate (خَبَرُ إِنَّ); hence, it takes the nominative case (مَرْفُوعٌ).	قَسَمٌ

6. The parenthesis is found between the first and second part of a إِضافةٌ (between the الْمُضافُ and the الْمُضافُ إِلَيْهِ).

This produces sophisticated constructions. Arabic learners are often told that they can't put anything between the two parts of a إِضافةٌ. So, you may find it difficult to identify the إِضافةٌ when it is mixed with a parenthesis. However, since the parenthesis is treated like an external, neutral thing (which does not have a place in the grammatical analysis as it is not governed by any word), it fits there.

This is, I swear, Zayd's book.	هذا كِتابُ - وَاللهِ - زَيْدٍ.
In this example, the oath (جُمْلَةُ الْقَسَمِ) serves as a parenthesis (جُمْلَةٌ مُعْتَرِضَةٌ) which has no place in إِعْرابٌ.	

7. If you have a prepositional phrase, you usually place the parenthesis between the preposition (الْجارُّ) and the genitive word (الْمَجْرُورُ).

I greeted Zayd, I swear to God.	سَلَّمْتُ عَلَى - وَاللهِ - زَيْدٍ.

8. A weird one: We squeeze it into the future tense. You can place the parenthesis between the future particle (حَرْفُ التَّنْفِيسِ) and the verb.

The diligent will, I am convinced, succeed.	سَوْفَ - أَنا مُوقِنٌ - يَنْجَحُ الْمُجِدُّ.

9. What we said about the future particle also works for قَدْ. You can squeeze the parenthesis into the construction (= before the verb).

Zayd, I swear, had come.	قَدْ - وَاللهِ - حَضَرَ زَيْدٌ.

10. Finally, the perhaps most confusing construction: between the negation particle (حَرْفُ نَفْيٍ) and the thing or verb being denied.

I swear to God, a careless person never succeeds.	مَا - وَاللهِ - أَفْلَحَ مُهْمِلٌ.

83. What is the weirdest function of the particle أَنْ؟

To introduce a paraphrase.

The paraphrase (الْجُمْلَةُ التَّفْسِيرِيّةُ) is a sentence that (further) explains or clarifies what is mentioned earlier and reveals its truth.

- It may follow unconnected (without a particle); in such situations, you will usually encounter a **comma (فَاصِلَةٌ)** – those sentences are easy to grasp.

- It may be accompanied by a particle (حَرْفُ تَفْسِيرٍ); usually أَيْ or أَنْ. The latter may lead to misunderstandings.

The particle أَيْ. This is the most common and easiest form.

I have Asgad, i.e., gold.	عِنْدِي عَسْجَدٌ أَيْ ذَهَبٌ.

أَيْ	*Particle of explanation* (حَرْفُ تَفْسِيرٍ). It does <u>not</u> have a place in إِعْرَابٌ and doesn't have governing power. It has a cemented shape and always looks the same (مَبْنِيٌّ عَلَى السُّكُونِ). What you see after this device is called a جُمْلَة تَفْسِيرِيّة (explanatory sentence) and does not have a place in إِعْرَابٌ as well.

The particle أَنْ can usually be interpreted as a <u>colon</u> (:) in English; it elaborates what was actually said, written, done, etc. This kind of أَنْ does not govern any word. It has the same meaning as أَيْ (*that is*). It is also a حَرْفُ تَفْسِيرٍ.

I wrote to him: "Send me back the book."	كَتَبْتُ إِلَيْهِ أَنْ أَرْسِلْ إِلَيَّ الْكِتَابَ.

أَنْ	Explanatory particle (حَرْفُ تَفْسِيرٍ). It has no place in إِعْرَابٌ. The verb right after أَنْ is <u>not influenced (governed)</u> by أَنْ. Notice the سُكُونٌ since we have an imperative! So, this is **not an interpreted** مَصْدَرٌ as such constructions would need a verb in the مَنْصُوبٌ-mood!
	The sentence that is placed after أَنْ is a جُمْلَةٌ تَفْسِيرِيّةٌ; therefore, it does

not have a place in إِعْرابٍ (لا مَحَلَّ لَها مِن الْإِعْرابِ).

This type of أَنْ is occasionally used in the Qur'an. In the following verse, don't get confused by the final vowel of أَنْ. ➡ It is a helping vowel for the pronunciation.

Sura 23:27	and so We revealed to him: "Build the Ark under Our watchful eye and according to Our revelation."	فَأَوْحَيْنَا إِلَيْهِ أَنِ اصْنَعِ الْفُلْكَ بِأَعْيُنِنَا وَوَحْيِنَا.
Sura 7:43	A voice will call out to them, "This is the Garden you have been given as your own on account of your deeds."	وَنُودُوا أَنْ تِلْكُمُ الْجَنَّةُ أُورِثْتُمُوهَا بِمَا كُنْتُمْ تَعْمَلُونَ.

84. How should we treat the content of an oath in Arabic?

We can ignore it. It does not have a place in إِعْرابٌ

The entire verbal sentence after an oath – the *complement* (جَوابُ الْقَسَم) – is **independent**. Its place is not governed by any word or device. W don't have to worry about case endings or place values.

I swear, the hard-working will succeed!	وَاللّهِ لَيُفْلِحَنَّ الْمُجِدُّ!

Lām that is pushed away from its proper place (اللَّامُ الْمُزَحْلَقةُ) – *see question #260.*	لَ
Verb in the present tense (فِعْلٌ مُضارِعٌ); energetic form. Notice the extra Nūn at the end, the so-called نُونُ التَّوْكيدِ.	يُفْلِحَنَّ
Subject (فاعِلٌ) of the verbal sentence; nominative case (مَرْفُوعٌ).	الْمُجِدُّ

85. What's the judgment on the 2nd part of a conditional sentence?

It depends on the conditional particle in the first part.

We first need to check whether the second part (الْجَوابُ) of a conditional sentence has a position in إِعْرابٌ or not.

Situation 1: The second part **doesn't** have a place in إِعْرابٌ if the conditional word (كَلِمَةُ الشَّرْطِ) **doesn't** trigger the jussive (مَجْزُومٌ) mood.

We call such particles غَيْرُ الْجازِمةِ. It comes down to four devices:

1	لَوْ
2	لَوْلا

3	إذا
4	لَمَّا

If you worked hard, you would have suc-ceeded.	إذا اِجْتَهَدْتَ نَجَحْتَ.
If I were in your position, I would be truly frightened of him.	لَوْ كُنْتُ مَكانَكَ لَخِفْتُ مِنْهُ حَقًّا.

The *response to the condition* (جَوابُ الشَّرْطِ) – the second part of the conditional or as linguists call it, the apodosis – is marked in gray. It holds no position in إِعْرابٌ.

Situation 2: The conditional word (كَلِمَةُ الشَّرْطِ) **triggers** the مَجْزُومٌ-mood (in both verbs) because it has operating power (جازِمةٌ), e.g., إِنْ.

What do we get then?

- The second part of the conditional sentence (جَوابُ الشَّرْطِ) has a place in إِعْرابٌ - but only if it is connected by فَ or a particle denoting surprise (إذا الْفُجائِيّةُ).

- If we don't use فَ or إذا (if the second part follows immediately), then the second part **won't** have a place in إِعْرابٌ.

If you work hard, you will succeed.	إِنْ تَجْتَهِدْ تَنْجَحْ.

Present tense verb, jussive mood (مَجْزُومٌ). The verb needs this mood to take on the job of the 2nd part of the conditional (لِوُقُوعِهِ فِي جَوابِ الشَّرْطِ). Its subject is a hidden pronoun (ضَمِيرٌ مُسْتَتِرٌ) with the implicit meaning of *you* (أَنْتَ). The verbal sentence is the جَوابُ الشَّرْطِ and **does not have a place** in إِعْرابٌ.	تَنْجَحْ

What happens, if we link the first and second part with فَ?

If you work hard, you will succeed.	إِنْ تَجْتَهِدْ فَأَنْتَ نَاجِحٌ.
أَنْتَ is the subject (مُبْتَدَأٌ) and نَاجِحٌ is the predicate (خَبَرٌ) of the nominal sentence (جُمْلَةٌ اِسْمِيّةٌ) which supplies the place of the جَوَابُ الشَّرْطِ. Thus, the جُمْلَةٌ اِسْمِيّةٌ supplies the position of a jussive (فِي مَحَلِّ جَزْمٍ); in other words, the **sentence does the job of a verb** in the jussive.	

This is **not** universally true for a جَوَابُ الشَّرْطِ connected by فَ. It all depends on the **first part**, especially on the conditional particle.

If you work hard, you will succeed.	إِذَا اِجْتَهَدْتَ فَأَنْتَ نَاجِحٌ.
Here, the **second part** of the conditional sentence (جَوَابُ الشَّرْطِ) does **not** have a place in إِعْرَابٌ. The location is not governed by a regent although we have فَ. Why? Because the particle إِذَا doesn't have the power to govern a verb in the مَجْزُومٌ-mood. It is غَيْرُ جَازِمةٍ (*see question #393*).	

86. How do grammarians treat the relative clause (جُمْلَةُ الصِّلةِ)؟

Pretty simple: it does not have a position in إِعْرَابٌ.

Let's see an example to see what the grammarians had in mind.

The man who is behind the mosque is married.	الرَّجُلُ الَّذِي خَلَفَ الْمَسْجِدِ مُتَزَوِّجٌ.

الَّذِي works as an adjective (صِفةٌ) for *the man* (الرَّجُلُ). The word الَّذِي is extra to the meaning. If we removed it from the sentence, the sentence would still make sense.

Arabic does not know a grammatical role for the part that follows الَّذِي. The صِلةُ الْمَوْصُولِ completes the meaning of the adjective الَّذِي – and not the meaning of the original sentence which consists of subject (مُبْتَدَأً) and predicate (خَبَرٌ), which in itself is quite sufficient.

For this reason, the grammarians says that the relative clause (صِلةُ الْمَوْصُولِ) is **not** influenced by other words. It does not have a position in the analysis of governance and cases (لَا مَحَلَّ لَهَا مِن الْإِعْرَابِ). The location of the relative clause is kind of a "neutral" space.

The individual of generous nature came.	جَاءَ الَّذِي خُلُقُهُ كَرِيمٌ.

The one who succeeded came.	جاءَ الَّذي نَجَحَ.

In both examples, the part after الَّذي (regardless of whether it is a nominal or verbal sentence) has no place in إِعْرابٌ; it is a relative clause (صِلةُ الْمَوْصُولِ).

PART TWO: LETTERS, FORMS, AND WORDS

Chapter 3: Secrets of Letters and Forms

87. What does the vowel on the second root letter of a verb tell us?

It reveals many things about the character and personality of the verb.

The **second radical** is the most important component of the past tense. Only the second root letter can have any of the three vowels ("*a*", "*i*", "*u*") in the past tense whereas the first and third must have فَتْحةٌ.

The second vowel can help us understand verbs better and may tell us more about the character and meaning of the verb. Let's see why.

	2nd vowel	pattern	What does it denote?	example	
1	"a"	فَعَلَ	an **act**; someone initiates something	قَتَلَ	to kill
				فَعَلَ	to do; to act
2	"i"	فَعِلَ	a **transitory state**;	لَبِسَ	to dress
				عَلِمَ	to know
3	"u"	فَعُلَ	a **permanent state**;	حَسُنَ	to be beautiful
				كَبُرَ	to be big

This is generally but not universally true. There are exceptions because neighboring consonants have influenced the vowels (or the other way round). There is a <u>rule of thumb</u> for verbs of **category 3** (فَعُلَ):

They usually **don't form an active participle** – but a pseudo, quasi participle that describes the state of things (صِفةٌ مُشَبَّهةٌ). For example: *big* (كَبِيرٌ), *nice* (لَطِيفٌ). See *Arabic for Nerds 1, question #143.*

If you know the vowel of the second root letter of the past tense, it will help you to predict the **correct middle vowel** of the **present tense**. In Arabic, there are only six possible patterns:

	past tense	present tense	الْمَاضِي	الْمُضَارِعُ	meaning
1	*a*	*u*	قَتَلَ	يَقْتُلُ	*to kill*
	a	*i*	ضَرَبَ	يَضْرِبُ	*to strike*
	a	*a*	فَتَحَ	يَفْتَحُ	*to open*
2	*i*	*a*	عَلِمَ	يَعْلَمُ	*to be wise*
	i	*i* *	حَسِبَ	يَحْسِبُ	*to suppose*
3	*u*	*u*	كَرُمَ	يَكْرُمُ	*to be precious*

* This vocalization is very rare. Despite يَحْسِبُ (which could also be used with "*a*": يَحْسَبُ), you only find it with verbs having a weak letter as the first radical (mainly و): *to inherit* (وَرِثَ - يَرِثُ); *to administer* (وَلِيَ - يَلِي).

88. In which position will you never find an Aleph?

The Aleph can never stand at the beginning of an utterance.

The Aleph (ا) is a sound of prolongation after فَتْحَةٌ (="*a*") and **can't carry any vowel** – which makes it different to و and ي since they are capable of that. The Aleph, although mostly unwritten, always has a سُكُونٌ on it (اْ). In Arabic, you can only start an utterance if the first letter has a vowel on it. Thus, you **can't start a sentence with an Aleph**.

But what about the letter أ which is often used at the beginning of a sentence? What you see is, in fact, a هَمْزَةٌ in the shape of an Aleph (أ) – and **not** a pure Aleph (ا).

The letter Aleph as a long vowel is used for prolongation – but also for softness – and is called *the quiet Aleph* (الْأَلِفُ الْهَادِئَةُ) or *the silent Aleph* (الْأَلِفُ السّاكِنة). Let's assume we want to make the Aleph "moveable" which means we want to put a vowel on it. How can we do that? We need an operation which **depends on the root**.

Option 1: The Aleph you see was transformed from the root letters و or ي. ➡ We restore the original letter which is either و or ي, e.g., *two* *batons* (عَصَوانِ). It would be impossible to write عَصَاآنِ.

Option 2: If it is not converted from an original و or ي (i.e., if it wasn't part of the root), you use a هَمْزَةٌ. In the word رَسائِلُ (*letters*), e.g., the هَمْزَةٌ is a substitute for the ا of the singular form رِسالةٌ.

Excursus: Is the Arabic word أَلِفٌ masculine or feminine? Most grammarians treat the term as feminine (like all other letters of the alphabet). Hence, the plural is أَلِفاتٌ. Sībawayhi had already noted that all letters of the alphabet are masculine <u>or</u> feminine. (*see question #25*).

89. Why is there an Aleph at the end of third-person plural verbs?

It is there for protection.

Have you ever thought why we spell كَتَبُوا (*they wrote*) with an Aleph at the end? When a conjugated verb has a و at the end, and when this و is preceded by ضَمّةٌ or by فَتْحةٌ, then the ا is often used (and written), particularly in the plural of verbs. Let's see some examples:

they (m.) reminded	ذَكَّرُوا		they (m.) saw	رَأَوْا
they (m.) wrote	كَتَبُوا		they (m.) visited	زارُوا

This Aleph, in itself superfluous (*Aleph otiosum*), is intended <u>to guard</u> the و. The Aleph protects it against the possibility that the و could be separated from the body of the word to which it belongs – and thus could be mistaken for the word *and* (i.e., the conjunction وَ). For this reason, this Aleph is called أَلِفُ الْوِقاية, *the guarding Aleph*, or الأَلِفُ الْفاصِلةُ, *the separating Aleph*.

90. Why is there sometimes an Aleph instead of و or ي in verbs?

The vowel before the Aleph is the reason.

To start our discussion, let's take two Arabic roots that both contain a final weak letter. From this root, we form the I-verb in both tenses.

verb in the present tense	verb in the past tense	root
يَغْزُو	غَزَا	غ-ز-و
يَرْمِي	رَمَى	ر-م-ي

Why do we write an Aleph (ا or ى)? It only appears because the final short vowel was dropped – otherwise, the pronunciation would be too heavy. However, if we delete the last vowel, this leaves us with a سُكُونٌ which is <u>not naturally</u> there. The سُكُونٌ shuts syllables and separates them. When the letters و or ي carry a سُكُونٌ, they either become a diphthong (*aw/ay*) or a long vowel (*uw/iy*) which is not what we want.

	how to pronounce	final result	Last letter is too heavy; so we drop the last vowel		last letter (theoretical)
1	"aa"	ا + ـَ	aw	وْ + ـَ	وَ
2	"aa"	ى + ـَ	ay	ئْ + ـَ	ئَ / ىَ
3	"uu"	و + ـُ	uw	وْ + ـُ	وُ
4	"ii"	ي + ـِ	iy	ئْ + ـِ	ئُ

	instead of	what we write	root	meaning
1	غَزَوَ	غَزَا	غ-ز-و	he invaded
	رَمَىَ	رَمَى	ر-م-ي	he threw
2	يُغْزَئ	يُغْزَى	غ-ز-و	he is invaded; *passive form*
	يُرْمَىُ	يُرْمَى	ر-م-ي	he is thrown; *passive form*
3	يَغْزُوُ	يَغْزُو	غ-ز-و	he invades
4	يَرْمِئُ	يَرْمِي	ر-م-ي	he throws

Let's turn to a tricky situation: the weak letter completely drops when the سُكُونٌ is found **naturally** **at the end of a word** (syllable). When does that happen? In the imperative (أَمْرٌ) and in the jussive (مَجْزُومٌ) mood. In such situations, the word finally ends with the middle vowel.

example	instead of	meaning
اُغْزُ!	اُغْزُوْ	Invade!
لَمْ يَغْزُ	يَغْزُوْ	Did not invade.
	We have to cut (جَزْمٌ) the last syllable. If we did not delete the weak letter, we would pronounce it as a long vowel: "uu".	
اِرْمِ	اِرْمِيْ	Throw!
لَمْ يَرْمِ	يَرْمِيْ	Did not throw.
اِرْضَ	اِرْضَىْ	Approve! (or: be satisfied!)
لَمْ يَرْضَ	يَرْضَىْ	Did not approve (was not satisfied).

91. The verb يدعون. What does it mean?

Without vowel markers (and further context), we can't tell.

Roots with weak letters may lead you into a wrong direction. Roots with three hard consonants do not produce double interpretations because none of the three radicals can disappear. This is different in roots with weak letters.

In the table below, without vowel markers, the following verbs in the present tense (الْمُضارِعُ) look the same in the plural form *they:* يدعون . However, they have different roots and mean different things!

verb	meaning	suffix	form	past/present	root
يَدَعُونَ	*they (people) let, put down*	وْنَ	I فَعَلَ	وَدَعَ يَدَعُ	و-د-ع
	The first root letter is weak. The و drops in the present tense. But why is that? Here, the فَتْحةٌ is the **characteristic vowel of the present tense** (الْمُضارِعُ). A rule says that verbs starting with و, which have a ضَمّةٌ or فَتْحةٌ as the characteristic vowel of the present tense (= vowel on second root letter), **retain** the و. For example: *to be afraid* (وَجِلَ - يَوْجَلُ); *to be a man of dis-*				

tinction (وَجَّهَ - يَوَجَّهُ). But why is the و deleted in our example? Why is it not يَوْدَعُ؟ It is an exception!

The reason lies in a different root letter. The فَتْحة of the present tense (imperfect) owes its existence only to the fact of the second or – in this example – third radical. This is true for **guttural** or **semi-guttural** consonants such as ع or ر. Remark: The verb وَدَعَ is <u>not</u> used in the past tense (only present and imperative!)

يَدَعُّونَ	*they (people; m.) rebuff*	وْنَ	I فَعَلَ	دَعَّ يَدَعُّ	د-ع-ع

يَدْعُونَ	*they (people; masc.) call*	وْنَ	I		
	The suffix needs a ضَمّة before وْنَ. Otherwise, we can't pronounce it. According to the rules, if we just added the suffix, we'd get يَدْعُوُوْنَ. This is impossible to pronounce. So, the 3rd radical is elided between th short vowel and the long vowel *"uu"*. Plus, the two vowels are contracted into a long vowel. So, we delete the weak letter of the root.			دَعَا يَدْعُو	
يَدْعُوْنَ	*they (women) call*	نَ	I		د-ع-و
	Nothing happens; you just add the suffix. Note that there is a سُكُونٌ on every long vowel: يَدْعُوْ.				
يَدَّعُّونَ	*they (people; m.) allege*	وْنَ	VIII إِفْتَعَلَ يَفْتَعِل	إِدَّعَى يَدَّعِي	
	This is a special situation. The suffix needs ضَمّةٌ before the وْنَ, otherwise you can't pronounce it. Therefore, we delete the weak letter which has the shape of ي because according to the pattern, we need a كَسْرةٌ in the middle root letter. Therefore, the weak letter at the end of يَدَّعِي must be ي. Since this ي can't carry a ضَمّة, we delete the ي, put a ضَمّةٌ on what is now the last letter – and add the suffix.				

92. What happens when ن and ب collide?

The ن is pronounced as م.

The phenomenon that consonants assimilate or even change due to phonetics has little to do with grammar, but since it sometimes irritates it, it is worth taking a look at. Let's check the word أَنْبا which denotes *bishop* in Arabic; more precisely, it is a high ecclesiastic title of the Coptic Church, preceding the names of bishops and saints. It is pronounced "*Amba*" and not "*Anba*". **Why is that?** It has to do with the assimilation of consonants in Arabic, in our example, with م and ن.

a) **The م is akin to a *labial*,** i.e., uttered with the participation of one or both lips. ➡ The ن becomes م **before** a dental (only in **pronunciation**). In Arabic, the ن is pronounced as م occasionally before ب like in our example أَنْبا ("*amba*").

b) **The ن is a *dental*;** a consonant articulated with the tongue against the upper teeth. ➡ The ن becomes م **before** a labial (in pronunciation). This is sometimes not pronounced as such – but **written**. For example: The ن in the VII-verb pattern (اِنْفَعَلَ) is getting absorbed by the first radical م: "immahā" (اِمَّحَى) instead of اِنْمَحَى for *to be obliterated*. Present tense: يَمَّحِي. The root is م-ح-ي.

In Qur'an reading styles, the ن is the most special letter. It often gets absorbed when it has a سُكُون on it and is followed by ب; this process is called الْإِقْلابُ. Let's check some examples.

root	remarks	meaning	how it is pronounced	word
ن-ب-ح	مَصْدَر of the IV-form	*making (a dog) bark*	'imbāh	إِنْباحٌ
ن-ب-ء	This is the plural of نَبَأٌ.	*news*	'ambā'	أَنْباءٌ
ن-ب-ش	Note that the plural أَنابِيشُ is pronounced with "*n*".	*torn out root or tree*	'umbuush	أُنْبوشٌ
ن-ب-و	This is the plural of نَبِيٌّ.	*prophets*	'ambiyā'	أَنْبِياءُ
ن-ب-ه	مَصْدَر of the II-form	*warning*	tambīh	تَنْبِيهٌ

ب-ر-ح	Used in Egyptian Arabic.	*yesterday*	*'imbārih*	إِمْبارِح
	The root means *to move* or *go away*; in Standard Arabic, the word الْبَارِحَة means *yesterday*.			

A dwarf; of small stature; plural form: تَنابِيلُ.		*timbāl*	تِنْبال
Pipe, tube; knot in a cane. The plural أَنابِيبُ is pronounced with "*n*" because the ن doesn't have سُكُونٌ; nor is it immediately followed by a ب.		*'umbuub*	أُنْبُوبٌ

Another example is the name *'Ahmad ibn Hanbal* (أَحْمَد بن حَنْبَل), occasionally pronounced *Hambal*. He was a Muslim theologian of the late 8th century and founded the strictest Islamic school of law.

93. What is the *Hā' of silence*?

The Hā' of silence (هاءُ السَّكْتِ) *is a* ه *with* سُكُونٌ. *It is an extra letter that is placed at the end of the last word of a sentence – when the reader pauses or stop there.*

We look at a letter that appears sometimes but has no grammatical meaning. The intriguing ه is found in seven verses of the Qur'an. When do we most likely encounter it? If a preposition (حَرْفُ الْجَرِّ) precedes ما, then the Aleph of the ما should (some say must) be deleted and shortened to مَ. In such a situation, the مَ and the preposition get united. We eventually get لِمَ, بِمَ, عَمَّ, etc.

The accent is transferred from مَ to the preceding syllable. Instead of, for example, "*bi-maa*", it is: "*bima*". If you stop at this word, you should compensate the deleted Aleph with a هاءُ السَّكْتِ – *the H of silence.*

why	لِمَهْ	pause + ما + لِ
with what	بِمَهْ	pause + ما + بِ
about what	عَمَّهْ	pause + ما + عَنْ
	Notice that ن plus م merge to a double م.	

Why do we need the ٥? You need it because you **can't stop at a vowel!**

If we had مْا, this would mean that we could stop at a سُكُونٌ. But we have a vowel now on the last letter of the word. That is the reason why we use the ٥ to compensate the deleted Aleph. This *H of silence* is not only applied to the vowel "*a*" (فَتْحَةٌ) – it can be used with any vowel.

| Sura 2:259 | God said, 'No, you stayed like that for a hundred years. Look at your food and drink: they have not gone bad. | قَالَ بَل لَّبِثْتَ مِائَةَ عَامٍ فَانظُرْ إِلَىٰ طَعَامِكَ وَشَرَابِكَ لَمْ يَتَسَنَّهْ. |

Remark: Scholars suggested that the هَاءُ السَّكْتِ could be the origin of the letter ة: the تَاءٌ مَرْبُوطَةٌ. This could have happened after the omission of the ت, i.e., the elision of the final consonant (تَرْخِيمٌ) for matters of euphony. This linguistic term denotes a harmonious succession of words having a pleasing sound). In some dialects, the ة is – regarding the pronunciation – close to a ٥ (*see question #48*).

Excursus: Why does Arabic use the letter ة? The ending "-*at*" is typical for Semitic languages, especially for feminine nouns. In many Semitic languages, however, the *t* is omitted when it is used as a final letter. This happens in Arabic, Hebrew, and Aramaic. Thus, we could say that the Arabic letter ة is a compromise between the original تـ ـ ending ("*at*"), the old pausal form ٥ ـ ("*ah*") and how we pronounce the ending until today: ٥ ـ ("*a*").

Arabic still knows some **remnants of the old "t"-ending.** In Arabic, it was common to keep the ت when it was preceded by an Aleph, resulting in ات. It is possible that this ات-form developed from an older ٥ا-form. The central square in Riyadh in Saudi-Arabia is called الصَّفاة but it is pronounced الصَّفات. It may have been the case that people once said الصَّفاه – but certainly not الصَّفا. Almost all words that should be spelled with ٥ا are spelled with ات. See *question #93* for a possible origin of the letter ة.

How do **other Semitic languages** treat the final *h* or *t*? In Hebrew, the *final t* had already disappeared in the earliest form of written texts and was substituted by the letter He (ה). However, in Biblical and Modern Hebrew, the letter Taf (ת) is written as well as pronounced in possessive constructions (סְמִיכוּת) instead of He (ה) – whereas in Arabic, in the corresponding إِضافةٌ-constructions, you only **pronounce** ة as "*t*" but **don't write** it as ت.

94. What is the energetic form of a verb?

The emphasis with the extra letter Nūn (نُون).

If you want to give a verb more force and emphasis, you can use the letter Nūn (ن). There's a *light* (نُونٌ خَفِيفَةٌ) and a *heavy Nūn* (نُونٌ ثَقِيلَةٌ):

1	I swear to God, the diligent will succeed.	وَاللهِ لَيُفْلِحَنَّ الْمُجِدُّ.
2	I will (for sure) seek goodness.	لَأَسْعَيَنَّ فِي الْخَيْرِ.

We have a verb in the present tense (مُضارِعٌ) which has an indeclinable, fixed shape (مَبْنِيٌّ عَلَى الْفَتْحِ), built on the vowel *"a"* (marked in gray). Verbs in the present tense usually get a case marker (in our examples, it would be a ضَمّةٌ).

This leads us to the grammatical implications. What will happen to a verb if it is connected to a ن for emphasis? Answer: You have to cement the **last root letter**. We say that the verb's last letter is structured, indeclinable (مَبْنِيٌّ) on the فَتْح ("a"-sound) if the verb is immediately connected to the *Nūn* (نُونُ التَّوْكِيدِ الْمُباشِرة). This means that it must not be separated by any kind of separation (فاصِلٌ).

So much for the theory. But what happens if the نُون does not follow immediately? First of all, this would mean that there must be "something" (فاصِلٌ) between the نُون and the verb stem. What could that be?

- the dual Aleph (أَلِف الْإِثْنَيْنِ);
- the وَاوٌ-suffix of the masculine plural (واوُ الْجَماعةِ);
- the ي-suffix (ياءُ الْمُخاطَبةِ) of the feminine singular (*you*);

Now hang on: In such situations the verb is **declinable** (مُعْرَبٌ)! It gets mood markers.

1	Oh diligent people, you will succeed!	لَتَنْجَحُنَّ أَيُّها الْمُجِدُّونَ!

How did we get the form تَنْجَحُنَّ? Well, we started from here:

نَّ	+	تَنْجَحُونَ

This, however, would mean that three *Nūn* (ن) collide:

1. The **marker for the indicative mood** (نُونُ الرَّفْعِ). In this example, since we have the plural form *they*, we get the ending ونَ.

2. The *heavy Nūn* (نُونُ التَّوْكِيدِ الثَّقِيلَةُ) which consists of **two** ن. The first one is "silent" (نُونٌ ساكِنةٌ). The second one carries a vowel; the نُونْ is "movable" (نُونٌ مُتَحَرِّكَةٌ); in grammar speech: **vowelled**.

Finally, we get:

emphasis				regular verb form: *you*, plural m.				
5		4		3		2		1
نَ	+	نْ	+	نَ	+	وْ	+	تَنْجَحُ

What should we do in such a situation? First, we delete the نُون الرَّفْع which is number 3 above. Arabic does not like the succession of two identical letters (تَوالِي حَرْفَيْنِ مِن جِنْسٍ واحِدٍ). We can't merge them because there is no "triple Nūn" in the shape of a single letter in Arabic. So, what is the function of this ن? It is the marker of the mood! Don't forget that the **nominative case has four markers**: ن – ا – و – ضَمّةٌ. The ن indicates the indicative mood in the so-called *five verbs* (الأَفْعالُ الْخَمْسةُ). We have such a form here (see *question #32*).

This, however, leads to another problem. → The situation that two سُكُونٌ would collide which Arabic doesn't like as well.

5		4		2		1
نَ	+	نْ	+	وْ	+	تَنْجَحُ

How can we fix that? As a second step, we delete the و (which is number 2). From a grammatical point of view, this means that we got rid of the visible subject in the word. What's the evaluation now? It becomes quite abstract.

We have a verb in the present tense, indicative mood (فِعْلٌ مُضارِعٌ مَرْفُوعٌ). Regarding the mood marker and the subject, for the analysis, we pretend that we have not deleted anything. What is the marker of the indicative mood (عَلامةُ الرَّفْعِ)? It is the firmness of the [**deleted**] Nūn, i.e., نَ. The Nūn had to be dropped because Arabic doesn't like the continuous succession of two similar letters (الأَمْثال). In Arabic, we'd say فِعْلٌ مُضارِعٌ مَرْفُوعٌ بِثُبُوتِ النُّونِ الْمَحْذُوفةِ لِتَوالِي الْأَمْثالِ.

What about the subject (الْفَاعِلُ)? It is the **deleted و**, i.e., the pronoun which is in the position of a nominative case. It had to be deleted to get rid of the collision of the two سُكُونٌ, a problem called اِلْتِقَاءُ السّاكِنَيْنِ. The final *Nūn* is indeclinable; it is only there for emphasis (حَرْفُ تَوْكِيدٍ). It does not have a place in إِعْرَابٌ. Finally, we arrive at تَنْجَحُنَّ.

Watch out: The vowel markers matter because there is a regular verb form that looks the same if all diacritical signs are left out.

You succeed.	تَنْجَحْنَ
This is the regular verb form for the plural *you* (fem.).	

Now, how do we arrive at لَتَنْجَحِنَّ (*verily, you (f.) succeed!*)? For this expression, we need the following ingredients:

1		2		3
نَّ	+	تَنْجَحِينَ	+	لَ

In fact, we have the same situation as above: three نُون would collide. So, we delete the ن which marks the (indicative) mood in the verb.

تَنْجَحِيْنٌ	←	تَنْجَحِيْ + نْ + نَ

However, this would mean that two سُكُونٌ collided: the one above the long vowel ي (above the يَاءُ الْمُخَاطَبةِ) and the other one above the first نْ of the doubled نُون (the so-called النُّونُ الْأُولَى مِن التَّوْكِيدِ).

How can we fix that? We delete the ي in exchange for a كَسْرةٌ on the letter before the ي. The complete analysis in Arabic sounds like this:

لَتَنْجَحِنَّ	فِعْلٌ مُضَارِعٌ مَرْفُوعٌ بِثُبُوتِ النُّونِ الْمَحْذُوفةِ لِإِلْتِقَاءِ الْأَمْثالِ، وَالْيَاءُ الْمَحْذُوفةُ لِإِلْتِقَاءِ السّاكِنَيْنِ فَاعِلٌ مَبْنِيٌّ عَلَى السُّكُونِ فِي مَحَلِّ رَفْعٍ، وَالنُّونُ حَرْفُ تَوْكِيدٍ مَبْنِيٌّ عَلَى الْفَتْحِ لا مَحَلَّ لَهُ مِن الْإِعْرَابِ.

95. Come to prayer! (حَيَّ عَلَى الصَّلاةِ). What form is حَيَّ؟

It is a so-called اِسْمُ الْفِعْلِ.

It is not so easy to find a suitable English term for the expression اِسْمُ الْفِعْلِ. Some call it *verbal noun*; let's call it *quasi-verb* or, more precisely, an *interjection denoting a sense of a verb*. Such **nouns point to the meaning of a verb** and carry its meaning as well as its time and function. We could say that we actually deal with a "**hybrid**". There are some important things you should know:

- Such words are **not pure nouns** (اِسْمٌ). Other than nouns, a اِسْمُ الْفِعْلِ conveys a meaning on itself only when it is linked to <u>time</u>.

- We also **don't call them pure verbs** because they don't carry the signs and markers of verbs (the usual endings).

- All forms of the اِسْمُ الْفِعْلِ are **indeclinable** (مَبْنِيٌّ).

- Furthermore, they are **not affected by other parts** of the sentence. In other words, they don't have an operator (عَامِلٌ) and don't have a position in إِعْرَابٌ.

- However, a اِسْمُ الْفِعْلِ has the **governing power** of a verb and works as an operator (عَامِلٌ). It induces cases in other words.

- Therefore, it **can carry a direct object** (مَفْعُولٌ بِهِ) which gets the accusative case (مَنْصُوبٌ). This object, however, can never precede but can **only follow** the اِسْمُ الْفِعْلِ. Note: In general, the direct object can only be brought forward if the regent is a "real" verb.

In grammar, the اِسْمُ الْفِعْلِ is classified by the time (tense) to which it relates. Therefore, we have **three types:**

A. Conveying the **imperative** (اِسْمُ فِعْلِ أَمْرٍ or اِسْمُ الْفِعْلِ مِنَ الْأَمْرِ).

This is the most common type. Many exclamations have a certain verbal force comparable to an imperative.

	equivalent	اِسْمُ الْفِعْلِ
Hush! Silence!	أُسْكُتْ!	صَهْ!
Stop! Give up! Let alone!	كُفَّ! or أُكْفُفْ!	مَهْ!
Come! Come to prayer! (حَيَّ عَلَى الصَّلَاةِ)	أَقْبِلْ! or عَجِّلْ!	حَيَّ!
Amen! (to hear/answer a prayer)	(اللَّهُمَّ) اِسْتَجِبْ!	آمِينَ!

Christians use the word *Amen* a lot. *Amen* is probably of Aramaic origin: אמין meaning *strong, enduring, true, lasting, eternal*. In Hebrew, אָמֵן (pronounced *"amén"*) denotes *so be it; truly*. From Hebrew, it perhaps entered ancient Greek (ἀμήν) from where it spread to other languages.

Muslims say *'Āmīn* as well, for example, after having read the first Sura *al-Fātiha* (سُورَةُ الْفاتِحَةِ). Linguists suggested that the ī, the *Aleph Madd* (أَلِفُ الْمَدِّ), in آمِين is there to provide the fullness of the sound *"a"* (فَتْحَةٌ). What supports this idea is the fact that there is no word in Arabic that follows the pattern فَاعِيلٌ.

Make haste! Hurry up to school! (هَيّا إِلَى الْمَدْرَسِةِ)	أَسْرِعْ!	هَيّا!
Come here! Bring here!	قَرّبْ! or إِقْتَرِبْ!	هَلُمَّ!

Let's analyze a sentence.

Karīm, hush!	صَهْ يا كَرِيمُ!

Quasi-verb (اِسْمُ فِعْلِ أَمْرٍ). It has an indeclinable shape (مَبْنِيٌّ عَلَى السُّكُونِ). It does not have a place in إِعْرابٌ which means it is not governed by anything. What about the subject (فاعِلٌ)? It is a hidden pronoun (ضَمِيرٌ مُسْتَتِرٌ) with the meaning of *you* (أَنْتَ).	صَهْ

Many common expressions fit into this category. Originally, they were **prepositional phrases** (الْجارُّ وَالْمَجْرورُ) or **adverbs of place** (ظَرْفُ مَكانٍ) but they now have the **meaning of an imperative**. Grammarians call such expressions a اِسْمُ فِعْلٍ مَنْقُولٌ (*transposed*).

translation	equivalent meaning	اِسْمُ الْفِعْلِ
There it is for you! (You take this!)	Take it (خُذْها إِلَيْكَ)!	إِلَيْكَها!
There is my hand for you!	Take my hand (خُذْ يَدِي)!	هاكَ يَدِي!
Take the book (said to a woman)!	You (f.) take (خُذِي)!	هاكِ الْكِتابَ!
		إِلَيْكِ الْكِتابَ!
Seize Karīm!	Seize Karīm who is in front of!	عَلَيْكَ كَرِيمًا!

	Seize Karīm who is beside you!	عِنْدَكَ كَرِيمًا!
	Get hold of K. who is close to you!	دُونَكَ كَرِيمًا!
Take him!	Take (خُذْ)!	دُونَكَهُ!
Get away from me!	Move away (إِبْتَعِدْ)!	إِلَيْكَ عَنِّي!
Take him!	Take (خُذْ)!	دُونَكَهُ!
Get away from me!	Move away (إِبْتَعِدْ)!	إِلَيْكَ عَنِّي!
You must be honest!	You have to (إِلْزَمْ)!	عَلَيْكَ الصِّدْقَ!
Move on! Forward!	Move forward (تَقَدَّمْ)!	أَمامَكَ!
Backward!	Fall behind! (تَأَخَّرْ)	وَراءَكَ!
Stay in your place!	Stand firm! (اُثْبُتْ)	مَكانَكَ!
It has several meanings: *Up! Come on! Onward!* With a word in the مَنْصُوب-case, it means: *Give me/us...! Bring...!*		هَلُمَّ!

Let's analyze عَلَيْكَ.

This is **not a preposition**! It is treated as a إِسْمُ فِعْلِ أَمْرٍ which is in-declinable (مَبْنِيٌّ) and fixed on the سُكُونٌ; no place in إِعْرابٌ.	عَلَى
Pronominal suffix (حَرْفُ خِطابٍ); no position in إِعْرابٌ. The subject (فاعِلٌ) is an implied pronoun (ضَمِيرٌ مُسْتَتِرٌ): *you* (أَنْتَ).	كَ

Another interesting pattern (وَزْنٌ) falls into this category: فَعالِ. This pattern has a fixed shape and can be **used for all I-form verbs** that can be fully conjugated (فِعْلٌ ثُلاثِيٌّ تامٌّ مُتَصَرِّفٌ). Note that this pattern also conveys the meaning of the imperative (أَمْرٌ).

translation	meaning	إِسْمُ الْفِعْلِ
Beware of doing... (أَنْ)!		
Beware of something (مِنْ)! Watch out for (مِنْ)!	إِحْذَرْ!	حَذارِ
Watch out for bad friends!		حَذارِ مِنْ صَدِيقِ السُّوءِ!

إِسْمُ فِعْلِ أَمْرٍ is derived from the root حَذِرَ (*to be cautious*). It is a إِسْمُ فِعْلِ أَمْرٍ which has an indeclinable shape (مَبْنِيٌّ عَلَى الْكَسْرِ) and always stays the same. It does not have a place in إِعْرَابٌ. What is the subject (فَاعِلٌ) here? It is a hidden, implied pronoun (ضَمِيرٌ مُسْتَتِرٌ) expressing *you* (أَنْتَ).

Other examples:

translation	meaning	إِسْمُ الْفِعْلِ
Go down!	إِنْزِلْ!	نَزَالِ
Listen!	إِسْمَعْ!	سَماعِ

Some words relate to the مَصْدَرٌ and can be difficult to grasp, for example, رُوَيْدَكَ (*Take it easy!*). In fact, this is a diminutive (تَصْغِيرٌ) of the مَصْدَرٌ of the root ر-و-د which conveys the meaning of *gentleness;* or *a leisurely manner of acting or proceeding.*

Calm down (slowly), my brother!	رُوَيْدَكَ يا أَخِي!
Slow down, Zayd!	رُوَيْدَكَ زَيْدًا!

The expression رُوَيْدَكَ is a إِسْمُ فِعْلِ أَمْرٍ and has the meaning of أَمْهِلْ. It has an indeclinable ending (مَبْنِيٌّ); it does not have a place in إِعْرَابٌ. The same is true for ك, a *particle of address* (حَرْفُ خِطابٍ). Subject (فَاعِلٌ) is a hidden pronoun (ضَمِيرٌ مُسْتَتِرٌ) which expresses *you* (أَنْتَ).

Notice that رُوَيْد is not always used in the meaning of an imperative.

Without the ك it is an *absolute object* (مَفْعُولٌ مُطْلَقٌ)	Take it easy, my brother. (In the meaning of: you give someone more time.)	رُوَيْدًا أَخِي.
Here, it is a حالٌ	They walked gently.	جاؤُوا رُوَيْدًا.
Used as a نَعْتٌ	They walked softly and slowly.	سارُوا سَيْرًا رُوَيْدًا.

Sura 86:17	فَمَهِّلِ الْكَافِرِينَ أَمْهِلْهُمْ رُوَيْدًا.

[Prophet], let the disbelievers be, let them be for a while. (*A. Haleem*).

رُوَيْدًا is an adjective for the **deleted absolute object** (نَعْتٌ لِمَفْعُولٍ مُطْلَقٍ مَحْذُوفٍ). The deleted part would be: إِمْهالًا رُوَيْدًا.

B. Conveying the meaning of the **past tense** (إِسْمُ فِعْلٍ ماضٍ).

There are not many.

translation	meaning	إِسْمُ الْفِعْلِ
What a difference between x and y! How different they are...	إِفْتَرَقَ or بَعُدَ or عَظُمَ!	شَتّانَ
It needs a **subject** that points to **two** things. The distance between the two things must be immense or distant. It can be followed by ما بَيْنَ or أَوْ, ما.		

Some examples:

How different are seriousness and carelessness! (Diligence and carelessness are two different things!)	شَتّانَ الْجِدُّ وَالْإِهْمالُ!
There is a great difference between Karīm and Zayd!	شَتّانَ ما كَرِيمٌ وزَيْدٌ!
How different they both are! (There is a great difference between the two! = They are not alike at all!)	شَتّانَ بَيْنَهُما!

What about the grammatical analysis?

This is a إِسْمُ فِعْلٍ ماضٍ which is indeclinable (مَبْنِيٌّ); thus, it always ends like this. It does not have a place in إِعْرابٌ.	شَتّانَ
Subject (فاعِلٌ) in the nominative case (مَرْفُوعٌ).	الْجِدُّ
Conjunction (حَرْفُ عَطْفٍ); it does not have a place in إِعْرابٌ (لا مَحَلَّ لَها مِن الْإِعْرابِ).	وَ
This is the مَعْطُوفٌ for the (coupled) noun that is placed before and (و). Therefore, it has to get the nominative (مَرْفُوعٌ) case too.	الْإِهْمالُ

Other examples:

How quickly…!	سَرْعَانَ or سُرْعَانَ or سِرْعَانَ!
How slowly…!	بُطْآنَ
How quickly is this coming forth! (meaning: سَرُعَ ذَا خُرُوجًا)	سَرْعَانَ ذَا خُرُوجًا!

How quickly were you doing that!	لَسَرْعَانَ مَا صَنَعْتَ كَذَا!

But oh! Wrong! What an idea! How absurd!	هَيْهَاتُ - هَيْهَاتَ - هَيْهَاتِ

The إِسْمُ فِعْلٍ مَاضٍ in the meaning of *to be distant* (بَعُدَ). Occasionally, ل plus مَا is inserted.

It is absolutely out of the question that...	هَيْهَاتَ أَنْ...
And how impossible is this to you!	وَهَيْهَاتَ لَكَ ذَلِكَ!
How far he is from doing so!	يَفْعَلَ كَذَا هَيْهَاتَ!

C. Conveying the meaning of **present tense** (إِسْمُ فِعْلٍ مُضَارِعٍ).

Such constructions are very rare.

translation	meaning of	إِسْمُ الْفِعْلِ
Oh!	I suffer pain (أَتَوَجَّعُ)	أَوَّهْ!
Ugh!	I am angry (أَتَضَجَّرُ)	أُفٍّ or أُفَّ or أُفِّ!

Oh from the rule of oppressors!	أَوَّهْ مِنْ حُكْمِ الظَّالِمِينَ!

This is a إِسْمُ فِعْلٍ مُضَارِعٍ which is indeclinable (مَبْنِيٌّ). Therefore, it always ends with سُكُونٌ; it doesn't have a place in إِعْرَابٌ. The subject is an implied pronoun (ضَمِيرٌ مُسْتَتِرٌ) having the meaning of *I* (أَنَا).	أَوَّهْ

96. *Give!* (هَاتِ). What form is that?

It is a quasi-verb (إِسْمُ فِعْلِ أَمْرٍ) conveying the imperative.

You will hear the expression هَات (masculine singular) in dialects (Egyptian Arabic) when people order in restaurants or at the market.

But the expression هَاتِ is also found in the Qur'an! The main meaning is *bring!* or *give!* (أَعْطِنِي) but it can also have other, figurative significations, e.g., قُلْ مَا عِنْدَكَ (*say it!*). **Watch out:** Never use this quasi-verb in a prohibitive matter! Now, let's see some examples.

Give me...! Bring me...!	هَاتِ لِي...
Bring me the cup!	هَاتِ الْفِنْجَانَ!
Man, say it! (Lit.: Give me what you have!)	هَاتِ يَا رَجُلُ مَا عِنْدَكَ!
What's on you? (Lit.: Give me what you have!)	هَاتِ مَا عِنْدَكَ؟
Come forward/hasten to the battle!	هَاتُوا يَا رِجَالُ إِلَى الْمَعْرَكَةِ!

هَاتِ cannot be used universally! This اِسْمُ فِعْلِ أَمْرٍ has different forms:

singular	masculine	لِلْمُفْرَدِ الْمُذكَّرِ	يَا رَجُلُ	هَاتِ
	feminine	لِلْمُفْرَدةِ الْمُؤَنَّثةِ	يَا امْرَأَةُ	هَاتِي
dual	masculine	لِلْمُثَنَّى بِنَوْعَيْهِ	يَا رَجُلَانِ	هَاتِيَا
	feminine		يَا امْرَأَتَانِ	
plural	masculine	لِجَماعةِ الذُّكُورِ	هَاتُوا يَا رِجَالُ	هَاتُوا
	feminine	لِجَماعةِ الْإِناثِ	هَاتِينَ يَا نِسَاءُ	هَاتِينَ

In the Qur'an, the plural forms of هَاتِ are used four times.

Sura 27:64	Say, "Show me your evidence then, if what you say is true."	قُلْ هَاتُوا بُرْهَانَكُمْ ن كُنْتُمْ صَادِقِينَ.

Excursus: The origin of هَاتِ is not entirely clear. Some trace it back to the Arabic root ه-ي-ت. The II-verb هَيَّتَ بِ denotes *to cry out*. Others suggested that it entered Arabic from Hebrew, Syriac, or Coptic. Some scholars indicated that the form relates to an imperative of the IV-form (أَفْعَلَ). This has to do with the first letter ه and its analogy to Hebrew.

meaning	regular form	
The original meaning is related to the verb *to come* (أَتَى). Today it has the meaning of *bring!*	آتِ	هَاتِ
to wish	أَرَادَ - يُرِيدُ	هَرَادَ

أَفْعَلَ corresponds in form and signification to the Hebrew verb pattern הִפְעִיל which takes the prefix ה in the imperative. So, what is the relation? In Hebrew, the prefix "h" (ה) is often used when Arabic (and Aramaic) would use an Aleph. Some traces of the *h* (ה) are still found in Arabic. Others suggested that هَاتِ is the imperative of the pattern فَاعَلَ assuming that the underlying verb is هتى.

97. Why does the Arabic word for *Caliph* (خَلِيفَةٌ) have a ة?

It is an old abstract noun which later was used to denote males. Others have suggested that the ة is there to intensify the meaning.

Morphemic gender is the visual gender sign of a word. Such signs are the ة or ات-plural suffix which are used for feminine nouns; وُنَ and يِنَ are used for masculine (plural) nouns. However, there is also the **natural gender.** According to Islamic sources, it is nearly impossible that a woman becomes the Caliph.[5] This means that خَلِيفَةٌ (plural: خَلَائِفُ or خُلَفَاءُ), the Arabic word for *Caliph* (= *successor*), is feminine in form but **semantically masculine** (masculine in meaning).

The تَاءٌ مَرْبُوطَةٌ doesn't always indicate the feminine gender. Instead, it may just signify **intensiveness** (لِلْمُبَالَغَةِ) or even strengthen the idea of intensiveness (لِتَأْكِيدِ الْمُبَالَغَةِ). Strangely many common words which you would consider masculine end in ة. Such a ة is also called التَّاءُ لِلْمُبَالَغَةِ. Three forms are capable of taking a ة to give more emphasis.

1. The **active participle** (فَاعِلٌ) – and its **intensifying form** فَاعِلَةٌ.

Active participle: One who hands down poems or historical facts by oral tradition.	رَاوٍ
The intensifying form of رَاوٍ denotes *a traditionary*.	رَاوِيَةٌ

2. **Forms of exaggeration** (صِيغَةُ الْمُبَالَغَةِ), let's call them **intensifying adjectives.** With the ة you can even add more intensity or emphasis.

- The form فُعَلٌ – and even more intensifying: فُعَلَةٌ.

fault-finder, captious critic, caviler, carper	لُمَزَةٌ

5   The Prophet said: *"A people who make a woman their ruler will never be successful."* (لَنْ يُفْلِحَ قَوْمٌ وَلَّوْا أَمْرَهُمُ امْرَأَةً). Saḥīḥ al-Bukhārī 7099

breaking in pieces, crushing to bits	حُطَمَةٌ
Remark: حُطَمَةٌ is a word for *hell* in the Qur'an. It describes *a crushing fire which causes everything to burst*.	

Sura 104:5	What will explain to you what the Crusher is?	وَمَا أَدْرَاكَ مَا الْحُطَمَةُ؟

- The form فَعَّالٌ – and more intensifying فَعَّالَةٌ.

A very learned	عَلَّامَةٌ

A great traveler	رَحَّالَةٌ

3. An adjective resembling the active participle (الصِّفَةُ الْمُشَبَّهَةُ بِاسْمِ الْفَاعِلِ) of the pattern فَعِيلٌ. The intensifying form is فَعِيلَةٌ.

successor; Caliph	خَلِيفَةٌ

the best, the pick: wife, spouse	عَقِيلَةٌ

Some scholars say that خَلِيفَةٌ would fit into this category; others have suggested that خَلِيفَةٌ is an old abstract which now denotes males.

What verb form (**gender**) should we use for خَلِيفَةٌ? The feminine or the masculine? خَلِيفَةٌ is **masculine** (هُوَ مُذَكَّرٌ وَفِيهِ عَلامَةُ تَأْنِيثٍ) and it applies to males. → Verbs and adjectives must get the masculine form.

That's also true for **proper names** such as *Muʿāwiya* (مُعَاوِيَةٌ) or *Zechariah* (زَكَرِياءُ). Masculine names with ة are usually <u>diptotes</u> (مَمْنُوعٌ مِنَ الصَّرْفِ) like *Talha* (طَلْحَةُ), *Hamza* (حَمْزَةُ), *Muʿāwiya* (مُعَاوِيَةُ). The same is true for **pre-Islamic (masculine) names**, e.g., *Ibrahīm* (إِبْرَاهِيمُ) or *Zechariah* (زَكَرِياءُ). See *Arabic for Nerds 1*, #240.

1	It has been narrated that the prophet said: "This order will continue to be dominant until there have been **twelve Caliphs**." (*Sahīh Muslim 1821*)	قَالَ النَّبِيُّ: "لَا يَزَالُ هَذَا الْأَمْرُ عَزِيزًا إِلَى اثْنَيْ عَشَرَ خَلِيفَةً."
	In the Arabic word for *twelve*, the units (اثْنا plus عَشَرَ for the masculine form) have normal gender agreement with the **following** noun! The 2 in 12 is a dual and follows the usual declension of a dual. For example: • *for twelve years* (مُنْذُ اثْنَيْ عَشَّرَ عَامًا) • *twelve trees* (اثْنَتا عَشْرَةَ شَجَرَةً)	

2	The Prophet said: "There will be no prophet after me, but **there will be** Caliphs who **will increase** in number." (*Sahīh al-Bukhārī 3455*)	وَإِنَّهُ لَا نَبِيَّ بَعْدِي، وَسَيَكُونُ خُلَفَاءُ فَيَكْثُرُونَ.
	Notice the verb forms! Both are used in the masculine form; in singular (سَيَكُونُ) and plural (يَكْثُرُونَ).	

98. What is the plural of the word عَالَمٌ?

The word عَالَمٌ *means* **world**. *The plural form is* عَالَمُونَ.

The word عَالَمُونَ is very famous. It appears in the very beginning of the Qur'an, in the first Sura *The Opening* (سُورَةُ الْفَاتِحَة):

1:2	Praise belongs to Allah, Lord of the Worlds.	الْحَمْدُ لِلّٰهِ رَبِّ الْعَالَمِينَ.

The word الْعَالَمِينَ looks strange. It seems to be a sound masculine plural (جَمْعُ الْمُذَكَّرِ السَّالِمُ). The Arabic word سَالِمٌ denotes *sound, perfect*, or *complete*. In grammar, the term means that all the vowels and consonants of the singular are retained in it.

Sound masculine plurals have the suffix ونَ attached to signify the plural in the nominative case (مَرْفُوعٌ). In the genitive (مَجْرُورٌ) and accusative (مَنْصُوبٌ) case, the ending is ينَ. The last vowel (فَتْحَة), written on top of the ن in these plurals (ونَ and ينَ), is <u>not</u> a case ending. It is a part of the plural. The و and the ي mark the case!

Sound masculine plurals are only used for words which refer to **male human beings**. In other words, a non-human noun like *book* (كِتابٌ) can never have a sound masculine plural. Fair enough, but the *world* is definitely not human as well. So, is this theoretically possible at all?

Let's check the prerequisites for a sound masculine plural:

1	A singular form of the word exists.	أَنْ يَكُونَ لَهُ مُفْرَدٌ.
2	The singular form is masculine.	أَنْ يَكُونَ الْمُفْرَدُ مُذَكَّرًا.
3	We talk about people and not things.	أَنْ يَدُلَّ عَلَى عاقِلٍ.
4	The singular does not break or lose parts when forming a plural.	أَنْ يَسْلَمَ هذا الْمُفْرَدُ عِنْدَ الْجَمْعِ.

Now let's get back to the word عالَمٌ. The plural form عالَمُونَ is violating **condition 3**. That is true, but it is usually okay to use the sound masculine plural form if one of the prerequisites is violated. Then we can still treat it grammatically as a sound masculine plural. We call such a situation مُلْحَقٌ بِجَمْعِ الْمُذَكَّرِ السّالِمِ.

Another example is أُولُونَ. You normally see it without a نْ at the end (أُولُو and not أُولُونَ) which is due to the fact that أُولُونَ exclusively works as the first part of a إِضافةٌ. The word means *possessors* (synonym: أَصْحابٌ) and does not have a singular form ➡ it violates **condition 1**.

The corresponding singular would be ذُو. It is counted as one of the *five (six) nouns* and therefore either ends in و or ي depending on the case it gets (يُرْفَعُ بِالْوَاوِ وَيُنْصَبُ وَيُجَرُّ بِالياءِ كَالْأَسْمَاءِ السِّتَّةِ). The word أُولُو is found many times in the Qur'an.

Sura 39:9	Only they will remember [who are] people of understanding.	إِنَّمَا يَتَذَكَّرُ أُولُو الْأَلْبَابِ.
Sura 40:54	As a guide and a reminder to people of understanding. (Note: Here we need the genitive case which is achieved by the ي.)	هُدًى وَذِكْرَىٰ لِأُولِي الْأَلْبَابِ.

Also some numbers don't have a singular form:

forty	أَرْبَعُونَ

twenty	عِشْرُونَ

Watch out: The first و in أُولُو is treated as a short vowel; و is only **written** in order to distinguish it from other words. In older texts, you may encounter أُلُو. This also happens in أُولَى (a plural of ذٰلِكَ - *that*).

that (singular)	اذ or ذِي	↔	*that* (plural); the و is pronounced as a **short** vowel.	أُولَى
			The و may have been inserted so that people don't confuse أُلَى with the preposition إِلَى (*to*).	
first (masculine form)	أَوَّل	↔	*first* (feminine); the و is pronounced as the **long** vowel "*ū*" (وُأ).	أُولَى

99. Can a feminine word form a sound masculine plural?

Yes, such words exist.

Of course, not every arbitrary feminine noun can form a sound masculine plural. Two important conditions must be met for this to work:

- The single form of the word ends in a ة and
- the third radical, mostly a و or ي, has been deleted.

Then, the letter ة disappears in the plural! One example is the Arabic word for *year*: سَنةٌ. This word is interesting because the third radical letter و has been gotten rid of at some time but still appears in plural forms. There are two main plural forms for سَنةٌ:

- سَنَواتٌ – following the pattern of a sound **feminine** plural
- سِنُونَ – which has the shape of a sound **masculine** plural

Sura 17:12	...and that you may know the number of years and the account [of time].	...وَلِتَعْلَمُوا عَدَدَ السِّنِينَ وَالْحِسَابَ.

Grammarians treat السِّنِينَ, which is the plural in the genitive case marked by ي, as a sound masculine plural (مُلْحَقٌ بِجَمْعِ الْمُذَكَّرِ السّالِمِ). How come? In question #98, we listed **four conditions** that have to be fulfilled in order to form a **sound masculine plural**. In this example, condition 2 is violated: the **single** form is feminine and **not masculine**.

We also said that it is okay to form such a plural form if only one condition is violated. Therefore, سَنةٌ follows the rules of a sound masculine plural which results in سِنُونَ in the nominative case (مَرْفُوعٌ) and gets a ي in the accusative (مَنصُوبٌ) and genitive case (مَجْرُورٌ) resulting in سِنِينَ. This brings us to a widespread mistake which is related to the plural forms سِنُونَ and سِنِينَ. Some people drop the ن in a إضافةٌ-construction and instead put a شَدّةٌ on the ي resulting in سِنِيّ. This is wrong! The only thing you have to do is to **drop the Nūn**.

	He was lazy during his years of studying.	كانَ كَسُولاً طِوالَ سِنِيّ دِراسَتِهِ.
incorrect	Our main interest is the word سِنِينَ (*years*). The doubling of the ي, so-called تَضْعِيفٌ, is wrong.	

	...during his years of studying.	...طِوالَ سِنِي دِراسَتِهِ
correct	If you use a sound masculine plural as the first part of a إِضافَةٌ, you only delete the ن and nothing else.	

Another example is the Arabic word for *lung* (رِئَةٌ). The plural form can either be the sound masculine form رِئُونَ or the sound feminine plural form: رِئاتٌ. If you form an adjective (نِسْبَةٌ) from the noun رِئَةٌ, the و suddenly appears resulting in رِئَوِيٌّ which means *pulmonary, pneumonic*.

Another example is the Arabic word for *ball* (كُرَةٌ). The usual plural forms are كُراتٌ or كُرًى. But there once was also the sound masculine plural form كُرُونَ which is not used anymore.

LINKING TWO NOUNS (الإِضافَةُ) – POSSESSION & BELONGING

100. Why does the first part of a إِضافَةٌ not get nunation?

Because the word is specified (further determined) by the following word and thus loses its pure indefiniteness and sign for it (= nunation/تَنْوِينٌ).

The إِضافَةٌ-construction can show various relationships:

- **Possession** (A of B): *the book of the teacher* (كِتابُ الْمُدَرِّسِ).
- **Being part of something:** *a piece of meat* (قِطْعةُ لَحْمٍ). However, you usually use مِن in such situations (قِطْعةٌ مِن لَحْمٍ).
- **Belonging to a time:** *the rain in summer* (مَطَرُ الصَّيْفِ); or **space:** *the road to Syria* (طَرِيقُ الشّامِ).
- **Denoting the material from which something is made:** *a chair made of wood = a wooden chair* (كُرْسِيٌّ خَشَبٍ). However, you usually use the preposition مِن in such situations (كُرْسِيٌّ مِن خَشَبٍ)

The إِضافَةٌ-construction consists of two parts:

It takes the case marker according to the position and function in the sentence. Watch out: It **never gets nunation:** you only put ُ or ٍ or ِ	مُضافٌ	first word; governing word
This part is **always** in the **genitive** case (مَجْرُورٌ).	مُضافٌ	following word(s);

If it is indefinite, it takes nunation (تَنْوِينٌ). This means that we either have ٍ or ً .	إِلَيْهِ	governed word

If you don't know the difference between a *pure* and *figurative* إِضَافَةٌ, see *Arabic for Nerds 1, question #192.*

But why does the first word lose the nunation (تَنْوِينٌ) although it doesn't have the definite article?

Because it is <u>more determined, better described</u> (تَخْصِيصٌ) by the word that follows which makes it not completely undefined/indefinite anymore. When this is the situation, the اِسْمٌ gets shortened in pronunciation by getting rid of the *"n"*-sound:

a) تَنْوِينٌ (= nunation: *"-un"*, *"-an"*, *"-in"*). In other words, it loses the sign of true indefiniteness. We use the same vowels (markers) that we also use for definite words.

b) You delete the endings نِ (dual) or نَ (sound masculine plural). By getting rid of them, the speaker can quickly pass on to the determining word which indicates the relation between the two words.

101. How do you know if a إِضَافَةٌ-construction is definite?

By looking at the <u>second</u> part (مُضَافٌ إِلَيْهِ).

Possessive constructions do not follow the typical rules. The biggest irritation is that you cannot apply the definite article as usual. You need to treat إِضَافَةٌ-constructions as if you looked at it as a single entity. Only then you will know whether the expression denotes *<u>a</u>* or *<u>the</u>* thing in question. Otherwise, you will struggle to translate the construction.

A rule of thumb: The <u>second</u> (the last) part of a إِضَافَةٌ-construction defines whether we talk about a definite or indefinite expression.

If we break it down, we would get either "*<u>a</u> of a*" or "*<u>the</u> of <u>the</u>*". Theoretically, we can never arrive at "*a of the*" or "*the of a*".

translation (notice the articles!)	example	second part is...
the professor of **the** university	أُسْتَاذُ الْجَامِعِةِ	definite (مَعْرِفَةٌ)

the university professor		
a professor of a university = a university professor	أُسْتاذُ جامِعةٍ	indefinite (نَكِرةٌ)

In general, the first part (مُضافٌ) never gets the visual signs of definiteness (definite article الـ or possessive pronoun). So, could we say that the **first word** in such constructions is **in**definite? Not really.

- If the **last word** of the إِضافةٌ is <u>definite</u> (مَعْرِفةٌ), the entire expression is definite. We call this process تَعْريفٌ which means *identification, determination*. Although there is no visual sign of definiteness, the **first word takes on definiteness (اكْتِسابُ التَّعْريفِ)**.

- If the **last word** in the إِضافةٌ is <u>indefinite</u> (نَكِرةٌ), the whole expression is **indefinite**. We call that تَخْصيصٌ which means *specification; itemization; more closely determined.*

This may cause some vagueness.

This can only mean: *Zayd's house <u>is</u> big.*	بَيْتُ زَيْدٍ كَبيرٌ

Why? We treat the first part as definite because *Zayd* is a proper name which makes the entire expression **definite**. So, كَبيرٌ can only be the **predicate (خَبَرٌ)** – but not an adjective for one of the nouns.

This could mean two things: *in the big house of Zayd.* Or: *in old Zayd's house.* (old in the meaning of age)	فِي بَيْتِ زَيْدٍ الْكَبيرِ

الْكَبيرِ is an **adjective** and can relate to both words: *Zayd or house* – since both nouns are treated as **definite** and both take the **genitive (مَجْرُورٌ)**.

Watch out: Be prepared to break these rules for the sake of translating. Even if the first term (مُضافٌ) is grammatically <u>indefinite</u>, it may be rendered as a definite word, i.e., with the article *the* instead of *a*.

the (a) son of a mother	إِبْنُ أُمٍّ

The same happens the other way round. If the first term (مُضافٌ) is grammatically treated as <u>definite,</u> you may render it as an <u>indefinite</u> word. This occurs when we talk about **general things** (a) or when the noun refers to something of which there is **only one** (b).

a)	**a cup of tea**	كُوبُ الشَّاي
b)	**a map of the world**	خارِطَةُ الْعالَم
	***one** of them.* You don't say: *the one of them.*	أَحَدُهُمْ
	This goes for to the words أَحَدٌ, and بَعْضٌ, and غَيْرٌ, and مِثْلٌ. They are *nouns that apply the indefiniteness intensively,* that are **impregnated with incertitude, obscurity** (مُتَوَغِّلٌ فِي الْإِبْهامِ). They are always considered <u>indefinite</u>. See *Arabic for Nerds 1, #216.*	

Remark: إِضَافَةٌ-constructions with ابْنٌ or صاحِبٌ or أَبٌ are often translated as *master of, endowed with, possessor of.*

master of learning = learned	صاحِبُ عِلْم

102. Should you use ابْن or بْن?

Both are correct – but you have to know when to use which one.

Both words ابْن and بْن mean the same: *son.* You will encounter both spellings, إِبْن written with an initial, connecting Hamza (هَمْزَةُ الْوَصْلِ) and sometimes without (بْن). What is correct? Both – but you have to know when you should apply which spelling.

You write بْن – **without I** – when the following things are fulfilled:

Requirement 1: بْن is found **between two proper nouns** (بَيْنَ عَلَمَيْنِ).

Requirement 2: The word بْن works as an **adjective/attribute** (نَعْتٌ) or stands in **apposition** (بَدَلٌ) to the preceding word. Simply put: as a whole, the expression **doesn't form a sentence.** Otherwise, ابْن would serve as the predicate (خَبَرٌ). For example:

Verily, Muhammad is the son of Abdallah.	إِنَّ مُحَمَّدًا ابْنُ عَبْدِ اللهِ.
ابْنُ here is the predicate (خَبَرُ إِنَّ). It is **not an adjective** for Muhammad. See also *Arabic for Nerds 1, question #30.*	
Is Yāsir the son of Tamīm?	هَلْ ياسِرٌ ابْنُ تَمِيمٍ؟

In questions, we have a sentence consisting of **subject and predicate**. There-fore, you have to use ابْن.

Requirement 3: You only write بن when the name before بن **doesn't get nunation**. This is possible and has the effect that it weighs down the word and pronunciation (غَيْرُ مُنَوَّنٍ لِلتَّخْفِيفِ). Most importantly, the final letter is a vowel now and not the سُكُونٌ of the nunation (تَنْوِينٌ).

That, however, would mean that most names could not be used with بن because most personal names do take nunation. No, it doesn't, be-cause there is a way out. Personal names that get the standard case end-ings (triptotes) lose the sign of indefiniteness (nunation) in **genealogi-cal citations** before the word بن (*son of*).

Ja'far, son of Muhammad, turned towards Sa'id ibn al-'Ās.	جَعْفَرُ بنُ مُحَمَّدٍ تَوَجَّهَ إِلَى سَعِيدِ بنِ العاصِ.
جَعْفَرُ is a proper name and does not take nunation. Furthermore, the expres-sion with بن has no predicative meaning – thus, we write بنُ.	

Zayd, son of Sa'd, son of Muhammad	زَيْدُ بْنُ سَعْدِ بْنِ مُحَمَّدٍ
You pronounce it: "*Zaydu-bnu-sa'di-bni-muhammadin*". It is not: Zaydun and sa'din. Here, the proper names dropped the nunation.	

Requirement 4: The proper name before بن denotes a **single** person.

Wasīm and Bāhir ibn Muhammad told me...	حَدَّثَنِي وَسِيمٌ وَباهِرٌ ابْنا مُحَمَّدٍ.
Here we must use the dual form of ابْن. Note that the Nūn (ابْنانِ) of the dual drops in إِضافةٌ-constructions when it is the first part (مُضافٌ).	

Things you should keep in mind:

- If you use بن, the preceding word (the last letter of it) takes only one vowel (ـُ instead of ـٌ). If you use ابْن, the preceding word takes nunation (تَنْوِينٌ), i.e., ـٌ. Otherwise, two سُكُونٌ would collide!

'Ali does not take nuna-	'Ali ibn Abū Tālib	عَلِيُّ بْنُ أَبِي طالِبٍ...

tion, so we write بن.	= ʿAlī, son of Abū Ṭālib,...	
ʿAlī takes nunation, so we have to write اِبْن.	ʿAlī **is** the son of Abū Ṭālib.	عَلِيٌّ ابْنُ أَبِي طَالِبٍ.

- In grammar, بن is a *follower* (تَابِعٌ). It "follows" the preceding word/name (regarding the grammatical position and case) and therefore takes the same case marker.
- The noun after بن is the second part of the إِضَافَةٌ; this is the reason why it takes the genitive case (مَجْرُورٌ).
- If the name after بن is the name of the **grandfather** or the **mother**, then usually the form اِبْن is used. Some grammarians say that this is necessary; others say its optional and you could also use بن.

Jesus, the son of Mary	عِيسَى ابْنُ مَرْيَمَ
ʿAmmār the (grand)son of Mansūr	عَمَّارُ ابْنُ مَنْصُورٍ

- If the series of names is interrupted in any way (for example, by a pronoun or an adjective), then you use اِبْن (with هَمْزَةُ الْوَصْلِ).

Yahya **the noble**, the son of Maymūn	يَحْيَى الْكَرِيمُ ابْنُ مَيْمُونٍ

- What about the nature of the names? It doesn't matter whether the names are proper (real) names, *kunyas* (كُنْيَةٌ) or *Laqabs* (لَقَبٌ). The كُنْيَةٌ (*teknonymy*) is a type of epithet, usually referring to the bearer's first-born son or daughter. It is a name for an adult derived from his/her eldest child's name. The لَقَب (*agnomen*) is what we call a *nickname*. The لَقَبٌ is typically a descriptive of the person.

Two كُنْيَةٌ	Abū Bakr ibn ʾAbu Shayba	أَبُو بَكْرٍ بْنُ أَبِي شَيْبَةٍ
Two لَقَبٌ	Saif al-Dawla ibn Zayn al-ʿĀbidīn.	سَيْفُ الدَّوْلَةِ بْنُ زَيْنِ الْعَابِدِينَ

Excursus: Many grammarians say that if the Arabic word for *son* happens to stand at the **beginning of a line**, then you should write it like اِبْن, i.e., with هَمْزَةُ الْوَصْلِ, provided that اِبْن is found between two proper names.

This was important in ancient times and had to do with the manufacturing of texts which used to be written on palm leaves, linen, or silk and which were put together producing lengthy material (this was often done in Khorasan using Chinese techniques). So people were afraid that they might forget that the word بِن was preceded by a proper name and wouldn't remember the last vowel (case ending) of the preceding word which is necessary to pronounce بِن. Don't forget that you can't start an Arabic sentence with بِن, i.e., with a سُكُونٌ. Nowadays, we switch to another line or page in less than a second – so this rule is not important anymore but, nonetheless, still often applied.

Let's check some examples of sentences with ابْن. Note: The number tells you also which prerequisite is violated and why we can't write بِن.

1	I am a farmer, the son of a farmer.	أَنا فَلَّاحٌ ابنُ فَلَّاحٍ.
	Why ابْن? Because the word ابْن is not found between two proper names.	
2	Tariq, who is the son of Ziyād, is the one who conquered Andalusia.	طارِقٌ هُوَ ابنُ زِيادٍ مَنْ فَتَحَ الْأَنْدَلُسَ.
	Why ابْن? Because there is something between them: the pronoun هُوَ.	
3	Saīd ibn al-Musayyab told us that...	حَدَّثَنَا سَعِيدٌ ابنُ الْمُسَيَّبِ...
	Why ابْن? Because the first proper name takes nunation (which is optional). ➡ We have to reinsert (إعادَةُ الْهَمْزَةِ) the هَمْزَةُ الْوَصْلِ resulting in ابْن. Without this helping letter, it would be impossible to pronounce بِن as two سُكُونٌ collided: the final نْ of the nunation and the بْ of بِن.	
4	I heard Ibn Abbās...	سَمِعتُ ابنَ عَبَّاسٍ...
	Why ابْن? Because ابْن is not preceded by a proper name.	

Additional remarks:

- If you use the vocative particle يا together with ابْن, oftentimes the first letter (هَمْزَةُ الْوَصْلِ) of ابْن is omitted. In such a situation, two spellings are possible: you merge the two words (يَابْنَ آدَمَ), or you keep a space between them (يَا ابْنَ آدَمَ).

- In transliterations, you often find the word *bin*. If you want to know why this is highly questionable, see *Arabic for Nerds 1, #30*.

103. *The king's sons and daughters.* How do you say that in Arabic?

We have to use a possessive pronoun to fix the construction.

First of all, let's get the problem straight: it is the possession of more than one thing, expressed by a إِضافةٌ.

Classical Arabic knows a fine solution for such problems:

- First step: we use a <u>standard</u> إِضافةٌ for the **first noun**.

- Second step: we add a <u>pronominal suffix</u> (possessive pronoun) to the **second noun** to indicate the relation to the مُضافٌ (= 1ˢᵗ part).

The king's sons and daughters.	بَنُو الْمَلِكِ وَبَناتُهُ.
Zayd's sword and spear.	سَيْفُ زَيْدٍ وَرُمْحُهُ.

In Modern Standard Arabic as well as in poetry, you might see a different construction: with the conjunction وَ.

A most pleasant and sweet sleep.	Classical A.	أَطْيَبُ نَوْمةٍ وَأَحْلاها.
	MSA/poetry	أَطْيَبُ وَأَحْلَى نَوْمةٍ.
Zayd's sword and spear	MSA/poetry	سَيْفُ وَرُمْحُ زَيْدٍ

104. بُيُوت الْقاهِرةِ الْقَدِيمة - What does it mean in English?

Without case endings, the sentence can mean two things: the old houses of Cairo or the houses of old Cairo.

The phrase بيوت القاهرة القديمة was part of a headline on the website of the news-channel al-'Arabīya. Since the text was written without vowels, we can only guess the translation.

What's the problem? We simply can't tell to which word the adjective belongs. We run into this situation if we have a إِضافةٌ-construction with a **definite second part**. This means that the **first** part is also considered **definite** and since both words (بُيُوت and الْقاهِرة) are feminine, we can't tell to which feminine word the feminine adjective relates.

There's a rule of thumb: The **adjective** usually belongs to the **first part** of the إِضافةٌ. In the following examples, have a close look at the case ending of the adjective (last word).

The new university professor.	أُسْتاذُ الْجامِعةِ الْجَدِيدُ.
The professor of the new university. (unlikely)	أُسْتاذُ الْجامِعةِ الْجَدِيدةِ.

However, there are examples with an ambiguous meaning.

The houses of **old** Cairo.	بُيُوتُ الْقاهِرةِ الْقَدِيمةِ.
The **old** houses of Cairo.	بُيُوتُ الْقاهِرةِ الْقَدِيمةُ.

The **small** gate of the house.	مَدْخَلُ الْبَيْتِ الصَّغِيرُ.
The gate of the **small** house.	مَدْخَلُ الْبَيْتِ الصَّغِيرِ.

How could you avoid possible misunderstandings? You could use the **preposition** لِ to mark the possession. If the possession is more metaphorically, you could use the **preposition** فِي.

The main entrance of the building.	الْمَدْخَلُ الرَّئِيسِيُّ لِلْمَبْنَى.

The houses of **old** Cairo.	الْبُيُوتُ فِي الْقاهِرةِ الْقادِمة.
The **old** houses of Cairo.	الْبُيُوتُ الْقَدِيمةُ فِي الْقاهِرة.

105. How do you say: *a son of the king?*

You shouldn't use a إِضافةٌ - *because it is impossible.*

The problem is the indefinite noun: <u>a son</u>.

We can't use a إِضافةٌ-construction here. The إِضافةٌ would make the first word (*a son*) automatically definite because the second word is definite (*the* king) – *see question #100.*

This also means that the first part of a إِضافةٌ doesn't possess the indefinite nunation (تَنْوِينٌ). In short: We are unable to use the genitive construction (إِضافةٌ) to express a truly indefinite regent.

How do we fix that? We can only **express** <u>a son</u> of the king **with the help of a preposition:** the لِ. → See also *#129* for a detailed analysis.

a son of **a** king (a king's son)	اِبْنُ مَلِكٍ
the son of **the** king (the king's son)	اِبْنُ الْمَلِكِ
a son to **the** king	اِبْنٌ لِلْمَلِكِ
a son from the sons of the king	اِبْنٌ مِنْ أَبْنَاءِ الْمَلِكِ

For the third and fourth rows, the middle cell spans both: meaning: *a son of the king*

An example of a Hadith (*Sunan ibn Mājāh*; 6/1556). It was narrated that Kurayb, the freed slave of ʿAbd Allah bin ʿAbbās, said:

A son of ʿAbd Allah b. ʿAbbās died, and he [ʿAbd Allah] said to me: 'O Kurayb! Get up and see if anyone has assembled (to pray) for my son.'	هَلَكَ ابْنٌ لِعَبْدِ اللّٰهِ بْنِ عَبَّاسٍ فَقَالَ لِي يَا كُرَيْبُ قُمْ فَانْظُرْ هَلِ اجْتَمَعَ لِابْنِي أَحَدٌ.

106. How do you express: *my (male) teachers?*

That's tough. When **my** *is used with the dual (*مُثَنَّى*) or a sound masculine plural (*جَمْعُ الْمُذَكَّرِ السَّالِمُ*), we will get pretty complex constructions.*

The ending of the dual and the sound masculine plural <u>can't</u> carry the vowel of إِعْرَابٌ (= case marker). Why? Because these forms express the **case by a letter** and not by a vowel. Now, if we add the possessive pronoun *my* (ي), the so-called يَاءُ الْمُتَكَلِّم, this will bring along some serious grammar issues. But there's a way out of this dilemma.

- The suffix ي (*my*) is cemented on the سُكُونٌ. This tells us to put a كَسْرَةٌ (vowel "*i*") under the preceding letter because only this combination turns the ي into a long vowel ("*ii/ee*").

- Now, what happens if the preceding letter can't carry a كَسْرَةٌ? We get that when the last letter of a word is an Aleph (ا) or a و. Then, the ي changes and becomes fixed on the vowel "*a*" (مَبْنِيٌّ عَلَى الْفَتْح). Eventually, we get: ـيَ. This has to be done to harmonize the sounds. It is exactly the situation when we have a **dual** or **sound masculine plural**.

My (male) teachers came.	حَضَرَ مُعَلِّمِيَّ.

Let's show all the steps that finally resulted in مُعَلِّمِيَّ.

1. You add ي to the word مُعَلِّمُونَ.

2. The final نَ drops.

3. We now get مُعَلِّمُويْ. That's a problem because two سُكُونْ collide.

4. The وْ is used to mark the case. It cannot carry a vowel. We fix that by putting a فَتْحةٌ on the ي resulting in يَ. So we get: مُعَلِّمُويَ

5. Finally, و and ي merge which means that the و first has to turn into a ي. So we get مُعَلِّمُيِيَ. This process is called اِنْقِلابٌ.

6. The ضَمّةٌ on top turns into كَسْرةٌ. So we get مُعَلِّمِيِيَ.

7. The two ي turn into a single يّ which for that reason gets a شَدّةٌ. The result is مُعَلِّمِيَّ.

Let's check more examples. We will deal with three problems:

1. We may have an Aleph (in the dual, nominative) which can't carry any vowel: (اْ).

2. We may have a وْ which will turn into a يْ to make it work. Once we did that, we will face the same problem as in number 3.

3. We have a collision of two ي: the ي of the dual or plural in the accusative/genitive case plus the ي of the pronominal suffix.

Dual, nominative (مَرْفُوعٌ)	صَدِيقانِ + ي
My two friends came.	جاءَ صَدِيقايَ.

Friends (صَدِيقانِ) is the subject (فاعِلٌ) of the verbal sentence; it takes the nominative case, marked by the Aleph (مَرْفُوعٌ بِالْأَلِفِ). There is **no assimilation** as we don't have a collision of two ي. We've cemented the يَ.

Dual, accusative (مَنْصُوبٌ)	صَدِيقَيْنِ + ي
I saw my two friends.	رَأَيْتُ صَدِيقَيَّ.

Here, **incorporation** or **assimilation** (إِدْغامٌ) happened. *Friends* (صَدِيقَيْنِ) is the direct object (مَفْعُولٌ بِهِ) and is مَنْصُوبٌ by the letter ي. We would have a collision of two ي: the يْ that marks the case, and the possessive pronoun يْ. We fix that by building the possessive pronoun on the vowel "a" (مَبْنِيٌّ عَلَى الْفَتْحِ). Afterwards both ي merge resulting in يَّ.

Sound masculine plural, nominative (مَرْفُوعٌ)	مُهَنْدِسُونَ + ي
My (male) engineers came.	جاءَ مُهَنْدِسِيَّ.

Engineers (مُهَنْدِسُونَ) is the subject (فاعِلٌ) of the verbal sentence and must be مَرْفُوعٌ which was originally achieved by the و. However, this و turns into a ي. In a second step, that ي assimilates with the second ي of the possessive pronoun. Originally, we had مُهَنْدِسُوي. Nevertheless, in the analysis, we would say about the case marker that it is مَرْفُوعٌ بالْواوِ (nominative by the و) with the addition that the و changed into a ي and finally merged (الْواوُ إِنْقَلَبَتْ ياءً ثُمَّ أُدْغِمَتْ فِي ياءِ الْمُتَكَلِّم).

Sound masculine plural, genitive/accusative	مُهَنْدِسِينَ + ي
I saw my engineers.	رَأَيْتُ مُهَنْدِسِيَّ.

Engineers is the direct object (مَفْعُولٌ بِه) and مَنْصُوبٌ by the ي. However, this ي merges with the following ي (the so-called ياءُ الْمُتَكَلِّم).

I greeted my engineers.	سَلَّمْتُ عَلَى مُهَنْدِسِيَّ.

Engineers is مَجْرُورٌ by ي which is also the marker for the genitive (جَرّ). It gets assimilated with the following ي to mark the possession. In Arabic, we say: مَجْرُورٌ بِالْياءِ وَعَلامةُ جَرِّه الْياءِ الَّتِي أُدْغِمَتْ فِي ياءِ الْمُتَكَلِّم.

A tricky example: What about the expression *my Mustafas*?

You can follow the same steps as in the example of مُعَلِّمِيَّ - with one difference. We will get فَتْحةٌ on the letter ف resulting in مُصْطَفيَّ, pronounced: Mustafayya. Why? The فَتْحةٌ remains because it points to the existence of an Aleph (the ى in مُصْطَفَى) which became deleted when forming the plural. Note that this form looks the same in any case: nominative, genitive, accusative.

What happens if we neither have a dual nor a sound masc. plural?

The ياءُ الْمُتَكَلِّم must be preceded by a كَسْرةٌ. To put it more practically, the last letter of the word (before the ي) must have a كَسْرةٌ, no matter, which position or function the word may have in the sentence. However, no letter can have two vowels at the same time. This means for us that the last letter can't take a كَسْرةٌ that fits to the ي (الْمُناسِبةُ لِلْياءِ) and the case marker of إِعْرابٌ at the same time.

In the following examples, the expression *my friend* has the same shape and vowels, but the grammatical function is different.

Nominative (مَرْفُوعٌ)	My friend came.	جاءَ صَدِيقِي.
Friend (صَدِيق) is the subject (فَاعِلٌ); therefore, it should get the nominative case (مَرْفُوعٌ). However, we can't use a visible ـُ to mark the case. Since the possessive pronominal suffix ي (*my*) needs a preceding كَسْرَةٌ, the كَسْرَةٌ is stronger and occupies the place of the ضَمّة. For the analysis, we use a virtual, estimated case marker "*u*" (ضَمّةٌ مُقَدَّرةٌ) on the ق.		
Accusative (مَنْصُوبٌ)	I saw my friend.	رَأَيْتُ صَدِيقِي.
Friend is the direct object (مَفْعُولٌ بِهِ). We can only use a virtual case marker for the accusative (فَتْحةٌ مُقَدَّرةٌ) which is neither written nor pronounced.		
Genitive (مَجْرُورٌ)	I greeted my friend.	سَلَّمْتُ عَلَى صَدِيقِي.
Friends is placed after a preposition; it is in the genitive case (مَجْرُورٌ). Even here, grammatically speaking, we have to use an assumed case marker because the كَسْرةٌ **for the ي is stronger**. We must say that the sign of the genitive is a كَسْرةٌ مُقَدَّرةٌ since the necessary and appropriate vowel (الْحَرَكةُ الْمُنَاسِبةُ) for the ي occupies the place to mark the case.		

107. How do you add *my* or *me* to verbs?

Contrary to nouns, you have to avoid any assimilation.

If we add a ي to a verb, we are able to express *to me, me,* or *my*. This is either the direct or indirect object in English. In order to achieve that in Arabic, we will have to insert an extra ن because we want to **avoid any assimilation (incorporation)** regarding the vowels.

This نُون is called *the supporting* (نُونُ الْعِمادِ) or *guarding or preventive Nūn* (نُونُ الْوِقاية). It is there to avoid the collision of two vowels without an intervening consonant. Linguists call that phenomenon *hiatus*. The *Nūn* prevents the final vowel of the verb from being absorbed by the long vowel ـِ + ي

However, **assimilation** (of vowel sounds) is exactly what happens when we have a <u>noun</u> (اِسْم). Let's see both problems in one sentence:

My (two) friends visited me.	زارَني صَديقايَ.

Past tense verb. The ن protects the last vowel (نُونٌ لِلْوِقايةِ).	زارَني

This ن has a fixed shape (مَبْنِيٌّ عَلَى الْكَسْرِ). It has no place in إعْرابٌ. The ي is a pronoun which serves as the **direct object**. It is indeclinable and always ends with a سُكُونٌ – as a result, we get the long vowel "ii/ee". We treat the ي as being located in the position of an accusative (فِي مَحَلِّ نَصْبٍ مَفْعُولٌ بِهِ).	

Subject (فاعِلٌ) of the verbal sentence; it takes the nominative case (مَرْفُوعٌ) which is marked by the dual Aleph.	صَديقايَ

→ We get rid of the ن of the dual Aleph to get the ي attached. The ي is a possessive pronoun which is fixed/built on the vowel "a" (for harmonization), resulting in يَ. The ي serves as the second part of the إضافةٌ (مُضافٌ إلَيْهِ) and must be genitive (مَجْرُورٌ). We can't show the marker of the genitive case; we can only say that it located in the position of a genitive case (فِي مَحَلِّ جَرٍّ).

108. What happens to a weak letter if it collides with *my*?

They merge (assimilation).

Nouns that end in a weak letter are either a اِسْمٌ مَقْصُورٌ (ends in permanent Aleph) or a اِسْمٌ مَنْقُوصٌ (ends in permanent ي); *see #40 and #43*. If we want to express *my*, we have to attach a possessive pronoun: the letter ي (ياءُ الْمُتَكَلِّمِ). This means that the noun with the weak letter serves as the first part of a genitive construction (إضافةٌ), the مُضافٌ.

The main problem here is how to put the appropriate case marker.

الْمَقْصُورُ	a young boy	فَتًى
This is my (young) boy.		هذا فَتايَ.

Boy is the subject (فاعِلٌ) of the verbal sentence; nominative case (مَرْفُوعٌ). However, here the case is marked by an assumed, virtual ـُ /"u" (ضَمّةٌ مُقَدَّرةٌ) as the Aleph, as shown in *question #88*, can't carry any vowel.

To make the construction work, the ي must have a fixed shape – otherwise, the Aleph would be forcefully transformed into a ي with a كَسْرةٌ.

The اِسْمٌ مَنْقُوصٌ is more complicated.

الْمَنْقُوص	a lawyer	مُحامٍ
My lawyer came.		جاءَ مُحامِيَّ.

Lawyer (مُحامٍ) is the **subject** (فاعِلٌ) and marked by a virtual, assumed vowel for the case (ضَمّةٌ مُقَدَّرَةٌ) on the ي which was assimilated/integrated by the possessive ي, the so-called ياءُ الْمُتَكَلِّم. In Arabic:

فاعِلٌ مَرْفوعٌ بِضَمّةٍ مُقَدَّرَةٍ عَلَى الْياءِ الْمُدْغَمةِ في ياءِ الْمُتَكَلِّم

I saw my lawyer.	رَأَيْتُ مُحامِيَّ.

Lawyer is the **direct object** (مَفْعولٌ بِه). It is مَنْصوبٌ by the visible فَتْحةٌ on the ي which was assimilated, incorporated by the ياءُ الْمُتَكَلِّم. In Arabic:

مَفْعولٌ بِه مَنْصوبٌ بِالْفَتْحةِ عَلَى الْياءِ الْمُدْغَمةِ في ياءِ الْمُتَكَلِّم

I greeted my lawyer.	سَلَّمْتُ عَلَى مُحامِيَّ.

In English, *lawyer* would be the direct object – but not in Arabic. It takes the **genitive case** (مَجْرورٌ) as it follows a preposition. We can't visibly put the sign for the genitive; we have to use an estimated marker (كَسْرةٌ مُقَدَّرَةٌ) on the ي which was merged with the possessive marker ي (ياءُ الْمُتَكَلِّم). In Arabic:

مَجْرورٌ بِعَلَى وَعَلامةُ جَرِّه كَسْرةٌ مُقَدَّرةٌ عَلَى الْياءِ الْمُدْغَمةِ في ياءِ الْمُتَكَلِّم

THE مَصْدَرٌ

109. What came first: مَصْدَرٌ or verb?

This was a famous debate – and there is no definite answer.

An Arabic verb denotes two things: an occurrence of an act (حَدَثٌ) and time (زَمانٌ). The verb ذَهَبْتُ (I went away) denotes the occurrence of the act of going away (الذَّهاب) and the fact that this act took place in the past. The majority of the grammarians hold the view that each verb form derives from the verbal noun, denoting the act expressed in it. So, ذَهَبَ (he went away) is derived from ذَهابٌ (the act of going away).

Simply put, a مَصْدَرٌ describes the meaning that is found in a verb **without pointing to time**. Since the grammarians believe that the verb is derived from tits verbal noun, they call the latter *the source* (الْمَصْدَرُ).

But it's not that simple.

- Sībawayhi treats the مَصْدَر as a *noun of the event* from which the verb originates – which is also the view of the grammarians of Basra (الْبَصْرِيُّونَ). I follow his view and treat the مَصْدَر as a word that may have the power of a verb but shows a noun-like behavior.

- The grammarians of Kūfa (الْكُوفِيُّونَ), on the other hand, regard the verb as the basis for deriving the noun.

The Greek view is that the noun precedes the verb. The noun came before the internal modification for the expression of tense, person, case, number (a process which linguists call *accidence*). Sībawayhi had a similar view.

Nowadays we translate the term مَصْدَر with *verbal noun, infinitive,* or *noun of event.* It is a اِسْم and therefore gets **case endings**. Speaking of Arabic patterns, مَصْدَر is the اِسْمُ الْمَكانِ of the I-verb صَدَرَ - يَصْدِرُ which means *to originate.* So, مَصْدَر denotes *the place from where anything goes forth, where it originates.*

110. Is عَطاءٌ the regular مَصْدَر of أَعْطَى؟

No, it is not.

The common word for *offer, gift* (عَطاءٌ) is a اِسْمُ الْمَصْدَرِ. It is not the actual مَصْدَر (original noun) of the IV-verb أَعْطَى (*to give*). It is difficult to find a good translation for the term اِسْمُ الْمَصْدَرِ; you might read *noun of action; noun of origin* – but the translations don't really help us if we want to understand it.

So, what is behind the Arabic term? The اِسْمُ الْمَصْدَرِ **focuses** more on the **state** than on the action – without any regard to the doer or circumstances of time and mood under which it takes place. Furthermore, some root letters may be left out – like in our example: عَطاءٌ which is a اِسْمُ مَصْدَرِ of IV-verb أَعْطَى → the first letter is gone.

Is there a difference (in meaning) to the regular مَصْدَر؟

- The اِسْمُ الْمَصْدَرِ consists of fewer letters than the underlying verb form because the اِسْمُ الْمَصْدَرِ is not derived from the actual verb form (لَيْسَ جَارِيًا فِي الْإِشْتِقَاقِ عَلَى فِعْلِهِ).

- It happens that you see a noun in the shape of a مَصْدَرٌ of a I-verb indicating an abstract meaning – although the underlying verb is not triliteral, but augmented.

- Furthermore, the اِسْمُ الْمَصْدَرِ does not really point to the meaning of an action (مَعْنَى الْحَدَثِ). A مَصْدَرٌ, on the other hand, does.

Let's take, for example, the VIII-verb *to wash; to perform the major ritual ablution, i.e., a washing of the whole body* (اِغْتَسَلَ - يَغْتَسِلُ).

- The standard مَصْدَرٌ of it is اِغْتِسَالٌ. The مَصْدَرٌ consists of the entire letters of the verb and points to the action (حَدَثٌ) without giving us information about the time (زَمَانٌ).

- The اِسْمُ الْمَصْدَرِ is غُسْلٌ. It has fewer letters than the verb it relates to (حُرُوفُهُ تَنْقُصُ عَنْ حُرُوفِ الْفِعْلِ). To put it more concretely, there is no ت (so-called تَاءُ الْإِفْتِعَالِ).

- غُسْلٌ does not necessarily point to the <u>action,</u> but it points to the <u>name</u> of the process which is *the washing* (الْغُسْلُ).

  Note: The مَصْدَر of the I-verb غَسَلَ - يَغْسِلُ (*to wash*) is غَسْلٌ with "a".

Another example: the II-verb كَلَّمَ - يُكَلِّمُ (*to talk*). The original مَصْدَرٌ (the الْمَصْدَرُ الْجَارِي) is تَكْلِيمٌ. However, كَلَامٌ is more frequently used. It is the اِسْمُ الْمَصْدَرِ and consists of fewer letters than the underlying verb. The doubling (تَضْعِيفٌ) of the ل is not shown. كَلَامٌ doesn't point to the action of speaking (التَّكْلِيمُ) but to <u>the spoken words</u> (الْكَلَامُ الْمَلْفُوظُ).

Let's check the IV-verb أَحَبَّ - يُحِبُّ (R2=R3; *to love*).

- The مَصْدَرٌ of أَحَبَّ is إِحْبَابٌ. You rarely come across that word. Instead, the word حُبٌّ is used. It is basically the difference between *loving* (إِحْبَابٌ; process) and *love* (حُبٌّ; state or result).

- The same is true for *to hate* (أَبْغَضَ). The original مَصْدَرٌ is إِبْغَاضٌ, but the common word is بُغْضٌ.

A hint: If you want to check whether a noun is a اِسْمُ الْمَصْدَرِ or an original مَصْدَرٌ, check if a deleted letter was compensated (تَعْوِيضٌ)! If there is some kind of compensation, it is **not** a اِسْمُ الْمَصْدَرِ.

اِسْمُ الْمَصْدَرِ - yes or no?	**noun**	verb	
No. We got rid of the و but compensated it with ة.	عِدَةٌ	to promise	وَعَدَ

Chapter 4: Pronouns and Prepositions

PRONOUNS (الضَّمِيرُ) AND WHAT WE CALL IN ENGLISH PRONOUNS

111. What turns an adjective into a predicate in Arabic?

The so-called pronoun of separation (ضَمِيرُ الْفَصْلِ).

This pronoun is used to distinguish between a predicate (خَبَرٌ) and an adjective (صِفَةٌ). Let's check an example to illustrate the problem.

The loyal/**sincere** Karīm	كَرِيمٌ الْمُخْلِصُ
This is not a complete sentence (جُمْلَةٌ غَيْرُ تامّةٍ) because it lacks a predicate (خَبَرٌ). The word الْمُخْلِصُ is an adjective (صِفَةٌ) for *Karīm*.	

The **sincere** Karīm **is** popular.	كَرِيمٌ الْمُخْلِصُ مَحْبُوبٌ.
This is a complete sentence.	

Now, imagine that you are talking to someone who says...

Zayd is sincere, Muhammad is sincere...	زَيْدٌ مُخْلِصٌ وَمُحَمَّدٌ مُخْلِصٌ...

... and you intervene:

... in fact, Zayd is the real sincere guy!	بَلْ زَيْدٌ الْمُخْلِصُ!
In the meaning of ➡	زَيْدٌ هُوَ الرَّجُلُ الْمُخْلِصُ حَقًّا!
Here, we understand الْمُخْلِصُ as the predicate and not as an adjective.	

Without knowing the context, الْمُخْلِصُ in زَيْدٌ الْمُخْلِصُ can be an attribute/adjective (صِفَةٌ) **or** the predicate (خَبَرٌ). If you want to settle this, you can use a trick.

An adjective (صِفَةٌ) always follows the noun which it describes. So we need something to separate them to create a predicate– which can be achieved by a pronoun (third person singular). Such *pronoun of separation* (ضَمِيرُ الْفَصْلِ) is also called *pronoun of support* (ضَمِيرُ الْفَصْلِ) because it is used to distinguish the predicate and clarify the subject.

Karīm **is** the sincere.	كَرِيمٌ هُوَ الْمُخْلِصُ.
We finally have achieved that *sincere* is the predicate (خَبَرٌ).	

When both – subject and predicate – are definite (مَعْرِفَةٌ), the pronoun between them prevents any possibility of the predicate being mistaken for an adjective or an apposition. This is done even if the subject itself is a pronoun (of the first or second person).

That man is I.	ذَلِكَ الرَّجُلُ هُوَ أَنَا.
Karīm is more excellent than Amr.	كَرِيمٌ هُوَ أَفْضَلُ مِنْ عَمْرٍو.

Let's get back to our example (كَرِيمٌ هُوَ الْمُخْلِصُ) and tear the sentence apart. There are two ways to analyze it (إِعْرَابٌ):

Approach I. The ضَمِيرُ الْفَصْلِ doesn't have a position in إِعْرَابٌ.

Subject (مَرْفُوعٌ); in the nominative case by ضَمّةٌ (nunation).	كَرِيمٌ
Pronoun of separation (ضَمِيرُ الْفَصْلِ); it does not have a place in إِعْرَابٌ. We treat it as neutral, it is more of an auxiliary word.	هُوَ
Predicate (خَبَرٌ) in the nominative case (مَرْفُوعٌ).	الْمُخْلِصُ

Approach II. The ضَمِيرُ الْفَصْلِ does have a position in إِعْرَابٌ.

Second subject (مُبْتَدَأٌ ثَانٍ). It should be in the nominative case, but since it is indeclinable (مَبْنِيٌّ), we can only assign the place value of a nominative case (فِي مَحَلّ رَفْعٍ).	هُوَ
Predicate of the <u>second</u> subject (خَبَرُ الْمُبْتَدَأِ الثَّانِي); therefore, it is in the nominative case (مَرْفُوعٌ بِالضَّمّةِ الظَّاهِرَةِ).	الْمُخْلِصُ
Now comes the crucial point: the entire sentence consisting of the second subject plus the predicate is the <u>predicate</u> of the <u>first</u> subject (كَرِيمٌ). Thus,	

we say that the extra sentence is located in the position of a nominative case (الْجُمْلَةُ مِنَ الْمُبْتَدَإِ الثّاني وَخَبَرِهِ في مَحَلِّ رَفْعٍ خَبَرَ الْمُبْتَدَإِ الْأَوَّلِ).

Does it matter which approach we use? Yes. The difference will get apparent if we add a verb that turns grammar rules upside down (فِعْلٌ ناسِخٌ) like كانَ. Then, the "subject" (اسْمُ كانَ) is in the nominative case as usual – but the predicate (خَبَرُ كانَ) is in the accusative (مَنْصُوبٌ).

Approach A. The ضَميرُ الْفَصْلِ **doesn't** have a place in إِعْرابٌ. It is **not governed** by anything and isn't inflected. We've analyzed that الْمُخْلِصَ is the predicate (خَبَرٌ), so it is in the accusative case (مَنْصُوبٌ).

Karīm was the faithful one.	كانَ كَريمٌ هُوَ الْمُخْلِصَ.

Approach B. An entire nominal sentence (جُمْلَةٌ اسْمِيّةٌ) serves as the predicate of the first subject.

Karīm was the faithful one.	كانَ كَريمٌ هُوَ الْمُخْلِصَ.

This is a complex sentence with two levels: the primary nominal sentence and a subsidiary which functions as the خَبَرٌ of the first subject (مُبْتَدَأٌ). Since the second sentence functions as the خَبَرُ كانَ, the entire sentence (as an entity) is located in the position of an accusative (في مَحَلِّ نَصْبٍ).

Both views are correct.

112. What is the *pronoun of the story* or *fact*?

A non-personal pronoun.

In general, we can say that Arabic has two types of pronouns:

- Personal pronouns (الضَّمائِرُ الشَّخْصِيّةُ): I, you, he, she, ...
- Non-personal pronouns (غَيْرُ شَخْصِيّةٍ): they don't refer to a specific person.

Let's examine the **non**-personal pronoun. It has several names in Arabic (their names relate to the thing or person they refer to):

ضَميرُ الْحِكاية or ضَميرُ الْقِصّة or ضَميرُ الْأَمْرِ or ضَميرُ الشَّأْن

Such a pronoun symbolizes the matter or affair, the situation or the action that will follow. The Kūfa grammarians (الْكُوفِيُّونَ) call it the *unidentified pronoun* (الضَّمِيرُ الْمَجْهُولُ). It is mainly used to express the neuter *this, it*, etc. The pronoun is masculine (= هُوَ) or feminine (= هِيَ) according to the gender of the subject of the sentence that **follows**.

The most famous example of a ضَمِيرُ الشَّأْنِ is found in Sura *The sincerity* (الْإِخْلَاصُ). The pronoun gives this verse an intensifying meaning:

Sura 112:1	**He** is God the One.	هُوَ اللّٰهُ أَحَدٌ.

Pronoun of the fact (ضَمِيرُ الشَّأْنِ). It is the **first subject** (مُبْتَدَأٌ). But since هُوَ is **in**declinable (مَبْنِيٌّ عَلَى الْفَتْحِ), we can only assign the place value of a nominative case (فِي مَحَلِّ رَفْعِ مُبْتَدَأٍ).	هُوَ
Second subject (مُبْتَدَأٌ ثانٍ); in the nominative case (مَرْفُوعٌ).	اللّٰهُ
Predicate of the <u>second</u> subject (خَبَرُ الْمُبْتَدَإِ الثَّانِي), nominative.	أَحَدٌ
What is the predicate of the first sentence? It is the entire nominal sentence which comes after the pronoun (الْجُمْلَةُ مِنَ الْمُبْتَدَإِ الثَّانِي وَخَبَرِهِ فِي مَحَلِّ رَفْعِ خَبَرُ الْمُبْتَدَإِ الْأَوَّلِ).	

- A ضَمِيرُ الشَّأْنِ must be placed at the beginning of a sentence (صَدْرُ الْجُمْلَةِ). It functions as the subject: the مُبْتَدَأٌ of a nominal sentence or as the إِسْمُ كَانَ or إِسْمُ إِنَّ.
- The pronoun is either singular masculine (يَدُلُّ عَلَى الشَّأْنِ), i.e., هُوَ, or singular feminine (يَدُلُّ عَلَى الْقِصَّةِ), i.e., هِيَ.
- When used as a **suffix**, the pronoun often represents or anticipates a whole subsequent clause.

Now let's check a sentence in which we use a pronoun suffix.

(Indeed), Zayd is generous.	إِنَّهُ زَيْدٌ كَرِيمٌ.

Particle for emphasis (حَرْفُ تَوْكِيدٍ وَنَصْبٍ); no position in إِعْرَابٌ.	إِنَّ
Pronoun of the fact (ضَمِيرُ الشَّأْنِ). It is indeclinable (مَبْنِيٌّ) and can't take any other vowel. In this sentence, it occupies the place of an accusative case (فِي مَحَلِّ نَصْبٍ) because it is the إِسْمُ إِنَّ.	ﻪ

Subject (مُبْتَدَأٌ) in the nominative case (مَرْفُوعٌ بِالضَّمّةِ الظّاهِرةِ).	زَيْدٌ
Predicate (خَبَرٌ) in the nominative case (مَرْفُوعٌ).	كَرِيمٌ

The <u>entire</u> sentence after إِنَّهُ (marked in gray) supplies the position of the **predicate** of إِنَّ. The whole sentence is grammatically in the position of a nominative case (فِي مَحَلِّ رَفْعٍ خَبَرُ إِنَّ).

113. ضَرَبَ الْأَبُ ابْنَهُ لِأَنَّهُ كانَ مَخْمُورًا – Who was drunk? Father or son?

We can't tell because the personal pronoun هـ in لِأَنَّهُ could theoretically refer to the father or to the son. The reference in the example is ambiguous. However, there is a rule of thumb in case the context doesn't tell you.

In Arabic, pronouns are fairly easy to handle compared to other languages. In Arabic, you basically only have two forms: the free, standalone form of the pronoun (ضَمِيرٌ بارِزٌ) and the abbreviated, connected form in the shape of a suffix (ضَمِيرٌ مُتَّصِلٌ).

The connected form may work as a possessive pronoun, a direct object, or can be the glue to link a relative clause to the main part, etc. If you encounter pronouns as suffixes, only هـ or ها can be tricky. They are called ضَمِيرُ الْغائِبِ, the *pronoun of the absent*. Such pronouns replace a preceding noun and are a substitute for the thing or person spoken about. Often they are used as a reference (ضَمِيرٌ عائِدٌ): as pronouns that refer to a word earlier in the sentence and thus link parts of a sentence.

Now, let's analyze our example:

ضَرَبَ الْأَبُ ابْنَهُ لِأَنَّهُ كانَ مَخْمُورًا.

The possessive pronoun هـ after ابْن refers to الْأَبُ (*father*). The pronoun is the second part of a إِضافةٌ-construction. It is located in the position of a genitive case (فِي مَحَلِّ جَرٍّ), but you can't see that since we can't mark it with the appropriate case. It has a fixed shape: هـ.

So far, so good. What about the expression لِأَنَّهُ? It is a combination of لِ plus أَنَّ. The هـ is a pronoun which is placed in the position of an accusative case (فِي مَحَلِّ نَصْبٍ) since it occupies the location of the إِسْمُ أَنَّ – and أَنَّ is a device that overthrows case endings (حَرْفٌ ناسِخٌ).

That's standard stuff. But there is still one question left: to what or whom does the pronoun ه relate? **There is a rule of thumb:**

> Without additional information, the **pronoun refers to the closest noun** (يَعُودُ إِلَى أَقْرَبِ اسْمٍ مَذْكُورٍ). What happens if that would be a إِضَافَةٌ-construction? Which part is targeted then? We can say that the pronoun usually refers to the **first part** – to the مُضَافٌ.

Even in the Qur'an, you may run into difficulties to find the appropriate reference of the pronoun. A famous example is found in Sura 48 – *The Victory/al-Fath* (سُورَةُ الْفَتْحِ).

Sura 48:9	...that you [people] may believe in Allah and His Messenger and honor **him** and respect **the prophet** and exalt **Allah** morning and afternoon.	...لِّتُؤْمِنُوا بِاللَّهِ وَرَسُولِهِ وَتُعَزِّرُوهُ وَتُوَقِّرُوهُ وَتُسَبِّحُوهُ بُكْرَةً وَأَصِيلًا.
Most commentators agree that the pronoun *Him* (the letter ه marked in gray) refers to Allah, while a few believe it refers to the Prophet Muhammad – and some translators just avoid using the pronoun and use the respective noun instead.		

Remark: For another notable example, see *question #17*.

114. What does a relative pronoun need?

Three things.

First of all, an important piece of information. In English, I use the term *pronoun*; in Arabic, however, we deal with a noun, which will be important for our analyses later on. The Arabic relative pronoun (إِسْمٌ مَوْصُولٌ) needs three things:

1. A relative **clause** (صِلَةُ الْمَوْصُولِ) carrying the information (جُمْلَةٌ خَبَرِيَّةٌ) – see *question #115*.

2. A **referential pronoun** (عَائِدٌ) that refers back to the relative pronoun (الْإِسْمُ الْمَوْصُولُ) – see *question #116*.

3. A (virtual) case since it has a **position** in إِعْرَابٌ. This means that the relative pronoun (e.g., الَّذِي) may serve as the direct object, etc.

Let's check some positions that the relative pronoun may cover:

subject (فَاعِلٌ)	**The one** came who...	...جاءَ الَّذي
adjective (نَعْتٌ)	The man **who came**...	...الرَّجُلُ الَّذي جاءَ
predicate (خَبَرٌ)	**What** did you do?	ماذا فَعَلْتَ؟

➤ We only have to check the position of the relative pronoun, e.g. الَّذي. What follows after الَّذي is of no interest, as it is only there to complete the meaning of الَّذي, which itself does not give us any real meaning.

115. What kind of relative pronouns does Arabic know?

Many. They are mainly classified as specific or unspecific.

The most common relative pronoun is الَّذي. It belongs to group A.

GROUP A: Relative pronouns that are specific (الأَسْماءُ الْخاصّةُ).

form	masculine	feminine
singular	الَّذي	الَّتي
plural	الَّذينَ	اللّاتي
		اللّائي
	الأُلى	
dual	اللَّذانِ	اللَّتانِ
dual, genitive/accusative	اللَّذَيْنِ	اللَّتَيْنِ
diminutive, singular	اللَّذَيّا	اللَّتَيّا
diminutive, plural	اللَّذَيُّونَ	اللَّتَيّاتُ

Why do we have two and sometimes three ل? The more common and usual forms – marked in gray – are corrupted forms. Nevertheless, they became the standard form as we don't use اللَّذينَ or اللَّتي or الَّذي. Some rarely used forms, however, contain the ل of the article and the demonstrative. Note that الَّذي as indicated by the definite article in the word itself is always definite and only refers to definite nouns.

Excursus: What is the origin of the relative pronoun (الَّذِي)?

It is not entirely clear. In Arabic, relative pronouns (اِسْمٌ مَوْصُولٌ) were originally demonstratives (اِسْمُ الْإِشَارَةِ). We can assume that الَّذِي is a compound of the **definite article** and the **demonstrative** ل plus ذِي or تِي which both also have a demonstrative meaning.

Sībawayhi said that the origin of الَّذِي was لَذِي. Later the definite article ال entered the expression to provide **determination** (لِلتَّعْرِيفِ). Then, the *Lām* (ل) of the definite article was incorporated by the other *Lām* (أُدْغِمَت اللَّمُ الَّتِي جاءَتْ مَعَ الْأَلِفِ فِي اللَّامِ الَّتِي فِي لَذِي). But do we really need the definite article? Well, some say that it is simply there to grammatically blueprint the definite word to which it relates. E.g.: **The** house that... (الْبَيْتُ الَّذِي). The word الَّذِي agrees in gender, number (singular/plural), case (although only virtual as you don't see it most of the time) and state of definiteness.

The Arabic grammarians call the definite article the *instrument of definition* (أَداةُ التَّعْرِيفِ). It consists of:

- the **Aleph** (l). This prefixed letter is a helping letter. It is a هَمْوةُ الْوَصْلِ. The Hamza is only there to lighten the pronunciation.

- The **letter** لامٌ; the *Lām of definition* or *determination* is called a حَرْفُ التَّعْرِيفِ. Note that the ل of the definite article isn't a preposition – it is the ل that is also found in الَّذِي. In fact, it is the demonstrative letter ل. Such *Lām of determination* cannot occur inseparably; it is found together with a connecting Hamza (هَمْزةُ الْوَصْلِ) which is placed before it. Finally, we will get ال.

Though ل has become *determinative* (making the expression *definite*), it was originally denoting a direction (demonstrative use). Its demonstrative meaning has survived in expressions like *tonight* (اللَّيْلَةَ) or *to-day* (الْيَوْمَ) expressing **to**-day (more of *this* day and not *the* day). Another example: *Who is the man there?* (مَن الرَّجُلُ؟) in the meaning of: *Who are you?* In Hebrew, the definite article ה works pretty similar. It was also used in such a way: "habaita" (הַבַּיְתָה) means *homeward*, literally **to** home (not: *the* home). It has also survived in Modern Hebrew.

Some scholars regard the Aleph as an integral part of the definite article. They suggest that it was originally أَلْ – with a pronounced Hamza

(أَلِفُ الْقَطْعِ) sharing the same pattern as هَل or بَل. Over time, it was probably gradually weakened to ال.

GROUP B: Relative pronouns that are unspecific – but point to a general state or being (الْأَسْماءُ الْعامّةُ).

		مَنْ
When used to convey a **definite** meaning, مَنْ is a **relative pronoun** (مَوْصُولٌ) and is followed by a relative clause.	*he or she who; whoever*	
When it conveys an **indefinite** meaning, it will be the **subject** followed by an adjective (صِفةٌ). مَنْ is the thing being described (مَوْصُوفٌ).	*one who; people who (collective meaning)*	
مَنْ is only used for **human beings** (عاقِلٌ) and can be used for any form (singular, dual, plural) or gender (masculine or feminine). **Watch out:** مَنْ is <u>never</u> used as an adjective.		

		ما
When used in a **definite** meaning, ما is a relative pronoun (مَوْصُولٌ).	*that which; whatever*	
When used to convey **indefiniteness**, it serves as the **subject** and must be followed by an adjective which describes the relative pronoun.	*something that; things that (collective meaning)*	
ما is used for **things**, animals, etc. It doesn't matter if what it refers to is singular, dual, plural, masculine or feminine. It is applied in the same way as مَنْ and is also <u>never</u> used as an adjective.		

	ذا
That	
For **people and things** – under the condition that ذا is placed after the question devices ما or مَنْ (so-called اِسْتِفْهامِيّةٌ). See *question #161*.	

	ذُو
What, who	
For **people and things**. ذُو was used in some variants of Classical Arabic, e.g., لَهْجةُ طَيِّءٍ. It is usually treated as an indeclinable word.	

Here is the one who succeeded.	جاءَ الَّذِي نَجَحَ = جاءَ ذُو نَجَحَ

he who; whoever	أَيّ
she who; whoever	أَيَّة
everything which; whatsoever	أَيُّما
every one who; whosoever	أَيَّمَن

For **people and things**. The above combinations of أَيّ are all treated as definite words (مَعْرِفةٌ) and take cases!

Watch out: أَيّ is treated as **indeclinable** (مَبْنِيٌّ) in one situation. When أَيّ is the first part of a إضافة (i.e., الْمُضاف) and the following relative clause (صِلة) is a **nominal sentence** (جُمْلةٌ اِسْمِيّةٌ) which starts with a deleted, personal pronoun (ضَمِيرٌ مَحْذُوفٌ) – see *question #116*.

In most other situations, it takes the singular form and is declined as it would be a normal noun (triptote/all three cases). Dual and plural are rarely found.

Let's check some examples (see *#161* to know more about ماذا).

Who (is the one who) succeeded?	مَنْ ذا نَجَحَ ؟

What's in the book?	ماذا فِي الْكِتابِ ؟
Literally: What is *this in the book?*	

Question word (اِسْمُ اِسْتِفْهامٍ). It functions as the **subject** (مُبْتَدَأٌ) of the nominal sentence but can't take any case marker since it is indeclinable (مَبْنِيٌّ); thus, it gets the place value of a nominative case (فِي مَحَلِّ رَفْعٍ).	*what*	ما
Relative pronoun which is the **predicate** (خَبَرٌ). Note that it has an indeclinable shape (اِسْمٌ مَوْصُولٌ مَبْنِيٌّ عَلَى السُّكُونِ); so, grammatically speaking, it serves in the position of a nominative case (فِي مَحَلِّ رَفْعٍ خَبَرٌ).	*that*	ذا
Preposition. It does not have a position in إعْرابٌ.	*in*	فِي
Noun in the genitive (مَجْرُورٌ) due to the preposition.	*the book*	الْكِتابِ

116. What is a *referential* or *fallback pronoun*?

Something you may need in a relative clause.

The *fallback pronoun or returner* (الْعائِدُ) may be confusing for learners of Arabic as they might think it doubles the information. This back-referring suffix has no equivalent in English because in English, we simply don't need it.

- If there is a returning, referential pronoun after الَّذِي, the verb in the relative clause is referring to an **object**.

- You **never** use such a pronoun if the information in the relative clause is referring to the **subject**. In other words, don't use it if the word before the relative pronoun and the verb in the relative clause relate to the same person or thing. This is also the situation if we have a prepositional or adverbial phrase (شِبْهُ الْجُمْلةِ).

I saw the **student** who **speaks** Arabic.	رَأَيْتُ الطَّالِبَ الَّذِي يَتَكَلَّمُ الْعَرَبِيَّةَ.

Let's check a sentence which has two different persons involved: *I helped the women.* Imagine that we turn the sentence around. Then, we would start with the direct object and get a relative clause:

Referential (fall back) pronoun attached to...		example
a verb	The **woman** whom **I helped** (her).	الْمَرْأَةُ الَّتِي ساعَدْتُها.
a preposition	This is **the book** that **you asked for** (lit: that you asked for it.)	هذا هُوَ الْكِتابُ الَّذِي سَأَلْتَ عَنْهُ.
a noun (direct object)	This is the **writer** whose **article I read** (lit. who I read his article).	هذا هُوَ الْكاتِبُ الَّذِي قَرَأْتُ مَقالَتَهُ.

What's the idea behind the *returner*? ➡ The relative pronoun الَّذِي actually belongs to the main clause. So, we need a personal pronoun, a referential pronoun, that relates to الَّذِي and thus links both clauses.

117. *The house which is big...* Why is the Arabic translation tricky?

The relative clause (صِلةُ الْمَوْصُولِ) *has to be a sentence* (جُمْلةٌ) *or at least a quasi-sentence* (شِبْهُ الْجُمْلةِ).

In English, you would normally say *the big house* and not *the house which is big...* You actually do the same in Arabic. However, let's assume you have such a construction and you start translating the sentence straightforward into Arabic. Then you will run into a problem, I guess.

	صِلةُ الْمَوْصُولِ	main sentence
Incorrect because this is not a sentence.	كَبِيرٌ...	الْبَيْتُ الَّذِي
Correct because this is a sentence.	هُوَ كَبِيرٌ...	الْبَيْتُ الَّذِي

What is the problem? It has to do with the nature of the relative pronoun – which is different from English.

- According to **English** grammar, the relative clause **includes** the relative pronoun.

- According to **Arabic** grammar, the relative clause (صِلةُ الْمَوْصُولِ or جُمْلةُ الصِّلةِ) does **not** include the relative pronoun. → The relative pronoun belongs to the main clause! Thus, the relative clause is a sentence on its own and could stand alone. The term جُمْلةُ الصِّلةِ does indicate that we need a **sentence** after the relative pronoun.

In Arabic, the relative clause (صِلةُ الْمَوْصُولِ) has to be a nominal or verbal sentence or a prepositional or adverbial phrase (شِبْهُ الْجُمْلةِ):

nominal sentence (جُمْلةٌ إِسْمِيّةٌ)	The ones who are my friends came.	حَضَرَ الَّذِينَ هُمْ أَصْدِقائِي.
	I like the one which is beautiful.	تُعْجِبُنِي الَّتِي هِيَ جَمِيلةٌ.
verbal sentence (جُمْلةٌ فِعْلِيّةٌ)	The student, who succeeded, traveled.	سافَرَ الطّالِبُ الَّذِي نَجَحَ.
	I hit the thief who entered the house. (Literally: I hit the thief, the one, he entered the house.)	ضَرَبْتُ اللَّصَّ الَّذِي دَخَلَ الْمَنْزِلَ.
adverbial phrase (ظَرْف)	The two men that (the two) are with you.	الرَّجُلانِ اللَّذانِ هُما عِنْدَكَ.
prepositional phrase (الْجارُّ وَالْمَجْرُورُ)	The man who is from Egypt...	الرَّجُلُ الَّذِي هُوَ مِنْ مِصْرَ...
	I picked the flowers that were in	قَطَفْتُ الْأَزْهارَ الَّتِي هِيَ

| the garden. | فِي الْحَدِيقةِ. |

How would the analysis of such a sentence look like? Let's do it.

| The one who was diligent was successful. | نَجَحَ الَّذِي هُوَ مُجْتَهِدٌ. |

Verb in the past tense (فِعْلٌ ماضٍ مَبْنِيٌّ عَلَى الْفَتْحِ).	نَجَحَ
Relative pronoun (إِسْمٌ مَوْصُولٌ) which supplies the position of the **subject of the verb** (فَاعِلٌ) here. However, it has an indeclinable shape (مَبْنِيٌّ عَلَى السُّكُونِ) and therefore doesn't get the case marker of the nominative. We can only apply a place value of a nominative case (فِي مَحَلِّ رَفْعٍ).	الَّذِي
Personal pronoun (ضَمِيرٌ مُنْفَصِلٌ) which **starts a new sentence**. It is indeclinable (مَبْنِيٌّ عَلَى الْفَتْحِ). It is located in the position of the **subject of the nominal sentence** (فِي مَحَلِّ رَفْعٍ مُبْتَدَأٌ).	هُوَ
This is the predicate (خَبَرٌ) of the nominal sentence. So it has to take the nominative case (مَرْفُوعٌ).	مُجْتَهِدٌ
The entire nominal sentence (هُوَ مُجْتَهِدٌ) serves as the relative clause (صِلةُ الْمَوْصُولِ). It has a "neutral" position in the sentence and doesn't fill a location that is guarded by another word (لا مَحَلَّ لَها مِن الْإِعْرابِ).	

However, the subject of the nominal sentence (مُبْتَدَأٌ) is usually deleted if you have a prepositional or adverbial phrase after الَّذِي.

Why is that possible? As often in such situations, we assume that something has been deleted and is tacitly understood. In this situation, it is a verb (فِعْلٌ مَحْذُوفٌ) expressing *to be stabilized* (اِسْتَقَرَّ). Since a verb has an implied subject, we don't need the pronoun anymore.

| The two men that are with you. | الرَّجُلانِ اللَّذانِ عِنْدَكَ. |
| I picked the flowers that were in the garden. | قَطَفْتُ الْأَزهارَ الَّتِي فِي الْحَدِيقةِ |

| This is how the sentence would look like with the virtual verb which is needed to make the relative clause work. However, the verb is implicitly understood anyway and therefore omitted. | قَطَفْتُ الْأَزهارَ الَّتِي اِسْتَقَرَّت فِي الْحَدِيقةِ. |

118. *The man from Beirut...* How do you translate that into Arabic?

You need a relative clause.

The man from Beirut... The sentence looks simple but can be a bit of a headache when translated into Arabic. Let's unravel the problem. In English, we have a definite noun (*the man*) which was modified by a prepositional phrase (*from Beirut*).

A direct translation will fail:

The man **is** from Beirut.	الرَّجُلُ مِنْ بَيْرُوتَ.
This doesn't work for us. This **sentence** is a nominal sentence (جُمْلة اِسْمِيّةٌ) with subject (مُبْتَدَأٌ) and predicate (خَبَرٌ). That's not what we need.	

The man from Beirut = The man **who is** from Beirut...	الرَّجُلُ الَّذي مِنْ بَيْرُوتَ...
This works! We need to modify a definite noun. Since we have a prepositional phrase, we have to use a relative pronoun to solve our task. Notice that *Beirut* (بَيْرُوت) in Arabic is a diptote; the genitive is marked by فَتْحةٌ.	

119. How can you get rid of a relative pronoun?

By using an active or passive participle instead.

The answer above may leave you amazed. Can we really get rid of the relative pronoun and the verb in the relative clause with the help of an active (اِسْمُ الْفاعِلِ) or passive participle (اِسْمُ الْمَفْعُولِ)? Yes, this is possible! The participle will then work as an adjective (صِفةٌ) describing the definite noun. This brings along that the صِفة gets the definite article and the same case endings. The meaning is more or less the same.

Rephrasing with the help of the **active participle:**

I saw the bus that is standing there.	رَأَيْتُ الْحافِلةَ الَّتي تَقِفُ هُناكَ.
Lit.: I saw the standing bus there.	= رَأَيْتُ الْحافِلةَ الْواقِفةَ هُناكَ.
In German, the difference is as follows: *Ich sah den Bus, der dort steht* (with the relative clause). *Ich sah den dort stehenden Bus* (with the participle).	

Rephrasing with the help of the **passive participle:**

I read the article **which** was published.	قَرَأْتُ الْمَقالَةَ الَّتِي نُشِرَتْ.
I read the **published** article.	= قَرَأْتُ الْمَقالَةَ الْمَنْشُورَةَ.

What should we do if the verb in the relative clause has a direct object?
→ We use the device لِ.

the countries **that** produce oil	الدُّوَلُ الَّتِي تُنْتِجُ النَّفْطَ
the oil **producing** countries	= الدُّوَلُ الْمُنْتِجةُ لِلنَّفْطِ

120. What are the rules for using أَيّ as a relative pronoun?

The discussion about the use of أَيّ as a relative pronoun goes back to the early phases of the development of Arabic grammar.

أَيّ may be used in the manner of الَّذِي and then also gets its status. This means that أَيّ works as a relative pronoun and denotes *he who; whoever*. As a relative pronoun it also requires a complement: a relative clause (قَدْ تَكُونُ بِمَنْزِلةِ الَّذِي فَتَحْتَاجُ إلَى صِلةٍ). To warn you in advance, you need a good understanding of Arabic grammar if you want to use أَيّ as a relative pronoun, because it may get case endings! You basically have to check one thing. Is there something else involved or not?

Without a pronoun: **indeclinable.**	Greet the one of them who is most excellent!	سَلِّمْ عَلَى أَيِّهِمْ أفْضَلُ!	A
If there is a (free) personal pronoun involved: **declinable.** (أَيِّهِمْ is in the genitive!)	(This example is from the book *al-Mufassal.*)	سَلِّمْ عَلَى أَيِّهِمْ هُوَ أفْضَلُ!	B

What is the difference between the two sentences? First of all, they both mean the same. It is only about the grammar.

Let's start with situation A. In Arabic, relative pronouns belong to the first part of the sentence (main clause) – except for أَيّ. The word أَيّ belongs to the relative clause! This means for us that we have to isolate the entire relative clause and treat it as one block. Therefore, the relative pronoun gets the <u>case ending</u> **according to the position in the relative**

clause – and not according to the position of the main clause.

In situation **B**, أيّ is used as a relative pronoun and is part of the main clause; it gets the case ending according to the position in the first part of the sentence. That would also be the situation if we used الَّذِي.

Let's illustrate the problem:

I will visit, who (**nominative**), of the two, studies Arabic.	سَأَزُورُ أَيُّهُما يَدْرُسُ اللُّغَةَ الْعَرَبِيَّةَ.	1
	سَأَزُورُ أَيُّهُما هُوَ يَدْرُسُ اللُّغَةَ الْعَرَبِيَّةَ.	2
I will visit the two who study Arabic.	سَأَزُورُ اللَّذَيْنِ يَدْرُسَا اللُّغَةَ الْعَرَبِيَّةَ.	3

In number 1, we didn't use the dual form of the verb, but instead the third person singular (يَدْرُسُ). Why? Well, the subject (مُبْتَدَأٌ), in fact, is the same as in number 2: it is the pronoun *he* (هُوَ, third person singular); in number 1, however, it was deleted. This will help us understand how we can use أيّ as a relative pronoun. In number 3, we use the standard relative pronoun to show the difference.

- أيّ **does not change with gender or number.** There is no dual or plural form. أَيّة may be used for feminine forms, but this is rare.

- أيّ is **declinable** (مُعْرَبٌ) like a triptote (i.e., it may get nunation and any of the three case endings) unlike the majority of the relative pronouns which are almost all indeclinable (مَبْنِيٌّ).

- You may treat أيّ as **indeclinable** <u>only in one situation</u>: أيّ is the first part of a إضافةٌ and what is placed after it is not the initial part (so-called صَدْرُ الصِّلةِ) of the relative clause. Simply put, you don't have a free pronoun such as هُوَ after أيّ. In such a situation, أيّ is cemented on the "*u*"-vowel (أَيُّ: مَبْنِيٌّ عَلَى الضَّمِّ). This is what the grammarian Sībawayhi proposed.

- If the relative clause (صِلةُ الْمَوْصُولِ) is a nominal sentence (جُمْلةٌ اِسْمِيّةٌ), then the **first word** (صَدْرٌ) of the relative clause serves as the subject (مُبْتَدَأٌ). If أيّ is indeclinable, the subject is usually a **deleted pronoun**. In our example: (أَيُّهُما (هُوَ

- Most grammarians say that أيّ can only work as a relative pronoun (اِسْمٌ مَوْصُولٌ) if it is governed by a word (mainly a verb) that **points to the future** – which means, that it has to be in the present tense (الْمُضارِعُ). The regent (عامِلٌ), usually the verb, has to be placed before أيّ. To put it in a nutshell: if the verb is in the past tense, you should better use الَّذي.

That was quite a lot of details and information. We should process it and analyze a sentence to get a feeling for the complexities:

He who strives (is diligent) will succeed.	سَيَفُوزُ أَيُّهُم مُجْتَهِدٌ.

Future particle (حَرْفُ تَسْوِيفٍ); no position in إِعْرابٌ.	سَ
Present tense verb in the indicative mood (مَرْفُوعٌ).	يَفُوزُ
Relative pronoun (اِسْمٌ مَوْصُولٌ). It serves as the **subject** (فاعِلٌ) of the verbal sentence. It is **indeclinable** (مَبْنِيٌّ عَلَى الضَّمِّ); it gets the place value of a nominative case (في مَحَلِّ رَفْعٍ). The word أَيّ is the first part of the إِضافةٌ, the so-called مُضافٌ.	أَيّ
Pronominal suffix (ضَميرٌ مُتَّصِلٌ); second part of the إِضافةٌ, i.e. مُضافٌ إِلَيْهِ. It is indeclinable; so we can't use a visible sign for the genitive (مَجْرُورٌ); we have to assign the place value of the genitive.	هُم
Predicate of the deleted (!) subject (خَبَرٌ لِمُبْتَدَإٍ مَحْذُوفٍ).	مُجْتَهِدٌ

How can we understand that the subject has been deleted?

This is the virtual, underlying meaning of the sentence – with هُوَ as the implied **subject** (مُبْتَدَأً).	أَيُّهُم هُوَ مُجْتَهِدٌ
The nominal sentence (جُمْلةٌ اِسْمِيّةٌ) serves as the relative clause (صِلةُ الْمَوْصُولِ); it does not have a position in إِعْرابٌ (لا مَحَلَّ لَها مِن الْإِعْرابِ).	

The word أَيّ is intriguing. What we have said so far was the topic of countless debates among the grammarians. Sībawayhi stated that أَيّ may be synonymous with الَّذي. In such a situation, Sībawayhi treated أَيّ as **indeclinable** and fixed on the ضَمّ resulting in أَيُّ.

But the Kūfa grammarians and a number of Basra grammarians disagreed with him, holding that أَيّ is always declined and therefore gets case endings. So, they suggested to treat أَيّ as a question word (اِسْمُ اِسْتِفْهامٍ) and not as a relative pronoun (الْإِسْمُ الْمَوْصُولُ).

The grammarian Abū 'Ishāq al-Zajjāj (الزَّجّاج), who was like Sībawayhi from the Basra school of grammar, even said: "It has not appeared to me that Sībawayhi has erred except in two instances, whereof this is one; for he has conceded that أَيّ is declinable when separated, and how can he say that it is indeclinable when it is a prefixed noun?"[6]

The grammarian Sālih al-Jarmī (صالِح الْجَرْمِيّ), who was from the Basra school too, allegedly said: "I have left Basra and have not heard, from my leaving the Khandak [the trench] to Mecca, anyone say, لَأَضْرِبَنَّ أَيُّهُمْ قَائِمٌ (I will assuredly beat him, of them, **who** is standing)"[7], with ضَمّة on أَيّ and not, as al-Jarmī proposed, with فَتْحة (أَيَّهُمْ) – implying hereby that Sībawayhi's analysis is wrong.

Let's see in detail what the grammarians said about أَيّ:

Sībawayhi (سيبويه)	I will assuredly beat him, of them, **who** is most excellent.	لَأَضْرِبَنَّ أَيُّهُمْ أَفْضَلُ.
	In the part أَيُّ (هُوَ) أَفْضَلُ (*him who is most excellent*), أَيّ would be **indeclinable** according to Sībawayhi. So, the verb doesn't trigger case endings. Note that we must suppress the pronoun هُوَ after أَيُّهُمْ; otherwise, the grammar would change.	
Al-Farrā' (الْفَرَّاء)	I will assuredly beat him, of them, or **whichever** of them, says that.	لَأَضْرِبَنَّ أَيُّهُمْ يَقُولُ ذلِكَ. لَأَضْرِبَنَّ أَيَّهُمْ يَقُولُ ذلِكَ.
	Al-Farrā' says that when أَيّ is governed by the preceding verb (= أَيّ gets cases), it loses its interrogative meaning and turns into a **relative pronoun** – which means: it works like الَّذِي. But unlike Sībawayhi, he permitted both: you treat it as indeclinable (أَيُّهُمْ) or as visibly governed by the verb (أَيَّهُمْ).	
Al-Kisā'i (الْكِسَائِيّ)	I will assuredly beat him, of them, or **whichever** of them, is in the house.	لَأَضْرِبَنَّ أَيَّهُمْ فِي الدَّارِ.
	Al-Kisā'i opposed Sībawayhi's and treated أَيّ as **declinable**.	

Watch out: Al-Kisā'i also stated that you can't treat أَيّ as a declinable relative pronoun if the	ضَرَبْتُ أَيَّهُمْ فِي الدَّارِ. *Such constructions are not*

---

6 مَا تَبَيَّنَ لِي أَنَّ سِيبَوَيْهِ غَلِطَ فِي كِتَابِهِ إِلَّا فِي مَوْضِعَيْنِ، هَذَا أَحَدُهُمَا" قَالَ" وَقَدْ أَعْرَبَ سِيبَوَيْهِ "أَيًّا" وَهِيَ مُفْرَدَةٌ لِأَنَّهَا مُضَافَةٌ، فَكَيْفَ يُبْنِيهَا مُضَافَةً"؟

7 خَرَجْتُ مِنَ الْبَصْرَةِ فَلَمْ أَسْمَعْ مُنْذُ فَارَقْتُ الْخَنْدَقِ إِلَى مَكَّةَ أَحَدًا يَقُولُ: " لَأَضْرِبَنَّ أَيُّهُمْ قَائِمٌ" بِالضَّمِّ بَلْ يَنْصِبُ

| verb inducing a case ending is in the **past tense**. | *permitted in Arabic.* |

| So al-Kisā'i distinguished between the actual occurrence and that which is expected (فَرَّقَ بَيْنَ الْوَاقِعِ وَالْمُنْتَظَرِ). Most scholars follow his view. For example, you don't say: أَعْجَبَنِي أَيُّهُمْ قَامَ. You can only use: يُعْجِبُنِي. |

We see from the examples that issue is not clear at all and terribly complicated. The famous grammarian Ibn Mālik (ابن مالك), an Andalusian scholar who lived in the 13th century, devoted five lines of his famous thousand verse Arabic grammar poem 'Alfīya (أَلْفِيّة) to أَيّ, siding with Sībawayhi and thus implying that it is a إِسْمٌ مَوْصُولٌ (*relative pronoun*). It starts in line 99. The first line is as follows:

| "The word أَيّ is like مَا [which also functions as a relative pronoun], and is **declinable** as long as it is not a مُضَاف (to anything). | أَيٌّ كَمَا وَأُعْرِبَتْ مَا لَمْ تُضَفْ. |
| and the initial part of its relative clause is not a ضَمِيرٌ [personal pronoun] that has been elided [otherwise it will be **indeclinable**]." | وَصَدْرُ وَصْلِهَا ضَمِيرٌ انْحَذَفْ. |

Is the whole discussion worth it? Yes, and as often, it has to do with the Qur'an (19:69). There is a verse that could be read in two ways (although nowadays, only option 1 is used).

Sura 19:69	According to the Basra reading, you pronounce the vowel "*u*" ➡	ثُمَّ لَنَنزِعَنَّ مِن كُلِّ شِيعَةٍ أَيُّهُمْ أَشَدُّ عَلَى الرَّحْمَنِ عِتِيًّا.	1
	According to the Kūfa reading, you pronounce the vowel "*a*" ➡	ثُمَّ لَنَنزِعَنَّ مِن كُلِّ شِيعَةٍ أَيَّهُمْ أَشَدُّ عَلَى الرَّحْمَنِ عِتِيًّا.	2
	Al-Farrā' said that he who reads أَيَّهُمْ (in the accusative case) in this verse makes أَيّ to be governed by لَنَنزِعَنَّ.		

| We shall seize out of each group **those who** were most disobedient towards the Lord of Mercy. (*Abdul Haleem*) |

| Then We shall pluck out from every sect **whichever of them** was most stubborn in rebellion to the Beneficent. (*Pickthall*) |

But even if you agree on pronouncing أَيُّ with "*u*", which most grammarians finally did, the analysis of verse 19:69 is nothing but trivial. It has to do with the nature of أَيِّ: is it a relative or an interrogative pronoun? That's not as easy as it might look like.

The following analysis shows what **Sībawayhi** had to say about it. It's the common view regarding the grammatical analysis.

Relative pronoun (اِسْمٌ مَوْصُولٌ); it is the **direct object** (مَفْعُولٌ بِهِ) of the verb نَنْزِعَنَّ. It should get the markers of the accusative case. Since we treat أَيُّ as **indeclinable** (مَبْنِيٌّ عَلَى الضَّمِّ), we can only assign a non-visible place value (فِي مَحَلِّ نَصْبٍ).	أَيُّ
This is a pronoun suffix (ضَمِيرٌ مُتَّصِلٌ مَبْنِيٌّ) in the position of the second part of a إِضَافَةٌ, the so-called مُضَافٌ إِلَيْهِ.	هُمْ
The word أَشَدُّ is the predicate (خَبَرٌ) of the deleted subject (مُبْتَدَأٌ مَحْذُوفٌ) which has the estimated meaning of *they* (هُمْ).	أَشَدُّ
The sentence (هُمْ أَشَدُّ) does not have a position in إِعْرَابٌ. Why? Because it is the relative clause (صِلَةُ الْمَوْصُولِ أَيّ)! See *question #86.*	

Now let's check what **al-Khalīl** (and other mainly Kūfan grammarians) proposed. The discussion was primarily about the object of the verb. Al-Khalīl said that the object was actually suppressed, and that the implied meaning is: *we will assuredly draw forth those of whom it will be said*, *"Which of them is most..."*

Al-Khalīl said that أَيِّ is an interrogative pronoun (اِسْمُ اِسْتِفْهامٍ) serving as the subject (مُبْتَدَأٌ); therefore, it is in the nominative.	أَيُّ
The pronoun suffix هُمْ is the second part of the إِضَافَةٌ and gets the place value of a genitive case (فِي مَحَلِّ جَرٍّ مُضَافٌ إِلَيْهِ).	هُمْ
The word أَشَدُّ is the predicate (خَبَرٌ). The entire sentence (أَيُّهُمْ أَشَدُّ) is set in the position of an accusative case as it serves as the **deleted object of the speech** (مَقُولُ الْقَوْلِ) of the missing, but implicitly understood expression: يُقالُ فِيهِم (*of whom it will be said*).	أَشَدُّ

121. What is the ل in the word ذٰلِكَ؟

This لام *is a so-called* لاَمُ الْبُعْدِ *and indicates that the person or thing pointed at (*الْمُشارُ إِلَيْهِ*) is far away.*

This type of *Lām* has a demonstrative meaning and denotes distance (اللّاَمُ الزّائِدَةُ). It is usually counted as an **extra letter** (للدَّلالةِ عَلَى الْبُعَدِ) that does not govern other words – which means that it doesn't induce any case ending. Note: The only part in ذٰلِكَ that can be charged with a function in a sentence (subject, object, etc.) is the word ذا.

That is Karīm.	ذٰلِكَ كَرِيمٌ.
Demonstrative word (اِسْمُ إِشارةٍ). It is in the position of the **subject** (فِي مَحَلِّ رَفْعٍ مُبْتَدَأٌ).	ذا
This letter (حَرْفٌ) points to distance (لاَمُ الْبُعْدِ); no place in إِعْرابٌ.	ل
Particle of address (حَرْفُ خِطابٍ); doesn't have a position in إِعْرابٌ.	ك
Predicate (خَبَرٌ) of the subject in the nominative case (مَرْفُوعٌ).	كَرِيمٌ

122. Can a demonstrative word (*this*) be an adjective?

Yes, this is possible.

هٰذا is usually translated as *this*. In fact, هٰذا is a combination of ها plus ذا which is written like هٰذا – with a dagger Aleph. Let's check the standard application:

This is Karīm.	هٰذا كَرِيمٌ.
Particle of attention (حَرْفُ تَنْبِيهٍ). It does not have a place in إِعْرابٌ (لا مَحَلَّ لَها مِن الْإِعْرابِ).	ها
Demonstrative noun (اِسْمُ إِشارةٍ) which is the subject (مُبْتَدَأٌ) in this sentence. We cannot visibly put case markers because the word is indeclinable (مَبْنِيٌّ عَلَى السُّكُونِ); we can only say that it holds the position of a nominative case (فِي مَحَلِّ رَفْعٍ).	ذا
Predicate (خَبَرٌ) in the nominative case (مَرْفُوعٌ).	كَرِيمٌ

Now, what about the function as an adjective (صِفَةٌ)?

If the اِسْمُ الْإِشارةِ is placed <u>after</u> the noun, the اِسْمُ الْإِشارةِ is just an adjective (صِفَةٌ) and nothing else. The crux of the matter: we often translate it into English as it would be a demonstrative pronoun. However, there are no demonstrative pronouns in Arabic. Arabic only has nouns (اِسْمٌ) that convey the meaning of demonstrative pronouns.

This book is useful. (The book, this one, is useful.)	الْكِتابُ هذا مُفيدٌ.

Subject (مُبْتَدَأٌ) of the nominal sentence in the nominative case.	الْكِتابُ
Particle of attention (حَرْفُ تَنْبيهٍ); doesn't have a place in إعْرابٌ.	ها
Demonstrative noun (اِسْمُ الْإِشارةِ). Here it functions as an adjective (صِفَةٌ) and therefore has to "follow" the noun which it describes regarding the case. In this example, we view it as holding the place of a nominative case (مَرْفوعٌ) like the subject (which it further describes). But you can't visibly see all that.	ذا
Predicate in the nominative case (خَبَرٌ مَرْفوعٌ).	مُفيدٌ

What would happen if we added كَ? ➡ We would get ذاكَ. This brings along a question. Would this كَ be the second part of a إضافةٌ? **No!**

Such كَ is a *particle* of address (حَرْفُ خِطابٍ). If it was indeed a pronoun, it would serve as the second part of a إضافةٌ: the مُضافٌ إلَيْهِ. Let's assume for a moment that we have a إضافةٌ. The اِسْمُ إشارةٍ would be the first part: the مُضافٌ. **BUT:** A demonstrative noun (اِسْمُ الْإِشارةِ) - *that* - is by its nature <u>definite</u> (مَعْرِفةٌ). A definite word, however, can never serve as the <u>first</u> part of a إضافةٌ. Let's continue with our analysis.

Could the word after the demonstrative (الْمُشارُ إلَيْهِ) work as an **apposition** (بَدَلٌ)? **Yes**, that's possible. If that word is definite by Aleph and Lām (الـ), then it is an attribute (نَعْتٌ) or apposition (بَدَلٌ). But we only see it as having the function of a بَدَلٌ. This is because the الْمُشارُ إلَيْهِ (the word after *this, that*) is the actual word what the speaker or writer intends to point at, and this is the function of the بَدَلٌ. If we see it as an attribute (نَعْتٌ), the word would not have a real meaning here.

I greeted these students.	سَلَّمْتُ عَلَى هؤُلَاءِ الطُّلابِ.

Particle of attention (حَرْفُ تَنْبِيهٍ)؛ no position in إِعْرابٌ.	ها
Demonstrative (اِسْمُ الْإِشارةِ). Don't get confused: This word is indeclinable and only by coincidence built on the same vowel as the appropriate case marker would be (كَسْرةٌ). We therefore have to assign a place value – that of a genitive case (جَرٌّ) since it is placed after the preposition عَلَى.	أُولاءِ
Apposition (بَدَلٌ)؛ it takes the same case as the word it refers to; therefore, it is مَجْرُورٌ by a كَسْرةٌ.	الطُّلابِ

PREPOSITIONS (حَرْفُ الْجَرِّ)

123. How many kinds of prepositions does Arabic know?

Mainly three.

The usual job of a preposition is to direct the reader or listener to a certain time or place – this type is easy to understand. But there are other kinds of prepositions which can easily be misunderstood. Let's look at the three main types in Arabic:

1. The original, unspoiled, real preposition (حَرْفٌ أَصْلِيٌّ).

Such words add a **new sub-meaning** to the sentence. They form a prepositional phrase and **can't be omitted**. You can only delete the entire prepositional phrase, but never just the preposition.

2. Extra (additional) prepositions or particles (حَرْفٌ زائِدٌ).

They **can be deleted** because they are mainly there to give (some) **emphasis**. The most common are بـ and مِن. They do <u>not</u> add a new sub-meaning. So, what is the meaning of *extra* (زِيادةٌ) here?

This does not mean that it is meaningless or that its presence in a sentence is as if it were not there. Its job is to **emphasize** and **strengthen the connection** between parts of the sentence. Such devices are not related to any word in the sentence. The following حُرُوفُ الْجَرِّ can either be used as أَصْلِيٌّ or زائِدٌ. So always double check to get the correct meaning.

بـ	لـ	كـ	مِن

3. Semi-optional prepositions (حَرْفٌ شَبِيهٌ بِالزّائِدِ). Roughly speaking, they're somewhere between type 1 and type 2.

If you add them, you add a new meaning. If you don't add them, the sentence still works, but the meaning is different. They convey a new meaning – but theoretically, they could be omitted and the sentence would still work; however, the meaning would be different. Examples are رُبَّ (*question #136*) and the particles of exclusion عَدا and خَلا and حاشا (#408). These devices are not related to any word in the sentence.

124. How many real prepositions does Arabic know?

Most grammarians say seventeen.

In Arabic, prepositions (حَرْفُ الْجَرِّ) are words that influence nouns or pronouns. Prepositions always precede the words they influence. You don't use them before verbs. A حَرْفُ الْجَرِّ *drags* or *pulls* a word into the genitive case which is literally the meaning of the II-verb جَرَّ - يَجُرُّ (R2=R3). Together with the *dragged* (مَجْرُورٌ) word, they form a prepositional phrase (الْجارُّ وَالْمَجْرُورُ). Although they do govern other words in the genitive, they themselves are never governed by anything. They don't have a position in إِعْرابٌ and never get case endings. Furthermore, all real prepositions are **indeclinable** (مَبْنِيٌّ) in Arabic.

Contrary to other languages, prepositions in Arabic can only rule over other words by inducing the genitive case. The words that are governed are called مَجْرُورٌ. In German, for example, you can have the Dativ (*auf dem Dach*) or Akkusativ (*durch den Garten*) after a preposition.

The grammarian Ibn Yaʿīsh al-Nahwī (ابن يَعيش النَّحْوِيّ), who was born in 1158 (553 AH) in Aleppo and became an adherent of the grammar school ob Basra (الْبَصْرِيُّونَ), named 17 prepositions in his famous work *Sharh al-Mufassal* (شَرْح الْمُفَصَّل).

مُنْذُ	13	عَنْ	7	ب	1
مُذْ	14	فِي	8	ت	2
عَدَا	15	عَلَى	9	ل	3
حاشا	16	مِن	10	ك	4

خَلَا	17		إِلَى	11		تَاءُ الْقَسَم	5
			حَتَّى	12		واوُ الْقَسَم	6

Note that حاشَا and خَلَا and عَدَا can be treated as verbs in the past tense – which is the situation if we use them to denote *exceptions* (see #408).

Ibn ʿAqīl (ابن عَقيل), who was born in 1294 (694 AH), said that there are **twenty**. He added the following three:

لَعَلَّ	20		مَتَى	19		كَيْ	18

Ibn ʿAqīl authored the most famous commentary on the *'Alfīya* (الْأَلْفِيّة) of Ibn Mālik (ابن مالِك). The 'Alfīya is a rhymed book of Arabic grammar written in the 13th century. It was one of the two major books on Arabic that were used to teach Classical Arabic until the 20th century. The other book was *al-Ājurrūmīya* (الْآجُرُّومية). It was also published in the 13th century and written in verse form to ease the memorization of rules. The author, Muhammad Ibn Ājurrūm (مُحَمَّد بن آجُرُّوم), was a Moroccan Berber.

125. Does a preposition have a meaning of its own?

That is disputed and has been debated for ages.

Some grammarians say that the حَرْفٌ does not express a meaning of its own. I do not fully agree with that. In my opinion, in Arabic, a preposition (حَرْفٌ) does indicate a slight meaning of its own. For example, the preposition مِنْ (*from*) is used for portioning (تَبعيضٌ) or to indicate a start (ابْتِداءٌ). The preposition إِلَى (*to*) serves to express an intention, but has also the meaning of utmost or extreme (غايَةٌ).

Moreover, a حَرْفٌ itself influences nouns and verbs in a way that it can change their meaning or even revert the meaning into the opposite or at least provide a contrast (نَقيضٌ). For example:

to desire, wish, crave something	فِي	يَرْغَبُ - رَغِبَ
to dislike, detest, loathe something	عَنْ	

The early Arabic grammarians checked what the Greeks had to say about that. Aristotle, the ancient Greek philosopher, used a different approach to analyze the particle:

- Aristotle says that the particle has a definite function but **no specific meaning**. We could say that he treated particles by looking at their **logical** relations (e.g. conjunction, negation).

- On the other hand, Sībawayhi, the great Arabic grammarian, says in the first chapter of *The Kitāb* (الْكِتَاب) that the حَرْف "**came for some meaning**" (جاءَ لِمَعْنًى) but has no specific function. Sībawayhi analyzes the حَرْف in relation to its **grammatical** function.

Sībawayhi's approach is founded on the principle that one element acts upon the other. What Western grammarians call a *regent* or *governor* is named by Sībawayhi "*element operating on*" (الْعامِلُ فِي).

For a preposition, this means the following. It is the operator for the genitive (جَرٌّ) which is also the reason why we call it حَرْفُ الْجَرِّ.

For the word on which a preposition operates, we use the term مَجْرُورٌ. We usually translate it as *genitive*.

126. Can you delete a preposition without changing the meaning?

Yes, this is possible – but only in a certain situation.

If we want to delete a preposition in a sentence, we need certain ingredients: the phrase after the now deleted preposition must be an **interpreted infinitive** (مَصْدَرٌ مُؤَوَّلٌ) molded by أَنْ plus a verb (subjunctive/مَنْصُوبٌ mood) or by أَنَّ and its governed factors (مَعْمُولَاها).

Let's see all this in action and use the I-verb طَمِعَ - لا يَطْمَعُ plus بِ or فِي which means *to desire, to crave something*.

I long for Zayd to visit me.	أَطْمَعُ أَنْ يَزُورَنِي زَيْدٌ.
equivalent meaning: →	أَطْمَعُ فِي زِيارَةِ زَيْدٍ.

Particle (حَرْفُ نَصْبٍ وَمَصْدَرٍ) to mold an interpreted مَصْدَرٌ.	أَنْ
Verb in the present tense (فِعْلٌ مُضارِعٌ) in the مَنْصُوب-mood (subjunctive) due to the particle أَنْ.	يَزُورَنِي

The resulting interpreted infinitive (مَصْدَرٌ مُؤَوَّلٌ) is placed in the position of a genitive case. It is governed by the **deleted** preposition (فِي مَحَلِّ جَرٍّ بِحَرْفٍ مَحْذُوفٍ).

This construction (without a preposition) is used in the Qur'an:

Sura 26:82	...and Who, **I hope** will forgive me my faults on the Day of Recompense, (the Day of Resurrection).	...وَالَّذِي أَطْمَعُ أَن يَغْفِرَ لِي خَطِيئَتِي يَوْمَ الدِّينِ.

Another example: I-verb سَعِدَ - يَسْعَدُ plus بِ; it means *to be happy.*

I am happy that you are successful.	سَعِدْتُ أَنَّكَ ناجِحٌ.
equivalent meaning ➡	سَعِدْتُ بِنَجاحِكَ.

أَنَّكَ	Particle of emphasis which operates on other words in the accusative (حَرْفُ تَوْكِيدٍ وَنَصْبٍ). The كَ is the إِسْمُ أَنَّ; so it is grammatically placed in the position of an accusative case (فِي مَحَلِّ نَصْبٍ).
ناجِحٌ	Predicate (خَبَرُ أَنَّ), in the nominative case (مَرْفُوعٌ).

What happened here? The interpreted مَصْدَرٌ, consisting of أَنَّ and its governed factors, is found in the position of a genitive case which is ruled upon by a **deleted preposition** (الْمَصْدَرُ الْمُؤَوَّلُ مِن أَنَّ وَمَعْمُولَيْها فِي مَحَلِّ جَرٍّ بِحَرْفٍ مَحْذُوفٍ).

The same happens when we delete لِ which is the type of *Lām to indicate the purpose or the reason why a thing is done* (لامُ التَّعْلِيلِ). Such a لِ is followed by a true مَصْدَرٌ. Finally, we are left with a كَيْ الْمَصْدَرِيَّة which produces an **interpreted** مَصْدَرٌ.

I traveled to Cairo to study.	سافَرْتُ إِلَى الْقاهِرَةِ كَيْ أَدْرُسَ.
equivalent meaning: →	سافَرْتُ إِلَى الْقاهِرَةِ لِلدِّراسَةِ.

كَيْ	Particle (حَرْفُ نَصْبٍ وَمَصْدَرٍ) to mold an interpreted infinitive.
أَدْرُسَ	Verb in the present tense (فِعْلٌ مُضارِعٌ); it is in the مَنْصُوبٌ-mood (subjunctive) due to the particle كَيْ.
	The interpreted مَصْدَرٌ consisting of كَيْ plus a following verb is in the po-

sition of a genitive case guarded by a deleted preposition.

This operation may also occur in an **oath** (حَرْفُ قَسَمٍ):

I swear (your life), I will be faithful to you!	حَيَاتِكَ لَأُخْلِصَنَّ لَكَ!
Equivalent meaning ➡	بِحَيَاتِكَ!
The word حَيَاة in the first example is in the genitive case by a deleted preposition (مَجْرُورٌ بِحَرْفٍ مَحْذُوفٍ), marked by a visible كَسْرَةٌ.	

EXTRA LETTERS & PREPOSITIONS TO EMPHASIZE THE MEANING

127. Can the بـ strengthen a word's meaning?

Yes, it can – as a superfluous augment (زَائِدةٌ).

The preposition بـ has a special character that is different from others that are otherwise very similar. Let's see what we mean by this.

- بـ merely indicates that a thing or person **is close to the other** or in contact with. Therefore, the preposition بـ can <u>be used to lay emphasis</u> (تَوْكِيـدٌ) on someone/something. In the language of grammarians: it may be used to emphasize the relation between subject and predicate or subject and object in a verbal sentence.

- فِي indicates that one thing is in the midst of another, surrounded by it **on all sides**. Therefore, the preposition فِي, since it is precise in meaning, <u>can't</u> be used additionally.

How can we use بـ to emphasize? We have many options. In all the following examples بـ is treated as follows:

Extra/additional preposition (حَرْفُ جَرٍّ زَائِدٌ)	بـ

1. The بـ is placed **before** the **subject** (مُبْتَدَأٌ) of a <u>nominal</u> sentence.

Knowledge is enough for you.	بِحَسْبِكَ الْعِلْمُ.
Allah is enough for you.	بِحَسْبِكَ اللّٰهُ.

Note: حَسْبُكَ is a اِسْمُ فِعْلٍ in the meaning of *to be sufficient* (كَفَى). See #153.	

Subject (مُبْتَدَأٌ) of the nominal sentence; it must be in the nominative (مَرْفُوعٌ) case. We can only use a ضَمَّةٌ مُقَدَّرَةٌ which is an imaginary, assumed and non-visible case marker, because the preposition prevents us from placing the actual case marker. For this reason, we see and pronounce a كَسْرَةٌ although the word is according to its grammatical function not in the genitive (مَجْرُورٌ).	حَسْبُ
Pronominal suffix (ضَمِيرٌ مُتَّصِلٌ); second part of the إِضَافَةٌ (the مُضَافٌ إِلَيْهِ). It has an indeclinable shape; it always stays the same and ends in فَتْحَةٌ (no matter what the case is). So, we can only say that it is located in the position of a genitive case (فِي مَحَلِّ جَرٍّ).	كَ
Predicate (خَبَرٌ) in the nominative case (مَرْفُوعٌ بِالضَّمَّةِ الظَّاهِرَةِ).	الْعِلْمُ

2. **The most common application:** A إِذَا الْفُجَائِيَّةُ, which introduces a person or thing that suddenly comes into the view, is placed before the subject (مُبْتَدَأٌ). Then, you insert a ب between إِذَا and the مُبْتَدَأٌ.

I went out and (suddenly) saw Zayd standing.	خَرَجْتُ فَإِذَا بِزَيْدٍ وَاقِفٌ.

Subject (مُبْتَدَأٌ) in the nominative case (مَرْفُوعٌ) – but only by a virtual, estimated case marker (ضَمَّةٌ مُقَدَّرَةٌ) because the preceding preposition drags the word visibly into the genitive (مَجْرُورٌ) case.	زَيْدٍ
Predicate (خَبَرٌ) in the nominative case (مَرْفُوعٌ).	وَاقِفٌ

3. The ب can also be placed **before** the **predicate** (خَبَرٌ) for emphasis.

Zayd is not stingy.	مَا زَيْدٌ بِبَخِيلٍ.

Negation particle (حَرْفُ نَفْيٍ); does not have a position in إِعْرَابٌ.	مَا
Subject (مُبْتَدَأٌ) of the nominal sentence; nominative (مَرْفُوعٌ) case.	زَيْدٌ
Predicate (خَبَرٌ) in the nominative case although you can't see that. The preposition, which precedes the word, drags the word visibly into the genitive case (جَرٍّ). Because of this we can only use an as-	بَخِيلٍ

sumed case marker (مَرْفُوعٌ بِضَمّةٍ مُقَدّرةٍ) for the nominative case.	

There is another possibility for the analysis of the above sentence which some consider even better. It all comes down to the function of ما.

Negation particle (حَرْفُ نَفْي) that works similarly to لَيْسَ and shares the same grammatical implications: it governs the predicate (خَبَر ما) in the accusative. This has the implication that although you only see the respective case marker due to the preposition, the **predicate** (i.e., بِخِيلٍ) is set in the position of an **accusative** case (فِي مَحَلّ نَصْبٍ).	ما

ما can be substituted by لَيْسَ; the ب actually often occurs with لَيْسَ.

Zayd is not stingy.	لَيْسَ زَيْدٌ بِبَخِيلٍ.

Defective past tense verb (فِعْلٌ ماضٍ ناقِصٌ). See *question #58* for more information why we call it *defective*.	لَيْسَ
This is the "subject" (اِسْمُ لَيْسَ) in the nominative case (مَرْفُوعٌ).	زَيْدٌ
Predicate (خَبَرُ لَيْسَ) in the accusative case (مَنْصُوبٌ). But watch out! We can't use the appropriate, usual case marker (nunation; فَتْحةٌ) because the additional preposition occupies the place of the case marker – and for this reason, you only see the genitive marker "-*in*" (كَسْرةٌ). However, regarding the grammatical skeleton, بَخِيل is located in the position of an accusative case (فِي مَحَلّ نَصْبٍ).	بَخِيلٍ

4. The ب can be put **before the subject** (فاعِلٌ) of a <u>verbal</u> sentence.

Sura 10:29	Allah is witness enough between us and you.	فَكَفَى بِاللّهِ شَهِيدًا بَيْننا وَبَيْنَكُمْ.

Past tense verb (فِعْلٌ ماضٍ). This verb doesn't need a preposition. If you see a preposition, it is just an extra preposition (only additional) like the ب in our example.	كَفَى
Subject (فاعِلٌ) in the nominative case (مَرْفُوعٌ) by a virtual, estimated case marker (ضَمّةٌ مُقَدّرةٌ).	اللّهِ
Specification (تَمْييزٌ); thus, it gets the accusative (مَنْصُوبٌ) case.	شَهِيدًا

5. The **بـ** <u>must</u> be put before the **subject** (فَاعِلٌ) when the form أَفْعِلْ **بِه** is used: the pattern for **surprise and wonder** (تَعَجُّبٌ).

What an excellent man Zayd is!	أَفْضِلْ بِزَيْدٍ!

Past tense verb which comes in the form of an imperative (فِعْلٌ ماضٍ جاءَ عَلَى صيغةِ الْأَمْرِ).	أَفْضِلْ
Subject (فَاعِلٌ) in the nominative (مَرْفُوعٌ) by a ضَمَّةٌ مُقَدَّرَةٌ. The preceding preposition forces the genitive case (مَجْرُورٌ).	بِزَيْدٍ

6. The **بِـ** can bet put before the **direct object** (مَفْعُولٌ بِه).

Zayd shared his opinion.	أَدْلَى زَيْدٌ بِرَأْيِهِ.

Direct object (مَفْعُولٌ بِه). It is in the position of an accusative case. You don't see the actual case marker. We can only apply a virtual marker (مَنْصُوبٌ بِفَتْحةٍ مُقَدَّرةٍ) because the preposition was first and occupies the place for the case marker. ➡ You see the genitive case.	رَأْي

128. The preposition مِنْ does not always mean *from*. Is it true?

Yes, this is true.

The **additional** preposition مِنْ usually conveys one of the following three things: *emphasis* and *strengthening* (التَّوْكِيدُ), *inclusion* (الشُّمُولُ), or *getting absorbed* (الْإِسْتِغْراق). What is the recipe to use مِنْ?

- It is necessary that the preposition must be **preceded by a negation** (نَفْيٌ) or at least by a **question particle** (e.g., هَلْ);
- The genitive noun (اِسْمٌ مَجْرُورٌ) after مِن <u>must</u> be **indefinite** (نَكِرَةٌ).
- مِنْ can **only** be placed **before the subject**, regardless of whether it is the subject of a nominal (مُبْتَدَأٌ) or verbal sentence (فَاعِلٌ).

In all the following examples مِنْ is treated as follows:

Extra/additional preposition (حَرْفُ جَرٍّ زائِدٌ).	مِنْ

1. مِنْ is placed before the **delayed subject** of a <u>nominal</u> sentence.

Do you have a father?	هَلْ لَكُمْ مِنْ أَبٍ؟
There is no success for a lazy man.	مَا لِلْكَسُولِ مِنْ فَلَاحٍ.

Negation particle (حَرْفُ نَفْيٍ). It does not have a place in إِعْرَابٌ.	مَا
The prepositional phrase (الْجَارُّ وَالْمَجْرُورُ) appears in the place of the fronted predicate and is connected to a word that is not mentioned in the sentence (مُتَعَلِّق بِمَحْذُوفٍ خَبَرٌ مُقَدَّمٌ). If all this sounds strange to you, have a look at *question #140* where we deal with the nature of a prepositional phrase in a nominal sentence.	لِلْكَسُولِ
Delayed subject (مُبْتَدَأٌ مُؤَخَّرٌ) of the nominal sentence in the nominative case (مَرْفُوعٌ). However, the marker of the nominative (ضَمّة) case is not shown. We use an estimated case marker (ضَمّةٌ مُقَدَّرَةٌ) because the preposition occupies the spot of the case marker (اِشْتِغَالُ الْمَحَلِّ بِحَرَكَةِ حَرْفِ الْجَرِّ الزَّائِدِ).	فَلَاحٍ

2. مِنْ can be used in a **sentence with كَانَ**.

Nobody was in the house.	مَا كَانَ فِي الْبَيْتِ مِنْ أَحَدٍ.

Negation particle (حَرْفُ نَفْيٍ). It does not have a place in إِعْرَابٌ.	مَا
Deficient verb in the past tense (فِعْلٌ مَاضٍ نَاقِصٌ).	كَانَ
Prepositional phrase (الْجَارُّ وَالْمَجْرُورُ). Also here, the شِبْهُ الْجُمْلةِ is linked to the deletion of the fronted predicate (خَبَرُ كَانَ مُقَدَّمٌ) that is still implicitly understood; so the prepositional phrase steps in and thus takes the place of an accusative case (فِي مَحَلِّ نَصْبٍ).	فِي الْبَيْتِ
The "subject" (اِسْمُ كَانَ); nominative case. But why do we see the ending "-*in*" (كَسْرةٌ)? The word أَحَدٍ is placed in the position of a nominative case, marked by hypothetical, virtual markers (مَرْفُوعٌ بِضَمّةٍ مُقَدَّرةٍ). The additional preposition drags it into the genitive which is why you see "-*in*" (كَسْرةٌ).	أَحَدٍ

3. مِنْ can be put **before** the **subject** of a <u>verbal</u> sentence (جُمْلَةٌ فِعْلِيّةٌ).

Did anyone come?	هَلْ جاءَ مِنْ أَحَدٍ؟

أَحَدٍ is the subject (فاعِلٌ) of the verbal sentence. It is in the nominative case by imaginary, virtual markers (مَرْفُوعٌ بِضَمَّةٍ مُقَدَّرةٍ) since the extra preposition ignites the genitive marker upon the word.

4. مِنْ can also be put **before** the **direct object** (مَفْعُولٌ بِه).

I have not forgotten any of it.	ما نَسِيتُ مِنْ شَيْءٍ.
Did you see anyone?	هَلْ تَرَى مِنْ أَحَدٍ؟

Direct object (مَفْعُولٌ بِه); therefore, it must be in the accusative case (مَنْصُوبٌ). But we can only use an estimated marker (مَنْصُوبٌ بِفَتْحةٍ مُقَدَّرةٍ) as the preposition prevents us from placing the actual case marker (اِشْتِغالُ الْمَحَلِّ بِحَرَكةِ حَرْفِ الْجَرِّ الزّائِدِ).	أَحَدٍ

5. مِنْ can also enrich the **absolute object** (مَفْعُولٌ مُطْلَقٌ).

Only the person who faithfully and sincerely worships Allah will find his reward.	ما أَخْلَصَ إِنْسانٌ مِنْ إِخْلاصٍ إلّا وَجَدَ جَزاءَهُ.

Absolute object (مَفْعُولٌ مُطْلَقٌ); therefore, it must be in the accusative (مَنْصُوبٌ). However, we can only assign a place value for the accusative (and not a visible marker) because the preposition drags the word into the genitive case (مَنْصُوبٌ بِفَتْحةٍ مُقَدَّرةٍ, مَنَعَ مِنْ ظُهُورِها اِشْتِغالُ الْمَحَلِّ بِحَرَكةِ حَرْفِ الْجَرِّ الزّائِدِ).	إِخْلاصٍ

Remark: مِنْ, used as a real preposition, has a specialty. If you refer to space or time, مِنْ will refer to a certain segment of that place or time.

(at a place) within the house	مِنْ داخِلِ الْبَيْتِ
at night (in a part of the night)	مِنْ اللَّيْلِ
the next morning	مِنْ الْغَدِ
She returned immediately (in a part of her time).	رَجَعَتْ مِنْ وَقْتِها.

129. Why is لِمُحَمَّدٍ (for Muhammad) with "i" but لَهُ (for him) with "a"?

Originally, the preposition ل *got "a"* (فَتْحَةٌ)*, i.e,* لَ*. However, if you could mistake it with another type of* ل*, it will get "i", i.e,* لِ*.*

The *Lām* (ل) is one of the most intriguing letters. There are many applications (perhaps up to 40). The *Lām* has two main types: one has operating power (عامِلةٌ); the other is a neutral device (غَيْرُ عامِلةٍ). Furthermore, it may appear with the vowel *a* (فَتْحةٌ) or *i* (كَسْرةٌ).

In this *question*, we will only focus on the ل that is used as a **preposition** (لامُ الْجارّةُ or حَرْفُ الْجَرِّ). Interestingly, this preposition has the original vowel *a* (فَتحةٌ), i.e., لَ, and not *i* (كَسْرةٌ). The *a* still appears in لَكَ (*for you*) or لَهُ (*for him*). How do you know which type to use?

- Whenever you add a **pronominal suffix**, it is لَ except for *my/me* when you necessarily need the كَسْرةٌ before ي resulting in لِي.

- When it occurs with an apparent noun, it is لِ. For example, لِمُحَمَّدٍ (*for Muhammad*).

But why was the original sound changed into the *i* (كَسْرةٌ)? It is quite simple. There was the danger of confusing it with the *corroborative, strengthening inceptive Lam* (لامُ الْإِبْتِداءِ). An example:

ل as preposition (لامُ الْجارّةُ)	(Verily,) this is _for_ Ali.	إِنَّ هذا لَعَلِيٍّ.	1
Here, we cannot use the original لَ because without case markers, we could not tell the meaning.			

ل as emphasizer (لامٌ مُزَحْلَقةٌ)	(Verily,) this _is_ (indeed) Ali.	إِنَّ هذا لَعَلِيٌّ.	2
After إِنَّ the predicate (خَبَرُ إِنَّ) is often marked by لَ. This type of لَ does not operate on any word; therefore, عَلِيٌّ gets the nominative case since it is the predicate of إِنَّ. See also *question #260*.			

Now, let's check the situations with the ل as a preposition (لامُ الْجارّةُ).

1. The ل to transfer things or possession (لامُ التَّمْلِيكِ).

تَمْلِيكٌ is the مَصْدَرٌ of the II-verb مَلَّكَ - يُمَلِّكُ which means *to make someone the owner; to put someone in possession; to transfer ownership.*

I bought a book for my friend.	إِشْتَرَيْتُ لِصَدِيقِي كِتابًا.

> Here, the ل indicates that a thing was physically transferred.

2. The *Lām to indicate possession* (لامُ الْمِلْكِ).

The word مِلْكٌ is the مَصْدَرٌ of the I-verb مَلَكَ - يَمْلِكُ (*to possess*).

The book belongs to my friend.	الْكِتابُ لِصَديقي.
The ل here indicates ownership. It may express the meaning of *to have*.	

3. ل can be used in complex إِضافةٌ-constructions (لامُ الْإِسْتِحْقاقٍ).

إِسْتِحْقاقٌ is the مَصْدَرٌ of X-verb اِسْتَحَقَّ - يَسْتَحِقُّ (R2=R3) and means *to deserve; to be entitled*. This *Lām* is used to claim possession (to show that someone has a right to it). There is an important practical side of this device. You need such a ل to fix a construction in which you want the **first part** of a إِضافةٌ to be **indefinite** (*see #104*).

For example, you want to say: *a* house of *a* teacher. We can express that with بَيْتٌ لِمُدَرِّسٍ. Here, we use a ل to make it beyond any doubt clear what we intend to express. But is that really necessary?

If you use a simple إِضافةٌ, the expression may be ambiguous and understood as: *the* house of *a* teacher (بَيْتُ مُدَرِّسٍ). Why? By following the basic rules of the إِضافةٌ, the expression بَيْتُ مُدَرِّسٍ would mean *a house of a teacher* – given that the indefiniteness of the مُضافٌ إِلَيْهِ is induced in the مُضافٌ. However, since it is usual that a person (a teacher) owns only one house, the expression بَيْتُ مُدَرِّسٍ would commonly be translated as *the house of a teacher*. See also #105.

Praise belongs to Allah.	الْحَمْدُ لِلَّهِ.
A house of **the** teacher	بَيْتٌ لِلْمُدَرِّسٍ
The ل here is used to claim the possession of the house.	

Furthermore, if a إِضافةٌ is interrupted, you can use the لامُ الْإِسْتِحْقاقِ to fix it. Note: In general, you can only add a demonstrative word after the first part of a إِضافةٌ, but nothing more. But it is not only used in possessive constructions (إِضافةٌ). As soon as we deal with abstract things, this type of ل will be very useful:

Sura 27:77	and it is guidance and grace for those who believe.	وَإِنَّهُ لَهُدًى وَرَحْمَةٌ لِلْمُؤْمِنِينَ.

Some linguists categorize this type of ل even further and speak of a لامُ الإِخْتِصاص (the Lām to show that something is ascribed to one; in a way they see this ل as a tool for **particularization**.

لامُ الإِخْتِصاص	Paradise is (only) for the believers.	الْجَنَّةُ لِلْمُؤْمِنِينَ.
لامُ الإِسْتِحْقاقِ	Hell is for the unbelievers.	النّارُ لِلْكافِرِينَ.

What we have seen so far is the core meaning and most frequently attested usage (أَصْلٌ) of the Lām. So, let's continue.

4. The Lām to indicate a certain moment in time. This type is called لامُ الْوَقْتِ or لامُ التّارِيخ.

This boy is one year old. (The expression لِسَنةٍ means to the completion of a year. The meaning here is: مَرَّتْ عَلَيْهِ سَنةٌ.)	هذا الْغُلامُ لِسَنةٍ.
She died on that same day.	ماتَتْ لِيَوْمِهِ.
for the first time	لِأَوَّلِ مَرَّةٍ
the homework for today	واجِبُ الْبَيْتِ لِهذا الْيَوْم

5. ل may be used to indicate to whom you talk, whom you inform, etc. This type is called Lām of notification (لامُ التَّبْلِيغِ).

I told him...	قُلْتُ لَهُ...
I authorized him to...	أَذِنْتُ لَهُ...

6. The Lām that is used to indicate the reason. This type is called Lām of justification (لامُ التَّعْلِيل). The grammarians assume that it stands for لِأَنْ or لِكَيْ (in order to). This explains why we have to use the subjunctive mood of a verb (فِعْلٌ مَنْصُوبٌ) after ل. Note that you don't neces-

sarily need a verb after لِ. You can also use a مَصْدَرٌ.

I came here to study.	جِئْتُ لِأَدْرُسَ = لِلدِّراسةِ.
We say that the entity consisting of the particle أَنْ plus the verb after لِ is grammatically located in the position of a genitive case (فِي مَحَلِّ جَرٍّ بِاللّامِ الْمَذْكُورةِ) due to the preposition لِ.	

7. It may indicate a direction (regarding place or time). This type of *Lām* has (almost) the same meaning as إِلَى (*to*) and is called the *Lām to designate the limit of the action* (لامُ الْإِنْتِهاء). *See also question #130.*

I read the book until the end.	قَرَأْتُ الْكِتابَ لِآخِرِهِ

Sura 7:57	... we drive them to a dead land...	سُقْناهُ لِبَلَدٍ مَيِّتٍ...

How do we treat all these kinds of لِ in a grammatical analysis? We simply call them *preposition* (حَرْفُ الْجَرِّ) or لامُ الْجارّةُ. In the إِعْرابٌ, only the grammatical implications matter. In practice, however, when you need to translate a sentence with such a لِ, recognizing the right type can be crucial to getting the right meaning.

Watch out! The preposition لِ may also convey the **meaning of other prepositions**. Such sentences can be tricky. Some examples:

meaning of عَلَى - *on, upon*		
Sura 17:109	They fall down on their faces...	وَيَخِرُّونَ لِلْأَذْقانِ...
Meaning of عَلَى الْأَذْقانِ.		

meaning of بَعْدَ - *after*		
Sura 17:78	So perform the regular prayers in the period from the time the sun is past its zenith till the darkness of the night	أَقِمِ الصَّلاةَ لِدُلُوكِ الشَّمْسِ إِلَى غَسَقِ اللَّيْلِ.
Meaning of بَعْدَ دُلُوكِ الشَّمْسِ.		

meaning of عِنْدَ - *at*		

Sura 50:5	But the disbelievers deny the truth when it comes to them.	...بَلْ كَذَّبُوا بِالْحَقِّ لَمَّا جَاءَهُمْ
Meaning of جَاءَهُمْ: عِنْدَما.		

130. ذَهَبْتَ لِمَنْزِلِي (*You went to my house.*) - Is there a mistake?

Yes, a tiny one. In the example, you should better use إِلَى *instead of* لِ.

The لِ, when it denotes *to* or *towards*, is called the *Lām to designate the limit of the <u>action</u>* (لامُ الْاِنْتِهاءِ). It is related to إِلَى in meaning and also etymologically. Both words may be used as synonyms when we talk about places or time. This brings us closer to the difference:

- إِلَى mostly expresses **concrete** relations, local or temporal; it <u>can't</u> be used for emphasis (تَوْكِيدٌ).
- لِ indicates **abstract** or ideal relations; it can be used for **emphasis**. If it is used in the meaning of إِلَى, it is called the *Lām to designate the limit of the action* (لامُ الْاِنْتِهاءِ).

Having all this in mind, you should say:

إِلَى	You went to my house.	ذَهَبْتَ إِلَى مَنْزِلِي.
	Here, the preposition إِلَى points to the direction (لِلدَّلالَةِ عَلَى اِتِّجاهِ حُدُوثِ الْفِعْلِ) of the action.	

We can make the difference even clearer.

إِلَى	You went to work.	ذَهَبْتَ إِلَى الْعَمَلِ.
	Here you express that you went to the **place of the job/work** (ذَهَبْتَ إِلَى مَوْقِعِ الْعَمَلِ). ➡ The preposition expresses the direction (الْاِتِّجاهُ).	

لِ	You went to (**for**) work.	ذَهَبْتَ لِلْعَمَلِ.
	Here, you express that you went for the purpose of work (ذَهَبْتَ مِنْ أَجْلِ الْعَمَلِ). The لِ is used to **indicate the cause** (*in order to*). ➡ The لِ expresses the meaning of التَّعْلِيلُ (*explanation, justification*).	

Hint: You should use إِلَى if you talk about directions and concrete places. In fact, the verb ذَهَبَ (*to go*) is almost exclusively used with إِلَى.

131. What is the *Lām of rejection* or *denial* (لامُ الْجُحُودِ) good for?

This device (لِ) is only used together with the negation of كانَ.

Such a لِ is found after ما كانَ or لَمْ يَكُنْ which may express **was not** or **will not** depending on the context. The *Lām of the rejection or denial* (لامُ الْجُحُودِ), which is written as لِ (with كَسرةٌ), **strengthens the negation** or even **expresses a complete denial** or rejection (تُفِيدُ الْإِنْكارَ الشَّدِيدَ). The term جُحُودٌ denotes *denial; rejection.*

Such type of لِ induces the **subjunctive mood** (مَنْصُوبٌ) in the verb which is found after لِ. For an analysis, see *Arabic for Nerds 1, #126.*

I did not treat people unjustly (=not tyrannize).		لَمْ أَكُنْ لِأَظْلِمَ النَّاسَ.
Sura 8:33	But Allah would not punish them while you, [O Muhammad], are among them.	وَمَا كَانَ اللَّهُ لِيُعَذِّبَهُمْ وَأَنتَ فِيهِمْ.
4:137	**never** will Allah forgive them	لَمْ يَكُنِ اللَّهُ لِيَغْفِرَ لَهُمْ...

Excursus: What about the negation of يَكُونُ in the present tense? The verb يَكُونُ is a rare guest anyway since we do not use it as a copula verb in Arabic when the event or state is happening or true now. Theoretically, in Arabic, it is almost impossible to deny the present tense or a fact that is currently true with لا يَكُونَ. Hence, لا يَكُونَ can only denote a future or conditional meaning: *will not be; might not be; would not be.* If you want to deny a state or fact that is true now, you should use لَيسَ.

132. Can you use an extra/redundant لِ to emphasize?

*Yes. The لِ can be used for emphasis (تَوْكِيدٌ) and indicates the **intention** of the subject or the object of the action.*

This لام is called the *Lām that strengthens the operator* (اللّامُ لِتَقْوِية الْعامِلِ). In a way, this device can activate some kind of extra power that is found in a conjugated verb. Such لِ helps the regent/operator to exercise its influence on its object – by expressing the **direction of the action** towards the object. By the way, this works for the subject as well.

When do we normally use an extra/additional لِ?

1. We can put the ﻝ before the **direct object** (مَفْعُولٌ بِهِ). You will encounter such a situation regularly after the verb *to want* (أَرادَ).

I want to specialize in this science field.	أُرِيدُ لِأَتَخَصَّص فِي هذا الْعِلْمِ.

Additional, extra preposition (حَرْفُ جَرٍّ زائِدٌ).	لِ
Present tense verb (فِعْلٌ مُضارِعٌ); subjunctive mood (مَنْصُوبٌ).	أَتَخَصَّص
In the end, we get a مَصْدَرٌ مُؤَوَّلٌ, an *interpreted* infinitive, consisting of أَنْ plus a verb. The entire expression serves as the direct object and is placed in the position of an accusative case (فِي مَحَلِّ نَصْبٍ مَفْعُولٍ بِهِ).	

Let's stop for a moment. Why is it an interpreted infinitive and why don't we use أَنْ? The grammarians assume that originally the particle أَنْ was found after ﻝ, but at some point was omitted. Linguists call that an *ellipsis*. Nevertheless, the insertion of أَنْ would still be possible:

I came to you to read.	جِئْتُكَ لِأَقْرَأَ = جِئْتُكَ لِأَنْ أَقْرَأَ.

This type of ﻝ is often used when the operator (عامِلٌ) immediately precedes the object. In the examples below, the operator is underlined.

Repent, that Allah may forgive you!	تُبْ لِيَغْفِرَ لَكَ اللهُ!
He said this only to do him honor.	إِنَّما قالَ ذلِكَ إِكْرامًا لَهُ.

2. A tough one: Some grammarians say that it is okay to place a ﻝ between the مُضافٌ and the مُضافٌ إِلَيْهِ. This construction, however, is almost only used in poetry.

Literal meaning: *Not your father! You have no father!*	لا أَبا لَكَ! = لا أَباكَ

The translation of this ancient proverb depends on the situation. It is an exclamation found frequently after imperatives, conveying the idea: *strive, bestir yourself.* It is usually not an insult as the literal meaning would imply.

Absolute negation (نافِيةٌ لِلْجِنْسِ).	لا
The اِسْمُ لا; therefore, in the accusative (مَنْصُوبٌ). Since أَبٌ is one of	أَبا

the *six (five) nouns* (الْأَسْماءُ السِّتَّة), *father* (أَب) is put into the accusative by an Aleph because it is the first part of the إِضافة.	
Additional preposition (حَرْفُ جَرٍّ زائِدٌ). Note: Since we add كَ, which has a fixed, indeclinable shape (مَبْنِيٌّ عَلَى الْفَتْح) and always ends in a فَتْحَة, the لَ must also carry a فَتْحَة.	لَ
Pronominal suffix (ضَمِير); it has an indeclinable shape (see above). It is the مُضافٌ إِلَيْهِ, i.e., the second part of the إِضافة. For this reason, it holds the position of a genitive case (فِي مَحَلِّ جَرٍّ).	كَ

Remark: The above expression is an ancient saying. When Arab people find themselves in difficult times, the father assists them. If you say that proverb, you express that you are not someone's father and can't help – the person relies on himself. The phrase is used to deter the listener from being a fool and to push or encourage him/her. (تَعْبِيرٌ يُقالُ لِلْمُبالَغَةِ فِي الْمَدْحِ لِاعْتِمادِهِ فِي حَياتِهِ

عَلَى ذاتِهِ لا عَلَى والِدِهِ؛ لِلْحَثِّ عَلَى الشَّيْءِ)

He said, "Come on! What is that?" He said, "Something I heard him saying." (Ṣaḥīḥ al-Bukhārī 6939)	قالَ ما هُوَ لاَ أَبا لَكَ. قالَ شَيْءٌ سَمِعْتُهُ يَقُولُهُ.

133. Is كـ a preposition?

Yes and no. The كـ is a tricky letter.

To better understand the كافُ, let's take a look at its three main uses.

1	Used to compare things (كافُ التَّشْبِيهِ). Such a كـ conveys a similar meaning to مِثْل; it is therefore usually translated as: *as, like*.	اسْمٌ مَبْنِيٌّ ⟶ Note: Some call it a حَرْف.
2	Possessive pronoun (for nouns) or pronominal suffix (for verbs).	ضَمِيرٌ مَنْصُوبٌ or مَجْرُورٌ
3	Particle of address; used for the demonstrative noun. It does not have a position in إِعْرابٌ.	حَرْفُ خِطابٍ مَعَ اسْمِ الْإِشارَةِ

1	Or [like people who, under] a cloudburst from the sky... (Sura 2:19)	أَوْ كَصَيِّبٍ مِّنَ السَّماءِ ...
2	Your Lord has not forsaken you. (Sura 93:3)	ما وَدَّعَكَ رَبُّكَ.

| 3 | That... | ...ذَلِكَ |

Let's return to our question: Is the كَ in number 1 a noun (اِسْمٌ) or a preposition (حَرْفٌ)? This has been a long debate.

- The grammarians agree that the كَ operates on another word and induces the genitive case (مَجْرُورٌ).
- If the كَ is a اِسْمٌ (noun), they say that the كَ is the **first part** of a إِضافةٌ. What comes after the كَ is the second part (مُضافٌ إِلَيْهِ) and therefore takes the genitive case (مَجْرُورٌ).
- If the كَ is treated as a حَرْفٌ (particle; preposition), then the كَ induces the genitive case in a following word. The result is the same.

Let's see what the grandmasters have to say about that:

- Sībawayhi (سيبويه) stated that the كافُ التَّشْبِيهِ is a حَرْفٌ and not a اِسْمٌ. Only in poetry, it can be treated as a اِسْمٌ.
- Al-Fārisī (الْفارِسِيّ) and al-'Akhfash al-'Akbar (الْأَخْفَش الْأَكْبَر) both said that the كَ could be treated as both, اِسْمٌ or حَرْفٌ.

Others say it must be a اِسْمٌ because it has the meaning of مِثْل. Nowadays grammarians like to avoid a clear definition and state that the كافُ substitutes a اِسْمٌ without calling it a اِسْمٌ. They call it an *instrument of comparison* (أَداةُ التَّشْبِيهِ). It is not a big deal anyway as most grammarians accept to treat the كَ in either way.

| As a اِسْمٌ, it must be **governed by another word or device** which sets the function of the كَ in the sentence. Therefore, the كَ gets the إِعْرابٌ according to that position. Furthermore, it is the first part of the إِضافةٌ, so a following word must get the genitive (مَجْرُورٌ) case. | اِسْمٌ بِمَعْنَى مِثْل
 عَلَى الْإِسْمِيّة | 1 |
| Here, the كَ **does not have a place** in إِعْرابٌ since a حَرْفٌ can't be governed. In order for such sentences to work, we look in the sentence (تَقْدِيرٌ) for a deleted part to which the كَ refers. As a حَرْفُ الْجَرِّ, the كَ governs a following word in the genitive case. | حَرْفُ الْجَرِّ
 عَلَى الْحَرْفِيّة | 2 |

Option 1: If we treat كَ as a اِسْمٌ, we have a certain problem. A noun

receives case markers, but we can't put case markers on كَ, because it is indeclinable and always looks the same. We can only analyze it according to its place value; so, it may be placed in the position of a subject, object, predicate, etc. In short: the كَ has a place in إِعْرابٌ.

Muhammad is like a lion.	مُحَمَّدٌ كَالْأَسَدِ.
Predicate (خَبَرٌ) of the nominal sentence (جُمْلَةٌ اِسْمِيَّةٌ). It is regarded as a noun expressing *likeness* (اِسْمٌ بِمَعْنَى مِثْل). We can't put case markers as the كَ is indeclinable (مَبْنِيٌّ عَلَى الْفَتْحِ); we treat it according to its location in the sentence which is that of a nominative case (فِي مَحَلِّ رَفْعٍ); also the first part of the إِضافةٌ.	كَ
Second part of the إِضافةٌ, i.e., the مُضافٌ إِلَيْهِ.	الْأَسَدِ

Option 2: If we treat the كَ as a حَرْفٌ, we will need some tricks to make the sentence work grammatically. This is a bit similar to the debate whether a prepositional or adverbial phrase (شِبْهُ الْجُمْلةِ) is the predicate of a nominal sentence or whether it only relates to the predicate that had to be deleted (see *question #219*).

If we want to call the كَ a *preposition* (حَرْفٌ), this will mean that we have to find a job for it in the sentence because a حَرْفٌ does not have a position in إِعْرابٌ. We could achieve that by treating كَ as an **adjective** (صِفةٌ). What would we achieve by doing that? Well, the صِفةٌ would describe an implicitly understood absolute object (مَفْعُولٌ مُطْلَقٌ). This would mean that the كَ is virtually in the accusative case (فِي مَحَلِّ نَصْبٍ). Sounds complicated, and indeed, it is.

You came like Zayd.	جِئْتَ كَزَيْدٍ.
Interpretation: You came a coming like the coming of Zayd.	جِئْتَ مَجِيئًا كَمَجِيءٍ (مِثْلَ مَجِيءٍ) زَيْدٍ.

There is another way to treat the كَ as a حَرْفٌ. We can regard the كَ as a حالٌ. In our example, the كَ would relate to the pronominal suffix of the verb (جِئْتَ) which is the subject (فاعِلٌ) of the verbal sentence.

| You came being like Zayd. | جِئْتَ كائِنًا كَزَيْدٍ (مِثْلَ زَيْدٍ). |

Picky scholars say that كَ is generally a حَرْفٌ (*particle of comparison*) and only a إِسْمٌ if the كَ is placed **after** a preposition. The following sentence is a line by the poet al-'Ajjāj (الْعَجَّاج), عَبْدُ اللَّهِ بن رُؤْبة), who was born just before Islam was established and later became a Muslim.

Laughing, they [the women] bare (teeth), white as fallen hail.	يَضْحَكْنَ عَنْ كَالْبَرَدِ الْمُنْهَمِّ (الذَّائِب).
كَ is treated as a إِسْمٌ in place of مِثْل since **a preposition can't immediately govern another preposition**. We need a إِسْمٌ after عَنْ, e.g., عَنْ مِثْلِ الْبَرَدِ. The كَ is in the position of a genitive (فِي مَحَلِّ جَرٍّ) as it follows the preposition عَنْ. It is the first part of a إِضافة and governs الْبَرَدِ in the genitive.	

134. Can you use an extra كَ to emphasize?

That's disputed.

Don't get confused: Our discussion is not about the كَ that is used as a possessive pronoun like in كِتابُكَ (*your book*). In this *question*, we will deal with the so-called كافُ التَّشْبِيهِ – the *Kāf of comparison*.

Muhammad is like a lion in his courage.	مُحَمَّدٌ كَالْأَسَدِ فِي شَجاعَتِهِ.
Subject (مُبْتَدَأً) of the nominal sentence. It is in the nominative case (مَرْفُوعٌ), marked by the usual case marker (ضَمّةٌ ظاهِرةٌ).	مُحَمَّدٌ
The كَ is a **noun** expressing *likeness* (إِسْمٌ بِمَعْنَى مِثْل) and serves as the **predicate** of the nominal sentence; so, it holds the place of a nominative case (فِي مَحَلِّ رَفْع خَبَرُ الْمُبْتَدَإِ). We don't see it because the كَ is cemented on the ـ. It is also the **first part** of the إِضافة.	كَ
Second part of the إِضافة; genitive case (مُضافٌ إِلَيْهِ مَجْرُورٌ).	أَلْأَسَد

Such a كَ is often combined with أَنَّ to express: *as* or *as if*.

Muhammad speaks German as if he was a Berliner.	مُحَمَّدٌ يَتَحَدَّثُ اللُّغةَ الْأَلْمانِيّةَ وَكَأَنَّهُ بَرْلِينِيٌّ.

Let's return to our question. Can you use an extra كَ for emphasis? The majority of the grammarians say that كَ **can't** be used to convey emphasis (الْكافُ لا تُزادُ). But that's perhaps only half of the truth. Occasionally it is used in such regard to emphasize the meaning of *someone like*. (German: *seinesgleichen*). It is mostly used with مِثْل. For example:

Sura 42:11	...فَاطِرُ السَّمَاوَاتِ وَالْأَرْضِ جَعَلَ لَكُم مِّنْ أَنفُسِكُمْ أَزْوَاجًا وَمِنَ الْأَنْعَامِ أَزْوَاجًا يَذْرَؤُكُمْ فِيهِ لَيْسَ كَمِثْلِهِ شَيْءٌ وَهُوَ السَّمِيعُ الْبَصِيرُ.

...the Creator of the heavens and earth. He made mates for you from among yourselves – and for the animals too – so that you may multiply. **There is nothing like Him**: He is the All Hearing, the All Seeing.

Let's only focus on the fragment لَيْسَ كَمِثْلِهِ شَيْءٌ and do an analysis.

Defective past tense verb (فِعْلٌ مَاضٍ نَاقِصٌ).	لَيْسَ
Extra, additional preposition (حَرْفُ جَرٍّ زَائِدٌ).	كَ
This is the خَبَرُ لَيْسَ (predicate). In grammar, a word in that position gets the accusative case (مَنْصُوبٌ). So, what can we do here? We can only use a virtual case marker (فَتْحةٌ مُقَدَّرَةٌ). We use the term مَجْرُورٌ لَفْظًا – *genitive by pronunciation* – as the preceding extra preposition drags the word forcibly into the genitive and the induced كَسْرةٌ occupies the location of the case marker (اِشْتِغالُ الْمَحَلِّ بِحَرَكةِ حَرْفِ الْجَرِّ الزَّائِدِ). It is the first part of the إِضافةٌ.	مِثْلِ
Second part of the إِضافةٌ, in the genitive (جَرٍّ) case.	٥
The "subject" (اِسْمُ لَيْسَ); therefore, it must be in the nominative case (مَرْفُوعٌ بِالضَّمّةِ الظَّاهِرةِ).	شَيْءٌ

EXCURSUS: The fear of comparing Allah

People who say that كَ is **extra** (زِيادة) in this verse often do that out of fear. If you treated the كَ as it would have its original meaning (الْإِعْرابُ الْأَصْلِيةُ) expressing *like*, this could perhaps express that **there is a** *like* (مِثْل) **of Allah** which is impossible to believe for Muslims. Therefore, they treat كَ as superfluous along with the synonymous مِثْل. However, is the fear of such a misunderstanding justified? Others argue that in this particular line, treating كَ as a particle expressing *like* would lead to a **contradiction**. The translation, in that case, would be *nothing is like that which is like him*. A simple logical proof can reveal the flaw:

- The original statement is: **(1)** *nothing is like that which is like X*
- Let Y denote: *that which is like X in* **(1)**:

- **(2)** Y is: *that which is like X*
- Substituting **(2)** in **(1)**, we get:
- **(3)** *nothing is like Y*
- Since from **(2)** we know that Y is like X, it follows that:
- **(4)** *X is like Y*
- But **(4)** contradicts **(3)**. ➡ This concludes the proof.

135. *Many a... How do you say that in Arabic?*

You can use رُبَّ.

رُبَّ is translated as *many a....* In German, it would be *so manche/er/ es*, in French *maint...*Most grammarians say that رُبَّ denotes a small number or decrease (لِلتَّقْلِيلِ) – and only in rare situations a large number or increase (لِلتَّكْثِيرِ).

رُبَّ is an unusual word. It resembles an extra preposition (الْحَرْفُ الشَّبِيهُ بِالزَّائِدِ). Why? Well, if we deleted it, the sentence would still work – but leave us with a different meaning. This brings us to the topic of the so-called حَرْفُ الْجَرِّ الشَّبِيهُ بِالزَّائِدِ, a *particle that resembles an additional preposition*. There are two important representatives of this type: رُبَّ and the letter وَ.

Many a poor is happier than a rich.	رُبَّ فَقِيرٍ أَسْعَدُ مِنْ غَنِيٍّ.
Many a harmful has its useful side.	رُبَّ ضَارَّةٍ نَافِعَةٌ.

Word resembling an extra preposition (حَرْفُ جَرٍّ شَبِيهٌ بِالزَّائِدِ).	رُبَّ
Subject (مُبْتَدَأٌ) of the nominal sentence. It is in the nominative case (مَرْفُوعٌ) by a virtual, estimated case marker (ضَمَّةٌ مُقَدَّرَةٌ). We can't show the case marker because رُبَّ – since it works like a preposition – governs a word in the genitive case (اِشْتِغَالُ الْمَحَلِّ بِحَرَكَةِ حَرْفِ الْجَرِّ الشَّبِيهِ بِالزَّائِدِ).	ضَارَّةٍ
Predicate (خَبَرٌ) of the nominal sentence; nominative (مَرْفُوعٌ) by the ضَمَّةٌ (nunation). This part functions as the complement of رُبَّ and serves as a description of *many*.	نَافِعَةٌ

Let's quickly check the letter وَ. You might find an indefinite word in the genitive case (مَجْرُورٌ) after the word وَ. How can that happen?

In such a situation, we assume that رُبَّ had originally been there but was deleted and substituted by وَ. Therefore, we call this letter the *Wāw of* رُبَّ, in Arabic: واوُ رُبَّ. It conveys exactly the same meaning as رُبَّ. That's pretty heavy stuff, so it is perhaps a good idea to see an example.

Many a glass have I boozed (drunk).	وَكَأْسٍ شَرِبْتُ!
Many a middle-aged man I met. (Case markers matter. This sentence doesn't mean: *And I met an old man*.)	وَرَجُلٍ كَهْلٍ قَابَلْتُ.

So-called واوُ رُبَّ. It is a particle that works similarly to an extra preposition (حَرْفُ جَرٍّ شَبِيهٌ بِالزَّائِدِ).	وَ
Direct object (مَفْعُولٌ بِه). Although you see the marker of the genitive due to the preposition, the word is grammatically in the accusative case (مَنْصُوبٌ بِفَتْحَةٍ مُقَدَّرَةٍ).	رَجُلٍ
Adjective (نَعْتٌ) for *man*; it has to agree (case!) with *man*.	كَهْلٍ
Verb plus subject (فَاعِلٌ).	قَابَلْتُ

This is all pretty old stuff that is rarely used nowadays. This construction was already known in pre-Islamic times (الْجَاهِلِيّةُ). The following sentence is a verse written by Imru' al-Qays (امْرُؤُ الْقَيْس), a poet of the 6th century AD and the son of one of the last *Kindah* kings (كِنْدة). *Kindah* was a tribal kingdom in the Najd in present-day central Saudi-Arabia. Imru' al-Qays is often considered the **father of Arabic poetry**.

Many a night, like (dark as) the waves of the sea, has let down its curtain upon me.	وَلَيْلٍ كَمَوْجِ الْبَحْرِ أَرْخَى سُدُولَهُ عَلَيَّ.

Word resembling an extra preposition (حَرْفُ جَرٍّ شَبِيهٌ بِالزَّائِدِ).	و
Subject (مُبْتَدَأٌ) of the nominal sentence. We have to use estimated case markers (ضَمّةٌ مُقَدَّرَةٌ) to mark the nominative case (مَرْفُوعٌ). The following verbal sentence (أَرْخَى) serves as the predicate (خَبَرٌ).	لَيْلٍ

Watch out: That's not all what وَ is capable of and may denote. The وَ may also introduce an oath: وَاللّٰه! (*I swear!*); see *question #447*. We may encounter the oppressing of رُبَّ, though it is rare, also after فَ or بَلْ.

Let's look at the following famous lines of Arab poetry:

| Nay, many a middle of a desert, like the back of a shield. | بَلْ جَوْزَ تَيْهَاءَ كَظَهْرِ الْحَجَفَتْ. |
| Many a one like you have I visited by night, pregnant and nursing a child. | فَمِثْلِكِ حُبْلَى قَدْ طَرَقْتُ وَمُرْضِعٍ. |

We could even delete these particles leaving the genitive alone.

| Many a deserted abode, amid the ruins of which I have stood. | رَسْمِ دارٍ وَقَفتُ فِي ظَلَلِهْ. |

We should now put رُبَّ under the microscope. First of all, it is a particle of signification (حَرْفُ مَعْنًى) which are words whose meaning is only completed if they are used with another noun.

Some grammarians say that رُبَّ is an accusative form (مَنْصُوبٌ) of the noun رُبٌّ. So, how come that رُبَّ has a فَتْحةٌ on top of the بّ? Early scholars, for example, Abū al-ʿAbbās al-Mubarrad (أَبُو الْعَبَّاس الْمُبَرِّد), a grammarian of the 9th century from Basra, stated that رُبَّ is originally the answer to a question.

| **Question:** Have you ever met a noble man? | هَلْ لَقِيْتَ رَجُلًا كَرِيمًا؟ |
| **Answer:** Many a noble man have I met. | رُبَّ رَجُلٍ كَرِيمٍ قَدْ لَقِيْتُ. |

Other grammarians say that it is dependent upon the interjection يا which is implicitly understood and only now and then expressed. There is a Hadith (حَدِيثٌ) narrated by ʾUmm Salama (أُمّ سَلَمة) which indicates this underlying idea. According to that tradition (*Sahīh al-Bukhārī 1126*), the Islamic Prophet Muhammad had said the following:

| Many (a woman who is) clothed in this world (will be) naked in the Hereafter. | يَا رُبَّ كَاسِيَةٍ فِي الدُّنْيَا عَارِيَةٍ فِي الآخِرَةِ. |

What's left for us now is to look at how we can use رُبَّ in practice. **You can use رُبَّ as follows:**

1. Add an **indefinite** noun (اسْمٌ نَكِرَةٌ) in the **genitive** case (مَجْرُورٌ).

2. Then, put an **indefinite** adjective (صِفةٌ or نَعْتٌ) after that noun.

This can be a single word (مُفْرَدٌ), a sentence (جُمْلةٌ), or a شِبْهُ الْجُمْلةِ (prepositional phrase). Grammarians call this صِفة the *answer* or *complement of* رُبَّ; the so-called جَوابُ رُبَّ.

Let's check an example: *Many a useful book.* Why is the Arabic translation tricky? The indefinite noun (اِسْمٌ نَكِرةٌ) after رُبَّ occasionally needs a description – an adjective (نَعْتٌ). The problem we have to solve is the case ending of the adjective. There are two options:

1. We use *"what we see and hear"* (عَلَى لَفْظِ الْإِسْمِ): the adjective follows the noun; the noun serves as the second part of a إضافةٌ and must be in the genitive case. So, the نَعْت gets the genitive case too.

2. We treat it according to its position (مَحَلّاً) in the sentence, which means that it can have any of the three case endings.

Many a useful books have I read.	رُبَّ كِتابٍ مُفيدٍ قَرَأْتُ.

رُبَّ	Preposition similar to an extra preposition. (حَرْفُ جَرٍّ شَبِيهٌ بِالزّائِدِ)
كِتابٍ	Fronted direct object (مَفْعُولٌ بِهِ مُقَدَّمٌ); in the accusative case by an estimated, virtual case marker (مَنْصُوبٌ بِفَتْحةٍ مُقَدَّرةٍ) because the preceding preposition induces the genitive on this word and occupies the spot for the case marker by nunation (كَسْرةٌ).

Now, what about the adjective (i.e., مُفيد)? Both of the following sentences are correct:

1	The adjective takes the case we see.	رُبَّ كِتابٍ مُفيدٍ قَرَأْتُ.
2	The adjective takes the case according to the position of the word it refers to: the direct object.	رُبَّ كِتابٍ مُفيدًا قَرَأْتُ.

Another example: *Many a correct Qur'an readings has 'Alī read.*

1	The adjective takes the case we see.	رُبَّ قِراءةٍ صَحيحةٍ قَرَأَ عَلِيٌّ.
2	The adjective takes the case according to the position of the word it refers to, i.e., the absolute object (مَفْعُولٌ مُطْلَقٌ).	رُبَّ قِراءةٍ صَحيحةً قَرَأَ عَلِيٌّ.

Remark: The root r-b is found in other Semitic languages as well. The Hebrew word *rov* (רֹב) means *multitude; most; much*. It is interesting that in Arabic, رُبَّ has lost its original signification of multitude (like in Hebrew) and now conveys the opposite, i.e., *not a great many*.

136. What type of pronoun is found in رُبَّهُ?

It is the pronoun of the unknown (الضَّمِيرُ الْمَجْهُولُ).

رُبَّ is a fascinating word. There is a special construction in which you add the pronominal suffix of the third person singular (ضَمِيرُ الْغَائِبِ), in other words, هُ. This pronoun is called *the pronoun of the unknown* (الضَّمِيرُ الْمَجْهُولُ) because the noun to which it relates has not previously been mentioned.

The pronoun is explained by the part that comes after the pronoun. Grammatically speaking, it is a *specification* (تَمْيِيزٌ). Therefore, the word after رُبَّهُ must get the accusative case (مَنْصُوبٌ).

Many a hero	بَطَلًا	
Many a two heroes	بَطَلَيْنِ	
Many heroes	أَبْطالًا	رُبَّهُ
Many a heroine (female hero)	بَطَلةً	
Many heroines	بَطلاتٍ	

Let's examine an example:

Semi-optional preposition (حَرْفٌ شَبِيهٌ بِالزَّائِدِ).	رُبَّ
Pronominal suffix (ضَمِيرٌ مُتَّصِلٌ).	هُ
The predicate (خَبَرٌ) is deleted (مَحْذُوفٌ) and has the underlying, virtual meaning of: مَوْجُودٌ or رُبَّهُ كائِنٌ.	
Specification (تَمْيِيزٌ); therefore, it takes the accusative (مَنْصُوبٌ).	بَطَلًا

137. What function has the ما in the expression رُبَّما؟

The ما has a huge grammatical impact.

رُبَّما is a frequently used expression that is usually translated as *perhaps, maybe; sometimes*. It literally means: *O that quantity of that which*. Given a context, it normally denotes *it is probable/likely that* (مِن الْمُحْتَمَل). Let's break down the expression رُبَّما:

- The ما hinders the regimen of رُبَّ which means all the reactions that are usually induced by رُبَّ are not working anymore – they are abolished. Such ما is therefore called a *hindering, neutralizing particle* (حَرْفُ كافٍّ).
- The word after رُبَّما must be a **definite** noun or a verb.

Therefore, رُبَّما may be prefixed to either...

- a nominal sentence (جُمْلةٌ اِسْميّةٌ). Then, the word after رُبَّما is in the nominative case (مَرْفوعٌ) because it is not governed by رُبَّ anymore due to the ما الْكافّةُ.
- a verbal sentence (جُمْلةٌ فِعْليّةٌ). This is the usual situation.

A liar may tell the truth.	رُبَّما صَدَقَ الْكَذُوبُ.
Particle that is similar to an additional, extra preposition (الْحَرْفُ الشَّبِيهُ بِالزّائِدِ).	رُبَّ
neutralizing letter (حَرْفُ كافٍّ)	ما
verb plus subject (فاعِلٌ)	صَدَقَ الْكَذُوبُ

With the **past tense**, رُبَّما expresses a <u>conditional</u> or <u>future</u> meaning.

Maybe I will leave the country. Perhaps I shall leave the country.	رُبَّما غادَرْتُ الْقُطَرَ.
Perhaps it won't be enough.	رُبَّما لَمْ يَكْفِ.
Perhaps Zayd is in the house.	رُبَّما زَيْدٌ في الْبَيْتِ.
He may (perhaps) travel to Egypt.	رُبَّما سافَرَ إلَى مِصْرَ.
Sura	The disbelievers may well come to	رُبَّما يَوَدُّ الَّذِينَ كَفَرُوا لَوْ كانُوا

15:2	wish they had submitted to God.	مُسْلِمِينَ

Watch out! What happens if the word after رُبَّما is an <u>indefinite</u> noun? The ما is a ما الزَّائِدَةُ (additional, extra) which means that ما is added without producing any effect, without affecting the regimen, government. Therefore, the word following رُبَّما is in the **genitive** case.

Many a stroke with a polished sword.	رُبَّما ضَرْبةٍ بِسَيْفٍ صَقيلٍ.

138. What does the word أَلَا signify?

Surely or *verily...*

أَلَا is a combination of the question device أ plus the negative device لا. Therefore, we get a compound word (كَلِمةٌ مُرَكَّبةٌ مِنْ هَمْزةِ الاسْتِفْهامِ وَلَا النَّافِيةِ) which grammarians call a *particle of opening* or *introduction* (حَرْفُ اسْتِفْتاحٍ) serving as an intensifying interjection. How come?

أَلَا is used to draw close attention to the certainty of a following statement and expresses *truly; verily; certainly*. It provides ascertainment or verification (تَحَقُّقُ مَا بَعْدَها) for the information that follows.

Sura 10:55	Unquestionably, to Allah belongs whatever is in the heavens and the earth. Unquestionably, Allah's promise is truth, but most of them don't know.	أَلَا إِنَّ لِلّهِ مَا فِي السَّمَاوَاتِ وَالْأَرْضِ أَلَا إِنَّ وَعْدَ اللّهِ حَقٌّ وَلَكِنَّ أَكْثَرَهُمْ لَا يَعْلَمُونَ.

Verily, many a poor is happier than a rich.	أَلَا رُبَّ فَقِيرٍ أَسْعَدُ مِنْ غَنِيٍّ.

Particle of opening (حَرْفُ اسْتِفْتاحٍ). It has no place in إِعْرابٌ.	أَلَا

THE QUASI-SENTENCE (شِبْهُ الْجُمْلةِ)

139. Why do we call some parts of a sentence *quasi-sentence*?

Because a so-called quasi-sentence (شِبْهُ الْجُمْلةِ) adds a sub-meaning.

The term شِبْهُ الْجُمْلةِ is used for what we call an adverb (ظَرْفٌ) or prepositional phrase (الْجارُّ وَالْمَجْرُورُ) in English. Such phrases **don't** convey an independent meaning in a sentence.

Instead, they lead to a sub-meaning (مَعْنًى فَرْعِيٌّ) as if they were an incomplete or semi sentence. We could say that they act on behalf of the sentence.

1	prepositional phrase (الْجارُّ وَالْمَجْرُورُ)	Zayd (is) at home.	زَيْدٌ فِي الْبَيْتِ.
2	adverb of place (ظَرْفُ مَكانٍ)	Zayd (is) at your place.	زَيْدٌ عِنْدَكَ.

What is the actual meaning of these sentences?

1	Zayd is present (located/settled) himself at home.	زَيْدٌ اِسْتَقَرَّ or كائِنٌ فِي الْبَيْتِ.
2	Zayd is present (located/is stabilized) at your place.	زَيْدٌ اِسْتَقَرَّ or كائِنٌ عِنْدَكَ.

Both – the prepositional phrase (الْجارُّ وَالْمَجْرُورُ) and the adverbial phrase (الظَّرْفُ) – are used as a **substitute for the predicate** (خَبَرٌ), which can be understood as having the underlying construction of a verb or a word working on its behalf plus a subject (فاعِلٌ). Therefore, we say that such phrases are *resembling a sentence* (شِبْهُ الْجُمْلةِ). The hidden, implied pronoun (ضَمِيرٌ مُسْتَتِرٌ) of the invisible verb has moved tacitly (= understood or implied without being stated) to the prepositional or adverbial phrase.

For this reason, both the adverb and the preposition must be linked to a verb or word with verbal power – regardless whether the verb is visible (verbal sentence) or hidden, but understood (nominal sentence). Let's check an example of a verbal sentence.

Zayd traveled from Cairo to Damascus by plane to attend the conference.	سافَرَ زَيْدٌ مِن الْقاهِرةِ إِلَى دِمَشْق بِالطّائِرةِ لِيَحْضُرَ الْمُؤْتَمَرَ.

بِالطّائِرةِ	إِلَى دِمَشْق	مِن الْقاهِرةِ

All three examples are prepositional phrases (الْجارُّ وَالْمَجْرُورُ). The respective prepositional phrases are linked (we could also say: attached) to the verb *to travel* (شِبْهُ الْجُمْلةِ مُتَعَلِّقٌ بِسافَرَ).

This لِ is a *Lām of justification* (لاَمُ التَّعْلِيلِ) which induces the subjunctive mood (مَنْصُوبٌ) in the present tense verb that imme- diately follows. It basically denotes *in order to*. It is understood as أَنْ and therefore molds an interpreted مَصْدَرٌ. Notice the ending of the verb which is ﹷ. See *question #132*.	لِ
The verb is in the present tense (فِعْلٌ مُضَارِعٌ) in the مَنْصُوبٌ- mood (subjunctive). This مَصْدَرٌ مُؤَوَّلٌ is in the position of a geni- tive case (فِي مَحَلِّ جَرٍّ بِاللاَّمِ) as it follows a preposition. This شِبْهُ الْجُمْلَةِ is grammatically linked to the verb سَافَرَ.	يَحْضُرَ-

140. What is the grammatical concept of التَّعَلُّقُ good for?

It is the glue that binds a preposition or adverbial phrase to a sentence.

Let's summarize the milieu in which a verb is actually located. The verb points to the action (حَدَثٌ). The action, however, does not happen in a vacuum (فَرَاغٌ). Moreover, the action occurs in a time frame (زَمانٌ) or at a place (مَكانٌ).

The adverb (ظَرْفٌ) and the prepositional phrase (الْجارُّ وَالْمَجْرُورُ) indi- cate a sub-meaning connected to the verb (يَتَعَلَّقُ بِهِ) and provide some extra information. Sounds abstract? Let's dig deeper.

▸ *Zayd traveled* (سافَرَ زَيْدٌ). This sentence has an independent mean- ing. We can enrich it: *Zayd traveled on Friday* (سافَرَ زَيْدٌ يَوْمَ الْجُمْعِةِ). Then the adverb conveys a sub-meaning that is connected with the verb (سافَرَ). We understand that the action (*to travel*) occurred on *Fri- day*, i.e., at a special time.

▸ *Zayd traveled from Cairo to Damascus* (سافَرَ زَيْدٌ مِن الْقاهِرةِ إِلَى دِمَشْقَ). The preposition مِنْ (*from*) initiates a new meaning; it also in- dicates that the action of the verb has already started to happen from this place. The preposition إِلَى (*to*) tells us at which place the action of the verb ends.

The term التَّعَلُّقُ denotes the **connection** of the شِبْهُ الْجُمْلَةِ **to the event** (حَدَثٌ) to which the verb or alike is pointed. Some grammarians also call it the "attachment" since a preposition is "attached" to a verb or a derived noun. The preposition not only drags the noun into the genitive case – it also links it to the verb. In addition to that, a شِبْهُ الْجُمْلة provides an indication of scope, domain, or sphere (الْحَيْزُ) in which the verb happens. Fine, but what happens when there is no verb?

Some grammarians call adverbs and prepositional phrases in nominal sentences simply the predicate itself. In their view, they are not linked to the deleted, "real" predicate (أَيْ لَيْسَ مُتَعَلِّقًا بِخَبَرٍ مَحْذُوفٍ). For native English speakers, this concept is easier to understand.

I wouldn't say that this view is wrong; in fact, there is some truth in it, but strictly speaking, adverbs and prepositional phrases are not the real predicate (لَيْسَ هُوَ الْخَبَرَ حَقِيقِيَّةً). They **must be connected with a word that conveys or points to an action** (حَدَثٌ). We call that ominous thing التَّعَلُّقُ.

Muhammad is at home (in the house).	مُحَمَّدٌ فِي الْبَيْتِ.

Here the شِبْهُ الْجُمْلة is placed in the position which apparently the predicate would hold: the place of a nominative case (شِبْهُ الْجُمْلةِ فِي مَحَلِّ رَفْعٍ خَبَرٌ). It would be acceptable to call it the *predicate*.

However, that is not entirely correct as the شِبْهُ الْجُمْلةِ must be connected with a word to which it gives meaning. We say that it is connected with the deleted, "real" predicate which could be, for example, كائنٌ. The idea of deletion is a hypothesized form (تَقْدِيرُ الْمَحْذُوفِ) which helps us to understand the structure and get our analysis right.

Muhammad studied at home (lit.: in the house).	ذاكَرَ مُحَمَّدٌ فِي الْبَيْتِ.

The شِبْهُ الْجُمْلةِ is connected to an optically visible verb (ذاكَرَ). Note: Have a look at *question #333* if you want to know which part of the sentence is actually the predicate. (*studied* only or *studied at home*).

The prepositional or adverbial phrase (شِبْهُ الْجُمْلةِ) is pictured as being connected with another word in the sentence. Sometimes that word in question – with which it is connected – is **not mentioned** in the sentence. This happens when the شِبْهُ الْجُمْلةِ appears in the position of the خَبَرٌ (predicate). ➡ Then, the "real" predicate has to be assumed.

So, if we don't have a verb in the sentence, the situation is actually not different – because although it is not mentioned, the verb *to be* is implicitly understood. Theoretically, a prepositional phrase relates to the deleted predicate of a nominal sentence. The predicate (خَبَر) of a nominal sentence, however, can be indicated by a prepositional phrase resembling a sentence (شِبْهُ الْجُمْلةِ), but it is not a sentence. Purist grammarians say that a شِبْهُ الْجُمْلةِ can neither be the subject nor the predicate of a sentence. Therefore, a verb or a word with verbal force is estimated before such phrases.

Nevertheless, we should not be too strict. Some grammarians say that the deleted word remains the one and only predicate. They say that the prepositional phrase is connected with the deleted word.

I prefer a mixture. I acknowledge that **the prepositional phrase is located in the position of a predicate**, but I also know that it needs a connection to another word in the sentence because it cannot just be there like a satellite. So we should assume that it is associated with a deleted word in the sentence so as not to violate the rules of our beloved Arabic grammar universe. See also *questions #140 and #219.*

We still need to solve one task. We need to look for an appropriate **underlying, estimated meaning** (تَقْدِير) of the connector (تَعَلُّق): the deleted word.

	شِبْهُ الْجُمْلةِ	assumed, virtual predicate		subject
active participle	فِي الْبَيْتِ.	being	كائِنٌ	زَيْدٌ
		settled, being stable	مُسْتَقِرٌّ	
past tense verb	أَمامَ الْبَيْتِ.	was	كانَ	
		was stabilized	إسْتَقَرَّ	
passive participle		is found	مَوْجُودٌ	

What does this mean for our analysis? In nominal sentences that contain a prepositional or adverbial phrase, you will encounter the expression مُتَعَلِّقٌ بِمَحْذُوفٍ in grammar books. Let's take the following sentence: زَيْدٌ فِي الْبَيْتِ.

فِي الْبَيْتِ is a prepositional phrase (الْجارُّ وَالْمَجْرُورُ) that **appears in the place of the predicate**. However, it is not the real predicate because that was deleted. We say that فِي الْبَيْتِ is connected/linked to a deleted word (مُتَعَلِّقٌ بِمَحْذُوفٍ), not mentioned in the sentence, which has the estimated, implicitly understood meaning of: كائِنٌ or مُسْتَقِرٌّ. It is this الْمَحْذُوفُ خَبَرُ deleted word which is the real predicate of the subject (الْمُبْتَدَإِ). *See also #369.*

الْجارُّ وَالْمَجْرُورُ ,مُتَعَلِّقٌ بِمَحْذُوفٍ، تَقْدِيرُهُ: كائِنٌ أَوْ مُسْتَقِرٌّ، وَهَذا الْمَحْذُوفُ خَبَرُ الْمُبْتَدَإِ.	فِي الْبَيْتِ

If we can sometimes do without a predicate, are we able to say when we will delete it in a nominal sentence?

- The predicate (*copula*) is only **deleted** if it points to a **general being** (كَوْنٌ عامٌّ). ➡ When it expresses the meaning of مَوْجُود or كائِنٌ or مُسْتَقِرٌّ.

- If it points to a **special being or state** (كَوْنٌ خاصٌّ), the predicate must be **shown**; otherwise, the meaning would be lost – see #224.

Zayd is sick at home.	زَيْدٌ مَرِيضٌ فِي الْبَيْتِ.
Here the predicate (مَرِيضٌ) must be shown! Otherwise, it does not transport the essence of the information, i.e., Zayd is **sick** and not only at home.	

Excursus: How do we treat such sentences in English? In fact, pretty similar. Let's take an example: *The boy is in the house.* What is the predicate? First of all, *the boy* ist the subject. The rest of the sentence is the predicate. The part *in the house* modifies the subject and is called a *predicative prepositional phrase*. The part *in the house* is **connected with** the subject by what is known as a **linking verb** (= *is*). Such verbs (e.g., *to be, to become*) are special because they connect the subject with the description. Note that the description is usually an adjective. For example: *The book is expensive.*

141. Do prepositional or adverbial phrases only relate to verbs?

No, a شِبْهُ الْجُمْلَةِ *can relate to many forms.*

We need to look at words that may resemble a verb in its force and convey the meaning of an action (حَدَثٌ). We have only one, but wonderful, option for this: **derived nouns of a root** (الْمُشْتَقّاتُ). Let's go through the most important options.

a) The original مَصْدَرٌ

I like traveling by train at night.	أُحِبُّ السَّفَرَ فِي الْقِطارِ لَيْلًا.

The prepositional phrase (جارٌّ وَمَجْرُورٌ) and the adverb of time (ظَرْفُ زَمانٍ) are linked to the مَصْدَرٌ which is السَّفَرَ.	فِي الْقِطارِ لَيْلًا

b) A quasi-verb; interjection denoting a sense of a verb (اِسْمُ الْفِعْلِ)

A اِسْمُ الْفِعْلِ is an indeclinable noun that never changes its shape. It replaces the verb by similarly expressing an action which may be combined with time. The intention of its use is usually that of a superlative. If you say *"ugh!"* (أُفٍّ), it stands for a sentence and action/event such as: *I am annoyed very much.*

Ugh! Away with the hypocrites!	أُفٍّ مِن الْمُنافِقِينَ!

Prepositional phrase (جارٌّ وَمَجْرُورٌ). The شِبْهُ الْجُمْلةِ is connected with the اِسْمُ الْفِعْلِ which is أُفٍّ.	مِن الْمُنافِقِينَ

c) The active participle (اِسْمُ الْفاعِلِ)

Zayd will travel tomorrow by plane.	زَيْدٌ مُسافِرٌ غَدًا بِالطّائِرةِ.

Adverb of time (ظَرْفُ زَمانٍ) and prepositional phrase (جارٌّ وَمَجْرُورٌ) are both connected with the active participle مُسافِرٌ.	غَدًا بِالطّائِرةِ

d) The passive-participle (اِسْمُ الْمَفْعُولِ)

This book is published in Egypt.	هذا الْكِتابُ مَنْشُورٌ فِي مِصْرَ.

Prepositional phrase (جارٌّ وَمَجْرُورٌ). The so-called شِبْهُ الْجُمْلةِ is connected with the passive participle مَنْشُورٌ.	فِي مِصْرَ

e) The adjective which resembles the active participle (الصِّفةُ الْمُشَبَّهةُ بِاسْمِ الْفاعِلِ) and which describes the constant state or condition.

| Zayd is generous and brave in every situation. | زَيْدٌ كَرِيمٌ وَشُجَاعٌ فِي كُلِّ مَوْقِفٍ. |

| Prepositional phrase (جَارٌّ وَمَجْرُورٌ); connected with two صِفَةٌ مُشَبَّهَةٌ, i.e., شُجَاعٌ and كَرِيمٌ. They convey a meaning of firmness. | فِي كُلِّ |

f) The noun of time (اِسْمُ الزَّمانِ) and place (اِسْمُ الْمَكانِ). This might be surprising but don't forget that both forms are derived from a root and are related to an action.

| This place was the playground for our children. | هَذِهِ الْأَرْضُ كَانَتْ الْمَلْعَبَ لِأَطْفَالِنا. |

| Prepositional phrase (جَارٌّ وَمَجْرُورٌ). The شِبْهُ الْجُمْلِةِ is connected with the noun of place (اِسْمُ الْمَكانِ) which is: الْأَرْضُ. | لِأَطْفالِنا |

g) A static (inert, rigid) noun that can be interpreted as a derived noun (اِسْمٌ جامِدٌ مُؤَوَّلٌ بِمُشْتَقٍّ). It is **not** connected with an action.

| Zayd is a lion in fighting. | زَيْدٌ الْأَسَدُ فِي الْقِتالِ. |

| Prepositional phrase (جَارٌّ وَمَجْرُورٌ). The شِبْهُ الْجُمْلِةِ is connected with the word الْأَسَدُ (lion), which can be interpreted as *courageous* (جَرِيءٌ - root: جَرُؤَ) or *audacious* (مِقْدامٌ). | فِي الْقِتالِ |

Now, let's check the situation when the شِبْهُ الْجُمْلِةِ relates to something that is not visibly found in the sentence, i.e., to a deleted word.

a) The (deleted) expression is understood anyway.

| My life for this country! (I will defend this homeland with my life.) | بِحَياتِي هَذا الْوَطَنَ! |

| Prepositional phrase (جَارٌّ وَمَجْرُورٌ). This شِبْهُ الْجُمْلِةِ is related to a **deleted verb** with the imaginary, implicit meaning (تَقْدِيرٌ) of: *I redeem* (أَفْدِي). This is the reason why الْوَطَنَ takes the accusative as it serves as the direct object of the implicitly understood verb. | بِحَياتِي |

b) If there is enough proof or information in the sentence (أَنْ يَدُلَّ عَلَيْهِ دَلِيلٌ) for the شِبْهُ الْجُمْلةِ to be correctly understood.

Today I am traveling to Cairo, as for the coming month, I will travel to Alexandria.	أُسَافِرُ الْيَوْمَ إِلَى الْقَاهِرَةِ، أَمَّا الشَّهْرَ الْقَادِمَ فَإِلَى الْإِسْكَنْدَرِيَّةِ.
Adverb of time (ظَرْفُ زَمانٍ). The شِبْهُ الْجُمْلـةِ is con-**nected with the verb** I travel (أُسَافِرُ).	الْيَوْمَ الشَّهْرَ
Prepositional phrase (جَارٌّ وَمَجْرُورٌ). The شِبْهُ الْجُمْلـةِ is **connected with a <u>deleted</u> verb** which has the virtual, estimated meaning of I travel (أُسَافِرُ).	إِلَى الْإِسْكَنْدَرِيَّةِ

c) The شِبْهُ الْجُمْلةُ is connected with the deleted predicate (خَبَرٌ).

Zayd is at home.	زَيْدٌ فِي الْبَيْتِ.
This prepositional phrase (جَارٌّ وَمَجْرُورٌ) appears to be located in the position of the predicate. But that is only half of the truth. The شِبْهُ الْجُمْلـةِ is connected (or let's say: attached) to the deleted predicate (مُتَعَلِّقٌ بِخَبَرٍ مَحْذُوفٍ), i.e., the "real" predicate that is implicitly understood and thus had to be deleted. Nevertheless, we need the deleted word in the sentence to connect the prepositional phrase to the sentence (to the predicate). *See #140 and #219.*	فِي الْبَيْتِ
Zayd was at home.	كَانَ زَيْدٌ فِي الْبَيْتِ.
Prepositional phrase (جَارٌّ وَمَجْرُورٌ). This شِبْهُ الْجُمْلةِ is connected with the deleted predicate (خَبَرُ كَانَ) which would be placed in the position of an **accusative** case (فِي مَحَلِّ نَصْبٍ). It is still implicitly understood; for example: *being* (كَائِنًا).	فِي الْبَيْتِ
Verily, Zayd is at home.	إِنَّ زَيْدًا فِي الْبَيْتِ.
Prepositional phrase (جَارٌّ وَمَجْرُورٌ) that some call the خَبَر إِنَّ (predicate of إِنَّ); But the more correct view is that it is connected with the deleted predicate of إِنَّ which would fill the location of a	فِي الْبَيْتِ

nominative case (فِي مَحَلِّ رَفْعٍ). This deleted word is implicitly understood; for example: the word كائِنٌ.	

d) If the شِبْهُ الْجُمْلةِ is connected with a deleted adjective (صِفةٌ).

This **is** a man *from Egypt*.	هذا رَجُلٌ مِنْ مِصْرَ.

The شِبْهُ الْجُمْلةِ is connected with a deleted adjective (مُتَعَلِّقٌ بِصِفةٍ مَحْذُوفةٍ) for *man* (رَجُلٍ). The deleted word could be estimated as كائِنٌ.	مِن مِصْرَ مِن مِصْرَ

This sentence actually means the following:

This is an Egyptian (man).	هذا رَجُلٌ مِصْرِيٌّ.

Watch out! This sentence does not mean: *This man **is** from Egypt*. For this, we would need to make رَجُلَ definite. Although the meaning is almost the same, the grammar would be different if we did that: هذا الرَّجُلُ مِنْ مِصْرَ.

e) The شِبْهُ الْجُمْلةِ is connected with a deleted حالٌ.

I respect the man for his loyalty.	أَحْتَرِمُ الرَّجُلَ فِي إِخْلاصِهِ.

Prepositional phrase (جارٌّ وَمَجْرُورٌ) that is related to a deleted circumstantial qualifier (حالٌ) for *the man* (الرَّجُلَ), which is still implicitly understood (see below).	فِي إِخْلاصِهِ

What is the meaning of the sentence?

I respect the man whose status of being is loyal.	أَحْتَرِمُ الرَّجُلَ حالةَ كَوْنِهِ مُخْلِصًا.

f) The شِبْهُ الْجُمْلةِ is connected with a deleted relative clause (صِلةٌ).

The man who is in the house is strange.	الرَّجُلُ الَّذي فِي الْبَيْتِ غَرِيبٌ.

Prepositional phrase (جارٌّ وَمَجْرُورٌ) that is placed where you would	فِي

| expect a relative clause (صِلَة). The relative clause is deleted, but we assume that the prepositional phrase is connected with this missing link which is implicitly understood and may have had the meaning of اِسْتَقَرَّ. | الْبَيْتِ |

g) A شِبْهُ الْجُمْلَةِ that conveys a self-sufficient meaning and is used alone.

(Be blessed) with healing!	Said to a sick person (when he drinks the medicine).	بِالشِّفَاءِ!
(Be blessed) with health!	Said to a guest who is eating.	بِالصِّحةِ!
(Be blessed) with harmony and children!	Said to a friend who gets married.	بِالرَّفَاءِ وَالبَنِينَ!

The above examples are prepositional phrases (جَارٌّ وَمَجْرُورٌ). The respective شِبْهُ الْجُمْلَةِ is connected with a deleted verb (مُتَعَلَّقٌ بِفِعْلٍ مَحْذُوفٍ), which has an imaginary meaning of...

you drank	شَرِبْتَ	بِالشِّفَاءِ
you ate	أَكَلْتَ	بِالصِّحةِ
you got married	تَزَوَّجْتَ	بِالرَّفَاءِ وَالبَنِين

The same is true for oaths (الْقَسَمُ) with و or تَ.

| Both are prepositional phrases (جَارٌّ وَمَجْرُورٌ). The respective شِبْهُ الْجُمْلَةِ is connected with a deleted verb having the virtual meaning of: I swear (أُقْسِمُ). | By Allah! | وَاللهِ! |
| | | تَاللهِ |

Chapter 5: Tiny Tricky Words

142. What functions can the word ما have?

There are many.

ما is a powerful Arabic word which has two natures: it can be a particle (حَرْفٌ) or a noun (اِسْمٌ) depending on the function in a sentence.

- When ما is a اِسْمٌ, it gets case endings. However, they are hidden as ما has an indeclinable shape. We can only assign a place value.
- When ما is a حَرْفٌ, it doesn't take any case ending because a حَرْفٌ doesn't have a place in إِعْرابٌ and is not governed by anything.

1	negation particle – without operating power	حَرْفُ نَفْي

Karīm did not come.	ما جاءَ كَريمٌ.

This type of ما does not have a position in إِعْرابٌ and **doesn't take case endings.** Furthermore, this ما **doesn't influence** (operate on) other words.

2	negation particle – with governing/operating power	حَرْفُ نَفْي

Sura 12:31	This is not a man. (He can't be mortal.)	مَا هٰذَا بَشَرًا.

This type of ما doesn't have a position in إِعْرابٌ. In contrast to number 1, this type of ما **works similarly to the verb** لَيْسَ which means that it does influence – govern – other words in the sentence.

We have a nominal sentence (جُمْلةٌ اِسْميّةٌ) with هٰذا as the subject (مُبْتَدَأٌ) in the nominative case (مَرْفُوعٌ). The word بَشَرًا is the predicate (خَبَرٌ). Since ما works similarly to لَيْسَ, the word بَشَرًا takes the accusative case (مَنْصُوبٌ). Remember that in sentences with لَيْسَ, the predicate has to be مَنْصُوبٌ.

3	*Neutralizing (hindering)* particle; only used with a nominal sentence (جُمْلةٌ اِسْميّةٌ).	حَرْفٌ كافٌّ/ ما الْكافّة

Verily, Muhammad is a messenger!	إِنَّما مُحَمَّدٌ رَسُولٌ!
The food is only for the poor.	إِنَّما الْأَكْلُ لِلْفُقَراءِ.

This type of ما doesn't have a position in إِعْرابٌ. When ما comes after إِنَّ, the ما hinders the so-called regimen of إِنَّ. This means that the operating power of إِنَّ doesn't extend beyond itself. ➞ It is neutralized. Therefore, the noun after إِنَّ is not in the accusative (مَنْصُوبٌ), but in the nominative case (مَرْفُوعٌ).

4	*Redundant, extra* ما which doesn't produce any	حَرْفٌ زائِدٌ بَيْنَ

effect. Such a ما is often placed after the preposi-	حَرْفِ الْجَرِّ
tions مِنْ, عَنْ, and بِ <u>without</u> affecting their power	وَالْمَجْرُور
of dragging a following word into the genitive.	

| Sura | By an act of mercy from Allah, you [Prophet] | فَبِمَا رَحْمَةٍ مِّنَ |
| 3:159 | were gentle in your dealings with them. | اللَّهِ لِنْتَ لَهُمْ. |

The ما is placed after the preposition بِ. The ما here doesn't produce any effect. This explains why the word after ما, i.e., رَحْمَةٍ, receives the genitive case (مَجْرُورٌ) because it is governed by the preposition بِ.

| 5 | Relative pronoun. Note: I use the term *pronoun* to build | اِسْمٌ مَوْصُولٌ |
| | a bridge to English, but in Arabic, it is a noun (اِسْمٌ). | |

| Sura | Whatever is in the heavens and what- | يُسَبِّحُ لِلَّهِ مَا فِي السَّمَاوَاتِ |
| 62:1 | ever is on the earth is exalting Allah. | وَمَا فِي الْأَرْضِ. |

This is a verbal sentence (جُمْلَةٌ فِعْلِيَّةٌ). The word ما is a noun (اِسْمٌ). Nouns by definition are inflected: they get case endings. However, ما is indeclinable (مَبْنِيٌّ) and can't receive visible case endings. The last vowel is per definition a سُكُونٌ because a long vowel always ends with سُكُونٌ; so we call it مَبْنِيٌّ عَلَى السُّكُونِ. In our example, ما serves as the subject (فَاعِلٌ) of the verb يُسَبِّحُ and is located in the position of a nominative case (فِي مَحَلِّ رَفْعٍ).

| 6 | Question word (serving as the subject). Notice: | اِسْمُ اِسْتِفْهَامٍ (فِي |
| | This type of ما is a noun (اِسْمٌ). | مَحَلِّ رَفْعٍ) |

| What tells you that Karīm is coming? (How | مَا أَخْبَرَكَ أَنَّ كَرِيمًا قَادِمٌ؟ |
| did you know that Karīm is coming?) | |

ما is treated as a noun (اِسْمٌ). Since ما is indeclinable (مَبْنِيٌّ), we cannot mark it with visible case endings. Nevertheless, regarding its function, it serves as the subject (مُبْتَدَأٌ) of a nominal sentence (جُمْلَةٌ اِسْمِيَّةٌ); we apply a place value. A subject without a predicate (خَبَرٌ) is not a complete sentence. The خَبَرٌ in our example is a verbal sentence (جُمْلَةٌ فِعْلِيَّةٌ): the sentence after ما.

| 7 | Question word (in the position of an object). | اِسْمُ اِسْتِفْهَامٍ (فِي |

Notice: This type of ما is a noun (اِسْمٌ).	مَحَلِّ نَصْبٍ)

| Did you drink anything? [(Didn't) drink + you + **what?**] | ما شَرِبْتَ ما؟ |

ما in this application is a noun (اِسْمٌ). It serves as the object of the verb *to drink*, so we have a verbal sentence (جُمْلَةٌ فِعْلِيّةٌ). Since we cannot put case markers due to its indeclinable shape, we can only say that it is grammatically occupying the location of an accusative case (فِي مَحَلِّ نَصْبٍ).

8	The ما as an expression of admiration.	اِسْمُ تَعَجُّبٍ - ما التَّعَجُّبِيّة

| What a beautiful sky! Remark: This is a famous Arabic sentence (see *question #5*). | ما أَجْمَلَ السَّماءَ! |

| What an excellent man Karīm is! | ما أَفْضَلَ كَرِيمًا! |

This is a nominal sentence (جُمْلَةٌ اِسْمِيّةٌ). The ما serves as the subject (مُبْتَدَأٌ) in the position of a nominative case (فِي مَحَلِّ رَفْعٍ). The entire verbal sentence (جُمْلَةٌ فِعْلِيّةٌ) after ما - now don't get confused - serves as the predicate (خَبَرٌ) of the nominal sentence.

Note: The sentence literally means *what has made Karīm excellent*. (In the meaning of: can anything make him more excellent than he is?)

| The same meaning could be achieved without ما by using the preposition ب plus the imperative of the verb. | أَفْضِلْ بِكَرِيم |

This sentence literally means: *Make Karīm excellent!* (In the meaning of: if you try, you can't make him more excellent than he is. A more literal translation could be: *try (your ability at) making excellent upon* (ب) *Karīm.*

9	The ما that has a vague intensifying force. Often used as an adjective/attribute for an indefinite noun to denote some emphasis.	اِسْمٌ / نَعْتٌ ما الإِبْهامِيّة

This ما is a noun (اِسْمٌ) and serves as a صِفةٌ/نَعْتٌ; it gets the place value (إِعْرابٌ) according to the position of the preceding word which may get all three cases. We use the expression فِي مَحَلِّ...

some (small) number or quantity	قَلِيلٌ ما
Give us some book (or other)!	أَعْطِنا كِتابًا ما!
You came for some purpose.	جِئْتَ لِأَمْرٍ ما.

You may know the expression هُوَ ما هُوَ or هِيَ ما هِيَ. In most situations, this is used to express that a person or a thing possesses a quality of a certain degree – either between the two extremes (A) or of an indefinitely high degree (B).

A	rather few than many	إِلَى الْقِلّةِ ما هُوَ
	blackish	أَسْوَدُ ما هُوَ
B	a very great need	حاجةٌ هِيَ ما هِيَ
	much more to the north	إِلَى الشَّمالِ أَقْرَبُ ما هِيَ

Watch out: Don't confuse the expression ما هُوَ with a grammatically different construction that happens to look exactly the same.

| Everybody knows what is the meaning of *hamd* (praise). | يَعْرِفُ كُلُّ واحِدٍ أَنَّ الْحَمْدَ ما هُوَ. |

| 10 | Conditional device. This ما governs verbs in the jussive mood (مَجْزُومٌ). Since this type of ما is a noun (اِسْمٌ), it gets cases – however, since it has an indeclinable shape, we can only assign "place values". | اِسْمُ شَرْطٍ |

| What you sow, you will reap. | ما تَزْرَعْ تَحْصُدْ. |

| 11 | This ما produces an interpreted infinitive. It is similar to the particle أَنْ, but with the difference that you use the **past tense** with ما (and not the present tense) to express an infinitive (مَصْدَرٌ). | حَرْفُ مَصْدَرٍ (حَرْفُ مَصْدَرِيّةٍ) |

Remark: The term مَصْدَرِيّةٌ is the artificial infinitive noun (مَصْدَرٌ صِناعِيٌّ) of the word مَصْدَرٌ (مِن مَصْدَر). See *Arabic for Nerds 1, question #78*. That is the reason why we have a إِضافةٌ and nunation (كَسْرةٌ). However, it could

also be the feminine form of the "relative" adjective/*Nisba* (نِسْبة) which is why you also encounter it, in other applications, in the nominative.	

I will work as long as I live.	سَأَعْمَلُ ما دُمْتُ حَيًّا.

The ما الْمَصْدَرِيّة does not have a place in إِعْرابٌ as it is a حَرْفٌ.	ما
Verb in the past tense. It is a special verb فِعْلٌ ماضٍ ناقِصٌ ناسِخٌ (مِن أَخَواتِ كانَ) and a sister of كانَ – see *question #241*.	دُمْتُ
Predicate (خَبَرُ ما دامَ); therefore in the accusative case (مَنْصوبٌ).	حَيًّا

143. When does the word ما lose the Aleph?

When it is preceded by a preposition.

The Aleph is a special letter that, although rare, sometimes appears additionally and sometimes just disappears. We will now look at situations in which it vanishes.

The ما, used as a question word (ما الْاِسْتِفْهامِيّة), is a noun (اِسْمٌ). If it is preceded by a preposition, it is dragged into the genitive case. We know that ما has an indeclinable shape. So, nothing should happen regarding the shape of ما in any case – unfortunately, its more complicated. In fact, you quite often get rid of the Aleph when ما is dragged into the genitive case by a preposition.

Rule of thumb: In questions words, you **must delete the Aleph if** there's a primary preposition before (ب - ل - عن - في - إلا). As soon as you have the word إذا after ما, this is not true anymore.

Why is that? The shortening of ما to مَ is necessary to avoid misunderstandings. It gets rid of a possible ambiguity between interrogative and relative clauses. The shortening distinguishes them from the ما used to introduce relative clauses (ما الْمَوْصولة).

What...?	بمَ	←→	that with which...	بِما
Why...?	لِمَ		that for which...	لِما

| What is your name? | ما اسْمُكَ؟ | 1 |

ما is a الْإِسْتِفْهامِيّةُ and the **subject**; in the position of a **nominative**.

| Why (for what) did you do this? | لِمَ فَعَلْتَ هذا؟ | 2 |

| Preposition (حَرْفُ الْجَرِّ); it does not have a position in إِعْرابٌ. | لِ |
| Question word (اِسْمُ اِسْتِفْهامٍ). It gets cemented, fixed on the سُكُونٌ on the **deleted Aleph** (مَبْنِيٌّ عَلَى السُّكُونِ عَلَى الْأَلِفِ الْمَحْذُوفةِ). It is located in the position of a genitive case due to the preposition. | ما |

Note: This is similar to the discussion ماذا or ما ذا (with space) – *see #161.*
Other examples are فِيمَ or بِمَ. See *Arabic for Nerds 1, question #131.*

144. Can وَ also mean *when, with, or while...?*

Yes, this is possible.

In certain constructions, وَ doesn't mean *and*. We need different English words like *when, with,* or *while*. This happens in two situations:

1. The وَ is a واوُ الْحالِ and part of a *circumstantial description.*

2. The وَ is part of a مَفْعُولٌ مَعَهُ, i.e., an *object of accompaniment.*

Situation 1: The *Wāw* is a واوُ الْحالِ – see *question #368.*

| Zayd traveled to Egypt **when** he was a student in the faculty of medicine. | سافَرَ زَيْدٌ وَهُوَ طالِبٌ في كُلِّيّةِ الطّبِّ إلَى مِصْرَ. |

This sentence **doesn't** mean *Zayd, who is a student in the faculty of medicine, traveled to Egypt.*
If you want to express that, you should use dashes (سافَرَ زَيْدٌ - وَهُوَ طالِبٌ - ...).

The child came **crying**.	جاءَ الطّفْلُ وَهُوَ يَبْكِي.
I graduated from university **when** I was 22 years old.	تَخَرَّجْتُ في الْجامِعةِ وَأَنا في الثّانِيةِ وَالْعِشْرِينَ مِنْ عُمْرِي.
I read a book **while** watching the news on the TV.	أَقْرَأُ كِتابًا وَأَنا أُشاهِدُ الْأَخْبارَ في التّلْفازِ.

Situation 2: The *Wāw* is part of the مَفْعُولٌ مَعَهُ.

He walked **along** the river.	سارَ وَالنَّهَرَ.

The *Wāw of company* or *Wāw of simultaneousness* expresses that something occurs with something else. It is called واوُ الصَّاحَبِة or واوُ الْمَعِيِّة (*Wāw of association*) or واوُ الْجَمْعِ. This وَ is best explained by مَعَ أَنَّ.

Don't eat **while** laughing!	لا تَأْكُلْ وَتَضْحَكَ!
Do not restrain (others) from any habit, **whilst** you yourself practice one like it!	لا تَنْهَ عَنْ خُلُقٍ وَتَأْتِي مِثْلَهُ!
The second verb expresses a simultaneous but subordinate action.	

145. What is the word كُلّ good for?

It can do many jobs, even provide some emphasis.

كُلّ means *the totality, the whole*; literally *what is rolled and gathered together*. It may be translated as *whole, all* (with a following definite word); or *each, every* (with an indefinite word). كُلّ conveys a meaning of vagueness; it needs another word to provide a full meaning since كُلّ doesn't point to a thing itself. For this reason, كُلّ must be part of a إِضافَةٌ. What we say here, by the way, is also true for بَعْضٌ (*some*).

كُلّ can do **many grammatical jobs**. Its function in a sentence depends on the **meaning** of the مُضافٌ إِلَيْهِ, i.e., the 2nd part of the إِضافَةٌ.

All students came.	جاءَ كُلُّ الطُّلابِ.	
Subject (فاعِلٌ) of the verbal sentence; therefore, it gets the nominative case (مَرْفُوعٌ بِالضَّمّةِ الظّاهِرةِ).		كُلّ

Every human being is mortal.	كُلُّ إِنْسانٍ فانٍ.	
Subject (مُبْتَدَأٌ) of the nominal sentence; nominative case (مَرْفُوعٌ).		كُلّ

I meet him every day.	أُقابِلُهُ كُلَّ يَوْمٍ.

| كُلّ | **Adverb of time** (ظَرْفُ زَمانٍ); so, it takes the accusative (مَنْصُوبٌ بِالْفَتْحةِ الظّاهِرةِ) case. Watch out: This is <u>not</u> the direct object! |

| أَحْبَبْتُهُ كُلَّ الْحُبِّ. | I loved him deeply. (I loved him with all the love.) |

| كُلّ | **Absolute object** (مَفْعُولٌ مُطْلَقٌ); so it takes the accusative (مَنْصُوبٌ). |

كُلّ can express **emphasis**. You just need to **attach a pronoun** (ضَمِير) that points to the thing that's supposed to get the booster (الْمُؤَكَّدُ).

| جاءَ الطُّلابُ كُلُّهُمْ. | All students came. |

| كُلّ | **Emphasis** (تَوْكِيدٌ) in the nominative case (مَرْفُوعٌ). A تَوْكِيدٌ is a fol-lower (تابِعٌ) in Arabic grammar. This means that it gets the same case as the word to which it refers. In our example, we **don't** con-sider كُلّ an adjective (نَعْتٌ) nor an apposition/substitution (بَدَلٌ). |

146. Can you say أَلْكُلُّ? Or is كُلّ already definite?

That's a difficult question.

Let's try to decode the problem. Arabic grammar tells us that if the second part of a إِضافةٌ is definite, the entire construction is treated as definite. Since كُلّ, when it denotes *all*, is part of a إِضافةٌ (with the sec-ond part having the definite article الـ), most grammarians consider كُلّ as a **definite** (مَعْرِفةٌ) word.

This would mean that الْكُلّ wouldn't make sense. However, many people use the expression الْكُلّ in the meaning of *all* when it is not fur-ther specified. Can we do that? Is that grammatically sound?

No, said the great grammarian Sībawayhi (سيبويه). He said that it is impossible to add the definite article (لا يَصِحُّ إِدْخالُ أَلْ) to كُلّ. In the Qur'an, for example, you can't find the expression الْكُلّ.

Sura 27:87	**All** will come to Him in utter humility.	كُلٌّ أَتَوْهُ داخِرِينَ.
Sura 2:116	**Everything** devoutly obeys His will.	كُلٌّ لَهُ قانِتُونَ.
Sura 21:33	**Each** floating in its orbit. (**All** [heavenly bodies] in an orbit are swimming.)	كُلٌّ فِي فَلَكٍ يَسْبَحُونَ.

But that is not the end of the story. Another famous grammarian, al-Fārisī (الْفَارِسِيّ), declared that the placement of the definite article before كُلّ (or بَعْض) is permissible (إِنَّ إِدْخَالَ أَلْ عَلَيْهِما جَائِزٌ).

Nowadays, most grammarians follow the view of the grammarian Ismāʿīl Hammād al-Jawharī (إِسْمَاعِيل ابْنُ حَمَّاد الْجَـوْهَري). He stated that both words (كُلّ and بَعْض) are **definite**, but that the Arabs **don't use it** with the **definite article**. Nevertheless, he said that it would be **permissible** to do so (كُلٌّ وَبَعْضٌ مَعْرِفَتَانِ, وَلَمْ يَجِئْ عَنِ الْعَـرَب بِـالأَلِـفِ وَاللّامِ, وَهُوَ جَائِزٌ). What's his idea?

We could justify the use of ال by assuming that the second part of the إِضَافَة is implicitly understood given the context. For example, the expression *all students* (كُلُّ الطُّلابِ) is treated as definite. If we deleted الطُّلابِ, we could add ال to the first word – which was not possible if the second part of the construction is there. So we get: الْكُلُّ. Thus, الْكُلُّ usually means *all* in relation to people. كُلٌّ has the meaning of وَاحِدٍ.

| All are ready (everyone is ready). | الْكُلُّ مُتَحَضِّرٌ. |
| Everyone knows you are clever. | الْكُلُّ يَعْرِفُ أَنَّكَ ذَكِيٌّ. |

Let's dig deeper. If we treat كُلّ as a definite word, despite not having ال prefixed, we will get certain grammar options. We could treat the word which is placed after كُلّ also as a حال because the صَاحِبُ الْحالِ must be مَعْرِفَة. This is rare, but possible, as some grammarians state.

| I passed (by) all who were reading. | مَرَرْتُ بِكُلٍّ قَارِئًا. |
| I passed (by) some who were writing. | مَرَرْتُ بِبَعْضٍ كاتِبًا. |

Remark: Al-Jawharī authored one of the most renowned Arabic lexical works: al-Sihāh (الصِّحاح). His date of birth is unknown. He was born in Fārāb (Otrar) in central Asia (today's Kazakhstan) and later moved to Baghdad. The sources differ as to the year of his death. Some say he died in 1003 (393 AH), others claim it was in the year 1010 (400 AH).

147. Can كُلّ be used as an adjective (نَعْتٌ)?

Yes, this is possible.

You can place the word كُلّ as a description/adjective (نَعْتٌ) if you want to express *perfection* (الْكَمَالُ). Such constructions are often quite difficult to understand.

He is a thorough scholar.	هُوَ الْعَالِمُ كُلُّ الْعَالِمِ.
You are a real man.	أَنْتَ الْفَتَى كُلُّ الْفَتَى.
Your brother is a true (perfect) hero.	أَخُوكَ بَطَلٌ كُلُّ الْبَطَلِ.
This is the meaning of the sentence:	بَطَلٌ كَامِلٌ فِي الْبُطولةِ.

One who believes in his country is the man of men.	الْمُؤْمِنُ بِوَطَنِهِ هُوَ الرَّجُلُ كُلُّ الرَّجُلِ.

Adjective (نَعْتٌ) in the nominative case (مَرْفُوعٌ) because it needs to be in grammatical agreement with the word to which it refers.	كُلُّ

148. Some students came. Should the verb be in the plural in Arabic?

No, you use the singular masculine form – but there is another option.

The whole issue is about the *logical subject*. Let's see what it means.

The verb refers to the **real subject**.	Some stu-	بَعْضُ الطُّلابِ جَاءَ.
The verb refers to the "**logical subject**".	dents came.	بَعْضُ الطُّلابِ جَاءُوا.

In our example, بَعْضٌ serves as the subject (فاعِلٌ) of the verbal sentence, clearly marked by the ـُ . Therefore, it has to agree with the verb. Since بَعْضٌ is a masculine, singular noun, the verb (or an adjective) should also be masculine singular. However, in Modern Standard Arabic, many times the verb refers to the *logical subject*.

The same is true for other quantifiers like كُلّ which is also a masculine singular noun. You will encounter two possibilities: verbs and adjectives agree in the masculine singular – or they follow the logical subject. The problem with quantifiers is whether they should be treated like real (masculine singular) nouns or ignored in verbal agreement.

In English, you ignore quantifiers. You say *some/a lot of people* **are** *here* – and not: *is here*. But in Arabic, quantifiers are true nouns (اِسْمٌ) and form compound constructions (إِضافةٌ) with the following اِسْمٌ, so they should be treated as the **main** اِسْمٌ. But since semantically they are not the salient part, people often make the verb agree with the following word. As a rule of thumb we can say:

- In **Classical Arabic**, the verb usually agrees with the <u>real subject</u>. Real here refers to the grammatical subject.

- In **Modern Standard Arabic**, the <u>logical subject</u> is often used for the agreement.

Let's take a look at the most common quantifiers. Note that what we say about the agreement is true for verbs (فِعْلٌ) and adjectives (صِفةٌ).

some (بَعْضٌ) and *all* (كُلٌّ)

Both بَعْض and كُلّ are masculine, singular nouns. So, a verb or adjective should also be masculine singular. But the verb may also refer to the logical subject with the result that we will have a plural form of the verb or adjective. Both views are common in Modern Standard Arabic.

The verb refers to the **real subject: بَعْضُ**. We use the **masculine**, singular form of the verb.	Some sources say...	يَقُولُ بَعْضُ الْمَصادِرِ...
The verb refers to the **logical subject: الْمَصادِرِ** is a non-human plural. We use the **feminine** (singular) form of the verb.		تَقُولُ بَعْضُ الْمَصادِرِ...

Should an adjective after كُلٌّ get the singular or plural form? As indicated, both treatments are possible. Nowadays, most people use the logical subject for the agreement. They treat كُلٌّ with respect to the actual meaning it conveys – and this is not necessarily the meaning of *all* but also *every*. So, كُلٌّ may express a singular or plural meaning. This becomes more complicated if we need to find the correct form of the predicate (خَبَرٌ) of a nominal sentence (جُمْلةٌ اِسْمِيّةٌ).

masculine plural	Every student is hard-working.	كُلُّ الطُّلابِ مُجْتَهِدٌ.
	All students are hard-working.	كُلُّ الطُّلابِ مُجْتَهِدُونَ.
pronoun referring to a plural	Every one of you is sincere.	كُلُّكُمْ مُخْلِصٌ.
	All of you are sincere.	كُلُّكُمْ مُخْلِصُونَ.
feminine plural	Every student (f.) is hard-working.	كُلُّ الطَّالِباتِ مُخْلِصةٌ.
	All students (f.) are hard-working.	كُلُّ الطَّالِباتِ مُخْلِصاتٌ.

If you want to express *every*, you usually use كُلّ plus a singular, indefinite noun. For example: *every student* (كُلُّ طالِبٍ). However, if you have to translate an Arabic sentence into English, you may use *all* or *every* depending on the context.

most, majority (مُعْظَمٌ)

مُعْظَمٌ is a masculine, singular noun – so, verbs and adjectives may be masculine singular too. However, **usually** the agreement is with the gender and number of the **logical subject** (the word after مُعْظَم).

| Agreement with the real (grammatical) subject – **correct**. | Most of the students come from Cairo. | مُعْظَمُ الطُّلابِ قادِمٌ مِن القاهِرةِ. |
| Agreement with the logical subject – **more common**. | | مُعْظَمُ الطُّلابِ قادِمُونَ مِن الْقاهِرةِ. |

totality, whole (جَمِيعٌ)

When جَمِيعٌ serves as the first part of a إضافةٌ-construction, usually the agreement is with the gender and number of the **logical subject** (i.e., the second part of the إضافة).

| Agreement with the logical subject – **more common**. | All the students rushed to the party. | هَبَّ جَمِيعُ الطُّلابِ مُتَّجِهِينَ إِلَى الْحَفْلةِ. |

When جَمِيعٌ is used independently, the verb corresponds to the masculine singular – since جَمِيعٌ is a masculine singular noun.

| Agreement with the **real** subject (الْجَمِيعُ). | Everybody knows. | الْجَمِيعُ يَعْلَمُ. |

most of; the greater portion (أَغْلَبُ)

In most situations, the verb agrees with the **logical subject**.

| The verb refers to the logical subject (الْمُسْتَخْدِمِينَ). | The majority of the users don't trust social media. (headline from *al-'Arabīya*) | أَغْلَبُ الْمُسْتَخْدِمِينَ لا يَثِقُونَ بِمَواقِعِ التَّواصُلِ. |

both (كِلا and كِلْتا)

Although both words are actually dual nouns, they are (grammatically) considered to be **singular**. Therefore, the agreement is **either in the masculine** or **feminine singular**.

| masculine | They (m.) both write. | كِلاهُما يَكْتُبُ. |
| feminine | Both (f.) travel to Egypt. | كِلْتاهُما تُسافِرُ إلى مِصْرَ. |

149. What can the word أَيّ be used for?

أَيّ is one of the more complicated words and can do many jobs.

When you want to analyze the function of أَيّ in a sentence, you should first check what is placed **after** أَيّ to get an idea of the **meaning.**

In other words, you have to look at the مُضافٌ إلَيْهِ because in most situations, أَيّ must be used in a إِضافةٌ-construction serving as the first part. However, if you want to identify the grammatical function of أَيّ, the first part of the إِضافةٌ represented by أَيّ is crucial. أَيّ is a اِسْمٌ and thus can be charged with a grammatical function.

What kind of jobs could أَيّ take on? It may be placed as a question word (اِسْمُ اِسْتِفْهامٍ), conditional particle (اِسْمُ شَرْطٍ), relative pronoun (اِسْمٌ مَوْصُولٌ), it may function as a particularization (الإِخْتِصاص), or even as work as a vocative (نِداءٌ).

Which man did you pass by today?	بِأَيِّ رَجُلٍ مَرَرْتُ الْيَوْمَ؟
Question word (اِسْمُ اِسْتِفْهامٍ), genitive (مَجْرُورٌ) by the preposition.	أَيِّ

Meet me any day you wish.	قابِلْنِي أَيَّ يَوْمٍ تَشاءُ.
Adverb of time (ظَرْفُ زَمانٍ); therefore, in the accusative (مَنْصُوبٌ).	أَيَّ

Zayd reads such a reading and writes such a writing.	يَقْرَأُ زَيْدٌ أَيَّ قِراءةٍ وَيَكْتُبُ أَيَّ كِتابةٍ.
Absolute object (مَفْعُولٌ مُطْلَقٌ); it gets the accusative case (مَنْصُوبٌ).	أَيَّ

150. Can you place أَيّ as an adjective (نَعْتٌ)?

Yes, this is possible.

Using أَيّ as an adjective (نَعْتٌ) is actually quite common, although it may look a little strange and is sometimes difficult to translate.

He is a true man. (Zayd is a man, such a man).	زَيْدٌ رَجُلٌ أَيُّ رَجُلٍ.
Adjective (نَعْتٌ) in the nominative case (مَرْفُوعٌ) referring to the predicate (خَبَرٌ) of the sentence; therefore, it gets the nominative case.	أَيُّ

I saw a knight, what a knight.	رَأَيْتُ فارِسًا أَيَّ فارِسٍ.
Adjective (نَعْتٌ) referring to the direct object (مَفْعُولٌ بِهِ). Therefore, it must also take the accusative case (مَنْصُوبٌ).	أَيَّ

151. Can the word غَيْر be cut off from the إِضافةٌ؟

Yes, this is possible.

غَيْرٌ is a noun (اِسْمٌ) and means *alteration, difference*. It is usually the first part of a إِضافةٌ (then losing nunation) and conveys the meaning of *differing from, the opposite of, other;* also: *not* or *else; un-* or *-non.* غَيْرٌ works like كُلّ or أَيّ and can be charged with various jobs in a sentence.

Not a single one attended.	حَضَرَ غَيْرُ واحِدٍ.	1
غَيْر is the subject (فاعِلٌ) of the verb; nominative (مَرْفُوعٌ) case.		
I didn't see anyone. (direct object)	رَأَيْتُ غَيْرَ واحِدٍ.	2

Now, let's return to our question. Can غَيْر stand alone at all?

Yes, there is a special construction that allows us to detach غَيْر, so that it is cut off from the إِضَافةٌ. This happens when it is **preceded by لَيْسَ** or **لا**. The expression لَيْسَ غَيْر conveys the meaning of *not otherwise, nothing more; nothing else, only this*. In English, you would often use an adverb at such a position. The characteristic feature of this construction is that the second part (مُضافٌ إِلَيْهِ) of the إِضَافةٌ is missing. But how should we treat غَيْر grammatically?

Let's analyze an example.

Muhammad came to us, (and) nobody else.	جاءَنا مُحَمَّدٌ لَيْسَ غَيْر.

There are three possibilities to treat غَيْر:

OPTION A – we use غَيْرُ. That's the preferred solution.

Muhammad came to us, nobody else.	جاءَنا مُحَمَّدٌ لَيْسَ غَيْرُ.

غَيْر is cut off visually (a missing second word) from the annexation, but **not regarding the meaning** since the second part is incorporated. Thus, we don't pronounce nor write Nunation. We assume that غَيْرُ is fixed and cemented on the "*u*" (مَبْنِيٌّ عَلَى الضَّمِّ).

➤ **Possibility 1:** غَيْرُ is the predicate of لَيْسَ which, by the rules, has to take the accusative case. However, we can't mark it as such. Thus, we need to assign a place value, i.e., that of an accusative case (فِي مَحَلِّ نَصْبٍ). In this approach, we assume that the subject was deleted.

estimated meaning (التَّقْدِيرُ) and literal translation	
The coming (= subject) is not other than him.	لَيْسَ الجائِي غَيْرَهُ.

➤ **Possibility 2:** غَيْرُ is the subject (اِسْمُ لَيْسَ), so it needs the nominative case. But the vowel *u* you see is not a case marker. It is part of the cemented – hence indeclinable – shape. We need to assign a place value, i.e., that of a nominative case (فِي مَحَلّ رَفْعٍ). Here, we assume that the predicate was deleted.

Not other than him is the coming (= predicate).	لَيْسَ غَيْرُهُ الْجائِيَ

The idea is deep. If we assume that غَيْر is declinable (مُعْرَبٌ) and not in-declinable, we would theoretically arrive at غَيْرًا in our example with Muhammad. This would mean that you cannot form an annexation. In order to signify that we do intend that, we need to drop the nunation. Since we got rid of the nunation (تَنْوِينٌ), it is clear that we do not want to express an indefinite meaning and that غَيْر incorporates a certain meaning. That's what the grammarian al-'Akhfash (الْأَخْفَش) suggested.

OPTION B – we use غَيْرَ.

Muhammad came to us, nobody else.	جاءَنا مُحَمَّدٌ لَيْسَ غَيْرَ.

The argumentation is similar to option B with one difference. We use the vowel "a" for fixing and cementing غَيْر. In the analysis, we say that it functions as the predicate of لَيْسَ. the estimated meaning is the same as in possibility 1.

OPTION C – we use nunation and get غَيْرٌ or غَيْرًا.

غَيْر is cut off from the إِضافةٌ visually **and** in terms of meaning (لَفْظًا وَمَعْنًى) due to the structure of a إِضافةٌ. If you see **nunation** (تَنْوِينٌ), it is clear that a word wants to be independent (= indefinite) and does not want any annexation. With nunation, it can't work as the first part of a إِضافةٌ anymore. The idea of the إِضافةٌ is gone. See *Arabic for Nerds 1*, #96.

| Muhammad came to us, nobody else. | جاءَنا مُحَمَّدٌ لَيْسَ غَيْرٌ. | a |
| | جاءَنا مُحَمَّدٌ لَيْسَ غَيْرًا. | b |

The "subject" (اسْمُ لَيْسَ); in the nominative (مَرْفُوعٌ).	غَيْرٌ	a
Predicate (خَبَرُ لَيْسَ); therefore in the accusative (مَنْصُوبٌ).	غَيْرًا	b

152. Can غَيْر be used as an adjective (نَعْتٌ)؟

Yes, this is possible.

Purist grammarians say that غَيْر doesn't accept the definite article (لا تُعَرَّفُ). If we believe them, which is what we should, we can conclude that غَيْر can't serve as an adjective for definite words.

To answer our question, yes, غَيْر can work as an adjective if غَيْر is placed **after** an <u>indefinite</u> noun. This leaves us with the following two situations:

a) غَيْر is **followed** by an **indefinite noun** or

b) غَيْر has a **pronoun attached**.

Wait! If we attach a pronoun (like in غَيْرُكَ) doesn't that make the entire expression definite? Well, similar to أَحَدٌ or مِثْلٌ, an expression with غَيْر is still considered **indefinite** even when you attach a personal pronoun or combine it with a definite genitive noun (إِضافةٌ). For example: *Men other than you* (رِجالٌ غَيْرُكُمْ). *A young man like me* (فَتًى مِثْلِي).

In both options, غَيْر is treated as **declinable** (مُعْرَبٌ). ➡ It gets case endings. We need to blueprint the case of the word to which غَيْر refers.

1	These are **uneducated people.** (It doesn't mean: *These people are uneducated* = هؤُلَاءِ النَّاسُ)	هؤُلَاءِ ناسٌ غَيْرُ مُهَذَّبِينَ.
2	**Another man** came.	جاءَ رَجُلٌ غَيْرُكَ.
3	I saw **another man.**	رَأَيْتُ رَجُلًا غَيْرَكَ.
4	I passed (by) **another man.**	مَرَرْتُ بِرَجُلٍ غَيْرِكَ.

1	Adjective (نَعْتٌ) for the predicate (خَبَرٌ); nominative (مَرْفُوعٌ).	غَيْرُ
2	Adjective (نَعْتٌ) for the subject (فاعِلٌ); nominative case (مَرْفُوعٌ).	غَيْرُ
3	Adjective for the direct object (مَفْعُولٌ بِهِ); accusative (مَنْصُوبٌ).	غَيْرَ
4	Adjective (نَعْتٌ), genitive case (مَجْرُورٌ) since the word it describes, رَجُلٍ, is under the control of the preposition ب.	غَيْرِ

153. What kind of word is حَسْب؟

Regarding its DNA, it is a noun (اِسْمٌ).

حَسْب conveys the meaning of *enough* (كَافٍ) or *only*. It is a **noun** with features of a verb, thus a quasi-verb (اِسْمُ فِعْلٍ), which conveys an imperative like in حَسْبُكَ! which means *(it is) enough for you!* Depending on the situation, it may mean: *hold on!* Since حَسْب is not a verb, it doesn't point to time (زَمانٌ) nor to a place (مَكانٌ).

We should look at how we can use حَسْب. The analysis is similar to what we have said about غَيْر in question #150. The central question is how do we deal with the fact that حَسْب usually forms a إِضافةٌ.

Option 1: حَسْب is the <u>first part</u> of a إِضافةٌ visibly (explicitly) and by meaning (لَفْظًا وَمَعْنًى). ➡ It gets case inflection.

It serves as the subject (مُبْتَدَأٌ) of a nominal sentence (جُمْلةٌ اِسْمِيّةٌ) or the predicate (خَبَرٌ). Most importantly, it gets **visible case endings**.

Allah is sufficient (enough) for us. (Sura 9:59)	حَسْبُنا اللهُ!

Fronted predicate (خَبَرٌ مُقَدَّمٌ); so it takes the marker of the nominative case (مَرْفُوعٌ بِالضَّمّةِ الظّاهِرةِ). First part of the إِضافةٌ.	حَسْبُ
Second part of the إِضافةٌ. It has an indeclinable shape (مَبْنِيٌّ); we say that it is located in the position of a genitive (فِي مَحَلِّ جَرٍّ).	نا
Delayed subject (مُبْتَدَأٌ مُؤَخَّرٌ), in the nominative case (مَرْفُوعٌ).	اللهُ

Faith is enough/sufficient for you.	بِحَسْبِكَ الإِيمانُ.

Additional (extra) preposition (حَرْفُ جَرٍّ زائِدٌ).	بِ
Delayed subject (مُبْتَدَأٌ مُؤَخَّرٌ), in the nominative case by a virtual, estimated marker (مَرْفُوعٌ بِضَمّةٍ مُقَدَّرةٍ). The additional preposition has the power over the place of the case marker as it drags the word into the genitive. ➡ We see a كَسْرةٌ.	حَسْبِ
Pronominal suffix (ضَميرٌ مُتَّصِلٌ); it has a fixed shape; nevertheless, it occupies the grammatical position of a genitive case (فِي مَحَلِّ جَرٍّ) since it is the مُضافٌ إِلَيْهِ, the 2nd part of the إِضافةٌ.	كَ

Predicate (خَبَرٌ); in the nominative case (مَرْفُوعٌ).	الإيمانُ

Verily, Allah is sufficient for you!	إِنَّ حَسْبَكَ اللهُ!

Particle of emphasis which has the power to operate on words in the accusative case (حَرْفُ تَوْكِيدٍ وَنَصْبٍ).	إِنَّ
"Subject" (اِسْمُ إِنَّ); accusative case (مَنْصُوبٌ بِالْفَتْحةِ الظَّاهِرةِ).	حَسْبَ
Predicate (خَبَرُ إِنَّ); therefore, it gets the nominative (مَرْفُوعٌ) case.	اللهُ

Option 2: حَسْب is cut off from the إِضافة visually (لَفْظًا), but not regarding the meaning. Then, it is **indeclinable** with a fixed ending on "*u*" (مَبْنِيٌّ عَلَى الضَّمِّ): i.e., حَسْبُ.

Only one student came.	جاءَ طالِبٌ حَسْبُ.

Adjective (نَعْتٌ). Since حَسْبُ is indeclinable (مَبْنِيٌّ عَلَى الضَّمِّ), we need to assign a "place value" – that of a nominative case (في مَحَلِّ رَفْعٍ). Note that حَسْبُ is an adjective/attribute (نَعْتٌ) because it refers to an <u>in</u>definite noun (*a student*).	حَسْبُ

Only Zayd came.	جاءَ زَيْدٌ حَسْبُ.

This is a حالٌ because it refers to a definite noun. Due to its indeclinable shape (مَبْنِيٌّ عَلَى الضَّمِّ), we can't put the markers of an accusative case and can only assign virtual markers according to its position, i.e., the place value of an accusative (في مَحَلِّ نَصْبٍ).	حَسْبُ

We saw in the above examples that حَسْب may serve as an adjective/attribute (صِفةٌ /نَعْتٌ) or a حالٌ. How can we identify its function? We already hinted at it, but it's worth going deeper again.

Let's start with the **adjective** (نَعْتٌ). ▷ The word حَسْب has to describe an <u>indefinite</u> noun.

Zayd is **a friend** sufficing you as a friend.	زَيْدٌ صَدِيقٌ حَسْبُكَ مِنْ صَدِيقٍ.

The expression حَسْبُكَ is an expression of praise, referring to the **indefinite** noun, denoting the following: *supplying to you the place of any other (by his excellent qualities).*

Placed as an **adjective** (نَعْتٌ); therefore, it also gets the nominative case (مَرْفُوعٌ) like the word to which it refers.	حَسْبُ
Extra (additional) preposition (حَرْفُ جَرٍّ زائِدٌ).	مِنْ
Specification (تَمْيِيزٌ) which is in the accusative case but only by virtual, estimated case markers (مَنْصُوبٌ بِفَتْحةٍ مُقَدَّرةٍ) because the additional preposition occupies this spot and drags the word apparently into the genitive case (مَجْرُورٌ).	صَديقٍ

I passed (by) a friend sufficing you as a friend.	مَرَرْتُ بِصَديقٍ حَسْبِكَ مِنْ صَديقٍ.

In the above examples, حَسْب is seen as an interpreted مُشْتَقٌّ (derived noun from the root). It has the function of an **active participle** (إِسْمُ الْفاعِلِ), كافٍ, e.g., كافِيكَ, i.e., *to be enough or adequate (for you).*

If the active participle functions as the first part of a إِضافةٌ, it **can't** have the definite article. Since the first part is not the word that specifies, it allows us to say that حَسْبُ is a نَعْتٌ for an **indefinite** noun (*a friend*).

Let's move on to حَسْب functions as a **circumstantial qualifier** (حالٌ). ⊳ حَسْب refers to a <u>definite</u> noun. Since we treat حَسْب as a حالٌ, it has to take the accusative (مَنْصُوبٌ) case.

حالٌ	This is Abdallah (definite!); being one sufficing you.	هذا عَبْدُ اللهِ حَسْبَكَ.	1
حالٌ	This is Abdallah (definite!); being one sufficing you as a man.	هذا عَبْدُ اللهِ حَسْبُكَ مِنْ رَجُلٍ.	2
نَعْتٌ	This is <u>a</u> man (indefinite!) sufficing you.	هذا رَجُلٌ حَسْبُكَ.	3

A حالٌ; so it takes the accusative case (مَنْصُوبٌ بِالْفَتْحةِ الظّاهِرةِ).	حَسْبَ
Additional/extra preposition (حَرْفُ جَرٍّ زائِدٌ).	مِنْ

Specification (تَمْييزٌ), it must take the accusative case. However, we can only apply estimated, virtual case markers because the word is indeclinable (مَنْصُوبٌ بِفَتْحةٍ مُقَدَّرةٍ).	رَجُلٍ

154. What does فَحَسْبُ mean? And what is the job of the فَ here?

فَحَسْبُ *means: and that's all. The* فَ *is just there for decoration.*

فَحَسْبُ and فَقَطْ mean the same and can usually be exchanged. It can convey many meanings, e.g., *and that is enough; and that's all*. In negations: *not only*.

If you use فَحَسْبُ, you must fix حَسْب on the vowel "*u*" (مَبْنِيٌّ عَلَى الضَّمِّ). Why is that? حَسْب normally works as the first part of a إِضافةٌ-construction. What happened is that the second part was deleted – visually and by pronunciation, but **not by meaning** (مَعْنًى لا لَفْظًا).

Put simply, we we incorporated the meaning (given by the context) in حَسْب and to make it clear that it is not an independent word, we deleted the nunation (تَنْوِينٌ) and fix the word on a single vowel. For that reason, it can only restrict the idea of exclusivity to words before, but not to words after it. Such an operation also happens in غَيْرُ or بَعْدُ; see *#151* & *Arabic for Nerds 1, #221.*

What about the grammatical treatment? In فَحَسْبُ, the word حَسْبُ works as the subject (مُبْتَدَأٌ) of a nominal sentence (جُمْلةٌ اِسْمِيّةٌ) under the prerequisite that it is combined with فَ.

I wrote three papers and that is all.	كَتَبْتُ ثَلاثَ وَرَقاتٍ فَحَسْب (=فَقَطْ).
➡ implicit meaning (تَقْدِيرٌ):	حَسْبُ الثَّلاثِ مَكْتُوبٌ.

Additional, extra particle used for **decoration, ornamentation** of the word (حَرْفٌ زائِدٌ لِتَزْيِينِ اللَّفْظِ). It doesn't have a place in إِعْرابٌ and does not have operating power (لا عَمَلَ لَهُ). It is also found in فَقَطْ, see *question #154.*	فَ
Subject (مُبْتَدَأٌ); the word حَسْبُ is indeclinable (مَبْنِيٌّ عَلَى الضَّمِّ); we can only virtually assign the nominative case (فِي مَحَلِّ رَفْعٍ). What about the predicate (خَبَرٌ)? It was deleted (مَحْذُوفٌ).	حَسْبُ

155. What kind of word is فَقَطْ?

فَقَطْ *is translated as* **only, solely, merely.** *Literally it means* **and enough.**

فَقَطْ has the same meaning as فَحَسْبُ. With that word it also shares the first letter, the *Fā' of embellishment* (الْفاءُ لِلتَّزْيِينِ). The second part قَطْ is usually treated as an indeclinable noun (اِسْمٌ مَبْنِيٌّ), but may also be seen as an interjection denoting a sense of a verb (اِسْمُ الْفِعْلِ).

قَطْ can be used alone. The two examples below basically mean the same – *A dirham is enough for Zayd.* –, but the idea of قَطْ is different.

Indeclinable noun (اِسْمٌ مَبْنِيٌّ بِمَعْنَى حَسْبُ); it is the subject (مُبْتَدَأ)	Lit: *The sufficiency of Zayd is a dirham.*	قَطْ زَيْدٍ دِرْهَمٌ.
Quasi-verb expressing to be enough (اِسْمُ فِعِلٍ بِمَعْنَى الْمُضارِع يَكْفِي). It governs the object in the accusative.	Lit.: *A dirham will suffice Zayd.*	قَطْ زَيْدًا دِرْهَمٌ.

Let's return to فَقَطْ. The expression is placed as an *adjective/attribute* (نَعْتٌ) or as a *circumstantial qualifier* (حالٌ). It can be placed **before or after** the word which is to be granted exclusivity.

Only one student attended.	حَضَرَ طالِبٌ فَقَطْ.

Additional, redundant particle used for ornamentation of the word (حَرْفٌ زائِدٌ لِتَزْيِينِ اللَّفْظِ).	فَ
Adjective (نَعْتٌ); it has an indeclinable shape, fixed on the سُكُونٌ; We can't mark the case and can only say that it is in the position of a nominative (فِي مَحَلِّ رَفْعٍ). Why is it an adjective? Because it refers to an <u>indefinite</u> noun. Otherwise, it would be a حالٌ (see below).	قَطْ

Only Zayd attended.	حَضَرَ زَيْدٌ فَقَطْ.

This is a حالٌ because it refers to *Zayd* (which is a proper noun and therefore treated as **definite**). It grammatically holds the position of an accusative case (فِي مَحَلِّ نَصْبٍ).	قَطْ

Some scholars use **different approaches.** and treat the expression فَقَطْ and its components differently. The following two options depend on the concept of *deletion* (الْحَذْفُ) and *interpretation* (التَّأْوِيلُ).

Option 1: We treat it as a <u>quasi-verb</u>; interjection (اِسْمُ الْفِعْلِ).

Additional, redundant particle (حَرْفٌ زَائِدٌ).	فَ
Quasi-verb (اِسْمُ فِعْلٍ) that expresses an imperative (أَمْرٌ) or the present tense (مُضَارِعٌ) of *enough for you* (يَكْفِيكَ). It is indeclinable and does not have a place in إِعْرَابٌ.	قَطْ

What would be the actual meaning of this approach?

His presence is enough for you.	فَيَكْفِيكَ حُضُورُهُ.

Option 2 is based on a hypothetical (virtual) <u>conditional sentence</u>.

Only Zayd attended.	حَضَرَ زَيْدٌ فَقَطْ.
Assumed, virtual meaning:	حَضَرَ زَيْدٌ، فَإِنْ عَرِفْتَ هذا فَهُوَ حَسْبُكَ.

Placed as the second part or **complement** of a (virtual, implicitly understood) **conditional sentence** (واقِعةٌ فِي جَوابِ شَرْطٍ مُقَدَّرٍ).	فَ
Predicate (خَبَرٌ) of the **deleted** subject (مُبْتَدَأٌ مَحْذُوفٌ). It is therefore placed in the position of a nominative case (فِي مَحَلِّ رَفْعٍ).	قَطْ

156. What is the word إِمَّا made of?

It consists of two words – if it is the conditional device.

إِمَّا is a tricky device that can be used for two things:

- to denote *either* (لِأَحَدِ شَيْئَيْنِ). It is placed at the predicate instead of أوْ (*or*). It occurs twice in sentence – see *question #156*.
- to indicate a conditional meaning (إِمَّا الشَّرْطِيّةُ); it denotes *if, whether* and is used like إِنْ. It occurs only once in the sentence.

For the conditional device, we have the following ingredients:

- إِنْ ➡ conditional particle (إِنْ الشَّرْطِيّةُ)
- ما ➡ additional particle (ما الزَّائِدةُ), it is there to strengthen the conditional meaning (ما لِتَأْكِيدِ مَعْنَى الشَّرْطِ).

➤ The result is إمّا. When a ن and a م collide, they usually merge. After that conditional particle, often the **energetic** is used (additional ن), but also the jussive (مَجْزُومٌ) mood would be possible.

إمّا تُعُدُّوا الصَّالِحاتِ فَإِنَّني أَقُولُ بِها.	If you ever count the good deeds, I shall also speak about them.

		إمّا يَبْلُغَنَّ عِندَكَ الْكِبَرَ
Sura 17:23	If either or both of them [your parents] reach old age with you, say no word that shows impatience with them, and do not be harsh with them, but speak to them respectfully.	أَحَدُهُمَا أَوْ كِلَاهُمَا فَلَا تَقُل لَّهُمَا أُفٍّ وَلَا تَنْهَرْهُمَا وَقُل لَّهُمَا قَوْلًا كَرِيمًا.

157. What does إمّا ... وَإمّا mean?

إمّا *is rarely used as a conditional particle in the meaning of whether. Usually* إمّا *is repeated and then conveys the meaning of:* **either... or.**

If you encounter إمّا ... وَإمّا, the analysis (إِعْرابٌ) may be challenging:

- The **first** إمّا is a **particle** (حَرْفٌ) which indicates a **specific meaning** (يَدُلُّ عَلَى مَعانٍ مُعَيَّنةٍ).
- The **second** إمّا is also a حَرْفٌ and like the first one, it points to the same specific meaning. That's no coincidence since it is always pre-ceded by وَ which is a عَطْفٌ ("coupler", coordinator). Some grammarians, however, suggested that the **second** إمّا is a حَرْفُ عَطْفٍ it-self. They treat وَ as an extra particle (حَرْفٌ زائِدٌ) and the entire the expression simply as one entity.
- Both إمّا don't have a place in إِعْرابٌ since they are a حَرْفٌ. The good news is that we don't have to think about their function/case.

What meanings can the expression إمّا ... وَإمّا convey?

a) Doubt (الشَّكُّ)

Either Zayd or Muhammad attended.	حَضَرَ إمّا زَيْدٌ وَإمّا مُحَمَّدٌ.

Particle of doubt (حَرْفُ شَكٍّ). Does not have a place in إِعْرابٌ.	إمّا

Subject (فَاعِلٌ) of the verbal sentence; nominative (مَرْفُوعٌ) case.	زَيْدٌ
Conjunction (حَرْفُ عَطْفٍ).	و
Again, this is a حَرْفُ شَكٍّ.	إمّا
Coupled word (مَعْطُوفٌ). Since it has to take the same case as the word to which it is linked, it is gets the nominative (مَرْفُوعٌ) too.	مُحَمَّدٌ

b) Giving a choice (التَّخْيِيرُ)

Sura 20:65	They said, "O Moses, either you throw or we will be the first to throw."	قَالُوا يَا مُوسَى إمّا أَن تُلْقِيَ وَإمّا أَن نَكُونَ أَوَّلَ مَنْ أَلْقَى.

c) Permission; authorization (الإِباحةُ)

Learn whether it is literature or grammar!	تَعَلَّمْ إمّا أَدَبًا وَإمّا نَحْوًا!

d) Giving details/elaboration (التَّفْصيلُ)

A man is either wise or unwise.	الإِنْسانُ إمّا عاقِلٌ وَإمّا غَيْرُ عاقِلٍ.

Remark: Is there a difference to أَوْ? Yes, but it is a finesse. أَوْ and إمّا are placed in a different location, which does matter as we will see. The following two sentences mean: *Zayd or Amr came to me.*

If we read it word by word, we first think that Zayd (جاءَنِي زَيْدٌ) did come. Only later, after the word Zayd, أَوْ informs us that this is perhaps not true.	جاءَنِي زَيْدٌ أَوْ عَمْرُو.
We know right after the verb that it is not clear who came as إمّا is placed before the first name.	جاءَنِي إمّا زَيْدٌ وَإمّا عَمْرُو.

158. What does the word أَمّا mean?

The word أَمّا has the meaning of: as for; concerning, as regards.

أَمّا is a particle (حَرْفٌ) and usually treated as a single word. Most grammarians assume that it is a contraction of أَمَّ and ما.

أَمَّا usually provides **emphasis** (التَّوْكِيدُ) or more **details** (التَّفْصِيلُ). Depending on the place and function in the sentence, أَمَّا can assist to express a **conditional meaning** (الشَّرْطُ) – note that it **doesn't put** the verb into the jussive mood (مَجْزُومٌ).

أَمَّا normally precedes a **noun** phrase presented with some emphasis as the **topic/subject** (often in contrast to some previous assertion). But you may also squeeze in a preposition or adverb, for example: أَمَّا بَعْدُ فَ (*now then on to*; used to introduce the main topic). The statement (comment/predicate) supplies more information about the noun and is usually a complete (nominal or verbal) sentence. It is introduced by فَ. Some examples:

noun (اِسْمٌ)	So as for the orphan, do not oppress him (Sura 93:9).	فَأَمَّا الْيَتِيمَ فَلَا تَقْهَرْ.
	As for the residents, they are well.	أَمَّا السُّكَّانُ فَهُمْ عَلَى ما يُرامُ.
preposition (حَرْفُ الْجَرِّ)	But as for the favor of your Lord, report it (Sura 93:11).	وَأَمَّا بِنِعْمَةِ رَبِّكَ فَحَدِّثْ.
conditional particle	So, as for him who in case he is of those brought near [to Us]. (Sura 56:88)	فَأَمَّا إِنْ كَانَ مِنَ الْمُقَرَّبِينَ.

| Sura 69:5 | So as for Thamūd, they were destroyed by the overpowering [blast]. | فَأَمَّا ثَمُودُ فَأُهْلِكُوا بِالطَّاغِيَةِ. |

Remark: Thamūd is the name of an ancient tribe, mentioned 26 times in the Qur'an, that rebelled against Allah and his messengers.

| As for Zayd, he is courageous. | أَمَّا زَيْدٌ فَشُجاعٌ. |

This construction is much stronger than the plain version:

| Zayd is courageous. | زَيْدٌ شُجاعٌ. |

| This particle is used to indicate a conditional meaning and to put emphasis (حَرْفُ شَرْطٍ وَتَوْكِيدٍ). It does not have a place in إِعْرابٌ. | أَمَّا |
| Subject (مُبْتَدَأٌ) of a nominal sentence; nominative (مَرْفُوع). | زَيْدٌ |

This فَ was placed before the estimated, virtual complement of the conditional sentence (الْفاءُ واقِعةٌ فِي جَوابِ شَرْطٍ مُقَدَّرٍ).	ف
Predicate (خَبَرٌ), in the nominative case (مَرْفُوعٌ).	شُجاعٌ

Why do we say that أَمّا has a **conditional** meaning? In order to show its force and meaning, we can rewrite such sentences with مَهْما. Let's see how the grammarians estimate the meaning of the above sentence.

No matter what it is, Zayd knows.	مَهْما يَكُنْ مِنْ شَيْءٍ فَزَيْدٌ عالِمٌ.

THE INQUIRY / QUESTION WORDS (كَلِماتُ الْإِسْتِفْهامِ)

If you see a question, you have two people involved: the one who asks (مُسْتَفْهِمٌ) and the one who answers (مُجِيبٌ). The question sentence is a request for understanding (طَلَبُ الْفَهْمِ). An interrogative sentence (جُمْلةُ الْإِسْتِفْهامِ) is a جُمْلةٌ طَلَبِيّةٌ, which means that it doesn't have a predicative meaning. It doesn't proclaim, declare, or affirm anything. Interrogative sentences are counted as *styles* (أُسْلُوبٌ) as they don't fit into the two main sentence structures in Arabic – see *chapter 12*. So, you may encounter the term أُسْلُوبُ الْاسْتِفْهامِ when you read about interrogative sentences.

159. Are all question words in Arabic nouns (إِسْمٌ)?

Yes, except for two.

In Arabic, words used to ask questions are nouns (إِسْمٌ) as the term already indicates: أَسْماءُ الْإِسْتِفْهامِ. But there are **two exceptions**.

Meaning: *does/do?* Or: *did?* Or: *is/are?*	أ	هَلْ
Both are indeclinable (مَبْنِيٌّ) particles (حَرْفٌ) and don't have a place in إِعْرابٌ.		

All the other question words are nouns (إِسْمٌ) and have a position in إِعْرابٌ: they get case endings! However, all of them except for one are **in**declinable (مَبْنِيٌّ) and never change their shape. The exception is أَيّ. It is usually the first part of a إِضافةٌ followed by a singular word.

Which (what) man came?	أَيُّ رَجُلٍ جاءَ؟

Question word (إِسْمُ اِسْتِفْهامٍ). It is the **subject** (مُبْتَدَأٌ) of the nominal sentence and therefore in the nominative case (مَرْفُوعٌ) – because أَيُّ is not مَبْنِيٌّ but مُعْرَبٌ. It serves as the مُضافٌ (first part of the إِضافةٌ).	أَيُّ
Second part of the إِضافةٌ (مُضافٌ إِلَيْهِ); in the genitive case (مَجْرُورٌ).	رَجُلٍ
Verb in the past tense. Its subject is an implied pronoun (ضَـمِـيرٌ مُسْتَتِرٌ) which has the meaning of *he* (هُوَ).	جاءَ

We identified the subject (مُبْتَدَأٌ). So, where's the **predicate** (خَبَرٌ)? It is the **verbal sentence** (جاءَ - *he came*) and has a hidden, implied pronoun as the subject (فاعِلٌ).

Remember that we deal with a complex sentence. We can say that the verbal sentence serves as the خَبَرٌ and is placed in the position of a nominative case (فِي مَحَلِّ رَفْعٍ خَبَرٌ).

part 2		part 1
جاءَ		أَيُّ رَجُلٍ
full verbal sentence: *he came.*	+	*which man*
predicate of the nominal sentence		**subject** of the nominal sentence

Which book did you read?	أَيَّ كِتابٍ قَرَأْتَ؟

Placed at the beginning of the sentence, أَيَّ serves as the **direct object** (مَفْعُولٌ بِهِ) of the verbal sentence (جُمْلةٌ فِعْلِيّةٌ) and is therefore in the accusative case (مَنْصُوبٌ). It serves as the first part of the إِضافةٌ.	أَيَّ
This is the second part of the إِضافةٌ (i.e., مُضافٌ إِلَيْهِ); thus مَجْرُورٌ.	كِتابٍ
Past tense verb. The تَ in form of a pronoun suffix (ضَمِيرٌ مُتَّصِلٌ) is the subject (فاعِلٌ). It is indeclinable (مَبْنِيٌّ) and only gets the virtual, estimated case marker of a nominative case (فِي مَحَلِّ رَفْعٍ فاعِلٌ).	قَرَأْتَ

160. What functions may مَنْ have in a sentence?

Quite some jobs.

It is not so easy to identify the function of the noun مَنْ because it is indeclinable and never changes its shape. Let's do a tour.

مَنْ	1. Subject (مُبْتَدَأٌ) of a nominal sentence (جُمْلةٌ اِسْمِيّةٌ)

1	Who will catch the train?	مَنْ مُدْرِكٌ الْقِطارَ؟
	This is the situation when مَنْ is followed by an **indefinite** noun.	

2	Who came?	مَنْ جاءَ؟
	When do we have such a situation? Answer: When you have an **intransitive** verb (فِعْلٌ لازِمٌ) after مَنْ. Such verbs **can't have an object**.	

3	**Whom** did you beat? (It is not: Who beat you?)	مَنْ ضَرَبْتَهُ؟

This is the situation when مَنْ is followed by a **transitive** verb (فِعْلٌ مُتَعَدٍّ).

This means that you need a direct object which is usually a pronoun in such constructions. Don't get confused: We have a **nominal sentence** here. So the **predicate** is the **verbal sentence**. In fact, what we got here is the following sentence: *Who (is) you beat him?*

It would also be possible to have the same sentence without a pronoun – but then we have a different underlying construction (see below). Note: You usually find these constructions when you play with the word order. For example: *in whose hands...* (بِيَدِ مَنْ = مَنْ بِيَدِهِ)

مَنْ	2. Fronted predicate (خَبَرٌ مُقَدَّمٌ)

Who is the writer?	مَنِ الْكاتِبُ؟
This is usually the situation when مَنْ is followed by a **definite** noun.	

مَنْ	3. Predicate of كانَ – in Arabic: خَبَرُ كانَ

Who was he?	مَنْ كانَ؟

4. Fronted direct object (مَفْعُولٌ بِهِ مُقَدَّمٌ)	مَنْ

Whom did you beat?	مَنْ ضَرَبْتَ؟

This is a verbal sentence (جُمْلَةٌ فِعْلِيَّةٌ)! We usually get such constructions when مَنْ is followed by a **transitive verb** (فِعْلٌ مُتَعَدٍّ) which **didn't take its object** (لَمْ يَأْخُذْ مَفْعُولَهُ).

Let's do some more analysis.

1	Who came?	مَنْ جَاءَ؟
2	Whose character is generous?	مَنْ خُلُقُهُ كَرِيمٌ؟
3	Who is at home?	مَنْ فِي الْبَيْتِ؟
4	Who is this?	مَنْ هذا؟
5	Who(m) did you see today?	مَنْ رَأَيْتَ الْيَوْمَ؟
6	Whose father is this?	أَبُو مَنْ هذا؟

مَنْ can be located in the position of a nominative (فِي مَحَلِّ رَفْعٍ), geni-tive (فِي مَحَلِّ جَرٍّ), or accusative case (فِي مَحَلِّ نَصْبٍ).

➤ **In examples 1, 2, and 3,** مَنْ is the **subject** (مُبْتَدَأٌ) of a nominal sen-tence, located in the position of a nominative case (فِي مَحَلِّ رَفْعٍ). What about the **predicate** (خَبَرٌ)؟

1	The verbal sentence is the predicate (خَبَرٌ); therefore, it is located in the po-sition of a nominative case (فِي مَحَلِّ رَفْعٍ).
2	Here we changed the word order. The whole part after مَنْ is a nominal sentence. This means that we deal with two nominal sentences. The sec-ond one (خُلُقُهُ كَرِيمٌ) is the predicate (خَبَرٌ) of the first and therefore in the position of a nominative case (فِي مَحَلِّ رَفْعٍ). Don't forget that as soon as we move مَنْ to the beginning, we need a *returner* (referential pronoun).
3	Here we have a prepositional phrase (شِبْهُ الْجُمْلَةِ) after مَنْ. Some call it the predicate. But that's not entirely correct; the predicate was deleted be-cause it is implicitly understood (e.g., مَوْجُودٌ). We say that the preposi-tional phrase is attached to that deleted predicate (مُتَعَلِّقٌ بِمَحْذُوفٍ واقِعٍ خَبَرًا). Note that a prepositional phrase can't stand alone in a sentence – it

> must be connected with a verb or a word with verbal force.

➤ Sentence 4: The structure of this sentence is not as easy as it may look. مَنْ is the **fronted predicate** (خَبَرٌ مُقَدَّمٌ) and therefore holds the position of a nominative case (فِي مَحَلِّ رَفْعٍ).

| 4 | Demonstrative noun (اِسْمُ الْإِشَارَةِ) which serves as the **delayed sub-ject** (فِي مَحَلِّ رَفْعٍ مُبْتَدَأٌ مُؤَخَّرٌ). This is because the answer to this sentence could be: .هٰذا كَرِيمٌ (*This is Karīm.*) | هٰذا |

➤ Sentence 5: Here we have a verbal sentence (جُمْلَةٌ فِعْلِيَّةٌ). How is that possible if we don't start with a verb? Because we moved the **direct object** (مَفْعُولٌ بِهِ) to the **front**, so it is just about word order! مَنْ can't take any case marker. Nevertheless, as the direct object, it is located in the position of an accusative case (فِي مَحَلِّ نَصْبٍ).

➤ Sentence 6: This is a nominal sentence. مَنْ is the second part of a إِضافةٌ and part of the fronted predicate (خَبَرٌ مُقَدَّمٌ).

6	This is the **fronted predicate** (خَبَرٌ مُقَدَّمٌ). It must get the nominative case (مَرْفُوعٌ) which is marked by the letter و and not by a ضَمّةٌ because *father* (أَب) is one of the *six nouns* (الْأَسْماءُ السِّتَّةُ). This word is also the first part of the إِضافةٌ.	أَبُو
	This is the second part of the إِضافةٌ, i.e., الْمُضافُ إِلَيْهِ; thus, it must be in the genitive (مَجْرُورٌ) case. مَنْ is indeclinable (مَبْنِيٌّ) and can't take any visible case marker. Therefore, we can only say that it is located in the position of a genitive case (فِي مَحَلِّ جَرٍّ).	مَنْ
	Demonstrative (اِسْمُ الْإِشَارَةِ) which functions as the delayed **subject** (مُبْتَدَأٌ مُؤَخَّرٌ); placed in the spot of a nominative case (فِي مَحَلِّ رَفْعٍ).	هٰذا

What we said about *who* (مَنْ) also works for *what* (ما). In the examples above, you could actually just delete مَنْ and use ما. Instead of *who/whose*, it then would be *what*.

Let's summarize our analysis and check the إِعْرابٌ for ما and مَنْ (the numbers correspond to the examples above):

In a <u>nominal sentence</u> (جُمْلةٌ اِسْمِيّةٌ) or a شِبْهُ الْجُمْلةِ, the words ما and مَن are the **subject** (مُبْتَدَأ).	3
If they are followed by a <u>verbal sentence</u> (جُمْلةٌ فِعْلِيّةٌ), then they are either the **subject** (مُبْتَدَأ) or **direct object** (مَفْعُولٌ بِهِ).	1, 5
If a (usually definite) **noun** (اِسْم) is placed after مَن (or ما), then مَن (or ما) serves as the **fronted predicate** (خَبَرٌ مُقَدَّمٌ).	2, 4, 6

161. The question word *what?* Is it ما or ماذا in Arabic?

That's not trivial. You will encounter both.

The more important word is **ما**; the more common perhaps **ماذا**.

ما		ماذا
used in **nominal** sentences	**what?**	Preferred in **verbal** sentences to avoid misunderstandings since ما can have many jobs when it occurs with verbs, e.g., starting a relative clause.

Let's start with **ما**. It can have various functions in a sentence

1	What is this?	ما هذا؟

| Question word (اِسْمُ اِسْتِفْهامٍ), located in the position of the **fronted, foregrounded predicate** (فِي مَحَلّ رَفع خَبَرٌ مُقَدَّمٌ). You can't visibly see the nominative (مَرْفُوعٌ) because ما is indeclinable (مَبْنِيٌّ). | ما |
| Demonstrative (اِسْمُ إشارةٍ), located in the position of the delayed **subject** (مُبْتَدَأ) that was put to the end of the sentence. | هذا |

2	What happened to you?	ما جاءَ بِكَ؟

| **Subject** (مُبْتَدَأ) of the nominal sentence (جُمْلةٌ اِسْمِيّةٌ). | ما |
| Verbal sentence (جُمْلةٌ فِعْلِيّةٌ); it supplies the place of the predicate (خَبَرٌ). | جاءَ بِكَ |

3	What do you intend?	ما فِي نِيَّتِكَ؟

Subject (مُبْتَدَأٌ) of the nominal sentence (جُمْلَةٌ اِسْمِيّةٌ).	ما
This prepositional phrase appears in the place of the predicate (خَبَرٌ فِي مَحَلِّ رَفْعٍ); it is connected to a deleted word (مُتَعَلِّقٌ بِمَحْذُوفٍ); see #224.	فِي نِيَّتِكَ

Let's now turn to ماذا. There are three different views about its nature.

Approach 1: You treat ماذا as one entity (a single word). The إعْرابٌ for the <u>entire</u> expression depends on the position in the sentence.

What is in your hands?	ماذا فِي يَدَيْكَ؟
Here, ماذا is an indeclinable interrogative noun which serves as the <u>subject</u> of the **nominal sentence** (اِسْمُ اِسْتِفْهامٍ مَبْنِيٌّ عَلَى السُّكُونِ فِي مَحَلِّ رَفْعٍ مُبْتَدَأً). What about the predicate (خَبَرٌ)? It is omitted because it is not necessary. The deleted خَبَرٌ could have been *being* (كائِنٌ), *being permanent* (ثابِتٌ), or *is/is found* (مَوْجُودٌ). The prepositional phrase is connected with the omitted word which is (still) implicitly understood.	
What did you do?	ماذا فَعَلْتَ؟
Here, we have a **verbal sentence** (جُمْلَةٌ فِعْلِيّةٌ). The word ماذا is placed as the fronted <u>direct object</u>; since ماذا is indeclinable (مَبْنِيٌّ), we can't use the case markers for the accusative (مَنْصُوبٌ). We can only say that ماذا holds the place of an accusative (فِي مَحَلِّ نَصْبٍ مَفْعُولٌ بِهِ لِلْفِعْلِ الآتِي).	

Approach 2: You treat the ذا as <u>extra</u> (زائِدٌ), so it does not have a position in إعْرابٌ. The ما, on the other hand, will be treated and analyzed according to its position in the sentence.

What is in your hands?	ماذا فِي يَدَيْكَ؟
This interrogative noun (اِسْمُ اِسْتِفْهامٍ) is indeclinable (مَبْنِيٌّ) and fixed on the سُكُونٌ. It is in the position of the <u>subject</u> of the **nominal sentence** (فِي مَحَلِّ رَفْعٍ مُبْتَدَأً).	ما
This word is additional (ذا زائِدَةٌ). What about the prepositional phrase (*in your hands*) that comes next? This شِبْهُ الْجُمْلةِ is related to the deleted predicate (*is*) which is implicitly understood anyway.	ذا

Approach 3: You treat the word ذا as a <u>relative pronoun</u> (اِسْمٌ مَوْصُولٌ)

expressing *which, that,* etc. ذا is also the predicate (خَبَّر) of ما.

What is in your hands?	ماذا فِي يَدَيْكَ؟

ما	Interrogative noun (إِسْمُ اِسْتِفْهامٍ); indeclinable (مَبْنِيٌّ). Although you can't mark the case visibly, ما is in the position of the <u>subject</u> (in the nominative) of the **nominal sentence** (فِي مَحَلِّ رَفْعٍ مُبْتَدَأً).
ذا	Here is the crucial point: ذا is a <u>relative pronoun</u> (إِسْمٌ مَوْصُولٌ) which does not change in any case as it is indeclinable (مَبْنِيٌّ) and always ends in سُكونٌ. It serves as the **predicate** (خَبَّر) of the nominal sentence (جُمْلَةٍ اِسْمِيّةٍ). Therefore, we say that it is located in the position of a nominative case (فِي مَحَلِّ رَفْعٍ).
فِي يَدَيْكَ	What about this prepositional phrase (الْجارُّ وَالْمَجْرورُ)? When you see a prepositional phrase and no verb in Arabic, it usually means that we have a nominal sentence. Nevertheless, this شِبْهُ الْجُمْلةِ needs to be connected with a verb (or a word with verbal power). We say that it is connected with a deleted word.
	What about the function of the شِبْهُ الْجُمْلةِ? It serves here as the **relative clause** (صِلةٌ). We have no problem to understand the phrase because we anticipate what is meant (which is exactly what was deleted). Note that فِي يَدَيْكَ doesn't have a position in إِعْرابٌ.

Which approach is best? The most accurate is probably the third view because ماذا is different from ما. Why does that matter? Well, we will see. The following sentences are <u>not</u> the same!

1	What was it that you read?	ماذا قَرَأْتَ؟
	This sentence actually expresses ما الَّذي. This means that the intention is to inquire about **something precise** and **determined**. In other words, the answer should include something with the **<u>definite</u>** article.	

2	What did you read?	ما قَرَأْتَ؟
	Watch out! This **can't be a negation** because for a *yes/no*-question (*"Didn't you read?"*), you would need a question particle such as هَلْ. Only in spoken Arabic, this would be acceptable and understandable.	

Possible answers to question number 1 are:

I read the newspaper.	قَرَأْتُ الْجَرِيدةَ.
I read the book which I bought yesterday.	قَرَأْتُ الْكِتَابَ الَّذِي اِشْتَرَيْتُهُ أَمْسِ.

What about question number 2 with **ما** alone? It usually inquires about an **in**definite noun (نَكِرَةٌ). The answer is more general or open and usually **indefinite** as well. For this reason, we **never** use **ماذا** (which is treated as having a definite touch) as a **fronted predicate** (خَبَرٌ مُقَدَّمٌ). Notice the difference:

1	incorrect	What is Karīm?	ماذا كَرِيمٌ؟
	correct		ما كَرِيمٌ؟
	possible answer	Karīm is an engineer.	كَرِيمٌ مُهَنْدِسٌ.

2	incorrect	What is this?	ماذا هٰذا؟
	correct		ما هٰذا؟
	possible answer	This is a book.	هٰذا كِتابٌ.

Sometimes **ماذا** is called the *intensified what*. But this is not really correct although it often conveys such a meaning.

Sura 34:23	"What did your Lord speak?"	مَاذَا قَالَ رَبُّكُمْ؟

WATCH OUT: Many Arabic speakers put a personal pronoun of the third person (ضَمِيرُ الْغائِبِ) between مَن or ما. According to the majority of the early grammarians, this type of construction is **not** correct.

incorrect	Who is Karīm?	مَنْ هُوَ كَرِيمٌ؟
incorrect	Who are the Fatimids?	مَنْ هُمُ الْفاطِمِيُّونَ؟
incorrect	What is the word?	ما هِيَ الْكَلِمةُ؟

Arabic does not know this type of construction. The pronoun here simply **does not have a function** (وَظِيفةٌ). Instead, you should say:

correct	Who is Karīm?	مَنْ كَرِيمٌ؟
correct	Who are the Fatimids?	مَن الْفَاطِمِيُّونَ؟
correct	What is the word?	ما الْكَلِمَةُ؟

Both the Qur'an and the Hadiths don't use the additional pronoun:

What is the Crashing Blow? (*Sura 101:2*)	مَا الْقَارِعَةُ؟
He was asked, "Who are the Mufarridun?" (*Sahīh Muslim 2676*)	وَمَا الْمُفَرِّدُونَ يَا رَسُولَ اللَّهِ؟
...(but) what is pure of heart? (*Sunan ibn Majāh, Book 37/4356*)	...فَمَا مَخْمُومُ الْقَلْبِ؟

But is it really wrong? It depends on whom you ask. I don't see a problem as language develops. In dialects and Modern Standard Arabic, you'll encounter the inserted pronoun pretty often.

| What is the solution? | ما هُو الْحِلُّ؟ |

The personal pronoun of the third person (ضَمِيرُ الْغَائِب) may follow the interrogative pronoun and could be interpreted as a presumptive repetition of the question word. Both مَنْ and ما are grammatically masculine singular, and any adjective or verb in agreement with them has to be **masculine singular** as well. But there is some flexibility:

• After مَنْ, the personal pronoun may be <u>singular</u> or <u>plural</u>.
• After ما, only the masculine or feminine <u>singular</u> is used.

What about the nature of such pronoun? It is neither a *pronoun of separation* or *support* (ضَمِيرُ الْعِمادِ or ضَمِيرُ الْفَصْلِ) nor a *pronoun for emphasis* (تَوْكِيدٌ). We may call it a *visiting pronoun* (ضَمِير زائِر) which does not have a position in إِعْرابٌ. It is just there to make the sentence easier to understand (تَسْهِيلٌ); to facilitate the sentence (تَيْسِيرٌ).

What about the structure? The question word would be placed as the **fronted predicate** (خَبَرٌ مُقَدَّمٌ); the single word (اِسْمٌ مُفْرَدٌ) would be the **delayed subject** (مُبْتَدَأٌ مُؤَخَّرٌ).

Predicate that was put to the front.	*what*	ما
ضَمِيرٌ زائِرٌ which does not have a position in إعْرابٌ.	---	هُوَ
delayed subject	*the solution*	الْحِلُّ

What	(it)	is	the solution?
	implicitly understood		

All this, by the way, is also true for مَنْ although it is not very common. For example, in the Qur'an, you don't find مَنْ هُوَ.... But you will find sentence constructions that contain the word ذا for emphasis.

Who is (there) at/with you?	مَنْ ذا عِنْدَكَ؟

Sura 2:255	Who is there that can intercede with Him except by His leave? (Who is it that can intercede with Him except by His permission?)	مَنْ ذا الَّذِي يَشْفَعُ عِنْدَهُ إلّا بِإذْنِهِ؟

To sum it up: You only use a personal pronoun if there is nothing else placed after ما or مَنْ:

What is it?	ما هِيَ؟

Who are you?	مَنْ أَنْتُمْ؟

162. What kind of words are *when* (مَتَى) and *where* (أَيْنَ)?

In Arabic, both question words are nouns (اِسْمُ اِسْتِفْهامٍ).

In Arabic, every noun (اِسْمٌ) needs case inflection. Since both مَتَى and أَيْنَ are nouns, but with a fixed, indeclinable ending, we cannot throw case markers on them. Is that a problem? Not really. It is no coincidence that both words end in فَتْحةٌ (fixed on the فَتْح) because both words serve in the position of a ظَرْفٌ (adverb).

- The question word *where* (أَيْنَ) always gets the إعْرابٌ of an adverb of place (ظَرْفُ مَكانٍ).
- The question word *when* (مَتَى) always gets the إعْرابٌ of an adverb of time (ظَرْفُ زَمانٍ).

Why do we say that these two words (اِسْمُ اِسْتِفْهَامٍ) are in the position of an **adverb** (ظَرْفٌ)?

➡ If the question word is followed by a اِسْمٌ or verb that doesn't form all tenses (فِعْلٌ نَاقِصٌ) like *to be* (كَانَ), then the adverb is the fronted predicate (خَبَرٌ مُقَدَّمٌ). However, the adverb isn't just miraculously there. It is invisibly related to a deleted verb: *to be*.

➡ If the question word is followed by a **full verb** (فِعْلٌ تَامٌّ), the adverb is connected with that (full) verb (ظَرْفٌ مُتَعَلِّقٌ بِهٰذَا الْفِعْلِ).

1	Where did Karīm go?	أَيْنَ ذَهَبَ كَرِيمٌ؟
2	Where were you (f.)?	أَيْنَ كُنْتِ؟
3	When is the departure? (When do you travel?)	مَتَى السَّفَرُ؟

أَيْنَ	1	Interrogative noun (اِسْمُ اِسْتِفْهَامٍ) that serves as an **adverb of place** (ظَرْفُ مَكَانٍ). It is indeclinable (مَبْنِيٌّ) and never changes its shape. Since we can't put any case marker on it, we can only say that it is located in the position of an accusative case (فِي مَحَلِّ نَصْبٍ). It is governed by the verb ذَهَبَ.
أَيْنَ	2	That's a complicated sentence because the predicate (خَبَرُ كَانَ) was deleted. The **adverb of place** (أَيْنَ) is linked to that deleted word (a verb) which we need to anticipate; otherwise, you can't explain why there is an adverb. (شِبْهُ الْجُمْلَةِ مُتَعَلِّقَةٌ بِمَحْذُوفٍ وَاقِعٍ خَبَرَ كَانَ). The "subject" (اِسْمُ كَانَ) is the pronoun تِ (*you*).
مَتَى	3	Here, the question word (اِسْمُ اِسْتِفْهَامٍ) serves as an **adverb of time** (ظَرْفُ زَمَانٍ). It is indeclinable (مَبْنِيٌّ) and ends in any case with سُكُونٌ (a long vowel always ends in سُكُونٌ). So, we can't put case markers but by looking at the structure, we can say that it is located in the position of an accusative (فِي مَحَلِّ نَصْبٍ). We treat this adverb as the **fronted predicate** (خَبَرٌ مُقَدَّمٌ). It is linked to a deleted word which is the verb *to be* (= *is*) in Arabic. There is only one word left which could be the subject of the sentence: السَّفَرُ. Although it is placed at the end of the nominal sentence, it is the **(delayed) subject** (مُبْتَدَأٌ مُؤَخَّرٌ).

163. Can the word *how* (كَيْفَ) be a حالٌ in Arabic?

Yes, this is possible.

In English sentences, the word *how* is pretty easy to handle. That's quite the opposite in Arabic. كَيْفَ is a pretty complicated fellow.

كَيْفَ is a noun (اِسْمٌ) and should get a case ending according to its function and place in the sentence – which won't happen visibly as the word is indeclinable (اِسْمُ اِسْتِفْهامٍ مَبْنِيٌّ عَلَى الْفَتْحِ). Nevertheless, we must analyze its job and apply virtual, estimated case markers.

1a)	How are you?	كَيْفَ أَنْتَ؟
1b)	How were you?	كَيْفَ كُنْتَ؟
2	How did you come?	كَيْفَ جِئْتَ؟

1a)	**Fronted predicate** (خَبَرٌ مُقَدَّمٌ). We can't put the nominative case marker (مَرْفُوعٌ). We can only say that it is located in the slot of such a case (فِي مَحَلِّ رَفْعٍ خَبَرٌ مُقَدَّمٌ).	كَيْفَ
	Personal pronoun (ضَمِيرٌ مُنْفَصِلٌ مَبْنِيٌّ عَلَى الْفَتْحِ) that never changes its shape. Here, it has the position of the **subject** of a nominal sentence which was placed further to the end of the sentence (فِي مَحَلِّ رَفْعٍ مُبْتَدَأٌ مُؤَخَّرٌ).	أَنْتَ
1b)	**Predicate** of كانَ; therefore, it is placed in the position of an accusative case (فِي مَحَلِّ نَصْبٍ خَبَرُ كانَ).	كَيْفَ
2	Here, we treat كَيْفَ as a حالٌ which brings along that it is placed in the location of an accusative (فِي مَحَلِّ نَصْبٍ) case. The حالٌ gives an answer to the question: **How did someone come?** كَيْفَ here is somehow a place holder because you actually use كَيْفَ itself to ask about the circumstantial situation.	كَيْفَ

Let's summarize:

- كَيْفَ is a حالٌ if it is placed **after a full verb** (فِعْلٌ تامٌّ);
- كَيْفَ is the **fronted predicate** (خَبَرٌ مُقَدَّمٌ) **after a noun** (اِسْمٌ) or an **incomplete verb** (فِعْلٌ ناقِصٌ) such as كانَ. What is the difference to a full verb? An incomplete verb needs a predicate. If there's a full verb, the subject (فاعِلٌ) is enough to provide a full meaning.

164. In Arabic, what do you need to express *how much/many*?

You use a specification (تَمْيِيزٌ).

كَمْ is an *abstract (vague) question word* (اسْمُ اسْتِفْهامٍ مُبْهَمٌ). It needs something to clarify the *vagueness* and *incomprehensibility* (إبْهامٌ). For this reason, we need a **specification** (تَمْيِيزٌ) after كَمْ. The specification has to be **singular** (مُفْرَدٌ) and must be in the **accusative case** (مَنْصُوبٌ).

In all the following examples, كَمْ means *how many* or *how much*. In Arabic, كَمْ is a noun (اسْمٌ) which means it should get case markers. كَمْ, however, has a fixed, indeclinable form (مَبْنِيٌّ عَلَى السُّكُونِ). We can't identify its function in the sentence just by looking at its ending.

1	How many students showed up?	كَمْ طالِبًا حَضَرَ؟
	Subject of the **nominal sentence** (أ مُبْتَدَأً فِي مَحَلِّ رَفْعٍ).	كَمْ
	This isn't the predicate. It is a **specification** (تَمْيِيزٌ) which gives meaning to the sentence. It is مَنْصُوبٌ, marked by فَتْحة (nunation).	طالِبًا
	This verbal sentence (جُمْلَةٌ فِعْلِيَّةٌ) - *he came/showed up* (حَضَرَ) - is the **predicate** (خَبَرٌ) of the nominal sentence.	حَضَرَ

2	How much money (do you have)?	كَمْ مالُكَ؟
	Here, we have a **nominal sentence** (جُمْلةٌ اسْمِيّةٌ) and كَمْ serves as the **fronted predicate** (فِي مَحَلِّ رَفْعٍ خَبَرٌ مُقَدَّمٌ).	كَمْ
	Subject, laced further back to the end of the sentence (مُبْتَدَأٌ مُؤَخَّرٌ).	مالُكَ

Watch out: Where is the **specification** (تَمْيِيزٌ) in sentence number 2? There is none. Sentences like this are common in Arabic. The grammarians say that the تَمْيِيزٌ was deleted because it is **implicitly understood** from the context anyway.

These specifications can be understood from the context:			تَمْيِيز
How many (*pounds*) do you own? (How much money do you have?)	كَمْ جُنَيْهًا مالُكَ؟		
How many (*houses*) do you own?			بَيْتًا

How many (*Feddan*) do you own? (1 Feddan=4.2 m²)	فَدّانًا

3	How many books have you read?	كَمْ كِتابًا قَرَأْتَ؟

كَمْ	We have a **verbal sentence** (جُمْلَةٌ فِعْلِيّةٌ). كَمْ holds the position of a **direct object** (فِي مَحَلِّ نَصْبٍ مَفْعُولٌ بِهِ) of the verb قَرَأْتَ. Note: كِتابًا is **not** the direct object – it is a specification (تَمْيِيزٌ).

4	(For) how many hours have you read?	كَمْ ساعةً قَرَأْتَ؟

كَمْ	This is also **verbal sentence**. However, this time كَمْ is in the position of an **adverb of time** (فِي مَحَلِّ نَصْبٍ ظَرْفُ زَمانٍ) of the verb قَرَأْتَ. Also here, the word ساعةً is **not** the direct object.

5	How many miles did you walk?	كَمْ مِيلًا سِرْتَ؟

كَمْ	Same as in example 4 – with one difference: كَمْ holds the position of an **adverb of place** (فِي مَحَلِّ نَصْبٍ ظَرْفُ مَكانٍ) for the verb that follows. Note that مِيلًا is **not** the direct object.

6	How (hard) did you hit him?	كَمْ ضَرْبةً ضَرَبْتَهُ؟

كَمْ	A special situation! Here, كَمْ occupies the position of an **absolute object** (فِي مَحَلِّ نَصْبٍ مَفْعُولٌ مُطْلَقٌ) of the verb that follows. Note that ضَرْبة is **not** the direct object.

What do we make out of that? كَمْ can <u>never</u> be used in إِضافةٌ-constructions. However, you may find a preposition (حَرْفُ الْجَرِّ) before كَمْ.

1. In such a situation, it is possible to treat the word **after** كَمْ as a تَمْيِيزٌ; therefore, it gets the accusative case (نَصْبٌ).

2. Alternatively and more common, the word **after** كَمْ gets the genitive (جَرٌّ). We don't have a إِضافةٌ, so why do we use the genitive? It is مَجْرُورٌ by مِنْ which is a hidden, implicit preposition (مُضْمَرةٌ).

1	For how many piasters did you buy this?	بِكَمْ قِرْشًا اشْتَرَيْتَ هٰذا؟

2	For how many Piasters did you buy it?	بِكَمْ قِرْشٍ اِشْتَرَيْتَهُ؟

1, 2	Preposition (حَرْفُ الْجَرِّ). Does not have a place in إِعْرابٌ.	ب
1, 2	Question word (اِسْمُ اِسْتِفْهامٍ); it has a fixed, indeclinable shape (مَبْنِيٌّ عَلَى السُّكُونِ). It is in the position of a genitive case due to the preceding preposition (في مَحَلِّ جَرٍّ بِالْباءِ).	كَمْ
1	**Specification** (تَمْييزٌ); therefore it must get the accusative case (مَنْصُوبٌ بِالْفَتْحةِ الظّاهِرةِ).	قِرْشًا
2	**Noun in the genitive case** (اِسْمٌ مَجْرُورٌ) governed by the preposition مِنْ which is not visible (nor pronounced) – but implicitly understood (مَجْرُورٌ بِمِنْ مُضْمَرةٍ وُجُوبًا).	قِرْشٍ

165. In Arabic, why can't you say: كَمْ عَدَدُ الطُّلابِ؟

Because this sentence contains a widespread grammatical mistake.

Let's start with the explanation. You can't use كَمْ together with عَدَد when عَدَد serves as the first part of a إِضافةٌ. You should say:

correct	How many students came?	كَمْ طالِبًا جَاؤُوا؟

incorrect	How many students came?	Lit.: *How is the number of students which came?*	كَمْ عَدَدُ الطُّلّابِ الَّذِينَ جَاؤُوا؟
This sentence is grammatically incorrect because كَمْ is a vague, undefined word and demands a **specification** (تَمْييزٌ): a singular (مُفْرَدٌ) word in the accusative case (مَنْصُوبٌ).			

How could we use عَدَد in the meaning of *number*? ➡ We don't use كَمْ. The word عَدَد can only be used in combination with ما.

Here is an example of a correct sentence:

Lit.: What is the number of students that came?	ما عَدَدُ الطُّلّابِ الَّذِينَ جَاؤُوا؟

166. What's the difference between هَلْ and أ in questions?

To put it simply, the Hamza (أ) is more flexible.

Both particles, هَلْ and أ, are used for questions that are answered by *yes* or *no* (طَلَبُ التَّصْدِيقِ).

1. The أ = the Hamza (الْهَمْزة)

Grammarians call the *Hamza* the origin of the inquiry (الْأَصْلُ فِي الْإِسْتِفْهامِ). The *Hamza* can be used...

* in a **non-negated, affirmative** sentence (الْجُمْلةُ الْمُثْبَتةُ);
* in a **negated** sentence (الْجُمْلةُ الْمَنْفِيّةُ) – *whereas* هَلْ *can't*;
* in a conditional sentence (الْجُمْلةُ الشَّرْطِيّةُ) – *whereas* هَلْ *can't*;
* with إنَّ – *whereas* هَلْ *can't*;

verbal sentence	Did Zayd travel?	أَسافَرَ زَيْدٌ؟
nominal sentence	Is Zayd traveling?	أَزَيْدٌ مُسافِرٌ؟
negated verbal sen.	Didn't Zayd travel?	أَلَمْ يُسافِرْ زَيْدٌ؟
negated nom. sent.	Isn't Zayd traveling?	أَلَيْسَ زَيْدٌ مُسافِرًا؟
conditional meaning	Would you reward Zayd if he succeeded?	أَإِنْ نَجَحَ زَيْدٌ تُكافِئُهُ؟
emphasis	Is he indeed a writer?	أَإِنَّهُ لَكاتِبٌ؟

2. The particle هَلْ

هَلْ can only be used in affirmative, **non-negated** sentences (الْجُمْلةُ الْمُثْبَتةُ). Furthermore, it can't be used together with emphatic particles. هَلْ usually introduces questions of a more lively sort.

verbal sentence	Did Zayd travel?	هَلْ سافَرَ زَيْدٌ؟
nominal sentence	Is Zayd traveling?	هَلْ زَيْدٌ مُسافِرٌ؟
not possible!	Didn't Zayd travel?	هَلْ لَمْ يُسافِرْ زَيْدٌ؟
	Isn't Zayd traveling?	هَلْ لَيْسَ زَيْدٌ مُسافِرًا؟
	Would you reward Zayd if	هَلْ إِنْ نَجَحَ زَيْدٌ تُكافِئُهُ؟

	he succeeded?	
	Is he indeed a writer?	هَلْ إِنَّهُ لَكَاتِبٌ؟

The correct **word order** of such constructions is not trivial if you deal with a conjunction (حَرْفُ الْعَطْفِ) like *and* (وَ) or *or* (أَوْ).

- Hamza (أ): The حَرْفُ الْعَطْفِ is placed <u>after</u> أ because the أ has the صَدارَةٌ. It has the precedence and always starts the sentence.
- هَلْ: The حَرْفُ الْعَطْفِ is placed <u>before</u> هَلْ.

	هَلْ	الْهَمْزَةُ - أَ
Did Zayd or 'Amr appear?	هَلْ حَضَرَ زَيْدٌ أَوْ هَلْ حَضَرَ عَمْرٌو؟	أَحَضَرَ زَيْدٌ أَوْ عَمْرٌو؟
Watch out: You don't use أَمْ together with هَلْ. If you insist on using it, you must repeat هَلْ after أَمْ.		
And so did 'Amr appear?	فَهَلْ حَضَرَ عَمْرٌو؟	أَفَحَضَرَ عَمْرٌو؟
And then did 'Amr appear?	ثُمَّ هَلْ حَضَرَ عَمْرٌو؟	أَثُمَّ حَضَرَ عَمْرٌو؟

Both particles share that they may be used in a nominal (جُمْلَةٌ اِسْمِيّةٌ) or verbal sentence. However, هَلْ is normally not used in nominal sentences when the predicate is a verbal sentence – except in poetry:

Has Zayd died?	هَلْ زَيْدٌ ماتَ؟

What is the answer to such questions? How do you say *yes or no*?

- For "*yes*": You can use نَعَمْ (a so-called حَرْفُ جَوابٍ) or more emphatic أَجَلْ or إِي expressing: *yes, indeed, certainly*. إِي is often used in oaths: *Yes, by Allah!* (إِي وَاللهِ).
- For "*no*": You simply use لا.

167. What is the answer to a negated question in Arabic?

This may be confusing (depending on your mother tongue).

- If you want to **confirm the negation**, you say: نَعَمْ.

- If you want to express a **positive, non-negated answer:** بَلَى.

Hasn't Zayd arrived?	أَلَمْ يَحْضُرْ زَيْدٌ؟

Your answer should express that Zayd has arrived and is now here: *oh yes, but of course, certainly* (بَلَى):

Oh yes, he has arrived.	بَلَى، حَضَرَ زَيْدٌ.

If he has not come yet (thus, he is not here), you say: "*yes*" followed by a negation:

Yes, he has not arrived.	نَعَمْ، لَمْ يَحْضُرْ زَيْدٌ.

168. Why does a question sometimes need a فَ?

فَ *links the second part of a question* (جَوابُ الْإِسْتِفْهامِ): *the part that completes the meaning.*

Such a فَ introduces a clause that expresses the result or effect of a preceding clause. The preceding clause must contain an imperative (affirmative or negative) or words which are equal to an imperative in meaning. Or it must express a wish or hope, **ask a question,** or even be a negative clause. Grammatically speaking, we apply the rules of a فاءٌ سَبَبِيّةٌ which is a conjunction; coupler (حَرْفُ عَطْفٍ).

Now comes the interesting part. We use the present tense verb in the **subjunctive** mood (مَنْصُوبٌ) after the فَ. Why is that?

This has to do with an implicitly included, concealed أَنْ (so-called مُضْمَرَةٌ). The device أَنْ is used to produce an interpreted مَصْدَرٌ which is placed in the position of an accusative case (فِي مَحَلِّ نَصْبٍ). This, by the way, is also true for the imperative form. In the following examples, notice the فَتْحةٌ on the final letter of the second verb.

Work hard and you will succeed!	إِجْتَهِدْ فَتَنْجَحَ!
If you work hard, you will succeed.	لَو تَجْتَهِدُ فَتَنْجَحَ.

Let's focus for a moment on the فَ in these sentences. We said before that we "couple" (عَطْفُ) the interpreted مَصْدَرٌ with the part which is found earlier in the sentence – because we assume that the فَ is a conjunction or connecting particle (حَرْفُ عَطْفٍ). What's the idea here?

The grammarians say that the interpreted مَصْدَرٌ in the second part harmonizes, or let's say, it depends on (مَعْطُوفٌ عَلَى) the virtual, hypothetical مَصْدَرٌ (مَصْدَرٌ مُتَخَيَّلٌ or مَصْدَرٌ مُتَوَهَّمٌ) of the preceding verb. In other words, instead of the verb in the first part, we assume a مَصْدَرٌ. Only then, we can harmonize both parts of the sentence: the مَصْدَرٌ with the interpreted مَصْدَرٌ. This is a necessary trick.

If we put all this together and stick to our example, *Work hard and you will succeed!* (اِجْتَهِدْ فَتَنْجَحَ), we will arrive at the following estimated meaning of the sentence:

Work hard and then you will succeed!	لِيَكُنْ مِنْكَ اِجْتِهادٌ فَيَكُونُ لَكَ نَجاحٌ!

Now let's return to our topic and check this type of structure in an interrogative sentence.

Will you work hard and succeed?	هَلْ تَجْتَهِدُ فَتَنْجَحَ؟

This would be the equivalent:	هَل يَكُونُ مِنْكَ اِجْتِهادٌ فَيَكُونُ لَكَ نَجاحٌ؟

حَرْفُ عَطْفٍ which conveys the meaning of a فاءٌ سَبَبِيَّةٌ.	فَ
Verb in the present tense (فِعْلٌ مُضارِعٌ); it is in the subjunctive mood (مَنْصُوبٌ). Why is it مَنْصُوبٌ؟ There is an unwritten أَنْ which is tacitly understood (مُضْمَرة) and helps to produce an interpreted مَصْدَرٌ (مَصْدَرٌ مُؤَوَّلٌ): أَنْ تَنْجَحَ This interpreted infinitive (أَنْ تَنْجَحَ) is coupled with the preceding, imagined interpreted مَصْدَرٌ reproduced by the preceding verb and keeping the meaning of the verb. Notice the words marked in gray – they would be the respective equivalent of the real مَصْدَرٌ.	تَنْجَحَ

Chapter 6: The follower (التَّابِعُ) – words that blueprint grammatical features

169. Why is it important to identify a *follower* (تابِعٌ)?

A "follower" needs to be in (grammatical) agreement with the word it is connected with. It blueprints the grammatical attributes of that word.

A *follower* or *appositive* (تابِع) doesn't have an own *grammatical identity* (شَخْصِيّةٌ إِعْرابِيّةٌ). A follower simply follows (and relates to) another word – and that word is called the مَتْبُوعٌ, *that which is followed.*

In Arabic grammar, a تابِع takes the same case as the مَتْبُوعٌ. The most famous examples of followers are the adjective (نَعْتٌ or صِفةٌ) and the apposition (بَدَلٌ). Just a quick reminder. In the following phrase, *Donald Trump* is an apposition: The US-president *Donald Trump* said...

Many *followers* must be in **agreement** (الْمُطابَقةُ) with the "other" word. This has nothing to do with the grammatical function of the word – but only with its shape.

We call it *full agreement* if two words share the following features:

1. **Gender** (التَّذْكِيرُ وَالتَّأْنِيثُ)
2. **Determination:** definiteness or indefiniteness (التَّعْرِيفُ وَالتَّنْكِيرُ)
3. **Number:** singular, dual, or plural (الْإِفْرادُ وَالتَّثْنِيةُ وَالْجَمْعُ)
4. **Case** (الْإِعْرابُ)

THE ADJECTIVE (الصِّفةُ OR النَّعْتُ)

170. Which words can serve as an adjective in Arabic?

Quite many forms.

In English, there is a certain word type called *adjective* (e.g., *beautiful*). This idea doesn't exist in Arabic, because there are only three types of words: إِسْمٌ (noun), فِعْلٌ (verb), and حَرْفٌ (particle). An adjective in Arabic is usually a **noun** (إِسْمٌ). When a إِسْمٌ *functions* as an adjective (which means it describes another noun), we call it نَعْتٌ or صِفَةٌ.

Usually such words are derived from a root (مُشْتَقٌّ). But it is even possible that they are not even related to a root. We call such words an *inert, static noun* (اِسْمٌ جامِدٌ). A اِسْمٌ جامِدٌ is *stationary* or *incapable of growth*. Though you may find it under a root in a dictionary, it cannot give birth to a مُشْتَقٌّ, e.g., an active participle. But there is good news. We can interpret such words as a مُشْتَقٌّ (see example below).

Derived forms (مُشْتَقٌّ) that may **function** as adjectives are the active (اِسْمُ الْفاعِلِ) and passive participle (اِسْمُ الْمَفْعُولِ), a word that resembles an active participle (الصِّفَةُ الْمُشَبَّهَةُ بِاسْمِ الْفاعِلِ), a comparative/superlative (اِسْمُ التَّفْضِيلِ) or a *Nisba* (اِسْمٌ مَنْسُوبٌ إِلَيْهِ) formed by the suffix ـِيّ. The *Nisba adjective* is used with place names, e.g., تُونِسِيٌّ (Tunisian), colors, e.g., بُرْتُقالِيّ (orange).

To *qualify* as an adjective in Arabic, the above mentioned forms need to be in agreement with the word to which they relate. Therefore, they usually "mirror" the following grammatical features: **number** (singular, plural, dual), **gender** (masculine, feminine), **determination** (definite or indefinite), and **case** (nominative - مَرْفُوعٌ, genitive - مَجْرُورٌ, accusative – مَنْصُوبٌ); see *question #173*.

Let's see a tricky, rare example of a **static noun** placed as an adjective:

Our enemy is courageous. (Word by word translation: *Our enemy - an enemy - a lion.*)	عَدُوُّنا عَدُوٌّ أَسَدٌ.

The word *lion* (أَسَدٌ) is a اِسْمٌ جامِدٌ and placed as a نَعْتٌ here.

Note: *Google Translate* rendered the sentence in March 2021 as follows: *Our enemy is an enemy of a lion.* What happened? Google could not process case endings properly and thought it is a إِضافَةٌ.

This sentence means the same as the one above. Instead of أَسَدٌ, we use a derived noun (مُشْتَقٌّ) of the root ش-ج-ع as an adjective. The I-verb شَجُعَ - يَشْجُعُ (*to be courageous*) produces a صِفَةٌ مُشَبَّهَةٌ following the pattern فُعالٌ. See *Arabic for Nerds 1*, #50, #143.	عَدُوُّنا عَدُوٌّ شُجاعٌ.

To sum it up: A singular adjective (النَّعْتُ الْمُفْرَدُ) must be a derived noun from the root (الْأَسْماءُ الْمُشْتَقَّةُ الْعامِلَةُ) or anything that can be interpreted as a مُشْتَقٌّ.

There are other words – also not derived from a root – which may do the job of an adjective too.

Let's look at the most important ones:

a) Demonstratives (اِسْمُ الْإِشارةِ)

I compensated/rewarded the student.	كافَأْتُ الطّالِبَ هذا.

Particle of attention (حَرْفُ تَنْبِيهٍ).	ها
Demonstrative (اِسْمُ إِشارةٍ). The noun ذا here serves as an **adjective** (نَعْتٌ), **describing** the **direct object** (*the student*). So it must "follow" the direct object regarding the case. But due to its fixed shape, it can't take case markers. We can only say that ذا is placed in the position of an accusative (فِي مَحَلِّ نَصْبٍ).	ذا

b) Relative pronouns (الْاِسْمُ الْمَوْصُولُ)

The student who worked hard succeeded.	نَجَحَ الطّالِبُ الَّذِي اِجْتَهَدَ.

Relative pronoun (اِسْمٌ مَوْصُولٌ), serving as an **adjective** (نَعْتٌ). It is actually a noun. The word الَّذِي has a fixed shape. It describes the (nominative) subject (*the student*) of the sentence. Hence, we say that it is placed in the position of a nominative case (فِي مَحَلِّ رَفْعٍ).	الَّذِي

c) Numbers (الْعَدَدُ)

I rewarded five students.	كافَأْتُ طُلّابًا خَمْسَةً.

The number – also a noun (اِسْمٌ) – serves as an **adjective** (نَعْتٌ). It has to be in the accusative case (مَنْصُوبٌ) because it has to take the same case as the word to which it refers: *students*.	خَمْسَةً

We can now compile a list of words that can function as adjectives.

description (نَعْتٌ)	described (مَنْعُوتٌ)		form working as adjective		#
الْفَاضِلُ	الرَّجُلُ	جاءَ	active participle	إِسْمُ فاعِلٍ	1
The virtuous man came.					
الْمَضْرُوبَةُ	الْمَوْعِدُ	حانَ	passive participle	إِسْمُ مَفْعُولٍ	2
Time has come for the meeting agreed upon.					
النَّسَبِ	شَرِيف	بِرَجُلٍ اِلْتَقَيْتُ	similar quality	صِفَةٌ مُشَبَّهَةٌ	3
I met a man of noble origin.					
الْأَقْوَم	الطَّرِيقَ	تَبِعْتُ	superlative; elative	أَفْعَلُ التَّفْضِيلِ	4
I followed the shortest way.					
هذا	الْفَتَى	أَكْرَمْتُ	demonstrative	إِسْمُ إِشارةٍ	5
I honored this young man.					
اِعْتَدَى	الَّذِي	الرَّجُلُ جاءَ	relative clause	مَوْصُولٌ بِأل	6
The man who was aggressive came. (The aggressive man came.)					
خَمْسَةً	رِجالاً	رَأَيْتُ	number	اِسْمُ عَدَدٍ	7
I saw five men.					
مِصْرِيٌّ	رَجُلٌ	أَنا	nisba	اِسْمٌ مَنْسُوبٌ	8
I am an Egyptian man.					
مَحْبُوبٌ	الْأَسَدُ	الرَّجُلُ	inert, static noun	اِسْمٌ جامِدٌ	9
The courageous (strong) man is popular.					
ثِقَةٌ	رِجالٌ		triliteral infinitive	مَصْدَرٌ ثلاثِيٌّ	10
Trustworthy men.					
فَضْلٍ	ذاتُ	امْرَأَةٌ هذِهِ	possessor of	ذُو ما	11
This is a woman of virtue.					
فارِس	أَيُّ	فارِسٌ أَنْتَ	what a; all	أَيّ - كُلّ	12
You are a knight, what a knight!					

Excursus: Always think twice when you translate adjectives from English into Arabic – often, the construction is entirely different. For example, how do you express **English adjectives ending in -able, -ive**? ➡ By using قابِلٌ لِ plus a مَصْدَرٌ with the definite article. The result corresponds to English adjectives ending in *-able, -ible, -ive, -al*. The I-verb قَبِلَ - يَقْبَلُ has many meanings: *to receive, to accept, to be disposed to.*

washable	قابِلٌ لِلْغَسِيلِ
mortal	قابِلٌ لِلْمَوْتِ
curable	قابِلٌ لِلشِّفاءِ
renewable	قابِلٌ لِلتَّجْدِيدِ

171. What is the difference between نَعْتٌ and صِفةٌ؟

Practically speaking, there is no difference.

In most grammar books about Modern Standard Arabic, نَعْتٌ and صِفةٌ are used like synonyms for **adjective** or **attribute (qualifier)**. Both words provide more information about the situation or quality of a person, thing, or place.

In the prime of Classical Arabic, the grammarians discussed a few subtleties (which are not really relevant for the grammatical analysis). The two schools of Arabic grammar used different terms to explain more or less the same thing:

- The Basra grammarians (الْبَصْرِيُّونَ) called it صِفةٌ.
- The Kūfa grammarians (الْكُوفِيُّونَ) called it نَعْتٌ.

We can say that صِفةٌ is the **more general concept** that includes the concept of نَعْتٌ. In other words, the نَعْتٌ (descriptive) is actually the one word that appears from all possible صِفاتٌ (qualities).

172. How many types of the descriptive (نَعْتٌ) does Arabic know?

There are two types.

1. The **true description** (نَعْتٌ حَقِيقِيٌّ) describes the **preceding** word. It usually refers to the described thing (مَنْعُوتٌ) **directly**. This is nothing but a simple adjective. For example: an *old* house.

2. The **causal description** or **semantically linked adjective** (نَعْتٌ سَبَبِيٌّ). This adjective **doesn't** describe the preceding word. سَبَبٌ denotes *cord* or *tent rope*. The grammarian Sībawayhi (سيبويه) used this term to refer that two elements of a sentence are connected in meaning – although the structure apparently would not suggest that. The grammar term سَبَبِيٌّ means *causal*.

The نَعْتٌ سَبَبِيٌّ is a *follower* and refers only **indirectly** to the word to which it is connected (logical head). Such an adjective is also called الْمُسَبَّبُ (*the connected*). What is important here?

- In Arabic, the "adjective" must follow the noun. In this construction, however, it is the opposite.

- The adjective (الْمُسَبَّبُ) belongs to the <u>following</u> noun. In other words, the adjective isn't for the person/the thing which we actually want to describe – but for something that is related to it.

- The noun after the adjective needs a *connector* (السَّبَبُ), a semantic link. We use a *returner* (referential, linking pronoun) to mark the relation with the word which comes earlier in the sentence.

- The two together (*the connected* and *the word after the adjective*) form the description (صِفةٌ) for the preceding noun (مَنْعُوتٌ).

  → The نَعْتٌ سَبَبِيٌّ structurally/visually (لَفْظًا) qualifies the **preceding** noun; however, **logically**, regarding the **meaning** (مَعْنًى), the نَعْتٌ سَبَبِيٌّ qualifies the noun which comes **after** it.

Let's see the difference and check both types:

1	I passed (by) a handsome man.	مَرَرْتُ بِرَجُلٍ حَسَنٍ.
	Standard adjective. The word حَسَنٍ agrees in gender, number, case, and determination (definiteness) with its **head** (رَجُلٍ).	
2	I passed (by) a man with a handsome mother (lit.: I passed a man beautiful his mother.)	مَرَرْتُ بِرَجُلٍ حَسَنةٍ أُمُّهُ.

The adjective حَسَنةٍ agrees only in **case** (مَجْرُورٌ) and **determination** (indefinite) with its <u>grammatical</u> **head** (رَجُلٌ). However, it agrees in **gender** (feminine) and **number** (singular) with its <u>logical</u> **head** (أُمُّهُ).

Here, the adjective (نَعْتٌ) has a dual function:

- Syntactically (regarding the grammatical arrangement), it is an attribute of *man* (رَجُل).
- Semantically (logically; in meaning) it is a predicate of *mother* (أُمّ).
- The connection (سَبَبٌ) is expressed by a referring pronoun: هـ.

In example 2, it appears that the word *handsome* (حَسَنةٍ) is placed as an adjective – but an adjective for which word? *Handsome* is **not** the real description/attribute for *man*. *Handsome* (حَسَنةٍ) is a نَعْتٌ سَبَبِيٌّ for a word that is somehow connected with *man* (رَجُل); in reality, however, حَسَنةٍ explains the word that follows رَجُل, i.e., *mother*.

Now comes the tricky part: The entire second part (حَسَنةٍ أُمُّهُ) is the adjective for *man* (رَجُلٌ). The word رَجُل is the مَنْعُوتٌ! We will deal with both types in the following *questions*. See also *Arabic for Nerds 1, #143*.

173. Does an adjective (نَعْتٌ حَقِيقِيٌّ) always need full agreement?

No, it only has to agree partly.

This happens when we use certain forms to work as an adjective.

A. The adjective (نَعْتٌ) is a مَصْدَرٌ.

The مَصْدَر can work as an adjective but only when the following two conditions are both fulfilled:

1. The مَصْدَر is based on a فِعْلٌ ثُلاثِيٌّ.
2. It is not a مَصْدَرٌ مِيمِيٌّ.

You can form a مَصْدَرٌ مِيمِيٌّ only from **I-verbs** using the patterns مَفْعَل or مَفْعِلٌ. A مَصْدَرٌ مِيمِيٌّ has the same meaning as the original مَصْدَرٌ, but it is characterized by strength and firmness in its expression; furthermore, poets needed it as we get another syllable and sound structure. Examples: مَطْلَبٌ (*search, pursuit*) instead of the original infinitive noun طَلَبٌ. *See Arabic for Nerds 1, question #76*.

What about the agreement? An adjective (نَعْتٌ) is a follower (تابِعٌ) which means it has to agree with the noun to which it relates in **all (four) kinds** (see #169). So, what happens to a مَصْدَرٌ؟

- The مَصْدَرٌ maintains the **singular** form (الْإِفْرادُ) and the **masculine** gender (التَّذْكِيرُ).
- But it follows the noun to which it relates (مَنْعُوتٌ) in the two remaining features of agreement: **case** (الْإِعْرابُ) and **definiteness/ indefiniteness** (التَّنْكِيرُ or التَّعْرِيفُ).

This is a **just** ruler.	هذا حاكِمٌ عَدْلٌ.
These are **just** rulers.	هؤُلاءِ حُكّامٌ عَدْلٌ.

B. The word which is described (مَنْعُوتٌ) is a **non-human masculine plural** (جَمْعٌ مُذَكَّرٌ غَيْرُ عاقِلٍ).

This gives us some flexibility. In such a situation, an adjective (نَعْتٌ) may take any of the following forms:

1. singular feminine (مُفْرَدٌ مُؤَنَّثٌ);
2. sound feminine plural (جَمْعُ الْمُؤَنَّثِ السّالِمُ);
3. feminine broken plural (جَمْعُ التَّكْسِيرِ لِلْمُؤَنَّثِ);

1	singular feminine		هذِهِ بُيُوتٌ عالِيَةٌ.
2	sound feminine plural	These are tall houses.	هذِهِ بُيُوتٌ عالِياتٌ.
3	feminine broken plural		هذِهِ بُيُوتٌ عَوالٍ.

C. The مَنْعُوتٌ is a **specification** (تَمْيِيزٌ) after a **number (11 to 99)**.

In concrete terms, this means that the مَنْعُوتٌ is a singular (مُفْرَدٌ) word in the accusative case (مَنْصُوبٌ).

How does this affect the نَعْتٌ, the adjective? You have two options. It can be singular (مُفْرَدٌ) or plural (جَمْعٌ).

singular	14 hard-working stu-	نَجَحَ أَرْبَعَةَ عَشَرَ طالِبًا مُجْتَهِدًا.
plural	dents succeeded.	نَجَحَ أَرْبَعَةَ عَشَرَ طالِبًا مُجْتَهِدِينَ.

174. What is the most important rule for the adjective?

The adjective (نَعْتٌ) is placed after the word it describes (مَنْعُوتٌ).

Especially in spoken Arabic, people play with words and often change the usual word order. Let's assume that the adjective (نَعْتٌ) is placed before the مَنْعُوتٌ. Can we still call it a نَعْتٌ? No, we can't – because in Arabic, the adjective has to be placed **after** the noun which it describes (i.e., the مَنْعُوتٌ). Fine, but if it occurs before, what is it then?

- If both words are **definite** (مَعْرِفَتانِ), we identify the grammatical function (إِعْرابٌ) of the نَعْتٌ according to its (**new**) position in the sentence. ▷ The مَنْعُوتٌ is an apposition (بَدَلٌ). For example:

The diligent, Zayd, succeeded.	نَجَحَ الْمُجْتَهِدُ زَيْدٌ.

Subject (فاعِلٌ) of the verbal sentence, nominative (مَرْفُوعٌ).	الْمُجْتَهِدُ
Apposition (بَدَلٌ); it must get the nominative (مَرْفُوعٌ) case too.	زَيْدٌ

- If both words are **indefinite** (نَكِرَتانِ), we treat the نَعْتٌ as a حالٌ. Therefore, it has to take the accusative case (مَنْصُوبٌ).

A diligent student succeeds. (A student succeeds while being diligent).	نَجَحَ مُجْتَهِدًا طالِبٌ.

Circumstantial qualifier (حالٌ), in the accusative case (مَنْصُوبٌ).	مُجْتَهِدًا
Subject (فاعِلٌ) in the nominative case (مَرْفُوعٌ).	طالِبٌ

Wait, isn't there a rule in Arabic that says that the صاحِبُ الْحالِ (the word that is being described by the حالٌ) has to be **definite**?

Yes, that's true. But there are exceptions. If the حالٌ is placed before the صاحِبُ الْحالِ, it is possible that the صاحِبُ الْحالِ is indefinite. We will analyze such constructions in depth in *question #371*.

A child came smiling.	جاءَ ضاحِكًا طِفْلٌ.
The word طِفْلٌ is the صاحِبُ الْحالِ which is placed **after** the حالٌ.	

175. Why is the causal description (نَعْتٌ سَبَبِيٌّ) hard to catch?

Because the adjective (نَعْتٌ) does not describe the preceding اِسْم in the true sense of a "real" adjective. It is only in some way related to it.

The **causal description** or **semantically linked adjective** (نَعْتٌ سَبَبِيٌّ) is a sophisticated construction which has nothing to do with the basic adjective. It provides a description for a thing that it connected with the main thing (مُرْتَبِطٌ بِالْمَوْصُوفِ).

This description is not an attribute for the main thing itself (لَيْسَ لِبَيَانِ الْمَوْصُوفِ نَفْسِهِ). Imagine three people. The one in the middle is holding hands with the other two and thus forms a chain of people. In grammar, the one in the middle would be the نَعْتٌ سَبَبِيٌّ.

Remark for specialists: That "middle man" always gets the independent case because it is the agent of the preceding participle.

We often use a relative pronoun to translate a causal description into English. Also in Arabic, the constructions are quite similar.

	literal translation	*The daughter whose father is sitting...*
causative description	the daughter the-sitting-down (masc. sing.) her father.	...الْبِنْتُ الْجَالِسُ أَبُوها
relative clause	the daughter, that one is sitting down (masc. sing.) her father.	...الْبِنْتُ الَّتِي يَجْلِسُ أَبُوها

Let's examine a sentence.

This is a man whose son is diligent (hard-working).	هذا رَجُلٌ مُجْتَهِدٌ اِبْنُهُ.

The word *diligent* (مُجْتَهِدٌ) is placed as an adjective (نَعْتٌ). However, it is clear that the نَعْتٌ relates to the اِسْم that follows. So we have a نَعْتٌ سَبَبِيٌّ as it provides a description for the اِسْم that comes **after** the adjective. The word مُجْتَهِدٌ has verbal power and is not just a neutral follower.

The noun after the نَعْتٌ سَبَبِيٌّ is *son*. It must include a pronoun (ضَمِيرٌ) to relate to the اِسْم which is placed **before** the نَعْتٌ سَبَبِيٌّ. This pronoun refers to the primary مَنْعُوتٌ (*man*) to make the relation understandable.

The whole phrase مُجْتَهِدٌ اِبْنُهُ serves as the "real" adjective for the first noun *man* (رَجُلٌ) which is grammatically the مَنْعُوتٌ.

Particle of attention (حَرْفُ تَنْبِيهٍ). Does not have a place in إِعْرابٌ.	ها
Demonstrative noun (اِسْمُ إِشارةٍ). It is the subject (مُبْتَدَأ) of the nominal sentence; since it is indeclinable, we can only assign the place value of a nominative case (فِي مَحَلِّ رَفْعٍ).	ذا
Predicate (خَبَرٌ) of the nominal sentence; nominative (مَرْفُوعٌ) case.	رَجُلٌ
Adjective (نَعْتٌ) in the nominative case (مَرْفُوعٌ). Regarding its morphological form, it is an active participle (اِسْمُ الْفاعِلِ).	مُجْتَهِدٌ
Subject (فاعِلٌ) in the nominative case (مَرْفُوعٌ). Wait?! Why is it the subject of a **verbal** sentence? Is there a verb? Well, yes, somehow. مُجْتَهِدٌ has similar power and can do the verb's job with all its implications (see #286). اِبْنُ is also the first part of the إِضافةٌ.	اِبْنُ
Pronominal suffix/connected pronoun (ضَمِيرٌ مُتَّصِلٌ) which has a fixed, indeclinable shape (مَبْنِيٌّ عَلَى الضَّـمِّ). Nevertheless, it is grammatically in the position of a genitive case (فِي مَحَلِّ جَرٍّ) because it is the second part of the إِضافةٌ, the so-called مُضافٌ إِلَيْهِ.	ﻪ

Another example:

This is a man whose son is popular.	هٰذا رَجُلٌ مَحْبُوبٌ اِبْنُهُ.

Adjective (نَعْتٌ) in the nominative case (مَرْفُوعٌ). The word مَحْبُوبٌ is the passive participle (اِسْمُ الْمَفْعُولِ) of the verb حَبَّ.	مَحْبُوبٌ
Subject of the passive (نائِبُ فاعِلٍ); thus, it has to be مَرْفُوعٌ.	اِبْنُهُ

To sum it up:

- The نَعْتٌ سَبَبِيٌّ agrees with the مَنْعُوتٌ (the **previous** noun – الْإِسْمُ السّابِقُ) in two things: **case** (إِعْرابٌ) and **determination** (definiteness/التَّعْرِيفُ or indefiniteness/التَّنْكِيرُ).

- The noun that comes **after** the نَعْتٌ سَبَبِيٌّ agrees with the نَعْتٌ only in one thing for sure: the **gender** (التَّأْنِيثُ or التَّذْكِيرُ). Regarding the number, it is more complicated – see below.

This is a man whose son is diligent.	هٰذا رَجُلٌ مُجْتَهِدٌ اِبْنُهُ.
This is a man whose daughter is diligent.	هٰذا رَجُلٌ مُجْتَهِدةٌ اِبْنَتُهُ.

Let's analyze some tricky situations. We will focus on the word that follows the نَعْتٌ سَبَبِيٌّ, i.e., the adjacent noun (الْإِسْمُ اللَّاحِقُ).

Situation 1: The noun after the نَعْتٌ سَبَبِيٌّ is **singular** (مُفْرَدٌ) or in the **dual** (مُثَنَّى). ➤ You must use the <u>singular</u> form of the نَعْت.

This is a man whose son is diligent.	هذا رَجُلٌ مُجْتَهِدٌ إِبْنُهُ.
This is a man whose two sons are diligent.	هذا رَجُلٌ مُجْتَهِدٌ إِبْناهُ.

Situation 2: The noun after the نَعْتٌ سَبَبِيٌّ is a masculine or feminine **sound plural** (جَمْعُ الْمُذَكَّرِ السّالِمُ or جَمْعُ الْمُؤَنَّثِ السّالِمُ). ➤ The best option in such situations is to use a <u>singular</u> adjective (نَعْتٌ).

This is a director whose employees are diligent.	هذا مُدِيرٌ مُجْتَهِدٌ مُوَظَّفُوهُ.
This is a man whose daughters are faithful.	هذا رَجُلٌ مُخْلِصَةٌ بَناتُهُ.

Remark: The plural of بِنْتٌ is بَناتٌ. It is, in theory, not a sound feminine plural, but is treated as such (مُلْحَقٌ بِالْجَمْعِ السّالِمِ) and also gets the case endings (إِعْرابٌ) of a sound feminine plural. The original Arabic word for *daughter* is اِبْنَةٌ. Over time, however, the word transformed into بِنْتٌ.

Situation 3: The noun after the نَعْتٌ سَبَبِيٌّ is a **broken plural** (جَمْعُ التَّكْسِيرِ). Then, you have two options. ➤ It is possible to use the adjective (نَعْتٌ) in the <u>singular</u> (إِفْرادٌ) or in the <u>plural</u> (جَمْعٌ) form.

This is a nation whose citizens (children) are generous.	هذا وَطَنٌ كَرِيمٌ أَبْناؤُهُ.
	هذا وَطَنٌ كُرَماءُ أَبْناؤُهُ.

In the second sentence, كُرَماءُ does not take nunation (تَنْوِينٌ) because it is a diptote (مَمْنُوعٌ مِنَ الصَّرْفِ).

176. Can an adjective describe another adjective?

In a way, yes.

Admittedly, what we are analyzing here sounds quite abstract and is mainly of importance for the analysis. Practically speaking, one understands such sentences quite well, as we will see. So what is it all about?

Some words may serve as the **first part of a إضافةٌ** and are **placed as an adjective (نَعْتٌ)** – but their actual function is different. They are not the real description regarding quality, manner, and kind – they are just there as an <u>amplifier</u>. Which words would fit into such a construction?

truth, reality, fact	حَقّ	all; true	كُلّ
any	أَيّ	diligence, effort, eagerness	جِدّ

How should we understand such constructions? These words are the first part of a إضافةٌ for a reason because the **utmost/extreme of the meaning** is reached in the **second part**, i.e. the مُضافٌ إلَيْهِ.

He is a true hero.	هُوَ الشُّجاعُ كُلُّ الشُّجاعِ.
He is a truly loyal friend.	هُوَ صَديقٌ جِدُّ مُخْلِصٍ.
This is a thorough (very learned) scholar.	هٰذا الْعالِمُ جِدُّ الْعالِمِ.
	هٰذا الْعالِمُ حَقُّ الْعالِمِ.
I treated him with the utmost deference.	أَكْرَمْتُهُ إكْرامًا حَقَّ إكْرامٍ.
'Umar is extremely just.	عُمَرُ عادِلٌ أَيُّ عادِلٍ.

The amplifiers are adjectives (نَعْتٌ) and serve as the first part of a إضافةٌ. Without the second part, they wouldn't convey much meaning. In English, such words are often adverbs (e.g., extremely).

THE EMPHASIS (التَّوْكيدُ)

177. What grammatical function do words used for emphasis have?

They are followers (تابِعٌ).

Like no other language, Arabic offers opportunities to emphasize and reinforce (تَوْكيدٌ). Sometimes it is just a word, sometimes a sophisticated technique that can be used to emphasize, confirm, authenticate or support a statement. In this *question* we'll check the basic forms.

There are two types:

1. The confirmation expressed by the **emphatic repetition** of the same word or a synonym (تَوْكِيدٌ لَفْظِيٌّ) - see *question #181*.

2. The **abstract, semantic emphasis** (تَوْكِيدٌ مَعْنَوِيٌّ). You use auxiliary words in this type of construction. For example:

eye, essence (of a thing); self	عَيْنٌ	totality; general	عامّةٌ
soul, self-	نَفْسٌ	both of – for masculine	كِلا
all	جَمِيعٌ	both of – for feminine	كِلْتا
	كُلٌّ		

The above words only work as amplifiers if the following four conditions are fulfilled:

1. The word which is **strengthened** (مُؤَكَّد) must be **definite** (مَعْرِفةٌ).

2. The helping words must be placed **after** the مُؤَكَّد.

3. You add a (*returner*) pronoun (ضَمِيرٌ) to the helping word.

4. The purpose of the pronoun is to connect the helping word with the مُؤَكَّد.

5. The helping words follow the مُؤَكَّد regarding the إِعْرابٌ.

In the following examples, check the case endings of the last word:

تَوْكِيدٌ مَرْفُوعٌ بِالضَّمّةِ	Zayd came himself.	جاءَ زَيْدٌ نَفْسُهُ.
تَوْكِيدٌ مَنْصُوبٌ بِالْفَتْحةِ	I saw Zayd himself.	رَأَيْتُ زَيْدًا نَفْسَهُ.
تَوْكِيدٌ مَجْرُورٌ بِالْكَسْرةِ	I passed (by) Zayd himself.	مَرَرْتُ بِزَيْدٍ نَفْسِهِ.

178. Can you reinforce an emphasis by adding an extra preposition?

Yes, this is possible.

However, this technique only works if you use نَفْس or عَيْن to convey emphasis (تَوْكِيدٌ). Let's analyze an example with an additional preposition (حَرْفُ جَرٍّ زائِدٌ).

Zayd came himself.	جاءَ زَيْدٌ بِنَفْسِهِ.
Extra, additional preposition (حَرْفُ جَرٍّ زائِدٌ); no place in إِعْرابٌ.	ب
نَفْس is used for strengthening (تَوْكِيدٌ).	نَفْس
نَفْس should be in the nominative since it must take the same case as the word which it emphasizes (= Zayd; the subject/فاعِل) because it is a **follower** (تابِعٌ). But we can only do that with a virtual case marker (مَرْفُوعٌ بِضَمَّةٍ مُقَدَّرةٍ) since the preposition induces the كَسْرة and occupies the spot of the case marker (اِشْتِغالُ الْمَحَلِّ بِحَرَكةِ حَرْفِ الْجَرِّ الزّائِدِ).	
Attached pronoun (ضَمِيرٌ مُتَّصِلٌ) that serves as the مُضافٌ إِلَيْهِ.	ﻩ
The pronoun should take the genitive case. Since it has a fixed shape (مَبْنِيٌّ عَلَى الْكَسْرِ), it can't receive a case marker. We can only say that it is placed in the position of a genitive (فِي مَحَلِّ جَرٍّ). Watch out: The كَسْرةٌ you see is not the case marker. It is only the vowel which is used to fix, cement the word.	

179. How can you emphasize the dual?

By using one of the following two words: كِلا *or* كِلْتا.

كِلا (for masculine dual words) and كِلْتا (for feminine dual words) are powerful devices. You can use them to confirm or emphasize things or events. In such constructions, كِلا or كِلْتا are placed after the word that you want to focus on.

There is one ingredient without which the whole thing won't work: you need a *returner*, a so-called **referential pronoun** (ضَمِيرٌ يَعُودُ إِلَى الْمُؤَكَّدِ) which has to be in the dual. Let's see some examples:

Both the professors came. (The two professors came, both of them).	حَضَرَ الْأُسْتاذانِ كِلاهُما.
I saw both the professors.	رَأَيْتُ الْأُسْتاذَيْنِ كِلَيْهِما.
I passed (by) both the professors.	مَرَرْتُ بِالْأُسْتاذَيْنِ كِلَيْهِما.
One of them or both of them.	أَحَدُهُما أَوْ كِلاهُما.

Note: كِلا and كِلْتا are extraordinary words. Both have a specialty that does not otherwise exist in Arabic. They are dual in form, but only show visible case inflections if they have a suffixed personal pronoun. For example: ذَهَبَ كِلاهُما (*They both went*); رَأَيْتُ كِلَيْهِما (*I saw both of them*). If a noun is added in a إِضافةٌ, they are not visibly inflected and have the same form in every case. For example: في كِلا الجانِبَيْنِ (*both parts*); في كِلا الجانِبَيْنِ (*on both sides*).

180. How can you stress on totality/the inclusive?

By using one of the following words: كُلٌّ *or* جَميعٌ *or* عامّةٌ.

Linguists call this type of emphasis the *global confirmation* (تَوْكِيدُ الشُّمُولِ). It intends to clear up the illusion of a lack of generalization. شُمُولٌ means *inclusion* or *containment*.

Similar to كِلا or كِلْتا, which also belong to the تَوْكِيدُ الشُّمُولِ, you need to attach a **referential pronoun** (ضَميرٌ يَعُودُ إِلَى الْمُؤَكَّدِ) to the amplifiers. Otherwise, the amplifiers would buzz around lost in space. Let's see some examples:

I read the entire book.	قَرَأْتُ الْكِتابَ كُلَّهُ.
All hard workers succeeded.	نَجَحَ الْمُجْتَهِدُونَ كُلُّهُم.
I rewarded all (of) the hard workers.	كافَأْتُ الْمُجْتَهِدِينَ كُلَّهُم.
I liked all the players. (A more literal translation: I liked the totality of the players.)	أَعْجَبْتُ بِاللّاعِبِينَ جَميعِهِم.
All students attended.	حَضَرَ الطُّلابُ عامّتُهُم.
The entire squad (team) was present.	حَضَرَت الْفِرْقَةُ عامّتُها.

Watch out: If you use جَميعًا without a referring pronoun, then it is <u>not</u> a تَوْكِيدٌ – it is a حالٌ! That's an important finesse that changes the meaning slightly. ▷ We should use an **adverb in the English translation**.

The students attended **altogether (entirely)**.	حَضَرَ الطُّلابُ جَميعًا.

جَميعًا is a حالٌ and must take the accusative (مَنْصُوبٌ). Notice that it doesn't take the case ending of the subject (*students*) which would be the nominative.

You can even emphasize the emphasis. Some words that convey the meaning of the تَوْكِيدُ الشُّمُولِ can be combined with كُلّ and are placed after it. As an amplifier of the emphasis, we usually opt for أَجْمَع (in its appropriate form). But there are other options as well. Note that some of these words are diptotes (مَمْنُوعٌ مِن الصَّرْفِ).

fem.	جَمْعاءُ	entire, whole, all	masc.	أَجْمَعُ
fem. plural	جُمَعُ		masc. plural	أَجْمَعُونَ

Some examples:

Sura 38:73	فَسَجَدَ الْمَلَائِكَةُ كُلُّهُمْ أَجْمَعُونَ.

- So the angels prostrated themselves, **all of them**. (*Muhsin Khan*)
- The angels all bowed down **together**. (*Abdul Haleem*)
- The angels fell down prostrate, **every one**. (*Pickthall*)
- So the angels prostrated - **all of them entirely**. (*Sahīh International*)

I read the entire book.	قَرَأْتُ الْكِتابَ كُلَّهُ أَجْمَعَ.

This is an example of a **masculine** word. The emphasis (تَوْكِيدٌ) is put on the direct object, so both words are مَنْصُوبٌ (accusative).	كُلَّهُ
	أَجْمَعَ

I read the entire story.	قَرَأْتُ الْقِصّةَ كُلَّها جَمْعاءَ.

An example of a **feminine** word. The emphasis (تَوْكِيدٌ) is put on the object; both words must be in the accusative (مَنْصُوبٌ).	كُلَّها
	جَمْعاءَ

All (of) the students came.	حَضَرَ الطُّلابُ كُلُّهُمْ أَجْمَعُونَ.

Emphasis (تَوْكِيدٌ) on the **subject**. Therefore, it must be in the nominative case (مَرْفُوعٌ), marked by a ضَمّة.	كُلُّهُمْ
Same here – but one thing is different: the marker of the nominative case (مَرْفُوعٌ) is expressed by the letter و.	أَجْمَعُونَ

All [of the (female)] students came.	حَضَرَتْ الطّالِباتُ كُلُّهُنَّ جُمَعُ.

Both words are used to lay emphasis (تَوْكِيدٌ) on the **subject** and	كُلُّهُنَّ

are thus in the nominative case (مَرْفُوعٌ), marked by the ضَمّةٌ. Note that جُمَعُ is a diptote.	جُمَعُ

There are several other expressions which are not used anymore. They all once conveyed the meaning of the تَوْكيدُ الشُّمُولِ after كُلّ and أَجْمَعُ. They are أَبْصَعُ - أَبْتَـعُ - أَكْتَـعُ and denote *all, altogether, whole, entire.* When they are used as a تَوْكيدٌ, they occur in a particular order: they are never placed before أَجْمَع. Here is a famous example:

All the people came.	جَاءَ الْقَوْمُ أَجْمَعُونَ، أَكْتَعُونَ، أَبْتَعُونَ، أَبْصَعُونَ.

Note that you have to use the correct and corresponding gender. The feminine form of أَبْصَعُ is بَضْعاءُ. For this reason, you say: جَمْعاءَ بَضْعاءَ. You also have to use the appropriate plural form:

I saw the women altogether.	رَأَيْتُ النِّسْوةَ جُمَعَ بُصَعَ.

181. Does repetition, repetition, repetition express emphasis?

Yes, it does.

In Arabic, repetition is a fine way to lay emphasis on words. You re-peat the مُؤَكَّدٌ (you use the same word two or three times in a row) or you use a synonym. In the English translation of such constructions, you don't necessarily have to translate the repeated words literally.

Grammarians call this style of emphasis *oral confirmation* (تَوْكيدٌ لَفْظِيٌّ). How does it work? The repeated words take the same gram-matical case and function as the thing/person on which you want to put the stress (i.e., مُؤَكَّدٌ). The repeated words do not influence other words.

Zayd is *at home.*	فِي الْبَيْتِ فِي الْبَيْتِ زَيْدٌ.
Where to, where to can I escape with my mule? The pursuers are come up to you, come up to you; Halt! Halt!	أَيْنَ إِلَى أَيْنَ النَّجَاةُ بِبَغْلَتِي أَتَاكِ أَتَاكِ اللَّاحِقُونَ احْبِسِ احْبِسِ.
Striving, striving is the way to success.	الْإِجْتِهادُ الْإِجْتِهادُ طَرِيقُ النَّجاحِ.

Subject (مُبْتَدَأٌ) of the nominal sentence; nominative (مَرْفُوعٌ).	الِاجْتِهادُ
Emphasis (تَوْكِيدٌ لَفْظِيٌّ). It has to agree with the preceding word which it aims to strengthen. Therefore, it takes the nominative case (مَرْفُوعٌ) as well.	الِاجْتِهادُ

You can use the **corresponding personal pronoun (ضَمِيرٌ مُنْفَصِلٌ)** in the standard form/nominative case (مَرْفُوعٌ) – whatever the case of the word it relates to may be. Such pronouns don't have a place in إِعْرابٌ. They are just there for stylistic reasons and give some emphasis.

nominative	*You* did this.	فَعَلْتَ أَنْتَ هذا.
accusative	You saw *us*.	رَأَيْتَنا نَحْنُ.
	I loved *you*.	أَحْبَبْتُكَ أَنْتَ.
	In this example the accusative of the pronoun could be used as well →	أَحْبَبْتُكَ إِيَّاكَ.
genitive	I sent the book to *him*.	أَرْسَلْتُ الْكِتابَ إِلَيْهِ هُوَ.
The personal pronouns (أَنْتَ - نَحْنُ - هُوَ) do not have a position in إِعْرابٌ.		

A famous example comes to mind, where the use of the extra pronoun is desired, if not necessary: *How are you? I am good. And how are you?*

وَكَيْفَ حالُكَ أَنْتَ؟   ←   أَنا بِخَيْرٍ.   ←   كَيْفَ حالُكَ؟

182. How can you express that you did something yourself?

You can use نَفْس plus a pronoun suffix (plus a separator after the verb).

You use this construction if you want to stress that you did something yourself. In Arabic, this type of emphasis/confirmation is called تَوْكِيدُ الضَّمِيرِ الْمُتَّصِلِ الْمَرْفُوعِ. The combination of نَفْس with the respective pronoun suffix is not enough. You also need a word that separates the verb from the amplifier (تَوْكِيدٌ). Grammarians call such a word a فَضْلَةٌ. What would be a good separator?

➤ You usually separate the verb from the amplifier (i.e., نَفْس) by a pronoun in the nominative case (ضَمِيرٌ مُنْفَصِلٌ مَرْفُوعٌ): the standard form of the personal pronoun. This **separation pronoun** is an *oral confirmation* (تَوْكِيدٌ لَفْظِيٌّ) and doesn't have a place in إِعْرابٌ. Instead of a pronoun, you may use another word.

I myself wrote this article.	كَتَبْتُ أَنا نَفْسِي هٰذِهِ الْمَقالةَ.

Past tense verb. Subject (فاعِلٌ) is the تُ which is a pronominal suffix (ضَمِيرٌ مُتَّصِلٌ) in the spot of a nominative (فِي مَحَلِّ رَفْعٍ).	كَتَبْتُ
Free personal pronoun (ضَمِيرٌ مُنْفَصِلٌ); no place in إِعْرابٌ.	أَنا
Emphasis (تَوْكِيدٌ). It is in the nominative case by an assumed case marker (مَرْفُوعٌ بِضَمّةٍ مُقَدَّرةٍ) since you cannot put the marker of the nominative on the final letter. Why? The ي must be preceded by a كَسْرةٌ. In Arabic, we'd say: اِشْتِغالُ الْمَحَلِّ بِالْحَرَكةِ الْمُناسِبةِ.	نَفْسِي

Let's see other pronouns in action:

second person singular	You (m.) did this yourself.	فَعَلْتَ أَنْتَ نَفْسُكَ هٰذا.
dual	You both did this yourselves.	فَعَلْتُما أَنْتُما أَنْفُسُكُما هٰذا.
second person plural, masc.	You (m. plural) did this yourselves.	فَعَلْتُم أَنْتُم أَنْفُسُكُم هٰذا.
second person plural, fem.	You (f. plural) did this yourselves.	فَعَلْتُنَّ أَنْتُنَّ أَنْفُسُكُنَّ هٰذا.

What we've analyzed so far works if the person (= the target of the emphasis) is the **subject** in the nominative (مَرْفُوعٌ). What happens if the person we focus on, expressed by a pronoun (ضَمِيرٌ), is the **direct object**? Then you <u>don't</u> need a *pronoun of separation*. The same is true if you already have a personal pronoun in the sentence (examples 3 and 4).

1	I saw him himself.	رَأَيْتُهُ نَفْسَهُ.
2	I passed (by) him personally.	مَرَرْتُ بِهِ نَفْسِهِ.
3	You yourself did this.	أَنْتَ نَفْسُكَ فَعَلْتَ هٰذا.
4	You (plural, m.) yourselves did this.	أَنْتُم أَنْفُسُكُم فَعَلْتُم هٰذا.

183. Can you use ثُمَّ to emphasize?

Yes, this is possible.

You can emphasize a preceding sentence (تَوْكِيدُ الْجُمْلةِ) by using ثُمَّ. The word ثُمَّ in such an application doesn't convey its typical meaning: *then, following that*. It does not indicate any kind of order (حَرْف عَطْفِ يَدُلُّ عَلَى التَّرْتِيب مَعَ التَّراخِي). Here, it is just an amplifier.

Sura 82:17	What will explain to you what the Day of Judgement is?	وَمَا أَدْرَاكَ مَا يَوْمُ الدِّينِ؟
Sura 82:18	• **Yes!** What will explain to you what the Day of Judgement is? (*Abdul Haleem*) • **Again**, what will make you know what the Day of Recompense is? (*Muhsin Khan*)	ثُمَّ مَا أَدْرَاكَ مَا يَوْمُ الدِّينِ؟

The only function of ثُمَّ in the above examples is to convey some emphasis (تَوْكِيدٌ). How should we treat this type of ثُمَّ grammatically?

Conjunction ("coupler", coordinator) whose grammatical power is disregarded (حَرْف عَطْفِ مُهْمَلٌ). It is just a device to emphasize.	ثُمَّ

The entire sentence after the تَوْكِيدٌ لَفْظِيٌّ does not have a position in إِعْرابٌ because this device can't exercise any grammatical force.

THE APPOSITION (الْبَدَلُ)

184. How does the apposition work in Arabic?

When we use two nouns (or noun phrases) next to each other, and they refer to the same person/thing, we call that an apposition.

Let's start with an example of an apposition in English:

• The US-president *Donald Trump* said...
• Donald Trump, *the US-president*, said...

In Arabic grammar, the expressions in italic would be a بَدَل which literally means *substitute; equivalent*. In grammar, an apposition denotes a noun (بَدَل) standing for another noun (الْمُبْدَل مِنْه, *the word that is substituted*). An apposition is a *follower* (تابِعٌ). *Follower* here means that together with the word it refers to, the entire expression (both words) can be regarded as one entity. For this reason, the بَدَلٌ "follows" (agrees with) the الْمُبْدَلُ مِنْهُ which is the noun that comes first.

How can we justify the grammatical position of a بَدَلٌ? First of all, we do not have a conjunction or coupling device. So we need another justification. We can apply a simple trick. We have to imagine that the operator/regent (عامِلٌ) of the "other" word (مُبْدَلٌ مِنْهُ) is repeated.

This regent governs the apposition and induces the case – the same case as the preceding word for which it works as a substitute.

The Caliph ʿUmar was just.	كانَ الْخَلِيفةُ عُمَرُ عادِلًا.

How did the original sentence, which justifies the grammatical position and case of the بَدَلٌ, look like?

The Caliph **was**, ʿUmar **was**, just.	كانَ الْخَلِيفةُ كانَ عُمَرُ عادِلًا.
The second regent (عامِلٌ) is needed to make the sentence work. However, it is almost never repeated since it is implicitly understood anyway.	

Note: Some grammarians call the الْبَدَلُ *permutative*. The permutative is a noun complement that follows the noun as the appositive and additionally explains it or even takes its place. Permutation refers to an exchange, a rearrangement; in linguistics, the rearrangement, shifting of words.

185. How many types of an apposition (بَدَلٌ) does Arabic know?

Four.

The concept of the apposition is quite complex in Arabic. There are four main types. We should analyze them step by step.

1	**The substitution of the whole for the whole.**	بَدَلُ الْكُلِّ مِن الْكُلِّ
	The apposition (permutative) is interchangeable and blueprints the grammatical implications of the "other" word. It does **not** need a رابِط. Sometimes, it is treated as an *explicative description* (عَطْفُ الْبَيانِ); #187		

This type of بَدَلٌ uses a word which is interchangeable with the مُبْدَلٌ مِنْهُ and is therefore completely equivalent:

الْخَلِيفَةُ (هُوَ) عُمَرُ	equals	عُمَرُ (هُوَ) الْخَلِيفَةُ
The Caliph, 'Umar, ...		'Umar, the Caliph, ...

Zayd, your brother, came.	أَتَى زَيْدٌ أَخُوكَ.
The words *Zayd* and *brother* are interchangeable.	

Visit him, Zayd, ...	زُرْهُ زَيْدًا...
Here we use a pronoun suffix which substitutes for a noun.	

2	**The substitution of the part for the whole.**	بَدَلُ الْبَعْضِ مِن الْكُلِّ

The apposition is part of the "main" word in question. In other words, this type of بَدَلٌ is a **real part** of the مُبْدَلٌ مِنْهُ. Therefore, it needs a bond (رَابِطٌ): a possessive pronoun that refers back to the مُبْدَلٌ مِنْهُ.

The pronoun can be shown or it is implicitly understood (unwritten). Watch out: The pronoun produces a إِضَافَةٌ-construction.

Some examples:

The doctor treated the patient, his stomach.	عَالَجَ الطَّبِيبُ الْمَرِيضَ بَطْنَهُ.

الْمَرِيضَ	Direct object (مَفْعُولٌ بِهِ), in the accusative case (مَنْصُوبٌ).
بَطْنَهُ	Apposition (بَدَلُ الْبَعْضِ مِن الْكُلِّ); therefore also in the accusative (مَنْصُوبٌ). The *pronoun suffix* (ضَمِيرٌ مُتَّصِلٌ) is indeclinable (مَبْنِيٌّ عَلَى الضَّمِّ); so we say that it is placed in the position of a genitive case as it serves as the second part of the إِضَافَةٌ.

I saw his parents; his mother and his father.	رَأَيْتُ وَالِدَيْهِ أُمَّهُ وَأَبَاهُ.
Your brother has a good heart.	طَابَ أَخُوكَ قَلْبُهُ.
Kiss him, his hand!	قَبِّلْهُ الْيَدَ!
I ate the bread, a third of it.	أَكَلْتُ الْخُبْزَ ثُلْثَهُ.

Now a specialty. If you have a sentence with *except* (أُسْلُوبُ الْإِسْتِثْناءِ), you can treat the word after إِلَّا as a بَدَلُ الْبَعْضِ مِنَ الْكُلِّ.

ما حَضَرَ الطُّلّابُ إِلَّا زَيْدٌ.	None of the students came, except (for) Zayd.

زَيْدٌ	Substitution of the part for the whole (بَدَلُ الْبَعْضِ مِنَ الْكُلِّ), in the nominative case (مَرْفُوعٌ) like the word it is linked to: *students*.

بَدَلُ الْإِشْتِمالِ	3 **The comprehensive substitution.** The apposition indicates a quality or circumstance possessed by or included in the preceding word.

This type of بَدَلٌ is **not a real part** of the مُبْدَلٌ مِنْهُ. There is a figurative connection. To avoid misunderstandings, also here, the بَدَلٌ needs a رابِطٌ: a (possessive) pronoun suffix. It may be expressed visibly; or it is unwritten (implicitly understood.)

أَعْجَبَتْ بِزَيْدٍ خُلُقِهِ.	I like Zayd's manners.

خُلُقِ	Comprehensive substitution (بَدَلُ الْإِشْتِمالِ). Since it is an apposition, it must take the same case as the word for which it works as a substitute (مُبْدَلٌ مِنْهُ), i.e., *Zayd*. Therefore, it also takes the genitive case (مَجْرُورٌ). The word *character, nature, temper* (خُلْقٌ) is not a real part of *Zayd*, but can be seen as a part of it.

ه	This suffix pronoun (ضَمِيرٌ مُتَّصِلٌ) has an indeclinable, fixed shape (مَبْنِيٌّ عَلَى الضَّمِّ). Nevertheless, it is placed in the location of a genitive case because it serves as the second part of a إضافةٌ.

يُعْجِبُنِي الرِّيفُ اِسْتِجْمامٌ فِيهِ.	I like recreating in the countryside. (I like the countryside, relaxation there.)

اِسْتِجْمامٌ	Comprehensive substitution (بَدَلُ الْإِشْتِمالِ); nominat. (مَرْفُوعٌ).

It is obvious that the word اِسْتِجْمامٌ can't be a part of الرِّيفُ nor some kind of it. Nevertheless, it is connected with it by the *place* because the relaxation happens there (in the countryside).

نَفَعَنِي زَيْدٌ عِلْمُهُ.	Zayd, his knowledge, benefited me.

Literally: *Zayd benefited me, his knowledge.*	
I liked your speech.	أَعْجَبَتْنِي كَلامُكَ.

Notice the verb in the second person singular (you). It has a direct object, i.e., *me* (ي). The sentence means literally: *You pleased me, your speech.*

Sura 2:217	They ask you [Prophet] about fighting in the prohibited month. [lit.: *about the sacred month, about fighting therein.*]	يَسْأَلُونَكَ عَنِ الشَّهْرِ الْحَرَامِ قِتَالٍ فِيهِ.

4 **The conflicting or contrast substitution.**	الْبَدَلُ الْمُبايِنُ لِلْمُبْدَل مِنْهُ

The *replacement* (بَدَلٌ) that is used in this type is totally different from the word for which it is substituted (مُبْدَلٌ مِنْهُ).

It can have two forms:

- **Retraction** (بَدَلُ الْإِضْرابِ). You give the listener or reader a hint that you turn away from the first word you mentioned. The بَدَل then is something you would like to substitute for the original statement (بَدَلُ الْبَداءِ). The preceding word (مَتْبُوعٌ) and the *follower* (تابِعٌ) – which is the extra word – are both there on purpose.

- **Error and forgetfulness** (بَدَلُ الْغَلَطِ وَالنِّسْيانِ). Here, the first word (i.e., the مَتْبُوعٌ) is uttered merely by mistake, and the correct word – the apposition or follower (تابِعٌ) – follows immediately.

1	*I ate bread,* (but then, preferring to state that I had eaten) *meat.*	أَكَلْتُ خُبْزًا لَحْمًا.
	This is a بَدَلُ الْإِضْرابِ. ➡ Its meaning is equivalent to the use of بَلْ: *I ate bread, in fact, meat.*	أَكَلْتُ خُبْزًا بَلْ لَحْمًا.
2	*I passed (by) a dog,* (*I meant to say:*) *a cat.*	مَرَرْتُ بِكَلْبٍ قِطّةٍ.

Type 4 is often used to correct mistakes:

Alexandria... (ah)... Cairo is the capital of Egypt.	الْإِسْكَنْدَرِيّةِ الْقاهِرةُ عاصِمةُ مِصْرَ.

Cairo here is a word that is used to correct the error (بَدَلُ الْغَلَطِ). Since it is an apposition, it also takes the nominative (مَرْفُوعٌ) case like the preceding word *Alexandria*.	الْقَاهِرةُ

186. What are the four most important rules for the بَدَلٌ?

They all deal with pronouns and verbs as we will see.

Rule 1: It is possible that the apposition (بَدَلٌ) is a plain, apparent noun (اِسْمٌ ظَاهِرٌ) and the مُبْدَلٌ مِنْهُ is a suffix pronoun (ضَمِيرُ الْغَائِبِ).

The students, the outstanding of them, succeeded. (This sentence does not mean: The students succeeded with excellence.)	الطُّلابُ نَجَحُوا مُتَفَوِّقُوهُمْ.

Apposition (بَدَلٌ); the substitution of the part for the whole (بَدَلُ الْبَعْضِ مِن الْكُلِّ); in the nominative (مَرْفُوعٌ) by the letter و. It is also the first part of the إضافةٌ.	مُتَفَوِّقُو (نَ)
Now, to which word does this بَدَلٌ refer? → To the و in the verb نَجَحُوا.	

Pronominal suffix/connected personal pronoun (ضَمِيرٌ مُتَّصِلٌ); it has an indeclinable shape; it is placed in the position of a genitive case because it serves as the second part of the إضافةٌ.	هُمْ

Another example:

You, all five of you, succeeded.	نَجَحْتُمْ خَمْسَتُكُمْ.

Substitution of the whole for the whole (بَدَلُ الْكُلِّ مِن الْكُلِّ) in the nominative case (مَرْفُوعٌ). The pronominal suffix كُمْ is the second part of the إضافةٌ.	خَمْسَتُكُمْ
What does the apposition (بَدَلٌ), the word خَمْسَتُكُمْ, refer to? It is connected with the pronominal suffix (تُمْ) which is the subject (فَاعِلٌ) of نَجَحَ.	

Rule 2: It is **impossible** that a pronoun (ضَمِيرٌ) serves as a بَدَلٌ for another pronoun. Moreover, a ضَمِيرٌ can't be a بَدَلٌ for an apparent noun (اِسْمٌ ظَاهِرٌ).

Rule 3: You will often encounter a بَدَل in questions (اِسْتِفْهامٌ) and in conditional sentences (شَرْطٌ) – but you perhaps never thought it was an apposition. We call it a بَدَلُ التَّفْصيلِ since it accompanies أ in questions and إِنْ in conditional sentences. The بَدَلُ التَّفْصيلِ clarifies – specifies; particularizes – what was mentioned earlier in the sentence.

Let's see what this means and start with an example of a **question**:

1	Who came today? (Was it) Muhammad or Zayd?	مَنْ حَضَرَ الْيَوْمَ؟ أَمُحَمَّدٌ أَمْ زَيْدٌ؟
2	Whom did you see today? (Was it) Muhammad or Zayd?	مَنْ رَأَيْتَ الْيَوْمَ؟ أَمُحَمَّدًا أَمْ زَيْدًا؟

أ	Question particle (حَرْفُ اِسْتِفْهامٍ). We could say that the question word includes the meaning of a Hamza (أ) already (اِسْمُ اِسْتِفْهامٍ مُتَضَمِّنٌ مَعْنَى هَمْزَةِ الْإِسْتِفْهامٍ), so the أ enters the second part.

1	Both are a بَدَلُ التَّفْصيلِ for the question word مَنْ which is the الْمُبْدَلُ مِنْهُ. The بَدَلُ التَّفْصيلِ adds details to the situation.	Nominative (مَرْفُوعٌ) as it refers to the subject of the preceding sentence.	مُحَمَّدٌ
2		Accusative (مَنْصُوبٌ) case because it is connected with the preceding question and the (unmentioned) direct object of it.	مُحَمَّدًا

A) Don't forget: If the الْمُبْدَلُ مِنْهُ is a question word (اِسْمُ اِسْتِفْهامٍ), there must be a هَمْزَةُ اِسْتِفْهامٍ before the بَدْلٌ.

Who visited you? Was it Zayd or Khālid?	مَنْ زارَكَ؟ أَزَيْدٌ أَمْ خالِدٌ؟

An example of a **conditional sentence**:

Those who work hard – be it a student or be it an employee – will succeed.	مَنْ يَجْتَهِدْ - إِنْ طالِبٌ وَإِنْ مُوَظَّفٌ - يُوَفَّقْ.

إِنْ	Conditional particle (حَرْفُ شَرْطٍ) which doesn't have a position in إِعْرابٌ. In our example, we could call it a حَرْفُ تَفْصيلٍ. Its only function is to indicate more details; it doesn't produce any gram-

matical effect.	
Apposition which provides more details (بَدَلُ التَّفْصِيلِ). It is in the nominative case (مَرْفُوعٌ). Why? Because it must be in grammatical agreement with the word to which it refers (= مَنْ).	طالِبٌ

B) Don't forget: If the الْمُبْدَلُ مِنْهُ is a conditional particle (اسْمُ شَرْطٍ), you must put the conditional device إِنْ الشَّرْطِيّةُ) before the بَدَلٌ.

Whatever you read – a book or a newspaper –, it will benefit you.	مَا تَقْرَأْ إِنْ كِتابًا وَإِنْ صَحِيفَةً يُفِدْكَ.
The word كِتابًا is an apposition (بَدَلٌ) and provides more details for the word ما which is the الْمُبْدَلُ مِنْهُ here. Note that if we use ما as a conditional particle (ما الشَّرْطِيّةُ), we need to put the verb into the jussive mood (مَجْزُومٌ) which is done by the سُكُونٌ at the end of the verb.	

Rule 4: In English, an apposition is a noun used as a synonym for another noun (or to provide more information).

In Arabic, however, it is possible that a <u>verb</u> (فِعْلٌ) is a replacement/synonym – an apposition – for another <u>verb</u>. It is even possible that a sentence (جُمْلةٌ) is a بَدَلٌ for a sentence.

We have two options:

Option 1: The first verb is the preparatory act (an introduction) for the second verb:

He stood up (and) prostrated before him.	قامَ سَجَدَ لَهُ.

Option 2: The second verb modifies the first:

He prostrated, he kept on doing it.	سَجَدَ أطالَ.

However, it is stylistically better to use a conjunction (وَ or فَ):

He stood up (and) prostrated before him.	قامَ فَسَجَدَ لَهُ.

CONJUNCTIONS –
COORDINATORS, CONNECTORS & COUPLERS (الْعَطْفُ)

In Arabic grammar, the term عَطْفٌ is used for conjunction. It is there for coordination and works as a connector, coordinator, or coupler. Such words connect clauses or sentences or coordinate words in the same clause (e.g.: *and, but, if*). They blueprint the grammatical case of the word they are linked with. Two grammar terms are important:

The word **before** the *coupler* is the الْمَعْطُوفُ عَلَيْهِ. It is the *attracting*.

The word **after** the device is called الْمَعْطُوفُ. It is the *attracted*. مَعْطُوفٌ means *feeling compassion; attracted; coupled* (joined together).

187. What is a *clarifying description* (عَطْفُ الْبَيَانِ)?

Practically speaking, it is the same as a بَدَلٌ – with a fine difference.

A noun that **replaces** another noun is a *substitution*, and that is more or less exactly what the Arabic term بَدَلٌ (*permutative*) means. The word that is substituted is called الْمُبْدَلُ مِنْهُ. E.g.: *Zayd, your brother, came to me.*

A noun that **specifies** another noun is an *explanatory insert; explicative* (عَطْفُ الْبَيَانِ). The word to which something is added is the مَعْطُوفٌ عَلَيْهِ. Example: *Your brother Zayd came to me.*

Now, what is the **difference** to the apposition (بَدَلٌ)?

- In the بَدَلٌ one can substitute the permutative (second word) for the modified (first word) with no change in meaning. In the عَطْفُ الْبَيَانِ, the modifier has the value of a descriptive adjective. I saw your brother *Zayd*. The عَطْفُ الْبَيَانِ specifies the modified noun by identifying one from a group, thus its name: the *explicative*.

- The عَطْفُ بَيَانٍ (= second word) is always **stronger in meaning**, more concrete or more clarifying (أَوْضَحُ مِنْ مَتْبُوعِهِ وَأَشْهَرُ). If this is not the situation, we will call it a بَدَلٌ.

- The عَطْفُ بَيَانٍ is usually a اِسْمٌ جَامِدٌ: a static, inert noun or a word that is not derived from a root. It **cannot** be a **pronoun** or a **verb** –

which is a big difference to the بَدَلٌ.

- The عَطْفُ بَيانٍ is usually a **single word**.

- If we delete the بَدَلٌ or the مُبْدَلٌ مِنْهُ, a sentence would still be a complete sentence. However, if we delete the عَطْفُ بَيانٍ, this is not always the situation.

- عَطْفُ بَيانٍ is a *follower* (تابِعٌ) and **resembles an adjective** (صِفةٌ).

This means that a عَطْفُ بَيانٍ is in **entirely** grammatical **agreement** with the word to which it refers (الْمَتْبُوعُ or الْمَعْطُوف عَلَيْهِ): num- ber (singular, plural, dual), determination (definite or indefinite), gender, case (الْإِعْرابُ). The بَدَلٌ, on the other hand, only mirrors the position and function in the sentence (الْبَدَلُ يَتْبَعُ فِي الْإِعْرابِ فَقَطْ). For example, it does not follow the word it refers to regard- ing definiteness/indefiniteness.

- What is the **difference** to the **adjective** (نَعْتٌ)? It's about morphol- ogy because function and meaning are actually quite similar. The عَطْفُ الْبَيانِ is a **frozen, static noun** whereas the adjective (نَعْتٌ) is usually a derived noun of a root (النَّعْتُ مُشْتَقٌّ أَوْ مُؤَوَّلٌ بِالمُشْتَقِّ).

1	عَطْفُ بَيانٍ	Your brother **Zayd** came to me.	جاءَنِي أَخُوكَ زَيْدٌ.	
		Zayd is more concrete and stronger in meaning than the ex- pression *your brother* (أَخُوكَ) which is the الْمَعْطُوفُ عَلَيْهِ.		
2	بَدَلٌ	Zayd, **your brother**, came to me.	جاءَنِي زَيْدٌ أَخُوكَ.	
		Your brother is less concrete and weaker in meaning than the first word *Zayd*. So we call it a بَدَلٌ.		

In English, we would call both examples an *apposition*. Indeed, many Arabic grammarians say that regarding its function in a sentence the عَطْفُ بَيانٍ is actually a بَدَلٌ.

The عَطْفُ الْبَيانِ, in fact, refers to the *substitution of the whole for the whole* (بَدَلُ الْكُلِّ مِن الْكُلِّ). However, there are situations in which it is not entirely correct to have a بَدَلٌ at such a position. For example:

I ate a fruit, an apple.	أَكَلْتُ فاكِهَةً تُفاحةً.

تُفاحةً	فاكِهَةً	أَكَلْتُ
عَطْفُ بَيانٍ	مَعْطوفٌ عَلَيْهِ	verb (فِعْلٌ) plus subject

Purist grammarians say that the عَطْفُ بَيانٍ is **stronger in terms of clarification** as the word to which it refers (مَتْبوعٌ), even if you treat it as a بَدَلٌ. What does that practically mean for us?

- The عَطْفُ الْبَيانِ may be **definite** (مَعْرِفةٌ). ➤ Then it is used for clarification (تَوْضيحٌ).
- The عَطْفُ الْبَيانِ may be **indefinite** (نَكِرةٌ). ➤ Then it is used for particularization or specification (تَخْصيصٌ).
- We need a definite article that goes along with the عَطْفُ بَيانٍ or, if it is indefinite, it must be at least more concrete than the word to which it refers (تَخْصيصٌ).

Let's check the difference:

تَخْصيصٌ	I wore a robe, a Jubba.	لَبِسْتُ ثَوْبًا جُبّةً.

Jubba (جُبّةٌ) is more specific than the word *robe, garment* (ثَوْبٌ). Therefore, we treat it as a عَطْفُ بَيانٍ.

	This man came.	جاءَ هذا الرَّجُلُ.

Man (الرَّجُلُ) is a بَدَلٌ. Why? Because the demonstrative *this* is stronger and "more definitive" than the word with the definite article (بَدَل مِن إسم الْإشارة لِأَنَّ إسمَ الْإشارة أَوْضَحُ مِن الْمُعَرَّفِ بِأَل).

188. How can you express a sequence in Arabic?

You use a "coupler", a coordinating device (عَطْفٌ): وَ *or* فَ *or* ثُمَّ.

In English, we don't connect sentences as much as we do in Arabic where the connection of sequence (عَطْفُ النَّسَقِ) is a common theme.

The Arabic term عَطْفُ النَّسَقِ is no coincidence because the word نَسَقٌ means *order, arrangement*. The three devices وَ and فَ and ثُمَّ coordinate words in relation to each other and are called حَرْفُ عَطْفٍ.

The word after such a device (= مَعْطوفٌ) gets the grammatical implications of the preceding word to which it refers (= مَعْطُوفٌ عَلَيْهِ). Simply put, we will deal with *followers* (تابِعٌ).

وَ – *and*

وَ conveys the meaning of the absolute association. This means that the مَعْطُوفٌ (= the word after وَ) shares every grammatical feature with the مَعْطُوفٌ عَلَيْهِ – even the moment when it happened.

Zayd and Muhammad came.	حَضَرَ زَيْدٌ وَمُحَمَّدٌ.
Both came. We don't know who came first or whether they came together.	

The الْفاءُ – *immediately after*

فَ conveys an arrangement or order (تَرْتِيبٌ). The grammatical power or verdict of the regent (الْحُكْمُ النَّحْوِيُّ) is first applied to the مَعْطُوف عَلَيْهِ (= the first word), but the period of delay, after which the مَعْطُوفٌ (= the second word) comes into the game, is not long.

Zayd and Muhammad came.	حَضَرَ زَيْدٌ فَمُحَمَّدٌ.
The فَ indicates that Zayd came first and Muhammad came closely after him (فِي عَقِبِهِ). The word عَقِب means *the last part of something* or *that which follows subsequently*: after a short period (فَتْرةٌ وَجِيزةٌ).	

ثُمَّ – *then, thereupon*

Also ثُمَّ conveys an arrangement (تَرْتِيبٌ). It denotes a succession after a certain interval, delay (الْمُهْلة) – or mitigation; passing time (التَّراخِي).

The regent (عامِل) applies its ruling power first to the مَعْطُوفٌ عَلَيْهِ for a period that isn't short and then operates on the other word too.

Zayd came, then (with a bit of laxity) Muhammad.	حَضَرَ زَيْدٌ ثُمَّ مُحَمَّدٌ.

Watch out: The three particles are not necessarily a حَرْفُ عَطْفٍ. They may convey the meaning of *exclusion* or *exception* (إِسْتِئْنافٌ). They may indicate a transition from the general to the more special. ثُمَّ, for example, can be used to convey the German expression *und zwar*. It may also be used to lay emphasis (see #183). Therefore, always make sure that the idea of *association* or *participation* (الْاِشْتِرَاكُ) is found which, in grammar, means that ثُمَّ works as a conjunction (عَطْفٌ).

189. Does the word حَتَّى always mean *until*?

No, it doesn't.

حَتَّى is normally used as a preposition (حَرْفُ الْجَرِّ) to convey the meaning of the utmost or extreme (الْغَايَة): *until*. In such a situation, حَتَّى has governing power and operates on the following word by inducing the genitive case.

However, حَتَّى may also be used as a **coordinating device** (حَرْفُ عَطْفٍ) in the sense of *even*. Then the word after حَتَّى remains under the same government as the preceding one – so it is not necessarily genitive, but takes the case of the word to which it refers.

When could حَتَّى work as a حَرْفُ عَطْفٍ? This is only possible when the word **after** حَتَّى, the so-called مَعْطُوفٌ, fulfills two conditions:

1. The مَعْطُوفٌ is an apparent noun (اِسْمٌ ظَاهِرٌ) which means it must be mentioned explicitly in the sentence – so the مَعْطُوفٌ can **never** be a pronoun.

2. The مَعْطُوفٌ must be **mentally or physically part of the word** that comes **before** حَتَّى (i.e., الْمَعْطُوف عَلَيْهِ). E.g., the tail is part of a fish.

In the following examples, notice the case endings of the word **before** حَتَّى (الْمَعْطُوفُ عَلَيْهِ) and **after** حَتَّى (الْمَعْطُوفُ عَلَيْهِ) – they both have the same case ending.

| Men have died, even the prophets. | مَاتَ النَّاسُ حَتَّى الْأَنْبِيَاءُ. |
| ...and they left him, even his brother. | ...وَفَارَقُوهُ حَتَّى أَخُوهُ. |

An example of a direct object (مَفْعُولٌ بِهِ):

| The mother loves her son – even his mistakes. | الْأُمُّ تُحِبُّ ابْنَهَا حَتَّى أَخْطَاءَهُ. |
| I have eaten the fish, even the tail of it. | أَكَلْتُ السَّمَكَةَ حَتَّى ذَيْلَهَا. |

In the first example, أَخْطاءَ is the مَعْطُوفٌ for the direct object *son*. In the second example, the *tail* is a kind of food, edible, and part of the fish. It is a اِسْمٌ ظاهِرٌ and functions as the مَعْطُوفٌ for the direct object السَّمَكَة, so it also takes the accusative case. The meaning is: *I ate the entire fish*.

Now, watch out!

I ate the fish **in order to leave only** its head. (= I ate the fish but not its head.)	أَكَلْتُ السَّمَكَةَ حَتَّى رَأْسِها.

Here, حَتَّى has a different job! It is a *particle of finality* (حَرْفُ غايةٍ), used to indicate an intention or the result plus its consequences. حَتَّى works as a preposition here (حَرْفُ جَرٍّ) which is the reason why we have the genitive case (مَجْرُورٌ) in the word *head* (رَأْسِها).

The meaning is: أَكَلْتُ السَّمَكَةَ مِن بِدايَتِها إلَى رَأْسِها. رَأْسُها غَيْرُ مَأْكُولٍ.

190. Is the word أَمْ only used in questions?

No, it isn't.

أَمْ is a coordinator (حَرْفُ عَطْفٍ) an may convey the meaning of:

A) **equalization** (التَّسْوِيةُ) between two things;

B) the appointing, **selecting** (تَعْيِينٌ) of one of two things.

A) The word أَمْ when it expresses equalization is used with a *Hamza of equalization* (هَمْزَةُ التَّسْوِية) expressed by أ.

This هَمْزَة does <u>not</u> introduce a question (اِسْتِفْهامٌ). Instead, it supports أَمْ in its function to connect two sentences. It is often used in sentences starting with *no matter whether..., regardless of whether...*

I won't care about him (be interested in him) *regardless of whether* he succeeded or failed.	لَنْ أَهْتَمَّ بِهِ سَواءٌ أَنَجَحَ أَمْ رَسَبَ.

In our example, the أ is a هَمْزَةُ التَّسْوِية. The sentence after it has a predicative meaning (خَبَرِيّةٌ). The أَمْ is a حَرْفُ عَطْفٍ. This is quite a complex structure. You need to mold two مَصْدَر to decode the proper meaning:

I won't be interested in his success or his failing both alike.	لَنْ أَهْتَمَّ بِهِ فَنَجاحُهُ وُرُسُوبُهُ عِنْدِي سِيَّانِ.

Such constructions are also used in the Qur'an. The هَمْزَةُ التَّسْوِيةِ occurs six times in the Qur'an.

Sura 2:6	As for those who disbelieve, it makes no difference *whether* you warn them or not: they will not believe.	إِنَّ الَّذِينَ كَفَرُوا سَواءٌ عَلَيْهِمْ أَأَنْذَرْتَهُمْ أَمْ لَمْ تُنْذِرْهُمْ لَا يُؤْمِنُونَ.
Notice that there is no spelling mistake in أَأَنْذَرْتَهُمْ. We need the two أأ. The first is a هَمْزَةُ التَّسْوِيةِ; the second belongs to the IV-verb أَنْذَرَ - يُنْذِرُ (*to warn*).		

Sura 63:6	It makes no difference *whether* you ask forgiveness for them or not, Allah will not forgive them.	سَواءٌ عَلَيْهِمْ أَسْتَغْفَرْتَ لَهُمْ أَمْ لَمْ تَسْتَغْفِرْ لَهُمْ لَنْ يَغْفِرَ اللّٰهُ لَهُمْ.

Let's move on and check the second and more common type:

B) أَمْ can convey the meaning of to **designate** or to **nominate one of two** (تَعْيِينٌ). It basically expresses the meaning of *or* (أَوْ).

This type of أَمْ also goes along with a أ, but with a different type: a so-called **interrogative Hamza** (هَمْزَةُ الْإِسْتِفْهامِ).

Did Zayd or Muhammad come?	أَحَضَرَ زَيْدٌ أَمْ مُحَمَّدٌ؟

Excursus: When analyzing أَمْ, you might encounter two other terms.

- أَمْ الْمُتَّصِلةُ. We talked about this type of أَمْ in this *question*. It is used with the هَمْزَةُ التَّسْوِيةِ and the هَمْزَةُ الْإِسْتِفْهامِ. This type of أَمْ is treated as a حَرْفُ عَطْفِ.

- أَمْ الْمُنْقَطِعة. This أَمْ separates two independent sentences. Usually it is not a حَرْفُ عَطْفِ but a *particle of introduction* or *inchoative particle* (حَرْفُ إِبْتِداءٍ), indicating a process of beginning or becoming. Imagine that there is a stop sign before أَمْ (in the form of a full stop) and then, a new sentence or clause starts with this device. Thus, it may convey the meaning of *yet*; *but rather*; *in fact* (بَلْ).

| Sura 32:2 | This scripture, free from all doubt, has been sent down from the Lord of the Worlds. | تَنزِيلُ الْكِتَابِ لَا رَيْبَ فِيهِ مِن رَّبِّ الْعَالَمِينَ. |
| Sura 32:3 | **Yet** they say, "Muhammad has made it up." No indeed! It is the truth from your Lord. | أَمْ يَقُولُونَ افْتَرَاهُ بَلْ هُوَ الْحَقُّ مِن رَّبِّكَ. |

191. Should you use لَكِنَّ or لَكِنْ for *but*?

It depends on the structure of the sentence.

لَكِنْ and لَكِنَّ are both[8] translated as *but; however; yet*. They transport the meaning of *to rectify or emend the previous statement* and are used for *correction* or *restriction* (الْإِسْتِدْرَاكُ). However, regarding the grammar, there is a huge difference between the two.

We need to check whether we can treat لَكِنْ as a conjunction or co-ordinating device (حَرْفُ عَطْفٍ). Only if a sentence meets the following three requirements, لَكِنْ will work as a حَرْفُ عَطْفٍ:

1) لَكِنْ is **followed by a <u>single</u>** word (مُفْرَدٌ) and not a sentence;

2) لَكِنْ is **not** preceded by وَ;

3) لَكِنْ must be **preceded by a negation**; therefore, it expresses denial (نَفْيٌ) or prohibition (نَهْيٌ);

I did not see the accident, but its effects.	لَمْ أَرَ الْحَادِثَةَ لَكِنْ آثَارَهَا.
Do not beat Zayd – but Amr!	لا تَضْرِبْ زَيْدًا لَكِنْ عَمْرًا!
I didn't drink milk, but water.	مَا شَرِبْتُ اللَّبَنَ لَكِنْ الْمَاءَ.

Notice in the examples the case endings before and after لَكِنْ. They must be of the same kind (nominative, genitive, or accusative) because in the examples, لَكِنْ is a conjunction, coordinator (حَرْفُ عَطْفٍ).

Why is that important? If لَكِنْ has the function of a عَطْفٌ, the word after لَكِنْ must (grammatically) **agree** with the preceding word. In all other situations, you use لَكِنَّ with a شَدّةٌ.

---

8 Notice that the dagger Aleph on top of ل which is actually a long vowel, i.e., an Aleph: لَاكِنَّ and لَاكِنْ.

The word لٰكِنَّ is used to convey *emphasis, assurance* (لِلتَّوْكِيدِ), or *re-traction* (لِلْإِسْتِدْرَاكِ). لٰكِنَّ must introduce a **complete** sentence. It can't immediately precede a verb and is usually followed by a noun or a pronoun suffix. Therefore, it introduces a <u>nominal</u> sentence: a pure one without a verb; or a more complicated one with inverted word order (subject + verb). لٰكِنَّ is a *sister of* إِنَّ (أَخَوَاتُ إِنَّ). ▷ A following noun must be in the **accusative case** (مَنْصُوبٌ).	لٰكِنَّ
لٰكِنْ, on the other hand, does **not** introduce a full sentence. It always stands between two opposing things. It **can't have a pronoun suffix**. Any word may follow; usually, it is a noun that takes the same case as the word before لٰكِنْ. But it may be immediately followed by a verb in the present tense, indicative mood (فِعْلٌ مُضَارِعٌ مَرْفُوعٌ) or a past tense verb.	لٰكِنْ

Now, what happens, if one of the **three conditions is violated**?

We can still use لٰكِنْ, but the grammatical analysis is different. Instead of a حَرْفُ عَطْفٍ, the word لٰكِنْ suddenly becomes a *particle of introduction* (حَرْفُ إِبْتِدَاءٍ) which starts a new sentence and works as a *device (particle) of correction* (حَرْفُ إِسْتِدْرَاكٍ). Sībawayhi (سيبويه) stated that in such an application لٰكِنْ has no operating power (إِهْمَالُها). However, other grammarians e.g., al-Mubarrad (الْمُبَرَّد), treated it like لٰكِنَّ.- More importantly, we have to fix the construction with a وَ.

We work in the morning, but then we shift at noon.	نَعْمَلُ صَبَاحًا وَلٰكِنْ نَقِيلُ ظُهْرًا.
The وَ intervenes and does the job of a "coupler" (حَرْفُ عَطْفٍ) now.	

Sura 2:12	but really they are causing corruption (they are the corrupters), **though** they do not realize it.	أَلَا انَّهُمْ هُمُ الْمُفْسِدُونَ وَلٰكِنْ لَا يَشْعُرُونَ.

Remark: The matter gets even more complicated because there is a **light** and a **bold** version of لٰكِنَّ. You can lighten لٰكِنَّ and basically strip off its governing power – which eventually turns it into لٰكِنْ; see question #266. However, the light version of لٰكِنَّ is not a conjunction and the type of لٰكِنْ we talked about in this *question*. See also #252 and #273 for the use of لٰكِنْ.

192. *You and Zayd went. How do you express this?*

You'd better not translate it word by word.

Let's start with what we don't need to discuss. We need the word *and* (وَ). This وَ is a conjunction (عَطْفٌ). So, let's try a translation.

This is **bad style** in Arabic. Some even say that it is incorrect.	You and Zayd went.	ذَهَبْتَ وَزَيْدٌ.

Generally, you may connect an apparent, visible noun (اِسْمٌ ظَاهِرٌ) with a pronoun by using a conjunction (عَطْفٌ). However, in our example, this has a weak point. The pronoun that is attached to a verb (ضَمِيرُ رَفْعٍ مُتَّصِلٌ) would function as the الْمَعْطُوفُ عَلَيْهِ.

How can we fix that?

Situation I: If the pronoun which is attached to the verb is in the <u>nominative</u> (ضَمِيرُ رَفْعٍ مُتَّصِلٌ), it is best to provide some space (فَصْلٌ). You can achieve this by throwing in a **personal pronoun** for emphasis (تَوْكِيدٌ مَعْنَوِيٌّ or تَوْكِيدٌ لَفْظِيٌّ) **after** the verb. Some grammarians state that this is necessary; others say that it does not need to be a pronoun and could be a different word as well.

personal pronoun (التَّوْكِيدُ اللَّفْظِيُّ)	You and Zayd went.	ذَهَبْتَ أَنْتَ وَزَيْدٌ.
abstract emphasis (التَّوْكِيدُ الْمَعْنَوِيُّ)	All of them and Zayd came.	حَضَرُوا كُلُّهُمْ وَزَيْدٌ.
none of the above (التَّوْكِيدُ بِغَيْرِهِما)	They attended today together with Zayd.	حَضَرُوا الْيَوْمَ وَزَيْدٌ.

Situation II: If the pronoun is located in the position of an <u>accusative</u> case (نَصْبٌ) or in the <u>genitive</u> case (جَرٌّ), you **don't** need an extra word to detach both parts. In short, you don't need a فَصْلٌ.

I saw you and Zayd.	رَأَيْتُكَ وَزَيْدًا.
I passed (by) you and Zayd.	مَرَرْتُ بِكَ وَزَيْدٍ.

193. How do you say: *Muhammad's book and pen?*

This is not as easy as it might look like.

You will quickly run into several grammatical issues. Let's try it.

Approach A: A **common solution** is the following idea. We use two first parts of a إِضافةٌ and place a conjunction (عَطْفٌ) in between: a وَ. Only after that, we let the 2nd part (مُضافٌ إِلَيْهِ) follow. Some consider this a weak construction. Some even say that it is not correct.

Approach B: That's the **better solution**. We use a basic إِضافةٌ-construction with first and second part, and then link the second word (in our example: *pen*) to the first word (*book*) by a possessive pronoun.

This is what we will get:

bad (incorrect)	Muhammad's book **and** pen.	كِتابُ وَقَلَمُ مُحَمَّدٍ.	A
better		كِتابُ مُحَمَّدٍ وَقَلَمُهُ.	B
bad (incorrect) Arabic	The council discussed the nature **and** reasons for the problems.	ناقَشَ الْمَجْلِسُ أَنْواعَ وَأَسْبابَ الْمُشْكِلاتِ.	A
better		ناقَشَ الْمَجْلِسُ أَنْواعَ الْمُشْكِلاتِ وَأَسْبابَها.	B

Chapter 7: The Numbers

194. How should we read numbers in Arabic? From right to left?

You can choose the reading direction.

If you want to write numbers, you really need to stick to special rules. If you want to read numbers, you can enjoy some flexibility. Most grammarians say that is correct to read **compound numbers** (الْأَعْدَادُ الْمَعْطُوفة), which are connected by وَ, from...

- left to right (مِن الْيَسارِ إِلَى الْيَمِينِ) _or_
- right to left (مِن الْيَمْينِ إِلَى الْيَسارِ).

Now, the fun starts: The reading direction has an impact on the case marker of the word that is described by the number. Look closely at the last word in the following examples and notice the cases.

The number **1924**: *In the city are 1,924 men.*

1	1000+900+4+20	فِي الْمَدِينةِ أَلْفٌ وَتِسْعُمِائَةٍ وَأَرْبَعةٌ وَعِشْرُونَ رَجُلًا.
2	4+20+900+1000	فِي الْمَدِينةِ أَرْبَعةٌ وَعِشْرُونَ وَتِسْعُمِائَةٍ وَأَلْفُ رَجُلٍ.

The number **2843**: *In the library are 2,843 books.*

1	2000+800+3+40	فِي الْمَكْتَبةِ أَلْفانِ وَثَمانِيمائةٍ وَثَلاثةٌ وَأَرْبَعُونَ كِتابًا.
2	3+40+800+2000	فِي الْمَكْتَبةِ ثَلاثةٌ وَأَرْبَعُونَ وَثَمانِيمائةٍ وَأَلْفا كِتابٍ.

The number **50404**: *In the region are 50,404 (female) teachers.*

1	50000+400+4	فِي الْمِنْطَقةِ خَمْسُونَ أَلْفًا وَأَرْبَعُمِائةٍ وَأَرْبَعُ مُدَرِّساتٍ.
2	4+400+50000	فِي الْمِنْطَقةِ أَرْبَعٌ وَأَرْبَعُمِائةٍ وَخَمْسُونَ أَلْفَ مُدَرِّسةٍ.

Remark: Some grammarians state that you can only choose the reading direction when you deal with numbers with **four or more digits**. In three-digit numbers, the hundreds would always be read first. It is generally advisable to **start with the biggest number first**.

195. What are the most important rules for numbers?

There are so many that we need a table.

إعْرابٌ	counted word (مَعْدُودٌ)		إعْرابٌ	number (عَدَدٌ)
	1 ; 2	These two are special. For number 1, use nunation; for 2 the dual.		
مُضافٌ إلَيْهِ	3 to 10	plural in the genitive case (جَمْعٌ مَجْرُورٌ)	for example: subject, direct object, absolute object, etc.	according to the position in the sentence;	opposite gender (مُخالِفٌ لِلْمَعْدُودِ)
تَمْيِيزٌ	20 to 90	singular in the accusative case (مُفْرَدٌ مَنْصُوبٌ)		only one shape for both genders, i.e., the shape of a sound masculine plural (جَمْعُ الْمُذَكَّرِ السَّالِمُ)
تَمْيِيزٌ	11 and 12	singular in the accusative case (مُفْرَدٌ مَنْصُوبٌ)		compound (مُرَكَّبٌ) consisting of the number 1 or 2 plus the number 10; both agree with the مَعْدُودٌ
تَمْيِيزٌ	13 to 99	singular in the accusative case (مُفْرَدٌ مَنْصُوبٌ)		opposite gender (مُخالِفٌ لِلْمَعْدُودِ)
مُضافٌ إلَيْهِ	100, 1000 - ...	singular in the genitive case (مُفْرَدٌ مَجْرُورٌ)		fixed, indeclinable shape; they never change their gender

Numbers are **triptotes** (apart from 8; *see #200*) and may take any of the three cases. Only when the numerals are used to express abstract numbers, they are treated as diptotes (مَمْنُوعٌ مِن الصَّرْفِ) like proper nouns.

Six is more than five.	سِتَّةُ أَكْثَرُ مِن خَمْسَةٍ.

Numbers are *vague, undefined words* (كَلِمَةٌ مُبْهَمَةٌ). In the following examples, the number (عَدَدٌ) works as the first part of a إضافة which means that it is the number that fills a certain position in the sentence. That's not really logical for English speakers. In Arabic, for example, the number may serve as a direct object (مَفْعُولٌ بِهِ) – and not the word that is counted (مَعْدُودٌ). In the following examples, we'll use the number *three* which means that the مَعْدُودٌ must be in the genitive case as it serves as the second part (مُضافٌ إِلَيْهِ) of the إِضافَةٌ.

Three men came.	جاءَ ثَلاثَةُ رِجالٍ.

Subject (فاعِلٌ) of the verbal sentence. It therefore takes the nominative case (مَرْفُوعٌ بِالضَّمَّةِ الظّاهِرةِ)	ثَلاثَةُ

I read for three hours.	قَرَأْتُ ثَلاثَ ساعاتٍ.

Adverb of time (ظَرْفُ زَمانٍ). Thus, it is located in the position of an accusative (مَنْصُوبٌ بِالْفَتْحةِ الظّاهِرةِ) and marked as such.	ثَلاثَ

I read three readings.	قَرَأْتُ ثَلاثَ قِراءاتٍ.

Absolute object (مَفْعُولٌ مُطْلَقٌ); therefore, it takes the accusative case (مَنْصُوبٌ بِالْفَتْحةِ الظّاهِرةِ). Notice: We use the مَصْدَرٌ of the same verb that is used in the sentence (here: قَرَأَ and قِراءةٌ) which is an indication for an absolute object – and not for a direct object!	ثَلاثَ

196. What is the key point in compound numbers?

The last number is essential for the correct treatment of the word which is numbered (مَعْدُودٌ).

If a number consists of more than one number, they are connected by وَ, which is a conjunction (عَطْفٌ). The important point regarding the grammar is that the مَعْدُودٌ only cares about the last number.

1	125 men came. (Notice the last	جاءَ مِائَةٌ وَخَمْسةٌ وَعِشْرُونَ رَجُلًا.
2	word رَجُل in the examples.)	جاءَ خَمْسَةٌ وَعِشْرُونَ وَمِائَةُ رَجُلٍ.

1	If you look at the table of *question #194*, you'll see that the counted word (مَعْدُودٌ) after 20 (عِشْرُونَ) is a specification (تَمْيِيزٌ). That is the reason for the accusative case (مَنْصُوبٌ) here.	رَجُلًا
2	Second part of the إِضافَةٌ (i.e., مُضافٌ إِلَيْهِ) because it is placed after 100 (مِائَةٌ). The word *hundred* in Arabic always forms a إِضافَةٌ. Here,	رَجُلٍ

the word مِائَةُ serves as the subject (فَاعِلٌ) of the verbal sentence.	
Both وَعِشْرُونَ and مِائَةُ serve as the subject (فَاعِلٌ) of the verbal sentence and take the nominative case (مَرْفُوعٌ), marked by و and ـُ respectively.	

197. Why are the numbers from 13 to 19 special?

They are made of two words (الْأَسْماءُ الْمُرَكَّبَةُ). Both parts have a fixed, cemented shape (مَبْنِيٌّ عَلَى الْفَتْحِ): they end in ـَ .

	the counted is masculine	the counted is feminine
13	ثَلاثَةَ عَشَرَ	ثَلاثَ عَشْرَةَ
14	أَرْبَعَةَ عَشَرَ	أَرْبَعَ عَشْرَةَ

Also the number 11 consists of two cemented parts. But there is a difference! Numbers from 13 to 19 have an **internal gender polarity** for the **unit** (not for *ten*). That doesn't happen in *eleven*. The first part for a counted word that is masculine is masculine too:

11	أَحَدَ عَشَرَ	إِحْدَى عَشْرَةَ

Let's see the difference:

You were 11 years old.	كانَ عُمْرُكَ أَحَدَ عَشَرَ عامًا.
after 18 years	بَعْدَ ثَمانِيَةَ عَشَرَ عامًا

Although these numbers change their shape, they do have a position in إِعْرابٌ depending on the place and function in the sentence. Therefore, we apply virtual, estimated case markers by assigning a place value.

What about *twelve* (12)? In Arabic, *twelve* observes the rules of the **dual** (الْمُثَنَّى) – see *Arabic for Nerds 1*, question #255.

198. How do you spell and pronounce *hundred* in Arabic?

The Arabic word for hundred is written مِائَة – but pronounced like مِئَة.

If we look at مِائَة, how is it possible to have a كَسْرَةٌ before an Aleph? Isn't that actually impossible in Arabic? Indeed, it looks like a spelling mistake. There are several ideas to justify the strange spelling of مِائَة.

- Some scholars date it back to the first writers of the Qur'an. The Aleph ﺍ was perhaps meant to indicate the vowel of the 2nd syllable but for whatever reason, it was placed **before** and not after ئ.

- Others say that it was used to differentiate between the words *hundred* (مِئَةٌ), *category* (فِئَةٌ), and *from him* (مِنْهُ). In ancient times, Arabic used to be written without vowel signs and dots; therefore, the words مِئَة and مِنْه would have looked exactly the same.

- The grammarians of the Basra school (الْبَصْرِيُّونَ) insisted on the extra Aleph (أَصَرَّ عَلى إِبْقاءِ الْأَلِفِ) – whereas their rivals from Kūfa (الْكُوفِيُّونَ) recommended omitting the Aleph (i.e., مِئَة).

مِائَة is an old word that is also found in other Semitic languages. In Hebrew, it is מֵאָה ("me-a"). You occasionally see the Hebrew letter Aleph (א) where you would find a Hamza in Arabic which may explain the spelling of the Arabic word مِئَةٌ. Whatever the reason is, the Aleph in مِائَة is extra (أَلِفُ زِيادَةٍ) and an ornament. Thus, don't pronounce the word as if it was written with a long vowel "aa" which would result in مَائَة ("māa"). This is wrong. The vowels are pronounced short and with "i", i.e., مِئَةٌ ("mi'a"). In many Arabic dialects, مِيّة ("meyya") is used.

مِائَةٌ usually serves as the first part of a إِضافَةٌ. A following word therefore has to be singular and in the genitive case. In written form, the numerals from 3 to 9 are often united with مِائَة into one word.

300 years	ثَلاثُمِائَةِ سَنَةٍ

That is acceptable. Purist grammarians, however, suggest that the very correct view is that you should separate the words.

199. Why do numbers from 3 to 10 need inverted agreement?

Probably to give them some importance.

The system for writing numbers from 3 to 10 is quite awkward. You have to use the opposite gender of the word to which the number refers

(الْعَدَدُ مُخالِفٌ لِلْمَعْدُودِ). This is called **inverted agreement**. The feminine form (مُؤَنَّثٌ) is used when referring to masculine (مُذَكَّرٌ) nouns and vice versa. The gender of the number is determined by the gender of the numbered/counted noun in the singular.

Numbers from 3 to 10 serve as the first part of a إِضافةٌ; the second part has to be in the plural.

Three men came.	جاءَ ثَلاثَةُ رِجالٍ.

Subject (فاعِلٌ) of the verbal sentence; nominative case (مَرْفُوعٌ). First part of the إِضافةٌ.	ثَلاثَةُ
Second part of the إِضافةٌ; thus, in the genitive case (مَجْرُورٌ). Note that we can't have a specification (تَمْيِيزٌ) here. In Arabic, a تَمْيِيزٌ must be a word in the accusative case (اِسْمٌ مَنْصُوبٌ).	رِجالٍ

This is also true when the counted is unnamed.

These three [men].	هٰؤُلَاءِ الثَّلاثَةُ.
Seven [nights] have passed.	مَضَتْ سَبْعٌ.

What could be the idea behind the opposite gender? It is not clear.

This phenomenon occurs in other Semitic languages too. In ancient times, numerals in Semitic languages only had one gender. No matter which gender the thing that was counted had, the numeral ruled over it in a possessive construction (إِضافةٌ), with the number being the first part. In **Hebrew**, scholars explain the opposite gender as follows. The primary original form of the numeral was an **abstract noun** (a so-called *nomen unitatis*, i.e., to indicate a single example of a class). This numeral was placed <u>before</u> the thing that was counted.

Such **abstract nouns** – and here comes the idea of the opposite gender – always take the **feminine ending** in Hebrew (similar in Arabic: *apples* – تُفّاحٌ, but: *an apple* – تُفّاحةٌ), regardless of the counted thing's gender. Later on, numbers were also used as adjectives or placed in apposition. Don't forget, adjectives (and words in apposition) need **agreement**! So, if the feminine form of the number is placed after a masculine noun, what should we do if the thing which we want to count, has the feminine gender? The same logic was applied! You use the opposite gender. Hence, new forms of the originally unisexual numeral were developed. This idea perhaps also works for Arabic.

Other scholars suggested that numbers are so important that they **should be given some prominence**, in other words, **an independent nature (of a substantive)**. This would make them different from a basic adjective (صِفةٌ/ نَعْتٌ) because an adjective in Arabic has to follow the gender of the noun to which it refers.

200. Why is the number 8 different from others?

It has to do with the spelling.

Let's put ثَمانٍ, the Arabic word for *eight*, under the microscope and focus on the **last letter**. Wait a second – what is the last letter? We deal with a so-called اِسْمٌ مَنْقُوصٌ, a noun with a reduced, imperfect ending, because the word has a final weak letter, the ي. Such words have a peculiarity: the last letter is *shortened* (مَنْقُوصٌ) in the indefinite form; it vanishes – see #40. This will become crucial in some situations.

What are possible **case endings** of ثَمانٍ? The noun is declined similarly to قاضٍ - الْقاضِي (*judge*).

a) If the number is the first part of a إِضافةٌ, you must **keep** the ي.

| Eight men came. | جاءَ ثَمانِيةُ رِجالٍ |
| I saw eight girls. | رَأَيْتُ ثَمانِيَ بَناتٍ |

b) If it is <u>not</u> the first part of the إِضافة and you refer to a <u>masculine noun</u> (مَعْدُودٌ مُذَكَّرٌ), you **keep** the ي in its <u>feminine</u> form (مَع تَأْنِيثِه). Sounds weird. Well, this happens if you change the word order.

| Eight men came. | جاءَ مِن الرِّجالِ ثَمانِيةٌ. |
| I saw eight men. | رَأَيْتُ مِن الرِّجالِ ثَمانِيةً. |

c) If it is <u>not</u> the مُضافٌ (the first part) and you refer to a <u>feminine</u>

noun (مَعْدُودٌ مُؤَنَّثٌ), you **delete** the ي in the nominative case (رَفْعٌ) and in the genitive (جَرٌّ) – which happens to any اِسْمٌ مَنْقُوصٌ.

Eight girls came.	جاءَتْ مِن الْبَناتِ ثَمانٍ.
I passed (by) eight girls.	مَرَرْتُ مِن الْبَناتِ بِثَمانٍ.
I saw eight girls.	رَأَيْتُ مِن الْبَناتِ ثَمانِيًا.

d) When it takes the accusative case (نَصْبٌ), it is possible to treat ثَمانٍ as a **diptote** (مَمْنُوعٌ مِن الصَرْفِ).

I saw eight girls.	رَأَيْتُ مِن الْبَناتِ ثَمانِيَ.

What about 18? It all depends on the noun to which 18 refers, i.e., the counted thing (مَعْدُودٌ).

➡ **The number refers to a <u>masculine</u> noun:** This means that we need the feminine form of 8 and the masculine form of the number 10.

I have with me eighteen men.	عِنْدِي ثَمانِيةَ عَشَرَ رَجُلًا.

➡ **The number refers to a <u>feminine</u> noun:** We need the masculine form of 8 and the feminine form of 10. Regarding 8, you may make the ي to have a فَتْحةٌ or you make it unvowelled, *quiescent* (سُكُونٌ).

I have with me, of women, eighteen women.	عِنْدِي مِن النِّساء ثَمانِي عَشْرةَ امْرَأةً.
	عِنْدِي مِن النِّساء ثَمانِيْ عَشْرةَ امْرَأةً.

And what about 800? This is a compound noun of ثَمانٍ and مِائة. You can merge <u>or</u> separate them: ثَمانِ مِائةٍ or ثَمانِيمائةٍ.

Excursus: Why is the number 8 spelled like this?

Some scholars say that it is a نِسْبة-noun (adjective) and that it is comparable in its form to the word يَمانٍ meaning *Yemenite* or *from Yemen*. يَمانٍ is an exception to the standard rules because the usual form (which, by the way, is also applied) is يَمَنِيّ. So, originally it was يَمَنِيٌّ derived from الْيَمَنُ which then became يَمانٍ (originally يَمانِيٌّ). As a compensation for the suppression of one of the two ي, the ا (Aleph) was inserted.

ثَمانٍ could also be the نِسْبةٌ-noun of الثُّمُنُ because it is the part or portion that makes seven to be eight; thus, it is its eighth. The first letter became to be pronounced with فَتْحةٌ. This sometimes happens. For example, سَهْل (*soft ground, level, plain*) has a different first vowel when used as a نِسْبةٌ. It is the form سُهْلِيّ which deviates from the standard rules; e.g., *ground cover* (نَباتٌ سُهْلِيّ). The word نَباتٌ is a collective noun and means *plants, vegetation*. It is related to the root ن - ب - ت which means *to grow (of plants)*.

More interestingly is the suppression of one of the two ي which could have been similar to the word يَمان. The Aleph (ا) of ثَمانٍ is a characteristic of such نِسْبةٌ-nouns because these words are not broken plurals like صَحارٍ. Note: The word for *desert* is صَحْراءُ and has the plural form صَحارٍ.

201. خمسة حَماماتٍ (*five pigeons*). Is there a mistake?

No, there isn't.

At first sight, it looks like that there is a mistake. Numbers from 3 to 10 observe abnormal rules because you have to use the opposite gender of the word (i.e., the مَعْدُودٌ) to which the number refers.

Okay, but isn't the مَعْدُودٌ in our example (حَماماتٍ) a feminine plural? Well, in order to apply the numbers correctly, we have to **check the singular form** as only the singular will tell us the correct gender.

These are five pigeons.	هٰذِهِ خَمْسةُ حَماماتٍ.

حَمامات has the shape of a sound feminine plural (جَمْعُ الْمُؤَنَّثِ السّالِمُ). However, the **singular form** (مُفْرَدٌ) is حَمامٌ which is **masculine** (مُذَكَّرٌ). Therefore, the <u>number</u> must be **feminine**.

For the same reason, we say:

singular	gender of the word	translation	example
a night (لَيْلةٌ)	feminine	seven nights	سَبْعُ لَيالٍ
a valley (وادٍ)	masculine	five valleys	خَمْسةُ أَوْدِية
a boy (فَتًى)	masculine	four boys	أَرْبَعةُ فِتْية

202. How do you say *some twenty* or *twenty odd* in Arabic?

You can use the word نَيِّفٌ *which literally means excess; surplus.*

Used with round numbers, نَيِّفٌ is rendered as *some...* or *...and odd*. In Arabic, we treat نَيِّفٌ as an **undefined number** (عَدَدٌ مُبْهَمٌ) in the degree of 1 to 9. It is always **masculine** (مُذَكَّرٌ). To link it with a number, you need a coupler/coordinator (حَرْفُ عَطْفٍ). ▷ The وَ.

Some thirty came.	جَاءَ ثَلَاثُونَ وَنَيِّفٌ.

Subject (فَاعِلٌ) in the nominative case (مَرْفُوعٌ), marked by the و.	ثَلَاثُونَ
Conjunction (حَرْفُ عَطْفٍ); it does not operate on other words.	وَ
The مَعْطُوفٌ (i.e., the word after وَ) gets the same case as the word before وَ, which is the subject here. Therefore, نَيِّفٌ takes the nominative case (مَرْفُوعٌ) as well.	نَيِّفٌ

I saw thirty and odd.	رَأَيْتُ ثَلَاثِينَ وَنَيِّفًا.
In this example, the number ثَلَاثِينَ is the direct object (مَفْعُولٌ بِهِ). Thus, it must take the accusative case (مَنْصُوبٌ); the case marker is expressed by the letter ي. The word نَيِّفًا gets the same case because it is coupled by وَ. That's the reason why نَيِّفًا is in the accusative case here.	

The same is true for the genitive case.

I passed (by) thirty and odd.	مَرَرْتُ بِثَلَاثِينَ وَنَيِّفٍ.

203. *The people came two by two?* How do you say that in Arabic?

Arabic knows a special pattern for so-called distributive adjectives.

A distributive adjective is one used to refer to each object in a group of things. Examples of distributive adjectives are *each, every, neither, either, any, one, both*. We need to solve how to express *two by two*. We have two options to express this special form of a **distribute adjective**:

1. We repeat the (cardinal) number once.

2. We use the pattern مَفْعَلُ (rarely فُعَالُ). These patterns are nor-

mally only used for the **first ten numbers**. Both patterns produce **diptotes** (مَمْنُوعٌ مِن الصَّـرْفِ) and are shared by masculine and feminine forms. They are usually placed as a حَالٌ.

		مَفْعَلُ	فُعالُ			مَفْعَلُ	فُعالُ
1	one by one	مَوْحَد	أُحَاد	6	six by six	مَسْدَس	سُداس
2	in pairs/2 by 2	مَثْنَى	ثُناء	7	seven by seven	مَسْبَع	سُباع
3	three by three	مَثْلَث	ثُلاث	8	eight by eight	مَثْمَن	ثُمان
4	four by four	مَرْبَع	رُباع	9	nine by nine	مَتْسَع	تُساع
5	five by five	مَخْمَس	خُماس	10	ten by ten	مَعْشَر	عُشار

The students entered four by four.	دَخَلَ التَّلامِيذُ رُباعَ.
This is the original meaning:	دَخَلَ التَّلامِيذُ أَرْبَعَةً أَرْبَعَةً.

Such patterns are called مَعْدُولٌ. In grammar, the term denotes *transformed*; *changed*. The process itself is called عَدْلٌ. You produce a word out of another having the same root, but according to a different pattern. We can say that such words were transformed from one pattern to another. Their original pattern was the number itself. The pattern helps to avoid repeating the numbers twice.

But that is not all. It gets even weirder. It is possible to repeat even such a pattern twice!

They came three by three.	جاءُوا مَثْلَثَ.
➡ Both sentences are correct.	جاءُوا مَثْلَثَ مَثْلَثَ.

How would you say *eight in number*? You could use the pattern فُعالُ.

They came eight in number.	أَتَوْا ثُمانَ.
This would be the meaning: →	أَتَوْا ثَمانِيَةً ثَمانِيَةً.

204. Is it possible to place the number after a word?

Yes, this is possible.

In practical terms, this would mean that you place the مَعْدُودٌ (i.e., the thing that is counted) before the number (عَدَدٌ). This operation can trigger severe grammatical changes.

What is striking: it is possible to either use the **masculine or feminine gender of the number** in such a situation. If you want to avoid any dishevelment, it is recommended to stick to the standard rules.

		standard rules
3 men came.	جاءَ رِجالٌ ثَلاثٌ.	جاءَ رِجالٌ ثَلاثَةٌ.
I saw 6 girls.	رَأَيْتُ بَناتٍ سِتَّةٌ.	رَأَيْتُ بَناتٍ سِتًّا.
I met 8 men.	قابَلْتُ رِجالًا ثَمانِيًا or ثَمانِي.	قابَلْتُ رِجالًا ثَمانِيَةً.
I met 8 girls.	قابَلْتُ بَناتٍ ثَمانِيَةً.	قابَلْتُ بَناتٍ ثَمانِيًا or ثَمانِي.
14 men came.	جاءَ رِجالٌ أَرْبَعَ عَشْرَةَ.	جاءَ رِجالٌ أَرْبَعَةَ عَشَرَ.
I saw 14 girls.	رَأَيْتُ بَناتٍ أَرْبَعَةَ عَشَرَ.	رَأَيْتُ بَناتٍ أَرْبَعَ عَشْرَةَ.

205. How do you make numerical expressions (3 to 10) definite?

You have three options.

Let's assume you want to say: *The three men came*. That's actually not that simple because you need to make the expression definite.

The whole issue is centered on the question of where to place the definite article (ال). Grammarians call it تَعْرِيفُ الْعَدَدِ. Numbers from 3 to 10 serve as the first part of a إِضافةٌ. So let's see what we could do.

OPTION 1 (preferred): Put ال before the **second** part (مُضافٌ إِلَيْهِ).

Why the second? Because the first part of a إِضافةٌ is per definition definite. The Basra grammarians (الْبَصرِيُّونَ) favored this approach.

nominative (مَرْفُوعٌ)	The 3 men came.	جاءَ ثَلاثةُ الرِّجالِ.
nominative (مَرْفُوعٌ)	The 3 girls came.	جاءَتْ ثَلاثُ الْبَناتِ.
accusative (مَنْصوبٌ)	I saw the 1000 books.	رَأَيْتُ أَلْفَ الْكِتابِ.

OPTION 2: You use ال **twice** – before the number (عَدَدٌ) **and** before the المُضافُ إلَيْهِ.

This is weird because it would violate some grammar rules. In Arabic, you are not allowed to use the definite article in the first part of a إضافةٌ. That's true, but the Kūfa grammarians (الْكُوفِيُّونَ) – except for al-Farrāʾ (أَبُو زَكَرِيّا الْفَرّاءُ) – approved it (but **only** for constructions with numbers). What's the idea behind? Imagine that the second part was originally the first part – which would make it an adjective.

nominative (مَرْفُوعٌ)	The 3 men came.	جاءَ الثَّلاثةُ الرِّجالِ.
nominative (مَرْفُوعٌ)	The 3 girls came.	جاءَتْ الثَّلاثُ الْبَناتِ.
accusative (مَنْصُوبٌ)	I saw the 1000 books.	رَأَيْتُ الْأَلْفَ الْكِتابِ.

OPTION 3: A rare and weird approach. You put ال only <u>before</u> the **number** (عَدَدٌ). You'll hardly encounter such constructions. How can we justify this construction? ➡ By assuming an omitted number!

nominative (مَرْفُوعٌ)	The 3 men came.	جاءَ الثَّلاثةُ رِجالٍ.
Where is the deleted number? ⊳ Before the word *men*: جاءَ الثَّلاثةُ ثَلاثةُ رِجالٍ.		
nominative (مَرْفُوعٌ)	The 3 girls came.	جاءَتْ الثَّلاثُ بَناتٍ.
accusative (مَنْصُوبٌ)	I saw the 1000 books.	رَأَيْتُ الْأَلْفَ كِتابٍ.

Let's see an example: *I bought the 5 books.* All three options are correct.

option 1	خَمْسةَ الْكُتُبِ.	
option 2	الْخَمْسةَ الْكُتُبِ.	اِشْتَرَيْتُ
option 3	الْخَمْسةَ كُتُبٍ.	

➡ What happens if the number is a compound number (عَدَدٌ مُرَكَّبٌ)? These are numbers from **13 to 19** which do not have a وَ. Then, it is best to add ال to the **first part of the number only**.

| nom. (مَرْفُوعٌ) | The 13 men came. | جاءَ الثَّلاثةَ عَشَرَ رَجُلًا. |

nom. (مَرْفُوعٌ)	The 13 girls came.	جاءَت الثَّلاثَ عَشْرَةَ بِنْتًا.
acc. (مَنْصُوبٌ)	I passed (by) the 15 men.	مَرَرْتُ بِالْخَمْسةَ عَشَرَ رَجُلًا.

➡ What happens if the number (عَدَدٌ) is 20, 30, 40, ... (أَلْفاظُ الْعُقُودِ)? In other words, we deal with numbers which resemble a sound masculine plural. Answer: you add الـ to the **number.**

nom. (مَرْفُوعٌ)	The 20 men came.	جاءَ الْعِشْرُونَ رَجُلًا.
acc. (مَنْصُوبٌ)	I saw the 20 girls.	رَأَيْتُ الْعِشْرِينَ بِنْتًا.

➡ Now let's combine all the nasty possibilities. What happens if we have a compound number with وَ and a أَلْفاظُ الْعُقُودُ? Then, you should add الـ to both, the مَعْطُوفٌ and the مَعْطُوفٌ عَلَيْهِ.

nom. (مَرْفُوعٌ)	The 23 men came.	جاءَ الثَّلاثةُ وَالْعِشْرُونَ رَجُلًا.
acc. (مَنْصُوبٌ)	I saw the 36 girls.	رَأَيْتُ السِّتَّ وَالثَّلاثِينَ بِنْتًا.

206. Can you use كَم as a substitute for a number?

Yes, this is possible.

كَم can be used to ask questions (اِسْتِفْهامٌ). It enables us to express *how many/much* but also to signify *many* (الْكَثْرَةُ). Grammarians call كَم a figure of speech or metonymy. A *metonymy* is a word which is a stand-in for other words; for example: *dish* for an entire plate of food or *hand* for help. كَم is a *metaphor* (كِنايَةٌ) for a number (عَدَدٌ). Similar words in this regard are كَأَيِّنْ or كَذا or كَيْتَ, as in كَيْتَ وَكَيْتَ which means *so and so, such and such, thus and thus.*

SITUATION 1: كَم used for **questions** (كَم الْإِسْتِفْهامِيّة).

Here, كَم inquires about a number. Most grammarians say that this type of كَم must be followed by a **specification** in the accusative case (تَمْييزٌ مُفْرَدٌ مَنْصُوبٌ). It takes precedence, the **forefront** (صَدارَةٌ) in questions except if it is preceded by a preposition (حَرْفُ الْجَرِّ).

كَم is a noun (اِسْمُ اِسْتِفْهامٍ) with a fixed, indeclinable shape (مَبْنِيٌّ)

(عَلَى السُّكُونِ). Since it is a اِسْم, we know that كَمْ has a position in إِعْرَابٌ and can do certain jobs depending on the position in the sentence.

How **many** students came today?	كَمْ طَالِبًا حَضَرَ الْيَوْمَ؟

Question word (اِسْمُ اِسْتِفْهَامٍ) serving as the **subject** (مُبْتَدَأٌ) of the **nominal sentence** (جُمْلَةٌ اِسْمِيَّةٌ). It has an indeclinable, fixed shape (مَبْنِيٌّ عَلَى السُّكُونِ), so we can only use virtual case markers and assign a "place value". In our example, as the subject, كَمْ is placed in the position that would get the nominative case (فِي مَحَلِّ رَفْعٍ).	كَمْ
Specification (تَمْيِيزٌ); accusative case (مَنْصُوبٌ بِالْفَتْحةِ الظَّاهِرةِ).	طَالِبًا
Now, where is the predicate (خَبَرٌ)? The verbal sentence (حَضَرَ) fills in for that and is located in the position of a nominative case (الْجُمْلَةُ مِنَ الْفِعْلِ وَالْفَاعِلِ فِي مَحَلِّ رَفْعٍ خَبَرٌ).	

How **many** students did you see today?	كَمْ طَالِبًا رَأَيْتَ الْيَوْمَ؟

Question word serving as the **direct object** (مَفْعُولٌ بِهِ). Therefore, it is located in the place of an accusative case (فِي مَحَلِّ نَصْبٍ).	كَمْ

How **many** hours did you read today?	كَمْ ساعةً قَرَأْتَ الْيَوْمَ؟

Question word serving as an **adverb of time** (ظَرْفُ زَمانٍ); therefore, it is located in the position of an accusative (فِي مَحَلِّ نَصْبٍ).	كَمْ

How **many** miles did the swimmers swim?	كَمْ مِيلًا سَبَحَ السّابِحُونَ؟

Question word serving as an **adverb of place** (ظَرْفُ مَكانٍ); therefore, it is located in the position of an accusative (فِي مَحَلِّ نَصْبٍ).	كَمْ

How **many** readings did I read today?	كَمْ قِراءةً قَرَأْتُ الْيَوْمَ؟

Question word serving as the **absolute object** (مَفْعُولٌ مُطْلَقٌ); therefore in the position of an accusative case (فِي مَحَلِّ نَصْبٍ).	كَمْ

In all the above examples, the words *students* (طالِبًا), *hours* (ساعةً), *miles* (مِيلًا), and *readings* (قِراءةً) have the same function:

> They are a **specification** (تَمْييزٌ)! According to the rules, a specification has to take the accusative case (مَنْصوبٌ بِالْفَتْحةِ الظّاهِرةِ). Furthermore, a specification has to be **indefinite** (نَكِرة) and **singular** (مُفْرَدٌ) – see #373.

If there is a **preposition** involved, you'll have two possibilities:

1	For how many piasters did you buy that?	بِكَمْ قِرْشًا اشْتَرَيْتَ هٰذا؟
2		بِكَمْ قِرْشٍ اشْتَرَيْتَ هٰذا؟

ب	Preposition (حَرْفُ الْجَرِّ).	
كَمْ	Question word that is placed in the position of a genitive case (في مَحَلِّ جَرٍّ بِالْباءِ) because it is governed by the preceding preposition. The prepositional phrase (شِبْهه الْجُمْلة) is linked to *to buy* (اِشْتَرَى).	
قِرْشًا	1	The **standard approach**: قِرْشًا serves as a specification (تَمْييزٌ) and gets the accusative case (مَنْصوبٌ بِالْفَتْحةِ الظّاهِرةِ).
قِرْشٍ	2	Noun in the genitive case (اِسْمٌ مَجْرورٌ) by the **virtual, as-sumed preposition** مِن. The prepositional phrase (الْجارُّ وَالْمَجْرورُ) is connected with the expression بِكَمْ. What's the im-plicit meaning of the entire sentence then? It is: بِكَمْ مِنْ قِرْشٍ **Note:** The genitive marker induced by the hypothetical, implicit مِنْ may give the sentence some kind of exclamation.

There is another possibility for the grammatical analysis. We could as-sume a إِضافةٌ!

كَمْ	مُضافٌ	**First part.** It is located in the position of a genitive case (في مَحَلِّ جَرٍّ) because it was dragged into this po-sition by the preposition بـ. However, all this is not visible because the word كَمْ can't take case markers.
قِرْش	مُضافٌ إِلَيْهِ	**Second part.** It is governed by the first part in the genitive case (مَجْرورٌ). We apply the usual case markers.

Remark: You will quite often deal with sentences in which the **specifi-**

cation (تَمْيِيزٌ) is omitted (marked in gray in the following table).

| How much money do you have? | كَمْ مالُكَ؟ |
| Implicitly understood: How many *dinars* do you own? | كَمْ دِينارًا مالُكَ؟ |

| How often has Zayd come to you? | كَمْ جاءَكَ زَيْدٌ؟ |
| How *many times* has Zayd come to you? | كَمْ مَرَّةً جاءَكَ زَيْدٌ؟ |

SITUATION 2: كَمْ does not inquire about a number. It itself expresses information (كَمْ الْخَبَرِيَّةُ) and takes over the job of a number, so to speak. We call this type **predicative** كَمْ. In most situations, such application of كَمْ expresses *much* or *many*.

- كَمْ is usually a metaphor for a **big number** (الْعَدَدُ الْكَثِيرُ) in a sentence that does not inquire, but gives us information (جُمْلَةٌ خَبَرِيَّةٌ). When used as an exclamation, it denotes *how many!*

- This type of كَمْ must **start the sentence** (صَدْرُ الْكَلامِ) and can only be preceded by a preposition (for example: بـ).

- The word after كَمْ is singular (مُفْرَدٌ) and in the genitive (مَجْرُورٌ) as most grammarians say. ▷ This is similar to the numbers *a hundred* (مِائَة) and *a thousand* (أَلْف).

- The final result of this construction is a إِضافَةٌ.

How many a dirham have I spent!	كَمْ دِرْهَمٍ أَنْفَقْتُ!
I saw many scholars!	كَمْ عالِمٍ رَأَيْتُ!
This is the meaning: →	رَأَيْتُ كَثِيرًا مِن الْعُلَماءِ!

A few subtleties you should know:

- It is permissible to delete the noun (اسْمٌ) after a كَمْ الْخَبَرِيَّةُ and place a verb there instead.

| A many has Zayd read and written! | كَمْ قَرَأَ زَيْدٌ وَكَمْ كَتَبَ! |

- It is permissible to have a plural form (جَمْعٌ) after كَمْ.
- كَمْ may be followed by the extra preposition مِن (which would be an ellipsis).

What about the grammatical analysis?

The predicative كَمْ الْخَبَرِيّة has a position in إِعْرابٌ depending on its function and place in the sentence – similar to what we have seen in the application of كَمْ as a question word.

Many a mile have the swimmers swum and did not feel tired.	كَمْ مِيلٍ سَبَحَ السّابِحُونَ وَلَمْ يَتْعَبُوا.
كَمْ here serves as an **adverb of place** (ظَرْفُ مَكانٍ). Therefore, it is located in the position of an accusative case (فِي مَحَلِّ نَصْبٍ).	

Many a book has Zayd read!	كَمْ مِنْ كِتابٍ قَرَأَ زَيْدًا!
Direct object (مَفْعُولٌ بِهِ). Since كَمْ has a fixed shape and can't carry apparent, visible case markers, we can only say that it occupies the position of an accusative case (فِي مَحَلِّ نَصْبٍ).	كَمْ
Prepositional phrase (جارٌّ وَمَجْرُورٌ); connected with كَمْ.	مِنْ كِتابٍ

PART THREE: THE SENTENCE

207. Does a verbal sentence always start with a verb?

No, it doesn't.

A sentence (جُمْلةٌ) consists of at least two words and has per defini-tion a meaning. The Arabic term جُمْلةٌ denotes *a sum* or *total of words*. In Arabic, there are only two types of sentences:

1. **Nominal sentence** (جُمْلةٌ اِسْمِيّةٌ): if the sentence starts with a noun (اِسْمٌ) originally, it is a nominal sentence.

2. **Verbal sentence** (جُمْلةٌ فِعْلِيّةٌ): if the sentence starts with a <u>full</u> verb (فِعْلٌ غَيْرُ ناقِص), we call it a verbal sentence. Therefore, a de-fective, deficient verb like كانَ doesn't produce a verbal sentence.

1	Karīm was standing.	كانَ كَرِيمٌ قائِمًا.
	This is **not** a **verbal sentence** because it doesn't point to an action (لا تَدُلّ عَلَى حَدَث) performed by the subject (فاعِلٌ). ➤ It is a **nominal** sentence that contains a special verb: كانَ. It is a defective, incomplete verb (فِعْلٌ ناسِخٌ ناقِصٌ) which overthrows the usual grammar rules.	

2	I read a book.	كِتابًا قَرَأْتُ.
	This is **not** a **nominal** sentence although it starts with a noun. Why? We only called a sentence a جُمْلةٌ اِسْمِيّةٌ if it had originally started with a noun. Here, the noun is the **direct object** (مَفْعُولٌ بِه) which was put in front of the verb. It is just a stylistic trick. ➤ It is a **verbal** sentence.	

Chapter 8: The Nominal Sentence

208. Why is the subject of a nominal sentence called مُبْتَدَأٌ?

Because the term describes what a subject, in fact, is: that with which a beginning is made (الْمُبْتَدَأ بِه).

In Arabic, the مُبْتَدَأ (subject) is a powerful function. It gives a word a superior rank and entitles it to priority. It signifies importance, for example, the start of a new thought, idea, story, or sentence (الْإِبْتِداءُ). Such primary jobs explain why it gets the nominative case (*see #52*).

The English term *subject* works in linguistic terms, but it fails to explain the philosophy of Arabic. Nevertheless, there is no good English translation of مُبْتَدَأٌ. So keep in mind that it is not just the subject. Practically speaking, it is the person or thing about which a statement is made. The subject (مُبْتَدَأٌ) is not a sentence. It is always just one word. If you see a مُبْتَدَأٌ in the form of a sentence, it is not the subject in form of a sentence. It is treated as an entity, as just one word (although it is a sentence). Sounds strange? Let's see:

"You (female) wasted the milk in summer" is an old proverb.	الصَّيْفَ ضَيَّعْتِ اللَّبَنَ مَثَلٌ قَدِيمٌ.

This ancient proverb goes back to pre-Islamic times (الْجاهِلِيّة). It denotes that someone lost his chance and is used to describe an opportunity willfully wasted or a good foregone.

The story is about a woman, Dakhtanūs (دَخْتَنُوس بِنْت لَقِيط), who is the wife of a wealthy old man called 'Amr (عَمْرُو بن عُداس). But she doesn't like him, mainly because he is too old. Hence, one day in summer, she leaves him (he divorced her), and a poor, young man married her.

When she suffered from poverty due to a drought, she sent a message to her former husband 'Amr asking him for milk – and he answered: *"You wasted the milk in summer"*. Usually, the story ends here. However, it continues.

After she heard this, the woman gave her husband a pat on the shoulder and said to herself: *"This and his watered milk are better."* (هذا وَمَذْقُهُ خَيْرٌ.). This sentence also became a proverb and is said to a person who is satisfied with a simple, poor thing or to someone who has to carry a heavy burden.

Remark: In the **first proverb**, you keep the verb form with كَسْرة even if you address a man or a group. In proverbs, verbs usually never change.

In the **second proverb**, مَذْقٌ is the مَصْدَرٌ of the I-verb يَمْذَق - مَذَقَ which means *to mix with water; dilute*. Some prefer to use مَذْقَة which is specifically related to milk and means *milk blended with water* (لَبَنٌ مَمْزُوجٌ بِالْماءِ).

Let's check the grammar of our example.

➔ The **entire expression** (quotation) is the subject	الصَّيْفَ ضَيَّعْتِ اللَّبَنَ

(مُبْتَدَأٌ). It is not just a single word.	

In fact, the whole expression is treated as an entity which is located in the position of a nominative case (مُبْتَدَأٌ مَرْفُوعٌ بِضَمّةٍ مُقدَّرةٍ).	

Predicate (خَبَرٌ) in the nominative case (مَرْفُوعٌ); marked by the usual case markers.	مَثَلٌ

Remark: In Classical Arabic, the subject (of a nominal or verbal sentence) is also called الْمُسْنَدُ إِلَيْهِ – *that upon which (the attribute) leans; or: by which it is supported.* The predicate is called الْمُسْنَدُ – *that which leans upon; or: is supported by* (the subject). Seen from that angle, we could call the predicate the attribute. The relation between them is termed الْإِسْنادُ, expressing *the act of leaning (one thing against another).*

209. What are the "usual suspects" that can work as a subject of a nominal sentence?

There aren't many.

First of all, the مُبْتَدَأٌ, that's what its name says, always starts a sentence. However, some devices may jump to the front and <u>precede</u> it:

- لَ which is called the *inceptive Lām* (لامُ الْإِبْتِداءِ). It does not have a grammatical function; it is only there to lay emphasis, to strengthen the meaning (وَظِيفةٌ مَعْنَوِيّةٌ لا إِعْرابِيّةٌ). Depending on the words used in the sentence, this *Lām* is also called لامُ التَّأْكِيد or, when used with إِنَّ, اللَّامُ الْمُزَحْلَقةُ.
- a negation particle (حَرْفُ نَفْيٍ);
- a question particle (حَرْفُ إِسْتِفْهامٍ);

Note: ➢ All of them do not influence the subject regarding the إِعْرابٌ.

By its nature, the subject (مُبْتَدَأٌ) is **definite** (مَعْرِفةٌ). The predicate (خَبَرٌ) is **indefinite** (نَكِرةٌ). So, which words can theoretically serve as a مُبْتَدَأٌ?

I. Nouns with a fixed, cemented shape (اسْمٌ مَبْنِيٌّ) can be the مُبْتَدَأٌ.

personal pronoun	He is generous.		هُوَ كَرِيمٌ.

demonstrative (اِسْمُ إِشارةٍ)	This is a book.	هذا كِتابٌ.
relative pronoun (اِسْمٌ مَوْصُولٌ)	What I said is correct.	ما (الَّذي) قُلْتُهُ صَحِيحٌ.
question word (اِسْمُ اِسْتِفْهامٍ)	What is your name?	ما اسْمُكَ؟
conditional device (اِسْمُ شَرطٍ)	He/the one who studies will succeed.	مَنْ يُذاكِرْ يَنْجَحْ.

II. The usual situation: A regular noun (اِسْمٌ صَرِيحٌ) works as the مُبْتَدَأ. For example: *the student* (الطَّالِبُ).

III. The rare situation: an **interpreted infinitive noun** (مَصْدَرٌ مُؤَوَّلٌ) works as the مُبْتَدَأ.

The construction with a مَصْدَرٌ مُؤَوَّلٌ can be difficult to grasp.

| Sura 2:184 | But to fast is best for you. (*Sahīh Internat.*) Fasting is better for you. (*Abdul Haleem*) | وَأَنْ تَصُومُوا خَيْرٌ لَكُمْ. |

| This is how we could rewrite the sentence: → | وَصِيامُكُمْ خَيْرٌ لَكُمْ. |

So, what did we do? We simply used the real, original مَصْدَرٌ which has exactly the same meaning as the interpreted مَصْدَرٌ.

Remark: خَيْرٌ works like a comparative (اِسْمُ التَّفْضِيلِ). A good example is the call of the muezzin in the morning in Sunni Islam which goes like: *"Prayer is better than sleep"* (الصَّلاةُ خَيْرٌ مِن النَّوْمِ). See *Arabic for Nerds 1*, question #54.

Let's analyze the grammar of the above sentence:

| This particle is a حَرْفُ نَصْبٍ وَمَصْدَرٍ, i.e., the place of the مَصْدَرٌ is supplied by this device. The particle triggers the مَنْصُوبٌ-mood in the verb that follows. It does not have a position in إِعْرابٌ. | أَنْ |
| Present tense verb (فِعْلٌ مُضارِعٌ) which is مَنْصُوبٌ due to the particle أَنْ. How is a verb put into مَنْصُوبٌ? Normally you put a | تَصُومُوا |

فَتْحَةٌ on the last letter. However, since we have a verb in the plu-ral form with the ending ون, we do it differently: we delete the final ن. Such verbs are called الْأَفْعالُ الْخَمْسةُ.

The و is an indeclinable pronoun and is the **subject** (فاعِلٌ) of the verbal sentence; it holds the position of a nominative case (الْوَاوُ ضَمِيرٌ مُتَّصِلٌ مَبْنِيٌّ عَلَى السُّكُونِ فِي مَحَلّ رَفْعِ فاعِلٍ).

Now, what about the **subject** (مُبْتَدَأٌ) of the **nominal sentence**? The entire interpreted infinitive noun (مَصْدَرٌ مُؤَوَّلٌ) supplies this job: أَنْ تَصُومُوا.

Predicate (خَبَرٌ) of the nominal sentence; nominative (مَرْفُوعٌ). This tells us that our analysis of the مُبْتَدَأٌ is correct. The predi-cate relates to *"fasting/to fast is..."* – and not to the pronoun *you* (which is the subject/فاعِلٌ of the auxiliary verbal sentence).	خَبَرٌ

Remark: The مَصْدَرٌ مُؤَوَّلٌ in our example consists of أَنْ plus verb. It is also possible to build it with ما instead of أَنْ. Such ما is called ما الْمَصْدَرِيّةُ.

210. Does every مُبْتَدَأٌ (subject) have a خَبَرٌ (predicate)?

No, it doesn't (grammatically speaking).

There is a situation in Arabic where grammarians say that the subject doesn't need a predicate (خَبَرٌ). What happens is that another word takes over the role of the predicate and completes the meaning together with the subject. This construction is called *the description of the nomi-native (subject) to complete its meaning* (الْوَصْفُ الرَّافِعُ لِمُكْتَفًى بِهِ).

The key is the term وَصْفٌ which means *description* What could be an appropriate وَصْفٌ? The grammarians understand by وَصْفٌ a **de-rived noun from the root** (اِسْمٌ مُشْتَقٌّ). In most situations, this will be the active particle (اِسْمُ الْفاعِلِ), the passive participle (اِسْمُ الْمَفْعُولِ), or quasi participles (صِفةٌ مُشَبَّهةٌ) – nouns that convey a meaning of firmness. See *Arabic for Nerds 1, #50, #143.*

Such words have verbal power and can do the job of a verb (also re-garding the governing power). Therefore, the term وَصْفٌ is a **morpho-**

logical (مُصْطَلَحٌ صَرْفِيٌّ) and not a grammatical term (مُصْطَلَحٌ نَحْوِيٌّ).

If the وَصْف is placed as the <u>subject</u> (مُبْتَدَأ), it needs a word in the nominative case (اِسْمٌ مَرْفُوعٌ) to complete its meaning. This word is placed later in the sentence. Now we have all ingredients:

- The مُبْتَدَأ is linked to a **negation** (نَفْي) or **question** (اِسْتِفْهامٌ).
- The word after the مُبْتَدَأ is another subject (فاعِلٌ), but one that is governed by a noun with verbal power; a اِسْمُ الْفاعِلِ for example.
- If we have a passive meaning, the second subject is the نائِبٌ عَن الْفاعِلِ; it is governed by a passive participle (اِسْمُ الْمَفْعُولِ).

The careless individual will not succeed.	ما ناجِحٌ الْمُهْمِلُ.
Literally: not successful the careless.	

There are two ways to analyze this sentence (regarding the إِعْرابُ):

Negation particle (حَرْفُ نَفْي); does not have a place in إِعْرابٌ.		ما
A	**Subject I** (مُبْتَدَأ) of the nominal sent.; nominative (مَرْفُوعٌ). This is the وَصْف.	ناجِحٌ
	Subject II (فاعِلٌ), governed by the active participle (اِسْمُ الْفاعِلِ) which does the job of a verb and has similar power. The فاعِلٌ **takes over the role of the predicate** (خَبَرٌ) and thus takes the nominative (مَرْفُوعٌ) case In Arabic, we'd say: فاعِلٌ سَدَّ مَسَدَّ الْخَبَرِ. → See *question #37* for a deeper explanation of the concept called سَدَّ مَسَدَّ.	الْمُهْمِلُ

B	**Fronted predicate** (خَبَرٌ مُقَدَّمٌ); in the nominative case.	ناجِحٌ
	Delayed subject (مُبْتَدَأ مُؤَخَّرٌ), in the nominative (مَرْفُوعٌ).	الْمُهْمِلُ

In the following two examples, only one إِعْرابٌ is possible.

The two careless individuals don't succeed.	ما ناجِحانِ الْمُهْمِلانِ.
(The) careless people will not succeed.	ما ناجِحونَ الْمُهْمِلُونَ.

Fronted predicate (خَبَرٌ مُقَدَّمٌ). It must get the nominative case which is marked by the Aleph of the dual (مَرْفُوعٌ بِالْأَلِفِ) and the و of the plural (مَرْفُوعٌ بِالْوَاو) respectively.	نَاجِحَانِ
	نَاجِحُونَ
Delayed subject (مُبْتَدَأٌ مُؤَخَّرٌ) of the nominal sentence; therefore, it is in the nominative case by the Aleph of the dual and by the و of the plural respectively.	الْمُهْمِلَانِ
	الْمُهْمِلُونَ

Let's take another look at what actually happened in the last example. The وَصْفٌ, which is placed as the مُبْتَدَأٌ, must agree with its supplement (مَرْفُوعُهُ) in the dual and plural. For this reason, we can't إِعْرَابٌ the word after ما as a وَصْفٌ and the part that follows as the one overtaking the role of the predicate (خَبَرٌ). Instead, we say that it is the fronted predicate and what follows must be the delayed subject.

Why is that? The وَصْفٌ with its nominative supplement (مَرْفُوعُهُ) follows the rules of a verb. This makes sense since we have an active or passive participle serving as a substitute for the verb and thus working as a regent, operator (عَامِلٌ). The **verb**, as the rules tell us, **does not agree in the dual or plural** with its subject except in some classical dialects (a concept which is known as أَكَلُونِي الْبَرَاغِيثُ – see #20.)

Now what about the following two sentences?

The two careless people are not successful.	مَا نَاجِحٌ الْمُهْمِلَانِ.
(The) careless people are not successful.	مَا نَاجِحٌ الْمُهْمِلُونَ.

Also here, we only have one possibility for the إِعْرَابٌ. This time we can only apply the approach of the وَصْفٌ. In other words, there is no خَبَرٌ!

Negation particle (حَرْفُ نَفْيٍ); doesn't have a place in إِعْرَابٌ.	مَا
Subject I of the nominal sentence (مُبْتَدَأٌ مَرْفُوعٌ).	نَاجِحٌ
Subject II (فَاعِلٌ) which **takes over the role of the predicate** (سَدَّ مَسَدَّ الْخَبَرِ) of the primary nominal sentence. We could also say that it is a **replacement of the predicate.** It is in the nominative case by the Aleph of the dual.	الْمُهْمِلَانِ
Subject (فَاعِلٌ) which serves as a replacement **of the predicate** (سَدَّ مَسَدَّ الْخَبَرِ); in the nominative case by the و.	الْمُهْمِلُونَ

This إِعْرابٌ is necessary because the two words don't share the agreement in number (singular, plural, dual) and gender (غَيْرُ مُتطابِقَتَيْنِ).

We can't say that the first word is a خَبَرٌ مُقَدَّم and the second a مُبْتَدَأٌ مُؤَخَّر because they do not agree! It is impossible that the مُبْتَدَأُ is a dual or plural noun and the predicate is singular (مُفْرَدٌ). The same is true for the passive participle (اسْمُ الْمَفْعُولِ).

Are your (two) brothers popular?	أَمَحْبُوبٌ أَخَواكَ؟

Question particle (حَرْفُ اسْتِفْهامٍ); doesn't have a place in إِعْرابٌ.	أ
Subject (مُبْتَدَأٌ) of the nominal sentence; nominative (مَرْفُوعٌ).	مَحْبُوبٌ
The subject of the passive that is *supplying the place of the predicate* (نائِبُ فاعِلٍ سَدَّ مَسَدَّ الْخَبَرِ مَرْفُوعٌ بِالأَلِفِ). It is governed by the مُبْتَدَأُ and takes over the role of the predicate; it is in the nominative case by the Aleph of the dual.	أَخَوا
The ن of the dual ending is deleted. This happens in إِضافةٌ-constructions when the dual serves as the first part. The pronominal suffix (مُضافٌ إِلَيْهِ) serves as the second part (the ضَمِيرٌ مُتَّصِلٌ). Thus, كَ is located in the position of a genitive (في مَحَلِّ جَرًّ).	كَ

What happens if we have a quasi-participle (صِفةٌ مُشَبَّهةٌ)? It is similar.

Carelessness does not do good.	ما حَسَنٌ الْإِهْمالُ.

Negation particle (حَرْفُ نَفْيٍ); doesn't have a place in إِعْرابٌ.	ما
Subject (مُبْتَدَأٌ) of the nominal sentence; nominative (مَرْفُوعٌ).	حَسَنٌ
Subject (فاعِلٌ), governed by the مُبْتَدَأُ. This subject takes over the role of the predicate (and replaces it); therefore, it is in the nominative case (فاعِلٌ سَدَّ مَسَدَّ الْخَبَرِ مَرْفُوعٌ بِالضَّمَّةِ الظّاهِرةِ).	الْإِهْمالُ

The **second subject** in such constructions (= فاعِلٌ) completes the meaning together with the مُبْتَدَأُ. Sometimes, this doesn't work and we don't get a meaningful sentence. In such a situation, we need to find another way to analyze the sentence structure (إِعْرابٌ).

Are Karīm's (two) brothers successful?	أَنَاجِحٌ أَخَوَاهُ كَرِيمٌ؟

We can't treat ناجِحٌ as the subject (أُمْبْتَدَأٌ) and أَخَوَاهُ as the فاعِلٌ which would replace the predicate in the nominative case (فاعِلٌ سَدَّ مَسَدَّ الْخَبَرِ). These two fragments (أَنَاجِحٌ أَخَوَاهُ) don't offer a complete meaning. They don't get by without outside supply; they are is not self-contained.	

So, how could we understand this sentence grammatically?

أ	Question particle (حَرْفُ اِسْتِفْهامٍ); doesn't have a place in إِعْراب.
ناجِحٌ	Active participle that serves as the **fronted predicate** (خَبَرٌ مُقَدَّمٌ); in the nominative case (مَرْفُوعٌ بِالضَّمَّةِ الظَّاهِرةِ).
أَخَوَا	Subject (فاعِلٌ), governed by the active participle (ناجِحٌ), which has a power similar to a verb; in the nominative case by the Aleph of the dual (مَرْفُوعٌ بِالْأَلِفِ). First part of a إِضافةٌ, so the ن drops.
هُ	Pronominal suffix/connected pronoun (ضَمِيرٌ مُتَّصِلٌ); fixed shape (مَبْنِيٌّ عَلَى الضَّمِّ). It is in the position of a genitive case (فِي مَحَلِّ جَرٍّ) because it is the second part of a إِضافةٌ (مُضافٌ إِلَيْهِ).
كَرِيمٌ	**Delayed subject** (مُبْتَدَأٌ مُؤَخَّرٌ); nominative case (مَرْفُوعٌ).

We could rearrange this sentence to better understand its meaning:

Are Karīm's (two) brothers successful? (Do Karīm's (two) brothers succeed?)	أَكَرِيمٌ ناجِحٌ أَخَوَاهُ؟

211. هَلْ مِنْ رَجُلٍ فِي الْبَيْتِ؟ – What is the subject here?
It is رَجُلٍ.

Let's start with a general advice: don't pay too much attention to the case endings you see. In several situations, they will mislead you.

The subject (مُبْتَدَأٌ), for example, may even carry the visible markers of the genitive case. This is the situation when there is an extra, additional preposition (حَرْفُ جَرٍّ زائِدٌ) involved which is mainly there for stylistic purposes, i.e., to give emphasis.

Is there *anyone* at home?	هَلْ مِنْ رَجُلٍ فِي الْبَيْتِ؟

Question particle (حَرْفُ إِسْتِفْهامٍ); doesn't have a place in إِعْرابٌ.	هَلْ
Extra (some call it: *expletive*) preposition (حَرْفُ جَرٍّ زائِدٌ) that does not convey the meaning of a real preposition (i.e., directing).	مِنْ
Subject (مُبْتَدَأٌ) of the nominal sentence. It is in the position of a nominative case (مَرْفُوعٌ), although you can't see that by the visible case markers. It is in the nominative case by a hidden, presumptive ضَمّة which in Arabic grammar is called ضَمّةٌ مُقَدَّرةٌ. This had to be done because you are not allowed to put the actual case markers. That spot on the final letter is preoccupied by the preposition which dragged رَجُلٍ into the genitive case (مَجْرُورٌ). We say that the noun after that preposition is indeed مَجْرُورٌ due to the preposition مِنْ. But if that extra preposition was not there, رَجُلٌ would be مَرْفُوعٌ since this is the subject of the sentence.	رَجُلٍ
Prepositional phrase (جارٌّ وَمَجْرُورٌ) which appears in the place of the predicate. It is linked to a word (مُتَعَلِّقٌ بِمَحْذُوفٍ) that had to be deleted as it is understood anyway; for example, *present, existing* (مَوْجُودٌ). See *question #219* for more details about that.	فِي الْبَيْتِ

Allah is sufficient for you! (It is enough to mention Allah.)	نَاهِيكَ بِاللّهِ!
Meaning of the sentence:	اللّهُ نَاهِيكَ عَنْ طَلَبِ غَيْرِهِ لِأَنَّهُ كَافِيكَ.

Fronted predicate; it is in the nominative case although you can't put the marker on it (خَبَرٌ مُقَدَّمٌ مَرْفُوعٌ بِضَمّةٍ مُقَدَّرةٍ) due to the *heaviness* of the last letter (الثِّقَلُ). First part of the إِضافةٌ.	نَاهِي
Pronoun (ضَمِيرٌ مُتَّصِلٌ); serving as the second part of the إِضافةٌ.	ك
Extra preposition (حَرْفُ جَرٍّ زائِدٌ) to provide emphasis.	ب
Delayed subject (مُبْتَدَأٌ مُؤَخَّرٌ) of the nominal sentence. It is placed in the location of a nominative, but is not visibly marked as such. We have to use estimated case markers (مَرْفُوعٌ بِضَمّةٍ مُقَدَّرةٍ) because the spot of the case marker is preoccupied by the additional preposition which triggers the genitive case (مَجْرُورٌ).	اللّهِ

212. السَّابِقُونَ السَّابِقُونَ – Is that a sentence?

Yes, this is a nominal sentence (جُمْلةٌ اِسْميّةٌ).

It is a verse of the Qur'an. The first word is the subject (مُبْتَدَأٌ), and the second word is the predicate (خَبَرٌ):

| Sura 56:10 | And those in front – ahead indeed. | وَالسَّابِقُونَ السَّابِقُونَ. |

The Qur'an is a stylistic marvel. In everyday life, however, it can be useful to make such constructions more user-friendly. We could add a *pronoun of separation* (ضَميرُ الْفَصْلِ) between the subject (first word) and the predicate – but only, if both, **subject and predicate**, are **definite**. The pronoun separates the major components, makes it easier to understand and lays some **emphasis on the subject**. Since the pronoun is used to distinguish the predicate and clarify the subject, it is also called *pronoun of support* (ضَميرُ الْفَصْلِ).

The form of the pronoun (gender; number: singular/plural) solely depends on the subject. In the following example, هُمْ *(they)* is used.

| Sura 39:33 | Those are the righteous. | أُولَئِكَ هُمُ الْمُتَّقُونَ. |

213. *A dog is in the house.* How do you say that in Arabic?

The sentence is more complicated as you might think.

Let's try the obvious.

| Grammatically **wrong**. | كَلْبٌ فِي الْبَيْتِ. |
| **Correct** (or let's say at least better). | فِي الْبَيْتِ كَلْبٌ. |

The subject (مُبْتَدَأٌ) in a nominal sentence is typically a noun which is specific, known – and **definite** (مَعْرِفةٌ). Only if we know a thing, we can pronounce a verdict – which is the predicate.

Consider the sentence "*a child is eating.*" It is a pretty useless information because *a* child is simply too general. That is why the subject is usually definite. Nevertheless, there are situations when the مُبْتَدَأٌ may be indefinite (نَكِرةٌ). The most common are:

1. The **subject** (مُبْتَدَأٌ) is a word that **expresses generality**. This is the case when we have a word that represents an abstract or general idea.

all	كُلّ		who	مَنْ		what	ما

Sura 30:26	And all are obedient to Him.	كُلٌّ لَهُ قَانِتُونَ.

Subject (مُبْتَدَأٌ); nominative case (مَرْفُوعٌ بِالضَّمّةِ الظّاهِرةِ).	كُلٌّ
This لـ is a preposition (حَرْفُ الْجَرِّ); it does not have a place in إِعْرابٌ. The ه is indeclinable (ضَمِيرٌ مُتَّصِلٌ), so you don't see the actual case marker according to the position in the sentence – which would be that of a genitive case (فِي مَحَلِّ جَرٍّ) since it follows a preposition. The prepositional phrase (الْجارُّ وَالْمَجْرُورُ مُتَعَلِّقٌ بِالْخَبَرِ الْآتِي) is connected with the predicate which comes next.	لَهُ
Predicate (خَبَرٌ) which is in the nominative case by the و.	قَانِتُونَ

2. The **subject** (مُبْتَدَأٌ) is preceded by a **negation** (نَفْيٌ) or a **question word** (اِسْتِفْهامٌ).

Is there a dog in the house?	هَلْ كَلْبٌ فِي الْبَيْتِ؟
There is no dog in the house.	ما كَلْبٌ فِي الْبَيْتِ.

Negation particle (حَرْفُ نَفْي). It doesn't have a place in إِعْرابٌ.	ما
Subject (مُبْتَدَأٌ) in the nominative case (مَرْفُوعٌ).	كَلْبٌ
Prepositional phrase; linked to the deletion of the predicate.	فِي الْبَيْتِ

3. The **subject** (مُبْتَدَأٌ) is placed **after** the predicate (خَبَرٌ). Thus, the predicate is either a sentence or a prepositional/adverbial phrase (شِبْهُ الْجُمْلةِ). When the subject (مُبْتَدَأٌ) is **in**definite and there is only a شِبْهُ الْجُمْلةِ, you translate such nominal sentences with *there is/are*.

There is a dog in the house.	فِي الْبَيْتِ كَلْبٌ.

The quasi-sentence (شِـبْهُ الْجُمْلـةِ) supplies the position of the fronted predicate (خَبَرٌ مُقَدَّمٌ), so it is in the position of a nominative case (فِي مَحَلِّ رَفْعٍ). Don't forget that a prepositional phrase must be connected with another word in the sentence – however, in our example, that word had to be deleted because it is implicitly understood anyway since it points to a general state of being. We can well imagine that the verb *to be* is indirectly present.	فِي الْبَيْتِ
Delayed subject (مُبْتَدَأٌ مُؤَخَّرٌ), i.e., it comes after the predicate. It is in the nominative case (مَرْفُوعٌ بِالضَّمّةِ الظّاهِرةِ).	كَلْبٌ

Now, let's analyze a complicated sentence structure.

It is to your benefit to have a loyal friend.	نَفَعَكَ وَفاؤُهُ صَدِيقٌ.

Verb in the past tense (فِعْلٌ ماضٍ مَبْنِيٌّ عَلَى الْفَتْحِ).	نَفَعَ
Pronoun (ضَمِيرٌ مُتَّصِلٌ) serving as the direct object; placed in the position of an accusative case (فِي مَحَلِّ نَصْبٍ مَفْعُولٌ بِهِ).	ك
Subject (فاعِلٌ) of the verbal sentence; nominative (مَرْفُوعٌ).	وفاؤُ
Suffix (possessive) pronoun (ضَمِيرٌ مُتَّصِلٌ); it has a fixed shape. So we can't mark the case and can only say that it is placed in the position of a genitive case (فِي مَحَلِّ جَرٍّ) as it serves as the second part of a إضافة (i.e., the مُضافٌ إلَيْهِ).	ه
The verbal sentence (verb plus subject) is the **fronted predicate**; therefore, it is in the position of a nominative case (فِي مَحَلِّ رَفْعٍ خَبَرٌ مَقَدَّمٌ).	
Delayed subject (مُبْتَدَأٌ مُؤَخَّرٌ), in the nominative case (مَرْفُوعٌ).	صَدِيقٌ

4. The **subject** (مُبْتَدَأٌ) is **indefinite** (نَكِرَةٌ) but specified by some additional information. We can achieve this with some tricks.

a) The subject gets an **adjective** (= the subject is مَوْصُوفٌ).

A generous man is in the house.	رَجُلٌ كَرِيمٌ فِي الْبَيْتِ.

Subject (مُبْتَدَأٌ) of the nominal sentence; nominative (مَرْفُوعٌ).	رَجُلٌ

A dog is in the house. How do you say that in Arabic?

361

| This is <u>not</u> the predicate. It is simply an adjective (نَعْتٌ) for the subject – which explains why it also must get the مَرْفُوعٌ-case. | كَرِيمٌ |
| Prepositional phrase (الْجارُّ وَالْمَجْرُورُ) that is connected with the deleted **predicate** which is implicitly understood; e.g., the verb *to be/is* (الْجارُّ وَالْمَجْرُورُ مُتَعَلِّقٌ بِمَحْذُوفٍ واقِعٌ خَبَرًا فِي مَحَلِّ رَفْعٍ). | فِي الْبَيْتِ |

b) The subject is a **diminutive** (تَصْغِيرٌ).

| A young (lit. *small*) man is speaking. | رُجَيْلٌ يَتَحَدَّثُ. |
| رُجَيْلٌ is the subject (مُبْتَدَأٌ). This diminutive is treated as a word with an "implied adjective". It is like saying: رَجُلٌ صَغِيرٌ – similar to the example given in *a)*. The verbal sentence يَتَحَدَّثُ holds the position of the predicate (فِي مَحَلِّ رَفْعٍ خَبَرُ الْمُبْتَدَإِ). | |

c) The مُبْتَدَأٌ is the first part of a إضافةٌ.

| Two educated men talk. | رَجُلا عِلْمٍ يَتَناقَشانِ. |
| Subject (مُبْتَدَأٌ) in the nominative case by the Aleph of the dual. Since it is the first part (مُضافٌ) of a إضافةٌ, the ن drops. | رَجُلا |

d) The مُبْتَدَأٌ is a word (form) signifying an **invocation** (دُعاءٌ).

Victory for believers!	نَصْرٌ لِلْمُؤْمِنِينَ!
Subject in the nominative case (مُبْتَدَأٌ مَرْفُوعٌ).	نَصْرٌ
Prepositional phrase that appears in the place of the predicate. We need to assume the deleted, "original" predicate because we need to have a connection to another word as otherwise the prepositional phrase would be a neutral block (جارٌّ وَمَجْرُورٌ) (مُتَعَلِّقٌ بِمَحْذُوفٍ خَبَرٌ فِي مَحَلِّ رَفْعٍ).	لِلْمُؤْمِنِينَ

e) The مُبْتَدَأٌ is part of a **circumstantial clause** (جُمْلةُ الْحالِ).

| He was working, helped by a friend (and a friend was helping him). | كانَ يَعْمَلُ وَصَدِيقٌ يُساعِدُهُ. |

This is a so-called وَاوُ الْحالِ; it does not have a position in إِعْرابٌ.	وَ
Subject (مُبْتَدَأٌ) of the nominal sentence in the nominative.	صَديقٌ
This verbal sentence is in the position of the predicate; thus, it is located in the position of a nominative case (في مَحَلِّ رَفْعِ خَبَرٌ).	يُساعِدُهُ

f) The مُبْتَدَأٌ comes after فَ in the second part (complement) of a conditional sentence (الْفاءُ الْواقِعةُ في جَوابِ الشَّرْطِ).

If you are loyal, you will get loyalty.	إِنْ يَكُنْ مِنْكَ إِخْلاصٌ فَإِخْلاصٌ لَكَ.

This device is used to introduce the second part of a conditional sentence (الْفاءُ الْواقِعةُ في جَوابِ الشَّرْطِ). No position in إِعْرابٌ.	فَ
This is the subject (مُبْتَدَأٌ) in the nominative case (مَرْفُوعٌ).	إِخْلاصٌ
Prepositional phrase that supplies the place of the predicate; therefore, it is located in the position of a nominative case.	لَكَ

g) The subject (مُبْتَدَأٌ) is found after the word لَوْلا.

If not for the stinginess...	لَوْلا بُخْلٌ لِ...

Denial particle (حَرْفُ إِمْتِناعٍ لِلْوُجُودِ); doesn't have a place in إِعْرابٌ.	لَوْلا
مُبْتَدَأٌ; in the nominative case (مَرْفُوعٌ). What about the predicate? It has to be deleted in such sentences (الْخَبَرُ مَحْذُوفٌ وُجوبًا).	بُخْلٌ

Note: Despite all these fine rules, you may see an indefinite subject at the beginning of a sentence for **emphasis reasons**. This happens, for example, on book titles, movies, signs, etc. Eventually, we'll have an indefinite, single word starting a nominal sentence:

Greetings to Egypt!	سَلامٌ عَلَى مِصْرَا!
Woe is to those who condemn!	وَيْلٌ لِمَنْ يُدينُ!

214. You have money. You have *a lot* of money. Why does *a lot* give us some leverage in grammar?

The adjective gives you the possibility to play with the word order.

The sentence *You have money* does not allow us to play with the word order. There is only one possibility:

You have money.	عِنْدَكَ مالٌ.
The expression عِنْدَكَ is the predicate (خَبَرٌ); *money* is the subject (مُبْتَدَأٌ) of the nominal sentence. As seen in the previous *question #213*, if the subject is a **single <u>indefinite</u> word**, you shouldn't start the sentence with it!	

The second sentence (*You have **a lot of** money*) gives us another option. Why? If the **<u>indefinite</u>** subject (in our example: *money*) is accompanied by an adjective, we can play with the word order – because it is further qualified and not entirely indefinite anymore (see *#213, no. 4*).

You have a lot of money.	Both sentences are correct.	عِنْدَكَ مالٌ كَثِيرٌ.
		مالٌ كَثِيرٌ عِنْدَكَ.

215. What does word order signify?

As soon as we intervene and change the usual word order, we do so mainly for reasons of emphasis.

The main source of emphasis is the intonation of the speaker. If you want to give a clear indication what you want to emphasize, you should use additional words or particles. Word order, however, may also give the reader some hints what you want to stress on. It is worth looking at some rules for the **natural emphasis** in Arabic sentences – see also *Arabic for Nerds 1, question #28*.

- The **defined part usually precedes the undefined** because experience tells us that the sentence develops from the better known to the less known.

- The **logical emphasis** normally falls on the **second part of the sentence**. What is the logical emphasis? We said that the better known usually comes first; we get the "important" information first. The second part, however, is more exciting because it classifies and supplements the first bit of information. In that way the *natural emphasis* is on the first, but the logical emphasis is on the second part.

Karīm is in the mosque (not elsewhere).	كَرِيمٌ فِي الْمَسْجِدِ.
In the mosque is Karīm (not anyone else).	فِي الْمَسْجِدِ كَرِيمٌ.

- We usually pay attention to the **natural emphasis**. Thus, many people say that the emphasis follows the word order: what comes first is the most important thing and gets the emphasis.

- In Arabic, you can give the **predicate** an emphatic effect by placing it at the beginning.

This human being is miserable!	مِسْكِينٌ هٰذا الْإِنْسانُ!
Smoking is forbidden!	مَمْنُوعٌ التَّدْخِينُ!

216. What does *anacoluthon* mean?

It is a grammatical trick and basically means that we interrupt the usual sentence structure.

The word *anacoluthon* is of Greek origin and literally means *unfollowing*. In grammar, it denotes an unexpected discontinuity.

You may interrupt the natural grammatical construction of a sentence to give priority to a word. (German: *Satzbruch*). How does it work? You start a sentence, but soon after, you suddenly break it and start with a new idea. In English, such constructions are often grammatically weak or even wrong and used in spoken language. In Arabic, they are totally fine regarding the grammar and are frequently used. We call them sentences with two faces (جُمْلةٌ ذاتُ وَجْهَيْنِ); *see #220*. The operation itself is called **particularization** (إِخْتِصاصٌ).

So what do we have to do? We need to isolate the noun from the construction and shift it to the beginning. The isolated noun is represented in its proper role by an appropriate personal (or possessive) pronoun. Such a pronoun is called a رابِطٌ (binder). The results can be quite sophisticated and are often not easy to grasp. Some examples:

Zayd [he - and nobody else] is generous.	زَيْدٌ هُوَ كَرِيمٌ.
Zayd [he - and no one else] died.	زَيْدٌ ماتَ هُوَ.
Zayd [is the one who] has a book.	زَيْدٌ لَهُ كِتابٌ.
To Zayd I said…	زَيْدٌ قُلْتُ لَهُ...
Zayd, him has Muhammad struck. (Note: The ه here is the direct object.) If you are not sure, why Zy is in the nominative case, see *question #220*.	زَيْدٌ ضَرَبَهُ مُحَمَّدٌ.

What's the grammatical job of the pronoun (إِعْرابٌ)? Two common options:

1) You treat it as a neutral device (لا مَحَلَّ لَهُ مِن الإِعْرابِ). The pronoun is just there as an amplifier.
2) You charge it with a grammatical role in the sentence – see *questions #112, #113*, and *#222*.

In many situations, you can achieve the same effect by **inserting a possessive pronoun**.

This is Zayd's [no one else's] book.	زَيْدٌ هذا كِتابُهُ.
Karīm's income is big.	كَرِمٌ دَخْلُهُ كَبِيرٌ.

This is how we could rewrite the last sentence:

The income of Karīm is big.	دَخْلُ كَرِيمٍ كَبِيرٌ.

217. Can you delete the subject of a nominal sentence?

You can only do that if it is obvious what the subject is.

The subject (مُبْتَدَأ) is the essential part of a sentence. You can't think of a nominal sentence (جُمْلَةٌ اِسْمِيّةٌ) without a subject, so there must be one. Always? Almost always; in rare situations the مُبْتَدَأ can be deleted!

Grammarians call such an operation an ellipsis: a word that is omitted from a sentence, but at the same time is also necessary to make the sentence work grammatically. In the end, we save the game by saying that the deleted word is implicitly understood from the context. This is the situation when you answer a question. For example: *What is he doing?* And you answer: *traveling* (مُسافِرٌ). Here you don't have to mention the subject: *he* (هُوَ). Another example:

deleted subject (الْمُبْتَدَأُ الْمَحْذُوفُ)	predicate (خَبَرٌ) This is what you actually say:	meaning
هذا	الْمَطْلَبُ الْأَوَّلُ (...)	*first demand*

There are constructions in Arabic that even demand the deletion of the subject. We will examine such sentences later in this book.

الْمُبْتَدَأُ الْمَحْذُوفُ	predicate (خَبَرٌ)	meaning
هُوَ	أُحِبُّ الْفَاكِهَةَ لا سِيَّما (...) الْمشْمِشُ.	I love fruits, particularly apricots.
هُوَ	نِعْمَ الرَّجُلُ (...) زَيْدٌ!	What a great man Zayd is!

How should we analyze such sentences? The grammarians use several approaches for the إِعْرابٌ. Let's check the most common one.

Negation particle; so-called *Lā that denies the whole / Lā of absolute negation* (لا النّافِيَةُ لِلْجِنْسِ). No place in إِعْرابٌ.	لا
"Subject" or, more correctly, the noun of the absolute negation (اِسْمُ لا النّافِيَةِ لِلْجِنْسِ). In such constructions, the noun must be in the accusative case (مَنْصُوبٌ), marked by a فَتْحةٌ. First part of the إِضافةٌ.	سِيَّ
Relative pronoun which is a noun in Arabic (اِسْمٌ مَوْصُولٌ مَبْنِيٌّ). It has a fixed (indeclinable) shape, so we cannot mark it with case markers. We can only use virtual markers and say that it is grammatically located in the place of a genitive case since it is the second part of the compound construction (فِي مَحَلِّ جَرٍّ مُضافٌ إِلَيْهِ).	ما
This is the **predicate** of the <u>deleted</u> subject (خَبَرٌ لِمُبْتَدَأٍ مَحْذُوفٍ وُجُوبًا). The deleted subject has the **presumed meaning** of هُوَ and must be omitted in such constructions.	المشْمِشُ

➜ The sentence starting with the (deleted) subject and ending with the predicate is the relative clause (الْجُمْلةُ مِنَ الْمُبْتَدَإِ وَالْخَبَرِ صِلَةُ الْمَوْصُولِ). Note that a relative clause does not have a position in إِعْرابٌ.

The above sentence is super tricky because there is something else missing that was also deleted (but is still understood). We need to look at the underlying meaning of the **relative clause** (تَقْدِيرُ جُمْلةِ الصِّلةِ).

In this sentence, the **predicate** of **the absolute negation** (خَبَرُ لا النّافِية لِلْجِنْسِ) was **deleted**. It has the estimated, underlying meaning of: مَوْجُود (*present*). We will examine لا سِيَّما in *question #283* in depth.	لا سِيَّما هُوَ الْمَشْمِشُ.

THE PREDICATE (الْخَبَرُ)

218. What is the nature of the predicate (خَبَرٌ) in Arabic?

It is essentially a description (وَصْفٌ).

Subject and predicate do not mean first and second. They mean **primary** (subject) and **descriptive** (predicate). The predicate (خَبَرٌ) completes the meaning of a sentence and gets the nominative case (مَرْفُوعٌ). When someone uses the term *predicate* in Arabic, he or she usually talks about a nominal sentence (جُمْلةٌ اِسْميّةٌ). Some grammarians prefer a more universal view: the **primary part** (subject) is called مُسْنَدٌ إِلَيْهِ and the **descriptive part** (predicate) is known as مُسْنَدٌ – see #208.

Let's take a closer look at the nature and essence of the predicate. First of all, the main property: the خَبَرٌ is **indefinite** (نَكِرةٌ). If this is not the case, you need to fix the construction with a pronoun of separation (ضَمِيرُ الْفَصْلِ) – see *question #112*.

There are two major types of predicates: the خَبَرٌ can be a word (مُفْرَدٌ) or a sentence (جُمْلةٌ).

OPTION 1. The usual situation: the predicate is a **word** (الْمُفْرَدُ) which means that the predicate is not a sentence.

The predicate can be a إِسْمٌ...

a) ...which is not derived from a root (جَامِدٌ);

b) ...which is derived from a root (مُشْتَقٌّ).

a)	الْخَبَرُ الْجَامِدُ	The Pleiades is a star (cluster).	الثُّرَيّا نَجْمٌ.
	The word نَجْمٌ (*star*) doesn't have a connection to an Arabic root. In this example, it serves as the predicate in the nominative case (خَبَرٌ مَرْفُوعٌ بِالضَّمّةِ الظّاهِرة).		
b)	الْخَبَرُ الْمُشْتَقُّ	Karīm is hard-working.	كَرِيمٌ مُجْتَهِدٌ.
	Hard-working (مُجْتَهِدٌ) is derived from the root ج-ه-د which denotes *to strive*. مُجْتَهِدٌ functions as the predicate in the nominative case.		

Why do grammarians distinguish between جَامِدٌ and مُشْتَقٌّ?

The إِسْمٌ جَامِدٌ is a (static, inert) noun that was not taken from any-where else. This could be a *concrete noun* (إِسْمُ ذاتٍ) like جَبَلٌ (*mountain*) or it could be an abstract noun (إِسْمُ مَعْنًى) which is the pure, original مَصْدَرٌ of a root.

The grammarians say that the type of الْخَبَرُ الْجَامِدُ is unoccupied by – or let's say free from – the concealed pronoun (ضَمِيرٌ مُسْتَتِرٌ), whereas the الْخَبَرُ الْمُشْتَقُّ in most situations is nominative by a hidden pronoun that refers to the subject.

In a nutshell: the الْخَبَرُ الْمُشْتَقُّ has to be in grammatical agreement with the subject – which is not true for the type الْخَبَرُ الْجَامِدُ.

What is this mysterious connection between a pronoun and a الْمُشْتَقُّ? Let's check the importance of that pronoun by looking at its estimated meaning (تَقْدِيرٌ).

Karīm is hard-working.	كَرِيمٌ مُجْتَهِدٌ (هُوَ).
Why is that important? Let's imagine that instead of هُوَ, we use something different like in the example on the right. We would get: *Karīm's brother is diligent.*	كَرِيمٌ مُجْتَهِدٌ أَخُوهُ.
Knowledge is useful.	الْعِلْمُ نافِعٌ.

This is what the above sentence actually means:	الْعِلْمُ نافِعٌ هُوَ.

In this situation, the pronoun is the subject (فاعِلٌ) for *useful* (نافِعٌ). The word نافِعٌ is an active participle (اِسْمُ الْفاعِلِ) which has some verbal force and therefore can govern the subject or objects.   Another option: It could be interpreted as an emphasis (تَوْكِيدٌ) for the hidden, implied pronoun contained in the word itself (ضَمِيرٌ مُسْتَتِرٌ فِيهِ).

OPTION 2. The predicate is not a single word, but a nominal (جُمْلةٌ اِسْمِيّةٌ) or verbal sentence (جُمْلةٌ فِعْلِيّةٌ). Grammarians say الْخَبَرُ الْجُمْلةُ.

Zayd's character is noble.	زَيْدٌ خُلُقُهُ كَرِيمٌ.

There are two subjects (of nominal sentences) in this sentence because we have two nested sentences.

First **subject** in the nominative case (مَبْتَدَأٌ أَوَّلٌ مَرْفُوعٌ).	زَيْدٌ
Second **subject** in the nominative case (مُبْتَدَأٌ ثانٍ مَرْفُوعٌ). Also first part of the إضافةٌ.	خُلُقُ
Pronoun that has a fixed shape; it takes, nonetheless, the position of a genitive case (ضَمِيرٌ مُتَّصِلٌ مَبْنِيٌّ عَلَى الضَّمِّ فِي مَحَلِّ جَرٍّ).	٥
This is the **predicate** of the **second** subject; therefore in the nominative case (خَبَرُ الْمُبْتَدَإِ الثَّانِي مَرْفُوعٌ بِالضَّمّةِ الظّاهِرةِ) as well.	كَرِيمٌ
Where is the predicate of the **first subject**? It is the sentence, starting from the second subject plus its predicate (= خُلُقُهُ كَرِيمٌ). The entire sentence is located in the slot of a nominative case (فِي مَحَلِّ رَفْعٍ خَبَرُ الْمُبْتَدَإِ الْأَوَّلِ).

Karīm speaks German.	كَرِيمٌ يَتَحَدَّثُ الْأَلْمانِيّةَ.

First subject of the **nominal sentence**; in the nominative (مُبْتَدَأٌ مَرْفُوعٌ بِالضَّمّةِ الظّاهِرةِ).	كَرِيمٌ
Present tense verb, indicative mood (مَرْفُوعٌ). The subject (فاعِلٌ) of the verbal sentence is a concealed, implied pronoun (ضَمِيرٌ مُسْتَتِرٌ) which has the implicit meaning of هُوَ.	يَتَحَدَّثُ

Notice: The **predicate** of this nominal sentence is supplied by the **verbal sentence** (الْجُمْلَةُ مِنَ الْفِعْلِ وَالْفَاعِلِ فِي مَحَلِّ رَفْعِ خَبَرٍ): *he speaks (German).*

Watch out: It is possible to have an exclamation (جُمْلَةٌ إِنْشَائِيَّةٌ) in the position of the predicate. Such a sentence is a more forceful version of a standard, declarative sentence (جُمْلَةٌ خَبَرِيَّةٌ). An exclamatory sentence makes a statement just like a declarative sentence, but it also conveys excitement or emotion. An exclamatory sentence usually ends with an exclamation mark: !

(Here is) the book, read it!	الْكِتَابُ إِقْرَأْهُ!

Subject (مُبْتَدَأٌ) of the nominal sentence; nominative (مَرْفُوعٌ) case.	الْكِتَابُ
Verb in the imperative mood (فِعْلُ أَمْرٍ) which is also the reason why the last letter is fixed on the سُكُونٌ. It also means that we have a verbal sentence with an implied pronoun (ضَمِيرٌ مُسْتَتِرٌ), standing for أَنْتَ, and functioning as the subject (فَاعِلٌ).	إِقْرَأْ
Pronoun (ضَمِيرٌ مُتَّصِلٌ) referring back to *the book*. The pronoun has an indeclinable form, however, it takes the position of an accusative (نَصْبٌ) because it serves as the **direct object** (مَفْعُولٌ بِهِ).	هُ
What about the predicate? It is إِقْرَأْهُ (verb+subject+[object]) which is placed in the location of a nominative (الْجُمْلَةُ مِنَ الْفِعْلِ وَالْفَاعِلِ فِي مَحَلِّ رَفْعٍ خَبَرٌ).	

The Crashing Blow! What is the Crashing Blow?	الْقَارِعَةُ، مَا الْقَارِعَةُ؟
Note: This is a reference to a story in the Qur'an (101:1-2). It deals with the coming of the Last Hour. Muslims believe that it will involve a terrifying transformation of the world.	

This is the **first subject** (مُبْتَدَأٌ أَوَّلٌ مَرْفُوعٌ).	الْقَارِعَةُ
This is a **question word** (اسْمُ اسْتِفْهَامٍ) and not a negation. Now, don't get confused! It takes the position of the **fronted predicate** of the <u>second subject</u>; therefore, it is located in the spot of a nominative (فِي مَحَلِّ رَفْعٍ خَبَرٌ مُقَدَّمٌ لِلْمُبْتَدَإِ الثَّانِي).	مَا
Delayed second subject (مُبْتَدَأٌ ثَانٍ مُؤَخَّرٌ); nominative case.	الْقَارِعَةُ

Now, we need to concentrate for a moment. The entire second part of the sentence (fronted predicate plus delayed [second] subject = مَا الْقَارِعَةُ) is the **predicate** of the **first subject**. Grammatically speaking, the entire second part takes the place of a nominative case (خَبَرُ الْمُبْتَدَإِ الْأَوَّلِ فِي مَحَلِّ رَفْعٍ).

219. Can a prepositional phrase (شِبْهُ الْجُمْلةِ) be the predicate?

Yes, it can – but it is complicated.

In a nominal sentence (جُمْلةٌ إسْمِيّةٌ), the prepositional or adverbial phrase (شِبْهُ الْجُمْلةِ) supplies the position of the predicate (خَبَر) and is often simply called the predicate. That's fine. But that's not all.

We also say that the prepositional phrase (شِبْهُ الْجُمْلةِ) is connected with a deleted word. There is a reasonable logic behind that. Let's imagine that a شِبْهُ الْجُمْلةِ is a detached block that needs to be connected with the sentence. It is like a trailer that carries important things, but is not part of the car. However, it is connected to the car by a trailer hitch, a rope or a chain. The prepositional or adverbial phrase (شِبْهُ الْجُمْلةِ) is like the trailer – and the connector that binds it to the main part is the word that conveys the action (usually the verb). The information that a شِبْهُ الْجُمْلةِ carries is usually related to time or place.

Sounds good. There is only one big problem: in a nominal sentence, there is no verb *to be*. The predicate was deleted because it points to a general state of being (كَوْنٌ عامٌ), i.e, *to be found, to be present*, and all variants of *to be*. But it is exactly this deleted word, the "original" predicate, to which a شِبْهُ الْجُمْلةِ relates.

How can we solve this elegantly? We need to look for an appropriate verb or word with verbal force that may stand for the deleted word (= the original predicate).

The student (...) in the class.	الطَّالِبُ (...) فِي الْفَصْلِ.
A tree (...) before the house.	أمامَ الْبَيْتِ (...) شَجَرَةٌ.
In your mind, you can fill the points (...) with *is, is found, is located*. These expressions would also be used in an English translation.	

Purist grammarians say that a prepositional phrase can neither be the subject nor the predicate of a sentence. They say that the **deleted word itself is the predicate**, and the prepositional phrase is just linked with it. Other scholars, on the other hand, say that it is okay if you say that the prepositional phrase *is* the predicate (خَبَرٌ) if you add the explanation that the خَبَر is *"connected with (attached to) a deleted word"*. At the end, it is an academic discussion.

What happens, if the predicate points to a special state of being or a special occurrence (كَوْنٌ خاصٌّ)? → The predicate must be mentioned!

Karīm is sleeping at home.	كَرِيمٌ نائِمٌ فِي الْبَيْتِ.
In the above example, you can't delete the predicate, unless you want to express a different meaning.	

Let's focus on the grammatical analysis if the predicate is omitted.

The student is in the class.	الطَّالِبُ فِي الْفَصلِ.
Subject in the nominative case (مُبْتَدَأٌ مَرْفُوعٌ).	الطَّالِبُ
Preposition (حَرْفُ الْجَرِّ); doesn't have a position in إِعْرابٌ.	فِي
Noun in the genitive case (مَجْرُورٌ) due to the preposition.	الْفَصلِ

The entire prepositional phrase (شِبْهُ الْجُمْلةِ) is linked to a deleted predicate which is implicitly understood in Arabic – the verb *to be* (*is*).

Is this all just an academic discussion? Yes and no. There is a difference between being a part of the predicate and being related or connected with it (مُتَعَلِّقٌ بِ). Let's analyze the following sentence:

Karīm ate at home.	كَرِيمٌ أَكَلَ فِي الْبَيْتِ.
Would you say that the predicate (خَبَرٌ) is أَكَلَ alone or أَكَلَ فِي الْبَيْتِ? This **is a debate**. The verb أَكَلَ is the predicate (خَبَرٌ), for sure.	
Some grammarians state that فِي الْبَيْتِ is the predicate too. Others suggest that it is not the predicate, but "only" related to the verb (مُتَعَلِّقٌ). I follow the latter view as it sounds more logical to me. Why?	

- In terms of meaning, they belong to each other for sure;

- In terms of grammar (إِعْرابٌ), the verb does nothing to the preposi-tional phrase (الْجارُّ وَالْمَجْرُورُ) because the verb does not govern it. The prepositional phrase is not a *patient* – it doesn't have a place in إِعْرابٌ.
- In this book, however, I occasionally call the prepositional phrase the predicate as I don't want to be over-academic.

There is another way to understand the logic of a شِبْهُ الْجُمْلةِ:

- Let's assume that both the verb أَكَلَ and the prepositional phrase فِي الْبَيْتِ are predicates. Then, we try to remove each of them in sequence and see what is left.
- By **removing the second "predicate"** (فِي الْبَيْتِ), the sentence be-comes: كَرِيمٌ أَكَلَ ➡ This is essentially the same as the original sentence, only with less details.
- By **removing the first predicate** (أَكَلَ), the sentence becomes: كَرِيمٌ فِي الْبَيْتِ ➡ This conveys a completely different meaning than the original sentence. This, in turn, shows that the prepositional phrase cannot be treated as a predicate. It must necessarily be connected to the true predicate and its only function is to provide more details about that predicate – and **not about the subject!**

Let's dig deeper. If we have an **adverb of time** (ظَرْفُ الزَّمانِ), it gets more complicated. It can only be linked to a predicate if the subject is a *noun of action* (اِسْمُ حَدَثٍ). This means that the subject must be a مَصْدَرٌ. Let's first look at a sentence that doesn't cause any issue.

| The test (the testing) is tomorrow. | الْإِخْتِبارُ غَدًا. |

إِخْتِبارٌ is the مَصْدَرٌ of the VIII-verb اِخْتَبَرَ - يَخْتَبِرُ (*to test*). The word إِخْتِبارٌ ex-presses at least some kind of action: *testing*.

However, the following sentences, which have a proper noun (name) as the subject (مُبْتَدَأٌ), are not correct and don't make sense at all.

| Muhammad (???) today. | مَحَمَّدٌ الْيَوْمَ. |
| Karīm (???) tomorrow. | كَرِيمٌ غَدًا. |

In general, adverbial phrases cannot be linked to proper nouns. As always, there are exceptions. The situation, for example, is different if the sentence can be interpreted:

The crescent (new moon) is tonight.	الْهِلالُ اللَّيْلَةَ.

This is the subject in the nominative case (مُبْتَدَأً مَرْفُوعٌ).	الْهِلالُ
Adverb of time (ظَرْفُ زَمانٍ) in the accusative case (مَنْصُوبٌ).	اللَّيْلَةَ

Some call the adverb (ظَرْفُ زَمانٍ) in the above example the predicate in the nominative case. That's understandable, but would leave the logical framework of Arabic grammar. I prefer to say that it appears in the place of the predicate (فِي مَحَلِّ رَفْعٍ خَبَرٌ). The adverb needs to be connected with a verb: an **action**. We should correctly say that the ظَرْفُ شِبْهُ الْجُمْلَةِ is related to the deleted predicate (مُتَعَلِّقٌ بِمَحْذُوفٍ). How can we mingle some action into this sentence? We need a مَصْدَرٌ!

The viewing of the crescent is tonight.	رُؤْيَةُ الْهِلالِ اللَّيْلَةَ.
Now everything is fine. The adverb is linked to an action.	

Remark: The prepositional or adverbial phrase is not a full sentence. It is *resembling a sentence* which is the reason why the grammarians use the general term شِبْهُ الْجُمْلَةِ because شِبْهٌ denotes *similar to, a kind of*.

220. When does the predicate have to be a sentence?

There are certain types of subjects (مُبْتَدَأٌ) that demand a sentence as a predicate (خَبَرٌ).

Examples are best for understanding the issues. So let's go through the most important situations.

SITUATION I. The **pronoun of the fact** (ضَمِيرُ الشَّأْنِ); also called *pronoun of general reference.*

Sura 112:1	• Say, "He is God, the One." (*Abdul Haleem*) • Say, "He is Allah, [who is] One." (*Sahīh Int.*) قُلْ هُوَ اللّٰهُ أَحَدٌ.

Pronoun of the fact (ضَمِيرُ الشَّأْنِ). The pronoun is indeclinable. It always looks the same no matter what function it has. Here, هُوَ serves as the **subject** and is located in the spot of a nominative (فِي مَحَلِّ رَفْعٍ مُبْتَدَأً). We assign the "place value" of a nominative case.	هُوَ
This is the <u>second</u> **subject** (مُبْتَدَأٌ ثَانٍ); nominative case.	اللهُ
Predicate of the <u>second</u> subject (خَبَرُ الْمُبْتَدَإِ الثَّانِي), in the nominative case (مَرْفُوعٌ بِالضَّمَّةِ الظَّاهِرَةِ).	أَحَدٌ
What about the predicate of the <u>first</u> subject? In our example, it is the clause consisting of the second subject plus its predicate (اللهُ أَحَدٌ) which serves as the predicate of the first subject (فِي مَحَلِّ رَفْعٍ خَبَرُ الْمُبْتَدَإِ الْأَوَّلِ).	

SITUATION II. Conditional words that are placed as the subject of a nominal sentence (اسْمُ الشَّرْطِ الْوَاقِعُ مُبْتَدَأً). The predicate of this kind of subject is a conditional sentence (جُمْلَةُ الشَّرْطِ).

Watch out for the correct mood of the verb!

Whoever (everyone who) studies, will succeed.	مَنْ يُذَاكِرْ يَنْجَحْ.

Conditional device (اسْمُ شَرْطٍ). It is indeclinable (مَبْنِيٌّ), you can't put a case marker on it. Nonetheless, it serves in the position of the **subject** in a nominative case (فِي مَحَلِّ رَفْعٍ مُبْتَدَأً).	مَنْ
Verb (فِعْلٌ مُضَارِعٌ) in the (مَجْزُومٌ)-mood (notice the سُكُونٌ) because it is a verb expressing a conditional meaning (فِعْلُ شَرْطٍ). Subject (فَاعِلٌ) is an implied pronoun (ضَمِيرٌ مُسْتَتِرٌ): *he* (هُوَ).	يُذَاكِرْ
The verbal sentence (= يُذَاكِرْ) serves as the **predicate** (الْجُمْلَةُ مِنَ الْفِعْلِ وَالْفَاعِلِ) for the subject مَنْ. (فِي مَحَلِّ رَفْعٍ خَبَرٌ)	

SITUATION III. The **verbs of praise and blame** (أَفْعَالُ الْمَدْحِ وَالذَّمِّ): the tricky words نِعْمَ and بِئْسَ when they don't start a sentence.

We get this situation when the word which is targeted by the verbs نِعْمَ or بِئْسَ (الْمَخْصُوصُ بِالْمَدْحِ أَوْ الذَّمِّ) is shifted to the front (مُقَدَّمٌ).

What an excellent leader Khālid is!	خَالِدٌ نِعْمَ الْقَائِدُ!

Subject (أُمُبْتَدَأٌ) of the <u>nominal</u> sentence in the nominative case.	خَالِدٌ
Past tense verb; by definition fixed on the *"a"* (مَبْنِيٌّ عَلَى الْفَتْحِ).	نِعْمَ
Subject (فَاعِلٌ) of the verbal sentence; nominative case (مَرْفُوعٌ).	الْقَائِدُ

Note: The **predicate** of the subject of the primary, <u>nominal</u> sentence is the entire verbal sentence (الْجُمْلَةُ مِنَ الْفِعْلِ وَالْفَاعِلِ فِي مَحَلِّ رَفْعٍ خَبَرٌ). Therefore, the expression نِعْمَ الْقَائِدُ is the predicate.

Question: In the above example, why don't we need a pronoun as a connector (رَابِطٌ)? The rules state that this is not required here because the **predicate** (خَبَرٌ) is wider, let's say, more general in its signification than the أُمُبْتَدَأٌ. This is true in our example: "What an **excellent leader** Khālid is".

SITUATION IV. كَأَيِّنْ (also written as كَأَيٍّ) serves as the subject (أُمُبْتَدَأٌ).

You may not encounter كَأَيِّنْ often, but the word is already used in the Qur'an. كَأَيِّنْ conveys the meaning of *many a...* or *how many a...* (تَكْثِيرٌ الْعَدَدِ). It basically means كَثِيرٌ مِنْ. The word كَأَيِّنْ is similar to كَمْ, the so-called كَمِ الْخَبَرِيَّةِ, which is not used in questions – see #206.

What kind of word is كَأَيِّنْ? It is a compound noun (اِسْمٌ مُرَكَّبٌ) produced by the letter كَ (so-called كَافُ التَّشْبِيهِ) plus the word *who/which* (أَيّ). The word أَيّ is a اِسْمٌ and gets case inflections (تَنْوِينٌ). Since it follows the letter ك, the word أَيّ is in the genitive case (مَجْرُورٌ). What about the نـ? It is a remnant. It is what's left of the nunation (تَنْوِينٌ) of the genitive case (تَنْوِينُ كَسْرٍ). Hence, the original word is كَأَيٍّ. In poetry, you may encounter even the spelling كَائِنْ.

Since we treat the word as a noun (اِسْمٌ), it takes the case ending according to its position in the sentence. كَأَيِّنْ may work as an absolute object (مَفْعُولٌ مُطْلَقٌ), a direct object (مَفْعُولٌ بِهِ), the subject of a nominal sentence (أُمُبْتَدَأٌ), an adverb (ظَرْفٌ), etc. In the following examples, the word كَأَيِّنْ serves in different positions:

مَفْعُولٌ بِهِ	I read many books.	كَأَيِّنْ مِنْ كِتَابٍ قَرَأْتُ.
ظَرْفُ زَمَانٍ	I have stayed up many nights.	كَأَيِّنْ مِنْ لَيْلَةٍ سَهِرْتُ.
مَفْعُولٌ مُطْلَقٌ	We have paid you many visits.	كَأَيِّنْ مِنْ زِيَارَةٍ زُرْنَاكَ.

What is placed after كَأَيِّنْ is a specification (تَمْيِيزٌ). This is similar to كَمْ. Why do we see the genitive case then? You will almost always see كَأَيِّنْ together with the preposition مِنْ dragging the word, which would otherwise take the accusative case of a *specification*, into the genitive case.

So far, so good. Now we need to look at a peculiarity. If كَأَيِّنْ serves as the subject (مُبْتَدَأٌ), then the predicate can never be just a word. It has to be a **sentence** or a **quasi-sentence** (شِبْهُ الْجُمْلةِ).

When do we get كَأَيِّنْ to serve as the subject (مُبْتَدَأٌ)?

A. If there is an intransitive verb (فِعْلٌ لازِمٌ) later in the sentence. Intransitive means that it cannot have a direct object.

Many a great men have died.	كَأَيِّنْ مِنْ عَظِيمٍ ماتَ.

كَأَيِّنْ is the subject (مُبْتَدَأٌ) and gets the place value of a nominative case.	كَأَيِّنْ
Additional preposition (حَرْفُ جَرٍّ زائِدٌ). It does not have a position in إِعْرابٌ. In Arabic, we say: لا مَحَلَّ لَهُ مِنَ الْإِعْرابِ.	مِنْ
The visible case endings tell us that it is in the genitive case (اِسْمٌ مَجْرُورٌ لَفْظًا) due to the preposition – according to its position, however, it is in the accusative because it is a specification for the word كَأَيِّنْ (اِسْمٌ مَجْرُورٌ لَفْظًا مَنْصُوبٌ مَحَلًّا عَلَى أَنَّهُ تَمْيِيزٌ لِكَأَيِّنْ).	عَظِيمٍ
Past tense (intransitive) verb. The verbal sentence (verb plus implied subject *he*) is located in the position of a nominative case because it is the predicate (فِي مَحَلِّ رَفْعٍ خَبَرُ كَأَيِّنْ).	ماتَ

B. We don't have a word. We only have a quasi-sentence (شِبْهُ الْجُمْلةِ).

Many a stars are in the sky.	كَأَيِّنْ مِنْ نَجْمةٍ فِي السَّماءِ.

C. We have a transitive verb that took its object إِذا جاءَ بَعْدَها فِعْلٌ (مُتَعَدٍّ اِسْتَوْفَى مَفْعُولَهُ).

| How many a sick people Allah healed! | كَأَيِّنْ مِنْ مَرِيضٍ شَفَاهُ اللَّهُ! |
| For a better understanding we can restate it: → | كَمْ مِنْ مَرِيضٍ شَفَاهُ اللَّهُ! |

This compound noun (اِسْمٌ مُرَكَّبٌ) serves as the **subject** (مُبْتَدَأٌ) of the جُمْلَةٌ إِسْمِيَّةٌ. It is located in the position of a nominative case (فِي مَحَلِّ رَفْعٍ). We can't mark the word as such because it has a fixed, indeclinable shape (مَبْنِيٌّ). We can only assign a place value, i.e., that of a nominative case.	كَأَيِّنْ
Prepositional phrase which is related to (جَارٌّ وَمَجْرُورٌ مُتَعَلِّقٌ) كَأَيِّنْ (بِكَأَيِّنْ) and is, in fact, placed as a specification (تَمْيِيزٌ).	مِنْ مَرِيضٍ
Past tense verb, third person singular. The last root letter ى of the I-verb يَشْفِي - شَفَى (R3 = ي; *to heal*) turns into ا when we attach a ه. So we can't use the usual فَتْحَةٌ as this is impossible (التَّعَذُّرُ) – see *question #39*. The ه is a pronoun suffix (ضَمِيرٌ مُتَّصِلٌ) and serves as the direct object (مَفْعُولٌ بِهِ); it is indeclinable; therefore, it is in the accusative case only by a "place value".	شَفَاهُ
Subject (فَاعِلٌ) of the verbal sentence, nominative.	اللَّهُ
Where is the predicate (خَبَرٌ) of the primary nominal sentence? It is the entire verbal sentence: شَفَاهُ اللَّهُ.	

Excursus: A special situation: what is the predicate (خَبَرٌ) if we have a particularization after the subject (الْمُبْتَدَأُ فِي أُسْلُوبِ الْإِخْتِصَاصِ)?

To put it more practically, we deal with a phrase in which a pronoun (usually of the first person: *we; I*) is followed by a noun. That pronoun functions as the subject (مُبْتَدَأٌ). It will be further determined by the next word: the **specification** or **particularization** of the pronoun.

| We Arabs (*literally: we, (I mean) the Arabs*) honor the guest. | نَحْنُ - الْعَرَبَ - نُكْرِمُ الضَّيْفَ. |

الْعَرَبَ is in the accusative (مَنْصُوبٌ) case which indicates that it is perhaps not the predicate (خَبَرٌ). Since we don't see a verb, why does الْعَرَبَ get the accusative case? The verb, which operates on it, is deleted! We have an ellipsis expressing: *I mean* (أَعْنِي) or *I specify* (أَخُصُّ).

The noun in the accusative case is, in fact, the direct object (مَفْعُولٌ بِهِ) of the omitted verb.

الضَّيْفَ	نُكْرِمُ	الْعَرَبَ	(...)	نَحْنُ
direct object of the verb *we honor*	verb (فِعْلٌ) with implied subject (فاعِلٌ مُسْتَتِرٌ)	direct object of the verb which we assume was deleted مَفْعُولٌ بِهِ لِفِعْلٍ مَحْذُوفٍ	**deleted verb;** implied subject (فِعْلٌ مَحْذُوفٌ)	subject (مُبْتَدَأٌ)
PREDICATE (خَبَرُ الْمُبْتَدَإِ)		circumstantial description of the subject; it gets the "place value" of an accusative case (فِي مَحَلِّ نَصْبٍ حالٌ).		**subject** (مُبْتَدَأٌ)

Personal pronoun (ضَمِيرٌ مُنْفَصِلٌ); placed in the position of the subject of a nominal sentence (فِي مَحَلِّ رَفْعٍ مُبْتَدَأٌ).	نَحْنُ
Direct object (مَفْعُولٌ بِهِ) of the **omitted** verb which would have the equivalent of *I specify* (أَخُصُّ); accusative case (مَنْصُوبٌ).	الْعَرَبَ
Present tense verb (فِعْلٌ مُضارِعٌ); indicative mood (مَرْفُوعٌ). The subject (فاعِلٌ) is an implied pronoun (ضَمِيرٌ مُسْتَتِرٌ): *we* (نَحْنُ).	نُكْرِمُ
The predicate is expressed by نُكْرِمُ, an **entire sentence** (verb plus implied subject)و which supplies the position of the predicate and is thus located in the spot of a nominative case (الْجُمْلَةُ مِنَ الْفِعْلِ وَالْفاعِلِ فِي مَحَلِّ رَفْعٍ خَبَرٌ).	

221. What is a sentence with two faces?

A sentence that may have a nominal or verbal nature.

Let's start with a quiz. Which of the two examples is correct?

Zayd's father slept, and I chased the dog away.	زَيْدٌ نامَ أَبُوهُ وَالْكَلْبُ طَرَدْتُهُ.	1
	زَيْدٌ نامَ أَبُوهُ وَالْكَلْبَ طَرَدْتُهُ.	2

Answer: **both are correct.** Two grammatical concepts compete here: primacy of the first word (الصَّدْرُ) versus missing verb (الْعَجْزُ). It is a matter of taste. The grammatical analysis, however, is entirely different and intriguing. It is a quite complicated structure.

- We have a nominal sentence (جُمْلةٌ اِسْمِيّةٌ) whose predicate is a verbal sentence (جُمْلةٌ فِعْلِيّةٌ).

- The second sentence الْكَلْبُ طَرَدْتُها has two "personalities". Grammarians call that a *sentence with two faces* or *aspects* (جُمْلةٌ ذاتُ وَجْهَيْنِ) as the sentence combines a nominal and verbal nature.

For the analysis (إِعْرابٌ), only the last part matters. There are two options. Both are correct. It is up to your taste.

Option 1. The last part is a **nominal** sentence: الْكَلْبُ طَرَدْتُهُ

الْكَلْبُ (*dog*) is the **subject** (مُبْتَدَأٌ) and the part with the <u>verb,</u> طَرَدْتُهُ (*to chase away, to expel*), is the **predicate**.

Together they form a **nominal sentence** (جُمْلةٌ اِسْمِيّةٌ) which is **coupled** with the **first nominal sentence** (:زَيْدٌ مَعْطُوفة عَلَى الْجُمْلةِ الْإِسْمِيّةِ نامَ أَبُوهُ). ▷ We are allowed to use the nominative case because it starts a nominal sentence (صَدْرُ الْجُمْلةِ).

Option 2. The last part is a **verbal** sentence: الْكَلْبَ طَرَدْتُهُ

الْكَلْبَ (*dog*) is the **direct object** (مَفْعُولٌ بِهِ). Wait a second!

Where is the verb that is responsible for that? Why are we allowed to use the accusative case here? If there wouldn't be a pronoun at the end of the verb (which serves as the direct object here already), it would be easy: the verb (طَرَدْتُ) is the regent (عامِلٌ) that operates on *dog* (الْكَلْب) and ignites the accusative case.

Since there's a pronoun connected to the verb, the regent or operator (عامِلٌ) is **occupied** and does not have enough power to deal with two direct objects. How can we fix that? Well, we assume, that the very same verb is implicitly there (again) to deal with the word *dog* (مَنْصُوبٌ بِفِعْلٍ مَحْذُوفٍ يُفَسِّرُهُ الَّذِي بَعْدَهُ). So, practically speaking, we assume the following verbal sentence: طَرَدْتُ الْكَلْبَ

This verbal sentence (جُمْلةٌ فِعْلِيّةٌ) is "coupled" (مَعْطُوفةٌ عَلَى الْجُمْلةِ) with the other verbal sentence: نامَ أَبُوهُ (الْفِعْلِيّةِ)

222. When can the predicate do without a connector (رابِطٌ)?

In three situations.

Let's start with the obvious: you never need a connector if a single word serves as the predicate (خَبَرٌ). Now, if the خَبَرٌ is made of a sentence (جُمْلَةٌ), the situation changes: you suddenly need to link this sentence with the subject. The خَبَر-sentence must contain a **binder** or **connector** (رابِط) that refers back to the subject (مُبْتَدَأٌ). Otherwise, it is not a correct Arabic sentence.

If we have a **verbal sentence** (جُمْلَةٌ فِعْلِيَّةٌ) serving as the predicate, it is an easy task because the verb itself contains a hidden pronoun (ضَمِيرٌ مُسْتَتِرٌ) which is the subject (فاعِلٌ) of the verb – and which also connects to the subject (مُبْتَدَأٌ) of the primary nominal sentence. This is possible because the two subjects refer to the same person:

Zayd **(he) writes a book.**	زَيْدٌ يَكْتُبُ كِتابًا.
Here, we don't need to insert an extra pronoun. The verb and its hidden, implied pronoun (= subject) does that job.	

The situation is different when the خَبَرٌ is a nominal sentence (جُمْلَةٌ اسْمِيَّةٌ). We need a quick surgery: we insert a connector in the خَبَرٌ that links both parts. This can be achieved by a *referential, returning pronoun* (ضَمِيرٌ عائِدٌ) that refers to the subject and agrees with it (*see #116*).

Zayd has a generous character.	زَيْدٌ خُلُقُهُ كَرِيمٌ.

The pronoun ه is the necessary binder (رابِط) to link both parts. The رابِط represents the word which works as the subject (مُبْتَدَأٌ). There are two situations when you can do without a رابِط.

SITUATION 1. You **repeat** the subject (إعادةُ الْمُبْتَدَإِ) and use **the same word** (تَكْرارُ الْمُبْتَدَإِ بِلَفْظِهِ) in the second part of the sentence. This is the strongest possible connector. A pronoun is a weaker connector. Why? Because the pronoun only **refers** to the مُبْتَدَأ. It is not the مُبْتَدَأ itself.

Sura 69:1-2	The Inevitable Reality, what is it [the Inevitable Reality]?	الْحَاقَّةُ، مَا الْحَاقَّةُ؟

The repetition of the مُبْتَدَأ is frequently used as a stylistic tool, mainly to amplify (تَفْخِيمٌ), but also for intimidation (تَهْوِيلٌ). The second repetition stands for: ما هُوَ؟ or ما هِيَ؟

الْحَاقَّةُ is the **first subject** (مُبْتَدَأ) of the primary (nominal) sentence. The second nominal sentence (= مَا الْحَاقَّةُ) is the predicate of the first subject. Now what about the ما? It is the subject of the second sentence (مُبْتَدَأ ثانٍ). This time, الْحَاقَّةُ serves as the **predicate** of the second subject. The connector between subject and predicate of the larger sentence is the apparent repetition of the subject (i.e., الْحَاقَّةُ).

SITUATION 2. The **referring (suffix) pronoun** can be **anticipated**. You can omit it when the sense is perfectly clear without it (مَعْلُومٌ).

An Ukka of grapes costs 5 lira.	الْعِنَبُ أُقَّةٌ بِخَمْسِ لِيراتٍ.

First subject in the nominative case (مُبْتَدَأ أَوَّلٌ مَرْفُوعٌ).	الْعِنَبُ
Ukka is a weight measure (1.248 kg in Egypt); here it is the second subject; nominative case (مُبْتَدَأ ثانٍ مَرْفُوعٌ).	أُقَّةٌ
ب is a preposition (حَرْفُ الْجَرِّ). The prepositional phrase (الْجارُ وَالْمَجْرُورُ) is linked to the deleted **predicate of the second subject** (مُتَعَلِّقٌ بِمَحْذُوفٍ: خَبَرُ الْمُبْتَدَإ الثّانِي). Imagine the verb *to be* although it would not fit into the English translation.	بِخَمْسِ لِيراتٍ
The sentence starting from the second subject (plus its predicate) is the predicate of the first subject.	

What would the sentence look like if the deleted predicate was written (تَقْدِيرُ الْجُمْلةِ)? It could be: الْعِنَبُ أُقَّةٌ مِنْهُ بِ

SITUATION 3. A **demonstrative noun** is linked to the subject (وُجُودُ اسْمِ إشارةٍ إِلَى الْمُبْتَدَإ). Then you also don't need a connector.

Success (that) is the hope of every student.	النَّجاحُ ذلِكَ أَمَلُ كُلِّ طالِبٍ.

First subject in the nominative case (مُبْتَدَأ أَوَّلٌ مَرْفُوعٌ).	النَّجاحُ
Demonstrative (اسْمُ إشارةٍ مَبْنِيٌّ) which is in the position of the	1ذ

second subject (في مَحَلِّ رَفْعٍ مُبْتَدَأً ثانٍ.).	
So-called اللَّامُ لِلْبُعْدِ; a حَرْفٌ; it does not have a place in إِعْرابٌ.	لِ
This is a حَرْفُ خِطابٍ. It does not have a place in إِعْرابٌ.	كَ
Predicate (خَبَرُ الْمُبْتَدَإِ الثَّاني) for the <u>second</u> subject; مَرْفُوعٌ.	أَمَلُ

Notice: The sentence consisting of the second subject (plus the respective predicate) is the predicate of the first subject.

223. When do you connect the predicate with فَ?

If you want or need to strengthen the connection to the subject.

The subject (مُبْتَدَأٌ) and the predicate (خَبَرٌ) are connected naturally by the structure of a nominal sentence. When فَ intervenes in the predicate, it is there to strengthen this connection.

The فَ is used on several occasions. Although rare, it may occur in a nominal sentence (جُمْلَةٌ اِسْمِيَّةٌ) before the predicate (خَبَرٌ). When does that happen? The فَ is added **after a nominal sentence** when the subject plus the predicate together resemble a conditional sentence (= the first part, جُمْلَةُ الشَّرْطِ). We could derive three important points that you may already know from the application of the فَ in a جَوابُ الشَّرْطِ.

1: The **subject** (مُبْتَدَأٌ) indicates ambiguity, uncertainty (الْإِبْهامُ), or generality (الْعُمُومُ). This is the situation when the subject is a relative pronoun (اِسْمٌ مَوْصُولٌ) or an indefinite noun (اِسْمٌ نَكِرَةٌ).

This sense of generality (indefinite noun) and vagueness (في إِبْهامِهِ وَعُمُومِهِ) explains why such a مُبْتَدَأٌ may resemble a conditional particle (اِسْمُ الشَّرْطِ). The same is true for الَّذي which comprises a **conditional meaning** (الْاِسْمُ الْمَوْصُولُ يَتَضَمَّنُ مَعْنَى الشَّرْطِ).

2: After the مُبْتَدَأٌ, either a **sentence** (جُمْلَةٌ) or a prepositional/adverbial phrase (شِبْهُ الْجُمْلَةِ) **has to follow**. This sentence must not contain a conditional particle (كَلِمَةٌ شَرْطِيَّةٌ).

3: Using the logic of a conditional sentence, we can say that the **predicate** (خَبَرٌ) represents the **result** of the **first part**. This explains why the predicate **must be connected** with the previous part. This cannot be achieved without a helper: the فَ. Only then, the خَبَر can resemble the 2nd part of a conditional sentence (جَوابُ الشَّرْطِ); the part without if.

Sounds quite complicated. Let's check an example:

He (the one) who strives succeeds.	الَّذِي يَجْتَهِدُ فَناجِحٌ.

- This sentence consists of a subject (مُبْتَدَأٌ): the relative pronoun الَّذِي. In Arabic, الَّذِي is noun (اِسْمٌ) that is not specified by itself because it does not refer to any particular person or thing itself. Therefore, it can be interpreted as a conditional particle.

- After الَّذِي, we have a sentence which doesn't contain a conditional particle (كَلِمَةٌ شَرْطِيّةٌ). It is a basic verbal sentence (=يَجْتَهِدُ) which is placed as the relative clause (صِلَةُ الْمَوْصُولِ). Thus, the verbal sentence doesn't have a position in إِعْرابٌ (لا مَحَلَّ لَها مِن الْإِعْرابِ). We don't need to look for its grammatical job in the sentence; it is like a neutral part that provides us with information.

- After that, we have the predicate (خَبَر): *succeeding* (ناجِحٌ). It is connected with the verbal sentence يَجْتَهِدُ. The خَبَر is placed as the جَوابُ الشَّرْطِ for the verb. We are allowed to treat it like that because *the success* (النَّجاحُ) is the consequence of *the effort* (الْإِجْتِهادُ).

- The most important ingredient: the فَ. It is there to strengthen the connection between subject and predicate. It links the subsequent predicate (the خَبَر after فَ) with the earlier part of the sentence.

Another example – this time without الَّذِي.

A student who strives will succeed.	طالِبٌ يَجْتَهِدُ فَناجِحٌ.

طالِبٌ	This is a nominal sentence. The subject (مُبْتَدَأٌ) is طالِبٌ; it is indefinite and doesn't point to a specific student. How can we start a nominal sentence with an indefinite word as the subject? It is possible because it is qualified by an adjective. See *question #213*.
يَجْتَهِدُ	After the indefinite noun, a verbal sentence (= يَجْتَهِدُ) is placed as an adjective for *student* (جُمْلَةٌ فِعْلِيّةٌ واقِعةٌ صِفةٌ لَهُ); it is located in the spot of a nominative case because it has to agree with the مُبْتَدَأُ (فِي مَحَلِّ رَفْعٍ صِفةٍ لِطالِبٍ). Subject (فاعِلٌ) of the verbal sentence is

an implied pronoun (ضَمِيرٌ مُسْتَتِرٌ) expressing *he* (هُوَ).	
Extra/additional particle (حَرْفٌ زَائِدٌ) which is placed before the predicate (الْفَاءُ وَاقِعةٌ فِي الْخَبَرِ) in order to link the predicate with the first part of the sentence. It does not have a place in إِعْرابٌ.	ف
Predicate (خَبَرٌ) of the nominal sentence; nominative (مَرْفُوعٌ) case.	ناجِحٌ

This leads us to the all-important question: is it necessary to use فَ? Or is it just a stylistic option? Well, it depends.

➜ **You must place the فَ...** when you use أَمّا (*as for; concerning*).

As for Zayd, he is generous; as for his brother, he is courageous.	أَمّا زَيْدٌ فَكَرِيمٌ وَأَمّا أَخُوهُ فَشُجاعٌ.

Conditional particle used for *elaboration* (حَرْفُ شَرْطٍ وَتَفْصِيلٍ); in-declinable form (مَبْنِيٌّ); it doesn't have a place in إِعْرابٌ.	أَمّا
Subject (مُبْتَدَأٌ) of the nominal sentence, nominative (مَرْفُوعٌ).	زَيْدٌ
Extra particle (حَرْفٌ زَائِدٌ). Does not have a place in إِعْرابٌ. The ف is placed before the predicate (خَبَرٌ). Some grammarians say that the ف is placed in the position of a *concealed, estimated second part* (i.e., the result) *of a conditional sentence* (جَوَابُ شَرْطٍ مُقَدَّرٌ). **This is probably the closest we could get in its function.**	ف
Predicate (خَبَرٌ) in the nominative case (مَرْفُوعٌ).	كَرِيمٌ

➜ **You may place the فَ...** if you don't have أَمّا in a sentence. In other words, except for أَمّا, the ف is optional.

224. When do you have to delete the predicate (حَذْفُ الْخَبَرِ)?

When the predicate points to a general state of being (كَوْنٌ عامٌّ).

It's actually quite trivial: we can get rid of the predicate (خَبَرٌ) – let's better say, we can leave it out – when the predicate conveys the general meaning of مَوْجُودٌ (*present; existing; found*) or كائِنٌ (*existing; located*), or مُسْتَقِرٌّ (*being stable, permanent*).

This means that the shape or form of this state of "*being*" is not further specified. There are situations in which you may (جَوَازًا) delete the predicate (خَبَرٌ) or in which you have to delete it (وُجُوبًا). Let's first examine the situations in which you **may** delete the predicate.

1. The خَبَرٌ **may** be omitted in the answer to a question if the deleted predicate can be anticipated (it is implicitly there anyway).

A asks:	"Who is loyal?"	مَنْ مُخْلِصٌ؟
B answers:	"Karīm."	كَرِيمٌ.

Karīm is the subject (مُبْتَدَأٌ). The predicate is deleted; the deletion replaced the word *loyal* (مُخْلِصٌ) because you still have in mind that it is Karīm who is loyal.

2. We have a sentence with the device إذا which *indicates something unexpected* (إذا الْفُجَائِيَّةُ). The word إذا must be followed by a nominal sentence and refers to the same time in which the preceding statement happened. In such constructions, the predicate *may* be deleted. Such sentences are sometimes difficult to understand.

I went out, and there was my friend.	خَرَجْتُ فَإذا صَدِيقِي.

صَدِيقِي	Subject (مُبْتَدَأٌ) in the nominative case (مَرْفُوعٌ), marked by an assumed case marker (ضَمَّةٌ مُقَدَّرَةٌ) on the letter <u>before</u> the possessive pronoun ي. You can't put the case marker because the vowel before the ي must be a كَسْرَةٌ. First part of the إضافةٌ.
ي	Pronominal suffix (ضَمِيرٌ مُتَّصِلٌ), serving as the second part of the إضافةٌ (مُضافٌ إلَيْهِ). It is located in the position of a genitive case (فِي مَحَلِّ جَرٍّ). It has a fixed, indeclinable shape (مَبْنِيٌّ) and always ends in سُكُونٌ.

What about the **predicate**? It was deleted (الْخَبَرُ مَحْذُوفٌ جَوَازًا) – but it is still understood. For example: *present* (مَوْجُودٌ) or *waiting* (مُنْتَظِرٌ).

Other examples of sentences in which you <u>may</u> delete the خَبَرٌ:

خَبَرٌ deleted	subject	example
كَذَلِكَ	...أَبُوكَ ناجِحٌ وَأَخُوكَ	Your father is successful, and so is your brother.
The deletion of the predicate is **optional** since it is implicitly understood.		

كامِنٌ	... خَرَجْتُ فَإذا الْعَدُوُّ	I went out and there was the enemy...
After the إذا الْفُجائِيَّةُ, the deletion is **optional**. The root ك-م-ن denotes *to hide, to be hidden; to ambush, to waylay.*		

عِنْدِي	مَنْ عِنْدَكَ؟ - أَبُوكَ ...	Who is there with you? Your father...
In the answer to a question (فِي جَوابِ الْإِسْتِفْهامِ), the deletion is **optional**.		

Let's move to more sophisticated constructions in which you **must** delete the predicate (خَبَرٌ).

1. We have a sentence with لَوْلا which means *if not for; had it not been for.* Then, after the subject (مُبْتَدَأٌ), you must omit the predicate (خَبَرٌ) if it points to a general state (كَوْنٌ عامٌّ): *to be, to be found, ...*

Note: Although you don't see it, scholars suggested that the condition that is introduced by لَوْلا includes the verbal idea of كانَ (*was/had not*).

It was reported that the Messenger of Allah said: "Had it not been for Eve, woman would have never acted unfaithfully towards her husband." (Were it not for Eve, no woman would ever betray her husband.) *Sahīh Muslim 1470; Sahīh al-Bukhārī 3399.*	قالَ النَّبِيُّ: لَوْلا حَوَّاءُ لَمْ تَخُنْ أُنْثَى زَوْجَها الدَّهْرَ.

If not for Islam, the Arabic language would not have spread.	لَوْلا الْإِسلامُ لَما انْتَشَرَتْ اللُّغَةُ الْعَرَبِيَّةُ.
If not for the mind, mankind would have been lost.	لَوْلا الْعَقْلُ لَضاعَ الْإِنْسانُ.

Particle of denial (حَرْفُ إمْتِناعٍ لِلْوُجُودِ); no place in إعْرابٌ.	لَوْلا
Subject (مُبْتَدَأٌ) of the nominal sentence; nominative (مَرْفُوعٌ).	الْعَقْلُ

Where is the **predicate**? It had to be deleted (الْخَبَرُ مَحْذُوفٌ وُجُوبًا). The empty space could have been filled by *present/is found* (مَوْجُودٌ).	
This لَ, an emphatic particle, is placed right before the second part (جَوابٌ) of the لَوْلا-sentence; doesn't have a place in إِعْرابٌ.	لَ
Past tense verb (indeclinable on the فَتْحٌ).	ضاعَ
Subject (فاعِلٌ); nominative case (مَرْفُوعٌ بِالضَّمِّةِ الظّاهِرةِ).	الْإِنْسانُ

Why do we need to delete the خَبَر in this sentence? The predicate points to a general or common state of being/existence (كَوْنٌ عامّ). In such situations, the deletion of the predicate is mandatory.

However, if the predicate points to a **special situation** or a **special state of being** (كَوْنٌ خاصٌّ), it should be placed and shown.

Hadn't the players been **skillful**, the team would not have won.	لَوْلا اللّاعِبُونَ ماهِرُونَ ما فازَ الْفَرِيقُ.

subject (مُبْتَدَأٌ)	اللّاعِبُونَ		predicate (خَبَرٌ)	ماهِرُونَ

➡ The predicate (خَبَرٌ) must be shown. It points to a special being (كَوْنٌ خاصٌّ) or special occurrence (وُجُودٌ خاصٌّ) which becomes clear when we do the counter check. The meaning of the sentence is not:

Hadn't the players **been present**, the team would not have won.	لَوْلا اللّاعِبُونَ مَوْجُودُونَ ما فازَ الْفَرِيقُ.

The reason is actually quite obvious: there is no team without players. Without players, the team can't win. Without a predicate that points to more than just *being*, the sentence wouldn't make sense. Instead, this sentence points to a special being/state regarding the players, and this is the skill/proficiency (الْمَهارةُ).

2. The **subject** (مُبْتَدَأٌ) in an __oath__ is displayed and explicit (إذا كانَ الْمُبْتَدَأُ صَرِيحًا فِي الْقَسَمِ).

By your life, the diligent will succeed!	لَعَمْرُكَ (...) لَيَنْجَحَنَّ الْمُجْتَهِدُ!

This is a **لامُ الْإِبْتِداءِ** which is often translated as *emphatic Lām*. Such a ل is placed before the **subject** (مُبْتَدَأ) to reinforce it (لامُ التَّوْكِيدِ). It is a حَرْفٌ (particle); so it does not have a position in إعْرابٌ.	ل
Subject (مُبْتَدَأٌ) of the nominal sentence; nominative (مَرْفُوعٌ). Since we deal with an oath, عَمْرُ is the person you swear by (مُقْسَمٌ بِهِ).	عَمْرُ
Pronominal suffix (ضَمِيرٌ مُتَّصِلٌ). You don't see the actual case marker as the ك is indeclinable (مَبْنِيٌّ). It is in the position of a genitive case (فِي مَحَلِّ جَرٍّ) since it is the second part of the إضافةٌ.	كَ
This is the place of the **deleted predicate** (الْخَبَرُ مَحْذُوفٌ وُجُوبًا). You are not allowed to express it there. It has the underlying, presumed meaning of: *my oath* (قَسَمِي).	(...)
Note: See *question #448* to learn more about the second *Lām*.	

Now, what about this sentence:

I swear by God, I will do it!	يَمِينُ اللهِ لَأَفْعَلَنَّ!
Remark: The noun يَمِينٌ in this context means *oath* like in the expression: *oath on the constitution* (الْيَمِينُ الدُّسْتُورِيّةُ).	

Here, we are allowed to delete the predicate, but it is not compulsory. If there is a **لامُ الْإِبْتِداءِ** at the beginning, we know something for sure: that the following word is the subject (مُبْتَدَأ) because that type of ل can only go along with the subject. Therefore, we know that it must have been the predicate which was omitted.

In the above example, however, it could be also the other way round. The expression يَمِينُ اللهِ could be treated as the predicate – with the effect that the deleted part was subject! Then, the sentence would have the following equivalent meaning: **لَعَمْرُكَ يَمِينِي or لَعَمْرُكَ قَسَمِي**

For this reason, we cannot say that you must delete the predicate because we cannot clearly detect the predicate in the sentence. That may be theoretical as the meaning is, practically speaking, the same. However, understanding the underlying construction will help you to decode and translate sentences better.

3. There is a و (واوُ الْعَطْفِ) after the subject (مُبْتَدَأٌ) of a nominal sentence. This و conveys the meaning of *with* (مَعَ). It is a *Wāw of accompaniment* or *togetherness* (واوُ الْمَعِيّةِ). For an analysis of this و, see #355.

What complicates the issue: we don't have a verb. If there was a verb, we would put the word after و into the accusative case. → Since there is no verb or something with verbal power, we use the nominative case.

Every person is associated with his deeds.	كُلُّ إِنْسانٍ وَفِعْلُهُ.
Every person is associated with his hometown.	كُلُّ رَجُلٍ وَضَيْعَتُهُ.

Note: This example was often used in early Classical Arabic grammar books. The sentence means that the place where you grew up is part of you, in the way you talk, behave, react, dress, etc.

Every man and his hometown are inseparable.	كلُّ رَجُلٍ وَضَيْعَتُهُ مُقْتَرِنانِ.
This is what we get if we rewrite it with مَعَ: →	كلُّ رَجُلٍ كائِنٌ مَعَ ضَيْعَتِهِ.

كُلُّ	Subject (مُبْتَدَأٌ), it takes the nominative case (مَرْفُوعٌ).
وَ	A conjunction (حَرْفُ عَطْفٍ) in the meaning of *with*, i.e., association (بِمَعْنَى مَعَ).
ضَيْعَتُهُ	This noun was "coupled" with the subject (مَعْطُوفٌ عَلَى كُلّ).

In the above examples, the و expresses two things at the same time: the meaning of a coordinator, "coupler" (واوُ الْعَطْفِ) and of *with* (واوُ الْمَعِيّةِ). We want to use it in the meaning of a واوُ الْمَعِيّةِ – but can we do that? Not really. The problem is that we don't have a verb. We can only coordinate two nouns (إِسْمٌ عُطِفَ عَلَى إِسْمٍ).

Let's see where the problem is rooted: the واوُ الْعَطْفِ makes the two things between the و equal in everything. But don't forget that the two nouns in our examples are not "equal" because *person* and *hometown* are not equal in their weight regarding the context. The *person* plays the more important part. We could say that *deeds* follow the *person*.

So, let's assume that we use the واوُ الْعَطْفِ and assume that the predicate, which gives us more or less the same meaning as a واوُ الْمَعِيّةِ,

was deleted. If we do that, we need to harmonize the cases. Therefore, the word before and after وَ will take the same case marker. The first word is the subject (مُبْتَدَأٌ), so the second word must also take the nominative case (مَرْفُوعٌ). What about the predicate? It **must** be deleted in such constructions because otherwise, it may convey a different meaning which would be wrong in this context – the meaning of *and*.

In our example, if we omit the predicate, the وَ is implicitly understood as كَائِنٌ مَعَ ضَيْعَتِهِ. It cannot be misunderstood as *and*. The predicate in such constructions has the hypothetical meaning of مُقْتَرِنانِ which is the active participle (dual form) of the VIII-verb اقْتَرَنَ - يَقْتَرِنُ and means *to be interconnected, to be linked together*. Another possible predicate would be مُتلازِمانِ which denotes more or less the same.

Although this is the view of the majority of the grammarians, you may find scholars who argue that you could use the accusative case (كُلُّ رَجُلٍ وَضَيْعَتَهُ) as well and treat the وَ as a واوُ الْمَعِيّةِ. In Classical Arabic grammar books, such treatment is rare. One of the very few grammarians who allowed the accusative case in such sentences is al-Saymarī. His full name is Abu Muhammad 'Abdallah bin 'Alī bin 'Ishāq al-Saymarī (أَبُو مُحَمَّد عَبْد الله بن عَلِيّ بن إسْحاق الصَّيْمَريِّ).

We know very little about his life. The only thing that was recorded was his move to Egypt. He died probably at the end of the 10th century (in the fourth or at the beginning of the fifth century AH). His most famous book is *al-Tabsira wa al-Tadhkira* (التَّبْصِرة وَالتَّذْكِرة), literally: *the instruction (enlightening) and the memento*.

In my opinion, only one thing counts: you should identify the correct meaning of the letter وَ which is *with* – and not: *and*. Let's make the difference clear between the two types of وَ.

Zayd and Muhammad are standing.	زَيْدٌ وَمُحَمَّدٌ قائمانِ.

Here, وَ denotes **participation** (الْإِشْتِراكُ) but not necessarily **association**. It does not convey the meaning of *with* because the action of Zayd's standing is not necessarily associated with Muhammad's standing at all times. They are both standing, and both actions are not interconnected – they just both do it. Therefore, we have to express the **predicate** (قائمانِ) and can't delete it.

> We could summarize the discussion as follows:
> وَ followed by an **accusative** case **doesn't** occur in **nominal** sentences.

Only if there is a word that may be interpreted as having some kind of verbal force (e.g., a demonstrative particle), you will encounter the accusative case. For example, if you want to warn someone (see *question #422*), you may say: *Watch out for the snake!* (إِيَّاكَ وَالْحَيَّة)

225. Can a subject have more than one predicate?

Yes, this possible and actually pretty common.

A subject can have several predicates (تَعَدُّدُ الْخَبَرِ) in a sentence. Sounds logical, but you have to watch out – mainly for two reasons:

1. The predicates are usually **not** connected by وَ (*and*). Arabs also don't use commas. Linguists have a term for this: *asyndetic*. In the English translation, however, you should use at least commas.

2. Some words may be mistaken for predicates, but are actually adjectives for the predicate. This can lead to ambiguous sentences:

Zayd is an Arab, courageous, and generous.	زَيْدٌ عَرَبِيٌّ شُجاعٌ كَرِيمٌ.
Subject (مُبْتَدَأ) in the nominative case (مَرْفُوعٌ).	زَيْدٌ
First predicate (خَبَرٌ); nominative case (مَرْفُوعٌ بِالضَّمّةِ الظّاهِرةِ).	عَرَبِيٌّ
Second predicate (خَبَرٌ ثانٍ) in the nominative case.	شُجاعٌ
Third predicate (خَبَرٌ ثالِثٌ) in the nominative case.	كَرِيمٌ

In this example, we could say that *brave* (شُجاعٌ) is an adjective (صِفةٌ) for the first predicate: *Arab* (عَرَبِيٌّ). Then, we would get: *Zayd is a **brave** Arab and generous.*

The same is true for *generous* (كَرِيمٌ) which could be a صِفةٌ for *Arab* as well. So we would get: *Zayd is a **generous** Arab and brave.* The case markers would be the same because an adjective for a word in the nominative case (صِفةُ الْمَرْفُوعِ) has to be مَرْفُوعٌ too. This grammatical approach, however, is not always possible.

226. When are we not allowed to bring the predicate forward?

In mainly six situations.

In general, the predicate (خَبَرٌ) of a nominal sentence should be placed **after** the subject (مُبْتَدَأٌ). This makes sense since the خَبَرٌ pronounces a verdict on the مُبْتَدَأ. Now, what about these sentences?

Karīm is standing.	كَرِيمٌ قَادِمٌ.	A
	قَادِمٌ كَرِيمٌ.	B
In example B, we place the **predicate before** the subject (تَقْدِيمٌ). This is grammatically correct because two things are fulfilled: the subject is **definite** and the predicate is __indefinite__ – see *question #213*.		

In some situations, it is necessary to place the predicate **after** the subject (تَقْدِيمُ الْخَبَرِ وُجُوبًا). When do we have to do that?

1. The subject (مُبْتَدَأٌ) is a اِسْمٌ that deserves the **priority** (صَدَارَةٌ).

Nouns deserving the primacy in a sentence are question words (أَسْماءُ الْإِسْتِفْهامِ), conditional words (أَسْماءُ الشَّرْطِ), words used for showing surprise (أَسْماءٌ تَعَجُّبِيَّةٌ), the كَمْ الْخَبَرِيّةُ, etc. In the following examples, the subject (مُبْتَدَأ) is marked in gray. Such words must start a sentence.

Who did that?	مَنْ فَعَلَ هٰذا؟
How good is honesty!	ما أَحْسَنَ الصِّدْقَ!

2. There is a so-called Lām of the beginning (لامُ الْإِبْتِداءِ) before the subject (مُبْتَدَأٌ). Such *Lām* is an emphatic particle and emphasizes the subject. It carries the vowel "*a*": لَ. Not that such type of ل doesn't trigger any case marker in other words

For the painstaking there will be success. (The painstaking is/will be successful).	لَلْمُجِدُّ ناجِحٌ.

▷ The لامُ الْإِبْتِداءِ always has the precedence; the predicate can't be put before the subject.

3. The subject (مُبْتَدَأٌ) and the predicate (خَبَرٌ) are on the same level regarding definiteness/indefiniteness. Practically speaking, this means that they **both** are **definite** (تَعْرِيفٌ) or **indefinite** (تَنْكِيرٌ).

My brother is my friend.	أَخِي صَدِيقِي.

subject (مُبْتَدَأٌ)	أَخِي		Predicate (خَبَرٌ)	صَدِيقِي

Both words (*brother* and *friend*) are a اِسْمٌ and serve as the first part of a إِضافةٌ, i.e., as the مُضافٌ. The second part is the pronoun *my* (ي). Being placed as the first part of a إِضافةٌ, they both are by definition definite, so they are on the same level regarding definiteness.

Why can't we change the word order here? Let's look at the meaning. If you want to strengthen that _my_ brother is my friend, the word *brother* must be the subject and *friend* must be the predicate. If you want to express the opposite, you should rearrange the sentence:

My friend is my brother.	صَدِيقِي أَخِي.

4. There is a فَ before the predicate (خَبَرٌ).

Whoever strives will succeed.	الَّذِي يَجْتَهِدُ فَناجِحٌ.
Remark: If you want to place the predicate before the subject, you would have to delete the فَ. We have analyzed this sentence in *question #223*.	

5. The predicate refers to a *pronoun of the fact* (ضَمِيرُ الشَّأْنِ).

Sura 112:1	Say, "He is Allah, *(who is the)* One."	قُلْ هُوَ اللهُ أَحَدٌ.
See *question #113* for more details on the ضَمِيرُ الشَّأْنِ.		

6. The predicate is disconnected/detached (الْخَبَرُ مَفْصُولٌ). It was isolated by a separate personal pronoun (ضَمِيرُ الْفَضْلِ).

God is gracious.	اللهُ هُوَ الْكَرِيمُ.

227. When do you have to place the predicate before the subject?

You might not always recognize it, but there are many situations in which you have to place the predicate before the subject.

Grammarians call such an operation تَقْدِيمٌ: *sending ahead*. There are situations when we are obliged to place the خَبَرٌ before the مُبْتَدَأٌ.

1. The predicate (خَبَرٌ) is entitled to have the **precedence**.

Some question words **function as the predicate** but demand that they are located right at the **beginning**.

Where is your house?	أَيْنَ بَيْتُكَ؟
When is the departure/journey?	مَتَى السَّفَرُ؟

خَبَرٌ	أَيْنَ		مُبْتَدَأٌ	بَيْتُكَ
	مَتَى			السَّفْرُ

B. The state, result, or attribute which the predicate is conveying is **limited to the subject** only. This happens when we have إنَّما or إلّا before the subject (أَنْ يَكُونَ الْخَبَرُ مَحْصُورًا فِي الْمُبْتَدَإِ بِإِلّا أَوْ إنَّما).

1	Only the hard-worker succeeds.	ما ناجِحٌ إلّا الْمُجِدُّ.
2	(Only) Karīm is at home. You limit the presence in the house to Karīm. → Only Karīm is there.	إنَّما فِي الْبَيْتِ كَرِيمٌ. = ما فِي الْبَيْتِ إلّا كَرِيمٌ

Note: If you started the sentence with the subject (مُبْتَدَأٌ) and let the predicate follow, you would spoil the meaning of *exclusiveness* (الْقَصْرُ).

C. When the subject (مُبْتَدَأٌ) is **indefinite** and consists of only one word, the predicate must be a sentence (جُمْلَةٌ) or quasi-sentence (شِبْهُ الْجُمْلَةِ), i.e., a prepositional or adverbial phrase.

If the subject (مُبْتَدَأٌ) is made of a single, indefinite word, you need to reverse the word order. You must move the predicate to the start. In other words, we can only start a sentence with an indefinite word if that word is the fronted predicate (see *question #213*). In the following examples, the predicate is marked in gray.

No entry.	مَمْنُوعٌ الدُّخُولُ.
There is a student in the classroom.	فِي الْفَصْلِ طالِبٌ.
You have a book.	عِنْدَكَ كِتابٌ.

Remark: If we place the singular subject at the beginning of a sentence without any additional information, it is possible to treat a following sentence (جُمْلةٌ) or prepositional phrase (الْجارُّ وَالْمَجْرُورُ) as an adjective (صِفةٌ) – and not as a predicate (خَبَرٌ).

228. How do you put emphasis on the predicate?

You move the predicate (تَقْدِيمُ الْخَبَرِ) forward.

Practically speaking, you place the خَبَرٌ before the subject (مُبْتَدَأٌ). In the following examples, the predicate is marked in gray:

| Smoking is forbidden. | مَمْنُوعٌ التَّدْخِينُ. |
| Men must not enter. | مَمْنُوعٌ دُخُولُ الرِّجالِ. |

It is actually pretty common to move a prepositional phrase to the front and start the sentence/utterance with it:

| It's hard to talk to this man. | مِن الصَّعْبِ التَّكَلُّمُ مَعَ هذا الرَّجُلِ. |

The same is true for adverbs:

| Certainly this is her. | أَجَلْ هذِهِ هِيَ. |

Chapter 9: Rule Breakers & Game Changers (النَّواسِخُ)

229. What is meant by the grammar term ناسِخٌ?

It means "abrogator".

Several scientific Arabic terms are derived from Islamic thoughts. Among them is the grammatical term **النّاسِخُ** (plural: النَّواسِخُ).

The root ن-س-خ conveys the meaning of *to abolish; to abrogate; to invalidate;* also *to replace* or *substitute.* For example, a Qur'anic verse which abrogates and supersedes another verse is called آيَةٌ ناسِخةٌ. The term **النَسْخُ** is an Islamic legal term (فِقْهِيٌّ) and means: *changing of a legal decision by another legal decision.*

When the pioneers of grammar thought about words like كانَ which invert several rules (especially case endings), they coined these words **النَّواسِخُ** – *the abrogators; abolishers.*

An "abrogator" can be a verb or a particle (حَرْفٌ). These special words add a new factor to the **nominal sentence** and change its common rules. The important thing is that the sentence retains its structure of a nominal sentence (جُمْلةٌ اِسْمِيّةٌ) – even if the new factor (النّاسِخُ) that encroaches on (enters) the nominal sentence is a verb (فِعْلٌ).

THE VERB كانَ (TO BE, TO EXIST)

230. What makes كانَ so special?

كانَ *implies the idea of being or existence. Verbs like* كانَ *are called non-attributive verbs. They do not contain the attribute in itself.*

Non-attributive verbs express an **independent** idea in the form of a predicate. In the case of *to be* (كانَ), the verb adds a circumstantial or modifying idea to the simple idea of existence. This extra information, which is in the accusative case (مَنْصُوبٌ), tells the reader or listener that the general idea of existence is limited and determined.

The verb كانَ is probably most famous for not being used in the present tense (الْمُضارِعُ). In fact, it is almost impossible that يَكُونُ expresses *is.* It can only express *will be* like in سَيَكُونُ الْجَوُّ بارِدًا (*The weather will be cold.*) The omission of the verb *to be* in the present tense – linguists call it *copula omission* – is typical for Semitic languages, but also for other languages (e.g., Turkish). See *question #64.*

231. Why don't we use the term فاعِلٌ (doer; subject) with كانَ؟

كان only points to time (زَمَنٌ) and not to an action (حَدَثٌ). Therefore, it doesn't need a subject (فاعِلٌ): the one who is doing the action.

Let's first check a normal I-verb: كَتَبَ (he wrote). This verb points to time (زَمَنٌ): the past tense. And it points to an action (حَدَثٌ): the process of *writing* (i.e., the مَصْدَرٌ which is الْكَتْبُ). What about كانَ؟

كانَ only points to time. The مَصْدَرٌ of كانَ is كَوْنٌ and does not convey any action. The idea of *being* or *existence*, when expressed by كان, is limited and determined by the **accusative case** (نَصْبٌ) - that's why the predicate of كان is in the accusative case.

In short, كان needs a nominal sentence with subject and predicate. This gives us an idea why كان is also called an *incomplete, defective verb* (فِعْلٌ ناقِصٌ). To tell you the difference, if we deal with a full verb, the subject (فاعِلٌ) is enough to provide a full meaning. كانَ necessarily needs a predicate. See #58 for the meaning of *defective* in this context.

Karīm was standing.	كانَ كَرِيمٌ قائِمًا.
The subject points to a state of being that is **absolute** (حُصُولٌ مُطْلَقٌ). The predicate points to a **certain** state of being (كَوْنُ الْقِيامِ). Note: Some grammarians don't agree that كان isn't capable of transporting any meaning of action.	

Note: There are rare situations in which كان is treated as a full verb and therefore has a subject (فاعِلٌ) – see the next *question #231*.

232. Can the verb كانَ be a full verb (فِعْلٌ تامٌّ)؟

Yes, this is possible.

In rare situations, كان can provide enough information and contains the **attribute** in itself; in other words, كانَ doesn't need a predicate (خَبَرُ كان). It is sufficient to only use كان plus a subject, which means that كانَ points to or indicates an action (حَدَثٌ) that demands a subject (فاعِلٌ).

This type of كانَ is used as a (syntactically) **full, complete verb** (فِعْلٌ تامٌّ) and is called in Arabic *the complete or absolute* كانَ (كان التّامّةُ). In such applications, the meaning of كانَ is *to happen, to take place* (حَدَثَ) or *to occur* (حَصَلَ). Sometimes it may convey *to be found* (وُجِدَ).

The sky was covered with clouds, the wind became stronger, and it started raining.	تَلَبَّدَتِ السَّماءُ بِالغُيُومِ وَاشْتَدَّتِ الرِّيحُ فَكانَ المَطَرُ.

Here, كانَ is a full verb in the past tense (فِعْلٌ ماضٍ تامٌّ).	كانَ
Subject of the complete verb (فاعِلٌ مَرْفُوعٌ بِالضَّمةِ الظّاهِرةِ); therefore, it is called فاعِلٌ and <u>not</u> اِسْمُ كانَ.	المَطَرُ

What is fated will come to pass. (Remark: This is a core belief in Islam. The decree must occur, and there is no escape from it even if you are cautious).	المَقْدُورُ كائِنٌ.
In the example, the active particle (اِسْمُ الْفاعِلِ) is used instead of the verb. This is possible because a اِسْمُ الْفاعِلِ has some verbal power.	

I will follow his news wherever he is.	سَأُتابِعُ أَخْبارَهُ أَيْنَما كانَ.
كانَ has the meaning of *to be found* (وُجِدَ). It has the power of a full verb.	

Note: What we have said so far is also true for the *sisters of* كانَ.

Sura 42:53	أَلَا إِلَى اللهِ تَصِيرُ الْأُمُورُ.

- Truly everything **will return** to God. (*Abdul Haleem*)
- Unquestionably, to Allah do [all] matters evolve. (*Sahīh International*)

Abdul Haleem translates the verb تَصِيرُ – which is the present tense of صارَ (*to become*) – with the meaning of *to return* (تَرْجِعُ). This shows that in this (rare) situation, we treat the verb صارَ as a full verb which does not need a predicate (attribute) to complete the meaning.

Watch out: If كانَ accompanies a word, to which the <u>pure idea of existence</u> (which is inherent in كانَ) is ascribed, then such a word works as the subject (فاعِلٌ) and gets the nominative case (مَرْفُوعٌ). It doesn't need a predicate. ▷ It works as a full verb.

| كانَ التّامّةُ | **There was** (or lived) a teacher, and he had | كانَ مُعَلِّمٌ وَكانَ |

	(lit.: *there were to him*) three sons.	لَهُ بَنُونَ ثَلاثةٌ.
كانَ النّاقِصةُ	He *was* a teacher.	كانَ مُعَلِّمًا.

233. Is a sentence with كانَ a nominal or verbal sentence?

The answer to that is more difficult than you might think.

Let's look at the two main views:

VIEW 1 The **Basra** grammarians (الْبَصرِيُّونَ) suggested that كانَ only abrogates the subject and predicate of a **nominal** sentence (ناسِخةٌ لِلْمُبْتَدَإِ وَالْخَبَرِ). A nominal sentence soaks up the meaning of time. Since a sentence with كانَ doesn't point to an action (حَدَثٌ) undertaken by the subject (i.e., الْفاعِلُ), it can't be a verbal sentence.

All sentences starting with a اِسْمٌ (the doer or subject; we don't talk about a fronted object here) or a فِعْلٌ ناقِصٌ are nominal sentences. Therefore, a sentence with كانَ is a nominal sentence which was transformed by a فِعْلٌ ناسِخٌ ناقِصٌ.

VIEW 2 The **Kūfa** grammarians (الْكُوفِيُّونَ), on the other hand, suggested that كانَ produces a **verbal** sentence (جُمْلةٌ فِعْلِيّةٌ). Why? It is rather simple: it is a verbal sentence because it starts with a verb – it doesn't matter whether the verb is defective (ناقِصٌ) or full (تامٌّ).

The Kūfa grammarians saw in the noun which goes along with كانَ a subject (فاعِلٌ) like in any other verb which was مَرْفُوعٌ, i.e., in the indicative mood. Furthermore, they saw in the predicate of كانَ a *circumstantial qualifier* (حالٌ) which has to get the accusative (مَنْصُوبٌ) case. Therefore, they assumed that كانَ did not enter a nominal sentence and does not have the power to abrogate rules (it is not ناسِخةٌ). They concluded that كانَ just follows the normal grammatical rules for verbs.

Most grammarians don't follow the Kūfa approach. They say that a sentence with كانَ is a nominal sentence (جُمْلةٌ اِسْمِيّةٌ) because it would be a nominal sentence in essence (أَصْلُها) if you deleted كانَ in your mind – which would leave us with a مُبْتَدَأٌ and a خَبَرٌ.

| Muhammad is diligent. | مُحَمَّدٌ مُجْتَهِدٌ. |
| Muhammad was diligent. | كانَ مُحَمَّدٌ مُجْتَهِدًا. |

كانَ changes a sentence consisting of مُبْتَدَأٌ and خَبَرٌ to a sentence with a
إِسْمُ كانَ and a predicate (خَبَرُ كانَ). Nevertheless, a sentence with كانَ
can still be regarded as a nominal sentence (جُمْلَةٌ اِسْمِيّةٌ) because the
verb كانَ is not a full verb (تامٌّ); it is defective/incomplete (ناقِصٌ).

Now, what about the following sentence:

| Karīm hit ʿUmar. | عُمَرَ ضَرَبَ كَرِيمٌ. |

Is this a nominal sentence? No, it isn't! Although it starts with a noun, it is a
verbal sentence (جُمْلَةٌ فِعْلِيّةٌ). The first word is the direct object (مَفْعُولٌ بِه)
which was moved to the beginning (التَّأْخِيرُ عَلَى فِعْلِه) for rhetorical reasons.

234. What does كائِنًا ما كانَ mean?

It means: whatever it may be.

كائِنٌ is the active participle (إِسْمُ الْفاعِلِ) of كانَ. It is now and then
used to denote *being, existing; a being, creature.*

كائِنٌ, however, is also part of the following expressions:

| 1 | **person; man** | Whoever it may be. | كائِنًا مَنْ كانَ. |
| 2 | **thing** | Whatever it may be. Be it what it may. | كائِنًا ما كانَ. |

| I will punish the thief whoever it may be. | سَأُعاقِبُ اللِّصَّ كائِنًا مَنْ كانَ. |
| I will pay the price for this thing whatever it may be. | سَأدْفَعُ ثَمَنَ هذا الشَّيْءِ كائِنًا ما كانَ. |

The underlying grammar is sophisticated. Let's do the إِعْرابٌ.

| كائِنًا | This is a حالٌ! It has to be in the **accusative** (مَنْصُوبٌ) which is the reason for the *"an"*-ending. اللِّصَّ is صاحِبُ الحالِ. An active participle (إِسْمُ الْفاعِلِ) carries a hidden pronoun (ضَمِيرٌ مُسْتَتِرٌ) |

which has the implied, estimated meaning of: *he* (هُوَ). That hidden pronoun is the **"subject"** (إسْمُ كائِن) and is therefore located in the position of a nominative case (فِي مَحَلِّ رَفْعٍ).	
This word, regarding its character, is an indefinite noun (إسْمٌ نَكِرَةٌ) which can't carry any case marker due to its indeclinable, fixed shape (مَبْنِيٌّ عَلَى السُّكُونِ). However, since مَنْ serves here as the **predicate** of كائِنٌ, it is placed in the location of an accusative case; so we assign the respective "place value" (فِي مَحَلِّ نَصْبٍ).	مَنْ
This is the exciting part: كانَ here is a **full/complete** past tense verb (فِعْلٌ ماضٍ تامٌّ). The subject (فاعِلٌ) is an implied pronoun (ضَميرٌ مُسْتَتِرٌ) conveying the meaning of *he* (هُوَ). ▷ So we have a verbal sentence (=كانَ) which is grammatically located in the position of an accusative case. Why is that? Because كانَ here servers as an **adjective** for مَنْ. In Arabic, we would say: فِي مَحَلِّ نَصْبٍ صِفَةٌ لِمَنْ.	كانَ

How can we understand the meaning of كانَ here? Let's rephrase it:

I will punish the thief no matter who he is.	سَأُعاقِبُ اللِّصَّ كائِنًا أَيَّ إِنْسانٍ وُجِدَ.

235. Can you change the word order in a sentence with كانَ?

If we focus only on the meaning, you can play with the word order. If we talk about the grammar, then your options are limited.

In a nominal sentence (جُمْلَةٌ إِسْمِيّةٌ) with subject (مُبْتَدَأٌ) and predicate (خَبَرٌ), it is possible to change the word order (تَرْتيبٌ). You may move the **predicate** (تَقْديمٌ) forward or **delay** the **subject** (تَأْخيرٌ).

The standard arrangement (تَرْتيبٌ) in a sentence with كانَ is as follows:

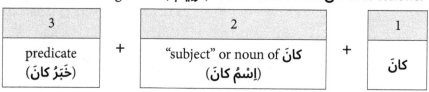

3		2		1
predicate (خَبَرُ كانَ)	+	"subject" or noun of كانَ (إسْمُ كانَ)	+	كانَ

- You place both subject & predicate after كانَ; after the الْفِعْلُ النّاسِخُ.
- You put the إسْمُ كانَ before the predicate (خَبَرٌ).

We can derive the following rule:

The إِسْمُ كانَ ("subject") can never be placed before the verb (النّاسِخُ)!

This needs some clarification as you will encounter many sentences like the following example.

Karīm was loyal.	كَرِيمٌ كانَ مُخْلِصًا.

What happened here? Well, we actually have **two** sentences:

sentence	مُخْلِصًا	كانَ	كَرِيمٌ
1	predicate (خَبَرٌ)		subject (مُبْتَدَأٌ)
2	predicate of كانَ (خَبَرُ كانَ)	verb plus hidden, implied subject (إِسْمُ كانَ)	

This is not the إِسْمُ كانَ that was moved to the beginning. It is the مُبْتَدَأٌ. We have a regular nominal sentence (جُمْلَةٌ اِسْمِيّةٌ).	كَرِيمٌ
The verb كانَ now starts a new sentence within the primary nominal sentence. كانَ has an implied, hidden subject – *he* – which is the إِسْمُ كانَ. This "subject" links both sentences.	كانَ
Predicate (خَبَرُ كانَ).	مُخْلِصًا

Note: The entire sentence (= كانَ مُخْلِصًا) serves as the خَبَرٌ for *Karīm*.

Does this mean that we can't change the word order in a sentence **starting with** كانَ? Not at all. You can adjust the word order – but you can only shift the **predicate,** which you may put to the front (تَقْدِيمٌ), to the end (تَأْخِيرٌ), or into the middle (تَوَسُّطٌ).

	تَأْخِيرُ		كانَ كَرِيمٌ قائِمًا.
خَبَرُ كانَ	تَوَسُّطٌ	Karīm was standing.	كانَ قائِمًا كَرِيمٌ.
	تَقْدِيمُ		قائِمًا كانَ كَرِيمٌ.

This is possible unless we have one of the following situations:

Situation 1: The predicate is a <u>question word</u>. Question words usually serve as the predicate and <u>always</u> **precede** the verb كانَ.

How was Karīm?	كَيْفَ كانَ كَرِيمٌ؟

Situation 2: The predicate must be placed **before** the اِسْمُ كَانَ ("sub-ject") if the اِسْمُ كَانَ <u>carries a pronoun</u> (ضَمِيرٌ) referring back to the predicate (or what was placed in the position of a predicate).

The owner of the home was inside the home.	كَانَ فِي الْبَيْتِ صَاحِبُهُ.

Situation 3: The predicate **must** come **at the end** (after كَانَ and the اِسْمُ كَانَ) if the predicate is <u>confined/limited</u> (إِذَا كَانَ الْخَبَرُ مَحْصُورًا بِإِلّا أَوْ إِنَّما) by إِلّا or إِنَّما. Otherwise, you'd produce the opposite meaning!

Karīm was only a poet.	إِنَّما كَانَ كَرِيمٌ شَاعِرًا.
Karīm has always been (was only) a poet.	= ما كَانَ كَرِيمٌ إِلّا شَاعِرًا.

Can we move the predicate if the خَبَر is a **whole sentence**? If the predi-cate (خَبَر) is a <u>sentence</u>, it **must be placed after** كَانَ and the اِسْمُ كَانَ.

Karīm's work was great.	كَانَ كَرِيمٌ عَمَلُهُ عَظِيمٌ.

The "subject" (اِسْمُ كَانَ) in the nominative case (مَرْفُوعٌ).	كَرِيمٌ
Subject (مُبْتَدَأٌ) of the nominal sentence (جُمْلَةٌ اسْميّةٌ), therefore in the nominative case (مَرْفُوعٌ). The ه is an indeclinable, pronominal suffix (ضَمِيرٌ مُتّصِلٌ); although we can't see it, the ه holds the posi-tion of a genitive case because it serves as the second part of the إِضافةٌ, i.e. the so-called مُضافٌ إِلَيْهِ.	عَمَلُهُ
Predicate (خَبَرٌ) for the مُبْتَدَأ of the nominal sentence; thus مَرْفُوعٌ.	عَظِيمٌ
The nominal sentence (عَمَلُهُ عَظِيمٌ) is the predicate (خَبَرُ كَانَ) of the primary sentence. We assign the "place value" of an accusative case (فِي مَحَلِّ نَصْبٍ).	

Remark: What we analyzed here works for the *sisters of* كَانَ as well.

236. Can كَانَ be redundant?

Yes, this is possible, but rare nowadays. Grammarians call it كَانَ الزَّائِدَةُ.

The *redundant* or *extra* كَانَ (كَانَ الزَّائِدَةُ) can be puzzling. If you want to understand such constructions correctly, you need to focus on case endings and the position of the extra كَانَ.

There are nine things you should know about the كانَ الزَّائِدةُ:

1. The extra كانَ has **no literal meaning**. It **does not affect the case ending** of any word in the sentence. If we deleted it, there would be no grammatical changes, nor would we (usually) curtail the meaning. In other words, it doesn't trigger grammatical changes (لا عَمَلَ لَها) and thus does not govern words – that is the core meaning of زَائِدة here. So good to know: the rules for cases aren't overthrown.

2. The purpose of the كانَ الزَّائِدةُ is to **lay emphasis** or to indicate the **past tense,** or even **both** (الإِشارةُ إلَى الـزَّمَنِ الْماضِـي أَوْ التَّوْكِيـدِ أَوْ كِلَيْهُما). It doesn't have a subject nor a predicate. Some grammarians say that the extra كانَ only occurs in sentences to lay emphasis. Others, among them the grammarian Sībawayhi, say it may indicate the past tense – but more in the sense of a general idea of the past because it doesn't refer to a special event.

3. كانَ الزَّائِدةُ **doesn't** denote **any action** (حَدَثٌ) because the main function of redundant, extra words is that of an amplifier.

4. It does not have a subject nor a predicate. So, there is no إِسْمُ كانَ, no خَبَرُ كانَ and also no فاعِلٌ.

5. Regarding the form, this type of كانَ is only used in the past tense form (الْماضِي). Nevertheless, it doesn't necessarily convey time.

6. The كانَ الزَّائِدةُ is **only** used in the **masculine form**: i.e., كانَ.

7. The كانَ الزَّائِدةُ is **never** added to the **beginning** of a sentence nor is it placed at its **end**. It is always found between two things that are connected/bound to each other (بَيْنَ جُزْءَيْنِ مُتَلازِمَيْنِ).

   Some remarks on the **spelling of the Hamza** (هَمْزةٌ): Why should you write the Hamza in the expression *two things* as a separate sign (i.e., جُزْءَيْنِ) and not in the shape of a كَسْرة (i.e., جُزْئَيْنِ)?

   Because the <u>letter before</u> the Hamza is a **non-vowel** (سُكونٌ) and **can't be connected** to another letter (which is true for ز or ر or و, ...). So you should write شيْءٌ (*thing*) in the dual as شَيْئانِ and in the accusative as شَيْئًا. On the other hand, you write ضَوْءٌ (*light*) in the dual as ضَوْءانِ and in the accusative as ضَوْءًا since the و can't be connected to another letter.

8. Because of its rigid form, we can treat it as a kind of حَرْفٌ (see below). We say that it is an **insertion** (حَشْوٌ).

9. The redundant كانَ is usually applied when you want to express **as-tonishment/admiration** (التَّعَجُّبُ). It is standard practice to use an extra كانَ in the التَّعَجُّبُ. In other situations, you rarely encounter it. In polished spoken Arabic, it may be used as a "filler".

Why is it possible that كانَ can be treated as extra/redundant? We said that we only use the third person singular of the past tense. Such forms are treated as **indeclinable** (مَبْنِيٌّ عَلَى الْفَتْحِ). ➤ Therefore, we can say that كانَ **resembles a particle** (حَرْفٌ) in its structure. This is the main reason why we can treat it as redundant.

The present tense, on the contrary, can be declined (مُعْرَبٌ) and therefore resembles a noun (اِسْمٌ). ➤ In general, a اِسْمٌ is **never used as a redundant word**.

There are exceptions, like always. A famous example is the following line of Classical Arabic poetry (Umm 'Aqīl/أمّ عَقيل) – notice that the extra كانَ is used in the present tense.

You will become a glorious and noble person if the north wind blows.	أَنْتَ تَكُونُ مَاجِدٌ نَبِيلٌ إذا تَهُبُّ شَمْأَلٌ بَلِيلٌ.
This is how we could understand the structure of the above sentence:	إذا تَهُبُّ شَمْأَلٌ بَلِيلٌ فَأَنْتَ ماجِدٌ نَبِيلٌ حِينَئِذٍ.

تَكُونُ is extra (زائِدَةٌ) and placed between the subject (مُبْتَدَأٌ) and the predicate (خَبَرٌ). Note: شَمْأَلٌ denotes a cold north wind, a wind cold with moisture (adjective: بَلِيلٌ). Here, the *north wind* stands for a time of hardship and tyranny.

Where can you place the كانَ الزَّائِدَةُ in a sentence?

1. Between the **subject** (مُبْتَدَأٌ) and the **predicate** (خَبَرٌ).

Zayd was standing.	زَيْدٌ كانَ قائِمٌ.

قائِمٌ gets the nominative case which is a sign that كانَ does not exercise its power and is redundant. Nevertheless, many grammarians say that it would be of better style to treat كانَ as a فِعْلٌ ناقِصٌ and let it do its usual job: to govern the predicate in the accusative case which would result in قائِمًا.

What about the following sentence?

| This sentence **does not** mean: *Zayd was standing.* | كانَ زَيْدٌ قائِمٌ. |

| كانَ is followed by two nominatives. The grammarians assume that كانَ here contains implicitly a *pronoun of the fact* (كانَ الَّذِي فِيها ضَمِيرُ الشَّأْنِ) – which is a pronoun of the third person singular, referring to the noun الشَّأْنُ or الْأَمْرُ (*the matter, the affair, or the story*) which does not appear in the sentence itself. It is implicitly understood as هُوَ. |

So far, all we've said is what the sentence doesn't mean. Let's move on and try to understand the missing links that are necessary to make the sentence actually work:

| The affair and the story was: Zayd is standing. | كانَ الشَّأْنُ وَالْحَدِيثُ زَيْدٌ قائِمٌ. |

| When someone says كانَ زَيْدٌ قائِمٌ, the speaker wants to express: *The affair and the story was: Zayd is standing.* We can assume that the implicit pronoun refers to الشَّأْنُ and serves as the subject (مُبْتَدَأٌ). The entire clause after كانَ (=زَيْدٌ قائِمٌ) is the predicate. Such constructions are mainly used in poetry. |

2. Between a **verb** and its **subject**.

| There was none like you. | لَمْ يُوجَدْ كانَ مِثْلُكَ. |

3. Between the **relative** pronoun and relative **clause** (الصِّلَةُ وَالْمَوْصُولُ).

| The one whom I met has come. | جاءَ الَّذِي كانَ قابَلْتُهُ. |

4. Between a **noun** and its **adjective** (الصِّفَةُ وَالْمَوْصُوفُ).

| I passed (by) a man who was standing. | مَرَرْتُ بِرَجُلٍ كانَ قائِمٍ. |

5. Such a كانَ often appears in an *exclamation of admiration or astonishment* (أُسْلُوبُ التَّعَجُّبِ). The indeclinable كانَ is placed before أَفْعَل. It indicates the past tense and functions as an amplifier.

| What a sweet nature he had! | ما كانَ أَطْيَبَ خُلُقَهُ! |

Word of amazement (اسْمُ تَعَجُّبٍ) that has the implied meaning of: *great thing* (شَيْءٌ عَظِيمٌ). It doesn't show any case inflection since it is indeclinable (مَبْنِيٌّ عَلَى السُّكُونِ). Even so, it is charged with the task of the **subject** of the nominal sentence, so it is located in the spot of a **nominative** (فِي مَحَلِّ رَفْعٍ مُبْتَدَأً).	ما
Redundant past tense verb (فِعْلٌ ماضٍ زائِدٌ). It does not have a position in إعْرابٌ. This type of كَانَ does not work as a regent or governor (لا عَمَلَ لَهُ) and does not invert case endings as usual.	كَانَ
Past tense verb. Its subject is a hidden pronoun (ضَمِيرٌ مُسْتَتِرٌ) having the meaning of *he* (هُوَ). This verbal sentence (consisting of verb and hidden, latent pronoun) is in the position of the **predicate** (فِي مَحَلِّ رَفْعٍ خَبَرٌ) of the subject ما of the nominal sentence.	أَطْيَبَ
Direct object of أَطْيَبَ in the accusative case (مَفْعُولٌ بِهِ مَنْصُوبٌ), marked by the فَتْحَةٌ. The ه here is an indeclinable pronominal suffix (ضَمِيرٌ مُتَّصِلٌ), located in the position of a genitive case as it serves as the second part of the إضافة (فِي مَحَلِّ جَرٍّ مُضافٌ إلَيْهِ).	خُلُقَهُ

So, is all this just theory what we're saying? No! The كَانَ الزَّائِدَةُ is also found in the Qur'an.

Sura 50:37	There truly is a reminder in this for whoever **has** a heart, whoever listens attentively. *(Abdul Haleem).*	إِنَّ فِي ذَٰلِكَ لَذِكْرَىٰ لِمَن كَانَ لَهُ قَلْبٌ أَوْ أَلْقَى السَّمْعَ وَهُوَ شَهِيدٌ.
Why does Abdul Haleem use the present tense? The entire verse is grammatically in the past tense but it doesn't specifically mean that the incidents happened in the past. In Arabic, you may use the past tense in certain occasions to indicate a general truth.		

237. Can you add و to the predicate of كَانَ?

Yes, this is possible.

For stylistic reasons, you can add و before the predicate of كَانَ. It works in both tenses, the past (الْماضِي) and present tense (الْمُضارِعُ). However, two things must be fulfilled to make it work:

1. The verb كَانَ must be negated (نَفْيٌ).

2. The predicate (خَبَرُ كانَ) must be interlinked with إلّا.

Sounds complicated? Let's analyze an example.

Every man has an end/his appointed term (i.e., death).	ما كانَ مِنْ إِنْسانٍ إِلّا وَلَهُ أَجَلٌ.

Negation particle (حَرْفُ نَفْيٍ). It does not have a place in إِعْرابٌ.	ما
Defective, incomplete past tense verb (فِعْلٌ ماضٍ ناقِصٌ).	كانَ
Extra preposition (حَرْفُ جَرٍّ زائِدٌ) – see *question #127*.	مِن
Although you see the genitive case marker (nunation; كَسْرةٌ) due to the additional preposition, this word is grammatically the "subject" (اِسْمُ كانَ) and thus in the location of a nominative case – but only by virtual case markers (مَرْفُوعٌ بِضَمّةٍ مُقَدّرةٍ) as the preceding preposition occupies the spot of the case markers (اِشْتِغالُ المَحَلّ بِحَرَكةِ حَرْفِ الجَرِّ الزّائِدِ).	إِنْسانٍ
Particle of exception (حَرْفُ اِسْتِثْناءٍ مُلْغًى) that doesn't exercise its operating power as its job as an operator was canceled; see #403.	إِلّا
Particle (حَرْفٌ) which jumps on – let's say, encroaches on – the predicate (خَبَرُ كانَ). It does not have a position in إِعْرابٌ.	وَ
This لـ is a real preposition (حَرْفُ الجَرِّ) and does not have a place in إِعْرابٌ. The ه is a pronominal suffix (ضَمِيرٌ), in the position of a genitive case (فِي مَحَلّ جَرٍّ). You can't put the actual case marker since ه is indeclinable. The prepositional phrase (الجارُّ وَالمَجْرُورُ) serves as the fronted **predicate** (خَبَرٌ مُقَدّمٌ) and is placed in the position of a nominative case (فِي مَحَلّ رَفْعٍ).	لَهُ
Delayed **subject** (مُبْتَدَأٌ مُؤَخَّرٌ); therefore, it is in the nominative case (مَرْفُوعٌ بِالضَّمّةِ الظّاهِرةِ).	أَجَلٌ
The sentence consisting of subject (مُبْتَدَأٌ) and predicate (لَهُ أَجَلٌ) gets the "place value" of an accusative (!) case because it is located in the position of the **predicate** of كانَ. In Arabic, we say: فِي مَحَلّ نَصْبِ خَبَرُ كانَ.	

Excursus: أَجَلٌ is not easy to translate. Basically, it denotes the *assigned, appointed term* or *period*; the *time of falling due; the time that something lasts for* (مُدّةُ الشَّيْءِ). The idea behind أَجَلٌ goes way beyond that. It comprises the whole duration of life in this world of every human being, decreed by Allah; in other words, the fixed period of time that will end – with *death*. Depending on the context, we can translate أَجَلٌ as *fate* or *destiny*. With the definite article, الْأَجَلُ denotes *the hour of death*. That's why the Arabs say: *His death drew near* (دَنَا أَجَلُهُ). أَجَلٌ is found many times in the Qur'an:

Sura 7:34	**There is a time set** for every people: they can't hasten it, nor, when it comes, will they be able to delay it for a single moment.	وَلِكُلِّ أُمَّةٍ أَجَلٌ فَإِذَا جَاءَ أَجَلُهُمْ لَا يَسْتَأْخِرُونَ سَاعَةً وَلَا يَسْتَقْدِمُونَ.
Sura 10:11	If God were to hasten on for people the harm [they have earned] as they wish to hasten on the good, **their time would already be up.**	وَلَوْ يُعَجِّلُ اللّٰهُ لِلنَّاسِ الشَّرَّ اسْتِعْجَالَهُم بِالْخَيْرِ لَقُضِيَ إِلَيْهِمْ أَجَلُهُمْ.
Sura 7:185	Have they not contemplated the realm of the heavens and earth and all that God created, and **that the end of their time** might be near?	أَوَلَمْ يَنْظُرُوا فِي مَلَكُوتِ السَّمَاوَاتِ وَالْأَرْضِ وَمَا خَلَقَ اللّٰهُ مِن شَيْءٍ وَأَنْ، عَسَىٰ أَن يَكُونَ قَدِ اقْتَرَبَ أَجَلُهُمْ.

238. Is it possible to delete the ن in كَانَ؟

Yes, although it looks weird in writing. But it is also found in the Qur'an.

Let's jump right in the water. You can only delete the ن of كان provided that the following prerequisites are fulfilled:

1. The verb كان is used in the **present tense** (فِعْلٌ مُضَارِعٌ).

2. The verb must be in the **jussive mood** (مَجْزُومٌ). ▷ We need to negate the verb with لَم or we need a conditional particle before it.

3. The jussive is marked by سُكُون on the final letter.

4. Since the verb in question is كان, we have to find a way how to deal with the weak letter (i.e., يَكُونُ). If we just add the سُكُون, we would get يَكُونْ – but the collision of two سُكُون is impossible in Arabic! Therefore, we drop the و of the present tense and get: يَكُنْ

5. There is **no pronoun** (ضَمِيرٌ مُتَّصِلٌ) attached.

I was not a believer. (This equals لَم أَكُنْ.)	لَمْ أَكُ مُؤْمِنًا.

لَمْ أَكُ أَفْعَلُ ذَلِكَ.	I was not doing that.

لَمْ	Negation particle (حَرْفُ نَفْيٍ) that triggers the jussive (جَزْمٌ).
أَكُ	Present tense verb, in the مَجْزُومٌ-mood by لَمْ. The marker for the جَزْمٌ is the سُكُونٌ on the **deleted** ن. The اِسْمُ أَكُنْ ("subject") is a hidden pronoun (ضَمِيرٌ مُسْتَتِرٌ) with the implied meaning of *I* (أنا).
أَفْعَلُ	Present tense verb, indicative mood (marked by a ضَمّة). The subject (فاعِلٌ) is an implied pronoun (ضَمِيرٌ مُسْتَتِرٌ) expressing *I* (أنا).
	أَفْعَلُ is an entire verbal sentence and placed in the position of an accusative case because it **serves as the predicate of** أَكُنْ. In Arabic: الْجُمْلةُ مِنَ الْفِعْلِ وَالْفاعِلِ فِي مَحَلِّ نَصْبٍ خَبَرُ أَكُنْ

Let's see two examples of the Qur'an.

Sura 4:40	...if there is a good deed, He multiplies it and gives from Himself a great reward.	..وَإِن تَكُ حَسَنَةً يُضَاعِفْهَا وَيُؤْتِ مِن لَّدُنْهُ أَجْرًا عَظِيمًا.
Sura 74:43	They will say, "We were not of those who prayed,	قَالُوا لَمْ نَكُ مِنَ الْمُصَلِّينَ
Sura 74:44	Nor did we used to feed the poor."	وَلَمْ نَكُ نُطْعِمُ الْمِسْكِينَ.

239. Is it possible to delete كانَ without changing the meaning?

Yes, this is possible.

Before we dig deeper into the topic, let us first think about the implications which such an operation will entail. كانَ is accompanied by a primary noun – the "subject" (اِسْمُ كانَ) – and a predicate (خَبَرُ كانَ). When we delete كانَ, can a sentence still be understood properly?

In principle, there are three ways to delete كانَ:

1. You only delete كانَ.
2. You delete كانَ together with its اِسْمٌ. → Only the predicate remains.
3. You delete كانَ with its predicate (خَبَرٌ). → Only the اِسْمٌ remains.

Option 1. You only delete كان.

This occurs occasionally in Modern Standard Arabic, but used to be very rare in Classical Arabic. For example:

Since you were generous, you are loved.	أَمَّا أَنْتَ كَرِيمًا فَأَنْتَ مَحْبُوبٌ.
Here, أَمَّا is not the usual conditional, corroborative particle أَمَّا which is translated as: *as for... is concerned; but; on the other hand.* See analysis below.	

QUESTION: Why can there be a مَنْصُوب-form when you don't have a verb? The grammarians say that this sentence used to be as follows:

You are loved because you were generous.	أَنْتَ مَحْبُوبٌ لِأَنْ كُنْتَ كَرِيمًا.

We can figure that أَمَّا أَنْتَ is for لِأَنْ كُنْتَ. But how is that possible? The letter ل and the verb (كُنْتَ) are suppressed for the sake of abridgment – with the effect that the pronoun (تَ in كُنْتَ) gets separated: أَنْتَ.

The ما is a substitute for the verb and is redundant (ما الزَّائِدَةُ); it does not have any operating power. The ن of أَنْ (which is a particle to produce an interpreted infinitive (أَنْ الْمَصْدَرِيَّة) is embodied in the م of ما – as a result, we get: أَمَّا. We call this process إِدْغامٌ.

This construction is all about **cause and effect** (الْعِلَّةُ والمَعْلُولُ). Let's first check the effect: أَنْتَ كُنْتَ كَرِيمًا. The cause for that is: لِأَنْ كُنْتَ كَرِيمًا. How can we put all this together to get a sentence without كان؟

Here are the steps:

1. Put the cause before the effect. ▷ We get the following sentence:

Because you were generous, you are loved.	لِأَنْ كُنْتَ كَرِيمًا فَأَنْتَ مَحْبُوبٌ.

2. Delete the لامُ الْجَرِّ. What is left now is أَنْ. It is a أَنْ الْمَصْدَرِيَّة which helps us to produce an interpreted مَصْدَر, a so-called مَصْدَرٌ مُؤَوَّلٌ. This means that we are ready now to connect a verb.

3. Delete كان and compensate/replace it with an extra device (حَرْفٌ زائِدٌ): a redundant ما. Then assimilate the ما with the ن of أَنْ, a process that is called تَدَغُّمٌ. Finally, the result is: أَمَّا.

4. The last remnant is the pronoun suffix of كُنْتَ: the ت. We change that into a free (separate) personal pronoun (ضَمِيرٌ مُنْفَصِلٌ) which is أَنْتَ. Why do we have to do this? When we deleted كانَ, the connecting idea between the two parts of the sentence got lost. ➢ We need a filler.

The final result is the following sentence which we are going to analyze in depth because sentences like these can give you a headache if you want to translate them properly.

Since you were generous, you are loved.	أَمَّا أَنْتَ كَرِيمًا فَأَنْتَ مَحْبُوبٌ.

أَمَّا	This "artificial" word was originally أَنْ + ما. The particle أَنْ is a (حَرْفُ مَصْدَرٍ) حَرْفُ مَصْدَرِيَّةٍ which doesn't have a place in إِعْرابٌ. The word ما is a redundant, extra particle (حَرْفٌ زائِدٌ) that compensates for the deletion of كانَ.
أَنْتَ	This is the noun ("subject") of the **deleted verb** كانَ, the اِسْمُ كانَ الْمَحْذُوفة. The personal pronoun (ضَمِيرٌ مُنْفَصِلٌ) has a fixed ending; grammatically, however, it is in the position of a nominative case (مَبْنِيٌّ عَلَى الْفَتْحِ فِي مَحَلِّ رَفْعٍ).
كَرِيمًا	Predicate of the deleted verb كانَ; therefore, it has to take the accusative case which is clearly visible by the ending "-an" (خَبَرُ كانَ الْمَحْذُوفةِ مَنْصُوبٌ بِالْفَتْحةِ الظّاهِرةِ).

Option 2. Delete كانَ and its "subject" (اِسْمُ كانَ).

This is only possible after the conditional particles إِنْ and لَوْ.

Every man is accountable for his work; good for good, and evil for evil.	كُلُّ اِنْسانٍ مُحاسِبٌ عَلَى عَمَلِهِ؛ إِنْ خَيْرًا فَخَيْرٌ وَإِنْ شَرًّا فَشَرٌّ.
We could also use a more literal translation: *If it was good, then it will be good (for him), and if it was bad then it will be bad (for him).*	

إِنْ	Conditional particle (حَرْفُ شَرْطٍ). Doesn't have a place in إِعْرابٌ.
خَيْرًا	**Predicate** of the **deleted** verb كانَ. That is why the word is in the accusative case (مَنْصُوبٌ) as indicated by the nunation "-an" خَبَرُ كانَ الْمَحْذُوفةِ مَنْصُوبٌ بِالْفَتْحةِ الظّاهِرةِ). ➡ Not only the verb, but also the "subject" (اِسْمُ كانَ) is deleted (إِسْمُها مَحْذُوفٌ أَيْضًا).

How did this sentence originally look like?

If their deeds are good, their set-off (i.e., reward) will be good. If their deeds are evil, their set-off (i.e., punishment) will be bad.	إِنْ كَانَ عَمَلُهُمْ خَيْرًا فَجَزَاؤُهُمْ خَيْرٌ ، وَإِنْ كَانَ عَمَلُهُمْ شَرًّا فَجَزَاؤُهُمْ شَرٌّ.

Some more examples:

The Messenger of Allah said, "Try (to find something), even if it were an iron ring." *Sahīh al-Bukhārī 5135*	قَالَ رَسُولُ اللهِ: الْتَمِسْ وَلَوْ خَاتَمًا مِنْ حَدِيدٍ.

The underlying meaning is: →	وَلَوْ كَانَ الَّذِي تَلْتَمِسُهُ خَاتَمًا مِنْ حَدِيدٍ.

Read every day even if it was a newspaper.	إِقْرَأْ كُلَّ يَوْمٍ وَلَوْ صَحِيفَةً.

Conditional particle (حَرْفُ شَرْطٍ); no position in إِعْرَابٌ.	لَوْ
Predicate of the deleted verb كَانَ; therefore, it takes the accusative case. The "subject" (اِسْمُ كَانَ) was deleted.	صَحِيفَةً

How would this sentence look like with كَانَ?

Read every day even if the read text was a newspaper.	إِقْرَأْ كُلَّ يَوْمٍ وَلَوْ كَانَ الْمَقْرُوءُ صَحِيفَةً.

Option 3. Delete كَانَ **and its predicate**; so only the اِسْمُ كَانَ remains. This is rare. It is only possible when كَانَ comes after إِنْ or لَوْ.

Every human being is accountable for his work; good for good, and evil for evil.	كُلُّ اِنْسان محاسِبٌ عَلَى عَمَلِهِ إِنْ خَيْرٌ فَخَيْرٌ وَإِنْ شَرٌّ فَشَرٌّ.

Conditional particle (حَرْفُ شَرْطٍ); doesn't have a position in إِعْرَابٌ.	إِنْ
This is the اِسْمُ كَانَ of the deleted verb كَانَ; therefore, it has to be in the nominative case (اِسْمُ كَانَ الْمَحْذُوفةِ مَرْفُوعٌ بِالضَّمَّةِ). The predicate of كَانَ is also deleted (خَبَرُها مَحْذُوفٌ).	خَيْرٌ

How did the sentence look like?

If there is good in their work, their set-off (= reward) will be good. If there is bad in their work, their set-off (= punishment) will be bad.	إِنْ كَانَ فِي عَمَلِهِمْ خَيْرٌ فَجَزَاؤُهُمْ خَيْرٌ وَإِنْ كَانَ فِي عَمَلِهِمْ شَرٌّ فَجَزَاؤُهُمْ شَرٌّ.

You may omit كان without any compensation when answering a question:

Will you travel even if (though) it will rain?	هَلْ سَتُسَافِرُ وَإِنْ كَانَ الْجَوُّ مُمْطِرًا؟
Yes, even if it rains.	نَعَم وَإِنْ.
In the meaning of (التَّقْدِيرُ): →	وَإِنْ كَانَ الْجَوُّ مُمْطِرًا.

THE SISTERS OF كانَ

240. Why are they called *sisters*?

Because they share similar grammatical implications and ideas.

All sisters of كانَ share the following: they add some circumstantial or modifying idea to the simple idea of existence. This may be the idea of duration or continuity, the idea of time, or the idea of negation (i.e., the existence itself is absolutely denied). Furthermore, many *sisters* are often just used to convey a similar meaning of كانَ.

This means that the additional idea of time (morning, night, etc.) which they could convey is neglected. In rare situations, they work as **full/complete verbs** (فِعْلٌ تَامٌّ) conveying their original meaning, except for the idea of negation (لَيْسَ - فَتِئَ - زالَ).

241. How many sisters does كانَ have?

Thirteen.

The verb كانَ is the most important *abrogator* (نَاسِخٌ) of the common rules. It is an *incomplete, abrogating verb* (فِعْلٌ نَاسِخٌ نَاقِصٌ). Incomplete here means that the verb is not satisfied with its subject alone. ➢ It needs a predicate. Let's get to know the family of كانَ.

1	كَانَ	to be; exist	9	لَيْسَ		not (denying of existence)
2	ظَلَّ		10	زَالَ		*still; not to stop doing* (when used with a negation)
3	بَاتَ		11	بَرِحَ		Usually grammarians do not cut these expressions into ما and the
4	أَصْبَحَ		12	فَتِئَ	ما	verb. So you don't say that the ما is a negation particle (حَرْفُ نَفْيٍ) or a
5	أَسْفَرَ	to become	13	إنْفَكَّ		particle to mold an infinitive (ما المَصْدَرِيَّةُ ظَرْفِيَّة). Instead, ما + verb
6	أَضْحَى		14	دَامَ		is treated as one entity.
7	أَمْسَى					
8	صَارَ		Note: لَيْسَ and دَامَ are the only two sisters of كَانَ that are only conjugated in the past tense.			

Many of these *sisters* are not used anymore. In fact, even in ancient times, in Classical Arabic, some of them were hardly used. Still, it's interesting to look at them to get a better feel for how Arabic actually works. The ideas that those verbs convey are similar to those of كَانَ:

- The idea of duration or continuity (دَامَ) or of *to cease* (with a negation particle).

- The idea of change or conversion (صَارَ).

- The idea of time: *to be or do during the whole day* (ظَلَّ), *during the whole night* (بَاتَ), *at daybreak* (أَسْفَرَ), *in the morning* (أَصبحَ), *in the forenoon* (أَضْحَى), *in the evening* (أَمْسَى).

- Many *sisters* are often used as synonyms of كَانَ without any regard to the secondary idea of time or negation.

The *verbs of approaching* or *beginning* (أَفْعالُ الْمُقارَبةِ) are **relatives of the sisters**. There are of two types:

TYPE 1: كَادَ and أَوْشَكَ and كَرَبَ. They indicate the **proximity of the predicate.** They convey: *almost; to be about to; to be on the verge of.*

The verb كَادَ is used in both tenses, present and past. Originally it went along with a إسْمٌ in the accusative case serving as the predicate (خَبَرُ كَادَ مَنْصُوبٌ); but it is more common now that كَادَ is used with a verbal sentence (indicative mood, مَرْفُوعٌ) serving as the predicate. In rare situations, an interpreted مَصْدَر is used, molded by أَنْ. For ex.: لا يَكادُ أَحَدٌ يَفْهَمُ ما يَقولُهُ (*Hardly anyone understands what he says*).

أَوْشَكَ generally goes along with أَنْ plus a verb in the subjunctive mood (مَنْصوبٌ); in rare situations, a verb in the present tense, indicative mood (مَرْفوعٌ), follows immediately. For ex.: أَوْشَكْتُ أَنْ أَنْسَى الأَمْرَ (*I almost forgot it*).

The verb كَرَبَ (sometimes: كَرِبَ) is only used in the past tense and is constructed with the present tense indicative; rarely you see it with أَنْ plus a verb in the مَنْصوبٌ-mood producing an interpreted مَصْدَرٌ.

> **TYPE 2:** عَسَى and إِخْلَوْلَقَ and حَرَى. They convey the **hope of the occurrence of the predicate**. Possible translations: *may be that; might; it could be that; possibly.* They imply eager desire or hope, sometimes also fear; rarely opinion or certainty.

These three verbs are **only used** in the **past tense** – but are translated into English with the **meaning** of the **present** or **future tense**.

Originally they were used like كادَ, i.e, with a noun in the accusative case (مَنْصوبٌ) serving as the predicate. But it is more common now to use them with أَنْ plus a verb in the مَنْصوبٌ-mood producing an interpreted مَصْدَرٌ. This interpreted مَصْدَرٌ serves as the subject (فاعِلٌ).

As for عَسَى the following construction is common: you use the third person masculine (i.e., عَسَى) and add a pronominal suffix in the accusative case (ضَميرُ نَصْبٍ) such as ك or ه or ها. For example: عَساكَ (*perhaps you*). For the details, see *question #242*.

حَرَى and إِخْلَوْلَقَ are rarely encountered. They are followed by أَنْ plus a verb in the مَنْصوبٌ-mood.

242. How do you know whether عَسَى is an incomplete or full verb?

By looking at the word order.

عَسَى is one of the most mysterious verbs in Arabic. Scholars are not sure about its nature and had several disputes. I will try to present the common ground. I want to send something ahead: the meaning of both verb forms (syntactically complete or incomplete) is in many situations almost the same – but the grammatical analysis is different.

SITUATION 1: عَسَى is a **full/complete verb** (فِعْلٌ تَامٌّ). It governs the subject (فَاعِلٌ) in the nominative case (مَرْفُوعٌ). The subject is an interpreted مَصْدَرٌ. This style is more eloquent and more common.

Such constructions are typical when عَسَى is **immediately** followed by أَنْ plus a verb in the subjunctive mood (مَنْصُوبٌ). So, there is nothing between عَسَى and أَنْ. We could say that we stripped off the اِسْمُ عَسَى.

- The interpreted مَصْدَرٌ serves as the **subject** (فَاعِلٌ) and is located in the position of a nominative case (فِي مَحَلِّ رَفْعِ فَاعِلٍ).

- As a full verb, عَسَى doesn't need a predicate (لَا يَطْلُبُ اِسْمًا وَخَبَرًا، بَلْ يَطْلُبُ فَاعِلًا).

It is time for Zayd to leave. The meaning is: **Zayd's departure** (= the subject) is near to being a fact/may be a fact.	عَسَى أَنْ يُغَادِرَ زَيْدٌ.

We have a III-verb which forms the مَصْدَرٌ following the pattern مُفَاعَلَةٌ. The part أَنْ يُغَادِرَ زَيْدٍ is equivalent to مُغَادَرَةُ زَيْدٍ. Here, the verb plus its subject (visibly expressed by a suffix or hidden in the verb عَسَى) are enough for us to know what is going on with *Zayd*.

Full/complete past tense verb (فِعْلٌ مَاضٍ تَامٌّ).	عَسَى
أَنْ is a device to mold an infinitive (حَرْفُ مَصْدَرِيَّةٍ). It is followed by a verb in the subjunctive mood (فِعْلٌ مُضَارِعٌ مَنْصُوبٌ بِأَنْ). The phrase أَنْ يُغَادِرَ serves as the **subject** (فَاعِلٌ) of عَسَى.	أَنْ يُغَادِرَ
Subject (فَاعِلٌ) of the verb يُغَادِرُ.	زَيْدٌ

▷ We have two subjects (فَاعِلٌ) because we have two verbs. What is the connection between them? The verb يُغَادِرُ has an implied, hidden pronoun (*he*) that functions as a link – because it refers back to the subject of عَسَى (فَاعِلُهُ ضَمِيرٌ يَعُودُ عَلَى فَاعِلِ عَسَى).

I am near to doing that.	عَسَيْتُ أَنْ أَفْعَلَ ذَلِكَ.
If I grant you that, **perhaps you** will	هَلْ عَسَيْتَ إِنْ أَعْطَيْتُكَ ذَلِكَ أَنْ

ask for more (*Sahīh Muslim 182 a*).	تَسْأَلَ غَيْرَهُ.

Sura 2:216	**You may** dislike something although it is good for you, or like something although it is bad for you: God knows and you do not.'	عَسَى أَنْ تَكْرَهُوا شَيْئًا وَهُوَ خَيْرٌ لَكُمْ وَعَسَى أَنْ تُحِبُّوا شَيْئًا وَهُوَ شَرٌّ لَّكُمْ وَاللهُ يَعْلَمُ وَأَنتُمْ لَا تَعْلَمُونَ.

Full/complete past tense verb (فِعْلٌ مَاضٍ جَامِدٌ تَامٌّ).	عَسَى
This interpreted مَصْدَرٌ مُؤَوَّلٌ) مَصْدَرٌ) functions as the subject (فَاعِلٌ) of the verb عَسَى. It is located in the position of a nominative case (فِي مَحَلِّ رَفْعٍ فَاعِلٌ).	أَنْ تَكْرَهُوا
Direct object (مَفْعُولٌ بِهِ) of the verb عَسَى; it therefore takes the accusative case (مَنْصُوبٌ).	شَيْئًا

SITUATION 2: عَسَى is an **incomplete, deficient** verb (فِعْلٌ نَاقِصٌ). It has the grammatical job and power of كَانَ.

Here, the **predicate** (which is highlighted in the translations below) is needed to understand the sentence, because without this information (i.e., the predicate), we would simply not know to which or where or what *Zayd* is close to (if we use the above example).

Let's first check some possible sentence structures if we use عَسَى as an incomplete, deficient verb. Notice the اِسْمُ عَسَى in the examples (the word after عَسَى. For the use of أَنْ, see *question #251*.

1	Khālid may travel.	عَسَى خَالِدٌ يُسَافِرُ.
2		عَسَى خَالِدٌ أَنْ يُسَافِرَ.
3	He may travel. (see *question #242*)	عَسَاهُ أَنْ يُسَافِرَ.

- If you use أَنْ after عَسَى, the **interpreted infinitive** (الْمَصْدَرُ الْمُؤَوَّلُ) will be the **predicate** (خَبَرُ عَسَى).

- If you don't use أَنْ, the **verbal sentence** will be the **predicate** (جُمْلَةُ الْفِعْلِ الْمُضَارِعِ).

| Zayd **is** near to departing (قَارَبَ زَيْدٌ الْقِيامَ). This is close to the meaning: I eagerly desire (I hope) that Zayd **may be** performing the act of departing/leaving (لَعَلَّ زَيْدًا أَنْ يَقُومَ). It may be that Zayd **is** (or **will be**) leaving. | عَسَى زَيْدٌ أَنْ يُغَادِرَ. (= عَسَى زَيْدٌ مُغَادَرَةً) |

Past tense verb, a so-called *verb of hope* (فِعْلٌ ماضٍ ناقِصٌ مِن أَفْعالِ الرَّجاءِ).	عَسَى
"Subject" (إِسْمُ عَسَى); nominative (مَرْفُوعٌ بِالضَّمَّةِ الظّاهِرةِ).	زَيْدٌ
The device أَنْ is a حَرْفُ نَصْبٍ. It is followed by a verb in the subjunctive mood (فِعْلٌ مُضارِعٌ مَنْصُوبٌ بِأَنْ), which is marked by a فَتْحةٌ. The subject (فاعِل) of this verb is a hidden pronoun expressing *he* (هُوَ) which refers back to *Zayd* (يَعُودُ عَلَى زَيْدٍ).	أَنْ يُغَادِرَ

| 17:8 | Your Lord may yet have mercy on you... | عَسَى رَبُّكُمْ أَنْ يَرْحَمَكُمْ... |

Incomplete past tense verb with the operating power of كانَ (فِعْلٌ ماضٍ جامِدٌ ناقِصٌ يَعْمَلُ عَمَلَ كانَ).	عَسَى
The "subject" (إِسْمُ عَسَى), in the nominative case (مَرْفُوعٌ); the pronoun suffix is the second part of the إضافةٌ.	رَبُّكُمْ
This is an interpreted مَصْدَر (مَصْدَرٌ مُؤَوَّلٌ) serving as the **predicate** (خَبَرُ عَسَى); we therefore assign the place value of an accusative case (فِي مَحَلِّ نَصْبٍ). The pronoun suffix is the direct object (مَفْعُولٌ بِه) of the verb. The subject of the verb (يَرْحَم) is concealed (فاعِلُه مُسْتَتِرٌ). The verb itself is in the subjunctive mood (فِعْلٌ مُضارِعٌ مَنْصُوبٌ بِأَنْ).	أَنْ يَرْحَمَكُمْ

Watch out: If we have a singular word as the subject, we can't really tell if عَسَى is a full or incomplete verb. In our first example (عَسَى أَنْ يُغَادِرَ زَيْدٌ), we could also treat it as an incomplete verb as most grammarians say. The analysis would be as follows:

| Past tense verb, incomplete (فِعْلٌ ماضٍ ناقِصٌ). | عَسَى |
| This expression takes over the role of the subject and the predicate (أَنْ وَما دَخَلَتْ عَلَيْهِ سَدَّتْ مَسَدَّ الْإِسْمِ وَالْخَبَرِ). See *question #37* for an explanation of the term سَدَّ مَسَدَّ. | أَنْ يُغَادِرَ زَيْدٌ |

Can you always choose whether you want to treat عَسَى as a full or incomplete verb? No, you can't!

As soon as there is a **dual or plural** involved, you have only **one option**. Let's analyze the sentence: *Both (two) Zayds are close to standing.*

1	**full verb (تَامَّةٌ)**	عَسَى أَنْ يُغَادِرَ الزَّيْدَانِ.
2	incomplete (نَاقِصَةٌ)	عَسَى أَنْ يُغَادِرَا الزَّيْدان.
	➢ This would mean that عَسَى can be interpreted as the **fronted predicate** (مُبْتَدَأٌ مُؤَخَّرٌ) and الزَّيْدانِ as the **delayed subject** (خَبَر مُقَدَّم).	

Is option 2 possible in Arabic? No, it isn't.

We will see why. Let's reverse the word order in our mind. Can you start a verbal sentence with a verb in the dual (or plural), in our example: (*they both leave*), يُغَادِرَا؟

Isn't there a rule that says that the verb must be singular (masculine or feminine) if it is placed before the subject? Yes, this is a rule in Arabic. Only in a certain, ancient Arabic dialect (أَكَلُوني الْبَراغِيثُ), it was possible to use the verb in the dual or plural when it starts a sentence (see *question #20*).

Remark: Some grammarians say that the following two sentences (with an <u>in</u>complete verb) are possible in Arabic. They both mean: *Zayd perhaps leaves/may depart.*

1	عَسَى زَيْدٌ مُغَادَرَتُهُ = عَسَى زَيْدٌ يُغَادِرُ.
	In this example, the مَصْدَر (the word مُغَادَرَتُهُ) is a *comprehensive apposition* (بَدَلُ اشْتِمالٍ) for زَيْدٌ. This type of apposition can't be a real part of the word to which it refers. As an apposition, it gets the same case marker as the الْمُبْدَلُ مِنهُ. This is similar to the application of كَادَ.

2	عَسَى زَيْدٌ مُغَادِرٌ.
	Here, عَسَى is treated as an incomplete verb. But where is the "subject" (اسْمُ عَسَى)? It is suppressed. It's a pronoun of the fact (ضَمِيرُ الشَّأْنِ), in our example: إنَّهُ. Therefore, the meaning is: *It may be that the case is this, Zayd is leaving.*

243. What is the job of the كَ in the phrase عَساك (perhaps you)?

It is not entirely clear. There are several ideas.

Let's start with two examples:

It may be that **he** will appear.	عَساهُ (أَنْ) يَحْضُرَ.
What could **he** possibly say?	ماذَا عَساهُ يَقُولُ؟
The meaning here is: مَاذَا بِإِمْكَانِهِ أَنْ يَقُولَ	

The DNA of عَسَى was the subject of many debates. Classical Arabic admits two forms of conjugation: عَسَيْتُ and عَساني for *I may*; عَسَيْتَ and عَساك for *you may, etc.*

In other words, you conjugate عَسَى as a regular past tense verb – or you treat it as a frozen device and add pronouns. We have noted in the previous *question #242* that عَسَى may work as a full **or** incomplete verb. Both approaches raise some questions. If it is a full verb (فِعْلٌ تامٌّ), we could say that the pronoun suffix (ه) is the direct object – but in the above examples, it is clearly the subject in the translation.

If it is an incomplete verb (فِعْلٌ ناقِصٌ), we run into another problem. عَسَى then behaves like a *sister of* كان which means that عَسَى governs the subject (اِسْمُ عَسَى) in the nominative (مَرْفُوعٌ) and only the predicate (خَبَرُ عَسَى) in the accusative case (مَنْصُوبٌ). Using this logic, how can we justify the pronoun suffix (ه) which would be placed in the location of an accusative? **There are three different opinions.**

APPROACH 1: The grammarian al-Mubarrad (الْمُبَرّد) said that the pronoun suffix is, in fact, a **fronted predicate** (خَبَرُ عَسَى مُقَدَّمٌ). After that, you will find the delayed "subject" (اِسْمُ عَسَى مُؤَخَّرٌ).

APPROACH 2: The grammarian al-'Akhfash (الْأَخْفَش) had another idea. He said that the pronoun in the accusative case is a **deputy** for the **pronoun** in the **nominative** (ضَمِيرُ النَّصْبِ نائِبٌ عَنْ ضَمِيرِ الرَّفْعِ).

APPROACH 3: This is what Sībawayhi (سيبويه) proposed. As soon as we attach a pronoun suffix, عَسَى is treated like a **particle** (حَرْفٌ). To justify that, we now use لَعَلَّ as a role model because لَعَلَّ (which denotes *perhaps*) is a *sister of* إِنَّ. Such words (إِنَّ وَأَخَواتُها) govern the "subject" (إِسْمُ لَعَلَّ) in the **accusative** case. عَسَى would convey pretty much the same meaning as لَعَلَّ. We have to use the accusative case for the pronoun. If we referred to ourselves (= *me*), we would have to use the suffix نِي because of the last letter ي. For example: لَعَلِّي or عَساني.

Is all that important? Actually, it is. Let's look at the following two sentences. Which one is correct?

correct	You may be fine. (Hopefully you are fine.)	عَساكُمْ طَيِّبُونَ.
incorrect		عَساكُمْ طَيِّبِينَ.
The evaluation depends on the **grammatical interpretation**. The probably **most correct view** is **APPROACH 3**. If we say that عَسَى works like إِنَّ regarding its governing power since it conveys the meaning of لَعَلَّ, then the pronoun suffix كُمْ is the "subject" (إِسْمُ عَسَى) which has to be in the accusative case (فِي مَحَلِّ نَصْبٍ). The predicate (خَبَرُ عَسَى) must be in the nominative case (مَرْفُوعٌ). Therefore, the answer is: طَيِّبُونَ.		

244. Many verbs mean *to become*. Can they convey other meanings too?

Yes, they can.

All verbs that express *to become* are *sisters* of كانَ.

Sometimes, however, they convey their original meaning and function as a (syntactically) **full verb** (فِعْلٌ تامٌّ). Then they are happy with just a subject and don't need a predicate to convey a meaningful sentence. This explains why all these verbs do not only mean *to become*.

1	*to be by day; to be or do during the whole day*	ظَلَّ
This verb conveys the meaning of continuation, continuity (إِسْتِمْرارٌ).		

Karīm stayed standing.	ظَلَّ كَرِيمٌ قائِمًا.

2	to be in the morning	أَصْبَحَ

The child became a man.	أَصْبَحَ الطِّفْلُ رَجُلًا.

أَصْبَحَ can be used as a **full verb** (فِعْلٌ تَامٌّ) conveying *that we entered the time of the morning* (يُفِيدُ مَعْنَى الدُّخُولِ فِي وَقْتِ الصَّباحِ).

He stayed awake until the morning.	ظَلَّ ساهِرًا حَتَّى أَصْبَحَ.

This is the meaning: →	ظَلَّ ساهِرًا حَتَّى دَخَلَ فِي وَقْتِ الصَّباحِ.

3	*to be in the forenoon*	أَضْحَى

The root ض-ح-و means *to become visible; to be struck by the sun's rays.* Notice that form II (ضَحَّى) means *to sacrifice;* form IV (أَضْحَى) *to bring to light, to become, to begin with* (followed by a verb in the present tense).

The worker became immersed in his work.	أَضْحَى الْعامِلُ مُسْتَغْرِقًا فِي عَمَلِهِ.

أَضْحَى can convey the meaning of صارَ, i.e., *to become* having the core meaning of change, transformation.

Science became necessary.	أَضْحَى الْعِلْمُ ضَرُورِيًّا.

أَضْحَى can also be used as a **full verb** (فِعْلٌ تَامٌّ).

He slept until forenoon.	ظَلَّ نائِمًا حَتَّى أَضْحَى.

This is the meaning: *...until he entered the time of forenoon.*	ظَلَّ نائِمًا حَتَّى دَخَلَ فِي وَقْتِ الضُّحَى.

4	*to be (or do) in the evening*	أَمْسَى

The man became worried.	أَمْسَى الرَّجُلُ مَهْمُومًا.
The unknown became known.	أَمْسَى الْمَجْهُولُ مَعْلُومًا.

As a full verb, it denotes *to do in the evening.* In the following examples, notice the word تُصْبِحُونَ which is the present tense of أَصْبَحَ and means *to be in the morning.*

Evening came upon you while you	أَمْسَى عَلَيْكَ الْمَساءُ وَ أَنْتَ ما زِلْتَ

| were still in Beirut. | في بَيْرُوتَ. |

| Sura 30:17 | So exalted is Allah when you reach the evening *(so celebrate Allah's glory in the evening)* and when you reach the morning. | فَسُبْحَانَ اللهِ حِينَ تُمْسُونَ وَحِينَ تُصْبِحُونَ. |

| 5 | *to be by night* | بات |

| The student stayed up throughout the night. | بات الطّالِبُ ساهِرًا. |

بات	Defective, incomplete past tense verb (فِعْلٌ ماضٍ ناقِصٌ).
الطّالِبُ	This is the "subject" (إسْمُ بات) in the nominative case (مَرْفُوعٌ).
ساهِرًا	Predicate of بات in the accusative case (خَبَرُ بات مَنْصُوبٌ).

بات can be used as a **full verb** (فِعْلٌ تامٌّ) as well:

| The stranger **spent** the night in our house. | بات الْغَرِيبُ فِي بَيْتِنا. |
| This is the meaning of the above sentence: | قَضَى الْغَرِيبُ لَيْلَهُ فِي بَيْتِنا. |

| بات | This is a **full** past tense verb (فِعْلٌ ماضٍ تامٌّ). |
| الْغَرِيبُ | Subject (فاعِلٌ); nominative case (مَرْفُوعٌ بِالضَّمّةِ الظّاهِرةِ). |

245. Which verbs convey change or transformation?

There are many verbs.

They are all *sisters of* كانَ and need a subject (إسْمٌ *of the respective verb*) and a predicate (خَبَرٌ *of the respective verb*) – and <u>not</u> a direct object (مَفْعُولٌ بِه) or a specification (تَمْيِيزٌ). Sometimes they are full verbs. The following verbs express the idea of change or conversion (التَّحَوُّلُ):

| 1 | *to become* | صارَ |

| The slave became free. | صارَ الْعَبْدُ حُرًّا. |

| 2 | *to turn out; to become* | رَجَعَ | عادَ | آضَ |

The boy became a man.	آضَ الْغُلامُ رَجُلًا.
"Subject" in the nominative case (إِسْمُ آضَ مَرْفُوعٌ).	الْغُلامُ
Predicate of آضَ in the accusative case (خَبَرُ آضَ مَنْصُوبٌ).	رَجُلًا

The village became/turned into a city.	عادَتْ الْقَرْيَةُ مَدِينةً.

Watch out: عادَ might look like a "regular" verb. In this application it conveys the meaning of change or transformation! Therefore, عادَ is a sister of كانَ here similar to all the other verbs that we present in this *question*.

Defective/incomplete verb in the past tense (فِعْلٌ ماضٍ ناقِصٌ). It is not satisfied with a subject, it also needs a predicate.	عادَتْ
This is the "subject" (إِسْمُ عادَ) in the nominative case (مَرْفُوعٌ).	الْقَرْيةُ
This is the **predicate** (خَبَرُ عادَ) in the accusative case (مَنْصُوبٌ).	مَدِينةً

An enemy never becomes a friend.	الْعَدُوُّ ما يَرْجِعُ صَدِيقًا.

3	to be transformed	تَحَوَّلَ	إِسْتَحالَ

The fire turned into ashes.	إِسْتَحالَتْ النَّارُ رَمادًا.

Defective, incomplete past tense verb (فِعْلٌ ماضٍ ناقِصٌ).	إِسْتَحالَتْ
"Subject" (إِسْمُ إِسْتَحالَ) in the nominative case (مَرْفُوعٌ).	النَّارُ
Predicate in the accusative case (خَبَرُ إِسْتَحالَ مَنْصُوبٌ).	رَمادًا

The wheat was turned/transformed into bread.	تَحَوَّلَ الْقَمْحُ خُبْزًا.

4	to turn into (also: to be/go in the morning)	غَدَا

The work became tiresome/boring.	غَدَا الْعَمَلُ مُمِلًّا.

246. Can you add the preposition ـب to the predicate of a *sister*?

Yes, you can.

All sisters of كانَ, **when negated**, are often seen with the letter ـب before the predicate (خَبَرٌ). The purpose of such extra/redundant preposition is to convey emphasis. The ـب is an intensifier.

Karīm did not use to be (wasn't) careless.	مَا كَانَ كَرِيمٌ بِمُهْمِلٍ.

Negation particle (حَرْفُ نَفْيٍ). It does not have a place in إِعْرَابٌ.	مَا
Defective, incomplete past tense verb (فِعْلٌ مَاضٍ نَاقِصٌ). It needs a predicate as the verb itself doesn't convey an action/description.	كَانَ
This is the subject (اِسْمُ كَانَ) in the nominative case (مَرْفُوعٌ).	كَرِيمٌ
Extra (redundant) preposition (حَرْفُ جَرٍّ زَائِدٌ).	ب
Predicate (خَبَرُ كَانَ); therefore, it is located in the position of an accusative case. But we can only assign estimated, virtual case markers (مَنْصُوبٌ بِفَتْحَةٍ مُقَدَّرَةٍ). Why? You cannot put the فَتْحَة (nunation) on the last letter since this position is occupied by the preceding preposition (اِشْتِغَالُ الْمَحَلِّ بِحَرَكَةِ حَرْفِ الْجَرِّ الزَّائِدِ) which governs the word and triggers the كَسْرَة.	مُهْمِلٍ

Pretty much the same is true for the predicate of لَيْسَ.

You are not there to control them. (Sura 88:22)	لَسْتَ عَلَيْهِم بِمُصَيْطِرٍ.

➤ Do you know why مُسَيْطِر is written as مُصَيْطِر? – see *question #41*.

Defective (incomplete) past tense verb (فِعْلٌ مَاضٍ نَاقِصٌ). The pronoun suffix ت takes the position of the "subject" (اِسْمُ لَيْسَ), it is located in the spot of a nominative case. We can't mark it as such because the ت is indeclinable.	لَسْتَ
Prepositional phrase (جَارٌّ وَمَجْرُورٌ) which is linked to the predicate of لَيْسَ, in our example to مُصَيْطِر.	عَلَيْهِمْ
Additional preposition (حَرْفُ جَرٍّ زَائِدٌ); no position in إِعْرَابٌ.	ب
Predicate (خَبَرُ لَيْسَ); it is in the accusative case – but only by assumed case markers (مَنْصُوبٌ بِفَتْحَةٍ مُقَدَّرَةٍ) because of the preceding preposition which triggers the كَسْرَة (nunation).	مُصَيْطِر

STILL, TO REMAIN

In Arabic, there are many ways to express that nothing has changed. All the verbs that can transport this idea are *sisters of* كانَ, i.e., these verbs are defective, incomplete (فِعْلٌ ناقِصٌ) which means that they are not satisfied with only their subject – they need a predicate (خَبَرٌ) which has to take the accusative case (مَنْصُوبٌ).

There are **four verbs** in Arabic that are *sisters of* كانَ **–** but only if they are preceded by a **negation particle** which is usually ما. For example, if زال is used with a negation, paradoxically, it doesn't express a negation. It conveys the meaning of *continuity* (اِسْتِمْرارٌ). So if we negate the negation, we get the **confirmation** (إِثْباتٌ).

Without negation: *to cease; stop being; stop doing.*	زالَ - يَزالُ

Note: Many grammarians don't cut the expression into ما and the verb (فِعْلٌ). They don't say that ما is a negation particle (حَرْفُ نَفْيٍ). Instead, ما+verb is regarded as an entity.

Karim is still standing.	ما زالَ كَرِيمٌ قائِمًا.

Defective, incomplete past tense verb (فِعْلٌ ماضٍ ناقِصٌ).	ما زال
This is the اِسْمُ ما زَال in the nominative case (مَرْفُوعٌ).	كَرِيمٌ
This is the predicate (خَبَرُ ما زال); it gets the accusative case.	قائِمًا

247. Is there a difference between لا يَزالُ and ما يَزالُ؟

Yes, there is.

If you want to be on the safe side, use لا with the present tense and ما with the past tense.

	don't say:	better say:
present tense	ما يَزالُ	لا يَزالُ
past tense	لا زالَ	ما زالَ

Nevertheless, you might encounter both expressions in texts; especially ما is used with both tenses. Let's see what the difference is.

PRESENT TENSE: If you use مَا with the **present tense** (مَا يَزَالُ), it expresses an **absolute continuation**.

God is still Forgiving, Merciful.	مَا يَزَالُ اللهُ غَفُورًا رَحِيمًا.
This expresses that Allah has these attributes always and forever.	

The construction مَا يَزَالُ isn't found in the Qur'an – but in the Hadiths.

"A person **continues** lying and trying hard to lie until he is recorded at Allah as a liar." (*Sahīh Muslim 2607 c*)	مَا يَزَالُ الرَّجُلُ يَكْذِبُ وَيَتَحَرَّى الْكَذِبَ حَتَّى يُكْتَبَ عِنْدَ اللهِ كَذَّابًا.

PAST TENSE: If you use مَا with the **past** (مَا زَالَ) or لَا with the **present tense** (لَا يَزَالُ), it expresses a **continuation until the time of utterance**. It may change right after the utterance or in the future.

The student is still in the exam. (Note: for sure he won't stay there forever...)	ما زالَ الطَّالِبُ فِي الْإِخْتِبارِ.
The people will remain on the right path **as long as** they hasten the breaking of the fast. (*Sahīh al-Bukhārī 1957*)	لَا يَزَالُ النَّاسُ بِخَيْرٍ مَا عَجَّلُوا الْفِطْرَ.
Sura 22:55	وَلَا يَزَالُ الَّذِينَ كَفَرُوا فِي مِرْيَةٍ مِّنْهُ حَتَّى تَأْتِيَهُمُ السَّاعَةُ بَغْتَةً أَوْ يَأْتِيَهُمْ عَذَابُ يَوْمٍ عَقِيمٍ.
The disbelievers **will remain (will not cease to be)** in doubt about it until the Hour suddenly overpowers them or until torment descends on them on a Day devoid of all hope.	

Excursus: What about using لَا with the **past tense**? The negation of a verb in the past tense with لَا is grammatically possible, but only in rare occasions. You mainly encounter it in **requests** or **invocations** (دُعَاءٌ). You need to be careful to get the correct meaning of such constructions. Let's check them.

1. You repeat what did not happen.

Sura 75:31	He neither believed nor prayed.	فَلَا صَدَّقَ وَلَا صَلَّى.

2. You express an invocation (دُعاءٌ).

May God neither give him wellness nor healing!	لا عافاهُ اللهُ وَلا شافاهُ!
May your brother never return! (And not: Your brother hasn't come back.)	لا رَجَعَ أَخُوكَ!
This is an invocation that the rain will keep on coming down (دُعاءٌ بِاسْتِمْرارِ نُزُولِ الْمَطَرِ).	لا زالَ الْمَطَرُ نازِلًا!

3. You express the future by using the past tense.

I swear, I will never do that!	وَاللهِ لا فَعَلْتُ ذلِكَ أَبَدًا.
Watch out: Such sentences are often mistranslated as some people, especially in spoken Arabic, don't use أَبَدًا correctly – see *question #350*.	

248. Are there alternatives to زالَ?

Yes, there are.

Some verbs work similar to زالَ and also express continuity. They have to be negated to be seen as a *sister of* كانَ.

1	without negation	with negation	إنْفَكَّ
	to be separated; to be disengaged	*to not stop doing; keep doing*	

Karīm is still standing.	ما إنْفَكَّ كَرِيمٌ قائِمًا.

2	without negation	with negation	فَتِئَ
	to cease; desist; stop	*not to cease to be*	

The child did not stop crying.	ما فَتِئَ الطِّفْلُ يَبْكَى.

Past tense defective/incomplete verb (فِعْلٌ ماضٍ ناقِصٌ).	ما فَتِئَ
This is the "subject" (اِسْمُ ما فَتِئَ) in the nominative (مَرْفُوعٌ).	الطِّفْلُ
Verb in the present tense, indicative mood (فِعْلٌ مُضارِعٌ مَرْفُوعٌ). We can't put the mood marker (ـُ) due to the final ى.	يَبْكَى

The expression يَبْكَى is a verbal sentence itself which supplies the position of the predicate (خَبَرٌ) of ما فَتِئَ and is therefore found in the location of an accusative case (مَنْصُوبٌ).	

3	without negation	with negation	بَرِحَ
	to quit; leave; finish; end	to continue to be	

He is still poor.	ما بَرِحَ فَقِيرًا.

There is one more common expression to express *still*: ما دامَ. This construction is different from what we have seen so far. We will examine it in the following *question #249*.

249. What is the function of ما in the expression ما دامَ؟

It is not a negation. It is a device to mold a مَصْدَرٌ.

The construction is quite complicated. We should take it apart.

without negation	negated	دامَ
to continue; persevere. As a full verb (تامٌّ), it conveys the meaning of بَقِيَ: *to last, to remain*.	If negated, the verb won't express *still, as long as*. It conveys *not to last* – see question #250.	root: د-و-م
If دامَ is a full verb, the verb is already satisfied with its nominative; thus, it would only need a subject (and no predicate). However, if it is ناقِصٌ, then a noun in the nominative would not be enough (لا يَكْتَفِي بِمَرْفُوعِهِ).		

So, why do people use ما دامَ to express *still, as long as*?

Because in such constructions, ما is **not a negation device** but a so-called ما الْمَصْدَرِيّةُ الظَّرْفِيّةُ. Such a ما helps to produce an interpreted verbal *noun, infinitive* (مَصْدَرٌ مُؤَوَّلٌ). The مَصْدَرٌ only focuses on the action of the verb, it isolates the action from the time frame. And there is more: the ما is also ظَرْفِيّةٌ (*adverbial meaning*).

ما works as a proxy for a *"temporal object"* (نائِبٌ عَنِ الْمَفْعُولِ فِيهِ): an adverb of time. ما conveys **duration** (الْمُدّةُ) which explains why we usually translate it as *as long as, still*. Note: Grammarians often do not cut ما دامَ apart and treat the expression as one entity.

Sura 19:31	He commanded me to pray, to give alms **as long** as I live.	أَوْصَانِي بِالصَّلَاةِ وَالزَّكَاةِ مَا دُمْتُ حَيًّا.

Here, we have an **incomplete/defective or deficient verb** (فِعْلٌ نَاقِصٌ). This means that a subject alone would not be enough; we need a predicate to complete the meaning. The تَ of the verb is the "subject" (اِسْمُ ما دامَ) and حَيًّا is the predicate (خَبَرُ ما دامَ).

as long as I remain alive…	...ما دُمْتُ حَيًّا

The original مَصْدَرٌ of دامَ is دَوَامٌ and means *duration; permanence*. An equivalent of the expression مـا دُمْتُ حَيًّا could be the expression on the right (note the فَتْحَةٌ on مُدَّةَ).	مُدَّةَ دَوَامِي حَيًّا or دَوَامَي حَيًّا

The interpreted مَصْدَرٌ is placed in the spot of an accusative case – as a temporal adverb (الْمَصْدَرُ الْمُؤَوَّلُ فِي مَحَلِّ نَصْبٍ عَلَى الظَّرْفِيَّةِ الزَّمَانِيَّةِ).

I will not sit during the continuance of your standing. (*as long as you stand; while you stand -* مُدَّةَ قِيامِكَ).	لَا أَجْلِسُ ما دُمْتَ قَائِمًا.

The student succeeds as long as he studies.	يَنْجَحُ الطَّالِبُ ما دامَ مُجِدًّا.
This is what the sentence expresses: →	يَنْجَحُ الطَّالِبُ مُدَّةَ دَوامِهِ مُجِدًّا.

Past tense verb. The "subject" (اِسْمُ ما دامَ) is an implied pronoun (ضَمِيرٌ مُسْتَتِرٌ) expressing *he* (هُوَ).	ما دامَ
Predicate (خَبَرُ ما دامَ); thus, it needs the accusative case (مَنْصُوبٌ) which is visibly marked by the usual case markers.	مُجِدًّا

The expression ما دامَ (lit.: *continuance*) points to the continuity of the **predicate** (اِسْتِمْرَارُ الْخَبَرِ). The parts before and after ما دامَ are connected. The construction acts as an **auxiliary** (verb) to show the **temporal connection between two events** (تَرْكِيبٌ لَفْظِيٌّ يَعْمَلُ كَفِعْلٍ مُساعِدٍ لِبَيانِ التَّرابُطِ الزَّمَنِيِّ بَيْنَ حَدَثَيْنِ).

The first event/action occurs only throughout the continuation of the second event/action. In other words, the verb in the first sentence remains valid for the period of time defined in the second sentence. This is the construction:

جُمْلةُ خَبَرٍ أَوَّلٍ + ما دامَ + الْكائِنُ أَوِ الشَّيْءُ + جُمْلةُ خَبَرٍ ثانٍ

I praise you as long as you volunteer and contribute.	أُثْني عَلَيْكَ ما دُمْتَ تَتَطَوَّعُ وَتَتَبَرَّعُ.
Praise is connected with the action of *volunteering* (الثَّناءُ مُرْتَبِطٌ بِالتَّطَوُّعِ).	

However, ما doesn't always provide an adverbial meaning. Sometimes, in a construction with دامَ, it is just a device to produce a مَصْدَرٌ which means that we have a (syntactically) **full verb**. Then, the subject (فاعِلٌ) is enough to provide a full meaning.

Sura 11:106	The wretched ones will be in the Fire, sighing and groaning,	فَأَمَّا الَّذينَ شَقُوا فَفِي النَّارِ لَهُمْ فيها زَفيرٌ وَشَهيقٌ
Sura 11:107	there to remain for as long as the heavens and earth **endure**, unless your Lord wills otherwise	خالِدينَ فيها مَا دامَتِ السَّماوَاتُ وَالْأَرْضُ إِلَّا ما شَاءَ رَبُّكَ.

We have a ما الْمَصْدَرِيّة. It **does not have an** adverbial meaning (غَيْرُ ظَرْفِيّةٍ).
ما does not have a position in إِعْرابٌ. The verb دامَتْ is a فِعْلٌ ماضٍ تامٌّ.
Now, where is the subject (فاعِلٌ)? The تْ of the verb and السَّماوَاتُ supply the position of the subject. What about وَالْأَرْضُ? This word is coupled with *heavens* (مَعْطوفٌ عَلَى السَّمَوات).

Remark: In Classical Arabic, ما may occasionally mean *while* or *as often as*, followed by the past tense. Yet it usually goes along with دامَ to make the meaning clear.

I shall not forget your crying as long as I walk on the earth.	ما أَنْسَى بُكاءَكُمْ ما مَشَيْتُ عَلَى الأَرْضِ.

250. What happens if ما in ما دامَ is, in fact, a negation?

If ما *before the verb* دامَ *is a negation* (ما النّافِيةُ), *the verb* دامَ *works as a full verb* (فِعْلٌ تامٌّ).

Let's start with a simple sentence.

Nothing remained.	.ما دامَ شَيْءٌ
This is the meaning if we rewrite the sentence: →	.ما بَقِيَ شَيْءٌ
If دامَ here was a *sister of* كانَ, it would need a predicate to produce a meaningful sentence. However, the subject (فاعِلٌ) is enough here.	

The grammatical analysis is different now:

Negation particle (حَرْفُ نَفْي). It does not have a place in إعْرابٌ.	ما
(Full) past tense verb (فِعْلٌ ماضٍ تامٌّ).	دامَ
Subject (فاعِلٌ) of the verbal sentence and therefore in the nomi-native case (مَرْفوعٌ بِالضَّمّةِ الظّاهِرةِ).	شَيْء

VERBS OF APPROACHING

251. Should you use أنْ after أوْشَكَ؟

It depends.

The question, whether you need أنْ after a *verb of approaching* can give students of Arabic a headache. In fact, it is pretty hard stuff. The topic of this *question* is not only about أوْشَكَ which denotes *to be on the verge of; to be about to; almost*. What we say here is true for many verbs that work similar to كانَ. Let's start with two important points:

- The original, underlying basis of the structures that we are going to analyze is a nominal sentence (→ important for the implications).
- All these verbs abrogate rules (فِعْلٌ ناسِخةٌ) similar to كانَ. They turn a nominal sentence into a special one: the subject (مُبْتَدَأٌ) is called noun (اسْمٌ) of the respective verb. The predicate (خَبَرٌ) does not get the independent nominative case, but the dependent case, i.e., the accusative case.

The verbs we are going to analyze fit into three groups:

1. *Verbs of approaching* (أَفْعالُ الْمُقارَبةِ). They indicate the **nearness** (proximity) **of the predicate:** كادَ - أوْشَكَ - كَرَبَ.

2. *Verbs of beginning* (أَفْعالُ الشُّروع). They underline the meaning of the **start, beginning of the action** of a verb. They are almost exclusively used in the past tense directly followed by a present tense verb: شَرَعَ - طَفِقَ - أَنْشَأَ - أَخَذَ - عَلِقَ - هَبَّ - هَلْهَـلَ - جَعَـلَ - بَـدَأَ. See Arabic for Nerds 1, *question #103*.

3. *Verbs of hope* (أَفْعالُ الرَّجاءِ). They convey the **hope or wish that the predicate will be accomplished**: عَسَى - حَرَى - اخْلَوْلَقَ.

What the three groups have in common: the predicate must be a verbal sentence (جُمْلَةٌ فِعْلِيّةٌ) in the present tense (مُضارِعٌ). They differ in one thing: some of these verbs can or must be followed by أَنْ plus a verb, other not. One would intuitively choose to use أَنْ since it is very rare that two verbs follow each other directly. Most of these verbs, however, connect the verb directly – without أَنْ.

A hint: If a verb can be fully conjugated in both tenses, it usually goes without أَنْ. Let's look at the rules:

- Group 1: **Verbs of approaching.** <u>Both options</u> – with or without أَنْ – are possible, i.e., with or without أَنْ.
- Group 2: **Verbs of beginning.** They are <u>**never**</u> used with أَنْ.
- Group 3: **Verbs of hope.** They are <u>**usually**</u> used with أَنْ.

Some verbs can be used in the past and present tense; some only in the past tense. أَوْشَكَ and كادَ can also be used as active participles (كائِدٌ مُوشِكٌ).

<u>never</u> with أَنْ	usually <u>not</u> with أَنْ	usually with أَنْ	<u>must</u> have أَنْ	verb	
		✔		أَوْشَكَ يُوشِكُ	1
	✔			كادَ يَكادُ	
	✔			كرب *	
✔				شَرَعَ	2
✔				طَفِقَ	
✔				أَنْشَأَ	

never with أَنْ	usually <u>not</u> with أَنْ	usually with أَنْ	must have أَنْ	verb
✔				أَخَذَ/بَدَأَ
✔				عَلِقَ
✔				هَبَّ
✔				هَلْهَلَ
✔				جَعَلَ
		⚠ ** - see below		عَسَى 3
			✔	حَرَى
			✔	اخْلَوْلَقَ

* This verb is only used in the past tense.

** Regarding عَسَى: Usually it goes along with أَنْ although stylistically it is better to use عَسَى without أَنْ. Some examples:

better style	*Perhaps Karīm succeeds.*	عَسَى كَرِيمٌ يَنْجَحُ.
weaker style (but more common)		عَسَى كَرِيمٌ أَنْ يَنْجَحَ.

Now let's enter the grammar world.

Karīm almost succeeded.	أَوْشَكَ كَرِيمٌ أَنْ يَنْجَحَ.

Defective/incomplete past tense verb (فِعْلٌ ماضٍ ناقِصٌ).	أَوْشَكَ
This is the "subject" (إِسْمُ أَوْشَكَ); nominative case (مَرْفُوعٌ).	كَرِيمٌ
Particle with operating power (حَرْفُ نَصْبٍ); this device induces the **subjunctive** mood (مَنْصُوبٌ) in the following verb. It does not have a position in إِعْرابٌ.	أَنْ
Present tense verb (فِعْلٌ مُضارِعٌ مَنْصُوبٌ). The preceding particle induced the subjunctive mood in this verb; notice the فَتْحةٌ on the last letter. However, this is more than just a verb. In Arabic, this is a verbal sentence as the subject is already implied, and this entire verbal sentence is placed in the position of the predicate of أَوْشَكَ (خَبَرُ أَوْشَكَ) and is therefore grammatically located in the position of an accusative case (فِي مَحَلِّ نَصْبٍ).	يَنْجَحَ

Now comes the interesting part. What **function** has the particle أَنْ in our example? Some grammarians don't consider the particle أَنْ here a حَرْفُ مَصْدَرِيَّةٍ that is used to produce an interpreted مَصْدَرٌ, a مَصْدَرٌ مُؤَوَّلٌ. Normally أَنْ plus a verb in the present tense equals a مَصْدَرٌ in meaning. For example:

He wants to go.	يُرِيدُ أَنْ يَذْهَبَ.
Both sentences have the same meaning.	يُرِيدُ الذَّهابَ.

So if we follow this logic, i.e., that we got an (interpreted) مَصْدَرٌ, we could also use the original مَصْدَرٌ, which would be in our above example نَجاحٌ. This word would be the predicate (خَبَرُ أَوْشَكَ). Let's try it.

Karīm almost succeeded. (Karīm is close to success.)	أَوْشَكَ كَرِيمٌ نَجاحَهُ.

So far, so good. Let's now use a trick which helps us to grasp the inner logic of these constructions: in all the sisters of كانَ or كادَ, you can simply delete the verb and the resulting nominal sentence (جُمْلةٌ اسْمِيّةٌ) would perfectly make sense. For example:

Karīm is on the verge to arrive.	كادَ كَرِيمٌ يَصِلُ.
Karīm arrives.	كَرِيمٌ يَصِلُ.

Let's try this operation in our example:

This is sentence doesn't make sense. It is not possible in Arabic.	كَرِيمٌ نَجاحَهُ.

For this reason, most grammarians say that in such constructions, أَنْ is "only" a حَرْفُ نَصْبٍ (particle inducing the subjunctive mood) and just there to **receive the verb**. Others, however, say that it is both: حَرْفُ نَصْبٍ وَمَصْدَرٍ, i.e., a particle to mold an infinitive which has the power to operate on verbs by inducing the subjunctive mood.

If we go with the majority, this would mean that if there is no verb in the sentence, we don't need أَنْ anymore as it was only there to receive the verb. In other words, the predicate can be re-interpreted as follows:

Karīm is about to become successful.	أَوْشَكَ كَرِيمٌ صاحِبَ نَجاحٍ.
This is possible in Arabic and does perfectly make sense.	

OPTICAL TWINS: إِنَّ AND أَنَّ

252. Which particles are *abrogators* (الْحُرُوفُ النّاسِخةُ)؟

All *sisters of* إِنَّ (أَنَّ).

Let's see what we count as *sisters*.

1	Both are used to express and convey some kind of **emphasis** (تَوْكِيدٌ).	حَرْفُ تَوْكِيدٍ وَنَصْبٍ	إِنَّ
2			أَنَّ
3	*As if;* for comparison (تَشْبِيهٌ).	حَرْفُ تَشْبِيهٍ وَنَصْبٍ	كَأَنَّ
4	*However;* used for correction or setting the record straight (إِسْتِدْراكٌ).	حَرْفُ إِسْتِدْراكٍ وَنَصْبٍ	لِكِنَّ
5	*If only;* for wish or desire (تَمَنٍّ).	حَرْفُ تَمَنٍّ وَنَصْبٍ	لَيْتَ
6	*Perhaps;* expressing expectation (رَجاءٌ).	حَرْفُ رَجاءٍ وَنَصْبٍ	لَعَلَّ
7	*There is no...;* absolute negation	حَرْفُ نَفْيٍ وَنَصْبٍ	لا

Before we examine the abrogating devices (الْحُرُوفُ النّاسِخةُ) in depth, let's recall what ناسِخةٌ means: *abolishing* (the rules). A summary:

- These devices can only enter a **nominal** sentence (جُمْلةٌ اِسْمِيّةٌ).
- Once they are part of a sentence, they operate on the **subject** (previously called مُبْتَدَأ) and induce the **accusative** case (مَنْصُوبٌ) with the effect that it gets emphasis. The "subject" is called اِسْمُ of the respective particle; for example: اِسْمُ إِنَّ.
- The **predicate** (خَبَرٌ) remains in the nominative (مَرْفُوعٌ) case and is called the predicate of the respective particle; for example: خَبَرُ إِنَّ.

Some linguists call these words and devices *particles that resemble verbs* (الْحُرُوفُ الْمُشَبَّهةُ بِالْفِعْلِ). There are several reasons for this:

- The last letter of these words and devices ends with فَتْحةٌ, similar to a past tense verb in the third person singular (فَعَلَ).
- The first word after such particles is مَنْصُوبٌ like in verbal sentences with inverted word order (► fronted object).
- Some of these particles embody the meaning of a verb. Some scholars have suggested that the force of *to see* (رَأَى) is embodied in these particles which is the reason for the accusative case.

Let's analyze an example:

Zayd is standing (is getting up).	إنَّ زَيْدًا قَائِمٌ.

Particle of emphasis that has governing power and triggers the accusative case (حَرْفُ تَوْكِيدٍ وَنَصْبٍ).	إنَّ
This is the "subject" which is now called إنَّ إسْمُ. It is in the accusative case (مَنْصُوبٌ بِالْفَتْحةِ الظَّاهِرة).	زَيْدًا
Predicate (خَبَرُ إنَّ) in the nominative case (مَرْفُوعٌ بِالضَّمّةِ الظَّاهِرة).	قَائِمٌ

A more complicated example:

Zayd has a generous nature.	إنَّ زَيْدًا خُلُقُهُ كَرِيمٌ.

This is the **subject of the nominal sentence** (مُبْتَدَأٌ) in the nominative case (مَرْفُوعٌ). The ه is a pronominal suffix (ضَمِيرٌ مُتَّصِلٌ) and serves as the second part of a إضافة. It is placed in the location of a genitive case (فِي مَحَلِّ جَرٍّ مُضافٌ إِلَيْهِ) but we can't mark it as such because the ه is indeclinable (مَبْنِيٌّ عَلَى الضَّمِّ).	خُلُقُهُ
This is the **predicate** of the subject of the nominal sentence (خَبَرُ الْمُبْتَدَإِ). It is in the nominative case (مَرْفُوعٌ بِالضَّمّةِ الظَّاهِرة).	كَرِيمٌ
The entire sentence خُلُقُهُ كَرِيمٌ is the **predicate of** إنَّ and is located in the position of a nominative case (فِي مَحَلِّ رَفْعٍ خَبَرُ إنَّ).	

Let's check another example of a predicate that is supplied by a whole sentence. This time we have a verbal sentence (جُمْلَةٌ فِعْلِيّةٌ):

The believer trusts in Allah.	إنَّ الْمُؤْمِنَ يَتَوَكَّلُ عَلَى اللهِ.
The verbal sentence (i.e., يَتَوَكَّلُ) is the **predicate of** إنَّ and is located in the position of a nominative case (فِي مَحَلِّ رَفْعٍ خَبَرُ إنَّ).	

What happens if we have a prepositional phrase?

Indeed, Karīm is at home.	إنَّ كَرِيمًا فِي الْبَيْتِ.
Where's the predicate of إنَّ? It is not mentioned/deleted, as it is a permanent state! The prepositional phrase (فِي الْبَيْتِ) is located in the place of the predicate; it is connected to that deleted word (شِبْهُ الْجُمْلَةِ مُتَعَلِّقٌ بِمحْذُوفٍ).	

253. Can you change the word order in a sentence with إِنَّ?

Your options are pretty limited.

إِنَّ really limits our flexibility. The subject (اِسْمُ إِنَّ) and the predicate (خَبَرُ إِنَّ) must be placed in a fixed order – no matter whether the predicate is a single word (مُفْرَدٌ) or a sentence (جُمْلةٌ). ➤ You **can't** change the word order! You can't place the predicate before the subject. The following examples (with the predicate marked in gray) don't work:

| not correct | Indeed, Zayd is standing (is getting up). | إِنَّ قَائِمٌ زَيْدًا. |
| not correct | Indeed, Zayd writes. | إِنَّ يَكْتُبُ زَيْدًا. |

Watch out: If the خَبَرُ إِنَّ is a prepositional or adverbial phrase (شِبْهُ الْجُمْلةِ), you **may** place the predicate before the اِسْمُ إِنَّ.

| correct | Indeed, Zayd is at home. | إِنَّ فِي الْبَيْتِ زَيْدًا. |

| Prepositional phrase (الْجارُّ وَالْمَجْرُورُ). It appears in the spot of the fronted predicate of إِنَّ and is connected with a deleted noun which is implicitly understood as *is* or *is found* (مَوْجُودٌ). We say: شِبْهُ الْجُمْلةِ مُتَعَلِّقٌ بِمَحْذُوفٍ خَبَرُ إِنَّ مُقَدَّمٍ فِي مَحَلِّ رَفْعٍ | فِي الْبَيْتِ |
| Delayed "subject" (اِسْمُ إِنَّ مُؤَخَّرٌ). *Zayd* is in the accusative case (مَنْصُوبٌ) since it is governed by إِنَّ. | زَيْدًا |

If a **referential pronoun** (ضَمِيرٌ يَعُودُ عَلَى شِبْهِ الْجُمْلةِ), a returner, is attached to the اِسْمُ إِنَّ, it will become even **necessary** to move the **predicate** (تَقْدِيمُ الْخَبَرِ) forward and place it before the subject (اِسْمُ إِنَّ). In these constructions, such pronouns refer to the prepositional phrase.

| The residents are in the house. (not: *his family*). | إِنَّ فِي الْبَيْتِ أَهْلَهُ. |

| اِسْمُ إِنَّ in the accusative case (مَنْصُوبٌ بِالْفَتْحةِ الظَّاهِرةِ). The ه is a pronominal suffix (ضَمِيرٌ مُتَّصِلٌ) and has an indeclinable shape. Therefore, you can't see that the pronoun is grammatically in the position of a genitive case (فِي مَحَلِّ جَرٍّ مُضافٌ إِلَيْهِ) as it serves as the second part of the إِضافةٌ. | أَهْلَهُ |

> ➤ The same is true for أَنَّ ...
...since أَنَّ has to be followed by a اسْمٌ in the accusative case or by a pronoun – but **never** by a verb or predicate (خَبَرُ أَنَّ).

254. What is the difference between إِنَّ and أَنَّ؟

It is the question of using a كَسْرَةٌ or a فَتْحَةٌ with the هَمْزَةٌ.

Both – إِنَّ and أَنَّ – are used for matters of emphasis (تَوْكِيدٌ).

- إِنَّ is often translated as *truly, certainly*.
- أَنَّ is often rendered as *...that*.

Throughout my reading of texts in Classical Arabic, I never got the impression that أَنَّ was more emphatic. Both share the same implications:

- The subject (اسْمٌ of the respective particle) is in the state of the accusative (نَصْبٌ) case.
- The predicate (خَبَرٌ) is in the state of the nominative (رَفْعٌ) case.

Zayd is standing. The second sentence is more emphatic and puts emphasis on the subject (*Zayd*).	زَيْدٌ قَائِمٌ.
	إِنَّ زَيْدًا قَائِمٌ.

What about أَنَّ؟

	ظَنَنْتُكَ مُسَافِرًا.
I assumed you were traveling.	ظَنَنْتُ أَنَّكَ مُسَافِرٌ.
Both sentences mean *I thought you were traveling*, but the one with أَنَّ is more emphatic. However, it doesn't necessarily mean you're strongly emphasizing how much you thought that the person was traveling.	

Some grammar books say that أَنَّ and إِنَّ could be referred to as the same particle: إِنَّ is regarded as a **particle of emphasis** (حَرْفُ تَوْكِيدٍ), so the same applies to the particle أَنَّ, they suggest. We should not make it too complicated. Basically, the only difference between إِنَّ and أَنَّ is the **Hamza** (هَمْزَةٌ). There are three possibilities:

A) The necessity of the *Kasra* (وُجُوبُ الْكَسْرِ).

B) The necessity of the *Fatha* (وُجُوبُ الْفَتْحِ) - question #255.

C) Both options are possible: *Kasra* or *Fatha* (جَوازُ الْكَسْرِ وَالْفَتْحِ) - question #256.

The necessity of the كَسْرة

The grammarians know many rules when our device has to be إِنَّ. They can be summarized in one rule: when the particle is placed at the beginning of a sentence, it has to be إِنَّ. When do we get this situation?

I. إِنَّ marks the beginning of speech (ابْتِداءُ الْكَلامِ).

Indeed, Zayd is standing.	إِنَّ زَيْدًا قائِمٌ.

II. إِنَّ is found at the beginning of a relative clause (صِلةٌ).

I appreciate the individual who is diligent.	أَقَدِّرُ الَّذِي إِنَّهُ مُجِدٌّ.
This all together is the relative clause (صِلةُ الْمَوْصُولِ); it does not have a position in إِعْرابٌ.	إِنَّهُ مُجِدٌّ

Watch out: In case إِنَّ is not placed at the beginning of the relative clause (جُمْلةُ الصِّلةِ), you have to use أَنَّ (with فَتْحةٌ).

I appreciate the individual who is diligent in his work.	أَقَدِّرُ الَّذِي فِي عَمَلِهِ أَنَّهُ مُجِدٌّ.

III. إِنَّ is placed at the beginning of an *attributive sentence* (جُمْلةُ الصِّفةِ). Such a sentence must refer to an indefinite word.

I appreciate a student who is diligent.	أَقَدِّرُ طالِبًا إِنَّهُ مُجِدٌّ.
The sentence is made of إِنَّ, subject (اسْمُ إِنَّ) and predicate of إِنَّ.	إِنَّهُ مُجِدٌّ
The entire phrase serves as an adjective for the direct object *student* (طالِبًا), an indefinite word in the accusative case. Adjectives have to agree with the word that they describe. Thus, the entire sentence is, grammatically speaking, placed in the position of an accusative case (فِي مَحَلِّ نَصْبٍ صِفةٌ لِطالِبٍ).	

→ **Watch out:** If إِنَّ is not placed at the beginning, you have to use أَنَّ. This is similar to the relative clause (see above).

I appreciate **a** student (of mine) who is diligent.	أُقَدِّرُ طَالِبًا عِنْدِي أَنَّهُ مُجِدٌّ.

IV. إِنَّ is placed at the beginning of a circumstantial clause (جُمْلَةُ الْحَالِ). What's important here? إِنَّ refers to a noun which has a <u>definite article</u>. For that reason, it can't be a جُمْلَةُ الصِّفَةِ (*see III*). Its a حَالٌ.

I appreciate **the** student who is diligent.	أُقَدِّرُ الطَّالِبَ إِنَّهُ مُجِدٌّ.

This sentence serves as a circumstantial clause (حَالٌ). Therefore, we find it in the position of an accusative case (فِي مَحَلِّ نَصْبِ حَالٍ مِن الطَّالِبِ). Notice: it is a حَالٌ and **not** a صِفَةٌ because a حَالٌ always refers to a definite noun (here: *the student*).	إِنَّهُ مُجِدٌّ

What happens if the حَالٌ is connected by و? Nothing special.

I appreciate the diligent student who cooperates with his classmates.	أُقَدِّرُ الطَّالِبَ الْمُجِدَّ وَإِنَّهُ مُتَعَاوِنٌ مَعَ زُمَلَائِهِ.

This is a so-called وَاوُ الْحَالِ.	و
This sentence serves as a حَالٌ and is located in the spot of an accusative case (فِي مَحَلِّ نَصْبٍ) since a حَالٌ has to be مَنْصُوبٌ.	إِنَّهُ مُتَعَاوِنٌ

➤ However, if إِنَّ is not placed at the beginning of the circumstantial clause (جُمْلَةُ الْحَالِ), you have to use أَنَّ (with فَتْحَةٌ).

The و here can't be a وَاوُ الْحَالِ.	أُقَدِّرُ الطَّالِبَ وَعِنْدِي أَنَّهُ مُجِدٌّ.
Why? Because the و has to be directly linked to the circumstantial sentence and can't be put somewhere else. → You have to use أَنَّ.	

V. إِنَّ is found at the beginning of an indirect (reported) speech.

➤ It must be إِنَّ – no matter if the device was placed directly after the utterance or not.

Muhammad said that Zayd is generous.	قَالَ مُحَمَّدٌ إِنَّ زَيْدًا كَرِيمٌ.

| This sentence serves as the **direct object** (مَفْعُولٌ بِهِ) of the verb *to say* – also called مَقُولُ الْقَوْل. Therefore, it serves in the location of an accusative case (فِي مَحَلِّ نَصْبٍ). | إِنَّ زَيْدًا كَرِيمٌ |

In such sentences, it doesn't matter how long the sentence is and where إِنَّ is placed.

| My friend told me last week (while we were at his house) that he will continue his studies. | قَالَ لِي صَدِيقِي وَنَحْنُ فِي بَيْتِهِ فِى الْأُسْبُوع الْمَاضِي إِنَّهُ سَوْفَ يُوَاصِلُ دِرَاسَتَهُ. |

VI. إِنَّ has an emphatic لَ before its predicate and is part of a primary sentence with a *verb of the heart* or *meaning* (more generally, a sister of ظَنَّ).

Such لَ is placed before the predicate (خَبَرُ إِنَّ). What is the idea behind such a لَ? The لَ is used with special verbs that can carry two direct objects in the accusative case (مَنْصُوبٌ).

These verbs are called *verbs of the mind* or *heart* (أَفْعَالُ الْقُلُوبِ) as they signify an act that takes place in your mind: *to think* (ظَنَّ), *to know* (دَرَى), *to see* in a figurative meaning (رَأَى), *to imagine* (تَوَهَّمَ), etc.

If there is إِنَّ involved, the verb can't do its job anymore and can't govern the two objects in the accusative case. So, we would run into a clash of operating power. For this reason, the لَ comes into the game.

We could say that such a لَ **suspends** the work of إِنَّ. This means: the second object is treated as it would be in a regular sentence with إِنَّ; thus, it receives the nominative case. For that reason, that kind of لَ is also called اللَّامُ الْمُعَلِّقَةُ (اللَّامُ فِي خَبَرِهَا وَهِيَ مُعَلَّقَةٌ لِمَا قَبْلَهَا). But the more general term for it is *inceptive Lām* (لَامُ الْإِبْتِدَاءِ).

| I knew that Zayd is diligent. | عَلِمْتُ إِنَّ زَيْدًا لَمُجِدٌّ. |

Particle of emphasis which puts the "subject" (of the second sentence starting with إِنَّ) into the accusative case (حَرْفُ تَوْكِيدٍ وَنَصْبٍ).	إِنَّ
"Subject" (اسْمُ إِنَّ); so it needs the accusative (مَنْصُوبٌ) case.	زَيْدًا
This is a لَامُ الْإِبْتِدَاءِ. It does not have a position in إِعْرَابٌ.	لَ

Predicate (خَبَرُ إِنَّ) in the nominative case (مَرْفُوعٌ).	مُجِدٌّ
The entire sentence إِنَّ زَيْدًا لَمُجِدٌّ supplies the two objects of the verb (عَلِمَ) and thus is located in the position of a نَصْبٌ-state (accusative).	مَفْعُولَا

63:1	Allah knows that you truly are His Messenger.	اللهُ يَعْلَمُ إِنَّكَ لَرَسُولُهُ.
Here we also have a لَامُ الْإِبْتِدَاءِ. It enable us to emphasize the content (like إِنَّ). Note that such ل only works in sentences with إِنَّ (and <u>not</u> أَنَّ).		

VII. إِنَّ is placed before the predicate of a concrete noun (خَبَرُ اِسْمِ ذَاتٍ).

A concrete noun is a noun that can be identified through one of the five senses (taste, touch, sight, hearing, smell). It is the opposite of an abstract noun (e.g., *courage*).

Zayd (= concrete noun) is diligent.	زَيْدٌ إِنَّهُ مُجِدٌّ.
This whole sentence serves as the predicate of the nominal sentence (فِي مَحَلِّ رَفْعٍ خَبَرُ الْمُبْتَدَإِ) and is located in the position of a nominative case.	إِنَّهُ مُجِدٌّ

Question: Is it possible to place an extra إِنَّ before the subject (مُبْتَدَأٌ) as well? Yes, this is possible, but it brings along a grammatical effect: it changes the case ending of the subject!

Zayd, he is diligent.	إِنَّ زَيْدًا إِنَّهُ مُجِدٌّ.

Particle of emphasis (حَرْفُ تَوْكِيدٍ وَنَصْبٍ).	إِنَّ
This is the "subject" (اِسْمُ إِنَّ) in the accusative case (مَنْصُوبٌ).	زَيْدًا
Again, a حَرْفُ تَوْكِيدٍ وَنَصْبٍ. The ه is an indeclinable pronoun suffix (ضَمِيرٌ مُتَّصِلٌ) serving as the اِسْمُ إِنَّ of the **second** إِنَّ; thus, it is located in the position of an accusative case (فِي مَحَلِّ نَصْبٍ).	إِنَّهُ
Predicate (خَبَرُ إِنَّ) in the nominative case (مَرْفُوعٌ). Okay, but the predicate of which إِنَّ? For the **second** one! And where is the **predicate of the first** إِنَّ (i.e., خَبَرُ إِنَّ الْأُولَى)? The entire expression إِنَّهُ مُجِدٌّ does that job. Therefore, it is placed in the position of a nominative case (فِي مَحَلِّ رَفْعٍ).	مُجِدٌّ

255. When do you have to use أَنَّ (with فَتْحَةٌ)?

If the part that comes after أَنَّ can be interpreted as a مَصْدَرٌ.

The concept of an interpretable, artificially generated infinitive is one of the most interesting and typical concepts in Arabic. It is really that simple: if أَنَّ is followed by a verb, the entire expression can be interpreted as an infinitive (مَصْدَرٌ).

Therefore, you must use أَنَّ (with فَتْحَةٌ on هَمْزَةٌ) if the two governed parts (مَعْمُولَاها) of the device have the meaning of a مَصْدَرٌ. This brings us to an **important rule** that tells us whether we should use أَنَّ or إِنَّ:

> If the result **can't** be understood as a مَصْدَرٌ,
> you most probably should use إِنَّ.

What is placed after أَنَّ may (grammatically, but not visibly) be located in the position of any case: the nominative (فِي مَحَلّ رَفْعٍ), genitive (فِي مَحَلّ جَرٍّ), or accusative case (فِي مَحَلّ نَصْبٍ).

Why is that important? This shows that أَنَّ plus its governed parts is a component that is needed in the sentence. We call that component مَصْدَرٌ مُنْسَبِكٌ, a *molded/cast* مَصْدَرٌ. ➤ This is different to إِنَّ which is mainly there for stylistic reasons.

Let's see some applications and functions of these *molded infinitives*:

I. The (interpreted) مَصْدَرٌ, molded by the device أَنَّ, is the **subject of the verbal sentence** (فَاعِلٌ).

It makes me happy that you are successful.	يُسْعِدُنِي أَنَّكَ مُوَفَّقٌ.

What is the meaning (= the virtual equivalent) of the sentence?

تَوْفِيقٌ is the real مَصْدَرٌ of the II-verb وَفَّقَ - يُوَفِّقُ (و=R1); to make successful. Pattern: تَفْعِيلٌ.	يُسْعِدُنِي تَوْفِيقُكَ.

Let's analyze our example:

Particle of emphasis which governs the "subject" (اِسْمُ أَنَّ), in the accusative case (حَرْفُ تَوْكِيدٍ وَنَصْبٍ).	أَنَّ

Pronoun suffix (ضَمِيرٌ مُتَّصِلٌ) which is placed in the position of the إِسْمُ أَنَّ and thus grammatically treated as occupying the position of an accusative case (فِي مَحَلِّ نَصْبٍ).	كَ
Predicate (خَبَرُ أَنَّ); nominative case (مَرْفُوعٌ بِالضَّمَّةِ الظَّاهِرَةِ).	مُوَفَّقٌ

We said that أَنَّ plus a verb serves as the **subject** (فَاعِلٌ) of the verb in this sentence… Well, what exactly is that subject made of? It is the entire expression starting with أَنَّ, in other words, the مَصْدَرٌ that was molded by أَنَّ and its (two) governed factors. We treat the entire expression as holding the position of a nominative (فِي مَحَلِّ رَفْعِ فَاعِلٌ).

II. The مَصْدَرٌ is a **direct object** (مَفْعُولٌ بِهِ).

I learned that Zayd is traveling.	عَرَفْتُ أَنَّ زَيْدًا مُسَافِرٌ.
This would be the equivalent of the above sentence if we express it by the original, "real" مَصْدَرٌ: →	عَرَفْتُ سَفَرَ زَيْدٍ.
Why do we use سَفَرٌ when, in fact, the مَصْدَرٌ of a III-verb (فَاعَلَ) follows the patterns فِعَالٌ (i.e., سِفَارٌ)? or مُفَاعَلَةٌ (i.e., مُسَافَرَةٌ)? Because these two forms are rarely used with the III-verb سَافَرَ - يُسَافِرُ (to travel). Instead, many people prefer the noun of origin (إِسْمُ الْمَصْدَرِ) which is: سَفَرٌ. It has the same meaning as the standard مَصْدَرٌ forms – see question #110.	

We have a verb in the past tense (عَرَفْتُ) with the suffix تُ serving as the subject (فَاعِلٌ) of the verbal sentence.

"Subject" (إِسْمُ أَنَّ); therefore, it is in the accusative (مَنْصُوبٌ).	زَيْدًا
Predicate (خَبَرُ أَنَّ); nominative case (مَرْفُوعٌ بِالضَّمَّةِ الظَّاهِرَةِ).	مُسَافِرٌ

Where is the direct object (مَفْعُولٌ بِهِ) of the verb عَرَفْتُ؟ The مَصْدَرٌ (which is molded by the two governed parts of أَنَّ) serves as the direct object. Therefore, we can say that it is placed in the position of an accusative case (فِي مَحَلِّ نَصْبٍ).

III. The مَصْدَرٌ is found **after a preposition** (حَرْفُ الْجَرِّ).

The following example works similarly to the sentences we have analyzed above. أَنَّ and its two governed parts get the place value of a genitive case (الْمَصْدَرُ الْمُنْسَبِكُ مِنْ أَنَّ وَمَعْمُولَيْها فِي مَحَلِّ جَرٍّ بِالْباءِ).

I rejoiced that Zayd is successful.	فَرِحْتُ بِأَنَّ زَيْدًا ناجِحٌ.
We could rewrite the sentence by using the original, "real" مَصْدَرٌ. This would be the result: →	فَرِحْتُ بِنَجاحِ زَيْدٍ.

IV. The molded مَصْدَرٌ serves in the position of the subject of a nominal sentence (فِي مَحَلِّ رَفْعٍ مُبْتَدَأٌ).

One of his qualities is that he helps the needy.	مِنْ صِفاتِهِ أَنَّهُ يُساعِدُ الْمُحْتاجَ.
This is the meaning of the sentence: →	مِنْ صِفاتِهِ مُساعَدةُ الْمُحْتاجِ.

What do we got here? There is the preposition مِنْ followed by a word in the genitive case (اِسْمٌ مَجْرُورٌ). The ه is an indeclinable pronoun suffix (ضَمِيرٌ مُتَّصِلٌ) placed as the second part of the إِضافةٌ.

The entire **prepositional phrase** (الْجارُّ وَالْمَجْرُورُ) is placed in the position of the <u>fronted predicate</u> (خَبَرٌ مُقَدَّمٌ) of the nominal sentence and takes the position of a **nominative case** (فِي مَحَلِّ رَفْعٍ). Now, what about the **subject** (مُبْتَدَأٌ)?

Particle of emphasis (حَرْفُ تَوْكِيدٍ وَنَصْبٍ).	أَنَّ
Indeclinable pronoun suffix (ضَمِيرٌ مُتَّصِلٌ), serving as the اِسْمُ أَنَّ; therefore, it is grammatically found in the position of an accusative case (فِي مَحَلِّ نَصْبٍ) – although you can't see that.	هُ
Verb in the present tense, indicative mood (فِعْلٌ مُضارِعٌ مَرْفُوعٌ). It has an implied subject (فاعِلٌ) expressing *he* (هُوَ). Now comes the fun part: this verbal sentence serves as the **predicate of أَنَّ** – thus, it is located in the position of a nominative (فِي مَحَلِّ رَفْعٍ).	يُساعِدُ
The **interpreted, molded** مَصْدَرٌ (مَصْدَرٌ مُؤَوَّلٌ), consisting of أَنَّ and its two governed parts, serves in the position of the **delayed subject** (مُبْتَدَأٌ مُؤَخَّرٌ) of the nominal sentence. It is thus located in the position of a nominative case (فِي مَحَلِّ رَفْعٍ).	

Direct object (مَفْعُولٌ بِهِ); in the accusative case (مَنْصُوبٌ).	الْمُحْتاجَ

IV. After *if not* (لَوْلا).

If you hadn't studied, you would not have suc-ceeded.	لَوْلا أَنَّكَ مُجِدٌّ ما نَجَحْتَ.
This is how the sentence would look like if we used the original, real مَصْدَرٌ:→	لَوْلا جِدُّكَ ما نَجَحْتَ.

Particle of negating the existence or of denial (حَرْفُ امْتِناعٍ لِلْوُجُودِ); it does not have a position in إِعْرابٌ.	لَوْلا
Particle of emphasis (حَرْفُ تَوْكِيدٍ وَنَصْبٍ).	أَنَّ
Pronoun suffix (ضَمِيرٌ مُتَّصِلٌ), indeclinable (مَبْنِيٌّ عَلَى الْفَتْحِ), so we can't put case markers. Grammatically, it is in the position of the "subject" (اِسْمُ أَنَّ) which means that it takes the "place value" of an accusative case (فِي مَحَلِّ نَصْبٍ).	كَ
Predicate (خَبَرُ أَنَّ) in the nominative case (مَرْفُوعٌ).	مُجِدٌّ

The interpreted مَصْدَرٌ (consisting of أَنَّ plus its two governed factors) is do-ing the job of the **subject** (فِي مَحَلِّ رَفْعٍ مُبْتَدَأٌ) of the **nominal sentence**; thus, it is grammatically in the position of a nominative case. What about the **predicate** (خَبَرٌ) of the **nominal sentence**?

It had to be deleted (مَحْذُوفٌ) because it is tacitly understood anyway. It may have the underlying, virtual meaning of: *present; existing, found* (مَوْجُودٌ).

The entire second part (= ما نَجَحْتَ) does not have a position in the analysis because it is the answer of the condition (جَوابُ الشَّرْطِ); *see #85*.

V. We have a nominal sentence, and the **subject** (مُبْتَدَأٌ) is an **abstract noun** (اِسْمٌ مَعْنًى). Then we use أَنَّ in the **second** part (predicate).

An abstract noun refers to something with which a person cannot physically interact. If the molded مَصْدَرٌ is placed as the predicate (خَبَرٌ) of such a nominal sentence, we use أَنَّ.

The truth is that he did it.	الثّابِتُ أَنَّهُ فَعَلَ ذلِكَ.

Meaning/equivalent of the sentence: →	الثّابِتُ فِعْلُهُ ذلِكَ.

Subject (مُبْتَدَأً) of the nominal sentence, nominative case (مَرْفُوعٌ).	الثّابِتُ
Particle of emphasis (حَرْفُ تَوْكِيدٍ وَنَصْبٍ).	أَنَّ
Pronoun suffix (ضَمِيرٌ مُتَّصِلٌ), serving as the "subject" (اِسْمُ أَنَّ); indeclinable, so we say that it gets the "place value" of an accusative case (فِي مَحَلِّ نَصْبٍ).	هُ
Past tense verb (فِعْلٌ ماضٍ). Its subject (فاعِلٌ) is a hidden pronoun expressing *he* (هُوَ). At the same time, فَعَلَ is also an entire (verbal) sentence which is located in the position of the predicate (خَبَرُ أَنَّ) of the sentence with أَنَّ. It is placed in the location of a nominative case (فِي مَحَلِّ رَفْعٍ).	فَعَلَ

Don't get confused: the primary sentence is a nominal sentence (جُمْلَةٌ اِسْمِيّةٌ) → notice the first word. Therefore, the **entire interpreted مَصْدَرٌ** serves as the **predicate** of the nominal sentence (خَبَرُ الْمُبْتَدَإِ). It occupies the place of a nominative case (فِي مَحَلِّ رَفْعٍ).

VI. The molded مَصْدَرٌ serves as **the thing excepted** (مُسْتَثْنَى).

I like his character although he is very forgetful.	تُعْجِبُنِي أَخْلاقُهُ إلّا أَنَّهُ كَثِيرُ النِّسْيانِ.
This is how we could rewrite the sentence without changing the meaning: →	تُعْجِبُنِي أَخْلاقُهُ إلّا كَثْرَةَ نِسْيانِهِ.

Present tense verb (فِعْلٌ مُضارِعٌ مَرْفُوعٌ), indicative mood. The attached ن is called *the guarding or preventive Nūn* (نُونُ الْوِقايةِ) because it prevents the final vowel of the verb (بُ) from being absorbed by the long vowel ي which must be preceded by a كَسْرَةٌ (the vowel "i"). The final ي is a pronoun suffix serving as the direct object (مَفْعُولٌ بِهِ); therefore, it is grammatically located in the position of an accusative case (فِي مَحَلِّ نَصْبٍ).	تُعْجِبُنِي
This is the subject (فاعِلٌ) of the verbal sentence, nominative case (مَرْفُوعٌ). The ه is an indeclinable pronominal suffix. It is also the second part of the إِضافةٌ. You can't mark the pronoun as such because the pronoun is fixed on the ضَمٌّ.	أَخْلاقُهُ

Particle of exception (حَرْفُ اسْتِثْناءٍ); no place in إِعْرابٌ.	إلّا
Particle of emphasis (حَرْفُ تَوْكيدٍ وَنَصْبٍ). The pronoun suffix ه (ضَميرٌ مُتَّصِلٌ) has a fixed shape (مَبْنِيٌّ عَلَى الضَّمِّ). It is placed as the اِسْمُ أَنَّ (the "subject"); so it is found in the location of an accusative case (مَنْصوبٌ).	أَنَّهُ
Predicate (خَبَرُ أَنَّ), nominative case (مَرْفوعٌ). Notice that this is also the first part of the إِضافةٌ, so you only have one ضَمّةٌ.	كَثيرٌ
Second part of the إِضافةٌ (مُضافٌ إِلَيْهِ); thus, it gets the genitive case (مَجْرورٌ بِالْكَسْرةِ الظّاهِرةِ).	النِّسْيانِ

Where is *the thing that is excepted* (مُسْتَثْنَى) in this sentence? It is the interpreted مَصْدَرٌ, consisting of أَنَّ plus its governed factors. This مُؤَوَّلٌ fills the position of a مُسْتَثْنَى; therefore, it is in the position of an accusative case (فِي مَحَلِّ نَصْبٍ).

VII. After the **conditional particle** لَوْ.

There is an issue we need to solve: لَوْ can only be used together with a verbal sentence (جُمْلةٌ فِعْلِيّةٌ). Why is that important? Well, it gets complicated: The interpreted مَصْدَرٌ serves as the subject for the <u>deleted verb</u> (فاعِلٌ لِفِعْلٍ مَحْذوفٍ).

Had he worked hard, he would have succeeded.	لَوْ أَنَّهُ اِجْتَهَدَ لَنَجَحَ.
Equivalent with a possible verb (ثَبَتَ = *to remain firm*) to make the sentence work grammatically: →	لَوْ ثَبَتَ اِجْتِهادُهُ لَنَجَحَ.

Conditional particle (حَرْفُ شَرْطٍ); no position in إِعْرابٌ.	لَوْ
Particle of emphasis (حَرْفُ تَوْكيدٍ وَنَصْبٍ). The ه functions as the اِسْمُ أَنَّ, it is indeclinable but grammatically located in the position of an accusative case (مَنْصوبٌ) - so we assign a "place value".	أَنَّهُ
Past tense verb (فِعْلٌ ماضٍ); implied subject (فاعِلٌ): *he* (هُوَ).	اِجْتَهَد

There are two things you should pay attention to:

- The verbal sentence (اِجْتَهَدَ) occupies the position of the خَبَرُ أَنَّ; thus, it is located in the position of a nominative (فِي مَحَلِّ رَفْعٍ).

- The entire مَصْدَرٌ مُؤَوَّلٌ (أَنَّ plus its governed parts), holds the position of the subject (فَاعِلٌ) of the <u>deleted</u> verb! Grammatically speaking, it is in the position of a nominative case (فِي مَحَلِّ رَفْعٍ فَاعِلٌ لِفِعْلٍ مَحْذُوفٍ).

VIII. After حَقًّا which means *really; truly; indeed*.

After حَقًّا it is a common mistake to use إِنَّ . You have to use أَنَّ. Although the sentences are usually easy to understand, the underlying grammar is quite high-level stuff.

Truly, he indeed is generous.	حَقًّا أَنَّهُ كَرِيمٌ.

There are two possibilities to view this sentence grammatically.

Option 1:

Absolute, inner object (مَفْعُولٌ مُطْلَقٌ), therefore, it is in the accusative case. Wait a second! There is no verb – so how can this be true? Well, we assume that the verb was deleted (فِعْلُهُ مَحْذُوفٌ). A possible estimated meaning would be: حُقَّ حَقًّا (passive voice of I-verb حَقَّ - يَحُقُّ; R2=R3; *to be true*).	حَقًّا
أَنَّ is an emphatic particle (حَرْفُ تَوْكِيدٍ وَنَصْبٍ). The pronoun is the إِسْمُ أَنَّ, in the position of an accusative case (فِي مَحَلِّ نَصْبٍ).	أَنَّهُ
Predicate (خَبَرُ إِنَّ); thus in the nominative case (مَرْفُوعٌ).	كَرِيمٌ
The interpreted مَصْدَرٌ molded by أَنَّ appears as the subject (فَاعِلٌ) in the place of a nominative (فِي مَحَلِّ رَفْعٍ). How can we understand the meaning of the sentence? → حُقَّ كَرَمُهُ حَقًّا (*His generosity was to be true indeed*).	

Option 2:

Adverb of time (ظَرْفُ زَمانٍ); the adverbial phrase appears as the fronted predicate, thus in the location of a nominative (شِبْهُ الْجُمْلَةِ فِي مَحَلِّ رَفْعٍ خَبَرٌ مُقَدَّمٌ).	حَقًّا
The interpreted مَصْدَرٌ appears in the place of the delayed subject (مُبْتَدَأٌ) of the nominal sentence, thus in the spot of a nominative case. How could we picture this sentence? فِي حَقِّ كَرَمُهُ. The adverbial character here is figurative (الظَّرْفِيَّةُ مَجازِيَّةٌ).	أَنَّهُكَرِيمٌ

256. In which situations can you use إِنَّ or أَنَّ؟

There are perhaps more than you might think of.

إِنَّ or أَنَّ is usually not a question of taste! But there are situations in which you have to choose one of the two. This is not trivial, because once you have made up your mind, you have to live with the consequences. Your choice has an impact on the grammar.

There is a rule we should always keep in mind. If you use أَنَّ, you will receive (produce) an interpreted مَصْدَرٌ, a so-called مَصْدَرٌ مُؤَوَّلٌ. **When can you choose between إِنَّ or أَنَّ؟**

SITUATION 1: The device is placed after the إِذا **of surprise** (إِذا الْفُجائِيّةُ), which indicates something unexpected.

A	I entered the room, and there was my friend sitting.	دَخَلْتُ الْغَرْفةَ فَإِذا إِنَّ صَدِيقِي جالِسٌ.
B	I entered the room, there was my friend sitting.	دَخَلْتُ الْغَرْفةَ فَإِذا أَنَّ صَدِيقِي جالِسٌ.

A	**Particle of surprise** (حَرْفُ مُفاجَأةٍ); no position in إِعْرابٌ.	إِذا
	Particle of emphasis (حَرْفُ تَوْكِيدٍ وَنَصْبٍ). When we use إِنَّ, we don't assume an interpreted infinitive.	إِنَّ
	This is the "subject" (إِسْمُ إِنَّ), so it has to take the accusative case (مَنْصُوبٌ بِفَتْحةٍ مُقَدَّرةٍ). However, you don't see the appropriate marker since there is the possessive pronoun *my* involved. This is expressed by ي which demands a preceding كَسْرةٌ. For this reason, the last letter of the word صَدِيق (which is also the first part of the إِضافةٌ) must carry a كَسْرةٌ, otherwise, *my* wouldn't work. The pronominal suffix is the second part of the إِضافةٌ; thus, in the spot of a genitive (فِي مَحَلّ جَرّ مُضافٌ إِلَيْهِ).	صَدِيقِي
	Predicate (خَبَرُ إِنَّ) in the nominative case (مَرْفُوعٌ).	جالِسٌ

Now, let's see the analysis for أَنَّ which is pretty different and resourceful. There are two interpretations (B1 and B2).

B1	**Particle of surprise** (حَرْفُ مُفاجَأةٍ); no position in إِعْرابٌ.	إِذا

صَدِيقِي وَاقِفٌ	B1	This is the اِسْمُ أَنَّ and the predicate (خَبَرُ أَنَّ).

What about the meaning of the interpreted أَنَّ؟ مَصْدَرٌ and its two governed factors serve as the **subject** (مُبْتَدَأ) in the position of a nominative case (مَرْفُوعٌ) of the _primary_ nominal sentence.

    The predicate (خَبَرٌ) of that nominal sentence is deleted. What could be a possible (estimated, underlying) meaning of the deleted predicate?

دَخَلْتُ الْغَرْفَةَ فَإِذا جُلُوسُ صَدِيقِي حَاصِلٌ.	I entered the room, and the sitting of my friend was happening.

That's not the end of the story. There is another possible interpretation of the sentence with أَنَّ.

إذا	B2	**Adverb of time or place** (ظَرْفُ زَمانٍ أَوْ مَكانٍ) depending on the meaning. We can't put any case marker on the Aleph as it has to carry a سُكُونٌ by definition. Since it serves as an adverb, it is placed in the position of an accusative case (فِي مَحَلِّ نَصْبٍ).

The adverbial phrase (شِبْهُ الْجُمْلةِ) appears in the position of the fronted **predicate** (خَبَرٌ مُقَدَّمٌ), which was deleted. It is this deleted word with which the adverbial phrase is connected (مُتَعَلِّقٌ بِمَحْذُوفٍ).

If there is a خَبَرٌ (predicate), there must be a مُبْتَدَأ (subject). The interpreted مَصْدَرٌ (consisting of أَنَّ plus governed factors = أَنَّ صَدِيقِي جالِسٌ) serves as the delayed **subject** (مُبْتَدَأ مُؤَخَّرٌ) in the nominative case of the nominal sentence.

There is one last thing we need to look at. What is the adverbial meaning that the word إذا may convey? The assumed, underlying meaning of analysis B2 could be for example:

دَخَلْتُ الْغَرْفَةَ فَفِي الْمَكانِ (or فِي الْوَقْتِ) جُلُوسُ صَدِيقِي.	I entered the room, and **at that very place**/moment, my friend was sitting.

SITUATION 2: إِنَّ or أَنَّ is placed after a _Fā' of sanction_ (فاءُ الْجَزاءِ or فاءٌ جَزائِيَّةٌ), also called _Fā' of the complement/answer_ (فاءُ الْجَوابِ). Such a ف is found in the 2nd part of a conditional sentence (جَوابُ الشَّرْطِ).

The final clause in a conditional sentence (جَوابُ الشَّرْطِ) is sometimes also called جَزاءُ الشَّرْطِ. The word جَزاءٌ means *reward* or *punishment* and is the مَصْدَرٌ of I-verb جَزَى - يَجْزِي (R3=ي; *to reward; to punish*).

A	Anyone who strives (works hard) will be suc-cessful.	مَنْ يَجْتَهِدْ فَإِنَّهُ ناجِحٌ.
B		مَنْ يَجْتَهِدْ فَأَنَّهُ ناجِحٌ.

What is the difference between A and B? Is there actually a difference? Let's start with what A and B have in common:

مَنْ	Conditional particle (اِسْمُ شَرْطٍ) supplying the place of the **subject** (مُبْتَدَأٌ) of a nominal sentence (جُمْلَةٌ اِسْمِيّةٌ); you don't see it, but it gets the place value of a nominative case (فِي مَحَلّ رَفْعٍ مُبْتَدَأً).
يَجْتَهِدْ	Verb in the present tense (فِعْلٌ مُضارِعٌ) that works as a conditional verb (فِعْلُ الشَّرْطِ). Therefore, we use the jussive mood (مَجْزُومٌ), marked by the سُكونٌ. The verbal sentence (verb plus implied فاعِلٌ *he*) is the **predicate** (خَبَرُ الْمُبْتَدَإِ) of the nominal sentence.
فَ	Particle (حَرْفٌ مَبْنِيٌّ عَلَى الْفَتْحِ) placed in the second part of the conditional sentence (جَوابُ الشَّرْطِ); does 't have a place in إِعْرابٌ.

Now let's analyze the differences.

إِنَّ	A	Particle of emphasis (حَرْفُ تَوْكيدٍ وَنَصْبٍ) with operating power.
هُ	A	Indeclinable pronoun suffix (ضَميرٌ مُتَّصِلٌ) serving as the sub-ject (اِسْمُ إِنَّ). This is the reason why it is located in the position of an accusative case (فِي مَحَلّ نَصْبٍ).
ناجِحٌ	A	Predicate (خَبَرُ إِنَّ), nominative case (مَرْفوعٌ بِالضَّمّةِ الظّاهِرةِ). The whole part after إِنَّ is grammatically treated as being in the state of جَزْمٌ (jussive mood) as it is the second part of the conditional sentence (الْجُمْلَةُ فِي مَحَلّ جَزْمٍ جَوابُ الشَّرْطِ).

This analysis is based on the concept that the particle إِنَّ is placed at the very beginning of the second part of the conditional sentence (صَدْرُ جُمْلَةِ الْجَوابِ).

أَنَّهُ ناجِحٌ	B	أَنَّ plus "subject" (اِسْمُ أَنَّ) plus predicate (خَبَرُ أَنَّ).
	B1	This time, we have an interpreted مَصْدَرٌ consisting of أَنَّ and its two governed factors. This interpreted مَصْدَرٌ does the job of the **subject**

	of the nominal sentence (مُبْتَدَأٌ). So, it gets the place value of a nominative case (فِي مَحَلِّ رَفْعٍ مُبْتَدَأً). What about the predicate (خَبَرٌ) of the nominal sentence? It was deleted (مَحْذُوفٌ).	
	How could the deleted predicate look like? Here is a possible reconstruction: →	مَنْ يَجْتَهِدْ فَنَجاحُهُ ثابِتٌ.
B2	The interpreted مَصْدَرٌ in B2 appears in the place of the **predicate** in the **nominative** (فِي مَحَلِّ رَفْعٍ خَبَرٌ) of the nominal sentence (جُمْلَةٌ اسْمِيّةٌ). And the subject (مُبْتَدَأً)? It was deleted (مَحْذُوفٌ).	
	How could the deleted subject look like? Here is a possible reconstruction: →	مَنْ يَجْتَهِدْ فَالثّابِتُ نَجاحُهُ.

Let's see both interpretations of option B next to each other and translate them literally. Pay attention to the position of the infinitive (نَجاحُهُ) which stands for أَنَّ and its governed factors:

B1	If one strives, then his success will be solid/enduring.	مَنْ يَجْتَهِدْ فَنَجاحُهُ ثابِتٌ.
B2	If one strives, then the constant factor will be his success.	مَنْ يَجْتَهِدْ فَالثّابِتُ نَجاحُهُ.

In the Qur'an, there are several verses that can be read in two ways – with إِنَّ or أَنَّ. For example:

Sura 6:54	any of you who does wrong out of ignorance and then repents after that and corrects himself - **indeed**, He is Forgiving and Merciful."	...مَنْ عَمِلَ مِنكُمْ سُوءًا بِجَهَالَةٍ ثُمَّ تَابَ مِن بَعْدِهِ وَأَصْلَحَ فَأَنَّهُ غَفُورٌ رَّحِيمٌ.

Why did we choose this example? Well, Instead of فَأَنَّهُ you could theoretically also read فَإِنَّهُ. Then, you'd assume a full sentence after فَ which would have the assumed meaning of: فَهُوَ غَفُورٌ

If you use فَأَنَّهُ, you treat أَنَّ plus its governed factors usually as the **predicate** (خَبَرٌ) with the subject being omitted (مُبْتَدَأً مَحْذُوفٌ). An assumed meaning could be the following sentence: *His fate is God's forgiveness and mercy* (فَمَصِيرُهُ غُفْرانُ اللهِ وَرَحْمَتُهُ).

257. What is the difference between إِنَّ and إِنَّما؟

When ما is attached, the operating, governing power of إِنَّ is neutralized.

Practically speaking, if there is a ما involved, the اِسْمُ إِنَّ will get the nominative case. This explains why such type of ما is called *the hindering Mā* or *neutralizing Mā* (ما الْكافَّة) because it hinders the operating power of the preceding device; it blocks the governing power of certain words. This is true for all *sisters of إِنَّ*, i.e., أَنَّ or كَأَنَّ or لٰكِنَّ. Note: كافّ is the active participle (اِسْمُ الْفاعِلِ) of I-verb كَفَّ - يَكُفُّ (R2=R3; *to stop; to abandon*).

Let's check the peculiarities of this type of ما. It is added without producing any major effect. ➤ We call it *redundant* (ما الزّائِدَةُ).

Even so, this حَرْفٌ زائِدٌ has a major grammatical impact. This type of ما abolishes the work of إِنَّ. Thus, such ما is called كافَّةٌ وَمَكْفُوفَةٌ.

- كافّ is the active participle (اِسْمُ الْفاعِلِ) of I-verb كَفَّ - يَكُفُّ (R2=R3; *to stop; to abandon*). This ما is كافَّةٌ (*stopping*) in a sense that it *stops* إِنَّ from doing its job. The ما itself does not work as a regent (عامِلٌ).

- مَكْفُوفٌ is the passive participle (اِسْمُ الْمَفْعُولِ) and denotes *stopped* (also: *blind*). This concerns إِنَّ which is *neutralized, hindered* (مَكْفُوفٌ) regarding its operating power since ما stopped it.

What is the purpose of such a ما? *Additional* or *redundant* here doesn't mean that it is useless. It just shows that it has a special function which is not similar to the usual ones.

The ما itself doesn't have a meaning; it is **only there to strengthen** or reinforce the sentence (تَقْوِيَةُ الْجُمْلَةِ): it adds (some) emphasis and normally **expresses some kind of limitation** (أَداةُ قَصْرٍ أَوْ حَصْرٍ). Thus, it is used to contradict or modify a previous assertion in the sense of *only, merely, simply*.

We can apply the formula *x is only y*; it denotes restriction of that which it precedes to that which follows it. We can translate إِنَّما with *nothing but, only; rather, much more, on the contrary*. إِنَّما occurs some 22 times in the Qur'an.

Sura 4:171	• God is only one God. (*Abdul Haleem*) • Indeed, Allah is but one God. (*Saheeh Int.*) • God is but One God. (*Muhammad Asad*)	إِنَّمَا اللَّهُ إِلٰهٌ واحِدٌ. *x is only y*

| 13:7 | • But you are only there to give warning. (*Ab-dul Haleem*)
• You are only a warner. (*Sahīh International*) | إنَّمَا أَنتَ مُنذِرٌ.

x is only y |

| The bird is (but) free. | إنَّما الطّائِرُ طَلِيقٌ. |

Particle of emphasis which usually governs the "subject" (اِسْمُ إنَّ) in the accusative case (حَرْفُ تَوْكِيدٍ وَنَصْبٍ). But watch out... Here, its power is neutralized (حَرْفٌ مَكْفُوفٌ يُفِيدُ التَّوْكِيدَ)!	إنَّ
Neutralizing particle (حَرْفُ كافٍّ زائِدٌ) that is redundant, extra here. It does not have a position in (لا مَحَلَّ لَهُ مِن الإِعْرابِ) إعْرابٌ.	ما
This is the **subject** (مُبْتَدَأٌ) of the nominal sentence; therefore, it is in the nominative case (مَرْفُوعٌ بِالضَّمّةِ الظّاهِرةِ).	الطّائِرُ
Predicate (خَبَرٌ) of the **nominal sentence**, nominative (مَرْفُوعٌ).	طَلِيقٌ

Why does ما neutralize the grammatical implications of إنَّ? It has to do with the nature and DNA of the sentence structure. It is perfectly fine to use إنَّما also in a verbal sentence (جُمْلةٌ فِعْلِيّةٌ) – but إنَّ alone, on the other hand, can only be used in **nominal** sentences.

| The one who strives (the hard-worker) will be (nothing but) successful. | إنَّما يَنْجَحُ المُجِدُّ. |
| He did it only because he didn't know the consequences. | إنَّما فَعَلَ ذلِكَ لِجَهْلِهِ بالعَواقِبِ. |

What we said in this *question* is also true for the *sisters of* إنَّ except for لَيْتَ (*if only..., ...would that*) – see next *question #258*.

258. In what way is the expression لَيْتَما special?

The ما *may (or may not) neutralize the ruling power of* لَيْتَ.

لَيْتَ (*if only..., ...would that; also: would God...*) normally expresses a wish impossible to be realized – and rarely a wish that is possible.

The origin of لَيْتَ is unclear. There are many ideas but none is really convincing. Some suggested that it is of Hebrew/Aramaic origin.

لَيْتَ **resembles a verb** in its force, its power of government, and shape. A main indication of this is that it consists of three letters and the last one carries a فَتْحَةٌ. What does that tell us about لَيْتَ?

First of all, لَيْتَ is not in the accusative case by the force of an omitted verb which would be the situation if we treat لَيْتَ as a اِسْمٌ in the accusative case (مَنْصُوبٌ).

Secondly, we can treat لَيْتَ as a حَرْفٌ ناسِخٌ, a **particle** with the power to operate on other words and overthrow some basic rules. The majority of grammarians treat لَيْتَ as a **particle of wish or hope** (حَرْفٌ ناسِخٌ يُفِيدُ التَّمَنِّي). ← لَيْتَ governs the "subject" (اِسْمُ لَيْتَ) in the accusative case (مَنْصُوبٌ) and the predicate (خَبَرُ لَيْتَ) in the nominative (مَرْفُوعٌ).

If only Zayd were here!	لَيْتَ زَيْدًا حاضِرٌ!

لَيْتَ can also take a pronominal suffix (similar to لَعَّلَ).

I wish; if only I had...	لَيْتَنِي... (or: لَيْتِي)
I wish I knew...! (If I had known...)	لَيْتَنِي أَشْعُرُ = لَيْتَ شِعْرِي.

Sura 19:23	She exclaimed, "I wish I had been dead and forgotten long before all this!"	قَالَتْ يَا لَيْتَنِي مِتُّ قَبْلَ هٰذَا وَكُنْتُ نَسْيًا مَّنْسِيًّا.

Now, what happens if ما enters the game? It gets complicated. If you attach ما to لَيْتَ, you will have two options regarding the grammatical treatment of ما:

- **Option A:** ما has the job of a *hindering, neutralizing particle*. This means that it does have a grammatical effect (إِعْمالُها) and strips-off the governing power of لَيْتَ. → You apply the rules of a standard nominal sentences (جُمْلَةٌ اِسْمِيّةٌ).

- **Option B:** You treat ما as a superfluous word (for emphasis) that is neutral (إِهْمالُها) and does not have any grammatical effect. → You apply the rules of لَيْتَ.

The following two sentences are both correct:

A	If only that Zayd was successful. (Hopefully Zayd	لَيْتَما زَيْدٌ ناجِحٌ.
B	is successful. *Or:* I wish Zayd was successful.)	لَيْتَما زَيْدًا ناجِحٌ.

A	Particle of wish (حَرْفُ تَمَنٍّ وَنَصْبٍ). Remark: تَمَنٍّ is the مَصْدَر of	لَيْتَ
B	the V-verb تَمَنَّى - يَتَمَنَّى (R3=ي; *to wish*). Pattern: تَفَعَّلَ	
A	<u>Neutralizing</u> (extra) particle (حَرْفُ كافٍّ زائِدٌ), no place in إعْرابٌ.	ما
B	Just a <u>redundant</u> particle (حَرْفُ زائِدٌ); no place in إعْرابٌ.	
A	Subject (مَبْتَدَأٌ) of the **nominal sentence,** nominative (مَرْفُوعٌ).	زَيْدٌ
B	"Subject" (اِسْمُ لَيْتَ); accusative (مَنْصُوبٌ بِالْفَتْحةِ الظّاهِرةِ).	زَيْدًا
A	Predicate (خَبَرٌ) of a regular **nominal sentence,** nominative.	ناجِحٌ
B	Predicate of لَيْتَ (خَبَرُ لَيْتَ); nominative case.	

259. What is the difference between إنَّما and إنَّ ما?

إنَّ ما *has some space between the two words, and this space matters.*

How can we "read" this space? Let's check them both.

- إنَّما **- without space:** ما may stop the grammatical implications of إنَّ. It is called a *hindering Mā* or *neutralizing Mā* (ما الْكافّةُ).

- إنَّ ما **- with space:** ما works as a relative pronoun (اِسْمٌ مَوْصُولٌ). This اِسْمٌ مَوْصُولٌ is virtually in the position of an accusative case. إنَّ is responsible for that as إنَّ is a حَرْفٌ ناسِخٌ and operates on the "subject" (here: the اِسْمٌ مَوْصُولٌ) in the accusative case (مَنْصُوبٌ). This also occurs in the Qur'an.

Sura 6:134	• **What** you are promised is **sure** to come, and you cannot escape. (*Abdul Haleem*) • **Surely, that** which you are promised will verily come to pass, and you cannot escape [Allah's punishment]. (*Muhsin Khan*)	إنَّ مَا تُوعَدُونَ لَآتٍ وَمَا أنتُم بِمُعْجِزِينَ.

What you did is indeed fruitful!	إنَّ ما عَمِلْتَهُ مُثْمِرٌ.
Why can't it be إنَّما? Because the "subject" (اِسْمُ إنَّ) would be missing.	

Particle of emphasis which governs the "subject" (اِسْمُ إنَّ) in the accusative case (حَرْفُ تَوْكِيدٍ وَنَصْبٍ).	إنَّ

ما	Relative pronoun (اِسْمٌ مَوْصُولٌ) that has the meaning of الَّذِي. It serves as the "subject" (اِسْمُ إِنَّ) here and is thus placed in the position of an accusative case (فِي مَحَلِّ نَصْبٍ).
عَمِلْتَهُ	Verb in the past tense (فِعْلٌ ماضٍ). The تَ is an indeclinable pronoun suffix (ضَمِيرٌ مُتَّصِلٌ) serving as the subject (فاعِلٌ); thus, it is (grammatically) in the position of a nominative (فِي مَحَلِّ رَفْعٍ). The ه is a **referential pronoun** (returner; عائِدٌ/). This suffix (ضَمِيرٌ مُتَّصِلٌ) takes on the job of a direct object (مَفْعُولٌ بِهِ) and is placed in the position of an accusative (فِي مَحَلِّ نَصْبٍ). The entire expression is a verbal sentence – it serves as the relative clause (صِلَةُ الْمَوْصُولِ). A relative clause doesn't have a position in إِعْرابٌ.
مُثْمِرٌ	**Predicate** (خَبَرُ إِنَّ), nominative case (مَرْفُوعٌ بِالضَّمّةِ الظّاهِرةِ).

Now, what about this sentence:

إنَّ ما عَمِلْتَ مُثْمِرٌ.	Indeed, what you did is fruitful.

How do you treat the ما here? You have two possibilities:

اِسْمٌ مَوْصُولٌ	1	It is a relative "pronoun" – like the previous example.
ما المَصْدَرِيّةُ	2	The ما produces an interpreted مَصْدَرٌ.
		In such a construction, the relative pronoun in Arabic would need a *referential, referring pronoun* (عائِدٌ). But the عائِدٌ was **deleted** (مَحْذُوفٌ) here! Why? Well, with the referrer pronoun, it would **not** be possible to treat it as an interpreted مَصْدَرٌ (مَصْدَرٌ مُؤَوَّلٌ).

For option 2, the إِعْرابٌ would be as follows:

إنَّ	Particle of emphasis (حَرْفُ تَوْكِيدٍ وَنَصْبٍ) that induces the accusative case.
ما	A particle of the infinitive noun (حَرْفُ مَصْدَرِيّةٍ), also called حَرْفٌ مَصْدَرِيٌّ, which is used to mold an interpreted مَصْدَرٌ (similar to أَنْ plus verb). It does not have a position in إِعْرابٌ.
عَمِلْتَ	Past tense verb. Its subject (فاعِلٌ) is the تَ. Together with ما, the verb forms an interpreted مَصْدَرٌ which takes the role of the اِسْمُ إِنَّ. For this reason, the entire verbal sentence (عَمِلْتَ) holds the position of an accusative (فِي مَحَلِّ نَصْبٍ). See *questions #142,*

#249, #291 for more information about molding a مَصْدَر with مَا.	
Predicate (خَبَر إِنَّ) in the nominative case (مَرْفُوعٌ).	مُثْمِرٌ

This would be the **meaning** of the sentence if we use the مَصْدَر + a possessive pronoun instead of the past tense verb:	إِنَّ عَمَلَكَ مُثْمِرٌ.

260. What is a *wandering* or *slipping Lām*?

A ل that has left its original position.

Have you ever heard about a letter that is wandering around? In Arabic, the letter ل is capable of doing that.

Such type of ل is called اللَّامُ الْمُزَحْلَقَةُ. It literally means *the Lām that is pushed away (from its proper place)*. The quadrilateral I-verb - يُزَحْلِقُ زَحْلَقَ denotes *to roll, slide*. The passive participle is مُزَحْلَق: *slid*.

This special Lām is originally a لَامُ الْإِبْتِداء which means that it is placed right at the beginning of a sentence. Regarding its purpose, it is an emphatic *Lām* (لَامُ التَّوْكِيدِ).

To understand the concept of the wandering Lām, we should start with the لَامُ الْإِبْتِداء, the *inceptive Lām*. The term الْإِبْتِداءُ means *the inchoative* (expressing the beginning of an action). In general, such ل may be prefixed to a noun or verb in the present tense.

- The *inceptive Lām* indicates a **process of beginning** or **becoming**.
- Like every affirmative ل, it has a *Fatha* (حَرْفٌ مَفْتُوحٌ) on top of it.
- This type of ل is used in the **front part** (صَدْرٌ) of a **nominal sentence** (جُمْلَةٌ اِسْمِيَّةٌ) to convey some **emphasis** (تَوْكِيدٌ).
- Such ل is frequently found in the Qur'an.

(Indeed,) Zayd is nice.	لَزَيْدٌ لَطِيفٌ.

Sura 16:124	And indeed, your Lord will judge between them on the Day of Resurrection.	وَإِنَّ رَبَّكَ لَيَحْكُمُ بَيْنَهُمْ يَوْمَ الْقِيَامَةِ.

Now, what happens to such a Lām, if إِنَّ النَّاسِخَةُ (إِنَّ) enters – encroaches on – a **nominal sentence**? ▷ Then, the ل moves towards the end (تَأْخِيرٌ). It **slides back a long way after** إِنَّ. That's where the name comes from: لَامٌ مُزَحْلَقَةٌ, *the Lām that is pushed away (from its proper place)*. Why does it have to move? It is actually quite simple: you have to avoid that two devices of emphasis meet/collide at the beginning, because Arabic doesn't like that (كَرَاهِيَّةُ اِبْتِداءِ الْكَلامِ بِمُؤَكِّدَيْنِ).

Only if a prepositional or adverbial phrase is immediately placed after إِنَّ, the ل doesn't have to slide but can be used with the "subject".

Let's see how this special kind of ل works. It can occur with the subject or predicate.

OPTION 1: The ل is attached to the subject (اِسْمُ إِنَّ). This is only possible under the condition that the اِسْمُ إِنَّ is **delayed** (مُؤَخَّرٌ) and therefore comes **after** the predicate (خَبَرُ إِنَّ).

Zayd is in the house.	إِنَّ فِي الْبَيْتِ لَزَيْدًا.
Particle of emphasis (حَرْفُ تَوْكِيدٍ وَنَصْبٍ).	إِنَّ
Preposition (حَرْفُ الْجَرِّ). It does not have a position in إِعْرابٌ.	فِي
Noun in the genitive case (اِسْمٌ مَجْرُورٌ) due to the preposition.	الْبَيْتِ
The شِبْهُ الْجُمْلةِ appears in the place of the **fronted predicate**. It is linked to a deleted word (مُتَعَلِّقٌ بِمَحْذُوفٍ). The true predicate (خَبَرُ إِنَّ) had to be deleted since it is implicitly understood (*to be*). However, the only way to fit the prepositional phrase into the sentence is to assume a deleted predicate since the شِبْهُ الْجُمْلةِ must be associated with some kind of action.	
This ل is a لَامٌ مُزَحْلَقَةٌ because it was pushed away from the beginning of the sentence. Note that it has a فَتْحةٌ on top ("la" - مَبْنِيٌّ عَلَى الْفَتْحِ). It does not have a position in إِعْرابٌ.	لَ
"Subject" (اِسْمُ إِنَّ); accusative case (مَنْصُوبٌ بِالْفَتْحةِ الظّاهِرةِ).	زَيْدًا

OPTION 2: The ل appears together with the predicate (خَبَرُ إِنَّ). This is the **usual situation**. There are many possible constructions.

In all of the following examples, ل has the same function and shape. It conveys the meaning of *certainly, surely*.

This is a لامٌ مُزَحْلَقَةٌ because it was pushed away from the beginning of the sentence. It doesn't have a position in إِعْرابٌ.	لـ

Situation 1: The predicate (خَبَرُ إِنَّ) consists of a single word (مُفْرَدٌ) and comes <u>after</u> the subject (اِسْمُ إِنَّ).

Zayd is indeed generous.	إِنَّ زَيْدًا لَكَرِيمٌ.

Predicate (خَبَرُ إِنَّ) in the nominative case (مَرْفُوعٌ).	كَرِيمٌ

Situation 2: The predicate (خَبَرُ إِنَّ) is a nominal sentence (جُمْلَةٌ اِسْمِيَّةٌ).

Zayd has certainly a generous nature.	إِنَّ زَيْدًا لَخُلُقُهُ كَرِيمٌ.

Subject (مُبْتَدَأٌ) of the nominal sentence; nominative (مَرْفُوعٌ) case.	خُلُقُ
Possessive pronoun serving as the second part (مُضافٌ إِلَيْهِ) of the إِضافةٌ, indeclinable; grammatically in the spot of a genitive case.	هُ
Predicate (خَبَرُ الْمُبْتَدَإِ) of the nominal sentence, nominative (مَرْفُوعٌ).	كَرِيمٌ
The nominal sentence consisting of subject (مُبْتَدَأٌ) and predicate (خَبَرٌ) functions as the خَبَرُ إِنَّ, so it gets the place value of a nominative (فِي مَحَلِّ رَفْعٍ).	

Situation 3: The predicate (خَبَرٌ) is a verbal sentence. The verb is in the present tense, indicative mood (جُمْلَةٌ فِعْلِيَّةٌ فِعْلُها مُضارِعٌ).

Zayd, indeed, honors the guest.	إِنَّ زَيْدًا لَيُكْرِمُ الضَّيْفَ.

Verb in the present tense (فِعْلٌ مُضارِعٌ مَرْفُوعٌ). Subject (فاعِلٌ) is an implied pronoun (ضَمِيرٌ مُسْتَتِرٌ) expressing he (تَقْدِيرُهُ هُوَ).	يُكْرِمُ
The verbal sentence (يُكْرِمُ) is in the position of the خَبَرُ إِنَّ. Therefore, it gets the "place value" of a nominative case (فِي مَحَلِّ رَفْعٍ).	

Situation 4: The place of the predicate (خَبَرُ إِنَّ) is filled by a prepositional or adverbial phrase (شِبْهُ الْجُمْلَةِ).

a	prepositional phrase	Zayd is certainly at home.	إِنَّ زَيْدًا لَفِي الْبَيْتِ.
b	adverbial phrase	You certainly have the book.	إِنَّ الْكِتابَ لَعِنْدَكَ.

a, b	The prepositional (a) or adverbial phrase (b) is called quasi-sentence (شِبْهُ الْجُمْلةِ) in Arabic. Here, it appears in the place of the predicate of إِنَّ (خَبَرُ إِنَّ) - however, it is not the real predicate, because the real predicate (e.g., "is") had to be deleted since it denotes a permanent state which is understood anyway. Grammatically, the شِبْهُ الْجُمْلةِ must be linked to this deleted word (مُتَعَلِّقٌ بِمَحْذُوفٍ), so that all parts of the sentence have a relationship to one another. *See #140.*

Situation 5: We have free, separate personal pronoun (ضَمِيرُ الْفَصْلِ) between the subject (اِسْمُ إِنَّ) and the predicate (خَبَرُ إِنَّ).

Correctness/integrity, certainly, is the way to success.	إِنَّ الِاسْتِقامةَ لَهِيَ الطَّرِيقُ إِلَى النَّجاحِ.

Personal pronoun (ضَمِيرُ الْفَصْلِ); doesn't have a position in إِعْرابٌ.	هِيَ

261. Why do we use different names for the emphatic Lām?

Because the name tells us more about the nature of the sentence.

اللَّامُ الْفارِقةُ and اللَّامُ الْمُزَحْلَقةُ and لامُ التَّوْكِيد and لامُ الْإِبْتِداء are different names for the same **emphatic** Lām (لـ) that is usually placed before the subject (مُبْتَدَأٌ). Why do we use different names? We choose them according to the position and character of the sentence. It would be okay, however, to call all of them simply emphatic *Lām*.

reason for the name	term
لـ that emphasizes the subject (لِأَنَّها تُؤَكِّدُ الْمُبْتَدَأَ). This is the generic name.	لامُ التَّوْكِيد
The emphatic particle إِنَّ and the emphatic لـ do not go along well and cannot stand next to each other (لِأَنَّ اللَّامَ وَإِنَّ لا تَجْتَمِعانِ); therefore, the *Lām* slides closer to the end. See *question #260*.	اللَّامُ الْمُزَحْلَقةُ
لـ that is interlinked with the subject (لِأَنَّها تَقْتَرِنُ بِالْمُبْتَدَإِ) of a nominal sentence. It marks the first word in a sentence or starts a new idea. See *question #262*.	لامُ الْإِبْتِداء

The *distinguishing* لـ. It tells you that إِنْ is not a negation particle but a softened إِنَّ (مِنَ الْمُخَفَّفَةِ إِنْ بَيْنَ تَفْرُقُ لِأَنَّها) – see *question #262*. (وَإِنْ الْأُخْرَى الثَّقيلةِ)	اللَّامُ الْفارِقةُ

262. Can you lighten (تَخْفيفٌ) the sisters of إِنَّ and أَنَّ?

Yes, you can.

To warm up, we should first look at four special and powerful words and devices that have one thing in common: a شَدَّةٌ.

لٰكِنَّ	كَأَنَّ	أَنَّ	إِنَّ
however	as if	that	that/indeed

They are called الْحُروفُ النّاسِخةُ الْمُشَدَّدةُ and have something else in common: the final نَّ. Is it possible to make the نَّ lighter, softer? Yes! An example:

Verily, Zayd is going away.	إِنْ زَيْدٌ لَمُنْطَلِقٌ.

What happened here? The *doubled Nūn* (نُونٌ مُشَدَّدةٌ), marked by a شَدَّةٌ, consists of two ن:

1. The first *Nūn* does not have a vowel; it is (ساكِنة): نْ.

2. The second *Nūn* has a vowel (مُتَحَرِّكة): نَ.

Arabic knows the concept of *dilution, softening* (تَخْفيفٌ) of these four particles (حُروفٌ). This can be done by deleting the ن with the vowel (i.e., the second نَ). After this process, إِنَّ will become إِنْ. Has the device lost its governing, operating power after the operation? We will see. We have two possibilities to treat إِنْ regarding its ruling power:

A) إِنْ **does its previous job.** This means that we apply the governing power (إِعْمالٌ) of the original word إِنَّ.

B) إِنْ does not have any governing power (إِهْمالٌ). It is just there for stylistic reasons. We apply the rules of a standard nominal sentence (جُمْلةٌ اِسْميّةٌ). ➡ The "subject" (اِسْمُ إِنْ) takes the **nominative** case (مَرْفوعٌ). This treatment of إِنْ is **more common.**

Now, don't get confused! إِنْ still conveys an **emphasis** – but only if we add لَ later in the sentence, the so-called لاَمُ الْاِبْتِداءِ. This is necessary! Without لَ, you could confuse the device with a إِنْ النّافِيَةُ: a negation conveyed by the particle إِنْ (see *question #275*). For this reason, grammarians call such a لَ a *distinctive, distinguishing Lām* (لاَمٌ فارِقة).

The entire construction is rare. If you encounter it, you will usually deal with option B. Here is an example of a softened إِنَّ, i.e. إِنْ, including the necessary لاَمٌ فارِقةٌ.

Sura 20:63	They said, "Indeed, these are two ma- gicians."	قَالُوا إِنْ هَذانِ لَسَاحِرَانِ.
Notice that هَذانِ is a dual form and the Aleph marks the nominative case!		

The case ending of the **subject** tells us which approach is used.

A	You apply إِنْ as it would be إِنَّ.	*Zayd is generous.*	إِنْ زَيْدًا لَكَرِيمٌ.
B	The governing force of إِنْ is neglected.		إِنْ زَيْدٌ لَكَرِيمٌ.

A	This particle (حَرْفٌ) was *lightened from the heaviness* (مُخَفَّفةٌ مِن حَرْفُ تَوْكِيدٍ وَنَصْبٍ الثَّقِيلةِ), but it is still a particle of emphasis (حَرْفُ تَوْكِيدٍ وَنَصْبٍ) which **governs the noun it lays emphasis on** in the accusative case (مَنْصُوبٌ). It does not have a position in إِعْرابٌ.	إِنْ
B	This is the **more common approach**. This particle (حَرْفٌ) was also lightened (مُخَفَّفةٌ مِن الثَّقِيلةِ), but in this sentence, we treat it as an idle particle (حَرْفٌ مُهْمَلٌ). It does not have a position in إِعْرابٌ. Don't forget that it is still a particle of emphasis!	

A	This is the اِسْمُ إِنَّ in the accusative case (مَنْصُوبٌ).	زَيْدًا
B	Subject (مُبْتَدَأٌ) of a **nominal sentence** (جُمْلةٌ اِسْمِيّةٌ); مَرْفُوعٌ.	زَيْدٌ

A, B	So-called لاَمٌ فارِقةٌ. This particle is necessary.	لَ

A	Predicate (خَبَرُ إِنَّ); nominative (مَرْفُوعٌ بِالضَّمّةِ الظّاهِرةِ).	كَرِيمٌ
B	Predicate (خَبَرٌ) of the (regular) nominal sentence.	كَرِيمٌ

263. Can you lighten إِنَّ in a sentence that starts with كانَ?

Yes, you can. But the idea is quite sophisticated.

> There is an important rule for the immediate part after إِنَّ:
> You **can't** place a <u>verb</u> after إِنَّ – only a <u>nominal sentence</u> (جُمْلَةٌ اسْمِيَّةٌ).

Let's complicate the matter. What happens if we have a verb like كانَ which is actually based on a nominal sentence? كانَ is a فِعْلٌ ناسِخٌ and abrogates some rules for cases endings (in nominal sentences). So, if we soften إِنَّ and arrive at إِنْ, how should we handle such a sentence? We have two options.

OPTION 1: Most grammarians say that you should **neglect** the power of إِنْ to abrogate rules (إِهْمالٌ). This is the common approach.

Indeed, Zayd was generous.	إِنْ كانَ زَيْدٌ لَكَرِيمًا.

This particle (حَرْفٌ) was softened (مُخَفَّفَةٌ مِن الثَّقِيلةِ). Its governing power is **neglected** (حَرْفٌ مُهْمَلٌ). No position in إِعْرابٌ.	إِنْ
Deficient verb of existence (فِعْلٌ ماضٍ ناقِصٌ) in the past tense.	كانَ
"Subject" (اسْمُ كانَ), nominative case (مَرْفُوعٌ بِالضَّمِّةِ الظّاهِرةِ).	زَيْدٌ
A so-called لامٌ فارِقةٌ which **must** be inserted in the sentence. We want to avoid that the reader regards إِنْ as a negation particle.	لَ
Predicate (خَبَرُ كانَ), accusative case (مَنْصُوبٌ بِالْفَتْحةِ الظّاهِرةِ).	كَرِيمًا

OPTION 2. Theoretically, we are allowed to apply the standard rules of such a device (إِعْمالٌ). ➡ We can **treat** إِنْ as it would be a bold إِنَّ.

Let's first think about the predicate (خَبَرُ إِنْ). It would be a verbal sentence (جُمْلَةٌ فِعْلِيّةٌ) which receives the "place value" of an accusative case (مَنْصُوبٌ). Now, it gets complicated...

The "subject" (اسْمُ إِنْ) is a *pronoun of the fact* (ضَمِيرُ الشَّأْنِ) – ضَمِيرُ or ضَمِيرُ الْقِصّةِ) which was **deleted** (مَحْذُوفٌ). That's pretty abstract. An example.

Verily, Zayd was generous.	إِنْ كانَ زَيْدٌ لَكَرِيمًا.

The same sentence with إِنَّ:	إِنَّهُ كانَ زَيْدٌ لَكَرِيمًا.

إِنْ	مُخَفَّفَةٌ مِن This particle (حَرْفٌ) was softened and is now lighter (الثَّقِيلةِ), but it is still a **particle of emphasis** (حَرْفُ تَوْكِيدٍ وَنَصْبٍ). It governs the noun – on which it lays emphasis – in the accusative. But where is that noun? Well, the "subject" (اِسْمُ إِنْ) here is an **eliminated** *pronoun of the fact* (ضَمِيرُ الشَّأْنِ) which would grammatically fit into the position of an accusative (ضَمِيرٌ مَحْذُوفٌ فِي مَحَلّ نَصْبٍ).

Let's focus on the last part of the sentence.

...كانَ زَيْدٌ لَكَرِيمًا.

This includes the "subject" (اِسْمُ كانَ) as well as the predicate (خَبَرُ كانَ). Both together serve as the **predicate of إِنْ** (خَبَرُ إِنْ) and are therefore placed in the position of a nominative case (كانَ وَاسْمُها وَخَبَرُها فِي مَحَلّ رَفْعٍ خَبَرُ إِنْ).

264. Can you lighten the particle أَنَّ?

Yes, you can do that.

If we soften the particle أَنَّ, it will become أَنْ. This form can be very ambiguous. For this reason, أَنْ can only be understood as أَنَّ in certain situations – namely, when we assume that the **"subject"** (اِسْمُ أَنْ) is deleted (مَحْذُوفٌ). Most grammar experts say that the **omitted** subject was originally a *pronoun of the fact* (ضَمِيرُ الشَّأْنِ).

And what about the **predicate** (خَبَرُ أَنْ)? There are two options.

Option 1: The predicate (خَبَرُ أَنْ) is a **nominal** sentence (جُمْلةٌ اِسْمِيّةٌ).

I ascertain that patience is the key to joy.	أُوقِنُ أَنْ الصَّبْرُ مِفْتاحُ الْفَرَحِ.
Equivalent (تَقْدِيرُ الْجُمْلةِ) with أَنَّ ←	أُوقِنُ أَنَّهُ الصَّبْرُ مِفْتاحُ الْفَرَحِ.

أُوقِنُ	Present tense verb (فِعْلٌ مُضارِعٌ مَرْفُوعٌ), first person singular of the IV-form verb أَيْقَنَ. The combination of the vowel "u" plus a following ي wouldn't work. → We have to convert the weak letter ي to و. The subject (فاعِلٌ) of this verbal sentence is a hidden/implied pronoun (ضَمِيرٌ مُسْتَتِرٌ) expressing *I* (أنا).

This particle (حَرْفٌ) was softened (مُخَفَّفَةٌ مِن الثَّقِيلةِ); nevertheless, it is still a particle of **emphasis** (حَرْفُ تَوْكِيدٍ وَنَصْبٍ) which governs the subject (on which it lays emphasis) in the accusative. In this example, the "subject" (اسْمُ أَنْ) is a **deleted** *pronoun of the fact* (ضَمِيرُ الشَّأْنِ مَحْذُوفٌ) which takes the position of an accusative case (فِي مَحَلِّ نَصْبٍ). Mind the <u>pronunciation</u>: You need to get rid of the سُكُونٌ of أَنْ. Otherwise, two سُكُونٌ would collide (الْتِقاءُ السّاكِنَيْنِ) which is impossible in Arabic. Therefore, you need a helping vowel: a كَسْرةٌ, resulting in أَنِ.	أَنْ (أَنِ)
Subject of the <u>nominal</u> sentence (مُبْتَدَأٌ), nominative (مَرْفُوعٌ) case.	الصَّبْرُ
Predicate (خَبَرٌ) of the <u>nominal</u> sentence in the nominative case. This is also the first part of the إضافةٌ.	مِفْتاحُ
Second part of the إضافةٌ (مُضافٌ إِلَيْهِ), in the genitive case.	الْفَرَجِ

We said that the subject (اسْمُ أَنْ) was deleted. What about the **predicate** of أَنْ (خَبَرُ أَنْ)? The **entire nominal sentence** (جُمْلةٌ اسْمِيّةٌ), consisting of subject (مُبْتَدَأٌ) and predicate (خَبَرٌ), serves as the خَبَرُ أَنْ and gets the place value of a nominative case (فِي مَحَلِّ رَفْعٍ).

Option 2. The predicate (خَبَرُ أَنْ) is a **verbal** sentence (جُمْلةٌ فِعْلِيّةٌ).

This is only possible if we have one of the following situations.

a) The **verb** implies an **invocation** or **wish**. For example:

Muslims called on Allah to grant victory to their armies.	نادَى الْمُسْلِمُونَ أَنْ نَصَرَ اللّهُ جُيُوشَهُمْ.
The verbal sentence starting with نَصَرَ is the **predicate** (خَبَرُ أَنْ) and gets the place value of a nominative case (فِي مَحَلِّ رَفْعٍ). And what about the "subject" (اسْمُ أَنْ)? It is a deleted pronoun (ضَمِيرٌ مَحْذُوفٌ).	

b) The **verb** has a special shape: It is a **solid/rigid verb**, also called *inert/unipersonal verb* (فِعْلٌ جامِدٌ). Usually, such verbs don't form the present tense nor do they have a مَصْدَرٌ. For example: نِعْمَ (used for praise in the meaning of: *how good/great...*).

Let's take a verse of the Qur'an to illustrate our discussion and, as a second step, add a softened particle.

Sura 3:136	How excellent is the reward of the [righteous] workers!	...وَنِعْمَ أَجْرُ الْعَامِلِينَ!

	We ascertain how excellent the reward of the [righteous] workers is!	نُوقِنُ أَنْ وَنِعْمَ أَجْرُ الْعَامِلِينَ!
	The entire part after نِعْمَ is the predicate (خَبَرُ أَنْ) and thus gets the place value of of a nominative case (فِي مَحَلِّ رَفْعٍ).	

c) The verb is separated by a **negation particle** (لَنْ or لا or لَمْ).

Sura 90:5	Does he think that never will anyone overcome him?	أَيَحْسَبُ أَنْ لَنْ (أَنْ لَنْ) يَقْدِرَ عَلَيْهِ أَحَدٌ.

Sura 90:7	Does he think that no one observes him?	أَيَحْسَبُ أَنْ لَمْ (أَنْ لَمْ) يَرَهُ أَحَدٌ.

	I realized that the diligent would not fail.	أَيْقَنْتُ أَنْ لا يَفْشَلَ الْمُجِدُّ
	Note: This sentence is tricky. Usually, when we have أَنْ plus لا, they get transformed and merge to أَلّا (*in order not to*). But this is not the meaning here. Instead, we have an emphasis!	

d) The verb is **separated by قَدْ**.

I realized that the diligent would succeed.	أَيْقَنْتُ أَنْ قَدْ أَفْلَحَ الْمُجِدُّ.

e) The verb **expresses the future** by the prefixes سَـ or سَوْفَ. Both are technically *particles of amplification* or *enlargement* (حَرْفُ التَّنْفِيسِ).

I am sure that the diligent will succeed.	أُوقِنُ أَنْ سَيُفْلِحِ الْمُجِدُّ.

f) The verb is **separated by لَوْ**.

I am sure (that) if a man strives, he will succeed.	أُوقِنُ أَنْ لَوْ جَدَّ الْإِنْسَانُ لَأَفْلَحَ.

➤ All the above examples have one thing in common. The part after أَنْ is the **predicate** (خَبَرُ أَنْ) and grammatically placed in the position of a nominative case (فِي مَحَلِّ رَفْعٍ). And the subject? We assume that it was a *pronoun of the fact* (ضَمِيرُ الشَّأْنِ) which was deleted.

265. Can you lighten the particle كَأَنَّ?

Yes, you can. It will finally become كَأَنْ.

When we lighten a particle of emphasis that has the power to abrogate rules (النَّاسِخُ), we have to can decide how to treat the lightened particle. We usually have two options. We apply the same grammar rules as if the device has operating, ruling power (إِعْمالٌ). Or we ignore the governing power (إِهْمالٌ) of the device. The purpose of the device, i.e., **emphasis**, remains anyway.

However, regarding كَأَنْ, we **do not have a choice**. We <u>must</u> apply the rules of a device with operating, governing power (إِعْمالٌ).

This means that كَأَنْ observes the rules of أَنْ, but with one special feature. The construction is built upon a اِسْمُ كَأَنْ ("subject") which is a **deleted pronoun** (ضَمِيرٌ مَحْذُوفٌ).

| He rages as if he was a wild beast. | يَثُورُ كَأَنْ حَيَوانٌ هائِجٌ. |
| This is how the sentence would look like with the original particle: → | كَأَنَّهُ حَيَوانٌ هائِجٌ. |

Particle of resemblance, comparison (حَرْفُ تَشْبِيهٍ وَنَصْبٍ) that was thinned (مُخَفَّفةٌ مِن الثَّقِيلةِ). Still, it is an *abrogator* (حَرْفُ تَشْبِيهٍ وَنَصْبٍ). It governs the "subject" (اِسْمُ كَأَنْ) – the part of the sentence on which the spotlight is turned – in the accusative case. Watch out: In the softened version, the اِسْمُ كَأَنْ is a **deleted pronoun** which is hypothetically placed in the position of an accusative case (ضَمِيرٌ مَحْذُوفٌ فِي مَحَلِّ نَصْبٍ).	كَأَنْ
Predicate (خَبَرُ كَأَنْ) in the nominative case (مَرْفُوعٌ).	حَيَوانٌ

Let's do some fine-tuning. If the **predicate** (خَبَرُ كَأَنْ) is a **verbal sentence** (جُمْلةٌ فِعْلِيّةٌ), it is better to separate كَأَنْ from the following verb by a noun or particle. We call such an operation or tool a فاصِلٌ. This could be قد before a past tense verb (فِعْلٌ ماضٍ) or the negation particle لَمْ before a verb in the present tense (فِعْلٌ مُضارِعٌ).

The weather is cold like (as if) winter **had (already)** come.	الْجَوُّ بارِدٌ كَأَنْ قَدْ أَتَى الشِّتاءُ.
The weather is hot as if summer **never ended**.	الْجَوُّ حارٌّ كَأَنْ لَمْ يَنْتَهِ الصَّيْفُ.

Remark: It is possible to leave the اِسْمُ كَأَنْ **unchanged.** This means that we do not have a deleted pronoun serving as such. Therefore, we will have a word in the accusative case in the sentence.

Like a shining full moon (= subject) is this face (= predicate).	كَأَنْ بَدْرًا مُشْرِقًا هذا الْوَجْهُ.

A more literal translation: *As if a shining full **moon** is this very face.*

➡ بَدْرًا (*moon*) is the اِسْمُ كَأَنْ (subject) in the accusative (مَنْصُوبٌ).

➡ مُشْرِقًا is an adjective (صِفةٌ) and has to agree with بَدْرًا. And the predicate (خَبَرُ كَأَنْ)? It is هذا, an indeclinable word. Since it serves as the predicate, it gets the "place value" of a nominative (فِي مَحَلِّ رَفْعٍ).

266. Can you lighten the particle لٰكِنَّ (*but*)?

Yes, you can. In the end, we will get the word لٰكِنْ.

The following discussion is about the Arabic word for *but*. There are two versions of the Arabic word, a **light** (لٰكِنْ) and a **heavy** (لٰكِنَّ) form.

In general, when should you use لٰكِنْ and when لٰكِنَّ?

- لٰكِنْ is used if a **verbal** sentence follows (more common).

- لٰكِنَّ is used if a **nominal** sentence follow.

→ In contradictions or contrasts, both are **mostly prefixed by** وَ (*and*).

For the analysis, we will focus on the heavy, emphatic لٰكِنَّ, *a sister of* إِنَّ.

لٰكِنَّ operates on the subject of the subordinate clause and induces the accusative case (حَرْفٌ مِن أَخَواتِ إِنَّ يُفِيدُ التَّوْكِيدَ).

لٰكِنَّ includes the emphatic particle إِنَّ which we may soften. This gets quite tricky. Contrary to كَأَنْ in the previous *question #265*, you <u>must</u> **neglect** the operating, governing power (إِهْمَالٌ) and thus the original grammatical implications when you use the softened version لٰكِنْ.

In short: لٰكِنْ conveys emphasis, but is like a neutral device regarding the case endings (لا تَعْمَلُ شَيْئًا). We apply the rules of a standard nominal sentence (جُمْلَةٌ اِسْمِيَّةٌ).

Karīm is diligent, but his brother is lazy.	كَرِيمٌ مُجِدٌّ لٰكِنْ أَخُوهُ كَسُولٌ.

Particle *to rectify* or *emend (correct) the previous statement* (حَرْفُ اِسْتِدْرَاكٍ مُهْمَلٌ) which lost its initial grammatical implication because it was softened and lost the نَ (مُخَفَّفَةٌ مِنَ الثَّقِيلَةِ). It does not have a position in إِعْرَابٌ.	لٰكِنْ
Subject (مُبْتَدَأٌ) of the nominal sentence (جُمْلَةٌ اِسْمِيَّةٌ), it takes the nominative case (مَرْفُوعٌ بِالْوَاو). The case marker is special. We have the word *brother* which is one of the five or *six special nouns* (الْأَسْمَاءُ السِّتَّةُ). → We mark the case by the letter و.	أَخُو
Pronoun suffix (ضَمِيرٌ مُتَّصِلٌ), serving as the 2nd part of a إِضَافَةٌ; thus, it is found in the position of a genitive case (فِي مَحَلِّ جَرٍّ).	هُ
Predicate (خَبَرٌ) of the nominal sentence; nominative case (مَرْفُوعٌ).	كَسُولٌ

Sura 19:38	...but the wrongdoers today are in clear error.	...لٰكِنِ الظَّالِمُونَ الْيَوْمَ فِي ضَلَالٍ مُبِينٍ.

Here, you would expect لٰكِنَّ since we have a nominal sentence (جُمْلَةٌ اِسْمِيَّةٌ) after it. How can we explain that? Answer: the ن lost some weight; the original device لٰكِنَّ was **softened**.

Particle to rectify the previous statement (حَرْفُ اِسْتِدْرَاكٍ). It was lightened (مُخَفَّفَةٌ مِنَ الثَّقِيلَةِ) and lost the نَ. It does not operate on other words and thus has no governing power.	لٰكِنِ
Subject (مُبْتَدَأٌ) of the جُمْلَةٌ اِسْمِيَّةٌ, in the nominative case by the ending ونَ. The و functions as the case marker!	الظَّالِمُونَ

Note: See #191 to know how لٰكِنْ works as a conjunction (عَطْفٌ).

THE REPORTED OR INDIRECT SPEECH

267. Does the indirect speech work differently in Arabic?

Yes, it does. If the reporting verb is in the past tense, we don't need to change the tenses in the reported speech.

The reported or indirect speech is used when we want to tell someone else what the first person said.

In English, the indirect speech is tricky because there might be a change of tenses or word order. Sometimes, you even need to convert words (*now* becomes *then/at that time*; *today* becomes *yesterday* or *that day*; *last week* becomes *the week before/the previous week*).

direct speech	reported/indirect speech (in English)
I bought a car yesterday.	She said (that) she had bought a car the day before.

Let's see how the indirect speech in Arabic works.

- If the direct speech is initiated by إِنَّ, the indirect speech is usually marked by بِأَنَّ. Why? You should use إِنَّ after قالَ if you **trust** the information that comes after it. If you <u>doubt</u> it, you should better use a construction with بـ and أَنَّ - to indicate that it may not be the absolute truth. See *Arabic for Nerds 1, #229*.

- In the direct speech, إِنَّ has the meaning of *verily, indeed* although you don't always have to translate it as such.

- In the indirect speech, بِأَنَّ (or إِنَّ) simply means: "*...that*".

- In the indirect speech in Arabic, tenses don't change nor does the word order.

direct speech	indirect speech
He said: "I wrote you a letter."	He said that he had written me a letter.
قالَ: (إِنِّي) كَتَبْتُ لَكَ رِسالةً.	قالَ إِنَّهُ / بِأَنَّهُ كَتَبَ لِي رِسالةً.
	He informed me that he had written me a letter.
	أَخْبَرَنِي بِأَنَّهُ كَتَبَ لِي رِسالةً.

What about **questions**? If we want to "report" a *when-*, *where-*, *who-* question, you don't need to change anything except for the correct form (person) of the verb.

direct speech	indirect speech
I asked him: "Where have **you** been?"	I asked him where **he** had been.
سَأَلْتُهُ: أَيْنَ كُنْتَ؟	سَأَلْتُهُ أَيْنَ كانَ؟

If we have a *yes-no* question, you will have the word *whether* in the in-direct speech. That's more complicated. You have two options. You can simply use أ or هَلْ, or you start the indirect question with one of the following two constructions to express *whether*:

construction 1			إنْ	
construction 2	verb	+	إذا	(ما)

Note: If the verb needs a preposition, the preposition and ما will merge.

to ask about	عَمَّا إذا	ما إذا + عَنْ	سَأَلَ عَنْ
to think about	فِيما إذا	ما إذا + فِي	فَكَّرَ فِي

If there is *whether* involved – what about the tenses in the part of the reported speech? Now, you have to watch out!

	tense that we use in English	construction in Arabic
1	present tense	فَعَلَ / كانَ يَفْعَلُ
2	past tense	كانَ قَدْ فَعَلَ
3	future tense	كانَ سَيَفْعَلُ
4	nominal sentence	كانَ + predicate

1	He thinks about whether he should take it or not.	يُفَكِّرُ فِيما إذا قَبِلَ (كانَ يَقْبِلُ) ذٰلِكَ أَمْ لا.
2	I asked him whether he had eaten or not.	سَأَلْتُهُ إنْ (عَمَّا إذا) كانَ قَدْ أَكَلَ أَمْ لا.

| 3 | I asked him whether he will come tomorrow. | سَأَلْتُهُ إِنْ (عَمّا إذا) كانَ سَيَأْتِي غَدًا. |
| 4 | I asked him whether he was sick. | سَأَلْتُهُ إِنْ (ما إذا) كانَ مَرِيضًا. |

THE NEGATION OF A NOMINAL SENTENCE

268. What kind of word is لَيْسَ?

لَيْسَ *is a special verb.*

لَيْسَ negates the existence of the predicate (خَبَرُ لَيْسَ). There are many ideas about its origin. Aramaic knows a similar word, *leita* (לֵית), expressing *there is no*. The famous grammarian Abū Zakarīya al-Farrāʾ (أَبُو زَكَرِيّا الْفَرّاء), who was born in 761 (144 AH) in Kūfa in present-day Iraq, claimed that لَيْسَ is a compound of *not* (لا) and the unused أَيْسَ, which is a noun (إِسْمٌ) and signifies *being, existence*. It seems that the corresponding Hebrew word for أَيْسَ is *"yesh"* (יֵשׁ), which is one of the most used expressions in Modern Hebrew and means *there is* or simply *existence*. Al-Farrāʾ gave the following example of أَيْسَ:

| Bring him from where he is or is not. | جِئْ بِهِ مِنْ حَيْثُ أَيْسَ وَلَيْسَ. |
| This is the meaning of the sentence: | مِنْ حَيْثُ هُوَ وَلَيْسَ هُوَ. |

لَيْسَ is a *rigid verb* (فِعْلٌ جامِدٌ) which means it can not be fully conjugated in all forms. لَيْسَ does **not** form the present tense (فِعْلٌ ماضٍ ناقِصٌ) and does **not** have a مَصْدَرٌ. Originally, it followed the pattern فَعِلَ resulting in لَيِسَ, but this is difficult to pronounce, so perhaps this is the reason why it became لَيْسَ. Some important characteristics:

- لَيْسَ goes along with a nominal sentence.
- لَيْسَ governs the subject (مُبْتَدَأٌ) in the nominative case (مَرْفُوعٌ). If لَيْسَ enters a nominal sentence, the subject is called إِسْمُ لَيْسَ.
- لَيْسَ governs the predicate (خَبَرٌ) in the accusative case (مَنْصُوبٌ). It is called خَبَرُ لَيْسَ. ➡ Because of all that, لَيْسَ is a *sister of* كانَ.
- If لَيْسَ is immediately placed before the predicate, the negation is is reinforced and is strongest.

But is لَيْسَ really a verb? It does not express an action, nor a time. Why can we treat it as a verb? لَيْسَ resembles a **verb in terms of force**. It is composed of at least three letters and the last letter has a فَتْحَةٌ. This is also true for لَيْتَ; see *question #258*.

Karīm is not standing.	لَيْسَ كَرِيمٌ قائِمًا.

Defective, incomplete past tense verb (فِعْلٌ ماضٍ ناقِصٌ). It is not enough to have only a subject; we need a predicate to produce a meaningful sentence.	لَيْسَ
This is the "subject" (اِسْمُ لَيْسَ) in the nominative case (مَرْفُوعٌ).	كَرِيمٌ
Predicate (خَبَرُ لَيْسَ), in the accusative case (مَنْصُوبٌ).	قائِمًا

269. Can you add وَ before the predicate of لَيْسَ?

Yes, this is possible.

Sometimes, you may see the letter وَ before the predicate of لَيْسَ. This works similar to كانَ (#237) and is mainly done for stylistic reasons. Can we always do that? No, this only works when the predicate is interlinked with إلّا.

Every man has his appointed term (death).	لَيْسَ إِنْسانٌ إِلّا وَلَهُ أَجَلٌ.

This is the اِسْمُ لَيْسَ in the nominative case (مَرْفُوعٌ).	إِنْسانٌ
Exception particle (حَرْفُ اِسْتِثْناءٍ مُلْغًى), Note that it does not exercise its governing power here. Does not have a place in إِعْرابٌ.	إِلّا
Particle that intervenes in the predicate (حَرْفٌ داخِلٌ عَلَى خَبَرِ لَيْسَ). This device does not have a position in إِعْرابٌ.	وَ
The لـ is a preposition (حَرْفُ الْجَرِّ), cemented on the فَتْحَةٌ. The هـ is a pronominal, indeclinable suffix (ضَمِيرٌ مُتَّصِلٌ); yet it is found in the position of a genitive case (فِي مَحَلِّ جَرٍّ) according to its job. What about the **predicate of the nominal sentence?** If we check the sentence, we see that the place of the fronted predicate (خَبَرٌ مُقَدَّمٌ) is empty. This happened for a reason. The fronted predicate is understood anyway because it points to generality.	لَهُ

Therefore, we say that the prepositional phrase (الْجَارُّ وَالْمَجْرُورُ) is linked to that deleted word (مُتَعَلِّقٌ بِمَحْذُوفٍ) because we need some glue to connect it to the sentence.	
Delayed subject (مُبْتَدَأٌ مُؤَخَّرٌ) in the nominative case (مَرْفُوعٌ).	أَجَلْ
Now, what about the **predicate of لَيْسَ؟** The sentence, consisting of subject (مُبْتَدَأٌ) and predicate (خَبَرٌ), fills that position which is grammatically, though not visibly, a location of an accusative case (فِي مَحَلِّ نَصْبٍ خَبَرُ لَيْسَ).	

Note: In general, the grammarians are not a big fan of the extra و since it can be confused with other types of و, for example, the و that initiates a circumstantial clause (وَاوُ الْحَالِ).

270. Why did the grammarians of Basra & Kūfa quarrel about لَيْسَ؟

They had a dispute whether the predicate of لَيْسَ could be placed at the very beginning.

Generally, it is possible to place the predicate of لَيْسَ before the noun of لَيْسَ, i.e., the subject. This if frequently done and it is also found in the Qur'an.

Sura 2:177	لَيْسَ ٱلْبِرَّ أَن تُوَلُّواْ وُجُوهَكُمْ قِبَلَ ٱلْمَشْرِقِ وَٱلْمَغْرِبِ.
It is not al-Birr (piety, righteousness, and each and every act of obedience to Allah, etc.) that you turn your faces towards east and (or) west (in prayers). *Abdul Haleem* renders it as follows: Goodness does not consist in turning your face towards East or West.	

In the above verse, الْبِرَّ is the fronted predicate (خَبَرُ لَيْسَ مُقَـدَّمٌ) which explains the accusative case (مَنْصُوبٌ). What about the subject? The interpreted infinitive (أَن تُوَلُّواْ) takes on this job and works as the delayed noun of لَيْسَ and thus gets the place value of a nominative case (الْمَصْدَرُ الْمُؤَوَّلُ فِي مَحَلِّ رَفْعٍ اسْمُ لَيْسَ مُؤَخَّرٌ).

In this example, the verb لَيْسَ was located in front of both parts which are governed by لَيْسَ, i.e. لَيْسَ was in the first position. In theory, could you put the predicate of لَيْسَ in front of the verb لَيْسَ itself? We will see.

We have seen in *question #235* that you could place the predicate of كَانَ before the verb (at the very beginning) to lay some emphasis. How-ever, it is way more complicated to do that in a sentence with لَيْسَ. The grammarians of Basra (الْبَصْرِيُّونَ) stated that this is impossible. In other words, you can't move the predicate (تَقْدِيمُ الْخَبَرِ) to the front. Let's try to understand their arguments by looking at an example:

| regular word order | The man is not present. | لَيْسَ الرَّجُلُ حَاضِرًا. |

Now, would the following sentence work?

| ➡ **No**, said the grammarians of Basra as it would mean that **another man is present**. | حَاضِرًا لَيْسَ الرَّجُلُ. |

According to their rivals, the grammarians of Kūfa (الْكُوفِيُّونَ), how-ever, such a sentence construction would be fine. They stated that you are allowed to move the predicate of لَيْسَ to the front.

They could not find proof for that in the spoken words of the Arabs. They analyzed the text of the Qur'an and found something that could indicate that fronting the predicate is permissible. It is some evidence, but not a proof. This is the line of the Qur'an:

| Sura 11:8 | أَلَا يَوْمَ يَأْتِيهِمْ لَيْسَ مَصْرُوفًا عَنْهُمْ وَحَاقَ بِهِم مَّا كَانُوا بِهِ يَسْتَهْزِئُونَ. |

But on the Day it comes upon them, nothing will divert it from them; what they mocked will be all around them.

| يَوْمَ يَأْتِيهِمْ | Adverb of time (ظَرْفُ زَمانٍ) which is connected (مُتَعَلِّقٌ) to the predicate of لَيْسَ, i.e., مَصْرُوفًا, which comes after it. |

يَوْمَ يَأْتِيهِمْ is the patient of the predicate (مَعْمُولُ الْخَبَرِ). The crucial point here is that the patient is placed before لَيْسَ. Since it is okay to bring the **patients of the predicate (تَقْدِيمُ مَعْمُولِ الْخَبَرِ)** to the front, this indicates that it may be also okay to front the predicate. Why? Because you are only allowed to bring the patient (الْمَعْمُولُ) to the front, if it is permissible to front the operator/regent (الْعَامِلُ) to that position as well.

Most grammarians, since this construction is used in the Qur'an, agree on the following. As long as لَيْسَ remains connected with the main predicate, you can move accessories (تَقَدُّمُ الْمُتَعَلِّقِ) forward since they both stay connected.

271. How many particles can do the job of لَيْسَ (as a negation)?

Arabic knows more or less four particles (حَرْف) that convey a negation – and they usually have the same governing power as لَيْسَ.

All of them were mainly used in (pre-)Classical Arabic. They negate a nominal sentence (جُمْلةٌ اِسْمِيّةٌ).

it is not..., this was not... this was no...	لاتَ	3	ما	1
	إِنْ	4	لا	2

If certain conditions are fulfilled, they share the same grammatical implications as their role model لَيْسَ:

- The subject (مُبْتَدَأٌ) will turn into the *noun of the negation particle* (اِسْمُ...) and takes the nominative case (مَرْفُوعٌ).
- There's a predicate (خَبَر...) which gets the **accusative case** (مَنْصُوبٌ).

However, the more common approach in Classical Arabic for ما, لا and إِنْ is different. They are "neutral" devices and don't have governing power. You'll end up with a negation – but the sentence structure and grammar stays the same. We'll examine that in the following *questions*.

272. Can you use ما to negate a nominal sentence?

Yes, this is found in (pre-) Classical Arabic, but it is very rare nowadays.

In Classical Arabic, ما is often used to negate a verbal sentence (present and past tense). In Modern Standard Arabic, you hardly encounter it and instead use لَم (plus jussive mood) for the past, لَن (plus subjunctive mood) for the future and لا (plus indicative mood) for the present tense. Though it was never really common, it is also possible to negate a nominal sentence with ما. In a nominal sentence (جُمْلةٌ اِسْمِيّةٌ), we usually don't find any indication of time. This is an important point because it tells us that we are able to negate the **predicate** in the present time (تُفِيدُ نَفْيَ الْمَعْنَى عَن الْخَبَرِ فِي الزَّمَنِ الْحالِي عَنْد الْإِطْلاقِ).

The tricky part is the word order because such a ما is placed at the beginning of a sentence which makes it occasionally difficult to understand. If you are not sure about the meaning of a sentence with ما, try to substitute ما by لَيْسَ and see if that would work. If yes, you most probably have to deal with a negation. Now, what are the grammatical implications if such a ما enters a sentence? There are two outcomes.

OPTION A: ما has the **governing power of** لَيْسَ, so we get the same grammatical implications. We use the grammar term إِعْمالٌ.

In that way it was applied in the Arabic of the Ḥijāz (لَهْجَةُ الْحِجازِيِّينَ) which is the reason why we call it ما الْحِجازِيّة. It was used especially in (pre-) Classical Arabic (but also in the Qur'an). This is the approach of the Basra school of grammar (الْبَصْرِيُّونَ).

In option 1, ما is a حَرْفُ نَفْيٍ ناسِخٌ. The word ناسِخٌ means that it inverts some rules. In any case, the grammatical implications are quite heavy. We call the الْمُبْتَدَأ the إِسْمُ ما which gets the nominative case (مَرْفُوعٌ). The predicate (خَبَرُ ما) takes the accusative case (مَنْصُوبٌ).

| Sura 12:31 | This is not a man (he can't be mortal). | ما هذا بَشَرًا. |

OPTION B: ما negates the predicate, but it is a **neutral device** regarding the grammatical implications. This ما **doesn't have governing power** and does not change the usual case endings (لا تَعْمَلُ شَيْئًا).

This was applied by the Banū Tamīm (لَهْجَةُ بَنِي تَمِيم). Thus, it is called ما التَّمِيمِيّة. This is the approach of the Kūfa school of grammar (الْكُوفِيُّونَ).

Even after ما has entered the sentence, we still have a standard nominal sentence with a مُبْتَدَأ and a خَبَرٌ (both in the nominative case). In other words, such ما negates the sentence but leaves the nominal sentence as it is. The underlying logic is intuitive. Since ما, when negating a verb, leaves the verb untouched, it does so with the إِسْم as well.

Both approaches are correct and have their merits. Let's compare them.

| A | Karīm is not standing. | ما كَرِيمٌ قائِمًا. |
| B | | ما كَرِيمٌ قائِمٌ. |

| A | Negation particle that operates on other parts of the sentence | ما |

	and induces cases (حَرْفُ نَفْيٍ ناسِخٌ)؛ no place in إِعْرابٌ.	
B	This is also a negation particle (حَرْفُ نَفْيٍ) but it *is negligent of its executive duties* (مُهْمِلٌ لِوَاجِبَاتِهِ)؛ no place in إِعْرابٌ.	
A	"<u>Subject</u>" (اِسْمُ ما), nominative case (مَرْفُوعٌ بِالضَّمَّةِ الظَّاهِرةِ).	كَرِيمٌ
B	This is the subject (مُبْتَدَأٌ) of a nominal sentence. Therefore, it is in the nominative case (مَرْفُوعٌ بِالضَّمَّةِ الظَّاهِرةِ).	
A	<u>Predicate</u> (خَبَرُ ما). Since it has the same power as لَيْسَ, it has to be in the **accusative** case (مَنْصُوبٌ بِالْفَتْحةِ الظَّاهِرةِ).	قائِمًا
B	The usual predicate (خَبَر) of a nominal sentence. Therefore, it takes the **nominative** case (مَرْفُوعٌ بِالضَّمَّةِ الظَّاهِرةِ).	قائِمٌ

Let's now focus on the ما الْحِجازِيّة. What features are necessary to equip ما with governing power? Several things have to be fulfilled:

- **Precondition I:** standard word order. The predicate (خَبَرٌ) must come <u>after</u> the subject (اِسْمُ ما). Otherwise, ما does not have any governing power.

Incorrect. You can't do that in Arabic.	ما قائِمًا كَرِيمٌ.
This works. The sentence means: *Karīm is not standing.* Here ما <u>doesn't have</u> governing power since we have a **fronted predicate** (خَبَرٌ مُقَدَّمٌ) and a delayed subject (مُبْتَدَأٌ مُؤَخَّرٌ).	ما قائِمٌ كَرِيمٌ.

Another example:

Karīm is not a writer.	ما كاتِبٌ كَرِيمٌ.
<u>Inverted</u> word order: The subject comes after the predicate; thus, ما can't exercise its governing power similar to لَيْسَ. ➡ We have a sentence with a delayed subject (مُبْتَدَأٌ مُؤَخَّرٌ) and fronted predicate (خَبَرٌ مُقَدَّمٌ), both in the **nominative** case. **Watch out:** Moving the predicate to the front is dangerous! This sentence could theoretically also mean: *What is a noble writer?*	

Karīm is not a writer.	ما كَرِيمٌ كاتِبًا.
<u>Standard</u> **word** order – now the ما can exercise governing power. The subject (اِسْمُ ما), in the nominative, is placed before the predicate (خَبَرُ ما). The	

predicate is in the **accusative** (مَنْصُوبٌ), similar to the predicate of لَيْسَ.

| The soldier isn't on the run. (was not defeated) | ما مُنْهَزِمٌ الْجُنْدِيُّ. |

Here, ما can't work like لَيْسَ. It can't exercise its ruling power (مُهْمَل) because the predicate comes before the subject (تَقَدُّمُ الْخَبَرِ عَلَى الْإِسْمِ).

| The soldier is not put on the run. | ما الْجُنْدِيُّ مُنْهَزِمًا. |

Here, ما serves as a negation similar to لَيْسَ and uses its operating power.

However, if the predicate is a **prepositional phrase** (شِبْهُ الْجُمْلَةِ), we have a choice: ما works like لَيْسَ (إِعْمالُها) or you treat ما just as a negation device without producing any grammatical changes (إِهْمالُها).

| Nobody is at home. | ما فِي الْبَيْتِ أَحَدٌ. |

ما	Negation particle (حَرْفُ نَفْيٍ ناسِخٌ) that has the power to overthrow the rules for cases. It does not have a place in إِعْرابٌ.
فِي	Preposition (حَرْفُ الْجَرِّ). It does not have a place in إِعْرابٌ.
الْبَيْتِ	Noun in the genitive (إِسْمٌ مَجْرُورٌ), marked by the كَسرةٌ due to the preposition فِي. The entire prepositional phrase (شِبْهُ الْجُمْلةِ) appears in the place of the predicate. The شِبْهُ الْجُمْلةِ is linked to an omitted word (مُتَعَلِّقٌ بِمَحْذُوفٍ) which is implicitly understood as the "real" predicate of ما (خَبَرُ ما), e.g, *to be*. Since it points to a general state of being, that word has to be deleted.
أَحَدٌ	"Subject" (إِسْمُ ما) in the nominative (مَرْفُوعٌ بِالضَّمّةِ الظّاهِرةِ).

How would the analysis look like if we applied option B, i.e., ما conveys a negation without producing any grammatical effect? In other words, if we regard ما as a التَّمِيمِيّة؟

| ما | Negation particle; it does not have the power to overthrow rules and guard words in a certain case (حَرْفُ نَفْيٍ مُهْمِلٌ لِوَاجِبَاتِهِ). |
| فِي الْبَيْتِ | Prepositional phrase (الْجَارُّ وَالْمَجْرُورُ) which appears in the place of the **fronted predicate** and thus gets the place value of a nominative case (شِبْهُ الْجُمْلةِ مُتَعَلِّقٌ بِمَحْذُوفٍ واقِعٌ خَبَرًا مُقَدَّمًا). It |

is connected with a deleted word, i.e, the "real" predicate which had to be deleted as it points to a general state of being (to be).	
Delayed subject (مُبْتَدَأ مُؤَخَّرٌ) of the nominal sentence and thus in the nominative case (مَرْفُوعٌ بِالضَّمَّةِ الظَّاهِرةِ).	أَحَدٌ

- **Precondition II:** It is <u>impossible</u> that the redundant, extra particle إِنْ (so-called إِنْ الزَّائِدةُ) is added after ما. If this happens, then ما has no governing power. This إِنْ is a device of augmentation and also called a *corroborative* or *supporting particle*; here, it emphasizes the negation. Usually, the extra إِنْ is used in verbal sentences with ما (for negation) and rarely with nominal sentences. For ex.: ما إِنْ أَتَيْتَ بِشَيءٍ أَنْتَ تَكْرَهُهُ (*I didn't do anything you dislike*).

This is a difficult construction because إِنْ itself may convey a negation.

Impossible in Arabic.	ما إِنْ كَرِيمٌ قائِمًا.
Possible. It means: *Karīm is not (at all) standing.*	ما إِنْ كَرِيمٌ قائِمٌ.

Negation particle (حَرْفُ نَفْيٍ مُهْمَـلٌ) with inoperative governing power regarding the grammar implications. No position in إِعْرابٌ.	ما
Extra particle (حَرْفٌ زائِدٌ). It does not have a position in إِعْرابٌ.	إِنْ
Subject (مُبْتَدَأٌ) of the nominal sentence in the nominative case.	كَرِيمٌ
Predicate (خَبَرٌ) of the nominal sentence, nominative case (مَرْفُوع).	قائِمٌ

- **Precondition III.** The predicate can't be interlinked with the particle of exception إِلَّا (*except*).

In other words, إِلَّا cannot not stand between the subject and the predicate because it would oppose the induced negation by ما and would bring about the meaning of a non-negated, affirmative sentence (إِثْباتٌ; جُمْلةٌ مُثْبَتةٌ). ما can't convey a negation in such a situation.

The ما has the meaning of a negation.	*The weather is not spring.*	ما الْجَوُّ رَبِيعًا.
Here, ما does not have the meaning of a negation.	*The weather is only (nothing but) spring.*	ما الْجَوِّ إِلَّا رَبِيعٌ.

Another example.

Sura 3:144	*Muhammad is only a messenger.*	مَا مُحَمَّدٌ إِلَّا رَسُولٌ.
	The sent. on the right is grammatically wrong. →	مَا مُحَمَّدٌ إِلَّا رَسُولًا.

Negation particle (حَرْفُ نَفْي مُهْمَلٌ) that does not have any governing power (unlike لَيْسَ). It does not have a position in إِعْرَابٌ.	مَا
Subject (مُبْتَدَأٌ) of the nominal sentence, nominative (مَرْفُوعٌ) case.	مُحَمَّدٌ
Particle of exception (حَرْفُ إِسْتِثْنَاءٍ مُلْغًى); its governing power is abrogated here. It does not have a position in إِعْرَابٌ.	إِلَّا
Predicate (خَبَرٌ) of the nominal sentence, nominative (مَرْفُوعٌ).	رَسُولٌ

- **Precondition IV**. If the predicate itself operates on a word (مَعْمُولُ الْخَبَرِ), for example, if it has a direct object (مَفْعُولٌ بِهِ), such word must **not** be put <u>before</u> the "subject" (اِسْمُ مَا). Let's see an example.

Incorrect as كِتَابًا was placed before the subject (اِسْمُ مَا). كِتَابًا is governed by the predicate *reader* (قَارِئًا); therefore, it is the مَعْمُولُ الْخَبَرِ.	ما كِتَابًا زَيْدٌ قارِئًا.
Correct. ➡ usual word order: subject + predicate. *Zayd doesn't read a book.* (lit.: Zayd is not a reader of a book.)	ما زَيْدٌ قارِئًا كِتَابًا.

Predicate of مَا, so-called خَبَرُ مَا; therefore in the accusative case.	قارِئًا
Direct object (مَفْعُولٌ بِهِ) of *reader* (قارِئًا). This is tricky because the active participle (قارِئًا) does the job of a verb. Thus, كِتَابًا is governed in the accusative by the active participle قارِئًا – see #286.	كِتَابًا

Can you change the position of prepositional or adverbial phrase (شِبْهُ الْجُمْلةِ) which is linked to the predicate? Could you put it right after the negation device? Yes, this is possible. You will get two options:

- **Option 1:** You let the مَا exercise the power of لَيْسَ (إِعْمالُها).

- **Option 2:** You treat مَا as a negation device without the power to operate on other words and induce case endings (إِهْمالُها).

Option 1:

| You are not a seeker of evil. | ما لِلشَّرِّ أَنْتَ ساعِيًا. |

| Negation particle (حَرْفُ نَفْي ناسِخٌ) that abrogates some of the standard rules for case endings. It doesn't have a place in إِعْرابٌ. | ما |

| Preposition (حَرْفُ الْجَرِّ). It doesn't have a place in إِعْرابٌ. | ل |

| Noun in the genitive case (اِسْمٌ مَجْرُورٌ), induced by the preposition. The entire prepositional phrase (الْجارُّ وَالْمَجْرُورُ) is linked to the predicate (مُتَعَلِّق بِخَبَرِ ما), i.e. ساعِيًا. | الشَّرِّ |

| Personal pronoun (ضَمِيرٌ مُنْفَصِلٌ), supplying the position of the اِسْمُ ما. We can't put case markers. Nevertheless, it is found in the location of a nominative case (فِي مَحَلِّ الرَّفْعِ). | أَنْتَ |

| Predicate (خَبَرُ ما) in the accusative case (مَنْصُوبٌ). | ساعِيًا |

Option 2:

| You are not pursuing evil. (same meaning as option 1) | ما لِلشَّرِّ أَنْتَ ساعٍ. |

| Negation particle (حَرْفُ نَفْي مُهْمَلٌ) that does not govern other words in the sentence. It doesn't have a place in إِعْرابٌ. | ما |

| Prepositional phrase (الْجارُّ وَالْمَجْرُورُ) that is related (connected) to the predicate of the nominal sentence (خَبَرٌ), i.e., ساعٍ. | لِلشَّرِّ |

| Personal pronoun (ضَمِيرٌ مُنْفَصِلٌ), serving as the **subject** (مُبْتَدَأٌ) of the nominal sentence. Although it has a fixed shape and cannot receive any case marker, it is grammatically treated as filling the position of a nominative case (فِي مَحَلِّ رَفْعٍ). | أَنْتَ |

| Predicate (خَبَرٌ) of the nominal sentence in the nominative case. | ساعٍ |

| Since we have to delete the final ي in such words (indefinite; weak letter), we cannot put the appropriate case marker on the last letter. We treat it as a word in the nominative case although it looks genitive. We use an estimated case marker (مَرْفُوعٌ بِضَمّةٍ مُقَدَّرةٍ عَلَى الْياءِ الْمَحْذُوفةِ) because the last letter can't carry the marker of the nominative case (الثِّقَلُ) – see #39. |

273. What happens if ما is used together with *but* (لَكِنْ or بَلْ)?

We will get a tricky grammatical situation.

Let's start with an example to illustrate the problem:

Karīm is not standing but sitting.	ما كَرِيمٌ قائِمًا بَلْ جالِسٌ.
	ما كَرِيمٌ قائِمًا لَكِنْ جالِسٌ.
Meaning of the last part: *but **he** is sitting*.	...بَلْ هُوَ جالِسٌ.

بَلْ or لَكِنْ are conjunctions. We can also call them coordinating, connecting devices or "couplers" (حَرْفُ عَطْفٍ).

According to the rules, the word after such devices (الْمَعْطُوف) takes the same case as the preceding word (الْمَعْطُوف عَلَيْهِ). Applied to our situation and example this means: the word after the conjunction (i.e., after *but*) – the الْمَعْطُوف – should get the same case marker as the predicate (خَبَرُ ما which is the الْمَعْطُوف عَلَيْهِ here).

However, this would produce a wrong meaning! If we did that, the negation would rule over this word too – which is not what we intended to express by *but*.

The الْمَعْطُوف after the predicate is جالِس. Before جالِس, there is a حَرْفُ عَطْفٍ. We can only kill the negation conveyed by ما if you do not use the accusative (مَنْصُوبٌ) case as well. If we use the same case marker, the meaning of the negation is extended to the word after *but* as well. The sentence would mean something different.

Karīm does not stand **nor** sit.	كَرِيمٌ لَيْسَ قائِمًا وَلا جالِسًا.

If we treat بَلْ or لَكِنْ as a conjunction (حَرْفُ عَطْفٍ), ما would have a second predicate – and the first and second predicate would be connected by an **opposing (adversative) particle** – like بَلْ or لَكِنْ.

If we run into such a situation, the second predicate must have the **nominative** case (مَرْفُوعٌ). For this reason, we need a different إِعْرابٌ and a trick to fix the construction. We have to assume a **deleted subject** (مُبْتَدَأٌ مَحْذُوفٌ) in order to convey the intended meaning.

Negation particle (حَرْفُ نَفْي ناسِخٌ) which overthrows some standard rules for cases. It does not have a position in إِعْرابٌ.	ما
مَرْفُوعٌ بِالضَّمّةِ الظّاهِرةِ). إِسْمُ ما in the nominative case	كَرِيمٌ

Predicate (خَبَرُ ما); accusative case (مَنْصُوبٌ بِالْفَتْحةِ الظّاهِرةِ).	قائِمًا
Conjunction (حَرْفُ عَطْفٍ). It does not have a place in إعْرابٌ.	بَلْ/لٰكِنْ
This is the critical point. This word is the <u>predicate in the nominal sentence</u> of a **deleted subject** (خَبَرٌ لِمُبْتَدَإٍ مَحْذُوفٍ), which in our example would be *he* (هُوَ). Now, since جالِسٌ is the **predicate** (خَبَرٌ) of a full, non-negated nominal sentence (*he is sitting*), it must be in the **nominative** case (مَرْفُوعٌ بِالضَّمّةِ الظّاهِرةِ).	جالِسٌ

274. Can you negate a nominal sentence with لا?

Yes, you can.

لا is a particle (حَرْفٌ) that negates a verb in the present tense and – in Modern Standard Arabic – also the future (سَ or سَوْفَ). In the old times, لا was also used to negate nominal sentences (جُمْلةٌ اسْمِيّةٌ) that don't have a verb. As always in such situations, we need to decide whether our device in question has the power to operate on words or remains neutrally. Regarding لا, it is usually seen as a "neutral" device: it conveys a negation, but leaves the sentence grammatically untouched. This was applied by the Banū Tamīm (لَهْجةُ بَنِي تَمِيمٍ).

There is another option. In the Arabic of the Hijāz (لَهْجةُ الْحِجازِيِّينَ), لا was applied in the way of لَيْسَ. Such لا is called لا الْحِجازِيّةُ. Generally, what we have said about ما to negate a nominal sentence in *question #272* is also true for لا. However, there are differences. Let's first look at an example when لا exercises its governing power:

A good deed is not lost.	لا خَيْرٌ ضائِعًا.

Negation particle (حَرْفُ نَفْي ناسِخٌ) which changes the usual case endings of the predicate; does not have a place in إعْرابٌ.	لا
This is the "subject" (اسْمُ لا) which therefore has to be in the nominative case (مَرْفُوعٌ بِالضَّمّةِ الظّاهِرةِ).	خَيْرٌ
Predicate (خَبَرُ لا); it has to be in the accusative case (مَنْصُوبٌ).	ضائِعًا

Now, what happens if we neglect its governing power?

A good deed is not lost.		لا خَيْرٌ ضائِعٌ.
Negation particle; its governing power is neglected (حَرْفُ نَفْي مُهْمَلٌ). It does not have a place in إعْرابٌ.		لا
This is the subject (مُبْتَدَأٌ) of the nominal sentence. That is why it has to be in the nominative case (مَرْفُوعٌ بِالضَّمَّةِ الظّاهِرةِ).		خيرٌ
Predicate (خَبَرٌ) of a standard nominal sentence which has to be in the nominative case as well (مَرْفُوعٌ بِالضَّمَّةِ الظّاهِرةِ).		ضائِعٌ

In which situations can لا do the job of لَيْسَ؟ **The following prerequisites must be met:**

- **Prerequisite I** (which is different to ما): Both – the اِسْمُ لا and its predicate (خَبَر لا) – must be **indefinite** (نَكِرةٌ).

If you try to use لا together with definite words, you would produce an incorrect Arabic sentence – even if only the "subject" (اِسْمُ لا) was definite (مَعْرِفةٌ) and the predicate indefinite. Exceptions to this rule are rare and only found in poetry.

- **Prerequisite II** (similar to ما): The **predicate** comes **after** the subject (اِسْمُ لا).

correct	A good deed is not lost.	لا ضائِعٌ خَيْرٌ.
The لا doesn't work like لَيْسَ and doesn't govern the خَبَرٌ in the accusative case. Therefore, we have the nominative case here (ضائِعٌ).		
incorrect	Note: such a sentence is not possible in Arabic.	لا ضائِعًا خَيْرٌ.

- **Prerequisite III** (similar to ما): The **predicate** is **not interlinked** with إلّا – otherwise, it would contradict the negation.

correct	Goodness (a good deed) is always fruitful.	لا خَيْرٌ إلّا مُثْمِرٌ.
incorrect	Such a sentence is not possible in Arabic.	لا خَيْرٌ إلّا مُثْمِرًا.

Let's analyze the above sentence:

Particle of negation (حَرْفُ نَفْي مُهْمَلٌ) conveying the meaning of a negation but not governing anything in the sentence. Therefore, it	لا

does not work like لَيْسَ; it does not have a position in إِعْرَابٌ.	
Subject (مُبْتَدَأٌ) of the nominal sentence; nominative (مَرْفُوعٌ).	خَيْرٌ
Predicate (خَبَرٌ) of the nominal sentence; nominative (مَرْفُوعٌ).	مُثْمِرٌ

- **Prerequisite IV** (similar to ما): A word governed by the predicate (مَعْمُولٌ) must **not be placed** <u>before</u> the "subject" (اِسْمُ لا). See #272.

correct	No believer is unjust to anyone.	لا مُؤْمِنٌ ظالِمًا أَحَدًا.
	أَحَدًا is the **direct object** (مَفْعُولٌ بِهِ) of ظالِمًا. The word ظالِمًا is the predicate of لا. Wait! There is no verb involved! Can the active participle ظالِمًا have a direct object? Yes. This is possible because the اِسْمُ الْفاعِلِ is doing the job of a verb – see *question #286*.	
incorrect	Such a sentence is impossible in Arabic.	لا أَحَدًا مُؤْمِنٌ ظالِمًا.

You are only allowed to move a prepositional or adverbial phrase (شِبْهُ الْجُمْلةِ) closer to the front. Such a phrase is an accessory; we assume that it stays connected with the predicate. Regarding the grammatical treatment, you have a choice:

1. You neglect (إِهْمالٌ) the governing power of the negation particle لا ➡ no grammatical implication.

2. You treat it as a negation particle with the governing power of لَيْسَ (إِعْمالٌ).

Zayd is not residing at your place.	لا عِنْدَكَ زَيْدٌ مُقيمًا.

Let's first check the second option which is more common: you treat لا as if it would do the job of لَيْسَ.

Negation particle (حَرْفُ نَفْيٍ ناسِخٌ) that operates on the predicate (and the subject). It does not have a place in إِعْرَابٌ.	لا
Adverb of place (ظَرْفُ مَكانٍ); therefore, it is found in the location of an accusative (مَنْصُوبٌ). The ك is a pronominal suffix (ضَميرٌ مُتَّصِلٌ) with an indeclinable, fixed shape and gets the "place value" of a genitive (في مَحَلِّ جَرٍّ) as it serves as the مُضافٌ إلَيْهِ, i.e., the second part of a إِضافةٌ. The entire adverbial phrase (شِبْهُ	عِنْدَكَ

(الْجُمْلَة) is linked to the predicate (خَبَرُ لا): the word مُقِيمًا.	
This is the "subject" (اِسْمُ لا) in the nominative case (مَرْفُوعٌ).	زَيْدٌ
Predicate (خَبَرُ لا) in the accusative case (مَنْصُوبٌ).	مُقِيمًا

Alternatively you can neglect the governing power (إِهْمالٌ) of لا:

Zayd is not residing at your place.	لا عِنْدَكَ زَيْدٌ مُقِيمٌ.
This is a **regular nominal sentence** (جُمْلَةٌ اِسْمِيّةٌ) with subject (مُبْتَدَأٌ) and predicate (خَبَرٌ) ➡ both take the nominative case.	

275. Can you negate a nominal sentence with إِنْ?

Yes, this is one of the very rare (and difficult) styles.

Such an application of إِنْ is only found in Classical Arabic – but not in Modern Standard Arabic. Nevertheless, you encounter it in old texts and in the Qur'an and should be able to decipher it.

The particle إِنْ may convey the meaning of a negation (in a nominal **or** verbal sentence). If it does, we call it إِنْ النّافِية. Such إِنْ is used in polished and sophisticated Arabic, in poems, and in the Qur'an.

He rules over nobody. *(a famous poetic verse)*		إِنْ هُوَ مُسْتَوْلِيًا عَلَى أَحَدٍ.
Sura 10:68	You have no authority to say this.	إِنْ عِنْدَكُم مِّن سُلْطَانٍ بِهذا.

An example of a verbal sentence: *I don't know.*	إِنْ أَدْرِي.

We will analyze the negation of the predicate (خَبَر) of a nominal sentence with إِنْ. We'll have to answer some questions: does the negation device إِنْ have a force similar to لَيْسَ? Does it induce case endings?

This was an issue between the grammarians of Basra (الْبَصْرِيُّونَ) and Kūfa (الْكُوفِيُّونَ). Most of the Basra experts, including al-Farrā' (الْفَرّاء), stated that إِنْ, when used as a negation device, is neutral and does not exercise any governing power (لا تَعْمَلُ شَيْئًا). The Kūfa grammarians, however, said the opposite: إِنْ has the grammatical force of لَيْسَ and does induce cases (تَعْمَلُ عَمَلَ لَيْسَ).

Some requirements must be met if we want إِنْ to work as a negation like لَيْسَ. They are all quite similar to ما and لا which we examined in depth in questions #272 and #274.

- **Prerequisite I.** The "subject" (اِسْمُ إِنْ) is <u>definite</u> (مَعْرِفةٌ) and the predicate (خَبَرُ إِنْ) is <u>indefinite</u> (نَكِرةٌ). Or both are <u>indefinite</u>.

The good deed is not lost.	إِنْ الْخَيْرُ ضائِعًا. = لَيْسَ الْخَيْرُ ضائِعًا.

The particle إِنْ is used as a negation particle (حَرْفُ نَفْي ناسِخٌ) that has governing power – which means that the predicate will be in the accusative case (مَنْصوبٌ). If you see the accusative case in a nominal sentence, is a sign to have a closer look at it. إِنْ, since it is a particle (حَرْفٌ), does not have a place in إِعْرابٌ.	إِنْ
"Subject" (اِسْمُ إِنْ) in the nominative case (مَرْفوعٌ), marked by the usual case marker.	الْخَيْرُ
Predicate of إِنْ (so-called خَبَرُ إِنْ), in the accusative case (مَنْصوبٌ) as clearly marked by the فَتْحة (nunation).	ضائِعًا

This construction also works if both – the "subject" (اِسْمُ إِنْ) and the predicate (خَبَرُ إِنْ) – are <u>indefinite</u>:

A good deed is not lost.	إِنْ خَيْرٌ ضائِعًا.

- **Prerequisite II.** The "subject" (اِسْمُ إِنْ) must be placed before the predicate – which is true for all negation devices. There is only one exception. You can put an adverbial or prepositional phrase (شِبْهُ الْجُمْلةِ) right after the negation particle and thus before the "subject" (اِسْمُ إِنْ). Why? Because we can assume that the شِبْهُ الْجُمْلةِ is still connected with the predicate.

- **Prerequisite III.** The predicate should **not** be used together with إِلّا. Otherwise, it does not convey the meaning of a negation.

Sentences with إِنْ and إِلّا are often misunderstood. They are also found in the Qur'an and often denote *only* or *except* - and **not** a negation.

Sura	It is God alone who will reward me (or:	إِنْ أَجْرِيَ إِلّا عَلَى اللهِ.

34:47	My payment is only from Allah).	
Judgment is for Allah alone. *(Sura 6:57, 12:40)*		إِنِ الْحُكْمُ إِلَّا لِلَّهِ.

Watch out! In elevated prose style as well as in poetry, the negative مَا is often prefixed to إِنْ. For example:

You have never seen (any) like them among men.	مَا إِنْ رَأَيْتَ لَهُمْ فِي النَّاسِ أَمْثَالًا.

Watch out! The particle إِنْ has various functions. Usually it introduces a conditional meaning. Let's see both, the conditional إِنْ and the negative إِنْ, in one sentence:

Sura 35:41	And [I swear that] **if** they did vanish, **no** one else could stop them.	وَلَئِن زَالَتَا إِنْ أَمْسَكَهُمَا مِنْ أَحَدٍ مِّن بَعْدِهِ.

276. Can you negate a nominal sentence with لَاتَ?

Yes, you can. لَاتَ *helps to express an exaggeration of the negation.*

لَاتَ is an old Semitic word that is also found in Aramaic conveying the same meaning. It can be rendered as *not the time* or *no longer; it is not; it was not; this was no...* لَاتَ negates a **nominal sentence** (جُمْلَةٌ اسْمِيَّةٌ). لَاتَ is a **forceful** and meaningful device if you want to lay emphasis on the negation (أَدَاةُ نَفْيٍ تُفِيدُ الْمُبَالَغَةَ فِي النَّفْيِ). لَاتَ was used in (pre-) Classical Arabic, but you also encounter it in the Qur'an and in poetry.

Sura 38:3	فَنَادَوا وَّلَاتَ حِينَ مَنَاصٍ. (= لَيْسَ الْحِينُ حِينَ مَنَاصٍ.)
• ...they [then] called out; but it was <u>not</u> a time for escape. *(Sahih Int.)*	
• ...they all cried out, once it was <u>too late</u>, for escape. *(Abdul Haleem)*	
• ...they cried out when there was <u>no longer</u> time for escape! *(Muhsin Khan)*	

The grammarians decoded the word as follows:

	Negation particle (حَرْفُ نَفْيٍ); we can call it لَا النَّافِيَةُ.	لا
a)	Particle to emphasize the negation (حَرْفٌ لِتَوْكِيدِ النَّفْيِ).	ت

or b)	A so-called *silent* ت (تاءُ التَّأْنِيثِ سَاكِنةٌ); it would result in لاتْ. Thus, it got a فَتْحةٌ on top of the ت; otherwise, there would be two سُكُونٌ in a row (إلْتِقاءُ السّاكِنَيْن). In the end, we get a تاءُ التَّأْنيثِ مَفْتُوحةٌ.

- Such a ت (تاءُ التَّأْنِيثِ مَفْتُوحةٌ) is occasionally added to particles. For this reason, some linguists also call it تاءُ الْحُرُوفِ.

not	لا	لاتَ
(so) many	رُبَّ	رُبَّتَ
perhaps	لَعَلَّ	لَعَلَّتَ
then	ثُمَّ	ثُمَّتَ

- Why do we use a ت and not a ة? A rule says that ة can only go along with nouns, but never with verbs or particles (لا تَكُونَ التَّاءُ الْمَرْبُوطةُ – هاءُ التَّأْنِيثِ – إلّا في الْأَسْماءِ). We have a particle.

- The ت here does not serve as a "subject" like in verbs. We don't speak of a تاءُ الفاعِلِ, also called تاءُ الضّمِيرِ, which is used in past tense verbs and always has a vowel on it (such a ت has a position in إعْرابٌ) In the conjugated verb form كَتَبْتُ, *I wrote*, the تُ serves as the subject ("I") – see *question #36*.

- To make it easier, لاتَ is usually treated as one entity: as a حَرْفٌ that conveys the meaning of a negation.

Depending on the other constituents, لاتَ may resemble لَيْسَ including its governing force – which is the view of the majority of the grammarians. So, you end up with a predicate (خَبَرُ لاتَ) in the accusative.

If لاتَ should work like لَيْسَ, two conditions need to be fulfilled:

- **Requirement I:** The "subject" (إسْمُ لاتَ) and the predicate (خَبَرُ لاتَ) do not appear in the same sentence. You **must** delete one of them – usually, you drop the "subject" (إسْمُ لاتَ).

- **Requirement II:** The government of لاتَ seems to be restricted to **nouns denoting time**. Therefore, لاتَ only works as a negation when it points to a <u>matter of time.</u> In many examples with with

لاتَ, you will find one of the following words. All of them are nouns (إِسْمٌ) and get inflected (case endings).

time, moment, when (this is the most common one)	حِينٌ
hour, time	ساعةٌ
time, moment	الْأَوْنُ

As for the required deletion, there are two general rules:

- If you delete the "subject" (إِسْمُ لاتَ), the above three words are in the مَنْصُوبٌ-case.

- If you delete the predicate (خَبَرُ لاتَ), the above words take the nominative case (مَرْفُوعٌ).

It is too late for repentance. (It expresses that regret is of no use anymore.) Notice the فَتْحَةٌ on ساعةَ.	لاتَ ساعةَ مَنْدَمٍ.
That's would be the meaning if we don't delete the "subject" (إِسْمُ لاتَ). Don't forget that لاتَ has the meaning of لَيْسَتْ.	لاتَ السَّاعَةُ ساعةَ مَنْدَمٍ.

Negation particle (حَرْفُ نَفْيٍ ناسِخٌ) that has the power to govern and induce case endings. It does not have a place in إِعْرابٌ.	لاتَ
Predicate of the negation particle (خَبَرُ لاتَ). So, it is in the accusative case (مَنْصُوبٌ). What about the "subject" (إِسْمُ لاتَ)? It was deleted (مَحْذُوفٌ)! First part of a إِضافةٌ-construction.	ساعةَ
This word takes the genitive case (مَجْرُورٌ), marked by the usual markers (كَسْرةٌ), because it serves as a مُضافٌ إِلَيْهِ, i.e., is the second part of a إِضافةٌ.	مَنْدَمٍ

How would the sentence look like if the predicate was deleted? The case markers would be different!

It is (or was) too late for repentance.	لاتَ ساعةُ مَنْدَمٍ.
This is the meaning of this sentence if we don't delete the predicate (خَبَرُ لاتَ): ➡	لاتَ ساعةُ مَنْدَمٍ مَوْجُودًا لَكَ.

Negation particle (حَرْفُ نَفْيٍ نَاسِخٌ) with governing power. It operates on the subject in the nominative case. No place in إِعْرَابٌ.	لَاتَ
"Subject" (اِسْمُ لَاتَ) in the nominative (مَرْفُوعٌ بِالضَّمَّةِ الظَّاهِرةِ). First part of the إِضافةٌ. In this example, the predicate was deleted.	سَاعَة
Noun in the genitive case (مَجْرُورٌ) as it serves as the مُضافٌ إِلَيْهِ.	مَنْدَمٍ

Excursus: Some grammarians, among them al-'Akhfash (الْأَخْفَش), treat لَاتَ as a neutral device without governing power (لا تَعْمَلُ شَيْئًا). So, how would al-'Akhfash possibly explain the accusative case in the verse of the Qur'an (Sura 38:3) which we showed above?

If there is a word in the accusative case like in the verse, he may say that it is governed by a tacit, implied verb (فِعْلٌ مُضْمَرٌ). We could assume, for example, that the meaning of the verb *I see* (أَرَى) is included:

لَاتَ أَرَى حِينَ مَنَاصٍ.

If someone used the nominative case instead, he may justify it as follows: the word in the nominative case is the subject (مُبْتَدَأٌ), and the predicate was deleted (الْخَبَرُ مَحْذُوفٌ). This is how the sentence would look like with the deleted predicate (notice the nominative case on the word حِينٌ as it is the subject!):

لَاتَ حِينُ مَنَاصٍ كَائِنٌ لَهُمْ.

THE ABSOLUTE NEGATION (THE CATEGORICAL DENIAL)

277. What is meant by *absolute negation*?

This type of لا (لا النَّافِيَةُ لِلْجِنْسِ) *denies the entire sort or category.*

The *Lā that denies absolutely* (لا النَّافِيَةُ لِلْجِنْسِ) is a special type of negation. We say that the "subject" (اِسْمُ لا النَّافِيَةِ لِلْجِنْسِ) of the negation **immerses** completely in the negation (اِسْتِغْراقٌ). Therefore, this type of لا is called *the categorical* or *absolute negation* (اِسْمُ لا النَّافِيةِ لِلْجِنْسِ). The word جِنْسٌ is an important term in this context. It means *kind, sort, variety* (but may also denote *sex* or *gender*).

In older books, you may encounter the term لا التَّبْرِئَةِ. The word تَبْرِئَةٌ

means *exemption, freeing; discharge.* Why was the لا called like that?
Because this لا exempts, acquits the subject from its predicate. This is
also the reason why the negation goes along with the subject (translation: *"No..."*) or even includes the denial which in English is usually expressed by: *"There is no..."*.

278. Why is the *absolute negation* grammatically interesting?

Because of the case endings.

The لا النّافِيةُ لِلْجِنْس is a device (حَرْف) that enters, encroaches on a
nominal sentence (جُمْلة اِسْمِيّة). Regarding the grammatical implications, this device works like the particle إنَّ. It is a حَرْفٌ ناسِخٌ. It abrogates rules.

The "subject" (اِسْمُ لا النّافِية لِلْجِنْس) gets the accusative case (نَصْبُ
الْمُبْتَدَإِ) – but only **one** vowel and not nunation – and the predicate (خَبَرُ
لا) takes the nominative case (رَفْعُ الْخَبَرِ). Some examples:

There is no man standing.	لا رَجُلَ قائِمٌ.
No striving man is deprived/needy.	لا مُجْتَهِدَ مَحْرُومٌ.
Don't mention it (There is no thanking for a duty).	لا شُكْرَ عَلَى واجِبٍ.
must (lit.: there is no avoiding of ...)	لا بُدَّ مِن...

Three conditions (شُرُوط) have to be fulfilled to make لا functioning as
a حَرْفٌ ناسِخٌ similar to إنَّ.

1. "Subject" (اِسْمُ لا) and predicate (خَبَرُ لا) must be **indefinite** (نَكِرة).

This is quite logical. If the اِسْمُ was definite (مَعْرِفةٌ), it could not be understood as being included in the category; it would leave its state to
deny the category and would become the negation of just **one** (نَفْيُ
الْواحِدِ); so, it would only refer to one specific thing.

If we have a definite word, how could we solve this?

- Regarding the grammar: In such a situation, the لا loses (إهْمالٌ) its
  force of a ناسِخٌ. We will end up with a regular, negated nominal

sentence (جُمْلةٌ اِسْميّةٌ).

- Regarding the meaning: If we want to express that the thing being denied is not the only thing/person that is denied, we need to reiterate similar words (تَكْرارٌ). For example:

Neither Zayd nor ʿAlī is standing.	لا زَيْدٌ قائِمٌ وَلا عَليٌّ.

"Neutral" negation particle that does not induce further grammatical implications (حَرْفُ نَفْي مُهْمَلٌ). It is the opposite to a حَرْفُ نَفْي ناسِخٌ. It does not have a position in إعْرابٌ.	لا
Subject (مُبْتَدَأٌ) of the nominal sentence (جُمْلةٌ اِسْميّةٌ), in the nominative case (مَرْفُوعٌ).	زَيْدٌ
Predicate (خَبَرٌ) of the nominal sentence in the nominative case.	قائِمٌ

2. There is **no word or letter between** لا **and the subject (**اِسْمُ لا**).**

Incorrect because you are not allowed to put stuff between لا and the "subject" (اِسْمُ لا).	لا في الْبَيْتِ رَجُلَ.

3. **Regular word order:** The predicate (خَبَرُ لا) comes <u>after</u> the اِسْمُ لا.

Incorrect because you can't place the predicate before the subject (اِسْمُ لا).	عِنْدَنا لا رَجُلَ مُقيمٌ.

Let's examine another example.

There is neither a man nor a woman in the house.	لا في الْبَيْتِ رَجُلٌ وَلا امْرَأةٌ.

The predicate is placed **before** the subject. This means that لا loses all its implications (إهْمالٌ) of a ناسِخٌ and just leaves us with a regular nominal sentence (جُمْلةٌ اِسْميّةٌ). We have regular case endings.

Negation particle (حَرْفُ نَفْي مُهْمَلٌ) that can't exercise its governing power. It does not induce any grammatical implication.	لا
Prepositional phrase (الْجارُّ وَالْمَجْرُورُ), supplying the position of a fronted predicate (خَبَرٌ مُقَدَّمٌ) in the nominative case.	في الْبَيْتِ

| Delayed subject (مُبْتَدَأٌ مُؤَخَّرٌ) of the nominal sentence; in the nominative case (مَرْفُوعٌ بِالضَّمّةِ الظّاهِرةِ). | رَجُلٌ |

How can we understand the اِسْمُ لا النّافِيةِ لِلْجِنْسِ (= the "subject")? There are two situations we need to look at.

Situation 1: The "subject" (اِسْمُ لا) is a **single** word (مُفْرَدٌ).

You consider the vowel on the last letter of the اِسْمُ لا as <u>fixed and unchangeable</u> (مَبْنِيٌّ عَلَى الْفَتْحِ). ➡ Although the word is **in**definite, there is only **one** فَتْحةٌ at the end. We say that we firm up the word (the "subject") in the location of an accusative case (الْبِناءُ فِي مَحَلِّ نَصْبٍ).

Words in such a position are treated as **indeclinable**. When we cement their shape, we use the role model of the accusative (يُبْنَى عَلَى مَا يُنْصَبُ بِهِ), i.e., the marker that it would get in such a position.

If you have, for example, a sound masculine plural or a dual, you use the ي to build the fixed ending (مَبْنِيٌّ عَلَى الْياءِ فِي مَحَلِّ نَصْبٍ), resulting in يْنَ or يْنِ. Simply, because the case marker for the accusative of such forms is the ي. However, this ending is not the case marker!

➤ To mark the case, we have to **assign a "place value"** because we treat the word as fixed/**indeclinable** (مَبْنِيٌّ). Note: For a sound feminine plural, you use the ending اتٍ.

| There is no man at home. | لا رَجُلَ فِي الْبَيْتِ. |
| There are no (two) men in the house. | لا رَجُلَيْنِ فِي الْبَيْتِ. |

Particle of absolute denial (نافِيةٌ لِلْجِنْسِ).	لا
This is the "subject", the اِسْمُ لا النّافِيةِ لِلْجِنْسِ; it is fixed on the last letter (مَبْنِيٌّ عَلَى الْفَتْحِ). Although we cannot put case markers, the word appears in the place of an accusative case (فِي مَحَلِّ نَصْبٍ).	رَجُلَ
Same as above – with a difference! The word's shape is not fixed by a vowel – but by the ي before the last letter. This ي, although it appears like that, does not mark the case, it is just there for the building of the word (مَبْنِيٌّ عَلَى الْياءِ). Talking about cases, we can only say that رَجُلَيْنِ occupies the location of an accusative case (فِي مَحَلِّ نَصْبٍ). The word can't visi-	رَجُلَيْنِ

bly take cases because we treat it as having a fixed shape.	
Prepositional phrase (الْجارُّ وَالْمَجْرُورُ) which is connected with an omitted word – the predicate (خَبَرُ لا) – which is implicitly understood (مُتَعَلِّقٌ بِمَحْذُوفٍ), i.e., the Arabic verb *to be, to be found*.	فِي الْبَيْتِ

Situation 2: The إِسْمُ لا is not just a single word. Then you treat the إِسْمُ لا as the first part of a إِضافةٌ-construction (مُضافٌ) or as something that resembles a إِضافةٌ (شَبِيهٌ بِالْمُضافِ).

If we follow this approach, the إِسْمُ لا النّافِيةِ لِلْجِنْسِ takes a <u>regular case ending</u> – which is the accusative case (مَنْصُوبٌ).

There is no newspaper seller around.	لا بائِعَ صُحُفٍ مَوْجُودٌ.

Let's summarize what we have analyzed so far:

- Situation 1: Usually the "subject" (إِسْمُ لا النّافِيةِ لِلْجِنْسِ) is a single word (مُفْرَدٌ), indefinite (نَكِرَةٌ), and **indeclinable** (مَبْنِيٌّ عَلَى الْفَتْحِ).
- Situation 2: The "subject" (إِسْمُ لا النّافِيةِ لِلْجِنْسِ) may be **declinable** and gets the مَنْصُوبٌ-case if the "subject" serves as the مُضافٌ.

Let's return to situation 2 and analyze an expression that resembles a شَبِيهٌ بِالْمُضافِ, so-called الشَّبِيهُ بِالْمُضافِ or إِضافةٌ. This means that we have a noun (إِسْمٌ) which is followed by another noun to complete its meaning. Therefore, the construction resembles a إِضافةٌ-construction. Note: What we are going to say works also for the *invocation* (النِّداءُ).

There is no generous man whose nature is disliked.	لا كَرِيمًا خُلُقُهُ مَكْرُوهٌ.
This would be the meaning of the sentence expressed by a regular إِضافةٌ:	لا كَرِيمَ الْخُلْقِ مَكْرُوهٌ.

Particle of absolute denial (نافِيةٌ لِلْجِنْسِ).	لا
"Subject" (إِسْمُ لا), in the accusative (مَنْصُوبٌ بِالْفَتْحِةِ الظّاهِرةِ).	كَرِيمًا
Subject (فاعِلٌ); therefore, it is in the nominative case (مَرْفُوعٌ).	خُلُقُهُ

Wait! We don't have a verb in this sentence – how can it be the فاعِلٌ (subject)? It is the subject of the صِفَةٌ مُشَبَّهَةٌ which means *similar quality*; to be more precise: *adjectives which are made like* or *assimilated to participles* (صِفةٌ مُشَبَّهَةٌ بِاسْمِ الْفاعِلِ or بِاسْــمِ الْمَفْعُولِ). It is a noun that indicates a meaning of firmness. We could say that كَرِيم does the job of an active participle (تَعْمَلُ عَمَلَ اسْمَ الْفاعِلِ), and the active participle can do the job of a verb – see *question #286*. What about the هُ? It is a pronominal suffix (ضَمِيرٌ مُتَّصِلٌ) serving as the second part of the إِضافة; thus, it is located in the position of a genitive case (فِي مَحَلِّ جَرٍّ مُضافٌ إِلَيْهِ).	
Predicate (خَبَرُ لا) in the nominative case (مَرْفُوعٌ).	مَكْرُوهٌ

That's not the only way to treat such sentences.

You could also use the accusative case (مَنْصُوبٌ) for both words after the الشَّبِيهِ بِالْمُضافِ because the second word doesn't serve as the subject – but as the **direct object!** This is usually the situation if the second noun doesn't have a pronoun attached to it.

There is no newspaper seller around.	لا بائِعًا صُحُفًا مَوْجُودٌ.

The اِسْمُ لا النّافِيةِ لِلْجِنْسِ; therefore, in the accusative (مَنْصُوبٌ).	بائِعًا
Direct object (مَفْعُولٌ بِهِ) in the accusative case (مَنْصُوبٌ بِالْفَتْحةِ الظّاهِرةِ). This direct object is the governed part (i.e., the *patient*; مَعْمُولٌ) of the active participle (اسْمُ الْفاعِلِ) which is in the position of the لا اسْمُ – but also does the job of a verb here.	صُحُفًا

Yet, there is even **another option** – but it is only possible if there is a prepositional phrase (الْجارُّ وَالْمَجْرُورُ) after the الشَّبِيهِ بِالْمُضافِ. Furthermore, both parts must be interlinked, for example, by a pronoun.

No hard-worker in his job fails.	لا مُجِدًّا فِي عَمَلِهِ فاشِلٌ.

The اِسْمُ لا النّافِيةِ لِلْجِنْسِ; in the accusative case (مَنْصُوبٌ).	مُجِدًّا
Prepositional phrase that is linked to مُجِدًّا and completes the meaning. Notice the pronoun ه which refers back to the "sub-	فِي عَمَلِهِ

ject": in the example, to the word مُجِدًّا.	
Predicate (خَبَرُ لا); nominative case (مَرْفُوعٌ).	فاشِلٌ

279. Can you use the absolute negation with the dual or plural?

Yes, this is possible and acceptable – although not really logical.

In contemporary Arabic, you see the absolute negation (لا النّافِيةُ
لِلْجِنْسِ) applied to singular (مُفْرَدٌ), dual (مُثَنّى), or plural (جَمْعٌ) nouns.

1	single word or broken plural	You get a fixed shape built on a vowel: one "a", i.e., ـَ .	مَبْنِيٌّ عَلَى الْفَتْحِ
2	dual or sound masculine plural	You get a fixed shape by using the letter ي to fix the construction.	مَبْنِيٌّ عَلَى الْياءِ
3	sound feminine plural	You get a fixed shape built on a vowel: one "i", i.e., ـِ .	مَبْنِيٌّ عَلَى الْكَسْرِ

1	There is no man...	masculine singular	لا رَجُلَ...
2	There are no two men...	masculine dual	لا رَجُلَيْنِ...
2	There are no painstaking men...	masculine plural	لا مُجِدّينَ...
1	There are no men...	masc. broken plural	لا رِجالَ...
3	There are no painstaking women...	feminine plural	لا مُجِدّاتٍ...

1	There is no newspaper vendor...	masc. sing.	لا بائِعَ صُحُفٍ...
2	There are no two newsp. vendors...	masc. dual	لا بائِعَيْ صُحُفٍ...
2	There are no male newsp. vendors...	masc. pl.	لا بائِعِي صُحُفٍ...
3	There are no female newsp. vendors...	fem. pl.	لا بائِعاتِ صُحُفٍ...

But is this logical? Not really.

The idea of the absolute negation clashes with the dual or plural. When the dual is used, it would limit the conveyed meaning only to things in pairs. But the absolute negation includes all members and de-

nies the whole genus! For this reason, the application of the لا النّافِيةُ
لِلْجِنْس should be limited to the **singular indefinite** (مُفْرَدٌ نَكِرَةٌ).

In poetry, the dual and plural may be used in the idea of *category*. A
good example is a sentence of *Sharh Shudhūr al-Dhahab* (شُذُور الذَّهَب)
which could be translated as *Nuggets of Gold/Particles of Gold*. It is a
book on Classical Arabic by the famous grammarian 'Abd Allāh ibn
Yūsuf Ibn Hishām (عَبْد الله بن يُوسُف ابن هِشام; died 1360/761 AH).

Be patient, no (two) people live together for-ever... Death comes (to them) one after another.	تَعَزَّ فَلا إِلْفَيْنِ بِالعَيشِ مُتِّعَا... وَلٰكِنْ لَوُرَّادِ الْمَنُونِ تَتَابُعُ.

إِلْفَيْنِ means *two companions* (صاحِبَيْنِ). Although it is in the dual, it doesn't
convey the meaning of the dual! Instead, as a matter of fact, it conveys the
meaning of the full category (الْجِنْسُ مِن الْبَشرِ). Why?

You can't imagine a *companion* (إِلْفٌ) alone. He needs another person (إِلْفُهُ)
as otherwise, the word wouldn't make sense. Therefore, the dual is used although it points to *one* or *unity* (الْواحِدُ).

280. What happens if you repeat the لا of the absolute negation?

You will get three options for the case markers.

Let's start with an example: *There is no man and no women present.*

option 1	one فَتْحةٌ: "*a*"	لا رَجُلَ مَوْجُودٌ وَلا امْرَأَةَ.
option 2	nunation; فَتْحةٌ: "*-an*"	لا رَجُلَ مَوْجُودٌ وَلا امْرَأَةً.
option 3	nunation; ضَمّةٌ: "*-un*"	لا رَجُلَ مَوْجُودٌ وَلا امْرَأَةٌ.

The first part is business as usual. We are only interested in the second
part. All three options have one thing in common:

This is a **conjunction** (حَرْفُ عَطْفٍ). But what do we connect and har-monize? A word? A sentence? This وَ is the crucial part in the con-struction and decides the case. It is the reason for the three options.	وَ

Let's focus on the **last word** and check the three options.

Option 1: The standard situation. The **second** لا is like the first لا: a
particle of **absolute denial** (لا النّافِيةُ لِلْجِنْس).

Particle of absolute denial (لا النّافِيةُ لِلْجِنْسِ).	لا
"Subject" (اِسمُ لا النّافِيةِ لِلْجِنْسِ); it has an indeclinable, fixed shape (مَبْنِيٌّ عَلَى الْفَتْحِ). We can only assign the "place value" of an accusative case (فِي مَحَلِّ نَصْبٍ). The predicate (خَبَرُ لا) of the **second** "subject" (اِسمُ لا) is **deleted** (مَحْذُوفٌ) and has the underlying meaning of مَوْجُودةٌ.	امْرَأَة

What is the job of the و? The term *coupling* (عَطْفٌ) in option 1 means that we connect and harmonize **both sentences** (عَطْفُ جُمْلةٍ عَلَى جُمْلةٍ). The **second sentence** with the repeated لا is a grammatical blueprint of the **first sentence** consisting of "subject" (اِسمُ لا) and predicate (خَبَرُ لا).

Option 2: The **second** لا doesn't have grammatical power (عاطِلةٌ) and is "neutral". We need to coordinate and couple it with و (الْعَطْفُ بِالْواو).

This is treated as a **redundant**, extra لا (so-called لا زائِدةٌ) to emphasize the negation (حَرْفٌ زائِدٌ لِتَّوْكيدِ النَّفْي). It does not have any grammatical impact.	لا
This is the coupled word for رَجُلَ. How do we harmonize the two words regarding the agreement? Since the second لا doesn't have any grammatical force, it leaves the word after it (امْرَأَة) untouched. This means that امْرَأَة is declinable and doesn't have a fixed shape.	امْرَأَة
What do we make of this? We need to check the place value of the first subject and copy that to the second "subject": accusative ▷ accusative. The **first** word (indeclinable; رَجُلَ) is in the **place** of an accusative but cannot be marked as such. The **second** word (declinable; امْرَأَةً) takes the **regular markers** of the accusative. In Arabic: الْمَعْطُوفُ عَلَى الْمَنْصُوبِ مَنْصُوبٌ.	

What does عَطْفٌ in option 2 mean? It implies that **a single word is coupled with a single word** (عَطْفُ مُفْرَدٍ عَلَى مُفْرَدٍ).

Option 3: The second لا resembles لَيْسَ (مُشَبَّهةٌ بِلَيْسَ).

This لا is treated as a **redundant/extra** لا in order to emphasize the negation (حَرْفٌ زائِدٌ لِتَّوْكيدِ النَّفْي).	لا
Subject (مُبْتَدَأٌ) of the nominal sentence (جُمْلةٌ اِسمِيّةٌ); in the nominative case because it initiates a new sentence (مَرْفُوعٌ عَلَى الْاِبْتِداءِ).	امْرَأَة

> Why can we do that? If we forget about the case endings for a moment and look at the **abstract position** of the word after لا, we can say that it is the subject – and the subject is entitled to receive the nominative case (مَرْفُوعٌ).

> So… what we do here is, in fact, the coupling of two sentences (عَطْفُ جُمْلةٍ عَلَى جُمْلةٍ). What about the predicate (خَبَرُ الْمُبْتَدَإِ) of the second sentence? It was deleted! Underlying, virtual meaning: مَوْجُودةٌ.

281. Which case marker does an adjective get after the لا of denial?

You have two options: put one فَتْحةٌ or treat it according to its position.

It happens quite often that the "subject" (اِسْمُ لا النّافِيةِ لِلْجِنْسِ) is described by an attribute (adjective). In such a situation, the لا اِسْمُ is the مَنْعُوتٌ and the adjective the نَعْتٌ. Now comes the interesting question: Which case marker should we use for the نَعْتٌ؟

Let's start our discussion with the standard form of a لا اِسْمُ: a single, indefinite noun (اِسْمٌ مُفْرَدٌ). In this construction, the لا اِسْمُ is an indeclinable word and has a fixed shape (مَبْنِيٌّ عَلَى الْفَتْحِ). ➡ The word always shows one فَتْحةٌ. Does that mean that the adjective also gets that ending? No, it doesn't. You have three options. Let's check an example:

There is no hard-working student that fails. (No diligent student fails.)

Opt. 1	One فَتْحةٌ – fixed on the last letter (الْبِناءُ عَلَى الْفَتْحِ)	فاشِلٌ.	مُجِدّ	لا طالِبَ
Opt. 2	nunation; فَتْحةٌ – accusative case (النَّصْبُ)		مُجِدّا	
Opt. 3	nunation; ضَمّةٌ – nominative case (الرَّفْعُ)		مُجِدّ	

Option 1: Just **mirror** what you see (i.e., the ending of the لا اِسْمُ).

Grammarians say that the adjective (نَعْتٌ) has to ride with the word it describes (مَنْعُوتٌ) with all implications. Note that this is grammatically <u>not</u> the same as putting a word into the accusative case (option 2). What we do: We fix the نَعْتٌ on the "*a*"-ending (فَتْحٌ) as well. By doing so, the adjective becomes indeclinable (مَبْنِيٌّ عَلَى الْفَتْحِ) and only receives the virtual "place value" of an accusative (فِي مَحَلِّ نَصْبٍ). If we didn't do that, the adjective would be declinable and would get the "-an"-ending (= option 2). This is a minor, but fine difference.

The نَعْت has a fixed, indeclinable shape (مَبْنِيٌّ عَلَى الْفَتْحِ); it mirrors all grammatical attributes of the thing it describes (مَنْعُوتٌ).	مُجِدّ
This is the predicate (خَبَرُ لا) in the nominative case (مَرْفُوعٌ).	فاشِلٌ

This approach is similar to what happens with numbers from 13 to 19. They are also fixed on the last letter (مَبْنِيٌّ عَلَى الْفَتْحِ), end in the vowel "a" (َ) and keep that shape in any case and position.

15	masculine	خَمْسةَ عَشَرَ
	feminine	خَمْسَ عَشْرَةَ

Remark: If the "subject" (اسْمُ لا) or the adjective (نَعْت) consists of more than one word (i.e., it is not مُفْرَدٌ), then it is not correct to arrange them like the numbers from 13 to 19. In other words, you can't cement them on the vowel "a" (مَبْنِيٌّ عَلَى الْفَتْحِ).

Option 2: The adjective (نَعْت) takes the regular مَنْصُوبٌ-case.

The adjective (نَعْت) follows the word it describes (مَنْعُوتٌ) regarding its **position** (عَلَى الْمَحَلِّ...) – and the position of the مَنْعُوت is the accusative case (نَصْبٌ). This is the **original way** of solving our problem.

Option 3: We check the actual **position** of the اسْمُ لا in the sentence.

If we only look at the word after the لا from a neutral perspective, we can say that it is the subject, and without the لا, it would the مُبْتَدَأ of a nominal sentence (جُمْلةٌ اسْمِيّةٌ) which takes the nominative case. If we apply this logic, the adjective (نَعْت) must be in the nominative (مَرْفُوعٌ).

➤ Let's see what will change if the اسْمُ لا doesn't have a fixed shape.

This means that the "subject" (اسْمُ لا; the word that is described; مَنْعُوتٌ) is **declinable** (مُعْرَبٌ) and gets case inflections. We get this situation if the اسْمُ لا serves as the مُضافٌ, i.e., the first part of a إضافةٌ.

Another option is a quasi-إِضافةٌ, a construction in which the اِسْمُ لا resembles a مُضافٌ, in Arabic called شَبِيهٌ بِالْمُضافِ.

Most importantly, you must refrain from fixing the adjective/attribute (نَعْتٌ) on the ending because this is only possible for a single word (مُفْرَدٌ). That leaves us with only two options:

A) We copy the visual ending and grammatical position of the "subject": the accusative (النَّصْبُ).

B) We look at it from a logical perspective and treat the اِسْمُ لا according to its actual function (i.e., the subject): the nominative case (الرَّفْعُ).

A) Let's start with the <u>accusative</u> (النَّصْبُ).

No rich employer is nice.	لا صاحِبَ عَمَلٍ غَنِيًّا لَطِيفٌ.
No student, who has exerted efforts to obtain knowledge, ended up with failure.	لا طالِبَ عِلْمٍ مُجِدًّا فاشِلٌ.

طالِبَ is the اِسْمُ لا and serves as the مُضافٌ. This has the effect that it gets the regular case ending of a اِسْمُ لا: so, it is in the accusative (مَنْصُوبٌ).

What about the adjective (نَعْتٌ), i.e., مُجِدًّا? Since a نَعْتٌ has to agree with the word it describes (مَنْعُوتٌ), it also has to be مَنْصُوبٌ.

B) The <u>nominative</u> case (الرَّفْعُ). We treat the adjective according to the position of the word which it describes, i.e., the subject. This is grammatically fine, but it may be confusing for the reader.

No student, who exerts efforts to obtain knowledge, ends up with failure.	لا طالِبَ عِلْمٍ مُجِدٌّ فاشِلٌ.

Watch out: The actual grammatical position of the اِسْمُ لا is that of the subject (مُبْتَدَأ) of a nominal sentence. This means that it takes the nominative case. Thus, also the adjective is in the nominative case.

Remark: It is also possible that مُجِدٌّ here is treated as the predicate of لا, and فاشِلٌ as an apposition of that predicate, thus resulting in the following inconceivable translation: *No student is diligent, unsuccessful.*

➞ What happens if an entire إِضَافَةٌ serves as an adjective (نَعْتٌ) and not just a single word (مُفْرَدٌ)? Nothing special. You can choose: accusative case (النَّصْبُ) or nominative case (الرَّفْعُ).

Let's have a look at an example: *No student of generous nature fails.*

accusative (النَّصْبُ) – فَتْحةٌ	لا طالبَ كَرِيمَ الْخُلْقِ فاشِلٌ.
nominative (الرَّفْعُ) – ضَمّةٌ	لا طالِبَ كَرِيمُ الْخُلْقِ فاشِلٌ.

282. *There is no God but Allah.* What got lost in the Arabic sentence?

In the sentence لا إِلَهَ إِلّا اللهُ the predicate (خَبَرُ لا) was deleted.

How is that possible? Well, the predicate may be omitted when it has already been sufficiently indicated (مَعْلُومٌ). The example we are going to analyze is one of the most famous sentences in Islam.

There is no God but Allah.	لا إِلَهَ إِلّا اللهُ.

Particle of absolute denial (نافِيَةٌ لِلْجِنْسِ); no place in إِعْرابٌ.	لا
"Subject" (اِسْمُ لا) which has a fixed shape, i.e., the last letter is cemented on the vowel "*a*" (مَبْنِيٌّ عَلَى الْفَتْحِ). So, we can only say that it is placed in the position of an accusative case (فِي مَحَلِّ نَصْبٍ).	إِلَهَ

Now, where is the **predicate** (خَبَرُ لا)? ➤ It was deleted (مَحْذُوفٌ)! The predicate is implicitly understood. The deleted word could have been, for example, *is found, existing* (مَوْجُودٌ).

There is no God existing but Allah.	لا إِلَهَ مَوْجُودٌ إِلّا اللهُ.

It is actually pretty common that the predicate is deleted in such constructions because it points to a general state (*is found; to be*). Here are some common expressions that use the absolute negation:

definitely; certainly; by all means; there is no way out...	لا بُدَّ...
No wonder...	لا عَجَبَ...
No good...	لا خَيْرَ...

The deletion of the predicate of an absolute negation (لا النّافِيةُ لِلْجِنْسِ) occurs occasionally in spoken Arabic. For example:

He will definitely (undoubtedly) succeed.	هُوَ ناجِحٌ لا شَكَّ.

Particle (حَرْفٌ) of absolute denial (لا النّافِيةُ لِلْجِنْسِ).	لا
"Subject" (اِسْمُ لا), it has a fixed shape (مَبْنِيٌّ عَلَى الْفَتْحِ). The word occupies the position of an accusative case (فِي مَحَلِّ نَصْبٍ).	شَكَّ

Also here, the predicate is omitted (مَحْذُوفٌ) but implicitly understood. Here is an example of a possible predicate (marked in gray):

… there is no doubt in that.	لا شكَّ مَوْجُودٌ فِي ذلكَ...
Note: I have inserted the word مَوْجُودٌ (the "real" predicate) because it is structurally needed so that the prepositional phrase (شِبْهُ الْجُمْلةِ) fits in.	

Another example:

Never mind! It doesn't matter. This is also said to a sick person. Note: Here, عَلَيْكَ is omitted and would appear in the place of the predicate (Lit.: It won't do you any harm).	لا بَأْسَ!

Let's return to the sentence لا إلَهَ إلّا اللهُ. Which case does the word after إلّا (= Allah) take? Well, constructions with إلّا are complex. Let's see.

1	This is an **apposition** for a **place** inside the sentence: the location of the لا plus the "subject" (اِسْمُ لا), in Arabic: بَدَلٌ مِن مَحَلِّ لا مَع اِسْمِها. Some grammarians even refer to the position before the device لا came into the sentence. Following that approach, the first word was *a God* which would have been the subject (مُبْتَدَأٌ). Since *Allah* is an apposition, *Allah* is in the nominative case as well (مَرْفُوعٌ بِالضَّمّةِ الظّاهِرةِ). Religious people reject this approach and say that the negation here means that you negate and deny *"false gods"* (الآلِهةُ الْباطِلةُ) – and Allah should not be connected with them. However, grammatically speaking, the analysis is sound.	اللهُ
2	Here, the word is an **apposition** for the **implied pronoun** which is found in the **deleted predicate** (بَدَلٌ مِن الضَّمِيرِ الْمُسْتَتِرِ فِي	اللهُ

الْخَبَر الْمَحْذُوفِ). Since the implied pronoun refers to the خَبَّر, it takes the nominative case (مَرْفُوعٌ بِالضَّمَّةِ الظَّاهِرةِ). This is the interpretation religious people prefer because the apposition refers to the deleted predicate.	
The underlying meaning could be: →	لا إِلَهَ مَوْجُودٌ "هُوَ" إلّا اللّٰهُ.

| 3 | The word *Allah* is *the excluded* or *excepted thing* (مُسْتَثْنَى), so it has to be in the accusative case (مَنْصُوبٌ بِالْفَتْحةِ الظَّاهِرةِ). | اللّٰه |

Excursus: The Arabic translation of *no one*.

In Classical Arabic, the direct negation of a verb was the norm. So, we would get: لا يَعْرِفُ أَحَدٌ (lit.: *not knows someone = no one knows...*). In Modern Standard Arabic, the absolute negation is used instead to express *no one*: لا أَحَدَ. E.g.: لا أَحَدَ يَدْرِي (*no one knows*). If we include the deleted predicate (e.g., مَوْجُودٌ), we'd get: *there is no one in existence who knows*. It's a matter of taste whether you use the Classical or Modern Arabic approach.

283. What does لا سِيَّما mean?

It means: above all, specially, in particular, mainly.

لا سِيَّما is a common expression in Modern Standard Arabic. You might also encounter the extended version لا سِيَّما وَأَنَّ which means *especially for the reason that..., particularly because...*

The expression is used when you mention two related things in a sentence and prefer the latter. What comes last in the sentence has more power (قُدْرةٌ) than the things mentioned earlier.

I love books, especially literature books.	أُحِبُّ الْكُتُبَ وَلا سِيَّما كُتُب الْأَدَبِ.
This sentence expresses that you love books in general, but that you love books of literature in particular. The word سِيَّ has the meaning of مِثْلَ.	

لا سِيَّما consists of three words and means (literally): *there is not the equal or like of.*

ما		سِيّ	لا
This is a مَا الْمُتَّصِلة.	**+**	This is the اِسْمُ لا.	**+** absolute negation النَّافِيةُ (لِلْجِنْس)
This ما can be • redundant/extra with no separate meaning (زائِدةٌ); • a relative pronoun (اِسْمٌ مَوْصُولٌ) expressing الَّذِي; • an indefinite, vague word (نَكِرةٌ مُبْهَمةٌ).		It expresses *equal, similar, alike* (for masculine & feminine). Synonyms are: هُوَ or هُوَ سِيُّكَ or مِثْلُكَ نَظِيرُكَ.	

- Watch out: It is quite common to use the word سِيّ in the dual form: سِيّ + سِيّ = سِيّانِ.

- The **predicate** (خَبَرُ لا) is <u>always deleted</u> (مَحْذُوفٌ دائِمًا) in such constructions. Its assumed, underlying meaning is مَوْجُودٌ.

Now comes the exciting part. What's the grammatical function and position of the noun (اِسْمٌ) after لا سِيَّمَا? There are three approaches.

option 1	nominative case (الرَّفْعُ)	...وَلا سِيَّما كُتُبُ الأَدَبِ.
option 2	accusative case (النَّصْبُ)	...وَلا سِيَّما كُتُبَ الأَدَبِ.
option 3	genitive case (الْجَرُّ)	...وَلا سِيَّما كُتُبِ الأَدَبِ.

First let's see what all three have in common:

Particle of resumption (لِلْإِسْتِئْنافِ); doesn't have a place in إِعْرابٌ.	و
Particle of the absolute negation (النَّافِيةُ لِلْجِنْسِ).	لا
This is the second (or even third) part of the إِضافةٌ (مُضافٌ إِلَيْهِ) and therefore takes the genitive case (مَجْرُورٌ بِالكَسْرةِ الظّاهِرةِ).	الأَدَبِ

Let's analyze the three options in depths.

Option 1: the nominative case (الرَّفْعُ)

This is the subject (اِسْمُ لا); it gets the accusative case (مَنْصُوبٌ). It also serves as the first part of a إِضافةٌ. The predicate is deleted; see above.	سِيّ

Regarding **ما**, there are two views:	**ما**
I	**Relative pronoun** (اِسْمٌ مَوْصُولٌ) that serves as the second part of the إِضافةٌ; thus, it is in the position of a genitive (فِي مَحَلِّ جَرٍّ مُضافٌ إِلَيْهِ).
II	It is treated as an **indefinite word** with the meaning of: *thing* (شَيْءٌ). The nominal sentence (جُمْلَةٌ اِسْمِيَّةٌ) after it serves as an adjective for **ما** and is placed in the position of a genitive case (فِي مَحَلِّ جَرٍّ صِفَةٌ لِما). The noun (اِسْمٌ) after **ما** takes the nominative case (مَرْفُوعٌ). This is because the relative pronoun **ما** needs a relative clause which is the nominal **sentence** (جُمْلَةٌ اِسْمِيَّةٌ) here. You could say that **ما** is indefinite (نَكِرَةٌ) and that the sentence that follows is the adjective (صِفَةٌ).

كُتُب is the **predicate** of the subject that had to be deleted (خَبَرٌ لِمُبْتَدَإٍ مَحْذُوفٍ وُجُوبًا). The deleted subject has the virtual meaning (تَقْدِيرٌ) of **هُوَ**. The nominal sentence (جُمْلَةٌ اِسْمِيَّةٌ) consisting of subject and predicate (الْجُمْلَةُ مِنَ الْمُبْتَدَإِ وَخَبَرِهِ) has no position in إِعْرابٌ as it is the relative clause (صِلةُ الْمَوْصُولِ).	**كُتُب**
Meaning: *I love books but not as much as those which are literature books.*	أُحِبُّ الْكُتُبَ لا مِثْلَ الَّذِي هُوَ كُتُبُ الْأَدَبِ.

Option 2: the accusative case (النَّصْبُ)

"Subject" (اِسْمُ لا) in the accusative case (مَنْصُوبٌ). Here, سِيَّ is **not** the first part of a إِضافةٌ. In other words, it is not the **مُضافٌ** nor resembling one. The خَبَرُ لا is deleted and could have the assumed, virtual, underlying meaning of مَوْجُودٌ.	**سِيَّ**
Extra particle (حَرْفٌ زائِدٌ). It does not have a position in إِعْرابٌ.	**ما**
This is the **direct object** (مَفْعُولٌ بِهِ) of the deleted verb with the underlying meaning of: *I mean* (أَعْنِي) or: *I specify/relate to* (أَخُصُّ).	**كُتُب**
The sentence means: *I love books but not as much as (the love I have for) literature books.*	أَحِبُّ الْكُتُبَ وَلا مِثْلَما أَخُصُّ كُتُبَ الْأَدَبِ.

Our analysis only works if we have a definite word (مَعْرِفةٌ) after لا سِيَّما. The trick is that the noun كُتُب has <u>by definition</u> a **definite char-**

acter because it is the first part of a إِضافةٌ that is followed by a definite word (*see #101*). If we had an **indefinite** word (نَكِرةٌ) after the expression, the إِعْرابٌ would follow the rules of a **specification** (تَمْيِيزٌ).

Note: Ibn Hishām (ابن هشام), one of the earliest Arabic grammarians, thought that the noun after لا سِيَّما is placed in the position of an accusative (the state of نَصْبٌ) because it was actually the مُسْتَثْنَى (*the thing excepted*). He suggested that لا سِيَّما has the meaning of إِلّا.

Option 3: the genitive case (الْجَرُّ)

I love books, particularly literature books.	أُحِبُّ الْكُتُبَ وَلا سِيَّما كُتُبِ الْأَدَبِ.

This is the "subject" (اسْمُ لا); it has to get the accusative (مَنْصُوبٌ بِالْفَتْحةِ الظّاهِرةِ). It is also the first part of a إِضافةٌ, i.e., the مُضافٌ.	سِيَّ
Extra particle (حَرْفٌ زائِدٌ). It does not have a position in إِعْرابٌ.	ما
Second part of the إِضافةٌ, so-called مُضافٌ إِلَيْهِ; therefore, it is in the genitive case (مَجْرُورٌ بِالْكَسْرةِ الظّاهِرةِ).	كُتُبِ

➤ This view **(option 3)** is the easiest and closest to the actual meaning of the sentence because the equivalent would be:

I love books, but not as much as literature books.	أُحِبُّ الْكُتُبَ وَلا مِثْلَ كُتُبِ الْأَدَبِ.

Summary:

If the word after لا سِيَّما is **in**definite (اسْمٌ نَكِرةٌ):

		reason for the case marker	
nominative	الرَّفْعُ	predicate of the deleted subject	خَبَرٌ لِمُبْتَدَإٍ مَحْذوفٍ
accusative	النَّصْبُ	specification	تَمْيِيزٌ لِلنَّكِرةِ الْمُبْهَمةِ (ما)
genitive	الْجَرُّ	second part of the إِضافةٌ	مُضافٌ إِلَيْهِ

If the word after لا سِيَّما is **definite** (اِسْمٌ مَعْرِفَةٌ):

		reason for the case marker	
nominative	الرَّفْعُ	predicate of the deleted subject	خَبَرٌ لِمُبْتَدَإٍ مَحْذُوفٍ
genitive	الْجَرُّ	second part of the إضافةٌ	مُضَافٌ إِلَيْهِ

The accusative is only possible with a trick. If we interpreted لا سِيَّما as *I specify* (أَخُصُّ), then it would work.

accusative	النَّصْبُ	direct object of the deleted verb	مَفْعُولٌ بِهِ لِفِعْلٍ مَحْذُوفٍ

Chapter 10: The Verbal Sentence

The verbal sentence is one of the two major types of sentences in Arabic. Most grammarians agree that a verbal sentence (جُمْلَةٌ فِعْلِيّةٌ) has to start with a full, complete verb (فِعْلٌ تامٌّ).

Conversely, this means that *incomplete/defective* verbs (فِعْلٌ ناقِصٌ) do not start a verbal sentence. A verb points to an action (حَدَثٌ) and therefore needs someone who carries out the action: the doer or subject (فاعِلٌ). When you see a verbal sentence, the most important thing is the identification of the doer: the subject (فاعِلٌ).

284. What do you express when you negate a verb with ما?

That the action never took place.

In Arabic, you have several options to negate a verb. Let's start with the **past tense** (الْماضِي): *did not; has not*

ما negates the occurrence of the action not for a particular situation, but **totally**: ما emphasizes that the action **never took place.**	ما
لَمْ negates the occurrence of a **single instance** (but may deny any realization of the action); it is generally used in a punctual context. The verb gets the jussive mood (مَجْزُومٌ).	لَمْ

May occur in negative wishes. Grammarians call that optatives. (thus the past does not express an action that already happened). The verb after لا is in the past tense form.	لا

She did not love him in the past nor does she love him at present.	ما أَحَبَّتْهُ فِي الْمَاضِي وَلا تُحِبُّهُ فِي الْحَاضِرِ.
I didn't go to school yesterday (single occurrence).	لَمْ أَذْهَبْ إِلَى الْمَدْرَسَةِ أَمْسِ.
Let us hope that his days will never return.	لا كانَتْ أَيَّامُهُ

In the following example, I use ما used instead of the perhaps more appropriate لَمْ to show the finesses.

The sun has not risen yet.	مَا طَلَعَتِ الشَّمْسُ بَعْدُ.
Note: Though it is understandable in a given context, strictly speaking, this could theoretically express that the sun has never risen so far.	

The negation of the **present tense** (الْمُضارِعُ): *does not*

The most common particle. It doesn't change the mood of the verb.	لا
You rarely encounter ما . If anything, it appears with verbs for mental states (ما أَظُنُّ - *I don't mean*) and to convey emotional intensity (see examples below).	ما

I don't know whether he is a friend of enemy.	ما أَدْرِي أَصَدِيقٌ هُوَ أَمْ عَدُوٌّ.
He does not listen to what I am saying.	ما يَسْمَعُ كَلامِي.

The negation of the future (الْمُسْتَقْبَلُ): *will not*

Almost always used. The verb gets the subjunctive mood (مَنْصُوبٌ).	لَنْ
Considered ungrammatical; but it occurs in Modern Standard Arabic: سَوْفَ plus لا plus verb.	لا

He will not be very late.	سَوْفَ لا يَتَأَخَّرُ كَثِيرًا.
	لَنْ يَتَأَخَّرَ كَثِيرًا.

285. What is the usual word order in Arabic?

You start with a verb.

Let's start with the normal word order in Classical Arabic:

> (1) verb + (2) subject + (3) object

Modern Standard Arabic is more flexible. It changes the aspect of the Arabic sentence to extremes, unknown to earlier periods. It is influenced by foreign languages. Nowadays, we often see the following word order which may have been influenced by English or German.

> (1) subject + (2) verb + (3) object + (4) adverbial expression
>
> Note that this word order produces a nominal sentence (جُمْلةٌ اِسْمِيّةٌ).

Playing with the position of words is mainly done to emphasize certain words. If you want to lay **emphasis** on the **object**, the object may **precede** the **verb**. Let's focus on that now.

The usual position of the direct object (مَفْعُولٌ بِهِ) is at the end, i.e., after the verb and subject. But you can play with the word order and move the direct object to the front (تَقْدِيمُ الْمَفْعُولِ بِهِ) or to the middle – provided that the meaning is not misleading.

In the language of grammar, this means that you place the direct object before its regent (عامِلٌ), also called governor, operator.

Whoever it may be. (see *question #234 for the analysis*)	كائِنًا مَنْ كان.
The student broke the **glass**.	كَسَرَ الزُّجاجَ التِّلْمِيذُ.
The student wrote the **lesson**.	دَرْسًا كَتَبَ الطّالِبُ.

Watch out: Sometimes you **have to** move the direct object to the front.

1. Words that have the precedence (صَدارةٌ) and must be placed at the beginning.

Such words are mostly questions words like مَنْ - *who(m)*.

Who(m) did you meet?	مَنْ لَقِيتَ؟

مَنْ is the fronted direct object (مَفْعُولٌ بِهِ مُقَدَّمٌ) - *see question #160.*

2. The **subject** (الْفَاعِلُ) of a verbal sentence is connected by a **possessive pronoun** that refers to the direct object (إِذا اتَّصَلَ بِالْفاعِلِ ضَمِيرٌ يَعُودُ عَلَى الْمَفْعُولِ بِهِ). Note: For a similar problem, see also #253.

Sometimes such sentences are rendered into English by using the passive voice. Two examples:

The owner took the **book**. (The book was taken by its owner.)	أَخَذَ الْكِتابَ صاحِبُهُ.

الْكِتابَ is the fronted direct object (مَفْعُولٌ بِهِ مُقَدَّمٌ) - *see question #410.*

Sura 2:124	وَإِذِ ابْتَلَى إِبْراهِيمَ رَبُّهُ بِكَلِماتٍ فَأَتَمَّهُنَّ قَالَ ...

- When **Ibrāhīm's Lord tested him** with certain commandments, which he fulfilled, He said,... *(Abdul Haleem uses the active voice.)*
- And [mention, O Muhammad], when **Ibrāhīm was tried** by his Lord with commands and he fulfilled them, [Allah] said, ... *(Sahīh International - passive)*

What about the position of adverbs?

The position of adverbs, especially when more than one is used, depends mainly on the specific importance or emphasis given to each of them. Unlike in English, **temporal** and **local adverbial modifications do not have a specific order.** They may follow each other or be separated by other elements in the sentence.

Just a moment ago, a new student was (came) here.	لَقَدْ جاءَ السَّاعَةَ هُنا طالِبٌ جَدِيدٌ.

Without case endings, you may have to read this sentence twice. السَّاعَةَ (with the definite article and the "*a*"/فَتْحَةٌ on the final letter) is an **adverb of time** and denotes *now, at present, by this time, at this moment, ...*

286. What else can do the job of a verb?

Five word forms.

We are concerned here with the following question. Which forms and words have the power to be the regent (عامِلٌ) in a verbal sentence?

Those types of words that cause grammatical states (cases) are known as عامِلٌ. The verb, for example, is the factor (عامِلٌ) that causes a word to be the subject (فاعِلٌ). Without a verb, there is no subject (in a verbal sentence). ▷ The verb is the governor, operator (عامِلٌ) of the subject and guards it in the nominative case (مَرْفُوعٌ). It can also govern the direct object (مَفْعُولٌ بِه) – but in the accusative case (مَنْصُوبٌ).

The verb is not unique in this power. There are **five** other kinds of words which can govern the subject of a verbal sentence.

1. Interjection denoting a sense of a verb (اِسْمُ الْفِعْلِ)

Such words resemble a verb by shape and meaning and point to action and time – but they are **not conjugated**. Don't confuse it with the *active participle* (اِسْمُ الْفاعِلِ).

Hush! (in the meaning of calling for silence: اُسْكُتْ)	صَهْ!

What are the grammatical implications? Even if we only use this single word without anything else, it is still a sentence.

صَهْ is a *verbal noun in the imperative* (اِسْمُ فِعْلِ أَمْرٍ) which never changes its shape (مَبْنِيٌّ) and always ends in سُكُونْ. It doesn't have a place in إِعْرابٌ. What about the **subject** (فاعِلٌ)? It is an **implied, hidden pronoun** (ضَمِيرٌ مُسْتَتِرٌ), expressing *you* (أَنْتَ).

Another example.

	هَيْهاتَ!
To what extent! How very far to achieve! How impossible! (بِمَعْنَى بَعُدَ).	occasionally also هَيْهاتُ or هَيْهاتِ
Success doesn't come with negligence!	هَيْهاتَ النَّجاحُ مَعَ الْإِهْمالِ!
النَّجاحُ is a Verbal noun with the meaning of a past tense verb (اِسْمُ فِعْلِ ماضٍ). the **subject** (فاعِلٌ) in the nominative case (مَرْفُوعٌ بِالضَّمّةِ الظّاهِرة).	

Ah! ; oh!	أَوَّهْ!

Interjection used to express surprise, anger, pain, admiration. It can also be used to lay emphasis or to attract somebody's attention.

أَوَّهْ is a verbal noun with the meaning of the present tense (اِسْمُ فِعْلٍ مُضارِعٍ). It has a fixed shape that never changes. **Subject** (فاعِلٌ) is an implied pronoun (ضَميرٌ مُسْتَتِرٌ) with the implied meaning (تَقْديرٌ) of: *I* (أَنا).

2. The active participle (اِسْمُ الْفاعِلِ)

This is very common and can be confusing because many people (especially in contemporary Arabic dialects) use participles instead of verbs to express an action. Let's look at an example to understand what we are talking about.

This man's son works hard (is diligent).	هٰذا رَجُلٌ مُجِدٌّ اِبْنُهُ.

Where is the **subject** (فاعِلٌ)? It is (اِبْنُهُ) اِبْن which is clearly apparent since it has the nominative case (مَرْفوعٌ بِالضَّمّةِ الظّاهِرةِ). Which word is responsible for this case ending? What is its عامِل؟ It is the active participle: مُجِدٌّ.

3. The form of exaggeration, noun of intensiveness (صيغةُ الْمُبالَغةِ)

This is a man of generosity.	هٰذا رَجُلٌ كَريمٌ خُلُقُهُ.

خُلُق is the subject (فاعِلٌ). It is governed by كَريم which makes it the regent, operator (عامِلٌ) of خُلْق.

4. The quasi- or pseudo participle (صِفةٌ مُشَبَّهةٌ); a derived noun which conveys a meaning of firmness. See *Arabic for Nerds 1*, #143.

This is a student who is excellent in his studies.	هٰذا طالِبٌ حَسَنٌ عَمَلُهُ.

عَمَل is the subject, clearly marked by the nominative case marker. The word حَسَنٌ is responsible for the case ending. It is the regent (عامِلٌ) of عَمَل.

5. The rigid or static/inert noun (اِسْمٌ جامِدٌ) that can be interpreted as a (يُؤَوَّلُ بِمُشْتَقٍّ) مَصْدَرٌ. That is very rare.

A اِسْمٌ جامِدٌ is a noun that is stationary and incapable of growth or action. It is a noun that is not derived from a root, e.g., *Egypt* (مِصْرُ),

woman (اِمْرَأَةٌ). Usually such nouns cannot be interpreted as a مَصْدَرٌ which means they do not have verbal power and cannot guard and operate on a subject.

But there are exceptions. Numbers (الْأَعْدادُ) are a good example. The idea behind this concept is quite sophisticated.

This is a man who has five sons.	هذا رَجُلٌ خَمْسةٌ أَبْناؤُهُ.
This would be the estimated meaning: →	هذا رَجُلٌ بالِغٌ أَبْناؤُهُ خَمْسةً.
Notice that we put the word *five* into the accusative case (مَنْصوبٌ) because the active participle (اِسْمُ الْفاعِلِ) governs the direct object (مَفْعُولٌ بِه) - which is *five* – in the accusative case.	
The subject (فاعِلٌ) is أَبْناؤُهُ; therefore, it is in the nominative case (مَرْفوعٌ بِالضَّمّةِ الظّاهِرة). It is governed by the word خَمْسةٌ.	

See also *questions #33, #218, #303, #327, #335.*

287. Does a verbal sentence have to start with a singular verb?

Yes, it has to.

In Arabic, the verb has to be singular (مُفْرَدٌ). Practically speaking, the verb lacks any sign of the dual or plural.

singular, masculine	The student came.	جاءَ الطّالِبُ.
dual, masculine	The two students came.	جاءَ الطّالِبانِ.
plural, masculine	The students came.	جاءَ الطُّلابُ.
plural, feminine	The (f.) students came.	جاءَتْ الطّالِباتُ.

Watch out! In ancient variants of Arabic, the sign of the dual and plural is added to the verb which starts the sentence. Grammarians have coined this phenomenon and call it أَكَلُوني الْبَراغيثُ (see *question #20*).

plural, masculine	The students came.	جاءُوا الطُّلابُ.
جاءُوا is a past tense verb in the third person plural (masculine).		

288. Can a verb end a sentence?

Yes, it can.

In Arabic, a verbal sentence (جُمْلَةٌ فِعْلِيّةٌ) normally starts with a verb. With some legal tricks, however, we can manage to put the verb at the end. It is just about word order. An example:

In war, everything is permitted.	كُلُّ شَيْءٍ فِي الْحَرْبِ يَجُوزُ.

289. When do you use the verb's feminine form to start a sentence?

If the subject is feminine.

The question of gender is a difficult issue when we are in the world of languages. Let's clarify first what *feminine* actually means. Basically, there are two categories of feminine words: real and figurative one.

You **should** (some say: must) start a sentence with the feminine, singular form of the verb if the subject is **in life, in realty feminine** and therefore *naturally feminine* (مُؤَنَّثٌ حَقِيقِيٌّ). This is true for humans and animals. For example: *mother* (أُمُّ); lioness (لَبُؤَةٌ) Related to that are words which are *semantically feminine* (مُؤَنَّثٌ مَعْنَوِيٌّ) without visual signs of feminization. For example, proper names like *Zaynab* (زَيْنَبُ); *Suad* (سُعادُ). The verb gets a feminine form.

Now, what happens if we have a word like شَمْسٌ (*sun*) which is *figuratively feminine* (مُؤَنَّثٌ مَجازِيٌّ) by tradition?

Or what should we do if the subject is a singular noun which is feminine (مُؤَنَّثٌ لَفْظِيٌّ) by form – but its gender can't be logically determined? We often get this situation when nouns end in ة or ى or اء and when this ending does not belong to the root. As a general rule, we can say that the **feminine verb form** is usually **applied**.

Let's look at the most common situations.

a) The subject (فاعِلٌ) is **figuratively feminine** (مَجازِيٌّ).

This happens when a noun is derived from a root and got a feminine marker for the ending. ▷ Then you use the **feminine verb form**.

The result appeared.	ظَهَرَتِ النَّتِيجَةُ.

Could you also use the masculine verb form?

Yes. But the feminine verb form is better style (الْأَفْصَحُ).	ظَهَرَ النَّتِيجَةُ.

b) The subject (فَاعِلٌ) is feminine **by nature** (التَّأْنِيثُ حَقِيقِيٌّ) but the verb is separated from the subject by another word.

Then you also use the **feminine verb form.**

Fātima appeared today.	حَضَرَتْ الْيَوْمَ فاطِمةُ.

Could you also use the masculine verb form?

Theoretically, yes. But the feminine verb form (like above) is considered a better style (الْأَفْصَحُ).	حَضَرَ الْيَوْمَ فاطِمةُ.

Watch out: If the connection between the verb and the feminine subject is interrupted by إِلَّا, the <u>masculine</u> verb form is better (التَّذْكِيرُ أَفْصَحُ)!

Only Fātima appeared today.	ما حَضَرَ الْيَوْمَ إلَّا فاطِمةُ.

Why is that? This has to do with the underlying, estimated meaning of the sentence:

No one appeared today except for Fātima.	ما حَضَرَ الْيَوْمَ أَحَدٌ إلَّا فاطِمةُ.

c) The subject (فَاعِلٌ)is a **broken plural** (جَمْعُ التَّكْسِيرِ) which is based on a **masculine** or **feminine singular.**

Your choice! Both verb forms (masculine or feminine) are possible.

| The students appeared. | حَضَرَتْ التَّلامِيذُ. |
	حَضَرَ التَّلامِيذُ.

In the following example, the word شَواعِر is the plural form of the singular word شاعِرَةٌ which is a female *poet*.

| The poets recited their poems (referring to female poets). | أَلْقَتِ الشَّوَاعِرُ قَصَائِدَهُنَّ. |
| | أَلْقَى الشَّوَاعِرُ قَصَائِدَهُنَّ. |

THE SUBJECT OF A VERBAL SENTENCE

290. Is the subject of a verbal sentence always a single word?

Purist grammarians would say yes.

The subject (فَاعِلٌ) is the one who is carrying out the (action) of the verb. Therefore, the subject must be in the most principle of states regarding cases: the state of the nominative (الرَّفْعُ).

Purist grammarians suggest that the subject **can't** be a sentence; it can only be a **word**. What we should understand here by the term *word* is that the subject is either a plain, apparent noun (إِسْمٌ صَرِيحٌ) or an interpreted مَصْدَرٌ, a so-called مَصْدَرٌ مُؤَوَّلٌ.

Other grammarians, however, say that the reality is a bit different. There are several structures and constructions in which you find a **sentence** working as the subject (فَاعِلٌ).

Let's check a verse of the Qur'an:

| Sura 14:45 | ...and it had become clear to you how We dealt with them. (*Sahīh Internat.*) | ...وَتَبَيَّنَ لَكُمْ كَيْفَ فَعَلْنَا بِهِمْ. |

What happened here? In this example, the subject (فَاعِلٌ) of the verb تَبَيَّنَ is a sentence (جُمْلَةٌ): كَيْفَ فَعَلْنَا بِهِم. How do we deal with this situation grammatically? We say that the entire sentence appears in the position of the subject and thus in the location of a nominative (فِي مَحَلِّ رَفْعِ فَاعِلٌ لِفِعْلِ: تَبَيَّنَ). In English, we would call that a *subject sentence*.

Such situations are very rare though. You usually encounter what the purist grammarians state: the subject is a single word.

291. Can an interpreted مَصْدَرٌ function as the subject (فَاعِلٌ)?

Yes, this is possible.

The subject (فَاعِلٌ) in a verbal sentence is not always just a single noun but may consist of various forms. Let's start with the most basic type of a sentence with a past tense verb plus a subject.

Karīm wrote.	كَتَبَ كَرِيمٌ.

Subject (فَاعِلٌ) of the verb كَتَبَ in the nominative case (مَرْفُوعٌ) as clearly marked by nunation (بِالضَّمَّةِ).	كَرِيمٌ

Let's jazz up the construction with a مَصْدَرٌ مُؤَوَّلٌ, an interpreted مَصْدَرٌ, that functions as the subject.

1. We have a مَصْدَرٌ مُؤَوَّلٌ, produced with the help of أَنْ.

I am happy that you visit me.	يُسْعِدُنِي أَنْ تَزُورَنِي.

Let's rewrite the English translation to understand what the subject in the Arabic sentence actually is: *Your **visit** to me pleases me.*

→ If we used the real مَصْدَرٌ: *Your **visit** made me happy.*	تُسْعِدُنِي زِيارَتُكَ.

Verb in the present tense (فِعْلٌ مُضَارِعٌ), indicative mood (مَرْفُوعٌ) (بِالضَّمَّةِ الظَّاهِرةِ).	يُسْعِدُ
The *guarding or preventive* نُونٌ; it got that name as it prevents the final vowel of the verb from being absorbed by the long vowel "*i*". (النُّونُ لِلْوِقايةِ حَرْفٌ مَبْنِيٌّ عَلَى الْكَسْرِ) – see *question #59.*	ن
Pronominal suffix (ضَمِيرٌ مُتَّصِلٌ); it has a fixed shape (مَبْنِيٌّ عَلَى السُّكُونِ). It serves as the direct object (مَفْعُولٌ بِهِ) of the verb; so, it is placed in the position of an accusative case (فِي مَحَلِّ نَصْبٍ).	ي
This is a so-called *infinitive particle* which has the power to form an interpreted مَصْدَرٌ. It also puts the following verb into the subjunctive mood (حَرْفُ نَصْبٍ وَمَصْدَرٍ).	أَنْ
Present tense verb (فِعْلٌ مُضَارِعٌ), in the subjunctive (مَنْصُوبٌ) due to أَنْ. The mood is marked by a فَتْحةٌ. The subject (فَاعِلٌ) is hidden (مُسْتَتِرٌ), the implicit meaning is: *you* (أَنْتَ).	تَزُورَ
Another *guarding or preventive* نُونٌ.	ن
Pronominal suffix, in the position of a direct object (مَفْعُولٌ بِهِ).	ي

There is one question left. What is the **subject** (فاعِلٌ) of يُسْعِدُ؟ Is it an implied pronoun? No, it isn't.

The interpreted مَصْدَرٌ consisting of أَنْ plus the verb does the job of the فاعِل. We say that the whole expression appears in the location of a nominative case (فِي مَحَلِّ رَفْعِ فاعِلٌ).

2. The مَصْدَرٌ مُؤَوَّلٌ, produced with the help of ما.

I liked what you did. (What you did pleased me.)	أَعْجَبَنِي ما فَعَلْتَ.
If we used the real مَصْدَر: *Your **doing** pleased me.*	أَعْجَبَنِي فِعْلُكَ.

ما is a حَرْفُ مَصْدَرِيَّةٍ and not a negation, nor a relative pronoun. The ما is followed by a past tense verb which has a subject (فاعِلٌ), i.e., the تَ. The entire expression, marked in gray, is a مَصْدَرٌ مُؤَوَّلٌ and works as the **subject of the verb** أَعْجَبَ; therefore, it is found in the position of a nominative case (فِي مَحَلِّ رَفْعِ فاعِلٌ).

3. The مَصْدَرٌ مُؤَوَّلٌ, produced with the help of أَنَّ.

I am happy that you are successful.	أَسْعَدَنِي أَنَّكَ ناجِحٌ.

Underlying meaning (تَقْدِيرٌ): *Your **success** pleased me.*	أَسْعَدَنِي نَجاحُكَ.

Pronoun for emphasis (حَرْفُ تَوْكِيدٍ وَنَصْبٍ) that has the power to govern the "subject" (اِسْمُ أَنَّ) in the accusative case.	أَنَّ
Pronominal suffix (ضَمِيرٌ مُتَّصِلٌ) serving as the اِسْمُ أَنَّ. Thus, the كَ is grammatically in the position of an accusative case (فِي مَحَلِّ نَصْبٍ). You can't mark or see the case marker since this pronoun is indeclinable and built on the فَتْح.	كَ
Predicate (خَبَرُ أَنَّ) in the nominative case (مَرْفُوعٌ).	ناجِحٌ

What about the **subject** of the verb أَسْعَدَ؟ It is the interpreted infinitive noun (مَصْدَرٌ مُؤَوَّلٌ) consisting of أَنَّ plus its two governed factors (أَنَّ وَمَعْمُولَاها). Since this expression functions as the subject, the whole expression is in the position of a nominative case (فِي مَحَلِّ رَفْعِ فاعِلٌ).

292. Which verbs tend to have an interpreted مَصْدَرٌ as a subject?

Not many verbs.

There are some Arabic verbs that usually have a مَصْدَرٌ مُؤَوَّلٌ (interpreted infinitive) as the subject (of the verbal sentence).

meaning	past tense	present tense	stem
to be possible; make possible for	أَمْكَنَ	يُمْكِنُ	IV
to be allowed; be possible	جازَ	يَجُوزُ	I
to be necessary; be incumbent	وَجَبَ	يَجِبُ	I
to be incumbent; be necessary	إِنْبَغَى	يَنْبَغِي	VII

In the following examples, the مَصْدَرٌ مُؤَوَّلٌ consisting of أَنْ plus a verb (marked in gray) serves as the subject (فاعِلٌ). It is therefore placed in the location of a nominative case (فِي مَحَلِّ رَفْعِ فاعِلٍ). Notice that the verb after أَنْ gets the **subjunctive** mood (مَنْصُوبٌ).

You can go now. (Lit.: Going/to go is possible for you now.)	يُمْكِنُكَ أَنْ يَذْهَبَ الْآنَ.
He may come today. (Lit.: His appearing is possible/allowed today.)	يَجُوزُ أَنْ يَحْضُرَ الْيَوْمَ.

What happens if we use a **negation**? Which part is negated?

You should not interfere in what is none of your business.	يَنْبَغِي أَلَّا تَتَدَخَّلَ فِيما لا يُعَنِّيكَ.

This is how we could rewrite the sentence having the same meaning: →	يَنْبَغِي عَدَمُ تَدَخُّلِكَ فِيما لا يُعَنِّيكَ.

This particle was originally أَنْ plus لا and means *not to*.	أَلَّا
This particle produces an infinitive and governs what follows in the accusative (حَرْفُ نَصْبٍ وَمَصْدَرٍ). No place in إِعْرابٌ.	أَنْ
Negation particle (حَرْفُ نَفْيٍ). Does not have a place in إِعْرابٌ.	لا
Present tense verb (فِعْلٌ مُضارِعٌ) in the subjunctive (مَنْصُوبٌ)	تَتَدَخَّلَ

mood due to the particle أَنْ. Its subject (فَاعِلٌ) is a hidden, implied pronoun (ضَمِيرٌ مُسْتَتِرٌ) expressing *you* (أَنْتَ).	

293. The subject is always in the nominative case, isn't it?

As far as its position in grammar is concerned, that's right.

As soon as we look at the case endings which you see or hear, this is not always true. A different, **visual** case ending can be misleading.

Oftentimes it is induced by an extra (superfluous) preposition (حَرْفُ جَرٍّ زَائِدٌ). The three most common particles (حَرْفٌ) that cause such situations are مِن and ب and ل. These devices are used to convey emphasis and have the effect that the word after the حَرْف takes the genitive case.

What does that mean for our analysis? Is the subject in the genitive case? No, it isn't! The subject is still located in the position of a nominative case (مَرْفُوعٌ) because of its function in the sentence. We can say that it appears in the place of a subject. Nevertheless, we have to mark the word with the genitive case (مَجْرُورٌ) due to the extra preposition. In the analysis, we need to use estimated, assumed markers (عَلامةٌ مُقَدَّرَةٌ).

If the subject is preceded by an extra preposition, two case markers are important:

- the **visible, apparent** marker: the genitive marker (مَجْرُورٌ لَفْظًا);
- the **actual** marker according to the position, i.e., the estimated, virtual marker for the nominative case (مَرْفُوعٌ مَحَلًّا عَلَى أَنَّهُ الْفَاعِلُ);

There was no one left in the place.	لَمْ يَبْقَ فِي الْمكانِ مِنْ أَحَدٍ.

Where is the subject in this sentence? Let's see.

Redundant, extra preposition (حَرْفُ جَرٍّ زَائِدٌ) mainly used for emphasis. It does not have a position in إعْرابٌ.	مِنْ
Subject (فَاعِلٌ) in the nominative case (مَرْفُوعٌ) – but only by an assumed, estimated, virtual case marker (ضَمَّةٌ مُقَدَّرَةٌ) because the spot of the case marker is occupied by the كَسْرة, induced by the additional preposition (إشْتِغالُ الْمَحَلِّ بِحَرَكةِ حَرْفِ الْجَرِّ الزّائِدِ).	أَحَدٍ

Especially the ب is likely to be mistaken as a mandatory preposition. A mandatory, "real" preposition **directs and changes the meaning**. Certain verbs use prepositions to express a specific action. If you spot a بـ, always ask yourself: is it necessary to indicate a direction; is it mandatory for the verb?

Let's see examples of verbs that must be used with a preposition. The بـ is mandatory – the بـ is not just there to polish the sentence.

to express something	أَدْلَى بِ
to express one's opinion	أَدْلَى بِرَأْيِهِ
to realize something, to feel something	شَعَرَ بِ

If بـ is not mandatory, it is *redundant* and only there to give emphasis. It is just an amplifier, a stylistic device.

| Sura 13:43 | Say, "Sufficient is Allah as Witness". | قُلْ كَفَى بِاللَّهِ شَهِيدًا. |

The بـ here is an extra, superfluous preposition (حَرْفُ جَرٍّ زَائِدٌ). *Allah* is the subject (فَاعِلٌ) and should get the nominative case marker. Grammatically, it remains located in the position of a nominative case – but you can't put the usual marker because the extra preposition gets in the marker's way. So we use an estimated, virtual, hypothetical marker (مَرْفُوعٌ بِضَمَّةٍ مُقَدَّرَةٍ).

Another example of a redundant preposition is the *Lām*. When used as an extra preposition, it has this shape: لِ – with the vowel "*i*".

| A negligent individual would never succeed! (How far is success for a negligent individual!) | هَيْهَاتَ لِنَجاحِ الْمُهْمِلِ! |

Although you see a genitive case marker, نَجاح is the subject (فَاعِلٌ) and found in the position of a nominative case (marked by an assumed ضَمّة).

294. When do you have to add a بـ before the subject?

If you use the form of admiration or astonishment (صِيغَةُ التَّعَجُّبِ).

The صِيغَةُ التَّعَجُّبِ is an interesting way to express that you are astonished or excited about something. There are two systems. This time, we will only focus on the construction with بـ. This is the formula:

3		2		1
the exclamative	+	بِ	+	أَفْعِلْ
"subject" of astonish-ment (الْمُتَعَجَّبُ مِنْهُ)		extra preposition (حَرْفُ جَرٍّ زَائِدٌ)		verb of astonishment (فِعْلُ التَّعَجُّبِ)

You'll end up with a verb in the shape of an imperative (2nd person sin-gular masculine), following the pattern أَفْعِلْ بِهِ. However, the meaning of the verb here is **not the imperative**, rather it conveys **astonishment**.

How generous the Arab is!	أَكْرِمْ بِالْعَرَبِيِّ!
Watch out! This sentence does not mean: *Be generous with the Arab!* It has the same meaning as مَا أَكْرَمَ الْعَرَبِيَّ	
What a beautiful moon!/How beautiful the moon is!	أَجْمِلْ بِالْقَمَرِ!

The analysis of the two examples (إِعْرَابٌ) solely depends on how you treat أَفْعِلْ. You have two options:

- **Option 1:** You treat أَفْعِلْ as an <u>imperative</u> (عَلَى أَنَّهُ فِعْلُ أَمْرٍ مَبْنِيٌّ عَلَى السُّكُونِ).

- **Option 2:** You treat أَفْعِلْ as a <u>past tense verb</u> (عَلَى تَقْدِيرِ أَنَّهُ فِعْلٌ مَاضٍ). ➡ This is more common.

Past tense verb (فِعْلٌ مَاضٍ) appearing in the form of an impera-tive (صِيغَةُ الْأَمْرِ).	أَكْرِمْ أَجْمِلْ
The بِ is an additional, extra preposition. The word that is placed after the بِ is called the الْمُتَعَجَّبُ مِنْهُ.	بِالْعَرَبِيِّ بِالْقَمَرِ

الْعَرَبِيِّ is the **subject** (فَاعِلٌ). It takes the genitive case (مَجْرُورٌ لَفْظًا) due to the preceding preposition. According to the position in the sentence, it should be in the nominative case, but we can only use a virtual, assumed marker (مَرْفُوعٌ بِضَمَّةٍ مُقَدَّرَةٍ). In Arabic, we say:

مَرْفُوعٌ مَحَلًّا عَلَى أَنَّهُ فَاعِلٌ لِفِعْلِ التَّعَجُّبِ بِاعْتِبَارِهِ فِعْلًا مَاضِيًا

Excursus: There is another possible form to express *surprise or wonder*, which is مَا أَفْعَلَ followed by a noun in the accusative case (مَنْصُوبٌ). We need to deal with a past tense verb (IV-form; أَفْعَلَ) in the third person singular (masculine). For a deep analysis, see #434 - #441.

What is the difference between the two forms of surprise? First of all, regarding the English translation, there is no difference. The following two examples can both be translated as: *What an excellent man Zayd is!* However, the inner, substantial meaning is slightly different.

1	Literal meaning: *What has made Zayd excellent!*	مَا أَفْضَلَ زَيْدًا!
	The idea behind this construction is the following question: can anything make Zayd more excellent than he is?	
2	The inner, literal meaning is: Try (your ability at) making excellent upon (ب) Zayd.	أَفْضِلْ بِزَيْدٍ!
	The idea behind this construction is the following: you can't make him more excellent than he is.	

295. Can you delete the subject of a verbal sentence?

No, you can't.

Nevertheless, there are rare situations in which one could assume that the subject was deleted. In fact, you hide the subject – or, to be more precise, you cover it (اِسْتِتَارٌ). We end up in such situations when we have the following two ingredients:

Ingredient 1. We need a verb in the present tense, having one of the following two forms:

- Masculine plural (*you*), so we will have a وَاوُ الْجَمَاعةِ: ونَ
- Feminine singular (*you*), so we'll have a يَاءُ الْمُخَاطَبةِ: ينَ

Ingredient 2. You need to add a ن for emphasis (نُونُ التَّوْكِيدِ).

➡ If we put that together, we will get the **energetic** form of a verb.

May you succeed, you hard-workers!	لَتَنْجَحُنَّ أَيُّهَا الْمُجِدُّونَ!
The actual form of the verb (on the right) would be difficult to pronounce – Arabic doesn't like that.	لتَنْجَحُونَ + نَّ

We have analyzed the form لَتَنْجَحُنَّ in depth in *question #94*. The special thing about it is the **missing subject** – because it was deleted.

- You first have to **delete** the ن of the ونَ or يـنَ-ending because Arabic doesn't like to have two ن in a row (كَراهةُ تَوالِي الْأَمْثالِ or كَراهةُ تَوالِي نُونَيْنِ زائِدَتَيْنِ).

- As soon as you have done this, you'll face another issue: the **problem of two** سُكُونٌ in a row which is called اِلْتِقاءُ السّاكِنَيْنِ. This is because the first نُون of the حَرْفُ التَّوْكِيدِ is constructed like this: نْ plus نَ. So, you would get: وْنَ - because a long vowel has always a سُكُونٌ although you normally don't write it.

- Therefore, you also need to delete the و (or the ي).

Now we have arrived at the problem. It's a dilemma. Once you delete the و, which is the subject (فاعِلٌ), we don't have a subject anymore. The only proof for the indicative mood (مَرْفُوعٌ) would be the fixed نَ at the end of the verb (ثُبُوتُ النُّونِ) as in other moods (مَجْزُومٌ or مَنْصُوبٌ), this ن is deleted. But we also got rid of that.

How do we get out of this dilemma? The solution: the vowel on the last letter of the verb serves as a **remnant of the subject**, which is fine and enough. The same is true for the feminine form:

| May you (female) succeed, you (f.) hard-worker! | لَتَنْجَحِنَّ أَيَّتُها الْمُجِدّةُ! |

296. Are there verbs that don't need a subject?

Yes, such verbs exist (as some grammarians suggested). But it is disputed.

Some grammarians state that verbs which bind a *hindering, neutralizing Mā* (ما الْكافّةُ) do not need a subject, because the ما hinders the so-called regimen of the verb (ما الْكافّةُ عَنِ الْفاعِلِ).

Therefore, the verb loses its power to operate on words and govern a word as the subject. To be more precise, the governing power of such a verb does not extend beyond itself.

Let's take the I-verb قَلَّ (R2=R3) which means *to be less; to decrease*. The present tense is يَقِلُّ.

| A (notorious) liar rarely tells the truth. | قَلَّما يَصْدُقُ الْكَذُوبُ. |

This is the meaning of the sentence:	قَدْ يَصْدُقُ الْكَذُوبُ.
Remark: كَذُوبٌ is an *exaggerated form* (صِيغَةُ الْمُبالَغةِ). A كَذُوبٌ is a person who lies a lot (كَثِيرُ الْكَذِبِ), similar to a كَذّابٌ.	

What about the grammatical analysis? There are two views. Let's first check what is common sense:

Present tense verb, indicative mood (فِعْلٌ مُضارِعٌ مَرْفُوعٌ).	يَصْدُقُ
Subject (فاعِلٌ) of the verb يَصْدُقُ.	الْكَذُوبُ

Interpretation 1. The ما is a hindering, neutralizing particle. Therefore, the verb قَلَّ can't have a subject because the governing power of the verb قَلَّ was stopped by the ما.

Past tense verb (فِعْلٌ ماضٍ). So far, nothing special.	قَلَّ
Hindering (neutralizing) particle (حَرْفٌ كافٌّ). No place in إِعْرابٌ.	ما

Interpretation 2. You treat ما as an infinitive particle (حَرْفُ مَصْدَرِيَّةٍ). Then, ما with a following verb (present tense: standard, indicative mood; or past tense) can be interpreted as a مَصْدَرٌ (مَصْدَرٌ مُؤَوَّلٌ). This interpreted infinitive is placed in the position of the subject (فاعِلٌ) of the verb قَلَّ! This is the **more common view** and it basically follows the standard rules. In this interpretation, we do have a subject for قَلَّ.

Underlying meaning (تَقْدِيرٌ) of this approach: →	قَلَّ صِدْقُ الْكَذُوبِ.

We treat ما as a حَرْفُ مَصْدَرِيَّةٍ; it does not have a position in إِعْرابٌ.	ما
What about the **subject** of قَلَّ? The **interpreted** مَصْدَرٌ (consisting of ما plus following verb) serves as the **subject** and is thus located in the position of a nominative case (الْمَصْدَرُ الْمُؤَوَّلُ مِنْ ما وَالْفِعْلِ فِي مَحَلِّ رَفْعٍ فاعِلٍ).	

Another example is طالَما. It is a compound of the I-verb طالَ (present tense: يَطُولُ) and ما. The ما can be interpreted as a hindering, neutralizing particle (interpretation 1) or a device to mold an infinitive (interpretation 2). The compound construction expresses *often* or *frequently* (=كَثِيرًا ما) if a verb clause is added. Usually, it immediately precedes a

verb in the past tense with a past tense meaning. In all <u>other</u> situations, it may express *as long as, while.*

He often helped his friends. (How often he...)	ظَالَما ساعَدَ أَصْدِقاءَهُ.
We have a past tense verb after ظَالَما. It is a common mistake to translate such constructions with *as long as* (As long as he helped his friends).	

297. Can you delete the regent (عامِلٌ) of the subject?

Yes, you can – and sometimes, you even have to delete it.

We do not want any misunderstandings to arise. We don't talk about the subject (فاعِلٌ) itself. We talk about the device which is responsible that a word serves as the subject: the *regent, operator, governor* (عامِلٌ). The regent may or even must be deleted in certain situations.

Let's start with the easy part.

a) You **may** delete the regent (عامِل) of the subject (فاعِلٌ) if the regent is understood anyway. This often happens in the answer to a question.

Question:	*Who came today?*	مَنْ حَضَرَ الْيَوْمَ؟
Answer:	*Ali.*	عَلِيٌّ.

Subject (فاعِلٌ) in the nominative case (مَرْفُوعٌ بِالضَّمّةِ الظّاهِرةِ).	عَلِيٌّ
Where is the verb? It was deleted, but is still implicitly understood: حَضَرَ عَلِيٌّ.	

Now let's move on to the more complicated part.

b) You **must** delete the عامِل (i.e., the verb) if there is a device involved which only works with a <u>verbal</u> sentence.

In order to make such a sentence work, there must be a verb later in the sentence which can interpret the deleted verb. Sounds complicated – an example:

If 'Ali comes, treat him with respect (honor him).	إِنْ عَلِيٌّ حَضَرَ فَأَكْرِمْهُ.

Conditional particle (حَرْفُ شَرْطٍ); no position in إِعْرابٌ.	إِنْ

Subject in the nominative case (فاعِلٌ مَرْفُوعٌ بِالضَّمّةِ الظّاهِرةِ). Why do we say فاعِلٌ (= subject of a verbal sentence!) since there is no verb earlier in the sentence? Shouldn't we call it مُبْتَدَأٌ؟ No! In fact, there was a verb. But this original **verb was deleted** and is interpreted now by a following verb: حَضَرَ.	عَلِيٌّ

Although superficially not much happened, such constructions are quite ingenious. The grammarians say that the deletion of the verb in sentences like our example is necessary! The reason for that is deeply rooted in the sentence structure of Arabic. The conditional particle إنْ only works with a **verbal sentence** (جُمْلةٌ فِعْلِيّةٌ). This means that إنْ stipulates the presence of a verb after it.

However, if a subsequent verb can explain the situation, it is not a problem anymore. But watch out! That verb (in our example حَضَرَ) does not take the مَجْزُومٌ-mood since it is not considered to be the verb after إنْ – because this verb (which would be in the jussive/مَجْزُومٌ) was deleted. You also find such a construction in the Qur'an:

Sura 9:6	If any one of the idolaters should seek your protection [Prophet], grant it to him.	وَإِنْ أَحَدٌ مِّنَ الْمُشْرِكِينَ اسْتَجَارَكَ فَأَجِرْهُ.

أَحَدٌ is the **subject** (فاعِلٌ) of the **deleted verb** (فِعْلٌ مَحْذُوفٌ) which is interpreted by the verb إسْتَجارَ – which is found later in the sentence.

298. *It was spring.* How do you say that in Arabic?

That's not easy since there is no impersonal subject (it is …) in Arabic.

English expressions like *it was; it became* have a so-called *impersonal subject*. Arabic does not know such thing. We have to find another way. Some ideas:

1. We use a verb with a passive meaning. Often, the VII-form (إنْفَعَلَ) is a good choice.

It was midnight.	إنْتَصَفَ اللَّيْلُ.
Literally: *The night reached the middle.*	

2. In temporal constructions with كانَ, the **subject is the temporal idea itself** that is implied in subjects like *the day, the month*.

It was Friday.	كانَ الْيَوْمُ يَوْمَ الْجُمْعةِ.
Literally: *The day was Friday.*	
It was spring.	كانَ الْفَصْلُ رَبِيعًا.
Literally: *The season was spring.*	
It was afternoon.	كانَ الْوَقْتُ عَصْرًا.
Literally: *The time was afternoon.*	

3. We may use verbs like أَصْبَحَ or أَمْسَى. Such verbs take the person (that is involved in the action) as the subject.

When **it** was morning...	لَمَّا أَصْبَحَ الصُّبْحُ...

Remark: Perhaps the closest you can get to an impersonal subject in Arabic is when you delete the subject of كانَ, i.e., the expressed إِسْمُ كانَ. This might sound a bit absurd, but it works: we are left with an implied, hidden subject in the verb كانَ which is not further specified – and this gives us the possibility to interpret the construction as *it*.

It was Friday.	كانَ يَوْمَ الْجُمْعةِ.

THE SUBJECT OF THE PASSIVE VERB (نائِبُ الْفاعِلِ)

299. Can something else step in for the actual *subject* (فاعِلٌ)?

Yes, the subject of a passive verb (نائِبُ الْفاعِلِ); *the deputy agent.*

In the passive voice (صِيغةُ الْمَبْنِيِّ لِلْمَجْهُولِ), the original subject is unknown by definition.

The passive is the form of the verb in which the regent (عامِلٌ) is not named. The regent is either **unknown** or **intentionally not identified**. The latter happens, for example, when Muslims want to express that a person has passed away (= died), because Muslims prefer the passive voice to express that. They say تُوُفِّيَ, *he was taken* (by Allah). It is the passive of V-verb يَتَوَفَّى - تَوَفَّى (R1=و; R3=ي; *to take; to let die*). See *Arabic for Nerds 1, question #85*.

This *subject of the passive* is usually a noun (اِسْمٌ) that **occupies the place of the deleted subject** (فاعِلٌ). Therefore, it becomes the main prop (عُمْدَةٌ) of the sentence. In grammar the term عُمْدَةٌ is used to describe a word which can't be deleted since it's essential for the meaning.

The نائِبُ الْفاعِلِ is placed in the location of a nominative case (رَفْعٌ) because the nominative always describes something essential. Like the regular subject of a verbal sentence, also the نائِبُ الْفاعِلِ is a plain noun (اِسْمٌ صَرِيحٌ) or may be an interpreted مَصْدَرٌ (مَصْدَرٌ مُؤَوَّلٌ).

1. The plain noun (اِسْمٌ صَرِيحٌ)

The lesson was understood.	فُهِمَ الدَّرْسُ.

2. The interpreted مَصْدَرٌ (مَصْدَرٌ مُؤَوَّلٌ)

The مَصْدَرٌ مُؤَوَّلٌ (the expression marked in gray in the following example) serves in the position of the subject of the passive (نائِبُ فاعِلٍ) and occupies the position of a nominative case (فِي مَحَلِّ رَفْعٍ).

It was written that Zayd is successful.	كُتِبَ أَنَّ زَيْدًا ناجِحٌ.
This is the equivalent of the above sentence: →	كُتِبَ نَجاحُ زَيْدٍ.
Particle of emphasis which governs the "subject" (اِسْمُ أَنَّ) in the accusative case (حَرْفُ تَوْكِيدٍ وَنَصْبٍ).	أَنَّ
"Subject" (اِسْمُ أَنَّ), so it has to be in the accusative case (مَنْصُوبٌ).	زَيْدًا
Predicate (خَبَرُ أَنَّ); in the nominative case (مَرْفُوعٌ).	ناجِحٌ

➤ Can a **redundant, extra preposition** (حَرْفُ جَرٍّ زائِدٌ) jump on a نائِبُ فاعِلٍ؟ Yes, that is not problematic at all.

Nobody was punished.	ما عُوقِبَ مِنْ أَحَدٍ.
Negation particle (حَرْفُ نَفْيٍ). It does not have a place in إِعْرابٌ.	ما

Past tense verb in the passive voice (فِعْلٌ مَبْنِيٌّ لِلْمَجْهُولِ).	عُوقِبَ
Additional preposition (حَرْفُ جَرٍّ زَائِدٌ); no place in إِعْرابٌ.	مِنْ
Subject of the passive voice (نائِبُ الْفاعِلِ).	أَحَدٍ

If we look at the position of أَحَد in the sentence, it is clear that it has to be in the nominative. But we can only apply an estimated, assumed marker (مَرْفُوعٌ بِضَمّةٍ مُقَدَّرةٍ) because the preposition comes in the way (اِشْتِغالُ الْمَحَلِّ بِحَرَكةٍ) and drags the verb visibly into the genitive case (حَرْفِ الْجَرِّ الزَّائِدِ مَجْرُورٌ).

➤ Can an **entire sentence** supply the position of the "passive subject"? In the prime of Classical Arabic, some grammarians stated that the نائِبُ الْفاعِلِ can't be a sentence. In principle, this is true. However, there are situations when a sentence can be interpreted as the *subject of the passive*. This is similar to the discussions about the nature of the subject (الْفاعِلُ) which we covered in *questions #209 and #290*. In the following examples, the نائِبُ الْفاعِلِ is highlighted in gray.

It was known how you came.	عُرِفَ كَيْفَ جِئْتَ.

Here, the sentence كَيْفَ جِئْتَ is interpreted as a **single entity** (الْجُمْلةُ الْمُؤَوَّلةُ بِالْمُفْرَدِ). It has the equivalent meaning of: عُرِفَ كَيْفِيّةُ مَجِيئِكَ (*The manner of your coming is known*).

In the Qur'an you also find such constructions.

Sura 2:11	When it is said to them, "Do not cause corruption in the land," they say, "We are only putting things right."	وَإِذَا قِيلَ لَهُمْ لَا تُفْسِدُوا فِي الْأَرْضِ قَالُوا إِنَّمَا نَحْنُ مُصْلِحُونَ.

Here, the subject of the passive is a verbal sentence which is placed in the position of a nominal case (فِي مَحَلِّ رَفْعِ نائِبِ فاعِلٍ بِضَمّةٍ مُقَدَّرةٍ).

300. What was the function of the نائِبُ الْفاعِلِ in the active voice?

Most probably it was a direct object.

The subject of a passive verb (نائِبُ الْفاعِلِ) often had a "previous life" before it was converted. Several jobs are possible. For our analysis we assume that the active voice was first.

A. The subject of the passive voice was the **direct object** (مَفْعُولٌ بِهِ).

I understood **the lesson** (= direct object).	فَهِمْتُ الدَّرْسَ.
The lesson (**subject of the passive**) was understood.	فُهِمَ الدَّرْسُ.

What happens, if a verb can have **two objects**? You usually use the first object as the نائِبُ الْفَاعِلِ. A good example of a verb with two objects is *to name* (سَمَّى). In the active voice, you have two choices:

1) You use the verb with two objects. This style is used in the Qur'an.

Sura 3:36	And I have named her Mary.	وَإِنِّي سَمَّيْتُهَا مَرْيَمَ.

Notice that the Arabic word *Mary* takes the accusative case since it is the second direct object – however, it is a diptote (female proper name, more than three letters); therefore, it gets only one فَتْحَةٌ. The first object is the pronoun *her*. Remark: *Mary* is probably of Aramaic origin (מרים).

2) You substitute the second object and add the preposition بـ in front of the *name* which you want to give to a person or thing. This option is common in spoken Arabic.

Let's check an example to illustrate option A:

active	The parents named the child 'Alī.	سَمَّى الْوَالِدانِ الطِّفْلَ عَلِيًّا.
passive	The child was named 'Alī.	الطِّفْلُ سُمِّيَ عَلِيًّا.

Let's analyze the sentence in the passive voice:

Subject (مُبْتَدَأٌ) of the nominal sentence, nominative (مَرْفُوعٌ).	الطِّفْلُ
Verb in the passive voice. The subject (نائِبُ الْفَاعِلِ) of the passive verb is a hidden pronoun (ضَمِيرٌ مُسْتَتِرٌ) expressing *he* (هُوَ).	سُمِّيَ
Second direct object (مَفْعُولٌ بِهِ ثانٍ), accusative case (مَنْصُوبٌ).	عَلِيًّا
Where is the **predicate** (خَبَرٌ) of the nominal sentence? This position is filled by the sentence consisting of the verb in the passive voice plus the نائِبُ الْفَاعِلِ; therefore, this sentence is placed in the position of a nominative case (فِي مَحَلِّ رَفْعِ خَبَرٍ).	

The same is true if you have **three objects** in a sentence. You choose the **first** object for the نائِبُ الْفاعِلِ.

1	Active voice (الْبِناءُ لِلْمَعْلُومِ)	أَعْلَمْتُ الطّالِبَ الْحُضُورَ مُهِمًّا.
	I informed the student that attendance is important.	
2	Passive voice (الْبِناءُ لِلْمَجْهُولِ)	أُعْلِمَ الطّالِبُ الْحُضُورَ مُهِمًّا.
	The student was informed that attendance is important.	

الطّالِبُ is the نائِبُ الْفاعِلِ. The word الْحُضُورَ is placed as the **second** object (مَفْعُولٌ بِهِ ثانٍ) and is in the accusative case (مَنْصُوبٌ). What about the last word (مُهِمًّا)? It serves as the third object (مَفْعُولٌ بِهِ ثالِثٌ); therefore, it is also located in the position of an accusative case.

What happens if the sentence in the active voice doesn't have a direct object? This is the situation when we deal with **intransitive** verbs (فِعْلٌ لازِمٌ). We will need some tricks and use words that are suitable for a نائِبُ الْفاعِلِ (see question #299).

In the examples so far, the subject of the passive was a transformed direct object. In all the following examples (C and D), this is **not** the case.

B. The نائِبُ الْفاعِلِ is represented by the مَصْدَر of the respective verb in the passive voice. This is tricky.

He was hit hard.	ضُرِبَ ضَرْبٌ شَدِيدٌ.
The word ضَرْبٌ is the نائِبُ الْفاعِلِ in the nominative case (مَرْفُوعٌ). It is the مَصْدَر of the I-verb ضَرَبَ - يَضْرِبُ.	

C. The نائِبُ الْفاعِلِ can be an **adverb** (ظَرْفٌ).

1	An enjoyable night was spent.	سُهِرَتْ لَيْلَةٌ مُمْتِعَةٌ.
2	Ramadan was fasted.	صِيمَ رَمَضانُ.
3	He was seated in front of the leader.	جُلِسَ أَمامَ الْقائِدِ.
	Note: The word أَمامَ is the first part of a إِضافةٌ; it is the نائِبُ فاعِلٍ.	

D. The نائِبُ الْفَاعِلِ can be a prepositional phrase (الْجارُّ وَالْمَجْرُورُ).

The matter was considered.	نُظِرَ فِي الْأَمْرِ.
It was regretted.	أُسِفَ عَلَيْهِ.

Preposition (حَرْفُ الْجَرِّ).	عَلَى
Pronominal suffix (ضَمِيرٌ مُتَّصِلٌ). What you see here is not a case marker! The ه has a fixed, indeclinable shape (مَبْنِيٌّ) due to the preceding letter ي. Regarding its position, the ه is placed in the position of a genitive case due to the preposition (فِي مَحَلِّ جَرٍّ بِعَلَى).	ه
What about the **subject of the passive**? The نائِبُ الْفَاعِلِ is the entire prepositional phrase (الْجارُّ وَالْمَجْرُورُ); visibly and acoustically we notice the genitive case (مَجْرُورٌ لَفْظًا), however, regarding its grammatical position in the sentence, the entire شِبْهُ الْجُمْلةِ is placed in the position of a nominative case (مَرْفُوعٌ مَحَلًّا).	

Watch out: Usually the passive verb takes the same gender as the نائِبُ الْفَاعِلِ. However, if the word after the preposition has the feminine gender, we don't use the feminine form of the passive verb. Instead, we use the **masculine verb form** (though it looks weird).

correct	Hind was passed by.	مُرَّ بِهِنْدٍ.
bad style; some consider it incorrect.		مُرَّتْ بِهِنْدٍ.

In the above example, it would be possible to put the prepositional phrase in front of the verb.

correct	Hind was crossed/passed by.	بِهِنْدٍ مُرَّ.

301. What is the regent (عامِلٌ) of the نائِبُ الْفَاعِلِ؟

It is either the verb or the passive participle (اسْمُ الْمَفْعُولِ).

The second option, the passive participle, may cause difficulties.

This is a man whose nature is liked.	هذا رَجُلٌ مَحْبُوبٌ خُلُقُهُ.

خُلْقُ is a نائِبُ فاعِلٍ in the nominative case (مَرْفُوعٌ), governed by the passive participle (مَحْبُوبٌ). The pronominal suffix (ضَمِيرٌ مُتَّصِلٌ), i.e., the ه, serves as the second part of the إضافةٌ.

302. Which verbs are almost only used in the passive voice?

There are at least a dozen of them.

Here are some common verbs which are only used in the **passive**:

to be confused	يُشْدَهُ I	شُدِهَ	to be astonished; to be surprised at	يُدْهَشُ I	دُهِشَ مِنْ or لِ
to be very devoted; to fall in love with	يُولَعُ IV	أُولِعَ بِ	to be passionately fond of; to be madly in love with	يُشْغَفُ I	شُغِفَ بِ
to faint; to lose consciousness	أُغْمِيَ IV	أُغْمِيَ عَلَيْهِ	to be hastened; to be hurried to	أُهْرِعَ IV	هُرِّعَ or أُهْرِعَ إِلَى
to turn pale	يُمْتَقَعُ VIII	أُمْتُقِعَ	to be concerned about	يُعْنَى I	عُنِيَ بِ

Interestingly those verbs were already listed by Abū Mansūr al-Thaʻālibī (الثَّعالِبِيّ), a grammarian of Persian origin (961/350AH - 1039/429AH), in his book *Fiqh al-Lugha* (فِقْه اللُّغة) and by Ibn Durayd (دُرَيْد), a grammarian from Basra, who lived in the 9th century.

Why are these verbs important? It has to do with the analysis of the sentence and the functions of the words (إعْرابٌ). Many classical grammarians thought that what is placed after those verbs is the regular **subject of a verbal sentence** (فاعِلٌ) and not the subject of the passive voice (نائِبُ عَن الْفاعِلِ). For example:

Zayd was taken care of in this regard/matter.	عُنِيَ زَيْدٌ بِهذا الْأَمْرِ.

Past tense verb in the passive voice.	عُنِيَ
Subject (فاعِلٌ) in the nominative case (مَرْفُوعٌ بِالضَّمّةِ الظّاهِرةِ).	زَيْدٌ

Scholars who favor this view state that these verbs were known to the Arabs in the passive voice only. Those scholars who state that these verbs had also been used in the active voice say that the word after the verb is actually the **subject of the passive voice** (نائِبٌ عَن الْفاعِلِ).

Chapter 11: The Objects (الْمَفاعِيلُ)

303. Is every verb capable of having a direct object?

No, it is not.

Every verbal sentence (جُمْلةٌ فِعْلِيّةٌ) consists of **two essential, constituents** (رُكْنانِ): a **verb** (فِعْلٌ) and a **subject** (فاعِلٌ; or the subject's substitute in the passive voice - نائِبُ الْفاعِلِ).

Without these two pillars, you can't produce a verbal sentence. The verb is the source or essence (أَصْلٌ) of all operator (عَوامِلُ) in Arabic. It is the verb that governs the subject in the state of the nominative (رَفْعٌ). Furthermore, it is the verb that governs all kinds of objects (مَفْعُولٌ), the adverb (ظَرْفٌ), and the circumstantial qualifier (حالٌ) in the state of the accusative (نَصْبٌ).

As soon as you have a verb and a subject, you have an independent, basic sentence (مَعْنًى مُسْتَقِلٌّ) which makes sense by itself. However, the sentence might need additional information to support or clarify the basic meaning (الْمَعْنَى الْأَساسِيُّ).

Grammarians call such words فَضَلاتٌ (singular فَضْلةٌ) which literally mean *surplus, overplus*. In grammar, we use this term for words that could theoretically be deleted without destroying the sentence. They are non-predicative elements of the sentence.

The most common object is the **direct object** (مَفْعُولٌ بِهِ). It is the thing or person which is immediately affected by the action of the verb. But is every verb capable of having a direct object? No, it isn't.

There are **verbs that don't need an object**. They are called *intransitive* verbs (فِعْلٌ لازِمٌ) or *limited, restricted* verbs (فِعْلٌ قاصِرٌ). The I-verb يَلْزِمُ - لَزِمَ means *to cling, to accompany*. The only job of a فِعْلٌ لازِمٌ is to bind the nominative case (رَفْعٌ) to the subject (فاعِلٌ); the governing power ends there. It is satisfied with a subject to convey a complete meaning and doesn't need an object.

If you want to add more information, it is necessary to *accompany* a preposition. The result is an indirect object. This explains why the passive participle (اِسْمُ مَفْعُولٍ) of intransitive verbs don't make sense. For example: *to laugh* (ضَحِكَ); the passive participle is مَضْحُوكٌ (*laughed*). You can't use it alone; you need to provide more information added by a preposition (*is laughed about*). What about the term قاصِرٌ (*limited*)? It expresses that it is impossible for such verbs to accept an object.

Arabic knows **verbs** that need **one, two**, or even **three** objects. They are called فِعْلٌ مُتَعَدٍّ. The term مُتَعَدٍّ means *transitive* and is the active participle of the V-verb تَعَدَّى - يَتَعَدَّى (R3=و) which means *to cross; to exceed*. Figuratively speaking, the influence of the verb extends beyond the subject and transposes to an object. Such verbs can form a passive participle. For example: *to write* (كَتَبَ) → *written* (مَكْتُوبٌ).

The word *transitive* entered English via Latin. The Latin word *transire* means *to cross, to go over*. In grammar, *transitive* basically describes that **activity is transferred from an agent** (doer) **to a patient** (object). It is helpful to imagine that the accusative state (نَصْبٌ) is the visualization of the relationship between the verb and another word (object).

The accusative case in a verbal sentence adds more information (meaning) to the verb/the action.

304. أَوَدُّ أَنْ أَزُورَهُ (*I want to visit him*) - Is there a direct object?

Yes, there is.

Let's start with an **important rule**:

> If there is **only one direct object**, it must either be a plain, pure noun (اِسْمٌ صَرِيحٌ) or an interpreted مَصْدَرٌ (a so-called مَصْدَرٌ مُؤَوَّلٌ).

pure noun	I understood the lesson.	فَهِمْتُ الدَّرْسَ.

الدَّرْسَ is the direct object (مَفْعُولٌ بِهِ) and therefore takes the accusative case (مَنْصُوبٌ بِالْفَتْحةِ الظّاهِرةِ), clearly marked by the vowel "a".

1	interpreted مَصْدَرٌ ➔	I want/would	أَوَدُّ أَنْ أَزُورَهُ.
2	original مَصْدَرٌ (same meaning) ➔	like to visit him.	= أَوَدُّ زِيَارَتَهُ.

In sentence 1, we have an interpreted infinitive noun (مَصْدَرٌ مُؤَوَّلٌ). The particle (أَنْ) is a حَرْفُ نَصْبٍ وَمَصْدَرٍ. After this device, you need to place a (present tense) verb in the subjunctive mood (مَنْصُوبٌ), marked by the فَتْحَةُ. What about the pronoun suffix ﻪ? This ضَمِيرٌ مُتَّصِلٌ is in the position of the **direct object**! But wait! It is **not the direct object** of the **main sentence** which started with أَوَدُّ, but of the second verb (*to visit*) as this is a sentence within the primary, larger sentence.

The pronoun has an indeclinable shape (مَبْنِيٌّ عَلَى الضَّمِّ), but since it serves as the direct object, it is placed in the position of an accusative case (فِي مَحَلِّ نَصْبٍ مَفْعُولٌ بِهِ).

What about the **direct object** of the **main verb** (*I want*)? The مَصْدَرٌ مُؤَوَّلٌ (consisting of أَنْ + verb) does the job of the direct object (مَفْعُولٌ بِهِ) and appears grammatically in the position of an accusative case (فِي مَحَلِّ نَصْبٍ).

305. Can only verbs have (direct) objects in Arabic?

No, there are other word forms as well (that do the job of verbs).

What does it mean when we say that a word does the job of a verb? Answer: the word has the power to operate on other words. Therefore, not only verbs can govern direct objects in the accusative case. Words that may have verbal power are the "usual suspects" (see #209).

1. The مَصْدَرٌ

In the following example, *lesson* (الدَّرْسَ) is in the accusative case although there is **no verb** in the sentence! It is governed by إِعْدَادٌ, a noun (مَصْدَرٌ), which has the power to be an operator, regent (عَامِلٌ).

Preparing your lesson is useful. (literal translation: Your preparation of the lesson is useful.)	إِعْدَادُكَ الدَّرْسَ مُفِيدٌ.

Subject (مُبْتَدَأٌ) of the nominal sentence; nominative (مَرْفُوعٌ بِالضَّمَّةِ الظَّاهِرَةِ). Regarding the form, this is a مَصْدَرٌ.	إِعْدَادُ

Pronominal suffix (ضَمِيرٌ مُتَّصِلٌ), serving as the second part of the إِضافةٌ. Thus, it is grammatically in the position of a genitive case – but since it has a fixed shape (مَبْنِيٌّ عَلَى الْفَتْحِ), you can't see the actual case marker.	كَ
Direct object (مَفْعُولٌ بِهِ), in the accusative case (مَنْصُوبٌ بِالْفَتْحةِ الظّاهِرة). It is governed by the مَصْدَرٌ, so we say that the word إِعْداد is the operator (عامِلٌ) of the word الدَّرْسَ.	الدَّرْسَ
Predicate (خَبَرٌ) of the nominal sentence, nominative (مَرْفُوعٌ).	مُفِيدٌ

2. The active (اِسْمُ الْفاعِلِ) and passive participle (اِسْمُ الْمَفْعُولِ)

Active and passive participles have the power to govern words in the accusative case (نَصْبٌ). This means that the active participle can go along with objects. If an active participle is <u>definite</u> (مَعْرِفةٌ) by الـ, it can work as a governor (عامِلٌ) without any restrictions. Why is that? Let's compare a regular sentence with a verb and its equivalent with an active participle: *The thief steals (will steal) the money.*

1	**with an active participle**		**with a present tense verb**	2
	هٰذا السّارِقُ الْمالَ.	↔	يَسْرِقُ اللِّصُّ الْمالَ.	

The definite article which you see in السّارِقُ is, in fact, more of a relative pronoun. We could say that الـ equals الَّذِي in the meaning of: *he who...* This special type of الـ only occurs with the active and passive participle as well as the الصِّفّةُ الْمُشَبَّهةُ which often expresses a quasi participle (in the meaning of an adjective). The sentence with the active participle can be understood as هٰذا الَّذِي سَرَقَ الْمالَ.

The relative "pronoun" (اِسْمٌ مَوْصُولٌ) acquires its definiteness not by الـ which is included in many of them (e.g. الَّذِي). It is the part which follows (صِلَتُهُ) that makes it definite – nevertheless, some grammarians hold the view that the اِسْمٌ مَوْصُولٌ already conveys some kind of definiteness and determination.

Now, if the الـ in the active participle would be there for determination and definition (لِلتَّعْرِيفِ), it would bring the active participle closer to a noun and away from its resemblance of a verb.

Eventually, it would be closer to a إِسْمٌ جَامِدٌ which can't work as a regent. Let's analyze a sentence.

He wrote the book yesterday.	هُوَ الْكَاتِبُ الْكِتَابَ أَمْسِ.
Personal pronoun (ضَمِيرٌ مُنْفَصِلٌ) which serves here as the subject (مُبْتَدَأٌ) of a nominal sentence. Hence, it occupies the position of a nominative case (فِي مَحَلِّ رَفْعٍ).	هُوَ
Predicate (خَبَرٌ) of the nominal sentence (جُمْلَةٌ اِسْمِيّةٌ), nominative case (مَرْفُوعٌ بِالضَّمّةِ الظّاهِرةِ). The word الْكَاتِبُ is an active participle (إِسْمُ الْفَاعِلِ).	الْكَاتِبُ
Direct object in the accusative case (مَفْعُولٌ بِهِ مَنْصُوبٌ), governed (مَعْمُولٌ) by the active participle (الْكَاتِبُ).	الْكِتَابَ
Adverb of time (ظَرْفُ زَمانٍ), indeclinable (مَبْنِيٌّ عَلَى الْكَسْرِ), so the last vowel is always "i". Nevertheless, أَمْسِ is placed in the position of an accusative case (فِي مَحَلِّ نَصْبٍ). It is **governed by the active participle**. An adverb adds information to the action which, in our example, is expressed by an active participle.	أَمْسِ

Now, what happens if the active participle is **in**definite? Then the إِسْمُ الْفَاعِلِ can work as a regent (عامِلٌ) if the active participle serves as a **circumstantial description** (حالٌ) or points to the **future** (الْإِسْتِقْبالُ).

حالٌ	I saw your brother carrying his luggage.	رَأَيْتُ أَخَاكَ حازِمٌ أَمْتِعتَهُ.
future tense	Zayd will understand the lesson tomorrow.	زَيْدٌ فاهِمٌ الدَّرْسَ غَدًا.

| Sura 18:18 | We turned them over, to the right and the left, with their dog stretching out its forelegs at the entrance. | وَنُقَلِّبُهُمْ ذَاتَ الْيَمِينِ وَذَاتَ الشّمَالِ وَكَلْبُهُم بَاسِطٌ ذِرَاعَيْهِ بِالْوَصِيدِ. |

ذِرَاعَيْهِ is the direct object (مَفْعُولٌ بِهِ); it is governed by the active participle (بَاسِطٌ) which serves as a حالٌ here. The حالٌ is not the main clause (which denotes something that happened in the past). The حالٌ serves only a description for the main action.

We need to talk about the **past tense** (الْماضِي). Can we use a إِسْمُ الْفاعِلِ (which operates on a direct object) for an action that is completed? Let's use a rather heavy sentence for the sake of illustration: *I killed Zayd yesterday.*

impossible	Is Zayd now dead or not?	أَنا قاتِلٌ زَيْدًا أَمْسِ.
	We don't have a confirmation. We can't know for sure. Since we assume that what happened – the action – is completed (الْماضِي = perfect tense = action is completed), most grammarians say that this construction is **not** possible in Arabic.	
theoretically possible	We can assume here that Zayd is dead – either after or before the statement.	أَنا قاتِلُ زَيْدٍ أَمْسِ.
	We want to convey more of a state than an action. We use a إضافةٌ-construction to indicate that.	

This shows that an active participle does **not work as a regent for an object** if the action conveyed by the active participle is related to the **past tense**. The past tense in Arabic expresses an aspect; i.e., an action is over or not, and not necessarily a tense in the notion of time. Therefore, we can say that if it targets the past tense, an active participle is closer to the **nature of a noun** – in the sense of effect or status (and not action). In such a situation, you should form a إضافةٌ-construction. For example: قاتِلُ النّاسِ which may be rendered as *one who killed; has killed; had killed.*

However, if we target the **present tense or future**, you have two options, because the character of the active participle is pretty much between a noun and verb. In fact, the term we use for present tense in Arabic is فِي الْمُضارِعِ لِاسْمِ الْفاعِلِ – see #62.

The phrase *one who kills people* could be rendered as قاتِلُ النّاسِ (if we treat the active participle closer to a noun → إضافةٌ) or as قاتِلٌ النّاسَ (if we see it closer to a verb → direct object).

Let's return to the question of **indefiniteness**. Can an indefinite active participle work as a regent for an object? Yes, but it is complicated.

The إسْمُ الْفاعِلِ can be indefinite, but it needs to depend on something that comes earlier in the sentence. In grammar, we call this concept إعْتِمادٌ (*reliance; dependence*). Certain devices and structures help us to achieve that. Basically, the active participle **cannot** be the first word in a sentence or utterance – but must be preceded by a subject, negation, etc. Put simply, we have one of the following situations.

a) the indefinite active participle is **negated** (نَفْيٌ) or...

b) used in **questions** (اِسْتِفْهامٌ) or...

c) serves as the **predicate** (خَبَرٌ) or is...

d) an **attribute/adjective** (صِفَةٌ) for the thing or person which it describes (مَوْصوفٌ).

a) The sentence is negated (نَفْيٌ).

Zayd is not reading a book.	ما قارِئٌ زَيْدٌ كِتابًا.
كِتابًا is the direct object (مَفْعولٌ بِهِ مَنْصوبٌ). The active particle قارِئٌ is its regent (عامِلٌ).	

b) The sentence is a question (اِسْتِفْهامٌ).

Does Zayd read a book?	هَلْ قارِئٌ زَيْدٌ كِتابًا؟
Same here: كِتابًا is the direct object (مَفْعولٌ بِهِ مَنْصوبٌ); the regent, operator, governor (عامِلٌ) is the active participle قارِئٌ.	

c) The indefinite اِسْمُ الْفاعِلِ serves as the predicate (خَبَرٌ) in a nominal sentence (جُمْلَةٌ اِسْمِيَّةٌ).

Muhammad is reading a book.	مُحَمَّدٌ قارِئٌ كِتابًا.

مُحَمَّدٌ	Subject (مُبْتَدَأٌ) of the nominal sentence, nominative (مَرْفوعٌ).
قارِئٌ	قارِئٌ is an active participle.. It serves as the predicate (خَبَرٌ) of the nominal sentence; nominative case (مَرْفوعٌ بِالضَّمّةِ الظّاهِرةِ).
كِتابًا	Direct object (مَفْعولٌ بِهِ); in the accusative case (مَنْصوبٌ بِالْفَتْحةِ الظّاهِرةِ). The word قارِئٌ is the operator, governor; كِتابًا is the patient (governed word).

What about an <u>indefinite</u> subject? If the active participle is purely indefinite, it struggles to serve as the subject (مُبْتَدَأٌ) of a nominal sentence. You can't start a جُمْلَةٌ اِسْمِيَّةٌ with a single, indefinite noun. You need to reverse the word-order or use some tricks. See *question #213*.

d) The active participle is an adjective (صِفةٌ).

I saw a man reading a book.	رَأَيْتُ رَجُلًا قَارِئًا كِتابًا.

Direct object, governed by the verb رَأَيْتُ.	رَجُلًا
This is an adjective that is describing the word *man*. Why is it an adjective and not a حالٌ? Because the حالٌ must refer to a word that is **definite** (and رَجُلٌ is indefinite). Adjectives must agree with the word they describe (with the مَوْصوفٌ); therefore, it also has to be in the accusative case (صِفةٌ مَنْصوبةٌ).	قَارِئًا
Another **direct object** (مَفْعولٌ بِهِ), also in the accusative (مَنْصوبٌ بِالْفَتْحةِ الظّاهِرةِ). Watch out! The عامِل of this direct object is the **active participle** – and **not** the verb at the beginning!	كِتابًا

3. The exaggerated noun (صيغةُ الْمُبالَغةِ)

The exaggerated noun can govern a direct object (مَفْعولٌ بِهِ) in the accusative case (مَنْصوبٌ). What we said earlier about the active participle (اِسْمُ الْفاعِلِ) here also applies to the صيغةُ الْمُبالَغةِ.

He is bearing their burdens.	هُوَ حَمّالٌ أَعْباءَهُم.
أَعْباءَ is the direct object (مَفْعولٌ بِهِ) in the accusative case (مَنْصوبٌ). It is governed by a form (noun) of exaggeration (صيغةُ الْمُبالَغةِ), in our example, by the word حَمّالٌ. Thus, the صيغةُ الْمُبالَغةِ works as the regent (عامِل) here.	

4. The اِسْمُ الْفِعْلِ (interjection denoting a sense of a verb).

Such words are abstract **nouns** which express an action, passion, or state – see *question #93*.

Here is the book!	هاكَ الْكِتابَ!
There is the book!	دُونَكَ الْكِتابَ!

Both words are a اِسْمُ فِعْلِ أَمْرٍ and can have the meaning of *Here you are! Take...! Watch out for! Beware of!* They do not have a po-	هاكَ دُونَكَ

sition in إِعْراب. Their subject (فاعِلٌ) is a hidden, implied pronoun (ضَمِيرٌ مُسْتَتِرٌ) expressing *you* (أَنْتَ).	
Direct object (مَفْعُولٌ بِهِ) in the accusative case (مَنْصُوبٌ). It is governed by هاكَ ; دُونَكَ which is the reason why it is مَنْصُوبٌ.	الْكِتابَ

Sura 5:105	You who believe, you are responsible for your own souls.	يَا أَيُّهَا الَّذِينَ آمَنُوا عَلَيْكُمْ أَنْفُسَكُمْ.
إِسْمُ أَنْفُسَكُمْ is the direct object, governed by عَلَيْكُمْ. The part عَلَيْكُمْ is a الْفِعْلِ. It has governing power which is the reason that أَنْفُسَكُمْ is مَنْصُوبٌ.		

5. Forms of astonishment and admiration (التَّعَجُّبُ) – see *question #434*.

VERBS WITH TWO (OR THREE) OBJECTS

306. Which verbs need two objects?

Verbs which express to give, to mean/think, and "transformation".

Verbs with two objects are difficult to handle for learners of Arabic. Arabic does not have a special case marker to distinguish between the two objects as other languages do, e.g., German (Dativ). In addition, unlike in English, verbs with two objects don't use a preposition for the second object, which would make the direction (= *to whom*) clearer.

There are three main categories of Arabic verbs with two objects:

1. Verbs that point to the meaning of *"to give"* (الْإِعْطاءُ).

to put on (clothes)	يُلْبِسُ	أَلْبَسَ	IV	to give (R3=ي)	يُعْطِي	أَعْطَى	IV
to dress (R3=و)	يَكْسُو	كَسا	I	to donate (R1=و)	يَهَبُ	وَهَبَ	I
to name (R3=و)	يُسَمِّي	سَمَّى	II	to grant	يَمْنَحُ	مَنَحَ	I
to decrease; to lack	يَنْقُصُ	نَقَصَ	I	to add (R2=ي)	يَزِيدُ	زادَ	I

2. Verbs of meaning (أَفْعالُ الْقُلُوبِ).

You will encounter many terms for the Arabic expression أَفْعالُ الْقُلُوبِ, among them are *verbs of meaning; mental verbs; verbs of affectivity (ability to experience affects: feelings, emotions, judgment, motivations); verbs of certainty and doubt.*

These verbs relate to certainty, truth, reality (الْيَقِينُ), doubt (الشَّكُّ), or denial (الْإِنْكارُ) and signify an act that takes place in your mind. They are a sub-category of the so-called ظَنَّ *and its sisters* (أَخَواتُ ظَنَّ).

These verbs have a peculiarity: the **origin** of their **two objects** is, in fact, a **nominal sentence** (جُمْلَةٌ إِسْمِيّةٌ) with a subject (مُبْتَدَأٌ) and a predicate (خَبَرٌ). These verbs abrogate (~ replace) the nominal sentence and are thus called فِعْلٌ ناسِخٌ; see #229 for the meaning of ناسِخٌ.

However, unlike كانَ they aren't defective, incomplete verbs (فِعْلٌ ناقِصٌ) because they convey and **point to an action** and therefore **need** a subject of a verbal sentence (فاعِلٌ). So it's no surprise that we're dealing with verbal sentences (جُمْلَةٌ فِعْلِيّةٌ) here. There are two categories (types) of *verbs of the heart:*

a) Verbs indicating **certainty** (الْيَقِينُ)

to see; to think; to believe (irregular verb)	يَرَى	رَأَى	I	to know; to find out	يَعْلَمُ	عَلِمَ	I
to know; to notice (R3=ي)	يَدْرِي	دَرَى	I	to find; to perceive (R1=و)	يَجِدُ	وَجَدَ	I
Learn! Know! (only in the imperative)	تَعَلَّمْ		V	to find (R3=و)	يُلْفِي	أَلْفَى	IV

Let's see the difference: عَلِمَ will get two objects if عَلِمَ denotes *to be convinced* (الْيَقِينُ), *to know a thing intuitively* – but it will only get one object if it conveys the meaning of *to become acquainted with, to possess learning, to know* in a literal sense, i.e., *to have knowledge* (مَعْرِفةٌ). Therefore, if it takes **two objects**, you usually translate عَلِمَ with: *to be convinced, to perceive, to understand, to be positive.*

The difference between عَرَفَ (*to known*) and عَلِمَ is that عَرَفَ refers to distinct and specific knowledge, while عَلِمَ is more general. The opposite of عَرَفَ is أَنْكَرَ (*to deny*). The opposite of عَلِمَ is جَهِلَ (*to be ignorant*).

Watch out: When you say وَجَدْتُ (*I found*; taking two objects), the verb doesn't convey *to find* (لَقِيتُ) in the literal sense – but the meaning of *to be ascertained, to be convinced* (أَيْقَنْتُ). The same is true for the other above mentioned verbs. Don't translate them literally!

I believed that diligence is the way to success.	رَأَيْتُ الْجِدَّ سَبِيلَ النَّجَاحِ.
I was convinced that diligence is the way to success.	عَلِمْتُ الْجِدَّ سَبِيلَ النَّجَاحِ.

Here, the verbs are not used in their literal sense. They convey the meaning of *I was convinced* (عَلِمْتُ) – and not: *I knew* (عَرَفْتُ); *I saw* (رَأَيْتُ).

الْجِدَّ is the first object (مَفْعُولٌ بِهِ أَوَّلٌ مَنْصُوبٌ) and سَبِيلَ is the second object (مَفْعُولٌ بِهِ ثَانٍ). Both objects were originally the subject (مُبْتَدَأٌ) and the predicate (خَبَرٌ):

Diligence is the way to success.	الْجِدُّ سَبِيلُ النَّجَاحِ.

b) Verbs which indicate **expectation** (الرُّجْحَانُ).

to think; believe (R2=R3)	يَظُنُّ	ظَنَّ	I	to imagine; think (R2=ي)	يَخَالُ	خَالَ *	I
to suppose; think	يَحْسَبُ	حَسِبَ	I	to think; deem	يَزْعُمُ	زَعَمَ	I
to consider; to count (R2=R3)	يَعُدُّ	عَدَّ	I	to think; assert (R3=و)	يَحْجو	حَجَا	I
Suppose! Think! (imperative only)	هَبْ!			to imagine; fancy (R1=و)	يَتَوَهَّمُ	تَوَهَّمَ	V
				to think; believe	تَجْعَلَ	جَعَلَ	I

I believed that Zayd is generous.	ظَنَنْتُ زَيْدًا كَرِيمًا.

* In old texts, the verb خَالَ occurs in two forms in the first person singular: the regular أَخَالُ and the more common إِخَالُ (which formed by using a كَسْرَة ("i") under the هَمْزَة). The past tense is, 1st person sing., is خِلْتُ.

I think Zayd is your brother.	إِخَالُ زَيْدًا أَخَاكَ.

Watch out! If you use these verbs in a literal sense, you will get a different grammatical assessment (see *question #312*).

3. Verbs of transformation (أَفْعالُ التَّحْويلِ), also called أَفْعالُ التَّصْيِيرِ

They convey a meaning of **conversion** or **transfer** (التَّحْويلُ).

to make; to bring about	يَجْعَل	جَعَلَ	I		to cause to be (R2=ي)	يُصَيِّر	صَيَّرَ	II
to leave; to render	يَتْرُك	تَرَكَ	I		to take, to adopt (R1=ء)	يَتَّخِذُ	إتَّخَذَ	VIII

This factory makes cheese out of milk.	هذا الْمَصْنَعُ يَجْعَلُ حَلِيبًا جُبْنًا.
The aggressors left the village in ruins.	تَرَكَ الْمُعْتَدُونَ الْقَرْيَةَ أَطْلالًا.
I made the rope strong (caused it to be strong).	تَرَكْتُ الْحَبْلَ شَدِيدًا.

307. Why do you sometimes use أَنَّ after verbs?

This only happens in verbs that take two objects.

If verbs can have two objects, what do these objects actually look like? After *verbs of transformation* (أَفْعالُ التَّحْويلِ or أَفْعالُ التَّصْيِيرِ), we need two nouns. As for the other verbs with two objects, we have two more, quite sophisticated options:

a) أَنَّ plus its two governed factors (أَنَّ وَمَعْمُولَاها);

b) أَنْ plus verb in the present tense, subjunctive mood (مَنْصُوبٌ);

Both options produce an **interpreted infinitive** (مَصْدَرٌ مُؤَوَّلٌ) which takes over the role of the two objects.

I thought that Zayd is generous.	ظَنَنْتُ أَنَّ زَيْدًا كَرِيمٌ.

The "subject" (اِسْمُ أَنَّ); it needs the accusative case (مَنْصُوبٌ).	زَيْدًا
Predicate (خَبَرُ أَنَّ); in the nominative case (مَرْفُوعٌ).	كَرِيمٌ
The *interpreted* مَصْدَرٌ consists of أَنَّ plus its two governed parts (مَعْمُولَاها). It	

takes the position of an accusative case **because it overtook the role of the two objects of** ظَنَّ and works as a replacement for them (فِي مَحَلِّ نَصْبٍ سَدَّ مَسَدَّ مَفْعُولَيْ ظَنَّ). See *question #37* for an explanation of the term سَدَّ مَسَدَّ.

Whoever thinks that he can succeed without work is delusional.	مَنْ ظَنَّ أَنْ يَنْجَحَ بِلا عَمَلٍ فَهُوَ وَاهِمٌ.

The interpreted مَصْدَرٌ (أَنْ يَنْجَحَ) is set in the location of an accusative case, overtaking the role of the two objects (فِي مَحَلِّ نَصْبٍ سَدَّ مَسَدَّ مَفْعُولَيْ ظَنَّ).

Remark: Some grammarians suggested that it is not correct to say that the مَصْدَرٌ مُؤَوَّلٌ would take over the role of both objects. They say that this is only true for the **first** object. Okay, but then what about the second object? They assume that it is deleted. If we use this logic and look for the missing part, we can interpret the above example as follows:

I believe (that) Zayd is generous.	ظَنَنْتُ أَنَّ زَيْدًا كَرِيمٌ.
→ Supposed meaning of the sentence with أَنَّ:	ظَنَنْتُ كَرَمَ زَيْدٍ ثَابِتًا.

308. Verbs with two objects - What's the nature of these objects?

There is only one "real" direct object.

Verbs that can get two objects are not easy to translate into English. Once you understand the different nature and origin of the two objects, you will develop a better understanding of these verbs. An example:

I gave Zayd a book.	أَعْطَيْتُ زَيْدًا كِتَابًا.

First object (مَفْعُولٌ أَوَّلٌ) in the accusative case (مَنْصُوبٌ).	زَيْدًا
Second (**direct**) object (مَفْعُولٌ بِهِ ثَانٍ), also in the accusative case.	كِتَابًا

In many situations, the second object is a "real" direct object. The first object is more of a "doer" (فَاعِلٌ). Let's continue with our example.

I gave Zayd a book...	...أَعْطَيْتُ زَيْدًا كِتَابًا
...and **Zayd** took the book.	...وَزَيْدٌ أَخَذَ الْكِتَابَ.

Notice: **Zayd** in the 2nd sentence is the subject (اَلْفَاعِلُ) → nominative (مَرْفُوعٌ)!

The famous grammarian Sībawayhi (سيبويه) suggested that the first object, in its origin, had actually been in the genitive case (مَجْرُورٌ).

In our example, this would mean: *I gave __to__ Zayd a book* (أَعْطَيْتُ لِزَيْدٍ كِتَابًا). For this reason, Sībawayhi suggested another term: *indirect object* (مَفْعُولٌ غَيْرُ مُباشِرٍ). This is the term other languages use as well. In German, the sentence would read like this: *Ich gab __dem__ Studenten das Buch.* In French, it would be: *Donnez-__lui__ les timbres.*

309. Verbs with two objects – can you delete one object?

Yes, you can.

You can delete one object if you have a verb pointing to the meaning of *to give* (الْإِعْطاءُ). Usually the **first object** of such verbs is deleted as otherwise the meaning might not be understood.

Second object was deleted	You don't specify **what** (ما) you gave Zayd.	I gave (to) Zayd.	أَعْطَيْتُ زَيْدًا.
First object was deleted	You don't specify **to whom** (مَن) you gave the book.	I gave money.	أَعْطَيْتُ مالًا.

Watch out: It is impossible to delete one of the two objects if the verb is a *verb of the mind* (أَفْعالُ الْقُلُوبِ) or a *verb of transformation* (أَفْعالُ التَّحْوِيلِ). Therefore, it is not correct to say:

I think (that) Zayd.	impossible	ظَنَنْتُ زَيْدًا.
The weaver caused the cloth to.		صَيَّرَ الْحائِكُ الْقُماشَ.

310. Why do *verbs of meaning* often lead to complicated structures?

It is all related to the second object.

Verbs of meaning (أَفْعالُ الْقُلُوبِ), also called *verbs of the heart*, take two objects, and the second one is not always easy to be identified as such. Why? Because it can be a single word (كَلِمَةٌ واحِدةٌ), but also a sentence (جُمْلة) or a prepositional/adverbial phrase (شِبْهُ الْجُمْلةِ).

I learned that diligence leads to success.	عَلِمْتُ الْجِدَّ يُؤَدِّي إلَى النَّجاحِ.

First direct object in the accusative case (مَفْعُولٌ أَوَّلَ مَنْصُوبٌ).	الْجِدَّ
Present tense verb in the indicative mood (فِعْلٌ مُضارِعٌ مَرْفُوعٌ), marked by an estimated, virtual case marker (ضَمّة مُقَدَّرةٍ) as the last letter ي can't carry any vowel. The subject (فاعِلٌ) is a hidden pronoun (ضَمِيرٌ مُسْتَتِرٌ) expressing *he* (هُوَ).	يُؤَدِّي

The verbal sentence (i.e., يُؤَدِّي) consisting of verb and subject is placed in the position of the second direct object and takes over that role. Thus, it is grammatically located in the place of an accusative case. The same would be possible for a prepositional phrase:

The stingy (person) thinks that happiness is to amass money.	يَظُنُّ الْبَخِيلُ السَّعادةَ فِي جَمْعِ الْمالِ.
The prepositional phrase (شِبْهُ الْجُمْلةِ ؛ الْجارُّ وَالْمَجْرُورُ) replaces (takes over) the role of the second direct object and is thus considered to be placed in the position of an accusative case (فِي مَحَلِّ نَصْبٍ سَدَّ مَسَدَّ الْمَفْعُولِ الثَّانِي). See *question #37* for an explanation of the term سَدَّ مَسَدَّ.	

There is another way we can treat the شِبْهُ الْجُمْلةِ grammatically. The prepositional or adverbial phrase is linked to the deleted second direct object (مُتَعَلِّقٌ بِمَفْعُولٍ ثانٍ مَحْذُوفٍ). Fair enough, but if it was deleted, what was there "before"? Let's see:

This is a possible (virtual) meaning of the deleted second object: →	يَظُنُّ السَّعادةَ كائِنَةً فِي جَمْعِ الْمالِ.

311. If there is a *verb of meaning*, can you change the word order?

Yes. But you have to expect some grammatical effects.

Arabic offers some flexibility in the grammatical treatment of sentences that are based on *verbs of meaning* and *of the mind* (أَفْعالُ الْقُلُوبِ), also called *verbs of certainty and doubt*. There are three possible rulings regarding the governing power of such verbs:

option 1	The verb has governing power and induces case endings on other words.	implementation (إِعْمالٌ)
option 2	The governing power of the verb (as a regent) is canceled; abrogated.	cancellation (إِلْغاءٌ)
option 3	The governing power of the verb (i.e., the regent) is suspended.	suspension (تَعْليقٌ)

OPTION 1: This is the <u>necessary</u> if the verb is placed **before** the two objects. In other words, when the verb starts the sentence.

OPTION 2: This is <u>possible</u> if the verb is found **between** the two objects or is placed after them. This happens, for example, when the verb is inserted as a parenthesis (sign in English: em dash). Then the verb can be treated as to exercise **no** grammatical influence upon the clause.

However, you can also apply the standard rules, i.e., the accusative case, which is preferable.

a)	preferred (= option 1)	Zayd is, I thought, gen-	زَيْدًا ظَنَنْتُ كَرِيمًا.
b)	possible (= option 2)	erous.	زَيْدٌ ظَنَنْتُ كَرِيمٌ.

Let's check sentence b) in detail:

Subject (مُبْتَدَأٌ) of the nominal sentence; nominative case (مَرْفُوعٌ).	زَيْدٌ
Past tense verb that **does not work as a regent** (فِعْلٌ غَيْرُ عامِلٍ) and therefore does not induce any case endings.	ظَنَنْتُ
Predicate (خَبَرٌ) in the nominative case (مَرْفُوعٌ).	كَرِيمٌ

What would happen if the verb was placed at the end of the sentence? This would mean that both two objects precede the verb.

Such sentences are tricky. Regarding the case endings, we can apply option 1 or option 2. Contrary to the above example, the **nominative case (option 2)** is preferable – with the effect that the governing power of the verb must be abrogated (إِلْغاءٌ).

| possible (= option 1) | Zayd is generous, I think. | زَيْدًا كَرِيمًا ظَنَنْتُ. |
| preferred (= option 2) | | زَيْدٌ كَرِيمٌ ظَنَنْتُ. |

OPTION 3: The <u>suspension</u> (تَعْلِيقٌ). What is that about? It means that the annulment (إِبْطَالُ عَمَلِها) of the regimen/government takes place only visibly (لَفْظًا). However, if we analyze the word according to its grammatical position in the sentence, the word will get the same "place value" as in option 1 (إِبْقاؤُه مَحَلًّا).

The reason (necessity) for option 3 is the **presence of something that separates the verb** from the two objects – under the condition that this word deserves the precedence in the sentence, the so-called صَدارَةٌ, which literally means *forefront; foremost part*.

All this is usually the situation when the verb is placed at the beginning of the sentence – and what follows is a **negation**, a **question particle**, or an affirmative clause introduced by the **particle** لَ.

The power of the verb as a regent is not killed, but rather suspended (التَّعْلِيقُ فِي اللَّفْظِ لا فِي الْمَعنَى). What is governed by the verb is still regarded as having the position of an accusative, although you might not see or hear it. The "space" (فاصِلٌ) that is used to separate the verb from its *patients* is called الْمانِعُ. It can be one of the following devices:

1. The لامُ الْإِبْتِداءِ: the *inceptive Lām*, also called *inchoative Lām*. It is prefixed (bound) to nouns or verbs in the present tense (see #260). This emphatic لَ accentuates the subject (topic) or predicate (comment); prefixed to verbs, it often strengthens an asseveration (claim, statement).

I was convinced that Zayd is generous.	عَلِمْتُ لَزَيْدٌ كَرِيمٌ.

This particle is a لامُ الْإِبْتِداءِ. It does not have a place in إِعْرابٌ.	لَ
Subject (مُبْتَدَأٌ) of the nominal sentence; in the nominative case.	زَيْدٌ
Predicate (خَبَرٌ) in the nominative case (مَرْفوعٌ).	كَرِيمٌ

The entire nominal sentence, consisting of subject and predicate, is placed in the position of an **accusative case** – because it takes over the role of the two objects of the verb عَلِمَ.

This different to option 2 (the *abrogation*) where we kill the job of the regent (and do not just suspend it). When we strip off the governing power and thus eliminate all implications (option 2), we also free the *patients* (the two objects) – with the result that both former "objects" simply become parts of a nominal sentence.

Now what would happen if we added more information? For example, if we add a conjunction, a coordinator/"coupler"? It will mirror the true case ending according to the place in the sentence. In other words, we will have the accusative case after the conjunction.

I thought that Zayd is laughing.	ظَنَنْتُ لَزَيْدٌ ضَاحِكٌ.
I thought Zayd is laughing **and** 'Amr is angry.	ظَنَنْتُ لَزَيْدٌ ضَاحِكٌ وَعَمْرًا غَاضِبًا.

The expression لَزَيْدٌ ضَاحِكٌ is virtually (عَلَى التَّقْدِيرِ) in the state of an accusative. Why is that? Well, if another object was added, without the particle ل being prefixed, it would get the accusative case.

2. The ل that is placed in the second part (i.e., the complement) of an oath (اللَّامُ الْوَاقِعَةُ فِي جَوَابِ الْقَسَمِ).

I was convinced that the diligent will succeed.	عَلِمْتُ لَيَنْجَحَنَّ الْمُجِدُّ.
This is the underlying meaning: →	عَلِمْتُ أُقْسِمُ لَيَنْجَحَنَّ الْمُجِدُّ.

The "hidden" part of the oath (جُمْلَةُ الْقَسَمِ الْمُقَدَّرَةُ), which is implicitly understood but unwritten, takes over the role of the two objects.

3. Question words (اِسْتِفْهَامٌ)

I do not know **whether** Zayd is present or absent.	لا أَدْرِي أَزَيْدٌ حَاضِرٌ أَمْ غَائِبٌ.

The أ is a question particle (حَرْفُ اِسْتِفْهَامٍ). زَيْدٌ is the subject (مُبْتَدَأٌ مَرْفُوعٌ) of the nominal sentence, حَاضِرٌ is the predicate (خَبَرٌ مَرْفُوعٌ); both get the nominative case. They both together form a جُمْلَة اِسْمِيّة which appears in the place of an accusative case because the entire sentence takes over the role of the two objects of the verb أَدْرِي. In Arabic, we'd say: الْجُمْلَةُ مِن الْمُبْتَدَإِ وَخَبَرِهِ فِي مَحَلِّ نَصْبٍ سَدَّتْ مَسَدَّ مَفْعُولَيْ أَدْرِيِ

4. The negation with إِنْ or لا or ما

I perceived that Zayd is not stingy (avaricious).	عَلِمْتُ ما زَيْدٌ بَخِيلٌ.

زَيْدٌ is the subject (مُبْتَدَأٌ مَرْفُوعٌ) and بَخِيلٌ is the predicate (خَبَرٌ مَرْفُوعٌ). Both form a nominal sentence which takes over the role of the two objects of the verb عَلِمْتُ and is thus placed in the position of an accusative case.

5. The word لَعَلَّ (perhaps) – see question #124 and #243

I do not know, maybe it is good.	لا أَدْرِي لَعَلَّ الْأَمْرَ خَيْرٌ.

The word لَعَلَّ is a so-called حَرْفُ رَجاءٍ ناسِخٌ. We use the term ناسِخٌ because لَعَلَّ has the power to operate on words with the effect that the common rules are overthrown (see #229). → لَعَلَّ follows the rules of إِنَّ.

الْأَمْرَ is the اِسْمُ لَعَلَّ in the accusative (مَنْصُوبٌ), and خَيْرٌ is its predicate (خَبَرٌ لَعَلَّ مَرْفُوعٌ). The sentence consisting of the اِسْمُ لَعَلَّ and its predicate takes over the role of the two objects of the verb أَدْرِي. In Arabic it would sound like this: الْجُمْلَةُ مِن اِسْم لَعَلَّ وَخَبَرِها فِي مَحَلِّ نَصْبٍ سَدَّتْ مَسَدَّ مَفْعُولَيْ أَدْرِي Usually لَعَلَّ is used after the present tense of دَرَى - يَدْرِي (R3=ي; to know).

6. The conditional particle لَوْ, so-called لَوُ الشَّرْطِيَّةُ

I'm positive that if Zayd strives, he will succeed.	أَعْلَمُ لَوْ جَدَّ زَيْدٌ لَنَجَحَ.

The sentence consisting of the verb (جَدَّ) and its subject (زَيْدٌ) takes over the role of the two objects. Thus, the sentence is (grammatically) located in the position of an accusative case (سَدَّتْ الْجُمْلَةُ مِن الْفِعْلِ وَالْفاعِلِ فِي مَحَلِّ نَصْبٍ مَسَدَّ مَفْعُولَيْ أَعْلَمُ).

7. The particle إِنَّ ➡ if there is a لِ before the predicate (خَبَرُ إِنَّ).

I am convinced that Zayd is indeed generous.	أَعْلَمُ إِنَّ زَيْدًا لَكَرِيمٌ.

Particle of emphasis (حَرْفُ تَوْكِيدٍ وَنَصْبٍ).	إِنَّ
This is the "subject" (اِسْمُ إِنَّ) in the accusative case (مَنْصُوبٌ).	زَيْدًا
Watch out! This is a *Lām that is slid* (لامٌ مُزَحْلَقَةٌ). Such لَ was originally at the beginning but has changed its position – see *#260*.	لَ
Predicate (خَبَرُ إِنَّ) in the nominative case (مَرْفُوعٌ).	كَرِيمٌ
The **sentence** consisting of the اِسْمُ إِنَّ and the خَبَرُ إِنَّ takes over the role of the **two objects** and is grammatically located in the position of an accusative.	

8. The word *how much* (so-called كَمُ الْخَبَرِيَّةُ)

I am aware how many books Zayd has read.	أَعْلَمُ كَمْ كِتابٍ قَرَأَ زَيْدٌ.
This is a so-called كَمُ الْخَبَرِيَّةُ. The word كَمْ is a noun (اِسْمٌ) which takes the position of an accusative case (فِي مَحَلِّ نَصْبٍ) because it **serves as the direct object** (مَفْعُولٌ بِهِ) of the verb *to read* (قَرَأَ).	كَمْ
Second part (مُضافٌ إِلَيْهِ) of the إِضافةٌ.	كِتابٍ
Subject (فاعِلٌ) of the verb قَرَأَ in the nominative case (مَرْفُوعٌ).	زَيْدٌ
The sentence consisting of the verb (قَرَأَ) and its subject (زَيْدٌ) takes over the role of the two objects and is positioned in the location of an accusative case (الْجُمْلَةُ مِنَ الْفِعْلِ وَالْفاعِلِ فِي مَحَلِّ نَصْبٍ سَدَّتْمَسَدَّ مَفْعُولَيْ أَعْلَمَ).	

What we have discussed so far in *question #311* can lead to tricky sentences. Let's analyze a sophisticated structure:

I perceived that Zayd is generous.	أَعْلَمُ زَيْدًا لَهُوَ كَرِيمٌ.
First direct object (الْمَفْعُولُ الْأَوَّلُ) in the accusative (مَنْصُوبٌ).	زَيْدًا
This device is a *Lām of the beginning/inceptive Lām* (لامُ الْإِبْتِداءِ). It starts a new sentence.	لَ
Personal pronoun (ضَمِيرٌ مُنْفَصِلٌ). It serves as the subject of the nominal sentence (جُمْلَةٌ اِسْمِيّةٌ) and is thus placed in the position of a nominative case (فِي مَحَلِّ رَفْعٍ مُبْتَدَأً).	هُوَ
Predicate (خَبَرٌ) of the nominal sentence, nominative (مَرْفُوعٌ).	كَرِيمٌ

> **Note:** The sentence consisting of subject (اَلْمُبْتَدَأ) and predicate (خَبَرٌ) is in the place of an accusative; it fills the spot of the **second direct object** of the verb (اَلْجُمْلَةُ مِنَ الْمُبْتَدَإِ وَخَبَرِهِ فِي مَحَلِّ نَصْبٍ سَدَّتْ مَسَدَّ الْمَفْعُولِ الثَّانِي لِأَعْلَمُ).

312. What happens if *to see* really means *to see*?

You will end up with a حَالٌ *in the sentence.*

If رَأَى (*to see*) or وَجَدَ (*to find*) are mere *verbs of sense and perception* (أَفْعالُ الْحِسِّ), i.e., they express nothing other than acts of the external organs of sense, they can still be connected with two words in the accusative (مَنْصُوبٌ) – but the second accusative is no longer for a second direct object (مَفْعُولٌ بِهِ ثانٍ). ➤ It is a **circumstantial qualifier** (حَالٌ).

In other words, when رَأَى means *to see* (in the literal sense), it has only one object; when it means *to know/to believe,* it takes two objects. That's also the reason why رَأْيٌ means *opinion* in Arabic. For example: *What's your opinion about this?* (مَا رَأْيُكَ فِي هَذَا؟).

Let's focus on the حَالٌ which expresses here a state or condition of the (first) object. The viewer sees the object in a certain state/condition.

I found him sick (i.e., in a state of sleep or sickness).	وَجَدْتُهُ مَرِيضًا.

Why is *him* (ه) an object and *sick* a حَالٌ؟

		Question to determine the function
مَفْعُولٌ بِهِ أَوَّلٌ	I saw *him* (رَأَيْتُهُ).	**What** did you see? (مَاذَا رَأَيْتَ؟)
	➡ This question word doesn't work here. Thus, it can't be a second object.	What did you see him? (مَاذَا رَأَيْتَهُ؟)
حَالٌ	I saw him *sick* (رَأَيْتُهُ مَرِيضًا).	**How** did you see him? (كَيْفَ رَأَيْتَهُ؟)

We translate such sentences in the same was as if there was a *verb of meaning* (أَفْعالُ الْقُلُوبِ), also called *verb of the heart* or *mind* – however, the **object** of a أَفْعالُ الْحِسِّ is **merely the individual.** If we had two objects, it is not only the individual, but the individual as the possessor of this quality: *he was sick.*

Two examples of *to see* and *to find*, used in the literal sense:

I saw him doing.	رَأَيْتُهُ يَفْعَلُ.
I found you doing that.	وَجَدْتُكَ فَعَلْتَ ذلِكَ.

313. *To consider*. Does this verb have two objects in Arabic?

It depends on which verb you use.

Nowadays people tend to use the VIII-verb إِعْتَبَرَ - يَعْتَبِرُ to express *to consider*. It is mostly used in the passive voice: اُعْتُبِرَ (*was considered*) and يُعْتَبَرُ (*is considered*). The verb is capable of carrying two (direct) objects. Let's see some examples in the active voice with two objects.

I considered Zayd a friend.	إِعْتَبَرْتُ زَيْدًا صَدِيقًا.
I consider Zayd a friend.	أَعْتَبِرُ زَيْدًا صَدِيقًا.
She considered the offer acceptable.	اِعْتَبَرَتْ الْعَرْضَ مَقْبُولاً.
We take (consider) your remark as an insult.	نَعْتَبِرُ تَعْلِيقَكَ إهانةً.

In Modern Standard Arabic, this is totally fine. However, the above examples are alien to Classical Arabic. The original meaning إِعْتَبَرَ بِ is *to take advice*. It is synonymous with اِتَّعَظَ بِ.

Let that be a warning!	هذِهِ عِبْرَةٌ لِمَنْ يَعْتَبِرُ!

Sura 59:2	• So take warning, O people of vision. (*Saḥīḥ Int.*) • Learn from this, all of you with insight! (*A. Haleem*)	فَاعْتَبِرُوا يَا أُولِي الْأَبْصَارِ.

What would be an alternative to إِعْتَبَرَ? Arabic knows the I-verb عَدَّ (R2=R3; present tense: يَعُدُّ) which literally means *to count*; but figuratively also *to consider, to think*. The verb is quite easy to handle – providing that you know that this verb takes **two** objects!

I consider Zayd a friend.	أَعُدُّ زَيْدًا صَدِيقًا.
I considered Zayd a friend.	عَدَدْتُ زَيْدًا صَدِيقًا.

Let's see an example of the Qur'an:

Sura 38:62	وَقَالُوا مَا لَنَا لَا نَرَىٰ رِجَالًا كُنَّا نَعُدُّهُم مِّنَ الْأَشْرَارِ.

- And they will say, "Why do we not see men whom we used to count among the worst?" *(Sahīh International)*
- They will say, "Why do we not see those we thought were bad?" *(A. Hal.)*

It depends on the context, but many times, when we use the word *consider* in English, you could use the Arabic I-verbs رَأَى *(to see)* and نَظَرَ *(to regard; to perceive with the eyes; to contemplate)*. For the conjugation of the irregular verb رَأَى, see *Arabic for Nerds 1, #251*.

Sura 59:18	You who believe! Be mindful of God, and let every soul **consider** carefully what it sends ahead for tomorrow.	يَا أَيُّهَا الَّذِينَ آمَنُوا اتَّقُوا اللَّهَ وَلْتَنظُرْ نَفْسٌ مَّا قَدَّمَتْ لِغَدٍ.

314. What is the mysterious thing about the word هَبْ?

There are several things. Among them: هَبْ *takes two objects.*

هَبْ is a solid ("frozen") imperative verb (فِعْلُ أَمْرٍ جَامِدٌ) that does **not** have a past tense form. Some people prefer the term *aplastic*, expressing that this verb doesn't have any other form except one.

Don't be confused: we don't talk about the imperative of the I-verb وَهَبَ - يَهَبُ (R1=و) which would have the meaning of *give me* (!أَعْطِنِي). Nor do we talk about the imperative of the I-verb هَابَ - يَهَابُ (R2=ي) which has the meaning of *to be scared!* For ex.: *Fear Allah!* (!هَبْ رَبَّكَ).

Our word in question is هَبْ. It conveys the meaning of: *assume (that); let's assume (that); let's suppose (that); supposing (that)*. It is a very interesting word also for another reason: هَبْ takes **two objects**!

Let's assume that he is an intelligent boy.	هَبْ وَلَدًا ذَكِيًّا.

Note: Many Arabic speakers use هَبْ with أَنَّ. This is possible, however, it is stylistically better (الْأَفْصَحُ) to use هَبْ without أَنَّ.

correct	I assume you are in good health!	هَبْ أَنَّ صِحَّتَكَ قَوِيَّةٌ!
better		هَبْ صِحَّتَكَ قَوِيَّةٌ!

315. Can the verb قَالَ have two objects?

Only when it does <u>not</u> denote to say.

Wait a second, but قَالَ does mean *to say*, right? Yes, it does. Arabic, however, is famous for assigning many meanings to a word. The grammarians who lived in the prime of Classical Arabic analyzed قَالَ thoroughly. They came to the conclusion that the verb may carry two objects in the accusative case (نَصْبٌ) – but only, when it conveys the meaning of ظَنَّ, i.e., *to think, to believe, to assume*. This is only possible when the following three conditions are fulfilled:

1. The verb قَالَ has to be in the present tense (مُضارِعٌ); it is usually restricted to the second person singular (*you*): تَقُولُ or تَقُولِينَ.

2. The indented meaning of the verb must be *to think; assume* (الظَّنُّ).

3. A question particle (حَرْفُ اِسْتِفْهامٍ) precedes the verb قَالَ.

Do you **think** that Zayd is coming today?	أَتَقُولُ زَيْدًا قادِمًا الْيَوْمَ؟
This is the meaning of the sentence:	أَتَظُنُّ زَيْدًا قادِمًا الْيَوْمَ؟

Question particle (حَرْفُ اِسْتِفْهامٍ); no position in إِعْرابٌ.	أ
Verb in the present tense (فِعْلٌ مُضارِعٌ), indicative mood (مَرْفُوعٌ).	تَقُولُ
First direct object (مَفْعُولٌ أَوَّلٌ) in the accusative case (مَنْصُوبٌ).	زَيْدًا
Second direct object (مَفْعُولٌ ثانٍ) in the accusative (مَنْصُوبٌ).	قادِمًا

Note: If قَالَ is used in the meaning of *to speak; utter* (نَطَقَ) or *to pronounce; express* (تَلَفَّظَ), the verb قَالَ will **only have one object** (مَفْعُولٌ واحِدٌ) which can be a word or a sentence.

You ask me about the road to success, and I **tell** you: "faith".	تَسْأَلُنِي عَنْ طَرِيقِ النَّصْرِ فَأَقُولُ الْإِيمانَ.

أَقُولُ in our example means that you actually utter or pronounce (أَنْطَقُ or أَتَلَفَّظُ) the word "*faith*" (الْإِيمان) – making the word الْإِيمانَ the direct object (مَفْعُولٌ بِهِ) of أَقُولُ and therefore مَنْصُوبٌ.

The following examples show how tricky the structure can be:

'Alī says that Zayd is generous.	يَقُولُ عَلِيٌّ زَيْدٌ كَرِيمٌ.

Subject (فاعِلٌ) of *to say* in the nominative case (مَرْفُوعٌ).	عَلِيٌّ
Subject (مُبْتَدَأٌ) of the **nominal sentence**, nominative case (مَرْفُوعٌ).	زَيْدٌ
Predicate (خَبَرٌ مَرْفُوعٌ) of the **nominal sentence**; nominative(مَرْفُوعٌ).	كَرِيمٌ

In the examples, why do we use the nominative case? The entire nominal sentence (marked in gray) is the *object of the speech* (مَقُولُ الْقَوْلِ), located in the place of an accusative case (فِي مَحَلِّ نَصْبٍ مَقُولُ الْقَوْلِ).

Grammarians call this sentence مَقُولُ الْقَوْلِ because in reality it cannot be a direct object (مَفْعُولٌ بِهِ). It is difficult to imagine what the action of *to say* could *do* with an object. That's different with, for example, *to write* as you can *write a book*. So it is much more logical to say that the *object of the speech* only takes over the role and place of the direct object (سَدَّ مَسَدَّ الْمُفْعُولِ بِهِ) and works as a replacement. See *question #37* for an explanation of the term سَدَّ مَسَدَّ.

Contemporary grammarians approve that the nominal sentence زَيْدٌ كَرِيمٌ functions as a direct object of the verb قالَ. This kind of structure, the so-called *object sentence* (الْجُمْلَةُ لِمَفْعُولٍ بِهِ), is quite common. Purist grammarians, however, say that the direct object cannot be supplied by a sentence (see also *questions #70 and #290*). What happens if we have a **verbal sentence**? We have the same situation. For example:

'Alī said that Zayd succeeded.	قالَ عَلِيٌّ نَجَحَ زَيْدٌ.

زَيْدٌ is the subject (فاعِلٌ) of the verb نَجَحَ. The entire verbal sentence (نَجَحَ زَيْدٌ) serves as the *object of the speech* (مَقُولُ الْقَوْلِ); therefore, it is found in the place of an accusative case (فِي مَحَلِّ نَصْبٍ).

316. Are there verbs with three objects?

Yes, there are – but they are rare.

Even though that constructions with three objects are rarely encountered nowadays, they do have a certain appeal. Verbs which may carry three objects (ثَلاثَةُ مَفاعِيلَ) are usually verbs of pattern IV (أَفْعَلَ),

rarely of pattern II (فَعَّلَ). The following verbs are the most common:

to inform; tell (R3=ﺀ)	or يُنبِئُ or يُنَبِّئُ	or أَنْبَأَ IV / نَبَّأَ II	to notify (somebody about something)	يُعْلِمُ	أَعْلَمَ IV
to relate; tell	يُحَدِّثُ	حَدَّثَ II	to notify; inform	or يُخْبِرُ or يُخَبِّرُ	or أَخْبَرَ IV / خَبَّرَ II
			to demonstrate; show	يُرِي	أَرَى IV

Normally, the stem I (فَعَلَ) of these verbs already demands two objects, e.g., عَلِمَ or رَأَى. Grammarians call them *verbs of the mind* (أَفْعالُ الْقُلُوبِ) or *meaning* – see *question #306*. For this reason, both the second and third object together were originally forming a nominal sentence consisting of subject (مُبْتَدَأ) and predicate (خَبَر). An example:

I told you that Zayd is generous.	أَعْلَمْتُكَ زَيْدًا كَرِيمًا.

What are the three objects of the verb أَعْلَمْتُ?

First object (مَفْعُولٌ أَوَّل); a pronominal suffix (ضَمِيرٌ مُتَّصِل). Since it has a fixed shape (مَبْنِيٌّ عَلَى الْفَتْح), we are not allowed to put case markers. Although it appears as being in the accusative (مَنْصُوبٌ), the فَتْحَة is not the case marker; it is just part of the fixed shape. We say that كَ appears in the place of an accusative (فِي مَحَلِّ نَصْبٍ).	كَ
Second object (مَفْعُولٌ ثَانٍ) in the accusative case (مَنْصُوبٌ).	زَيْدًا
Third object (مَفْعُولٌ ثَالِثٌ) in the accusative case (مَنْصُوبٌ).	كَرِيمًا

Watch out: It is possible to interpret the **third object** as a حال:

Sura 2:167	Allah will make them see their deeds as a source of bitter regret.	يُرِيهِمُ اللهُ أَعْمَالَهُمْ حَسَرَاتٍ عَلَيْهِمْ.

Let's adjust this verse a little for our analysis. Note that يُرِي is the past tense form of أَرَى.

Allah will make the evildoers see their deeds as a source of bitter regret.	يُرِي اللهُ الْمُذْنِبِينَ أَعْمَالَهُمْ حَسَرَاتٍ عَلَيْهِم.

	حَسَرَاتٍ	أَعْمَالَهُمْ	الْمُذْنِبِينَ	اللّٰهُ	يُرِي
I	3rd object	2nd object			
	originally the خَبَرٌ	originally the مُبْتَدَأٌ	1st object	subject (فاعِلٌ)	verb
II	circumstantial qualifier (حالٌ)	2nd object			

These verbs are often used in the **passive voice** (مَبْنِيّةٌ لِلْمَجْهُولِ). As a rule we could say that the **first** of the **three accusatives** in the active voice becomes the **subject** of the passive (نائِبُ الْفاعِلِ). In the following example, *Muhammad* (مُحَمَّدٌ) is the نائِبُ الْفاعِلِ.

Muhammad was informed that 'Amr was coming/approaching.	أُعْلِمَ مُحَمَّدٌ عَمْرًا قادِمًا.

Zayd's success was foreseen by me.	نُبِّئْتُ زَيْدًا ناجِحًا.

Past tense verb in the passive voice. The pronoun suffix (تُ) serves as the **subject** of the passive voice (نائِبُ الْفاعِلِ).	نُبِّئْتُ
Second object (مَفْعُولٌ ثانٍ) in the accusative case (مَنْصُوبٌ).	زَيْدًا
Third object (مَفْعُولٌ ثالِثٌ) in the accusative case (مَنْصُوبٌ).	ناجِحًا

317. Can you change the word order if there are three direct objects?

Yes, but such an operation may stir up case endings.

The *verbs of the mind or meaning* (أَفْعالُ الْقُلوبِ) can take three objects. The longer a sentence is, the trickier it becomes. This is especially the case as soon as we mess up the usual word order because some rules may be abrogated (إِلْغاءٌ).

In the end, it depends on whether we have a nominal or verbal sentence. Only in a verbal sentence, we may get three words with مَنْصُوبٌ-endings. It is quite complex. All of the following sentences mean the same and are fine in Arabic. Let's start with the usual word order:

I told you that Zayd is generous.	أَعْلَمْتُكَ زَيْدًا كَرِيمًا.

1	إِعْمَالٌ	Verbal sentence. The second object was placed at the beginning. The verb is treated as a **parenthesis** – nevertheless, it still exercises its grammatical job as a regent.	زَيْدًا أَعْلَمْتُكَ كَرِيمًا.
2	إِلْغَاءٌ	Nominal sentence. This verb does not work as a regent (فِعْلٌ غَيْرُ عَامِلٍ)! It is inserted as a **parenthesis**.	زَيْدٌ أَعْلَمْتُكَ كَرِيمٌ.
3	إِعْمَالٌ	Verbal sentence. Both, the second and third object, are moved to the front. The verb has kept its governing power and executes it.	زَيْدًا كَرِيمًا أَعْلَمْتُكَ.
4	إِلْغَاءٌ	Nominal sentence. The verb loses its influence on the nominal sentence which is, in fact, made of the second and third direct object. In other words, they serve now as the subject (مُبْتَدَأٌ) and the predicate (خَبَرٌ).	زَيْدٌ كَرِيمٌ أَعْلَمْتُكَ.

Another example:

| I informed Zayd that his brother succeeded. | أَنْبَأْتُ زَيْدًا أَخَاهُ نَاجِحًا. |

1st **object** in the accusative case (مَفْعُولٌ أَوَّلٌ مَنْصُوبٌ).	زَيْدًا
2nd **object** (مَفْعُولٌ ثَانٍ). Note that the Aleph marks the accusative case (مَنْصُوبٌ بِالْأَلِفِ) here because أَخٌ is one of the *five* (some say six) *nouns* (الْأَسْمَاءُ السِّتَّةُ) – see *question #32*.	أَخَا
Pronominal suffix (ضَمِيرٌ مُتَّصِلٌ) serving as the second part of the إِضَافَة. We can only assign the "place value" of a genitive case (فِي مَحَلِّ جَرٍّ مُضَافٌ إِلَيْهِ) because we cannot put the appropriate case marker due to its indeclinable shape (مَبْنِيٌّ عَلَى الضَّمِّ).	ه
3rd **object** (مَفْعُولٌ ثَالِثٌ); accusative case (مَنْصُوبٌ بِالْفَتْحَةِ الظَّاهِرَةِ).	نَاجِحًا

Does an extra particle or device have an effect on the cases? Yes, it does. As seen in *question #310*, there are letters, particles, or words which – when placed between the verb and its object – may cause the suspension (تَعْلِيقٌ) of the verb's ruling power. In other words, although we pronounce the objects with case markers other than the accusative case (مَنْصُوبٌ), we still treat them grammatically as occupying the grammatical place of an accusative case.

أَعْلَمْتُكَ لَزَيْدٌ كَرِيمٌ.	I told you that Zayd is generous.

ك	Pronominal suffix; first direct object (ضَمِيرٌ مُتَّصِلٌ). It takes the position of an accusative case (فِي مَحَلّ نَصْبٍ).
ل	*Inceptive Lām* (لامُ الْإِبْتِدَاءِ). It does not have a place in إِعْرَابٌ.
زَيْدٌ	Subject (مُبْتَدَأ) of the nominal sentence, nominative case (مَرْفُوعٌ).
كَرِيمٌ	Predicate (خَبَرٌ) in the nominative case.

What's crucial: The **entire nominal sentence** (consisting of subject and predicate) takes over the role of the **two direct objects** and is treated as being located in the place of an accusative case (الْجُمْلَةُ مِن الْمُبْتَدَإِ وَخَبَرِهِ فِي مَحَلّ نَصْبٍ سَدَّتْ مَسَدَّ الْمَفْعُولَيْنِ الثَّانِي وَالثَّالِثِ لِأَعْلَمَ).

THE ABSOLUTE OR INNER OBJECT (الْمَفْعُولُ الْمُطْلَقُ)

318. How did the absolute object get its name? And is it an object?

It is not really an object. "Absolute" may be interpreted as general; core.

When you say ضَرَبْتُ (*I hit*), the sense of this utterance is: أَحْدَثْتُ ضَرْبًا (*I brought into existence [an act] of hitting*) or فَعَلْتُ ضَرْبًا (*I performed [an act] of hitting*). The مَصْدَر denotes the real act which is performed by the subject/agent. Therefore, Sībawayhi (سِيبَوَيْهِ) and al-Mubarrad (الْمُبَرَّد) state that the مَصْدَر is a مَفْعُولٌ in the sense of *something which is performed*. Al-Mubarrad gave an example.

ضَرَبْتُ زَيْدًا.	*I hit Zayd*: the direct object (*Zayd*) is **not** brought into existence by the doer (فاعِلٌ), although it suffers the act performed by him.	الْمَفْعُولُ بِهِ
ضَرَبْتُ ضَرْبًا.	*I hit a hitting*: the absolute object denotes the sense of *the act performed by the doer*. ➤ In fact, it **does not** denote an object!	الْمَفْعُولُ الْمُطْلَقُ

The term مَفْعُولٌ in this connotation means *what is done* and the term مُطْلَق denotes *free, general* – in the sense of a noun which is not restricted by anything, e.g., an adjective or a preposition. A possible translation could be: *unqualified thing done*. We could say that the مَفْعُولٌ مُطْلَقٌ is free from any kind of restrictions or stipulations that other types of objects might have.

The **absolute object** (مَفْعُولٌ مُطْلَقٌ) signifies what (action) is done free from any idea of being done <u>to</u> something (بِهِ), <u>in</u> something (فِيهِ), out of or for the purpose of something (مِنْ أَجْلِهِ) or with or in the company of something (مَعَهُ). The مَفْعُولٌ مُطْلَقٌ emphasizes (usually) the core meaning of the verb. It may show its nature and number. Let's see all different kinds of objects together in one sentence:

Zayd read with Muhammad (in his company) the book today in front of the teacher well (lit.: a good reading) out of a desire for progress.	قَرَأَ زَيْدٌ وَمُحَمَّدًا الْكِتابَ الْيَوْمَ أَمامَ الْمُعَلِّمِ قِراءةً جَيِّدةً فِي التَّقَدُّمِ.

مَعَهُ	مَفْعُولٌ	with/in the company of Muhammad was the act of reading done;	مُحَمَّدًا
بِهِ	مَفْعُولٌ	to the book was the act of reading done;	الْكِتابَ
فِيهِ	مَفْعُولٌ	in the time of today was the act of reading done;	الْيَوْمَ
		in front of the teacher (place) was the act done;	الْمُعَلِّمِ
مُطْلَقٌ	مَفْعُولٌ	what was actually done was the act of reading;	قِراءةً
لِأَجْلِهِ	مَفْعُولٌ	out of a desire (رَغْبة) for progress was the act of reading done;	التَّقَدُّم

319. What is the purpose of the absolute object?

It adds greater force to the verb.

Some people call the مَفْعُولٌ مُطْلَقٌ just مَصْدَرٌ. This is the reason why in dictionaries, you may see the مَصْدَر written with the ending "*-an*", the indefinite accusative ending. For example: *sitting* (جُلُوسًا). The idea is the following: the signification lies in the indefiniteness of the مَصْدَر which leaves the verbal idea quite unlimited in its force and effect.

When a مَصْدَر stands alone and is undefined (مُبْهَمّ), the مَصْدَر is used for *strengthening* (تَأْكِيدٌ) or *magnifying* (تَعْظِيمٌ) – **to add greater force to the verb**. This is the idea of the مَفْعُولٌ مُطْلَقٌ. It serves to emphasize the fact of the verb's occurrence. This is only possible if the مَصْدَر is the *patient* of a verb, which means that a verb governs and operates on it which is exactly the situation if we have a مَفْعُولٌ مُطْلَقٌ.

In very old books on Arabic grammar, you will rather find the term مَنْصُوبٌ عَلَى الْمَصْدَرِيَّةِ. This term conveys pretty much the same as the more modern term مَفْعُولٌ مُطْلَقٌ.

What are the functions of a مَصْدَر in the accusative (مَنْصُوبٌ) case?

Such a مَصْدَر may emphasize (تَأْكِيدٌ) the **regent** (عَامِلٌ), provide a *specification* (تَمْيِيزٌ) or *distinction* (تَبْيِينٌ), denote the type of action or its kind (نَوْعٌ), or it is used for *enumeration* (عَدَدٌ) – to denote the number of times an act has been carried out. For stylistic purposes, it may be used to convey a command (positive or negative), a wish, a reproach (question), praise, or salutation. It often conveys the meaning of *really*.

Emphasis	I bestowed (the utmost) honors upon the diligent.	أَكْرَمْتُ الْمُجْتَهِدَ إِكْرَامًا.
Indicating or clarifying its kind; often translated as *like* (مِثْلَ).	I walked quite well.	سِرْتُ سَيْرًا حَسَنًا.
	The people defend their freedom like heroes.	يُدَافِعُ الشَّعْبُ عَنْ حُرِّيَّتِه دِفَاعَ الْأَبْطالِ.
Enumeration. We use a special form of the مَصْدَر: the اِسْمُ الْمَـرّةِ (see *Arabic for Nerds 1*, question #120).	I sat on the beach twice.	جَلَسْتُ عَلَى الشَّاطِئِ جَلْسَتَيْنِ.
	I hit him three times.	ضَرَبْتُهُ ثَلاثَ ضَرَباتٍ.
	I read the book twice.	قَرَأْتُ الْكِتابَ قِراءَتَيْنِ.

What is the grammatical job of the words marked in gray? All of them are placed as an **absolute object** (مَفْعُولٌ مُطْلَقٌ) which is the reason why they are located in the position of an accusative case. For example:

Absolute object (مَفْعُولٌ مُطْلَقٌ), accusative case; it serves as a confirmation (مُؤَكِّد) of the regent (عَامِلٌ), i.e., the verb أَكْرَمَ.	إِكْرَامًا

320. Why do we say "shukran" (شُكْرًا) and not "shukrun" (شُكْرٌ)?

The word شُكْرًا *(thankfulness) is, in fact, an object and thus in the accusative case* (مَنْصُوبٌ).

Students of Arabic learn شُكْرًا at the very beginning. Have you ever wondered why we don't say *shukr* (شُكْرٌ) or *shukrun* (شُكْرٌ)?

The answer it quite startling: there is a "hidden" **verb** which is responsible that شُكْرٌ gets the accusative case, i.e., شُكْرًا. We say that the verb is hidden, because it was, in fact, **deleted.**

Speaking in grammar terms, شُكْرًا is an **absolute object** (مَفْعُولٌ مُطْلَقٌ). Words that are assigned to have this function provide emphasis and force. We mentioned that the verb (i.e., the regent, عامِلٌ) was deleted. To logically understand such a construction, we have to reconstruct the verb that implicitly governs the object, but was deleted.

We can do that by using the مَصْدَر in the مَنْصُوبٌ-case, check its root and use the root to form an appropriate verb.

translation	actual meaning	مَفْعُولٌ مُطْلَقٌ
Thanks!	أَشْكُرُكَ شُكْرًا	شُكْرًا!
As well	آضَ or يَئِيضُ أَيْضًا	أَيْضًا!
Really, truly, indeed	أُحِقّ حَقًّا	حَقًّا!
Gently! Softly! Slowly!	أَمْهِلْ مَهْلًا	مَهْلًا!
Best regards	أُحَيِّيكُمْ تَحِيَّةً طَيِّبةً	تَحِيَّةً طَيِّبةً
Sit!	إِجْلِسوا جُلُوسًا!	جُلُوسًا!
Shut up!	أُسْكُتُوا سُكُوتًا!	سُكُوتًا!
With patience, not with panic! (Be patient and do not give way to immoderate grief!)	إِصْبِرْ صَبْرًا وَلا تَجْزَعْ جَزَعًا!	صَبْرًا، لا جَزَعًا!

Let's look at some invocations (دُعاءٌ). Many of them are famous expressions in Arabic and in Islam.

translation	actual meaning	مَفْعُولٌ مُطْلَقٌ
Help us! (Grant us a great victory!)	اُنْصُرْنا نَصْرًا!!	اللَّهُمَّ نَصْرًا!!
May Allah give you rain!	سَقاكَ اللّٰهُ سَقْيًا!	سَقْيًا لَكَ!

Many common expressions in Arabic have a مَفْعُولٌ مُطْلَقٌ serving as the **first** part of a إضافةٌ-construction:

translation	Arabic meaning	expression
Allah be praised! (exclamation of surprise)	تَنْزِيهُهُ تَعَالَى وَتَعْظِيمُهُ وَإِجْلَالُهُ، أيْ أَبَرِّئُ اللّٰه عَنْ كُلِّ سُوءٍ	سُبْحَانَ اللّٰه!
God forbid! (I seek the refuge of Allah. Or: Allah, save me/us from that!)	أَعُوذُ مَعاذَ اللّٰهِ! or اِسْتِعانةً بِهِ وَلُجُوءًا إِلَيْهِ	مَعاذَ اللّٰهِ!
Have mercy on me, o my lord!	جِنْ or تَحَنَّنْ عَلَيَّ حَنانًا	حَنانَيْكَ يا رَبِّ!
I wait intent up your service, o Allah.	أُلِبُّ لَكَ إِلْبابًا or أَلَبُّ لَكَ لَبًّا.	لَبَّيْكَ اللَّهُمَّ!
Another way to make that expression work is أُلَبِّي لَبَّيْكَ = تَلْبِيَة بَعْدَ تَلْبِيَةٍ.		

How do you إِعْرابٌ **the expression** لَبَّيْكَ؟ The word fraction لَبَّي is the absolute object and therefore takes the accusative case (الْكَلِمَةُ مَنْصُوبَةٌ عَلَى أَنَّها مَفْعُولٌ مُطْلَقٌ). The letter ي is the marker for the accusative case since it is a dual (مَنْصُوبٌ بِالْياءِ). The ك is a pronominal suffix and is the second part of the إضافةٌ which is also the reason why the ن of the dual drops. What about the regent (عامِلٌ), i.e., the verb? It was deleted (الْعامِلُ مَحْذُوفٌ).

In the expressions حَنانَيْكَ and لَبَّيْكَ, the **dual** (التَّثْنِيَةُ) is used – but not to express two occasions, but rather **to indicate repetition** and **frequency** (لِلتَّكْرِيرِ وَالتَّكْثِيرِ). See *Arabic for Nerds 1, question #204*.

لَبَّيْكَ frequently appears together with another expression of the same grammatical nature: لَبَّيْكَ وَسَعْدَيْكَ. The saying وَسَعْدَيْكَ signifies: *aiding You after aiding* [i.e., time after time]; or *aiding you and then aiding*. The dual here conveys the idea of *repeating*: إِسْعَادًا لَكَ بَعْدَ إِسْعادٍ.

321. Can a مَصْدَرٌ govern another مَصْدَرٌ؟

Yes, this is possible.

The original operator (الْعامِلُ الْأَصْلِيُّ) of the absolute object is a verb that can be fully conjugated (أَنْ يَكُونَ مُتَصَرِّفًا تامًّا) and denotes an action. What happens if the verb is deficient, for example, كانَ؟ Let's see.

impossible in Arabic	I was under the tree.	كُنْتُ تَحْتَ الشَّجَرَةِ كَوْنًا.
You cannot use the absolute object of the verb *to be* – because *to be* is not an action. كان is not a "full" verb: it is *deficient* (فِعْلٌ ناقِصٌ).		

Now, what happens if we don't even have a verb in the sentence? Can another word step in and govern the indefinite مَصْدَر in the accusative case making it an absolute object (مَفْعُولٌ مُطْلَقٌ)? Yes, there are substitutes for the verb which have similar powers.

a) The مَصْدَر. It may sound strange that a مَصْدَر governs and operates on another مَصْدَر, but this happens actually quite often.

Trusting Allah with a true trust leads you to success in the two worlds.	إِنَّ التَّوَكُّلَ عَلَى اللهِ تَوَكُّلًا حَقِيقِيًّا يَقُودُكَ إِلَى الْفَوْزِ فِي الدَّارَيْنِ.
Remark: الدَّارانِ (literally *the two houses*) expresses the worldly existence and the hereafter (الدُّنْيا وَالْآخِرةِ).	

This is the مَصْدَر of the V-verb يَتَوَكَّلُ - تَوَكَّلَ (*to trust*; R1=و). It supplies the job of the "subject" (اِسْمُ إِنَّ) and therefore takes the accusative case (مَنْصُوبٌ).	التَّوَكُّلَ
Predicate (خَبَرُ إِنَّ) in the nominative case (مَرْفُوعٌ).	يَقُودُكَ
Absolute object (مَفْعُولٌ مُطْلَقٌ) in the accusative (مَنْصُوبٌ).	تَوَكُّلًا
Adjective; thus, it is also in the accusative case (صِفةٌ مَنْصُوبةٌ).	حَقِيقِيًّا

What caused تَوَكُّلًا to be in the accusative case (نَصْبٌ)? It is the مَصْدَر of the very same word: التَّوَكُّلُ تَوَكُّلًا. What is the purpose of the مَفْعُولٌ مُطْلَقٌ here? It indicates a certain **kind** (of *trust*) as the *trust* is further described (مُبَيِّنٌ لِلنَّوْعِ لِأَنَّهُ مَوْصُوفٌ).

b) The active participle (اِسْمُ الْفَاعِلِ)

The individual who trusts Allah with a true trust is successful in the two worlds.	إِنَّ الْمُتَوَكِّلَ عَلَى اللهِ تَوَكُّلًا حَقِيقِيًّا فَائِزٌ فِي الدَّارَيْنِ.

Active participle, serving as the اِسْمُ إِنَّ; therefore, it gets the accusative case (مَنْصُوبٌ). It exercises governing power and functions as the regent (عَامِلٌ) for the absolute object.	الْمُتَوَكِّلَ
Predicate (خَبَرُ إِنَّ) in the nominative case (مَرْفُوعٌ).	فَائِزٌ
Absolute object (مَفْعُولٌ مُطْلَقٌ مَنْصُوبٌ) in the accusative.	تَوَكُّلًا

c) The passive participle (اِسْمُ الْمَفْعُولِ)

This man is deeply loved by his people.	هٰذا الرَّجُلُ مَحْبُوبٌ حُبًّا شَدِيدًا بَيْنَ قَوْمِهِ.

The analysis of this sentence is interesting.

Particle of attention (حَرْفُ تَنْبِيهٍ). Doesn't have a place in إِعْرابٌ.	ها
Demonstrative (اِسْمُ إِشارةٍ); placed in the position of a nominative case (فِي مَحَلِّ رَفْعٍ) as it serves as the subject (مُبْتَدَأٌ) of the nominal sentence (جُمْلَةٌ اِسْمِيَّةٌ). The word has an indeclinable shape (مَبْنِيٌّ عَلَى السُّكُونِ); we can't put case markers.	ذا
This is an apposition (بَدَلٌ); therefore, it has to be in the nominative (مَرْفُوعٌ) like the word to which it refers (i.e., the subject).	الرَّجُلُ
Passive particle. It is placed as the predicate (خَبَرٌ) of the nominal sentence (جُمْلَةٌ اِسْمِيَّةٌ) and gets the nominative (مَرْفُوعٌ). This word works as the regent (عَامِلٌ) and governs the مَفْعُولٌ مُطْلَقٌ.	مَحْبُوبٌ
Absolute object (مَفْعُولٌ مُطْلَقٌ); in the accusative case (مَنْصُوبٌ) (بِالْفَتْحَةِ الظَّاهِرَةِ). In grammar, we also call it the *patient* (مَعْمُولٌ) of the passive participle since the passive participle is the عَامِلٌ.	حُبًّا
Adjective for the absolute object (صِفَةٌ مَنْصُوبَةٌ); so, it must take the same case as the word it describes (here: حُبًّا).	شَدِيدًا

Watch out: What about the comparative, superlative (اِسْمُ التَّفْضِيلِ)

and the pseudo active-participle (الصِّفةُ الْمُشَبَّهةُ بِاسْمِ الْفَاعِلِ)؟

For a final judgment we need to follow two important rules:

➤ If a word points to an action and is associated with **renewal** (التَّجَدُّدُ), it <u>may govern</u> an absolute object (which is used to provide emphasis).

➤ However, if it points to **steadiness** (الثُّبُوتُ), it <u>can't</u> govern an absolute object.

Regarding the اسْمُ التَّفْضِيلِ, it is pretty much impossible that such a word governs an inner object. There is no action nor revival, renewal involved. Most grammarians say that this is also true for the صِفةٌ مُشَبَّهةٌ. For example, you can't say:

The use of an absolute object (أَمَانَةٌ) here **wouldn't make sense!**	Muhammad's son is faithful.	مُحَمَّدٌ أَمِينٌ اِبْنُهُ أَمَانَةً.

322. Can you repeat the absolute object?

Yes; if you want to lay greater emphasis, you may repeat the مَصْدَرٌ.

It demands some creativity and a good feeling for words to translate such sentences in a good way. The results are often intriguing.

Sura 89:21		كَلَّا إِذَا دُكَّتِ الْأَرْضُ دَكًّا دَكًّا.

No indeed! When the earth is **pounded to dust, pounded and pounded.** (*Abdul Haleem*)
Nay, but when the earth is **ground to atoms, grinding, grinding.** (*Pickthall*)
No! When the earth has been **leveled - pounded and crushed.** (*Sah. Int.*)
Keineswegs! Wenn die Erde **eingeebnet, ja platt eingeebnet wird.** (*Bub. & Ely.*)

323. Can you delete the absolute object and keep its idea?

Yes, this is possible.

The absolute object (مَفْعُولٌ مُطْلَقٌ) often occurs with an attribute or adjective (صِفةٌ/نَعْتٌ). Sometimes, however, we get the strange situation that we only see the adjective. For example:

Production progresses quickly.	يَتَقَدَّمُ الإنْتاجُ سَرِيعًا.

For English speakers, the above sentence looks totally normal. You have an adverb at the end: *quickly*. In Arabic, it is a bit more complicated. So, what happened? The **absolute object** (مَفْعُولٌ مُطْلَقٌ), which was the مَصْدَر of the V-verb يَتَقَدَّمُ, was deleted. Now,, an **adjective/attribute** (صِفةٌ/نَعْتٌ) appears in this place now. In English, we would call that an adverb of manner. Originally the sentence looked like this:

Production progresses in a quick progression.	يَتَقَدَّمُ الإنْتاجُ تَقَدُّمًا سَرِيعًا.

تَقَدُّمًا is the مَصْدَر of the V-form-verb *to advance* (تَقَدَّمَ). This means that the word سَرِيعًا is just an adjective, description (وَصْفٌ) for the absolute object. If we delete the absolute object, we are left with the adjective.

What about the إعْرابٌ? Could سَرِيعًا be the direct object (مَفْعُولٌ بِهِ) here? No way! That is merely impossible because the verb تَقَدَّمَ is **intransitive** (فِعْلٌ لازِمٌ) and therefore can't carry any direct object. We often get such situations with **verbs that have a reflexive or passive meaning**, especially the **V-form** (تَفَعَّلَ), **VI-form** (تَفاعَلَ) and **VII-form** (انْفَعَلَ). These three verb forms are usually <u>intransitive</u>.

Moreover, numbers and significations of quantity are often involved.

He often came.	كانَ يَحْضُرُ كَثِيرًا.
I gave him twenty blows.	ضَرَبْتُهُ عِشْرِينَ.

324. Which words are suitable to function as an absolute object?

Normally it is a type of مَصْدَرٍ. *But there are other options too.*

An absolute object (مَفْعُولٌ مُطْلَقٌ) is used to support and confirm the meaning of the verb – or any word which does the job of a verb. In Arabic, the absolute object is usually a مَصْدَر in the accusative. Now, could we also place other forms in such a position? In other words, what could be a substitute for the مَصْدَر? There are actually quite many.

a) The *noun of origin* (اِسْمُ الْمَصْدَرِ) is suitable to be placed as a مَفْعُولٌ مُطْلَقٌ. For more information about the اِسْمُ الْمَصْدَرِ, see #110.

I gave you generously.	أَعْطَيْتُكَ عَطاءً.
عَطاءً is the absolute object. Notice that this is the اِسْمُ الْمَصْدَرِ because the original مَصْدَر of أَعْطَى, which is a IV-form verb, follows the pattern إِفْعالٌ and thus would be إِعْطاءٌ.	

It is common to use the اِسْمُ الْمَصْدَرِ in Modern Standard Arabic. The following examples use the اِسْمُ الْمَصْدَرِ instead of the original مَصْدَرٌ.

to wash (oneself); to take a bath	اِغْتَسَلَ - يَغْتَسِلُ غُسْلًا.
to listen carefully	اِسْتَمَعَ - يَسْتَمِعُ سَماعًا حَسَنًا
to perform the ritual ablution before prayer	تَوَضَّأَ - يَتَوَضَّأُ وُضوءًا.
to get separated	اِفْتَرَقَ - يَفْتَرِقُ فُرْقةً.

b) Expressions pointing to **generality** (الْعُمُومُ): كُلٌّ and بَعْضٌ

The student worked really hard.	جَدَّ الطّالِبُ كُلَّ الْجِدِّ.
كُلَّ is the absolute object (مَفْعُولٌ مُطْلَقٌ) in the accusative case (مَنْصُوبٌ); الْجِدِّ is the second part of the إِضافةٌ in the genitive case (مَجْرُورٌ).	

What is the meaning of the above sentence?

This is how we could rewrite the sentence to get the same meaning by using the مَصْدَرٌ as the absolute object and كُلّ as an attribute (صِفةٌ): →	جَدَّ الطّالِبُ الْجِدَّ كُلَّهُ.

Let's try to understand the logic here. Both words, كُلّ and بَعْض, must be connected with a مَصْدَرٌ in such constructions. This مَصْدَرٌ was originally (فِي الْأَصْلِ) the absolute object. كُلّ and بَعْض can only be determined and convey a concrete meaning by the word that follows (i.e., مُضافٌ إِلَيْهِ) which in this construction has to be a مَصْدَرٌ.

However, the **second part** of a إِضافةٌ **can never** function as an object (or any other job). The second part is just the word to which an-

nexation is made, which is the reason for the genitive case (مَجْرُورٌ).
Only the first part, the *determining noun* (مُضافٌ), gets the marker of
a specific function such as an absolute object. An example with بَعْض.

I loved her to a certain extent.	أَحْبَبْتُها بَعْضَ الْحُبِّ.

c) The demonstrative noun (اِسْمُ الْإِشارةِ) can appear in the position of
the absolute object.

مَفْعُولٌ مُطْلَقٌ standard	I hit Zayd (harshly).	ضَرَبْتُ زَيْدًا ضَرْبًا.
substituted form		ضَرَبْتُ زَيْدًا ذٰلِكَ الضَّرْبَ.

1	Demonstrative (اِسْمُ إِشارةٍ), functioning as the absolute object (مَفْعُولٌ مُطْلَقٌ); therefore, we find it in the position of an ac-cusative case (فِي مَحَلِّ نَصْبٍ).	ذٰ
	So-called اللَّامُ لِلْبُعْدِ – a حَرْفٌ. It indicates remoteness.	لِ
	Particle of address (حَرْفُ خِطابٍ); no position in إِعْرابٌ.	ك
2	Apposition (بَدَلٌ مَنْصُوبٌ) for the absolute object.	الضَّرْبَ

We indicated in the analysis that there is an apposition (بَدَلٌ) in the
form of a مَصْدرٌ after the اِسْمُ الْإِشارةِ. It is the word ذا that is meant to
be the مَفْعُولٌ مُطْلَقٌ. This will become clearer if we look at the grammatical structure of the sentence above and skeletonize the sentence.

I hit Zayd with a such strike that...	ضَرَبْتُ زَيْدًا ضَرْبًا كَذٰلِكَ الَّذِي ...

d) **Numbers** (الْعَدَدُ)

I read three readings.	قَرَأْتُ ثَلاثَ قِراءاتٍ .

Absolute object (مَفْعُولٌ مُطْلَقٌ) in the accusative case (مَنْصُوبٌ).	ثَلاثَ
Second part of the إِضافةٌ (i.e., the مُضافٌ إِلَيْهِ); therefore, it is in the genitive case (مَجْرُورٌ بِالْكَسْرةِ الظَّاهِرةِ).	قِراءاتٍ

This is the meaning of the sentence if we rewrite it with the مَصْدَر serving as an absolute object: →	قَرَأْتُ قِراءاتٍ ثَلاثًا.
Note that the marker for the accusative (and genitive) case of a sound feminine plural is the same: كَسْرة (-"in").	

Let's take a look at more complex structures. What happens, if we also have a direct object in the sentence? Nothing special.

I met him 50 times.	قابَلْتُهُ خَمْسِينَ مُقابَلةً.

Verb plus subject (تُ) plus **direct object** (هُ).	قابَلْتُهُ
Absolute object (مَفْعُولٌ مُطْلَقٌ) which is in the accusative case (مَنْصُوبٌ بِالْياءِ).	خَمْسِينَ
This is the *specification* of the number (تَمْيِيزٌ); therefore, it takes the accusative case (مَنْصُوبٌ بِالْفَتْحةِ الظّاهِرةِ).	مُقابَلةً

The number here doesn't know its position and function in the sentence without the thing that is counted (مَعْدُودٌ).

This would be the equivalent of the sentence: →	قابَلْتُهُ مُقابَلاتٍ خَمْسِينَ.

e) A **sort** or **kind of** مَصْدَر

This is frequently used in spoken Arabic. Instead of the مَصْدَر of the respective verb, you could use one of the following:

a) the مَصْدَر of the **same** verb – but you use a form other than the original, standard pattern/form;

b) the مَصْدَر of **another** verb which conveys the same meaning;

c) a **concrete noun.**

Let's check the most difficult one: **c)**

Zayd sat in the squatting position.	جَلَسَ زَيْدٌ الْقُرْفُصاءَ.

Absolute object (مَفْعُولٌ مُطْلَقٌ) in the accusative (مَنْصُوبٌ). This word describes a **kind** of *sitting* (نَوْعٌ مِن الْجُلُوسِ). Note:	الْقُرْفُصاءَ

قُرْفُصاءَ is a diptote (مَمْنُوعٌ مِن الصَّرْفِ).	

The enemy retreated backward.	رَجَعَ الْعَدُوُّ الْقَهْقَرَى.

Absolute object (مَفْعُولٌ مُطْلَقٌ) in the accusative case; however, the case marker is virtual because the last letter can't carry any vowel (تَعَذُّر). The word الْقَهْقَرَى describes a way of *reverting/re-turning* (مِن الرُّجُوعِ).	الْقَهْقَرَى

f) The returning pronoun (الضَّمِيرُ الْعائِدُ عَلَى الْمَصْدَرِ)

I studied so diligently that no one else had done so other than me.	اِجْتَهَدْتُ اِجْتِهادًا لَمْ يَجْتَهِدْهُ غَيْرِي.
I love Zayd like I love no one else.	أُحِبُّ زَيْدًا حُبًّا لَا أُحِبُّهُ أَحَدًا غَيْرَهُ.

Direct object in the accusative case (مَفْعُولٌ بِهِ مَنْصُوبٌ).	زَيْدًا
Absolute object in the accusative case (مَفْعُولٌ مُطْلَقٌ مَنْصُوبٌ).	حُبًّا
Negation particle (حَرْفُ نَفْيٍ). Doesn't have a place in إِعْرابٌ.	لا
Verb; present tense, indicative mood (فِعْلٌ مُضارِعٌ مَرْفُوعٌ بِالضَّمِّةِ الظاهِرة). Its subject (فاعِلٌ) is a hidden, implied pronoun (ضَمِيرٌ مُسْتَتِرٌ وَجُوبًا) expressing *I* (أَنا).	أُحِبُّ
Pronominal suffix (ضَمِيرٌ مُتَّصِلٌ) which serves in the position of an **absolute object** (فِي مَحَلّ نَصْبٍ مَفْعُولٌ مُطْلَقٌ). You can't mark the case (indeclinable shape); nevertheless, the word is placed in the place of an accusative case.	هُ
Direct object in the accusative case (مَفْعُولٌ بِهِ مَنْصُوبٌ). It is the direct object of the second verb أُحِبُّ.	أَحَدًا

325. What is a so-called نائِبُ مَفْعُولٍ مُطْلَقٍ؟

A somewhat strange, misleading term.

In some Arabic language books, the term نائِبُ مَفْعُولٍ مُطْلَقٍ is used for words that can be placed as a مَفْعُولٌ مُطْلَقٌ, but are not the original مَصْدَرٌ – see previous *question #324*. The term could be translated as *substitute for the absolute object.* This term, in my opinion, does not make sense in Arabic grammar. Why?

The مَفْعولٌ مُطْلَقٌ is a grammatical **function** in a sentence (وَظيفةٌ نَحْويّةٌ) for which the مَصْدَرُ is used. However, words which could do the job instead of the مَصْدَرُ **do not substitute** the مَفْعولٌ مُطْلَقٌ.

They only substitute the مَصْدَرُ in its function as a مَفْعولٌ مُطْلَقٌ. Some of these words are abstract and have nothing in coming with a مَصْدَرٌ. For example, كُلّ is only filled with real meaning by the word which follows كُلّ. Furthermore, words like كُلّ may function as a subject (فاعِلٌ), object (مَفْعُولٌ), or adverb (ظَرْفٌ).

1	I ate all the sweets.	أَكَلْتُ كُلَّ الْحُلْوَياتِ.
2	He works few hours.	هُوَ يَعْمَلُ بَعْضَ الْوَقْتِ.
1	Direct object (مَفْعُولٌ بِهِ). We do not say: نائِبُ مَفْعُولٍ بِهِ.	كُلّ
2	Adverb of time (ظَرْفُ زَمانٍ). We don't say: نائِبُ ظَرْفِ زَمانٍ	بَعْض

So, there is no reason why we should use the term نائِبُ مَفْعُولٍ مُطْلَقٍ.

THE PURPOSE OF THE ACTION (الْمَفْعُولُ لِأَجْلِهِ)

326. What is the so-called مَفْعُولٌ لِأَجْلِهِ؟

An object that indicates why the action of a verb is being performed.

The الْمَفْعُولُ لِأَجْلِهِ has many names in English: *that on account of which something is done* (مَفْعُولٌ لِأَجْلِهِ), *causative/causal object* (مَفْعُولٌ لَهُ), or *adverbial accusative of reason.* It gives an answer to the question: *why?* (لِمَ؟) Thus, it has the underlying sense of *because of* or *out of.*

The nature of the object is a مَصْدَرٌ that is used to show the reason for the action (لِبَيانِ سَبَبِ الْحَدَثِ). The مَصْدَرُ relates to the verb which is the reason why it is in the accusative case (مَنْصُوبٌ) because the verb operates on this object and functions as its regent (عامِلٌ).

The idea of the مَفْعُولٌ لِأَجْلِهِ is to show the **feeling that pushes the subject to perform the action.** An appropriate مَصْدَرٌ for such an object must be a *mental* or *intellectual infinitive* (مَصْدَرٌ قَلْبيٌّ) that touches *intrinsic* motives and inner feelings (أَفْعالُ النَّفْسِ الْباطِنِة): desire (رَغْبَةٌ), courage (جُرْأَةٌ), fear (خَوْفٌ), impertinence (وَقاحةٌ), contempt (تَحْقِيرٌ), glorification (تَعْظِيمٌ), eeriness (رَهْبةٌ), apprehension (خَشْيةٌ), or sympathy (شَفَقةٌ).

➢ Thus, never use the مَصْدَر of a root that expresses a non-feeling, an *extrinsic* meaning. Such roots convey actions like *reading* (قِراءةٌ), *writing* (كِتابةٌ), *stopping* (وُقُوفٌ).

What you intend to say here: *I bought the pen for writing down the lesson.*	إِشْتَرَيْتُ الْقَلَمَ كِتابةً لِلدَّرْسِ.
This sentence (construction) doesn't really make sense – unless you entertain a **feeling** to it!	

Instead, you should avoid using a مَفْعُولٌ لِأَجْلِهِ and use a slightly different construction.

I bought the pen to write the lesson.	إِشْتَرَيْتُ الْقَلَمَ لِكِتابةِ الدَّرْسِ.
Notice the position of the ل <u>before</u> the مَصْدَر. Such ل is used to indicate the **purpose** for which something is done or the reason why something is done (لامٌ لِلتَّعْلِيلِ). It must precede the action (مَصْدَر). Note that such ل actually stands for the expression لِكَيْ or لِأَنْ.	

We can derive an important rule from this:

The accusative of cause (= مَصْدَر) must happen **at the very same time** (زَمانٌ) when the subject (فاعِلٌ) is performing the action.

How can we implement the idea of the purposive object?

1. The مَفْعُولٌ لِأَجْلِهِ can be a **singular, indefinite** (نَكِرةٌ) noun.

I am not saying it to be nice.	لا أَقُولُهُ مُجامَلَةً.
I stood up in honor of the teacher.	قُمْتُ إِجلَالًا لِأُسْتاذِي.

إجلالًا is a مَصْدَر which serves as the مَفْعُولٌ لِأَجْلِهِ. It explains or justifies the action or even (حَدَثٌ): in our example, *carrying out, undertaking*, الْقِيام, which is the مَصْدَر of I-verb قامَ - يَقُومُ; R2=و; *to do; to rise*.

Both actions (الْقِيامُ and الْإِجْلالُ) take place at the same time. Both also share the same subject since الْقِيامُ and الْإِجْلالُ were done by the same (and one and only) subject.

Purposive object (مَفْعُولٌ لِأَجْلِهِ), accusative case (مَنْصُوبٌ).	إجْلالا
Preposition (حَرْفُ الْجَرِّ). It does not have a place in إِعْرابٌ. Notice the position of the لِ; it is placed **after** the مَصْدَر. This لِ expresses the direction of the action towards the object. The grammarians call it the *Lām that strengthens the regent*, i.e., the verbal power which it possesses (اللّامُ لِتَقْوِيةِ الْعامِلِ). Why? The verbal power in the مَصْدَر is less than that in the corresponding verb, so by the لِ (by annexing a preposition) it exercises its influence on its object.	لِ
Noun in the genitive case (إِسْمٌ مَجْرُورٌ), governed by the preposition. The كَسْرةٌ here is not a case marker. We have a إِضافةٌ-construction: أُسْتاذ is the first, the pronoun ي the second part → which means that in any case, a كَسْرةٌ must precede ي. Therefore, أُسْتاذ can't receive a case marker since it has a fixed shape built on the "*i*": أُسْتاذِ. For this reason, we can only apply an assumed, hypothetical genitive marker (كَسْرةٌ مُقَدَّرةٌ).	أُستاذ
The ي is the مُضافٌ إلَيْهِ; it is placed in the position of a genitive case (فِي مَحَلِّ جَرٍّ) but can't receive any case marker because a long vowel must end in سُكُونٌ in Arabic.	ي

2. The causal object is the مُضافٌ: the first part of a إِضافةٌ.

I took a walk to relax (lit: asking for rest).	تَنَزَّهْتُ طَلَبَ الرّاحةِ.
I slowed down (on the way) in fear of slipping.	تَمَهَّلْتُ فِي السَّيْرِ خَوْفَ الْإِنْزِلاقِ.
Fear (خَوْفٌ) is the first part of the إِضافةٌ and serves as the object telling the reason (مَفْعُولٌ لِأَجْلِهِ); thus, it must be in the accusative case.	

327. Can only a verb have an object telling the reason?

No, also other words can have (and govern) a purposive object.

The primary and original regent (الْعَامِلُ الْأَصْلِيُّ) in verbal sentences is the verb. Thus, it is the verb which operates on the object that gives us the reason and motive for the action (مَفْعُولٌ لِأَجْلِهِ) and induces the accusative case (مَنْصُوبٌ). But that's not all. Other words too can do the verb's job of a *regent* (عَامِل). Let's call them the "usual suspects".

1. The مَصْدَرٌ

Staying at home to rest is necessary after hard work.	لُزُومُ الْبَيْتِ طَلَبَ الرّاحةِ ضَرُورةٌ بَعْدَ الْعَمَلِ الشّاقِ.

Subject (مُبْتَدَأٌ) of the nominal sentence (جُمْلةٌ اِسْمِيّةٌ); nominative case (مَرْفُوعٌ); first part of the إِضافة. The word لُزُومُ, a مَصْدَرٌ, **governs the purposive object** (مَفْعُولٌ لِأَجْلِهِ) in the accusative.	لُزُومُ
Second part of the إِضافة; so it needs the genitive case (مَجْرُورٌ).	الْبَيْتِ
This is **not** a verb. It is طَلَبٌ which is the مَصْدَرٌ of the verb *to request* (طَلَبَ) and coincidentally looks the same as the verb – because it is the **purposive object** and thus takes a فَتْحةٌ to mark the accusative case (مَفْعُولٌ لِأَجْلِهِ مَنْصُوبٌ بِالْفَتْحةِ الظّاهِرةِ). It is the first part of the إِضافة; so it only gets one فَتْحةٌ.	طَلَبَ
Second part of the إِضافة, in the genitive case (مَجْرُورٌ).	الرّاحةِ
Predicate (خَبَرُ الْمُبْتَدَإِ) of the nominal sentence, مَرْفُوعٌ.	ضَرُورةٌ

2. The active participle (اِسْمُ الْفاعِلِ)

Zayd works hard, seeking success.	زَيْدٌ مُجْتَهِدٌ طَلَبًا لِلتَّوَفُّقِ.

زَيْدٌ is the subject (مُبْتَدَأٌ مَرْفُوعٌ) of the nominal sentence. مُجْتَهِدٌ is an **active participle** and functions as the predicate (خَبَرٌ مَرْفُوعٌ) of the nominal sentence. طَلَبًا is the **purposive object, indicating the reason**. It is governed by the active participle which is responsible for the accusative case. So, the active participle plays the role of the regent similar to a verb.

3. The passive participle (اِسْمُ الْمَفْعُولِ)

He is beloved in honor of his brother.	هُوَ مَحْبُوبٌ إِكْرامًا لِأَخِيهِ.

The passive participle مَحْبُوبٌ is the predicate (خَبَرٌ مَرْفُوعٌ) of this sentence and governs the purposive object إِكْرَامًا in the accusative case.

4. The exaggerated form (صِيغَةُ الْمُبَالَغَةِ)

He is courageous in the war seeking martyrdom or victory.	هُوَ مِقْدَامٌ فِي الْحَرْبِ طَلَبًا لِلشَّهَادَةِ أَوِ النَّصْرِ.

مِقْدَامٌ is an *intensified, exaggerated form* (صِيغَةُ الْمُبَالَغَةِ) and is placed as the predicate (خَبَرٌ مَرْفُوعٌ) of the nominal sentence (جُمْلَةٌ اِسْمِيَّةٌ). The exaggerated form governs the purposive object (طَلَبًا) in the accusative case. The prepositional phrase (فِي الْحَرْبِ) is linked to the predicate.

5. The اِسْمُ الْفِعْلِ (interjection denoting a sense of a verb – see #110)

Keep silent as a tribute to the Qur'an!	صَهْ إِجْلَالًا لِلْقُرْآنِ!

صَهْ is a اِسْمُ فِعْلِ أَمْرٍ; doesn't have a place in إِعْرَابٌ. The subject (فَاعِلٌ) of this verbal sentence (جُمْلَةٌ فِعْلِيَّةٌ) is implied/hidden (مُسْتَتِرٌ) conveying the meaning of *you* (أَنْتَ). The word صَهْ governs إِجْلَالًا (i.e., the object indicating the reason; مَفْعُولٌ لِأَجْلِهِ) in the accusative case (مَنْصُوبٌ).

328. Can you move the مَفْعُولٌ لِأَجْلِهِ to the beginning?

Yes, you can place the purposive object before its regent (عَامِلٌ).

This works similarly to the direct object (مَفْعُولٌ بِهِ) which can also be fronted and placed at the start – see *question #285*. An example:

Striving to succeed, Zayd works hard.	طَلَبًا لِلتَّوَفُّقِ يَجْتَهِدُ زَيْدٌ.

329. Can a مَفْعُولٌ لِأَجْلِهِ be mistaken for a حَالٌ?

Yes, this can happen.

The difference between a *purposive object* (مَفْعُولٌ لِأَجْلِهِ) indicating the reason/cause and a *circumstantial accusative* (حَالٌ) is often subtle. ➤ A مَفْعُولٌ لِأَجْلِهِ **can't** be modified by an adjective, but a حَالٌ **may** be.

That's it. In general, the difference is up to interpretation. In the following example, pay attention to جُوعًا and how it can be interpreted.

$$لا يَمُوتُ كَثِيرٌ مِن النَّاسِ جُوعًا.$$

This would be the translation if we understand جُوعًا as a **purposive object** (مَفْعُولٌ لِأَجْلِهِ). It gives us information **why** the action (verb) is happening.	Not many people die **of/due to hunger.**
This would be the translation if we understand جُوعًا as a **circumstantial accusative** (حَالٌ). It gives us more information **how** the action is performed.	Not many people die **hungry.**

ADVERBIAL EXPRESSION OF TIME AND PLACE (الْمَفْعُولُ فِيهِ)

330. Why do we call an adverb in Arabic ظَرْفٌ؟

It is probably an idea borrowed from the Greeks.

ظَرْفٌ denotes *circumstance; vessel, container*. Linguists suggested that the term ظَرْفٌ goes back to a Greek idea. It is the Greek borrowing from the word *anggeíon* (*vessel, container*), which was used by Aristotle to indicate temporal/local circumstances.

The famous grammarian Sībawayhi stated about it: "This is the chapter of those locations and times that receive an accusative; this is because they are **containers** in which things happen and exist; the reason they receive the accusative ending is that they are that in which something happens and in which something exists."[9]

In some of his writings, Sībawayhi treats the ظَرْفٌ as a category of words. He sometimes distinguishes between words that are neither إِسْمٌ nor ظَرْفٌ. Later on, the grammarians of the Basra school avoided the term ظَرْفٌ and started to introduce the concept of the مَفْعُولٌ فِيه (*that in which the act is done*) in line with a new logical framework that **all accusative endings** are, in fact, **objects**.

The Kūfa grammarians (الْكُوفِيُّونَ) took the word *container* (ظَرْفٌ)

---

9   هذا بابٌ ما يَنْتَصِبُ مِن الْأَماكِنَ وَالْوَقْتِ وَذَاكَ لِأَنَّها ظُرُوفٌ تَقَعُ فِيها الْأَشْياءُ
وَتَكُونُ فِيها (*al-Kitāb* I; 201.8-9)

almost philosophically. In his book *Kitāb al-ʿAyn*, al-Khalīl writes about ظَرْفٌ: "It is a **container** of anything, just as a jug is a container of something in it; ظُرُوفٌ; you say صِفاتٌ like أَمامَ and قُدّامَ are called ظُرُوفٌ; you say خَلْفَكَ زَيْدٌ (*behind you is Zayd*) and it is put in the accusative because it is a container of what is in it and it is a place for something else."

Let's check the three most important features of the ظَرْف in Arabic:

- A ظَرْفٌ has to be a **noun** (اِسْمٌ) and never a verb. It defines the time or the place when or where the action takes place.

- A اِسْمٌ which cannot indicate time or place cannot be a ظَرْفٌ.

- **Case:** the accusative (مَنْصُوبٌ) or a cemented form with the place value of the accusative (الْبِناءُ فِي مَحَلِّ نَصْبٍ).

Further remarks:

- The Kūfa grammarians used the term صِفةٌ (*attribute, adjective, descriptive*) also for adverbs (which explains the term in the above quote).

- Grammarians suggested that certain adverbs have an indeclinable shape (مَبْنِيٌّ) to prevent them from being governed by a preceding word.

- Adverbs of time (ظَرْفُ زَمانٍ) and place (ظَرْفُ مَكانٍ) can either be undefined, vague (مُبْهَمٌ) or specific (مُخْتَصٌّ), limited (مَحْدُودٌ). For ex.:

specific	Thursday	يَوْمَ الْخَمِيسِ
specific	at sunrise	ساعةَ الشُّرُوقِ
vague	never	أَبَدًا

Note: If the words يَوْم and ساعة are connected with a **pronoun** referring to the subject, they will denote *immediately; at once*.

| We'll start right away. | نَبْدَأُ بِهِ يَوْمَنا. |
| He immediately entered the room. | دَخَلَ مِنْ ساعَتِهِ الْغُرْفَةَ. |

331. Is the مَفْعُولٌ فِيهِ the same as an adverb of time or place?

We can say that without hesitation, yes.

The مَفْعُولٌ فِيهِ (*that in which the act is done*) is what we would call in English an adverb of time (ظَرْفُ الزَّمانِ) or place (ظَرْفُ الْمَكانِ).

Why is it called مَفْعُولٌ فِيهِ? The existence of a place or a time is unthinkable without the action (= the verb), happening during or at them. Adverbs of time or place are used to determine the time and place of an action. We call it مَفْعُولٌ فِيهِ because the adverbial phrase (i.e., the شِبْهُ الْجُمْلةِ) is initiated with a **virtual, estimated فِي**:

| Muhammad appeared on Friday. | حَضَرَ مُحَمَّدٌ يَوْمَ الْجُمْعةِ. |
| The underlying basis of the sentence is: → | حَضَرَ مُحَمَّدٌ فِي يَوْمِ الْجُمْعةِ. |

Why can we call يَوْمَ an adverb?

- First of all, it is related to a verb: to the action (حَدَثٌ). The action is enfolded and surrounded (مَظْرُوفٌ فِيهِ) by this information: يَوْمَ.

- Secondly and more important, the underlying meaning of يَوْمَ is virtually connected with فِي which removes the ambiguities.

332. Why is the adverb in the accusative case (مَنْصُوبٌ)?

Because it is seen as a certain type of object (مَفْعُولٌ فِيهِ).

The Basran grammarians (الْبَصْرِيُّونَ) suggested that each and every accusative ending (مَنْصُوبٌ) is the result of the governance of a verb. This implies that the adverbs of time and place need to be analyzed as objects due to their accusative ending.

The central idea behind analyzing **adverbs as objects** is that a verb by itself implies the existence of several things: an agent (subject; the one who is doing the action), an object (patient), the action itself, the circumstances, and the time and location. For this reason, some grammarians speak of the **heaviness of the verb** compared to the lightness of the noun.

The adverb is in the accusative case (مَنْصُوبٌ) visibly (لَفْظًا) or by a place value (مَحَلًّا) due to its location in the sentence. It is usually governed by the verb (عامِلٌ).

Now, watch out: If the word that usually functions as an adverb is <u>not included</u> or <u>enfolded in the action</u> (حَدَثٌ), we don't treat it as a

ظَرْفٌ - but according to its position in the sentence.

A day has 24 hours.	الْيَوْمُ أَرْبَعٌ وَعِشْرُونَ ساعةً.

This is a nominal sentence (جُمْلَةٌ اِسْمِيّةٌ). The word *the day* (الْيَوْمُ) is the subject (مُبْتَدَأٌ) and gets a ضَمّة for the nominative case – and not a فَتْحةٌ as usual, when it is used as an adverb (الْيَوْمَ) expressing *today*. Why?

Because in the example, it is not enfolded in the action. In fact, there is no action at all. The word الْيَوْمُ is a اِسْمٌ and serves as the **subject** (مُبْتَدَأٌ) of the nominal sentence (جُمْلَةٌ اِسْمِيّةٌ)

The believer is afraid of Judgment Day.	الْمُؤْمِنُ يَخْشَى يَوْمَ الْقِيَامَةِ.

Here, we do have a verb (يَخْشَى), but the word يَوْمَ is not tangled up in the action of the verb. It inflicts a punishment, because the believer does not wait until Judgment Day comes in order to be afraid of it. Instead, he is **now** afraid of the Judgment Day, and for this reason, the word is the **direct object** (مَفْعُولٌ بِه) – and not an adverb (مَفْعُولٌ فِيه).

Remark: A specific measurement may also work as an adverb of place.

I walked for miles.	سِرْتُ مِيلًا.

مِيلًا is an **adverb of place** in the accusative case that is attached to the verb (مَفْعُولٌ فِيه ظَرْفُ مَكَانٍ مَنْصُوبٌ بِالْفَتْحَةِ الظَّاهِرَةِ مُتَعَلِّقٌ بِالْفِعْلِ سِرْتُ).

333. Can an adverb of time or place be the predicate (خَبَرٌ)?

That's still a debate. Purist grammarians say no; pragmatists yes.

Let's start with a sentence (which we will also use in *question #336*):

The departure/journey **is** tomorrow.	السَّفَرُ غَدًا.
This would be the sentence with a predicate (خَبَرٌ):	السَّفَرُ حاصِلٌ غَدًا.

Some people say that the adverb غَدًا itself is the predicate (خَبَرٌ) of the nominal sentence (جُمْلَةٌ اِسْمِيّةٌ). However, this is not entirely correct.

In nominal sentences, we have a special situation. We do not have a word which operates on the ظَرْف; we are missing the action for which the circumstances (the place or time of occurrence) are mentioned, to which the adverb is attached (التَّعَلُّقُ).

Such a word was deleted since it was a mere description of a general state or being. This could be an active or passive participle. For ex.: *occurring/taking place* (حاصِلٌ), *being/existent* (كائِنٌ), *enduring* (مُسْتَقِرٌّ). We could even imagine that there was a verb: *to find* (وَجَدَ), *to occur/ happen* (حَصَلَ), *to endure* (اِسْتَقَرَّ); *see #330.*

Let's return to our question: can the adverb of time or place serve as the predicate (خَبَرٌ) in a nominal sentence (جُمْلةٌ اِسْمِيّةٌ)? You read that in many grammar books. I prefer to say that the ظَرْف **appears** in the **place** of a predicate. When we look at the idea of the شِبْهُ الْجُمْلةِ, it makes sense to follow the view of the classical grammarians, which means: we need to focus on the necessary **deletion** of the predicate (because it points to generality) and **assume a relation** (مُتَعَلِّقٌ بـ) to it. → For a deep discussion see question #229.

334. What's the difference between an adverb and a prepositional phrase?

The adverb (ظَرْفٌ) has a grammatical place in the sentence.

We can use the term شِبْهُ الْجُمْلةِ (*quasi-sentence*) as a generic term for the adverb (ظَرْفٌ) and the prepositional phrase (الْجارُ وَالْمَجْرُورُ).

A شِبْهُ الْجُمْلةِ indicates a sub-meaning and does not convey an independent meaning – instead, it only completes the meaning. The adverb and the prepositional phrase share that they both need a connection to an event or action to which they can relate (اِرْتِباطُ شِبْهِ الْجُمْلةِ بِالْحَدَثِ) and to which they are attached. Otherwise, the prepositional or adverbial phrase would be like a detached satellite. Here, however, the similarities between the ظَرْفٌ and the الْجارُ وَالْمَجْرُورُ end.

In grammar, the ظَرْفٌ and the الْجارُ وَالْمَجْرُورُ are different concepts:

- The **adverb** (ظَرْفٌ) is a **noun** (اِسْمٌ) and is governed in the accusative case – we need to look for the operator (عامِلٌ). *See #335.*
- The **prepositional phrase** (الْجارُ وَالْمَجْرُورُ), as its name says, starts with a حَرْفٌ, and a حَرْفٌ **never has a place** in the **analysis** (إِعْرابٌ). It is not governed and never gets a case ending.

335. Which words can govern an adverb?

Many.

In Arabic, the adverb (ظَرْفٌ) is a **noun** (اِسْمٌ) and therefore gets a case marker: the accusative case. The regent or governor (عامِلٌ) of the adverb (الْعامِلُ فِي الظَّرْفِ) is quite sophisticated: it is the word (الْمُتَعَلَّقُ) to which the ظَرْفٌ is attached, connected to (مُتَعَلِّقٌ بِهِ).

The verb (فِعْلٌ) is the principal governor (عامِلٌ) in Arabic, and this is true for the adverb too. The verb is responsible for the case marker.

Muhammad will come tomorrow.	سَيَأْتِي مُحَمَّدٌ غَدًا.
غَدًا (*tomorrow*) is an adverb of time (مَفْعُولٌ فِيهِ, ظَرْفُ زَمانٍ مَنْصُوبٌ). The adverbial phrase (شِبْهُ الْجُمْلةِ) is related to the verb (مُتَعَلِّقٌ بِسَيَأْتِي).	

However, there are many possible regents (عَوامِلُ): the "usual suspects".

1. The مَصْدَرٌ

Staying awake during the night is tiresome.	السَّهَرُ لَيْلًا مُرْهِقٌ.

Subject (مُبْتَدَأ) of the nominal sentence (جُمْلةٌ اِسْمِيّةٌ); مَرْفُوعٌ.	السَّهَرُ
Adverb of time (ظَرْفُ زَمانٍ مَنْصُوبٌ). It is connected with the infinitive noun (شِبْهُ الْجُمْلةِ مُتَعَلِّقٌ بِالسَّهَرِ) السَّهَرُ.	لَيْلًا
Predicate (خَبَرٌ مَرْفُوعٌ) in the nominative case.	مُرْهِقٌ

2. The active participle (اِسْمُ الْفاعِلِ)

Muhammad will come tomorrow.	مُحَمَّدٌ قادِمٌ غَدًا.

The adverb of time (غَدًا) is in the accusative case. The adverbial phrase (شِبْهُ الْجُمْلةِ) is linked and attached to the active participle (which does the job of a regent similar to a verb).

3. The passive participle (اِسْمُ الْمَفْعُولِ)

The shop is opened in the morning and closed at night.	الْمَحَلُّ مَفْتُوحٌ صَباحًا وَمُغْلَقٌ مَساءً.

The passive participle مَفْتُوحٌ (*opened*) is linked to the adverb of time (صَبَاحًا) and shows this connection by inducing the accusative case. The other passive participle مُغْلَقٌ (*closed*) is linked to the other adverb of time (مَسَاءً).

4. The form of exaggeration (صِيغَةُ الْمُبَالَغِةِ)

Zayd has been lying (has been a notorious liar) throughout his life.	زَيْدٌ كَذَّابٌ طُولَ حَيَاتِهِ.

The word كَذَّابٌ (*someone who lies a lot*) is a صِيغَةُ الْمُبَالَغِةِ. The adverb of time (طُولَ), in the state of an accusative (نَصْبٌ), is attached/linked to it.

5. The noun resembling an active participle – the pseudo participle working as an adjective (صِفَةٌ مُشَبَّهةٌ). See also *Arabic for Nerds 1, #143*.

A generous individual is generous throughout his life.	الْكَرِيمُ كَرِيمٌ طُولَ حَيَاتِهِ.

كَرِيمٌ (*generous*) is a صِفَةٌ مُشَبَّهةٌ. It conveys the permanency or constancy of a characteristic (تَدُلُّ عَلَى الثُّبُوتِ مِن كَرُمَ), in our example: *generousness*. It is connected with and attached to طُولَ, i.e., the adverb of time (طُولَ), which is in the state of an accusative case (نَصْبٌ).

336. Can it be required to delete the regent (عامِلٌ) of an adverb?

Yes, it can – and this happens quite often.

Usually people don't realize that there is something missing in a sentence because they understand the meaning anyway (implicitly). This is also the main reason and justification why we can delete certain words.

Knowing that a word has been left out in a sentence can be of great help when translating difficult sentences. So, let's check the most common **situations in which the regent of an adverb has to be deleted.**

1. Originally, the **predicate** (خَبَرٌ) was the regent (عامِلٌ).

The traveling/journey is tomorrow.	السَّفَرُ غَدًا.

This would be the sentence with a predicate (خَبَرٌ): →	السَّفَرُ حاصِلٌ غَدًا.

Subject (مُبْتَدَأٌ) of the nominal sentence, nominative (مَرْفُوعٌ).	السَّفَرُ
Adverb of time (ظَرْفُ زَمانٍ); in the accusative case (مَنْصوبٌ). The adverb appears in the place of the predicate and is related to the deleted predicate (e.g.: حاصِلٌ) which had to be deleted since it is implicitly understood (شِبْهُ الْجُمْلةِ مُتَعَلِّقٌ بِمَحْذوفٍ خَبَرٌ) from the context and structure.	غَدًا

2. Originally, the **circumstantial qualifier** (حالٌ) was the عَامِلٌ.

The book is the best solace in times of loneliness.	الْكِتابُ ساعةَ الْوَحْدةِ خَيْرُ جَليسٍ.

Supposed meaning (تَقْديرٌ): →	الْكِتابُ مُصاحَبًا ساعةَ الْوَحْدةِ خَيْرُ جَليسٍ.

Subject (مُبْتَدَأٌ) of the nominal sentence; nominative (مَرْفوعٌ).	الْكِتابُ
It is an adverb of time (ظَرْفُ زَمانٍ مَنْصوبٌ) in the accusative case; first part of the إضافةٌ. The adverbial phrase (شِبْهُ الْجُمْلةِ) is related and connected to a deleted circumstantial qualifier (شِبْهُ الْجُمْلةِ مُتَعَلِّقٌ بِمَحْذوفٍ واقِعٍ حالًا); see supposed meaning above.	ساعةَ
Second part of the إضافةٌ; genitive case (مُضافٌ إلَيْهِ مَجْرورٌ).	الْوَحْدةِ
Predicate, nominative case (خَبَرٌ مَرْفوعٌ بِالضَّمّةِ الظّاهِرةِ). This is also the first part of another إضافةٌ.	خَيْرُ
(مَجْرورٌ بِالْكَسرةِ); thus, it takes the genitive case مُضافٌ إلَيْهِ.	جَليسٍ

3. Originally, an **adjective** (صِفةٌ) was the regent. ▷ <u>indefiniteness</u>

I bought the book from **a** library in front of the university.	إشْتَرَيْتُ الْكِتابَ مِنْ مَكْتَبةٍ أمامَ الْجامِعةِ.

This is the assumed meaning (تَقْديرٌ): →	مِنْ مَكْتَبةٍ كائِنةٍ أمامَ الْجامِعةِ.

أمامَ is an adverb of place (ظَرْفُ مَكانٍ مَنْصوبٌ). This adverbial phrase (شِبْهُ الْجُمْلةِ) is connected with the deleted **indefinite** (نَكِرةٌ) **adjective** because the word *library* is also indefinite. Which word could have served in the position of the deleted indefinite adjective? It could have been an **active participle**, e.g., *being existent* (كَائِنة).

4. Originally, a **relative clause** (صِلة) was the regent. ➤ <u>definiteness</u>

I bought the book from **the** library **which** is in front of the university.	إِشْتَرَيْتُ الْكِتابَ مِن الْمَكْتَبةِ الَّتِي أَمامَ الْجامِعةِ.

supposed meaning	I	...مِن الْمَكْتَبةِ الَّتِي تَقَعُ أَمامَ الْجامِعةِ.
(تَقْدِيرٌ); two possibilities	II	...مِن الْمَكْتَبةِ الَّتِي هِيَ واقِعةٌ أَمامَ الْجامِعةِ.

The adverb of place (أَمامَ) is in the accusative and is related to the deleted relative clause (صِلةٌ) which doesn't have a place in the analysis. In Arabic:

ظَرْفُ مَكانٍ مَنْصُوبٌ بِالْفَتْحةِ الظَّاهِرةِ, وَشِبْهُ الْجُمْلةِ مُتَعَلِّقٌ بِمَحْذُوفٍ, صِلةٌ لا مَحَلَّ لَهُ مِن الْإِعْرابِ

337. Can one regent (عَامِلٌ) govern two adverbs?

Yes, this is possible.

But it's not that simple after all. Purist grammarians state that this is only possible if the two adverbs are of different types. In other words, one is an adverb of **place** (ظَرْفُ مَكانٍ), the other one is an adverb of **time** (ظَرْفُ زَمانٍ).

I waited for you on Saturday in front of the house.	إِنْتَظَرْتُكَ يَوْمَ السَّبْتِ أَمامَ الْبَيْتِ.

Both adverbs – the adverb of time (يَوْمَ) and of place (أَمامَ) – are connected with the same verb. This verb, إِنْتَظَرَ (*to wait*), governs both of them in the accusative case. At the same time, each of the adverbs functions as the first part of the إِضافةٌ.

What happens if the two adverbs are of the same type (الظَّرْفانِ مِن نَوْعٍ واحِدٍ)? The grammatical analysis (إِعْرابٌ) is surprisingly different.

- the first word is an adverb (ظَرْفٌ);

- the second word is an apposition (بَدَلٌ) for the first adverb;

I waited for you for an hour on Saturday.	اِنْتَظَرْتُكَ يَوْمَ السَّبْتِ ساعةً.
Adverb of time (ظَرْف زَمانٍ مَنْصُوبٌ). The adverbial phrase is connected with (attached to) the verb *to wait* (اِنْتَظَرَ).	يَوْمَ
Apposition (بَدَلٌ مَنْصُوبٌ بِالْفَتْحةِ الظّاهِرة). It relates to the first adverb; thus, it is also in the accusative as it must take the same case.	ساعةً

Many grammarians, however, say that it is possible to have two adverbs of the same kind governed by the same verb – provided that both adverbs coincide in time with the action/process, in our example: *waiting* (الإنْتِظار). The above sentence is a good example of that.

338. Where in the sentence should you place an adverb of time?

Actually, you can place it wherever you want.

The adverb of time or place (ظَرْفُ مَكانٍ or زَمانٍ) doesn't have to be necessarily placed after the verb.

Changing the word order and thus moving an adverb of time/place has an effect, but it is subtle. It conveys nuances of emphasis, but it is more up to intonation at the end. So, an adverb (of time or place) in Arabic can theoretically appear anywhere in the sentence. It is my feeling that in verbal sentences, it sounds more natural at the end of the sentence and not between the verb and the direct object.

The following sentences mean basically the same:

Tomorrow, Muhammad will come.	غَدًا سَيَأْتِي مُحَمَّدٌ.
Muhammad, he will come tomorrow.	مُحَمَّدٌ سَيَأْتِي غَدًا.
Tomorrow Muhammad will come.	سَيَأْتِي غَدًا مُحَمَّدٌ.
Muhammad is coming tomorrow.	مُحَمَّدٌ غَدًا قادِمٌ.

339. What does سارَ الْيَوْمَ mean?

If you only see this sentence (fragment), then it is not quite clear.

The sentence can mean two things – and both are correct.

1	adverb of time	He went **today**.	سارَ الْيَوْمَ.
2	direct object	He spent **the day** going.	

There is a trick to find out which of the two options is meant. → Try to transform the sentence into the passive voice. The direct object will become the subject of the passive (option 2).

1	adverb of time	He was walked **today**.	سِيرَ الْيَوْمَ.
2	direct object	**The day** was spent.	سِيرَ الْيَوْمُ.

What happened in example 1? If we have an adverb, the adverb remains in the accusative case! The passive sentence with the adverb has an underlying meaning: سِيرَ سَيْرُ الْيَوْمِ.

In the end, it all boils down to one question: which element is responsible for the accusative ending?

- If الْيَوْمَ is a **direct object**, then it is directly <u>governed</u> by the **verb**.
- If it is an **adverb**, the accusative case is explained differently. It is **independent of the construction of the sentence**. The adverb can be seen as separated from the verb, but it remains related to it in meaning. → See also *question #340* (number 3).

340. What can act as a substitute for an adverb (نائِبٌ عَن الظَّرْفِ)؟

In fact, you don't need a substitute.

Many words that we call adverbs in English are in Arabic basic nouns (اسْمٌ) that do the job of adverbs. Let's look at forms that may be placed as adverbs and are located in the spot of an accusative (نَصْبٌ).

1. The مَصْدَرٌ

I waited for you after the students left.	إِنْتَظَرْتُكَ إِنْصِرافَ الطُّلابِ.
Underlying meaning of the sentence: →	إِنْتَظَرْتُكَ وَقْتَ إِنْصِرافِ الطُّلابِ.

إنْصِرافَ	**Adverb of time** in the accusative case (ظَرْفُ زَمانٍ مَنْصُوبٌ). The adverbial phrase is connected with the verb *to wait* (شِبْهُ الجُمْلةِ مُتَعَلِّقٌ بِالْفِعْل انْتَظَرَ).

The star appeared for the twinkling of an eye, then it vanished.	ظَهَرَ النَّجْمُ طَرْفَةَ عَيْنٍ ثُمَّ اخْتَفَى.
This is the meaning of the sentence: →	ظَهَرَ النَّجْمُ مُدَّةَ طَرْفةِ عَيْنٍ.

طَرْفَةَ	طَرْفَةَ serves as an adverb of time (ظَرْفُ زَمانٍ مَنْصُوبٌ); thus, it is in the accusative case; the adverbial phrase is related to the verb ظَهَرَ.

2. **Quantifiers** can convey the meaning of an adverb. They serve as the 1ˢᵗ part of a إضافةٌ; the second part gives them a full meaning.

like	مِثْل		all	كُلّ		any	أَيّ
what, that	ما		some	بَعْض			

Muhammad appears/comes every day.	يَحْضُرُ مُحَمَّدٌ كُلَّ يَوْمٍ.

كُلَّ here is an adverb of time (ظَرْفُ زَمانٍ مَنْصُوبٌ) and the first part of a إضافةٌ. The adverbial phrase (شِبْهُ الْجُمْلةِ) is related to the verb حَضَرَ.

I read sometimes.	قَرَأْتُ بَعْضَ الْوَقْتِ.

Also here, بَعْضَ is an **adverb of time**, connected with the verb *to read* (شِبْهُ الْجُمْلةِ مُتَعَلِّقٌ بِالْفِعْل قَرَأَ).

He walked for a mile and then returned.	سارَ مِثْلَ مِيلٍ ثُمَّ عادَ.

مِثْلَ is an adverb of place (ظَرْفُ مَكانٍ) and is connected with *to go*.

Go anytime you wish!	اذْهَبْ أَيَّ وَقْتٍ تَشاءُ!

The word أَيَّ is an adverb of time in this sentence. The adverbial phrase is linked to the verb *to go* (شِبْهُ الْجُمْلةِ مُتَعَلِّقٌ بِالْفِعْل ذَهَبَ).

3. **Numbers** (عَدَدٌ) ➜ if they are followed by a time or a place.

I read for three hours.	قَرَأْتُ ثَلاثَ ساعاتٍ.

The word ثَلاثَ is an adverb of time, connected with the verb *to read*.

Why can't ثَلاثَ be the direct object in the above example? The direct object would indicate that I **physically** read three hours (which is merely impossible). I can **only physically read a book**. I can only read for (the duration of) three hours (which would convey the meaning of an adverb of time). This is the difference between the adverb and the direct object.

341. Can a *noun of place* (اِسْمُ الْمَكانِ) fill the place of an adverb?

Yes, this is possible – but only under conditions.

What do we mean by the اِسْمُ الْمَكانِ؟ The اِسْمُ الْمَكانِ is used to indicate the **place** where the core meaning of the verb is carried out. It is the noun (اِسْمٌ) which indicates the place of doing a action.

There are two patterns: مَفْعِلٌ or مَفْعَلٌ; they form broken plurals: مَفاعِلُ and مَفْعَلةٌ. E.g., the place of *prostrating* is a *mosque* (مَسْجِدٌ; pl. مَساجِدُ), the place where *damaging* occurs is a *battlefield* (مَعْرَكةٌ; pl. مَعارِكُ). The اِسْمُ الْمَكانِ – unlike other derived nouns (مُشْتَقّاتٌ) – only works for a standard 3-lettered verb (ثُلاثِيٌّ). See *Arabic for Nerds 1*, #170.

So, can such a word do the job of an adverb? Yes, a اِسْمُ الْمَكانِ can function as an adverb of place – but only if the اِسْمُ الْمَكانِ was derived from the same root as the regent (عامِلٌ).

I sat on Zayd's place.	جَلَسْتُ مَجْلِسَ زَيْدٍ.

مَجْلِسَ functions as an adverb of place (ظَرْفُ مَكانٍ مَنْصُوبٌ بِالْفَتْحةِ الظّاهِرةِ, وَشِبْهُ الْجُمْلةِ مُتَعَلِّقٌ بِالْفِعْلِ جَلَسَ). This is possible since مَجْلِسَ and its regent (جَلَسْتُ) are derived from the same material (مِنْ مادّةٍ واحِدةٍ), i.e., ج-ل-س.

342. When is إذْ treated as an adverb?

Usually when it denotes: when, while.

Many common words may be used as an adverb in Arabic. إِذْ is one of them, although that is not its most common function. When used as an adverb, إِذْ usually goes along with the **past tense** (ظَرْفٌ لِلْماضِي مِن الزَّمانِ) and expresses *when, while*. A possible synonym would be حِينَ.

Now, if إِذْ is placed as an adverb, will it get a فَتْحَةٌ to mark the accusative (مَنْصُوبٌ)? No, it won't. إِذْ has a fixed shape (مَبْنِيٌّ) and always ends in سُكُونٌ. However, for the analysis, we need to assign an estimated, virtual place value. We say that إِذْ is placed in the position of an accusative case (فِي مَحَلِّ نَصْبٍ).

إِذْ is mostly used to add/connect a sentence and usually precedes a verb (= introducing a verbal sentence) or occasionally a noun (= introducing a nominal sentence). Before we analyze إِذْ as an adverb of time, let's check the most common functions of إِذْ. Note that in some situations, the ending changes - but this never happens when إِذْ works as an adverb of time as such إِذْ is indeclinable.

particle of surprise	حَرْفُ مُفَاجَأَةٍ	While I was walking, it (**suddenly**) started raining.	بَيْنَمَا أَنَا سَائِرٌ إِذْ أَمْطَرَتِ السَّمَاءُ
particle of causality	حَرْفُ تَعْلِيلٍ	I rewarded my son **for his** success.	كَافَأْتُ وَلَدِي إِذْ نَجَحَ.
adverb of time	ظَرْفُ زَمانٍ	I was born **when** the war started.	وُلِدْتُ إِذْ بَدَأَتِ الْحَرْبُ.
annexed part	مُضافٌ إِلَيْهِ	You returned, **then** you came in.	رَجَعْتُمْ وَبَعْدَئِذٍ دَخَلْتُمْ.

➤ Here, وَ is a conjunction (to couple/coordinate two sentences). Why do we have the ending ٍ? The nunation (تَنْوِينٌ) is regarded as a **substitution and compensation** (عُوِّضَ بِالتَّنْوِينِ عَنْ جُمْلةٍ مَحْذُوفةٍ) for the deleted sentence (in gray) because the estimated meaning is: رَجَعْتُمْ، وَبَعْدَ إِذْ رَجَعْتُمْ دَخَلْتُمْ

| direct object | مَفْعُولٌ بِهِ | Remember **how you used to be few** (*Sura 7:86*). | وَاذْكُرُوا إِذْ كُنْتُمْ قَلِيلًا. |
| | | إِذْ (here in the meaning of وَقْتَ) serves as the direct object; it gets the place value of an accusative case (فِي مَحَلِّ نَصْبٍ). The nominal sentence after إِذْ is placed as the second part of the إِضافةٌ; it is in | |

| | | the place of a genitive case (الْجُمْلَةُ الْإِسْمِيّةُ بَعْدَهَا (فِي مَحَلِّ جَرٍّ بالإِضافةِ). |

Let's focus on the situation when إذْ does the job of an adverb of time:

| How happy we were as children! | كَمْ سَعِدْنا إذْ نَحْنُ أَطْفالٌ! |

Adverb of time, for the past (ظَرْفٌ لِما مَضَى مِن الزَّمان). It is fixed, cemented (مَبْنِيٌّ) on the سُكُونٌ. Nevertheless, it is located in the grammatical place of an accusative case (فِي مَحَلِّ نَصْبٍ). The adverbial phrase (شِبْهُ الْجُمْلةِ) is connected with the verb *to be happy* (سَعِدَ).	إذْ
Personal pronoun (ضَمِيرٌ مُنْفَصِلٌ) which serves as the subject of the nominal sentence (فِي مَحَلِّ رَفْعٍ مُبْتَدَأً).	نَحْنُ
Predicate (خَبَرٌ) in the nominative case (مَرْفُوعٌ).	أَطْفالٌ

- Regarding إذْ: In the above sentence, it is the first part of a إضافةٌ. The entire nominal sentence consisting of subject and predicate is located in the place of the second part (مُضافٌ إلَيْهِ) and therefore set in the position of a genitive case (فِي مَحَلِّ جَرٍّ).

- Regarding كَمْ: Usually after a كَمْ الْخَبَرِيّةُ (predicative *how much* – not the كَمْ to inquire about a number). It is used in **exclamations**; a noun in the genitive case follows. However, if the meaning is implicitly understood, you can delete the genitive part – and put a verb immediately after كَمْ. For this reason, it is possible to delete the noun that specifies the sentence (تَمْيِيزٌ).

| How often did you disobey (break) my order! | كَمْ عَصَيْتَ أَمْرِي! |
| Implicit meaning: How many times did you disobey it! | كَمْ مَرّةٍ عَصَيْتَهُ! |

Another example of إذْ:

| He succeeded because he studied. | نَجَحَ إذْ ذاكَرَ. |
| إذْ is an adverb of time for the past (ظَرْفٌ لِما مَضَى مِن الزَّمان) in the meaning of: "*when you have studied*". Note that some prefer to treat it as a particle in place of a causative ل and translate it with *because* (see above). The verbal | |

> sentence ذاكَر is in the place of the second part of the إضافةٌ of إذْ.

Excursus: The most common job of إذْ is that of a direct object (مَفْعُولٌ بِه). We get this situation when the verb is transitive (which basically means that it can have an object).

Remember [the time] when we were in the village!	اُذْكُرْ إذْ كُنَّا فِي الْقَرْيَةِ!
In this example, إذْ is **not an adverb** (ظَرْفٌ) because the action – remembering (الذِّكْر) – **does not fall into the time when we <u>were</u> in the village.** Instead, the action of *remembering* is happening **now** which means: *I remember that time* (أنا أذْكُرُ هذا الْوَقْتَ) = direct object!	
Remember when you were little!	اُذْكُرْ إذْ كُنْتَ صَغِيرًا!!

Such application of إذْ is found many times in the Qur'an. In these situations, إذْ is the **direct object of a deleted verb** (فِعْلٌ مَحْذُوفٌ) with the estimated, implicitly understood meaning (تَقْدِيرٌ) of: *Remember! Mention!* (اُذْكُرْ). For example:

Sura 2:30	وَإذْ قَالَ رَبُّكَ لِلْمَلَائِكَةِ إنِّي جَاعِلٌ فِي الْأَرْضِ خَلِيفَةً.

- And [**mention, O Muhammad**], when your Lord said to the angels, "Indeed, I will make upon the earth a successive authority." *(Sahīh Int.)*
- And (**remember**) when your Lord said to the angels: "Verily, I am going to place (mankind) generations after generations on earth." *(Muh. Khan)*

Many translators, however, ignore it:

- [Prophet], when your Lord told the angels, "I am putting a successor on earth." *(Abdul Haleem)*

What is the underlying meaning/structure of such a sentence?

Remember now, oh Allah's Prophet, when your Lord said...	اُذْكُرْ يَا نَبِيَّ اللهِ الْآنَ إذْ قالَ رَبُّكَ ...

343. Can إذْ work as the second part of a إضافةٌ?

Yes, it can.

Let's take the expression وَقْتَئِذٍ which is usually translated as *at that time*. In this expression, إِذْ receives as **special treatment**:

- إِذْ here is the **second** part of a إِضَافَةٌ (i.e., the مُضَافٌ إِلَيْهِ).
- Therefore, إِذْ is <u>not</u> placed as an adverb (ظَرْفٌ) since the second part in a possessive construction can't carry out jobs like the direct object, adverb, etc. Only the first part is capable of that.
- The only job of the مُضَافٌ إِلَيْهِ is to indicate possession (*A of B*; with *B* being the second part).
- Now comes the interesting point: <u>another</u> adverb (ظَرْفٌ) serves as the <u>first</u> part (الْمُضَافُ) of the إِضَافَةٌ-construction.
- Only in that situation, the word إِذْ takes **nunation** (تَنْوِينٌ).

The treatment of إِذْ in such constructions is complicated. The nunation here is **not** a تَنْوِينُ التَّنْكِيرِ; it is not the typical nunation for an indefinite word. The nunation which إِذْ gets is a **compensation** for a deleted part (التَّنْوِينُ عِوَضُ الْجُمْلَةِ الْمَحْذُوفَةِ) **after** إِذْ. What we finally get is the ending "*-in*" (كَسْرَةٌ). How can we understand the deleted part after إِذْ؟

Sura 69:16	The sky will be torn apart **on that Day**, it will be so frail.	وَانْشَقَّتِ السَّمَاءُ فَهِيَ يَوْمَئِذٍ وَاهِيَةٌ.
يَوْمَئِذٍ	يَوْمَ is an adverb of time and serves as the first part of the إِضَافَةٌ. The word إِذْ is the second part (مُضَافٌ إِلَيْهِ).	

What does the nunation here compensate? The nunation stands for the deleted sentence after إِذْ which would grammatically be a مُضَافٌ إِلَيْهِ.

What is the deleted part after يَوْمَ إِذْ...؟ What could be a possible virtual, estimated meaning (تَقْدِيرٌ)? It could be (for example): *...when the soul of a dying man comes up to his throat.* (...إِذْ بَلَغَتِ النَّفْسُ الْحُلْقُومَ)

Sura 27:89	Whoever comes with a good deed will be rewarded with something better, and be secure from the terrors **of that Day** (Abdul Haleem) ...from the horror **on that Day** (Mustafa Khattab)	مَن جَاءَ بِالْحَسَنَةِ فَلَهُ خَيْرٌ مِّنْهَا وَهُم مِّن فَزَعٍ يَوْمَئِذٍ آمِنُونَ.

What does the nunation here compensate and stand for? There are many ideas. E.g.: يَوْمَ إِذْ جَاءَ الْحَسَنَةِ *(when the reward of good deeds will come)*.

Some remarks on the translation. Abdul Haleem is a highly respected translator. However, in this verse, يَوم cannot be a مُضافٌ إلَيْهِ because the word فَزَع gets nunation (تَنْوِينٌ). Instead, يَومَ is an adverb of time (مَفْعُولٌ فِيهِ, ظَرْفُ زَمانٍ) and works as the first part of a إضافةٌ.

If يَوم was the مُضافٌ إلَيْهِ as the translation of Abdul Haleem suggests, it would be genitive (مَجْرُورٌ) by a visible كَسرةٌ like in 11:66: ...مِنْ خِزْيِ يَوْمِئِذٍ which Abdul Haleem (correctly) translated as: *from the disgrace of that day.* ▸ Therefore, the translation of يَوْمَئِذٍ in 27:89 cannot be *of that day.* It should be: *on that day.*

at that time	وَقْتَئِذٍ	then, at the time	حِينَئِذٍ
then, at that time/hour	ساعَتَئِذٍ	then, on that day	يَوْمَئِذٍ

Note: The word الآنَئِذِ does not exist because الآنَ (*now*) denotes the nearest present time.

My brother married when I was young. (at the time that I was young.)	تَزَوَّجَ أَخِي وَكُنْتُ حِينَئِذٍ صَغِيرًا.
What you see here marked in gray is what the nunation actually compensates for.	تَزَوَّجَ أَخِي وَكُنْتُ حِينَ تَزَوَّجَ أَخِي صَغِيرًا.

We then traveled. (After we got up, we traveled.)	وَحِينَئِذٍ سافَرْنا.
حِينَئِذٍ is a compensation for the deleted verb قُمْنا: *when we got up, we traveled* (أَتَى التَّنْوِينُ كَتَعْوِيضٍ عَنْ جُمْلةِ قُمْنا).	...حِينَ قُمْنا سافَرْنا.

344. Can إذا function as an adverb?

Yes, it can – when the sentence talks about the future.

إذا can denote several things. The most common application is perhaps to denote *if; when.* If we have such a sentence, إذا is treated as an **adverb of time** for the future (ظَرْفٌ لِلْمُسْتَقْبَلِ) or more correctly ظَرْفٌ (لِما يُسْتَقْبَلُ مِن الزَّمانِ). This explains why إذا is often used as a conditional particle (إذا الشَّرْطِيّةُ).

إذا produces quite complicated structures. The second part of the conditional clause is, roughly said, the reason why إذا is located in the position of an adverb in the place of an accusative case (فِي مَحَلِّ نَصْبٍ بِجَوابِهِ). Moreover, what we get is, in fact, a إضافةٌ-construction.

We say that the second part of the conditional clause (جُمْلَةُ الشَّرْطِ) is treated as the second part of the إضافةٌ (i.e., the مُضافٌ إلَيْهِ) because the **adverb إذا** serves as the **first part** of the إضافةٌ-construction. Sounds complicated? Let's check an example.

| If you work hard, you will succeed. | إذَا اجْتَهَدْتَ نَجَحْتَ. |

So, what does this sentence actually mean?

| Your success is conditioned by your diligence. | نَجاحُكَ مَشْرُوطٌ بِاجْتِهادِكَ. |

Let's analyze the interesting parts:

Adverb of time for the future (ظَرْفٌ لِمَا يُسْتَقْبَلُ مِن الزَّمانِ). It occupies the grammatical place of an accusative case (فِي مَحَلِّ نَصْبٍ). Notice: This adverb is connected with the **second verb** (i.e., نَجَحْتَ) and <u>not</u> the first verb.	إذا
Verb plus subject (فاعِلٌ). The entire sentence serves as the second part of the إضافةٌ; thus, it is grammatically located in the place of a genitive case (فِي مَحَلِّ جَرٍّ مُضافٌ إلَيْهِ).	اجْتَهَدْتَ

However, إذا does not always function as a particle for the conditional. It can also be used to **simply denote time**.

| Sura 92:1 | By the night when it covers! | وَاللَّيْلِ إذَا يَغْشَى! |
| Sura 92:2 | And [by] the day when it appears! | وَالنَّهارِ إذَا تَجَلَّى! |

In both examples, إذَا is an **adverb of time** (ظَرْفُ زَمانٍ) which is connected with the verb يَغْشَى (and تَجَلَّى respectively). Since إذَا can't take any case marker, we have to use a place value; we say that إذَا takes the position of an accusative case (فِي مَحَلِّ نَصْبٍ).

345. What happens if إذا denotes surprise?

Then إذا is not an adverb (ظَرْفٌ); we treat it as a particle (حَرْفٌ).

إذا can also denote **surprise** (إذا الْمُفاجَأةِ) in the sense of: *Lo! See! Behold!* It indicates something unexpected (أَمْرٌ غَيْرُ مُتَوَقَّعٍ).

- Such إذا is treated as a حَرْفٌ. Therefore, it does not have a position in إعْرابٌ similar to any other حَرْفٌ.

- This type of إذا must be followed by a nominal sentence (جُمْلةٌ اسْميّةٌ) and refers to the **same time** as the preceding statement.

I entered the house, and – **lo!** – there was the woman mourning.	دَخَلْتُ الدَّارَ فَإذَا الْمَرْأَةُ تَنُوحُ.
I went out and – **behold!** – the dog was at the door.	خَرَجْتُ فَإذَا الْكَلْبُ بِالْبابِ.

Sura 7:107	So he [Moses] threw his staff and – **lo and behold!** – it was a snake, clear to all.	فَأَلْقَى عَصاهُ فَإذَا هِيَ تُعْبانٌ مُّبِينٌ.

Conjunction; Coordinating, "coupling" *Fa* (الْفاءُ عاطِفةٌ).	فَ
Particle of surprise (حَرْفُ مُفاجَأةٍ). It does not have a position in the analysis of case (and mood) endings (لا مَحَلَّ لَهُ مِن الْإعْرابِ).	إذا
Subject (مُبْتَدَأٌ) plus predicate (خَبَرٌ) of the nominal sentence. The sentence is coordinated with the preceding one (الْجُمْلةُ مَعْطُوفةٌ).	هِيَ تُعْبانٌ
Adjective (صِفةٌ); thus, it is also in the nominative case.	مُبِينٌ

346. Can the word مَع function as an adverb?

Yes, it can.

In English, the word *with* is a preposition. Some people think that in Arabic, مَع is a preposition too and can only express the meaning of *with*. Far from it, مَع is quite a versatile and tricky word.

In Arabic, it is a اسْمٌ (noun) which may be followed by the second part of a إضافةٌ in the genitive case. This is the reason why people think it is a preposition. In such a situation, مَع is placed as an **adverb** (ظَرْفٌ) of time or place and has a fixed, cemented shape (مَبْنِيٌّ عَلَى الْفَتْحِ).

- مَع may indicate **accompaniment** (مُصاحَبةٌ) – but only if used with people. Then it denotes *with; together with*.

- مَعَ may indicate **possession** similar to لَدَى.

- مَعَ may indicate **association** or a **connection regarding time** or **place** (وَقْتُهُ or مَكَانُ الْإِصْطِحَابِ). In other words, مَعَ can also describe the time when the action happens; in this sense, it would usually be synonymous with عِنْدَ. Therefore, مَعَ can also indicate a certain time (German: *Zeitpunkt*). For ex.: *at dawn* (مَعَ الْفَجْرِ).

Let's look at some possibilities.

adverb of time (ظَرْفُ زَمَانٍ) always مَنْصُوبٌ	I played (together) with the children.	لَعِبْتُ مَعَ الْأَوْلَادِ.
	I came to you **when** the sun was rising (with the rising of the sun).	جِئْتُكَ مَعَ طُلُوعِ الشَّمْسِ.
	I came to you **in** the afternoon.	جِئْتُكَ مَعَ الْعَصْرِ.
adverb of place (ظَرْفُ مَكَانٍ)	He sat **with** him.	جَلَسَ مَعَهُ.

مَعَ, when used as an adverb, has a fixed, indeclinable shape and therefore never changes the vowel at the end. All adverbs have to be located in the place of an accusative case (مَنْصُوبٌ) which is also true for مَعَ if it functions as an adverb – therefore, we apply a "place value" due to its indeclinable shape. In such applications, مَعَ is also the first part of a إِضَافَةٌ; what follows is the second part which must be in the genitive case.

Declined noun (إِسْمٌ مُعْرَبٌ); according to its position	He went away from beside him = مِنْ عِنْدِهِ.	هَبَّتْ مِنْ مَعِهِ
	That's a weird construction. We treat مَعَ as a إِسْم which conveys the meaning of عِنْدَ here. As a noun, it gets a case ending, i.e., the كَسْرَةٌ due to the preceding preposition مِنْ. (This example was recorded by Sībawayhi; I 177, 14-15)	
Circumstantial qualifier (حَالٌ)	We came **together**.	جِئْنَا مَعًا.
	Since مَعَ functions as a حَالٌ, it must be in the accusative case (مَنْصُوبٌ); eventually, we get: مَعًا.	

Notice the difference:

- An adverb (ظَرْفٌ) in Arabic provides additional information about the **place or time** when the **action** happens.

- A حالٌ tells you more information **about the state or condition** of the **subject** (or object) whilst the act is taking placeو

Let's check some examples. We start with a verse of the Qur'an.

94:6	Truly where there is hardship there is also ease.	إِنَّ مَعَ الْعُسْرِ يُسْرًا.

Muhammad traveled at dawn.	سافَرَ مُحَمَّدٌ مَعَ الْفَجْرِ.

مَعَ is an **adverb of** <u>time</u> in the accusative case (مَنْصُوبٌ). The شِبْهُ الْجُمْلةِ, which is initiated by مَعَ, is associated with the verb سافَرَ.

I sat with Zayd.	جَلَسْتُ مَعَ زَيْدٍ.

Here مَعَ is an **adverb of** <u>place</u> (ظَرْفُ مَكانٍ مَنْصُوبٌ); it gets the place value of an accusative case; the adverbial phrase (شِبْهُ الْجُمْلةِ) is connected with the verb جَلَسَ. In Arabic: شِبْهُ الْجُمْلةِ مُتَعَلِّقٌ بِجَلَسَ.

Watch out: Some people think that in the above example, مَعَ is a preposition (حَرْفُ الْجَرِّ), but this is <u>not</u> correct. In Arabic, مَعَ is a noun (إِسْمٌ) which is underlined by the fact that it will get nunation (تَنْوِينٌ) if it is found in the place of a حالٌ. The nunation is a sign which **only** a إِسْمٌ can get! See *Arabic for Nerds 1*, #36.

Remark: مَعَ can be followed by هذا or ذلِكَ to express contrast in the sense of *yet* or *nevertheless*. If it is followed by أَنَّ, it expresses *although*.

347. مَعًا and جَمِيعًا both mean *together*. But what is the difference?

It depends on the word which you use to express together.

The two most common words to express *together* are مَعًا and جَمِيعًا. Is there a difference? Yes, there is. Let's look at an example: *We came together.* How would you translate that?

The following sentences mean more or less the same in English – in Arabic, however, there is a tiny, but fine difference.

This means that we all came together (as a group) **at the same time** (الْمَجِيءُ فِي صُحْبَةٍ واحِدةٍ).	جِئْنا مَعًا.

| This means that we all came together, but (perhaps) **not at** the same time (دُونَ اِشْتِراكٍ فِي زَمَنِ الْحَدَثِ). | جِئْنا جَمِيعًا. |
| Note that both words, مَعًا and جَمِيعًا, are placed as a حالٌ. This explains why they are indefinite and take the accusative case. | |

It is important to know what مَعًا actually denotes: that people did something at the same time or at the same place! In other words, مَعًا gives the meaning of being together when the action happened. The word جَمِيعًا can express both (الْإِفْتِراقُ or الْإِجْتِماعُ).

| We were together (in the same place). | كُنّا مَعًا. |
| We left together (at the same time). | خَرَجْنا مَعًا. |

348. How do you say: I have money?

It all depends on whether you have the money with you or not.

Two Arabic words are suitable for the translation, and they both denote more or less the same: لَدَى and عِنْدَ.

لَدَى means *beside, near, at* or *by, in the possession of.* It is an adverb of place (ظَرْفُ مَكانٍ جامِدٌ). It is possible to attach a pronoun to لَدَى.

| I sat at your place. | جَلَسْتُ لَدَيْكَ. |

Now, let's move on to our question: *I have money.*

| Only use لَدَى if the money is **really present**. This means that you actually have the money with you. | لَدَيَّ مالٌ. |
| This generally expresses that you have money – it doesn't matter if the money is with you right now or not. | عِنْدِي مالٌ. |

لَدَى differs from عِنْدَ in being restricted to **material objects** which are with the speaker (or the person spoken of).

| This assertion is right in my opinion. | هٰذا الْقَوْلُ عِنْدِي صَوابٌ. |
| Muhammad knows about it. | عِنْدَ مُحَمَّدٍ عِلْمٌ بِهِ |

> ➤ **Don't** use لَدَى because we don't talk about a materialistic thing.

However, you may use لَدَى as an **adverb of time** similar to مَعَ:

| I came to you at sunrise. | جِئْتُكَ لَدَى طُلُوعِ الشَّمْسِ. |

Notice! If the second part of the إِضافةٌ is a pronoun, the Aleph of لَدَى will change into ي.

| The book is with you/me/her. | الْكِتابُ لَدَيْكَ or لَدَيَّ or لَدَيْها |

349. Which part of بَيْنَما (while) is an adverb?

It is بَيْنَ *which literally means between.*

بَيْنَ can be connected with...

- ...an extra/redundant Aleph (أَلِفٌ زائِدةٌ) resulting in بَيْنا; or

- ...an extra ما, so-called ما زائِدةٌ, resulting in بَيْنَما. This ما may also work as a device to form an infinitive (see below).

Both words share many things. They are usually translated as *while, whereas*. They do not influence the clause which comes after them, and they have to be followed by a sentence (normally a nominal sentence).

Originally بَيْنَ was followed by an expression denoting time. This word, however, **was deleted and compensated** by ما. For example: ... بَيْنَ أَوْقاتِ قِراءَتِنا → originally, this was: ...بَيْنَما نَحْنُ نَقْرَأُ

What about the nature of the ما?

- This (extra) ما should be placed at the beginning of a sentence.

- We have a إِضافةٌ-construction. What is placed after ما functions as the second part of the إِضافةٌ and is located in the place of a genitive case (فِي مَحَلِّ جَرٍّ).

The expression بَيْنَما is more frequently used. بَيْنَما can join two statements which express a situation or an action occurring at the same time. It may be followed by a nominal or a verbal sentence. The verb can be in the present or past tense.

If a **verb** comes after ما, we treat ما as a device to mold an **infinitive** (مَا الْمَصْدَرِيَّةُ). The actual tense – time – is determined by the main clause. This becomes important if you have to translate a sentence.

بَيْنَما often denotes a surprise or exclamation (مَعْنَى الْمُفَاجَأَةِ) when the subsequent main clause is introduced by إِذْ or فَ or فَإِذا.

While we **were** walking, the bell **rang**.	بَيْنَمَا نَحْنُ نَسِيرُ إِذْ دَقَّ الْجَرَسُ.
The actual meaning is: *at the time during which we **were** walking.*	...فِي الْوَقْتِ الَّذِي كُنَّا نَسِيرُ فِيهِ.
What happened to the structure of the sentence? The word *time* (الْوَقْت) was deleted (مَحْذُوفٌ) and substituted by the (undefined) word مَا.	

Let's analyze more examples.

While I was reading, a friend came.	بَيْنَمَا أَقْرَأُ حَضَرَ صَدِيقِي.

بَيْنَما	Adverb of time (ظَرْفُ زَمَانٍ). It has a fixed shape (مَبْنِيٌّ عَلَى السُّكُونِ) because an Aleph can't carry any vowel. Grammatically it is located in the place of an accusative case (فِي مَحَلِّ نَصْبٍ). The adverb is connected with the verb حَضَرَ.
أَقْرَأُ	This verbal sentence (جُمْلَةٌ فِعْلِيَّةٌ) serves as the second part of the إِضافةٌ and is thus placed in the position of a genitive (فِي مَحَلِّ جَرٍّ). The adverb serves as the first part of the إِضافةٌ (مُضافٌ إِلَيْهِ).

1	Whilst Zayd was sleeping, his brother showed up.	بَيْنَما زَيْدٌ نائِمٌ حَضَرَ أَخُوهُ.
	The adverb of time بَيْنَما is linked to حَضَرَ (verb). زَيْدٌ is the subject of the nominal sentence (مُبْتَدَأٌ مَرْفُوعٌ); نائِمٌ is the predicate (خَبَرٌ مَرْفُوعٌ). The entire nominal sentence is in the place of the second part of the إِضافةٌ.	
2	Allah's Messenger said: "While I was sleeping, I was given the treasures of the earth." (*Sahīh al-Bukhārī 4375*)	قَالَ رَسُولُ اللهِ ﷺ: "بَيْنَا أَنَا نَائِمٌ أُتِيتُ بِخَزَائِنِ الأَرْضِ."

Watch out: It is common to put the expression بَيْنَما into the <u>middle</u> of a sentence – however, this is not correct!

| incorrect | Muhammad came whilst Farīd was working. | حَضَرَ مُحَمَّدٌ بَيْنَما كَانَ فَرِيدٌ يَعْمَلُ. |

If you want to put such an expression into the middle of a sentence, then you should use the expression عَلَى حِينَ.

| correct | Muhammad came whilst Farīd was working. | حَضَرَ مُحَمَّدٌ عَلَى حِينَ كَانَ فَرِيدٌ يَعْمَلُ. |

350. *I have never done that.* How do you say that?

You include قَطُّ.

Let's open the discussion with a famous mistake in Arabic:

| incorrect | I have never done that. | لَمْ أَفْعَلْ ذَلِكَ أَبَدًا. |

Why is there a mistake? ➤ أَبَدًا is an adverb for the **future** (ظَرْفُ زَمانٍ) (لِلْمُسْتَقْبَلِ) only. أَبَدًا conveys the meaning of continuity (اِسْتِمْرارٌ) in the future and may express *always, forever; ever.* The translation, however, depends on the context and – more importantly – whether there is a negation involved or not. أَبَدًا may receive case inflections (مُعْرَبٌ).

| **With a negation** (نَفْيٌ) ➡ | *never (in the future); not at all; on no account* |

If there is a negation involved, it will usually be the particle لَنْ because a sentence with أَبَدًا needs a **future meaning**.

| **Without a negation** (إِثْباتٌ) ➡ | *never; not at all; by no means!* |

| correct | I will never do that. | لَنْ أَفْعَلَ ذَلِكَ أَبَدًا. |

أَبَدًا is an adverb that has to target the future; the adverbial phrase (شِبْهُ الْجُمْلةِ) is related to the verb أَفْعَلَ.

Let's check some verses of the Qur'an:

| Sura 98:8 | Their reward with Allah will be gardens of perpetual residence beneath which rivers flow, wherein they will abide for- | جَزَاؤُهُمْ عِندَ رَبِّهِمْ جَنَّاتُ عَدْنٍ تَجْرِي مِن تَحْتِهَا الْأَنْهَارُ خَالِدِينَ فِيهَا أَبَدًا رَضِيَ اللّهُ |

	ever, Allah being pleased with them and they with Him.	عَنْهُمْ وَرَضُوا عَنْهُ.
Sura 5:24	They said, "O Moses, indeed we will not enter it, **ever**, as long as they are within it; so go, you and your Lord, and fight. Indeed, we are remaining right here."	قَالُوا يَا مُوسَىٰ إِنَّا لَن نَدْخُلَهَا أَبَدًا مَّا دَامُوا فِيهَا فَاذْهَبْ أَنتَ وَرَبُّكَ فَقَاتِلَا إِنَّا هَاهُنَا قَاعِدُونَ.

In the above examples, أَبَدًا is an **adverb of time** and visibly in the accusative case (مَنْصُوبٌ بِالْفَتْحَةِ الظَّاهِرَةِ). The adverbial phrase in the first example is connected with the word خَالِدِين, which does the job of a verb and is enfolded by the adverb.

Now, how would you say: "*I have **never done** that*"?

correct	I have never done that.	لَمْ أَفْعَلْ ذلِكَ قَطُّ.

قَطُّ means *never; at all*. It is an **adverb of time** (ظَرْفُ زَمانٍ) that engages in the **past tense** (لِاسْتِغْراقِ الْماضِي).

قَطُّ has an indeclinable, fixed shape (مَبْنِيٌّ) and thus never changes its form. قَطُّ <u>must</u> be **used with the negation** (نَفْيٌ). Since we have to use the past tense, we negate the verb with لَمْ or with ما.

He has never lied to me.	لَمْ يَكْذِبْ عَلَيَّ قَطُّ.

قَطُّ is an adverb of time. It has a fixed shape, so we can't put the actual case marker which would be the accusative (مَنْصُوبٌ). Therefore, we say that it is placed in the position of an accusative case (فِي مَحَلِّ نَصْبٍ). The adverbial phrase is related to the verb *to lie*.

Some examples to underline the difference:

incorrect	I have never visited him.	ما زُرْتُهُ أَبَدًا.
correct	I have never visited him.	ما زُرْتُهُ قَطُّ.
correct	I will never visit him.	لَنْ أَزُورَهُ أَبَدًا.

Since قَطُّ must be used with a negated past tense verb, you can't express "*I won't do that at all*" with قَطُّ since you imply a future meaning.

incorrect	I won't (don't) do that at all.	لا أَفْعَلُهُ قَطُّ.
correct		لا أَفْعَلُهُ أَبَدًا.

There is a word that looks similar: **قَط**. What is the difference?

قَط (with **سُكُونٌ** on the final letter) has the same meaning as **حَسْبُ**: *to be enough, you only need...*

You only need sincerity in your work.	قَطْكَ الْإِخْلاصُ فِي الْعَمَلِ.
Same sentence (and meaning) with **حَسْبُ**: →	حَسْبُكَ الْإِخْلاصُ فِي الْعَمَلِ.

Subject (**مُبْتَدَأٌ**) of the nominal sentence (**جُمْلَةٌ إِسْمِيّةٌ**). The word has an indeclinable shape. So, we can only assign a place value: **قَط** is located in the place of a nominative (**فِي مَحَلِّ رَفْعٍ**).	قَط
Predicate (**خَبَرٌ**) in the nominative case (**مَرْفُوعٌ**).	الْإِخْلاصُ

351. What is the job of the adverb لَمّا?

It binds/connects two sentences.

لَمّا is translated as *when* or *after*. It is an **adverb of time** (**ظَرْفُ زَمانٍ**) and has a fixed, cemented shape (**مَبْنِيٌّ**). **لَمّا** has several applications. It may work as a conditional particle (see *question #85*) or as a particle of exception (**حَرْفُ إِسْتِثْناءٍ**) denoting the meaning of **إِلّا**.

Let's focus on the type of **لَمّا** that works as an **adverb of time** (**ظَرْفُ زَمانٍ**). It relates to verbal sentences in the <u>past tense</u> and has the meaning of **حِينَ** or **حِينَما**.

Sura 28:14	When Moses reached full maturity and manhood, We gave him wisdom and knowledge: this is how We reward those who do good.	وَلَمّا بَلَغَ أَشُدَّهُ وَاسْتَوَىٰ آتَيْنَاهُ حُكْمًا وَعِلْمًا وَكَذَلِكَ نَجْزِي الْمُحْسِنِينَ.

When he came, I treated him with respect (hospitably).	لَمّا جَاءَ أَكْرَمْتُهُ.

This sentence is pretty complex. Don't get confused:

- The **first sentence** is the **second part** of a إِضَافَةٌ-construction; in Arabic: الْجُمْلَةُ الْأُولَى تَقَعُ مُضافًا إِلَيْهِ.

- It is the **second sentence** (i.e., the <u>first</u> part of the إِضَافَةٌ) that governs the adverb لَمَّا in the accusative case (فِي مَحَلِّ نَصْبٍ بِجَوابِهِ). This is similar to إذا – see *question #344*.

first sentence (after لَمَّا)	second sentence
Second part of the إِضَافَةٌ; it is (grammatically) in the genitive. Since it has a fixed shape, we have to assign the place value of a genitive case.	First part of the إِضَافَةٌ. It governs the adverb in the accusative case.

Another example:

When Muhammad came, his family went out to greet him.	لَمَّا حَضَرَ مُحَمَّدٌ خَرَجَ أَهْلُهُ لِاسْتِقْبالِهِ.
لَمَّا is an **adverb of time** (ظَرْفُ زَمانٍ). It has a fixed shape; we can only use a "place value" and say that لَمَّا occupies the place of an accusative case (فِي مَحَلِّ نَصْبٍ). Note that لَمَّا is linked to the verb – خَرَجَ – and not to حَضَرَ.	
The verbal sentence حَضَرَ مُحَمَّدٌ (as an entity) is found in the place of the **second part** of the إِضَافَةٌ. All of that is not visible, but it is implicitly understood in the grammar of the sentence (الْجُمْلَةُ فِي مَحَلِّ جَرٍّ مُضافٌ إِلَيْهِ).	

352. Are مُنْذُ and مُذْ prepositions or adverbs?

They may function as both: as a حَرْفٌ or as a ظَرْفٌ.

Depending on their position in the sentence and the context, we can say that both words generally denote *since, for; ago*. Grammarians have suggested that مُنْذُ is produced by the assimilation of مِنْ and إِذْ; or by the assimilation of مِنْ and ذ.

Arabic does not know many "real" prepositions (see *question #124*). Most of the words that we call prepositions in English are in Arabic adverbs of time or place. Does this difference matter? Let' see.

- مُنْذُ and مُذْ express *since, ever since, from the time when*.

- They signify the duration of an **event that has started in the past**

and endures to the present. → Therefore, we deal with **adverbs of time** (ظَرْفُ زَمانٍ).

- We will usually have a verbal **clause** (in the past tense) after مُذْ or مُنْذُ when they are used as adverbs.

- What about the regent/operator (عامِلٌ)? Both must be governed by **a verb in the past tense.**

- Both have an **indeclinable**, fixed shape (مَبْنِيٌّ) and can't take cases. We can only check the position in the sentence and use a place value – which is the location of an accusative case (في مَحَلِّ نَصْبٍ).

- Furthermore, both serve as the **first part** of a إضافةٌ. The second part can be a verbal or nominal sentence. In most situations, it is a verbal sentence.

verbal sentence	I came since Zayd	حَضَرْتُ مُذْ or مُنْذُ سافَرَ زَيْدٌ.
nominal sentence	traveled.	حَضَرْتُ مُذْ or مُنْذُ زَيْدٌ مُسافِرٌ.

مُنْذُ is an **adverb of time** and is found in the location of an accusative case (في مَحَلِّ نَصْبٍ). It is connected with the verb حَضَرَ. The entire verbal sentence (سافَرَ زَيْدٌ) is in the position of the second part of a إضافةٌ and thus in the position of a genitive case (الجُمْلَةُ في مَحَلِّ جَرٍّ مُضافٌ إلَيْهِ). The same is true for the nominal sentence (زَيْدٌ مُسافِرٌ).

What would happen if we treated مُذْ - مُنْذُ as **prepositions** (حَرْفٌ)?

- Grammarians say that مُذْ and مُنْذُ should be treated as a **preposition** only when they refer to an **unexpired period of time.**

- As prepositions, they denote مِنْ or في (*from*) if the act endures until the present. They are usually translated as *since (then), since that time, from that time on, ever since.*

- Or they may denote من - إلى (*from – until*) if an enumerated time is given.

- Usually you will only have a **single word** (and **not** a clause/sentence) after مُذْ or مُنْذُ when they are used as prepositions.

meaning of مِنْ	
He traveled long ago.	سَافَرَ مُنْذُ عَهْدٍ بَعِيدٍ.

| He has not attended for two days. | مَا حَضَرَ مُنْذُ يَوْمَيْنِ. |

meaning of فِي	
I will not visit him from the time of today.	لَنْ أَزُورَهُ مُنْذُ الْيَوْمِ.
He has not attended ever since that day.	مَا حَضَرَ مُنْذُ يَوْمِنا هذا.

meaning of مِنْ - إلى	
Used for a specified time frame. It expresses the duration from the beginning of this period until its end (مِن ابْتِداءِ هٰذِهِ الْمُدّةِ حَتَّى نِهايَتِها).	
I have not attended the lesson for three days.	مَا حَضَرْتُ الدَّرْسَ مُنْذُ ثَلاثَةِ أَيّامٍ.

Now, let's analyze a rare and special construction. There are sentences with a noun in the **nominative** case (اسْمٌ مَرْفُوعٌ) after مُذْ - مُنْذُ. How is that possible? ➡ مُذْ - مُنْذُ are constructed with a **noun of time** (اسْمُ زَمانٍ) in the nominative case to designate the **lower limit of dating**, as of the earliest plausible date at which a fact could have occurred (terminus a quo).

In the following examples, we use the nominative case after مُذْ - مُنْذُ.

Since it was Friday (meaning: since **last** Friday).	مُنْذُ يَوْمُ الْجُمْعةِ
It is a year since.	مُنْذُ سَنَةٌ
I attended two days ago.	حَضَرْتُ مُذْ يَوْمانِ.

How can we justify that in grammar? You have two possibilities for the إعْرابٌ. We use the last example for the analysis.

Option 1. You **convert** مُذْ يَوْمانِ (*two days*) into a **nominal sentence**.

You would get the following estimated, underlying meaning which is the basis for our analysis:

| I was present, the duration of the presence was two days. | حَضَرْتُ، أَمَدُ الْحُضُورِ يَوْمانِ. |

Subject (مُبْتَدَأٌ) of the nominal sentence (جُمْلَةٌ اِسْمِيَّةٌ). Since the word has an indeclinable shape (مَبْنِيٌّ عَلَى السُّكُونِ), we can't mark the case – nevertheless, the word is located in the position of a nominative case (فِي مَحَلِّ رَفْعٍ) and gets that "place value".	مُذْ
Predicate in the nominative case, marked by the Aleph due to the dual (خَبَرٌ مَرْفُوعٌ بِالْأَلِفِ).	يَوْمانِ

Option 2. You treat مُذْ يَوْمانِ as the **delayed subject** (خَبَرٌ مُقَدَّمٌ) of a nominal sentence.

Adverb of time (ظَرْفُ زَمانٍ). The adverbial phrase (شِبْهُ الْجُمْلةِ) is linked to the **deleted fronted predicate** (خَبَرٌ مُقَدَّمٌ مَحْذُوفٌ); thus, it occupies the position of a nominative case (فِي مَحَلِّ رَفْعٍ).	مُذْ
This is the delayed subject (مُبْتَدَأٌ مُؤَخَّرٌ). It is in the nominative case by the letter Aleph because we have a dual (مَرْفُوعٌ بِالْأَلِفِ).	يَوْمانِ

However, you use the **genitive case** with a definite اِسْمُ زَمانٍ to mark a yet <u>unexpired</u> period.

Since the beginning of this day (= today)…	مُنْذُ الْيَوْمِ…

353. How do you express *while*? Should you use بَيْنَما or a حالٌ?

If you use بَيْنَما, it conveys a sense of surprise and randomness.

Both, the حالٌ and بَيْنَما (which is an adverb of time) describe the state of the subject or object during the happening of an action: *while*.

مَفْعُولٌ فِيه	As I was walking, I suddenly heard a scream.	بَيْنَما أَنا أَمْشِي إِذْ سَمِعْتُ صَرْخةً.
	Here, بَيْنَما, an *adverb of time*, indicates that the hearing of the scream was completely random and unexpected.	
حالٌ	I heard a scream while I was walking.	سَمِعْتُ صَرْخةً وَأَنا أَمْشِي.
	The scream wasn't really surprising or unexpected. The sentence أَنا أَمْشِي is a حالٌ in form of a nominal sentence.	

Let's dig deeper and check the nuances:

حالٌ	بَيْنَما - مَفْعُولٌ فِيهِ
You'll very rarely find the circumstantial qualifier (حالٌ) before the verb. ➤ The حالٌ comes **after the verb**.	بَيْنَما usually **precedes** the verb (i.e., the الْمُتَعَلَّقُ) to which it is connected.
The حالٌ **doesn't** convey randomness nor any kind of surprise.	بَيْنَما conveys a sense of **randomness** and **surprise**.
There is no sub-ordination.	In a sentence with بَيْنَما, we will have a main and subsequent part.
The حالٌ needs a subject or object to which it refers: the صَاحِبُ الْحالِ. The circumstantial description is **valid** for the <u>entire</u> duration of the action (of the verb).	بَيْنَما is an adverb of time for the main verb. The description is **not** necessarily valid **throughout** the performance of the action. Usually it only refers to a certain time frame or a certain point of time during the action.
In the above example, *I heard a scream while I was walking*, we have to assume that you heard the scream throughout the entire time of walking. This is probably not realistic and the context will define it.	In our example, *As I was walking I heard a scream*, it means that I was walking and suddenly (after some time), I heard a scream. But I did not hear the scream right from the beginning until the end of the walk.

354. What does يَوْمَ يَوْمَ mean?

It basically means every day (day after day).

Arabic, like other languages, knows the concept that **two separate nouns** are treated as one expression (الْأَسْماءُ الْمُرَكَّبَةُ) – a compound or composite. If you merge two Arabic nouns so that they can be seen as one entity, you have to be careful. You change their grammatical DNA. Both words lose their nunation (تَنْوينٌ) and become **indeclinable** and cemented on the vowel "a" (مَبْنِيٌّ عَلَى الْفَتْحِ).

This approach is used with **numbers** (13 to 19), **adverbs** (الظُّرُوفُ

الْمُرَكَّبَةُ) and the **circumstantial description**. For example (number): *fourteen* (أَرْبَعَةَ عَشَرَ). Here, we will focus on adverbs and the حالٌ.

Situation I: We have **two adverbs**.

1	He visits us every morning and evening,	يَأْتِينا صَباحَ مَساءَ.
2	He visits us every day (literally, *day after day*).	يَأْتِينا يَوْمَ يَوْمَ.
3	He has taken a path in his life between good and bad.	يَنْهَجُ فِي حَياتِهِ بَيْنَ بَيْنَ.
	Note: The expression بَيْنَ بَيْنَ denotes that *something is between good and bad, a mixture, neither good nor bad, medium.*	

All expressions marked in gray are **adverbs**, to be precise: combined, compounded adverbs (ظَرْفٌ مُرَكَّبٌ).

- Examples 1 and 2 are **adverbs of time** (ظَرْفُ زَمانٍ).
- Example 3 is an **adverb of place** (ظَرْفُ مَكانٍ).
- They all have a fixed, indeclinable shape (مَبْنِيٌّ عَلَى الْفَتْحِ); there-fore, we cannot put case markers.
- Instead, we can only assign them the place value of an accusative case as we deal with adverbs in Arabic. For example, both words in ex. 1, صَباحَ مَساءَ, appear in the place of an accusative (نَصْبٌ).

Situation II: We have two **circumstantial qualifiers** (حالٌ) that can be combined and blended (الْأَحْوالُ الْمُرَكَّبَةُ).

1	Zayd is my next-door (literally, house to house) neighbor.	زَيْدٌ جارِي بَيْتَ بَيْتَ.
2	They fell apart. (Scattered, one after another; like as sparks are scattered from iron.)	تَساقَطُوا أَخْوَلَ أَخْوَلَ.
		= تَساقَطُوا مُتَفَرِّقَيْنِ.
	The sparks flew about scattered.	تَطايَرَ السَّرَرُ أَخْوَلَ أَخْوَلَ.

1	Both are placed in the place of a حالٌ. They are indeclina-ble. Grammatically, they are placed in the position of an	بَيْتَ بَيْتَ
2	accusative case (نَصْبٌ) and get that "place value".	أَخْوَلَ أَخْوَلَ

THE TRICKY وَ - THE OBJECT OF ACCOMPANIMENT
(الْمَفْعُولُ مَعَهُ)

355. Why does و not always mean *and*?

*Because a وَ can also denote the meaning of **with**.*

Arabic knows a kind of object which denotes *that with whom the act [expressed in the verb] is done* (مَفْعُولٌ مَعَهُ). Such an object is initiated with وَ, a so-called *Wāw of association* or *accompaniment, concomitance* (وَاوُ الْمَعِيّةِ). Simply said, such a وَ expresses the meaning of **with** (مَعَ); also: *along; at the same time*. A noun (اِسْمٌ) after و will become an object, and this object is something or someone that occurs at the same time as the subject. In essence, this و is between two nouns (اِسْمٌ) and connects them – in a way that the **second** اِسْمٌ is <u>subordinate</u> to the first اِسْمٌ and **not** in coordination with the first one.

The مَفْعُولٌ مَعَهُ is constructed as follows:

1. The regent (عَامِلٌ) must be placed before the وَ. → So, there must be a verb before the و (or a word that does the job of a verb).

2. The وَ conveys the meaning of accompaniment (مُصَاحَبَةٌ).

3. After the وَ, we will have a noun in the accusative (اِسْمٌ مَنْصُوبٌ) – and **never** a sentence or شِبْهُ الْجُمْلةِ.

I woke up with (*at the same time of*) the call to prayer.	اِسْتَيْقَظْتُ وَأَذَانَ الْفَجْرِ.
Muhammad walked along (*at the same place of*) the beach.	مَشَى مُحَمَّدٌ وَالشّاطِئَ.

So-called وَاوُ الْمَعِيّةِ. This particle has a fixed shape (حَرْفٌ مَبْنِيٌّ عَلَى الْفَتْحِ). It does not have a position in إِعْرَابٌ.	وَ

مَفْعُولٌ مَعَهُ; accusative case (مَنْصُوبٌ بِالْفَتْحةِ).	أَذَانَ الْفَجْرِ/الشّاطِئَ.

In Arabic sentences, a **preceding verb** works as the operator (عَامِلٌ) that governs the مَفْعُولٌ مَعَهُ in the accusative case (نَصْبٌ). However, there are other words that can convey the meaning of a verb and are capable of doing the job of a governor (عَامِلٌ).

1. The active participle (اِسْمُ الْفَاعِلِ)

I am walking along the beach.	أَنَا سَائِرٌ وَالشّاطِئَ.

Personal pronoun (ضَمِيرٌ مُنْفَصِلٌ) which is the subject (مُبْتَدَأٌ) of the nominal sentence (جُمْلَةٌ اِسْمِيّةٌ). It is indeclinable, however, regarding the function in the sentence, it occupies the position of a nominative case (فِي مَحَلّ رَفْعٍ).	أَنَا
Predicate (خَبَرٌ), nominative (مَرْفُوعٌ). It is an active participle, and as such, it works as the regent (عَامِلٌ) for the مَفْعُولٌ مَعَهُ.	سَائِرٌ
So-called واوُ الْمَعِيّةِ. It does not have a position إِعْرَابٌ.	وَ
Object of accompaniment (مَفْعُولٌ مَعَهُ), accusative (مَنْصُوبٌ).	الشّاطِئَ

2. The passive participle (اِسْمُ الْمَفْعُولِ)

Muhammad is honored along with his brother.	مُحَمّدٌ مُكْرَمٌ وَأَخَاهُ.

Subject (مُبْتَدَأٌ مَرْفُوعٌ) of the nominal sentence.	مُحَمّدٌ
Passive participle of the verb أَكْرَمَ; it is the predicate (خَبَرٌ مَرْفُوعٌ) of the sentence and is the regent (عَامِلٌ) of the object.	مُكْرَمٌ
مَفْعُولٌ مَعَهُ in the accusative case (مَنْصُوبٌ) by the Aleph – as *brother* is one of the *five*, some say, *six nouns* (الْأَسْمَاءُ السّتّةِ).	وَأَخَاهُ

3. The مَصْدَرٌ

Walking along the beach in the morning is useful.	سَيْرُكَ وَالشّاطِئَ فِي الصّباحِ مُفِيدٌ.

سَيْرٌ is the مَصْدَرٌ of سَارَ. It is the subject of the nominal sentence (مُبْتَدَأٌ مَرْفُوعٌ). The word مُفِيدٌ is the predicate (خَبَرٌ). The مَصْدَرٌ (i.e., سَيْرٌ) works as the governor (عَامِلٌ) of the مَفْعُولٌ مَعَهُ which is: الشّاطِئَ.
---

4. The so-called اِسْمُ الْفِعْلِ (interjection denoting a sense of a verb)

| Be gentle with the sick person! | رُوَيْدَكَ وَالْمَرِيضَ! |
| This is the meaning of the sentence: | أَمْهِلْ نَفْسَكَ مَعَ الْمَرِيضِ! |

| رُوَيْدَكَ is a *noun of the verb* in the imperative (اِسْمُ فِعْلِ أَمْرٍ); an interjection. It has the same meaning as the regular imperative أَمْهِلْ: *slow(ly)! Go easy!* رُوَيْدَكَ has an implied pronoun (ضَمِيرٌ مُسْتَتِرٌ) as the subject (فَاعِل), i.e., *you* (أَنْتَ). The regent (عَامِلٌ) of the مَفْعُولٌ مَعَهُ is the اِسْمُ الْفِعْلِ. |

Excursus: The problem of identifying the regent (عَامِلٌ).

We said that the regent (عَامِلٌ) of an *object of accompaniment* is the verb or a word that has enough power to do that. This is the view of the majority of the grammarians (and of the Basra school) because it fits best into the framework of Arabic grammar. But this doesn't mean that it is also the most logical view. There are other interesting ideas.

Approach 1: The grammarians of Kūfa (الْكُوفِيُّونَ) had an extraordinary idea. They explained the accusative by claiming that such a word (i.e., the object) needs the opposite case (مَنْصُوبٌ عَلَى الْخِلَافِ). There is a famous example that is often cited in books:

| The water became even with the piece of wood. (The water has risen with the piece of wood.) | اِسْتَوَى الْمَاءُ وَالْخَشَبَةَ. |
| It wouldn't make sense to repeat the same verb in the sentence: *The water was leveled, and the wood became even* (اِسْتَوَى الْمَاءُ وَإِسْتَوَت الْخَشَبَةُ). Why? Because the wood was neither turned upside down nor was it uneven. |

Another example: *Zayd came with Amr.* You can't repeat the verb as it would mean that *Zayd came, and 'Amr came.* (جَاءَ زَيْدٌ وَجَاءَ عَمْرُو). That's why the Kūfa grammarians suggested that a word after this type of وَ needs the opposite case (قَدْ خَالَفَ الثّانِي الْأَوَّلَ).

Approach 2: The Basra grammarian Abū 'Ishāq al-Zajjāj (الزَّجّاج) explained the accusative case by **reconstructing the operator** (تَقْدِيرُ الْعَامِل), i.e., searching for an appropriate verb. In the example, it could be: لَابَسَ الْخَشَبَةَ (the III-verb لَابَسَ means *to accompany; to associate with*).

Approach 3: Other grammarians used another approach to find an explanation. They stated that the *object of accompaniment* is an **inter-**

preted مَعَ. If we apply this logic, the powerful وَ was originally the word مَعَ, which is a noun (إِسْمٌ). When مَعَ is placed as an *adverb of time* or *place* (ظَرْفٌ زَمَنِيٌّ أَوْ مَكَانِيٌّ), it serves as the first part of the إِضَافَةٌ.

They came at sunset.	وَصَلُوا مَعَ غُرُوبِ الشَّمْسِ.
Adverb of time (ظَرْفُ زَمانٍ), connected with the verb; it is placed in the position of an accusative case. It serves as the first part of the إِضَافَةٌ.	

Now it gets complicated. If we replace مَعَ (the adverb) in the above sentence by وَ, we will get a problem. The وَ is a particle (حَرْفٌ) and as such, by definition, does not have a position in إِعْرابٌ. We need a trick. We have to say that the word **after** وَ gets the "place value" of a ظَرْفٌ (adverb), i.e., an accusative case. That's the reason why the مَفْعُولٌ مَعَهُ receives the accusative case – if you follow the logic of approach 3.

356. How do you know that وَ starts a مَفْعُولٌ مَعَهُ?

The case marker will tell you whether the وَ expresses accompaniment.

Let's analyze the following sentence to start our discussion.

I am traveling along the sea.	أَنا سائِرٌ وَالْبَحْرَ.

A *Wāw of accompaniment* (واوُ الْمَعِيّةِ) **cannot** share the action that is found in the first part of the sentence (i.e., the verb before وَ). Practically speaking, this means: *the sea doesn't travel.* So we know that the وَ introduces an **object** to which the subject (in our example: *I*) is doing actions on the side. Therefore, we call it *an object in connection with which something is done* (مَفْعُولٌ مَعَهُ).

Nevertheless, the most common application of the وَ is to convey the meaning of *and* (واوُ الْعَطْفِ). Even if you don't understand the words in a sentence, you can get closer to the meaning by looking at the cases.

1	مَفْعُولٌ مَعَهُ	I walked **with** Zayd.	سِرْتُ وَزَيْدًا.
2	مَعْطُوفٌ	I and Zayd walked.	سِرْتُ وَزَيْدٌ.

Which one is correct? Both are correct (although example 2 is grammatically shaky – see #192). **There is the following rule of thumb:**

➡ In this situation, it is better to treat the وَ as a مَفْعُولٌ مَعَهُ (no. 1). Why? If we want to treat وَ as a coordinator/"coupler" (عَطْف), we will need some adjustments. In our example, there is a verb which has a hidden subject included (الْعَطْفُ عَلَى الضَّمِيرِ الْمُتَّصِلِ). For this reason, we need some space (فَاصِلٌ) between the verb and the مَعْطُوف which can be achieved by repeating the **personal pronoun** (ضَمِيرٌ مُنْفَصِلٌ).

I walked with Zayd.	سِرْتُ أَنَا وَزَيْدٌ.

Sura 2:35	And We said, "O Adam, dwell, you and your wife in Paradise".	وَقُلْنَا يَا آدَمُ اسْكُنْ أَنتَ وَزَوْجُكَ الْجَنَّةَ.

Now, let's look at this sentence: مَشَى مُحَمَّدٌ وَالشَّاطِئ .

Without case markers, the sentence can have two grammatical interpretations – but only one makes sense:

1	*with* ➡ what follows takes the accusative case	Muhammad walked **along** the beach.	مَشَى مُحَمَّدٌ وَالشَّاطِئَ.
2	*and* ➡ case-matching with the word that is placed before وَ	Muhammad walked **and** the beach walked.	مَشَى مُحَمَّدٌ وَمَشَى الشَّاطِئُ.
الشَّاطِئ (*beach*) must get the accusative case since it can only be a مَفْعُولٌ مَعَهُ. It is not correct to say that it is a مَعْطُوفٌ for مُحَمَّدٌ.			

In some situations, however, you only have the option of a مَعْطُوفٌ. The وَ then has the effect that the cases of the words before and after وَ are coupled/mirrored.

Muhammad came, and Zayd came before him.	حَضَرَ مُحَمَّدٌ وَزَيْدٌ قَبْلَهُ.
You must treat *Zayd* as a مَعْطُوفٌ (coupled word) for *Muhammad* which means it gets the same case as Muhammad: the nominative (مَرْفُوعٌ). Why? It is impossible to treat it as a مَفْعُولٌ مَعَهُ due to the presence of the expression *before him* (قَبْلَهُ) which prevents the وَ from conveying the meaning of accompaniment (مُصَاحَبَةٌ).	

Watch out if there is a verb with a reflexive meaning (*each other*).

| Zayd and ʿAlī fought (**with**) each other. | تَضارَبَ زَيْدٌ وَعَلِيٌّ. |

ʿAlī is a مَعْطوفٌ and takes the nominative case (مَرفُوعٌ) like *Zayd*. It is impossible to treat it as a مَفْعُولٌ مَعَهُ. The V-verb *to fight* (تَضارَبَ) needs more than one subject (فاعِلٌ) since it points to participation (الْإِشْتِراكُ). To translate such a sentence, ironically, you might use *with* or *each other*.

357. Can you use a مَفْعُولٌ مَعَهُ in questions?

Yes, this is actually pretty common. But there is a problem.

Let's first look at some examples to get an idea of the issue.

How about your exam?	كَيْفَ أَنْتَ وَالْإِمْتِحانَ؟
What is it with you and Zayd?	ما أَنْتَ وَزَيْدًا؟
What's the matter with you and Ali?	ما لَكَ وَعَلِيًّا؟
How are you these days?	مَا أنتَ وَالأَيَّامَ؟

Here's the problem. The مَفْعُول مَعَهُ needs the **presence of a (verbal) sentence** before the وَ. In other words, there has to be a verb (فِعْلٌ) involved whose job is to govern the object (مَفْعُولٌ مَعَهُ) in the accusative case (نَصْبٌ). Can we fix that?

Some grammarians have suggested that in such a situation, the question word (إِسْمُ الْإِسْتِفْهامٍ) is the operator (عامِلٌ) of the مَفْعُولٌ مَعَهُ. Most grammarians, however, have another (perhaps better) idea. They say that the part with the question contains a deleted verb. This "hidden", estimated, virtual verb would "secretly" do the job of the regent.

Which verbs would be suitable for that?

	تَكُونَ	
وَالْإِمْتِحانَ؟	تَصْنَعُ	كَيْفَ
	تَفْعَلُ	

THE STATE OR CIRCUMSTANCE (الْحالُ)

The Arabic word حالٌ means *condition, state; situation; circumstance; circumstantial expression* (in grammar). The term can be treated as a masculine **or** feminine noun in Arabic.

358. To which question does the حالٌ give an answer?

It is the question: How did the action happen? (كَيْفَ حَدَثَ الْفِعْلُ؟).

The حالٌ gives an answer to the question word *how* (كَيْفَ) in regard to the state or circumstance/condition of the subject or object (or both) while the act is taking place. The حالٌ is a *redundancy* (فَضْلةٌ) because without the حالٌ, the sentence would still be complete and intelligible. Linguists also call it a non-predicative element. The حالٌ is one of the most important chapters of the accusative case (نَصْبٌ). But why does it get the accusative case (مَنْصُوبٌ)؟

Some grammarians suggest that the حالٌ **resembles an object** and in some ways has the **nature of an adverbial expression of time or place** (= مَفْعُولٌ فِيهِ). In the English translation, the حالٌ would often play the part of a participle *(e.g., laughing)* that is used as a modifier. The حالٌ may also be rendered into English as *as, while; for (because of)*.

Let's introduce another important term to understand the logic behind the حالٌ: the صاحِبُ الْحالِ (*concerned by the status*). It is the entity (subject and/or object) whose circumstances are described by the حالٌ. The word صاحِبٌ literally means *holder, possessor, companion*. Therefore, the حالٌ describes the shape of the صاحِبُ الْحالِ at the time of the occurrence of the action. This brings us to the most important rule:

- The حالٌ is almost always **<u>indefinite</u>** (unless it is a sentence).
- The صاحِبُ الْحالِ should be **definite**.

باكِيًا	مِن الطَّبِيبِ	الطِّفْلُ	عادَ
crying	*from the doctor*	*the child*	*returned*
الْحالُ	الْجارُّ وَالْمَجْرُورُ	صاحِبُ الْحالِ	الْعامِلُ

The child returned from the doctor **crying**.

359. What is suitable as a صَاحِبُ الْحالِ؟

Mainly the subject and the object. But there is more.

The صَاحِبُ الْحالِ has to be defined (= definite word or, if indefinite, it should be additionally described by another word) since we need a clear target for the status (مَحْكُومٌ عَلَيْهِ). What kind of forms and words would work as a صَاحِبُ الْحالِ in a sentence?

1. The **subject** (فَاعِلٌ) of a verbal sentence.

The student came smiling.	جاءَ الطّالِبُ مُبْتَسِمًا.
مُبْتَسِمًا is the حالٌ and describes the state of the subject (فَاعِلٌ) - *the student* (الطّالِبُ) - during the time of the action (*to come*).	

2. The direct **object** (مَفْعُولٌ بِه).

Muhammad drove the car speeding.	رَكِبَ مُحَمَّدٌ السَّيّارَةَ مُسْرِعةً.
Watch out! The sentence doesn't mean: Muhammad drove the *fast car.* But: Muhammad *drove* the car *fast.* The صَاحِبُ الْحالِ is *the car* (السَّيّارَةَ).	

Note: Also other type of objects may function as the صَاحِبُ الْحالِ.

3. The **subject** (فَاعِلٌ) and the direct **object** (مَفْعُولٌ بِه) together.

This can be tricky because the English translation is often different from the Arabic structure.

Zayd and 'Alī met smiling.	إِسْتَقْبَلَ زَيْدٌ عَلِيًّا ضاحِكَيْنِ.
The صَاحِبُ الْحالِ consists of two persons: *Zayd* (زَيْدٌ), which is the subject. And *'Alī* (عَلِيًّا), which is the direct object. This is because we use the **dual**-form ضاحِكَيْنِ indicating that both were smiling.	

4. The **subject** (مُبْتَدَأٌ) of a nominal sentence (جُمْلَةٌ إِسْمِيّةٌ).

The vegetables – fresh (ones) – are useful.	الْخَضْرَواتُ - طازِجَةً - مُفيدةٌ.
Notice صَاحِبُ الْحالِ. *Vegetables* (الْخَضْرَواتُ) is the subject (مُبْتَدَأٌ) and the	

> that the word طَازِجَةً is <u>not</u> an adjective/attribute because adjectives always have to share the characteristics of the thing they describe (case, gender, negated or not, definite or not). This is not the situation here.

Let's now check constructions that are more challenging. They are often difficult to translate. You may need a helping construction.

5. The <u>second</u> part of a إِضافةٌ (i.e., الْمُضافُ إِلَيْهِ) is the صاحِبُ الْحالِ.

How can we achieve that the **second** part of a إِضافةٌ functions as the صاحِبُ الْحالِ؟ That's possible in three situations:

SITUATION 1: The first part of the إِضافةٌ is a **real** part or piece of the **second** part. For example:

I liked the balcony of the house, with the spacious atmosphere.	أَعْجَبَتْنِي شُرْفَةُ الْبَيْتِ فَسِيحًا.
The second part of the إِضافةٌ - *the house* (الْبَيْتِ) – is the صاحِبُ الْحالِ. The first part of the إِضافةٌ is *balcony* (شُرْفَةُ) which is a piece of the house.	

SITUATION 2: The first part of the إِضافةٌ is – by status, degree, or position – a **piece of the second** part (بِمَنْزِلةٍ جُزْءٌ مِن الْمُضافِ).

The first part (مُضافٌ) is virtually or metaphorically a part of the مُضافٌ إِلَيْهِ – for this reason, we could theoretically delete the <u>first</u> part, and the sentence would still make sense.

I liked the article of Zayd who was explaining [the matter].	أَعْجَبَتْنِي مَقالةُ زَيْدٍ مُوَضِّحًا.

The صاحِبُ الْحالِ is the second part of the إِضافةٌ, in our example: *Zayd* (زَيْدٍ). The first part (مُضافٌ) is the word *article* (مَقالةُ). This is certainly not a piece, nor a part of *Zayd*. Nevertheless, the phrase would still be quite clear and correct even without the word *article*. Thus, it is okay to delete مَقالةُ. If we did so, we would get the following sentence:

I liked Zayd, explaining [the matter].	أَعْجَبَنِي زَيْدٌ مُوَضِّحًا.

Sura 4:125	...follow the religion of Abraham, **inclining toward truth...** (Sah. Int.)	...وَاتَّبَعَ مِلَّةَ إِبْرَاهِيمَ حَنِيفًا...

حَنِيفًا depends on the expression مِلَّة إِبْرَاهِيم being metaphorically a part of *Ibrahim*. However, the phrase would be quite clear even without it.

SITUATION 3: The first part of the إِضافةٌ has verbal power and functions as the **regent** (عامِلٌ) of the second part (الْمُضافُ إِلَيْهِ). This means that the **first** part naturally needs to be capable of being the عامِلٌ of the حالٌ (see *question #361* for a possible عامِلٌ of a حالٌ).

I liked to write the book in a clarifying style.	أَعْجَبَتْنِي كِتابةُ الْكِتابِ واضِحًا.

The صاحِبُ الْحال is the second part of the إِضافةٌ: *the book* (الْكِتاب). The 1ˢᵗ part is the عامِلٌ of the second part since *the book* (الْكِتاب) in its origin is, in fact, the **direct object** (مَفْعُولٌ بِه) of the process of *writing* (الْكِتابة).

Sura 10:4	To Him is your return all together.	إِلَيْهِ مَرْجِعُكُمْ جَمِيعًا.

All together (جَمِيعًا) is the حالٌ and refers to the صاحِبُ الْحالِ: *you* (كُمْ).

360. Can the حالٌ refer to any kind of object?

Yes, it can.

In principle it is simple. Any kind of object can serve as the صَاحِبُ الْحالِ (which is marked in gray below). Let's look at some examples:

direct object	الْمَفْعُولُ بِه	I avoid the wind from the north.	أَجْتَنِبُ الرِّيحَ شَمالِيّةً.
absolute object	الْمَفْعُولُ الْمُطْلَقُ	I was totally tired.	تَعِبْتُ التَّعَبَ شَدِيدًا.
object of result (cause)	الْمَفْعُولُ لِأَجْلِهِ (لَهُ)	I fled out of (naked) fear.	هَرَبْتُ لِلْخَوْفِ مُجَرَّدًا.
adverbial exp. of time/place	الْمَفْعُولُ فِيهِ	You fasted the entire month.	صُمْتَ الشَّهْرَ كامِلًا.
object of accompaniment	الْمَفْعُولُ مَعَهُ	I walked along the rough sea.	سِرْتُ وَالْبَحْرَ هائِجًا.

361. What is the regent of the حالٌ؟

Usually the verb – but that is not the end of the story.

The حالٌ depends on a regent (عامِلٌ) which is the reason why the حالٌ is in the accusative case (نَصبٌ). The grammarians say that both the حالٌ and the صاحِبُ الْحالِ **share the same** عامِلٌ, which is usually the verb. The original عامِلٌ for the حالٌ is the verb (فِعْلٌ). As usual, there are also other words that can work as regents (عَوامِلُ). In the following examples, the حالٌ is marked in gray.

I. Regents that <u>resemble</u> verbs and have verbal power.

a) The plain, regular infinitive (مَصْدَرٌ صَرِيحٌ)

Your early presence (coming) is important.	حُضُورُكَ مُبَكِّرًا أَمْرٌ مُهِمٌّ.

What is the regent (عامِلٌ) of the صاحِبُ الْحالِ؟ It is the مَصْدَرٌ: *attending* (حُضُورٌ). The صاحِبُ الْحالِ is the pronoun suffix (كَ) which serves as the second part of the إِضافةٌ.

b) The active participle (إِسْمُ الْفاعِلِ)

This is a student who writes his article understandably.	هٰذا طالِبٌ كاتِبٌ مَقالَتَهُ واضِحةً.

The operator of the حالٌ is كاتِبٌ. The word كاتِبٌ has verbal power and governs the direct object (*article* - مَقالةٌ) in the accusative (مَنْصُوبٌ) – the word مَقالةٌ is also the صاحِبُ الْحالِ.

c) The passive participle (إِسْمُ الْمَفْعُولِ)

Zayd is hit whilst standing. (Zayd is beaten standing.)	زَيْدٌ مَضْرُوبٌ قائِمًا.
This is an article whose topic was understandably written.	هٰذه مَقالةٌ مَكْتُوبٌ مَوْضُوعُها واضِحًا.

The passive participles مَضْرُوبٌ and مَكْتُوبٌ are the regents of the حالٌ.

They both have verbal power: مَكْتُوبٌ governs مَوْضُوع in the nominative case (رَفْعٌ) since it is the subject of the passive. The word مَوْضُوع is also the صاحِبُ الْحالِ.

d) The pseudo/quasi participle (صِفةٌ مُشَبَّهةٌ) and the noun of preference (اِسْمُ التَّفْضِيلِ).

In the following table, the underlined words act as the regents for the حالٌ and resemble a verb in this regard.

| صِفةٌ مُشَبَّهةٌ | Zayd looks handsome standing. | زَيْدٌ حَسَنٌ قائِمًا. |
| إِسْمُ التَّفْضِيلِ | Zayd looks more handsome standing than sitting. | زَيْدٌ قائِمًا أَحْسَنُ مِنْهُ قاعِدًا. |

e) The اِسْمُ الْفِعْلِ (interjection denoting a sense of a verb)

| Write in an explanatory way! | كَتابِ شارِحًا! |
| Leave quickly! | نَزالِ مُشرِعًا! |

The regent of the حالٌ is the اِسْمُ فِعْلِ أَمْرٍ which is كَتابِ. This word governs the subject (فاعِلٌ) in the state of the nominative (رَفْعٌ); subject is a hidden pronoun in the imperative (expressing you/أَنْتَ). This hidden, implied subject (أَنْتَ) is the صاحِبُ الْحالِ.

Usually the اِسْمُ فِعْلِ أَمْرٍ is a word (with a fixed shape) that is not derived from a verb. For example, هَيّا or عَلَيْكَ. The form used in the examples above conveys the meaning of the imperative of a I-verb (الْفِعْلُ الثُّلاثِيُّ). Thus, كَتابِ means the same as أُكْتُبْ (write!). The pattern فَعالِ has a cemented shape (مَبْنِيٌّ عَلَى الْكَسْرِ) and never changes its shape

II. Covert governors that carry the __meaning__ of a verb (عامِلٌ مَعْنَوِيٌّ).

These are words which include (implicitly) the meaning of a verb without having its root letters (دُونَ حُرُوفِهِ).

a) Demonstratives (اِسْمُ الْإِشارةِ), e.g., *this* (هذا)

| This work of yours is excellently done. | هٰذا عَمَلُكَ مُمْتازًا! |
| This is Zayd, standing. | هٰذا زَيْدٌ قائِمًا. |

In both examples, the عامِلٌ for the حالٌ is the اِسْمُ الْإِشارةِ because it includes the meaning of a verb which is أُشِيرُ (*I point to*). We could rewrite the second sentence as follows:

| I point at Zayd whose status of being is standing. | أُشِيرُ إِلَى زَيْدٍ حالَ كَوْنِهِ قائِمًا. |

Let's examine another possible supposed meaning of هٰذا.

| This is 'Amr (in the act of) going away. | هٰذا عَمْرُو مُنْطَلِقًا. |

The word هٰذا has the virtual meaning of:

| Look at him going away! | اُنْظُرْ إِلَيْهِ مُنْطَلِقًا! |
| I point to him going away. | أُشِيرُ إِلَيْهِ مُنْطَلِقًا. |

| Sura 27:52 | So those are their houses, desolate because of the wrong they had done. | فَتِلْكَ بُيُوتُهُمْ خاوِيَةً بِمَا ظَلَمُوا. |

The demonstrative تِلْكَ includes (virtually) the following meaning: أُشِيرُ إِلَى بُيُوتِهِمْ.

b) Particle of wish (حَرْفٌ لِلتَّمَنِّي)

| perhaps | لَعَلَّ | | if only; would that | لَيْتَ |

Watch out! Both particles govern the subject in the accusative case because they are *abrogators* (حَرْفٌ ناسِخٌ). That's why the Arabic word for *citizen* gets the accusative case (مَنْصُوبٌ) in the following example.

| Would only the citizens, the cultured, return one day. | لَيْتَ الْمُواطِنَ - مُثَقَّفًا - يَعُودُ يَوْمًا. |

لَيْتَ is a حَرْفٌ لِلتَّمَنِّي and functions as the regent of the حالٌ. Why? Because it includes the meaning of the verb *I wish for* (أَتَمَنَّى). Another example:

| Let the young come back! | لَيْتَ الشَّبَابَ يَعُودُ! |

c) A so-called حَرْفُ التَّشْبِيهِ, a particle that introduces a comparison. Most famous example: the expression *as if* (كَأَنَّ).

| It is as if the full moon was rising. | كَأَنَّهُ الْبَدْرُ طَالِعًا. |
| كَأَنَّ is the regent of the حَالٌ. Why? Since it is a حَرْفُ التَّشْبِيهِ, it includes the meaning of the verb *to resemble* (أَشْبَهَ). | |

d) Prepositional or adverbial phrase (شِبْهُ الْجُمْلةِ)

| Zayd is in the house, standing. | زَيْدٌ فِي الْبَيْتِ قَائِمًا. |
| فِي الْبَيْتِ has the underlying meaning of: → | مُسْتَقِرٌّ فِي الْبَيْتِ |

Some more examples:

What are you about, standing (there)?	مَا لَكَ وَاقِعًا؟
Beside you is Zayd, sitting.	عِنْدَكَ زَيْدٌ جَالِسًا.
The subject is clear in front of you.	الْمَوْضُوعُ أَمَامَكَ وَاضِحًا.

➤ The regent (عَامِلٌ) of the حَالٌ is the شِبْهُ الْجُمْلةِ (underlined words) because these prepositional or adverbial phrases relate implicitly to a (deleted) verb or a word with verbal force. In a way, the شِبْهُ الْجُمْلةِ in-cludes the meaning of that verb since it is implicitly understood (شِبْهُ الْجُمْلةِ يَتَعَلَّقُ بِمُتَعَلِّقٍ أَصْلُهُ الْفِعْلُ، فَهُوَ يَتَضَمَّنُ مَعْناهُ).

362. What is the regent of the حَالٌ in a nominal sentence?

The position of the subject (مُبْتَدَأٌ).

Let's start with the problem: The verb is normally the regent of the حَالٌ. But this cannot work for a حَالٌ that relates to the subject (مُبْتَدَأٌ) of a nominal sentence (جُمْلةٌ اسْمِيّةٌ) simply because there is no verb.

The regent of the subject (مُبْتَدَأٌ) in a nominal sentence is nothing but the **beginning** (الإِبْتِداءُ): the start of the utterance. If there is an abrogator (ناسِخٌ), it is the word that has abrogating power, for example, إِنَّ or كانَ *and its sisters*. Now comes the interesting question. Can the subject govern the حالٌ?

Some grammarians state that this cannot work. They say that it is impossible that the حال is governed by the subject (مُبْتَدَأٌ) because this operator does not have enough power (عامِلٌ ضَعِيفٌ).

The famous grammarian Sībawayhi (سيبويه) claimed the opposite and said that the مُبْتَدَأٌ is capable of that – namely, that a حالٌ can be governed by the مُبْتَدَأٌ because this had been proven by examples of Classical Arabic.

Let's analyze the chain of reaction:

step 3	step 2	step 1
الْحالُ	الْمُبْتَدَأُ	الإِبْتِداءُ
Due to the governing power of the subject, such a word takes the accusative case because it tells us more about the state or condition of the subject while the act (*) is taking place. ←	The regent assigns the job of the subject to a word and governs it in the nominative case. ←	The regent here is abstract. It is simply the position: the beginning of the sentence.

(*) Note: The act here is implicitly understood as a deleted active participle, for example: مُسْتَقِرّ.

Most grammarians follow Sībawayhi's view. The regent of the مُبْتَدَأُ is simply its position in the sentence, i.e., the beginning. And the regent of the حالٌ is the مُبْتَدَأُ.

363. Which forms of a word can be used to work as a حالٌ?

Usually the حالٌ has the form of a derived noun (مُشْتَقٌّ).

A مُشْتَقٌّ (derived noun) is a variable noun (اِسْمٌ مُتَصَرِّفٌ) which means that it can form the dual, plural, or nisba (يُنْسَبُ إِلَيْهِ) and does not have a cemented shape (مَبْنِيٌّ). A مُشْتَقٌّ has a root from which it was derived. The مُشْتَقّ is close to its root in meaning and action.

A derived noun, when placed as a حالٌ, expresses a **temporary state** (حالٌ مُنْتَقِلةٌ). The word مُنْتَقِلٌ literally means *movable, mobile*.

However, the حالٌ can also be expressed by a **static, inert noun** (إِسْمٌ جَامِدٌ) that is not derived from a root and therefore the opposite of a مُشْتَقّ. If we want to use a static noun in the location of a حالٌ, we need to interpret the static word as a مُشْتَقّ. Such a structure is called حالٌ جَامِدةٌ and not, as usual, حالٌ مُشْتَقةٌ.

Remark: If you are wondering why we use the feminine forms for the adjective, don't forget that the word حالٌ can be treated as masculine or feminine. If you are not familiar with the term مُشْتَقّ, see *Arabic for Nerds 1, #75*.

Which words can be **interpreted as derived nouns** (الْمُؤَوَّلةُ بِالْمُشْتَقّ)؟

a) The **regular infinitive noun** (مَصْدَرٌ صَرِيحٌ)

Zayd ran scared.	جَرَى زَيْدٌ خَوفًا.
I killed him in cold blood.	قَتَلْتُهُ صَبْرًا.

In both examples, a مَصْدَرٌ is placed as the حالٌ. Both words, خَوفًا and صَبْرًا, can be interpreted as a مُشْتَقّ (e.g, the active participle):

steadfast	صابِرًا		being afraid, fearful	خَائِفًا

---

b) The حالٌ may be a **static, inert** noun (إِسْمٌ جَامِدٌ). This happens if the word conveys **likeness** or **resemblance** (أَنْ تَدُلَّ الْحالُ عَلَى تَشْبِيهٍ).

The moon rose full.	طَلَعَ الْقَمَرُ بَدْرًا.
Zayd attacked (like) a lion.	كَرَّ زَيْدٌ أَسَدًا (= كَأَسَدٍ).

The حالٌ in the last example is *lion* (أَسَدًا), in the meaning of *resembling a lion* (i.e., مُشْبِهًا الْأَسَدَ). The word أَسَد may be interpreted as:

ravenous	مُفْتَرِسًا		bold	جَرِيئًا		audacious	مِقْدَامًا

c) The noun points or suggests **participation** (مُشَارَكَةٌ or مُفَاعَلَةٌ).

I met him face to face (fair and square).	لَقِيتُهُ كَفَّةً كَفَّةً.
Remark: كَفَّةً كَفَّةً has the meaning of confronting (مُوَاجَهَةٌ). You could also express it by لَقِيتُهُ كَفَّةً عَنْ كَفَّةٍ or كَفَّةً لِكَفَّةٍ	

I personally gave him the book.	سَلَّمْتُهُ الْكِتَابَ يَدًا بِيَدٍ.
I dealt (traded, with him) for ready money.	بِعْتُهُ يَدًا بِيَدٍ.

يَدًا is the حَالٌ in the accusative (مَنْصُوبٌ). Here, we don't have a derived noun of a root; we don't have an action. We have a static noun that does the job of a circumstantial qualifier (حَالٌ جَامِدَةٌ هِيَ فِي مَعْنَى الْمُشْتَقِّ).

What about the word بِيَدٍ؟ It is a prepositional phrase (جَارٌّ وَمَجْرُورٌ) that is in the location where you would expect an adjective in the accusative case (صِفَةٌ فِي مَحَلِّ نَصْبٍ) for the word يَدًا. We assume that the place of the prepositional phrase is reserved for a صِفَةٌ. Therefore, the *thing that is described* (الْمَوْصُوفُ) would be the word يَدًا which is placed as a حَالٌ. Since a prepositional phrase needs a connection, we assume that it is associated with a deleted word (مُتَعَلِّقٌ بِمَحْذُوفٍ), in fact, imagine an adjective. Sounds complicated, but this is how we make such sentences work.

Note: The expression يَدًا بِيَدٍ conveys the meaning of مُقَابَضَةٌ (*exchanging commodities, bartering*) or مُنَاجَزَةٌ (lit., *struggle, contention*). You could also say: بِعْتُهُ نَاجِزًا بِنَاجِزٍ

Remark: In Islamic Finance, تَقَابُضٌ denotes the reciprocal taking possession of a commodity and its monetary equivalent by buyer and seller respectively (against immediate payment of the price or a counter-value).

Such types of حَالٌ-constructions can be interpreted as a مُشْتَقٌّ. Often, the pattern مُفَاعَلَةٌ is used which is the مَصْدَرٌ of a III-verb (فَاعَلَ). E.g.:

Bartering; exchanging goods with each other	مُقَابَضَةٌ

d) The word points to a **price** (سِعْرٌ) - *at the rate of.*

I bought the wheat at the rate of ninety per bag (Kaila).	اِشْتَرَيْتُ الْقَمْحَ كَيْلَةً بِتِسْعِينَ.

Remark: It is not *kilogram* (كيلو). One *Kaila* (كَيْلَةٌ) is a dry measure and equals 16.72 liters.

The word كَيْلَةً is the حَالٌ. The prepositional phrase (بِتِسْعِينَ) here is placed where you would expect an adjective (صِفَةٌ) in the position of an accusative – see the example of c). But that adjective was deleted, so we say that the prepositional phrase is connected with that deleted word which is implicitly understood. The الْمَوْصُوف is the word كَيْلَة. This word is interpreted as a مُشْتَقّ: as the مَصْدَر of the II-verb (سَعَّرَ).

مُسَعِّرًا	setting a price; quoting on the market.

e) The word points or suggests an **arrangement** or **order** (تَرْتِيبٌ).

سَمَّاهُم رَجُلًا رَجُلًا.	He named them man for man.
دَخَلُوا الْقَاعَةَ ثَلاثَةً ثَلاثَةً.	They entered the court in groups of three.
هُوَ جَارِي بَيْتَ بَيْتَ.	He is my next-door neighbor.
بَيَّنْتُهَا لَهُ بَابًا بَابًا.	I explained it to him, item by item.

In the second example, ثَلاثَةً is the حَالٌ. The following word ثَلاثَةً is a مَعْطُوفٌ relating to a **deleted conjunction** which could be either فَ or ثُمَّ. We could also treat the entire phrase as an emphasis (تَوْكِيدٌ لَفْظِيٌّ).

All the above examples (the words in the accusative case) work as a حَالٌ and can be interpreted as a مُشْتَقّ in the overall meaning of:

مُتَرَتِّبِينَ	arranged; organized

Note that this word is a sound masculine plural – which is put into the accusative case by the ي before the ن (instead of the ending ونَ).

364. What happens if the حَالٌ can't be interpreted as a مُشْتَقّ?

Well, in many situations we can still treat it as a حَالٌ.

We will now turn to very peculiar constructions of a حَالٌ. Neverthe-less, they occur frequently. So it's worth taking a look at a few sentences. Remember that a حَالٌ **qualifies the state of a noun** and never of an action (for an action we would most probably use a مَفْعُولٌ مُطْلَقٌ).

a) The حَالٌ is a **branch** or **subdivision** (فَرْعٌ) of the صَاحِبُ الْحَالِ.

This is your money in gold.	هٰذا مَالُكَ ذَهَبًا.
He wears gold, in the form of a ring.	يَلْبَسُ الذَّهَبَ خَاتِمًا.
In sentence 2, the word خَاتِمًا is a حَالٌ جَامِدةٌ. The word *ring* is a branch of the material *gold* (الذَّهَبِ). The word *gold* is the صَاحِبُ الْحَالِ.	

b) The صَاحِبُ الْحَالِ is a **branch** or **subdivision** (فَرْعٌ) of the حَالٌ; the reverse situation to a).

He wears a ring, made of gold.	يَلْبَسُ الْخَاتِمَ ذَهَبًا.
The word *gold* (ذَهَبًا) is the حَالٌ جَامِدةٌ. It is a kind (نَوْعٌ) of the word *ring* which is the صَاحِبُ الْحَالِ.	

c) We have a **noun of comparison** (أُسْلُوبُ التَّفْضِيلِ). The مُفَضَّلٌ (the word before the comparative) is the صَاحِبُ الْحَالِ. The regent (عَامِلٌ) in such constructions is the إِسْمُ التَّفْضِيلِ (i.e., the comparative, superlative) and is usually placed between the two حَالٌ.

Muhammad (when) walking, is faster than Zayd, (when) riding.	مُحَمَّدٌ مَاشِيًا أَسْرَعُ مِنْ زَيْدٍ راكِبًا.
As a fruit an apple is better than a date.	الْفَاكِهةُ تُفَّاحًا أَحْسَنُ مِنها بَلَحًا.
Two words, تُفَّاحًا <u>and</u> بَلَحًا, are placed as a حَالٌ جَامِدةٌ. They are both subordinates of *fruits*. And what is the صَاحِبُ الْحَالِ? ➡ It is الْفَاكِهةُ.	

d) The حَالٌ is expressed by a **number** (عَدَدٌ).

The number of students was 30.	تَمَّ عَدَدُ الطُّلابِ ثَلاثِينَ طالِبًا.
The حَالٌ جَامِدةٌ is ثَلاثِينَ. Note: Some grammarians say that we could interpret the حَالٌ as a مُشْتَقٌّ which would be بَالِغِينَ (*reaching*).	

e) The حَالٌ is further described by a **derived noun** (مَوْصُوفَةٌ بِمُشْتَقٍّ).

The sea (level) rose a great deal.	إِرْتَفَعَ الْبَحْرُ قُدْرًا كَبِيرًا.
The حَالٌ جَامِدَةٌ here is قُدْرًا. That word is further described by a derived noun (مَوْصُوفَةٌ بِمُشْتَقٍّ), a صِفَةٌ مُشَبَّهَةٌ: it is the word كَبِيرًا.	

365. Is the حَالٌ always indefinite?

Almost always.

In Arabic grammar books, you often read that the حَالٌ has to be in-definite (نَكِرَةٌ) by definition. This is true but there are very few excep-tions in which you may find the حَالٌ taking a the definite form (مَعْرِفَةٌ). This usually happens when we have the expression وَحْدَ (lit.: *as one of*), which is always followed by a pronoun suffix. It is then translated as *alone; by ...self.*

I traveled alone/by myself.	ذَهَبْتُ وَحْدِي.
He traveled alone.	ذَهَبَ وَحْدَهُ.
They traveled alone.	ذَهَبُوا وَحْدَهُمْ.

The word وَحْدَ is the حَالٌ. Now comes the finesse: وَحْدَ can't be used alone. It must be part of a إِضَافَةٌ-construction. This has a huge gram-matical implication. وَحْدَ is the first part of the إِضَافَةٌ. Now, when the first part (مُضَافٌ) is followed by a possessive pronoun, the first part is, by definition, **definite** (مَعْرِفَةٌ)!

So we are in a dilemma, but the grammarians have found a way out. A possible interpretation (تَأْوِيلٌ) of a singular form (نَكِرَةٌ) of that ex-pression could be the following:

I went alone.	ذَهَبْتُ مُنْفَرِدًا.

But that is not all. There are some other special situations:

Go in one by one/one after the other! (Lit. mean-ing: *each time the first available*).	اُدْخُلُوا الْأَوَّلَ فَالْأَوَّلَ!

Interpretation of the حالٌ: →	اُدْخُلُوا مُتَرَتِّبِينَ.
The first appearance of الْأَوَّلَ is the حالٌ. The second is coupled with the first one (مَعْطُوفٌ). Both are definite (مَعْرِفةٌ) by the Aleph and the Lām (ال).	

They came, every single one of them = large crowd. Lit.: its gravel with its pebbles; i.e., small and great, one and all.	جاءُوا قَضُّهُمْ بِقَضِيضِهِمْ.
قَضُّهُمْ is the حالٌ. We also have a إضافةٌ making the expression definite. Note: قَضِيضٌ means *gravel; pebble* but is mostly used figuratively: بِقَضِّهِ وَقَضِيضِهِ (*as a whole; in its entirety*); النَّاسُ بِقَضِّهِمْ وَقَضِيضِهِمْ (*every single one of the people*).	
This is the meaning: *A large crowd came*.	جاءُوا الْجَمَّاءَ الْغَفِيرَ = مُجْتَمِعِينَ كَثِيرِينَ

The traveler returned to the start.	رَجَعَ الْمُسافِرُ عَوْدَهُ عَلَى بَدْئِهِ.
The word عَوْد is the حالٌ. It is used in a إضافةٌ with a pronoun (ضَمِيرٌ). So the word is, grammatically speaking, definite. Note: the expression عَوْداً على بَدْءٍ means *going back to the beginning; starting over*.	
This is the interpretation: →	رَجَعَ عائِدًا عَلَى بَدْئِهِ.

366. Is it correct to use the expression لِوَحْدِي to translate *alone*?

No, it isn't.

Today, the word وَحْد is often used with لِ. Such a construction is incorrect according to the rules of Arabic.

incorrect	I went alone/by myself.	ذَهَبْتُ لِوَحْدِي.
	He went alone/by himself.	ذَهَبَ لِوَحْدِهِ.
correct	I traveled alone/by myself.	ذَهَبْتُ وَحْدِي.
	He traveled alone.	ذَهَبَ وَحْدَهُ.

Why is it incorrect? The word وَحْد here can **only** be used in one way: in the meaning of a حالٌ as explained in the previous *question*. Therefore, وَحْد has to take the accusative case (مَنْصُوبٌ) which means that it cannot be preceded by a لَامٌ (ل)! What is the solution? Just drop the ل and use وَحْد in the accusative case (مَنْصُوبٌ) which results in وَحْدَ – finally, add a pronoun suffix. There are other words that follow the same logic.

I tried my best.	حاوَلْتُ جُهْدِي.
This would be the interpretation of the حالٌ: →	حاوَلْتُ جاهِدًا.

I did my best in this matter.	سَعَيْتُ فِي الْأَمْرِ طاقَتِي.
Interpretation of the حالٌ: →	سَعَيْتُ فِي الْأَمْرِ مُطِيقًا.
Remark: مُطِيقٌ is the active participle (اِسْمُ الْفاعِلِ) of the IV-verb - أَطاقَ (to master; to be able to; to bear; R2=و) يُطِيقُ	

The words جُهْدٌ and طاقةٌ are used in إِضافةٌ-constructions serving as the first parts what makes them definite since the second part is a pronoun. Unlike وَحْدَ, both words **can be interpreted as indefinite** (نَكِرةٌ). Anyway, you don't necessarily have to use them in a إِضافةٌ.

367. Is the status of the حالٌ only temporary?

Yes, normally it is only temporary.

Let's look again at the basic, original idea of a حالٌ. We can say that it does **not** express a fixed and stable description for the صاحِبُ الْحالِ.

The grammarians use the term مُنْتَقِلةٌ (see *question #363*) which literally means *movable, mobile*. It basically denotes that the status which the حالٌ describes is not inherent to the صاحِبُ الْحالِ.

The *circumstantial description* (حالٌ), as the name already indicates, is only valid for a certain, specific amount of time. We could say that it is valid for the time/duration of the action only.

Zayd came, laughing.	جاءَ زَيْدٌ ضاحِكًا.
Zayd was **only** laughing at the time he was coming (وَقْتُ الْمَجِيءِ).	

If we need something more durable (ثابِتٌ لِصاحِبِها), what should we do? There are several options. The حالٌ then conveys emphasis.

a) We use an **assuring, strengthening** description (حالٌ مُؤَكِّدَةٌ) for the content that is found earlier in the sentence. In such constructions, the regent/governor/operator (عامِلٌ) of the حالٌ is usually deleted.

The description may refer to the verb (which would then be the regent) or to an entire preceding sentence (which is reassured by the حالٌ).

- If it refers to a preceding clause, this clause must be a **nominal sentence** (جُمْلَةٌ اِسْمِيّةٌ), consisting of <u>two definite</u> **static nouns** (اِسْمانِ مَعْرِفَتانِ جامِدانِ). The حالٌ reassures the information before.

- If the description refers to the **verb** itself (though this is rare), it **may be derived** from the verb itself.

Zayd is your father, as kind/compassionate.	زَيْدٌ أَبُوكَ عَطُوفًا.	1
Note: The nominal sentence زَيْدٌ أَبُوكَ comprises the meaning of compassion (عَطْفٌ). The حال here is not adding much extra meaning; it reaffirms the fatherhood.		
He is Zayd, as (well-)known. (Note: The حالٌ is used to reassure that the man is Zayd.)	هُوَ زَيْدٌ مَعْرُوفًا.	2
I am Zayd, as (well-)known.	أَنا زَيْدٌ مَعْرُوفًا.	3
This is the truth, as manifest.	هُوَ الْحَقُّ بَيِّنًا.	4

In such sentences, some grammarians interpret the صاحِبُ الْحالِ as a **deleted pronoun** (ضَمِيرٌ مَحْذُوفٌ). We therefore would get the following estimated (supposed) meanings (تَقْدِيرٌ):

example 1	زَيْدٌ أَبُوكَ أَحُقُّهُ عَطُوفًا.
	We could say that the حالٌ is explained by an ellipsis of the I-verb حَقَّ - يَحُقُّ (R2=R3). So we get: *I affirm it; I know it to be true* (أَحُقُّهُ); *I know him/it* (أَعْرِفُهُ or أَعْلَمُهُ); *I know him/it for certain* (أُثْبِتُهُ).
example 2	هُوَ زَيْدٌ أَعْرِفُهُ مَعْرُوفًا.
example 3	أَنا زَيْدٌ أَحَقُّ مَعْرُوفًا.
	Notice: Since we talk about the first person *"I"*, we use the passive voice (indicative): *I am known* (أُعْرَفُ) or أَحَقُّ.

In such constructions, you are not allowed to move the حال closer to the front or even place it before the nominal sentence.

impossible	fronted (تَقْدِيمُ الْحالِ)	عَطُوفًا زَيْدٌ أَبُوكَ.
	in the middle (تَوَسُّطُ الْحالِ)	زَيْدٌ عَطُوفًا أَبُوكَ.

b) The regent (عامِلٌ) points to **creation** (خَلْقٌ) or **renewal** (تَجَدُّدٌ).

God created the neck of the giraffe long.	خَلَقَ اللّٰهُ رَقَبَةَ الزَّرافةِ طَويلةً.
طَويلةٌ is the حال for رَقَبة which describes a permanent shape (هَيْئَةٌ ثابِتةٌ).	

c) There is a **linkage** (قَرينةٌ) that points to the **constancy** (ثَباتُ الْحالِ) of the حال.

Sura 6:114	It is He who has revealed to you the Book explained in detail.	وَهُوَ الَّذِي، أَنزَاَ، إِلَيْكُمُ الْكِتَابَ مُفَصَّلًا.
مُفَصَّلًا is the حال for الْكِتَاب. Here, the حال does not describe a temporary state. Instead, it points to the steadiness of the shape which can't change – because Muslims believe that the Qur'an is perfect forever.		

368. Can the حال be a full sentence, and what would happen then?

Yes, this is possible. But you will need a binder or connector (رابِطٌ) which connects the حال with the صاحِبُ الْحالِ.

In general, the حال consists of one singular, **indefinite** word only. This means that it is not a sentence nor a prepositional phrase (شِبْه الْجُمْلةِ). However, you will see a sentence quite often instead.

The حال indeed can be a full sentence: a nominal or verbal sentence (as well as a شِبْهُ الْجُمْلةِ, see *question #369*).

A	nominal sent.	I saw Zayd while he was leaving.	رَأَيْتُ زَيْدًا وَهُوَ خارِجٌ.
B	verbal sentence	I saw Zayd leaving.	رَأَيْتُ زَيْدًا يَخْرُجُ.

Sentence A:

This particle (حَرْفٌ مَبْنِيٌّ) is a وَاوُ الْحالِ. No position in إِعْرابٌ.	و
Personal pronoun (ضَمِيرٌ مُنْفَصِلٌ); it is the subject (مُبْتَدَأٌ) of the nominal sentence; in the position of a nominative (فِي مَحَلِّ رَفْعٍ).	هُوَ
Predicate (خَبَرٌ مَرْفُوعٌ) of the nominal sentence (جُمْلَةٌ إِسْمِيّةٌ).	خارِجٌ
Watch out: The entire nominal sentence consisting of the subject and the predicate appears in the location of the حالٍ. Therefore, it takes the place of an accusative case (الْجُمْلَةُ مِن الْمُبْتَدَإِ وَخَبَرِهِ فِي مَحَلِّ نَصْبِ حالٍ).	

Sentence B:

Verb in the present tense, indicative (فِعْلٌ مُضارِعٌ مَرْفُوعٌ). The sub-ject (فاعِلٌ) is an implied pronoun (ضَمِيرٌ مُسْتَتِرٌ): *he* (هُوَ).	يَخْرُجُ
The verbal sentence (i.e., يَخْرُجُ) is in the position of the حالٍ; it occupies the position of an accusative case (الْجُمْلَةُ مِن الْفِعْلِ وَالْفاعِلِ فِي مَحَلِّ نَصْبِ حالٍ).	

Now, why should we be careful when the حالٍ is a sentence?

➤ We need a <u>binder</u> or <u>connector</u> (رابِطٌ) which connects the حالٍ with the صاحِبُ الْحالِ. Such a sentence is placed in the location of a *circumstantial description* (حالٍ) and therefore occupies the place of an accusative case (فِي مَحَلِّ نَصْبٍ).

The connector is a subordinator and is usually translated as *while; as*. In some situations, we can delete the connector. Some grammarians say if the connector is deleted, it may indicate a closer connection between the situation (= action) of the main clause and the circumstantial qualifier. For example:

1	The child returned from the doctor crying.	عادَ الطِّفْلُ مِن الطَّبِيبِ باكِيًا.
	There is a close connection between the action of *returning* and *crying*.	
2	The child returned from the doctor and/while it was crying.	عادَ الطِّفْلُ مِن الطَّبِيبِ وَهُوَ يَبْكِي.
	Here, the structure is different: two actions occur simultaneously.	

What could work as a رابِطٌ?

- the letter وَ: the *Wāw of the circumstantial description* (وَاوُ الْحالِ);
- a *referential, returning pronoun* (ضَمِيرٌ عائِدٌ عَلَى صاحِبِها);
- both together;

A. The حالٌ is a **nominal sentence** (جُمْلةٌ اِسْمِيّةٌ).

Usually you **add** a وَ before the جُمْلةُ الْحالِ (when it is a nominal sentence). However, in two situations, you **have to** put a وَ:

1. There is no pronoun (earlier in the sentence) to which we could relate. In other words, we have a different subject in the main clause. For example:

I was sleepless/stayed up the night while the people were sleeping.	سَهِرْتُ وَالنّاسُ نائِمُونَ.

2. The subject (مُبْتَدَأٌ) of the sentence serving as the حالٌ is a personal pronoun. This is the usual situation. For example: وَهُوَ...

There are also situations when you normally <u>don't use</u> a وَ.

- If the nominal sentence working as the حالٌ contains an **absolute negation** with لا, it is usually not connected with the main clause by وَ.

He slept without moving.	نامَ لا حَراكَ فِيهِ.

- You don't use a و if the حالٌ is confirming/**guaranteeing** the information in the main clause (إذا كانَتِ الْجُمْلةُ الْحالِيّةُ مُؤَكِّدةً لِمَضْمُونِ الْجُمْلةِ السّابِقةِ).

This right is unquestionable.	هذا الْحَقُّ لا رَيْبَ فِيهِ.

B. If the حالٌ is a **verbal sentence** (جُمْلةٌ فِعْلِيّةٌ).

- You normally **don't use a connector** when the main clause and the حالٌ (a verbal sentence) **share the same subject**. The subject could even be an implied, hidden pronoun.

I went into the room laughing.	دَخَلْتُ إِلَى الْغُرْفةِ أَضْحَكُ.

In several situations, you should or even __must__ use وَ:

- If you **repeat the subject** in the circumstantial clause, you need a free, separate personal pronoun and **must place** وَ before that pronoun. → The حالٌ becomes a nominal sentence with a separate personal pronoun serving as its subject, so the rules described above (under A) apply. Therefore, the وَ is mandatory.

I went into the room laughing.	دَخَلْتُ إِلَى الْغُرْفةِ وَأَنا أَضْحَكُ.

- You use وَ when the verbal sentence serving as the حالٌ is **negated** by لا or ما plus a verb in the present tense, indicative mood, or by لَمْ plus a verb in the jussive mood (فِعْلٌ مَجْزُومٌ). In such a situation, you may repeat the subject (which is the common approach), but you don't necessarily have to.

- You use وَ plus قَدْ in a **non-negated** (affirmative), **past tense** sentence which serves as the حالٌ. This construction indicates an action or situation that started in the past but continues to have results concurrent with the action that is found in the main clause.

  Note: If you have كانَ in the circumstantial clause, you don't use قَدْ.

Watch out! If you place a verbal sentence as a حالٌ, you cannot use the **future** tense therein because it would contradict the idea (لِلْمُنافاةِ بَيْنَ الزَّمانَيْنِ الْحالِ وَالْمُسْتَقْبَلِ). For example, you can't translate *Zayd came without hurry* into Arabic using the following sentence: جاءَ زَيْدٌ لَنْ يُسْرِعَ ➡ The particle لَنْ here indicates a future meaning!

369. Can a prepositional/adverbial phrase be understood as a حالٌ?

Strictly speaking: no. Practically speaking: yes.

This is similar to the debate whether a prepositional phrase may serve as the predicate of a nominal sentence (*see qu. #140*). Let's check how we could understand a semi-sentence (شِبْهُ الْجُمْلةِ) as a حالٌ.

A شِبْهُ الْجُمْلةِ, used as a حَالٌ, does <u>not</u> need a connector (رابِطٌ). It is added directly. If the adverbial (الظَّرْفُ) or prepositional phrase (الْجارُّ وَالْمَجْرُورُ) is located in the place of a circumstantial description (فِي مَوْقِعِ الْحالِ), there has to be a definite word earlier in the sentence. That is nothing special. So, what's the issue? In such situations, it is not trivial to determine the word or clause which functions as the حَالٌ.

Approach 1: Some (mostly modern) grammarians say that the prepositional or adverbial phrase itself can be seen as the حَالٌ. We would get the following analysis: شِبْهُ الْجُمْلةِ فِي مَحَلِّ نَصْبٍ حال

Approach 2: Other (mostly classical) scholars say that the actual حَالٌ was deleted and that the prepositional/adverbial phrase is linked to the deleted word and associated in meaning: شِبْهُ الْجُمْلةِ مُتَعَلِّقٌ بِالْحالِ الْمَحْذُوفِ

The whole issue is similar to the nominal sentence (جُمْلةٌ اِسْميّةٌ) and the "glue" (الْمُتَعَلِّقُ or التَّعَلُّقُ) which we need to connect a prepositional or adverbial phrase to the sentence – see *question #219*.

In such constructions, we say that the quasi-sentence (شِبْهُ الْجُمْلةِ) is related to a word which had to be deleted because it points to generality. For example: مُسْتَقِرًّا (*stable; permanent*) or اِسْتَقَرَّ. That deleted word is the actual circumstantial qualifier (الْمُتَعَلَّقُ الْمَحْذُوفُ فِي الْحَقيقةِ وَهُوَ الْحالُ) and the prepositional or adverbial phrases **appears** in the place of a حَالٌ, because the "real" حَالٌ was omitted as it is implicitly understood. Logically, I prefer what the old grammarians suggested. In practical terms, I find both solutions okay and use them. The important thing is to realize that there is a حَالٌ in the sentence.

Let's look at an example and use approach 2 for the analysis:

Summer in the mountains is more beautiful than on the beach.	الصَّيْفُ عَلَى الْجِبالِ أَجْمَلُ مِنْهُ عَلَى الشّاطِئِ.

How do we bring this sentence into line with our grammar? We need to understand that the actual, original حَالٌ was deleted, which is weird. If we included the deleted حَالٌ (in gray below), this would be the result:

الصَّيْفُ كائِنًا عَلَى الْجِبالِ أَجْمَلَ مِنْهُ عَلَى الشّاطِئِ.

For this reason, the grammarians say that the prepositional phrase is linked to the deleted حالٌ and can be seen as a remnant that is implicitly understood even without the original حالٌ.

Prepositional phrase (الْجارُّ وَالْمَجْرُورُ) that appears in the place of a circumstantial qualifier (جارٌّ وَمَجْرُورٌ مُتَعَلِّقٌ بِمَحْذُوفٍ حالٌ في مَحَلِّ نَصْبٍ). In other words, it is connected with a deleted word which was placed as a حالٌ.	عَلَى الْجِبالِ

Two more examples:

A ship on the waves is like a feather in the wind.	السَّفينَةُ بَيْنَ الْأَمْواجِ كَالرِّيشةِ في مَهَبِّ الرِّيحِ.

Adverb of place (ظَرْفُ مَكانٍ مَنْصُوبٌ).	بَيْنَ
Second part of the إضافةٌ in the genitive case (مَجْرُورٌ). The entire شِبْهُ الْجُمْلةِ (adverbial phrase) is linked to the deletion of the circumstantial qualifier and appears in the place of a circumstantial qualifier (شِبْهُ الْجُمْلةِ مُتَعَلِّقٌ بِمَحْذُوفٍ حالٌ في مَحَلِّ نَصْبٍ).	الْأَمْواجِ

Sura 28:79	He went out among his people **in all his pomp.**	فَخَرَجَ عَلَى قَوْمِهِ في زينَتِهِ.
The prepositional phrase (في زينَتِهِ) is located where you would expect a circumstantial clause. We say that it is connected with the deleted حالٌ (مُتَعَلِّقٌ بِحالٍ مَحْذُوفٍ). How could we understand the deleted word working as the حالٌ? A possible, hypothetical meaning (تَقْديرٌ) could be: كائِنًا في زينَتِهِ		

370. Does it matter whether a verb or a participle serves as the حالٌ?

Not really. However, there are some subtle differences.

The answer whether you should use a participle or a verb as a حالٌ mainly depends on the kind of action that the sentence expresses.

- Actions that involve a **process** such as *reading, writing, eating* are better described by a verb (فِعْلٌ مُضارِعٌ). ➡ Therefore, you should prefer a verbal sentence to express the حالٌ.
  For example: I saw Zayd *writing* (رَأَيْتُ زَيْدًا يَكْتُبُ).

- **States of being** such as *sleeping, laughing, wearing* and states of motion such as *walking, heading for* are better described by an active or passive participle (إِسْمُ الْمَفْعُولِ or إِسْمُ الْفَاعِلِ). ➡ Therefore, you should prefer a participle to express the حَالٌ.

For example: Zayd came *laughing* (جَاءَ زَيْدٌ ضَاحِكًا).

371. Can you move the حَالٌ closer to the front?

Yes, this is possible. In some situations, it is even necessary.

Usually, the حَالٌ is placed **before** the صَاحِبُ الْحَالِ and comes at the end of a sentence. Sometimes, however, it is necessary to move the حَالٌ closer to the front.

Three situations demand to **move the حَالٌ** to the front (تَقْدِيمٌ).

SITUATION 1: You <u>must</u> place the حَالٌ before the صَاحِبُ الْحَالِ if the صَاحِبُ الْحَالِ is a plain <u>indefinite</u> word (not negated, no إِضافةٌ).

Such constructions are rare exceptions because according to the rules, the صَاحِبُ الْحَالِ has to be definite (مَعْرِفةٌ).

| A man came speeding. | قَدِمَ مُسْرِعًا رَجُلٌ. |
| I saw a lion lurking. | رَأَيْتُ رابِضًا أَسَدًا. |

SITUATION 2: If there is an indefinite direct object involved and the حَال refers to subject: then you must not place the حَال at the end but before the direct object (to avoid confusion).

Why? With the new arrangement, you make it clear that the word in question is a حَالٌ and not an adjective for the direct object:

| Circumstantial description of the subject (حَالٌ). | I saw, **when I was riding**, a man. | رَأَيْتُ راكِبًا رَجُلًا. |
| Adjective (نَعْتٌ) for the direct object (مَفْعُولٌ بِه). | I saw a **riding man**. | رَأَيْتُ رَجُلًا راكِبًا. |

SITUATION 3: If the sentence is a **question**, you <u>must</u> move the حالٌ to the front, i.e., you place it before the صاحِبُ الْحالِ.

Here is an example of Hāfiz Ibrāhīm (حافِظ إبْراهِيم). Hāfiz Ibrāhīm (1871 - 1932) was a famous Egyptian poet, known as the *Poet of the Nile*.

How pleasing is the revenge on the powerful?	كَيْفَ يَحْلُو مِن الْقَوِيِّ التَّشَفِّي؟
What happened here? كَيْفَ is a **question word** (اِسْمُ اِسْتِفْهامٍ) **placed as a** حالٌ and thus located in the place of an accusative case (فِي مَحَلِّ نَصْبٍ). You have to place the حالٌ before its regent (عامِلٌ) as the question word must always stand at the beginning of an utterance (لَهُ صَدارةُ الْكَلامِ).	

This is the reason why you find the answer usually also in the accusative case. For example:

Question:	How did you return?	كَيْفَ عُدْتَ؟
Answer:	Riding (driving).	راكِبًا.

Let's examine situations when the حالٌ is occasionally placed before the صاحِبُ الْحالِ - but at the **very beginning!** This happens, for example, if you want to **stress on the importance of the situation** (of the circumstance). Then, you should place the حالٌ before the verb:

Laughing, the girl came in.	ضاحِكةً جَلَسَت الْفَتاةُ.
Quickly came the answer.	مُسْرِعًا جاءَ الرَّدُّ.

That's also why the following expressions are usually treated as a حالٌ:

firstly	أَوَّلًا		secondly	ثانِيًا
generally	عامّةً		especially	خاصّةً
similarly	مُساوِيًا		suddenly	فَجْأةً
always	دائِمًا		together	مَعًا

In all other situations, you can choose:

Both are correct and mean the same.	I visited the neighborhood, crowded with people.	زُرْتُ الْحَيَّ عَامِرًا.
		زُرْتُ عَامِرًا الْحَيَّ.

Watch out if the regent of the حَالّ is **not derived from a root**! This will limit your ability to move the حَالّ.

correct	That is the Hijab wearing Hind!	تِلْكَ هِنْدٌ مُتَحَجِّبَةً!
incorrect	Why can't we front the حَالّ and place it before its regent? The demonstrative تِلْكَ is an *abstract regent*, a covert governor (عَامِـلّ مَعْنَوِيٌّ), whose verbal meaning (= أُشِيرُ) can only be understood virtually.	مُتَحَجِّبَةً تِلْكَ هِنْدٌ!

correct	As if Zayd is riding a lion. ← تَشْبِيهُ زَيْدٍ فِي حالٍ رُكُوبِهِ بِأَسَدٍ.	كَأَنَّ زَيْدًا راكِبًا أَسَدٌ.
incorrect	Same reason as above. We have an abstract regent, i.e., كَـأَنَّ (see #265). Its verbal meaning (= أُشَبِّهُ) can only be estimated and understood virtually.	راكِبًا كَأَنَّ زَيْدًا أَسَدٌ.

372. How do you know whether a word is a حَالّ or an adjective?

You need to check the grammatical differences.

The حَالّ is a powerful tool in Arabic. It is a quite sophisticated idea, not found in English to this extent, which makes it a major source of translation errors. As a matter of fact, the circumstantial description/ qualifier (حَالّ) and the adjective (صِفَةٌ - نَعْتٌ) are easily confused.

Let's check the major differences.

1: case endings

- The main difference between the adjective (نَعْتٌ) and the حَالّ is the following: the **adjective does not have a special place in** إعْرابٌ. It gets the same case as the word to which it refers.

- The حَالّ, on the other hand, has a place in إعْرابٌ and is always in the **accusative** case (مَنْصُوبٌ).

2: definite vs. indefinite

- The **adjective** can be **definite** or **indefinite,** depending on the word it describes.

- The حالٌ is **always** <u>in</u>**definite** (نَكِرةٌ). The صاحِبُ الْحالِ is almost always **definite**.

3: permanent vs. temporary

- Usually the **adjective** is a **permanent description.**

- The حالٌ is a description that is usually valid **only for the time during which the action occurs.**

Let's see the difference: a *fast car* (which is always fast ➡ adjective), but he *drove fast* (which he does not necessarily always do ➡ circumstantial description - حالٌ).

حالٌ	The car came **speeding**.	أَقْبَلَتِ السَّيّارةُ مُسْرِعةً.
	Easy to recognize as a حالٌ because if it was an adjective, the adjective would need to be definite as well.	
نَعْتٌ	The fast (**speeding**) car came.	أَقْبَلَتِ السَّيّارةُ الْمُسْرِعةُ.
	Two definite articles usually mean that it can't be a حالٌ. It is almost certainly an adjective.	
نَعْتٌ	I looked at a **fast** car.	نَظَرْتُ إِلَى سَيّارةٍ مُسْرِعةٍ.
	Easy to recognize as an adjective as a حالٌ would have to be in the accusative (مَنْصوبٌ). Moreover, the صاحِبُ الْحالِ is usually definite.	

373. Can an adjective become a حالٌ?

Yes, it can.

Such constructions are tricky. If the adjective (صِفةٌ) should turn into a حالٌ, we need the following situation: the صِفةٌ must be placed <u>before</u> the **indefinite** word (thing, person) it describes (مَوْصوفٌ).

Let's see an example:

The book is useful to Zayd.	لِزَيْدٍ مُفِيدًا كِتابٌ.

Preposition (حَرْفُ الْجَرِّ). It does not have a position in إعْرابٌ.	لِ
Noun in the genitive (إسْمٌ مَجْرُورٌ). The prepositional phrase (الْجُمْلةِ - الْجارُّ وَالْمَجْرُورُ) appears in the position where you would expect the fronted predicate (خَبَرٌ مَقَدَّمٌ). However, that predicate was deleted and is implicitly understood. The prepositional phrase still needs to relate to that deleted word. This is because the actual predicate (= copula: the verb *to be*) has to be deleted.	زَيْدٍ
The حالٌ for كِتابٌ; thus, it needs the accusative case (مَنْصُوبٌ).	مُفِيدًا
Delayed subject (مُبْتَدأً مُؤَخَّرٌ) in the nominative case (مَرْفُوعٌ).	كِتابٌ

Here is a rule of thumb: If the actual adjective (صِفةٌ) precedes the word it describes (i.e., the مَوْصُوفٌ) and is **indefinite** (نَكِرَةٌ), then it has to be in the **accusative** (مَنْصُوبٌ) and **becomes a** حالٌ.

374. Can a حالٌ also express an intention?

Yes, this is possible.

Let's imagine the following situation. We talk about something that happened in the past with the intention (expectation) that something else will happen in the future. How can we express that? We use a حالٌ!

Wait! How is that possible? Well, the حالٌ usually indicates a simultaneous state, but it may indicate a future state as well. To be more precise: an act which was regarded as future in relation to the past time of which we speak. When this is the situation, the **present tense** is used after the past tense directly.

So, we do not use any particle or special mood, etc. The verb in the present tense forms a secondary, subordinate clause expressing the state (حالٌ) in which the subject of the preceding past tense verb was, when the subject completed the action. This action was expressed by the past tense. For this reason, we call this type an *interpreted, estimated* حالٌ, a so-called حالٌ مُقَدَّرٌ.

| He came to him to visit him. | جَاءَ إِلَيْهِ يَعُودُهُ. |
| He came to a spring of water to drink. | أَتَى إِلَى عَيْنِ مَاءٍ يَشْرَبُ. |

The same happens after the verbs بَقِيَ (*to remain*), دَامَ (*to last*), and لا يَزالُ (*will not cease*).

| He did not cease sitting. | لَمْ يَزَلْ قَاعِدًا. |

Let's check a verse of the Qur'an:

Sura 4:14	وَمَن يَعْصِ اللَّهَ وَرَسُولَهُ وَيَتَعَدَّ حُدُودَهُ يُدْخِلْهُ نَارًا خَالِدًا فِيهَا.
And whoever disobeys Allah and His Messenger and transgresses His limits - He will put him into the Fire **to abide eternally therein**.	
The expression خَالِدًا فِيهَا is a حَالٌ مُقَدَّرٌ as it indicates a future state.	

THE SPECIFICATION (التَّمْيِيزُ)

375. Why do we need specifications?

The specification (تَمْيِيزٌ) helps us get rid of the vagueness in a sentence. It answers the question, "What exactly?"

In grammar, we call the تَمْيِيزٌ (*specification; distinguishing element*) a supplement of the sentence, a فَضْلَةٌ, which means *remnant* or *surplus*. We don't necessarily need it to produce a meaningful sentence; if we deleted the تَمْيِيزٌ, the sentence would still work. The specification is used to **clarify the meaning** of a noun, verb, or nominal sentence which may otherwise remain ambiguous.

Let's examine the main characteristics of a تَمْيِيزٌ:

- The تَمْيِيزٌ must be an <u>in</u>definite **noun** (اِسْمٌ نَكِرَةٌ). It cannot be a verb, nor a particle.

- The تَمْيِيزٌ **cannot** be a **sentence** that is reinterpreted as a noun – which, for example, is possible for the حَالٌ.

- The تَمْيِيزٌ clarifies an abstract, vague, ambiguous, or undefined word (كَلِمةٌ مُبْهَمةٌ). It may classify a summarized meaning (مَعْنًى

مُجْمَلٌ). Most importantly it can qualify nouns, adjectives, or verbs.

- The تَمْييزٌ must be in the state of an **accusative** (نَصْبٌ).

- The تَمْييزٌ is **placed immediately** after the word which it defines.

- The English translation of a specification depends on the context. It may be an adverb of manner (ending -*ly*), a direct object, or a prepositional phrase. Other suitable translations could be: *in regard to; in terms of; as.*

There are two main types of specifications:

Type 1. We have an **evidently undefined word** in the sentence. Without the specification, we are still in the area of the intended meaning.

The specification clarifies a preceding <u>singular word</u>. We call this type a تَمْييزُ الْمُفْرَدِ; other common terms are التَّمْييزُ الْمَلْفُوظُ or تَمْييزُ الذَّاتِ.

Such a تَمْييزٌ clears up the vagueness, ambiguity that is found in words expressing **numbers and measurements** (kilo, liter, weights, areas). This type is often used with مِن (see *question #384*).

In the sentence *I bought 10 cows*, we can delete *cow* and it would still be a correct, valid, and meaningful sentence. However, it would leave room for misinterpretation – since it is not clear what I bought.

I bought a meter of silk.	إِشْتَرَيْتُ مِتْرًا حَرِيرًا.
	إِشْتَرَيْتُ مِتْرًا مِن الْحَرِيرِ.

Type 2. We **don't** have an undefined word – but we need to clarify what we intend to say. It is used to clarify the entire sentence.

If we deleted the تَمْييزٌ, the meaning would be corrupted. Although we still had a valid sentence, it would not be accurate at all. It would not only give us room for misinterpretation, it would **completely distort** the meaning.

Such specifications clarify the ambiguity. This type helps sharpen the meaning of a sentence. It is called *distinctive of the sentence* (تَمْييزُ الْجُمْلةِ); also *distinctive of the relation* (تَمْييزُ النِّسْبةِ) or *substantial specification* (التَّمْييزُ الْمَلْحُوظُ). It is not regarded as a detail of the sentence – but constitutes a top-level component along with the subject (plus predicate). Often such a clarification was originally a مُضافٌ.

1	Egypt is the largest country of the world...	مِصْرُ أَكْثَرُ بِلادِ الْعالَم...
	This is a meaningful sentence which would be fine regarding the grammar. However, the information it provides is not true – unless we specify it.	
2	Egypt is the biggest country of the world **in terms of antiquities** (Egypt is the country with the most antiquities).	مِصْرُ أَكْثَرُ بِلادِ الْعالَم آثارًا.
	Now we know in which discipline Egypt is best. We could also have stated that Egypt is the biggest country in terms of inhabitants, companies, etc.	

We will examine both types in the following *questions*.

376. When do you have to specify a word?

After a measure of capacity (كَيْلٌ), weight (وَزْنٌ), area (مِساحَةٌ) or after the numbers from 11 to 99.

Such a specification (تَمْيِيزٌ) clarifies a preceding abstract word (= the measurement), which is an indefinite noun and gets the case ending according to its function in the sentence. The تَمْيِيزٌ is easy to build: you only have to add an indefinite noun (اِسْمٌ) in the accusative (مَنْصُوبٌ).

In the following table, we see some examples of measurements and tools. I present them in the nominative (مَرْفُوعٌ), however, these words usually serve as the direct object and take the accusative (مَنْصُوبٌ).

a bucket of water	ذَنُوبٌ ماءً	a pound of oil	رَطْلٌ زَيْتًا
a skin of ghee/fat	نَحْيٌ سَمْنًا	a pot of honey	حُبٌّ عَسَلًا

I bought one Okka of grapes. (1 Okka = 1.248 kg in Egypt)	اِشْتَرَيْتُ أُقّةً عِنَبًا.

أُقّةً	Direct object in the accusative case (مَفْعُولٌ بِهِ مَنْصُوبٌ); this vague, undefined word (كَلِمَةٌ غامِضَةٌ) doesn't give us a full meaning. So far, we don't know what I have actually bought.
عِنَبًا	Now, we know what I have bought – thanks to the **specification**.

Thus, *grapes* gets the accusative case (تَمْيِيزٌ مَنْصُوبٌ بِالْفَتْحةِ الظّاهِرةِ).
It lifts the vagueness of the word *Okka*. Without the word *grapes*, we
wouldn't know what I have actually bought.

An example of a **number**:

I saw 15 students.	رَأَيْتُ خَمْسةَ عَشَرَ طالِبًا.
This is the direct object (مَفْعُولٌ بِه مَنْصُوبٌ); it is a vague, ambiguous word (كَلِمةٌ غامِضةٌ). If we stopped here, we would not know what I had actually seen.	خَمْسةَ عَشَرَ
This is <u>not</u> the direct object – it is the **specification**. Thus, it must be in the accusative (تَمْيِيزٌ مَنْصُوبٌ بِالْفَتْحةِ الظّاهِرةِ).	طالِبًا

Watch out: Numbers from 3 to 10 as well as 100 or 1000 do not work
with a تَمْيِيزٌ. They use a إِضافةٌ-construction. The **second** part (مُضافٌ
إِلَيْهِ) is a singular or plural noun in the **genitive case** (اِسْمٌ مُفْرَدٌ - جَمْعٌ
مَجْرُورٌ). See #195 and #197. It would be a mistake to treat them as a
تَمْيِيزٌ. Why? Because the تَمْيِيز must be a word in the accusative case.

Remark: The specification is not the only possibility to lift the mystery
of a vague noun. There are four options:

specification; accusative	النَّصْبُ عَلَى التَّمْيِيزِ	عِنْدِي رَطْلٌ زَيْتًا.
genitive by إِضافةٌ	الْجَرُّ بِالْمُضافِ	عِنْدِي رَطْلٌ زَيْتٍ.
genitive by an extra مِنْ	الْجَرُّ بِمِنْ	عِنْدِي رَطْلٌ مِن الزَّيْتِ.
apposition; nominative	الرَّفْعُ عَلَى الْبَدَلِيّةِ	عِنْدِي رَطْلٌ زَيْتٌ.

377. What is the grammatical DNA of a *specification* of a sentence?

Generally we can say that such a تَمْيِيزٌ is a transferred subject or object.

The تَمْيِيزُ النِّسْبةِ is a **specification** that does not clarify measurements or numbers (see previous *question #376; type 2*). This specification helps to clear up the ambiguity of the sentence and not just of a
word. The grammarians say that such a تَمْيِيزٌ is usually a word that was

transposed and *transferred* (مُحَوَّلٌ and مَنْقُولٌ) to another place in the sentence. But transferred from where?

We get closer to an answer if we look at the regent (عَامِلٌ) of the تَمْيِيزٌ. The grammarians regard the *specification* as governed by the verb that is found earlier in the sentence.

We start the analysis by assuming that the sentence looked differently. We assume that the word which serves as a تَمْيِيزٌ was either the **subject** (general term: مُسْنَدٌ إِلَيْهِ) or an **object** (general term: مَعْمُولٌ لِلْفِعْلِ) and was governed by the verb.

Then, such word was shifted to the location of a specification (تَمْيِيزٌ) which is a place of an accusative case. A word in that position limits or defines what was left undefined earlier in the sentence (الْمُمَيَّزُ). It explains the proportion and relation (of what we call the predicate in English), often with respect to quantity or measure.

Let's make it less abstract. We could rewrite a sentence that includes a تَمْيِيزٌ by using a إِضَافةٌ-construction. In the إِضَافةٌ, we will use the original subject or object. This works perfectly if the original clause contains a verb that can be conjugated (مُتَصَرِّفٌ).

SITUATION 1: The تَمْيِيزٌ is a transferred **subject** (تَمْيِيزٌ مُحَوَّلٌ عَنْ فَاعِلٍ) of a <u>verbal sentence</u>.

Sura 19:4	... وَاشْتَعَلَ الرَّأْسُ شَيْبًا.

- and my head has filled with white (*Sahīh International*)
- and my hair is ashen grey (*Abdul Haleem*)
- and my head is shining with grey hair (*Pickthall*)
- and grey hair has spread on my head (*Muhsin Khan*)
- und in Altersgrauheit entfacht ist der Kopf (*Bubenheim & Elyas*)

...and my hair turned ashen grey.	...وَاشْتَعَلَ الرَّأْسُ شَيْبًا.	specification (تَمْيِيزٌ)
Lit.: The gray hair of my head has spread.	...وَاشْتَعَلَ شَيْبُ الرَّأْسِ.	إِضَافةٌ-construction

The word شَيْب means *gray hair*, metaphorically: *old age*. The VIII-verb اشْتَعَلَ usually denotes *to catch fire, ignite; to blaze*. But it is also used to describe that one's hair turned white, in the meaning of *to be filled* (اِمْتَلَأَ).

That is why we can say that the specification is *transformed* (مُحَوَّلٌ) *from the doer of the action* (subject: شَيْب). This is the reason why the specification here points to the subject of the verbal sentence (فاعِلٌ or نائِبٌ عَن الْفاعِلِ).

SITUATION 2: The تَمْييزٌ is a transferred **subject** (مُبْتَدَأٌ) of a <u>nominal sentence</u>.

| I have more wealth (I am greater than you in wealth) - *Sura 18:34*. | أَنَا أَكْثَرُ مِنْكَ مَالًا. | specification (تَمْييزٌ) |
| My wealth is more than your wealth. | مالِيْ أَكْثَرُ مِنْ مالِكَ. | إِضافةٌ-con-struction |

Let's analyze how we transformed the إِضافةٌ-construction into a specification. The word مالٌ is the subject (مُبْتَدَأٌ) and serves as the first part of the إِضافةٌ; the pronoun ي is the second part.

Let's assume that the إِضافةٌ-construction was the original sentence. We start the transformation by deleting both instances of *wealth* (مالٌ) from مالِيْ (subject) and مالِكَ; so we are left with the pronouns ي and ك. If we now convert the pronoun ي into a subject, we get أَنَا.

The last step is to add a specification, and we will finally arrive at the sentence that is used in Sura 18:34.

SITUATION 3: The تَمْييزٌ is the transferred **(direct) object**.

| The government developed the country economically. | طَوَّرَت الْحُكُومةُ الْبِلادَ اِقْتِصادًا. |

If we excluded the تَمْييزٌ in the above sentence (i.e., اِقْتِصادًا), we wouldn't know what is meant by *the government developed the country*. The word *economy* demystified it. For this reason, grammarians say that the تَمْييزٌ clarified the relation to the process/action of *development* (تَطْويرٌ) which furthermore is related to the *government* (الْحُكُومةُ).

In our example, the تَمْييزٌ does not support the subject (فاعِلٌ), but the **direct object** (مَفْعُولٌ بِه). Following the logic of the specification, the verb operates on the تَمْييزٌ, i.e., the word that once (originally) had been the direct object before it was transferred to the place of a specification (مُحَوَّلٌ عَنِ الْمَفْعُولِ بِهِ). Let's see the underlying, virtual meaning:

The government developed the economy of the country.	ظَوَّرَتِ الْحُكُومةُ إِقْتِصادَ الْبِلادِ.

Another example of a direct object:

Sura 54:12	And we caused the earth to burst with springs.	وَفَجَّرْنَا الْأَرْضَ عُيُونًا.

If the word عُيُون (*springs*) was dropped, we would be left with a direct object: الْأَرْض (*the earth*). That wouldn't make a lot of sense, so we need a clarification; a specification (تَمْيِيزٌ). We could rewrite this sentence as follows: *And we caused the springs of the earth to burst* (وَفَجَّرْنا عُيُونَ الْأَرْضِ).

SITUATION 4: The تَمْيِيزٌ can also be a **new word** which is added to learn more or to identify the direction of the vagueness.

Therefore, it is <u>not transformed/transposed</u> from any part of the sentence (غَيْرُ مَنْقُولٍ عَنْ شَيْءٍ). In this situation, we **can't** rewrite it as a إِضافةٌ.

We usually have to deal with such a construction in two situations:

a) We have an **intransitive verb** which cannot have a direct object. Then, the specification is not transformed.

Since such verbs are incapable of having a direct object, it is impossible that the specification has undergone a transformation. Let's take, for example, the VIII-verb اِمْتَلَأَ - يَمْتَلِئُ (R3=ء; *to be filled*) of the pattern اِفْتَعَلَ. Verbs of that pattern have a special connection to the تَمْيِيزٌ as the specification is frequently used after such verbs.

The streets became crowded with people.	اِزْدَحَمَتِ الشَّوارِعُ ناسًا.
The hall filled up (was filled) with students.	اِمْتَلَأَتِ الْقاعةُ طُلّابًا.

- In both examples, we can't do the trick and form a إِضافةٌ-construction since this would not make sense. For example: *The students of the hall filled up* (اِمْتَلَأَ طُلّابُ الْقاعةِ).

> • Remark: The last letter of the above verbs would need a helping vowel to avoid two colliding سُكُون. I just wanted to highlight the form of the verb and therefore have put the سُكُون.

Let's focus on the words طُلَّابًا and نَاسًا. First of all, they are **not** a **direct object.** They are a specification (تَمْيِيزٌ) and get the accusative (مَنْصُوبٌ).

Can these two words be interpreted as the subject (فَاعِلٌ)? In other words, does the تَمْيِيزٌ here convey the meaning of the subject (فَاعِلٌ)? Some grammarians have suggested that because *the students* is the **"visible" subject,** the actual people who fill the hall. If we followed this logic, the sentence would have the following meaning (*the students* would then be the subject).

The students filled the hall.	مَلَأَ الطُّلَابُ الْقَاعَةَ.

However, the majority of the grammarians reject this approach and say that it is not correct to interpret the تَمْيِيزٌ as the subject.

b) The verb **can't be conjugated** (غَيْرُ مُتَصَرِّفٍ).

This happens, e.g., in the *form of astonishment* (تَعَجُّبٌ). In such a situation, you can also use the preposition مِن to express the specification.

Honor Muhammad as a scientist! (Honor in Muhammad his being a scientist!)	أَكْرِمْ بِمُحَمَّدٍ عَالِمًا!
	أَكْرِمْ بِمُحَمَّدٍ مِن عَالِمٍ!

378. Why is the word that is placed as a تَمْيِيزٌ in the accusative?

The reason is not as clear as it might look like.

Let's start with the obvious. Since we deal with an accusative case, there must be an operator (عَامِلٌ) somewhere which governs the تَمْيِيزٌ in that position (نَصْبٌ), that is for sure. But what is the regent?

Situation 1: The word raising the vagueness is a single **noun** (اِسْمٌ).

➤ The **regent** (عَامِلٌ) of the تَمْيِيزُ الْمُفْرَدِ (specification of the <u>isolated</u>) is an **vague word** (الْكَلِمَةُ الْمُبْهَمةُ) which precedes the specification.

Situation 2: The تَمْيِيزٌ specifies an **entire sentence** (تَمْيِيزُ الْجُمْلة).

Such constructions are usually called تَمْيِيزُ النِّسْبة (specification of the relation). ▷The regent is a **verb** (فِعْلٌ) or a word resembling a verb.

In the following examples, the **regent** is marked in gray:

1	I have a pint of oil.	عِنْدِي رَطْلٌ زَيْتًا.
	I bought a pint of oil.	إِشْتَرَيْتُ رَطْلًا زَيْتًا.
	The specification (زَيْتًا) clarifies the **ambiguity of the subject** (first sentence) and of the **direct object**. Now we know what *I have* or what *I bought*: oil. The تَمْيِيزٌ is governed by the abstract noun (*pint*).	

زَيْتًا	رَطْلًا	إِشْتَرَيْتُ
specification (تَمْيِيزُ الْمُفْرَد)	direct object (مَفْعُولٌ بِهِ)	فِعْلٌ + subject (تُ)

زَيْتًا	رَطْلٌ	عِنْدِي
specification (تَمْيِيزُ الْمُفْرَد)	subject (مُبْتَدَأٌ)	predicate (خَبَرٌ)

2	Zayd has a good soul (is cheerful in spirit).	طابَ زَيْدٌ نَفْسًا.
	So-called تَمْيِيزُ النِّسْبة. It clarifies the **vagueness of the verb**, the ambiguities that exist between the verb and the subject or object (يُبَيِّنُ الْإِبْهامَ الْحاصِلَ عَنْ نِسْبةِ الْفِعْلِ).	

نَفْسًا	زَيْدٌ	طابَ
specification (تَمْيِيزُ النِّسْبة)	subject (فاعِلٌ)	**verb** (فِعْلٌ)

Let's focus on situation 2. The grammarians regard this type of a *specification* to be governed by the verb. The idea is that the تَمْيِيزٌ was originally the **subject** or **object**. If we rewrite the sentence in the form of a إِضافةٌ, it becomes evident (see *question #377*).

Zayd has a good soul.	طابَ زَيْدٌ نَفْسًا.
The soul of Zayd is good.	طابَ نَفْسُ زَيْدٍ.

379. إِزْدَادَ زَيْدٌ عِلْمًا – Is the word عِلْمًا here the direct object?

No, it is a specification (تَمْيِيزٌ).

Let us first put the sentence in question under the microscope:

Zayd grew in knowledge.	إِزْدَادَ زَيْدٌ عِلْمًا.
إِزْدَادَ is a VIII-verb (اِفْتَعَلَ). This pattern can be tricky. The root of إِزْدَادَ is ز-ي-د and not ز-د-د. To facilitate the pronunciation, the ت was turned into د. Furthermore, in the past tense, the ي becomes an Aleph.	

Let's analyze the first part of the sentence:

Zayd increased.	إِزْدَادَ زَيْدٌ.
This sentence gives us an abstract, overall meaning. We don't learn from it what kind of thing was growing in or on Zayd.	

A specification (تَمْيِيزٌ) can help us to clarify an already included *incomprehensibility* (الْإِبْهَامُ) in the verb. This type of specification has several names, among them are *distinctive of the sentence* (تَمْيِيزُ الْجُملةِ or التَّمْيِيزُ النِّسْبِةِ) or *the substantial, noticeable specification* (التَّمْيِيزُ الْمَلْحُوظُ). It helps clear up the ambiguity of the sentence. In our example, *knowledge* is the demystifying تَمْيِيزٌ. In the language of the grammarians: the تَمْيِيزٌ explains the intended part of the increase (النِّسْبةِ الْمَقْصُودةُ مِن الزِّيادةِ) assigned to Zayd.

Such sentences are often difficult for non-native speakers of Arabic. The English translation – which is often *to increase* – uses a different grammatical concept. The verb إِزْدَادَ means *to grow; to increase, to be growing; to do more and more*. In Arabic, however, it **does not have a transitive meaning** – you will struggle to place a direct object after it, because this is impossible.

The specification perfectly solves this problem. The sentence, when applying the idea of the specification, had the following (original) virtual meaning (تَقْدِيرٌ):

Zayd's knowledge increased.	إِزْدَادَ عِلْمُ زَيْدٍ.
The word عِلْمُ is the subject (فاعِلٌ) of the verbal sentence.	

Let's see some more examples.

She grew in beauty and magnificence. (She became more beautiful).	اِزْدَادَتْ جَمالًا وَبَهَاءً.
The road became wider.	اِزْدَادَ الطَّريقُ اتِّساعًا.
Something increased for him = he increased it himself.	اِزْدَادَ شَيْئًا لَهُ = زَادَهُ لِنَفْسِهِ.

Such constructions are frequently used in Modern Standard Arabic. The تَمْييزٌ is marked in gray in the following examples:

The air of the city became better.	طابَتْ الْمَدينةُ هَوَاءً.
Zayd is of generous nature.	كَرُمَ زَيْدٌ خُلْقًا.
'Alī is good (improved) in literature.	حَسُنَ عَلِيٌّ أَدَبًا.
The industrial sector of the country advanced.	تَقَدَّمَتْ الْبِلادُ صِناعةً.

380. What is the difference between a حالٌ and a تَمْييزٌ؟

The main difference: a حالٌ is a state – the تَمْييزٌ is a result.

Let's start with the things they both share.

- both are nouns (اِسْمٌ);
- both are indefinite (نَكِرةٌ);
- both are not necessary for a meaningful sentence, they are supplements (فَضْلةٌ);
- both get the accusative case (مَنْصُوبٌ);
- both clarify ambiguities and a vagueness (رافِعةٌ لِلْإِبْهامِ);

Let's see the differences now.

specification (تَمْييزٌ)	circumstantial description (حالٌ)
It can only be a **noun** (اِسْمٌ).	It may be an entire sentence (جُمْلةٌ).
It **cannot** be placed <u>before</u> its regent.	It may precede its regent (تَتَقَدَّمُ عَلَى

	عامِلُها).
It is almost **never a derived word**, but a static word (حَقُّهُ الْجُمُودُ).	It is usually a derived noun, e.g., an active participle.

381. Can you use a تَمْيِيزٌ together with a comparative?

Yes, this construction is pretty common.

You will often encounter Arabic sentences that are based on the construction of the following example:

Zayd has more knowledge than ʿAlī.	زَيْدٌ أَفْضَلُ مِن عَلِيٍّ عِلْمًا.
The word عِلْمًا is the تَمْيِيزٌ in the accusative case (مَنْصُوبٌ).	

In many situations it is necessary to use a تَمْيِيزٌ after a comparative or superlative (اِسْمُ التَّفْضِيلِ). This happens when the **comparative** serves as the **predicate** (خَبَرٌ) of the sentence – but it does not provide us with the necessary information to express the intended meaning.

In the above example, the predicate (أَفْضَلُ) does not tell us the reason why Zayd is better than ʿAlī. Here, the تَمْيِيزٌ enters the game. It tells us the grade or share of why Zayd is better. See *Arabic for Nerds 1, #189*.

How should we understand the this sentence structure? Let's imagine that the specification had a "previous life" in the sentence. It worked as the subject (مُحَوَّلٌ عَن الْفاعِلِ), but was eventually transposed to the place of a specification: to the spot of an accusative. Sounds a bit weird, so, let's rewrite the sentence for a better understanding of the idea.

The knowledge of Zayd surpluses (is superior to) the knowledge of ʿAlī.	فَضَلَ عِلْمُ زَيْدٍ عَلَى عِلْمِ عَلِيٍّ.

382. Does the تَمْيِيزٌ go along with surprise and wonder (تَعَجُّبٌ)?

Yes, but such constructions are pretty sophisticated.

A تَمْيِيزٌ can be used with the following two patterns which are used to express **astonishment** (تَعَجُّبٌ):

| أَفْعِلْ بِ ... | 2 | | مَا أَفْعَلَ ... | 1 |

Mind that the "subject" of the *surprise* in formula 1 must be in the accusative (مَنْصُوبٌ) and in formula 2 in the genitive case – see #434.

| How generous is Zayd! | مَا أَكْرَمَ زَيْدًا!! |

Let's enrich this sentence. We use a specification.

| 1 | How generous is Zayd's nature! (Zayd is endowed | مَا أَكْرَمَ زَيْدًا خُلُقًا! |
| 2 | with a generous nature!) | أَكْرِمْ بِزَيْدٍ خُلُقًا! |

In both sentences, خُلُقٌ is a تَمْيِيزٌ in the accusative case (مَنْصُوبٌ). How could we interpret these sentences regarding the structure? We could say that the specification had been the subject before it was transferred to the position of the specification (مُحَوَّلٌ عَنِ الْفَاعِلِ). Therefore, we could rewrite the sentence as follows:

| Zayd's nature has become generous. | كَرُمَ خُلُقُ زَيْدٍ. |

The تَعَجُّبٌ before the تَمْيِيزٌ does **not** clarify in which thing Zayd is generous/noble (كَرِيمٌ). It is the تَمْيِيزٌ that gives us this information, i.e., the relation or amount of the generosity (نِسْبَةُ الْكَرَمِ عِنْدَ زَيْدٍ). Don't get the translation wrong because it **does not mean** the following:

| Zayd did not bestow honors upon anyone. | مَا أَكْرَمَ زَيْدٌ أَحَدًا. |

| This is not a تَعَجُّبٌ – it is just a standard, negated sentence in the past tense! Notice the case marker on *Zayd*: it is the subject (فَاعِلٌ). |

There are certain phrases and expressions which use a تَمْيِيزٌ.

| God, how knowledgeable is Zayd! | لِلّٰهِ دَرُّ زَيْدٍ عَالِمًا! |

| The expression لِلّٰهِ دَرُّهُ alone means: *how capable, how good, how excellent he is!* Lit.: *his achievement is due to God.* The word دَرٌّ means *achievement, accomplishment.* Also here, the تَمْيِيزٌ clears up the vagueness included at the beginning of the sentence. |

| This expression is frequently used with a pronoun (ضَمِيرٌ). For example: |

How much knowledge has God given him! (!لِلّٰهِ دَرُّهُ عالِمًا)	

Allah is the best witness! (Allah suffices as...)	كَفَى بِاللّٰهِ شَهِيدًا!!
Allah is the best protector!	كَفَى بِاللّٰهِ وَكِيلًا!

Allah suffices as a protector!	حَسْبُكَ بِاللّٰهِ وَكِيلًا!
The word حَسْبُكَ is a إسْمُ فِعْلٍ and has the meaning of كَفَى. The indeclinable expression حَسْبُكَ means *enough for you* and can be used with the preposition بـ as well. حَسْبُكَ أَنْ may also convey *it suffices to say that.... you need only...*	

But enough of all these negative aspects!	وَحَسْبُكَ بِهذا كُلِّهِ شَرًّا!!

Note: وَكِيلًا - شَهِيدًا - عالِمًا are a تَمْيِيزٌ in the **accusative** case (مَنْصُوبٌ).

383. Does the تَمْيِيزٌ work with *praise and blame*?

Yes, it does.

The *verbs of praise and blame* (أَفْعالُ الْمَدْحِ والذَّمِّ) are نِعْمَ (*to be good*) and بِئْسَ (*to be bad*). They have a fixed, cemented shape and are used as exclamations – see *question #443*.

There are two ways to add more details to such exclamations:

OPTION 1: The noun (إسْمٌ) following such verbs must be definite: by the article الـ or by serving in the position of the first part of a إضافةٌ - *see question #101.* ▷This approach is **not** a specification (تَمْيِيزٌ).

OPTION 2: This approach uses the تَمْيِيزٌ. The *verb of praise and blame* is followed by a noun in the accusative (مَنْصُوبٌ) – which is a تَمْيِيزٌ. The specification is used to clarify the direction (جهةٌ).

Let's examine the two options:

1	Zayd is an excellent companion/friend (Lit.: Excellent is the companion Zayd).	نِعْمَ الصّاحِبُ زَيْدٌ.

	اَلصّاحِبُ is the subject (فَاعِلٌ) and زَيْدٌ stands in apposition (بَدَلٌ) to it.	

2	Excellent as a companion is Zayd.	نِعْمَ صاحِبًا زَيْدٌ.
	Here, صاحِبًا is a تَمْيِيزٌ. The word زَيْدٌ is the **delayed subject** (مُبْتَدَأٌ مُؤَخَّرٌ); the whole sentence before *Zayd* is the predicate (خَبَرٌ). Now, where is the subject (فَاعِلٌ) of the verb? We will deal with that now...	

Let's focus on the **word order** in the second approach by using this example: *(How) excellent as a companion is Zayd!*

1	This is the standard version because the تَمْيِيزٌ has to be placed **after** the word it defines.	نِعْمَ زَيْدٌ صاحِبًا!
2	The تَمْيِيزٌ in *praise and blame*-constructions may be placed **before the predicate** which it defines. This is done especially in poetry.	نِعْمَ صاحِبًا زَيْدٌ!

But is option 2 correct? Yes, it is. In fact, it is no exception to the ordinary rules because the actual, virtual meaning is the following:

This hidden personal pronoun (ضَمِيرٌ مُسْتَتِرٌ) is understood in option 2 as serving as the **subject** (فَاعِلٌ).	نِعْمَ هُوَ صاحِبًا زَيْدٌ.

384. What will happen to a تَمْيِيزٌ if you place the word مِن before it?

The case ending will change.

It is quite common to put the preposition مِنْ before the specification (تَمْيِيزٌ). This preposition is not there to point to a direction.

It is considered to be **extra/additional** (زائِدٌ) and is primarily used for **emphasis** and sometimes just for stylistic reasons – with the effect that the word after the preposition is still a specification (تَمْيِيزٌ). Using مِنْ before a specification is only possible in one situation: the تَمْيِيزٌ must relate to the (direct) **object** (مَنْقُولٌ مِن الْمَفْعُولِ)!

If the تَمْيِيزٌ refers to the subject (مَنْقُولٌ مِن الْفاعِلِ), you won't be able to use an additional مِنْ.

| direct object | *I planted the land with trees.* Both sentences are correct and make sense. | غَرَسْتُ الْأَرْضَ شَجَرًا. |
| | | غَرَسْتُ الْأَرْضَ مِنْ شَجَرٍ. |

| subject | Zayd is cheerful in spirit. | طابَ زَيْدٌ نَفْسًا. |
| | The sentence with مِنْ doesn't make sense: → | طابَ زَيْدٌ مِنْ نَفْسٍ. |

The تَمْيِيزٌ sharpens the meaning of the preceding verbal sentence (جُمْلَة فِعْلِيَّة). Why do some people prefer the variant with the extra preposition? Some say it sounds better (stylistic reasons), others want to lay some extra emphasis, and there are people who do it for both reasons. How does the preposition مِنْ change the grammatical analysis?

In general, the كَسْرَةٌ is stronger than the other vowels. This means that we will visibly get a noun in the genitive case (اسْمٌ مَجْرُورٌ). Nevertheless, the word (= the specification) still keeps its place value of an accusative case since it is located as a specification.

with مِنْ	We planted two acres of wheat.	زَرَعْنا فَدّانَيْنِ مِنْ قَمْحٍ.	1
تَمْيِيزٌ	We planted two acres of wheat.	زَرَعْنا فَدّانَيْنِ قَمْحًا.	2
إضافَةٌ	We planted two acres of wheat.	زَرَعْنا فَدّانَيْ قَمْحٍ.	3

➤ The word مِنْ is a redundant preposition (حَرْفُ جَرٍّ زائِدٌ).

| In the **first sentence**, the word serves as a **specification** (تَمْيِيزٌ) in the accusative case (مَنْصُوبٌ) by an assumed case marker (فَتْحَة مُقَدَّرَة) since the position is occupied by the marker induced by the extra preposition (اشْتِغالُ الْمَحَلِّ بِحَرَكَةِ حَرْفِ الْجَرِّ الزّائِدِ). | قَمْح | 1 |
| In the **last example**, the word قَمْح is the second part of the إضافَةٌ and thus in the genitive case. | | 3 |

Chapter 12: Fine Ways of Wording (الْجُمَلُ الْأُسْلُوبِيّةُ)

The word أُسْلُوبٌ (plural: أَساليبُ) has many meanings. It may denote *method, way, manner* – in Arabic grammar books, it is often translated as *style*. This is a misleading because these constructions have usually nothing to do with "good style". The term أُسْلُوبٌ actually aims at a specific part of a sentence that leaves the scope of the two classical types of Arabic sentences: the nominal and verbal sentence. So, what are we dealing with? It's important stuff, for example: the *vocative* (أُسْلُوبُ النِّداءِ), *praise and blame* (أُسْلُوبُ الْمَدْحِ وَالذَّمِّ), or the conditional sentence (أُسْلُوبُ الشَّرْطِ).

THE CONDITIONAL SENTENCE (جُمْلةُ الشَّرْطِ)

385. What are the main ingredients of a conditional sentence?

The condition and the answer.

The conditional sentence is one of the most difficult sentence structures in any language. In Arabic, a conditional sentence (جُمْلةُ الشَّرْطِ) consists of **three things**:

1. The **condition** (الشَّرْطُ) or "if"-clause. This is the first part of the sentence, the subordinate clause (*Nebensatz*), also called *protasis*.

2. The **answer** (الْجَوابُ), also called complement, consequent to the condition, main sentence (*Hauptsatz der Bedingung*), *apodosis*. Another term is الْجَزاءُ which literally means *reward; punishment* or *penalty* and is often translated as *final clause*. For some readers, الْجَزاءُ might be easier to remember because the Arabic expression for *penalty kick* in soccer is ضَرْبَةُ جَزاءٍ. Important: the جَوابُ الشَّرْطِ does not have a place in إِعْرابٌ. In Arabic, no grammatical function is assigned to it (لا مَحَلَّ لَها مِن الْإِعْرابِ); *see #85*.

3. Both parts are linked (we could also say bound) by a **conditional device or word** (كَلِمةٌ شَرْطِيَّةٌ). Don't get confused by the English term conditional "particle"; in Arabic they can be a حَرْفٌ or a اِسْمٌ.

The choice of a suitable conditional word depends on the relationship between the two parts of the conditional sentence. You need to check whether there is a real condition or whether the hypothetical situation is possible or impossible. The subordinate clause (الشَّرْطُ) and the main clause (الْجَوابُ) take the place of a single sentence.

Why do we call such sentences *conditional sentences*? Because the actual validity of a statement is "conditioned" by another statement which is given along with it. The information in the second (final) clause has no validity in itself (عَلاقةٌ عِلِّيّةٌ) without the restriction in the subordinate clause. It may be the situation that the meaning of the second part (جَوابٌ) is included in the first part already.

Notice: Sometimes the condition is pure temporal (زَمَنِيّةٌ). We get this situation if we link both parts with لَمّا (when) or كُلَّما (whenever).

| Whenever Zayd appears, 'Amr is traveling. (Every time Zayd comes, 'Amr leaves.) | لَمّا حَضَرَ زَيْدٌ سافِرٌ عَمْرٌو. |
| | كُلَّما حَضَرَ زَيْدٌ سافِرٌ عَمْرٌو. |

The relationship of both parts does not depend on a condition. The presence or coming of Zayd is not the reason for the traveling of 'Amr.

386. Does the first part of a conditional sentence need a verb?

Yes, it does. We need a فِعْلُ الشَّرْطِ.

The idea of a condition (شَرْطٌ) includes the requirement of an action (حَدَثٌ) leading to whatever result. Thus, there has to be a verb – a full, complete verb (فِعْلٌ مُتَصَرِّفٌ). It cannot be an *inert* or *static* verb (فِعْلٌ جامِدٌ) like عَسَى (perhaps) or لَيْسَ (negation). What about كانَ? That's possible if you put it immediately after the conditional word.

The main sentence (الْجَوابُ), of course, may be of any nature.

The following sentence is incorrect because a **nominal sentence can't form the condition** or subordinate clause (شَرْطٌ) in Arabic.

| impossible in Arabic | If you succeed (are succeeding), I will reward you. | إِنْ أَنْتَ ناجِحٌ فَسَوْفَ أُكافِئكَ. |

However, there are exceptions when a nominal sentence may be placed after لَوْ. The following example is a line of the famous Arab Christian poet 'Adīy ibn Zayd (عَدِيُّ بْنُ زَيْدٍ) who lived in the 6th century in al-Hīra (الْحِيرة), an ancient city in Mesopotamia located south of Kūfa (الْكوفة) in present-day Iraq. He died in 587/35 BH.

| If my throat had trouble swallowing due | لَوْ بِغَيْرِ الْماء حَلْقِي شَرِقَ كُنْتُ |

to lack of water (dehydration), I would take water to me like someone choking.	كَالْغَصّانِ بِالْماءِ اغْتِصاري.

A remark on اغْتَصَرَ which conveys *to press out, squeeze out something.* The expression اغْتَصَرَ بِالْماء means *to swallow the water by little and little in order that some food by which he was choked might be made to descend easily in his throat.* (شَرِبَهُ قَلِيلًا قَلِيلًا لِيُسِيغَ ما غَصَّ بِهِ مِن طَعامٍ).

▸ Usually the construction لَوْ أَنَّ instead of لَوْ alone is used if you have a nominal sentence involved because أَنَّ itself has some verbal force. This often happens when you deal with "inverted verbal sentences" in which you have a construction consisting of subject followed by a verb. Another fine option would be to use كانَ after لَوْ.

Excursus: Why is the second verb in the مَجْزُومٌ-mood?

Grammarians disagree about which operator/regent causes the جَزْم-mood in the second verb of conditional clauses. The dispute goes back to the early times of Arabic grammar. The **Basra school** (الْبَصْرِيُّونَ) claimed that the conditional particle affects both verbs; in other words, the conditional particle governs **two verbs** in the state of جَزْم. Other scholars suggested a kind of domino effect. The first verb governs the second one. So, the conditional particle triggers the مَجْزُومٌ-mood in the first verb, and this verb, in turn, governs the following verb in that state. This is similar to what the **grammarians of Kūfa** (الْكُوفِيُّونَ) suggested. The verb expressing the main clause/complement/consequence (جَوابٌ) is governed in the جَزْم by its proximity (مَجْزُومٌ بِالْجَوارِ) to the first verb that describes the condition.

For this reason, the Kūfa grammarians were convinced that if the **subject** of the first verb is placed **after the verb**, then the **second verb** should be used in the **indicative** mood (مَرْفُوعٌ) because the "proximity" to the first verb is ruined.

If you come to me, Zayd will respect you.	إِنْ تَأْتِيني زَيْدٌ يُكْرِمُكَ.

The Basrans, on the other hand, said that this would not interrupt the governance – which means that the second verb should also be مَجْزُومٌ.

387. How many types of *if* are there in Arabic?

While there are many words for "if" in Arabic, there are only two general
types with varying degrees of influence.

Arabic conditional devices and words (أَسْماءُ الشَّرْطِ) differ from
those in English. In Arabic, they are either a particle (حَرْفٌ) or – which
is the normal situation – a noun (اِسْمٌ).

The following three words are a حَرْفٌ, a so-called حَرْفُ شَرْطٍ. They
are all indeclinable (مَبْنِيٌّ) and never change their shape. They do not
have a place in إِعْرابٌ which is typical for a حَرْفٌ.

1	*When, if,* etc. إِنْ simply indicates a condition. It ties the second part of the sentence (الْجَوابُ) by the condition. Watch out: إِنْ describes the "realness" (actual happening) of an event as **uncertain**.	إِنْ

2	*If not; if it were not for...* It is a synonym of أَلَّا.	لَوْلا

لَوْلا points to the **refusal** of the information that is presented in the second part of the sentence (اِمْتِناعُ الْجَوابِ). The first part of the sentence, which is placed after لَوْلا (protasis), includes the verbal meaning of كانَ, although you don't see a verb in the first part. لَوْلا is usually followed by a single noun (or pronoun) in the nominative as a statement of the noun's existence which the particle hypothetically denies: "*If it were not for...*"
The predicate here is deleted. The second part normally begins with لَ.

Had it not rained, the plants would have dried up.	لَوْلَا الْمَطَرُ لَهَلَكَ الزَّرْعُ.

This is the actual meaning of the sentence:

The plants were prevented from drying up thanks to the rain that fell.	اِمْتِناعُ هَلاكِ الزَّرْعِ بِسَبَبِ نُزُولِ الْمَطَرِ.

3	*"Put the case that..."*. This particle, in contrast to إِنْ, implies that what is supposed either **doesn't take place** (حَرْفُ اِمْتِناعٍ) or isn't likely to be so.	لَوْ

The inner meaning of لَوْ denotes that something is refused due to other
refused things (يَدُلُّ عَلَى اِمْتِناعِ شَيْءٍ لِامْتِناعِ غَيْرِهِ). In other words, لَوْ indi-

cates that due to a certain performed or non-performed action, something else was prevented from happening. لَوْ doesn't necessarily signify complete impossibility, it may be just stronger than the mere imagination of a situation.

If you had come in time, I would have treated you with deference (respect).	لَوْ جِئْتَ فِي الْوَقْتِ الْمُنَاسِبِ لَأَكْرَمْتُكَ.

This is the actual meaning of the sentence:

I **refuse** to honor you for your **refusal** of coming in time.	قَد امْتَنَعَ إِكْرَامِي إِيَّاكَ لِامْتِنَاع مَجِيئِكَ فِي الْوَقْتِ الْمُنَاسِبِ.

Remark: لَوْ has sparked some debates. Since لَوْ postulates a situation that is entirely impossible, this would theoretically mean that even God would not be able to make it happen. Thus, the theological dispute arose whether a believer may use لَوْ at all and under what circumstances.

388. What are the most common indeclinable conditional words?

There are many.

The term **indeclinable** (مَبْنِيٌّ) will be the main topic in this *question*. It is the common theme of the following conditional devices.

1	All three get the إِعْرَابٌ **depending on the position** and function in the	whoever; (any) who; for people only	مَنْ
2	sentence (place value). Although you don't visually see the case marker as they are مَبْنِيٌّ, you should	whatever; whatsoever; for non-humans (غَيْرُ الْعَاقِلِ)	مَا
3	think about the function and position to grasp the correct meaning.	no matter what; whatever; (wie sehr auch immer)	مَهْمَا

4	All of them are always treated as an **adverb of time** (ظَرْفُ زَمانٍ). What about their regent (عامِلٌ)? They are	when	مَتَى
		with مَا it means *whenever*	مَتَامَا
5	governed by the verb (فِعْلُ الشَّرْطِ) in the first part (conditional).	when, whenever	أَيَّانَ

6	They are always treated as an **ad-verb of place** (ظَرْفُ مَكَانٍ). Their operator (عَامِلٌ) is the verb in the first part (فِعْلُ الشَّرْطِ), the conditional part.	*where*	أَيْنَ
		wherever	أَيْنَمَا
7		*in whatever way; however*	أَنَّى
8		*wherever*	حَيْثُمَا

9	*When; whether; as often as; if.* The event will happen, but the time (German: *Zeitpunkt*) is not clear.	إذا

Mostly followed by a verb in the past tense. The past tense here conveys the meaning of the present tense. Therefore, إذا is often used for the **conditional I** in English (*If you do, I will*). See *question #393* for details.

Some examples:

1	Whoever studies will succeed.	مَنْ يُذَاكِرْ يَنْجَحْ.

The word مَنْ is in the position of the **subject** (مُبْتَدَأٌ) of the nominal sentence (فِي مَحَلِّ رَفْعٍ). The second part of the sentence is the predicate (خَبَرٌ).

2	Whatever good you do, Allah is well aware of it (*Sura 2:197*)	وَمَا تَفْعَلُوا مِنْ خَيْرٍ يَعْلَمْهُ اللّٰهُ.

Notice that both verbs are in the مَجْزُومٌ-mood. The first verb تَفْعَلُوا is put into the jussive by deleting the final ن (the present tense indicative is تَفْعَلُونَ). The second verb يَعْلَمْهُ is put into the مَجْزُومٌ-mood by cutting the usual ending (vowel) and replacing it by a سُكُونٌ.

3	They said, "We will not believe in you, **no matter what** signs you produce to cast a spell on us". (*Sura 7:132*)	قَالُوا مَهْمَا تَأْتِنَا بِهِ مِنْ آيَةٍ لِتَسْحَرَنَا بِهَا فَمَا نَحْنُ لَكَ بِمُؤْمِنِينَ.
	Be that as it may; in any case...	مَهْمَا يَكُنْ مِنَ الْأَمْرِ...
	Whatever it may cost...	مَهْمَا كَلَّفَ الْأَمْرُ....

Notice that you can also use the past tense – nevertheless, you still consider the verb to hold the position of a verb in the مَجْزُومٌ-mood.

4	When you go, I will also go.	مَتَى تَذْهَبْ أَذْهَبْ.

| 5 | Wherever you may go, I will go with you. | أَيْنَما تَذْهَبْ أَذْهَبْ مَعَكَ. |

مَتَى and أَيْنَما are conditional words (اِسْمُ شَرْطٍ). They are indeclinable, fixed (مَبْنِيٌّ) nouns and are in the place of an accusative case (نَصْبٌ): the particle مَتَى is in the position of an adverb of time; أَيْنَما in the position of an adverb of place (فِي مَحَلِّ نَصْبٍ ظَرْفِ زَمانٍ/ مَكانٍ لِفِعْلِ الشَّرْطِ).

6	Wherever he goes, people (will) respect him.	أَيْنَ يَذْهَبْ يَحْتَرِمْهُ النَّاسُ.
7	If you work, you will produce.	أَنَّى تَعْمَلْ تُنْتِجْ.
8	Wherever he goes, he finds (will find) a friend.	حَيْثُما يَذْهَبْ يَجِدْ صَدِيقًا.

All three conditional words are in the location of an adverb of place (فِي مَحَلِّ نَصْبٍ ظَرْفُ مَكانٍ) and are linked to the verb in the first part of the conditional sentence (لِفِعْلِ الشَّرْطِ).

389. Why do we need a فـ in a conditional sentence?

The فَ in a conditional sentence is used to separate the 1st from the 2nd part for grammatical reasons. But at the same time, it links both parts.

The فَ is necessary when the **conditional device** of the first sentence **cannot extend its power** to the verb of the second part. This may need some thought process. The condition (الشَّرْطُ) and the consequent (الْجَوابُ) are closely linked. **This is done by...**

1. the conditional device plus two verbs in the مَجْزُومٌ-mood. ➡ You don't use فـ;

2. by connecting the first to the second part using the letter فَ, a so-called حَرْفٌ رابِطٌ لِلْجَوابِ. This فَ has the grammatical effect that the nature of the second part (past tense or present tense in the مَجْزُومٌ-mood; verbal or nominal sentence) becomes independent of the first part.

So, when do we use فَ? In the **basic form** of a conditional sentence, you <u>don't</u> use فَ. This means that you have two verbal sentences without anything extra (no negation, no pronouns).

Whoever works hard, will succeed.	مَنْ يَجْتَهِدْ يَنْجَحْ.

In all other situations, you should better use a فَ, no matter what kind of sentence the second part is (nominal sentence, verbal sentence, imperative, نِعْمَ). The فَ is used to show the relationship between the two parts. If we use فَ, does it induce any grammatical changes?

Whoever works, will succeed.	مَنْ يَعْمَلْ يَنْجَحْ.	1
	مَنْ يَعْمَلْ فَسَوْفَ يَنْجَحُ.	2

In a construction with فَ, the verb can be in the indicative (مَرْفُوعٌ), subjunctive (مَنْصُوبٌ) or jussive mood (مَجْزُومٌ). It depends on the function and position in the sentence. In example 2, it is the indicative.

If we have a conditional word such as إِنْ or مَنْ inducing the jussive mood in the second part, we say that the entire sentence after فَ gets the "place value" of a jussive (الْجُمْلَةُ بَعْدَهُ فِي مَحَلِّ جَزْمٍ جَوابُ الشَّرْطِ).

Verb in the indicative mood (فِعْلٌ مُضارِعٌ) by the ضَمّةٌ.	يَنْجَحُ
The entire sentence gets the place value of a jussive mood because it is located in the position of the second part of the conditional sentence (فِي مَحَلِّ جَزْمٍ جَوابُ الشَّرْطِ).	سَوْفَ يَنْجَحُ

As a rule of thumb, we could say: Use فَ if the second part (الْجَوابُ) is not suitable to be a condition (شَرْطٌ) for إِنْ or other conditional words.

Let's look at some possibilities for the **second** part (main clause).

1. Nominal sentence (جُمْلَةٌ اِسْمِيّةٌ); negated (مَنْفِيّةٌ) or non-negated/ affirmative (مُثْبَتةٌ)

If you say this, you are one of the un-believers.	إِنْ قُلْتَ هذا فَأَنْتَ مِن الْكافِرِينَ.
If you strive, you are successful.	إِنْ تَجْتَهِدْ فَأَنْتَ ناجِحٌ.

Sura 27:89	Whoever comes with a good deed [at Judgment Day] will be rewarded with something better.	مَن جَاءَ بِالْحَسَنَةِ فَلَهُ خَيْرٌ مِّنْهَا.

2. **Verbal sentence** (جُمْلَةٌ فِعْلِيَّةٌ) expressing a **desire, wish, command** or **prohibition** (فِعْلٌ طَلَبِيٌّ). So we have an imperative (أَمْرٌ), a question (اِسْتِفْهامٌ), or a prohibition (نَهْيٌ).

a) Imperative

If you want success, work hard!	إِنْ تُرِدِ النَّجاحَ فَاجْتَهِدْ!

b) Prohibition

If you strive, do not fear anything!	إِنْ تَجْتَهِدْ فَلا تَخْشَ شَيْئًا!
Notice the مَجْزُومٌ-mood in the verb *to fear* (خَشِيَ) induced by لا! In the present tense indicative, *you frighten* would be تَخْشَى. Thus, in the مَجْزُومٌ-mood, the weak letter drops and gets substituted by a vowel that is put on the now last letter (i.e., a فَتْحَةٌ).	
If you ask for excellence, don't be negligent!	إِذا طَلَبْتَ التَّفَوُّقَ فَلا تُهْمِلْ!

c) Question

If you strive, will you get anything but success?	إِنْ تَجْتَهِدْ فَهَلْ لَكَ إِلَّا النَّجاحُ؟
Do you insult someone who did a good deed to you?	مَنْ يُحْسِنْ إِلَيْكَ فَهَلْ تُهِنْهُ؟

3. **Verbal sentence** (جُمْلَةٌ فِعْلِيَّةٌ) consisting of an **inert, static, rigid** verb (فِعْلٌ جامِدٌ). It doesn't form the present tense nor a مَصْدَرٌ.

If you strive, this is the best you can do.	إِنْ تَجْتَهِدْ فَنِعْمَ الْعَمَلَ.
Sura 3:28	Anyone who does such a thing will isolate himself completely from God – except when you need to protect yourselves from them.	وَمَنْ يَفْعَلْ ذَلِكَ فَلَيْسَ مِنَ اللهِ فِي شَيْءٍ إِلَّا أَنْ تَتَّقُوا مِنْهُمْ تُقاةً.

4. The verb of the <u>second</u> part of the conditional sentence has an **affirmative** particle preceded: سَوْفَ - س for the future or قَدْ for the past.

If you work hard, you will succeed.	إِنْ تَجْتَهِدْ فَسَتَنْجَحُ.
If you work hard, you will succeed.	إِنْ تَجْتَهِدْ فَسَوْفَ تَنْجَحُ.
If you work hard, you will definitely succeed.	إِنْ تَجْتَهِدْ فَقَدْ أَفْلَحْتَ.

Sura 8:19	[Disbelievers], if you were seeking a decision, now you have witnessed one.	إِن تَسْتَفْتِحُوا فَقَدْ جَاءَكُمُ الْفَتْحُ.

5. The <u>second</u> part is a verbal sentence **negated** by مَا or لَنْ.

If you work hard, you won't fail.	إِنْ تَجْتَهِدْ فَلَنْ تَفْشَلَ.

Sura 10:72	But if you turn away, I have asked no reward from you.	فَإِن تَوَلَّيْتُمْ فَمَا سَأَلْتُكُم مِّنْ أَجْرٍ.

What about other negation devices? For example, لَمْ? The grammarians say that the use of فَ is optional then. The same is true for . But watch out! If فَ is inserted, لا requires a present tense verb, indicative mood (مَرْفُوعٌ).

6. Two **special** situations in the second (= main) part.

a) **Another device does the job of the فَ.** What could that be?

The so-called إذا *of the unexpected* (إذا الْفُجَائِيّة) can occupy the place as a connector (see *question #168*). In order to charge the إذا الْفُجَائِيّة with the job of the فَ, two things have to be fulfilled:

- The 2ⁿᵈ part (جَوابُ الشَّرطِ) is a **nominal** sentence (جُمْلةٌ اِسْمِيّةٌ).
- The nominal sentence is **not negated** (غَيْرُ مَنْفِيّةٍ) and is not emphasized by إنَّ (غَيْرُ مَنْسُوخةٍ).

If you strive, then you will be outstanding.	إِنْ تَجْتَهِدْ إِذَا أَنْتَ مُتَفَوِّقٌ.

Sura 30:36	...وَإِنْ تُصِبْهُمْ سَيِّئَةٌ بِمَا قَدَّمَتْ أَيْدِيهِمْ إِذَا هُمْ يَقْنَطُونَ.

- ...but when something bad happens to them - because of their own actions - they fall into utter despair. (*Abdul Haleem*)

- ...but if evil afflicts them for what their hands have put forth, imme-diately they despair. *(Saḥīḥ International)*

b) Inverted word order. When the second (= main) clause precedes the conditional ("*if-*") clause, we <u>do not</u> use فَ.

| I'll die if I remain here. | إِنِّي أَمُوتُ إِنْ مَكَثْتُ هُنا. |
| For what reason would she summon him if not for this? | لِأَيِّ سَبَبٍ تَدْعُوهُ إِنْ لَمْ يَكُنْ لِهٰذا؟ |

Remark: Don't confuse this type of فَ with a فَاءٌ سَبَبِيَّةٌ. Such a فَ intro-duces a clause that expresses the **result** or **effect** of a preceding clause. The preceding clause must contain an imperative (affirmative or negative) or it expresses a wish or hope, a question, or it contains a negation. *See #168.*

390. Does it matter whether you use the present or the past tense in a conditional sentence?

No, it doesn't.

In Arabic, a past tense verb is often used in the first part (شَرْط) of the conditional sentence. Could you also use a present tense verb in the مَجْزُومٌ-mood instead? Yes, you could.

The consequence clause (جَوابٌ), i.e., the second part, is often in the same tense as the شَرْط. Nevertheless, a change of tenses is possible – if that is the situation, the particle فَ normally precedes the جَوابٌ.

Let's assume we have an if-clause starting with a conditional device that demands the مَجْزُومٌ-mood. What would be the necessary form (tense and mood) of the verb then?

| If you work hard, you will succeed. (Both sen-tences mean exactly the same.) | إِنْ تَجْتَهِدْ نَجَحْتَ. |
| | إِنْ اجْتَهَدْتَ نَجَحْتَ. |

Watch out! Neither the verb in the if-part (فِعْلُ الشَّرْطِ) nor the verb in the second part (جَوابُ الشَّرْطِ) must be in the present tense, jussive mood (مَجْزُومٌ).

Instead, it is possible that one verb is in the past tense (which cannot be put visibly into the مَجْزُومٌ-mood) and the other verb in the present tense مَجْزُومٌ-mood.

It is even possible that both verbs are in the past tense. How come? We can't put a past tense verb visibly into the مَجْزُومٌ-mood for one specific reason: the past tense verb has a fixed, indeclinable, cemented shape (مَبْنِيٌّ) and therefore doesn't get any mood-marker. ➡ You can't see that a past tense verb is in the *jussive* mood.

The same applies to the imperative which also has a fixed shape. Only in the present tense, you can see the jussive mood, marked by a سُكُونٌ (ـْ). The key word here is **visible, apparent marker** – as grammatically speaking, we can treat a past tense verb as holding the place of a مَجْزُومٌ-mood (فِي مَحَلِّ جَزْمٍ). See *question #391*.

391. How do you mark a past tense verb in the jussive mood?

You assign a "place value".

In other words, we say that the past tense verb occupies the place of *a state of* جَزْمٌ (jussive). In Arabic, a verb in the past tense has a fixed, indeclinable shape (مَبْنِيٌّ) and therefore does not receive any mood marker as seen in the previous *question*. Some examples:

1	If you study, you will succeed.	إِنْ تَدْرُسْ نَجَحْتَ.
2	If you study, be awake!	إِنْ تَدْرُسْ كُنْ واعِيًا!
3	If you study, you will succeed.	إِنْ دَرَسْتَ نَجَحْتَ.
4	If you study, you will succeed.	إِنْ دَرَسْتَ تَنْجَحْ.
5	If you study, you will succeed.	إِنْ دَرَسْتَ تَنْجَحُ.

1	Past tense verb in the place of a jussive mood (الْماضِي فِي مَحَلِّ جَزْمٍ).	نَجَحْتَ
2	Imperative in the position of a jussive mood (الْأَمْرُ فِي مَحَلِّ جَزْمٍ).	كُنْ

3	Both are past tense verbs in the place of a jussive (الْماضِي فِي مَحَلِّ جَزْمٍ);	دَرَسْتَ نَجَحْتَ
4	Past tense verb in the place of a jussive mood (الْماضِي فِي مَحَلِّ جَزْمٍ). The present tense verb is مَجْزُومٌ by the سُكُونٌ.	دَرَسْتَ تَنْجَحْ
5	This is tricky! Why do we see the **indicative** mood (مَرْفُوعٌ) and not a سُكُون at the end which would be the marker for the jussive mood (مَجْزُومٌ) like in example 4? The present tense verb in the indicative (مُضارِعٌ مَرْفُوعٌ) is the predicate (خَبَرٌ) for the deleted subject (مُبْتَدَأ مَحْذُوف) of the nominal sentence (جُمْلَة اِسْمِيّةٌ). The entire sentence is the جَوابُ الشَّرْطِ. If we inserted the deleted subject, the sentence would look like this: إِنْ دَرَسْتَ فَأَنْتَ تَنْجَحُ	تَنْجَحُ

A past tense verb in the place where you would expect a verb in the jussive mood – that happens frequently in the Qur'an.

Sura 41:52	Say [Prophet], 'Have you ever thought, what if this revelation really **is** from God and you still reject it? Who could be more astray than someone who cuts himself off so far [from God]?'	قُلْ أَرَءَيْتُمْ إِن كَانَ مِنْ عِندِ ٱللَّهِ ثُمَّ كَفَرْتُم بِهِۦ مَنْ أَضَلُّ مِمَّنْ هُوَ فِى شِقَاقٍ بَعِيدٍ

The conditional device إِنْ induces the jussive mood in a following verb. However, the past tense verb كانَ has a fixed shape. We can only say that it appears in the place of a jussive mood (فِي مَحَلِّ جَزْمٍ فِعْلُ الشَّرْطِ).

392. Why is the conditional particle إِنْ often tricky?

The word إِنْ has some flexibility and specialties as we will see.

Specialty I: after إِنْ two verbs in the مَجْزُومٌ-mood have to follow.

The first verb is the فِعْلُ الشَّرْطِ and the second the جَوابُ الشَّرْطِ; the second is the result depending upon the first.

However, it is possible that a noun (اِسْمٌ) is placed after إِنْ. In such a situation, we assume that there was a verb in the مَجْزُومٌ-mood immediately after the particle إِنْ, but it was deleted.

| If Karīm comes, treat him well (honor him). | إِنْ كَرِيمٌ جَاءَ فَأَكْرِمْهُ. |
| Assumed/virtual meaning of the sentence: | إِنْ جَاءَ كَرِيمٌ (جَاءَ) فَأَكْرِمْهُ. |

| Conditional particle. It does not have a position in إِعْرَابٌ. | إِنْ |
| **Subject** (فَاعِلٌ) of the <u>deleted</u> verb (فِعْلٌ مَحْذُوفٌ). Therefore, we treat this sentence as a **verbal sentence**. The deleted verb is interpreted by the actual verb that is found in the sentence (i.e., جَاءَ). In principle, we don't do anything other than mentally push the verb forward so that it comes right after إِنْ. | كَرِيمٌ |

The actual verb that follows كَرِيمٌ is understood as being virtually in the مَجْزُومٌ-mood. Since it is not immediately following إِنْ, this verb <u>cannot</u> be in the present tense مَجْزُومٌ-mood because this only works when a verb is placed right after the particle. So, we are in a dilemma.

We cannot use a present tense verb in the indicative mood – we do need a conditional meaning! But there is a nice trick. We must use a **past tense** verb to avoid any misunderstanding! Past tense verbs have an indeclinable shape (مَبْنِيٌّ); even if we wanted to, it would be impossible to visibly put it into the jussive mood (جَزْمٌ). From the structure of the sentence, however, we understand that this verb has the same meaning as a present tense verb in the مَجْزُومٌ-mood. An example:

| Sura 9:6 | If any one of the idolaters should seek your protection [Prophet], grant it to him so that he may hear the word of Allah... | وَإِنْ أَحَدٌ مِّنَ الْمُشْرِكِينَ اسْتَجَارَكَ فَأَجِرْهُ حَتَّىٰ يَسْمَعَ كَلَامَ اللَّهِ ... |

Specialty II: the word إِمّا. The word ما is often added after إِنْ.

The ما is redundant, extra (مَا الزَّائِدَةُ). It is mainly there to strengthen the conditional meaning (مَا لِتَأْكِيدِ مَعْنَى الشَّرْطِ). Now, why do the two words merge? ➡ The ن is embodied which frequently happens when م and ن collide. We finally get إِمّا. This process is called إِدْغَامٌ.

| If you see Muhammad, treat him with respect! | إِمّا تَرَ مُحَمَّدًا فَأَكْرِمْهُ! |

| The word إِمّا was originally إِنْ مَا. | إِمّا |

1	Conditional particle (حَرْفُ شَرْطٍ) which is indeclinable (مَبْنِيٌّ).	إِنْ
2	Additional particle (حَرْفٌ زَائِدٌ); indeclinable (مَبْنِيٌّ).	ما
Both particles – إِنْ and ما – do not have a position in إِعْرَابٌ.		

In constructions with إِمَّا, the verbs are often strengthened by the نُونُ التَّوْكِيد. This type of construction occurs quite often in the Qur'an.

Sura 7:200	If Satan should prompt you to do something (if an evil suggestion comes to you from Satan), seek refuge with Allah.	وَإِمَّا يَنزَغَنَّكَ مِنَ الشَّيْطَانِ نَزْغٌ فَاسْتَعِذْ بِاللَّهِ.

Specialty III: the negation. If إِنْ is used with a negation, the negation is achieved by لَمْ plus a verb in the present tense, مَجْزُومٌ-mood.

You should **not use** لا for the negation! If you do so, the إِنْ will change into a different word: إِلَّا denoting *if not, unless*. What happens here is that the ن is embodied in the لا.

If you don't read, you won't understand.	إِنْ لَمْ تَقْرَأْ لا تَفْهَمْ.
If you don't read, you won't understand.	إِلَّا تَقْرَأْ لا تَفْهَمْ.

Sura 9:39	If you do not go out and fight, Allah will punish you severely and put others in your place (will replace you with another people).	إِلَّا تَنفِرُوا يُعَذِّبْكُمْ عَذَابًا أَلِيمًا وَيَسْتَبْدِلْ قَوْمًا غَيْرَكُمْ.
Note that both verbs are in the مَجْزُومٌ-mood.		

393. Why is the word إِذَا special?

The word إِذَا is different from the other conditional particles.

إِذَا is a noun (اِسْمٌ) which points to the **future (time)**. Why? Because it is clear that the event will happen, but it is uncertain when this is going to be (German: *Zeitpunkt*). This is the difference to إِنْ which conveys the idea that the action/event itself is uncertain (and not only the time).

إِذَا implies some note of expectancy, as if the one who tells the information (the speaker of the sentence) is anticipating that the action will

take place. Sometimes the note of expectancy is strong and إذا is therefore translated as **when**.

In Arabic (as in other languages too), temporal and conditional
clauses are closely related. This is especially true when a temporal circumstance is understood as being essential or necessary for the actual
occurrence of the action (expressed by the main clause). Therefore, إذا
is also frequently found with a meaning equivalent to that of a conditional particle (i.e., **if**).

The basic conditional significance of إذا normally remains so closely
related to its temporal one that even in its conditional application, it
only introduces a statement whose eventual occurrence will happen
without doubt.

What is the original meaning of إذا as a **temporal demonstrative**?

1. Parallelism. Sometimes the past tense after إذا does express an event
in the past. We call that a temporal meaning of the <u>past</u> (parallelism).

Whenever he **roamed** through the village, he was always **seen** alone.	إذا جَالَ فِي الْقَرْيةِ لَمْ يُرَ إلّا مُنْفَرِدًا.

Usually, however, إذا is used in sentences expressing a meaning that
has nothing to do with the past tense in the sense of time. It expresses a
conditional meaning. Nevertheless, you express it by a past tense verb
denoting the <u>future</u>. By doing this we are getting close to the meaning
of a conditional sentence.

When(ever) I **get** in touch with any (of them), they **answer** me coldly.	إذا اتَّصَلْتُ بِأَحَدٍ رَدَّ فِي جَفَافٍ.

2. Unexpected moment. إذا may also present a <u>statement at a definite
moment</u> during a given action. As a result of this meaning and its
demonstrative function, إذا must follow another statement containing a
temporal idea to which the إذا refers. *See #345.*

Let's check the grammar now. إذا produces quite complex sentences.
This is mainly related to the function of إذا which serves as the first part

of a إِضَافَةٌ. The second part is an entire sentence (مُضافٌ إِلَى جُمْلةٍ)!

➡ (فِعْلُ الشَّرْطِ) The regent (عامِلٌ) in sentences with إِذا is not a verb it is the **second part** of the conditional (الْجَوابُ). إِذا is an adverbial device having a conditional as well as temporal function, receiving its meaning from the future (ظَرْفٌ لِمَا يُسْتَقْبَلُ مِن الزَّمانِ).

➡ In other words, إِذا is a particle for the **future** (ظَرْفٌ لِلْمُسْتَقْبَلِ) which conveys the meaning of the **conditional** (يُفِيدُ مَعْنَى الشَّرْطِ).

When (if) you work, you will succeed.	إِذا اجْتَهَدْتَ نَجَحْتَ.
The word إِذا here is a ظَرْفٌ لِلْمُسْتَقْبَلِ which includes/incorporates the meaning of a condition (يَتَضَمَّنُ مَعْنَى الشَّرْطِ).	
This is the meaning of the sentence: ➡	نَجاحُكَ مَشْرُوطٌ بِاجْتِهادِكَ.

When Karīm comes, treat him with respect!	إِذا جَاءَ كَرِيمٌ فَأَكْرِمْهُ!

إِذا	Adverbial particle that has a conditional as well as temporal function (ظَرْفٌ لِما يُسْتَقْبَلُ مِن الزَّمانِ خافِضٌ لِشَرْطِهِ). The particle إِذا limits, let's say, it makes the situation concrete. It has a fixed, indeclinable shape; as an adverb, however, we treat it as holding the place of an accusative case, governed by the second part of the if-clause (مَنْصوبٌ بِجَوابِهِ).
جاءَ	Past tense verb (فِعْلٌ ماضٍ مَبْنِيٌّ عَلَى الْفَتْحِ).
كَرِيمٌ	Subject (فاعِلٌ) of the verbal sentence; nominative case (مَرْفُوعٌ). The verbal sentence *Karīm came* (جَاءَ كَرِيمٌ) is placed in the location of a **genitive** case since it serves as the second part of the إِضافةٌ introduced by إِذا (فِي مَحَلِّ جَرٍّ بِالْإِضافةِ).

The expression أَكْرِمْهُ is the second part (جَوابٌ) of the conditional sentence. The جَوابٌ is the regent (عامِلٌ) that governs the word إِذا in the accusative case (نَصبٌ). How could we picture such a construction?

We could say that إِذا takes grammatically an accusative case (adverb of time; giving the temporal circumstances of the action) due to the second part of the conditional sentence (مَنْصوبٌ بِجَوابِهِ). Therefore, we could rewrite the sentence as follows: أَكْرِمْهُ إِذا جَاءَ

Remark: أَكْرِمْ is the imperative of the IV-verb أَكْرَمَ which uses the pattern أَفْعِلْ for the imperative. Form IV is the only verb form whose imperative begins with أ (which must be always pronounced as a glottal stop).

If you want to express the **conditional I** (real condition; present or future), which is the main application of إِذَا, this is the recipe:

- After إِذَا you almost exclusively use the past tense.

- If negated, you use لَمْ plus a verb in the مَجْزُومٌ-mood.

- So, the most common situation is that you end up with two past tense verbs (see below marked with *), but these verbs express the present tense or even future.

- In rare situations you may use كَانَ plus a verb in the present tense or كَانَ plus past tense.

English tenses		Arabic tenses		translation	Arabic sentence
part 1	part 2	**part 1**	part 2		
PRESENT TENSE	present tense	**PAST TENSE**	past tense	If you ask, (then) you will understand.	إِذا سَأَلْتَ.. فَهِمْتَ.
			present tense		إِذا سَأَلْتَ..تَفْهَمُ.
	future II		يَكُونُ قَدْ فَعَلَ	If you ask, you will have understood.	إِذا سَأَلْتَ.. تَكُونُ قَدْ فَهِمْتَ.
	future I		فَسَوْفَ يَفْعَلُ	If you ask, (then) you will understand.	إِذا سَأَلْتَ.. فَسَوْفَ تَفْهَمُ.
	imperative		فَافْعَلْ	If you ask, (then) understand!	إِذا سَأَلْتَ.. فَافْهَمْ!

Notice! The second part of the conditional sentence is connected by فَ - no matter if the second part is a nominal (جُمْلَةٌ اِسْمِيّةٌ) or verbal sentence (جُمْلَةٌ فِعْلِيّةٌ). The verb can also be preceded/connected by قَدْ or سَوْفَ. or س or لَنْ or ما.

If the people one day will (want) to live, then destiny must respond.	إِذَا الشَّعْبُ يَوْمًا أَرَادَ الْحَيَاةَ فَلَا بُدَّ أَنْ يَسْتَجِيبَ الْقَدَرُ.

Remark: This is the first line of a poem (قَصيدةٌ) called *"The Will To Live"* (لَحْنُ الْحَياةِ) by Abū al-Qāsim al-Shābbī (أَبُو الْقَاسِم الشّابّيّ). These lines serve as the final two verses of the current National Anthem of Tunisia. Some suggested that these lines were a source of inspiration for the most famous slogan (شِعارٌ) of the Arab Spring 2011:

The people want the fall of the regime!	الشَّعْبُ يُرِيدُ إِسْقاطَ النِّظامِ!

394. What is the difference (in meaning) between إذا and إنْ?

It is subtle.

The temporal clause introduced by إذا is often (almost) identical in meaning with a conditional clause introduced by إنْ. **But there are differences.**

- إنْ denotes **what is possible**. It states a fact or an event that one **cannot** be sure will occur - but one which is always possible.

- إذا denotes **what is ascertained**. Through its conditional meaning, it only conveys uncertainty about the time when the action will take place (but not about whether the action will take place at all). We could say that إذا seems to give a greater degree of certainty to the statement presented in the clause.

- إذا often conveys a conditional meaning and may even be used in hypothetical constructions; in such situations, it is close to become a **synonym for إنْ**.

- إنْ, on the other hand, can never be used when the sentence has a temporal meaning. It **can't be a synonym** for a temporal إذا.

For this reason you say:

إنْ	If Karīm comes... (He might not come...)	إنْ جاءَ كَرِيمٌ...
إذا	When Karīm comes... (He will definitely come.)	إذا جاءَ كَرِيمٌ...
	When the beginning of the month will come (= when the month starts). This event will happen for sure.	إذا جاءَ رَأْسُ الشَّهْرِ...

The right choice of the conditional word is essential to transport the correct meaning. The action (i.e., the verb) can relate to a different event or moment; to a certain time – due to the conditional device. The following examples make the difference clear:

When he dies (when that comes to happen, and it will)...	...إذا ماتَ
If he dies (today, for example, of his present illness)...	... (إنْ تَمُتْ (or مات)

395. What is the difference between إذا and إِذْ؟

The time to which they relate.

It basically comes down to the following difference:

إذا conveys the meaning of the **future**. You can only use a verbal sentence (إذا لا تُضافُ إلّا جُمْلةٍ فِعْلِيّةٍ) after it; *see #396*.

I will come to you at sunrise.	أتَيْتُكَ إذا طَلَعَتِ الشَّمْسُ.

إذْ signifies the **past tense**. You can use a nominal or verbal sentence after it (إذْ تُضافُ إلَى الْجُمْلةِ الْإسْمِيّةِ وَالْفِعْلِيّةِ).

In Modern Standard Arabic, إذْ often expresses a reason and is translated as *since; because*.

I came to you when the sun rose.	جِئْتُكَ إذْ طَلَعَتِ الشَّمْسُ.
	جِئْتُكَ إذْ الشَّمْسُ طالِعةٌ.

إذْ may be followed by **a verb in the present tense**, nevertheless, the verb then <u>denotes</u> the **past tense**. In the following example, you see the present tense in Arabic, but the translator uses the past tense for the English translation.

| Sura 2:127 | As Abraham and Ishmael **built** up the foundations of the House [they prayed], 'Our Lord, accept [this] from us. You are the All Hearing, the All Knowing. | وَإِذْ يَرْفَعُ إِبْرَاهِيمُ الْقَوَاعِدَ مِنَ الْبَيْتِ وَإِسْمَاعِيلُ رَبَّنَا تَقَبَّلْ مِنَّا إِنَّكَ أَنتَ السَّمِيعُ الْعَلِيمُ. |

In the Qur'an, إذْ occasionally starts the main clause and indicates a time in the past (*once, at one time; when*). It may be left untranslated.

Sura 2:126	وَإِذْ قَالَ إِبْرَاهِيمُ رَبِّ اجْعَلْ هَٰذَا بَلَدًا آمِنًا وَارْزُقْ أَهْلَهُ مِنَ الثَّمَرَاتِ مَنْ آمَنَ مِنْهُم بِاللَّهِ وَالْيَوْمِ الْآخِرِ.
And [mention] **when** Abraham said, "My Lord, make this a secure city and provide its people with fruits - whoever of them believes in Allah and the Last Day." (*Saḥīḥ International*)	

In the following verse of the Qur'an, إذْ is used three times. Notice the different tenses in Arabic and English.

Sura 9:40	إِلَّا تَنصُرُوهُ فَقَدْ نَصَرَهُ اللَّهُ إِذْ أَخْرَجَهُ الَّذِينَ كَفَرُوا ثَانِيَ اثْنَيْنِ إِذْ هُمَا فِي الْغَارِ إِذْ يَقُولُ لِصَاحِبِهِ لَا تَحْزَنْ إِنَّ اللَّهَ مَعَنَا.
[Even] If you do not aid the prophet - Allah has already aided him **when** those who disbelieved **had driven** him out [of Mecca] as one of two, **when** they **were** in the cave and he **said** to his companion, "Do not grieve; indeed Allah is with us." (*Saḥīḥ International*)	

396. Can you place a noun (اسمٌ) after إذا؟

Yes, but this is only possible with a trick.

Although the rules dictate that إذا has to be followed immediately by a verb, the verb after إذا is sometimes deleted. It is explained by the verb that comes later in the sentence. ➡ As a result, you might find a noun (اسمٌ) after إذا. For example:

When Karīm comes, treat him politely!	إذا كَرِيمٌ جاءَ فَأَكْرِمْهُ!
Virtual (underlying) structure of the sentence: ➡	إذا جاءَ كَرِيمٌ جاءَ فَأَكْرِمْهُ!

What happened? *Karīm* is the subject (فَاعِلٌ) of the **deleted verb** (فِعْلٌ مَحْذُوفٌ). If we check the underlying, assumed construction of the sentence, we see that the verb (again) is placed after إذا.	كَرِيمٌ
Therefore, we can say that the verb after إذا can be interpreted by the verb that is actually found in the second part of the conditional sentence. If we assume all this, then the sentence is grammatically correct.	

397. What is the peculiar thing about the conditional particle أَيّ؟

Arabic nouns that work as conditional devices (أَسْماءُ الشَّرْطِ) are inde-clinable (مَبْنِيٌّ) - except for أَيّ (who, whoever).

أَيّ is declinable (مُعْرَبٌ) and receives visual case endings. It serves as the first part of a إِضافةٌ is connected with a singular noun (مُفْرَدٌ).

Any man who (whoever) does good deeds will find his reward.	أَيُّ رَجُلٍ يَعْمَلْ خَيْرًا يَجِدْ جَزاءَهُ.

أَيُّ	Conditional word (اِسْمُ شَرْطٍ). It serves as the **subject** (مُبْتَدَأٌ) and gets the nominative case (مَرْفُوعٌ), marked by the ضَمّة. It also serves as the مُضافٌ (i.e., the first part of the إِضافةٌ).
رَجُلٍ	This word is the مُضافٌ إِلَيْهِ (i.e., the second part of the إِضافةٌ); therefore, it takes the genitive case (مَجْرُورٌ).

Another example to illustrate that أَيّ gets the case marker according to its place in the sentence:

Any deeds you do, you will be accounted for.	أَيَّ عَمَلٍ تَعْمَلْ تُحاسَبْ عَلَيْهِ.

أَيَّ	**Fronted direct object** (مَفْعُولٌ بِهِ مُقَدَّمٌ) of the verb تَعْمَلْ which serves as the فِعْلُ الشَّرْطِ. Therefore, أَيّ must be in the accusative (مَنْصُوبٌ). Remark: Whenever you struggle to translate a sentence, check the case marker as it will give you a hint. In the above example, أَيّ can't be the subject (مُبْتَدَأٌ) as the subject has to take the nominative case (مَرْفُوعٌ).

398. Which tense should you use with لَوْ in Arabic?

The past tense.

As a rule of thumb, we can say:

- The **first part** of a conditional sentence after لَوْ may have a verb in the present <u>or</u> past tense. Usually, the past tense is used.

- The **second part** (جَوابُ الشَّرْطِ) doesn't give you a choice: you <u>must</u> use a past tense verb. But... such past tense verb **doesn't convey** the meaning of the past tense!

In English, we call it conditional II (*would, could*) and in German *Konjunktiv II* (*würde, könnte, wäre*).

The past tense is used to express a **hypothetical condition**. In rare situations, the past tense does convey a past meaning when the statement involves a condition contrary to fact. How can we know the correct tense in English? The meaning of the verb (and of the condition) is only given by the context.

If you gave me the letter, I would read it immediately.	لَوْ أَعْطَيْتَنِي هذِهِ الرِّسالَةَ قَرَأْتُها فَوْرًا.

- If you want to stress that something is impossible, you should add the emphatic particle لـ to the beginning of the second part of the sentence. It is a so-called لامُ جَوابِ لَوْ. You also find لـ in the second part of لَوْلا. See *Arabic for Nerds 1, question #126*.

- If you want to stress on the past tense, you could use the **past perfect tense**, expressed by: كانَ قَدْ فَعَلَ.

If I had known that, I would have come with you.	لَوْ (كُنْتُ قَدْ) عَرَفْتُ ذلِكَ لَذَهَبْتُ مَعَكَ.

Occasionally, لَوْ plus أَنَّ plus a nominal sentence (جُمْلَةٌ اِسْمِيّةٌ) is used. In such a situation, the following noun (اِسْمُ أَنَّ) gets the accusative case (مَنْصُوبٌ).

(Allah's Messenger said:) "If Adam's son had a valley full of gold, he would like to have two valleys, for nothing fills his mouth except dust. And Allah forgives him who repents to Him." (*Sahīh al-Bukhārī 6439*)	لَوْ أَنَّ لِابْنِ آدَمَ وادِيًا مِنْ ذَهَبٍ أَحَبَّ أَنْ يَكُونَ لَهُ وادِيانِ، وَلَنْ يَمْلَأَ فاهُ إلاَّ التُّرابُ، وَيَتُوبُ اللهُ عَلَى مَنْ تابَ
If the student had been diligent, he would have been successful.	لَوْ أَنَّ الطّالِبَ كانَ مُجْتَهِدًا لَنَجَحَ.

399. How do you negate a sentence that starts with لَوْ?

You use لَمْ *or occasionally* لَمّا.

Here is the recipe to make the negation work.

- In the **first part** of the conditional sentence, you use لَمْ plus a present tense verb in the jussive mood (مَجْزُومٌ).

- In the **second part** of the sentence, you could use the same negation tool. If you have the device لـ involved, the negation works as follows: you use مَا + لـ resulting in لَمَا (*certainly not*) plus a past tense verb. You don't use لَمْ because you need to avoid two لـ in a row which is not only ugly but would also produce a cacophony.

- If there is **no verb** involved, we use لَوْ لا – see *question #387*.

If the student had not been diligent, he would not have been successful.	لَوْ لَمْ يَكُنْ الطَّالِبُ مُجْتَهِدًا لَمَا نَجَحَ.
Note that in this example, يَكُنْ is only written with a سُكُونٌ to illustrate the jussive mood. In fact, it needs a helping vowel here resulting in يَكُنِ.	

Let's see the difference (negated/non-negated):

non-negated	If he had been rich, he would have been able to help you.	لَوْ كَانَ غَنِيًّا لَاسْتَطاعَ أَنْ يُساعِدَكَ.
negated	If he hadn't been rich, he would not have been able to help you.	لَوْ لَمْ يَكُنْ غَنِيًّا لَمَا اسْتَطاعَ أَنْ يُساعِدَكَ.

400. Can the 1ˢᵗ part of a conditional sentence work as an adjective?

Yes, it can.

Let's start with the obvious: the first part of a conditional sentence introduces the **condition** (جُمْلَةُ الشَّرْطِ). Therefore, the first part can be treated as a **subordinate clause** (جُمْلَةٌ فَرْعِيَّةٌ).

Why do we state that? This grammatical reality makes it possible that the first part can be placed as a predicate (خَبَرٌ), as an adjective (صِفةٌ), or as a relative clause (صِلةٌ). Let's see some concrete examples.

a) The جُمْلةُ الشَّرْطِ serves as the **predicate** (خَبَرٌ).

Zayd, if he works hard, will succeed.	زَيْدٌ إِنْ يَجْتَهِدْ يَنْجَحْ.

Subject (مُبْتَدَأٌ) of the nominal sentence; nominative case (مَرْفُوعٌ).	زَيْدٌ
Conditional particle (حَرْفُ شَرْطٍ).	إِنْ
Present tense verb (فِعْلٌ مُضارِعٌ) in the مَجْزُومٌ-mood in order to be a فِعْلُ الشَّرْطِ. The subject of the verb (فاعِلٌ) is a hidden pronoun (ضَمِيرٌ مُسْتَتِرٌ) with the implied meaning of *he* (هُوَ).	يَجْتَهِدْ
Present tense verb (فِعْلٌ مُضارِعٌ) in the مَجْزُومٌ-mood. The subject of the verb (فاعِلٌ) is a hidden pronoun (ضَمِيرٌ مُسْتَتِرٌ) with the implied meaning of *he* (هُوَ). This sentence is the جَوابُ الشَّرْطِ, and does <u>not</u> have a position in إِعْرابٌ. See *question #85*.	يَنْجَحْ

Where is the **predicate** (خَبَرٌ) of the nominal sentence? The entire conditional sentence (جُمْلَةُ الشَّرْطِ وَالْجَوابِ; marked in gray) serves as the predicate (خَبَرٌ): إِنْ يَجْتَهِدْ يَنْجَحْ ➡ Thus, it grammatically appears in the place of a nominative case (فِي مَحَلِّ رَفْعٍ).

b) The جُمْلَةُ الشَّرْطِ is an **adjective** (صِفَةٌ).

A man, who will tell you the truth if you ask him, came.	جاءَ رَجُلٌ إِنْ تَسْأَلْهُ يَصْدُقْكَ.

Verbal sentence with a verb (فِعْلٌ) and a subject (فاعِلٌ).	جاءَ رَجُلٌ
Conditional particle (حَرْفُ شَرْطٍ).	إِنْ
Verb + subject (فاعِلٌ) *you* + direct object (مَفْعُولٌ بِهِ) *him*.	تَسْأَلْهُ
Verb + subject (فاعِلٌ) *he* + direct object (مَفْعُولٌ بِهِ) *you*. This sentence is the جَوابُ الشَّرْطِ; it does not have a place in إِعْرابٌ.	يَصْدُقْكَ

Where is the **adjective** (صِفَةٌ)? The entire conditional sentence (جُمْلَةُ الشَّرْطِ وَالْجَوابِ), in gray, serves as an adjective (صِفَةٌ) for *a man* (رَجُلٌ), which is the subject. It is set in the location of a nominative (فِي مَحَلِّ رَفْعٍ) as it must get the same case marker as the word to which it refers.

c) The جُمْلَةُ الشَّرْطِ is a **relative** clause (صِلَةٌ).

The one, who speaks the truth if you ask	جاءَ الَّذِي إِنْ تَسْأَلْهُ يَصْدُقْكَ.

him, has come.	
The entire conditional sentence (جُمْلةُ الشَّرْطِ وَالْجَوابِ) after الَّذِي doesn't have a position in إعْرابٌ because it is the relative clause (صِلةُ الْمَوْصُولِ –) see *question #86*.	

THE EXCLUSION (جُمْلةُ الإسْتِثْناءِ)

401. Why does the excluded thing take the accusative case?

It is governed by a verb – but you usually don't see that verb.

The *exclusion* or *exceptive sentence* (جُمْلةُ الإسْتِثْناءِ) helps to extract a noun (إسْمٌ) from another noun. It often conveys the meaning of *except* or *only*. We need **two grammar terms** for our analysis:

- *the thing that is extracted* (الإسْمُ الْمُخْرَجُ): the الْمُسْتَثْنَى;
- *that from which the exclusion/exception is made* (الْمُسْتَثْنَى مِنْهُ);

The players came except for Khālid.	جاءَ اللّاعِبُونَ إلَّا خالِدًا.

الْمُسْتَثْنَى	خالِدًا	الْمُسْتَثْنَى مِنْهُ	اللّاعِبُونَ

The grammarians regard the الْمُسْتَثْنَى as a **variety of the direct object** (مَفْعُولٌ بِه). Why a direct object? Because indirectly, virtually there is a verb included which takes the الْمُسْتَثْنَى as the direct object and governs it in the accusative case (مَنْصُوبٌ). But which verb?

In the above example, it is not the verb جاءَ. It is another verb which you normally don't see: a virtual verb that governs the الْمُسْتَثْنَى and has the assumed meaning (تَقْدِيرٌ) of *I except* or *I exclude* (أَسْتَثْنِي). E.g.:

The students came except for Zayd.	جاءَ الطُّلابُ إلَّا زَيْدًا.
The students – **I exclude Zayd** – came.	جاءَ الطُّلابُ أَسْتَثْنِي زَيْدًا.

In the second example, the regent (عامِلٌ) for the الْمُسْتَثْنَى is the verb أَسْتَثْنِي. What about the first example? Most grammarians accept the view that it is actually the particle (كَلِمةُ الإسْتِثْناءِ) which functions as the regent and governs the excluded thing/person. We assume that the particle (إِلَّا) has a verbal force. I also use this approach in this book.

402. Does the word إِلَّا only mean *except*?

No, it can also mean "if not".

Normally إِلَّا (regarded as a single word) is used as a **particle of exception** (حَرْفُ إِسْتِثْناءٍ) expressing *unless, saving, except; but.*

But there is also another application: the meaning of *if not.* Such kind of إِلَّا is used in Classical Arabic to introduce negative conditional clauses. It is also used in the Qur'an. In contemporary texts, it is rare.

How does it work? The conditional particle إِنْ (*if*) is united with the negative لا (*not*). The result looks exactly like the *exceptive* إِلَّا. It is regarded as a **negation particle** (حَرْفُ نَفْيٍ). We eventually have a compound word (حَرْفٌ مُرَكَّبٌ) consisting of two parts:

1. إِنْ, a so-called إِنَّ الشَّرْطِيَّةُ الْجازِمَةُ, which denotes *if.*

2. لا which is a negation particle (لا النَّافِيَةُ).

Note that in such an application, إِلَّا must be followed by a verb in the jussive mood (مَجْزُومٌ) because of إِنْ - but the verb can be suppressed.

If you don't study, you will fail.	إِلَّا تَدْرُسْ تَرْسُبْ.
Sura 9:39	If you **do not** go out and fight, God will punish you severely.	إِلَّا تَنفِرُوا يُعَذِّبْكُمْ عَذَابًا أَلِيمًا.
Sura 8:73	The disbelievers support one another. **If you do not** do the same, there will be persecution in the land and great corruption.	وَالَّذِينَ كَفَرُوا بَعْضُهُمْ أَوْلِيَاءُ بَعْضٍ إِلَّا تَفْعَلُوهُ تَكُن فِتْنَةٌ فِي الْأَرْضِ وَفَسَادٌ كَبِيرٌ.

إِلَّا introduces a **negation** + a **conditional** meaning. Note the jussive mood!

Sura 81:29	➡ إِلَّا denotes an **exception** (حَرْفُ إِسْتِثْناءٍ)!	وَمَا تَشَاءُونَ إِلَّا أَن يَشَاءَ اللَّهُ رَبُّ الْعَالَمِينَ.

But you will **only** wish to do so by the will of God, the Lord of all people.

> (Abdul Haleem)
>
> And you **do not will** except that Allah wills – Lord of the worlds. (Sahīh International)

Watch out: You may encounter وَإِلّا – *if not, otherwise* – when you have two if-clauses in a row. Although it is not written, the first if-clause transports the message: *then it is good, all well and good*. The grammarians would say that the *apodosis* is left unexpressed. The second if-clause, starting with وَإِلّا, usually contains a warning or punishment.

If you do such a thing (*excellent will it be*) but **if not**, I will kill you.	اِنْ فَعَلْتَ كَذا (فَنِعِمّا هُوَ) وَإِلّا قَتَلْتُكَ.

The part in brackets (فَنِعِمّا هُوَ) is implicitly understood. If ما is added to نِعْمَ, we finally get فَنِعِمّا. For example, Sura 2:271: *If you give charity openly, **it is good*** (إِن تُبْدُوا الصَّدَقَاتِ فَنِعِمّا هِيَ).

403. Is there only one possible case marker for the الْمُسْتَثْنَى؟

No, you usually have several options to choose from.

This is one of the most difficult topics for Arabic students as will you only understand what's going on if you have a solid understanding of how the language works. What are the options?

1. You use the **accusative case** (نَصْبٌ) for the الْمُسْتَثْنَى. You regard إِلّا as the regent (عامِلٌ). ➡ This is the common approach.

2. You use the **same case** as the الْمُسْتَثْنَى مِنْهُ and treat the الْمُسْتَثْنَى as an apposition – *the substitution of the part for the whole* (بَدَل الْبَعْضِ مِن الْكُلّ). Therefore, the particle إِلّا does not govern a word in the accusative case. ➡ The governing power of the word إِلّا is neglected (حَرْفٌ مُهْمَلٌ).

1	No students came, except for Zayd.	ما حَضَرَ الطُّلابُ إِلّا زَيْدًا.
2	No students, except for Zayd, came.	ما حَضَرَ الطُّلابُ إِلّا زَيْدٌ.

Let's analyze both approaches thoroughly:

Negation particle (حَرْفُ نَفْيٍ). No place in إِعْرابٌ.	1+2	ما
Past tense verb (فِعْلٌ ماضٍ).	1+2	حَضَرَ
Subject of the verb; nominative case (فاعِلٌ مَرْفُوعٌ).	1+2	الطُّلابُ
Particle of exception (حَرْفُ اِسْتِثْناءٍ).	1	إِلّا
Particle of exception (حَرْفُ اِسْتِثْناءٍ مُلْغًى) that does not exercise its grammatical (governing) power. Therefore, it just conveys the meaning of *except*.	2	
The *thing excepted* (الْمُسْتَثْنَى); accusative case (مَنْصُوبٌ).	1	زَيْدًا
Apposition; substitution of the part for the whole (بَدَلُ الْبَعْضِ مِن الْكُلِّ); thus, it takes the nominative case (مَرْفُوعٌ) like the word it accompanies (الطُّلابُ) (بِالضَّمّةِ الظّاهِرةِ).	2	زَيْدٌ

The same is true if there is a preposition involved – you either use the accusative (مَنْصُوبٌ) or you "copy" the case (example 2).

I didn't pass by the students, except Zayd.	1	ما مَرَرْتُ بِالطُّلابِ إِلّا زَيْدًا.
I didn't pass by the students except (by) Zayd.	2	ما مَرَرْتُ بِالطُّلابِ إِلّا زَيْدٍ.

Prepositional phrase (الْجارُّ وَالْمَجْرُورُ).	1+2	بِالطُّلابِ
Particle of exception (حَرْفُ اِسْتِثْناءٍ).	1	إِلّا
Particle of exception (حَرْفُ اِسْتِثْناءٍ مُلْغًى); it does not use its governing power and does not induce case endings.	2	
The *thing excepted* (الْمُسْتَثْنَى); accusative case (مَنْصُوبٌ).	1	زَيْدًا
Substitution of the part for the whole (بَدَلُ الْبَعْضِ مِن الْكُلِّ); in the **genitive case** (مَجْرُورٌ) because an apposition must get the same case as the word to which it refers.	2	زَيْدٍ

Watch out! There are exceptions!

1. Word order: If the word order is reversed, you don't have a choice: the الْمُسْتَثْنَى must get the **accusative case** (مَنْصُوبٌ). This is the situation when the الْمُسْتَثْنَى is placed before the الْمُسْتَثْنَى مِنْهُ.

The only friend I have is Zayd.	مَا لِي إِلَّا زَيْدًا صَدِيقٌ.
Negation particle (حَرْفُ نَفْي).	مَا
Prepositional phrase (الْجَارُّ وَالْمَجْرُورُ), which appears in the place of the fronted predicate (خَبَرٌ مُقَدَّمٌ). The actual predicate, to which it is attached and linked to, was deleted.	لِي
Particle of exception (حَرْفُ إِسْتِثْنَاءٍ).	إِلَّا
The *thing excepted* (الْمُسْتَثْنَى) in the accusative case (مَنْصُوبٌ).	زَيْدًا
Delayed subject (مُبْتَدَأٌ مُؤَخَّرٌ) in the nominative case (مَرْفُوعٌ).	صَدِيقٌ

2. Mismatch: If the thing excepted (الْمُسْتَثْنَى) is **completely different** from the general term in its kind, the preference is usually given to the **accusative case** (مَنْصُوبٌ). In early times, this approach was common among the people of the Hijāz (اللَّهْجَةُ الْحِجَازِيَّةُ).

No one (i.e., *no person*) came to me, but an idiot (lit. *donkey*).	مَا جَاءَنِي أَحَدٌ إِلَّا حِمَارًا.

However, such constructions were not used by the Banū Tamīm (لَهْجَةُ بَنِي تَمِيم), another ancient tribe that was important for the standardization of Classical Arabic. They favored **case mirroring**. In other words, they treated the الْمُسْتَثْنَى as a permutation (**apposition**).

No one came to me, but an idiot.	مَا جَاءَنِي أَحَدٌ إِلَّا حِمَارٌ.

404. What happens if the الْمُسْتَثْنَى مِنْهُ is missing?

The word إِلَّا loses its governing power.

When grammarians say that a sentence expressing an exclusion (جُمْلَةُ الْإِسْتِثْنَاءِ) is incomplete, it normally means that the **general term** (الْمُسْتَثْنَى مِنْهُ) is **missing.** This has some impact: إِلَّا loses its grammatical power and also somehow its original meaning of *except*. It has more the **function of an emphasis**, i.e., conveying the meaning of *only*.

Grammarians call this type a *vacated, exhaustive exclusion* (الْإِسْتِثْنَاءُ الْمُفَـرَّغُ) because the sentence starts as a negation, but misses the negated thing (= there is no antecedent). In other words, the part before إلّا is made free and available for what follows – and gets its actual meaning by إلّا. **What can be placed after إلّا in such a construction?**

When the sentence starts with a negation, but does not convey a complete meaning, إلّا loses its grammatical force. Therefore, the word after إلّا gets the case ending according to the place and function in the sentence – which can easily be identified if you imagine the sentence without the negation and without إلّا.

subject (مُبْتَدَأٌ)	The Messenger's duty is only to deliver the message clearly. (24:54)	مَا عَلَى الرَّسُولِ إلّا الْبَلَاغُ الْمُبِينُ.
subject (فَاعِلٌ)	Only Muhammad came.	ما حَضَرَ إلّا مُحَمَّدٌ.
passive subject (نَائِبُ فَاعِلٍ)	Only a book was sold.	ما بُيِعَ إلّا كِتَابٌ.
direct object (مَفْعُولٌ بِهِ)	I only saw Muhammad.	ما رَأَيْتُ إلّا مُحَمَّدًا.
prepositional phrase	I only passed (by) a garden.	ما مَرَرْتُ إلّا بِحَدِيقةٍ.
predicate (خَبَرٌ)	Muhammad is only a messenger. (Sura 3:144)	ما مُحَمَّدٌ إلّا رَسُولٌ.
predicate of لَيْسَ, in the accusative	Smoking is nothing but a harm to your health.	لَيْسَ التَّدْخِينُ إلّا ضَرَرًا لِصِحَّتِكَ.
circumstantial description (حَالٌ)	The student arrived (indeed, nothing but) happily.	ما وَصَلَ الطَّالِبُ إلّا سَعِيدًا.
	We sent you only to give good news and warning. (Sura 17:105)	ما أَرْسَلْناكَ إلّا مُبَشِّرًا وَنَذِيرًا.
purposive object (مَفْعُولٌ لَهُ)	I only honored (paid homage to) my professor.	ما قُمْتُ إجْلَالًا إلّا لِأَسْتَاذِي.

Let's analyze two examples.

Only Muhammad appeared.	ما حَضَرَ إلّا مُحَمَّدٌ.

Exception particle that does not exercise its governing power as a	إلّا

regent (عاطِلٌ or حَرْفُ إِسْتِثْناءٍ مُلْغًى).	
Subject (فاعِلٌ) of the verb حَضَرَ, in the nominative case (مَرْفُوعٌ).	مُحَمَّدٌ

I only saw Muhammad.	ما رَأَيْتُ إِلّا مُحَمَّدًا.
Direct object (مَفْعُولٌ بِهِ) in the accusative case (مَنْصُوبٌ).	مُحَمَّدًا

Most grammarians say that you can place an **entire sentence** (جُمْلَةٌ) after إِلّا – introducing a *vacated, exhaustive exclusion* (الْإِسْتِثْناءُ الْمُفَرَّغُ).

A loyal person works for none but his homeland.	ما الْمُخْلِصُ إِلّا يَعْمَلُ لِوَطَنِهِ.

Negation particle (حَرْفُ نَفْيٍ).	ما
Subject (مُبْتَدَأٌ) of the nominal sentence; nominative (مَرْفُوعٌ).	الْمُخْلِصُ
Exception particle, but it does not exercise its governing power (عاطِلٌ or حَرْفُ إِسْتِثْناءٍ مُلْغًى).	إِلّا
This verbal sentence (verb + hidden subject *he*) is located in the place of a nominative case: it appears in the place of the predicate of the nominal sentence (فِي مَحَلِّ رَفْعٍ خَبَرٌ).	يَعْمَلُ

Remark: In the standard application you can use a sentence after إِلّا. For example, you connect it with الَّذِي which denotes *except the one that...*

405. Can you use إِلّا to combine sentences?

No, you can't. Or, let's say, you shouldn't.

In Modern Standard Arabic, often in newspapers, إِلّا is not always used to express *only; except* (الْإِسْتِثْناءُ). Instead, إِلّا does the job of ...

- ...joining two conditional sentences (رَبْطُ جُمْلَتَيِ الشَّرْطِ);
- ...joining sentences starting with *although, nevertheless* (مَعَ أَنَّ or عَلَى الرَّغْمِ مِن);

Classical Arabic **does not know such** applications of إِلّا. In fact, it is regarded as bad (linguistically weak) style. It is better to link these sentences by فَ. If you use فَ, don't forget that you need the particle إِنَّ (instead of أَنَّ which is used with إِلَّا) – see *question #256*.

Although the exam is difficult, I am sure I will succeed.	
bad style	مَعَ أَنَّ الْإِمْتِحانَ صَعْبٌ إِلَّا أَنَّنِي مُتَأَكِّدٌ مِن النَّجاحِ.
better style	مَعَ أَنَّ الْإِمْتِحانَ صَعْبٌ فَإِنَّنِي مُتَأَكِّدٌ مِن النَّجاحِ.

If the issue is thorny, even then we will fix it (we can address it).	
bad style	إِذا كانَتْ الْقَضِيّةُ شائِكَةً إِلَّا أَنَّنا نَسْتَطِيعُ مُعالَجَتَها.
better style	إِذا كانَتْ الْقَضِيّةُ شائِكَةً فَإِنَّنا نَسْتَطِيعُ مُعالَجَتَها.

Although the situation is difficult, even then we will be able to face it. Even though the situation is difficult, we can confront it.	
bad style	مَعَ أَنَّ الْمَوْقِفَ صَعْبٌ إِلَّا أَنَّنا نَسْتَطِيعُ مُواجَهَتَهُ.
better style	مَعَ أَنَّ الْمَوْقِفَ صَعْبٌ فَإِنَّنا نَسْتَطِيعُ مُواجَهَتَهُ.

406. Are there alternatives to إِلَّا؟

Yes, there are.

إِلَّا is a <u>particle</u> of exception (حَرْفُ الْإِسْتِثْناءِ) which has a cemented shape (مَبْنِيٌّ) and does not get case inflections. But there are also <u>nouns</u> (اِسْمٌ) that can do the same job. These words are called أَسْماءُ الْإِسْتِثْناءِ.

Two examples of such words are غَيْرُ and سِوَى. Since they both are a اِسْمٌ, we suddenly deal with different grammatical topics. Both words form the first part of a إِضافَةٌ, and you treat and mark them according to their function/place in the sentence. Let's see how it works.

1	All students came except for Zayd.	حَضَرَ الطُّلابُ غَيْرَ زَيْدٍ.
2		حَضَرَ الطُّلابُ سِوَى زَيْدٍ.

| 1+2 | Subject (فاعِل) of the verb حَضَرَ and therefore in the nomi- | الطُّلابُ |

	native case (مَرْفُوعٌ بِالضَّمَّةِ الظَّاهِرةِ).	
1	The الْمُسْتَثْنَى, therefore in the accusative case (مَنْصُوبٌ). It is the first part of a إِضافةٌ.	غَيْرَ
2	This is the الْمُسْتَثْنَى in the accusative (مَنْصُوبٌ), marked by an imaginary, virtual فَتْحةٌ since the last letter cannot carry (التَّعَذُّر) the case marker. It is also the first part of the إِضافةٌ.	سِوَى
1+2	2nd part of the إِضافةٌ, genitive case (مُضافٌ إِلَيْهِ مَجْرُورٌ).	زَيْدٍ

Let's play with this construction.

1. What will happen if we use a **negation**? Then we have two options.

The students did not come, except for Zayd. (None of the students came but Zayd.)	مَا حَضَرَ الطُّلابُ غَيْرِ زَيْدٍ.

In this example, we use the device ما (a حَرْفُ نَفْي) to negate the sentence followed by the verb plus its subject (فَاعِلٌ). Which final vowel should we put on غَيْر? **You have the choice:**

option 1	The الْمُسْتَثْنَى; it takes the accusative case (مَنْصُوبٌ).	غَيْرَ
option 2	Apposition: the substitution of the part for the whole (بَدَلُ الْبَعْضِ مِن الْكُلّ). It is aimed at the subject, so it also takes the nominative case (مَرْفُوعٌ).	غَيْرُ
	Second part of the إِضافةٌ; genitive case (مُضافٌ إِلَيْهِ مَجْرُورٌ).	زَيْدٍ

2. What happens if غَيْر is **connected with a direct object**?

Also then we have **two options**. But watch out! You don't see the difference because they look the same on paper.

I did not see the students, except for Zayd.	مَا رَأَيْتُ الطُّلابَ غَيْرَ زَيْدٍ.
الطُّلابَ is the direct object (مَفْعُولٌ بِهِ) in the accusative case (مَنْصُوبٌ).	

option 1	الْمُسْتَثْنَى, therefore in the accusative case (مَنْصُوبٌ).	غَيْرَ
option 2	Apposition; substitution of the part for the whole (بَدَلُ	

الْبَعْضِ مِنَ الْكُلِّ) for the **direct object**! Thus, it also has to be in the **accusative** (مَنْصُوبٌ) because an apposition al-ways takes the same case as the word it refers to.

3. What happens if the الْمُسْتَثْنَى مِنْهُ is **not there**?

No one came, except for Zayd.	مَا حَضَرَ غَيْرُ زَيْدٍ.
The مَا is a negation particle (حَرْفُ نَفْيٍ), followed by a past tense verb.	

Where is the subject in this sentence?

Subject (فَاعِلٌ) in the nominative case (مَرْفُوعٌ). This word is also the first part of a إِضَافَةٌ.	غَيْرُ
Second part of the إِضَافَةٌ; genitive case (مُضَافٌ إِلَيْهِ مَجْرُورٌ).	زَيْدٍ

4. What happens if there is a **preposition** (حَرْفُ الْجَرِّ) **involved**? For example, the preposition بـ?

As usual, the preposition drags the word (in our situation: غَيْر) into the genitive case (مَجْرُورٌ).

Note that in the following example, بـ is needed by the verb and is thus not redundant (extra).

I only passed (by) Zayd.	مَا مَرَرْتُ بِغَيْرِ زَيْدٍ.

407. What does the word بَيْدَ mean?

It conveys the meaning of although, whereas; but, however, yet.

بَيْدَ (in older texts also مَيْدَ) can be used as a synonym for غَيْر. There-fore, it is treated as a device to convey an exception or exclusion. بَيْدَ conveys the meaning of *although, whereas*. When it introduces a sen-tence, it denotes *yet; however*.

Three requirements must be fulfilled to use بَيْدَ:

1. بَيْدَ has to be the first part of a إِضَافَةٌ. It is only found in the position

of an **accusative case**.

2. The second part of the إضافةٌ is an interpreted مَصْدَرٌ. This مَصْدَرٌ **مُؤَوَّلٌ** is molded by أَنَّ and its governed parts (مُلازِمٌ لِلْإِضافةِ إِلَى أَنَّ **وَمَعْمُولَيْها**).

3. It must be an *interrupted, discontinuous exception* (اِسْتِثْناءٌ مُنْقَطِعٌ). This means that the excluded/extracted word is <u>not</u> of the same kind as the overall group to which it refers. Let's look at an example:

The travelers arrived, except for their luggage (belongings).	وَصَلَ الْمُسافِرُونَ إِلّا أَمْتِعَتَهُمْ.
Note: the words *travelers* and *luggage* are not of the same kind.	

Let's quickly check an example in which the main group and the extracted are of the same kind (اِسْتِثْناءٌ مُتَّصِلٌ):

The students came, but not Zayd.	حَضَرَ الطُّلابُ إِلّا زَيْدًا.

That's it for the rules. Let's analyze an example of بَيْدَ.

Zayd is intelligent, but he is negligent.	زَيْدٌ ذَكِيٌّ بَيْدَ أَنَّهُ مُهْمِلٌ.

Subject (مُبْتَدَأٌ) of the nominal sentence; nominative case (مَرْفُوعٌ).	زَيْدٌ
Predicate (خَبَرٌ) in the nominative case (مَرْفُوعٌ).	ذَكِيٌّ
الْمُسْتَثْنَى, in the accusative (مَنْصُوبٌ). First part of the إضافةٌ.	بَيْدَ
Particle of emphasis/strengthening which governs another word in the accusative case (حَرْفُ تَوْكِيدٍ وَنَصْبٍ).	أَنَّ
Pronominal suffix (ضَمِيرٌ مُتَّصِلٌ), serving as the اِسْمُ أَنَّ; thus, it is grammatically placed in the position of an accusative case (فِي مَحَلِّ نَصْبٍ). Nevertheless, we can't put the case marker because the pronoun has a fixed shape.	هُ
Predicate (خَبَر أَنَّ) in the nominative case (مَرْفُوعٌ).	مُهْمِلٌ

Now, where is the second part of the إضافةٌ? ➡ It is the **interpreted** مَصْدَرٌ (مَصْدَرٌ مُؤَوَّلٌ) consisting of أَنَّ and its governed parts (مَعْمُولَاها). This مَصْدَرٌ مُؤَوَّلٌ serves in the position of the **second part** of the إضافةٌ.

Therefore, we treat the entire expression as appearing in the place of a genitive case (فِي مَحَلِّ جَرٍّ مُضافٌ إلَيْهِ).

Two more examples:

| He went but did not arrive. | ذَهَبَ بَيْدَ أَنَّهُ لَمْ يَصِلْ. |
| He has a lot of money (is rich), but he is un-generous/stingy. | هُوَ كَثِيرُ الْمَالِ بَيْدَ أَنَّهُ بَخِيلٌ. |

408. What function has the ما in the expression ما خَلَا or ما عَدا?

It is not a negation. It is a device to mold an infinitive noun.

In the previous *questions*, we have examined particles (حَرْفٌ) and nouns (اِسْمٌ) that can be used for an *exception* or *exclusion* (اِسْتِثْناءٌ). But there are other words too, also verbs (فِعْلٌ), which can denote *except* and express an exception. We will examine three words which may change their own nature (verb or particle) depending on the application. Let's see what makes them really special.

1. They may be interpreted as **verbs** that govern a direct object in the **accusative** case. This happens when we use them with ما. ➡ It is the most common application.	عَدا خَلَا
2. They may be interpreted as **prepositions** (حَرْفُ الْجَرِّ) which drag a following word into the **genitive** case (مَجْرُورٌ). This is the situation when we use them without ما.	حاشا
3. You put a ما (so-called ما الْمَصْدَرِيّةُ) before them and interpret the entire expression as a مَصْدَرٌ (infinitive noun). ➡ We get a verbal meaning. Note that some grammarians say that this is only possible with عَدا and خَلَا - but not with the verb حاشا.	

Let's focus on the ما which is the most confusing part of these words. Some readers may assume that ما is a negation – but it is not. Why? ➡ The الْمُسْتَثْنَى, which comes after ما, is in the **accusative** (مَنْصُوبٌ) and expresses the **direct object** (مَفْعُولٌ بِهِ).

| The students came, except for Zayd. | حَضَرَ الطُّلابُ ما عَدا زَيْدًا. |

	حَضَرَ الطُّلابُ ما خَلا زَيْدًا.
➡ Note that حاشا does **not** work with ما!	حَضَرَ الطُّلابُ (ما) حاشا زَيْدًا.

Strict grammarians would consider the expression ما حاشا as incorrect; others approve it and say that it is of weak style, but understandable.

What is the actual meaning of these constructions?

The students appeared leaving behind Zayd.	حَضَرَ الطُّلابُ مُجاوِزِينَ زَيْدًا.

مُجاوِزٌ is the passive participle (اسْمُ الْمَفْعُولِ) of the III-verb جاوَزَ - يُجاوِزُ (R2=و; *to exceed; to go beyond*). It does the job of a verb.

This is **not** a device for the negation! It is a particle that has the power to form an interpreted مَصْدَرٌ, so we call it a حَرْفُ مَصْدَرِيَّةٍ. The resulting مَصْدَرٌ مُؤَوَّلٌ consists of ما and the verb عَدا (or خَلا). Note that the ما does not have a position in إِعْرابٌ.	ما
Past tense verb (فِعْلٌ ماضٍ). Its subject (فاعِلٌ) is a hidden pronominal suffix (ضَمِيرٌ مُسْتَتِرٌ) expressing *he* (هُوَ). The interpreted مَصْدَرٌ is in the **place of a** حالٌ linked to the verb حَضَرَ; thus, it is grammatically located in the position of an accusative (فِي مَحَلِّ نَصْبٍ حالٌ).	عَدا خَلا
Direct object (مَفْعُولٌ بِهِ) of the verb حَضَرَ, accusative case (مَنْصُوبٌ).	زَيْدًا

What happens if you use these words without ما? You get **two options**:

1. You treat them as **verbs** (like in the previous analysis).

2. Or you treat them as a **preposition** (حَرْفُ الْجَرِّ).

1	The students came, except for Zayd.	حَضَرَ الطُّلابُ عَدا زَيْدًا.
2		حَضَرَ الطُّلابُ عَدا زَيْدٍ.

1+2	Verb plus subject (فاعِلٌ).	حَضَرَ الطُّلابُ

| 1 | Past tense verb (فِعْلٌ ماضٍ). Its subject (فاعِلٌ) is a hidden pronominal suffix (ضَمِيرٌ مُسْتَتِرٌ) expressing *he* (هُوَ). This verbal sentence is in the place of a حال connected with the verb حَضَرَ; | عَدا |

		thus, it is in the position of an accusative case (فِي مَحَلِّ نَصْبٍ).	
	2	Preposition (حَرْفُ جَرّ). It does not have a position in إِعْرابٌ.	
	1	Direct object (مَفْعُولٌ بِهِ) of حَضَرَ; accusative case (مَنْصُوبٌ).	زَيْدًا
	2	Noun in the genitive by the preposition عَدا. The prepositional phrase (الْجارُّ وَالْمَجْرُورُ) is linked to the verb حَضَرَ.	زَيْدٍ

THE PARTICULARIZATION (أُسْلُوبُ الْإِخْتِصاصِ)

409. What is a *particularization* in Arabic?

The particularization is a noun which clarifies a pronoun.

This type of construction is common in contemporary Arabic. Let's look at an example to see what it is about.

We, the students, ...	... نَحْنُ الطُّلابَ

The *particularization* or *specification* (الْإِخْتِصاصِ) is a grammar term given to a noun in the accusative case (اِسْمٌ مَنْصُوبٌ) which follows a free personal pronoun, usually *I* or *we*. The noun in the accusative is a type of direct object.

The اِسْمٌ مَنْصُوبٌ is used to **clarify** the preceding **pronoun**. It lifts its built-in *obscurity, incomprehensibility* (إِبْهامٌ) or *lack of clarity* (غُمُوضٌ).
→ The *particularization* explains what is actually meant (مَخْصُوصٌ) by the preceding pronoun.

Why is the *particularization* regarded as a direct object and therefore takes the accusative case (مَنْصُوبٌ)? We assume that there is a hidden, virtual verb in the sentence which was deleted (قَبْلَهُ فِعْلٌ مَحْذُوفٌ وُجُوبًا) as it is implicitly understood: أَعْنِي (*I mean*) or *I specify* (أَخُصُّ). Grammarians call that an ellipsis. The particularization – the word in the accusative case – was the direct object of those verbs. That is how it got the accusative case ending (مَنْصُوبٌ) and explains why we use the term *direct object* (الْمَفْعُولُ بِهِ عَلَى الْإِخْتِصاصِ).

Where should the *specification* be placed in the sentence?

The اِسْمٌ مُنْصُوبٌ is placed between the subject (مُبْتَدَأٌ) and the predicate (خَبَرٌ). We have a primary, nominal sentence (جُمْلةٌ اِسْمِيّةٌ). The
personal pronoun supplies the position of the subject (مُبْتَدَأٌ), followed
by the اِسْمٌ مُنْصُوبٌ, which clarifies the intention of the pronoun. Then
comes the predicate (خَبَرٌ).

Let's analyze the word in the accusative case (اِسْمٌ مَنْصُوبٌ). We said
that we need to assume a virtual, estimated verb. It is good to stop here
and think about what that means. If there is a verb, then there is also a
subject! But where is the فاعِلٌ of the deleted verb? We assume that the
subject is hidden (فاعِلٌ مُسْتَتِرٌ). All in all, we had a verbal sentence (
جُمْلةٌ فِعْلِيّةٌ), but this verbal sentence **doesn't impact other parts of the
sentence**; it does not have a place in إِعْرابٌ since it is inserted neutrally
between the مُبْتَدَأٌ and the خَبَرٌ. ➡ It is as a **parenthesis** – see #82.

What needs to be fulfilled to make such a construction work?

1. In most situations, the الْإِسْمُ الْمَنْصُوبُ is used in <u>nominal</u> sentences (جُمْلةٌ اِسْمِيّةٌ).

2. The الْإِسْمُ الْمَنْصُوبُ must be <u>definite</u> which can be achieved by ال
   or by serving as the first part of a إِضافةٌ (followed by a definite word
   with ال, a proper name, a pronoun, etc.)

3. The الْإِسْمُ الْمَنْصُوبُ has to be preceded by a <u>pronoun</u>, generally of
   the first person – *I* or *we* (ضَمِيرُ الْمُتَكَلِّم) –, rarely of the second
   person (ضَمِيرُ الْمُخاطَبِ; *pronoun of the person spoken-to*): *you*. It is
   impossible to use it with *he, she, it, they* (ضَمِيرُ الْغائِبِ).

4. The الْإِسْمُ الْمَنْصُوبُ must specify the pronoun.

5. There is <u>no verb</u> that interferes with the construction.

Let's go into the details and analyze some examples.

1. The اِسْمٌ is <u>definite</u> (مَعْرِفةٌ) by ال which is the common application.

We Muslims are united. (We, I mean the Muslims, are united.)	نَحْنُ - الْمُسْلِمِينَ - مُوَحِّدُونَ.

| Personal pronoun (ضَمِيرٌ مُنْفَصِلٌ) which is placed as the sub- | نَحْنُ |

ject (مُبْتَدَأٌ) of the nominal sentence (جُمْلَةٌ اسْمِيّةٌ). Since it has a fixed shape (مَبْنِيٌّ), what you see is not the case marker although coincidentally, it would be the correct one. We assign a "place value" and say that the pronoun is located in the place of the subject (فِي مَحَلِّ رَفْعٍ مُبْتَدَأً) of the nominal sentence, occupying the position of a nominal case.	
Noun in the accusative because it does the job of the **specification** (مَنْصُوبٌ عَلَى الإِخْتِصَاصِ). The case marker of the accusative (مَنْصُوبٌ بِالْياءِ) is the letter ي of the sound masculine plural. We can say that it is the direct object (مَفْعُولٌ بِهِ) of the deleted verb (فِعْلٌ مَحْذُوفٌ); thus, it has to be in the accusative as the verb has the estimated meaning of, for example, أَخُصُّ. The subject (فَاعِلٌ) is the hidden, implied pronoun (ضَمِيرٌ مُسْتَتِرٌ). The sentence consisting of the deleted verb and the direct object does not have a place in إِعْرابٌ because it is a **parenthesis** (جُمْلَةٌ اعْتِراضِيّةٌ).	الْمُسْلِمِينَ
Predicate (خَبَرٌ) of the nominal sentence; nominative by the و since we have a sound masculine plural (مَرْفُوعٌ بِالْواوِ).	مُوَحِّدُونَ

2. The اسْمٌ is the <u>first part</u> of a إِضافةٌ (مُضافٌ) to a definite word.

We – the students of science – strive to learn.	نَحْنُ - طُلّابَ الْعِلْمِ - نَجْتَهِدُ فِي التَّحْصِيلِ.
طُلّابَ is the direct object of the deleted verb which expresses (implicitly) *I specify* (أَخُصُّ); *I mean*. The verbal sentence (starting with نَجْتَهِدُ) is in the place of the predicate of the nominal sentence (فِي مَحَلِّ رَفْعٍ خَبَرٌ).	

3. The اسْمٌ is a <u>proper noun</u> (عَلَمٌ). This is rare.

I – Zayd – defend the truth.	أَنا زَيْدًا أُدافِعُ عَنِ الْحَقِّ.

4. A special situation: the الإِسْمُ الْمَنْصُوبُ is represented by the (indeclinable) word أَيّ or أَيّة (feminine) <u>combined with the word</u> ها which is a particle of attention (ها التَّنْبِيهِ). This type of أَيّ is used by a

speaker to call attention to himself or to himself and his companions.

This combined expression **must be followed by a definite noun**, usually definite by الـ. ➡ أَيُّها has to be preceded by the personal pronoun to which أَيُّها refers. Note that this pronoun is never prefixed by يا.

The use of أَيّ and أَيّة in the أُسْلُوبُ الإِخْتِصاصِ is more common in Modern Standard Arabic than in Classical Arabic.

1	...and so we remained behind, O three [we three].	...فَتَخَلَّفْنا أَيَّتُها الثَّلاثَةُ.
2	As for me I will do so and so, O man [meaning himself].	أَمّا أَنا فَأَفْعَلُ كَذا أَيُّها الرَّجُلُ.
3	Allah's Messenger said: "Every Umma [nation] has a man of trust, and the man of trust of this [i.e., Muslim] nation is Abū ʿUbayda bin al-Jarrāḥ." *(Ṣaḥīḥ al-Bukhari 3744)*	إِنَّ لِكُلِّ أُمَّةٍ أَمِينًا، وَإِنَّ أَمِينَنَا أَيَّتُها الأُمَّةُ أَبُو عُبَيْدَةَ بْنُ الْجَرّاحِ.
4	As for me as an Arab, I am generous.	أَنا - أَيُّها الْعَرَبِيُّ - كَرِيمٌ.
	This is the actual meaning of the above construction: ➡	أَنا - مَخْصُوصًا مِن بَيْنِ النّاسِ بِالْعَرَبِيِّ - كَرِيمٌ.

أَنا	Subject (مُبْتَدَأٌ) of the nominal sentence (جُمْلَةٌ إِسْمِيّةٌ).
أَيّ	**Direct object** (مَفْعُولٌ بِهِ) which does not receive the actual case marker because it is indeclinable (مَبْنِيٌّ عَلَى الضَّمِّ). Thus, we say that it occupies the place of an accusative case (فِي مَحَلِّ نَصْبٍ). It is governed by a deleted verb, e.g., أَخُصُّ, which has a hidden/implied (مُسْتَتِرٌ) subject (فاعِلٌ). The verbal sentence does not have a position in إِعْرابٌ ➡ because it is a parenthesis.
ها	Particle of attention (حَرْفُ تَنْبِيهٍ). Doesn't have a place in إِعْرابٌ.
الْعَرَبِيُّ	You have two ways to treat this word grammatically: 1) **Apposition** (بَدَلٌ) to the subject أَنا. As an apposition it takes the same case marker as the word to which it refers; thus, it receives the nominative case (مَرْفُوعٌ بِالضَّمّةِ الظّاهِرَةِ). 2) **Adjective** (صِفةٌ). Since an adjective has to agree with the word it describes (which is the subject أَنا), it has to be in the

nominative case (مَرْفُوعٌ) as well.	
Predicate (خَبَرٌ) in the nominative case (مَرْفُوعٌ).	كَرِيمٌ

Remark: In older texts, أَيّ or أَيّة were often used after **verbal sentences** (جُمْلةٌ فِعْلِيّةٌ). This would mean that the **specification** would be in the place of a حال for the preceding pronoun; therefore, it would grammatically also get the accusative case (فِي مَحَلِّ نَصْبٍ).

O our Lord, forgive us, the poor!	رَبَّنَا اغْفِرْ لَنَا أَيُّها الْمَسَاكِينُ!
This is the meaning of the sentence: ➡	رَبِّ اغْفِرْ لَنَا مَخْصُوصِينَ مِنْ بَيْنِ النَّاسِ بِالْمَساكِينَ.

Did you notice that there is no ي in the last sentence (first word)? Well, in the vocative, the suffix of the first person singular *my* (ي) is usually shortened to a كَسْرةٌ. For example: "*Oh my lord!*" (يا رَبِّ). If you use the vocative without an interjection particle (which is possible, see *question #412*), you could also omit the ي: "*My lord, show me!*" (رَبِّ أَرِني).
We need the كَسْرةٌ before the ي (see *question #37* for a detailed explanation). Therefore, we must use a كَسْرةٌ and nothing else. Nevertheless, we still treat this word as a vocative in the accusative case (مُنادًى مَنْصُوبٌ).

The verb اغْفِرْ in the above example is an imperative form and used as an **invocation** (فِعْلُ دُعاءٍ). The word الْمَساكِينُ is an **apposition** (بَدَلٌ) in the nominative case.

THE OCCUPIED REGENT (الْإِشْتِغالُ)
OR: EMPHASIS BY WORD ORDER

410. هَلْ زَيْدًا ضَرَبْتَهُ؟ - Why is Zayd here in the accusative case?

Because it is the direct object. But not of the verb you see.

هَلْ زَيْدًا ضَرَبْتَهُ؟ means: *Did you hit Zayd?*

Such constructions are among the most difficult for non-native speakers of Arabic. It is mainly used to lay emphasis by word order and repetition. In Arabic, such constructions are called إِشْتِغالٌ (lit.: *state of being busy, occupied*). In books, you will find the terms *verbal occupation* or *syntactical distraction*. اِشْتِغالٌ is known by grammarians from al-Mubarrad (الْمُبَرّد) on and by Sībawayhi (سيبويه) as سَبَبٌ (*link*).

What is happening? The object is fronted and its original position (after the word) is occupied by a pronoun – with the result that *one regent* (عامِلٌ واحِدٌ) would **face two patients** (مَعْمُولانِ); thus, we have to take the pressure off the regent. Either we use a different case for the first noun, or we need to find an invisible, underlying operator so that we can explain the accusative case. We need to introduce three terms:

- الْمَشْغُولُ عَنْهُ (lit: the distracted): the noun at the beginning. This is the fronted noun that is replaced by a pronominal suffix in the accusative case that indicates the previously mentioned noun.

- الْمَشْغولُ: the operator (الْعامِلُ). This is the verb that governs the pronominal suffix.

- الْمَشْغولُ بِه or شاغِلٌ (lit: the busy one; processed): the pronominal suffix = the referential pronoun, the returner. It replaces the fronted noun and establishes a link to it.

In our example, the noun at the beginning (زَيْدًا) is followed by a verb (ضَرَبْتَ). This verb, however, does not govern زَيْدًا, but the attached pronoun (ه). The pronoun then refers back to the noun (زَيْدًا) at the beginning.

So, how can we explain the accusative case in زَيْدًا? First of all, you don't have to. Regarding the noun, you can apply the nominative or accusative case. Let's focus on the accusative case first.

The interesting thing here is the following: the word at the beginning (زَيْدًا) would be in the accusative case if the pronoun wasn't there. Then it would simply be a sentence with inverted word order, and we would have a fronted direct object:

You hit Zayd.	زَيْدًا ضَرَبْتَ.
Zayd, you hit him. (German: Den Zayd, du hast ihn geschlagen).	زَيْدًا ضَرَبْتَهُ.

Let's make the problem a little clearer:

- If you say قَرَأْتُ الْكِتابَ (*I read the book*), you have one sentence.
- If you say الْكِتابَ قَرَأْتُهُ (*The book, I read it*), you suddenly have two sentences!

Let's dig deeper and use the above introduced grammar terms.

Did you hit Zayd? (Zayd, did you hit him?)	هَلْ زَيْدًا ضَرَبْتَهُ؟

How do you explain the accusative (زَيْدًا)? If we only use the verb ضَرَبَ for the analysis, we get a problem as this verb can only take **one** object.

Let's do the test, change the word order in our mind and put زَيْدًا at the end: ضَرَبْتُهُ زَيْدًا – no, this sentence would not work in Arabic.

But does this mean that our sentence with the **fronted direct object** is incorrect? No, it doesn't! We just have to find a way to do it.

First of all, we already attached a pronoun to the verb which functions as the direct object (هُ). What can we do with the other direct object (زَيْدًا)? Linguists know the concept of *implication of a missing (syntactical) part*, the Arabic concept of تَقْدِيرٌ. We need to imagine a word in our mind that would fit into the sentence and make it work. The easiest solution is to use the same verb again.

Did you hit Zayd, did you hit him?	هَلْ ضَرَبْتَ زَيْدًا ضَرَبْتَهُ؟

	Question word (حَرْفُ إِسْتِفْهامٍ); this word does not have a position in إِعْرابٌ.	هَلْ
deleted verb (فِعْلٌ مَحْذُوفٌ)	The verb ضَرَبْتَ had to be deleted because it is explained by the occupied regent (مُشْتَغِلٌ).	...
distracted from the regent (مَشْغُولٌ عَنْهُ)	Direct object of the deleted verb (مَفْعُولٌ بِهِ لِفِعْلٍ مَحْذُوفٍ). It is the **first patient** (مَعْمُولٌ أَوَّلُ) of the verb which usually only governs one.	زَيْدًا
occupied or busy regent (عامِلٌ مُشْتَغِلٌ) or (عامِلٌ مَشْغُولٌ)	This verb (as an operator) is busy with governing the pronoun. Usually, the word that follows the standard rules has the priority over other words. The standard rule in Arabic is: the direct object follows the regent.	ضَرَبْتَ
occupied by	Returning pronoun (ضَمِيرٌ عائِدٌ) serving as the di-	هُ

| the regent (مَشْغُولٌ بِه) | rect object of the verb ضَرَبْتَ. It is the **second patient** (مَعْمُولٌ ثَانٍ). Since the first object denotes the same meaning as the second, we can say that the regent of the first object (*Zayd*) is explained by the second part of the sentence (verb plus returning pronoun). | |

Now, what will happen if we have an **intransitive verb** (فِعْلٌ لَازِمٌ) which are verbs that do **not** have a direct object?

| I passed Khālid. (Khālid, I passed him.) | خَالِدًا مَرَرْتُ بِهِ. |

We cannot assume that the verb, which governs the first word in the accusative, is the verb مَرَّ because this verb always needs to go along with the preposition ب which induces the genitive case. What should we do? How could we explain this sentence grammatically? We need to think about a **different verb** which could do the job. For example:

| I met Khālid. (Khālid, I met him.) | خَالِدًا لَقِيتُهُ. |

In general, there are two ways to treat اِشْتِغَالٌ-constructions.

Option A. You bring the noun forward and place the verb after it. This verb works as a regent for the *referential, returning pronoun* (فِعْلٌ عَامِلٌ فِي الضَّمِيرِ الْعَائِدِ) that is attached to the verb. The pronoun refers back to the fronted noun. For example: *You hit Zayd* (زَيْدٌ / زَيْدًا ضَرَبْتَهُ).

Option B. You bring the noun (تَقْدِيمُ الْاِسْمِ) forward and let the verb follow it. However, the verb then is the regent for another noun that works as the first part of a إِضَافَةٌ and follows the verb. The second part of the إِضَافَةٌ is a *referential, turning pronoun* that refers back to the very first noun. For example: *You hit Zayd's boy* (زَيْدٌ / زَيْدًا ضَرَبْتَ وَلَدَهُ).

Let us now focus on the possible case endings.

| 1. The accusative case |

| I hit Zayd. (Zayd, I hit him.) | زَيْدًا ضَرَبْتُهُ. |

Here we say that *Zayd* is the **fronted direct object** (مَفْعُولٌ بِهِ مُقَدَّمٌ). Some call that an *isolated accusative*. What about the pronoun (ه)? It is located in the place of an accusative case (فِي مَحَلِّ نَصْبٍ). The pronoun serves as a **confirmation/emphasis** (تَوْكِيدٌ) and is governed by the verb.

The pronoun – regarding its meaning – denotes the same as the fronted noun. There is only one problem which especially occurs with option B. The verb ضَرَبَ can only govern **one** object. But here, we have two. How can we explain that there are two accusatives? We assume that the verb, that governs the first noun, is deleted. The actual meaning of the sentence would be: *I hit Zayd, I hit him.* (زَيْدًا ضَرَبْتُ ضَرَبْتُهُ.)

Note: In reality, it is not allowed to repeat the (implicitly understood) verb because we would ruin the rhythm and purpose (confirmation) of the construction.

We can derive **three points** which you should keep in mind if you want **to apply the accusative case** in such constructions:

- You **can't insert anything** between the fronted noun and the verb.

  Therefore, you <u>cannot</u> say: زَيْدًا أَنْتَ ضَرَبْتَهُ.

  Instead, you <u>must</u> say: زَيْدٌ أَنْتَ ضَرَبْتَهُ.

- The accusative case only works if the **verb can be conjugated** (فِعْلٌ مُتَصَرِّفٌ). In other words, the fronted noun can't take the accusative case if the regent (الْعَامِلُ) is a comparative or superlative (تَفْضِيلٌ), a pseudo participle that indicates firmness (صِفَةٌ مُشَبَّهَةٌ), an infinitive noun (مَصْدَرٌ), or a simple letter or particle (حَرْفٌ).

  ➡ This is because such words may work as a regent in a standard sentence (with standard word-order), however, they do not extend their governing power to what precedes them!

- If the الْمَشْغُولُ عَنْهُ is in the accusative, it is usually the direct object (مَفْعُولٌ بِهِ) of a verb that had to be **deleted** (فِعْلٌ مَحْذُوفٌ وُجُوبًا).

Watch out: There are situations in which you **have to use** the accusative case. This happens if you have a device that is followed by a verb:

- **conditional particles** (أَدَواتُ الشَّرْطِ) like إِنْ;
- **question particles** (الْإِسْتِفهامُ) like هَلْ;
- **requests** (الْعَرْضُ and التَّحْضيضُ) like هَلّا.

Why is that? ➡ You are <u>not</u> allowed to use the **nominative** case and treat the word after the particle as the subject (مُبْتَدَأٌ) because this wouldn't work in Arabic – the particles have to go along with a verb. Therefore, you need the accusative case:

If you use your knowledge, it will benefit you.	إِنِ الْعِلْمَ خَدَمْتَهُ نَفَعَكَ.

In the above example, the verb was in the past tense. Coincidence? No! Now comes a finesse. Such constructions don't work if you have a conditional particle that puts verbs into the **jussive** mood (مَجْزُومٌ), and if this is done **visibly** (لَفْظًا). In other words, you have a conditional particle such as إِنْ and the verb is in the present tense (مُضارِعٌ) and ends in سُكُونٌ (jussive mood).

This is different, however, if the verb is in the **past tense** and therefore, the jussive mood (مَجْزُومٌ) cannot be marked visibly but only by a "place value" (مَحَلّا). This is because you cannot put a past tense verb visibly into the jussive mood as past tense verbs are مَبْنِيٌّ; *see #43*. Let's make the difference clear:

correct	past tense	If you meet Zayd, treat him with respect! (honor him)	إِنْ زَيْدًا لَقِيْتَهُ فَأَكْرِمْهُ!
incorrect	present tense, jussive		إِنْ زَيْدًا تَلْقَهُ فَأَكْرِمْهُ!

One last note about the conditional particles. You should only use this construction with the particles إِنْ and لَوْ and إِذا.

2. The nominative case

As for Zayd, I hit him.	زَيْدٌ ضَرَبْتُهُ.

We treat *Zayd* as the subject (مُبْتَدَأٌ) of a nominal sentence which has to be in the nominative case (مَرْفُوعٌ). The verbal sentence (ضَرَبْتُهُ) is the predicate.

Watch out: In some situations, you **have to use** the **nominative case**.

→ This happens when you find the fronted noun (الْمَشْغُولُ عَنْهُ) before certain devices. We will examine them now.

A. After words that **start** a **nominal sentence** (اِبْتِداءً).

The إذا الْفُجائِيّة, which indicates something unexpected, is such a particle. After this device, the subject (مُبْتَدَأً) must follow immediately.

I came out - and behold! - the thief, beaten by the police!	خَرَجْتُ فَإذا اللِّصُّ يَضْرِبُهُ الشُّرْطِيُّ.
اللِّصُّ is the subject (مُبْتَدَأ) of the nominal sentence because after the إذا الْفُجائِيّة, a noun **must** follow. The verbal sentence (يَضْرِبُهُ الشُّرْطِيُّ) serves as the predicate (خَبَر).	

The same logic is applied to the *circumstantial description* (حالٌ) that is introduced by a واوُ الْحالِ. You must use the nominative case after وَ because you cannot place a verb after the وَ. An example of the واوُ الْحالِ:

I traveled while the regime restrained the people from an uprising.	سافَرْتُ والشَّعْبُ يَنْهاهُ النِّظامُ عَنِ الْإِنْتِفاضةِ.

B. Before words that have the **precedence** (صَدارةٌ).

- The relative pronoun (أَدَواتُ الْمَوْصولِ):

It was Zayd that I hit.	زَيْدٌ الَّذي ضَرَبْتُهُ.

- The *Lām of the beginning* (لامُ الْإِبْتِداءِ):

The professor, I honor him!	الْأُستاذُ لَأَنا مَكْرِمُهُ!

- Requests (تَحْضيضٌ):

Your mother, you should respect her!	أُمَّكَ هَلّا اِحْتَرَمْتَها!

- Question words (أَدَواتُ الْإِسْتِفهامِ):

Do you master the language?	اللُّغةُ هَلْ أَتْقَنْتَها؟

Note: If you use the nominative case, then the الْمَشْغُولُ عَنْهُ is usually the subject (مُبْتَدَأ) of a nominal sentence. Two examples of the Qur'an:

Sura 54:24	They said, 'What? A man? Why should we follow a lone man from amongst ourselves? (A. Haleem)	فَقَالُوا أَبَشَرًا مِّنَّا وَاحِدًا نَّتَّبِعُهُ.
	Is it one human being among us that we should follow? (Sahīh International)	

The word بَشَرًا is in the accusative case (مَنْصُوبٌ عَلَى الْإِشْتِغَالِ). If the pronoun wasn't there, the regent (= the verb) would govern the word بَشَرًا. Theoretically, you could also use the nominative case. However, some grammarians say that it is much better to use the accusative after the so-called هَمْزَةُ الْإِسْتِفْهَامِ, i.e., the initial أ used to ask questions.

Sura 36:39	And for the moon, we have determined for it phases. (We have determined phases for the moon.)	وَالْقَمَرَ قَدَّرْنَاهُ مَنَازِلَ.

The word *moon* (الْقَمَرَ) is the direct object of the deleted verb. The omitted verb is explained by the word that follows.

Let's check a quite difficult sentence:

54:52	Everything they did is in their records.	وَكُلُّ شَيْءٍ فَعَلُوهُ فِي الزُّبُرِ.

Note: The word الزُّبُرُ basically means *anything written, scripture* (الْكُتُب).

So, is this a إِشْتِغَالٌ-construction? No, it isn't, although it looks like it at first glance. The verbal sentence فَعَلُوهُ does not control the word كُلُّ; it does not govern كُلُّ as a direct object in the accusative. Why? Because the verbal sentence is an adjective (صِفَة), and an adjective never governs the word it describes (مَوْصُوفٌ).

Thus, كُلُّ necessarily must be the subject (مُبْتَدَأ) and the prepositional phrase (الْجَارُّ وَالْمَجْرُورُ), i.e., the expression فِي الزُّبُرِ, appears in the place of the predicate (خَبَرٌ) – and is connected with the deleted actual predicate (e.g., ثَابِتٌ). We get the following reconstructed meaning:

Everything they did is permanently there in the records.	وَكُلُّ شَيْءٍ فَعَلُوهُ ثَابِتٌ فِي الزُّبُرِ.

That's for the grammar part. But what about the meaning? Would there be any difference? Yes! If the sentence would use a اِشْتِغَالٌ-construction, the meaning would be the following:

They did everything in the records.	وَفَعَلُوا كُلَّ شَيْءٍ فِي الزُّبُرِ.

This would express that the الزُّبُرُ (register) is a place for all things they did. This is not what the Qur'an intended to say.

Excursus: The اِشْتِغَالٌ-construction in the Qur'an.

There are mainly two ideas why it is used. First, there is its **function to bind content**. Its role is to link verses and phrases. The logical relations are as follows: the linked parts may represent opposites or nouns belonging to the same category such as the sun and the moon. In Sura 36:39, the word *moon* is fronted (see above). This indicates a logical relation between the sun (36:38 and 36:40) and the moon. Furthermore, a اِشْتِغَالٌ-construction may denote a **contrast** or a relation of **case and effect**. Very common is also that it marks the **beginning or the end of an idea**.

Secondly, it is a **stylistic device**. The Qur'an uses the اِشْتِغَالٌ-construction to lay **emphasis**; but also to **avoid repetition** of a particular thought through the same structure. Moreover, this structure is used for intonation and **rhythm**. In Sura 80:20, the noun is fronted to prevent deficiency in the rhyme: ثُمَّ ٱلسَّبِيلَ يَسَّرَهُ - (*Then) He makes the way easy for him.*)

Remark: The equivalent to اِشْتِغَالٌ in Biblical Hebrew is called *casus pendens*. The Kūfa grammarians (الْكُوفِيُّونَ) suggested that the fronted accusative noun in اِشْتِغَالٌ-constructions is governed by the visible verb, which then exceptionally governs two objects.

TWO REGENTS WANT TO RULE OVER ONE PATIENT (التَّنَازُعُ)

411. What do you do if you have two verbs but only one subject?

You choose one of the two verbs.

That two verbs wrestle with a subject sounds strange at first. Nevertheless, sentences of this kind do not cause any problems in terms of understanding. Nevertheless, we should know how to use such sentences grammatically; after all, we want to produce sentences that are also correct and not just somehow understood. An example:

Zayd traveled and returned.	سَافَرَ وَعَادَ زَيْدٌ.

Looks logical, so what is the big deal here? Well, both verbs need a subject (فَاعِلٌ): which is *Zayd* (زَيْدٌ). But it is **not allowed that two regents rule over one patient**. The grammarians have a name for this situation: التَّنَازُعُ, which literally means *contention; struggle*.

It describes the situation when **both possible governors (عَامِلٌ)** come **before** the *patient* (the subject or object; مَعْمُولٌ). To make it clear, in a situation of التَّنَازُع, **two** regents point to **one** patient.

You need to do the following: you choose one regent to be the governor of the visible word that comes at the end (الْمَعْمُولُ الْمُتَأَخِّرُ مُتَنَازَعٌ فِيهِ), i.e., after both regents. Which one should you choose?

- The grammarians of the **Kūfa** school (الْكُوفِيُّونَ) assigned the job of the governor to the **first verb**. ➡ In general, they said that the first of all possible governors has the power.

- The grammarians of **Basra** (الْبَصْرِيُّونَ) said that the **second verb** is the governor, because it is closer to the object. ➡ Thus, the regent is the one which is closest to the object.

What should you do with the remaining regent once you have selected one?

- If the contested word is the **subject**, we treat the other governor as ruling over the implied pronoun (الْعَامِلُ الْآخَرُ عَامِلٌ فِي الضَّمِيرِ).

- And if the contested word is the **direct object**, we treat it as not exercising its ruling power (أَنْ يُهْمَلَ الْآخَرُ عَنِ الْعَمَلِ فِيهِ).

Speaking in grammar terms, we have the following construction:

زَيْدٌ	وَعَادَ	...	سَافَرَ
Delayed *patient* (here: subject). زَيْدٌ is fought over by two operators: it is **the contested word** (الْمَعْمُولُ الْمُتَأَخِّرُ مُتَنَازَعٌ فِيهِ). By assuming a *deleted patient* ear-	**Second** operator الْعَامِلُ الثَّانِي	**Deleted** *patient* (here: the subject). In Arabic: الْمَعْمُولُ الْمَحْذُوفُ. It is the word *Zayd* (زَيْدٌ),	**First** operator الْعَامِلُ الْأَوَّلُ

lier in the sentence we can say that it is the **subject** (فاعِلٌ) of the verb عادَ.	however, it is not repeated here as it is explained later in the sentence.

The same idea also works for a direct object.

Sura 18:96	• Bring me molten metal (copper) to pour over it! (*Abdul Haleem*) • Bring me, that I may pour over it molten copper! (*Sahīh Int.*)	آتُوني أُفْرِغْ عَلَيْهِ قِطْرًا! meaning: آتُوني قِطْرًا أُفْرِغْ عَلَيْهِ قِطْرًا

Two verbs (آتُوني and أُفْرِغْ) compete for the control over **one** direct object (قِطْرًا). Both verbs (in the imperative here) demand an object, and this is the word قِطْر which means (*melted*) *copper*.

THE VOCATIVE (النِّداءُ)

412. Why does the word after يا take the مَنْصُوبٌ-case?

Because we assume that it is the direct object of a deleted verb.

The *call/vocative* (جُمْلةُ النِّداءِ) is a special construction in Arabic that is often initiated with يا. What is simple in English can fill entire dissertations in Arabic, because the vocative in Arabic is really complicated.

We have to deal with a sentence as it would give us a full meaning if we stopped at the end of the utterance. It consists of a vocative particle (حَرْفُ النِّداءِ) and a noun – *the one who is being called* (مُنادًى). A sentence cannot just consist of a حَرْفٌ and a اِسْمٌ. Usually we need two parts. A nominal sentence consists of a subject and a predicate; we usually have two اِسْمٌ. The verbal sentence consists of a verb and a subject. The relation between the two parts is termed إِسْنادٌ, *the act of leaning* (one thing against another) or *the relation of attribution* – see #208.

So, is the إِسْنادٌ broken in the vocative? Some grammarians affirm this and therefore call the vocative a جُمْلةٌ غَيْرُ إِسْنادِيّةٍ.

Nevertheless, most grammarians say that the vocative (جُمْلةُ النِّداءِ) is a **full sentence** (جُمْلةٌ تامّةٌ). The components are, in fact, connected, so there is a إِسْنادٌ – but the relationship is not visible (إِسْنادٌ غَيْرُ ظاهِرٍ).

How does it work? The grammarians say that the الْمُنادَى has a kind of **direct object** (مَفْعُولٌ بِهِ), governed in the accusative case (مَنْصُوبٌ) by a <u>deleted verb</u>. This deleted verb has the **equivalent meaning** of *I announce; I call* (أُنادِي) or *I call; I invite* (أَدْعُو). If we use the estimated meaning (= *I call*), we can convert the vocative clause into a جُمْلَةٌ خَبَرِيَّةٌ (*declarative sentence*) – with the effect that we are able to explain the إِسْنادٌ now. But these verbs **never** show up in vocatives. They are substituted by the vocative particle (حَرْفُ النِّداءِ) which takes on their job. Sounds logical, but there is another view.

Many grammarians of the prime of Classical Arabic stated that the جُمْلَةُ النِّداءِ is an *order* or *request* (جُمْلَةٌ طَلَبِيَّةٌ) which means that the vocative doesn't have a predicative meaning. Hence, we don't need to check how these parts are related, in other words, we don't need a إِسْنادٌ. There is no final judgment.

There seven vocative particles (حَرْفُ النِّداءِ). They are distinguished according to how far the addressed person is from the caller.

- for the person that is near (لِلْقَرِيبِ): the Hamza (أ) or يا
- for the person that is neither close nor far (لِلْمُتَوَسِّطِ): أَيْ
- for the person that is far away (لِلْبَعِيدِ): يا or أَيا or هَيا or وَآ
- for the lamentation (نُدْبَةٌ); to express sadness, impatience: وَا

    Note: In practice, you will only encounter يا nowadays.

Vocative particles don't necessarily have to be linked to a person. They may figuratively "address" a **time** (زَمانٌ) or **place** (مَكانٌ). Moreover, they can be interpreted in an **abstract, semantic way** (مَعْنَوِيّ), for example, *the son* (الْاِبْن), *the friend* (الصَّدِيق), *the enemy* (الْعَدُوّ).

Remark: Why don't we use **nunation** (تَنْوِينٌ) in the vocative? Some scholars suggest that this is related to the energy with which the word is spoken. It is shorter and sharper because the ending is clipped. The imperative and the مَجْزُومٌ-mood of the verb follow a similar idea.

413. Which case marker should you use for the person called?

It's complicated.

الْمُنادَى denotes *the person that is being called; called upon.* How should we treat a word serving as the الْمُنادَى grammatically?

We have two options:

a) We assume that the word has a fixed, cemented shape (مَبْنِيٌّ). This means that the الْمُنادَى has one ضَمّة ("*u*") but is considered to be located in the place of an accusative case (فِي مَحَلِّ نَصْبٍ.). There are two different types; we will check them later.

b) The الْمُنادَى gets the regular case inflection. It is مُعْرَبٌ.

---

a) **The fixed shape** (مَبْنِيٌّ). We use the form which the word would get in the nominative case. Nevertheless, the word is located in the place of an accusative case.

Let's start with the **single proper noun** (الْعَلَمُ الْمُفْرَدُ): a proper name of a person. This means that the الْمُنادَى is not part of a إِضافةٌ nor resembling a إِضافةٌ.

1	**singular**	O 'Alī, come closer!	يا عَلِيُّ أَقْبِلْ!
2	**dual**	O you (two) 'Alīs, come closer!	يا عَلِيَّانِ أَقْبِلا!
3	**plural**	O you 'Alīs, come closer!	يا عَلِيُّونَ أَقْبِلُوا!
4	**singular**	O Fātima, come closer!	يا فاطِمةُ أَقْبِلِي!
5	**dual**	O you (two) Fātimas, come closer!	يا فاطِمَتانِ أَقْبِلا!
6	**plural**	O you Fātimas, come closer!	يا فاطِمَاتُ أَقْبِلْنَ!

Watch out! We used the IV-verb أَقْبَلَ (*to approach*). ➡ Never delete the initial Hamza of the IV-pattern أَفْعَلَ if you use the imperative! Form IV is the **only form whose command begins with** أ (= a pronounced glottal stop).

	Vocative particle (حَرْفُ نِداءٍ); it does not have a position in إِعْرابٌ.	يا
1	The *person called upon* (الْمُنادَى). This word, due to its function, has a fixed shaped (مُنادَى مَبْنِيٌّ عَلَى الضَّمِّ). You see the	عَلِيُّ

	"*u*" (ـُ), however, grammatically, we treat the word as being placed in the position of an accusative case (فِي مَحَلِّ نَصْبٍ).	
2	This word is in the dual form. The الْمُنادَى is fixed on the Aleph (مُنادَى مَبْنِيٌّ عَلَى الْأَلِفِ). Nonetheless, we treat it as being located in the place of an accusative case.	عَلِيَّانِ
3	Here the الْمُنادَى is fixed on the و (مُنادَى مَبْنِيٌّ عَلَى الْواوِ). Regarding its position in the sentence, it is in the place of an accusative case (فِي مَحَلِّ نَصْبٍ).	عَلِيُّونَ

The same applies to the *specific call* (النَّكِرَةُ الْمَقْصُودَةُ). This is the situation when the الْمُنادَى is **by its shape and nature <u>indefinite</u>** – but acquires definiteness (التَّعْرِيفُ) by the act of calling the person.

O man, turn forward!	يا رَجُلُ أَقْبِلْ!
O (two) men, turn forward!	يا رَجُلانِ أَقْبِلا!
O (young) woman, turn forward!	يا فَتاةُ أَقْبِلِي!

But that's not all. If an **indefinite مُنادَى** is further described by an adjective (مَوْصُوفَةٌ), then usually it is put into the accusative case (نَصْبٌ) and gets nunation (فَتْحَةٌ).

Allah will help you, oh great leader!	نَصَرَكَ اللهُ يا قائِدًا عَظِيمًا!

Watch out: If you use a demonstrative, you express a derogatory meaning!

Listen, you!	إِسْمَعْ يا هذا! اسْمَعِي يا هذِهِ!

414. How do you call سَعِيد بن زَيْد (*Said son of Zayd*) correctly?

You need to deal with some grammatical problems.

Let's decode the problem:

- We have a **singular proper noun** (الْعَلَمُ الْمُفْرَدُ) – *Said*;
- which is **described** (مَوْصُوفٌ) by the word *son* (ابن) – or *daughter* (بِنْت) – in a إِضافَةٌ-construction.

- The result is that the expression *son of* is placed **in-between two proper names**.

➔ You have two options for the **first proper name** (الْمُنادَى).

In both options, the word, originally a declinable noun, is transformed into one with a fixed, indeclinable shape – but with different last vowels:

1. The word ends in ـُ / "*u*" (الْبِناءُ عَلَى الضَّمِّ).

2. The word ends in ـَ / "*a*" (الْبِناءُ عَلَى الْفَتْحِ).

1	O Saīd son of Zayd, come forward!	يا سَعِيدُ بنَ زَيْدٍ أَقْبِلْ!
2		يا سَعِيدَ بنَ زَيْدٍ أَقْبِلْ!

1	Don't be frightened, o Zayd, son of Amr!	لا تَخَفْ يا زَيْدُ بنَ عَمْرٍو!
2		لا تَخَفْ يا زَيْدَ بنَ عَمْرٍو!

The first approach follows the standard rules for a singular proper noun in the vocative. You will end up with a single ضَمّةٌ since you address a specific person.

1	The الْمُنادَى is **fixed, cemented** (مَبْنِيٌّ عَلَى الضَّمِّ), the last vowel is the "*u*" (ـُ); nevertheless, it is grammatically placed in the position of an **accusative case** (فِي مَحَلِّ نَصْبٍ). For this reason, the word which follows (i.e., بنَ) – an apposition – is in the accusative case as well. Why was the initial letter ا dropped? See *question #100*.	سَعِيدُ
2	The الْمُنادَى has a fixed shape and is built upon an **assumed** "*u*" (مَبْنِيٌّ عَلَى الضَّمِّ الْمُقَدَّرِ). The ضَمّةٌ can't be shown because we have a *follower* here: an apposition. Thus, the "*a*" (فَتْحةٌ) on the proper noun سَعِيدَ "follows" the فَتْحةٌ which is found on the adjective (صِفةٌ): the word ابْن. Therefore, both words need to have the same vowel (grammarians call that حَرَكةُ الْإِتِّباعِ). Therefore, the فَتْحةٌ on top of the proper noun سَعِيدَ in this application follows the فَتْحةٌ found on the last letter of بنَ.	سَعِيدَ
	But that is not all. Other grammarians say that the الْمُنادَى follows a similar pattern as the numbers from 13 to 19.	

	The number 15, for example, is always written as follows: خَمْسةَ عَشَرَ. Both words are fixed/built on the فَتْح regardless of the position in the sentence and thus the case ending.	
1 + 2	Adjective in the accusative case (صِفةٌ مَنْصُوبةٌ), marked by the usual case marker in such a position, i.e., a فَتْحة.	بنَ

Watch out: If you don't find ابن or بِنْت between <u>two</u> **proper** nouns, you don't have a choice. ➡ You must fix the word on the ضَمّ, i.e., it must end with ـُ.

O Yusuf, son of my brother!	يا يُسُفُ ابْنَ أَخِي!

The Hadiths are a good source for studying the vocative. In many sayings and traditions of the Prophet Muhammad, vocatives are used. Here is an example in which you see our discussed topics in action:

The Messenger of Allah said: "O Fātima, daughter of Muhammad. O Safiya, daughter of 'Abd al-Muttalib, O sons of 'Abd al-Muttalib. I have nothing which can avail you against Allah!" (*Sahīh Muslim 205*)	يَا فَاطِمَةَ بِنْتَ مُحَمَّدٍ يَا صَفِيَّةُ بِنْتَ عَبْدِ الْمُطَّلِبِ يَا بَنِي عَبْدِ الْمُطَّلِبِ لا أَمْلِكُ لَكُمْ مِن اللهِ شَيْئًا!

Remark: Once a word is fixed on ـُ in a vocative, this shape will pass on if it is repeated. Even if you call another person, the name of that person will function as an apposition.

O Zayd, Zayd!	يا زَيْدُ زَيْدُ!
O you man there, Zayd!	يا رَجُلُ زَيْدُ!
O Zayd and Amr!	يا زَيْدُ وَعَمْرُو!

415. Can you call someone whose name ends in a weak letter?

Sure. But in order to call him or her correctly, you need to know the rules for a إِسْمٌ مَنْقُوصٌ *or a* إِسْمٌ مَقْصُورٌ.

Many common names, in fact, end in a weak letter:

type		**active** part.	meaning	verb	name
إِسْمٌ مَنْقُوصٌ	الرَّاضِي	رَاضٍ	to be pleased	رَضِيَ	Rādī
	الْهادِي	هادٍ	to guide	هَدَى	Hādī

type		**passive** part.	meaning	verb	name
إِسْمٌ مَقْصُورٌ	الْمُصْطَفَى*	مُصْطَفَى	to choose	إِصْطَفَى	Mustafā

* al-Mustafā is an epithet for the Islamic prophet Muhammad and means *the chosen*.

There are two ways to call a person whose name has such a morphology.

OPTION 1: You **keep** the ي of the إِسْمٌ مَنْقُوصٌ. ➡ This is the more frequent and better option (easier to understand). The same is true for the إِسْمٌ مَقْصُورٌ. ➡ Then, you **keep** the Aleph.

O Rādi, come forward!	يا راضِي أَقْبِلْ!
راضِي	The one called upon (الْمُنادَى); it is fixed/built on the imaginary, estimated ضَمّ-position; in Arabic we say مَبْنِيٌّ عَلَى ضَمٍّ مُقَدَّرٍ. The word can't end in a *"u"*-vowel due to the "heaviness" (الثِّقَلُ) of the last letter, i.e., the ي. But it gets even more complicated. The word راضِي occupies the grammatical place of an accusative case (فِي مَحَلِّ نَصْبٍ) since it serves as the الْمُنادَى.

Two examples of the إِسْمٌ مَقْصُورٌ:

O Mustafā, come forward!	يا مُصْطَفَى أَقْبِلْ!
مُصْطَفَى	The one being called (الْمُنادَى); it is fixed on the imaginary, estimated ضَمّ-position: مَبْنِيٌّ عَلَى ضَمٍّ مُقَدَّرٍ ➡ because the last letter can't carry any vowel (التَّعَذُّرُ). It grammatically serves in the place of an accusative case (فِي مَحَلِّ نَصْبٍ).

| Sura | When he came to the fire, he was | فَلَمَّا أَتَاهَا نُودِيَ يَا مُوسَى! |

20:11	summoned, "Moses!"

OPTION 2: You **delete** the ي.

O Rāḍi, come forward!	يا راضِ أَقْبِلْ!
The one called upon (الْمُنادَى) is fixed on an assumed, virtual position: the "*u*" (مَبْنِيٌّ عَلَى ضَمٍّ مُقَدَّرٍ). But fixed on what and where? ➡ It is on the **deleted** letter ي (عَلَى الْياءِ الْمَحْذُوفَةِ). Indeed, that's quite abstract. But apart from that everything is pretty standard. We treat the word as being placed in the position of an accusative case (فِي مَحَلِّ نَصْبٍ).	راضِ

Let's analyze the situation if you have an **indefinite word** (نَكِرَةٌ) with a **weak letter**. This means: we don't deal with a proper name.

➡ You keep the Aleph in the اِسْمٌ مَقْصُورٌ and the ي in the اِسْمٌ مَنْقُوصٌ as shown in the previous examples of the proper noun (الْعَلَمُ الْمُفْرَدُ). Watch out if you add the possessive pronoun *my* (ي)!

O youth, move forward!	يا فَتَى أَقْبِلْ!
O inattentive, watch out!	يا لاهِي تَنَبَّهْ!
O **my** young boy, move forward!	يا فَتايَ أَقْبِلْ!
O (my) judge!	يا قاضِيَّ

416. How does a blind man call someone?

He uses nunation (تَنْوِينٌ).

Let's check situations in which the الْمُنادَى is **not** treated as an **inde**clinable word with a fixed, cemented ending. Translated into grammar: When does the الْمُنادَى get the case that it would naturally get due to its position, i.e., the accusative (الْمُنادَى الْمُعْرَبُ الْمَنْصُوبُ)?

There are **three situations**.

a) The الْمُنادَى is **indefinite** (النَّكِرَةُ).

This means that the one who is called is not a specific person (غَيْرُ الْمَقْصُودةِ); we say that the call is **not intentional**. The most common example is the **call of a blind man** (قَوْلُ الْأَعَمَى).

O man, take my hand! (said by a blind man)	يا رَجُلًا خُذْ بِيَدِي!
The one being called (الْمُنادَى) is treated as an **indefinite direct object** in the accusative case (مُنادًى مَنْصُوبٌ بِالْفَتْحةِ الظّاهِرةِ).	رَجُلًا

This construction is not only used by blind people. It is frequently found nowadays – when people don't have a specific person in mind.

O repentant, blessed are you!	يا تائِبًا طُوبَى لَكَ!

b) What happens if we have a more complex construction: a إضافةٌ with the الْمُنادَى serving as the first part (الْمُضافُ)?

This type of vocative is quite common.

O doer of good deeds, come!	يا فاعِلَ الْخَيْرِ أَقْبِلْ!
The one being called (الْمُنادَى); مَنْصُوبٌ by an apparent فَتْحةٌ.	فاعِلَ
Second part of the إضافةٌ; in the genitive case (مَجْرُورٌ).	الْخَيْرِ

c) The الشَّبِيهُ بِالْمُضافِ (resembling a possessive construction).

That is a tricky one. We dealt with this topic already in the discussion about the absolute negation (لا النّافِيةُ لِلْجِنْسِ) – see *question #278*.

O generous of nature, please help!	يا كَرِيمًا خُلُقُهُ ساعِدْ!
The one being called (الْمُنادَى), accusative (مَنْصُوبٌ); nunation.	كَرِيمًا
Subject (فاعِلٌ) in the nominative case (مَرْفُوعٌ) by a visible ضَمّةٌ. The pronominal suffix (ضَمِيرٌ مُتَّصِلٌ) is located in the place of a genitive case since it is the second part of the إضافةٌ.	خُلُقُهُ

Remark: In poetry, the vocative may be used with an indefinite word in the accusative case. But this only works if the accusative is followed by additional information!

| O you who would kindle a fire! | يا مُوقِدًا نارًا! |
| O you heroic horseman! | يا رَاكِبًا كَمِيًّا! |

417. What does يا أَبَتِ mean?

It means: O my father!

The possessive pronoun *my* (يَاءُ الْمُتَكَلِّم) is a tricky word that touches many grammatical topics. Some people yell يا أَبِي to express *"O my father!"* Is that wrong? Well, you will struggle to put any sign of a vocative on the expression أَبِي which only means *my father*.

As soon as you use a vocative and add the possessive pronoun *my* to the person you call (الْمُنادَى), you will face several grammatical issues, among them are the topics of compensation and shortening. The إِعْرابٌ of the يَاءُ الْمُتَكَلِّم in the vocative is tough and some rulings are disputed. Let's start the discussion.

a) The most **common solution** (as used also in the headline of this *question*). This works for most vocatives with *my*.

Here is the recipe:

1. First, you **delete** the ي of أَبِي (*my father*) and compensate it with a ت (تاءُ التَّأْنِيثِ). Here the ت doesn't denote a feminine form. ➡ It is only a compensation (للتَّعْوِيضِ عَن ياءِ الْمُتَكَلِّم الْمَحْذُوفةِ). Some scholars say that it conveys some kind of emphasis similar to the idea that the feminine ة amplifies the meaning (see *question #95*).

2. Then you get rid of the "i" (كَسْرةٌ) under the ب since this was only necessary for the possessive pronoun ي. Notice that you still have a إِضافةٌ-construction. ➡ We now arrive at: أَبت.

3. Now you put a فَتْحة on the ب of أَب resulting in أَبَت.

4. Finally, you put a كَسْرة under the additional ت and get the following result: يا أَبَتِ

| أَبَ | *The one being called* (الْمُنادَى) in the accusative by a visible فَتْحةٌ. |

This letter (حَرْفٌ) is used to **compensate for the deleted** ي. The ت does not have a position in إِعْرابٌ. The **deleted** ي is a pronoun that serves in the position of the second part of the إِضافةٌ and virtually takes the place of a genitive case (فِي مَحَلِّ جَرٍّ مُضافٌ إِلَيْهِ).	تِ

My teacher, …!	يا أُستاذِ, …
O (my) father, …!	يا أَبَتِ, …
If you stopped at the end (**pause**), you'd say it this way: ➡	يا أَبَهْ!

When Allah's Messenger came to Medina, Abu Bakr and Bilāl got fever, and I ['Ā'isha] went to both of them and said, "**O my father**, how do you feel?" (*Sahīh al-Bukhārī 3926*)	لَمَّا قَدِمَ رَسُولُ اللهِ الْمَدِينَةَ وُعِكَ أَبُو بَكْرٍ وَبِلَالٌ ـ قَالَتْ ـ فَدَخَلْتُ عَلَيْهِمَا فَقُلْتُ يَا أَبَتِ كَيْفَ تَجِدُكَ

I said to him: "Father, do you prostrate yourself in the path?" (*Sahīh Muslim 520b*)	فَقُلْتُ لَهُ: يَا أَبَتِ أَتَسْجُدُ فِي الطَّرِيقِ؟

The same construction is used for: *Oh my mother!*

O (my) mother, …!	يا أُمَّتِ, …!
In pause, you would say it this way: ➡	يا أُمَّهْ!

If you have a complex إِضافةٌ with three parts, you <u>cannot</u> substitute the ي and must keep it.

3		2		1
my		*heart*		*joy*
Second مُضافٌ إِلَيْهِ ياءُ الْمُتَكَلِّم	+	First مُضافٌ إِلَيْهِ	+	الْمُنادَى
ي or يْ		قَلْبِ		فَرْحةَ

Regarding the vowel of ي, you have a choice: it can be سُكُونٌ or فَتْحةٌ.

O joy of my heart!	يا فَرْحةَ قَلْبِيْ !
	يا فَرْحةَ قَلْبِيَّ !

b) The الْمُنادَى is one of the following words in the table. Then you do **not** keep the ي.

daughter	إِبْنة		son	ابن
niece	ابْنة عَمّ		nephew	ابن عَمّ

You have two options:

1. Delete the possessive pronoun *my* and just keep the كَسْرةٌ on the preceding letter which means: you will have a كَسْرةٌ at the end.

O (my) nephew!	يا بْنَ أُمِّ!

2. Convert the ي into an Aleph (ا). An Aleph needs the vowel "a" before, so we also convert the كَسْرةٌ into a فَتْحةٌ. Then delete the Aleph – but keep the "a" (فَتْحةٌ). *About the Aleph, see also #427.*

O (my) nephew!	يا بْنَ أُمَّ!

Sura 7:150	(Aaron) said, "Son of my mother, these people overpowered me!"	قَالَ ابْنَ أُمَّ إِنَّ ٱلْقَوْمَ ٱسْتَضْعَفُونِى...

418. Is it true that the person called upon can't have ال?

Yes, this is true – but there are exceptions.

The noun (اسْمٌ), which immediately follows the vocative particle, does not admit the definite article. In other words, *the one that is addressed* (الْمُنادَى) **can never be definite** by ال.

Why is that? ➡ Because it is already definite by definition as you call a **specific** person. It is impossible in Arabic two use two devices of definiteness (لا يَصِحُّ الْجَمْعُ بَيْنَ "يا" وَبَيْنَ الْ) at the same time. Similar to that is the first part of a إِضافة which is also by definition definite (if the second part is regarded as definite). But there is a famous exception: the word **Allah** (اللهُ).

This leaves us with a problem. How should we pronounce the ال, i.e.,, the هَمْزةٌ of the word Allah? Should we pronounce it as a glottal stop? The following two options are both correct.

1	You **don't pronounce** the Hamza. You treat it as a هَمْزةُ وَصلٍ which is ا. The word *Allah* = *the God* is definite by ال. When it is placed in the position of the الْمُنادَى, it gets a fixed, indeclinable shape (مَبْنِيٌّ عَلَى الضَّمِّ): it must end with ـُ. From a grammatical point of view, since it serves as the الْمُنادَى, it occupies the place of an accusative case (نَصْبٌ).	يا اللهُ !
2	You **pronounce** the Hamza (= glottal stop) and treat it as a هَمْزةُ قَطْع, i.e., أ. Actually this would be incorrect according to the rules of Arabic – but is fine with the word for *the God*.	يا أَللهُ !

There is another possibility to use ال in the vocative: when the الْمُنادَى is implicitly understood as a compound noun (إِضافةٌ), although the first part of the إِضافةٌ, the الْمُضافُ, is deleted.

O lion's courage!	يا الْأَسَدُ جُرْأَةً!
The مُضافٌ of the الْمُنادَى was deleted – in other words, the first part of the إِضافةٌ is missing. Which word could have been the first part? ➡ مِثْلَ	يا مِثْلَ الْأَسَدِ جُرْأَةً
This is the الْمُنادَى; it has a fixed shape and has to end with ـُ. Grammatically speaking, it fills the position of an accusative case (فِي مَحَلِّ نَصْبٍ).	الْأَسَدُ

419. By which trick can you use ال in the vocative?

By inserting أَيّ or أَيّةَ after the يا.

If the الْمُنادَي is definite by ال, you must insert أَيّ or أَيّةَ to fix the construction. Furthermore, you can also add a ها التَّنْبِيهِ.

O learned man!	يا أَيُّها الْعالِمُ!

| O soul! (Note: *soul* is feminine in Arabic.) | يَا أَيَّتُهَا النَّفْسُ! |
| [But] you, soul at peace! *(Sura 89:27)* | يَا أَيَّتُهَا النَّفْسُ الْمُطْمَئِنَّةُ! |

Vocative particle (حَرْفُ نِداءٍ). It does not have a place in إِعْرابٌ.	يا
The one being called (الْمُنادَى). It has a fixed ending: ـُ (مَبْنِيٌّ عَلَى الضَّمِّ). Grammatically, however, it is located in the place of an accusative case (فِي مَحَلِّ نَصْبٍ).	أَيُّ
Particle of attention (حَرْفُ تَنْبِيهٍ). Does not have a place in إِعْرابٌ.	ها
This is an attribute/adjective (نَعْتٌ). It mirrors the visual case of the word it refers to: the الْمُنادَى – and not the actual case ending according to the position in the sentence.	الْعالِمُ

Watch out: If we use a static, inert noun (اسْمٌ جامِدٌ) instead of a derived noun from a root (like الْعالِمُ, an active participle; اسْمُ الْفاعِلِ), then we treat it as an **apposition** (بَدَلٌ) – and not as a نَعْتٌ:

| O man! | يا أَيُّها الرَّجُلُ! |

The word أَيُّ serves as the الْمُنادَى. It is fixed on the "*u*" (مَبْنِيٌّ عَلَى الضَّمِّ); nevertheless, according to the place, we assign the "place value" of an accusative case (فِي مَحَلِّ نَصْبٍ).	أَيُّ
Particle of attention; it does not have a position in إِعْرابٌ.	ها
Apposition (بَدَلٌ); it takes the same visible case ending as the word that is placed before the apposition and to which it would be interchangeable.	الرَّجُلُ

The same is true for a relative clause that begins with ال, which is actually ال + ذي resulting in الَّذِي.

| O you who are prepared – come! | يا أَيُّها الَّذِي اسْتَعَدَّ أَقْبِلْ! |

| Relative pronoun (اسْمٌ مَوْصُولٌ). It is an apposition (بَدَلٌ) and in the grammatical position of a nominative case (فِي مَحَلِّ رَفْعٍ). | الَّذِي |
| Past tense verb; the hidden pronoun *he* is the subject (فاعِلٌ). This verbal sentence serves as the relative clause (صِلَةُ الْمَوْصُولِ). It | اسْتَعَدَّ |

does not have a place in إِعْرابٌ.	

Sura 3:102	**O you who** believe, fear Allah as He should be feared and do not die except as Muslims [in submission to Him].	يَا أَيُّهَا الَّذِينَ آمَنُوا اتَّقُوا اللَّهَ حَقَّ تُقَاتِهِ وَلَا تَمُوتُنَّ إِلَّا وَأَنتُم مُّسْلِمُونَ!

Remark: A <u>demonstrative particle</u> (اِسْمُ الْإِشارةِ) would also do the job.

Hey (you) man!	يا هذا الرَّجُلُ!
Hey (you) men!	يا هؤُلَاءِ الرِّجالُ! (= يا أَيُّها الرِّجالُ!)

The structure of the sentence remains the same: the word الرَّجُلُ is an apposition (بَدَلٌ) – see above. The demonstrative particle is indeclinable.

But it is quite complicated. We say that it is fixed on the estimated, virtual "u" (مَبْنِيٌّ عَلَى ضَمٍّ مُقَدَّرٍ), because the word itself has a fixed shape already and ends in a non-vowel (حَرَكَةُ الْبِناءِ الْأَصلِيَّةُ هِيَ السُّكُونُ). Now, what is the actual "place value" of the location in which the word is placed? It is the accusative case (فِي مَحَلِّ نَصْبٍ).

420. What is the finest way to call God (Allah)?

You use the word اللَّهُمَّ.

If Muslims want to call *God*, they usually don't use the word *Allah*. They prefer اللَّهُمَّ which has the same meaning as يا اللهُ. What is the difference? Grammatically speaking, it is a big one. ➡ If you use اللَّهُمَّ, you **don't use a vocative particle** to call God.

The origin of the expression اللَّهُمَّ is not entirely clear. For some etymological ideas, see *Arabic for Nerds 1, question #204*. Regarding the **morphology**, اللَّهُمَّ is probably the result of the following process:

- As a first step, the vocative particle (حَرْفُ النِّداءِ) is deleted.
- Then the omitted part is compensated by enhancing the word الله with a مِيمٌ مُشَدَّدةٌ resulting in: اللَّهُمَّ.
  - ➡ Since part of this process was to delete the vocative particle, you cannot use يا with اللَّهُمَّ.

| This is the الْمُنادَى; its shape is fixed on the last vowel ـُ "*u*" (الضَّمّ). Regarding its position in the sentence, it is located in the place of an accusative case (فِي مَحَلِّ نَصْبٍ). | اللهُ |
| This letter is a substitute/compensation for the deleted vocative particle (حَرْفُ النِّداءِ الْمَحْذُوفُ). The م itself has a fixed shape, i.e., it is built on the فَتْح. It does not have a position in إِعْرابٌ. | م |

| Sura 39:46 | Say, 'God! Creator of the heavens and earth! Knower of all that is hidden and all that is open (visible)! | قُلِ اللَّهُمَّ فاطِرَ السَّماواتِ وَالْأَرْضِ عالِمَ الْغَيْبِ وَالشَّهادَةِ. |

WARNINGS (التَّحْذِيرُ) AND INSTIGATIONS (الإِغْراءُ)

421. *The road! The road!* **Which case do we use to warn people?**

The accusative case (مَنْصُوبٌ) because the issued warning is treated as a direct object of a deleted verb.

Warnings and instigations are grammatically of the same kind. The **warning** (تَحْذِيرٌ) tells the addressed person (الْمُخاطَبُ) what he or she should avoid or be aware of. The **instigation** or **incitement** (إِغْراءٌ) is a message for the addressed about something that is laudable (مَحْمُودٌ) to be involved with. So, a person is urged to do something/a certain thing.

Some examples of **warnings**:

The road! The road!	الطَّرِيقَ الطَّرِيقَ!
The dog! The dog!	الْكَلْبَ الْكَلْبَ!
(Beware of) negligence, negligence!	الإِهْمالَ الإِهْمالَ!

| **Direct object** (مَفْعُولٌ بِهِ) in the accusative case (مَنْصُوبٌ). If we have a direct object, there should be a verb – but where is it? The **verb** (an imperative) **was deleted** and had the meaning of *be cautious!* (إِحْذَرْ). Its subject (فاعِلٌ) was an implied/hidden pronoun (ضَمِيرٌ مُسْتَتِرٌ) with the implied meaning of *you* (أَنْتَ). | الإِهْمالَ |
| This is an **emphasis** (تَوْكِيدٌ مَنْصُوبٌ). Since it is used as a repeti- | الإِهْمالَ |

tion (تَكْرِيرٌ), we treat the repeated word (اسْمٌ مُكَرَّرٌ) as a *corroboration/confirmation* (تَوْكِيدٌ لَفْظِيٌّ). The emphasis consists of the emphatic repetition of the word itself since it is not emphasized by a special word.	

An example of an **instigation**.

Work hard, it is the way to success!	الْجِدَّ الْجِدَّ فَإِنَّهُ طَرِيقُ النَّجاحِ!
Direct object (مَفْعُولٌ بِهِ) in the accusative case (مَنْصُوبٌ). The verb (i.e., the governor/عامِلٌ) here is deleted, but still understood. It had the meaning of: *keep doing!* (الْزَمْ).	الْجِدَّ
Repetition – used for emphasis (تَوْكِيدٌ مَنْصُوبٌ).	الْجِدَّ

Let's analyze the **direct object** of a warning and instigation (مَفْعُولٌ بِهِ فِي التَّحْذِيرِ وَالْإِغْراءِ). The verb governing such an object may be deleted; sometimes it even must be deleted (فِعْلٌ مَحْذُوفٌ وُجُوبًا).

When does the verb have to be deleted?

a) If the direct object (مَفْعُولٌ بِهِ) itself is repeated (مُكَرَّرٌ) – see above;

b) or if it is followed by a conjunction (حَرْفُ عَطْفٍ) plus **another** word (مَعْطُوفٌ). The extra word is coupled (coordinated) which means that it gets the grammatical implications (case marker) of the preceding word (مَعْطُوفٌ عَلَيْهِ).

Beware of (= I warn you of) negligence and perversion, as they are the way to failure.	الْإِهْمالَ وَالْإِنْحِرافَ فَإِنَّهُما طَرِيقُ الْفَشَلِ.
The word الْإِنْحِرافَ is the مَعْطُوفٌ.	

Nowadays the direct object (مَفْعُولٌ بِهِ) of such constructions is often used in the style of a إِضافةٌ. Technically speaking, this means that the direct object is connected with a personal pronoun which serves as the second part of a إِضافةٌ (مُضافٌ إِلَى ضَمِيرِ الْمُخاطَبِ).

Your head, watch out for the wall!	رَأْسَكَ وَالْحائِطَ!
The كَ here is a pronominal suffix (ضَمِيرٌ مُتَّصِلٌ) which has a fixed, indeclin-	

able shape (مَبْنِيٌّ عَلَى الْفَتْحِ). Since it is the second part of the إِضافة, it grammatically holds the position of a genitive (فِي مَحَلِّ جَرٍّ مُضافٌ إِلَيْهِ).

422. What is the purpose of the word إِيَّا؟

This word is often used to warn people.

The word إِيَّا is an undefined **noun** (اسْمٌ مُبْهَمٌ) that does not convey a specific meaning of its own. We can treat it as an independent pronoun in the **accusative case** (ضَمِيرٌ مُنْفَصِلٌ مَنْصُوبٌ) which gets connected with a pronoun suffix (تَتَّصِلُ بِهِ جَمِيعُ الضَّمائِرِ). What we finally get – for example: إِيَّاكَ, إِيَّاكِ, ... – means *beware...!* or *take care not to...!*

Where does that meaning come from? ➡ Well, there is an underlying verb (*I warn*) which was deleted – but is still implicitly understood.

Take care! (If there is no other word involved, this expression only issues a general warning: *watch out, take care!*)	إِيَّاكَ إِيَّاكَ!
This is how the expression would look like without deleting the verb: *I warn you!* ➡	إِيَّاكَ أُحَذِّرُ!

If you want to be more specific, you can also include the reason for the warning. You have three options for that:

a) You can directly add a word in the accusative case (مَنْصُوبٌ).

Beware of negligence! (I warn you not to be negligent.)	إِيَّاكَ إِيَّاكَ الْإِهْمالَ!

This اسْمٌ مُبْهَمٌ serves as the **first direct object** (مَفْعُولٌ أَوَّلٌ). Since it is indeclinable (مَبْنِيٌّ عَلَى السُّكُونِ, i.e., إ), we can only assign the "place value" of an accusative (فِي مَحَلِّ نَصْبٍ) but no visible case marker. The **deleted verb** – which is the reason why we have put this expression into the accusative – could be, for example, *I warn* (أُحَذِّرُ). The hidden subject therein is: *I* (أنا).	إِيَّا
Particle of address (حَرْفُ خِطابٍ); no position in إِعْرابٌ.	كَ
Repeated word which conveys emphasis (تَوْكِيدٌ). It is placed in the position of an accusative case (فِي مَحَلِّ نَصْبٍ).	إِيَّاكَ

Second direct object of the deleted verb (مَفْعُولٌ ثانٍ لِلفِعْـلِ الْمَحْذُوف). Why the second? Because the verb حَذَّرَ takes <u>two</u> objects! In such situations, you could also use just one direct object and a preposition to connect the second object (*see #309*).	الْإِهْمال

b) You could add the object of the warning by a و. The expression is often translated as *do not*.

Don't be negligent! Be careful not to be negligent!	إِيَّاكَ وَالْإِهْمالَ!

The meaning is the same as in option a) – but the grammatical analysis is slightly different. This has to do with the deleted verb and the و. We do not coordinate, "couple" (عَطْفٌ) a single word, but a whole sentence! Since the verb is deleted, it appears like a single word, but grammatically it is treated as a sentence.

Direct object (مَفْعُولٌ بِهِ). The deleted verb is أُحَذِّرُ. So far, we have the same situation as in option a).	إِيَّاكَ
Conjunction (حَرْفُ عَطْفٍ).	و
Direct object (مَفْعُولٌ بِهِ) in the accusative (مَنْصُوبٌ). Now we see the difference to a) because this is <u>not</u> the second object! Why? We have another (second) deleted verb which is *I disfigure* (أُقَبِّح) or *I make hateful* (أُبَغِّض).	الْإِهْمالَ

c) You could use the preposition مِنْ.

Stay away from negligence!	إِيَّاكَ مِن الْإِهْمالِ!
The prepositional phrase (الْجارُّ وَالْمَجْرُورُ) is connected with the deleted verb.	

423. Can the object of a *warning* take the nominative case?

Yes, this is possible – but then it is not an object anymore.

The best thing to do is to construct an example. At the beginning, we will use a word in the nominative case, which will be the subject (مُبْتَدَأ)

of a nominal sentence (جُمْلة اسميّة). Now, we need a predicate. But do we? Well, yes and no! We can assume that the predicate is **deleted** (خَبَرٌ مَحْذُوفٌ)! Note that what we say here works for instigations as well.

Diligence is needed, for it is the way to success.	الْجِدُّ فَإِنَّهُ طَرِيقُ النَّجاحِ.
This would be the equivalent if we use a nominal sentence with subject and predicate. Note that the predicate (مَظْلُوبٌ) was omitted in the above sentence.	الْجِدُّ مَظْلُوبٌ فَإِنَّهُ طَرِيقُ النَّجاحِ.

Nevertheless, the **accusative** is the standard approach for interpreting such sentences. We assume that there is an underlying (deleted) **verb**.

Diligence is needed, for it is the way to success.	الْجِدَّ فَإِنَّهُ طَرِيقُ النَّجاحِ.
Direct object in the accusative case (مَفْعُولٌ بِهِ مَنْصُوبٌ بِالْفَتْحـةِ الظّاهِرة). In such constructions, the verb (فِعْلُهُ مَحْذُوفٌ جوازًا) could be interpreted as: الْزِم. But you don't have to mention it. It is totally fine and common to delete it.	الْجِدَّ

Let's return to our topic. Could we also delete the **subject** (مُبْتَدَأ) of the nominal sentence instead of the predicate? Yes, that is possible.

The lion, the lion!	الْأَسَدُ الْأَسَدُ!

In this example, two interpretations are theoretically possible:

Assumed (underlying) meaning of the word in the nominative case:	
We assume (عَلَى تَقْدِيرٍ) that we **deleted the subject** (مُبْتَدَأ مَحْذُوفٌ): *this*.	هذا الْأَسَدُ.
We assume that we **deleted the predicate** (خَبَرٌ مَحْذُوفٌ): *in your way*.	في طَرِيقِكَ الْأَسَدُ.

SORROW AND PAIN (النُّدْبة)

424. How do you lament in Arabic?

You use a special particle: وا.

The النُّدْبَةُ (lamentation) is a special form of an invocation (النَّداءُ). It turns one's attention to the one who is painfully affected or tormented. نُدْبَةٌ means *dirge* or *funeral song*.

This type of construction is also used to lament for the dead. The person which is *bewailed* or *bemoaned* (الْمَنْدُوبُ) is the الْمُنادَى in grammar. For example, if you want to mourn (worry) intensely about a person who died and whose name was *Zayd*, you say:

Alas, (O) Zayd!	وا زَيْدُ!

This is a *particle of lamentation* (حَرْفُ نُدْبَةٍ) which is, in fact, a vocative particle (حَرْفُ نِداءٍ). It does not have a place in إِعْرابٌ.	وا
The one being called (الْمُنادَى). Why do we have the ending ـُ? Because it has a fixed, cemented shape (مَبْنِيٌّ عَلَى الضَّمّ). But it is quite complicated. Since we say that the vocative particle transports a verbal meaning (= I call), زَيْدُ is grammatically in the place of a direct object and located in the place of an accusative case (فِي مَحَلّ نَصْبٍ).	زَيْدُ

"O my father, he has answered the call of his Lord." *Sunan ibn Majāh (Book 6, 1698)*	وَا أَبَتاهْ! أَجابَ رَبًّا دَعاهُ.

Let's assume you have a terrible headache and want to lament about it. What would you say?

Alas, (oh) my head!	وا رَأْسِي!

We have the typical situation that the كَسْرَةٌ is needed before the pronoun *my* (ي) – see *question #106*. Nevertheless, the word *head* (i.e., the الْمُنادَى) occupies the position of an accusative case (مَنْصُوبٌ); but you can't put the respective vowel marker as you need the كَسْرَةٌ.
And what about the ي? The ي must take a سُكُونٌ because a long vowel always ends in this quiescent (non-vowel) sound. Here too, you don't mark it visibly according to its position, i.e., the second part of a إِضافَةٌ. ➡ We use a hidden, assumed marker for the genitive case (فِي مَحَلّ جَرّ مُضافٌ إِلَيْهِ).

The particle that is used in the النُّدْبَةُ is usually وا. Oftentimes, you put a superfluous/extra Aleph at the end of the الْمَنْدُوبُ plus a so-called هاءُ السَّكْتِ in case you stop there. Such ه is used to give emphasis as this sound fits more to the actual process of moaning.

Alas, Zayd!	وا زَيْدَاهْ!

	زَيْدَ
The one that you call (الْمُنادَى). Now it gets complicated: this word is built on a hypothetical (assumed/estimated), fixed "u" (مَبْنِيٌّ عَلَى ضَمٍّ مُقَدَّرٍ); the fixed ending "u" (ُ) is normal in the vocative. However, here it is can only be virtually because you have to put another vowel on the last letter, i.e., a فَتْحة, otherwise you would not be able to add an Aleph. In other words, we have an imaginary ُ that was changed, for reasons of pronunciation, into a َ. This َ however is **not** the marker of the accusative case. It is just there to facilitate the pronunciation. Thus, we can only assign the "place value" of an accusative since زَيْدَ is located in the place of an accusative case (فِي مَحَلِّ نَصْبٍ), but isn't visibly marked as such.	
Redundant, extra letter (حَرْفٌ زائِدٌ).	ا
Letter of pause (هاءُ السَّكْتِ).	ةْ

What happens with the اه if you have a name that is made of a إِضافةٌ? The Aleph and the ه move to the second part of the إِضافةٌ. The first noun therefore gets the accusative case.

Alas, Abd al-Majid!	وا عَبْدَ الْمَجِيدَاهْ!

What happens to اه if there is a pronoun at the end? This is more complicated. The Aleph is added under the condition that it does not lead to confusion ➡ which means it should not lead to a final long vowel (حَرْفُ مَدٍّ)! Let's take the word *brother* (أَخ) and assume you want to express: *alas, your (f.) brother!* We start with: وا أَخاكِ

In such a construction, the possessive pronoun كَ is the <u>second</u> part of the إِضافةٌ which would carry the extra Aleph. Let's try to add an extra Aleph. Theoretically, you would get this: وا أَخاكِا.

This would be impossible in Arabic! You would need a فَتْحةٌ on the last letter. This would result in أَخاكَا which is confusing – because it may indicate that we talk to a man (masculine form of *you*), but we want to express the feminine pronoun **you**. But there is a trick. We can use another letter that will help us: the ي!

Alas, your (f.) brother!	وا أَخاكِي!

This also works for other pronouns.

Alas, his brother!	وا أَخاهُوْ!

What happened if we added an Aleph only? We would get: وا أَخاها. This would be confusing (ها = *her*). What do we do? ➡ We adapt it and use وْ.

Let's check the most confusing situation. You want to express *my* by the pronoun suffix ي (ياءُ الْمُتَكَلِّم). At the same time, you want to add an Aleph. Then, you have three possibilities:

1	You simply keep the ي without anything else.	وا رَأْسِي!
2	You put a فَتْحةٌ on the ي. (Notice that it had originally a سُكُونٌ on it: يْ). Then you add an (extra) Aleph after the ي. This is quite difficult to pronounce, but it works.	وا رَأْسِيَا!
3	Delete the ي and simply add the additional Aleph.	وا رَأْسَا!
You may add a هاءُ السَّكْتِ when you pause after the utterance in no. 2 and 3.	

THE CALL FOR HELP (الْإِسْتِغاثةُ)

425. How do you call someone for help in Arabic?

By using one or two Lām (ل).

The *call for help* (الْإِسْتِغاثةُ) is a subgroup of the *vocative* (النّداءُ). The term is the مَصْدَرٌ of the X-verb اسْتَغاثَ - يَسْتَغِيثُ ب (R2=و, to *ask somebody for help*). It is a complicated construction:

5	4	3	2	1
عَمْرو	لِ	زَيْدٍ	لَ	يا
الْمَعان مُسْتَغاثٌ لَهُ	الْمَصْدَرُ مَحْذُوفٌ	الْمُعِينُ مُسْتَغاثٌ بِهِ	العامِلُ مَحْذُوفٌ	حَرْفُ النِّداءِ
The **person or reason why** help is being	The deleted infinitive noun could	The **helper**. It takes the visible marker of the genitive case, dragged into this state by the	The regent (verb) was deleted.	

sought. Often: The one to be helped. It is a noun in the genitive case.	express *supporting, aiding, assisting* = إعانة.	preceding ل. However, according to its position, it is placed in the location of an accusative case (مَفْعُـولٌ بِـهِ مَحَلًّا) since it serves as the direct object.	E.g.: *I call* (أَدْعُو).

(1) Vocative particle (حَرْفُ النِّداءِ). It <u>must</u> be يا and no other.

(2) You have to insert the letter ل. In most situations, it is considered to have a fixed shape, built on the فَتْحٌ ← لَ. Note: You could compensate the ل with an Aleph, see *question #427*.

(3) Then comes a noun (اِسْمٌ): the name of the **person that is called to help** (الْمُسْتَغاثُ بِهِ or الْمُسْتَغاثُ). It gets the genitive (مَجْرُورٌ) due to the preceding ل. It is usually definite. See example 1.

(4) Watch out: If you want to add another person's name, you use وَ plus ل before the second person. ➡ The وَ is **crucial** here to get the correct meaning. See example 2.

(5) If you want to add **why the aid is required** (الْمُسْتَغاثُ لَهُ or الْمُسْتَغاثُ مِنْ أَجْلِهِ), then again you have to insert the letter ل. This Lām has a different shape (built on the كَسْرٌ ← لِ. The following word is مَجْرُورٌ due to that ل. See example 3 and 4. **Watch out**: It depends mainly on the context how you translate this part. Instead of the person's name for whom help is being sought, you can also give the reason for the distress, for example, a fire, etc. – see example 5.

1	Help, Zayd! (= Zayd, come to help!)	يا لَزَيْدِ!
2	Zayd and Amr, (come to) help!	يا لَزَيْدِ وَلَعَمْرِو!

Amr here is a مَعْطُوفٌ. Although you see the genitive ending, it is grammatically placed in the position of an accusative (فِي مَحَلِّ نَصْبٍ) and, like the preceding word, appears in the location of an accusative (**direct object** of the vocative particle which is being interpreted as a verb: "*I call*").

3	Zayd! Help Amr!	يا لَزَيْدِ لِعَمْرِو!

| 4 | O people, help the unfairly treated! | يا لَلنّاسِ لِلْمَظْلُومِ! |
| 5 | O firefighters, help against the terrible fire! | يا لَرِجالِ الْمَطافِئِ لِلْحَرِيقِ الْمُرَوِّعِ! |

Let's analyze an example in depth:

| O people, help the tyrannized! | يا لَلنّاسِ لِلْمَظْلُومِ! |

Vocative particle (حَرْفُ نِداءٍ). It doesn't have a place in إِعْرابٌ.	يا
Preposition (حَرْفُ جَرٍّ مَبْنِيٌّ عَلَى الْفَتْحِ) fixed on the فَتْح. It does not have a position in إِعْرابٌ.	لَ
Noun in the genitive (إِسْمٌ مَجْرُورٌ) by the لَ. The prepositional phrase (الْجارُّ وَالْمَجْرُورُ) is connected with the vocative particle. We assume that the vocative particle has a verbal force; we implicitly find the meaning of a verb: *I call* (أَدْعُو).	النّاس
Preposition (حَرْفُ جَرٍّ مَبْنِيٌّ عَلَى الْكَسْرِ) fixed on the كَسْر. It does not have a position in إِعْرابٌ.	لِ
Noun in the genitive case (إِسْمٌ مَجْرُورٌ) by لِ. The prepositional phrase (الْجارُّ وَالْمَجْرُورُ) is linked to the vocative particle.	الْمَظْلُوم

We said that the first *Lām* before the الْمُسْتَغاثُ has to be a لَ and the second a لِ. But there are exceptions, for example, if you use a personal pronoun that is already fixed on a certain vowel (مَبْنِيٌّ). So, it must be...

- لَنا and <u>never</u> لِنا
- لَهُ and <u>never</u> لِهُ
- لَي and <u>never</u> لِي

Excursus: The construction with لَ and لِ is also used to a) invite people or b) to express surprise and wonder:

a)	O you men, come to the water!	يا لَلرِّجالِ لِلْماءِ!
b)	Oh, what a surprise!	يا لَلْعَجَبِ!
	Oh, what a misfortune!	يا لَلدّاهِيَةِ!

| Oh, how terrible! How dreadful! | يا لَلْهَوْلِ! |

You can use لـ and add personal suffixes (لَكَ, لَهُ, etc.) which turns it into لَ. The pronoun suffix refers to the person that is called. The indefinite noun in the accusative case describes the reason for the astonishment. Alternatively, you can use the preposition مِنْ.

Oh, what a man! (What a man he was!)	يا لَهُ مِنْ رَجُلٍ!
	يا لَهُ رَجُلًا!
Oh, what a (splendid) night!	يا لَكِ مِنْ لَيْلةٍ!
	يا لَكِ لَيْلًا!
What seriousness there was!	يا لَهُ مِن جِدٍّ!

426. What was the war-cry of the *time of ignorance*?

Ask someone else but Allah for help.

The term *war-cry of the time of ignorance* (دَعْوَى الْجَاهِلِيَّة) was used by the Islamic Prophet Muhammad when people called someone other than Allah (or the Muslims) for help. Concerning the grammar, it is a **call for help** (الْإِسْتِغاثَةُ).

The grammarians of Kūfa (الْكُوفِيُّونَ) stated that the first لـ in these types of construction – resulting in يا لـ – with a following word in the genitive was originally يا آلَ followed by the name of the kinsmen of the man who called for aid. The word آلَ means *family* or *clan*. A Hadith documents that Muhammad had coined this type of construction:

We were in the company of the prophet in a battle. A large number of the Muhājirūn [those who followed the prophet from Mecca to Medina] joined him and among the Muhājirūn there was a person who used to play jokes (or play with spears); so he hit a man from the 'Ansār [people in Medina who helped the prophet] on the hip/back.

The 'Ansāri man got so angry that both of them called their people. The 'Ansāri man shouted: "Help, O 'Ansār!" And the man of the Muhājirūn shouted: "Help, O Muhājirūn!" The Prophet came out and said: "What is wrong with the people (as they are calling) this call of the Time of Igno-rance?" (*Sahīh al-Bukhārī 3518*)

> يَقُولُ غَزَوْنَا مَعَ النَّبِيِّ وَقَدْ ثَابَ مَعَهُ نَاسٌ مِنَ الْمُهَاجِرِينَ حَتَّى كَثُرُوا، وَكَانَ مِن
> الْمُهَاجِرِينَ رَجُلٌ لَعَّابٌ فَكَسَعَ أَنْصَارِيًّا، فَغَضِبَ الْأَنْصَارِيُّ غَضَبًا شَدِيدًا، حَتَّى
> تَدَاعَوْا، وَقَالَ الْأَنْصَارِيُّ يَا لَلْأَنْصَارِ. وَقَالَ الْمُهَاجِرِيُّ يَا لَلْمُهَاجِرِينَ. فَخَرَجَ النَّبِيُّ
> فَقَالَ:"مَا بَالُ دَعْوَى أَهْلِ الْجَاهِلِيَّةِ!"

Muhammad forbade such expressions. He substituted it by يا لِلَّهِ and يا لَلْمُسْلِمِينَ. Notice the لَ in both expressions!

O Allah, (help us) against the enemy!	يا لِلَّهِ لِلْعَدُوِّ!

427. What is the strange additional ending ٱ good for?

The ٱ might occur in a call for help (الْإِسْتِغَاثَةُ).

You can tweak the construction of a **call for help** (الْإِسْتِغَاثَةُ). The formula: you delete the لَ after the يا, which is the لَامٌ before the person that is asked <u>for</u> help (الْمُسْتَغَاثُ).

Once you did that, you have to add an Aleph (optional an extra ه if you pause) as a compensation.

O believer, help the oppressed!	يا مُؤْمِنَا لِلْمَظْلُومِ!

Since we got here a special form of an invocation, this is the *person being called* (الْمُنَادَى). The word, as common in the vocative, is fixed on an assumed, virtual ضَمٌّ (مَبْنِيٌّ عَلَى ضَمٍّ مُقَدَّرٍ) – which is not shown because you need a فَتْحَة before the final (additional) Aleph (الْفَتْحَةُ الْمُنَاسِبَةُ لِلْأَلِفِ). This word is, nonetheless, in the place of an accusative case (فِي مَحَلِّ نَصْبٍ).	مُؤْمِن
This Aleph **compensates for the deleted preposition** لَ. It has no position in إِعْرَابٌ.	Aleph (١)

If you don't continue after the last word (pausal form), you add the *Hā' of silence or pause* (هاءُ السَّكْتِ).

O believer, help!	يا مُؤْمِنَاهْ!

428. How can you turn a call for help into a call for destruction?

By adding a preposition.

The preposition مِنْ can change the meaning of an invocation dramatically. It may transform a **call for help** (الْإِسْتِغاثَةُ) into a **call for destruction**. Basically, we name the problem, the reason for the call for help. Watch out: This happens in the **second part** of the construction which normally gives the name of the person that <u>needs</u> help.

The X-verb اِسْتَغاثَ means *to appeal for help* or *to seek the aid*. It is one of those verbs in which a following preposition is decisive. Note that we also use these prepositions for the appropriate grammar terms.

to call for help **of** someone.	بِ	اِسْتَغاثَ
to seek the aid **against** someone.	عَلَى	

If the person (whose name is given after the person that is asked for help) should not be helped, but rather **ruined** (الْمُسْتَغاثُ عَلَيْهِ), you delete the لِ and use مِنْ instead.

O Allah, help us against (save us from) the hypocrites!	يا لَلَّهِ مِنَ الْمُنافِقِينَ!
O heroes, help us against the corrupt people!	يا لَلْأَبْطالِ مِنَ الْعُتاةِ الْمُفْسِدِينَ!
What misery and deprivation!	يا لَها مِنْ تَعاسَةٍ وَحِرْمانٍ!

PROHIBITION (النَّهْيِ) AND PROPOSAL (الْعَرْضُ)

429. How do you call upon a person who is absent (الْغائِبُ)؟

You use the so-called Lām of the command (لامُ الْأَمْرِ).

This Lām is a لامٌ مَكْسُورَةٌ ("li": لِ) which is normally prefixed to the **third person singular** in the jussive mood (مَجْزُومٌ) to give it the sense of an imperative. It is usually translated as: "*Let…*"

Let Zayd write!	لِيَكْتُبْ زَيْدٌ!

| Let Fātima write! | لِتَكْتُبْ فاطِمةُ! |
| Let your heart be at ease! | لِيَطِبْ قَلْبُكَ! |

Now, what happens if there is a وَ or فَ before the verb? Then the *Lām* becomes سَاكِنةٌ which practically means that you drop the vowel *"i"* and put a سُكُونْ on it. The final result will be: لْ.

| Let Zayd write and let him perfect his book! (and let him write well!) | لِيَكْتُبْ زَيْدٌ وَلْيُتْقِنْ كِتابَتَهُ! |
| Let Zayd go and inform them of the news, and then let him wait there. | لِيَذْهَبْ زَيْدٌ فَلْيُخْبِرْهُمْ بِالْخَبَرِ ثُمَّ لِيَنْتَظِرْ هُناكَ! |

430. *Let's...!* How do you say that in Arabic?

There are many ways (but some are grammatically dubious).

One of the most common constructions in contemporary Arabic is probably an import from English. Although that's just a natural process in any language, being aware of it doesn't hurt. It's all about this:

➡ This doesn't sound like good Arabic, but it is understandable. The construction is presumably an import from English or German. In English, it is common to use the verb *let* in the imperative of the absent (3rd person; أَمْرُ الْغائِبِ) or the imperative of the speaker (1st person; أَمْرُ الْمُتَكَلِّم).	*Let them go!*	دَعْهُمْ يَذْهَبُوا!
	Let him go!	دَعْهُ يَذْهَبْ!
	Let us go!	دَعْنا نَذْهَبْ!
	Let me go!	دَعْنِي أَذْهَبْ!

How do you express that in sophisticated (others may say: old-fashioned) Arabic? ➡ You use a *Lām* with *"i"* underneath (لِ), a so-called لامُ الْأَمْرِ, and add a verb in the مَجْزُومٌ-mood (jussive); see #429.

| imported | Let's speak Arabic! | دَعْنا نَتَكَلَّمُ الْعَرَبِيَّةَ! |
| better style | | لِنَتَكَلَّمْ الْعَرَبِيَّةَ! |

The Classical Arabic construction is frequently found in the Qur'an:

| Sura 2:186 | So **let** them respond to Me, and believe in Me, so that they may be guided! | فَلْيَسْتَجِيبُوا لِي وَلْيُؤْمِنُوا بِي لَعَلَّهُمْ يَرْشُدُونَ. |

Watch out: If you have a verb with a weak letter (حَرْفُ الْعِلّةِ), always check the root. The position and the type of the weak letter has a huge impact on the conjugation.

	imperative	present tense	past tense	meaning
1	دَعْ!	يَدَعُ	وَدَعَ	to let
2	أُدْعُ!	يَدْعُو	دَعا	to call

431. Can words other than verbs also express an imperative?

Yes, some words are capable of that.

In Arabic, there are indeclinable forms that can be used to express an imperative. They are called اِسْمُ فِعْلٍ لِلْأَمْرِ and usually follow the pattern فَعَالِ, but there are other forms too.

The pattern فَعَالِ is mainly used in (pre-) Classical Arabic as a command form. Except for some common expressions, this pattern is almost extinct nowadays.

Go ahead! Let's get going!	إِيهِ!		Hush, quiet!	صَهْ!
Beware!	حَذَارِ!		Listen!	سَمَاعِ!

| Watch out for that! (be careful of that!) | حَذَارِ مِن ذَلِكَ! |

432. Can you put a negation particle ("don't") before an imperative?

No, you can't.

Unlike in English, in Arabic it is **impossible** to place a negation device before the imperative. So, how can you express "Don't ...!" in Arabic? Grammarians call such an expression a *prohibition* (النَّهْي).

In Arabic, you do use the negation particle لا; but regarding the verb, you use the **present tense** in the مَجْزُومٌ-mood (jussive) – and not the imperative. This type of لا is called لا النّاهِية and is used for **orders** and **requests of stopping** or **refraining**. It can be used with the energetic form (you add a نُونٌ for emphasis).

Don't go!	لا تَذْهَبْ!
Don't (you two) go! Remark: This verb in the dual form is put into the مَجْزُومٌ-mood by deleting the last letter نِ.	لا تَذْهَبا!

Sura 2:132	So **do not** die except while you are Muslims!	فَلَا تَمُوتُنَّ إِلَّا وَأَنتُم مُّسْلِمُونَ!

Remark: What would happen if we applied the prohibition to the speaker himself (i.e., to myself)? In grammar, we would call that a الْمُضارِعُ الْمُسْنَدُ إِلَى الْمُتَكَلِّم. This is understandably rare but it may be acceptable if the verb is in the passive form:

I am not to be placed in a position that I don't like!	لا أُوضَعْ مَوْضِعًا لا أُحِبُّهُ!

433. How can you demand something with urgency?

There are several particles that can do the job.

These particles are هَلَّا – أَلَّا – أَلا – لَوْلا – لَوْما. They are called *particles of suggestion and proposals*. The translation depends on the context. The punctuation is not always a reliable guide. Sometimes you use an exclamation mark; sometimes, a question mark is used instead because the context tells us that it is a **rhetorical question** ("why not"). These particles can be used to express that you....

a) ... demand something with **gentleness** (حَرْفُ الْعَرْضِ);

b) ... demand something with **urgency** (حَرْفُ التَّحْضِيضِ). More urgency usually means more heaviness in articulation, as we will see.

The tense is crucial for the correct meaning. The particles are placed...

- before the **present** tense to <u>incite</u> a person to perform an action;
- before the **past** tense to <u>blame</u> a person for neglecting to act.

a) The concept of الْعَرْضُ is used when you ask a person – in **friendliness** (رِفْقٌ) and **gentleness** (لِينٌ) – to perform an action.

Normally you use the particles لَوْ or أَلَا because these particles have less force than the particles used for urgency (see below). This type is mostly used with the **present tense**. Note that in this application, لَوْ is not a device for the conditional.

	equivalent meaning	example
Why aren't you diligent?	إِجْتَهِدْ!	أَلَا تَجْتَهِدُ!
Why don't you think about this matter?	فَكِّرْ!	لَوْ تُفَكِّرُ فِي هذا الْأَمْرِ!
Why don't you visit your relatives?	زُرْ!	أَلَا تَزُورُ أَقارِبَكَ؟

Sura 24:22	**Do you not** wish that Allah should forgive you?	أَلَا تُحِبُّونَ أَنْ يَغْفِرَ اللّهُ لَكُمْ؟

Sura 9:13	How **could you not** fight a people who have broken their oaths, who tried to drive the Messenger out, who attacked you first?	أَلَا تُقَاتِلُونَ قَوْمًا نَّكَثُوا أَيْمَانَهُمْ وَهَمُّوا بِإِخْرَاجِ الرَّسُولِ وَهُم بَدَءُوكُمْ أَوَّلَ مَرَّةٍ؟

b) The التَّحْضِيضُ describes the **request** (الطَّلَبُ) with force.

If you want to underline the urgency of your demand, you can use particles that are similar to the ones we have already examined in a) – but are heavier.

These particles are هَلَّا (*is not...? Why not...?*) and لَوْلَا as well as أَلَّا. You could translate them as *why wouldn't/couldn't you...!*) Note that هَلَّا is a compound (كَلِمَةٌ مُرَكَّبَةٌ) of هَلْ and لَا. This type is mostly used with the <u>past tense</u>.

	equivalent meaning	example
Why didn't you inform me?	أَعْلِمْ!	هَلَّا أَعْلَمْتَنِي!

Why aren't you diligent?	اِجْتَهِدْ!	هَلَّا اِجْتَهَدْتَ!
Why don't you pay attention?	اِنْتَبِهْ!	لَوْلا اِنْتَبَهْتَ
Why don't you sit down?	اِجْلِسْ!	هَلَّا جَلَسْتَ!
Wouldn't you agree that...!	وافِقْ!	هَلَّا وافَقْتَ عَلَى أَنَّ

| Sura 63:10 | My Lord, if You **would only** reprieve me for a little while, I would give in charity and become one of the righteous. | لَوْلا أَخَّرْتَنِي إِلَى أَجَلٍ قَرِيبٍ فَأَصَّدَّقَ وَأَكُنْ مِّنَ الصَّالِحِينَ. |

| Sura 27:46 | Why **do you not** ask forgiveness of Allah, so that you may be given mercy?' | لَوْلا تَسْتَغْفِرُونَ اللَّهَ لَعَلَّكُمْ تُرْحَمُونَ. |

Sometimes the verb can be omitted.

| Why not better than this? | هَلَّا خَيْرًا مِنْ ذلِكَ! |

Let's see an example of Classical Arabic, from a time before Islam appeared. A line of the poet ʿAntara ibn Shaddād.

| Inquire, o daughter of Mālik, from knights of high renown * whatever of me, to you, as yet, is still unknown. | هَلَّا سَأَلْتِ الْخَيْلَ يا ابْنةَ مالِكِ إِنْ كُنْتِ جَاهِلةً بِما لَمْ تَعْلَمِي. |

Remark: **ʿAntara ibn Shaddād** (عَنْتَرة بن شَدّاد), born in ~525 AD (~106 BH), was an Arab knight and poet, famous for his poetry and his adventurous life. Although I give his birth date, we have to acknowledge that we know next to nothing about him.

The person is more of a legend. His mother was perhaps an Ethiopian woman, his father an Arab. ʿAntara grew up in slavery as a shepherd. He may have lived in an isolated region in Arabia.

His poems deal with a society in turmoil and are full of bravery and blood. There was unrest among the tribes of Arabia, and there was a big clash between two superpowers, Byzantium and Persia. ʿAntara won his freedom in battle and loved a woman called ʿAbla, his cousin, who refused him. Legend has it that parts of his poems were hung up in the Kaaba in Mecca (before Islam). He died, allegedly aged 83, in 608 AD (14 BH).

EXCLAMATIONS: ADMIRATION & ASTONISHMENT (جُمْلَةُ التَّعَجُّبِ)

434. How can you express admiration or astonishment?

You have the choice between two formulas.

Arabic knows two constructions to express **admiration** or **astonishment** which are known in grammar as التَّعَجُّبُ. The term literally means *astonishment; amazement.* You can apply one of the following two formulas. Both denote *how* plus the *predicated quality.*

		3		2		1
I	nominal sentence	"object" in the accusative	+	أَفْعَلَ	+	ما
II	verbal sentence	"subject" in the genitive	+	بِ	+	أَفْعِلْ

Note: The بِ here is extra/redundant and mainly there to convey emphasis. Construction II is very rare and is almost extinct.

Both constructions are now completely fossilized, cemented.

I	**nominal sentence**	What a beautiful sky! (How beautiful the sky was!)	ما أَجْمَلَ السَّماءَ!

This is the assumed, virtual meaning: *A great thing* has made the sky beautiful.	شَيْءٌ عَظِيمٌ جَعَلَ السَّماءَ جَمِيلةً!

Let's put the sentence under the microscope.

This is a إِسْمُ تَعَجُّبٍ which is the subject (مُبْتَدَأٌ) of the nominal sentence (جُمْلةٌ إِسْمِيّةٌ). Therefore, ما is grammatically located in the position of a nominative case (فِي مَحَلِّ رَفْعٍ).	ما
This word has the form of a past tense verb. It has a fixed shape and never changes its form (فِعْلٌ ماضٍ مَبْنِيٌّ عَلَى الْفَتْحِ). Its subject (فاعِلٌ) is a hidden, implied pronoun (ضَمِيرٌ مُسْتَتِرٌ) which expresses *he* (هُوَ) and refers back to ما. أَجْمَلَ is a verbal sentence that serves as the **predicate** (خَبَرٌ) of the primary (larger), nominal sentence and is thus grammatically located in the place of a nominative case (فِي مَحَلِّ رَفْعٍ).	أَجْمَلَ

السَّماء	This is the مُتَعَجَّبٌ مِنْهُ. It is the direct object of the verb (أَجْمَلَ); therefore, it takes the accusative case (مَفْعُولٌ بِهِ مَنْصُوبٌ).

What is the function of ما in this sentence? It is neither a question word (اِسْمُ اِسْتِفْهامٍ) nor a relative pronoun (اِسْمٌ مَوْصُولٌ). ➡ It has a special job and is a so-called اِسْمُ تَعَجُّبٍ.

We don't treat such a ما as definite (مَعْرِفةٌ). We say that it is **indefinite in all aspects** (نَكِرةٌ تامّةٌ) because the underlying meaning of the ما here is: *thing* (شَيْءٌ). In other words, *a big thing* (شَيْءٌ كَبِيرٌ), *a wonderful thing* (شَيْءٌ هائِلٌ), *a great thing* (شَيْءٌ عَظِيمٌ), ...

II	verbal sentence	أَجْمِلْ بِالسَّماءِ!
	assumed (virtual) meaning I *	جَمُلَتْ السَّماءُ
	assumed (virtual) meaning II (= *make something beautiful with the sky!*)	يا جَمالُ أَجْمِلْ بِالسَّماءِ!
* Note that *sky* in Arabic is feminine. See *Arabic for Nerds 1, question #56*.		

You have two options for the grammatical analysis (إِعْرابٌ). Note that you cannot mix them.

Option I: You treat أَجْمِلْ as if it was a past tense verb (جَمُلَتْ). ➡ This is the preferred and more common approach.

أَجْمِلْ	Past tense verb (فِعْلٌ ماضٍ) which comes in the form of an imperative (صِيغةُ الأَمْرِ).
بِ	**Redundant/extra** preposition (حَرْفُ جَرٍّ زائِدٌ).
السَّماء	Subject (فاعِلٌ); in the nominative case (مَرْفُوعٌ) by a virtual, estimated ضَمّةٌ (ضَمّةٌ مُقَدَّرةٌ). We cannot put the actual case marker because the كَسْرةٌ, induced by the preposition, occupies the place. So what you see and hear (لَفْظًا) isn't the same as the location would demand (مَحَلًّا) – which would be the nominative case because the word السَّماء supplies the position of the subject (فاعِلٌ).

Option II: You treat أَجْمِلْ as if it was a regular imperative.

Verb in the imperative (فِعْلُ أَمْرٍ). The subject (فاعِلٌ) is a hidden pronoun (ضَميرٌ مُسْتَتِرٌ) expressing *you* (أَنْتَ).	أَجْمِلْ
Redundant/additional preposition (حَرْفُ جَرٍّ زائِدٌ).	بِ
Noun in the genitive case (مَجْرُورٌ), marked by the usual case marker (كَسْرةٌ). The prepositional phrase (الْجارُّ وَالْمَجْرُورُ) is connected with the imperative verb (أَجْمِلْ).	السَّماء

435. Why do we use a past tense form to express astonishment?

The past tense form shows, in fact, the present result of a past event.

The verb patterns أَفْعَلَ and أَفْعِلْ are special. We call them static past tense verbs (فِعْلٌ ماضٍ جامِدٌ) which means that they do not form the present tense nor do they have a مَصْدَرٌ.

They are **not conjugated** and do not take a feminine, dual, or plural marker. And, which might be confusing, they usually do not convey time (زَمَنٌ) although you use a past tense pattern (see *question #438* for the past tense of *verbs of admiration*).

How can we understand the past tense form in such constructions? Here, the past tense (also called perfect tense) has a so-called resultative present tense meaning. In other words, it shows the present result of a past event, of an activity that took place in the past.

		literal meaning	
1	What a beautiful nature!	What has made nature beautiful!	ما أَجْمَلَ الطَّبِيعةَ!
2		Try your ability at making beautiful upon the nature!	أَجْمِلْ بِالطَّبِيعةِ!

In these examples, we are not amazed about the *beauty* of the *nature* in a specific time or event. What is meant here is a **general astonishment**. For this reason, the grammarians say that the جُمْلةُ التَّعَجُّبِ does not have a predicative meaning (جُمْلةٌ خَبَرِيّةٌ). Instead, it is a جُمْلةٌ إِنْشائِيّةٌ which points to the creation/foundation of the astonishment (إِنْشاءُ التَّعَجُّبِ) and therefore to the emotion/excitement of something (عَلَى الْإِنْفِعالِ بِشَيْءٍ ما).

436. *What a pretty blue!* How do you say that?

You need an auxiliary construction.

Let's start with a question: can you use every Arabic verb to express *astonishment, admiration* (التَّعَجُّبُ) by a special pattern? No, you can't.

In *questions #142* and *#434*, we analyzed the sentence *What a beautiful sky!* (ما أَجْمَلَ السَّماءَ). We took the root *to be beautiful* (جَمُلَ) and applied the pattern أَفْعَلَ. It was possible because our construction fulfilled the **following conditions**:

- The pattern أَفْعَلَ is only compatible with triliteral verbs (فِعْلٌ ثُلاثِيّ); therefore, you can only use it for I-verbs (فعل).

- The verb must be in the active voice (مَبْنِيٌّ لِلْمَعْلُومِ).

- The verb is not negated (تامٌّ مُثْبَتٌ).

- The verb can be fully conjugated (فِعْلٌ مُتَصَرِّفٌ).

- The verb expresses an act or state in which one person may compete with or surpass another (قابِلٌ لِلْمُقابَلةِ). For example, you can't be more than *dead* (مات). Also verbs that signify colors are not suitable because they already follow a similar pattern: أَفْعَلُ. For example, the word for *black* is أَسْوَدُ.

What happens if you have a verb that doesn't have all these characteristics? ➡ You need a **helping verb** (فِعْلٌ مُساعِدٌ) and put a مَصْدَرٌ after it. Which words are suitable to do the auxiliary job? Some examples:

to signify the amount	أَكْثَرَ	to signify quality	أَجْوَدَ
to signify a certain degree	أَشَدَّ	to signify pureness	أَنْقَى
to signify beauty or quality	أَجْمَلَ	to signify greatness	أَعْظَمَ

Regarding the مَصْدَرٌ, you can use the regular, standard form (مَصْدَرٌ صَرِيحٌ) or an interpreted infinitive (مَصْدَرٌ مُؤَوَّلٌ) of the **verb** that can't be used to form the التَّعَجُّبُ.

What a reply of him!	ما أَجْوَدَ جَوابَهُ!
	أَجْوِدْ بِجَوابِهِ!

Why did we use a helping verb (أَجْوَدَ)? Couldn't we just take the root of
the III-verb *to answer* (جاوَبَ) and use one of the two patterns for surprise? No, that would not work!

Impossible in Arabic.	ما أَجْوَبَهُ!
	أَجْوِبْ بِهِ!

The helping construction is quite common with colors.

What a magnificent blue color!	ما أَشَدَّ زُرْقَهُ!
What a pretty red it is!	أَحْبِبْ بِحُمْرَتِهِ!
What a pure white!	ما أَنْقَى بَياضَهُ!

How should we treat such sentences grammatically? Let's take the verb
to beg forgiveness (إِسْتَغْفَرَ) and do the analysis.

What a plea for forgiveness of the believer! (How great that the believer asks for forgiveness!)	ما أَجْمَلَ إِسْتِغْفارَ الْمُؤْمِنِ!

اِسْمُ تَعَجُّبٍ denoting *a great thing* (شَيْءٌ عَظِيمٌ). It has an inde-clinable shape. ما here serves as the subject (مُبْتَدَأٌ); thus, it oc-cupies the position of a nominative case (فِي مَحَلِّ رَفْعٍ).	ما
Past tense verb that has a fossilized shape (فِعْلٌ ماضٍ مَبْنِيٌّ عَلَى الْفَتْحِ). The hidden pronoun (ضَمِيرٌ مُسْتَتِرٌ) is the subject (فاعِلٌ) expressing *he* (هُوَ) and referring to ما. The entire verbal sen-tence functions as the predicate (خَبَرٌ) and is grammatically seen as being located in the place of a nominative case (فِي مَحَلِّ رَفْعٍ).	أَجْمَلَ
Direct object (مَفْعُولٌ بِهِ) in the accusative case (مَنْصُوبٌ). This is also the first part of the إِضافةٌ.	إِسْتِغْفارَ
Second part (مُضافٌ إِلَيْهِ) of the إِضافةٌ and therefore in the geni-tive case (مَجْرُورٌ بِالْكَسْرَةِ الظّاهِرَةِ).	الْمُؤْمِنِ

The same sentence – but with the other pattern of the التَّعَجُّبُ:

What a plea for forgiveness of the believer!	أَجْمِلْ بِاسْتِغْفارِ الْمُؤْمِنِ!

Past tense verb (فِعْلٌ ماضٍ) which comes in the form of an imperative (صِيغةُ الأَمْرِ).	أَجْمِلْ
Redundant/extra preposition (حَرْفُ جَرٍّ زائِدٌ).	بِ
Subject (فاعِلٌ); thus, it is located in the place of a nominative case (مَرْفُوعٌ), but only marked by an imaginary, virtual ضَمّةٌ. It can't be shown because the كَسْرةٌ occupies that place which is necessary due to the preceding redundant preposition. This word serves as the first part of the إضافةٌ.	اسْتِغْفارِ
Second part (مُضافٌ إلَيْهِ) of the إضافةٌ. It is in the genitive case (مَجْرُورٌ بالكَسْرةِ الظّاهِرةِ) by the usual marker.	الْمُؤْمِنِ

Watch out: Some people use the pattern of *astonishment* or *admiration* even though they violate one of the conditions. These constructions are often not a real التَّعَجُّبُ since the underlying verb is <u>not</u> a ثُلاثِيٌّ-verb – but languages develop... Remark: What we discussed here is closely related to the comparative/superlative – see *Arabic for Nerds 1*, #189.

437. Can you delete the بِ in the التَّعَجُّبُ-form of أَفْعِلْ بِهِ؟

Yes, this is (theoretically) possible.

You will encounter أَفْعِلْ بِهِ only in ancient texts. If some part of it is obviously missing, we have to be careful to understand the meaning correctly. You can only delete the بِ in أَفْعِلْ بِهِ in one special situation. The governed part of the verb (الْمَعْمُولُ), i.e., the object, <u>must</u> be an **interpreted** مَصْدَرٌ. Only then, you can get rid of the بِ. This مَصْدَرٌ مُؤَوَّلٌ is produced by أَنْ plus verb or أَنَّ plus its governed parts (مَعْمُولَها).

How great that Zayd visits us!	أَجْمِلْ أَنْ يَزُورَنا زَيْدٌ!
This would be the standard form with بِ: ➡	أَجْمِلْ بِزِيارةِ زَيْدٍ!

Let's check the difference:

Verb (فِعْلٌ ماضٍ) in the form of an imperative (صِيغةُ الأَمْرِ).	أَجْمِلْ
Particle of the infinitive that has the power to operate on a follow-	أَنْ

ing verb in the subjunctive mood (حَرْفُ نَصْبٍ وَمَصْدَرٍ).	
Verb in the present tense (فِعْلٌ مُضَارِعٌ) which is put into the مَنْصُوبٌ-mood (subjunctive) by adding a فَتْحَةٌ on the final letter of the verb. The مَصْدَرٌ مُؤَوَّلٌ, which is molded by أَنْ and this verb, **together** with **the imaginary, implied extra preposition** (مَعَ تَقْدِيرِ حَرْفِ جَرٍّ زَائِدٍ), serves as the <u>subject</u> (فَاعِلٌ) of the verb. It thus gets the place value of a nominative case (فِي مَحَلِّ رَفْعٍ).	يَزُورَنَا

Another example:

How great (it is) that you are our guest!	أَجْمِلْ أَنَّكَ ضَيْفُنَا!
This is the meaning of the above sentence: ➡	أَجْمِلْ بِكَوْنِكَ ضَيْفُنَا!

Particle of emphasis and accusative (حَرْفُ تَوْكِيدٍ وَنَصْبٍ).	أَنَّ
Pronominal suffix (ضَمِيرٌ مُتَّصِلٌ) which functions as the "subject" (اِسْمُ أَنَّ); therefore, it is located in the position of an accusative case (فِي مَحَلِّ نَصْبٍ) following the rules of أَنَّ.	كَ
Predicate (خَبَرُ أَنَّ), nominative case (مَرْفُوعٌ). The pronominal suffix (نا) is the مُضَافٌ إِلَيْهِ (the second part) of the إِضَافَةٌ; therefore, it occupies the position of a genitive case (فِي مَحَلِّ جَرٍّ). But you don't see the case marker as the pronominal suffix has an indeclinable shape (مَبْنِيٌّ عَلَى السُّكُونِ).	ضَيْفُنَا
The interpreted مَصْدَرٌ consists of أَنَّ plus its governed words (مَعْمُولَاها), i.e., the اِسْمُ أَنَّ and the predicate. The interpreted مَصْدَرٌ – together with **the estimated extra preposition** (مَعَ تَقْدِيرِ حَرْفٍ زَائِدٍ) – serves as the <u>subject</u> (فَاعِلٌ), occupying the place of a nominative case (فِي مَحَلِّ رَفْعٍ).	

438. How excellent Zayd was! How do you say this in Arabic?

The problem with this sentence is the past tense.

The verb pattern we use to express **admiration** (التَّعَجُّبُ) may have the shape of a past tense verb, but it does not express the notion of time. So the first thing that comes to mind would be a construction with كَانَ? Does that work? Yes, it does. It is the most practical solution.

You have to put the verb كانَ between the ما التَّعَجُّبِيَّةُ and the verb of astonishment (فِعْلُ التَّعَجُّبِ). In other words, if you want to form the past tense of a *verb of astonishment*, you must use كانَ and place it before the *verb of astonishment*.

How often **has** he **drunk** wine!	ما كانَ أَكْثَرَ شُرْبَهُ لِلْخَمْرِ!

→ The letter لام is often found in such constructions. Why is the لِ here? You use لِ plus a genitive noun after the exclamation if there is a مَصْدَرٌ involved (*to drink*) that itself governs an object (*wine*) in the accusative.

How excellent Zayd **was**! (What an excellent man Zayd was!)	ما كانَ أَفْضَلَ زَيْدًا!

There is another, more complex solution which also works:

The literal meaning is confusing: What has made excellent that which Zayd was? What has produced the past excellence of Zayd?	ما أَفْضَلَ ما كانَ زَيْدٌ!

Let's see how we could treat this sentence grammatically.

How generous 'Alī **was**!	ما كانَ أَكْرَمَ عَلِيًّا!

كانَ	**Additional** past tense verb (فِعْلٌ ماضٍ زائِدٌ). It does not have a place in إِعْرابٌ. Additional here means that we do not apply the usual grammatical implications of كانَ. See *question #236*.
أَكْرَمَ	Starting from here, the analysis is similar to a regular form of astonishment. أَكْرَمَ is a static/frozen past tense verb (فِعْلٌ ماضٍ) that forms a verbal sentence with its implied subject. This جُمْلةٌ فِعْلِيّةٌ supplies the location of the predicate (فِي مَحَلِّ رَفْعٍ خَبَرٌ) of the primary (larger) nominal sentence (جُمْلةٌ إِسْمِيّةٌ) with ما as the subject (مُبْتَدَأٌ).
عَلِيًّا	Direct object (مَفْعُولٌ بِهِ مَنْصُوبٌ) of the verb أَكْرَمَ.

439. What happens if we negate an exclamation of surprise?

We need an auxiliary construction.

We have said in *question #434* that the form of admiration and as-tonishment (اَلتَّعَجُّبُ) cannot be negated. So, that's it? No! There is a way out. We use an auxiliary construction and need a مَصْدَرٌ for that. We opt for a مَصْدَرٌ مُؤَوَّلٌ, an interpreted مَصْدَرٌ, formed by أَنْ plus لا which finally results in أَلّا. This device is followed by a verb.

Let's start with a regular negated sentence in the past tense.

The careless did not succeed.	مَا نَجَحَ الْمُهْمِلُ.

Now let's produce a form of admiration and astonishment (اَلتَّعَجُّبُ):

How fair that the careless doesn't succeed!	مَا أَعْدَلَ أَلّا يَنْجَحَ الْمُهْمِلُ!

1	اِسْمُ تَعَجُّبٍ serving as the subject (مُبْتَدَأٌ) of the nominal sen-tence. It can't take case markers; grammatically speaking, it is located in the place of a nominative case (فِي مَحَلِّ رَفْعٍ).	مَا
2	Past tense verb (فِعْلٌ مَاضٍ مَبْنِيٌّ عَلَى الْفَتْحِ). The hidden pro-noun (ضَمِيرٌ مُسْتَتِرٌ) is the subject (فَاعِلٌ). It expresses *he* (هُوَ) referring to مَا. The entire verbal sentence serves as the predi-cate (خَبَرٌ) of the primary (larger) nominal sentence; thus, it is placed in the position of a nominative case (فِي مَحَلِّ رَفْعٍ).	أَعْدَلَ
3	The word أَنْ plus the word لا – which results in أَلّا.	أَلّا
	Particle (حَرْفُ نَصْبٍ وَمَصْدَرٍ) used to produce an interpreted infinitive. It governs the following verb in the مَنْصُوبٌ-mood.	أَنْ
	Negation particle (حَرْفُ نَفْيٍ); doesn't have a place in إِعْرَابٌ.	لا
4	Present tense verb (فِعْلٌ مُضَارِعٌ) in the subjunctive (مَنْصُوبٌ بِأَنْ). The mood is marked by a فَتْحَةٌ.	يَنْجَحَ
5	Subject (فَاعِلٌ) of the verb, in the nominative case (مَرْفُوعٌ بِالضَّمَّةِ الظَّاهِرَةِ).	الْمُهْمِلُ
→ The interpreted مَصْدَرٌ (i.e., أَلّا يَنْجَحَ) serves in the place of the **direct ob-ject of the first verb** (أَعْدَلَ). Regarding its position in the sentence, we can say that it is located in the place of an accusative case (فِي مَحَلِّ نَصْبٍ).		

Now, we use this sentence again and modify the construction.

It is fair that the negligent does not succeed!	أَعْدِلْ بِأَلَّا يَنْجَحَ الْمُهْمِلُ!

Past tense verb (فِعْلٌ ماضٍ) which appears in the form of an imperative (صِيغَةُ الْأَمْرِ).	أَعْدِلْ
Redundant/additional preposition (حَرْفُ جَرٍّ زائِدٌ).	بِ
Subject (فاعِلٌ) of the verb in the nominative case (مَرْفُوعٌ).	الْمُهْمِلُ

What is the difference? Here, the interpreted مَصْدَرٌ (i.e., أَلَّا يَنْجَحَ) serves as the **subject of the first verb** (أَعْدَلَ); regarding its place value, it occupies the place of a nominative case (فِي مَحَلِّ رَفْعِ فاعِلٌ).

440. Can you use a passive verb to express astonishment?

Yes, but we need some tuning – and use a ما الْمَصْدَرِيّةُ.

Let's take the III-verb كافَأ - يُكافِئُ (ء=R3) which means *to reward*. The passive form is كُوفِئَ (*he was rewarded*) and يُكافَأُ (*he is rewarded*).

The hardworking was rewarded.	كُوفِئَ الْمُجِدُّ.

Let's spice up the sentence with an *exclamation* (التَّعَجُّبُ). For this we need an interpreted infinitive built by ما (a ما الْمَصْدَرِيّةُ). Note that an interpreted infinitive doesn't relate to time or tenses.

Let's start with **construction 1**: ما أَجْمَلَ

How great that the hardworking is rewarded!	ما أَجْمَلَ ما كُوفِئَ الْمُجِدُّ!

This is the إِسْمُ تَعَجُّبٍ serving as the subject (مُبْتَدَأٌ). Thus, it occupies the position of a nominative case (فِي مَحَلِّ رَفْعٍ).	ما
Verb in the shape of the past tense (فِعْلٌ ماضٍ مَبْنِيٌّ عَلَى الْفَتْحِ). The hidden pronoun (ضَمِيرٌ مُسْتَتِرٌ) is the subject (فاعِلٌ), expressing *he* (هُوَ) and referring to ما. The verbal sentence is set as the predicate (خَبَرٌ) in the place of a nominative (فِي مَحَلِّ رَفْعٍ).	أَجْمَلَ
This is a حَرْفُ مَصْدَرِيّةٍ. It does not have a position in إِعْرابٌ.	ما
Past tense verb in the **passive** form. Together with ما, it forms an	كُوفِئَ

interpreted infinitive (مَصْدَرٌ مُؤَوَّلٌ). This **interpreted** مَصْدَرٌ serves as the <u>direct object</u> (مَفْعُولٌ بِهِ); therefore, it is located in the place of an accusative case (فِي مَحَلِّ نَصْبِ) and we assign the "place value" of an accusative case.	
Subject of the passive (نَائِبُ فَاعِلٍ), in the nominative (مَرْفُوعٌ).	الْمُجِدُّ

Construction 2: أَجْمِلْ بِ. That's a pretty complex construction.

How great that the hardworking is rewarded!	أَجْمِلْ بِما كُوفِئَ الْمُجِدُّ!
فِعْلٌ ماضٍ, appearing in the form of an imperative (صِيغَةُ الْأَمْرِ).	أَجْمِلْ
Additional, redundant preposition (حَرْفُ جَرٍّ زائِدٌ).	بِ
Particle producing an interpreted infinitive (حَرْفُ مَصْدَرِيَّةٍ).	ما
Past tense verb in the passive form.	كُوفِئَ
The **interpreted** مَصْدَرٌ (i.e., ما كُوفِئَ) serves as the <u>subject</u> (فاعِلٍ) of أَجْمِلْ; thus, it is in the spot of a nominative case (فِي مَحَلِّ رَفْعِ فاعِلٍ).	
Passive subject (نَائِبُ فَاعِلٍ) of the passive verb كُوفِئَ; in the nominative case (مَرْفُوعٌ).	الْمُجِدُّ

What happens if we have a verb that is (almost) exclusively used in the passive tense (مُلازِمٌ لِلْبِناءِ الْمَجْهُولِ)? Then it is better to use a standard form of the التَّعَجُّبُ. In Arabic, e.g., the verb *to hurry, hasten* (هُرِعَ) is almost only used in the passive – but when translated into English, often the active voice is used.

Zayd hastened.	هُرِعَ زَيْدٌ.

We should apply one of the standard patterns of the التَّعَجُّبُ:

What a hurry by Zayd!	ما أَهْرَعَ زَيْدًا! or أَهْرِعْ بِزَيْدٍ!

441. How do you express admiration with the verb *to be*?

It is difficult to imagine something that is greater than being.

The good news is: there is a solution. Verbs like *to be* (كانَ) or *to be-*

come (أَصْبَحَ) are verbs of existence. In Arabic, we call them *incomplete* or *defective, deficient* verbs (فِعْلٌ نَاقِصٌ) – see *question #58*.

If the defective verb has a مَصْدَر, it is simple. You put the مَصْدَر after the صِيغَةُ التَّعَجُّبِ. The مَصْدَر serves as the direct object and as well as the first part of a إِضافة. Let's first look at a regular sentence with كانَ.

Zayd was generous.	كانَ زَيْدٌ كَرِيمًا.

The verb كانَ has a مَصْدَرٌ: *being* (كَوْن). So let's try to build an exclamation of astonishment, admiration or wonder (التَّعَجُّبُ):

1	How great that Zayd is generous! (Watch out: Don't treat *great* as an adverb for *generous*. It does not mean *greatly generous*.)	مَا أَعْظَمَ كَوْنَ زَيْدٍ كَرِيمًا!
2		أَعْظِمْ بِكَوْنِ زَيْدٍ كَرِيمًا!

Now, what should we do if the verb does not have a مَصْدَرٌ? For example, the verb كادَ which expresses *almost; to be about to*. Before we go straight into the analysis, let's first analyze the nature of كادَ. The verb كادَ (which was originally كَوِدَ) is weaker than *to be* (كانَ).

Sībawayhi (سيبويه) suggested that we we do not use the active participle (اِسْمُ الْفَاعِلِ) of كادَ for that reason whereas with كانَ this is possible without a problem. We also don't use the imperative of كادَ – but we do it with كانَ. However, in ancient times as well as in poetry, though rarely, the مَصْدَرٌ of كادَ was used:

I will not do that, nor will I be near to doing it.	لَا أَفْعَلُ ذلِكَ وَلَا كَوْدًا.

The main difference between كانَ and كادَ is the following:

→ كادَ needs a **verbal sentence** as a predicate (خَبَرُ كادَ) whereas كانَ (*to be*) can easily take a simple noun. This is the underlying problem of not having a مَصْدَرٌ, of not expressing any kind of action. So there is no مَصْدَرٌ of كادَ. How can we fix that? Is there a way out?

- We need <u>another</u> ما to form an interpreted مَصْدَرٌ.
- We apply the صِيغَةُ التَّعَجُّبِ by putting the original verb (which doesn't have a مَصْدَرٌ) before the ما. By doing this, we produce an interpreted مَصْدَرٌ, which serves as the direct object. The مَصْدَرٌ مُؤَوَّلٌ consists of ما plus verb (and its implied subject).

The negligent almost perished.	كادَ الْمُهْمِلُ يَهْلِكُ.

1	How plentiful are the negligent who almost perished!	ما أَكْثَرَ ما كادَ الْمُهْمِلُ يَهْلِكُ!
2		أَكْثِرْ بِما كادَ الْمُهْمِلُ يَهْلِكُ!

Analysis of construction 1:

اِسْمُ تَعَجُّبٍ. It is the subject (مُبْتَدَأٌ) of the nominal sentence; thus, it is located in the place of a nominative case (فِي مَحَلِّ رَفْعٍ).	ما
Past tense verb (فِعْلٌ ماضٍ). Its subject (فاعِلٌ) is hidden and refers back to **ما**. The entire verbal sentence is the predicate (خَبَر) of the nominal sentence, thus in the place of a nominative (فِي مَحَلِّ رَفْعٍ).	أَكْثَرَ
Infinitive particle (حَرْفُ مَصْدَرِيَّةٍ). Does not have a place in إِعْرابٌ.	ما
Defective past tense verb (فِعْلٌ ماضٍ ناقِصٌ). This verb, together with the preceding particle, forms a مَصْدَرٌ مُؤَوَّلٌ. The interpreted مَصْدَرٌ is the **direct object** of the verb أَكْثَرَ. Therefore, it is grammatically located in the place of an accusative case (فِي مَحَلِّ نَصْبٍ).	كادَ

What is the difference to construction 2? In construction 2, the interpreted مَصْدَرٌ serves as the **subject** (فاعِلٌ) of the **verb** أَكْثَرَ. Therefore, it is located in the place of a nominative case (فِي مَحَلِّ رَفْعٍ).

PRAISE AND BLAME (جُمْلَةُ الْمَدْحِ وَالذَّمِّ)

442. Which words do you use for praise and blame?

Two indeclinable, static verbs (فِعْلٌ جامِدٌ) in the past tense form are used for exclamations of praise and blame.

Arabic has a fine way (أُسْلُوب) to express **praise** (الْمَدْحُ) or **criticism/blame** (الذَّمُّ). There are fossilized verbs whose purpose is to express the **confirmation** of praise or blame.

1	What a perfect...! Wonderful...! How good...!	نِعْمَ
2	What a bad...! How bad...!	بِئْسَ

| Sura 5:63 | How evil their deeds are! (How wretched is what they have been practicing!) | لَبِئْسَ مَا كَانُوا يَصْنَعُونَ. |

Let's jump into the grammar and see how we can apply them. First of all, what kind of sentence do we get? We may get a nominal **or** a verbal sentence. There are two ways to treat them (إِعْرَابٌ). Let's see why.

| What a wonderful leader Khālid is! | نِعْمَ الْقَائِدُ خَالِدٌ! |

OPTION 1: nominal sentence (جُمْلَةٌ اِسْمِيَّةٌ)

Indeclinable past tense verb (فِعْلٌ مَاضٍ جَامِدٌ).	نِعْمَ
Subject of the verb (فَاعِلٌ) in the nominative case (مَرْفُوعٌ).	الْقَائِدُ
The verbal sentence (consisting of a verb and a subject) appears in the position of the **fronted predicate** (خَبَرٌ مُقَدَّمٌ) of the nominal sentence. We apply the usual case marker of a nominative case (فِي مَحَلِّ رَفْعٍ).	
Delayed subject (مُبْتَدَأٌ مُؤَخَّرٌ) of the nominal sentence, مَرْفُوعٌ.	خَالِدٌ

Why do we say it is a nominal sentence? ➡ The one who is targeted by the praise (الْمَخْصُوصُ بِالْمَدْحِ) functions as the **delayed subject** (مُبْتَدَأٌ مُؤَخَّرٌ). The entire verbal sentence (جُمْلَةٌ فِعْلِيَّةٌ) appears as the fronted predicate (خَبَرٌ مُقَدَّمٌ). We could rewrite the sentence as follows:

| Khālid is the best leader! (What an excellent leader...) | خَالِدٌ نِعْمَ الْقَائِدُ! |

OPTION 2: verbal sentence (جُمْلَةٌ فِعْلِيَّةٌ)

Indeclinable past tense verb (فِعْلٌ مَاضٍ جَامِدٌ).	نِعْمَ
Subject (فَاعِلٌ) of the verb; nominative case (مَرْفُوعٌ).	الْقَائِدُ
Predicate of the **deleted subject of the nominal sentence** (خَبَرٌ لِمُبْتَدَإٍ مَحْذُوفٍ). What does the deleted subject stand for? It has the imaginary, estimated meaning (تَقْدِيرٌ) of *he* (هُوَ).	خَالِدٌ

Why is it regarded as a verbal sentence (جُمْلَةٌ فِعْلِيَّةٌ)? ➡ The one who is targeted (الْمَخْصُوصُ بِالْمَدْحِ) is placed as the **predicate** (خَبَرٌ) of the deleted subject (مُبْتَدَأٌ مَحْذُوفٌ). The estimated, virtual meaning (تَقْدِيرٌ) of option 2 could be the following:

Literally: What an excellent leader *(he)* is Khālid.	نِعْمَ الْقَائِدُ هُوَ خَالِدٌ.

There is even a third way (إِعْرَابٌ). We also assume a verbal sentence, but one word is treated differently.

Apposition, also called **permutative** (بَدَلُ كُلٍّ مِن الْقَائِد). A بَدَلٌ re-ceives the same case as the word it refers to(i.e., الْقَائِدُ). Therefore, it takes the **nominative** case (مَرْفُوعٌ بِالضَّمّةِ الظّاهِرةِ).	خَالِدٌ

443. Why are نِعْمَ and بِئْسَ regarded as verbs?

To be honest, it's not entirely clear if they are verbs at all.

Are the نِعْمَ and بِئْسَ nouns or verbs? The debate goes back to the prime of Classical Arabic. You will find supportive ideas for both views.

The **grammarians of Kūfa** (الْكُوفِيُّونَ) stated that these words are nouns (اِسْمٌ). The Kūfans, for example al-Farrā' (الْفَرّاء) came to this conclusion for several reasons. One of the main reasons was that these two words, نِعْمَ and بِئْسَ, are used with prepositions. Note that only a noun (but certainly not a verb) can immediately follow a preposition. Here is an example:

What a beautiful trip on such a miser-able donkey!	نِعْمَ السَّيْرُ عَلَى بِئْسَ الْعَيْرُ!

However, this is not the view of the majority of grammarians. The most common handling of these two words is what the **Basran grammari-ans** (الْبَصْرِيُّونَ) proposed. They suggested that نِعْمَ and بِئْسَ are verbs, to be precise: **indeclinable, frozen, aplastic, fossilized verbs** (فِعْلٌ جَامِدٌ). Why fossilized verbs? Because the present tense (مُضارِعٌ) and the imperative (أَمْرٌ) are not used; moreover, derived nouns (مُشْتَقّات) of both roots do not exist, e.g., you can't form the active participle.

So, why did the Basrans say that نِعْمَ and بِئْسَ are verbs? Theoretically both verbs may get a final ت to produce the feminine form (إِلْحاقُ تاءٍ التَّأْنِيثِ السّاكِنةِ). For ex.: *What an excellent woman!* (نِعْمَتُ الْمَرْأَةُ). This is, however, extremely rare because usually they are treated as frozen/fossilized verbs (only one form).

Furthermore, their shape resembles a verb in the past tense. Now we come closer to the crucial point. How would the Basrans explain sentences with a preposition which was the main reason why their rivals, the Kūfans, opted to regard them as nouns? The Basrans would explain such an application by an underlying, virtual attribute (قَوْلٌ مُقَدَّرٌ):

What a beautiful trip on a donkey **about which it is said:** such a miserable donkey!	نِعْمَ السَّيرُ عَلَى عَيْرٍ مَقولٍ فِيهِ: بِئْسَ الْعَيْرُ!

In this book, I follow the view of the Basrans and treat them as **pseudo-verbs**. This has huge implications. It automatically means that we need a **subject** (فاعِلٌ). We will discuss that in the next *question*.

444. How does the subject of a *praise and blame*-sentence look like?

You have three options.

Let's take a look at how we can solve the question of the subject.

OPTION 1. This is the most common approach. The subject (of these pseudo-verbs) is a **single, definite** (مَعْرِفةٌ) **noun**.

The subject could be a proper noun. Or it is definite by ال or by serving as the first part of a إِضافةٌ.

What an excellent leader of the Muslim army Muhammad is!	نِعْمَ قائِدُ جَيْشِ الْمُسْلِمِينَ مُحَمَّدٌ!
Indeclinable past tense verb (فِعْلٌ ماضٍ جامِدٌ).	نِعْمَ
Subject of the verb (فاعِلٌ); therefore it is in the nominative case (مَرْفوعٌ بِالضَّمّةِ الظّاهِرةِ). It is also the first part of a complex إِضافةٌ-construction (مُضافٌ إِلَى مُضافٍ).	قائِدُ
Second and third part of the إِضافةٌ-construction. The third	جَيْشِ

part (i.e., الْمُسْلِمِينَ) is put into the genitive case by the ي.	الْمُسْلِمِينَ
The sentence consisting of a verb and a subject serves as the fronted predicate (خَبَرٌ مُقَدَّمٌ) and is thus located in the place of a nominative (فِي مَحَلِّ رَفْعٍ).	
Delayed subject (مُبْتَدَأٌ مُؤَخَّرٌ) of the nominal sentence, it is in the nominative case (مَرْفُوعٌ).	مُحَمَّدٌ

OPTION 2. The subject is a **hidden pronoun** (ضَمِيرٌ مُسْتَتِرٌ). Then, the subject we will get a **specification** (تَمْيِيزٌ) after the verb.

What a great leader Khalid is!	نِعْمَ قَائِدًا خَالِدٌ!
Indeclinable past tense verb (فِعْلٌ مَاضٍ جَامِدٌ). Subject (فَاعِلٌ) is a hidden pronoun (ضَمِيرٌ مُسْتَتِرٌ); the implied meaning is *he* (هُوَ).	نِعْمَ
The sentence consisting of verb + subject serves as the fronted predicate (خَبَرٌ مُقَدَّمٌ); it is located in the place of a nominative case (فِي مَحَلِّ رَفْعٍ).	
Specification (تَمْيِيزٌ); in the accusative case (مَنْصُوبٌ). The specification defines *he*, i.e., the hidden pronoun.	قَائِدًا
Delayed subject (مُبْتَدَأٌ مُؤَخَّرٌ) in the nominative case (مَرْفُوعٌ).	خَالِدٌ

Note that you could also use a تَمْيِيزٌ with a visible, normal subject.

What a hardworking student Zayd is!	نِعْمَ الطَّالِبُ مُجْتَهِدًا زَيْدٌ!
Subject; in the nominative case (فَاعِلٌ مَرْفُوعٌ). The verbal sentence (verb plus subject) serves as the fronted predicate and occupies the place of a nominative case.	الطَّالِبُ
Specification (تَمْيِيزٌ); therefore, it is in the accusative (مَنْصُوبٌ).	مُجْتَهِدًا

OPTION 3. The noun ما (or مَنْ) is the subject.

Note that you could also use ما instead of مَنْ.

What a deed that you do for the good!	نِعْمَ ما تَفْعَلُ الْخَيْرُ!
Relative pronoun (اِسْمٌ مَوْصُولٌ) which means *which/that* (الَّذِي).	ما

The indeclinable noun **مَا** serves as the **subject** (فَاعِلٌ), so it is located in the place of a nominative case (فِي مَحَلِّ رَفْعٍ).	
Verb in the present tense, indicative mood (فِعْلٌ مُضَارِعٌ مَرْفُوعٌ). The subject (فَاعِلٌ) of this verb is a hidden pronoun (ضَمِيرٌ مُسْتَتِرٌ) having the implied meaning of: *you* (أَنْتَ).	تَفْعَلُ
The sentence consisting of verb (تَفْعَلُ) and subject is the **relative clause** (صِلَةُ الْمَوْصُولِ). It does not have a position in إِعْرَابٌ.	
The sentence consisting of نِعْمَ plus subject (مَا) serves as the fronted predicate (خَبَرٌ مُقَدَّمٌ); it occupies the place of a nominative case (فِي مَحَلِّ رَفْعٍ).	
Delayed subject (مُبْتَدَأٌ مُؤَخَّرٌ مَرْفُوعٌ) of the nominal sentence in the nominative case.	الْخَيْرُ

Watch out: There is another way to analyze (إِعْرَابٌ) the above sentence.

Indeclinable past tense verb (فِعْلٌ مَاضٍ جَامِدٌ). It has an implied hidden pronoun (ضَمِيرٌ مُسْتَتِرٌ) serving as the subject and expressing *he* (هُوَ). The verbal sentence takes over the role of the fronted predicate (فِي مَحَلِّ رَفْعٍ خَبَرٌ مُقَدَّمٌ); thus, it is grammatically positioned in the place of a nominative case.	نِعْمَ
Specification (تَمْيِيزٌ). It has a fixed shape (مَبْنِيٌّ عَلَى السُّكُونِ); therefore, it can't visibly express the accusative. We can only say that it is found in the place of an accusative case (فِي مَحَلِّ نَصْبٍ).	مَا
Verb in the present tense, indicative mood (فِعْلٌ مُضَارِعٌ مَرْفُوعٌ). The sentence consisting of the verb plus the hidden subject serves as an **adjective** (صِفَةٌ) for مَا.	تَفْعَلُ
An adjective gets the same case as the word it describes. In our example, the accusative case. But we can only assign a "place value". We say that the entire verbal sentence is set in the position of an accusative (فِي مَحَلِّ نَصْبٍ).	
Delayed subject (مُبْتَدَأٌ مُؤَخَّرٌ مَرْفُوعٌ) in the nominative case.	الْخَيْرُ

That's some pretty heavy grammar stuff. Let's try to summarize the most important points. The dispute is about the character (type) of مَا. Is it a relative pronoun (إِسْمٌ مَوْصُولٌ)? Or is it an indefinite noun (إِسْمٌ نَكِرَةٌ)? This question is not trivial at all.

- If ما works as a اِسْمٌ مَوْصُولٌ, then ما is the subject (فَاعِلٌ) and the sentence after it is the relative clause (صِلَةٌ لَهُ). Sometimes, the verb and ما become fused resulting in نِعِمَّا or بِئْسَمَا

- If ما works as a اِسْمٌ نَكِرَةٌ, then it is a تَمْيِيزٌ. Note that a specification has to be indefinite by definition. This brings along that the sentence after it is placed as an adjective (صِفَةٌ لَهُ). The sentence, which fills the place of an adjective, could have the following virtual, assumed meaning:

What a deed for the good you do!	نِعْمَ شَيْئًا تَفْعَلُ الْخَيْرُ!

Excursus: *Zaynab is an excellent woman!* Which verb form would you use? In general, نِعْمَ and بِئْسَ prefer to be used in the **masculine** form, even if the subject is clearly feminine (by signification).

Zaynab is an excellent woman!	نِعْمَ الْمَرْأَةُ زَيْنَبُ!
You use the masculine form and not the feminine which would be نِعْمَتْ.	

445. What does the pattern فَعُلَ express?

It can express the meaning of نِعْمَ or بِئْسَ.

Most I-verbs of triliteral roots (فِعْلٌ ثُلاثِيٌّ مُجَرَّدٌ) can apply the pattern فَعُلَ to express the meaning of نِعْمَ or بِئْسَ. Such verb forms can be used in the **praise and blame**-style with the result that they express good or bad stuff.

	contracted form*				cont. f.*	
to be quick	سَرْعَ or سُرْعَ	سَرُعَ		to be far off	بُعْدَ	بَعُدَ
to be good	حُسْنَ	حَسُنَ				

* Note: the contracted form (سُكُونٌ in the middle) is more common.

What a great man Zayd is!	حَسُنَ زَيْدٌ!
What a good student Zayd is!	حَسُنَ الطَّالِبُ زَيْدٌ!

Indeclinable past tense verb (فِعْلٌ ماضٍ جامِدٌ).	حَسُنَ
Subject (فاعِلٌ) of the verb in the nominative case (مَرْفوعٌ).	الطّالِبُ
The sentence consisting of verb plus subject is the fronted predicate (خَبَرٌ مُقَدَّمٌ). It is located in the place of a nominative case (في مَحَلِّ رَفْعٍ).	زَيْدٌ
Delayed subject (مُبْتَدَأٌ مُـؤَخَّرٌ) of the nominal sentence; it is therefore in the nominative case (مَرْفوعٌ بِالضَّمّةِ الظّاهِرةِ).	زَيْدٌ

An example that uses a specification (تَمْييزٌ).

What a good student Zayd is!	حَسُنَ طالِبًا زَيْدٌ!

Indeclinable verb, past tense (فِعْلٌ ماضٍ جامِدٌ). Its subject (فاعِلٌ) is a hidden, implied pronoun (ضَميرٌ مُسْتَتِرٌ) expressing *he* (هُوَ). This verbal sentence serves as the fronted predicate (خَبَرٌ مُقَدَّمٌ) of the primary nominal sentence (جُمْلةٌ اِسْمِيّةٌ); thus, it holds the place of a nominative case (في مَحَلِّ رَفْعٍ).	حَسُنَ
Delayed subject (مُبْتَدَأً مُؤَخَّرٌ) of the nominal sentence, مَرْفوع.	زَيْدٌ

446. Is the verb حَبَّ used for praise or for blame?

It can be used for both – as a synonym for نِعْمَ or بِئْسَ.

The I-verb حَبَّ (*to love*) can be used to express praise or blame. We assume that it is a contracted form of حَبُبَ (#445), because Arabic does not like it when two letters of the same kind are next to each other;.

- If حَبَّ is **not negated** (مُثْبَتٌ), it is used for **praise** (الْمَدْحُ): *How adorable is… how nice, lovely, charming, excellent, is…*

- If حَبَّ is preceded by لا, the negative particle (حَرْفُ نَفْيٍ), it is used to express **blame** (الذَّمُّ): *How not adorable is…*

Note: A noun that follows it is in the **nominative** case (مَرْفوعٌ).

No matter what you want to express, both applications share the following grammatical implications. The translation depends on the context. Normally, an exclamation such as *"What a…!"* or *"How lucky that…"* work quite well in most situations.

a) The **subject** (فَاعِلٌ) is a demonstrative noun (إِسْمُ الْإِشارَةِ): ذا. We finally get the <u>indeclinable</u> word حَبَّذا – *lovely, charming, excellent is…*

With the demonstrative ذا, it becomes the fossilized verb حَبَّذا. It is completely cemented (invariable) and used to introduce sentences expressing a strong wish, usually with لَوْ (*how nice it would be if…*).

How lovely you are!	حَبَّذا أَنْتَ!
That's just wonderful!	يا حَبَّذا الْحالُ!
That's fantastic! (How lovely the solution is!)	حَبَّذا الْحالُ!
How disgusting the lie is! (Lying is not good!)	لا حَبَّذا الْكِذْبُ!

Let's analyze the sentence حَبَّذا الْحالُ. If we dissect the sentence, we get the following ingredients: *This is adored + the solution.*

Indeclinable past tense verb (فِعْلٌ ماضٍ جامِدٌ).	حَبَّ
Demonstrative (إِسْمُ إِشارَةٍ). It is the subject (فَاعِلٌ) of the verb. Since it has a fixed shape, we can't visibly mark the case. We can only assign a "place value": that of a nominative (فِي مَحَلِّ رَفْعٍ).	ذا
Both words are usually written together. The verbal sentence consisting of the verb (حَبَّ) and the subject (ذا) serves as the fronted predicate (خَبَرٌ مُقَدَّمٌ); it appears in the place of a nominative case (فِي مَحَلِّ رَفْعٍ).	
This is the delayed subject (مُبْتَدَأٌ مُؤَخَّرٌ مَرْفُوعٌ بِالضَّمَّةِ الظّاهِرَةِ) of the nominal sentence, marked by the usual case marker ـُ.	الْحالُ

It is possible to use a **specification** (تَمْييزٌ) after ذا.

What a loyal guy Zayd is!	حَبَّذا صادِقًا زَيْدٌ!

If we dissect the sentence, we get the following ingredients: *This is adored + in terms of being loyal + Zayd.*

Verb plus subject (ذا) serving as the fronted predicate (خَبَرٌ مُقَدَّمٌ), placed in the location of a nominative case (فِي مَحَلِّ رَفْعٍ).	حَبَّذا
Specification (تَمْييزٌ مَنْصُوبٌ). It must get the accusative according to the rules of a تَمْييزٌ. Note that the تَمْييزٌ must be **indefinite**.	صادِقًا

Delayed subject (مُبْتَدَأٌ مُؤَخَّرٌ) of the nominal sentence; marked in the nominative case (مَرْفُوعٌ بِالضَّمَّةِ الظَّاهِرةِ).	زَيْدٌ

b) The subject (فاعِلٌ) is any noun (اِسْمٌ) other than ذا.

This allows us to use different **vowels** for the **first letter** of حبّ. You have the choice: a فَتْحةٌ ("a" = ـَ) resulting in حَبَّ or a ضَمَّةٌ ("u" = ـُ) resulting in حُبَّ. The variant with فَتْحةٌ is more common.

Watch out: If you use the ضَمَّةٌ, you still treat the word after it as the subject (فاعِلٌ) of a regular, **active voice** because حُبَّ here is <u>not</u> the passive form (هُوَ لَيْسَ فِعْلًا مَبْنِيًّا لِلْمَجْهُول) although it looks like that.

1	What an honest guy Zayd is!	حَبَّ الصَّادِقُ زَيْدٌ!
2	Ingredients: *The loyal is adored + Zayd.*	حُبَّ الصَّادِقُ زَيْدٌ!

الصَّادِقُ is the subject (فاعِلٌ) of the indeclinable past tense verb حَبَّ. Together with the subject, it serves as a fronted predicate (خَبَرٌ مُقَدَّمٌ) which takes the grammatical place of a nominative case (فِي مَحَلِّ رَفْعٍ).

The word Zayd (زَيْدٌ) is the delayed subject (مُبْتَدَأٌ مُؤَخَّرٌ مَرْفُوعٌ) of the primary, larger nominal sentence in the nominative case. Also here, the verbal subject (فاعِلٌ) might be dragged into the genitive case (جَرٌّ) by an extra/redundant preposition ب, a so-called بَاءٌ زائِدَةٌ.

How great Zayd is loyal!	حَبَّ or حُبَّ بِالصَّادِقِ زَيْدٌ!
Additional preposition (حَرْفُ جَرٍّ زائِدٌ); no place in إعْرابٌ.	ب
Subject of the verbal sentence (فاعِلٌ مَرْفُوعٌ), marked by a virtual case marker (مَرْفُوعٌ بِضَمَّةٍ مُقَدَّرةٍ) because the كَسْرةٌ occupies the place of the case marker.	الصَّادِقِ
The whole sentence consisting of verb and subject serves as the fronted predicate (خَبَرٌ مُقَدَّمٌ); therefore, it is grammatically treated as holding the place of a nominative case (فِي مَحَلِّ رَفْعٍ).	
Delayed subject (مُبْتَدَأٌ مُؤَخَّرٌ); therefore, it is marked in the nominative case (مَرْفُوعٌ بِالضَّمَّةِ الظَّاهِرةِ).	زَيْدٌ

c) It is possible that the subject (فاعِلٌ) is a **hidden pronoun** (ضَمِيرٌ مُسْتَتِرٌ) that is further described by a **specification** (تَمْيِيزٌ).

What an honest guy Zayd is!	حَبَّ صادِقًا زَيْدٌ!

If we dissect the sentence, we get the following ingredients: *He is adored + in terms of being loyal + Zayd.*

Indeclinable past tense verb. The subject (الْفاعِلُ) is a hidden pronoun (ضَمِير مُسْتَتِر وُجُوبًا) with the implied meaning of *he* (هُوَ). This verb with its implied subject is a whole sentence that is placed as a fronted predicate (خَبَرٌ مُقَدَّمٌ); thus, it is grammatically in the place of a nominative case (فِي مَحَلِّ رَفْعٍ).	حَبَّ
This word describes the implied subject further. It is a specification (تَمْيِيزٌ) in the accusative case (مَنْصُوبٌ بِالْفَتْحةِ الظّاهِرةِ).	صادِقًا
Delayed subject (مُبْتَدَأً مُؤَخَّرٌ) of the nominal sentence; therefore, it is in the nominative case (مَرْفُوعٌ بِالضَّمّةِ الظّاهِرةِ).	زَيْدٌ

THE OATH – TAKING A VOW (جُمْلةُ الْقَسَمِ)

447. How can you swear *by Allah* in Arabic?

You have several options.

The oath (قَسَمٌ) is a complicated construction (أُسْلُوبٌ) in Arabic. An oath is technically made of the following parts:

1. A verb (فِعْلُ الْقَسَمِ); so, we have a verbal sentence (جُمْلةٌ فِعْلِيّةٌ) which is called جُمْلةُ الْقَسَمِ.

2. This verb (فِعْلُ الْقَسَمِ) can be visible/pronounced (مَذْكُورٌ) or it is deleted (مَحْذُوفٌ). If it is not there, it is implicitly understood.

3. After the verb, we have a prepositional phrase (شِبْهُ الْجُمْلةِ). It consists of the particle of oath (a preposition/حَرْفُ الْجَرِّ) plus a noun in the genitive case (مَجْرُورٌ), the الْاِسْمُ الْمُقْسَمُ بِهِ, which is the person you swear by. You cannot use an oath without a *particle of oath*, (e.g.: بِ.) The prepositional phrase is linked to the فِعْلُ الْقَسَمِ, no matter if the verb is pronounced or not.

4. Usually you also find the information which should be confirmed by the oath (جَوابُ الْقَسَم).

I swear by Allah!	أُقْسِمُ بِاللهِ!	←	*to take an oath by*	أَقْسَمَ بِ	1
	أَحْلِفُ بِاللهِ!		*to swear by*	حَلَفَ بِ	2
	بِاللهِ!		*without a verb*		3

Three swear particles may provide the force of a verb:

بِ	وَ	تَ

The تَ is very rare and only used when people swear by Allah/God. It was especially used in Mecca in ancient times.

The بِ is the original particle of the oath. The بِ usually goes along with the verb (فِعْلُ الْقَسَم) which means that you pronounce the verb. On the contrary, وَ and تَ are used without the verb – therefore, the verb must be deleted and is not pronounced.

I swear by God!	وَاللهِ	equals	أُقْسِمُ بِاللهِ!
	تَاللهِ		بِاللهِ!

not correct		أُقْسِمُ وَاللهِ لَأَفْعَلَنَّ الْيَوْمَ!
correct	I swear, I will do it today!	أُقْسِمُ بِاللهِ لَأَفْعَلَنَّ الْيَوْمَ!

بِ can be used with a **separate noun** (اِسْمٌ ظاهِرٌ) or just with a pronoun (ضَمِيرٌ). For example, the sentence *I swear by him* (أُقْسِمُ بِهِ) is correct. However, وَ and تَ can only be used with a اِسْمٌ ظاهِرٌ.

بِ can be **followed by a question** (جُمْلَةٌ اِسْتِفْهامِيّةٌ) which is used as the complement of the oath (جَوابُ الْقَسَم). However, this is not possible with وَ and تَ.

correct		بِاللهِ، هَلْ أَدَّيْتَ واجِبَكَ؟
not correct	By God, did you fulfill your duties?	وَاللهِ، هَلْ أَدَّيْتَ واجِبَكَ؟
not correct		تَاللهِ، هَلْ أَدَّيْتَ واجِبَكَ؟

448. What are the specialties of the complement of the oath?

In some situations, you might need to add إِنَّ *plus* لَ *or just* لَ.

An oath wouldn't make sense without the information you want to swear on (i.e., to confirm). This information is called the **complement of an oath** (جَوابُ الْقَسَمِ). It can be a nominal or verbal sentence. Like any other جَوابٌ, the جَوابُ الْقَسَمِ doesn't have a position in إِعْرابٌ.

Now comes the interesting stuff.

Situation 1. What happens if the جَوابُ الْقَسَمِ is an affirmative, nominal sentence (جُمْلةٌ اِسْمِيّةٌ)?	* non-negated * nominal sentence

➡ Then, the جَوابُ الْقَسَمِ is almost always accompanied by إِنَّ and لَ (a لامٌ مُزَحْلَقةٌ) which is placed later in the sentence. This construction helps to convey some emphasis. At least one of the two (إِنَّ or لَ) is usually found in such sentences.

By God, verily Muhammad is His apostle!	وَاللهِ إِنَّ مُحَمَّدًا لَرَسُولُهُ!

Particle (حَرْفُ الْجَرِّ) that is used for an oath, followed by a noun in the genitive case (مَجْرُورٌ).	وَ
The whole expression وَاللهِ is a quasi-sentence (شِبْهُ الْجُمْلةِ) which is connected with a deleted verb (فِعْلٌ مَحْذُوفٌ), having the underlying, assumed meaning of *I swear* (أُقْسِمُ).	
Particle of emphasis; it governs a following word in the accusative case (حَرْفُ تَوْكِيدٍ وَنَصْبٍ).	إِنَّ
This is the اِسْمُ إِنَّ, so it has to be in the accusative case (مَنْصُوبٌ).	مُحَمَّدًا
Lām (used for emphasis) that is pushed away from its proper place (لامٌ مُزَحْلَقةٌ). It is originally a لامُ الْإِبْتِداءِ which means that it is placed right at the beginning of a sentence. However, the لَ is slid (مُزَحْلَقةٌ) and put closer to the end if we have a sentence with إِنَّ in order to avoid that two devices of emphasis meet at the beginning (كَراهِيةُ ابْتِداءِ الْكَلامِ بِمُؤَكِّدَيْنِ).	لَ
Predicate (خَبَرُ إِنَّ); nominative (مَرْفُوعٌ). First part of the إِضافةٌ.	رَسُولُ
The sentence starting from إِنَّ is the جَوابُ الْقَسَمِ; no place in إِعْرابٌ.	

We could also express this sentence by إِنَّ or لَ only.

Only with إِنَّ ➡	وَاللهِ إِنَّ مُحَمَّدًا رَسُولُهُ!
Only with لَ ➡	وَاللهِ لَمُحَمَّدٌ رَسُولُهُ!

Situation 2. What happens if the complement after the oath is a negated, nominal sentence (جُمْلَةٌ إِسْمِيّةٌ مَنْفِيّةٌ)؟	* negated * nominal sent.

➡ Then, the complement (جَوابُ الْقَسَم) is **not connected** with anything but the **negation particle** (حَرْفُ نَفْيٍ).

I swear to Allah, no one is immortal!	وَاللهِ ما إِنْسانٌ مُخْلِدٌ!
By Allah, Muhammad is not a liar!	وَاللهِ ما مُحَمَّدٌ كاذِبٌ!

Situation 3. What happens if the جَوابُ الْقَسَم is a non-negated (affirmative) verbal sentence (جُمْلَةٌ فِعْلِيّةٌ مُثْبَتَةٌ) with a verb in the present tense (فِعْلٌ مُضارِعٌ)؟	* non-negated * verbal sentence * present tense

➡ Then, the complement is connected with a لَ and a نُونُ التَّوْكِيدِ.

Sura 38:82	Iblis (Satan) said, "I swear by Your might! I will tempt all! (I will surely mislead them all!)"	قَالَ، فَبِعِزَّتِكَ لَأُغْوِيَنَّهُمْ أَجْمَعِينَ!

I swear to God, the diligent will succeed!	وَاللهِ لَيَنْجَحَنَّ الْمُجْتَهِدُ!

لَ	*Lām for emphasis* that is placed before the جَوابُ الْقَسَم.
يَنْجَحَنَّ	Present tense verb (فَعْلٌ مُضارِعٌ). The last letter is fixed on the فَتْحٌ which helps to attach the نُونٌ **for emphasis** (result: نَّ).
الْمُجْتَهِدُ	Subject (فاعِلٌ) of the preceding verb.

Situation 4. What happens if the complement (جَوابُ الْقَسَم) is a non-negated verbal sentence (جُمْلَةٌ فِعْلِيّةٌ مُثْبَتَة) with a verb in the past tense?	* non-negated * verbal sentence * past tense

➡ Then, the جَوابُ الْقَسَم is connected by لَ and the particle قَدْ.

| I swear by Allah that **I saw them lying slain in the battlefield** of Badr. It had been a hot day, their complexion had changed (showing signs of decay). *(Sahīh Muslim 1794)* | أُقْسِمُ بِاللهِ لَقَدْ رَأَيْتُهُمْ صَرْعَى عَلَى بَدْرٍ. قَدْ غَيَّرَتْهُمُ الشَّمْسُ وَكَانَ يَوْمًا حَارًّا . |

| By Allah, Abū Jahl is dead indeed! | وَاللهِ لَقَدْ هَلَكَ أَبُو جَهْلٍ! |
| I swear to God, the truth has won! | وَاللهِ لَقَدْ إِنْتَصَرَ الْحَقُّ! |

| *Lām for emphasis* that is placed in the جَوابُ الْقَسَمِ. | لَ |
| Particle of verification (حَرْفُ تَحْقيقٍ). | قَدْ |

Note: If the past tense verb is a verb that does not exist in the imperative or as an active participle (invariable inert verb: فِعْلٌ جامِدٌ), e.g., كانَ or نِعْمَ, then the جَوابُ الْقَسَمِ is usually only accompanied by a لَ.

| I swear to God, the best character of men is honesty! | وَاللهِ لَنِعْمَ خُلْقُ الْمَرْءِ الصِّدْقُ! |

| **Situation 5..** What happens if the جَوابُ الْقَسَمِ is a negated, verbal sentence? | * negated
* verbal sentence |

Then, the complement (جَوابُ الْقَسَمِ) is only accompanied by the negation particle and nothing else.

| I swear to God, no believer betrays his homeland! | وَاللهِ ما خانَ مُؤْمِنٌ وَطَنَهُ! |
| I swear to God, a true believer will strive for nothing but goodness! | وَاللهِ لا يَسْعَى مُؤْمِنٌ حَقٌّ إِلّا إِلَى الْخَيْرِ! |

449. Can you use a conditional clause (شَرْط) with an oath?

Yes, you can.

It is actually pretty common to use the first part of a conditional sentence (شَرْط) and then add an oath (قَسَم). There is one grammatical issue we need to solve. Both constructions need a **complement** (جَوابٌ)

which poses the following problem. Which complement belongs to which part?

> The **general rule** says that the complement (الْجَوابُ) is linked to the **part that comes first** (لِلسّابِقِ).

If you work hard, I swear, you will succeed.	إِنْ تَجْتَهِدْ واللهِ تَنْجَحْ.

تَنْجَحْ is a verb in the present tense (فِعْلٌ مُضارِعٌ), jussive mood (مَجْزُومٌ), because it is placed as a complement (second part) for the conditional sentence (جَوابُ الشَّرْطِ). Why does it refer to the conditional sentence and not to the oath? Because the الشَّرْط is the first of the two which demand a complement.

What about the complement for the oath? It is not there. The جَوابُ الْقَسَم is deleted, but its meaning is implicitly included. Let's see the difference:

1	If you work hard, I swear, you will be successful!	إِنْ تَجْتَهِدْ واللهِ فَأَنْتَ ناجِحٌ.

The complement (جَوابٌ) is connected by فَ because it is the complement for the conditional (جَوابُ الشَّرْطِ). Why? Because the الشَّرْط precedes the oath.

2	I swear, if you work hard, you will definitely succeed!	واللهِ إِنْ تَجْتَهِدْ لَتَنْجَحَنَّ!

The complement belongs to the oath – because it comes first. Notice the لَ before the verb in the present tense and the emphasis by نَّ; see #448.

Therefore, we say that the phrase *to be successful* (لَتَنْجَحَنَّ) does not have a place in إِعْراب as it is the complement for the oath (جَوابُ الْقَسَم). In this example, the complement for the conditional (جَوابُ الشَّرْطِ) is deleted; its meaning is implicitly included in the جَوابُ الْقَسَم.

450. Can you express an oath by combining لَ and إِنْ?

Yes, this is quite common.

If you place لَ before the conditional particle إِنْ, the two devices will merge. The result will be لَئِنْ which is translated as *verily, if* or *if indeed*.

Now comes a finesse! This *Lām* is not the type of لِ that is placed before the complement of an oath (جَوابُ الْقَسَم).

Instead, grammarians call this لِ the *Lām that smooths the way for the oath* (اللَّامُ الْمُوَطِّئَةُ لِلْقَسَم). This لِ is a sign indicating the presence of an oath <u>before</u> the conditional sentence. In a way, this لِ is a place holder for an oath. For that reason, the complement (جَوابٌ) in such sentences belongs to the oath (قَسَمٌ). For example:

If you strive (I swear), you will succeed!	لَئِنْ اِجْتَهَدْتَ لَتَنْجَحَنَّ!

Lām that is indicating an oath here (اللَّامُ الْمُوَطِّئَةُ لِلْقَسَم).	لَ
Conditional particle (حَرْفُ الشَّرْطِ).	إِنْ
Verb plus the subject.	اِجْتَهَدْتَ
Affirmative Lām that relates to the complement of an oath (لامُ جَوابِ الْقَسَم).	لَ
Verb in the present tense (فِعْلٌ مُضارِعٌ); it is fixed on the last letter resulting in ـَ so that the emphasis (the نّ) can be added.	تَنْجَحَنَّ

What about the complements (جَوابٌ) of both parts?

The **complement** of the **oath** (جَوابُ الْقَسَم) is **given** in the sentence (marked in gray) because the oath came first. Although the oath is not expressed, it is understood. The جَوابُ الْقَسَم does not have a position in إِعْرابٌ.

The **complement** of the **conditional** (جَوابُ الشَّرْطِ) starting with *if* was **deleted**; its meaning is already pointed out by the جَوابُ الْقَسَم.

An example in which the oath is shown:

By God, if, indeed, you treat me with deference, I will honor you.	وَاللهِ لَئِنْ أَكْرَمْتَنِي لَأَكْرِمَنَّكَ!

Let's quickly check a complex construction. What if both – the first part of a conditional sentence (شَرْطٌ) **and** the oath (قَسَمٌ) – are placed after the subject (مُبْتَدَأٌ) of a nominal sentence?

In such a situation, the complement (الْجَوابُ) **always** stands for the **conditional** - regardless of whether it is before or after the oath.

Zayd, I swear, if he works hard, he will succeed!	زَيْدٌ وَاللهِ إنْ يَجْتَهِدْ يَنْجَحْ!

The word *Zayd* (زَيْدٌ) is the subject (مُبْتَدَأٌ) of the nominal sentence (جُمْلَةٌ إِسْمِيّةٌ). The complement of the oath (جَوابُ الْقَسَمِ) was deleted – as it is pointed out already by the complement of the conditional (جَوابُ الشَّرطِ).

EPILOGUE

What is the function of the وَ in كُلُّ عامٍ وَأَنْتُمْ بِخَيْرٍ؟

A dubious one. Most grammarians say that you don't need it – and that it would be stylistically better to go without it.

Our journey ends here. Grammar is the only way to understand and appreciate the beauty of a language. Good writers (and readers) are aware of the options grammar gives us to build sentences, to explain and understand them, to choose the most effective among them. Once you have developed a feeling for stylistic finesses, you start appreciating well written texts and speeches. Let's analyze a last sentence:

كُلُّ عامٍ وَأَنْتُمْ بِخَيْرٍ.

This sentence is used in Modern Standard Arabic and in Arabic dialects (with some modifications) to congratulate at birthdays, weddings, etc. The translation depends on the context: *Congratulations! Happy birthday! Happy new year!* Have you ever thought about the reason why there is a وَ in this sentence? Let's give it a try.

We need to find a function for the وَ. This discussion is not just a thought process. The job of the وَ determines the case ending of كُلّ:

1	فَصيحةٌ	Better style – without وَ.	كُلُّ عامٍ أَنْتُمْ بِخَيْرٍ.
2	صَحيحةٌ	Correct - with وَ. To make the sentence work grammatically, we need some tricks.	كُلُّ عامٍ وَأَنْتُمْ بِخَيْرٍ.

> The grammarians have stated that both versions are correct.

Let's examine both approaches.

1 | كُلّ serves as an **adverb of time** (إِسْمُ نائِبٍ عَن ظَرْفِ الزَّمانِ مَنْصُـوبٌ
بِالْفَتْحةِ), therefore it gets the **accusative case** (مَنْصُوبٌ).

The sentence that follows (i.e., أَنْتُمْ بِخَيْرٍ) is a nominal sentence consisting of a subject (مُبْتَدَأٌ) and a predicate (خَبَرٌ). If we change the word order, it will become clear:

$$\text{أَنْتُمْ بِخَيْرٍ كُلَّ عامٍ.}$$

2 | كُلّ is the **subject** (مُبْتَدَأٌ) of the nominal sentence and is thus in the **nominative** case (مَرْفُوعٌ). The **predicate** (خَبَرٌ), however, was **deleted**. The sentence could have the assumed, underlying meaning of:

$$\text{كُلُّ عامٍ مُقْبِلٌ وَأَنْتُمْ بِخَيْرٍ.}$$

The word مُقْبِلٌ means *next* or *coming (year, month, ...)*. The وَ functions as a وَاوُ الْحالِ. Therefore, the sentence after it (i.e., أَنْتُمْ بِخَيْرٍ) is placed as a حالٌ. Grammatically speaking, it occupies the place of an accusative case (فِي مَحَلِّ نَصْبٍ) since a حالٌ has to be مَنْصُوبٌ.

Even the *Academy of the Arabic Language in Cairo* (مَجْمَعُ اللُّغةِ الْعَرَبِيّةِ) analyzed this sentence and published a communiqué on the topic which was later published in a book[10]. The function of the *Academy* is the reform of Arabic grammar, script, and vocabulary.

It is said that discussions may take years until a problem is fixed and eventually finds its way into dictionaries.

---

10   1978 - 1934 مِن الْأَلْفاظ وَالْأَساليب فِي الْقَرارات المَجْمَعِيَّة (p. 147)

ISLAMIC SALUTATIONS AFTER CERTAIN NAMES

After mentioning Allah, Muhammad, other Islamic prophets or companions of Muhammad, Muslims are supposed to praise them by uttering specific expressions. I don't use these expressions in the book, however, Muslims are supposed to say them. Here is a list of complimentary phrases that are used after certain names:

ALLAH (اللهُ):

After mentioning Allah, Muslims say *subhānahu wa ta'ālā* (سُبْحانَهُ وَتَعالَى) which means: *Glorious and exalted is He (Allah).* This is exclusively used with Allah. Abbreviation in English texts: SWT.

MUHAMMAD (مُحَمَّدٌ):

After mentioning the Prophet's name, Muslims say *sallā Allāhu 'alayhi wa sallam(a)* (صَلَّى اللّهُ عَلَيْهِ وَسَلَّمَ). It means: *Allah bless him and grant him peace.*

You may also hear: *(May) Allah pray for him and save him!* The abbreviation is, SAAS or SAAW or in its English translation: *peace be upon him* (PBUH).

MESSENGERS, PROPHETS and ARCHANGELS:

After their names, Muslims say: *'alayhi al-Salām* (عَلَيْهِ السَّلامُ) which means: *Peace be upon him.* It is said after mentioning, e.g. Noah (نُوح) or Gabriel (جِبْرِيل). Abbreviation in English: AS.

COMPANIONS (الصَّحابةُ) of the Prophet Muhammad:

After mentioning one of Muhammad's companions, Muslims say the wish *radiya Allāhu 'anhu* (رَضِيَ اللّهُ عَنْهُ).

It means: *May Allah be pleased with them.* This is said, for example, after Muhammad's father-in-law 'Abū Bakr (أَبُو بَكْر) or Muhammad's wife 'Ā'isha (عائشة بِنْت أَبِي بَكْر). Abbreviation in English: RA.

INDEX

RELATIVE CLAUSE.........120,
191FF., 197, 199, 201F., 243F.,
278, 367, 442, 461, 597, 696, 776

Printed in the USA
CPSIA information can be obtained
at www.ICGtesting.com
LVHW022032181123
764024LV00031B/85/J